GENERAL WALKER
AND THE MURDER *OF*
PRESIDENT KENNEDY

GENERAL WALKER
AND THE MURDER OF
PRESIDENT KENNEDY

THE EXTENSIVE NEW EVIDENCE
OF A RADICAL-RIGHT CONSPIRACY

JEFFREY H. CAUFIELD, M.D.

MORELAND PRESS

CONTENTS

Contents

Contents

INTRODUCTION

I have long had an interest in the assassination of President Kennedy and have read every book on the subject I could lay my hands on, including those from the Warren Commission, the writings on the 1967 assassination investigation of Jim Garrison—the district attorney of New Orleans—and Congress's 1977 House Select Committee on Assassinations. In 1994, two years after Garrison's death, I had the good fortune to join other researchers in New Orleans to obtain and copy Garrison's personal investigative files, courtesy of his son Lyon Garrison—thus beginning a twenty-year path of intense research, investigation and discovery, among other things. *General Walker and the Murder of President Kennedy* was never intended to (and does not) directly address all of the previous theories put forth in other works about the assassination. Rather, it is designed as an evidence-based academic textbook that provides an in-depth analysis of the people and organizations—almost all violent right-wing extremists—behind the world-changing event and serves as a rich resource for further academic study of the crime.

What quickly became evident in 1994 while digging through Garrison's files—most of which had rarely been seen before—was that the vast majority of the documents in no way supported his well-publicized, still-popular claims that U.S. intelligence operatives were behind the murder of President Kennedy. Rather, they suggested that the people behind the president's alleged assassin, Lee Harvey Oswald, were southern segregationists and radicals tied to the Citizens' Council, the John Birch Society, and related extremist groups.

With suspicions of a radical right plot, I undertook an exhaustive investigation of the matter that involved frequent trips to the South—particularly Louisiana—and intensive study of the relative documents in the National Archives and FBI documents obtained through the Freedom of Information Act, as well as over fifty interviews with people who had knowledge of Lee Harvey Oswald or the individuals he was involved with. Much of this research led to suspicions about General Edwin A. Walker of Dallas, Texas, the city which was the location of the president's 1963 murder. Exhaustive research ultimately tied Walker to the extremist elements behind Lee Harvey Oswald in New Orleans—the city where Oswald was born and raised and in which he resided the summer before the assassination.

When Major General Edwin A. Walker was relieved by President Kennedy of his command of the 24th Army Infantry Division in Germany in 1961, he returned to the States and joined forces with fellow radical rightists to plot assassinations and insurrection against the United States of America. While much of their activity during the era fell under the guise of anti-Communism and preventing the Communist menace from taking over the country—a continuation of 1950s McCarthyism—their primary motivation and irritation stemmed from the growing racial integration/civil rights movement. By attempting to link Communism to the American civil rights movement at every opportunity, through whatever means available, the radical right had an effective—though short-lived—strategy to halt the southern integration effort: the Communist Control Act of Louisiana. Under the law, any organization with ties to "known" Communists, like Lee Harvey Oswald, would face unprecedented fines and jail time. In essence, every group associated with the integration effort was to be targeted under the law, making it nearly impossible for these groups to operate—or even exist—in the South. However, when the strategy became gravely endangered by President Kennedy's proposed Civil Rights Act, the radical right turned to their last resort—something they knew all too well: violence.

In mid-1962, Walker joined other disgruntled former military officers and oversaw a plot to assassinate a large number of people in power positions in the government and in industry. They were convinced that Communists had infiltrated the power structure of the U.S. and that selective assassinations would save the country from imminent Communist takeover. The FBI knew full well about the plot, which was aborted in early 1963 after low-level members of the conspiracy were brought in for questioning. They did not, however, question Walker, an ardent racist who they knew was involved, who—in the fall of 1962—put out a clarion call for other southern extremists to join him at the University of Mississippi to block the admission of African American James Meredith to the then all-white university.

By order of President Kennedy, Walker was arrested and charged with insurrection against the United States for fomenting a riot that led to two deaths and the wounding of scores of U.S. Marshals. As was customary for the era, an all-white southern jury refused to indict him, but the FBI continued to monitor Walker and the other extremists and discovered, in October of 1963, that members of the group planned to murder President Kennedy. Thirteen days before Kennedy's murder, the FBI learned the plot was in the works, in what would turn out to be the exact detail in which the Dallas murder was carried out. The information was never provided to the Warren Commission, which led the government's official investigation of the assassination.

After the president's death, General Walker became a part of the assassination story when it was determined that the president's accused assassin, Lee Harvey Oswald, had attempted to shoot Walker at his home in April of 1962. The Warren Commission questioned Walker about the shooting, but the FBI concealed from the Warren Commission the aforementioned 1962 broad-based assassination plots that Walker was involved in, as well as the later plot by other extremists in the group to kill Kennedy.

Jack Ruby murdered Lee Harvey Oswald after the assassination, for which he received the death penalty. Ruby testified before the Warren Commission and alluded to General Walker's role in the assassination, but he was not taken seriously. Ruby's verdict was overturned in 1966 and he won a change of venue for the retrial. When the sheriff of Wichita Falls came to transfer Ruby to the new venue, he found him too ill to be moved and Ruby was instead taken to the hospital where he was treated for cancer. At about that time, in a personal letter, Walker wrote to a friend and warned him that Ruby, who was now out of the Dallas County jail, might talk. He vowed he would not allow Ruby to leave the hospital alive. After all, he had been able to compel Ruby's silence while Ruby was in the Dallas jail, but now that Ruby was out of his influence, Walker feared he might talk.

The life and times of General Walker are woven within the pertinent history of the Kennedy assassination, which took place in Walker's hometown. No matter how many other titles you may have read on the topic, *General Walker and the Murder of President Kennedy* offers a massive amount of new, well-documented information that will only be found here, including substantial evidence of Walker's role in the broad-based assassination plots and his plan to murder Jack Ruby. Unlike many other works on this subject, *General Walker* is meticulously referenced with documents obtained from the FBI and other archival sources. As such, this is a dense, voluminous work intended to inform—rather than merely entertain— and generate renewed interest in one of the biggest unsolved crimes of the last century.

CHAPTER ONE

LEE HARVEY OSWALD AND GUY BANISTER

He didn't even have the satisfaction of being killed for civil rights . . .
it had to be some silly little Communist.
— *Jacqueline Kennedy*

A t least eleven people witnessed Lee Harvey Oswald, the presumed assassin of President Kennedy, with W. Guy Banister in New Orleans in the summer of 1963, just months prior to the November 22 assassination of the president. A relationship between the two men was extremely unlikely, since their avowed views on Communism were diametrically opposed. Guy Banister was a career FBI agent, and former head of the FBI's Chicago office, who dedicated his life to hunting Communists and preserving segregation of the races. Oswald, on the other hand, had spent three years in the Communist Soviet Union and publicly declared himself a Marxist. Several more people also saw Oswald with a number of close associates of Guy Banister. Unfortunately, the seven-member Warren Commission appointed by President Johnson to investigate the assassination—and headed by Supreme Court Chief Justice Earl Warren—had no knowledge of Banister or his association with Oswald. Accordingly, they did not investigate the matter.

The office of the District Attorney of New Orleans, headed by Jim Garrison, first uncovered Banister's ties to Oswald during the enigmatic investigation of the assassination that began in 1966. The House Select Committee on Assassinations took up the matter somewhat further in their re-investigation of the Kennedy assassination in 1977 and determined that Lee Harvey Oswald and Banister could have been associated. The paradox of why a fanatical anti-Communist like Banister and a declared, dedicated Communist like Lee Harvey Oswald were seen so many times together has never been adequately explained. District Attorney Jim Garrison claimed Oswald was not a true Communist but, rather, that he traveled to the Soviet Union and participated in anti-Castro demonstrations as an agent of the Central Intelligence Agency, Office of Naval Intelligence, or some other federal government spy agency—claims which he failed dismally to substantiate. The assassination, therefore, he concluded, was the work of those federal spy agencies. Assassination writers took Garrison's claims further and offered various sophistical explanations claiming many of Oswald's activities were related to government intelligence.

Guy Banister maintained close contact with FBI director J. Edgar Hoover after his tenure with the agency. Although there is no evidence that the FBI was involved in the assassination, there is an abundance of evidence that Director J. Edgar Hoover deliberately concealed from the Warren Commission a plot to murder the president by the radical right wing and segregationist elements. Finally, the FBI's investigation of Oswald's activities in New Orleans was of poor quality, suggesting FBI malfeasance in failing to uncover Oswald's ties to the Banister operation.

The allegation of the eleven or more witness who saw Banister and Oswald together, and those who saw Oswald with close associates of Banister, will be presented in this chapter along with an examination of the Banister operation.

The Law Enforcement Career of Guy Banister

The life and times of these two strange bedfellows, Guy Banister and Lee Harvey Oswald, will be presented briefly here and expanded throughout this work. Guy Banister's career in law enforcement began when he served on the Monroe, Louisiana, Police Department from 1929 to 1934. On November 5, 1934, he became a special agent of the FBI, a post he held until 1938 when he was appointed Special Agent in Charge, SAC, in 1938. As a SAC, he served in Butte, Montana, from 1938 to 1941, when he was transferred to Oklahoma City. In 1943, he was transferred back to Butte. In 1953, he was transferred to the Minneapolis division, then to the Chicago, Illinois, division until 1954 when he retired.[1]

Banister had an adopted daughter named Mary Jane who married Donald Duvio. According to her son Ken Duvio, Mary Jane was the product of one of Banister's affairs in Butte, Montana, whom Banister—and his apparently forgiving wife Mary—adopted.[2] Banister's seventeen years as a Special Agent in Charge was the longest ever served by a SAC at that time. At the Chicago office, he supervised 500 agents, which represented the second-largest FBI office in the country next to New York. In addition to a wide array of crimes, he investigated espionage and subversive activity. On June 14, 1953, J. Edgar Hoover wrote Banister at the Chicago FBI office and congratulated him on his successful investigation of the Nationalist Party of Puerto Rico, as well as the arrest of several party members, which Hoover called "a source of much satisfaction."[3, 4, 5] During his career in law enforcement, Banister was also involved in several gunfights. He once shot and killed a man who was a suspect in the murder of a police officer.[6]

After his retirement, he accepted an invitation from Mayor deLesseps Morrison to join the New Orleans Police Department to clean up graft in the department. From 1955 to 1957, Banister served as secretary and assistant superintendent of the department. As a result of his graft investigations, many police officers were indicted for corruption. In connection with his investigation, he even prepared cases of malfeasance against Mayor Morrison, and others. A Grand Jury was convened to consider the charges. Unfortunately for Banister, no indictments were returned. Banister was understandably not pleased with the outcome.[7]

On March 2, 1957, Banister visited the Absinthe House bar in the French Quarter with two attorney friends visiting from Chicago. Banister became involved in a confrontation with the bartender and reached across the bar, grabbed his jacket, and cursed him. He boasted he had killed two men already and another wouldn't make any difference. Moments later, a customer shouted, "look out, he has a gun." Banister's close aide, Sergeant Hubert Badeaux, investigated the incident for the police department. Badeaux provided a statement in defense of Chief Banister. Badeaux stated that he happened to be nearby when he heard the sound of a nightstick and investigated the incident. He took the gun from Banister who denied pulling a gun, saying, "Good God, no. I wouldn't do a thing like that." Banister denied all charges and his two friends signed statements supporting his innocence.

Police Superintendent Provosty Dayries drew up charges against Banister and laid them out in a letter. He charged that: Banister assaulted a bartender without provocation and drew a gun without jurisdiction; witnesses saw him drinking and cursing the bartender; and he permitted a citizen, his Chicago friend, to drive a police car at an excessive rate of speed. Additionally, it was noted that Banister had previously made speeches and given press releases without approval, and, in 1955, Banister had assaulted a newspaper reporter while carrying a gun. Based on the Absinthe House incident, Superintendent Dayries removed Banister from the payroll on June 1, 1957. However, Banister would have been retained on the force if he had accepted certain conditions.[8]

A third violent incident was reported in the press when Banister was arrested for aggravated assault following a scuffle with three youths on a city bus. He threatened one of them with a gun, which was knocked out of his hand and broke a window. Banister said one of them insulted him. The gun was not found when police arrived.[9]

Guy Banister and Associates, Inc.

After being fired from the police department, Banister opened a private detective agency called "Guy Banister and Associates" in Room 434 of the Balter Building. George Singelmann, one of his closet friends, was the personal assistant to Judge Leander Perez and directed his Citizens' Council organization in the office just below Banister's. In promoting his detective agency, Banister touted his ability to conduct fixed and mobile surveillance and provide complete photographic coverage.[10] As we'll see in later chapters, the Balter Building was not only the center of operations for the pro-segregation Citizens' Council, but also of neo-Nazi and Cuban exile activities in New Orleans.

A young former New Orleans police officer, Joseph Oster, became a partner. Oster told the author he eventually left the operation because Banister spent most of his time doing things that didn't bring any money into the office. Joseph Oster was also an FBI informant and, in 1967, he furnished a great deal of information to the FBI about the Jim Garrison assassination investigation. This information was initially communicated to the FBI on January 4, 1967, more than a month before the investigation became public. Oster's information was valued by the FBI, which commented that it could not have been obtained by any other source.[11]

Garrison's chief investigator, Lou Ivon, may have been a source of Oster's information. Ivon told the author he served on the police force with Oster in the 1950s and that they had been boyhood friends.[12]

INTRODUCING

Guy Banister Associates, Inc.

Photos of Guy Banister (left) and Joseph Oster (right) in a rare Guy Banister Associates, Inc. brochure, circa. 1958. Source: deLesseps Morrison Papers, New Orleans Public Library

Lester Ottilio took Joseph Oster's place at Guy Banister and Associates. When asked if he thought Banister was a radical, he replied, "No. He wasn't a radical but he did hate Communism with a passion."[13] Contrary to Ottilio's opinion, Banister *was* a radical, as we shall see from the accounts that follow. A glimpse into Banister's radical activities and his relationship with Lee Harvey Oswald is provided by the following accounts from those who knew him.

Vernon Gerdes told Garrison's investigators that he worked in Banister's office in the Newman Building at the corner of Camp and Lafayette Streets between 1960 and 1963. Gerdes recalled some of the individuals involved with the office. He related that David Ferrie frequented the office and was involved with right-wing political activities. He knew Joe Newbrough, another Banister employee, who was nicknamed "The Fat Man." Gerdes recalled seeing large quantities of ammunition in a back room, with the name "Schlumberger" printed on the boxes. Banister told Gerdes he was not worried about getting in trouble for obtaining the armaments, because the officials at Schlumberger knew about it. Gerdes quit Banister's operation when Ivan Nitschke came to work for him. According to Gerdes, Nitschke was an ex-FBI agent and had worked with Banister in Chicago.

The armaments reported in the office by Nitschke were procured or stolen from the Schlumberger warehouse in Houma, Louisiana, by Banister, David Ferrie, and Gordon Novel, and reportedly were intended for use in the anti-Castro effort.[14, 15] Nitschke told Garrison's investigators that Hugh Ward, a partner in the Banister operation, was a friend of David Ferrie and they were running guns to Miami and other places. Hugh Ward was a pilot who was flying former New Orleans Mayor deLesseps Morrison and his son when a fatal crash occurred in Mexico.[16, 17] According to Delphine Roberts, Banister had been the one to train Hugh Ward as an agent. She noted that Ward was running guns to Cuba to fight Castro.[18] Nitschke was the Western Vice President of the Society of Former Special Agents of the FBI, Inc., in 1959.[19] He was the director of the National Rifle Association and a lifetime member.[20] Nitschke recalled that Richard Lauchli, a high-ranking aide to Robert DePugh—national leader of the Minutemen—brought a load of arms through Mississippi during the 1962 integration crisis and insurrection led by Banister associate, and former army major general, Edwin Walker.

The Minutemen were a radical civilian militia formed to fight the purported Communist takeover during the Red Scare. Lauchli was connected with the right-wing and anti-Castro training camp north of New Orleans. The training camp was located on the property of a man named McLaney that became the scene of an FBI raid according to a Garrison memo.[21]

Jerry Brooks was another top aide to DePugh in the Minutemen and worked out of Banister's office from 1961 through 1964. Brooks traveled back and forth from New Orleans in his duties as an aide to DePugh. Brooks worked without pay, mainly investigating "anti-Communist" matters. Brooks identified Banister and his colleagues Hugh Ward and Maurice Gatlin as Minutemen. He said he had placed DePugh in touch with Banister. Brooks later defected from the Minutemen and testified against DePugh in a federal firearms trial. DePugh told the author he did not know Banister personally, but recalled that Brooks called him frequently from Banister's office and told DePugh about Banister's work in the Anticommunist Crusade of the Caribbean. DePugh was probably lying, however, since the FBI documented that Banister did not belong to the group and his ties to the group were limited. Banister told the FBI his only connection to the Anticommunist Crusade of the Caribbean was his investigation into the sale of Jeeps to Cuba through the Port of New Orleans for the organization.[22]

Hugh Ward, not surprisingly—and like Banister—was a member of the Minutemen.[23, 24] Nitschke was in Banister's office before the assassination and he saw 24-inch by 18-inch placards with slogans painted on them or drawn on with Magic Marker. It was his impression that they were stored in Banister's office because they had just been used or were about to be used. Nitschke was vague about a more definitive description. He said the presence of the signs "tended to convince me further that I was glad I had not stayed in that office on a permanent basis." He described them as "sloganistic." Castro's name may have been written on them. He could not recall exactly what they said, but stated, "It didn't make sense to him how Guy got tied up to those signs." Nitschke's surprise stemmed from the fact the signs were probably pro-Castro, when Banister was vehemently anti-Castro. The signs were likely those used by Oswald in his public demonstrations in support of his one-man pro-Castro organization, Fair Play for Cuba Committee, which the Warren Commission described as a "product of his Oswald's imagination."

Nitschke was with Delphine Roberts, Banister's love interest, when they discovered Guy Banister dead at his home in June 1964. Delphine Roberts told Nitschke that Banister had told her he was concerned about certain papers that "would hurt an awful lot of big people" if they were discovered by the wrong individuals. Banister asked her to take possession of the so-called special papers, which were not located in the regular offices files, in the event something happened to them. Roberts initially told a Garrison investigator that the papers were lost. Later, she said she found some of them in an old box of Christmas tree ornaments and handed them over to Garrison's investigators.

Nitschke observed a constant flow of Cubans and armaments in and out of the office.[25] Nitschke, in another statement to the D.A.'s office, stated that he was invited by Guy Banister to participate in a bid to perform security operations at the Michoud NASA assembly facility in New Orleans in 1961. While awaiting the awarding of the contract, he maintained a desk at Banister's office at Camp and Lafayette. At one time, the Cubans in the office asked him for advice on obtaining arms and automatic weapons. Garrison showed Nitschke a photo of a tall Cuban man standing in a group with Lee Harvey Oswald. Nitschke recognized him as a Cuban who had been in Banister's office and who had asked Nitschke—a former FBI arms expert—about where he could obtain silencers for rifles.[26]

Joe Newbrough was an employee of Guy Banister from 1959 to 1964. He anecdotally told Garrison's investigators that he saw Banister on the day of the Bay of Pigs invasion (April 17, 1961). Banister reportedly told him the invasion took him by surprise, which is difficult to believe since all of the people who had been involved locally in the anti-Castro effort had disappeared.[27] Newbrough implied that the New Orleans Cubans were involved in the invasion. Newbrough later told the House Select Committee on Assassinations (HSCA) that he believed that Oswald was an agent of the CIA and was acting under orders.[28] An informant of the Louisiana State Police identified Newbrough as a homosexual with a criminal record. The informant reported that on the eve of the assassination General Walker, from Dallas, Texas, met with a group of individuals at the Jung Hotel—including Joe Newburgh, an employee of Guy Banister. It would be very surprising if Banister weren't with them. (As we shall see later, General Walker was a right-wing radical and bitter enemy of President Kennedy, who relieved him of his Army command in 1961.) Days earlier, Walker had met in New Orleans with close Banister associates Kent Courtney and Judge Leander Perez.[29]

Walker's appearance in New Orleans on the eve of the assassination is suspicious, because he, too, had a relationship with Lee Harvey Oswald. In April 1963, while Oswald was in Texas, he supposedly fired his rifle at Walker, as will be discussed in detail later. As will also be shown, Walker's appearance in New Orleans is even more suspicious in view of the fact that Walker and Banister, two men in different cities who had a connection to Lee Harvey Oswald, were close associates.

Mary Brengel, a staunch conservative, also worked as a secretary for Banister in the months before and after the assassination. She revealed to the author that Delphine Roberts told her that Lee Harvey Oswald was at the office when she was there. According to Brengel, she did not recall seeing Oswald, because there were so many young men coming in and out of Banister's office seeking employment. Banister was hiring pier watchmen under a contract he had procured, one of the few endeavors that brought money into the office. She recalled Delphine Roberts brought a radio to work on the day of the assassination, something she had not done before. When the murder was announced on the radio, Roberts jumped out of her seat and pirouetted in delight.

Guy Banister and David Ferrie worked as investigators for G. Wray Gill, the attorney for New Orleans mob boss Carlos Marcello. Marcello was not a U.S. citizen and Attorney General Robert Kennedy worked vigorously for his deportation. Brengel recalled that, one day, Banister asked her to dictate a letter about the Marcello case. She expressed her disapproval of Banister's dealing with an organized crime figure. Banister told her Marcello had the right to defend himself like any one else. As a result of the incident, she was never asked by

Banister to take a letter again. Brengel stated there was never much money coming into the office. As a result, Banister never paid her for the four months she worked for him.[30]

A confidential informant, whose information appears credible, wrote a letter to Garrison describing the Banister operation. He told him that Banister employed Hugh Ward, an electronics expert and a photographer with a lab. Banister was one of the FBI's greatest room search and electronics "bag men," an individual who surreptitiously planted listening devices. Banister gained intra-Bureau fame and J. Edgar Hoover's undying gratitude for a World War II operation, which he commanded in Mexico City. The operation was a "bag job" on the safe of the German Embassy. Banister was said to have obtained the codebook of the German diplomatic service. As a reward for the operation, Banister was given the SAC job in Chicago. Reportedly, Banister then broke with the FBI in order to perform underground intelligence work. His subsequent position with the New Orleans police was allegedly a single-step phase in "sterilizing" him from government connections. The second phase of this long-range "sterilization" process was his move into the private detective field. Banister accepted cases as a private investigator for fees considerably below the market price. He had connections with sources that could provide him with master passkeys to any locks. He also reportedly had very strong connections to the Office of Naval Intelligence through a man named Kirsch. Banister twice bagged the office of Aaron Kohn of the New Orleans Metropolitan Crime Commission because he considered Kohn to be a member of the Jewish underground movement. Next to the statement about Aaron Kohn, Garrison wrote about Banister in the margin: "Banister orientation = Nazi." Banister's connection with the Nazis (described in Chapter Three of this work, *Lee Harvey Oswald and the Nazis*) will bear out Garrison's claim.[31]

Emile Stopper had business dealings with Guy Banister in 1963. Banister mentioned several times his bitterness towards President Kennedy. Stopper heard Banister remark on several occasions that someone should do away with Kennedy. He believes Banister belonged to several segregation groups, which was Banister's true principal preoccupation.[32, 33]

Louise Decker McMullen worked in Banister's office in the Newman Building from October 1961 to January 1962, and recalled seeing Carlos Quiroga, David Ferrie, and David Lewis in the office. She noted that Banister was an "arch-conservative" and once received a direct call from J. Edgar Hoover.[34, 35] Another secretary, Mary Brengel, and former partner Joseph Oster confirmed to the author that J. Edgar Hoover telephoned Banister at his office from time to time. Decker told Garrison's investigators that her job consisted mainly of clipping articles about racial problems throughout the country and articles on Communism. She noted that Banister was "a fanatic on these two subjects." Banister felt integration was a Communist-inspired effort and devoted his efforts to fighting it.[36]

Festus Brown introduced Lawrence Melville to Guy Banister. Melville told Garrison's investigators that Banister had papers on Americanism, congressional reports on counter subversives of the House Un-American Activities Committee, and other materials in his possession. Banister offered Melville a desk and typewriter in his office and told him it would be a good idea to investigate those people who were mixed up in integration. Melville used

Banister's files to check those involved in local integration activities. He recalled Banister possessed numerous publications related to his anti-subversion work. Melville worked in Banister's office for six to eight months. Banister's preoccupation with the civil rights movement was a primary recollection of many who had worked with him.[37]

The HSCA interviewed Banister's brother, Ross Banister, in 1978. He told them that when Guy retired from the FBI he desired to return to the South. Ross Banister contacted Mayor deLesseps Morrison and Guy got the job of Assistant Superintendent of Police as an outsider to assist in the investigation of ongoing scandals in the police department. He told them Guy got fired—or quit—because he was a controversial figure. He mentioned several times that Guy was a dedicated anti-Communist and maintained extensive files on all sorts of subversive activity. He said that he felt Guy was cooperating with the FBI throughout his retirement, and that Guy Banister never mentioned the CIA to him. Guy told him he saw Lee Harvey Oswald handing out FPCC literature. He advanced the theory that Oswald stamped the 544 Camp Street address of the office above Banister's on one of his handouts in an attempt to embarrass Guy over his publicity campaign to kill the sale of Jeeps to Cuba.[38] Ross Banister identified William Irwin as a friend of his brother.

William Irwin told the HSCA, in 1978, that he began an association with Banister in the late 1950s or early 1960s through the American Legion. He told them that Banister was a dedicated anti-Communist, maintaining extensive files on known Communists at his office at Camp and Lafayette.[39] The southern strategy to align integration efforts with Communism was a major weapon in the arsenal of the segregationist's attempts to preserve white supremacy.

Guy Banister and the Communist Inquisitions of Senator James O. Eastland, 1956
Although Banister's involvement with anti-Castro Cubans was highly touted and emphasized by Garrison and other assassination writers, the efforts of Guy Banister and David Ferrie on behalf of the anti-Castro effort were meager at best. Preservation of segregation was Banister's principal preoccupation—a fact that Jim Garrison ignored, or more likely concealed. Garrison, like Banister, was a member of the segregationist Citizens' Council. The Citizens' Council endorsed Garrison's bid for the district attorney's office in 1962 at a Council meeting he attended.[40]

Banister participated in a number of inquisitions aimed at integrationists, who were accused of being Communists. Banister became enlightened regarding the Communist menace during his friendship with Elizabeth Bentley, one of the nation's best-known FBI Communist Party informants. Banister first met Bentley shortly after she testified that Harry Dexter White and other prominent government officials had Communist affiliations. Banister sought a $10,000 "red probe" fund (a fund to investigate Communists) to employ Bentley with the police intelligence unit. The City Council Vice President called it a "crackpot idea" and said investigation of Communism "is a job for the federal government."[41]

Arch segregationist Senator James O. Eastland anticipated the ominous outcome for segregationist of the 1954 *Brown v. Board of Education* Supreme Court decision, which held that segregation in the public schools was unconstitutional. In response to that decision, Eastland held hearings of the Senate Internal Security Subcommittee (SISS) on the Southern Conference Education Fund (SCEF), a New Orleans integration group. Testimony from a former Communist purportedly showed that the integration movement was directed by the Soviet Union and was infested with U.S. Communists. His chief witness, later found out to be a serial perjurer, was a "former Communist" and—like Lee Harvey Oswald—spent time in the Soviet Union. Eastland's strategy was to tie integration to Communism during the Red Scare era, and show that the true motivation behind the civil rights movement was a Communist plot to divide and conquer America.

Buoyed by the success of the 1954 SISS hearing, Eastland held another hearing in New Orleans, in March 1956, that was given the dubious title of "Scope of Soviet Activity in the United States," an important event in the Kennedy assassination history.[42] Eastland called several witnesses to testify, including civil rights activist, and African American, Hunter Pitts O'Dell who later became an advisor to Dr. Martin Luther King, Jr. Robert Morris was Eastland's chief counsel who asked his witnesses, in McCartheyesque style, "Are you now a Communist?"[43] Mayor deLesseps Morrison ordered Superintendent Guy Banister to conduct an investigation into subversive activities in New Orleans after Eastland's findings of Communist activities in the city. He called Banister "an expert in the field."[44] Banister announced that he planned to add another man to the police "Red Squad" in addition to Sergeant Hubert Badeaux, the lone officer in the intelligence department at the time.[45] Banister and Mayor Morrison flew to Greenwood, Mississippi, to confer with Senator Eastland on subversive activity in New Orleans—and segregation.[46] Morrison stated, "Mr. Banister has complete liaison with the committee's staff, which was the main object of our trip."[47] Judge Leander Perez offered his support.

Banister's liaison with Senator Eastland and Robert Morris marked the beginning of his career outside of the FBI of hunting both real and supposed Communists; in reality, simply searching out those who opposed the sacred southern institution of segregation. After the triumphant hearings, Sergeant Badeaux wrote his friend Willie Rainach that he was grooming an individual to infiltrate leftist organizations. At the same time, Lee Harvey Oswald first began acting like a Communist. The year was 1956.

These critical events will be discussed in detail in Chapter Twenty-two. Eastland summarized his committee's case against integrationists like Hunter Pitts O'Dell: "Our evidence here in New Orleans indicates very clearly that Communist leaders in Moscow . . . are reaching down into this part of the United States for agents willing to do their mischievous work." It would not be surprising if young Lee Harvey Oswald watched the hearings on TV.[48] After the proceedings, Banister announced that he would seek to have O'Dell tried under the state Communist laws—or, as historians have called them, "little Smith Acts"—through the district attorney's office. The law required Communists to register, and violations carried stiff jail time and fines.[49] Under similar—but far stiffer—laws in 1963, any person or organization associated with a supposed Moscow Communist like Lee Harvey Oswald could face fines and jail time that were so severe they would have the effect of abolishing or severely curtailing the civil rights movement in the South.

Soviet Premier Nikita Khrushchev fanned the flames of anti-Communism when he threatened the U.S. in November 1956, declaring, "We will bury you."[50] Through the 1950s and early 1960s Eastland's committee and racial extremists on the House Un-American Activities Committee conducted witch hunts on integrationists throughout the South. The cooperation between Senator Eastland, Guy Banister, Robert Morris, Hubert Badeaux, and Judge Leander Perez was shaping events in history leading up to the assassination.

Guy Banister and the State of Louisiana Joint Legislative Committee on Segregation, 1957
On March 6–9, 1957, the State of Louisiana Joint Legislative Committee held public hearings with the exaggerated title of "Subversion in Racial Unrest; An Outline of a Strategic Weapon to Destroy the Governments of Louisiana and the United States." Since the 1954 Supreme Court *Brown* decision, southern leaders had followed Eastland's strategy and also endeavored to tie the civil rights movement to Communism during the Red Scare. Leander Perez, Hubert Badeaux, and Guy Banister were the star New Orleans witnesses in the state hearings. These individuals had also been brought together during Eastland's earlier SISS hearings. Committee Chairman, and state senator, Willie Rainach began the hearings with a review of Banister's credentials. He stated that Banister was a Communist hunter, noting that during World War II and in the Cold War Banister's principal commitment was to combating subversion. Banister, he noted, "devoted considerable study to Communist history, theory, strategy and tactics." Banister testified that he had become familiar with the Communist Party through a fellow agent—a Russian emigrant—while working in the New York office of the FBI in 1935. Banister testified, "It was also my duty to develop and supervise those people called informers. To be more specific, we might say they were the counter spies sent in to report on the activities of the party members. That was part of my duties throughout the nearly seventeen years I served as Special Agent in Charge." He went on to say, "I regretted getting out of counter-espionage, counter-sabotage, counter-subversive activity." (In fact, in 1963, Banister was engaged in counter-subversive activities with Lee Harvey Oswald.) Banister told the committee, "Every member of the Louisiana Communist Party, a component part of the Communist Party of the United States of America, is a Soviet agent." (The committee on segregation hearings will be detailed in Chapter Twenty-two.) Kent Courtney, a close Banister associate, personally delivered a copy of the 1957 Subversion in Racial Unrest hearings transcripts to Eastland's SISS chief counsel, J. G. Sourwine in Washington, D.C.[51]

In October 1959, Lee Harvey Oswald departed New Orleans for the Communist Soviet Union, which is extraordinary, since he was later closely tied to Banister who dedicated his life to hunting Communists. He returned to the U.S. in June 1962, and to New Orleans in May 1963.

Guy Banister and the Hearings on the "Communist Subversion

Behind Racial Trouble in Arkansas," 1958

President Eisenhower's 1957 deployment of federal troops to uphold the court-ordered integration of Little Rock, Arkansas, schools was the first major federal assault on segregation under the *Brown v. Board of Education* decision that eventually led to the abolition of segregation in the public schools. The Arkansas legislature decided to use the same strategy that linked integration to Communism that had been successful for the State of Louisiana. They called on Guy Banister to appear before the Special Education Committee of the Arkansas legislature on December 16–17, 1958. Banister told them that the Little Rock school integration crisis was a result of the "subversive influence in this part of the country." A news article summed up Banister's testimony: "unrest blamed on Reds" was written with the byline "Half of Commy trained Americans were of the Negro race."[52] Also in 1958, Banister appeared before the American Legion Un-American Committee and discussed supposed subversive activities at Louisiana State University.[53]

Guy Banister and the Louisiana State Sovereignty Commission

Banister applied with the state-run Sovereignty Commission in Baton Rouge in 1960 for a job supervising the work of their investigators.[54] "Sovereignty" was a code word meaning the states' right to maintain segregation without the outside interference of the federal government. "Segregation Commission" would have been more to the point. Banister offered the use of his library, "one of the largest of its kind" on subversives.[55] The Commission was a state-funded, semi-secret organization created to preserve segregation by spying on integrationists. Although all of the Louisiana Sovereignty Commission files were—suspiciously—destroyed, Banister's name shows up on a Mississippi Sovereignty Commission file—which was preserved by the state—suggesting he had indeed been retained as their investigator, since the two state agencies cooperated with each other.[56] Delphine Roberts, Banister's secretary, told the HSCA that she worked for the Sovereignty Commission to expose several groups in New Orleans that were anti-American, evidence that, in all probability, Banister had been retained to work for the Commission.[57]

The Sovereignty Commissions of Mississippi, Louisiana, and Virginia agreed to cooperate in matters of equal interest and share their intelligence. The Louisiana Sovereignty Commission was created during the regular session of the Louisiana Legislature in 1960, and was composed of Governor Jimmie Davis, the attorney general, and others in state government. The stated mission of the Sovereignty Commission was "to exercise every legal means to preserve and protect for the State and its people those rights, which are traditionally, and legally theirs," in other words, the right to maintain segregation. They pledged to keep the people of Louisiana "informed as to the activities of organizations or individuals within the State who are propagandizing or working toward decreasing state powers."

The "Information Division" of the Sovereignty Commission investigated and kept records on many such organizations and individuals and, from time to time, submitted confidential reports to members of the legislature. Put simply, the "Information Division" was a surveillance operation which used informants and other means to spy on individuals and groups advocating integration in order to enjoin, arrest, and otherwise stifle the civil rights movement in the state.

The "Registration Division" was concerned with voter registration. They advised voters that successful testing of their knowledge of the Constitution was required for them to vote. In short, the "Registration Division" was designed to deny African Americans the right to vote in order to maintain white supremacy.

The "Education Division" was a professed advisory group composed of constitutional lawyers, elected officials, and others organized to develop a program to inform the people of the state's best interest of preserving states rights. In other words, the "Education Division" sought to propagandize and create solidarity among its citizens. The Louisiana Sovereignty Commission could not have found a more determined and qualified person to supervise their investigators than Guy Banister.[58]

Guy Banister and the Louisiana Un-American Activities Committee

The most significant of all of Banister's efforts in relationship to Lee Harvey Oswald was his position with the Louisiana Un-American Activities Committee (LUAC). LUAC primarily concerned itself with integrationists and leftists. In 1960, Guy Banister was hired as an investigator for LUAC. In his interview for the position, he claimed that white left-wingers were behind the civil rights movement because blacks lacked the leadership and organizational skills needed to steer the movement. Furthermore, he noted gratuitously (expressing his contempt for African Americans) that they never made great criminals either. He told LUAC members that agitators from New York were behind the civil rights group called the Congress of Racial Equality, or "CORE." (As we will see in Chapter Twenty-one, Lee Harvey Oswald had ties to that group.) Banister lamented the lack of anti-subversive efforts in the state since his involvement in the investigations for the Subversion in Racial Unrest hearings in 1957, which had also involved his close associates Hubert Badeaux and Judge Leander Perez.[59]

LUAC was an outgrowth of the American Legion's Un-American Activities Committee, and was formed to gather intelligence on Communists. Banister associate Festus Jerry Brown, headed the Legion committee.[60] Banister's close friend Kent Courtney was the head of the American Legion Americanism Committee representing thirty posts.[61] William Irwin told the HSCA, in 1978, that Banister was an advisor to the American Legion Anti-Communist Committee. Banister's brother Ross told Garrison's investigators that Festus Brown "was either a client or investigator for him [Banister]. Mr. Brown was closely related to him in some phase of his work."[62] Part of Brown's work with Banister (as we shall see in Chapter Twenty-one) was related to Lee Harvey Oswald affecting an association with the so-called Communist-front group known as the New Orleans Committee for Peaceful Alternatives (NOCPA).

James H. Pfister was elected to the Louisiana state house of representatives in 1960 and introduced a bill that established the formation of LUAC the same year. Pfister was the commander of the First District American Legion in 1959.[63] In the course of LUAC's subversive hearings, members were empowered to charge their witnesses with contempt, just like their congressional counterparts in Washington.[64] Banister's relationship with Pfister goes back to at least 1958, when James Pfister, Kent Courtney, Festus Brown, and Banister—all members of the American Legion—voiced opposition to a New Orleans student's plan to attend the Communist-sponsored World Youth Festival in Vienna to promote America. They organized a seminar to warn students about the threat of Communism. Guy Banister, Douglas Caddy, and Medford Evans spoke at the seminar.[65] Courtney and Evans are important figures, since both of these close Banister associates were, in turn, closely associated with General Walker, a purported near victim of a Lee Harvey Oswald bullet

When Lee Harvey Oswald returned to the U.S. from the Soviet Union in June of 1962, two seminal events occurred in the Oswald saga. First, the Louisiana State Legislature enacted the Communist Control Act and the Propaganda Act, the brainchildren of Banister's colleague Judge Leander Perez. The laws provided that anyone advocating integration or other leftist causes tied to a Communist or Communist-front group cited by the attorney general or a congressional committee could face decades in jail—and tens of thousands of dollars in fines. So severe were the penalties that imposing them would have the effect of wiping out the civil rights movement, a clearly desired goal. Senator Eastland's committee labeled nearly every civil rights group as a Communist front, which meant almost anyone in the civil rights movement could be prosecuted under the new laws. Other southern states were expected to follow suit and adopt similar laws as well. The sacred institution of segregation, which was facing extinction through the work of the Kennedy administration, would be saved.

In the introductory wording of the Communist Control Act, warnings about the possible Soviet infiltration and direction of civil rights groups were set forth. The law meant that any individual or group associated with someone like Lee Harvey Oswald, a purported Soviet agent, could incur the same penalties as a murderer or rapist. As will be shown, Oswald affected a relationship with three so-called Communist-front groups: the Fair Play for Cuba Committee, the New Orleans Committee on Peaceful Alternatives, and the Congress of Racal Equality; all of which were tied to the integrationist organization known as the Southern Conference Education Foundation, SCEF. If an investigative agency such as LUAC were to have "uncovered" Oswald's association with those groups, it would have been the kiss of death for them under the state's brutal anti-subversion laws.

The second seminal event in the Oswald saga occurred in June 1962, when collaboration between LUAC and Senator Eastland's Senate Internal Security Subcommittee began. LUAC, and presumably Guy Banister, began planning a raid on the headquarters of the Southern Conference Education Foundation in downtown New Orleans in June 1962, which took place over a year later. Investigators from Eastland's Communist-hunting committee flew to New Orleans in the summer of 1962 to plot strategy for the raid with LUAC, Thomas Burbank of the state police, and—most likely—Banister. (As LUAC's chief investigator, Banister must have been involved.) The raid occurred on October 4, 1963, and involved more than 100 members of law enforcement.

Following the raid, LUAC leaders announced that they not only planned to hold hearings on the purported evidence uncovered of Communist infiltration of SCEF, but they also had obtained the membership list of the New Orleans Committee for Peaceful Alternatives, and planned to investigate the Fair Play for Cuba Committee and the Congress of Racial Equality. Coincidentally, Oswald had purposely begun to engage in activities with all three groups in the summer of 1963. If LUAC could prove any one of those organizations had ties to a known Communist like Oswald it would have meant their dissolution and death under the Communist Control Act. At the same time that the staunch anti-Communist Banister was directing individuals to spy on so-called Communist-front groups, he was seen by eleven or more witnesses with the self-declared Communist himself, Lee Harvey Oswald.

When Banister applied for the investigator's role with LUAC, Festus Brown also recommended Guy Johnson and Jack N. Rogers for the job. Guy Johnson, a close friend of Banister, was a former member of the Office of Naval Intelligence. Jim Garrison claimed in his 1991 book about his investigation that Banister was also a member of the Office of Naval Intelligence (when he was not), in an effort to tie him to a purported U.S. government intelligence operation he claimed was responsible for the Kennedy assassination. Since Johnson was formerly with Naval Intelligence, Banister was too, Garrison implied. What Johnson and Banister actually had in common was that they were two ardent southern racists who investigated integrationists under the guise of searching out Communists.[66] Jack N. Rogers, like James Pfister, began hunting Communists in 1959 while serving on the American Legion Post and National Americanism Committee. Soon after, he became the chief counsel for LUAC under chairman Pfister. Rogers "exposed" the American Friends Service Committee, in 1959, which he called, "a very dangerous foe of segregation." He condemned the ACLU for backing integration.[67] (As we shall see, the ACLU was another leftist organization Oswald had maintained a superficial relationship with.)

Officers from the Louisiana State Police were assigned to assist in the work of the Sovereignty Commission and LUAC and presumably worked with Banister in his position as an investigator. Banister's brother Ross was interviewed by Andrew Sciambra of the D.A.'s office on February 1, 1967, weeks before Garrison's investigation into the assassination became public. Ross Banister may not have been aware they were investigating his brother in connection with the assassination when he told Sciambra he had some materials from his deceased brother, "and would be more than happy to cooperate . . . in the fight against Communism," suggesting he may have believed the D.A.'s office was working in the field of subversion like Guy. Ross told them he would locate the material from his brother and deliver it to the D.A.'s office the next day. He told them of "some other people who may have some material which his brother was working on" and named Colonel Burbank of the Louisiana State Police, (LUAC's) James Pfister, John Garrett, and John McKinley, who was an attorney in Monroe, Louisiana, and former law partner of Governor McKeithen.

By the next day, Ross Banister may have communicated with other members of the far right who had been contacted by Garrison's office and caught wind of their still-secret investigation of the assassination. For whatever reason, he was less forthcoming the next day, telling Sciambra that he did not have much luck finding the papers from his brother. He did tell them one important piece of information: that, on September 15, 1964, Major Wylie of the Louisiana State Police spoke to him about acquiring Guy Banister's files after his death. He told them that Guy's wife, Mary Banister, obtained and Photostatted the files and the expenses were paid by John McKinley. Ross told them that an "ex-agent" was helping her to sell or dispose of his files "or something of that nature." Sciambra concluded, "He was rather hesitant and skeptical about revealing everything that he may know or have had access to."[68] As will be shown in this work, the officers from the state police acquired Banister's files—in all likelihood to conceal his association with Lee Harvey Oswald.

State Police Major Russell M. Willie was interviewed by the HSCA in 1978 and told them about obtaining Banister's files. He stated that the Sovereignty Commission and the Louisiana State Police had employed him. (The state police were assisting the Sovereignty Commission's investigations in the New Orleans area.) He told them that the files that were kept by Banister covered many organizations and individuals that were of interest, but did not further specify, which was more evidence that Banister probably worked for the Sovereignty Commission. Willie said that he and Joseph Cambre of the state police purchased some files in 1964 or 1965, for 500 dollars—approximately one five-drawer file cabinet, which was about half full of manila folders and three-by-five cards. He suggested they contact Joseph Cambre, Ray Thomas, and Billy Joe Booth, who had contacts with "Senator Eastland's Un-American Activities Committee." He stated that Banister had some files on SCEF, and noted that many entities investigated that civil rights group. He told them that SCEF was formerly called the "Southern Regional Communist Party U.S.A., or a title like that." He believed some files pertained to FPCC.[69] When Willie retired from the state police, he went to work as an investigator for Ross Banister, who was employed as an inspector for the State Highway Department.[70]

State Police Officer Joseph Cambre told the HSCA, in 1978, a similar story of assisting Russell Willie to obtain Guy Banister's records from Mary Banister. He later remembered them being destroyed in compliance with the Privacy Act. Cambre had been assigned to the records section of investigations and intelligence in the state police. He worked for the Sovereignty Commission in 1970 and 1971. Cambre confirmed that Banister's files were contained in a five-drawer filing cabinet that was partially full. He recalled the files contained the news of organizations and individuals that were considered subversive or Communistic. He said Banister had extensive records on the integration group Southern Conference Education Fund. There were also many newspaper clippings—he saw files on the Fair Play for Cuba Committee that were mostly news clippings. He remembered a transcription of Oswald's radio debate. (Oswald "debated" Ed Butler, a radical right winger and close associate of Guy Banister, in August 1963, on the radio and Oswald declared he was a Marxist.) He remembered that the FPCC literature had an address on Camp Street and was surprised to learn that 544 Camp was the same address of the building Banister had his office in.[71]

The HSCA interviewed State Police Officer Ray William Thomas in 1978. Thomas was assigned to the Sovereignty Commission in 1960 and 1961 and procured Guy Banister's files after his death in 1964. He told the HSCA that the Sovereignty Commission's interest in the files was to use them to check on people who might cause violence during the period of integration in the state. He said that he believed the Sovereignty Commission files were destroyed or misplaced. He had witnessed the burning of some files from the Louisiana State Police in 1970. He remembered that some of the Banister files contained information on the Fair Play for Cuba Committee.[72]

Banister, LUAC, the State Police, and Senator Eastland's Committee held ongoing investigations into the integrationist Southern Conference Education Fund, which had close ties to several purported Communist-front groups tied to Lee Harvey Oswald. Those critical events in the Oswald story will be discussed at length later within this work.

The Guy Banister Files

Like many right-wing extremists of his day, Guy Banister collected files on American citizens who were supposed Communists or members of Communist-front groups. Banister's files rivaled those of the House Committee on Un-American Activities (HUAC), and its Senate counterpart, the Senate Internal Security Subcommittee (SISS)—the same subcommittee that Banister eagerly assisted in a 1956 inquisition. Banister's "Communists" were the voices of dissidence or supporters of civil rights, voting rights, labor, or the peace movement. According to a Banister friend, Cecilia Pizzo, Banister brought many of the Communist files with him from the Chicago FBI office when he left for New Orleans. According to Joe Newbrough, a detective with Guy Banister from 1958 to 1964, Guy Banister had one of the "last remaining files and indexes on 27,000 Communists in the United States."[73]

After his dismissal from the New Orleans Police Department, Banister took his collection of files to his new office in the Balter Building, a stable for Nazis, segregationists and—later—anti-Castro Cuban activities. In the year 2000, the author located Banister's former partner from the 1950s, Joseph Oster, busily working at his own detective agency in Monroe, Louisiana. Oster commented, about Banister's files, "I always thought he was doing it for the FBI." Oster disliked the practice of filing and Banister's other political activities. "I didn't like doing things that didn't bring money into the office," he stated. It was this problem that resulted in Oster leaving Banister. However, he remained in close contact with Banister until Banister's death in 1964.

According to Oster, Banister's filing system was patterned after the FBI's.[74] Director J. Edgar Hoover learned his filing skills as a young man working as a cataloguer at the Library of Congress. Hoover had an enormous file of newspaper clippings, from over 625 newspapers.[75] Similarly, clipping articles on subversion was one of the main duties of Banister's former secretary Mary Brengel.[76] Hoover's most important ally in Congress was segregationist, Communist hunter, and Banister friend, Senator James O. Eastland of Mississippi, whose Senate duties involved FBI oversight.[77] Hoover's obsession with collecting files on dissidents was such that 35,000 square feet of FBI space was devoted to domestic intelligence, while a mere 23,000 square feet of space was devoted to all other FBI matters.[78]

Another member of the radical right engaged in private sector espionage was Edgar Bundy of the Church League of America. Bundy acquired the Communist files of famed House Committee on Un-American Activities Chief Council J. B. Mathews, and kept them in a library in Wheaton, Illinois. The files were referenced on over seven million index cards. They were kept in a bombproof bunker, surrounded by attack dogs and barbed wire.

The American Security Council (ASC), staffed by former FBI agents, was another repository of files on Communists. The ASC kept extensive files on subversives and performed name checks for employers.[79] One of the goals behind collecting files and performing background checks was largely to put so-called Communists on blacklists for the purpose of barring them from employment. Congress joined the blacklisting effort, and well-known "Communists" were paraded before inquisitions led by Congressmen Martin Dies and Richard Nixon and Senators James O. Eastland and Joseph McCarthy, among others.

Robert DePugh, leader of the ultra-right Minutemen kept extensive files on those he judged to be Communists. Collecting the files was the main focus of his endeavors, not any militia activities, he told the author. DePugh collected files of so-called Communists so that—in the event of a Communist takeover of the U.S.—he could eliminate them by assassination. "Even now the crosshairs are upon you," he wrote in the Minutemen newsletter *On Target*. "If a Communist ever comes into office he will be removed by ballot or bullet." Because of DePugh's long incarceration for weapons violations in the 1960s, the building housing the files fell into disrepair and became ruined by exposure to the weather. DePugh frequently traded files with Dan Smoot of Dallas, and others.[80] Smoot was a friend of Guy Banister and also was a former FBI man and an assistant to J. Edgar Hoover in the early 1950s. Smoot worked on H. L. Hunt's *Life Lines* radio propaganda program and, later, on *Facts Forum* that was co-written by yet another former FBI man, Paul Rothermel—Hunt's security chief. Rothermel was friendly with Guy Banister, and worked with him when his agency provided detective services for Hunt's oil operations—the majority of which were located in Terrebonne and Plaquemines Parishes in Louisiana. Rothermel was also a personal friend of Senator Joseph McCarthy.[81] Smoot eventually published his own radical right-wing propaganda sheet, *The Dan Smoot Report*, and became a prominent member of the John Birch Society (JBS), the Liberty Lobby, and the Minutemen.

DePugh told the author that right-wing publisher Frank Capell had an extensive collection of private files on "Communists." DePugh sought to acquire the collection, but to his dismay, Capell's files ended up at the John Birch Society's headquarters in Belmont, Massachusetts. (Frank Capell wrote the book *The Strange Case of Marilyn Monroe*, in which he advanced the theory that Robert Kennedy was in some way involved in the actress's tragic death due to a drug overdose in 1961. Capell's book fueled wild speculation about Monroe's death and the Kennedys that continues to this day.) Capell also penned derogatory articles on President Kennedy in his *Herald of Freedom* propaganda sheet, and Banister had a copy of Capell's paper in his files. Capell was a great admirer of J. Edgar Hoover, and there are inferences from his correspondence with Hoover that Capell was a recipient of Bureau files.[82]

The John Birch Society's Communist files were kept in what was referred to as the Research Department in Belmont, Massachusetts. In June 1961, Robert Welch called upon JBS members to help compile "the most complete and most accurate files in America on the leading Comsymps, Socialists and liberals."[83] They invited members to submit briefs on subversives in the form of a program known as Members Monthly Messages, or MMM. Banister sent one directly to JBS Director Robert Welch on purported Communist activities at NASA's Mississippi Test Site.[84] Author Frank Donner described the JBS thusly: "The linkages between the intelligence community and the private sector are best illustrated by the John Birch Society. The JBS embrace of intelligence spookery complements its conspiracy obsession." In Chicago, the John Birch Society infiltrated the leftist Students for a Democratic Society, the DuBois Clubs, and other leftist groups.[85]

Billy James Hargis, who was aligned with the JBS and other far-right-wing organizations—and was the nationally known leader of the Christian Crusade—purchased the anti-Communist files of Allen Zoll, a right-wing publisher and notorious anti-Semite.[86] Banister's secretary, Mary Helen Brengel, told the author that Hargis was a friend of Guy Banister who met with him in New Orleans, probably around October 30, 1963, when he was in town for a speech.[87]

George W. Wackenhut was a high-ranking member of the FBI's Domestic Intelligence Unit when he left the Bureau to form the Wackenhut Detective Agency with three other former FBI agents in 1952. His company led the counter-subversive private detective industry, boasting 2.5 million name files with 10,000 additions a week—second only to the FBI. Wackenhut acquired the files of Karl Barslaag, the former HUAC and McCarthy Committee member. George Wackenhut appointed prominent members of the JBS and other right-wingers to the Wackenhut Board of Directors.[88] According to author Frank Donner, file keepers like Banister, Wackenhut, and the others were part of "an ever growing political espionage system that had become an institutional response to dissent."[89]

When District Attorney Garrison learned that the state police received some of Guy Banister's files, he sent his chief investigator, Lou Ivon, to the state capital to retrieve them. Ivon found the files missing, but found the titles of a number of files, recorded them, and relayed the information to Garrison. The author asked Ivon what was the main reason for Garrison's claim that Banister was involved with the CIA. He replied, "it seemed that way by the titles on the files." Garrison listed the titles in his book *On the Trails of Assassins*, claiming they were evidence of Banister's involvement with national intelligence operations, as follows:

AMERICAN CENTRAL AGENCY 20–10
AMMUNITION AND ARMS 32–1
ANTI-SOVIET UNDERGROUND 25–1
B-70 MANNED BOMBER FORCE 15–16
CIVIL RIGHTS PROGRAM OF JFK 8–41
DISMANTLING OF BALLISTIC MISSILE SYSTEM 15–16

DISMANTLING OF DEFENSES, U.S. 15–16
FAIR PLAY FOR CUBA COMMITTEE 23–7
INTERNATIONAL TRADEMART 23–14
ITALY, U.S. BASES DISMANTLED IN ASSEMBLY OF THE UNITED NATIONS 15–16
LATIN AMERICA 23–1
MISSILE BASES DISMANTLED—TURKEY AND ITALY 15–16

At a superficial glance, the files have the intriguing appearance—as Lou Ivon suggested—of government intelligence. However, they were not. Jim Garrison smugly wrote in *On the Trail of Assassins*, after presenting the twelve file titles in the book: "Thus ended the myth of Guy Banister's Private Detective Agency."[90] Garrison suggested that Banister was involved in far more that performing local private detective work, but was actually part of a national intelligence operation concerning military and global matters. In doing so, Garrison, in turn, created another myth—and one with many devotees. His claim is simply contrary to fact. Garrison committed wholesale fraud and deception when he selected the twelve titles without mentioning the existence of over 400 other titles that would have led a reasonable person to conclude that these were the files of a rabid anti-Communist, racist, and anti-Semite engaged in private sector anti-subversive espionage and blacklisting.

The complete list was in the possession of the House Select Committee on Assassinations, although there is no evidence in their report that they took any interest in it. The author obtained the complete list from the National Archives. Former Banister partner Joseph Oster was adamant when he told the author that the titles of Banister's files were always *about* the individual or organization being investigated. It did not mean he had a working relationship with the group listed on the file. In other words, the CIA file would be *about* the CIA and does not imply the CIA collaborated with Banister. The titles referring to the military and disarmament all appear in the "15" series. Importantly, Garrison omitted the fact that most—if not all—of the provocative military titles (for example "Dismantling of Defenses" and "SAC Strategic Air Command, U.S.") came directly from articles in the blacklisting publication called *Counterattack*, and were cited as such in the list of files obtained by Garrison. Banister's file titles on President Kennedy, Helen Gahagan Douglas, Eleanor Roosevelt, Adlai Stevenson, and CIA Director John McCloy were drawn from the same far-right publication. All of these individuals were liberals or New Dealers, considered pro-Communist by the radical right. Scores of other file titles were taken directly, and so indicated on each title, from the racist newsletter *Citizen Report*, the organ of the Southern Louisiana Citizens' Council (where Jackson Ricau, a former investigator for Banister from 1960–61, was the publisher). Banister's close associate Hubert Badeaux was an officer in the group. The overlapping of the topics presented in the *Citizens' Report* and the titles of Banister's files are so distinctive it is more than likely Banister furnished information directly from his files to Ricau to write the articles—or he wrote them himself.

Other files were about the American Friends Service Committee, Harry Bridges, the

Abe Lincoln Brigade, the Anti-Defamation League, and many other individuals and organizations considered leftist or pro-Communist. A number of files were about local integrationists, for example: Dr. Albert D'Orlandi, Rabbi Julian Feibelman, and others connected to integration and SCEF. Other files were about fellow radical rightists or Banister friends, such as Louis Bundez, the *Dan Smoot Report*, Reverend James Parker Dees, General Edwin A. Walker, Robert Welch, Hubert Badeaux, Festus Brown, and the JBS, to name a few. Cubans from the former 544 Camp Street office were title subjects.[91, 92] Further proof of Banister's activities was confirmed by Banister's secretary Mary Brengel, who told Garrison that Banister kept files on integrationists, which is corroborated by his file headings.[93]

Three former FBI special agents founded and published *Counterattack* and its companion book *Red Channels*. The agents' first effort was a monthly magazine called *Plain Talk*, written in collaboration with Isaac Don Levine and Alfred Kohlberg, a founding council member of the John Birch Society. *Counterattack* was described as "a four-page weekly newsletter containing an up-to-the-minute pin pointed and documented exposé of important Communist and Communist 'United front' activities with an unmasking of individuals participating in such activities."[94] Others called it a "blackmail sheet" or "hate sheet;" or "a weekly news sheet which lists names of person it suspects of leftist leanings." *Red Channels* was described as "a vicious publication that destroys character by innuendo and veiled accusations" and "a discredited unofficial publication" that committed "character assassination for profit."[95]

Garrison asserted that the state police went though Banister's files after his death in a "routine check," possibly because Banister's brother had been connected to the state—which was not the case at all. There was nothing "routine" about Banister, his files, and his relationship to the state police. As we shall see in several later chapters, members of the state police were working with LUAC, which Banister was connected with, as well as being connected to Senator Eastland's Committee in an elaborate scheme to show that integrationists and other leftist groups had been infiltrated by Communists from Moscow. It is no coincidence that the groups they intended to prove were Communist-backed were all those that Lee Harvey Oswald had managed to affect an association with in the summer of 1963.

While the Warren Commission was in the midst of their assassination inquiry, Banister (far right), whom they did not investigate, was eulogized in June 1964 in *The Grapevine*, published by the Society of Former Special Agents of the FBI. Dallas County district attorney and former FBI SA Henry Wade was pictured and praised on the cover of the same edition for successfully prosecuting Jack Ruby for the slaying of Lee Harvey Oswald. Source: *The Grapevine*, June 1964, with permission from Executive Director Nancy Savage of the Society of Former Special Agents of the FBI, Inc.

Delphine Roberts went to Banister's house with Ivan Nitschke on the day Banister died in June

1964 while the Warren Commission was in the midst of its deliberations. She told Nitschke she was worried about his files, since Banister cautioned her they would "hurt an awful lot of big name people" if they got into the wrong hands. Banister told her to take possession of the files if "something happens to him."[96] Nitschke recalled the first thing Roberts did after the two discovered Banister had died was to recover his files. The unidentified "big name people" were most likely prominent anti-Communist extremists tied to the Banister operation, like General Walker, H. L. Hunt, Leander Perez and Dr. Alton Oschner, to name a few. Upon Banister's death, his files were procured by—in addition to the Sovereignty Commission—close Banister associates G. Wray Gill, Kent Courtney, Delphine Roberts, Guy Johnson, and others.[97] The files were reportedly sent to Atlanta and microfilms of the complete files were sent to Augusta, Georgia—the home of one of the nation's leading segregation figures, Roy V. Harris, a close Leander Perez associate.[98]

Guy Banister and the Citizens' Council

Guy Banister was a member of the South Louisiana Citizens' Council that published the newsletter the *Citizens' Report*. His friend Hubert Badeaux was the first vice president of the group.[99] Banister was also involved in the Greater New Orleans Citizens' Council directed by his close associates Leander Perez and George Singelmann, whose operation was housed a floor below Banister's Agency in the Balter Building in the late 1950s. The Citizens' Councils were first organized in response to the *Brown* decision in 1954 and supported by arch segregationist Senator James O. Eastland. In Louisiana, leaders also included close Banister associates Willie Rainach and Leander Perez. Some referred to the Councils as the "white-collared Klan." District Attorney Jim Garrison attended the Councils' public meetings at the municipal auditorium.

Banister orchestrated the picketing of the Federal Fifth Circuit Court in New Orleans for the Citizens' Council during court proceedings in connection with African-American James Meredith's attempt to enroll in the then all-white University of Mississippi. At this event, Delphine Roberts and others carried signs bitterly critical of President Kennedy.[100]

Banister eventually ran for New Orleans councilman at large in the April 15, 1961, Democratic primary and declared he was in favor of segregation.[101]

While the activities of the Citizens' Council will be discussed extensively in later chapters, for now let us simply be clear that the leadership, membership, and interests of the Citizens' Councils, LUAC, and the Sovereignty Commission overlapped.

Guy Banister and the Student Spy Apparatus

Guy Banister hired students to infiltrate leftist groups at Tulane University and other colleges. The FBI was aware of one such instance and learned from Banister in 1961 that he had hired William R. Martin, a Tulane Law student, in a part-time position to ascertain the political sympathies of Cubans and other foreign students at Tulane and for the purpose of "ferreting out subversive activities in the State of Louisiana." According to the FBI, "He explained that

Martin would be interested in ascertaining whether or not any pro-Castro people had infiltrated either the FRD or the Friends of Democratic Cuba, Inc." The FRD was an anti-Castro group. They noted further, "This is of interest to Banister in connection with his interest and position in the Louisiana State organization known as the State Joint Legislative Committee on Un-American Activities."[102] This is just one example of Banister's extensive student surveillance operation.

Guy Banister and the National Far Right

Guy Banister was affiliated with most of the prominent national far right organizations of his time, which will be briefly mentioned here and detailed in later chapters. Banister was a member of the John Birch Society, which was founded in 1958 by Robert Welch, who published works openly contemptuous of democracy. Welch famously called President Eisenhower "a dedicated conscious agent of the Communist conspiracy." Banister sent a letter to Welch in Belmont, Massachusetts, in the form of a Members Monthly Messages (or MMM, as noted previously). On August 14, 1963, Robert Welch's secretary, in Welch's absence, sent Banister a letter thanking him for submitting the MMM.[103] Banister colleague General Edwin A. Walker, was a prominent national figure in the group, while Banister's close friend Kent Courtney was the Louisiana state coordinator for the JBS. Jack Ruby, Oswald's murderer, alluded to the involvement of the JBS in Kennedy's assassination in his Warren Commission testimony, as will be presented later.

The author has also found that, unknown until this time, Guy Banister attended the meeting of the Congress of Freedom, COF, in New Orleans in April 1963. The Congress of Freedom was a radical group heavily comprised of members of the John Birch Society, the Citizens' Council, and other groups. At the meeting, an informer for the FBI learned that a plot was underway to assassinate people considered to be Communist-oriented in the Council on Foreign Relations, prominent Jewish figures, and leaders in government and industry. Attending the meeting was Revilo Oliver, an original council member of the JBS; as well as Banister's close friend Kent Courtney, the state JBS coordinator. General Walker's attorney and friend Clyde Watts was a speaker. Because of the importance of this event, an entire chapter is devoted to the landmark 1963 meeting of the Congress of Freedom.

Guy Banister and his close friends Festus J. Brown and Hubert Badeaux were on the Advisory Committee for the New Orleans Indignation Committee (NIC), in 1961, a branch of the national organization.[104] The NIC evolved in Dallas, Texas, and was formed to protest the Kennedy administration's sale of obsolete U.S. jets to Yugoslavia, a Communist bloc country. General Edwin Walker, a Banister friend, used the National Indignation Committee as a vehicle to publicly criticize the Kennedy administration at NIC rallies, while elevating his stature to a leadership position in the national radical right.

Banister subscribed to a number of far-right radical publications, including *The Thunderbolt*, the monthly newspaper of the Nazi-oriented and racist group, the National

States' Rights Party, (NSRP). His secretary, Mary Brengel, recalled seeing reams of Gerald L. K. Smith's publication, the *Cross and Flag*, at Banister's office.[105] Since the 1940s Smith had been the country's most notorious anti-Semite, who also was a leading printer of anti-Semitic tracts. Among Guy Banister's files was a copy of Richard Cotton's June 11 and 12, 1964, newsletter, *Conservative Viewpoint*, that reprinted a letter from General Walker to members of Congress. In the letter, Walker was critical of the 1964 civil rights bill, calling it illegal and destructive to the government of the fifty states.[106] Banister also had a copy of Frank Capell's *Herald of Freedom* in his files. Capell was a friend of General Walker whose name was mentioned in the Warren Commission testimony of Revilo Oliver, a founding council member of the JBS.

Banister was a supporter of the Free Electors campaign scheme, which was the pet project of Leander Perez. The Free Electors scheme was a way to deprive President Kennedy of the state's electoral college votes in an attempt to defeat him in the 1964 election. A Free Elector rally was held at the Capitol House Hotel in Baton Rouge on May 10, 1963. Guy Banister attended the rally, and was named as a representative to the First District.[107] It should come as no surprise that the Sovereignty Commission backed the Free Electors scheme.[108]

In 1961, members of George Lincoln Rockwell's American Nazi Party descended upon New Orleans in a Volkswagen bus dubbed the "Hate Bus" to counter-protest the arrival—also by bus—to the South of the Freedom Bus Riders. (The Freedom Bus rides were organized by the Congress of Racial Equality, and carried integrationists and college students south to protest segregation and to publicly disobey Jim Crow laws.) The Nazis were invited and funded by members of the Banister operation. When the Nazis were arrested for picketing, Banister came to their aid by paying their bail. Nazi Commander Rockwell also visited Banister at his Newman Building office. As evidence presented in Chapter Three will show, Lee Harvey Oswald associated with at least one member—and likely a second member—of Rockwell's Nazi storm troopers in the summer of 1963.

Banister was a member of the American Institute For Freedom Project (AIFP), along with William Irwin. Several others in that group were members of the Information Council of America (INCA), including Dr. Alton Oschner. The AIFP was a collaboration of both the Chamber of Commerce and INCA. Their purpose was to assist INCA in the development of "freedom tapes" which were to be distributed to Latin America to combat Communism. Local Congress of Freedom leader George Soule was also a member.[109] As we shall see later, Lee Harvey Oswald proclaimed he was a Marxist when he debated INCA officer Ed Butler—who supported the anti-Communist position—on the radio. Butler, once a John Birch Society member, was a close associate of Guy Banister. The Oswald-Butler debate (which will be detailed later in this work) is one of several examples of Oswald publicly flaunting his supposed Communist credentials with a far-right-wing member of the Banister operation acting as his adversary.

Banister was also a member of the Advisory Committee of the Greater New Orleans School of Anti-Communism directed by Dr. Fred Schwartz of California from October 21 to

27, 1961, along with other local notables. Serving on the faculty were national figures of the far right Herbert Philbrick, Phyllis Schlafly, W. Cleon Skousen, and others. The press wrote of Philbrick, the featured speaker: "It was obvious that Philbrick himself was doing an excellent job of winning youthful hearts and minds. So many college students pressed around him as the conference progressed, it was hard to carry on at times. They asked for his autograph." Philbrick defended the John Birch Society, stating, "I never met a John Birch Society member who was advocating overthrow of the government."[110] (It should be noted that Philbrick was, actually, a spy for the FBI who pretended to be a Communist. An exaggerated book and a television show entitled *I Led Three Lives* were produced based on Philbrick's experiences. The TV show, which aired from 1953 to 1955 was Lee Harvey Oswald's favorite and may have been a model for his career as a Communist, or for his life posing as one.) Robert Morris was also on the faculty of the Anti-Communist School. Morris's relationship with Guy Banister dates back to their mutual participation in Eastland's 1956 hearing on the purported Soviet influence of leftist and integrationist groups in New Orleans. Morris represented General Walker in his troubles with the Kennedy administration which arose from accusing President Truman and former First Lady Eleanor Roosevelt of being pro-Communist. (After an investigation, General Walker was relieved of his command.) Morris and Guy Banister's close friend Medford Evans represented Walker in the hearings that followed. As we shall see later, Morris was a member of General Walker's Dallas Minutemen in 1963, a group that plotted violence against their enemies on the left.

Banister was also a member of Meyer Lowman's Circuit Riders. Lowman compiled massive files on presumed Communists. He provided his files and expertise in sworn testimony, like Banister, to state and congressional Communist inquiries, as well as to the Citizens' Councils.[111]

As noted, Banister and his close associates Hugh Ward and Maurice Gatlin were Minutemen. The Minutemen funded Cuban exile leader Rudolph Ricardo Davis, a Banister associate who had an encounter with Lee Harvey Oswald. Two out-of-state Minutemen, Jerry Milton Brooks and Richard Lauchli—top-ranking aids to Minuteman leader Robert DePugh—worked in New Orleans with the Banister operation, making it a virtual satellite office of the national Minutemen organization located in Norborne, Missouri.

Guy Banister and the Anti-Castro Cubans

Guy Banister told the FBI, on February 3, 1961, that he served on the first board of directors of the Friends of Democratic Cuba, whose mission was to solicit funds to obtain field hospital materials, medical supplies, and other items to assist the anti-Castro Cuban effort. (As of February 1961, their main accomplishment was providing fifty Cuban exile girls residing in the Ursulines Convent with toothpaste, bedding, and other small items.) Banister told the FBI he was not a member of a group called the Anti-Communist League of the Caribbean, but had done some investigative work for its director, Maurice Gatlin, regarding trucks allegedly scheduled for shipment to Cuba.[112] New Orleans FBI Special Agent Regis Kennedy, a Banister associate, was involved with Friends of Democratic Cuba (primarily a public relations and fundraising operation to assist the Cuban Revolutionary Council) and reportedly met with a former Banister employee, Bill Dalzell, to discuss the operation.[113] Banister was also an officer in the Free Voice of Cuba, also known as Radio Cuba Libre, with Festus Brown.[114]

Carlos Bringuier is the first of six anti-Communist Cubans presented here who had direct contact with Lee Harvey Oswald in 1963. Bringuier had ties to the Cuban Revolutionary Council which was formerly housed at the 544 Camp Street address and helped obtain supplies for the Friends of Democratic Cuba.[115] He claimed Oswald entered his clothing store in August 1963 and offered to train anti-Communist Cubans in the fight against Castro. Later, Bringuier, a staunch anti-Castro Cuban, got into a half-hearted scuffle with Oswald while he was passing out pro-Castro literature with the 544 Camp Street address of Banister's office building stamped on it. The two were arrested, and Bringuier went to Banister's close friend Kent Courtney for advice. After that, the two agreed to a radio debate wherein Oswald admitted he was a Marxist. Ed Butler, a Banister colleague, also debated Oswald, taking the opposing view on Communism. A characteristic of Oswald's activities in 1963 was that whenever he was engaged in some kind of act or demonstration, someone with ties to the Banister operation played the adversary.

Numerous witnesses saw Sergio Arcacha Smith with Oswald in the summer of 1963. Smith was the second of six Cubans tied to the 544 Camp Street office address just above Guy Banister's office. Arcacha Smith, however, denied knowing Oswald, claiming he had left the city by the summer of 1963. Arcacha Smith was closely associated with Guy Banister and was seen many times with him. Arcacha Smith operated the Crusade to Free Cuba and Cuban Revolutionary Council formerly based at the 544 Camp Street office, as well.[116] On January 21, 1962, a parade was held on Canal Street followed by a door-to-door campaign to raise funds for the Crusade.[117] John Irion, who served with Oswald in David Ferrie's Civil Air Patrol Unit in 1956, recalled that, in the summer of 1963, Ferrie and his cadets collected money on Canal Street for the anti-Castro effort.[118] Remarkably, that same summer, former Ferrie cadet Oswald passed out *pro*-Castro literature on Canal Street. According to unnamed Cuban exiles interviewed by Jim Garrison, local Cubans despised Arcacha Smith and saw him as their enemy. Ferrie was a key associate in Arcacha Smith's organization and played a substantial role. In fact, one of Ferrie's former CAP cadets, Layton Martens, became second in command to Arcacha Smith in 1961.[119] Many of the Cuban exiles were aware of Ferrie's homosexuality and morals charges and, as a result, thought Arcacha Smith's association with him was an embarrassment that undermined the operation. Arcacha Smith was terminated from the CRC, for stealing funds for his own use, on September 18, 1962.[120] In 1967, Jim Garrison fraudulently tried to pass off the ragtag anti-Castro operation run by the odd couple of Ferrie and Arcacha Smith as a capable, CIA-backed operation for the second invasion of Cuba.

Arnesto Rodriquez, Jr. is the third of six Cuban exiles presented here with ties to the Crusade to Free Cuba at 544 Camp Street, and who had direct contact with Lee Harvey Oswald in 1963. After Kennedy's assassination, the FBI and the Secret Service descended upon the 544 Camp Street office in the Newman Building when they discovered one of the booklets Oswald had handed out in his FPCC demonstration bore the 544 Camp Street address of the office above Banister. Corliss Lamont, a well-known target of the anti-Communists, wrote the booklet Oswald passed out, called *The Crime Against Cuba*. They learned that Arnesto Rodriquez, Jr. and his father, Arnesto Rodriquez, Sr., were both members of the Cuban Revolutionary Council and the Crusade to Free Cuba that had once operated out of the 544 Camp Street office.[121] Building owner Sam Newman said he rented the office to the CRC and the Crusade from October 1961 to February 1962.[122] The Secret Service interviewed Arnesto Rodriquez, Sr. after the assassination, and he told them he had never seen Oswald before. He related that Sergio Arcacha Smith once worked out of the office at 544 Camp Street, but left before the assassination because he had lost favor in the Cuban exile community. He reported Smith stole from the group's funds for his personal use. As a result, he was fired from the CRC and left town.[123] On November 26, 1963, Dr. Guillermo Aguirre of Mexico told an officer of the United States Information Service that Maria Rodriquez de Lopez told him that her son-in-law, Arnesto Rodriquez, Jr., was well acquainted with Lee Harvey Oswald and that they were friends. She told them he ran a language school and had tape-recorded a conversation with Oswald.[124, 125] The Secret Service secured the tape and found out it was from Oswald's radio debate with Carlos Bringuier after the two scuffled during Oswald's pamphleting.[126] On November 25, 1963, Arnesto Rodriquez, Jr. (who happened to be an FBI informant on Latin American matters) told the FBI that Oswald approached him at his Modern Language School on St. Charles Street sometime after July 24, 1963, and asked him about taking a course in Spanish, and about Cuban affairs in general. Rodriquez purportedly told Oswald he was busy and to come back at another time. He claimed Oswald never did.[127] Oswald was out of work and trying to support a wife and two children at the time—he could ill afford to take Spanish lessons. It can be assumed that Rodriquez was likely providing an alibi as to why he had contact with the would-be presumed murderer of the president. Rodriquez was authorized to sign checks for the CRC. Carlos Bringuier was once a member of the CRC, but left to become the New Orleans delegate of the Directorio Revolucionario Estudiantil (DRE).[128] In a 1979 interview with Anthony Summers (author of the book *Conspiracy* that theorized that President Kennedy might have been assassinated by a rogue element of the CIA), Rodriquez admitted meeting Oswald, but had forgotten the Spanish language school story he told years before. He said Oswald came to him offering to help train anti-Castro Cuban exiles in guerilla techniques—something he neglected to tell law enforcement in 1963. Carlos Bringuier also claimed Oswald offered to train anti-Castro Cubans, allegations which are completely contradictory to Oswald's professed pro-Castro sentiment.[129] Arnesto Rodriquez, Jr. gave Carlos Bringuier a sign he hung in his French Quarter clothing store, Casa Roca, that read, "Cuba lies in chains."[130]

Andrew Sciambra, from Garrison's office, interviewed Arnesto Rodriquez, Jr. on February 13, 1967, noting that his name appeared on the letterhead of Crusade to Free Cuba. Rodriquez repeated the story that Oswald talked to him about taking a Spanish language course, and about Cuba in general. In a new wrinkle, he told Sciambra that Oswald knew about the training camps across Lake Pontchartrain from talking to Carlos Bringuier. There is nothing, however, in Bringuier's numerous statements to law enforcement noting that he told Oswald about the training camps. Rodriquez also told Sciambra that Bringuier knew David Ferrie.[131]

A week later, on February 20, 1967, Rodriquez briefed the FBI about his interrogation by Garrison's office. He told them Garrison's interest in him stemmed from his name being on FRD letterhead. He told them that Garrison had information that Arcacha Smith, Carlos Quiroga, and Richard Davis had offices at 544 Camp Street. Rodriquez was asked about the training camps across the lake and he told them that Richard Davis directed the camp, which involved a dozen or so anti-Communist Cubans. He told them some Cubans were angry with Davis for diverting funds for his own use, when they were intended to feed the Cubans. He repeated his story about Oswald and the language school, now watered down, telling them "a man" came to him about taking a language course who might have been Oswald. Garrison asked Rodriquez about his FBI duties, and he said the FBI would call upon him from time to time with questions about Latin America.

In the midst of Rodriquez's briefing of the FBI on questions posed by Garrison's office on the intriguing matters of the anti-Castro movement and Oswald, Rodriquez reported that Garrison changed the subject 180 degrees to the issue of the integration movement, without expressly saying so. He related that Garrison had asked him if he knew attorneys Benjamin Smith or Bruce Walzer, not mentioning the fact that they were two of New Orleans' best known integrationists. Rodriquez told them he knew Walzer because his wife had worked for him. Investigators asked him if he knew of any connection between Walzer and Smith and the Fair Play for Cuba Committee, Crusade to Free Cuba, or any of the notable Cuban exiles tied to Guy Banister.[132]

The integrationist Southern Conference Education Fund housed in the central business district of New Orleans was Guy Banister's arch nemesis; his files overflowed with intelligence on SCEF and its leaders. Unlike other integrationist groups, SCEF had no membership, which made it difficult for Banister to penetrate. As we shall later see, one of Banister's young informants was able to break into the SCEF office in 1959. Remarkably, Banister associate Arnesto Rodriquez, Jr. did manage to penetrate the SCEF operation when his wife went to work for Bruce Walzer, who was closely associated with SCEF. The odds that Oswald's alleged visit to Rodriquez's St. Charles Street language school was a coincidence are slim. More likely, the story was fabricated as a pre-emptive alibi should witnesses come forth and identify the two together at the school or elsewhere. Rodriquez's mother-in-law's comment that Rodriquez and Oswald were close friends more likely represents the truth of the matter.

Carlos Quiroga was the fourth of six Cuban exiles with ties to the Crusade to Free Cuba who had direct contact with Lee Harvey Oswald. On August 16, 1963, after Oswald handed out his pro-Castro literature on Canal Street, Carlos Bringuier purportedly told Carlos Quiroga to visit Oswald at his Magazine Street apartment to inquire about his

Fair Play for Cuba Committee chapter and his motives. Quiroga, accompanied by Rudolph Ricardo (Richard) Davis, allegedly met with Oswald at his apartment for about an hour, and Oswald gave him an application to join his FPCC chapter.[133] Bringuier told the FBI that Carlos Quiroga was not formally a member of Crusade to Free Cuba, but simply participated in the group's meetings for the purpose of creating unity between the CRC and the Student Revolutionary Directorate. Quiroga claimed he had no idea why Oswald used the CRC/544 Camp Street address on the booklet he passed out. After the Cubans vacated the 544 Camp Street office, Quiroga and Arcacha Smith ran the operation out of Banister's office, according to the building owner. Banister, Smith, and Quiroga were often seen having coffee at Mancuso's restaurant in the front of the building.[134] Quiroga failed a lie detector test given to him by Garrison about his knowledge of Oswald. His claim that he met with Oswald to determine his motives was likely a cover story, as well.

A fifth anti-Castro Cuban had admitted contact with Lee Harvey Oswald. Frank Bartes, a CRC delegate (and FBI informant), got into a heated public argument with Oswald following Oswald and Bringuier's court appearance for the scuffle. When the media surrounded Oswald for a statement, Bartes got into an argument with them because he felt they were not granting enough time for the Cubans to present their anti-Castro views. The incident garnered more publicity for Oswald.[135] Bartes addressed a crowd with Carlos Bringuier in May of 1963, on the sixty-first anniversary of the founding of Cuba, and told them that the Cubans had the feeling that the American people had let them down. He declared that the Cubans would take back their own country.[136] Bartes told the HSCA he had never visited the 544 Camp Street office of Arcacha Smith between 1961 and 1962. It's not known if they asked him about Guy Banister, or if he had visited the Newman Building in 1963. HSCA investigator Gaeton Fonzi concluded that the New Orleans chapter of the CRC had no relationship with, and/or knowledge of, the activities of Lee Harvey Oswald, other than Bartes's brief encounter with him at the courthouse. He refused to disclose to the HSCA the agent's name that he frequently reported to, which is odd, to say the least, but it would not be surprising if it were Regis Kennedy, Banister's friend.[137]

Before the Kennedy assassination, the FBI checked on Oswald's possible Communist and Cuban ties in New Orleans. On September 9, 1963, they asked one of their informants who was familiar with some phases of Communists Party activity if he knew Oswald. They also asked Frank Bartes, an FBI informant on Cuban affairs, if he knew Oswald. Both told them Oswald was unknown to them.[138] Bartes has now been caught in a lie, missed by the Warren Commission, FBI, and HSCA. A month before he reported to the FBI that he did not know Oswald, he had been standing beside him with the media in the courtroom after the sentencing in the Bringuier scuffle. There were no consequences of lying to the FBI on September 9, 1963, because they would probably never know the truth. But lying to them after the November 22 assassination and the scrutiny that followed would cast certain suspicion on Bartes. After all, plenty of witnesses were there in the courtroom while Oswald, Bringuier, and Bartes talked to the media after the sentencing for the scuffle.

Rudolph Ricardo (Richard) Davis, Jr., the sixth of six Cubans tied to the Banister operation and the CRC who had direct ties to Oswald, knew Guy Banister, David Ferrie, and Sergio Arcacha Smith. He told Garrison's investigators that he witnessed Oswald handing out leaflets on Canal Street and that he had seen his scuffle with Carlos Bringuier. He also told Jim Garrison he saw Oswald with Layton Martens, David Ferrie's roommate. Later, he said that Oswald held a meeting at Lee Circle to protest the treatment of Cuba. Davis recalled that he and Carlos Quiroga went to Oswald's house on Magazine Street one night and were introduced to Oswald by Quiroga, who told Davis—who was involved in the training camps north of Lake Pontchartrain—that he wanted to infiltrate Oswald's organization.[139]

Setting aside the cover stories given by the Cubans in contact with Oswald, a 1967 FBI report gives a more telling account of the anti-Castro effort and the Banister operation. According to an FBI report dated July 3, 1967, C. P. H. Bell of Traveler's Insurance Company of Houston, where Ricardo Davis worked, learned of information relative to the Kennedy assassination from a coworker and friend of Davis. When Jim Garrison's assassination investigation became public in February 1967, Bell was prompted to report the incident to the FBI. The co-worker related that Rudolph Ricardo Davis told him an anti-Castro group known as the Minutemen paid for his living expenses. Davis allegedly stated that Lee Harvey Oswald was connected in some manner with the Minutemen organization. (In early pronouncements about the assassination, Garrison claimed the Minutemen were involved. That rapidly changed after the investigation became public and, instead, Garrison claimed that U.S. intelligence was involved.) The FBI interviewed Ricardo Richard Davis on July 17, 1967, and he denied any association with the Minutemen, but admitted that he did receive financial assistance from the John Birch Society. Davis told the FBI he met Lee Harvey Oswald on two occasions in connection with his anti-Castro activities. He encountered him when Oswald was pamphleting and when he went to Oswald's apartment with Carlos Quiroga to obtain information regarding Oswald's pro-Castro campaign. (As noted, Davis and Quiroga were both tied to the Crusade to Free Cuba in Banister's office building that once had offices at the 544 Camp Street address.) Davis told them that the training of the Cubans took place on the estate of De La Barre, who was closely associated with the John Birch Society. Davis had set up the training site for the Cubans with the assistance of the JBS. Occasionally, they would put on demonstrations for wealthy members of the JBS and solicit funding from them. Davis envisioned one day obtaining one million dollars from the JBS to assist him in overthrowing Castro's government.[140] Minutemen leader Robert DePugh told the author that he was involved with procuring armaments for the anti-Castro effort.[141]

Davis's claim that Oswald was a Minuteman is not surprising, considering so many witnesses saw him coming and going from Banister's office, as we shall see. Furthermore, Banister and his partner Hugh Ward were both Minutemen. Two prominent out-of-town members of the Minutemen were tied to Banister's operation, as well. A top aide to the leader of the Minutemen, Jerry Brooks, worked out of Banister's office. According to Davis and several other witnesses, high-ranking Minuteman Richard Lauchli attended the training camps.[142] Davis also recounted that prominent members of the John Birch Society were invited to watch the camp spectacle. Other sources noted that two members of the American Nazi Party were also at the training camps.[143] Banister was clearly tied to all of these ultra-rightist groups or individuals.

During Garrison's investigation, an anonymous informant wrote him a letter regarding the Banister operation and Cuba. The informant stated that he was traveling around the country when he settled in New Orleans in 1961. He visited the office of Friends of Democratic Cuba, which he learned was a front for a scheme to invade Cuba. Through that connection, he met Guy Banister and learned he was a former FBI man and private investigator. He related that Banister "had some kind of delusion of grandeur" about obtaining a high office in Cuba after Castro was overthrown. He supposedly had a grand scheme to organize a "black brigade" of anti-Communist *banditos*, which was to be named "Banister's bastards" to fight South and Central American Communists "anywhere and everywhere" with funding from the governments of the countries involved. He identified Sergio Arcacha Smith as the chief spirit in New Orleans for the organization's plans for invasion. The anonymous informant identified several men connected to Banister, including Dr. Jose Del Haya, "Tiger Jim," and Joseph Moore, whose names were mentioned by others in the Garrison investigation lending credibility to his allegations.[144]

Armaments and Cubans flowed in and out of Banister's office, described as a "Cuban Grand Central Station." However, there is no evidence that the efforts of Banister, Ferrie, and their motley assortment of John Birch Society, Minutemen, American Nazi Party members, and a dozen or so Cubans amounted to much in the final analysis. Dysfunction ran throughout their meager anti-Castro operation. The leader of the New Orleans Cuban effort, Sergio Arcacha Smith lost respect among his followers for stealing the movement's funds, forcing him to resign and leave town. Rudolph Ricardo Davis who had been in charge of the militia camps north of Lake Pontchartrain was similarly disgraced for stealing the movement's funds. David Ferrie, who trained a group of teenage boys for action against Castro, was considered a joke among many Cubans as a result of his arrests for crimes against nature, homosexuality, and freakish appearance. Evidence of government or CIA sponsorship of the camps—as Jim Garrison and many conspiracy theorist's claim—is lacking. It's known that the CIA considered using Guy Banister and Associates for the collection of foreign intelligence, but had second thoughts.[145] Banister's history of violence and far-right extremism may have been factors in their decision.

Guy Banister after the Assassination

After the Kennedy assassination, the FBI investigated the 544 Camp Street address found on one of Oswald's handouts. FBI Special Agent Earnest C. Walls, Jr. telephoned Guy Banister on November 25, 1963. Banister told him that Sergio Arcacha Smith had an office at the 544 Camp Street address. He said he saw a young Cuban man with Smith on a number of occasions but could not recall his name. Astonishingly, the synopsis of the interview consisted of two sentences, and there was no indication that Banister was asked anything about Oswald or his FPCC literature bearing the address of the office above his.[146] That was the full extent of the FBI's dealings with Guy Banister in connection with the assassination. It's not known if the Warren Commission took notice of the memo on Banister, since Banister's name is not mentioned anywhere in the Warren Commission Report—or in its twenty-six volumes of supporting evidence.

Five days after President Kennedy's assassination, the New Orleans Police Department interviewed building owner Sam Newman asking about the office space that was being leased to FPCC. Newman told investigators that about fifteen months earlier he had leased the office to the "Cuban Revolutionary Society" and that "Guy Banister was well acquainted with this organization." He claimed to know nothing about Lee Harvey Oswald, a man named Hidell (Oswald's alias), or FPCC. He told them Louis Rabel headed the Cuban organization.[147] Newman recalled being introduced to Sergio Arcacha Smith and Carlos Quiroga.[148] Newman related that Arcacha Smith ran the Cuban Revolutionary Democratic Front from the 544 Camp Street office in the last three months of 1961. The group never paid rent, although they pledged to pay with money expected to come from Miami. Guy Banister talked Newman into letting them use the space for free. They had a shortwave radio that Carlos Quiroga operated. After they vacated the 544 Camp Street office, Arcacha Smith and Quiroga congregated at Banister's office and often had coffee at Mancuso's in the building. When Banister died in 1964, he owed eight months rent.[149] Newman recalled that Banister and Arcacha Smith were very close and he saw them together most times he visited the building. He also saw David Ferrie at the 544 Camp Street office, as well as at Banister's office below it.[150] Despite plentiful information to the contrary, the Warren Commission came to the conclusion that, "neither the Fair Play for Cuba Committee nor Lee Harvey Oswald ever maintained an office at that address."[151]

Guy Banister was at Delphine Roberts's home the evening before his death. While there, he told her he did not feel well and made her aware of the fact that he'd had a heart attack two years earlier.[152] The next day, Roberts tried to contact Banister by phone several times. When he didn't answer, she contacted Ivan Nietzsche and they went to the residence and found him lying dead in bed.[153] Mary Brengel told the author that she and Delphine Roberts had planned to meet Banister at Audubon Park to counterprotest the peaceniks on the day he died, but all she knew at the time was that he didn't show up. Guy Banister died on June 6, 1964, at age sixty-three, in his apartment at 1031 Moss Street in New Orleans. An autopsy revealed a thrombosis of the left coronary artery, with evidence of recent and old heart attacks.[154]

The Communist

In stark contrast to the rabid anti-Communist Guy Banister, Lee Harvey Oswald was a Communist, or at least posed as one. Oswald was named after the Confederate General Robert E. Lee, who commanded Southern rebels in the war with the Union, and fought to preserve slavery. Oswald liked the name so much he planned to name a future son "Lee Lee." His father and brother were both named Robert Lee Oswald. According to fellow marine Peter Connor, Oswald "claimed to be named after Robert E. Lee, whom he characterized as the greatest man in history."[155]

Oswald's father died before he was born. An impoverished and overbearing mother, Marguerite Oswald, who worked as a practical nurse, raised him. Difficult economic conditions forced Mrs. Oswald to move in with her other son John Pic in New York City, where Oswald often refused to attend school with African Americans. According to his brother John Pic, "Lee Harvey Oswald did not like the school because Negroes attended along with white children."[156] The truant young Oswald passed his time riding the subways and visiting the Bronx Zoo. In 1953, a truancy officer described Oswald as "surly" and noted he had referred to the officer as a "damned Yankee."[157] Mrs. Oswald and her son Lee moved back to New Orleans in 1954.

Oswald's favorite TV show was *I Led Three Lives*, which aired from 1953 to 1956. The show was essentially a work of fiction loosely based on Herbert Philbrick's career posing as a Communist and infiltrating leftist or Communist groups as an informant for the FBI. If anyone aspired to be a phony Communist for the purpose of infiltrating and identifying supposed Communists in leftist groups, then Philbrick's exaggerated TV show provided a terrific how-to guide.

From 1955 to 1956, Oswald belonged to Captain David Ferrie's Civil Air Patrol. Ferrie was a brilliant, yet bizarre, airline pilot and fanatical anti-Communist who often threw parties for—and had sex with—the teen cadets. Nonetheless, many of Ferrie's cadets had an intense loyalty toward him; he was often described as "mesmerizing." As part of the Civil Air Patrol, Ferrie taught the cadets advanced aeronautics. Oswald had a passionate desire to follow in his brother Robert's footsteps and join the marines. Robert recalled his mother telling him about a man in a uniform coming to her house and encouraging her to allow Lee to join the marines. It is more than likely that that man was David Ferrie, the only person Oswald knew who wore a military-style uniform. Oswald began to act like a Communist in 1956, at the same time, paradoxically, that he was under the guidance of Ferrie, who was a fanatical anti-Communist. Around that time, when he was sixteen, he also lied about his age and tried—but failed—to join the marines. Oswald yearned to join the marines, who ostensibly trained to fight the Communists in the ongoing Cold War with the Soviet Union—which was also clearly contradictory and noteworthy for a supposed budding Communist. In 1956, Oswald tried to join William Wulf's Astronomy Club. He told Wulf he admired Communism and wanted to join a Communist cell. It appears David Ferrie had a hand in nurturing Oswald in this Communist-posing escapade. Immediately after the assassination, Ferrie contacted Wulf to ask him about his recollections of Oswald at that time.

Also in 1956, Guy Banister and Hubert Badeaux assisted Senator Eastland's New Orleans inquisitions on the so-called Soviet infiltration of the integration movement. Following the hearings, Badeaux wrote to a prominent segregation leader, saying that he was grooming an individual to infiltrate leftist groups on college campuses. Oswald fit the unnamed individual's description, as we shall see in subsequent chapters. Badeaux, like Banister, was well versed in Communist methods.

Former Ferrie CAP cadet James R. Lewallen exemplified the fierce allegiance some cadets had to Ferrie. Lewallen met Ferrie in 1948 in his CAP unit at the Cleveland, Ohio, municipal airport. At the time, Ferrie was a teacher at Benedictine High School and taught aeronautics. After Ferrie left Cleveland for New Orleans in 1951, Lewallen remained in touch with him. In 1953, Lewallen followed Ferrie to New Orleans and moved in with him. In 1958, Lewallen went on active duty in the air force for a year and returned to New Orleans. While the FBI was investigating Ferrie after the Kennedy assassination, they asked Lewallen to accompany them to Ferrie's apartment to look for photos of Oswald, based on the allegation made by Banister employee Jack Martin that Ferrie knew Oswald and had a CAP photo of him at his apartment.[158]

On his seventeenth birthday, in 1956, Oswald joined the marines, where he chose to work in the field of aeronautics. It would not be surprising if his choice was the result of the teachings and mentorship of David Ferrie. After serving three undistinguished years in the marines, Oswald arrived in Moscow in October of 1959. He entered the American Embassy, tossed his passport down, and renounced his American citizenship. He told them he intended to share with the Soviets all his knowledge from his tenure in the marines. One of the American Consular officials noticed something peculiar about Oswald's phrasing and had the feeling, "he was following a pattern of behavior in which he had been tutored by a person or people unknown . . . seemed to be using words he had learned, but did not fully understand. In short, it seemed to me there was a possibility that he had been in contact with others before or during his Marine Corps tour who had guided him and encouraged him in his actions."[159] Correspondent Pricilla Johnson interviewed Oswald in Moscow in 1959 and he told her, "I was brought up like every southern boy, to hate Negroes." He claimed Socialism changed his view. While describing the racial strife in the U.S., he used the term "nigger," a term egalitarian Communists did not use.[160]

When he returned, in June 1962, from the Soviet Union to Fort Worth, Texas, Oswald's first order of business was to write a renunciation of Communism, which he paid to have professionally typed with what little money he had. No sooner than that was accomplished he began writing to various U.S. Communist organizations, including the Communist Party U.S.A., the Socialist Labor Party and the Socialist Workers Party, embellishing his credentials as a Communist in the U.S. He corresponded with the head of the Fair Play for Cuba Committee in New York, and established his own one-man chapter in New Orleans— which the Warren Commission called "a product of his imagination." Banister's colleague, Senator James O. Eastland, had already established in hearings of his Senate Internal Subversion Subcommittee that FPCC was a Communist-front organization financed by Castro.

Still again, paradoxically, the only friends Oswald made upon his return to the U.S. were White Russians, Russian aristocrats who were fanatically *against* Communism. Thomas

Beckham claimed to know Oswald. He reported that Oswald told him Communism was Jewish because Karl Marx was a Jew, a favorite claim of anti-Semites.

Most, if not all, of Lee Harvey Oswald's public theatrics involved an associate of Guy Banister acting as his adversary. In April 1963, Oswald was involved in some way with a shooting at General Edwin Walker's Dallas home, and admitted his involvement to his wife. He ostentatiously handed out pro-Castro literature in downtown New Orleans and got into a scuffle with anti-Castro Carlos Bringuier. He debated Ed Butler, a staunch anti-Communist on the radio. In each of those instances, his supposed adversaries (General Walker, Carlos Bringuier, and Ed Butler) were all close associates of Guy Banister. Oswald engaged in two other public incidents involving the New Orleans Committee for Peaceful Alternatives and the Congress of Racial Equality in the seventeen-month period from his return to the U.S. until his death, which follow a similar pattern. (Those incidents will be detailed in later chapters.) Another characteristic of Oswald's public acts, as in the case of the Walker shooting incident, the Bringuier scuffle, and the Kennedy assassination itself, was that Oswald *expected to get arrested*. (A full explanation for that remarkable claim will be forthcoming in later chapters.) All things considered, when a closer look at Oswald is taken, he begins to look a lot more like Guy Banister and a lot less like Karl Marx.

Lee Harvey Oswald and Guy Banister: The Witnesses

At least eleven witnesses saw Lee Harvey Oswald with Guy Banister in the summer of 1963. Each allegation will be described here, and their stories will be expanded upon in later chapters.

Guy Banister was not a subject of the FBI's investigation of the assassination for the Warren Commission, a fact likely the result of his close association with Director J. Edgar Hoover and New Orleans FBI SA Regis Kennedy. It was New Orleans District Attorney Jim Garrison who first began investigating Banister in 1966. David F. Lewis was the first witness to attest that he saw Lee Harvey Oswald in the company of Guy Banister. On December 15, 1966, before Garrison's assassination investigation became public, Lewis gave a statement to Garrison's office about meeting Lee Harvey Oswald in the late summer of 1963. He had never been questioned by the FBI or any other law enforcement agency prior to this time. Lewis had been employed by Banister from January 1961 through January 1962 as a private investigator. In the summer of 1963, Lewis was out of work and reported to the Louisiana State Employment office at 601 Camp Street. At the time, he could only find work doing odd jobs. He stopped in several times at Banister's office in the Newman Building at Camp and Lafayette Streets to see if they had any "legwork" to be done. On one occasion, he stopped in at Mancuso's restaurant, which occupied the front—or Camp Street—side of Banister's office building before going to Banister's office. He noticed Sergio Arcacha Smith, a man named Carlos, and a man he was introduced to as "Lee Harvey" in the restaurant. Later, after watching the murder of Oswald on TV, he identified the man in the restaurant as Lee Harvey Oswald. Lewis recalled that Oswald didn't talk much and appeared eager to get on his way. Lewis stated that he appeared highly nervous and with boundless energy. Oswald and Arcacha Smith were involved in some business that dealt with Cuba, which Lewis stated was more or less a racket to acquire funds. Lewis recalled seeing Oswald "three or four times in the neighborhood of Lafayette and Camp Street and Banister's office in the Newman Building." A few days before or after meeting Oswald at Mancuso's, he saw a young man with sandy hair in Banister's office with David Ferrie who "could have very well been Oswald." Each time he saw Oswald in the company of Carlos. Lewis stated that "Carlos" had quite a few closed-door meetings with Banister.[161] Garrison later identified "Carlos" as Carlos Quiroga, a friend of Carlos Bringuier. Lewis was given a lie detector test, regarding whether or not he had seen Oswald at Banister's office, and passed.[162] In a story printed in the *New Orleans Times–Picayune,* Lewis told the paper that he met with Garrison and singled out four to five men he felt were involved in the assassination. He told them he feared for his life and his family's lives.[163] On January 2, 1967, Lewis claimed that while he was driving through the French Quarter a man with a dark complexion in a car shot at him with a small revolver.[164]

Tom Bethell was an Englishman serving on Garrison's staff who kept a behind-the-scenes diary of the Garrison case. On September 9, 1967, he asked Garrison what he thought of Lewis as a witness. Garrison replied that he didn't have much of an opinion. Bethell pointed out a problem with Lewis's recollection, noting that when he was initially interviewed by Garrison on December 14, 1966, he was quite sure he saw "Lee Harvey" at Mancuso's restaurant in 1961 at the time when Oswald was in the U.S.S.R. Garrison told Bethell that Lewis later corrected the date.[165] Bethell subsequently wrote a summary of his investigation entitled "Recapitulation of activity in New Orleans." Bethell interviewed David Lewis again on December 16, 1967, and during the interview Lewis's wife reminded him that they both had seen David Ferrie and "Lee Harvey" at Mancuso's restaurant. Garrison was excited about Mrs. Lewis's revelation and noted in the margin "IMP!.....!! See Lou!!!" a reference to his chief investigator Lou Ivon.[166] Jack Mancuso told the HSCA that Banister was a regular at his restaurant on the ground floor of the 544 Camp Street building. Other regulars were Jack Martin and three or four Cubans from "upstairs."[167] There was no obvious personal gain for Lewis in telling his story, nor for the other witnesses that follow. His claim does not appear to be anything but honest.

Delphine Roberts was Guy Banister's secretary, mistress, and ideological twin. Roberts told author Anthony Summers she believed Oswald's wife Marina once accompanied him to Banister's office.[168] Many times, she saw David Ferrie at the office. She said Oswald came in to the office in 1963 seeking an application to work as one of Banister's "agents." (As will be shown in Chapter Twenty, Banister employed young men to infiltrate leftist groups on college campuses.) In talking to Oswald, Roberts had the impression that he and Banister already knew each other. (As we shall see later, there is evidence suggesting Banister's relationship with Oswald dates back to 1956.) After Oswald filled out the application for Roberts, Banister called him into his office. Roberts assumed Oswald was there to act undercover. She stated that Oswald came back a number of times and was on familiar terms with Banister and the office. She knew he used an office upstairs, which bore the 544 Camp Street address. One time, she went to the office and saw various Fair Play for Cuba Committee leaflets, which were part of Oswald's one-man operation. She said Banister became upset when various people brought pro-Castro material downstairs, because he did not want the material in his office. She later saw Oswald passing out the materials on the street. Oswald made a spectacle of himself passing out the pro-Castro leaflets in busy downtown New Orleans in the summer of 1963. Allen Campbell, who worked for Banister, recalled him saying about Oswald's handing out leaflets, "Don't worry about him. He's a nervous fellow; he's confused. He's with us; he's associated with the office." Delphine told the HSCA that Banister not only met Oswald in the office, but he also took him to an anti-Castro training camp outside of New Orleans.[169]

Roberts disclosed to reporter Earl Golz on December 20, 1979, in a phone interview, "I had (interviewed Oswald). At least I was under the impression that it was he. But I am pretty sure it was Oswald. He was introduced to me by Mr. Bannister [sic]." She recalled that Banister had talked with Oswald just prior to her meeting him. She stated again that Oswald used the office upstairs and Banister had taken her up there once. Roberts stated that Oswald's wife probably did not know of his political activities and Roberts thought Oswald kept many things from her. Similarly, Banister reportedly told Roberts there were some things Banister did not want Roberts to know for her own protection. Golz asked Roberts about Oswald's trip to the Cuban and Soviet Embassies in Mexico City in September 1963 (he tried to get visas for travel to Cuba and the U.S.S.R.), but she told him she would not talk to him over the phone about it.[170]

Roberts told the HSCA that she interviewed Oswald for an investigator position, but did not remember the details. She told them Oswald came in several times and went right into Banister's office. She made up files on Oswald for Banister. Although she was introduced to Oswald and his wife by Banister, she had no conversations with either of them. She had been to the 544 Camp Street upstairs office that Oswald used for FPCC and saw boxes of FPCC literature and pro-Castro slogans painted on the walls. She heard Banister holler at Sam Newman for letting Oswald keep literature in the second-floor office. She recalled that, after Oswald left New Orleans, Newman brought the boxes to Banister to get rid of them. She believed Oswald did not act alone in the assassination and that he was working for the FBI at the time. She stated that she saw FBI Special Agent Regis Kennedy at the office.[171] (Regis Kennedy admitted to Garrison that he had visited Banister in his office, corroborating her claim.[172])

Delphine Roberts's daughter, also named Delphine, used the offices above Banister's to do photographic work. She told author Anthony Summers that she and a photographer friend saw Oswald there occasionally. She knew he had his pamphlets and other materials up in the second-floor office. She never saw him talking to Guy Banister, but knew he worked in his office. She stated, "I got the impression Oswald was doing something to make people believe he was something he wasn't. I am sure Guy Banister knew what Oswald was doing . . . ."[173] The younger Delphine was astute in her observations. She had no obvious reason to tell that story if it was not true.

William Gaudet, a source for the Central Intelligence Domestic Contact Division in New Orleans, is the fourth witness who saw Lee Harvey Oswald with Guy Banister. Gaudet told author Anthony Summers that he saw Oswald handing out pamphlets on several occasions. He stated, "I do know I saw him (Oswald) one time with a former FBI agent by the name of Guy Banister. Guy of course is now dead. What Guy's role in all of this is I really don't know. I did see Oswald discussing various things with Banister at the time, and I think Banister knew a whole lot of what was going on . . . ." Gaudet also saw David Ferrie with Oswald and knew Sergio Arcacha Smith was acquainted with Oswald. He saw the two near his own office at Camp Street and Common, not far from the 544 Camp Street building. From the staff at the 544 Camp Street building, Summers confirmed that Banister knew Gaudet and that Gaudet would occasionally visit his office in the Newman Building. Gaudet did not believe the CIA was behind the assassination, nor that Oswald killed the president. He told Summers, "I think he was a patsy. I think he was set up on purpose."[174] The HSCA concluded that there was no evidence that Oswald had any contact with Gaudet on behalf of the CIA.[175]

On May 13, 1975, veteran assassination researcher Bernard Fensterwald interviewed William Gaudet, who was sixty-seven years old and in poor health. Gaudet told Fensterwald that he was a secret agent for Nelson Rockefeller in Latin American during World War II and switched to the CIA in 1947, working for them until 1969. During that time, Gaudet published the *Latin American Newsletter* and *Latin American Report*, which he claimed were 100 percent commercial ventures and not CIA fronts. He traveled extensively in Latin America and combined his commercial work with his CIA assignments, which were largely uncompensated. Gaudet admitted to Fensterwald that he was a right winger and generally did not like President Kennedy. He said he kept his CIA relationship secret and did not even tell his wife. Both the CIA and the KGB subscribed to his fifteen-dollar-per-week *Latin American Newsletter*, which netted him fifteen thousand dollars annually—a tidy sum at the time. Gaudet stated that he never met Oswald, but that he observed him on occasion, calling him a "miserable little creature" who would do anything for money. He believed Oswald worked both sides of the "Cuban Street" and that his FPCC outfit was nothing but a front. Gaudet related that David Ferrie was a friend of many homosexuals, including Clay Shaw. Gaudet said that he observed Oswald handing out pamphlets on several occasion and thought he was a nut. Gaudet also commented on Oswald's scuffle with Carlos Bringuier while handing out his pro-Castro literature, which led to Oswald's appearance in the radio debate with Ed Butler and his announcement of his supposed Marxist beliefs. Gaudet felt Bringuier's altercation with Oswald was on purpose and that Ed Butler put on the whole thing.[176, 177] As we shall later see, Carlos Bringuier and Ed Butler, like Oswald, were both tied to the Banister operation. At the same time, all of Gaudet's suspicions that Oswald was not who he pretended to be will be corroborated with evidence from completely different sources.

Another essential part of the Gaudet-Oswald story is the fact that Gaudet purchased a tourist card, number 824084, for entrance into Mexico on September 17, 1963; and Oswald purchased the next tourist card in sequence after Gaudet, number 824085, on the same day.[178] Gaudet denied having anything to do with that coincidence. Many who believe the CIA was behind the assassination of President Kennedy feel that the incident was more than a quirk of fate, however, and feel that it was evidence that Oswald was tied to the CIA. The HSCA determined that Gaudet was a source for the New Orleans CIA Domestic Contact Division, providing information on political and economic conditions in Latin America, but was not involved in clandestine activities. The HSCA concluded, finally, that there was no evidence that Oswald had contact with Gaudet on behalf of the CIA.[179]

Allen Campbell told the author that he saw Lee Harvey Oswald at Banister's office in 1963. He stated, "This man [Banister] actually believed he was in the forefront of a battle against Communism." Campbell went on to say that people had the wrong perception of his role at Banister's office. Campbell told the author he developed a relationship with Banister to learn "what his perceptions were of Communism in the U.S., especially his 1013 file." The 1013 file was on the Communist Party U.S.A., a file which Banister took from the Chicago FBI office when he retired. Banister reportedly told Campbell, "Communism is the philosophy of materialism, but having the force and effect of religion." He related that, until about 1994, Dan Campbell had the power of attorney over Delphine Roberts and her daughter, who became an invalid in later life. He stated that Leander Perez and Bluford Balter came by Banister's office all the time, and he recalled that Kent Courtney came into Banister's office quite a bit and that they were the best of friends. Ed Butler, who debated Oswald on the radio in September of 1963, was very close to Banister. Campbell stated that Banister, Ebahard Deutch, and Alton Oschner worked closely together, and called them the "triumvirate." He said Leander Perez could be included with that group. He affirmed that Klan leaders Jack Helm and Roswell Thompson were at the office. Campbell had no particular theory on the assassination, other than to say most of what was out there was "nonsense."[180] Anthony Summers interviewed Campbell, who recalled seeing Oswald handing out his pro-Castro material on the street, and that when Campbell told Guy Banister about it, he laughed.[181]

Allen Campbell told Garrison's investigators he worked for Banister around 1958 or 1959, and again around 1962 and 1963. He said he did everything for Banister, which ranged from investigating to undercover work trying to get information on Communist groups in the city. Campbell told them that Banister worked closely with the CIA and had a lot to do with the overthrow of Arbenz in Guatemala in 1959. Campbell was with Kerry Thornley—a former member of Oswald's marine unit—on the night of the assassination, and Thornley told him that he had known Oswald in New Orleans in 1963. Thornley coldly remarked on the night of the assassination, "It could not have happened to a nicer guy." Campbell told the investigators that he knew David Ferrie, and that when Ferrie's picture was printed in the newspaper in connection with Garrison's investigation, Ferrie told Campbell, "I'm a dead man." Campbell related that he and his brother Dan were in the Bethlehem Children's home at the same time Oswald was there, around 1946.[182]

The author interviewed Dan Campbell at the Napoleon House in the French Quarter in New Orleans in 1996. Dan Campbell, like his brother Allen, was a frequent visitor to Banister's office as a young man. As the author was introduced to Campbell, Campbell demanded, "Are you a Jew?" Thus it was clear from the onset that Campbell shared Banister's anti-Semitic tendencies. When informed that the author was not Jewish, he settled down and said that he and his brother Allen had both seen Lee Harvey Oswald at Banister's office. He stated that he saw Oswald one day while he was working on a skip search or skip trace for Banister. Dan and Allen Campbell were watching television when they saw Oswald's picture after the assassination. Dan said to himself, "My God. I remember his face." A day or two later, when it came out that Oswald was from New Orleans, it dawned on him where they had seen him: Banister's office. After placing Oswald with Banister, Campbell "realized the inconsistencies of Oswald being where he was, and on the streets representing who he was and also having access to and obviously functioning out of Banister's office." Campbell indicated that that wasn't anything odd for Banister, because he associated with all kinds of people from different political persuasions, "but not . . . you know, friends of Cuba for Christ Sake! It was totally anathema to Banister." He realized Oswald was pretending to be what he wasn't, something the Warren Commission and the HSCA did not realize. Commenting on the non-descript appearance of Lee Harvey Oswald, he stated, "The most extraordinary thing about Lee Harvey Oswald was just how ordinary he looked." Aside from his public demon-strations, Oswald's appearance was ordinary and he did not stand out. Dan Campbell told the author that, in 1963, New Orleans was "a city of one hundred people," meaning everyone knew everyone. Dan Campbell was close to David Ferrie and, as a pilot, relished serving as his copilot and flew with him any time he could.[183] He also admitted seeing Oswald with Banister in a guarded interview with Anthony Summers.[184]

Raymond Broshears, the seventh witness presented here, was a friend and former lover of David Ferrie in the summer of 1963. Like Ferrie, he was a radical right winger and somewhat bizarre in his own right. Broshears saw Lee Harvey Oswald with Guy Banister in the Newman Building. He saw Oswald another time at Ferrie's apartment. (Those credible allegations will be discussed further in Chapter Nineteen.) What makes Broshears's allegations compelling is their rich detail, reflecting his firsthand knowledge of the Guy Banister operation. Broshears also named other, somewhat more obscure, figures connected to the assassination that are cor-roborated by completely separate sources first uncovered in this work and detailed later.

Adrian Alba owned the Crescent City Garage at 618–28 Magazine Street, a service station adjacent to Reily Coffee, where Oswald worked in the summer of 1963. Alba ate his lunch at Mancuso's restaurant and saw Oswald there many times, but could not remem-ber anyone with him. As discussed earlier, Mancuso's occupied the Camp Street side of the Newman Building where Banister had his office. Above Mancuso's was the 544 Camp Street office. Alba was a gun enthusiast and maintained three stacks of magazines on guns, fishing and hunting. He said Oswald would come into his waiting room almost daily and drink a lot of Coke. Alba held many conversations with Oswald, mostly about guns, but claimed they never talked politics. During that time, the Secret Service stored their cars in Alba's garage. He recalled a man from the FBI borrowed a car for few days with the permission of the Secret Service. A few days later, the car stopped outside of Reily Coffee and someone in the car gave Oswald a legal-sized envelope, which he tucked under his T-shirt. He last saw Oswald somewhere between a week and two months before the assassination, and Oswald told him he would be leaving soon for a "pot of gold in Gentilly" (a nearby suburb of New Orleans). Garrison and the HSCA pointed out that the NASA base of Michoud was located in Gentilly. Garrison claimed several people connected with his ongoing investigation of David Ferrie became employed at Michoud, suggesting their employment was arranged by government intelligence. Former Banister employee and close friend Ivan Nitschke was the chief of security at the operation. Nitschke—and not government intelligence—may have been the one who promised the alleged lucrative job at the facility to Oswald.[185, 186]

Michael L. Kurtz, a professor of history at Southwestern University in Hammond, Louisiana, also witnessed Lee Harvey Oswald in the presence of Guy Banister. Kurtz developed other "confidential sources" who saw Oswald with David Ferrie. In 1980, Kurtz published an article in *Louisiana History* entitled, "Lee Harvey Oswald in New Orleans: A Reappraisal." Citing a "confidential source," he wrote that twice Ferrie and Oswald were seen conversing in Mancuso's restaurant. One source saw the two at a Citizens' Council meeting in the late spring of 1963. In August of 1963, they were seen at a party in the French Quarter and both expressed disapproval of the Kennedy administration's failure to overthrow the Castro regime. Kurtz wrote that Oswald accompanied an unidentified prominent leader of the White Citizens' Council to Baton Rouge six or eight times in July and August of 1963. The two engaged in discussions critical of Kennedy's policies on civil rights and Communism. Kurtz revealed to the author in a 1996 letter that the individual was Kent Courtney, a close associate of Banister, who will be discussed further in the next chapter.[187, 188]

Kurtz also authored the 1982 book *Crime of the Century* and wrote of his extensive research indicating that Oswald was actually engaged in right-wing activities in New Orleans in 1963. Kurtz wrote of three possible scenarios as to those responsible for the assassination and presented the supporting evidence for each: the CIA, the Cuban government, and the Mafia. He did not consider a right-wing scenario, in spite of credible evidence presented— and his own account that Oswald was engaged in right-wing activity. He did not feel there was sufficient evidence to identify exactly who was responsible for the assassination, although in a television interview he stated that the Cuban government was the culprit. He wrote in his book, "On numerous occasions, Oswald associated with Guy Bannister [sic], an ex-FBI official and private investigator. Militantly anti-Castro and rabidly segregationist, Bannister was well known in New Orleans for his extremist views. Twice, Bannister and Oswald visited the campus of Louisiana State University in New Orleans, LSUNO and engaged students in heated discussion of federal racial policies. During these discussions, Oswald vehemently attacked the civil rights policies of the Kennedy administration." However, in his book, he did not identify the witness to the event. In a 1996 letter to the author, Kurtz admitted he had witnessed the event himself and actually had seen Oswald and Banister together on two separate occasions. He explained that, in the summer of 1963, he attended LSUNO and worked across the street from Banister's office at the *New Orleans Times–Picayune* building. While a student at the university, Kurtz was introduced to Oswald by Banister. Banister had employed his fellow student George Higganbotham to spy on college students political activities, who was present at the time. A discussion on racial policies took place with the students, including Kurtz. Kurtz saw Banister and Oswald again in Mancuso's restaurant.[189] In his book, Kurtz expanded upon the claims made in *Louisiana History* that several times Oswald and David Ferrie were seen together. He wrote that they were seen at Pontchartrain Beach, an amusement park. They frequented the Napoleon House, where they debated Kennedy's foreign policies with students. The two were seen together in Baton Rouge, where they openly denounced Kennedy's foreign and domestic policies. Another witness told Kurtz he saw the two dressed in military fatigues carrying automatic rifles and conducting military training maneuvers at Bedico Creek near Lake Pontchartrain. Kurtz did not identify his sources, and wrote that the relationship of these accounts to the assassination was unclear.

Garrison's investigation determined, from an interview with George Higganbotham that he did indeed know Guy Banister, adding further credence to Kurtz's claims. Higganbotham declined to tell the D.A. that he saw Banister with Oswald on the campus of the University of New Orleans. He told them he was an investigator for Banister in 1960–61, but was only a social contact of Banister in 1962–63. He showed the D.A. investigator three letters from Banister to him, in which Banister provided him with false credentials for infiltrating Communist groups. His code name was "Dale." Higganbotham kidded Banister about sharing a building with people passing out leaflets on the street and Banister said, "Cool it . . . one of them is mine." Higganbotham suggested the possibility of a connection between Rich Lauchli and Banister. He told Garrison's team that Lauchli was arrested for selling weapons to Latin America and that he published a paper called the "Counter Insurgency Council." Higganbotham was cooperative with Garrison, because he was in trouble for possession of marijuana and wanted the D.A.'s help. Wray Gill, Jr. represented him in the matter.[190, 191] Several other individuals also tied Rich Lauchli to the Banister operation. Like Ferrie and Banister, Lauchli was in the business of procuring armaments for the anti-Castro effort. Robert DePugh told the author that he and Lauchli undertook a cross-country tour through the South ending in Miami, soliciting weapons for the anti-Castro Cuban cause.[192]

Jack Martin, a tenth person to see Oswald with Guy Banister, was a shady character with a criminal past who was employed by Banister as an investigator. In a signed statement to the New Orleans district attorney's office on December 26, 1966, Martin stated that in the late summer of 1963 he was sitting in Guy Banister's office in the rear of Mancuso's Restaurant and David Ferrie walked in with three or four young men in their twenties who were dressed in sport shirts. One man was Morris Brownlee. Another they referred to as "Lee." All of them went into Banister's office and the door was shut. He told the D.A. that Oswald, Ferrie, and Banister all knew each other. After the assassination, Martin recognized one of the men as Lee Harvey Oswald.[193] Like others, Martin called Banister "the chief." Martin recalled that Banister "voiced total hatred for the Communists above all the most liberal factions . . . and the Jews." Martin told the HSCA in an affidavit that Banister often stated, referring to unpopular politicians, that "[s]omeday, someone is going to poke a rifle out of a window." He recalled that Banister and Delphine Roberts entered Katzenjammers bar on the evening of the assassination in high spirits. Banister's exuberance was completely out of context for him. Martin stated that, on the night of the assassination, he told Banister he had "seen things" around the office. Banister became enraged and struck Martin twice in the head with his pistol. After that, Martin did not see Banister again until shortly before Banister's death in June 1964. On that occasion, Banister quizzed Martin to find out if he had been circulating anything about him he shouldn't have, adding "[his] old FBI buddy Regis Kennedy had pretty well taken care of things to protect [him and his] interests on that score." Martin claimed that New Orleans FBI SA Regis Kennedy, who was a frequent visitor to Banister's office, protected Banister. Martin related that he saw a Civil Air Patrol photo of Oswald with Ferrie. He said the gun Oswald used might have belonged to David Ferrie or he may have purchased it at the same place Ferrie purchased his. Martin further related that the training camps north of Lake Pontchartrain were designed for the purpose of training for an invasion of Cuba and that Minuteman Rich Lauchli was present at the camp.[194] Martin was guarded about what he would say about Banister, because he admired and had worked for him for a long time. However, the same was not true of David Ferrie, whom Martin despised. In 1994, author Gus Russo located a former Ferrie CAP cadet who had a photo of Ferrie with young Oswald and others at a CAP encampment. The photo was shown on a 1994 Public Broadcasting Service program.

Thomas Beckham, an eleventh witness, saw Oswald with Guy Banister at both his Newman Building office and at a local cafeteria.[195] Beckham was an aspiring teenage singer and met Banister through Jack Martin, and worked for Banister running small errands. He, like others, called Banister "the chief." Beckham stated that he knew Lee Harvey Oswald and they had become "good buddies." Beckham had, as we shall see later, the correct assessments of Oswald's true identity when he told the HSCA, "I can't understand this Russia thing, because he was always 100% American he seemed like." He stated that Oswald was anti-Castro and that he told him that Communism was Jewish because "Karl Marx was a Jew." Beckham saw Oswald leafleting on Canal Street, which he called "some of his crazy stuff." When Beckham asked Oswald what he was doing, Oswald told him he wasn't worried, "The Chief [Banister] would take care of him." Afterwards, he joined Oswald for a Coke.[196] Beckham testified in Garrison's 1968 New Orleans Grand Jury proceeding, in which Clay Shaw was accused of conspiracy in the assassination of the president. Beckham later told the HSCA that Roswell Thompson, a Klansman-friend of Guy Banister, told him to keep his mouth shut during the proceedings if he wanted to live. (Beckham's credible story will be presented in detail in Chapter Nine.)

A *New Orleans States–Item* reporter interviewed an unidentified witness who reporting seeing Oswald with Banister, Arcacha, and Ferrie at 544 Camp Street.[197] This individual may be a twelfth witness, or could be someone already named—perhaps David Lewis, whose story was covered in the press.

Many of the witnesses who saw Lee Harvey Oswald with Guy Banister were strange characters with checkered pasts, inviting skepticism about anything they might say. Nonetheless, they were all telling the truth. As will be shown next, in 1963, Lee Harvey Oswald was seen coming and going from Guy Banister's office repeatedly by an agent of the United States Border Patrol whose eyewitness account is unimpeachable. Unfortunately, though, his observation never came to the attention of the Warren Commission, Jim Garrison's investigation, or the House Select Committee on Assassination.

The United States Senate Select Committee to Study Governmental Operations with Respect to Intelligence Activities, a U.S. Senate committee, was created in 1975 and chaired by Senator Frank Church (D-ID). Dubbed the Church Committee, it was formed to investigate abuses in U.S. intelligence operations, and its findings were published in fourteen reports. The Church Committee investigated the U.S. involvement in the assassination plots of foreign leaders including Patrice Lumumba of Congo, Fidel Castro, and Rafael Trujillo of the Dominican Republic. One report, Book V, was entitled "The Investigation of the Assassination of President John F. Kennedy: Performance of the Intelligence Agencies." The Church Committee investigated the relationship between the CIA, FBI, the Warren Commission, and the assassination. They did not investigate Guy Banister or David Ferrie, and may not have known anything about them.[198]

Wendall Roache was in charge of the Immigration and Naturalization Service's Border Patrol division in New Orleans in 1963. He contacted an investigator from the Church Committee in 1975 and related his astonishing story. He explained that his job with the INS was to keep watch on various Cuban groups in New Orleans. Roache had never before been interviewed and was eager and relieved to relate his story telling them, "I've been waiting twelve years to talk to someone about this." He told them that, through the course of his work he had placed David Ferrie and his Cuban associates—a group he referred to as a "group of nuts"—under surveillance at the Newman Building. Inspectors for the INS saw Lee Harvey Oswald repeatedly going in and out of the office of David Ferrie's group, which was described as being on a side street entrance between St. Charles and Camp. This same side entrance was the sole and exclusive entrance to Guy Banister's office. The other offices in the Newman Building could only be accessed from the front, Camp Street, entrance. Banister's name was never mentioned, nor did the Church Committee investigators ask Roache about him. The INS had in-depth knowledge of Ferrie's bizarre and checkered background. They were aware of his dismissal from Eastern Airlines, his homosexuality, and his "perverse tendencies," and called him "nuttier than a fruitcake." Roache knew Ferrie was anti-Castro and owned an airplane. He believed Ferrie was going to take his brigade to a camp at Lake Pontchartrain where training was directed by a six-foot-tall ex-marine. He told them Ferrie liked young men and was known to "give these guys all sorts of pills at the training camp and take movies of them." According to Roache, when Oswald was arrested after his scuffle with Carlos Bringuier he spoke only Russian to the New Orleans police, who assumed he was Russian. As they were accustomed to doing, the police called the INS to verify an alien. The INS sent over inspector

Ron L. Smith. The INS was aware of Oswald's pamphleting and knew before his arrest that he was American, not Russian. Smith told the Church Committee investigators that he interrogated Oswald for five minutes before Oswald admitted he was American and Smith left. Smith did not recall discussing the incident with anyone. Roache described their record-keeping habits and explained that most of their reports were oral, so they had no written reports of the described events.[199] The unheralded and little-known Church Committee, who in 1975 knew of Roache's startling evidence, apparently had no idea of its significance and made nothing out of it. Neither the Warren Commission, HSCA, nor Jim Garrison knew anything about Roache's statement linking Oswald to Ferrie and Banister's office, which is a truly a stunning piece of documentary evidence that corroborates the accounts of the eleven witnesses presented above.

Wendall Roache notified the FBI of his surveillance of Banister's office, although Banister's name was not mentioned, perhaps due to Banister's friendship with SA Regis Kennedy. The FBI incorrectly spelled his name as "Windle Roach." In 1961, Roache told the FBI about Ferrie, his Cuban exploits, his dealings in armaments, and his manipulation of teenage boys. According to FBI documents "Windle Roach" of the U.S. Border Patrol advised the FBI, on October 20, 1961, about allegations furnished to them by John Harris about David Ferrie. Harris stated, "Captain Ferrie has a group of young boys whom he supports and controls completely." The INS reported, "Ferrie had been holding something over the heads of the boys in this group and suspects he is keeping them doped up with narcotics, liquor, and hypnotism. Ferrie has taken pornographic pictures of the various boys in this group, which he is holding over their heads to make them cooperative with him." Ferrie asked Harris if he would help him purchase an XC47 airplane for $35,000 and to determine whether the purchase had to be reported to the proper officials. Harris reported that Ferrie had a cache of arms located in several places around New Orleans. He observed Ferrie with hand grenades in the trunk of his car. Ferrie helped the boys obtain passports and Harris suspected they planned to leave the U.S. During the investigation of Ferrie on morals charges, the police found he had an assortment of rifles and ammunition. Ferrie told the officers that he purchased the ammunition at Crescent Gun and he was working for the Cuban Revolutionary Front. On October 25, 1961, an individual (name redacted by the FBI) supplied information to the FBI about Ferrie and his Cuban activities. The individual told the FBI that Ferrie behaved at times like he had "gone off the deep end." The FBI reported they interviewed Ferrie on August 22, 1961, and knew he was active in the Cuban Revolutionary Front and possessed arms at his home. He was described as a "crackpot."[200] There are no other reports from a Roache (or "Roach") in the JFK Collection in the National Archives. Had the HSCA known about the INS information, they probably would have been able to obtain direct testimony from INS agents Roache and Smith tying Banister to Oswald, and Oswald to the six Cubans from the CRC, formerly of 544 Camp Street. They likely would have found out that the Cubans had more contacts with Oswald than they admitted to—and for reasons other than those that they claimed.

Jim Garrison and the HSCA on Oswald and the Banister Operation

Jim Garrison deserves credit for bringing David Ferrie and Guy Banister into key aspects of the assassination story. Days after the assassination, Garrison alerted the FBI and Secret Service about the allegations that Ferrie knew Oswald from the Civil Air Patrol, as well as having had contact with him in the summer before the assassination. He also told them of Jack Martin's allegation that Ferrie taught Oswald how to shoot a rifle. However, after interviewing Jack Martin, the FBI and Secret Service dismissed him as a drunk and a liar. They released David Ferrie after they were satisfied with his convoluted story and after making their determination that Jack Martin's claims were without merit. It would not be surprising if the FBI's cursory dismissal of the allegations against David Ferrie had something to do with Guy Banister's close relationship with FBI Director J. Edgar Hoover and New Orleans FBI SA Regis Kennedy.

A second astute and valuable contribution Jim Garrison made to history was his observation that Oswald was not a Communist but had been used by Banister as an agent provocateur. Unfortunately, Garrison claimed he did not know why Oswald had been used or what his role was. After the story broke that he was secretly investigating the assassination, Garrison announced that ultra rightists were behind the murder. Soon after, he abruptly changed course and announced that government intelligence was responsible for the murder. His case and credibility sharply dropped thereafter. He falsely claimed that Banister had worked for the Office of Navel Intelligence in WWII, and he noted that Banister's office was across from the post office where CIA offices were located. Garrison pointed out that Adrian Alba's garage—where Lee Harvey Oswald spent his lunch breaks—provided parking services for the Secret Service and the Office of Naval Intelligence, and at one time the FBI, while the CIA office was just a few blocks away. On that basis, Garrison concluded that Oswald chose to spend his spare time within the U.S. government's intelligence complex. Therefore, Garrison reached the improbable and unsubstantiated conclusion that the intelligence community in New Orleans used Oswald as an agent provocateur. Garrison called Oswald's presence amidst the federal government centers in downtown New Orleans the "propinquity factor"—a farfetched sort of "guilt by geographical association." As was previously mentioned, the CIA considered using Guy Banister Associates for collection of foreign intelligence, but didn't—that was the extent of any possible proven relationship with the CIA.[201]

Claiming still more evidence of a government plot, Garrison cited a news article about an FBI raid on a home with a cache of bombs and weapons in St. Tammany Parish. Garrison alleged that the home and weapons were connected to U.S. government intelligence—without supporting evidence. Garrison provided no explanation as to why the FBI would raid the supposed operation of another government agency.[202] Even one of his own investigators, Bill Boxley, a.k.a. William Wood—who was formerly with the CIA—told Garrison, "There was little possibility Banister was CIA."[203] Garrison failed to reveal even a hint of Banister's consuming and passionate fight against integration. Despite its terrible flaws, Garrison's actual investigation of Oswald in New Orleans, his raw investigative files—

especially those pertaining to Guy Banister and David Ferrie—provided invaluable pieces of the puzzle. (The same cannot be said for the implausible conclusions put forth in his book *On the Trail of Assassins*.[204])

Unfortunately for history and justice, FBI Director J. Edgar Hoover wanted nothing to do with Garrison, neither the good nor the poorly conceived parts of his case. A few weeks after Garrison's investigation became public, an FBI memo revealed that Hoover had instructed the FBI offices to make "No inquiries concerning the investigation being conducted by New Orleans district attorney Jim Garrison . . . ."[205] Had Hoover's agents investigated Garrison's leads, Hoover would have had a lot of explaining to do about his friend and former high-ranking FBI SAC Guy Banister and his business with Lee Harvey Oswald.

Guy Banister and the 544 Camp Street matter were investigated for the HSCA chiefly by Gaeton Fonzi and summarized in seven pages in the HSCA Report. The findings were grossly deficient and rudimentary, at best. Largely based on the evidence of the 544 Camp Street office address printed on Oswald's pamphlet and Delphine Roberts's testimony that Oswald was in Banister's office applying for a job, "The committee determined there was at least a possibility that Oswald and Guy Banister were acquainted." That is as far as they went with the matter, and they drew no further inferences. Banister's name was mentioned less than a dozen times, and little was revealed about him other than that he was formerly with the FBI, had an association with the anti-Castro Cubans, and ran a detective agency. The implication was that Banister's possible relationship to Oswald was a one-time event simply related to Oswald seeking employment. To the contrary, the evidence presented in this work indicates Oswald was a frequent visitor to Banister's office and was seen with him by eleven or more witness. None of the witnesses—other than Delphine Roberts—presented herein were mentioned in Fonzi's report. None of the large number of radical rightist and segregationist groups Banister associated with were reported by the HSCA, despite the fact that they all bitterly opposed President Kennedy.[206]

Interestingly, the HSCA investigated the murders of both President Kennedy and Martin Luther King, Jr. at the same time. The HSCA believed there was a likelihood that James Earl Ray murdered King for the standing reward offered by members of a St. Louis "secret southern organization" aligned with the Citizens' Council and another segregationist organization.[207] Yet, at the same time, they failed to even acknowledge Banister's fanaticism about segregation and membership in several racist organizations—including the Citizens' Council—in their JFK investigation.

In 1993, Gaeton Fonzi wrote a book based on his experiences with the HSCA called *The Last Investigation*. "The Least Investigation" would have been a more fitting title. To give an idea of how little he thought of the Oswald-Banister relationship, Fonzi mentioned Banister's name but once in his over 400-page book. Fonzi claimed that Oswald was being handled by a CIA spymaster, David Phillips—an idea based on an allegation by Antonio Veciana, a militantly anti-Castro Cuban who claimed that he saw Oswald with the agent in Dallas. When the HSCA arranged a surreptitious placing of Veciana in the same room with

CIA agent Phillips, Veciana was unable to identify him as the CIA handler he had supposedly seen with Oswald. Nonetheless, the substance of Fonzi's book was that the CIA was involved with Oswald and the Kennedy assassination.[208] Senator Gary Hart served on the Church Committee and investigated the Veciana allegation. Hart felt Veciana probably saw Oswald with George de Mohrenschildt, Oswald's older White Russian friend, who resembled the CIA agent. He concluded Veciana's claim was a case of mistaken identity.[209] Fonzi's personal belief in the CIA's involvement in the assassination may account for the exceedingly poor investigation by the HSCA of the Banister-Oswald matter. Fonzi became bitter and cynical over the conclusion of the HSCA investigation and stated that the government had failed everyone.

G. Robert Blakey was the chief counsel for the HSCA, who—as a result of their investigation—pointed to the Mafia as the only group who had the motive, means, and opportunity to murder the president. A conclusion like that is problematic, because a lot of individuals and groups had the motive, means, and opportunity to murder the president. Even so, the HSCA failed to provide direct and proximate evidence of a Mafia conspiracy in the murder of the president. Blakey wrote in his book *The Plot to Kill the President* that he was not persuaded by the allegations of Jack Martin and Delphine Roberts that Oswald had been in Banister's office. Blakey stated that the committee was unable to document a Banister-Oswald relationship, but did establish correctly an association between Ferrie and Banister, who, in turn, were linked to New Orleans Mafia leader Carlos Marcello. Blakey showed no awareness of the numerous witnesses who saw Oswald with Banister or of the Border Patrol's observation of Oswald constantly coming and going from the Banister office, and no information of this kind was presented in his HSCA Report. He failed to note Banister's affiliation with a large number of radical fringe groups, all of whom bitterly opposed the president. Blakey was dependent upon Gaeton Fonzi for the performance of a proper investigation of the Banister-Oswald matter, which, unfortunately, was not done.[210] The HSCA noted in their report, "The committee candidly acknowledged, for example, that it could not explain Oswald's associations—nor at this late date fully determine their extent—with anti-Castro Cubans. The committee remained convinced that since Oswald consistently demonstrated a left-wing Marxist ideology, he would not have supported the anti-Castro movement."[211] The HSCA missed the boat entirely. The answer to their dilemma as to why a professed Communist was in contact with so many anti-Communists was that Oswald was neither a Marxist nor a Communist. He was only posing as one.

The problem with the theories that the CIA or Mafia was behind the assassination is that Lee Harvey Oswald, the one constant in the assassination story, had no demonstrable ties to either organization.

Conclusions

Eleven or more witnesses saw Lee Harvey Oswald in the presence of Guy Banister. Still others saw him in the company of close Banister associates Sergio Arcacha Smith, David Ferrie, and—as we shall see in the next chapter—Kent Courtney. Corroborating the witnesses' accounts was an Immigration and Naturalization Border Patrol agent who reported, unknown to the Warren Commission, Garrison investigation, or HSCA, that he had observed Oswald coming and going from Banister's office with David Ferrie, on a frequent basis.

Neither Jim Garrison nor the HSCA, the only ones to investigate Guy Banister, made note of Banister's extensive and all-consuming career as a segregationist. They failed to note his role in the southern states' inquisitions on the integration movement. Banister's role with Senator Eastland's Senate Committee that persecuted those who challenged the sacred southern institution of segregation—which faced extinction under the Kennedy administration—was also somehow missed. The various assassination investigations and few, if any, conspiracy writers made note of Banister's position on the racist State Sovereignty Commission and Un-American Activities Committee.

It became an ingrained myth initiated by Jim Garrison—and carried on in conspiracy books—that Guy Banister's extensive files were related to CIA activities, when there is no evidence that they were. Banister's files, like those of his radical right-wing contemporaries and the primitive racists on the SISS and HUAC, were on integrationists, liberals, and others deemed crudely as "un-American." There was a failure to note Banister's association with a large number of ultra-right-wing and segregationist organizations that passionately hated President Kennedy.

While suspecting the convicted murderer of Martin Luther King, Jr. may have been enticed by a bounty placed on King by the Citizens' Council, the HSCA failed to note Banister's involvement with the same racist organization.

Six anti-Castro Cubans, five of whom admitted contact with Lee Harvey Oswald—while the sixth was seen with him by witnesses—all had direct ties to Banister's anti-Castro operation, which were not appreciated by those who have studied the case. That is not to suggest that any of them were involved in the assassination. They would have been pretty foolhardy to consort with Lee Harvey Oswald and would have had little to gain knowing that he was going to be involved in the assassination of an American president. As we shall see, none of Oswald's demonstrations as a Marxist/Communist had anything to do with the assassination, but were related to matters of critical importance to the southern states during that era.

Outside of the initial perceptions that the radical right wing was involved in the assassination, after Oswald was identified as the Communist murderer no one who has written about the assassination considered that Kennedy's death might have been at the hands of the segregationists. His widow, however, found the explanation that a Communist murdered her husband to be un-fulfilling. When Robert Kennedy told Jacqueline Kennedy, "They think they've found the man who did it. He says he's a Communist," Mrs. Kennedy replied, "That's absurd. It even robs his death of any meaning. He didn't even have the satisfaction of being killed for civil rights. It's—it had to be some silly little Communist."

CHAPTER TWO

CIRCLE OF FRIENDS: DAVID FERRIE, KENT COURTNEY,
AND DELPHINE ROBERTS

Kennedy is no good, Kennedy is a nigger lover.
– David Ferrie

The life and times of three close friends of Guy Banister—David Ferrie, Kent Courtney, and Delphine Roberts—provide further insight into the Banister operation. A
closer look at these three individuals is explored in this chapter.

David Ferrie

As documented in Chapter One, David Ferrie's ties to Lee Harvey Oswald, both while in
the New Orleans Civil Air Patrol in the period of 1955–1956 and in the summer of 1963,
are beyond dispute. Ferrie, like Banister, was a fanatical right-winger and segregationist. Jim
Garrison failed to note his involvement in those radical groups and portrayed Ferrie as a
government agent—a claim for which evidence is lacking. As we shall see, Ferrie was a bright
but deeply disturbed individual and a serial pedophile. Even so, Guy Banister maintained a
tremendous allegiance to Ferrie and defended him vigorously during the legal proceedings
for sexual crimes charges. Banister, who saw Communists everywhere, believed the charges
against Ferrie were trumped up by the so-called Communist conspiracy as a result of his outspoken anti-Communist position.

David William Ferrie grew up in an Irish Catholic neighborhood on the west side of
Cleveland, Ohio, where he was educated in parochial schools. His uncles were battalion commanders in the fire department, which, along with the police department, was dominated by
Irish Catholics. Ferrie's father—who later became an attorney—began his career as a Cleveland police detective during the period when famed crime fighter Eliot Ness served as the
safety director of the city. At the prestigious St. Ignatius High School in Cleveland, Ferrie had
a recognized gift for public speaking, winning the school's debating award in four consecutive
years. After graduation, he attended St. Mary's seminary from 1938–40, St. Charles seminary
in 1941, and John Carroll University, before graduating from Baldwin Wallace College with
a degree in education. At St. Mary's seminary in Cleveland he suffered a nervous breakdown;

he eventually left the school because of "emotional instability," before moving on to his next school. He was diagnosed with *alopecia areata* in 1944, a condition that caused patches of his hair to fall out.

Ferrie joined the Civil Air Patrol in Cleveland in 1947. He maintained a close relationship with the boys in his unit, trying to influence them to enter the priesthood. Ferrie allegedly was jailed for taking several boys from the Cleveland CAP to a home of prostitution in Sandusky, Ohio, in 1949—an incident which was kept out of the newspapers through his father's influence.[212]

Ferrie's younger brother Parmely served in the army air force in Europe during World War II, and was shot down over France and parachuted to safety. A long-time family friend of the Ferries, Brother Greg Franz, told the author that he fondly recalled driving to a public square in downtown Cleveland on V. J. Day to celebrate along with David and Parmely. At Parmely's wedding, his bride wore the parachute that had saved his life, which had been made into a dress. David and Brother Greg played in the orchestra during the ceremony. Overshadowed by his brother's heroics—and having failed miserably in two attempts at the priesthood—the older Ferrie was given, by his father, an airplane to take his mind off his problems. He learned to fly at Cleveland Municipal Airport, which was located about a mile from his home.

By 1948, Ferrie was teaching aeronautics at Benedictine High School in Cleveland. (On one occasion, while driving out of the school driveway at an apparent high rate of speed, he rolled his car over.[213]) After school, he often took his students to the Cleveland airport for flying lessons.[214] In 1951, Ferrie applied for a pilot's job with Eastern Airlines, was accepted, and moved to New Orleans. (It is important to note that Lee Harvey Oswald became proficient as an Aviation Electronics Operator while in the marines. Later, he was stationed at the Marine Air Control Squadron One at Atsugi, Japan, home of the U2 spy plane.[215] It would not be surprising if the influence of David Ferrie led Lee Harvey Oswald to choose work in the field of aeronautics as a marine.)

David Ferrie and the Jim Garrison Investigation

Jim Garrison started his carreer as district attorney of New Orleans during the 1962 term. When, after Kennedy's assissination, he learned that Oswald had resided in New Orleans during the previous summer, he asked his staff to remain vigilant for any leads they might develop in the case. Through no effort of the D.A.'s office, allegations of involvement of David

David Ferrie in an Eastern Airlines uniform in the early 1950s (left). Marguerite Oswald recalled that a man in a uniform came to her home and urged her to allow her son to join the service. The man was probably Ferrie. Ferrie in a 1957 passport application photo (middle). Ferrie in a 1961 passport application photo (right). By 1961, he had suffered complete hair loss and wore painted-on eyebrows and a homemade wig. Source: Richard Billings Papers, Georgetown University

Ferrie in the assassination came to the doorstep of the D.A.'s office, in the person of Jack Martin. Martin was an employee of Guy Banister at his Camp and Lafayette Street office. He was in charge of the meager, legitimate private detective work that came into the office while Banister engaged in Citizens' Council activities, blacklisting, anti-Castro Cuban affairs and spying on leftist students on campus, among other far-right endeavors. After the assassination, Martin approached a member of the district attorney's office and told him that Ferrie had taught Lee Harvey Oswald how to shoot a rifle in the Civil Air Patrol—a story Martin also told to the media. Garrison had met both Ferrie and Martin in the past. Martin had grown to despise Ferrie over a dispute the two had had while involved in the Anglican Orthodox Church. (Martin, it should be noted, did not tie Banister—whom he admired—to Oswald, and kept him out of the story.) Martin's allegation has corroboration. Thomas Clark, another youthful associate of David Ferrie, told Garrison's office that Ferrie told him he had taught Oswald to use a rifle.[216]

Ferrie had driven to Houston, Texas, from New Orleans shortly after the assassination, further raising suspicions of his involvement in the assassination. Upon Ferrie's return from Texas, two days after the assassination, on Sunday, November 24, he was taken into custody by the D.A.'s office. Ferrie explained that he and two companions had traveled to Houston to do some duck hunting, but didn't take any weapons. He had then changed his plans and decided to go ice skating in Galveston, but spent his time on the telephone and never skated. The story lacked credibility and Garrison held Ferrie for questioning by the FBI and the Secret Service.[217]

The FBI interviewed Ferrie, at Garrison's request, four days after the assassination as a result of the allegations by Jack Martin. Ferrie told the FBI that he became a member of the CAP serving as an instructor in 1952. The students were taught to shoot .22-caliber rifles without sights. He told them he did not know Lee Harvey Oswald. Ferrie also related that he had been employed as an investigator and law clerk since March of 1962 with attorney G. Wray Gill and worked on the case of New Orleans mob boss Carlos Marcello. He explained that, one time, Martin visited him at attorney G. Wray Gill's office. Gill did not want Martin—a shady, disreputable person—in his office. Ferrie claimed he put him out in an undiplomatic fashion, which led to their feud.[218] He told them that the trip to Houston was a vacation for him and his two companions.

Martin was questioned by the FBI on November 26 and recanted his previous story about Ferrie and Oswald and Martin stated that he had made up the whole story.[219] However, in another account, Martin told investigators that he was in Ferrie's home, and in addition to the photo of Oswald in the CAP, he saw Fair Play for Cuba materials, as well.[220] Martin's allegations about David Ferrie and Lee Harvey Oswald never came to the attention of the Warren Commission. Garrison, based on the FBI and Secret Service finding a lack of credence to Martin's allegations, gave the incident no further consideration until three years later.

Garrison claimed that, in November 1966 while on an airline flight with Senator Russell Long, Long's doubts on the validity of the Warren Commission findings renewed his interest in the case. Garrison purchased a copy of the Warren Commission's twenty-six volumes of evidence and began to study it. Garrison came upon the Commission testimony of New Orleans attorney Dean Andrews who stated that he had handled some legal matters for Lee Harvey Oswald in the summer of 1963, and had been called after the assassination by a mystery man named Clay Bertrand, requesting that Andrews represent Oswald after the assassination. As Garrison read the Warren Commission's findings, he became appalled at their shoddy work, missed leads, and unsubstantiated conclusions. Based on the deficiencies of the Warren Commission, the Dean Andrews story, and Martin's David Ferrie allegations, Garrison began a formal, but secret, investigation into the assassination in late 1966.[221]

On December 15, 1966, Garrison's office re-interviewed David Ferrie. Ferrie told them that, to his knowledge, he did not know Lee Harvey Oswald. Ferrie explained that he had told FBI SA Walls that, after the assassination, a former CAP cadet told him that Oswald—at roughly the age of fifteen—was in his CAP group. Ferrie stated that Jack Martin was a psychopath and had created the accusation of his relationship with Oswald as a vendetta. Ferrie repeated the story that he had left for Houston on the day after the assassination on vacation, to do some ice skating and hunting with two companions. He called his attorney from Houston, G. Wray Gill, who told him to get back in town because he was in major trouble. He denied the allegation that he taught Oswald to shoot a rifle, although he admitted he did teach the cadets to shoot with a .22-caliber rifle, and sometimes larger caliber rifles.[222]

Joseph S. Newbrough was an employee of Guy Banister and provided some details on Ferrie's life for Garrison investigators. He told them that he was an employee, associate, and investigator with Guy Banister at the time David Ferrie had been charged by the police with sodomy or some other homosexual charge. He insisted that Ferrie was in Banister's office on a daily basis, and told them that Ferrie had all the mannerisms of a person with a psychological maladjustment and that he had lost all the hair on his head, including his eyebrows. To cover up for it, he used theatrical makeup and crepe hair on his head and eyebrows. Newbrough pointed out that there were several rumored explanations for his hair loss. Newbrough had heard that Ferrie lost it from working with radioactive material; in a dynamite explosion prospecting for gold in Latin America; and that he had it removed purposely so Eastern Airlines would fire him and give him an excuse to sue them. He related that Ferrie was a clerk in the law office of G. Wray Gill and did investigation and legal research for Gill, frequenting all of the courts in New Orleans and—on one occasion—Gill sent Ferrie to Washington to discuss a case with an Associate Justice of the Supreme Court. Ferrie had become friendly with Carlos Marcello—an ardent racist and segregationist—and was a confidant and legal advisor. Guy Banister also did investigative work for Marcello. Newbrough claimed Jack Martin had antipathy toward Ferrie that could cause him to imagine all types of crimes that Ferrie might take part in. Ferrie practiced the Catholic religion and was extremely knowledgeable, but also believed that he was a saint and could cause the appearance of saints and demons. Martin had put Ferrie in contact with the Orthodox Church in Kentucky. Newbrough also pointed out that Ferrie was dismissed from Eastern Airlines, where he was a pilot, after the crimes against nature charges were filed against him, in a case which had involved a boy who was once in

Ferrie's Civil Air Patrol unit. Ferrie once asked Newbrough to sign a false statement against a former CAP cadet involved in the morals case, attesting that he had personally witnessed the teenager habituating homosexual hangouts, but Newbrough refused. Ferrie asked several others to do the same thing.[223]

In 1961, the FBI investigated Ferrie in connection with a possible violation of the Neutrality Act, but none were found. Ferrie was interviewed by the FBI and told investigators that he had worked for the Cuban Revolutionary Front about three days a week since the end of April 1961 collecting food, medicine, clothing, and money for them. Ferrie also gave talks to several clubs, such as the Rotary and Kiwanis Clubs, beginning late in 1960. He also informed the FBI that he started the New Orleans Cadet rifle club in 1959. The FBI was told by a source that Ferrie started a group called the Omnipotents, whose purpose was to train for a possible all-out attack on the United States. A source told the FBI that, in 1955, Ferrie was "very popular and an excellent leader among the boys of the Civil Air Patrol, that he used considerable profanity." Another source told the FBI that Ferrie was critical of the Roosevelt and Truman administrations because they were "trying to drive us into Communism."[224] The FBI report suggests Ferrie was running a Minutemen-like organization for teens.

Jules Ricco Kimble told Garrison investigators that he met David Ferrie at a bar in the French Quarter in 1960, when he was about eighteen years old, and that he flew with Ferrie on several occasions. He recalled taking a plane trip to Canada with Ferrie, Clay Shaw, and a Cuban. Two or three weeks after Ferrie's 1967 death, Kimble received a call from Jack Helm of the Ku Klux Klan, who asked him to take a ride to Ferrie's apartment to pick up papers. Helm went to the back of Ferrie's apartment, exited with a briefcase, and then they drove off. The briefcase was later taken to a "big black box" in St. Bernard Parish that belonged to the Ku Klux Klan. Kimble acquired some of the papers from the briefcase and found they pertained to Klan matters.[225] (Allen Campbell—one of the witnesses described in Chapter One who worked for Banister and saw Oswald at the office—told the author that Jack Helm was a frequent visitor to Banister's office.) Kimble's account suggests that Ferrie, like Banister, had ties to the Ku Klux Klan.[226] It can be noted that Helm served on the State Citizens' Council Board of Directors with close Banister associates Leander Perez and George Singelmann.[227] Helm was also the leader of Perez's Parents and Friends of Catholic Children and the Citizens' Council.[228, 229]

Banister's career as a racist—his ties to the Klan will be described in detail later on—dates back to at least 1956 and is well documented since he was a public figure. Ferrie's track record as a racist is more obscure, but is evident nonetheless. As noted, Ferrie allegedly attended a meeting of the segregationist Citizens' Council. An investigator for Garrison noted that Ferrie once told his cadets "Kennedy is no good, Kennedy is a nigger lover."[230] According to a friend, Ferrie once stated after the assassination: "President Kennedy is the first, they're not going to stop until they kill every nigger in this country."[231] Ferrie had ties to the John Birch Society that advocated segregation and, on one occasion, he invited Cuban exile Julian Buznedo to speak at a JBS meeting.

David Ferrie and the New Orleans Civil Air Patrol

Sidney Edward Voebel attended Beauregard Junior High School with Lee Harvey Oswald and provided an account of his experience to the Warren Commission. Voebel joined the CAP in 1954 or 1955 and invited Oswald to join. He believed, incorrectly, that Oswald only lasted one month. He stated Oswald attended a party at David Ferrie's home after the cadets received their stripes.[232] According to another cadet, Ferrie "completely mesmerized" the cadets in his squad.[233]

John Irion met Ferrie between the period of 1956 and 1957 and told Garrison's investigators that Ferrie's cadets had "personal loyalty to him." Irion recalled that Oswald had been in his squadron. Ferrie—and his cadets in later years—worked with Cuban refugees to raise funds. In the summer on 1963, Ferrie, his CAP cadets, and a few Cuban exiles collected money on Canal Street in New Orleans for the anti-Castro effort. The Cubans and cadets were being trained in five-member, guerilla, small-weapons teams—under what Ferrie claimed were the auspices of the U.S. Marine Corps—for action in Cuba. Ferrie told Irion that the U.S. State Department unofficially asked him to train the units for the purpose of freeing hostages in the Sierra Maestra mountains of Cuba, the training for which took place in Abita Springs, Louisiana.[234] There is no documentary evidence that Ferrie and the marines—or the State Department—had any actual ties whatsoever. The allegation likely represents another of Ferrie's grandiose tall tales. Abita Springs, on the other hand, is in the same area as the training camp used by the John Birch Society, Minutemen, and anti-Castro Cubans, and may have been one and the same. Perry Russo, a friend of Ferrie, corroborated Irion's account. Russo told the press that one of Ferrie's cadets had told him that Ferrie was training them in jungle warfare, "to help bring about more democratic government [in Cuba]."[235] Ferrie's involving the CAP cadets with anti-Castro Cuban activities was not only bizarre, but was completely outside of the scope and mission of the CAP as a national organization.

The FBI documented another instance in which David Ferrie involved his CAP cadets in the anti-Castro effort. On November 26, 1963, the FBI learned that—in July of that same year—several individuals affiliated with the CAP, including Ferrie, went on an overnight campout where they met some Cubans in military training at an undisclosed location.[236] Arnesto Rodriguez, Jr. told Garrison's investigators on February 13, 1967, that he was acquainted with Ferrie and that he was supposed to have formed a small commando unit that held classes in his apartment. He related that the Cubans knew of Ferrie's homosexual tendencies and believed the only reason he wanted to form a commando group was to lure young boys into his apartment.[237]

Another source reported that Ferrie "had a group of boys he played around with . . . ." He said Ferrie had pornographic photographs of the boys, which he used as a threat to keep them in line. In 1959, Ferrie had an organization known as the New Orleans Cadet Rifle Club and obtained .30-caliber rifles from the Crescent Gun Shop for use. The Rifle Club members were also in the CAP. In 1959, as noted above, Ferrie was alleged to have organized a group of boys known as the "Omnipotents." The group was supposed to be planning an invasion of

Cuba—or at least support for one. The mother of a boy in the group looked up "omnipotent" in the dictionary and, after learning of its meaning, told her son not to have anything to do with it.[238] In 1959, Ferrie slept in the same barracks with the cadets during a summer training session.[239] In 1961, Ferrie hosted parties for boys and girls with liquor. Al Landry, who knew Ferrie for five years as a cadet in the CAP, recalled attending a number of stag parties at Ferrie's home where hard liquor was served. Ferrie's perverse behavior continued up to the year he died. In 1967, one source reported Ferrie showed nude motion pictures to young boys.[240] Al Cheramie told Garrison's investigators that he was closely associated with Ferrie as a cadet in the CAP from 1956 to 1959—a period of time shortly after Oswald left. When Cheramie became a marine in 1960, he stayed in contact with Ferrie. He recalled that many of the boys were very close to Ferrie and were called "Dave's boys." Ferrie would spend five days a week with some of the cadets and he often helped them with their homework, and also tried to instill patriotism in his cadets. Cheramie stated that the cadets had no knowledge of Ferrie's homosexuality, but knew he hated women. He felt Ferrie was unstable and was capable of conspiring to assassinate President Kennedy.[241]

Tommy Compton, who was in Ferrie's CAP outfit from 1954 to 1958, told Garrison's investigators in 1967 that he had known Ferrie off and on for ten years. He stated that, sometime before the Kennedy assassination, he drove Ferrie to Banister's Camp Street office, where Ferrie and Banister had a beverage at the restaurant in the front of the building. At 5:00 a.m. on Sunday, after Ferrie returned from his trip to Houston following the assassination, he stayed with Compton in his dormitory room at Southeastern Louisiana State University. According to Compton, Ferrie was hysterical and knew the police had been to his house where they had taken some of his things. He told Compton that he was afraid to return. He placed telephone calls, which Compton believed to be to G. Wray Gill, then left at 8:30 a.m. Compton did not know Lee Harvey Oswald and could not connect him with the CAP. The only knowledge Compton had of Oswald "was from Bill Wulf who headed the New Orleans Astronomers Club." Wulf related that, in 1956, Lee Harvey Oswald attempted to join the club and submitted an application, which was refused. Compton stated that shortly, after the assassination, Ferrie called Wulf and inquired if he knew anything about Oswald. Compton related that he couldn't figure how Ferrie had "knowledge of Mr. Wulf and the Astronomy Club and connecting this with Lee Harvey Oswald."[242] As we shall see later, though it was not noted by Compton, the reason Wulf would not allow Oswald to join his club in 1956 was because Oswald had told him that he was a Communist and was trying to join a Communist cell. Wulf told the Warren Commission about the incident, which was the first time Oswald began acting like a Communist. Not coincidentally, it occurred at the time he was in David Ferrie's CAP unit. Ferrie's call to Wulf after the assassination, asking about his recollections of Oswald, suggests Ferrie had known of Oswald's encounter with Wulf and had something to do with Oswald's professing to be a Communist in 1956.

Roy Tell, the executive Secretary of the CAP "Moisant Division" was closely associated with Ferrie in the late 1950's. He recalled Ferrie was "a devout Catholic and insisted that the boys attend their church." Ferrie often referred the boys to Father Sebastian Argonello.[243]

The HSCA found several witnesses who had knowledge of Lee Harvey Oswald's participation in the CAP with Ferrie. All remaining doubts of their relationship were put to rest in 1994, when a photo of Ferrie and Oswald pictured together at a CAP outing was discovered by author Gus Russo.

David Ferrie's Morals Charges

Between August 5 and August 18, 1961, Ferrie was arrested twice and charged with indecent behavior involving three juvenile boys. According to the press, Ferrie used alcohol, hypnotism, and the excitement of flying, to lure the youngsters into committing indecent acts; all three accusers were former CAP cadets. Afterward, Ferrie visited one of them, sixteen-year-old Eric Crouchet, and threatened him. Ferrie made Crouchet sign a paper stating that he made the accusations up out of anger and revenge and that he would not press charges against him. Ferrie told Crouchet that if he didn't sign the paper, "A Cuban friend would take care of him." Cuban exile Sergio Arcacha Smith who rented the office at 544 Camp Street, later visited Crouchet and threatened him. Crouchet said he signed the paper out of fear, after which Ferrie was charged with intimidation of a witness by the D.A.'s office.[244]

In another case, Ferrie was charged with delinquency in the runaway of Al Landry, a minor. Landry's parents claimed that after their son joined Ferrie's CAP at age fifteen he was not the same. The parents filed a complaint and stated they had seen Ferrie take cadets into a bar on several occasions, including an incident where he took fifty boys to Graci's lounge. According to the Juvenile Police Bureau, another boy, Richard Dumas, slept at Ferrie's house on two occasions. On one occasion, Ferrie masturbated Dumas while masturbating himself. He masturbated Crouchet on four or five occasions, and Landry three times. He showed the boys obscene literature, as well.[245]

Ferrie provided a written statement regarding the morals charges. He stated that, on August 5, 1961, Al Landry of the Civil Air Patrol appeared at his home and told him of the increasing difficulties he was having with his parents. Ferrie claimed that Landry's mother had made an arrangement with his grandfather—who carried a sawed-off shotgun under the front seat of his auto—to beat him with it, supposedly when he found out his grandson had run away from home. The next day, Mrs. Landry and the police appeared at Ferrie's home. On August 12, the police searched Ferrie's house and, on August 14, he was arrested. Ferrie alleged officials told him the only way to get out of his trouble was to pay them off with five thousand dollars. In his affidavit, Ferrie accused Al Landry of associating with Perry Russo—whom he described as a "hard character"—and Lefty Petersen—who hung out at a known homosexual bar. In defense of the morals case brought against him by Landry, Ferrie accused Landry of soliciting "blow jobs" from homosexuals and other criminal offenses. He also accused Crouchet of engaging in crimes against nature with a male nurse, giving "blow jobs" for money, and other misdeeds. Ferrie insisted that Al Landry and Eric Crouchet were the criminals and that their accusations were made to blackmail him.[246]

Robert E. Lee was an attorney and pilot who occasionally flew with Ferrie for Eastern Airlines in 1967. He also worked in the D.A.'s office and told Jim Garrison that Ferrie wanted to retain his legal services to adopt then-seventeen-year-old Albert Cheramie in the early 1960s. Three weeks later, Cheramie joined the Marine Corps, which terribly upset Ferrie. He wanted Lee to help him get Cheramie out of the marines, and was prepared to pay any amount. Ferrie told him that he and Cheramie had had homosexual relations and suggested to Lee that he use that to get him out of the marines. In Lee's presence, Ferrie hastily typed a three-page letter to the marines, relating Cheramie's alleged homosexuality. Lee tore it up and told Ferrie to get out of his office and to never come back. Ferrie, on one occasion, confided to Lee that he flew in and out of Cuba with passengers from Tampa and the Florida Keys. He mentioned that he trained Cuban guerillas.[247] (According to one source, Ferrie and Arcacha Smith were scheming to sabotage machinery in Cuba through a plot named "Operation Mosquito." Ferrie even told a friend he was training people to go in and out of Cuba at nighttime.[248])

Ferrie kept handwritten notes for his defense of the morals charges and the resultant FAA hearings on the matter that led to his dismissal from Eastern Airlines. Ferrie wrote that, in 1959, he gave a lot of talks on Communism—often giving talks on career days and regularly speaking about the deterioration of the schools. Ferrie stated that it became apparent to him that Castro was a Communist in 1959 and, as a result, that spurred him to assist Cuban refugees in the area.

On August 16, 1961, Ferrie was hit with a crime against nature charge in regard to the Crouchet case, and a second charge of public intimidation. Ferrie wrote that he was making the same type of speeches that Captain Rickenbacker (a radical-right national figure) was making throughout the country. Explaining the reason for his legal problems, he stated, "I felt I was getting too close to something and my fangs were pulled."[249] Ferrie further implied that the Communists were behind the charges because of his anti-Communist views.

Ferrie sought help in his legal troubles in connection with the morals cases from Guy Banister. Ferrie stated that Banister knew he was giving two or three speeches a week against Communism and Castro. Banister checked his files and found out that Richard Dowling, the prosecuting district attorney at the time of the charges, was a member of "the legal arm of the Communist Party" which he had determined from congressional documents in his files. Ferrie claimed the district attorney brought charges against him because he was an outspoken anti-Communist and the D.A. was associated with the Communist Party.[250] Banister's close associate Judge Leander Perez despised Dowling, and had worked for his ouster from office. (Perez had helped Garrison defeat Dowling and take over the D.A.'s office in 1962 by financially backing his campaign.) On two occasions while Perez addressed a Citizens' Council rally, he pointed out Garrison—his new, handpicked district attorney—to the crowd. Ferrie was eventually exonerated when Eric Crouchet withdrew the charges against him.

The Eastern Airlines Grievance Hearings

Ferrie was fired from Eastern Airlines as a result of the morals charges against him. Eric Crouchet wrote the president of Eastern Airlines on January 1, 1963, and told him that he wanted to exonerate Captain Ferrie, after which Ferrie filed a grievance against the airline for his reinstatement. Guy Banister testified at the grievance hearings held on July 15, 1961, in Miami, where G. Wray Gill served as Ferrie's attorney. At the onset, Banister and Ferrie complained that someone had rifled through their baggage at the Miami airport.

The counsel for Eastern noted that Ferrie had eleven charges against him. A member of the New Orleans Police testified that several boys in Ferrie's CAP squad often slept at his house and had been molested by him. The officer recalled that one boy was not returned to his parents until he signed a statement given to him by Sergio Arcacha Smith stating that he would not press charges against Ferrie.

Ferrie testified that Communists and fellow travelers at Eastern were out to get him. He blamed the Communists for his arrests on morals charges and for his dismissal from Eastern Airlines. He told the grievance committee, "At this time we do not know the chain of command of the Communists at the local level. However, my problem has been traced with certainty to highly-placed local officials." He explained further, "We have been beset in New Orleans with members of the Communist Party and/or their agents."

Guy Banister testified on Ferrie's behalf after presenting his impressive credentials in law enforcement. G. Wray Gill examined Banister. Banister told him he had been retained by Ferrie to reinvestigate the morals charges brought against Ferrie by Eric Crouchet. He said that Crouchet was unstable and was the type who would frighten easily and—under the circumstances—would do anything that he was told. Banister told the grievance hearing that Mrs. Landry was the instigator of the charges against Ferrie regarding her son Al, testifying, "Behind Mrs. Landry there was most certainly the influence of Communism. The tactics of the Communists is the big smear and the attempt to place a moral turpitude label on those they wish to 'get' . . . . You see, by accident, Captain Ferrie stumbled onto something big the Communists were doing in this port city of New Orleans. In his patriotism he meant to stop it. The charges resulted." Banister cited fourteen individuals he had interviewed in regards to the charge of moral turpitude who told him that Ferrie was highly moral and a credit to his community.

Despite their best efforts, Ferrie was not reinstated.[251] Regardless, many of Ferrie's cadets displayed tremendous loyalty towards him. His serial sexual molestations of the cadets suggests he had the ability to get them do practically anything he asked of them. (In Chapter Twenty-two evidence will be presented that Ferrie, a fanatical anti-Communist, was likely responsible for Oswald's posing as a Communist in 1956—and his move to the Soviet Union in 1959.)

Mrs. Oswald recalled that a man in a uniform came to her home and urged her to allow her son to join the service. The man may have been Ferrie. Oswald wrote the name of his wife and the name of his son, David Lee Oswald, in his diary while he was in the in the

Soviet Union. Oswald didn't have a son, but perhaps he was bestowing the name of David on his future son in honor of David Ferrie.[252]

Kent Courtney and Lee Harvey Oswald

Kent Courtney was a close associate of Guy Banister and there is a credible witness account that he, like Banister, was seen with Lee Harvey Oswald on numerous occasions. Courtney's relationship with Banister dates to 1958, when the two men joined with other members of the American Legion, James Pfister, and Festus J. Brown, and expressed opposition to a New Orleans student's plan to attend the Communist-sponsored World Youth Festival in Vienna. A seminar planned to warn students about the threat of Communism included Guy Banister and Medford Evans as the featured speakers.[253] (Kent Courtney and Medford Evans are important figures, since both were close to Guy Banister as well as General Walker, a purported near-victim of a Lee Harvey Oswald bullet in April 1963. As will be discussed later, it is unlikely that Oswald actually tried to kill Walker, given the mutual association of both men with Guy Banister and Kent Courtney.)

In the early 1970s, in an attempt to secure a job as an instructor of political science at Northwestern State University of Louisiana, Courtney donated a large number of tape recordings from his radio programs and assorted writings, pamphlets, and copies of his right-wing newspaper to the University's Special Collections. Courtney wrote a three-page letter of introduction to his political collection and stated, "At one time I acquired the library of a friend of mine who had been a member of the anti-Red squad of the FBI and who later was Assistant Superintendent of the New Orleans Police Department. These books are by and about members of the Communist Conspiracy." Courtney was clearly referring to Guy Banister. Included in the collection was a book from Banister's library, which was stamped with his name on the cover. The book was *The Twilight of Capitalism* by William Z. Foster, former chairman of the American Communist Party. (Foster died in the Soviet Union in 1961 and was memorialized in Red Square.)

Kent Harbinson Courtney was born in Minnesota and moved to New Orleans as a boy. He graduated from Tulane University and eventually became an instructor at the university. Courtney considered himself a "Taft-MacArthur-McCarthy conservative," and he and his wife Phoebe were fervent admirers of Senator Joseph McCarthy. In 1954, Courtney held a rally in New Orleans to protest McCarthy's censure in the U.S. Congress. Dismayed by McCarthy's political demise, Courtney was inspired to publish a far-right newspaper on January 1, 1955, called *Free Men Speak*. *Solid South* was its successor, printed by Courtney in 1959 with an emphasis on states' rights and the formation of a new, third political party. Courtney ran for governor of Louisiana under the states' rights banner in 1960 and did poorly.[254] The paper's name was changed again to the *Independent American*, reflecting Courtney's desire to form an ultra-conservative third party. In support of that goal, Courtney wrote letters to General Douglas MacArthur, Clarence Manion, and Senators James O. Eastland, and Strom Thurmond urging the formation of a "New Party."

Courtney, unlike Banister and Ferrie, tried to maintain a veneer of mainstream respectability. He avoided being associated with the various far-right fringe groups like the Klan or the Nazis, if for no other reason than expediency. Courtney, instead, tried to draw mainstream politicians to his proposed conservative third party. Nonetheless, Harold Lord Varney, an admitted Nazi, sat on the board of his Conservative Society of America.

Courtney was a national leader of the radical right in the 1950s and 60s and networked across the country with other national right-wing figures. As a result of his stature in the national far-right movement, Courtney most likely placed Guy Banister in touch with other prominent members of the national far-right movement, such as General Walker. On October 29, 1959, Revilo Oliver, Dan Smoot, William F. Buckley, Tom Anderson, and Robert Welch spoke at Courtney's Chicago "New Party" meeting. (All but Buckley, a moderate, are important figures in the assassination story presented in this work.)[255] Retired Lieutenant General Pedro del Valle was named "Temporary Chairman" of Courtney's New Party at its inception.[256] Del Valle, like Banister, saw Communists everywhere and had a violent disposition. (Del Valle is also an important figure in the assassination conspiracy as will be detailed in Chapter Eight.) The New Party effort led to Courtney hosting an annual spring meeting in Chicago called the "Congress of Conservatives," which featured various speakers including Robert Welch of the John Birch Society and General Walker. Welch, Walker, and Harry Everingham spoke at the May 1963 meeting in Chicago.[257] Courtney operated *Let Freedom Ring* in New Orleans, an operation that consisted of a pre-recorded far-right-wing message that could be listened to by dialing the organization's phone number.[258]

Courtney also had ties to the ultra-right Constitution Party. An FBI informant who attended the October 1963 Constitution Party convention in Indianapolis notified the FBI that he learned of threats to assassinate President Kennedy, which, as will be seen later, were the same plots behind the assassination. Courtney was not, however, at that meeting. Kent Courtney did attend the Constitution Party meeting on September 20, 1956,[259] and he was invited to speak before the Constitution Party of Florida in Pensacola in 1966.[260]

Guy Banister's relationship with General Walker was described as "tight" by one Garrison investigator and may have developed through Courtney. Banister was also an associate of Medford Evans and Robert Morris of Dallas, Texas, who came to Walker's defense after he was relieved of his command of the twenty-fourth infantry division in Germany in 1961 by the Kennedy administration. General Walker had been censured by the Kennedy administration for publicly stating that former first lady Eleanor Roosevelt and President Truman were "pink" or pro-Communist. (Walker eventually resigned from the army.) Kent and Phoebe Courtney wrote a book about the Walker affair in 1962 that was also bitterly critical of President Kennedy, entitled *The Case of General Walker.* (A pre-release edition was published on August 16, 1961.)[261]

Although long prominent in radical-right circles, Courtney came to national attention in the mainstream media when the widely sold *Look* magazine published a story on the far right on March 13, 1962, entitled "Rightist Revival: Who's on the Far Right?" Featured were biographies of prominent members of the radical right, including wealthy dog food maker D. B. Lewis, Dan Smoot, Robert Welch, Patrick J. Frawley, and General Walker. A full-page photo of Walker standing behind a rostrum,which was taken from the floor, made Walker appear larger than life. Dan Smoot's remarks to a reporter succinctly described the consensus sentiment of the far right at the time: "I wondered when I was a member of the FBI Commy squad, why those who opposed Communism were vilified and slandered. I learned the reason. It was because people were blindly following the philosophy of the New Deal, which stands for the total transfer of power from the individual to the Federal Government under the claim of using the power beneficently. This is the same philosophy of the Fair Deal, the New Frontier and modern republicanism. It is also the basic philosophy of Communism, Fascism and Nazism." The story featured numerous pictures of Courtney and his wife Phoebe, who Courtney described as "so far right the only thing beyond is outer Space." The article quoted Mrs. Courtney as saying she preferred her steaks cooked "Communist blood red." Phoebe Courtney, commenting on the subject of President Kennedy, stated that Kennedy "gives aid and comfort to the enemy, and that's the Constitutional definition of treason." Phoebe was pictured applauding a speech by General Walker, in which he called for the impeachment of Chief Justice Earl Warren. Kent Courtney stated that there were "hidden Communists in Congress who vote 100 percent for what the Communists want." Other associates of Guy Banister mentioned in the article were Fred Schwartz, Billy James Hargis, and Edward Hunter. The article concluded with Kent Courtney stating, "People are going to be surprised and stunned in 1964 when all these groups and organizations are coordinated. There may be enough to take powerful political action."[262]

In 1962, Courtney was on the state board of the Citizens' Council with Banister colleagues George Singelmann, Leander Perez, Willie Rainach, and an up-and-comer in the segregation and anti-Communist movement, John Rarick.[263]

Michael Kurtz, Professor of History and Government at Southeastern Louisiana University, observed Oswald and Guy Banister sitting together at Mancuso's Restaurant in the infamous Newman Building at 544 Camp Street. In 1980, Kurtz reported his Banister-Oswald sightings in an article in *Louisiana History*. As intriguing as the Banister-Oswald sightings, Kurtz wrote about a Courtney-Oswald connection as well, without disclosing Courtney's name, as follows:

One feature of Oswald's five-month sojourn in New Orleans that has never been revealed is the fact that he made several trips to Baton Rouge in the summer of 1963. According to witnesses, Oswald accompanied a prominent leader of the White Citizens' Council and other segregationist organizations to Baton Rouge six or eight times in July and August. These witnesses met Oswald, who was introduced to them as "Leon" Oswald. Oswald's companion, who was a personal friend of two of these witnesses, stated he was employing "Leon" to do construction work for him. Oswald, however, was not dressed in work clothes; he was wearing what appeared to be "dressy clothes." Furthermore, Oswald and his companion engaged in discussions which included criticism of American foreign policy as being "soft on Communism" and of United States civil rights programs. On their last visit to Baton Rouge, the two men were accompanied by two "Latins," neither of whom said anything to them.[264]

Kurtz cited his sources as "confidential interviews." The author wrote to Kurtz in 1996 and asked him the name of the prominent member of the Citizens' Council. Kurtz responded that it was Kent Courtney, which he felt he could now reveal with the passage of time. (Courtney's name has never been disclosed heretofore.) The reasons for Courtney's trips with Oswald to Baton Rouge were not disclosed. However, Courtney, like Banister, was active in the Free Electors movement trying to oust President Kennedy from office, spearheaded by Leander Perez, which had intensified its activities that summer in Baton Rouge.[265]

At a major meeting of the Free Electors on September 4, 1963, at the Capitol House Hotel in Baton Rouge, Guy Banister was seen in the company of General Walker and Clinton, Louisiana, attorney, Richard Van Buskirk. Lee Harvey Oswald, not coincidentally, was in Clinton, Louisiana—outside of Baton Rouge—around the same time, standing in a Congress of Racial Equality voter registration line with African-Americans attempting to register to vote before a hostile racist registrar. Oswald's appearance in Clinton with members of CORE may have been the reason for his reported visits to Baton Rouge with Kent Courtney. (Oswald's association with CORE during the height of racial tensions will be discussed in detail.) Kurtz's allegation is not without additional support.

Raymond Broshears, a close friend of David Ferrie, related that Ferrie told him that Courtney was involved in the Kennedy assassination. Broshears referred to Courtney as a "financier in New Orleans." Broshears made additional extraordinary claims[266] that appear credible, and will be examined thoroughly in Chapter Nineteen.

After Carlos Bringuier and Lee Harvey Oswald were arrested, Bringuier went to Courtney for advice on legal counsel. A characteristic consistent of all of Oswald's public demonstrations is that his assumed adversaries were always tied to Banister's operation. Bringuier, Oswald's adversary in the scuffle, was one of several Cubans connected with Cuban exile efforts at Banister's office building. Courtney, whom he consulted, was close to Banister and a regular visitor to his office. A similar phenomenon occurred when Oswald infiltrated the leftist group New Orleans Committee for Peaceful Alternatives (NOCPA): Kent Courtney, Carlos Bringuier, Banister's secretary Mary Brengel, and others tied to the Banister operation were the group's adversaries—and counter-demonstrated against them.

Courtney was also a member of the advisory board of the Committee to Free Cuba of Arcadia, California. The group was chaired by Cuban Tirso del Junco, a frequent speaker with Billy James Hargis of the Christian Crusade. Other notable luminaries on the national far right were Herbert Philbrick and Matt Cvetic (two "former Communists"), Walter Knott, John H. Rousselot, General Sumter Lowry, J. B. Mathews, and Phyllis Schlafly. Listed as a supporter was Robert Surrey, a Dallas Nazi and close associate of General Walker.[267] Surrey is best known for circulating a "Wanted for Treason" poster featuring a mug-shot-like photo of President Kennedy just prior to Kennedy's assassination, and he was called to testify before the Warren Commission because of that poster.

Courtney, like Banister, was present at the infamous Congress of Freedom (COF) meeting in April 1963 in New Orleans, a fact which is being disclosed for the first time in this work. The COF held annual meetings and featured speakers from the national far right. It was estimated that the majority of attendees were members of the John Birch Society, like Courtney and Banister. An FBI informant at the meeting learned that there was a plot to assassinate high-ranking members of government and industry, as well as members of the Council on Foreign Relations. (An entire chapter is devoted to this critical event.)

Courtney was the director of the American Legion Americanism Committee, representing thirty posts. On one occasion, he objected to a lecturer's appearance at the Louisiana State University Law School because Courtney claimed the lecturer was associated with several pro-Communist groups.[268] Not surprsingly, the Louisiana Committee on Un-American Activities was spawned from the American Legion Americanism Committee—and Guy Banister served as a special advisor.

Kent Courtney and Marguerite Oswald

On October 27, 1964, not long after the Warren Commission Report was published, the mother of Lee Harvey Oswald, Marguerite Oswald, telephoned Kent Courtney. A concerned Courtney wrote to J. Edgar Hoover and provided a transcript of the call. The letter from Courtney read as follows:

> Dear Mr. Hoover,
>
> At approximately 5:45 p.m. on October 27, 1964, I answered my home telephone (University 5-1613) and a woman's voice introduced herself saying, "Is this Kent Courtney? This is Mrs. Oswald." I did not know any Mrs. Oswald, so I said, "What are your initials?" She replied, "I am the mother of Lee Oswald. My first name is Marguerite."
>
> She said that she wanted to know if I had ever had any contact with her son.
>
> I answered at no time had I any direct contact with her son.
>
> Mrs. Oswald went on for several minutes in an apparently well-rehearsed statement in which she attempted to prove that her son was not the assassin of President Kennedy.
>
> She pointed out what she considered several errors in the Warren Commission Report, while at the same time telling me that if her son killed the president he would have been proud to tell everyone that he did and tell them why. At the same time she said that she was wrongly accused, that she did not alter her son Lee's birth certificate; but in a sort of double-talk she indicated that he might

have altered the birth certificate.

At one point Mrs. Oswald asked me if my printing company had ever printed anything for the Fair Play for Cuba Committee. I told her that I had not printed anything, and that if he had come and asked me to print it I would have refused. I have no idea why she called me or how she got my name, and I terminated the conversation as quickly as I could by repeating again, "I have had no personal contact with your son and therefore I don't think there is anything I can do for you."

I did volunteer the information that I thought the Warren Commission Report was incomplete and that I did hope after the election of Barry Goldwater that the new Congress would set up a special joint committee for further investigation into the assassination.

Knowing that Mrs. Oswald has been talking before audiences, arranged in some cases by individuals with Communist-front affiliations, and knowing that Mrs. Oswald is doing everything to confuse the issue, I would not be a bit surprised to see it reported that Mrs. Oswald might be saying things on the lecture platform claiming that she learned these things from me as a result of a telephone conversation with me, giving the hour, the date and time.

Therefore, this is the reason I am informing you by this letter, and your Field Agents in Charge at the New Orleans and Dallas offices, concerning this conversation.

As you know, I have always made it a practice to send the Washington office and local New Orleans office copies of all our publications, and I wish to reaffirm the fact that we here at THE INDEPENDENT AMERICAN shall always support the Federal Bureau of Investigation in its effort to control crime and the agents of the international, atheistic Communist conspiracy.

Constitutionally yours,

Kent Courtney, Publisher
THE INDEPENDENT AMERICAN

Courtney may have suspected that Mrs. Oswald might inform the FBI of her suspicion that her son had worked for him. Courtney therefore may have alerted the FBI about the accusation to preemptively reduce any likelihood of suspicion from the FBI of a relationship with Oswald. It's conceivable that Director J. Edgar Hoover knew Courtney was close to Guy Banister and would overlook any other allegations that might arise about a Courtney-Oswald relationship.[269] It's worth noting that Courtney qualified his denial of a relationship with Oswald stating he had no "personal" and no "direct" relationship with him. (Chapter Twenty will describe Courtney's counter demonstration with two other Banister associates against a campus peace group that Oswald had infiltrated.)

Oddly enough, in 1968, after the capture of the later-convicted assassin of Martin Luther King, Jr.—James Earl Ray—Ray's brother Jerry approached Courtney in New Orleans. Curiously, Courtney tape recorded the unexpected meeting as he had a habit of doing, and the recording still exists today. (In 1958, Courtney taped a phone conversation with Robert Welch, insisting on his appearance at the Congress of Conservatives that year. The two alluded to Welch's preoccupation with a new important undertaking—presumably the formation of the John Birch Society in that same year. Courtney also tape recorded a debriefing of Carlos Bringuier after his interrogation by Jim Garrison.) During Courtney's conversation with Jerry Ray, Courtney sounded anxious. The two were extremely vague, but Ray stated that he had approached Courtney because of instructions from his brother, James Earl. Jerry Ray alluded to the fact that James Earl had been in New Orleans before King's assassination, and seemed to be trying to get Courtney to volunteer anything he might know about his brother's activities while in Courtney's hometown. No specifics came from the conversation. James Earl Ray had spent some time at the Los Angeles John Birch Society offices in 1968, which doubled as the George Wallace for President campaign office. At the same time, Courtney was the Louisiana Coordinator of the John Birch Society and was close to George Wallace and his campaign. There is no known evidence that Courtney alerted the FBI to his meeting with Jerry Ray. However, the simple fact that family members of two of the most notorious presumed assassins in American history approached Kent Courtney regarding the assassinations is stunning.[270]

Delphine Roberts

Delphine Roberts was Guy Banister's secretary and love interest at the time of the Kennedy assassination and shared his radical-right philosophies. Louise Kombar, who knew Delphine Roberts through her husband Marvin, told the FBI, "Mrs. Delphine Roberts's extreme right-wing group would make the John Birch Society look like Communists." Kombar's husband, who belonged to one of Roberts's groups, once remarked, "Throw all the niggers to the alligators; line them up and machine gun them down."[271] Lester Ottilio, who once worked for Banister, told a Garrison investigator that Delphine Roberts was Banister's girlfriend, whom he described as, "radical, way out, I think she was a nut."[272]

Roberts told Garrison's investigators in 1967 that she began to work for Guy Banister around March of 1962 when he trained her as a "confidential secretary."[273] Her political activism began when President Roosevelt and the first lady, whom she referred to as "his Negro wife, Eleanor," got the United States into the United Nations, whose charter she stated was based on the Communist Manifesto.[274] Roberts addressed the New Orleans City Council and asked them to remove the United Nations flag from the council chamber of City Hall, remarking that Communists has drawn up the U.N. charter.[275] Roberts announced that she planned to run for councilman-at-large in the January 27, 1962, primary election on a platform of segregation and anti-Communism. She pledged she would work to remove the U.N. flag from all public buildings and move the U.N. out of the U.S., and stated she was a proud member of the John Birch Society.[276] (Most on the far right during that era despised the United Nations.) Roberts, like Banister, saw Communists everywhere. She wrote to J. Edgar Hoover on December 9, 1959, and told him, "the Russian secret police, their agents and informers are in swarms in our National Capitol and throughout our whole country and have been infiltrating so many of our Organizations and Clubs . . . ." She added, "I also know that many of our patriotic as well as civic clubs have been infiltrated by the Communists . . . ."[277]

Roberts was a member of a far-right group called Discussion Unlimited that hosted many prominent national figures on the far right, who are important figures who are extremely relevant to this work.[278] General A. C. Wedemeyer, a close associate of H. L. Hunt, spoke before Discussion Unlimited on November 13, 1956.[279] Senator Eastland addressed the group on the Communist menace, on December 14, 1958, two years after his New Orleans Communist inquisition in which he was assisted by Guy Banister and Hubert Badeaux.[280] Revilo Oliver addressed Discussion Unlimited on May 8, 1959, on the dangers of Communism.[281] Oliver was also a Warren Commission witness and founding member of the John Birch Society. He went before the Warren Commission and presented his far-fetched theory as to why a Communist, Lee Harvey Oswald, killed President Kennedy, the most liberal president in modern times who strove to bring about détente with the Communist Soviet Union. Robert Morris, counsel during Eastland's 1956 inquisition of New Orleans integrationists, spoke before Discussions Unlimited on May 6, 1960, and declared that Cuban revolutionary Fidel Castro was a Communist.[282] Tom Anderson, another founding member of the John Birch Society, and a close associate of General Walker, was invited to address Discussion Unlimited on January 19, 1961.[283]

Roberts, like Banister, also hated African Americans and integrationists. In the early sixties, she became involved with the anti-integration movement. She gained fame by picketing schools undergoing integration and, as a result of her efforts, the Soviet newspaper *Pravda* took note and wrote about them.[284] She admired southern leaders who fought to preserve segregation. She stated, "Men like Governor Faubus and Senator Eastland are the Patrick Henrys of today."[285]

In addition, Roberts hated the Kennedy brothers. On July 27, 1963, she urged "Congress to demand the removal of the Kennedy brothers and impeachment against both be begun immediately."[286] She was also the chairwoman of the far-right Women for Constitutional Government, which adopted a resolution opposing the Kennedy administration and the civil rights bill, "on the grounds of usurpation of power and malfeasance in office."[287]

Roberts joined the White Citizens' Council and spoke at PTA meetings on the Communist plot behind integration of the schools. She knew Leander Perez and, like Perez, was excommunicated from the Catholic Church. Roberts told the HSCA she worked for the

Sovereignty Commission on several groups in New Orleans that were anti-American, no doubt in conjunction with Banister's own work with the Commission. The Commission was interested in Black Muslims and other un-American groups, but particularly those felt to be aligned with Communism. Roberts corresponded with Senator Eastland and his committee and another congressional committee she did not identify. She recalled corresponding with one of J. Edgar Hoover's assistants—Ed or John Sullivan—after he came to New Orleans and spoke to the American Legion. She related that Sullivan talked with arch-segregationist Leander Perez, who told him that he was very concerned about the activities in New Orleans.

In 1961 or 1962, she opened a patriotic booth on Canal Street after she decided the American flag was not getting enough respect. She flew the confederate flag and played patriotic music. The police were called by Canal Street merchants, whom she noted were all Jews. That's when she first met Banister. He came into the booth wearing a suit, hat, and gun and told the police that if they were going to arrest her they would have to arrest him. She recalled that Banister had one of the largest and most complete files on Communists and fellow travelers, stating that Banister was very upset because Sam Newman and his building janitor, James Arthus, let Oswald use the office upstairs at 544 Camp. She related that Banister stated, "how is it going to look for him to have the same address as me?" She told the committee that she took a radio to work on the day of the assassination, and she said that Guy Banister accused Jack Martin of stealing some files and pistol-whipped him.[288]

Roberts obviously shared completely Banister's racist and radical right wing views. According to police reports furnished to D.A. Garrison, Roberts appeared in a photograph, in 1961, in front of the New Orleans Federal Building with a placard declaring her opposition to President Kennedy because of his stance on integration. On one side, the sign stated that Kennedy and others in government were Socialists and they should get out of government. On the other side, she called Martin Luther King, Jr. a "racist agitator" whom she described as a "Socialist agent." The sign stated that Kennedy "was planning to use New Orleans as the place from which to issue the second Emancipation Proclamation." Also in 1961, Roberts handed out an anti-integration booklet with "The National States' Rights Party La. Branch Box 4342 N.O. La." stamped on it. She also handed out John Birch Society and anti-United Nations literature stamped, "Council on American Relations, 710 Summit Boulevard, West Palm Beach, Fla." (The Council on American Relations was a group that, in 1962, began plotting the assassination of prominent figures in the Council of Foreign Relations and members of government and industry. After the FBI learned about it, the plot narrowed to the assassination of the president. Those plots will be detailed in later chapters.)

On April 16, 1962, Roberts also picketed a Camp Street church protesting integration. On April 30, 1962, she picketed City Hall in protest of President Kennedy's upcoming visit to New Orleans (on May 5, 1962). Then, on May 2, she again picketed Kennedy's upcoming visit with a sign declaring there was treason in the government for allowing Castro to come into power in Cuba. On the day of Kennedy's 1962 New Orleans visit, Roberts picketed the event. The police noted that most of her demonstrations involved two or three people—usually members of the John Birch Society. In the first sentences of her campaign platform—published when she ran in the Councilman-at-large primary on January 27, 1962—she declared that she was a "strong segregationist and strong believer in white supremacy." She opposed the NAACP, CORE, "and other organizations that has [sic] for its prime goal, cramming down the White people's throats, integration, mongrelizing and all social mixing of the negro [sic] race with Caucasians. . . I am opposed to integration of any kind, shape or form, because it is an integral part of the International Communist Conspiracy."

Roberts opposed eminent domain and likened it to provisions set forth in Karl Marx's Communist Manifesto.[289] She summed up the worldview she shared with Guy Banister to author Anthony Summers: "He and I were against the way they were going about it, which ignored the civil rights of the white person . . . It was taking away from whites and giving it all to the Negroes . . . ."[290] Summers did not figure Banister's radical right and segregationist activities into his theory that the assassination was perhaps committed by a rogue element of the CIA that included Banister and his associates. Summer's investigation of the Banister operation is invaluable, however—as we shall see—the widely held theory of CIA involvement is unsubstantiated.

Leander Perez

Perhaps none of Banister's close associates was more important than Judge Leander Perez. Perez was the wealthy district attorney of Plaquemines Parish, adjacent to New Orleans. (An entire chapter, Chapter Ten, will be devoted to Perez. He will only be mentioned briefly here.) Perez's relationship with Guy Banister dates back to 1956, when he pledged to help Banister ferret out Communists in the state. Perez was a fanatical segregationist and devoted his life to the battle to preserve it.

Perez had an iron grip on the state legislature and was responsible for two pieces of legislation designed to defeat President Kennedy and his civil right initiatives. The first was the "Free Electors" legislation that was designed to withhold Louisiana's electors from the Kennedy slate in the 1964 election. By doing so, they expected other southern states to join them and throw the election into the House of Representatives. They would use their resultant bargaining power to quash civil rights legislation. The second law—contrived by Perez and the chairman of the Louisiana Un-American Activities Committee, Representative James Pfister—was the Communist Control Act of 1962. The law was enacted at the same time of Oswald's return from the Soviet Union in June of 1962. Under the law, members of so-called Communist-front groups like Fair Play for Cuba Committee, the Congress of Racial Equality, and other organizations tied to the civil rights movement could be arrested and sentenced up to thirty years in jail. The law called for any members of those groups who associated with someone like Lee Harvey Oswald, a "known" Communist, to face the same penalty. The law would have the effect of stopping the integration movement in its tracks.

Perez, like Banister, was close to General Walker, who gave speeches around the country bitterly critical of President Kennedy's stance on Communism and integration.

Conclusions

A number of documented accounts of Ferrie's tawdry, criminal behavior are cited as examples of his ability to mesmerize his cadets as well as to highlight his impressive power of persuasion. Like the Oswald-Banister relationship, the Ferrie-Oswald relationship presents a paradox in view of Ferrie's anti-Communist fanaticism, juxtaposed with Oswald's professed allegiance to Communism, but evidence that will be presented in later chapters resolves this dilemma. There are good reasons to suspect that Ferrie molded Lee Harvey Oswald, especially in the early years, and was responsible for Oswald posing as a Communist in 1956 while in the CAP—as well as his Herbert Philbrick-like portrayal of a Communist later.

Kent Courtney was closely tied to Guy Banister. Their relationship dates back to at least 1958 when they worked together on the American Legion Un-American Activities Committee. He was often in Banister's office during the same time as Oswald. The allegation that he was seen multiple times with Oswald gains added credibility from Raymond Broshear's allegation that Courtney had some connection to the assassination. Mrs. Oswald's suspicions about a relationship between Courtney and her son only support the allegations of an Oswald-Courtncy relationship. Moreover, the fact that Courtney provided Carlos Bringuier with advice after his scuffle with Oswald raises further suspicions.

Kent Courtney was one of Guy Banister's conduits to the national radical right and may have been the one who introduced Banister to General Walker, an event of tremendous historical importance. Oswald was involved in some way in the Walker shooting incident, and also the Bringuier scuffle during his FPCC pamphleting. In each of those cases, his adversaries—Bringuier and Walker—were associates of Kent Courtney, as well as Guy Banister. In a third incident, Courtney and Bringuier, along with other associates of Guy Banister, protested against a peace group that Oswald had infiltrated, which will be discussed in Chapter Twenty.

Delphine Roberts's worldview mirrors Banister's, and provides a reflection of his political philosophy during Oswald's time in New Orleans. However, there is no evidence that Roberts had anything to do with Oswald's parading around as a Communist in the summer of 1963 or his role in the assassination. She simply may not have understood the meaning of the whole Oswald affair.

CHAPTER THREE

LEE HARVEY OSWALD AND THE NAZIS

*Above the operational level, insulated and removed to the point of being
very nearly invisible, appeared to have been individuals whose political
orientation can only be described as Neo-Nazi. Even as I have described
this Neo-Nazi aspect, I am sure that it sounds somewhat fanciful. Because of the unbelievability of this part of the picture, I have found it
necessary to refrain from mentioning it . . . . Nevertheless, the essentially
Fascist origin of the assassination is inescapable.*
— D.A. Jim Garrison's Letter to Lord Bertrand Russell,
August 27, 1967

Evidence of Lee Harvey Oswald's ties to two members of the American Nazi Party and
others of a Nazi philosophical belief and orientation during his residence in New
Orleans in the summer of 1963 will be presented in this chapter. Those contacts were
identified in documents from the FBI, as well as the subsequent investigation of New Orleans district attorney Jim Garrison. Oswald's ties to the Nazis are at odds with the Warren
Commission's conclusion that Oswald was a Communist, an ideology at the opposite end of
the political spectrum from Nazism. Clues that Oswald and his family were of a radical right,
racist, and anti-Semitic orientation will be presented, here, as well.

Guy Banister, George Lincoln Rockwell, and the American Nazi Party

Eleven witnesses identified Lee Harvey Oswald in the company of Guy Banister in New
Orleans in the summer of 1963, as was noted in Chapter One. Two of Guy Banister's former
employees, Lester Ottilio and Louise Decker, told investigators for District Attorney Jim
Garrison that a meeting of Commander George Lincoln Rockwell of the American Nazi Party
(ANP) and Guy Banister took place in Banister's office in 1961. Years later, Ottilio, a member
of the New Orleans Police Department, was assigned to a special detail assisting the D.A.'s
office during Garrison's assassination investigation.[291]

Banister's Nazi orientation may come as a surprise to those who accepted Jim Garrison's unsupported depiction of Banister as a CIA or government agent, but Banister's an-

ti-Semitism was well documented. In a letter he wrote to segregationist leader Willie Rainach, he stated, "International Communism is controlled and completely subservient to Jewish leaders: therefore the greater danger to the country is from the Jews."[292]

George Lincoln Rockwell, a former Naval Commander, founded the American Nazi Party in Arlington, Virginia, in 1958, at approximately the same time as the birth of the John Birch Society.[293] Like many in the John Birch Society, Rockwell identified General Douglas MacArthur, Charles Lindberg, and Senator Joseph McCarthy as inspirational influences. Rockwell saw his enemies as Jews, race mixers, and Communists. "Jews are through in 1972!" was his motto. Like many of Banister's associates, Rockwell was opposed to democracy, calling it "mob rule." He believed in an authoritarian republic and a "back-to-Africa" movement for Negroes. Rockwell sold "Hatenanny" records, which were a spin on the beatnik and hippie-era folk concerts known as Hootenannies. One recording crudely entitled "Ship Them Niggers Back," sold for ninety-nine cents.[294]

Rockwell housed his storm troopers in barracks at the American Nazi Party headquarters in Virginia, where they spent their time reading Nazi literature, performing calisthenics, and completing military drills. Dressed in full Nazi regalia, the storm troopers picketed Jewish gatherings and the White House. Funding was scarce, however, and the storm troopers often subsisted on rations of cornflakes and water, and boredom and frustration with Commander Rockwell led to a high membership turnover.[295]

The FBI identified one of Guy Banister's close associates, Colonel Bluford Balter, and Ray James Leahart as leaders of the New Orleans American Nazi Party. Balter was the owner of the Balter Building on 403 Camp Street, a short distance from the infamous 544 Camp Street address where Oswald was seen on numerous occasions. The Balter Building was the center of radical right-wing activity in New Orleans in the 1950s and early 1960s. The offices of the segregationist Citizens' Council operated by close Banister associates George Singelmann and Leander Perez were housed in the Balter Building in Suite 323. Guy Banister and Associates occupied the office above them in Rooms 432–34 from 1958 to 1960. Friends of Democratic Cuba, which was incorporated by Banister, was housed there before moving to the Newman Building. A fundraising operation for Little Rock, Arkansas, private white schools as an alternative to the public schools integrated by force in 1957 by President Eisenhower, was located in the Balter Building, as well. Ross Buckley, who frequently ran for local public office—and once denounced President Kennedy at a Citizens for a Free Cuba meeting—had an office in the Balter Building. G. Wray Gill, the attorney for Carlos Marcello (who employed David Ferrie) also had an office in the Balter Building at one time.[296]

The Balter Building was plagued with vacancies and perennially advertised its office space as "luxurious but inexpensive." Bluford Balter apparently revered Huey Long, and on each floor near the elevator hung a portrait of the assassinated Louisiana governor. Two close associates of Long, who was murdered in 1936—Leander Perez and Maurice Gatlin—were also close to Banister. Balter was a partner with Banister in a local newspaper called the *West Bank Herald*. The weekly ran local stories, a column by Banister, and also commentary from syndicated writer, and alleged Banister friend, Paul Harvey. Oddly, a third partner was Federal Judge John Minor Wisdom, whose life was later frequently threatened for making decisions favorable to integrationists.[297, 298] In addition to his alliance with the American Nazi Party, Balter was a staunch anti-Communist and once exhorted, "Bomb Russia! Why did the heavenly father . . . give us the atomic bomb? . . . to use it judiciously to destroy Communism, Bomb Stalingrad and Moscow!"[299]

The City of New Orleans planned to seize the Balter Building by eminent domain to facilitate the construction of the Hotel International, which may have been a factor in Banister's move to the nearby Newman Building at Camp and Lafayette Streets. In response, Balter published a newspaper entitled *The Federationist* in which he railed against the City of New Orleans' plan to seize his property.[300]

The Congress of Racial Equality sent buses with civil rights workers, dubbed Freedom Riders, to the segregated South from the north as part of an integration drive in the spring of 1961. They planned to test the laws mandating separation of whites and blacks in bus station waiting rooms in the most aggressively segregated areas of the Deep South. The Supreme Court had ruled, in 1946, that segregation of waiting rooms in bus stations was an unconstitutional burden on interstate travel, which was bolstered by the 1954 *Brown v. Board of Education* decision that had ruled that segregation in the public schools was unconstitutional. The southern segregationists in the Citizens' Council and the American Nazi Party knew in advance of CORE's plans through well-developed intelligence sources in the north. One source was Roy Frankhouser, a Reading, Pennsylvania, Klan leader, Minuteman, Nazi associate, and officer in the Citizens' Council of America.[301] The CORE Freedom Buses planned to leave Washington on May 2, 1961, and arrive in New Orleans on May 17, 1961. Along the way, they intended to integrate bus stations and restaurants.

Banister's close associates Louis P. Davis and Bluford Balter were involved in a scheme to send a minibus packed with Rockwell's storm troopers from Virginia, as a public counter-demonstration against the Freedom Riders as they entered the South. Michael Slatter, the son of British Nazi Party member Martin Slatter and a New Orleans Nazi, traveled to Arlington and convinced Rockwell to support the plan. Bluford Balter, Louis P. Davis and another unknown individual each raised six hundred dollars, to purchase a Volkswagen minibus, which they dubbed the "Hate Bus." The FBI learned of the plan from an informant within the Nazi Party. According to FBI documents, the third individual involved in the Hate Bus purchase, whose name was redacted, appears—by the context of the report—to have been Leander Perez, a third Banister associate.[302] Banister employee Jack Martin reported Banister's relationship with Rockwell to Senator Russell Long and incurred the wrath of Leander Perez and George Singelmann when they learned about it.[303]

Many of Banister's close associates had Nazi orientations. Louis P. Davis, who owned a construction and dredging business, was a leader in the local Citizens' Council. Davis rose quickly in the ranks of the national Citizens' Council and, on October 10, 1956, he was a featured speaker at the national convention of the Citizens' Council in Jackson, Mississippi. Davis was close to Ross Barnett, who headed the Mississippi Citizens' Council at its inception in 1956. (In 1960, Barnett was elected governor of the State of Mississippi.)[304] "Captain" Davis, as he was known, had infiltrated a number of integrationist groups with some of his friends. He spoke of the "Zionist" influence in the NAACP and the Congress of Racial Equality.[305] Davis was close to Roswell Thompson, a Klan leader and frequent visitor to Banister's Camp and Lafayette Street office.[306, 307] Davis was also close to General Walker, as well as Governor Barnett, and was with the two in the governor's mansion during the autumn 1962 integration crisis at the University of Mississippi. Davis reportedly bragged of his influence over General Walker, remarking, "He owns Walker."

Davis was also a friend of D.A. Jim Garrison, who was aware that Davis, like Banister, engaged in the infiltration of leftist groups. During Garrison's initial assassination investigation, when he pointed to the radical right as the culprits, Davis told Garrison that he was going "in the wrong direction," from the commonly accepted story that President Kennedy was killed by a Communist. Another young Nazi, Tommy Baumler, worked undercover for Banister searching for subversives at Tulane University.[308] Banister investigator and author Harold Weisberg told the author that Baumler had lost the use of his legs and was able to ambulate with the assistance of a dolly.[309] Baumler was a person of interest in Garrison's investigation. He bragged that he and Davis were Nazis and talked about the big takeover to come. Baumler knew David Ferrie's godson, Morris Brownlee. (Ferrie, whose Nazi connections will be examined later, successfully converted Brownlee, a Jew, to Catholicism.)

The Hate Bus rolled in to New Orleans after earlier stops in strife-torn Montgomery, Alabama, and Mobile, Alabama, the next day, on an avowed campaign against integration and Communism.[310] According to the Nazi Party, the Hate Bus was sent, "to symbolize the fact that decent Americans do hate and should hate Communism and race mixing."[311] The Nazis followed the itinerary of the Freedom Riders—equal numbers of black and white civil rights workers—who began their journey south from Washington, D.C.

Rights advocates, many of them college students, set out in two regularly scheduled buses. Minor fighting erupted during two stops in North Carolina. Outside of Anniston, Alabama, one bus was set on fire and destroyed. The Freedom Riders were pummeled and bloodied. College students joined the Freedom Riders in Tennessee, but were quickly taken back to the Tennessee border by Birmingham Police Chief Bull Connor as they entered Alabama. Connor made a name for himself during the Birmingham race riots by using dogs and fire hoses on black demonstrators. Connor had been a representative at the States' Rights Party meeting in 1948, which was formed after southern members of Congress, dubbed Dixiecrats, bolted from the 1948 Democratic Convention in protest of the party's civil rights plank. Banister's close associates, Leander Perez and Alvin Cobb attended the Dixiecrat meeting, along with the elite of the southern segregation defense movement.[312]

Close Banister associate and New Orleans Citizens' Council director, George Singelmann, was quoted in the *New York Times* as noting that the Freedom Bus campaign, "could lead to violence or death." His prediction came true. When Attorney General Robert F. Kennedy called Alabama governor Robert Patterson and asked him to provide protection for the Freedom Riders, Patterson refused. Instead, a call from the Klan went out for white protestors to meet the Freedom Buses in Birmingham, and a riot broke out. (Two Alabama newspapers reported that the Klan had supported Patterson's 1958 election.) Reverend Fred Shuttlesworth, whose home was dynamited during the Montgomery Bus Boycott, backed the Riders, and was arrested. Bus drivers refused to drive the Freedom Riders to Montgomery, and they were forced to fly to New Orleans, instead.

On May 21, 1961, Mississippi governor Ross Barnett offered Alabama governor Patterson the assistance of the Mississippi National Guard to aid those "who refuse to be rolled over and stomped" by the federal government. The Hate Bus arrived in Montgomery after a stop in Birmingham on May 23. The National Guard kept the Nazis, dressed in full Nazi regalia, under close watch, and escorted them to the outskirts of the city. An Associated Press photographer took their picture when they stopped to fuel the minibus. As they reached the outskirts of New Orleans, the Hate Bus was stopped again. They were not permitted to enter the city until they removed the hate signs plastered on it.

On May 23, 1961, another bus of CORE Freedom Riders reached Montgomery, the first capital of the "Old Confederacy." A white mob of one thousand assembled and violence followed. The Montgomery police were nowhere to be found. A representative of United States Attorney General Robert Kennedy was beaten, and Kennedy subsequently asked a Federal Judge in Montgomery to enjoin the Ku Klux Klan and the National States' Rights Party (NSRP) from interfering with the peaceful interstate travel of the Freedom Riders, sending 400 armed U.S. Marshals to protect them.

The storm troopers on their way to New Orleans in the Hate Bus in counter-protest of the CORE Freedom Riders bus trip opposing segregation. Guy Banister bailed them out of jail after their arrest. Dan Burros (right front), John Patler (second from right front). (John Patler murdered George Lincoln Rockwell in 1967.) Source: Corbis

When a mob threatened a black rally at a church led by Dr. Martin Luther King, Jr., King called Robert Kennedy for help and told them, "They're moving in on the church." Kennedy assured that the U.S. Marshals would protect them; Martial law was declared.

Commander Rockwell did not travel on the Hate Bus, but instead flew to New Orleans and joined them. Rockwell informed the New Orleans Police of his intention to picket the Civic Theater's showing of the movie *Exodus* on May 24. The Civic Theater had already received phone calls and literature from the Greater New Orleans American Nazi Party, protesting the showing of the movie. The storm troopers protested the screening of the movie for obvious reasons—it favorably depicted the repatriation of Jews to the new Jewish state of Israel. The storm troopers held similar protests at the Boston showing of the movie.[313] (Dalton Trumbo, one of "The Hollywood Ten" film directors who had been blackballed after the House Committee on Un-American Activities held a probe of Communist influence in the motion picture industry, directed the film.)

The storm troopers arrived at the theater in the Hate Bus and began to picket. They were promptly arrested for disturbing the peace and were subsequently tried and found guilty in state court. It was ruled that wearing Nazi uniforms with swastika armbands was enough to unduly alarm the public.[314] Guy Banister negotiated the sureties and L. P. Davis provided the bond money, and bail bondsman Hardy Davis bailed out Rockwell.[315] (Interestingly, Hardy Davis was the first person told by Banister employee Jack Martin that Lee Harvey Oswald was in the Civil Air Patrol with David Ferrie. Davis relayed the Oswald-Ferrie story to Jim Garrison on the day of the Kennedy assassination, which began Garrison's assassination inquiry.)

Rockwell departed the scene after the arrests, but returned on June 14, 1961, to "get my boys out on bond today." On June 13, 14, and 15, the storm troopers were released on bond. L. P. Davis provided Rockwell with "the sanctuary of his home." Rockwell returned to New Orleans in 1962 to affect the merger of the Nacerima, the New Nazi National, and the Ku Klux Klan, according to FBI documents.[316]

Lee Harvey Oswald and Daniel Burros

After Oswald's arrest following the Kennedy assassination, the FBI discovered the name of Daniel Burros, a Queens, New York, Nazi, listed in Oswald's notebook. Burros was one of those involved in the Hate Bus incident. Oswald's notebook entry in his handwriting appears as follows:[317]

Lee Harvey Oswald wrote the name of the American Nazi Party secretary, Dan Burros, in his notebook. Source: Warren Commission

The information contained in Oswald's notation was so obscure that it would have had to come from either Burros or someone close to him. It is not known when Oswald made the entry in his notebook. Burros left the American Nazi Party and their Arlington, Virginia, barracks in November 15, 1961, after a disagreement with Commander Rockwell. Burros was angered to learn that Rockwell sent three storm troopers to terrorize two former ANP members who were organizing a new party opposed to Rockwell.[318] Burros entered the ANP headquarters, removed his file from Rockwell's office, and then slipped out a window. In 1963, he mended his rift with Rockwell.

Oswald jotted down that Burros was the national secretary of the ANP ("Nat sec")—a detail he did not need to write down if he wanted to write a letter to him. Rockwell was publicly known as George Lincoln Rockwell—both the ANP monthly newsletter, *The Rockwell Report* and Rockwell's published books always used his full name George Lincoln Rockwell—but privately his friends knew him as Lincoln Rockwell. Oswald's entry of "Lincoln Rockwell" reflects a familiarity with Rockwell by using the name his friends commonly employed.

Oswald's "American Nationalist Party" notation follows the American Nazi Party entry, also abbreviated ANP. Burros founded the American Nationalist Party in Queens, New York, after he left Rockwell's outfit. There were six members at most and the group was short lived. John Patler, a Hate Bus alumnus, was one of those who joined the party. Patler was so enamored with Nazism that he named his son after the well-known Nazi "martyr," Horst Wessel. The impact of Burros's group was termed "almost non-existent." Together, Patler and Burros wrote a publication entitled *Kill! Magazine.* The magazine was "dedicated to the annihilation of the enemies of the white people." The back cover featured a hangman's noose and the inscription, "Impeach the TRAITOR John F. Kennedy for giving aid and comfort to the enemies of the U.S.A." Anyone aware of Burros's little Nazi group in New York, as Oswald was from his entry in his notebook, would have been close to either Burros or one of his associates.

The notation "Hollis sec. of Queens N.Y." also shows a special knowledge of Burros's operation. While Oswald used the abbreviation "sec." for secretary in the beginning of the entry he used "sec." as an abbreviation for "section" of New York in the later entry. The Hollis section of Queens, New York, was the location of Burros's Nazi group, the America Nationalist Party, which operated out of a one-room wooden shanty at 97–15 190th Street. Oswald's Hollis notation would serve no useful purpose as a mailing address, rather it was a personal comment about the area that might be mentioned to someone familiar with New York—hardly useful to anyone in New Orleans. The notation further suggests a unique and specific knowledge of Burros and his operation. Oswald lived in the Bronx, New York, from 1952 to 1954, and was familiar with the city from riding the subways all day while he was frequently absent from school. Oswald may have made the Hollis section notation because he was familiar with the area from the time he spent there as a boy.

The last notation in Oswald's notebook, "(Newspaper) Nat. Socialist Bulletin" highlighted the name of Rockwell's publication. The bulletin featured accounts and photos of the storm trooper's activities. Rockwell considered the Arlington headquarters primarily a printing operation, and prized Burros's high IQ and printing skills. Burros prepared a propaganda booklet for Rockwell on January 1, 1963, wrote for the *National Socialist Bulletin,* and published a newsletter entitled *The International Nazi Fascist,* which enabled him to keep in touch with various Fascist groups throughout the world. Burros also enjoyed corresponding with former Nazi Germany military officers.[319]

Oswald's entry of Burros's name—and his entire notebook—were published in the Warren Commission's twenty-six volumes of evidence, but the Commission made no attempt to explain it, perhaps considering it a red herring. The FBI knew about Burros and his position in the ANP but apparently made no attempt to relay the information to the Warren Commission. The New York City FBI had opened a file on Burros in January 1963,[320] and was in receipt of information about him from the New York City police. They were aware that Burros had been arrested for pasting Swastikas on the walls of the Anti-Defamation League in 1960. Burros had also been arrested in July 1960 for counter-picketing CORE demonstrators who were protesting against the discriminatory hiring practices at a White Castle restaurant in the Bronx. The Secret Service, however, took note of Oswald's Burros entry and, on December 12, 1963, asked the Washington Field Office to investigate the matter.[321] It is not known if they followed through. In July of 1964, he was convicted on a "charge to riot" and was sent to Sing Sing prison.

The 1976 U.S. Senate Select Committee on Intelligence Activities showed slightly more interest in the Burros entry in Oswald's notebook when they asked for the FBI files on Burros. On February 2, 1976 the committee requested from the Justice Department "Delivery of all materials . . . pertaining to Dan Burros, an alleged member of the National States' Rights Party in 1963."[322] The House Select Committee, on the other hand, did not apparently take the enigmatic Burros notation matter into consideration.

District Attorney Jim Garrison was aware of Banister's connection with Rockwell— and the Burros entry in Oswald's notebook. Jim Garrison also knew of Burros's and Patler's participation in the Hate Bus incident from Rockwell's New Orleans police file #E-11897-61, which was part of the D.A.'s radical right-wing file. Burros avoided arrest when he was instructed by Rockwell to stay at the hotel and await orders from him and the New Orleans' Nazis. Garrison noted that the ANP in Dallas operated out of P.O. Box 22071, Dallas, Texas, 75202, and the ANP and NSRP membership rolls were similar. Garrison wrote a confidential memo to file entitled "Probable NSRP make-up for three cites." He listed the Los Angeles NSRP as consisting of Colonel William Gale, Edgar Bradley, Clinton Wheat, Dr. Stanley Drennan, and Jim Bradley. He named Guy Banister, David Ferrie, Louis Davis, Kent Courtney, Carlos Bringuier, Tommy Baumler, Delphine Roberts, Dr. Gerald Mauterer, Dr. Fredrick Doughty-Beck, Tommy Compton, and Dr. Gustav Von Herr as New Orleans NSRP. Garrison claimed the Dallas NSRP was composed of Edwin A. Walker, individuals on the Dallas police force, Joe Cody, Reverend O. B. Graham, Fredrick Lorenz, J. D. Tippit, and Warren Reynolds. Although he did not provide corroborating evidence, he was likely correct about many of those he named as NSRP members. It's less likely that Kent Courtney or Carlos Bringuier were involved in the NSRP. Garrison pursued the radical right, Nazis, and the NSRP as suspects in the early stages of his assassination investigation. However, after his investigation became public, he did an abrupt about-face and instead blamed the government intelligence.[323]

Dan Burros enlisted in the army in 1955 and served under the command of General Walker. Walker was ordered to Little Rock, Arkansas, to enforce the federally mandated integration of the public schools. Walker objected to the order and tried to get relieved of his command, but was refused. Private Burros appeared on television escorting a black child to school. He later left the army over the Little Rock deployment, stating he didn't like "protecting niggers."[324] Burros described Walker as "a man of destiny." Regarding the origins of his right-wing leanings, Burros stated, "I think Little Rock was the turning point."[325]

Influenced by an Irish teacher sympathetic to Senator Joseph McCarthy, Burros became an admirer of the anti-Communist senator and grew concerned about the "Communist menace" in high school. One of his favorite books was *Under Cover*, which exposed many well-known right wingers as Nazis, like Banister's friend Edward Hunter, who was as an admitted Nazi before WWII. It also exposed a Kent Courtney and Edwin Walker associate, Harold Lord Varney—the publisher of the well-known far-right magazine, *The American Mercury*—as a Nazi.[326]

After the Kennedy assassination, Burros wore a button he designed that read, "Lee Harvey Oswald Fan Club." He became interested in the Ku Klux Klan at a Klan rally in Bear, Delaware. Roy Frankhouser introduced Burros to the Imperial Wizard (National leader) of the United Klans of America, Robert Shelton, who cherished Klan members from the north. Frankhouser was the Grand Dragon of the State of Pennsylvania. Shelton swore in Burros as Kleagle (organizer) and, later, as provisional Grand Dragon of the State of New York. Frankhouser, whose first ties to the Klan were in 1958, reportedly assaulted a police captain during a segregationist rally in October of 1961 in Atlanta. Attorneys and prominent leaders in the Klan and NSRP, J. B. Stoner and James Venable respectively, defended Frankhouser.[327] Interestingly, Venable intimated—not long before he died in the 1990s—that Lee Harvey Oswald had visited his Stone Mountain, Georgia, home in 1963.[328] It is also worth noting that Stoner served as the attorney for the convicted assassin of Dr. Martin Luther King, Jr., James Earl Ray.

Prompted by the wave of racial violence that gripped the South, the House Committee on Un-American Activities began an investigation of the Klan in 1965. When they named Dan Burros as a member of the New York Klan, a member of the Jewish community informed the FBI that Burros was Jewish, having been bar mitzvahed at the Temple Talmud Torah in the Richmond Hill section of Queens—not far from Hollis, which later would become home to Burros's Nazi activities. A *New York Times* reporter learned about Burros's Nazi and Klan activities and Jewish background. When approached by the reporter, Burros stated: "If you publish this I'll come and get you and I'll kill you." Burros retreated to Frankhouser's home in Reading, Pennsylvania, where—upon reading the article exposing his Jewish background—shot himself in the head. After Burros's death, Frankhouser told the *New York Times* that Burros had offered the FBI Photostats that connected Lee Harvey Oswald to the Socialist Workers Party.[329] In a May 18, 1967, FBI memo, an informant told the FBI that Frankhouser had, in a secure place, letters concerning the assassination of President Kennedy from a person known as "Payne." The letters apparently were intended to be given by the informant to Garrison during his investigation, but they never materialized.[330] The information was, however, passed along from the FBI to the Secret Service. "Payne" was determined to be a reference to Michael Paine, whose wife shared their home with the Oswald's before the assassination. Frankhouser, in a 1975 interview, claimed that Ruth and Michael Paine had infiltrated the Socialist Workers Party when he had infiltrated the party in 1960, and that he had met Oswald when the Paines took him to New York for an international science meeting. Frankhouser's story remains unverified and was likely fabricated.[331]

Lee Harvey Oswald and Ray James Leahart

On December 16, 1963, after the Kennedy assassination, the New Orleans FBI investigated a tip that Lee Harvey Oswald had been seen with Ray Leahart during the previous summer. Leahart was a New Orleans Nazi whom Banister had bailed out of jail in the Hate Bus incident. The report is presented here for the first time:

> MUNCY PERKINS, Clerk Carrolton Avenue Station, New Orleans Public Service, Inc., residence address 5320 Camp Street, New Orleans advised that occasionally individuals have been observed by him at the Carrollton Avenue Station in the early morning hours waiting for RAY JAMES LEAHART, one of the bus drivers. MR. PERKINS thought that possibly LEE HARVEY OSWALD may have been among these persons waiting for LEAHART.

The FBI interviewed Leahart and accepted his denial of knowing Oswald. The FBI sent the report of the Oswald-Leahart allegation to the Warren Commission, which apparently also saw no value in any further investigation. The author obtained the thirty-four pages of FBI files on Leahart from the New Orleans FBI, through the Freedom of Information Act. The date of the first report was June 11, 1965, and covered an investigatory period between November 10, 1964, and May 20, 1965.[332] The author also received 600 pages on Leahart from FBI Headquarters in Washington that covered a period of time beginning on October 8, 1964.[333] Oddly, there were no overlapping documents. Each set of documents contained separate information and all began at a period of time after the assassination. No documents mentioned the Oswald-Leahart allegation of Muncy Perkins. However, the FBI cited the records of the New Orleans Police Department and found that Leahart had an FBI reference number 841767D—apparently in connection with Leahart's arrest for the 1961 Hate Bus incident on May 24, 1961.

No FBI documents, other than the New Orleans police mug shots from the Hate Bus arrest, were in the FBI record obtained from either FBI Headquarters or the New Orleans FBI. Its absence in the FBI record raises the question of what happened to FBI reference 841767D (Leahart's arrest record in the Hate Bus incident) and why it did not accompany the allegation and substantial likelihood of an Oswald-Leahart association when sent to the Warren Commission. Banister's close friendship with New Orleans FBI SAC Regis Kennedy may have had something to do with the critical omission.

Garrison's investigators were aware of Leahart, but not of the allegation that he was seen with Lee Harvey Oswald. They had information that Ray Leahart, a city streetcar or bus driver, pasted ANP slogans and posters on the walls of the Magazine Street bus depot where he worked. Investigators were aware that Leahart had been to the training camp across Lake Pontchartrain with Derek Frier who was a courier for the Nazi Party (several allegations that Oswald had been to the camp were noted in Chapters One and Two), and that Frier's friend Loren Butler was a high-ranking official in the Nazi party.[334]

The New Orleans Police photo of Ray Leahart after his arrest in the 1961 Hate Bus incident. Source: FBI file number 157-2965, AX 157-624

According to FBI documents, Ray Leahart and Bluford Balter were organizers of the New Orleans American Nazi Party. Leahart personally knew George Lincoln Rockwell and had at least twelve personal discussions with Rockwell—and even visited him on one occasion in Virginia. Rockwell also met with Leahart, the head of the New Orleans National States' Rights Party, in New Orleans in September 1964. In 1961, a "Special New Orleans Edition" of the NSRP newspaper *The Thunderbolt* was issued with the front page headline, "PEREZ TURNS SPOTLIGHT ON THE ENEMY", and appeared with a story written by Ray James Leahart above a large photograph of Leander Perez, Banister's close friend. In the story, Leahart urged Governor Jimmie Davis to close the public schools, rather than integrate them, until private all-white schools could be opened. Leahart quoted Perez, "Zionist Jews are leaders in forcing communistic racial integration." Leahart and the NSRP distributed 100 copies of *The Thunderbolt* around each of six schools which were to be integrated. The article noted a recent speaking appearance of Roy Frankhouser before a New Orleans NSRP meeting, and a photo showed Frankhouser adorned with a thunderbolt on his armband.[335] Given the close relationship between northerners Frankhouser and Burros, Burros's prior trip to New Orleans and FBI evidence that he traveled to Klan rallies in the South, an encounter with Lee Harvey Oswald in 1963 (thus spurring Oswald's notebook entry) would not have been out of the question.

In 1961, Leahart was on a first-name basis with Banister's close associate Willie Rainach, a well-known defender of segregation.[336]

In an October 8, 1964, report from FBI Headquarters, a confidential informant revealed that Leahart had opened a post office box in the name of the National States' Rights Party in 1961. This unknown individual, whose name was redacted by the FBI, was a member of the NSRP and gave them a copy of the NSRP newspaper, *The Thunderbolt*, which listed Leahart as the New Orleans representative. Guy Banister subscribed to *The Thunderbolt*.

Leahart began working as a bus operator for the New Orleans Public Service, Inc., in 1961, but was dismissed in 1964 for distributing NSRP literature and cartoons "critical of Negroes," while operating his bus. In a document characterizing the NSRP in Louisiana and Mississippi, a confidential informant advised the FBI, on November 18, 1963, that Leahart and another individual—name redacted—were the only known active members of the NSRP. The actual report from the confidential informant's statement was not found in the FBI files, but was only alluded to in a summary of the NSRP. The FBI had investigated the NSRP—and knew of Leahart's involvement in the NSRP before the assassination and before the alleged Oswald-Leahart sighting—yet did not connect the two (or did not wish to).

The FBI had investigated all the groups Leahart belonged to (the Klan, NSRP, and ANP), due to their known track records of violence. All three groups were rabidly opposed to President Kennedy. It is not clear if the FBI knew of Leahart's arrest in the Hate Bus incident before the Oswald-Leahart allegation. Most likely they did, however, because at some point they obtained Leahart's mug shot from the New Orleans Police Department, which was taken from the 1961 incident. Had the Warren Commission known of Leahart's NSRP, Nazi, or Klan associations, they may have shown more interest in him and called him to testify.

On November 17, 1964, Leahart was interviewed by the FBI and refused to provide names of other members of the New Orleans ANP. The FBI noted that Leahart had been a member of the New Orleans Citizens' Council since 1959 (as were Banister and all of the New Orleans figures involved in the Hate Bus incident). Leahart told the FBI that he had been arrested for handing out handbills on the street in 1961, reminiscent of Oswald's 1963 pamphleting. (It will be recalled from Chapter One that Lee Harvey Oswald allegedly attended a Citizens' Council meeting with David Ferrie.)

On October 8, 1964, copies of a letterhead memorandum concerning FBI information on James Ray Leahart were sent to the Secret Service. No reason for this was expressed in the memoranda of the FBI file. It is reasonable to assume, however, that the FBI felt Leahart was a threat to the president's security in 1964. An agreement had been made between the FBI and the Secret Service to share protective responsibilities for the safety of the president. The agreement was the result of the Warren Commission's finding that the FBI had failed to notify the Secret Service that Oswald was a subject of investigation by the agency before Kennedy's assassination. On January 31, 1972, FBI Director J. Edgar Hoover—apparently for the second time—notified the Secret Service under their agreement and advised them that Leahart was a threat to President Nixon's life. They noted that Leahart met the agreement criteria for notification for being a subversive, ultra rightist, racist, and Fascist and based on prior acts, conduct, or statements indicating a propensity for violence and antipathy toward good order and government.

Leahart was next interviewed by FBI in March 1965 and claimed that he no longer belonged to the NSRP nor did he any longer subscribe to its newspaper, *The Thunderbolt*. Even so, upon Leahart's death in 1997, Dr. Edward Fields—editor of *The Thunderbolt*—eulogized him.

The FBI sought to establish Leahart's whereabouts on March 20 and 21, 1965, in connection with an FBI investigation into what they referred to as "the Greenbombs case," which was not further described in their report. In connection with their inquiry, Leahart told them he had not left the state of Louisiana.

Leahart was the head of the Louisiana Fighting American Nationalists (FAN), an ANP front that received its literature from George Lincoln Rockwell. FAN was devoid of swastikas and other overt Nazi trappings and was created to attract supporters who otherwise might be turned off by Nazi symbolism. FAN, which began in Chicago in 1960 and was defunct by 1964, served as a training ground for "frustrated Nazis."

The Dallas FBI office was aware of correspondence linking Leahart to ANP activities in Texas.[337] One Dallas ANP member, Robert Surrey, was a close associate of General Walker. Surrey's wife Mary was Walker's personal secretary. Wealthy oilmen reportedly funded Surrey's Nazi outfit.[338] Surrey printed the infamous "Wanted for Treason" poster which had circulated in Dallas before the assassination. The poster pictured mug-shot-styled photos of President Kennedy and accused him of treason. Surrey and Walker were Warren Commission witnesses, and, of course, Walker was close to both Guy Banister and Kent Courtney.

In 1966, Leahart was present at an anti-Vietnam War rally in New Orleans, called a "Love In" at Audubon Park.

Each year, Leahart synchronized his vacation time to coincide with the Congress of the World Union of National Socialists in Virginia so he could attend. In 1970, he was a featured speaker at the September 5–7 event, their second annual meeting.[339]

In the 1970s, Leahart became a leading member in the National Socialist White People's Party—a reconfigured ANP and Ku Klux Klan outfit—along with David Duke, perhaps the best-known white supremacist in America in the 21st century. Leahart peddled his propaganda along with Duke in what was known as a "Free Speech Rally" at Louisiana State University in Baton Rouge. On September 9, 1972, Leahart became the best man at Duke's wedding. Leahart may have known Duke as early as 1964, the year that then fourteen-year-old Duke visited Banister's close associate, George Singelmann, at the Citizens' Council office and read their literature.[340]

At a 1972 National Socialist White People's Party meeting, A. Roswell Thompson spoke with Duke. Thompson, as noted, was close with Guy Banister and was a regular visitor at the Lafayette and Camp Street office that Oswald had frequented in 1963. Thompson ran for local office on the ticket of the CDO, or Conservative Democratic Organization, a far-right version of the better-known RDO—or Regular Democratic Organization—along with Guy Banister.[341]

Finally, Leahart attended a 1974 Metairie, Louisiana, Klan meeting with Ned Touchstone, editor of the *Councilor*, and David Duke. In 1975, Leahart was at a New Orleans Klan rally at Lee Circle, also with Duke, which armed members of the local mafia also attended.[342]

The FBI and the Nazis

Nearly all of the individuals involved in the neo-Nazi activities in New Orleans were under FBI investigation. Moreover, most of the individuals under investigation were placed under the shared presidential protection list of the FBI and the Secret Service and considered risks to the president of the United States of America. Dan Burros was one of the first to be considered under the protective services agreement. On May 26, 1965, and again on October 20, 1965, Burros was placed on the presidential protection list by FBI Director J. Edgar Hoover as an "ultra rightist, racist and fascist" and meeting the criteria of "emotional instability and prior acts . . . indicating a propensity for violence . . . ."[343] Ray James Leahart earned a place on the presidential protection list on June 23, 1972, placed there by Director L. Patrick Gray,

III, and again on March 3, 1976, placed by Director Clarence M. Kelley who felt Leahart was "potentially dangerous because of background, emotional instability or activity in groups engaged in activities inimical to the U.S."[344]

The FBI opened a file on New Orleans Nazi financier Bluford Balter who helped bring the Hate Bus to town. As we know, Banister's office was in the Balter Building, where he met with Rockwell on July 28, 1961. On October 12, 1964, the New Orleans FBI forwarded to the Secret Service a copy of a letter sent to President Kennedy on March 1, 1961, in which Balter voiced criticism of federal corporations for "invading some private enterprises" and "promiscuous lending to foreign nations." The subject of the letter was "Travel of the President in the United States and the Commonwealth of Puerto Rico" and suggests Balter was considered a security risk to President Kennedy in 1961, as well as to President Johnson in 1964.[345]

The FBI opened a file on Louis P. Davis on December 12, 1960. Davis was close to Guy Banister and had helped with the of purchase the Hate Bus. Davis was noted to be involved in obstruction of a court order when he protested against the integration of New Orleans schools. State senator Willie Rainach, Banister's close associate—along with an investigator for the Louisiana Sovereignty Committee, whose name was redacted but perhaps was Guy Banister—joined in the protest with Davis.

The FBI also reported on a meeting of the New Orleans Citizens' Council. Leander Perez, Banister mistress Delphine Roberts, and Louis P. Davis were in attendance. Although Davis did not make the presidential protection list, the FBI recognized his potential for violence. On July 7, 1968, the FBI learned that Davis, a member of Pipefitters Local #50 in New Orleans, threatened Edward Grady Partin to influence his testimony against Teamster leader Jimmie Hoffa. It is not clear if the threat was made directly to Partin, a juror, or someone else, since the FBI documents were heavily redacted. Davis had called someone connected to the case—perhaps Partin—and stated on the phone: "You are on the spot. There is a contract out for you." Then an unidentified person took the phone and stated: "If you go back to Baton Rouge, you are dead."[346]

John Patler was no doubt under the watch of the FBI. Patler was a member of the Hate Bus crew and was Rockwell's "minister of propaganda," but later became disillusioned with Rockwell. In 1967, Patler called Rockwell "the biggest fake that ever came down the pike."[347] On August 8, 1967, Patler assassinated Rockwell in the parking lot of an Arlington, Virginia, laundromat, using a high-powered rifle and firing from the roof of a building—an act reminiscent of the events in Dealey Plaza. And, like Oswald, Patler left the scene of the crime on a city bus.[348]

A. Roswell Thompson, who was a frequent visitor to the Banister operation at Camp and Lafayette and an associate of Ray Leahart, was also a subject of FBI interest. J. Edgar Hoover placed Thompson on the presidential protection list on September 18, 1967, for "Prior acts . . . indicating a propensity for violence and antipathy toward good order and government." The FBI investigated Thompson under the heading of "Racial Matters" for his activities in the Ku Klux Klan.[349] Thompson, although he was not a lawyer, "represented" Thomas Beckham, a subject of Garrison's assassination investigation. Beckham claimed years later that he knew Lee Harvey Oswald and Guy Banister well, but kept silent about them because Thompson threatened his life. Thompson attended NSRP meetings at Holsum's Cafeteria in New Orleans in 1967, a restaurant that Oswald frequented in 1963, according to Beckham.[350]

Judge Leander Perez, a close Banister associate who apparently helped finance the Hate Bus and whose Citizens' Council office was at one time in the Balter Building, was not considered a presidential threat. The FBI file on Perez was over two hundred pages long and was related to his opposition to school integration, his stand on black voter's rights, and his criticism of the actions of the federal government and Supreme Court.[351] Perez was extremely wealthy and wielded tremendous political power across the Deep South. One informant—who reported, in detail, a JFK assassination plot before the murder—credited Perez with financing the assassination. (That plot will be discussed in greater detail later.)

It is worth noting that Jimmy Arthus was placed on the protective services list, as well. Arthus was the custodian of the 544 Camp Street office building, which was the office address above Banister's operation. Arthus, a member of the New Orleans Citizens' Council, sent President Kennedy a dead pigeon—and included his return address.[352, 353]

Even with all of these connections, the FBI conducted a search to see if Oswald had any ties to the American Nazi Party and concluded that there were "No known associations"—a monumental error of history and justice.[354]

George Lincoln Rockwell and J. Edgar Hoover

One prominent leader of the radical right wing, Robert DePugh of the Minutemen, revealed to the author that George Lincoln Rockwell was "a 100% FBI informant." He may have been correct.[355] Five days after the assassination of President Kennedy, Rockwell wrote the following letter to FBI Director J. Edgar Hoover on ANP stationery:

Dear Mr. Hoover,

As I am sure you know, this organization not only does not believe in force and violence as a method of achieving our ends, but believes that force and violence is the surest way to suicide for our tiny, anti-Communist forces. We believe in the Constitution and government by law. We also believe that these things are under deadly attack by world Communism, and that it will take a more extreme political movement than "conservatism" to stop the red revolutionaries and killers. We thus believe that the only way to save our race and Nation is by a LEGAL counter-revolution, which is the open course of the American Nazi Party.

Inevitably, however, such an extreme political movement attracts

irresponsible and lunatic elements, who are not welcome, but who
force themselves upon the movement and are very hard to get rid of.

The assassination of the president was, I believe, the work of
such a "nut" over on the other side from us. As vile and evil as I
believe our Communist opponents to be, I do not think that they
would be stupid enough to have shot the president as part of their
filthy plans.

Such bloody and violent events tend to generate further violence
and bloodshed by deranged and violent people. For this reason I
have made a list of persons [. . .] whom I believe might conceivably
be involved in further incidents [. . . .][356]

Rockwell then provided the names of twenty-seven of his storm troopers whom he
felt were capable of violence. Burros and Leahart were not mentioned. (One individual who
was named, Frank Rotella, was in the New York National Renaissance Party with Dan Burros.
Burros felt that Rotella insulted Hitler's honor when Rotella expressed distaste for photos of
German atrocities against Poles, which he was shown by Burros.[357]) It is not entirely clear
what Rockwell meant in the letter. A case can be made that Rockwell was implying that
Oswald was a "nut" (from the other side) who associated with the ANP. Rockwell may have
known of Oswald through Banister, Burros, or Leahart. Oswald may have corresponded with
the ANP and perhaps Rockwell felt it might only be a matter of time until the FBI found
out. Perhaps Rockwell was seeking preemptive redemption. On the other hand, Rockwell
may have been implying that Oswald, as a genuine Communist, did not do the shooting, but
perhaps a nut known to the ANP did.

In any case, it seems Rockwell was raising the possibility that one of his men was
involved. Rockwell further expressed his feelings about the assassination in a press interview,
saying, "I'm not heartbroken but it louses up the political picture for preservation of the white
race. The president brought it on himself, the way he has been pillorying the white race. The
people of the South hated that man with a passion and I don't blame them." The reporter
noted, "Rockwell, himself a member of the extreme right wing believes the president was shot
by a right winger."[358] Rockwell apparently had not been placed on presidential protection list.

David Ferrie and the Nazis

Jim Garrison discovered evidence that David Ferrie was Nazi-oriented. In a memo to his staff,
he wrote, "The lines are gossamer lines, but when you find them they lead from David Ferrie
to Nazi-ism, Fascism."[359] Jim Garrison also considered privately that Oswald might have been
a "civilian Nazi."[360] David Ferrie was, perhaps, the first Nazi in Lee Harvey Oswald's life. After
Ferrie's death in 1967 he left behind a note to his friend, Al Beauboef, which Garrison dubbed
a suicide note. It read:

Dear Al,

When you read this I will be quite dead, so no answer will be possible. I wonder how you are going to justify and rationalize things. Tommy said you treated me as you did because I was the one who always got you trouble:

> The police arrests
> The stripped car charge
> The deal at Kohn school
> Flying Baragona in the Beech.
> ETC

Well I guess that helps ease your conscience, even if it is not the truth.

All I can say is that I offered you love and the best I could. All I got in return, in the end, was a kick in the teeth, Hence, I die alone and unloved.

You would not even straighten out Carol about me though this <u>you</u> started when you were going steady.

I wonder what your last days and hours are going to be like. As you sow, so shall you reap.

Goodbye
Dave

Garrison did not provide an explanation for all of the note's subject matter. However, he did know the meaning of "Flying Baragona in the Beech." "Beech" refers to the model of Ferrie's airplane, a Beechcraft. Baragona was a Nazi, from Fort Sill. Although Garrison publicly referred to the note as a sinister "suicide note," he jotted on the Baragona documents that it was a "Farewell letter," perhaps admitting that Ferrie knew he was ill when he wrote it, shortly before he died of a ruptured brain aneurysm.

Garrison also obtained a transcript of a letter written by Ferrie to Baragona. Next to Baragona's name, Garrison wrote: "Note: Baragona <u>is</u> important." The letter had been sent to Garrison by Glenn Pinchback, and a carbon copy was sent to Mendel Rivers, a congressman from Georgia. (Pinchback worked in the Operations Command at Fort Sill, where he intercepted mail.) In the letter, Ferrie shared his dream of the re-unification of Germany and living in a world where all the currency was in Deutschmarks. Pinchback's summation of the letter described a "Neo-Nazi plot to enslave America in the name of anti-Communism," and "a neo-Nazi plot gargantuan in scope." The Ferrie letter spoke of the need to kill all the Kennedys and Martin Luther King, Jr. Ferrie wrote that he was being "suffocated by the niggers and Jews," saying he felt that they could "absolutely depend on Welch and Wallace." (Robert

Welch was the leader of the John Birch Society. George Wallace was the governor of Alabama, a critic of President Kennedy and outspoken defender of segregation.) Throughout the letter, Ferrie complained of terrible headaches, a sign that his cerebral aneurysm was leaking before it ultimately ruptured and killed him. Pinchback reportedly also obtained a letter from David Ferrie to Baragona confessing his role in the assassination of Robert Gehrig, who was a Nazi and Fort Sill soldier. Garrison did not have the letter, but felt that Pinchback was entirely reliable.[361]

The Oswald Family, Racism, and Anti-Semitism

Lee Harvey Oswald grew up in a household marked by an atmosphere of racism and anti-Semitism. In one conversation, his mother referred to a friend of Attorney Fred Korth as a "Negro Jew" who owned a Negro newspaper. (Korth later became Secretary of the Navy.) The FBI interviewed Oswald's mother, Marguerite Oswald, and reported, "At several points, Marguerite displayed an unmistakable prejudice against Jews and Negroes, and speculated as to why Negroes have not been implicated in the case (the assassination)."[362] According to her son Robert, Marguerite Oswald held a "conspiratorial view of the world."[363]

According to the FBI, Marguerite Oswald worked in the home of a Jewish individual named Leon Brachman in Fort Worth, Texas. She stated that Brachman lost a lot of money in the stock market and blamed it on JFK. She attended Brachman's grandson's circumcision party and believed that her son's killer, Jack Ruby, was present. The FBI summed up her claims: "It is her theory that the Jewish people hired Jack Ruby to kill President Kennedy then they shot her son, Lee Harvey Oswald, and the Jewish are now going to free Jack Ruby, their executioner."[364]

Lee Harvey Oswald adored his older brother Robert and joined the marines in 1956, following in Robert's footsteps. After the assassination, the FBI interviewed Robert. The FBI had already come out and let their findings be known that Oswald was indeed a Communist and acted alone in killing the president. On February 19, 1964, Robert Oswald shared with the FBI a diary in his own handwriting, which contained six paragraphs from Thomas Jefferson's autobiography. The following entry was made on August 28, 1963, well before the assassination. Several of the noteworthy paragraphs are presented as follows:

> Thomas Jefferson
> Born April 2, 1743 o.s. (April 13th)
> Died July 4th 1826
>
> From his Autobiography.
>
> "Nothing is more certainly written in the book of fate, than these people (Negroes) are to be free; nor is it less certain that the two races, equally free, cannot live in the same government."

"I do not judge with willful & ill-intentioned error, but honest error
must be arrested, where its toleration leads to public ruin."
"But it saves the Republic, which is the first & Supreme law."

Following his quotes of Thomas Jefferson, Robert Oswald offered his own written opinion on the matter stating, "Jefferson spoke of impeachment of judges but I believe this should apply to all public offices whether state or Federal."[365] Clearly Robert Oswald was defending segregation and invoking Jefferson to sanction his view. He may well have been referring to Kennedy's proposed civil rights bill, which the segregationists felt vehemently would lead to public ruin, when he cited "honest error must be arrested." He proposed impeachment of state and federal officials and may have been pointing directly at President Kennedy and Supreme Court Chief Justice Earl Warren. Both the Warren Supreme Court's 1954 *Brown v. the Board of Education* decision that called for abolition of segregation in the public schools and President Kennedy's proposed June 1963 sweeping Civil Rights Act that would end segregation had outraged the South. The tensions between the South and the federal government that followed had not been seen since the Civil War. As a direct result of the *Brown* decision, southern segregationists and the John Birch Society embarked on an "Impeach Earl Warren" campaign. (Jack Ruby was fully aware of the campaign. He apparently felt that a billboard in Dallas that read "Impeach Earl Warren"—paid for by the John Birch Society—was of such importance that he left his apartment at 4:00 a.m. to photograph it on the night of the assassination. That event will be detailed in Chapter Seventeen.) Taking another shot at the federal government, Robert Oswald also wrote a long passage on the right of the states to do what was in their best interest and not that of "a distant authority." Clearly, he was alluding to the federal government's efforts to enforce the provisions of the *Brown* decision.

Lee Harvey Oswald displayed signs of being a racist and a segregationist, as noted in Chapter One. While in the marines in 1956, a fellow marine in Oswald's platoon in San Diego, Alan R. Felde, recalled that Oswald continually wrote to senators about issues that he felt strongly about, although Felde was unaware of the letters' subjects. A number of letters were sent to Senator Strom Thurmond, the outspoken segregationist leader from South Carolina who led the Dixiecrat revolt at the Democratic National Convention in 1948. Felde recalled that Oswald found fault with both Eisenhower and Truman, and felt nothing was accomplished in the Korean War. Felde and Oswald were transferred together to Aviation Electronics School in Memphis, Tennessee, in 1957.[366] In June 1957, Oswald was then transferred to a marine base in El Toro, California.[367] *Los Angeles Times* reporter Peter Noyes learned from an unknown source that Oswald attended far-right meetings while at El Toro.[368]

In October of 1959, Oswald traveled to the Soviet Union and denounced his American citizenship. Then, on November 13, 1959, reporter Aline Mosby interviewed Oswald at the Metropole Hotel in Moscow where he was staying. Mosby asked Oswald about his views on life in America. Oswald told him, "I am against conformism in such matters, such as fashionably hating minority groups. Being a southern boy, I've seen poor niggers. That was a lesson, too. People hate because they are told to hate. Like school kids. In Little Rock they don't know the difference between a nigger and a white man but it was the fashion to hate niggers so they hated them. People in the United States were like that in everything." Mosby asked him if he was a member of the Communist Party. Oswald replied with a look of surprise, "Communist? I've never met a Communist. I might have seen a Communist once in New York, like the old lady who gave me a pamphlet, Save the Rosenbergs." Contrary to his comments, Oswald's use of the term "nigger" three times in any context suggests he was a racist like his mother and brother Robert.[369] On November 16, 1959, the reporter's notes on her interview with Oswald read: "Segregation, I was brought up like every southern boy, to hate Negroes—Then Socialist lit. opened my eyes to reconsider reasons for hating Negroes . . ."[370]

Oswald was eager to find a wife while in the Soviet Union. His first marriage overtures, which were rebuffed, were made to his tour guide. Oswald took a job at a Minsk radio factory and became interested in twenty-three-year-old Ella German in June 1960. He wrote in his notebook, "Ella German—silky black-haired Jewish beauty." Ella felt that Oswald was aware that she was Jewish from the beginning of their friendship. Lee began to drop hints of marriage, but Ella was not interested. Oswald told her, "I know you are Jewish and people, you know, don't like Jewish people, but I don't care about that." Oswald asked her to marry him, and she refused. After a long friendship, they parted ways in January 1961. On March 17, 1961, Oswald met his future bride, Marina, and on April 30, 1961, they were married. Lee told Marina he wanted her to get pregnant, have a boy, and name him David—perhaps in honor of Captain David Ferrie. Oswald had been working towards returning to America a month before he met Marina.

The marriage was troubled from the beginning, but Marina quickly became pregnant. In May of 1962, they departed Moscow for America.[371] Oswald's hasty attempt to marry three different women in less than three years' time suggests he may have had an agenda in mind. It would not be surprising if Oswald's quest for a Russian bride was to ostentatiously demonstrate that he was a Communist with ties to the Soviet Union. Had he married a Jewish-Soviet Communist, like Ella German, it would have been the icing on the cake, since the radical right claimed that Communism was a Jewish phenomenon.

The Oswalds had a second child, born at Parkland Hospital in Dallas, after their return to America. Lee asked Marina what she would like to name the baby girl, and she replied "Rachel," but Lee quickly objected noting, "It sounds too Jewish." The child was named Audrey Marina Rachel Oswald, but Marina prevailed and she was called Rachel, an important figure in the Jewish Tanakh and Christian Old Testament.[372]

Joseph Milteer and Ray James Leahart

Ray James Leahart wrote to Joseph Milteer of Quitman, Georgia, in 1959, evidenced by an empty envelope addressed to Milteer from Leahart which was found in Milteer's residence after his death. There is nothing further known about their relationship. It is known, however, that the two had similar far-right backgrounds with ties to the Klan, NSRP, Nazis, and other far-right organizations.

Envelope addressed to Joseph Milteer from Ray J. Leahart in 1959 found in Milteer's home after his death by HSCA investigators (left). Ray Leahart speaking at the 1971 annual Congress of the National Socialist White People's Party as the National Commander (right). A witness told the FBI he saw Lee Harvey Oswald with Leahart, and it has been shown that Milteer knew in exact detail how the assassination was to occur thirteen days before it happened. Source: Envelope, HSCA, Boxes 48-49. Leahart Photo: FBI file number 157-2965, AX 157-624

Joseph Milteer was a violent far-right extremist and an individual of monumental importance in the Kennedy assassination story. He told an FBI informant, on November 9, 1963—thirteen days before the assassination—that the murder of the president was in the works. Milteer described in detail how it was to occur, and correctly—as it did occur as he predicted, as we shall see in the next two chapters. As the evidence will show, Milteer not only knew in advance of the plot, but he was also in Dealey Plaza during the murder.

Milteer had extensive ties to the radical right of New Orleans, as did Leahart. Unfortunately, however, the HSCA conducted a flawed investigation of Milteer and his foreknowledge of the murder. Milteer died before their investigation, but his house and belongings remained. HSCA investigators searched his home and found the envelope from Leahart, but were completely unaware of the FBI report of the sighting of Oswald with Leahart by Muncy Perkins. Furthermore, they had no knowledge of the FBI investigation of Leahart, his racist activities that dovetailed Milteer's, or his subsequent placement on the presidential protection list. These were all tremendous blunders of historical proportions.

Conclusions

Credible evidence presented herein suggests Lee Harvey Oswald was tied to at least one leader of the American Nazi Party, Ray Leahart, if not a second, Dan Burros. The allegations are not unexpected, since Oswald came from a racist and anti-Semitic household and had close ties to two Nazi-oriented individuals, Guy Banister and David Ferrie.

As more and more information is presented, the picture becomes clear that Oswald was not an authentic Communist, but he began acting like a Communist in 1956. Adding to the complexity of the story, though, his reasons for beginning to pose as a Communist in 1956 were in no way related to President Kennedy's assassination years later, nor was his posturing as a Communist in 1963 related to the murder, as we shall see later.

In the 1940s, 1950s, and 1960s, false Communists—or repentant "ex-Communists"—were frequently paraded before congressional and state committees led by ardent anti-Communist politicians during the Red Scare. At those heralded proceedings, they accused leftist political dissidents of being Communists. The false and "ex-" Communists enjoined a celebrity status and made a handsome living in doing so. Those who once lived in the Soviet Union, like Oswald, were the most prized witnesses. Eventually, some of the "ex-Communist" witnesses were found guilty of perjury, while others admitted that they were never Communists at all.

The Guy Banister operation, like Rockwell's ANP, the Klan, and others that opposed CORE and the Freedom Buses, also targeted CORE. In September 1963, Lee Harvey Oswald infiltrated a CORE voter registration drive. Under the State of Louisiana Communist Control Act, any civil rights worker or group associated with someone with a Communist background like Lee Harvey Oswald could spend decades in prison. The law was designed by Banister's close associate Leander Perez and was introduced into law by another Banister colleague and head of the Louisiana Un-American Activities Committee, LUAC State Representative James Pfister. (Banister was the chief investigator for Pfister and LUAC as noted in Chapter One.) Chapter Twenty-one is devoted to Lee Harvey Oswald's infiltration of CORE.

The envelope sent by Ray Leahart to Joseph Milteer in 1959, both far-right radicals, reflects the existence of an underground network that stretched across the South that was organized to defend the sacred southern institution of segregation against the assault of the federal government and the Kennedy administration. As we will see in the next chapters, Ray Leahart's associate, Joseph Milteer, was part of a far-right cabal consisting of disgruntled ex-military officers, northern reactionaries, and southern segregationists who were responsible for the murder of the president. Oswald's Communist persona was part of a separate and distinct segregationist plot apart from that of the assassination effort, as we shall see.

CHAPTER FOUR

JOSEPH A. MILTEER AND THE PLOT TO MURDER THE PRESIDENT

He is the most violent-minded man in America.
– William A. Somersett

Joseph Adams Milteer was a violent Klansman from Quitman, Georgia. An envelope found in his home in 1977—three years after his death—dates a relationship with New Orleans Nazi James Ray Leahart to 1959. As presented in the last chapter, Guy Banister bailed Leahart out of jail after his arrest in the Hate Bus incident. A citizen reported a possible meeting of Leahart with Lee Harvey Oswald that occurred before the assassination. Milteer told a law enforcement informant thirteen days *before* the assassination the precise manner in which the murder would be carried out—a description that turned out to be correct down to the smallest details. Milteer had the same far-right credentials as Guy Banister and Ray Leahart. Evidence found in his home after his death, along with the accounts of an FBI informant, document his ties to the Citizens' Council, John Birch Society, Ku Klux Klan, American Nazi Party, Minutemen, Gerald L. K. Smith's anti-Semitic organization, and other far-right groups. Guy Banister had ties to the very same groups.[373]

Rise of the Southern Resistance to Integration

The May 17, 1954, *Brown v. the Board of Education* Supreme Court decision, which spelled the end of legalized segregation, was a watershed event in American history. *Brown* ushered in the second reconstruction of the South—and the second Southern rebellion. During the reconstruction of the defeated South after the Civil War, the advancement of the lot of African-Americans was short-lived. White Southerners enacted a series of state laws that led to "Jim Crow" and legalized apartheid. African-Americans were "put back in their place" and progress toward equal rights was nearly non-existent until after World War II. The *Brown* decision led to the rise of an organized Southern resistance against the court-ordered desegregation, which gave birth to the White Citizens' Council in 1955 and led to the rebirth of the Ku Klux Klan. The subsequent reign of terror that began in the South in the 1950s was characterized by waves of murders and bombings across the region, wherein even synagogues were targeted, because Jews were widely viewed as a significant force behind the integration movement.

The Radical Right Plots to Kill the President

Joseph Milteer's revelation of a plot to kill President Kennedy, not made public until 1967, has been mentioned—but largely discounted—in a number of books about the Kennedy assassination. Milteer told an informant that the murder would take place from an office building, with a high-powered rifle that could be taken apart, and that a patsy would be picked up to throw authorities off. That was just how the assassination happened.

Simply put, the FBI and Secret Service knew of the plot in advance, but failed to act on it. After the fact, the FBI was tasked with investigating the assassination on behalf of the Warren Commission and furnishing them with pertinent evidence. The FBI failed to hand over the voluminous files—related to the astounding Milteer prophecy—to the Warren Commission until after their deliberations were already complete.[374] It is difficult to conceive of an explanation for the omission, other than an act of deliberate concealment by FBI director J. Edgar Hoover.

Hoover had kept in touch with former FBI SAC Guy Banister after his departure from the agency. The FBI was aware that Banister was at a meeting in April 1963 in New Orleans—attended by Milteer—where the assassination of members of the left was discussed. (Banister's friend Kent Courtney also attended the meeting.) Unfortunately, the House Select Committee on Assassinations, which reinvestigated the assassination in 1977, was not aware of this. At the meeting, Milteer told FBI informant Willie Somersett of a broad-based plot that involved assassination of members of the Council of Foreign Relations serving in the Kennedy administration, prominent Jewish figures, and leaders of business and industry who were felt to be advancing the Communist agenda (the plot will be discussed in detail in the next chapter). In October 1963, the FBI learned from Somersett that the plot had narrowed to a plan to murder the president by the same group of far-right radicals. A photo surfaced in the 1970s of Milteer, or a look-alike, standing in Dealey Plaza during the assassination.

The HSCA took the matter into consideration in 1978, deciding to undertake a scientific investigation of the photo to determine whether or not the figure in Dealey Plaza was in fact Milteer. Based on a flawed anthropological height analysis, they determined that the subject was too tall to be Milteer. No analysis of the volumes of documents retrieved from Milteer's house—nor the hundreds of investigative documents generated from the informant—were given any consideration by the Committee in the published volumes whatsoever. None of those associated with Milteer, or associated with the plotting, were called to testify. Few, if any, gave the Milteer allegation further consideration after the HSCA investigation of the evidence rendered it seemingly irrelevant.

Willie Somersett and the Miami Bombing

In the 1960s, a rash of synagogue bombings plagued Florida, particularly South Florida, home to the majority of the state's Jewish population. In response to the bombing of the home of Donald C. Shoemaker, editor of the *Miami Herald*, on February 18, 1962, the state attorney general's office and Miami Police Intelligence Department redoubled their efforts to catch the perpetrators. (Although Shoemaker was not Jewish, the *Herald* was viewed as a Jewish mouthpiece by the radical segregationists.) A five-thousand-dollar reward for information about the bombing was offered. Soon thereafter, Miami resident William "Willie" Augustus Somersett, a Ku Klux Klan insider, responded, and implicated James Keithley—who was eventually arrested for the crime. The Miami police and *Miami Herald* had high praise for Somersett for his indispensable help in solving the bombing, one of the few in the state of Florida that were ever solved.

Somersett had been a reliable FBI informant since 1949. He infiltrated and rose to the highest levels of leadership in the national Ku Klux Klan, and did not reveal his position as an FBI informant to the Miami police. The FBI highly regarded Somersett as an informant and wrote, "this informant is one of the few Klan informants that possesses the ability, incentive and appropriate cover to go anywhere in the southeast section of the United States concerning Bureau matters. He is also personally acquainted with a large number of various political figures throughout the southeast portion of the United States, as well as a large number of Klansmen and hoodlums." Somersett was even in contact with Commander Rockwell's Miami unit of the American Nazi Party. William Somersett is an unsung hero in his efforts against the terrorist campaign of racial violence in the South in the 1950s and 1960s. His work likely prevented untold numbers of bombings, burnings, and murders. "Racial matters informants," as the FBI referred to them, were often racists themselves, but deplored violence. However, Somersett may not have been a racist, as evidenced by a 1964 dispute which Somersett had with the Miami AFL-CIO in an attempt to stop race discrimination in the hiring of black mechanics in the city.

When the HSCA began their investigation of the Milteer matter they requested—from the FBI—all intelligence reports that had been gathered from Willie Somersett. The FBI's documents concerning Somersett were so extensive—and retrieving them so laborious—that they bargained with the HSCA and agreed to deliver only the documentation gathered after 1960. In the end, the HSCA received only two-fifths of Somersett's informant documents and, even then, they did not receive the raw reports, instead receiving brief capsule summaries. In 1960, Somersett had provided summaries of Klan activities to the FBI almost on a daily basis. He made as many as twenty trips per month on Klan business at the urging of the FBI, putting his life on the line as an informant. On June 8, 1963, the FBI learned that a group of Miami supporters of the National States' Rights Party had planned to murder Somersett because he opposed their presence in Miami. (As was discussed earlier, Guy Banister, Ray Leahart, and the others involved with Lee Harvey Oswald in New Orleans were associated with the National States' Rights Party.)

Somersett, born March 27, 1903, in Wilmington, North Carolina, was an imposing, "mountainous figure" and reminded the Commanding Officer of the Intelligence Unit of the Miami police, Charles H. Sapp, of an Oldsmobile Rocket 88—one of the largest automobile models of the time. Hence, he was dubbed "bucket-ass 88," or just "88," by the Miami police. Somersett was a member of the Northern League, the National States' Rights Party, and the

National Knights of the Ku Klux Klan, NKKK—the leading Klan organization in the U.S. in 1960. Somersett held the high office of National Adjutant of the National Grand Council of Klans, and was appointed to the three-man finance committee, which substantially raised his informant potential. The NKKK was later incorporated into Grand Wizard Robert Shelton's United Klans of America, or UKA.

Both Milteer and Somersett traveled extensively to KKK meetings. In 1960, Somersett attended Klan meetings in Stone Mountain, Georgia; Chattanooga, Tennessee; Atlanta, Georgia; Columbia, South Carolina; Orlando, Florida; and Montgomery, Alabama. Somersett was an honorary member of the Association of South Carolina Klans (ASCK), and belonged to the Association of Georgia Klans. Somersett attended a meeting of the "Hidden Hand" in 1960 in Jackson, Mississippi. He reported to the FBI that at the Hidden Hand meeting it was announced "any future attempts by the Congress of Racial Equality, CORE, to force integration in Mississippi and Louisiana would result in serious injury to those participating." The Hidden Hand appears to be the same as—or related to—a group called the "flying squad," which was a rapid-response, on-call collection of extremist volunteers prepared to commit retaliatory acts of racial or anti-Jewish violence, on command. One FBI report described an Association of South Carolina Klans request for the flying squad to take care of a "job," not further described, which was apparently carried out in early 1963.

The FBI sent Somersett to New Orleans during the period of November 15–28, 1960, to monitor the Catholic school integration crisis. In doing so, he landed right in the heart of the operation of Guy Banister and his associates. As part of his cover, Somersett joined the New Orleans Citizens' Council, in which Ray Leahart, Guy Banister, and Kent Courtney were active members. As was noted previously, Lee Harvey Oswald allegedly attended a meeting of the Citizens' Council with David Ferrie. Jack Helm, a Klan leader and associate of David Ferrie and Guy Banister, was in the forefront in the fight against the Catholic school integration campaign ordered by the diocese. Banister's secretary (and love interest), Delphine Roberts, was a vocal opponent of the Catholic school integration and was apparently photographed by Somersett for the FBI. Photos of Roberts picketing the newly integrated school also appeared in the local newspapers. Leander Perez, a devout Catholic, was the leader of the integration resistance movement and was close to Guy Banister, as well as Joseph Milteer (his role in the assassination of President Kennedy will be discussed in detail later). Perez, Roberts, and Jackson Ricau (who collaborated with Banister in publishing the *Citizens' Report*), were excommunicated for their opposition to the archbishop's integration order.[375]

Somersett was also the leader of a small labor union in Miami and published a union newsletter, *The National Federation of Labor News*. In 1963, Somersett was arrested (and acquitted) for assaulting a union member over disputed union funds. Somersett's display of violent temperament further enhanced the radical right's respect for him.

Unfortunately, in another attempt to increase his stature among the radical groups he infiltrated, Somersett bragged that the FBI interviewed him on the suspicion that he had committed acts of racial violence. The FBI learned—through another of its informants—of

Somersett's false and unsanctioned statements about the FBI, and he was discontinued as an informant on November 13, 1961.[376] Nonetheless, now unwanted and unpaid, Somersett felt a deep-seated allegiance to the FBI and his cause and continued to send reports on the far right to them.

Somersett consorted with some of most dangerous characters in the Klan for over a decade and called Milteer "the most violent-minded man in America." Somersett had no doubt that Milteer blew up a house in Chattanooga and "knocked out a colored man and his wife." He felt Milteer was guilty of a lot of bombings in Georgia and Tennessee, and stated, "He had a taste for terror by bombing." He reported that Milteer agreed, if necessary for the cause, to murder an African-American Morehouse College student.

Joseph A. Milteer

Joseph Adams Milteer was born in the small town of Quitman, Georgia, located near the Florida border, on February 22, 1902, and continued to live in his parents' home in the 1960s after they died. He also often stayed with his common-law wife, Lula Belle (Mrs. C. C.) Cofield, in nearby Valdosta, Georgia.

Little is known about his upbringing. His mother was from Peekskill, New York, and he attended school for a time in Poughkeepsie, New York. In 1938, he operated a lunch stand in Cleveland, Ohio, and at some point operated concessions around military installations. He was involved in some capacity in the construction of the Supreme Court building in Washington, D.C., for three and a half years. However, the death of his father in 1962, and a 200,000 dollar inheritance—a tidy sum at the time—allowed him to pursue his personal agenda.

Milteer was a well-known character in the Quitman and Valdosta region as a prolific pamphleteer and perennial candidate for local office. He was unemployed, and devoted his efforts to traveling and networking with extremists across the country. In letters from his friends, found after his death, he recounted numerous trips taken that covered three to six thousand miles at a time, from south to north and coast to coast on the trail of radical right-wing meetings (he tape recorded and sold the speeches at the meetings). His far-right political activism can be traced back to 1955. In 1956, he belonged to the far-right group We the People in Chicago. In 1957, he belonged to For America, the Constitution Party, and the Federation for Constitutional Government, which operated out of New Orleans. Banister's close associate Leander Perez was a principal in the Federation, as was J. Evetts Haley, a close ally of General Walker.[377]

In 1957, Milteer traveled from Maine to Florida promoting a conservative third party and, in 1958, he tape recorded speeches in Kansas City.[378] In a 1968 letter to a friend, Milteer described the earlier days of his political activism, writing, "Back in 1958 I went around to many parts of the country trying to get the Right Wing Groups to get together and form one big front and select men for public office and we all work together to that end."

He wrote that he ran into Kent Courtney at a meeting he sponsored in Chicago and noted that Courtney was doing the same thing he was doing: trying to organize the various right-wing organizations into a "New Party." He wrote that he did not know much about Courtney and his followers and was not too "hep" about him. Milteer felt America needed men like Tom Anderson and Dan Smoot leading the country and offered them the Presidency and Vice Presidency respectively on the Constitution Party ticket at one time.[379] In 1960, Milteer tape recorded a speech of Billy James Hargis, an associate of Guy Banister and General Walker (as noted in Chapter One), and Hargis later contacted Milteer and asked him to delete one statement on the tape he made that was factually incorrect.[380] In 1960, Roy V. Harris discussed with Milteer his efforts to get the Free Electors movement going in Georgia.[381] (It will be recalled from Chapter One that Guy Banister and Leander Perez were active in the Free Elector Movement in Louisiana. All of the individuals mentioned by Milteer in his early foray into the radical right are critically important in this work and will be discussed in depth later.)

Milteer was the leader of the Dixie Klan of Georgia, which was an affiliate of the Dixie Klan of Tennessee—who were noted for their violence—though neither group was apparently affiliated with the Georgia Klan run by Stone Mountain attorney James Venable.[382]

Revelation of the Plot to Assassinate President Kennedy

In October of 1963, Milteer visited Willie Somersett in Miami for the purpose of distributing his far-right pamphlets to "trusted people" and promoting the upcoming Indianapolis meeting of the Constitution Party on October 10, 1963. Titles of the various pamphlets were: "End of Kennedy, King, Khrushchev Dictatorship"; "Operation Survival"; "David Goes Forth to Meet Goliath"; "Why? Defender or Defectors"; "Liars and Easter"; "War Time Emergencies"; "Is term 'Cold War' a Lie"; and "When They Take Over." The leaflets were generally critical of integrationists, the Supreme Court, and the Federal Government. Milteer explained that the purpose of the Constitution Party meeting to be held at the Marott Hotel (not to be confused with "Marriott" hotels) in Indianapolis was to "put an end to the Kennedy, Khrushchev and King dictatorship." Milteer told Somersett, "Next year there is going to be a lot of killing, and it may be necessary to go right into the State Department and place several traitors under citizens' arrest. If these traitors resist they will be killed right on the spot."

At the meeting, the formation of a violent underground army was planned. Milteer used various other terms to describe the violent underground including "hardcore underground," "policy group" and "international underground." Somersett attended the meeting with Milteer, and reported to the FBI that there was talk of killing President Kennedy by those in attendance (as will be discussed at length in the next two chapters).

Milteer told Somersett he planned to visit him at his Miami apartment on November 9, 1963. Somersett alerted the Miami police, and they planted a tape recorder in Somersett's broom closet. In particular, they were interested in ascertaining whether Milteer knew the identities of those responsible for the bombing of the Birmingham Sixteenth Street Baptist Church on September 15, 1963, in which four black Sunday school children were killed.

They were also interested in finding out if any violence was planned for President Kennedy's upcoming visit to Miami on November 18, 1963. Somersett remarked, "The Miami Police were not about to have him [Kennedy] killed here." When Milteer arrived at his apartment, Somersett discovered that the tape recorder had accidentally become unplugged. Thinking quickly, Somersett excused himself from the living room, explaining he needed to unplug his refrigerator to prevent it from frosting, a common problem at the time, and he plugged the tape recorder back in. The transcript begins with Somersett asking Milteer about two notoriously violent Klansmen, Jack Brown and Kenneth Adams, whom he suspected might have been involved in the Birmingham church bombing. Lee McCloud, an Atlanta Klansman whom Milteer drove to the Constitution Party meeting, was mentioned.[383] The transcript of the surreptitious taping of the Somersett-Milteer conversation is as follows:

> Somersett: Now we are going to, you are going to take, Kenney, what do you call his last name?
>
> Milteer: Kenneth Adams.
>
> Somersett: Yeah, you are going to take him in, he is supposed be one of the hardcore underground, are you going to invite him into that, too? What about Brown now, are you going to invite Brown in? You are going to have Brown in it?
>
> Milteer: Yeah.
>
> Somersett: Now, I will tell you between you, and me because we are talking, we are not going to talk to every body like we are talking here. Now, you know this, I like Brown, he is a good fellow, you know him, now here is something, when he was in his house, now, he knows me and you, but he don't know Lee McCloud, well I think he done too much talking in front of a man he didn't know. Brown trusts a lot of people, he figures everybody is good.
>
> Milteer: Yeah.
>
> Somersett: And you know when he was telling him about blowing up all those churches and, you know, I don't think he should have said all that in front of McCloud.
>
> Milteer: That is exactly the way I feel about it, too. And I didn't talk about it anymore after we left there.
>
> Somersett: No, I see you didn't, you see, these things come to my mind, I don't know McCloud well and Brown never seen him before in his life, that I know of, now you seen this boy, Jackie [Brown's son], didn't open his mouth he just sit there and listen. Jack Caulk [Brown's son] he is a very quiet boy, Brown it just seems, well, he, I guess he has gotten by

with so much he just don't care. He come out with all that about going over to Atlanta carrying that stuff, and showing them how to operate, I didn't want to say anything to him, but I don't think it is a good idea for people to discuss things like that in front of strangers. What do you think about it?

Milteer: No I—He should operate that, the same as he does the rest of us.

Somersett: That's right, damn right that is right. Now you take like Birmingham—

Milteer: Any conclusion they come up with, that's them, not him.

Somersett: That is true.

Milteer: He didn't give them anything.

Somersett: Well, he didn't give them nothing.

Milteer: Just like me at home these folks want to know, "Joe, where do you get all of your information?" "Well, I get it, that is all you are interested in," and that is a far as it goes, see. And the same guy will turn around and give me some information, but he doesn't know where I am getting my information. The same guy who asks me where I get my information will turn around and give me information.

Somersett: Well, sure, of course, I realize that.

Milteer: That is the way you have got to operate.

Somersett: Well, that is what I say, if you are going to take Brown in, and Brown is going to be one of the head men, the man behind you, then you have got to talk to Brown a little bit, and tell him, you know, "You have got to be a little more conscientious, especially on these bombings and killings." After all he comes right out with it.

Milteer: We have got to let him understand, that, that is his operation, and not ours.

Somersett: Yeah, that is true. We don't care if he wants to go to Birmingham and blow up a church, let him.

Milteer: If he wants to blow up the National Capital, that is alright with me. I will go with him, but not as a party, it is an individual, you are going to have to make him understand that.

Somersett: Well, if you want to go with him and help him blow it up, that is not the party, it is an individual, you are going to have to make him understand that.

Milteer: There is a party movement and also an individual movement.

Somersett: Yeah, that is right.

Milteer: And they are distinct and separate.

Somersett: Well, you are going to have to make him understand that, right there, he didn't exactly admit it, but Jesus Christ, he intimated, he indicated it right there, he backed the bombings of killing the Negroes in Birmingham, well, you know damn well we don't want anybody talking like that.

Milteer: Can't afford it.

Somersett: Well, you damned well that it is bad talk especially to somebody you don't know. He could have said that to me, and you would have been alright, it would have been between you and me then.

Milteer: That is true.

Somersett: But go and say it in front of McCloud, what the hell . . .

[Milteer interrupts]

Milteer: Well, I don't think that he thought that he [McCloud] would have been with us, if he had not have been all right. But that is still not enough.

Somersett: Hell, no, that is no good, at least before he made all those statements, he should have called you outside, or consulted about this man a little bit.

Milteer: You have to have reservations, you know.

Somersett: That is right. Hell, he didn't say these things in any way to try to get us in trouble, because the only one who could be in trouble would be him, he was confessing on his damn self, he wasn't confessing on us, because we hadn't done a damned thing.

Milteer: You and I would not get up there on the stand and say that he told us a cotton picking thing either.

Somersett: Well, he knows that, but how about the other man.

Milteer: Well, that is what I say.

Somersett: Yeah, hell yes. I tell you something, you take Kenneth Adams over there, he is a mean damned man, like Brown was saying, the guy he was sending him to, well Kenneth is real mean, and the way Brown indicated they *[unintelligible? killing, bombing, blowing up]* the Negroes, well, we don't care anything about that. I would rather he wouldn't tell us those stories.

Milteer: You sure can't repeat them.

Somersett: Yeah. That is the set-up we are in now, I mean, we have to work with them, but let them operate their . . . *[unintelligible]*

Milteer: I have a man who is the head of his underground of his own up there in Delaware, and since I worked on the Supreme Court, he wanted me to give him the lay-out there so they could go over there and do some things there, you know. But he called it off, I don't know why, I didn't even ask him why. That was his affair, but he called it off. But I was ready to go with him. I gave him the damn information he wanted.

Somersett: You worked on the Supreme Court?

Milteer: Yeah, three and a half years.

Somersett: Well, that is why he wants you to go, then, well, them things have got to be done, but outside the Party, we have got to be mighty careful who the hell we let know anything. Now, here is one thing you have got to realize, transporting dynamite across the state line is a federal offence, well you better let them know that.

Milteer: Well, there is a way to beat that, you know. All you have to do is pull up to the state line, unload it there, slide it across the line, get in the car and load it again, and they can't accuse you of transporting it then, because you didn't do it. I have done the same thing with a woman. I had one, then I had a woman frame me on it. I got to the state line, and I said, "Listen, Toots, this is the state line, get out and I'll meet you over there," she got out, walked across the line, got in my car in the other state, I didn't transport her, there wasn't a fucking thing she could do about it, I had her ass for a long time.

Milteer: I was talking to a boy yesterday, and he was in Athens, Georgia, and he told me, that they had two colored people working in the drug store, and that them, uh, they went into the basement, and tapped them small pipes, I guess that they were copper together, and let that thing accumulate and blowed that drug store up. He told me that yesterday, do you think that is right?

Somersett: It could have happened that way.

Milteer: Well. That is what he told me, and he is in town right now.

Somersett: Does he know who did it? Do they think these Negroes did it?

Milteer: Oh, no, they killed the Negroes, because they had two Negroes working in the place, that is what he told me. He is in town now, he is from Chattanooga. He knows Brown, he knows them all, and his uncle is in the Klan there. He is a young boy, he has been in the marines, and he really knows his business. He went there, he went down and looked, and he told me that is what happened. So he has been involved in quite a little bit of stuff, according to his story about Nashville, Chattanooga and Georgia. I have no reason not to believe him, because he told me too much about Brown's operation, that is the reason . . . *[unintelligible]*

Milteer: Yeah. You take this boy Conde McGinley, a boy up there in Union, New Jersey, of course he doesn't go to anything like that, but he is on our side, he is one that puts out that *Common Sense*. He is an ex-marine. He is all man, too.

Somersett: Now, you see, we will talk to these other people, you have made up your mind that you are going to use the Constitutional Party as a front.

Milteer: Yeah, Constitutional Party States Rights.

Somersett: Yeah, and it will be strictly secret, and nobody will be exposed except you.

Milteer: Yeah.

Somersett: Because when we talk to them today, you want to know exactly what to tell them, how it operates.

Milteer: Yeah, and we got to set up a little fund there to get it operating.

Somersett: Oh, yeah, sure.

Milteer: And I am going to devote my time to it, I don't have any idea of getting elected to that City Commission, but I am making it cost them bastards, it costs them as it is, it cost them between $1,500 and $2,000 to beat me before, so I want to make it cost another couple of thousands of dollars. If they want to get rid of me, they can buy my fucking property, and I will get out of the damn town. In other words they will save money. I am going to put that out in one of these little bulletins, like a typewriter page, eight and a half by eleven and brother don't you think they ain't waiting for them, when I don't put them out, "Joe, where is the bulletin?" Bill that could go all over the country, the same way. That was just a trial proposition, if it would work in a little stinking town like that, it will work anywhere.

Somersett: I don't know, I think Kennedy is coming here on the 18th, or something like that to make some kind of a speech, I don't know what it is, but I imagine it will be on TV, and you can be on the look for that, I think it is the 18th that he is supposed to be here. I don't know what it is supposed to be about.

Milteer: You can bet bottom dollar he is going to have a lot to say about the Cubans, there are so many of them here.

Somersett: Yeah, well he will have a thousand bodyguards, don't worry about that.

Milteer: The more bodyguards he has, the easier it is to get him.

Somersett: What?

Milteer: The more bodyguards he has the easier it is to get to him.

Somersett: Well how in the hell do you figure would be the best way to get him?

Milteer: From an office building with a high-powered rifle, how many people *[room noise—tape not intelligible]* does he have going around who look just like him? Do you know about that?

Somersett: No, I never heard that he had anybody.

Milteer: He has got them.

Somersett: He has?

Milteer: He had about fifteen. Whenever he goes anyplace they *[not intelligible]* he knows he is a marked man.

Somersett: You think he knows he is a marked man?

Milteer: Sure he does.

Somersett: They are really going to try and kill him?

Milteer: Oh, yeah, it's in the working. Brown himself, Brown is just as likely to get him as anybody. He hasn't said so, but he has tried to get Martin Luther King, yeah..

Somersett: He did?

Milteer: Oh yes, he followed him for miles and miles, and couldn't get close enough to him.

Somersett: You know exactly where it is in Atlanta don't you?

Milteer: Martin Luther King, yeah.

Somersett: Bustus Street [phonetic]

Milteer: Yeah, 530.

Somersett: Oh Brown tried to get him huh?

Milteer: Yeah.

Somersett: Well he will damn sure do it, I will tell you that. Well that is why, look, you see, well that is why we have to be so careful, you know that Brown is operating strong.

Milteer: He ain't going for play you know.

Somersett: That is right.

Milteer: He is going for broke.

Somersett: I never asked Brown about his business or anything, you know just what he told me, told us you know. But after the conversation, and the way he talked to us, there is no question in my mind who knocked the church off in Birmingham, you can believe that, that is the way I figured it.

Milteer: That is right, it is about the only way you can figure it.

Somersett: That is right.

Milteer: Not being there, not knowing anything.

Somersett: But just from his conversation, as you and me know him, but if they did it is their business, like you say . . .
[subject breaks in]

Milteer: Its up to the individual.

Somersett: That is right. They are individual operators, we don't want that within the party. Hitting Kennedy this Kennedy is going to be, a hard proposition, I tell you. I believe, you may have figured out a way to get him, you may have figured out the office building, and all that. I don' know how them Secret Service agents cover all them office buildings, or anywhere he is going, do you know whether they do that or not.

Milteer: Well, if they have any suspicions they do that of course. But without suspicion chances are they wouldn't. You take there in Washington, of course it is the wrong time of the year, but you take pleasant weather, he comes out on the veranda, and someone could be in a hotel room across the way there, and pick him off just like . . . [fades out]

Somersett: Is that right?

Milteer: Sure, disassemble a gun, you don't have to take a gun up there, you can take it up in pieces, all those guns come knock down, you can take them apart.

Somersett: They have got a damn, this boy was telling me yesterday about, they have got an explosive that you get from the army, it is supposed to be like putty or something, you stick it up, and use a small fuse, you just stick it like that, he told me, and I think that is what happened in the church in Birmingham, they stuck this stuff, somebody stuck it under the steps with a short fuse, and went on home.

Somersett: This boy is pretty smart, demolition is that what you call it?

Milteer: Demolition, that is right.

Somersett: I am going to talk with him some more.

Milteer: Yeah, I would.

Somersett: I am going to talk with him some more, and find out a lot more about his operation, because he knows a hell of a lot.

Milteer: You need a guy around like that too. Where we can put or finger on him, when we want him.

Somersett: Yeah. Well, you have got somebody up there in that country now, if you need them.

Milteer; Well, we are going to have to get nasty . . . *[not intelligible]*

Somersett: Yeah, get nasty.

Milteer: We have got to be ready, we have got to be sitting on go, too.

Somersett: Yeah, that is right.

Milteer: There ain't any count down to it, we have just got to be sitting on go. Count down they can move in on you, and on go they can't. Count down is alright for a slow prepared operation, but in an emergency operation, you have got to be sitting on go, we have got to know where we are at. Because you know that that will be a real shake, if they do that.

Somersett: Boy, if that Kennedy gets shot, we got know where we are at. Because you know that will be a real shake, if they do that.

Milteer: They wouldn't leave any stone unturned there's no way. They will pick up somebody within hours afterwards, if anything like that would happen just to throw the public off.

Somersett: Oh, somebody is going to have to go to jail, if he gets killed.

Milteer: Just like that Bruno Hauptman in the Lindbergh case you know.

[At this point Somersett interrupts to make a phone call and the transcript ends][384]

After the taped conversation, Milteer left Somersett's Miami apartment on the evening of November 9, 1963, and attended the Political Rally for Goldwater in Fort Lauderdale. Milteer despised Goldwater because he was part Jewish, noting incorrectly that he was half Jewish, when Goldwater was only one-eighth Jewish. Milteer referred to him as "Goldwasser," the original family name, which had been changed to Goldwater in the nineteenth century. Goldwater was a member of the NAACP; however, he was strongly supportive of states' rights and sanctioned the state's right to maintain segregation.

The recorded conversation began with Somersett asking Milteer if he was going to invite "Kenney" into the "hardcore underground." "Kenney" was Kenneth Lamar Adams, the Secretary and Treasurer of the Anniston Alabama Citizens' Council, a member of the National States' Rights Party, and the leader of the Anniston Klan.

Adams had a long history of committing racial violence—on April 10, 1956, the then thirty-five-year-old Adams attacked legendary singer Nat "King" Cole while Cole was performing at the Birmingham Municipal Auditorium. During Cole's performance, two white assailants knocked Cole to the stage floor. The plot reportedly involved 150 others planted in the audience, who were expected to join the melee but ultimately did not. It was learned that the plot was hatched in Adams's Anniston service station. Only six arrests were made, including plot leader Kenneth Adams, who was charged with assault with intent to kill and ultimately fined fifty dollars. The police had received advanced notice of a planned demonstration by the assailants, but felt no action was warranted. Later, President Eisenhower praised the white Alabama citizenry who condemned the act.[385, 386]

Adams gained further national notoriety for torching the Congress of Racial Equality Freedom Bus in Anniston, Alabama, on May 14, 1961. Segregationists were outraged when they learned that CORE was sending the integrated Freedom Buses from Washington on May 2, 1961, with plans to end up in New Orleans on May 17, 1961. Kenney Adams led the assault against the Freedom Bus in Anniston. Although the informant's name was redacted in the FBI documents, Somersett is certainly the informant described as a union leader from Miami. National Klan leader Robert Shelton, along with Adams, formulated the original plan to attack the bus. Adams was to slow the bus down in Anniston and, when it was to arrive in Birmingham, some of the riders were to be killed. However, Adams went too far by driving a pickup truck in front of the bus as it made its way to Anniston on the highway, repeatedly putting on the brakes in an effort to wreck it. Adams then flattened the front tire of the bus and it came to a halt at a grocery store. The riders were kept on the bus as the rear of the bus was set on fire and smoke billowed from the windows, overcoming many of the riders. A hostile crowd gathered, a window was broken, and one rider was hit in the face with a chain. The highway patrol arrived, fired shots into the air, and the mob was dispersed. Adams and three others were arrested—and later acquitted for lack of evidence.[387] (Willie Somersett's high position in the national KKK earned him the honor of an invitation to attend the trial of Adams.[388])

Adams had prior arrest records for assault and battery on a Negro who tried to obtain service at his gas station. Adams displayed a sign at his service station, where he stored explosives guns and other weapons, that read "We serve white customers only." He carried an automatic .45 pistol with him, and was considered armed and dangerous with a past record of larceny, resisting arrest, shooting into a house and church, and assault with intent to murder. Before a Birmingham Citizens' Council meeting, Adams proposed the formation of a new Klan dedicated to action. To emphasize his message, he had men carrying revolvers surround him on stage.[389]

In October of 1958, the FBI suspected Adams was involved in the bombing of the Atlanta Temple and asked him of his whereabouts on the day of the event. They also asked if he was involved in a Confederate underground, or if he had a problem with Jews. J. B. Stoner, another Milteer associate, was arrested for the crime.[390] An FBI informant, who appears to have been Willie Somersett, was told by Adams that he was in the process of manufacturing explosives equivalent to several sticks of dynamite and, in 1961, Adams purchased fifty riot-type shotguns. The FBI believed Adams traveled to Tennessee, and suspected his involvement in a bombing there.[391]

Adams and members of his Klavern drove to Oxford, Mississippi, on September 27, 1962, to join General Walker in protest of the admission of the first African American, James Meredith, to the University of Mississippi.[392] President Kennedy sent U.S. Marshals to secure Meredith's enrollment, and a riot led by General Walker ensued. Walker was arrested for insurrection against the United States of America (an entire chapter will be dedicated to this critically historical event). A number of close associates of Guy Banister—as well as associates of Milteer—responded to General Walker's call for men from all over to join him in protest of President Kennedy's forced integration of the hallowed, all-white University of Mississippi.

Adams attended Klan meetings in Mississippi, Tennessee, Florida, California, Ohio, and Illinois. He attended a Klan rally in New Orleans on May 12, 1962. On December 5, 1962, the FBI approached Adams and told him to desist from taking any action during Martin Luther King, Jr.'s planned visit to Anniston.[393] On May 12, 1963, shots were fired at the homes of two African Americans, for which Kenneth Adams was arrested and found guilty of the crime.[394] Prior to this arrest on May 2, 1963, Adams traveled to Fort Payne, Alabama, to meet with a Klansman arrested for killing a white postman from Baltimore named William Moore (he was walking through the South with a placard advocating racial tolerance)—an event emblematic of the era. On May 27, 1965, pursuant to the presidential protection agreement, FBI director J. Edgar Hoover notified the Secret Service that Adams was a threat to the life of President Johnson based on his prior acts. Later that same year, on July 23, Adams traveled to a Bogalusa Louisiana Citizens' Council and Klan-led rally protesting integration. However, Adams had been drunk for the entire month leading up to the event and was not permitted to speak at the rally. On November 9, 1969, Adams was sentenced to two years in prison for being found guilty of intent to murder in the shooting of an eighteen-year-old black man, Albert Satcher.[395]

Milteer and Somersett also discussed the merits of letting another violent Klansman,

Jack Brown, into their hardcore underground. In 1957, members of Eldon Edwards's U.S. Klans in Tennessee broke away to form the Dixie Klan Knights of the KKK under Jack W. Brown. Kenneth Adams became the Dixie Klan Alabama Grand Dragon.[396] (The author has not viewed Brown's FBI file.) Brown, who was involved in the National States' Rights Party, died in 1965. The FBI learned that Brown was the Imperial Wizard of the KKK in Chattanooga, Tennessee, and was responsible for five house bombings in Hamilton County in August 1960.[397] Brown was a presidential elector for the National States' Rights Party (which met at the meeting hall of the Dixie Klan of Tennessee) that selected Orval Faubus and John G. Crommelin—a Milteer associate—as their candidates for president and vice president, respectively, in 1960.[398] Jack Brown told Milteer that he attempted to murder Martin Luther King, Jr. at King's home in Atlanta.[399]

As utterly violent and murderous as Kenney Adams and Jack Brown were, Willie Somersett reserved the distinction of being described as "the most violent-minded man in American" for Joseph Milteer. In a travesty of justice, the FBI ignored the warning—and the Warren Commission was never told of Milteer and the advance knowledge of a plot to kill the president.

The Accurate Prediction

The details of Milteer's predictions as to how the assassination would take place were accurate on all counts:

His prediction that the shooting would take place in an office building was borne out. The Texas School Book Depository was an office building as well as depository for schoolbooks.

Milteer's statement that the murder rifle could be disassembled and surreptitiously brought into the office building was also correct. The Warren Commission determined that the rifle could be disassembled and was brought into the Texas School Book Depository in a brown paper wrapping fabricated by Oswald. Wesley Frazier, who drove Oswald and the package to work on the morning of the assassination, told the Warren Commission that Oswald grasped one end of the package, which Oswald said contained curtain rods, with his hand and tucked the other end under his armpit.

Oswald's Manlicher Carcano was a high-powered rifle, another correct prediction.

The prediction that a suspect would be picked up shortly after the assassination was also correct. Oswald was picked up within hours of the murder and, later, charged with the crime.

Milteer's precise predictions on four specific events in the case were far too accurate to be the result of chance alone. Moreover, his predictions alone should have raised grave suspicions that he had knowledge of the actual conspiracy to kill the president and may have been an accessory. (Overwhelming documentation of this conspiracy and the identity of the other conspirators will be presented in later chapters.)

Reaction to the Plot by Law Enforcement

After the assassination, FBI Director J. Edgar Hoover quickly announced that a lone Communist gunman—Lee Harvey Oswald—committed the murder. The Warren Commission came to the same conclusions. However, unlike Hoover, the Warren Commission did not know about the Milteer evidence or prediction. Milteer's dead-on foreknowledge was never revealed to the Warren Commission by Hoover and, accordingly, was never taken into consideration by them. The FBI Director failed to deliver the investigative files on Milteer's prediction to the Warren Commission until just weeks before their investigation ended—when their findings were already written and awaiting publication. From there, the files were buried in the National Archives where they became "classified."[400]

It is hard to conceive of any explanation for Hoover's failure to deliver this compelling evidence of conspiracy, other than that it was an act of deliberate concealment. As will be shown later, when the trails of evidence left by Milteer and others on the radical right are followed, they lead to prominent figures in the anti-Communist movement, fostered by Hoover and his former SAC of the Chicago office, Guy Banister. The wife of Congressman Hale Boggs, who served on the Warren Commission before he died in 1973 in an airplane crash, told a friend that Hale felt "very, very torn during his work on the [Warren Commission] . . . he wished he had never been on it or signed it [The Warren Report]." A former aide to Boggs reported, "Hale always returned to one thing: Hoover lied his eyes out to the Commission—on Oswald, on Ruby, on their friends, the bullet, the gun, you name it . . . ."[401]

The Milteer evidence was not made public until 1967. By that time, a number of books and articles had surfaced doubting the conclusions of the Warren Commission. William Somersett was unwavering in his conviction that Milteer was a part of the conspiracy that led to the killing of the president. That conviction drove Somersett to take it upon himself to go public with the Milteer story and tell his local newspaper about it. Certainly, he did so at great personal risk—considering that Milteer and his violent cohorts were alive and well at the time—but Somersett was a tough and fearless individual who had stood up to a number of threats in the past. Before going forward, Somersett asked for the Miami FBI's permission on January 26, 1967, to release the transcript of his taped exchange with Milteer. Somersett advised the FBI that a *Miami News* reporter was planning a story on the assassination in which he would be critical of the U.S. attorney general and the Secret Service, but not the FBI. The FBI reminded Somersett of the confidentiality agreement he had with them, which meant that Somersett was not permitted to reveal his role as an informant with the Bureau.

In a February 2, 1967, FBI memorandum, a somewhat vague account of the Milteer saga was recounted and an incorrect statement was made, stating that Somersett was discontinued as an FBI informant because of his unreliability. On the contrary, the FBI had praised Somersett in the past for his reliability. Somersett insisted that he was discontinued as an informer because he made the false claims in an effort to enhance his status in the eyes of those he was informing on. (As noted, Somersett had falsely told individuals in a group he had infiltrated for the FBI that the FBI questioned him on suspicions he, too, was involved in racial hate crimes.) Compared to the wealth of information Somersett had provided, his trivial indiscretion would have been an extremely poor reason to discontinue their relationship. Somersett had been the FBI's most valuable weapon against the reign of terror that existed during the civil rights movement in the 1950s and '60s, a movement that J. Edgar Hoover had complete contempt for.

Somersett read the stories in the national press raising doubts about the Warren Commission's conclusions. When asked what his motivation to speak publicly was, Somersett responded, "Because the FBI and the Secret Service knew about the threat to kill the president and they didn't protect him from it. They knew how it was to be done and they didn't protect him." Somersett also advised the Miami police of his intention of going public with the tape and, on February 1, 1967, the Miami police played the tape recording for a group of newsmen. Assistant State's Attorney Arthur Huttoe discounted any relation between the tape and the Kennedy assassination. Huttoe's name, curiously, was not found in the volumes of Miami police, state attorney general, FBI, or Secret Service documents on the Milteer matter—and he does not appear to have been a principal in that investigation. However, Huttoe stated "in our opinion, there is no connection between the death of President Kennedy and this [Milteer's] group." He stated, rather, that the Miami police investigation was related to the Shoemaker bombing in which individuals were investigated "who used to sit around and threaten to kill a lot of people."[402] Huttoe's opinion of a doubtful relationship between the tape and the assassination runs contrary to the sentiments conveyed to the author by then-principal law enforcement figures in the case, Assistant Dade County Attorney General Seymour Gelber and Detective Everett Kay. They both told the author that they were certain that Milteer and a hate group were behind the assassination of President Kennedy.[403]

On February 2, 1967, the relative parts of the transcript of Milteer's taped assassination conversation were published in the *Miami News*. Neither Milteer's nor Somersett's name was mentioned. Milteer was referred to as a "States' Rights organizer" and Somersett as "the informer." In addition to the taped meeting, the story divulged that the man (Milteer) traveled to Dallas on November 10, 1963 on a political trip and had also discussed a possible plot to bomb the Supreme Court Building in Washington. This was Milteer's third visit to Dallas before he traveled there for the assassination. He also visited in June–July 1963, and just prior to the October 10, 1963, Constitution Party meeting. (He also traveled to Dallas in December 1963 and June 1964, as we shall see in later chapters.) It was further reported that it was the conviction of the informer (Somersett) that the "States' Rights man" (Milteer) knew who was responsible for the heinous Sixteenth Street Baptist Church bombing in Birmingham, Alabama, that resulted in the death of four young black girls. The newspaper story noted that the FBI questioned the man (Milteer) on November 27, 1963. The following day (February 3rd), the *Miami Herald* reported the dismissive comments of Florida Assistant Attorney General Huttoe.

New Orleans district attorney Jim Garrison had begun a secret investigation into the New Orleans connection to the assassination in 1966. Garrison's investigation was leaked by the press on February 17, 1967, and may have provided additional impetus for William Somersett to publish an account of the Milteer affair in his union newsletter, the *National Federation of Labor News*. The paper was published on February 22, 1967, which was also the day key Garrison suspect, David Ferrie—Lee Harvey Oswald's former Civil Air Patrol instructor—was found dead of a ruptured cerebral aneurysm. The headline of the *Labor News* read: "DID THE FRICTION BETWEEN ROBERT F. KENNEDY AND J. EDGAR HOOVER CAUSE THE DEATH OF PRESIDENT JOHN FITZGERALD KENNEDY IN DALLAS ON NOVEMBER 22, 1963?" Somersett did not identify the names of any individuals in his story. But certainly, if Milteer had read the *Labor News* story, he would have known that Somersett was the mentioned Miami police informant. Nonetheless, any threat of retaliation did not deter Somersett from publishing the story.

The Miami revelations, surprisingly, stirred little interest—perhaps because the idea of a segregationist plot was such a foreign concept as compared to the prevailing conspiracy theories that the U.S. intelligence community was responsible for Oswald and the assassination. Somersett probably didn't help his cause when he published a brazen headline blaming Robert Kennedy for his brother's murder in the *Labor News* on March 26, 1967, that read, "I CHARGE ROBERT F. KENNEDY WITH MURDER." Somersett stated that it was Attorney General Kennedy's fault for not assigning adequate FBI manpower to protect the president in Dallas. Somersett stated that Robert Kennedy was aware of the taped plot but did nothing to prevent the crime (it should be noted that is not clear if Robert Kennedy knew anything at all about the Milteer tape). When *Miami News* reporter Bill Barry requested a copy of the tape recording from the Miami FBI, they advised him, on February 7, 1967, "the Bureau did not have such a tape and could make no comment." Assistant State District Attorney Seymour Gelber told the author that the Miami police did, in fact, give the FBI a copy of the tape in 1963, but the FBI never acknowledged receiving it. One member of the Miami police summed up the relationship between the Miami police and the FBI, saying: "They take but do not give."[404]

Harold Weisberg, a prolific, sensational writer and early critic of the Warren Commission, was the first to mention the Milteer plot in his book *Frame-Up: The Assassination of Martin Luther King*, published in 1971. Weisberg, of Frederick, Maryland, may have learned of the affair from reading the *Baltimore Sun*, which picked up the story on the wire and published it on February 3, 1967. Weisberg offered no new information in his book other than providing the transcript of the tape recording. Weisberg later told the author that he didn't put any stock in the Milteer story, stating that Milteer was just some crackpot shooting off his mouth.

Weisberg liberally spread the blame around in his early books on the assassination. He blamed the FBI and Secret Service for covering up evidence in his 1966 book *Whitewash II: the Secret Service FBI Cover-up*. He named the CIA in his book *Oswald In New Orleans: Case for Conspiracy with the CIA*, a year later. Jim Garrison endorsed the latter book, and even wrote the foreword. Weisberg's *Frame-Up* account of the Milteer affair gained little attention, probably because it was about the assassination of Martin Luther King, Jr.—rather than that of Kennedy—and the Milteer material appeared almost entirely in the appendix. Whether or not it was because of the overshadowing of the Milteer affair by the Garrison investigation, which was revealed fifteen days after Somersett's 1967 Milteer disclosure, or the minimizing of the Milteer case by Florida Attorney General Huttoe, the matter remained dormant until Dan Christensen investigated the case for *Miami Magazine* in 1976.

The Milteer Miami Police and FBI Files

The Miami Police Department and FBI files on Milteer obtained by the author through the Freedom of Information Act provide additional compelling suspicion of Milteer's involvement in the assassination in some way. The additional Milteer evidence contained herein was never made public in the earliest news accounts of the story—and a significant amount is revealed for the first time in this writing.

Miami police obtained a letter Milteer wrote to Somersett, from the home of his girlfriend Lulu Belle Cofield, dated November 18, 1963, and postmarked Valdosta, Georgia. It was thought the letter was sent as pretense to establish Milteer's whereabouts before the assassination. Incidentally, Miami authorities could not find the letter when requested by *Miami Magazine*—both the police and the state district attorney's files were missing. However, reporter Bill Barry had retained a copy given to him by Somersett. In the letter, Milteer told Somersett that he had arranged a meeting with "our man in South Carolina" (code for Klansman Belton Mims) for Sunday morning, November 24, at the Wade Hampton Hotel. Milteer told Somersett to meet him at the Jacksonville train station late Saturday night, and that they would drive late into the night to the Wade Hampton, which would "save you a few pennies" on hotel costs. Somersett told reporter Barry, "And I got the idea that it was supposed to be setting up his alibi. He told me later to keep the letter to prove he was home . . ."[405]

On the morning of the Kennedy assassination, Milteer telephoned Somersett and told him, "I'm down here in jackrabbit country. I guess you won't be seeing your boy again"—a clear clue that he was in Texas. Milteer's presence in Texas on the day of the assassination was never revealed in the early public accounts (evidence that Milteer was actually in Dallas, at the scene of the murder will be presented in the next chapter). Milteer's establishment of an alibi on the days around the assassination, his admitted presence in Texas on the day of the assassination, and his prediction that Kennedy ("your boy") wouldn't be seen again is compelling evidence of conspiracy.

After the assassination, two associates of Guy Banister, Carlos Bringuier and Ed Butler, approached the press and told them of their contact with Lee Harvey Oswald. Butler told them he had debated Oswald on the radio and Oswald admitted he had been to the Soviet Union and was a Marxist. Bringuier told them Oswald was pro-Castro and had tried to infiltrate his anti-Castro group. (Both incidents were phony, concocted schemes of the Banister operation as will be shown later.) The two (Bringuier and Oswald) were later arrested for fighting over their ideological differences later that August. Their stories and photos were featured on Saturday, November 23, in the New Orleans *Times–Picayune*. Also that Saturday, Ed Butler flew to Washington, D.C., and appeared before Senator Eastland's Senate Internal Security Subcommittee on Sunday. There, he presented the tape-recorded admission that Oswald, now the presumed assassin of the president, was a Marxist. It is interesting to note that Banister's relationship with Eastland dated back to 1956, when Banister raided the home of black civil rights advocate Hunter Pitts Odell in connection with Eastland's probe of what he called the "Soviet influence" of the integration movement, an event which will be discussed in detail in Chapter Twenty-two.

On December 2, 1963, Miami Police Detective Everett Kay debriefed Somersett. Somersett told him about his meeting—arranged by Milteer—with Belton Mims, the leader of the Association of South Carolina Klans. Somersett also told Kay that, on November 23, 1963, he left Miami by train at 9:00 a.m. and met Milteer at the Jacksonville Union Train Station at 4:15 p.m. From there, the two set out in Milteer's car for Columbia, South Carolina.

That Saturday morning, Somersett related, Milteer was jubilant over the Friday murder of the president, and that Lee Harvey Oswald had been charged with the crime and was now secure in jail. Milteer told Somersett, "Everything ran true to form. I guess you thought I was kidding you when I said he would be killed from a window with a high-powered rifle." When asked by Somersett whether he was guessing or not, Milteer stated, "I don't do any guessing." In another account of Somersett's Saturday meeting with Milteer, he related that Milteer was happy and shook Somersett's hand saying, "Well I told you so, it happened like I told you, didn't it? It happened from a window with a high-power rifle." Somersett replied, "I don't know if you were guessing or not, but you hit it on the head pretty good." At that point, Milteer said he did not want to talk about the assassination because the next step was for the underground to work on the Jews. Somersett stated, when being debriefed, "This Milteer says he doesn't want too much talk about Kennedy any more, now he is alleging he is against the Jews, and their associates." (It may not be a coincidence that Milteer turned the subject to the "Jews" the day before Jack Ruby, a Jew, murdered Lee Harvey Oswald.) Milteer was reluctant to talk further about the assassination, and Somersett decided not to push him on the matter.

In a second debriefing of Somersett by the Miami police, on December 12, 1963, he again told them of the conversation he had with Milteer about the assassination on the Saturday ride from Jacksonville to South Carolina. He stated that Milteer told him he was connected with the "International Underground" and that he planned to put out propaganda that would prove that the Jews murdered President Kennedy. The pair arrived at the Wade Hampton Hotel in Columbia, South Carolina, around midnight. About 9:00 a.m. Sunday morning, Milteer awoke and stepped out for coffee. Upon returning, Milteer had in his hand about a dollar and a half worth of quarters and dimes and a cup of coffee, giving Somersett the distinct impression that Milteer had just made a long distance call on a pay phone. Milteer reported, "Oswald has not said anything and he will not say anything." Somersett responded, "Why do you think that?" "Well, he will just not say anything, and nobody has any worry." Milteer went on to say, "The right wing had no worry whatsoever, because there would never be nothing to get out, because it was a small job, and very few people knew anything about it." Milteer clearly knew about the plot to murder the president before the event. It is less clear if he knew the particulars of Lee Harvey Oswald's journey to the Soviet Union and his portrayal of a Communist, or of Jack Ruby's motives and position in the murder of Lee Harvey Oswald.

Milteer's Statements on Oswald's Pro-Castro Group and Infiltration

While awaiting the arrival of the South Carolina Klansmen to the hotel on Sunday, Milteer turned his attention to Oswald and his connection with the Fair Play for Cuba Committee. It's not clear if Milteer fully understood the meaning of Oswald's ties to FPCC as he tried to relate it to Somersett. If he did, it's not clear whether Somersett interpreted it correctly in his somewhat confusing statement to the Miami police. According to Somersett's statement, Milteer told Somersett, in regard to "infiltration," that "the underground had no worries as to being exposed, because this group that this Oswald belonged to which was pro-Castro had been promptly infiltrated, and of course, money had been put into the right hands, furnished to the right people to do the right job without throwing anything onto the patriots." (Evidence that will be presented in later chapters will show that Oswald's affiliation with the Fair Play for Cuba Committee was one of a number of phony schemes concocted by the Banister operation to further the far right and segregationist agenda of Louisiana and the South. They were not schemes related to the assassination or to Milteer's operation.)

The second mention of infiltration was made when Milteer was departing the meeting with the Klansmen at the Wade Hampton. As he left the group, Milteer called for a December secret meeting. Somersett noted, "It was agreed, before we left, that Milteer would set the date, and the place where everybody would meet and that they would invite people that were highly trusted, but we were not under no circumstances to give the impression to our people that we had infiltrated this pro-Castro organization and had the job done, let it go just like it is, and we would work right on down the line and our objectives now was to get rid of the Jews." What Milteer might have tried to convey was that Oswald was not genuine in his involvement in FPCC, but had infiltrated the group as a pretense that they wanted to keep secret.

The subject of infiltration was brought up a third time when Somersett was debriefed by the Miami authorities. They asked him, "Do you think he knows this Oswald person, or knows anything about him?" Somersett replied, "Well, I believe that he does, I believe that if he doesn't know Oswald in person, he knows the people in Miami or New Orleans that was doing business with the group which he belonged to. And that is where the infiltration was made into it, into this man's group, it was either Miami or New Orleans." Noting the confusion of the far right involved with the left, they asked him, "These are two separate groups are they not? They are separate widely in their beliefs so to speak. How do you think they could be coming together?" Somersett replied, "From the impression he gives me, and what he told me, was that Oswald group was pro-Castro, and they were infiltrated, and their leaders, somebody close to them was given money to infiltrate their group, and pay them to kill Kennedy, and they would throw, if anybody did get caught, that would throw the entire case into the laps of the Communists." Milteer told him, "Money was put in the right hands to do the job without throwing anything on the patriots."

A fourth reference to infiltration was made when Somersett was asked, "Did he ever make mention of any persons that this Oswald may have contacted or may have known?" Somersett replied, "No, he didn't mention Oswald directly being acquainted with anybody. The only thing that he was down on was that this group [FPCC] had been infiltrated by the "Patriot Underground" and arranged from there to have the execution carried out, and drop the responsibility right into the laps of the Communists, their association, or Castro."

Ostensibly, the Miami police were trying to comprehend the contradiction of a far-left Communist, Oswald, and his involvement in a far-right assassination plot. It is not clear that Somersett completely understood the paradox, either. What Somersett does make clear is that Oswald's leftist Fair Play for Cuba Committee was indeed infiltrated by the right-wing "Patriots." However, what Somersett probably did not realize or understand was that the infiltrator, from the right wing, *was* Oswald. Compelling evidence that Oswald infiltrated, or better stated, *created* the phony New Orleans chapter of FPCC, not to further its agenda but to destroy it. That was ultimately done when the FPCC disbanded in 1964 after the damaging publicity resulting from Oswald's ties to the organization. Milteer probably did not wish to divulge how the supposed-Communist Oswald was used as a weapon of the far right when he demurred, saying, "let it go just like it is." What Milteer could not make clearer was that the conspiracy was aimed at laying the assassination on the laps of Castro, the Communists, and the Jews.

At 10:20 a.m. on Sunday, November 24, 1963, Association of South Carolina Klans members Belton Mims, Grand Dragon A. D. Boling, and Jack D. Hendricks, arrived at Milteer and Somersett's Wade Hampton Hotel room. A general discussion followed and Milteer told the group the right-wing underground had no worries in regard to the assassination, alluding to the far right's involvement. Milteer explained that the purpose of the meeting with the Klan leaders was to get their help and circulate his blame-the-Jews pamphlet. It's not clear if Milteer came out and directly told them that the assassination was the work of the far right, but it was implied in their conversations.

Mims stated, in regards to the president's murder, "Well it wouldn't have been so bad if it was Martin Luther King." Milteer countered that King was just one of Kennedy's race agitators and was not important, since if they did kill King, the Jews would just set up another race agitator, adding, "There's still time to get him [King]." Milteer told the group that what was important "was to get out a pamphlet laying the murder of Kennedy at the foot of the Jews." Milteer then wrote out the text for his pamphlet on hotel stationery, as follows:

Notice to all Christians

The Zionist Jews killed Christ 2,000 years ago and on November 22, 1963, they killed President Kennedy. You Jews killed the president. We're going to kill you.

–The International Underground

He added, "We the Christian people must push the Jews from the continental United States. Unless they did get out, that we would kill them . . ." Milteer then ordered the Carolina Klansmen to distribute the pamphlet as soon as he sent them an official copy. Milteer, Somersett, and the contingent of Klansmen then traveled together to the Anchor Restaurant, which they found fully occupied by a group of "church people." Just outside the restaurant, Mims ran into a friend who told him that Lee Harvey Oswald had just been shot. The group then rode to the Piggy Park Drive-in and sat at an outside table and ate.

The slaying of Oswald was confirmed on the car radio on the way to the drive-in. Milteer reacted to news of the shooting of Oswald, saying, "That makes everything perfect now, the Jews killed Kennedy and the Jews killed Oswald. Now we have no worry." Immediately upon Ruby's detention for the murder of Oswald, the Dallas police announced that the assailant was Jack Rubenstein—despite the fact that Ruby had legally changed his name years earlier. It is not known if Ruby's Jewish background was relayed on the car radio report or not. If not, then Milteer's quick identification of Ruby as a Jew indicates prior knowledge of Ruby—and that he is in some way related to the conspiracy.

Somersett knew the Carolina Klan contingent well, but Milteer did not, even though he had corresponded with them and talked to them before on the phone. Milteer had simply met Mims at another time with Jack Brown. Milteer appeared emboldened when, after the success of the assassination, he ordered the Carolina Klansmen to circulate the pamphlet implicating the Jews, which was the next phase of the Underground's plan. Mims and Boling were not pleased with the murder of the president, however, because they felt it made the U.S. look bad in the eyes of the world. Milteer countered that President Kennedy's appointment of "all the Jews" was a conspiracy. The Carolina Klansmen were more in accord with eliminating Martin Luther King, Jr. and the other Negro leaders, but not Kennedy. Hendricks and Will Ulmer, who was also in attendance, on the other hand, were enthused by the assassination.

Milteer told the group he wanted them each to have a copy of Conde McGinley's right-wing magazine, *Common Sense*, and went to his car to get some copies. Milteer was a friend of McGinley and was a distributor for his magazine (McGinley died before the assassination). In Milteer's brief absence, Mims asked Somersett to call him at another time and let him know more about Milteer's knowledge of the assassination and his future plans. Somersett's impression was that some of the Carolina Klansmen were in shock and disbelief from what Milteer had told them, and his implication of the right wing. At 6:00 p.m., Mims announced that he had to leave on other business and appeared eager to get away from Milteer. When Milteer returned with the magazines, Mims dropped a bombshell on Somersett. Mims read Milteer a letter from NSRP leader J. B. Stoner, the prime suspect in the 1958 Atlanta Temple bombing, stating that Somersett was an FBI informant. The allegation appeared to stem, not from Stoner's actual knowledge of Somersett's informant status, but instead from a desire to settle a score with Somersett. Stoner and Somersett had been at a national KKK board meeting when Stoner tried to place a delegate of his preference on the board. Somersett objected, stating that Stoner's group accepted foreign-born members and Catholics—a practice objectionable to most Klansmen and an argument found persuasive by the board. Stoner's delegate was dismissed. In what had to be a relief to Somersett, Milteer was quick to scoff at the idea that Somersett was an informant. Milteer seemed to be aware that Stoner had an axe to grind with Somersett, and his immediate response was "Stoner probably put this out." Milteer stated that he felt Stoner's associate in the NSRP, Edward Fields, was too smart to let Stoner put out the letter, because it tarnished the NSRP's credibility (Fields told the author, in 1999, that he knew Milteer and that he also knew Somersett was a lifelong FBI informant).[406]

Having returned to Miami, Somersett provided a transcript of the November 24, 1963, meeting with the Klansmen to the Miami FBI. Later, he received an airmail letter postmarked "9:30 p.m. 11-26-63 Valdosta, Georgia", containing an apparent revision of the Milteer pamphlet, that read: ·

> It now becomes the solemn duty of every true red-blooded Ameri-
> can to seek, find, expel, drive out from our country every traitor be
> he Zionist Jew, Communist, or what have you.
> Give us liberty or we'll give you death.
>
> –International Underground

Somersett quoted Milteer's message from memory and there are slight variations in different reports of the wording of the pamphlet. Milteer's message was tantamount to a call for a pogrom against the Jews, which was the oft-repeated fear of Jack Ruby.

The Miami FBI office's apparent main interest in Milteer's revelations was what Somersett found out about the Birmingham Baptist Church bombing in the November 24, 1963, meeting. The FBI instructed Somersett to contact the Miami or Birmingham bureau using the code name "Bill Southport" if he heard anything more about the bombing.

When asked by the Miami police his opinion of Milteer and his revelations, Somersett told them, "I am satisfied that this man beyond doubt knew that this was going to happen, and from the impression I got from him this conspiracy originated in New Orleans, probably some in Miami and different parts of the country, probably in California. And I am pretty sure California had a lot to do with it, because he mentioned Dr. Swift very often, what a great man he was and he'd already be killed before he got out of office." Somersett stated that Milteer knew the groundwork for the assassination was being laid in five or six different states. Milteer told Somersett that Kennedy could have been killed in Miami, but someone had called the FBI and "give the thing away." After the failed Miami plot, Milteer told him "everybody kept quiet and waited for Texas." Somersett was again asked if he was able to determine what was the nature of the relationship between Oswald and Milteer. He replied, "I believe he doesn't know Oswald personally, he knows the people in Miami or New Orleans that was doing business with the group he belonged to."

When asked about funding of the Underground, Milteer told Somersett that Reverend Billy James Hargis raised a lot of money for the Underground. Milteer recorded Hargis's speaking engagement in Jacksonville in 1963, at which Hargis can be heard urging the crowd to give generously when the collection plate was passed around. (Hargis was an associate of Guy Banister and General Walker in Texas as noted in Chapter One, and both men were associated with Lee Harvey Oswald.) Milteer told Somersett that Reverend Wesley Swift of California, Kenneth Goff of Colorado, both two close Milteer associates, and Billy Estes of Texas also raised money for the Underground. Goff was a former high-ranking member of the American Communist Party, who later had a change of heart (whether or not Goff was ever a genuine Communist will be discussed later). Milteer told Somersett that Goff headed an organization "fighting the Kennedys and the Communists and the Jews and the negroes [sic]." He added that there was a "good underground in Texas and California," and that "Illinois is very strong." Milteer told him that the amount of money involved in the assassination was substantial. Milteer again told him that the conspirators had "planned to drop the assassination in the laps of Castro or the Communists" (Oswald's trip to the Cuban and Russian Embassies in Mexico City in September 1963 fit that plan). Somersett stated that "there was probably a lot of Catholic money" going to the Underground, which was, perhaps, a reference to New Orleans, which had a sizeable Catholic population. Milteer told Somersett that, in the period of around June and July of 1963, he visited New Orleans, Dallas, Gulfport, Biloxi, and Jackson (Mississippi), as well as spending considerable time in Alabama. (The individuals tied to Milteer in some of those locales will be identified in the next chapter.)

Somersett told the FBI that those in the hardcore underground that especially needed watching included R. E. Davis, Jack Brown, James Finnaman of the NSRP, and Kenneth Adams. Somersett advised, "Now, if we closely observed their activities [with this pamphlet blaming the Jews], it may bring us closer to the fact that Milteer was directly connected [to the assassination]. At this point we have nothing. But if we cover this man the way he should be covered, and the charges he [Milteer] is going to make against the Jews, the propaganda campaign that he is going to start, it seems to me we can lead back and sooner or later identify some people close to him and this conspiracy who killed this man [the president]."[407]

FBI director J. Edgar Hoover may not have wanted Somersett to reveal those behind the conspiracy and there is no evidence that the FBI took Somersett's advice to observe the activities of those men. To the contrary, on November 27, 1963, the FBI sent Special Agent Donald Adams to Milteer's house to interrogate him. It's difficult to conceive of a rational reason for sending Adams, other than to blow Somersett's cover. Somersett told the FBI that with time and close observation those behind the conspiracy would be sooner or later identified. That all ended when the FBI sent Adams to interrogate Milteer, which was an act tantamount to silencing him.

Former FBI SA Donald Adams told the author that he feels without doubt he was used for the purpose of exposing Somersett as an FBI informant to keep Milteer from further revealing those behind the murder of the president. (Adams's encounters with Milteer will be detailed later.)

Conclusions

Joseph Milteer had precise knowledge of how the assassination was to occur thirteen days in advance. The FBI and the Secret Service knew about it, but nothing was done to protect the president in Dallas. Milteer knew the plot would take place in an office building with a high-powered rifle that could be broken down. He knew a patsy would be picked up within hours to throw authorities off. He was dead-on accurate on all four points.

Milteer was in Dallas three times before the assassination, as well as on the day of the assassination. Milteer attended seemingly every radical-right meeting in the country, tape recorded the speakers, and offered the tapes for sale beginning in at least 1958. His long, extensive ties to the national far right and his willingness to commit violence for the cause made him a valuable and trusted figure that put him in a position to know about the far-right plot to kill the president. While some felt that Milteer was just a crackpot shooting off his mouth, the evidence presented in this chapter alone should have been sufficient to seriously consider his involvement—it is just the tip of the iceberg and more evidence of conspiracy will follow in the next chapters.

Willie Somersett's characterization of Milteer as "the most violent-minded man in America" who had "a taste for terror by bombing" gave law enforcement all the reasons they needed to take his prediction with grave concern. Further, they knew he associated with at least two of the most violent Klansmen in the country, Kenneth Adams and Jack Brown. The segregationists and the extremists in the Ku Klux Klan and related groups had as much motive as any group to kill the president at the time, based on their militant opposition to President Kennedy and his plan to put an end to the Southern institution of segregation. Murder as a weapon was not new for the racist extremists in the country at the time. Bombings, beatings and shootings of black citizens took place on a daily basis during the civil rights-era reign of terror that took place at the time of the assassination.

Milteer, like Guy Banister, had ties to the Citizens' Council, John Birch Society, National States' Right Party, Minutemen, American Nazi Party, Ku Klux Klan, and Gerald L. K. Smith's anti-Semitic organization. They were birds of a feather. Milteer associated with two members of the American Nazi Party, Robert Surrey and Ray Leahart (remember, Banister bailed Leahart out of jail in the 1961 Hate Bus incident). Surrey, a Warren Commission witness, was the top aide to General Walker, a close associate of Guy Banister. More evidence of Milteer and the far right's involvement in the assassination of President Kennedy follows in the next chapter.

CHAPTER FIVE

MILTEER IN DEALEY PLAZA

I didn't go to kill him. But I didn't mind seeing him killed.
— Joseph A. Milteer

P ublic skepticism regarding the Warren Commission's findings grew after a spate of books and articles raised doubt about the official story that a lone Communist killed the president. Despite marked opposition, Congress voted to reopen an investigation into the murder of President Kennedy in 1977. In conjunction with Congress's planned reinvestigation, CBS national news anchor Dan Rather mentioned the Milteer tape prediction on television in April of 1976. It piqued the interest of *Miami Magazine* reporter Dan Christensen, who contacted Circuit Judge Seymour Gelber, who—in his former role as Dade County Florida assistant attorney general—had investigated the Milteer case in 1963. Gelber provided Christensen with the primary investigative documents and a copy of the Somersett-Milteer tape recording.

Milteer died on February 28, 1974, without heirs, and his estate went into probate. In July 1976, working with probate judge James R. Knight, Christensen gained access to Milteer's dilapidated home in Quitman, Georgia. The judge was told by a neighbor of Milteer that other men had arrived in a vehicle that bore Texas license plates, ransacked the house, and carted boxes of Milteer's belongings away. Milteer had been a prolific letter writer, and left carbon copies behind when he died. Suspiciously, few copies from 1963 were among them when Christensen first viewed them. Christensen gathered up and saved some of the letters and a number of personal photos of Milteer, and took them with him to study. He later gave the materials to HSCA investigator Gaeton Fonzi, who was a firm believer that the CIA was behind the president's murder. In the September 1976 edition of *Miami Magazine*, Christensen published the pertinent parts of the Milteer/Somersett tape transcript.

In a follow-up article in October 1976, Christensen revealed astonishing new evidence that not only had Willie Somersett informed authorities of a plot to kill the president in 1963, but he that also had had advance knowledge of a plot to kill Martin Luther King, Jr. in 1968. Willie Somersett contacted Miami Police Lieutenant Charles H. Sapp at his home on the evening before the April 4, 1968, assassination of King and told him that he had learned—on April 1, 1968—that King was going to be murdered. Somersett felt that, because of his own background as a Klansman, he might be blamed—and did not want to be connected to the crime. Somersett's prediction was correct, again.

On the evening of April 3, 1968, as if anticipating his fate, King addressed a crowd and stated, "It really doesn't matter to me because I've been to the mountain top! And I don't mind. Like anybody I would like to live a long life; longevity has its place. But I'm not concerned about that now. I just want to do God's will! And he's allowed me to go up to the mountaintop, and I've looked over and seen the Promised Land . . . So I'm happy tonight: I'm not worried about anything; I'm not fearing any man!" Twenty-two hours later, King was shot in the head and killed on the balcony of the Lorraine Motel in Memphis, Tennessee. Afterwards, on April 9, 1968, Seymour Gelber wrote a letter to United States Attorney General Ramsey Clark and informed him of Somersett's call and advance knowledge of Dr. King's murder.

An assistant to Attorney General Clark confirmed receipt of the letter, but Clark did not contact or further pursue the matter with Miami authorities. The FBI was asked to comment on the information reported in *Miami Magazine* of the foreknowledge of the two assassination plots, but declined.

In December of 1976, after publishing the two-part magazine series, Christensen began to look over the documents and photos of Milteer, which were taken from his home, and made a remarkable discovery. Christensen studied the photo, taken by UPI photographer James Altgens, of President Kennedy's limousine on Houston Street in Dealey Plaza moments before its turn in front of the Texas School Book Depository (and the murder). He found the photo in the hardcover edition of the book *Six Seconds in Dallas*. He noticed that one of the motorcade spectators in the crowd bore a strong resemblance to Joseph Milteer. Christensen wrote in the January 1977 *Miami Magazine* of the discovery and stated, "If this mysterious look-alike is actually Milteer, it strains credibility to suggest that this man, who only 13 days before had predicted the murder, could have been at the scene of the crime and not have been involved in some way." When the HSCA learned of Christensen's discovery, they sealed Milteer's house and later sent investigators to the home.[408][409]

The Altgens photo. The motorcade suspect stands to the right of a taller man wearing a hat. The top of Jacqueline Kennedy's hat can be seen on the bottom right. The top of the president's limousine windshield appears across the bottom of the photo. Source: National Archives, JFK Collection

Three photos of Joseph Milteer obtained from his home. The motorcade spectator in the Altgens photo is at the top left. Milteer's characteristic plume of hair on the right scalp (best seen in the photo at the top right) is similar to that of the motorcade spectator. Source: National Archives, JFK Collection

Photos of Milteer through the years showing the right hair plume similar to the Dealey Plaza figure's hair. Top left photo is dated 1921. Bottom right photo is from 1938. The others are undated. Source: Brooks County Probate Court

The author discovered a photo of Melvin Sexton in a Happy New Years card greeting from Robert Shelton that bears a resemblance to the tall man with the hat standing to "Milteer's" right. Melvin Sexton was the Klan's Imperial Kligrapp (Treasurer) and was a next-door neighbor of Robert Shelton in Northport, Alabama. Shelton was the Imperial Wizard of the United Klans of America in 1963, the largest Klan group in America. Ironically, Sexton—who led the Klan fundraising effort for the defense of the accused King murderer James Earl Ray—was questioned in 1978 in an executive session of the HSCA during their investigation of the King assassination.[410]

Klan leaders Robert Shelton (left) and Melvin Sexton (right). The identity of the female (center) is unknown. Sexton bears a likeness to the tall man with a hat standing to the immediate right of the Milteer look-alike in the Altgens photo. They are both tall men with similar raccoon-type eyes, similar noses, lips, jowl lines, cheeks, left ears, and jutting jaws. On September 14, 1963, the eve of the Birmingham Sixteenth Street Baptist Church bombing, Joseph Milteer met with Shelton. Given that the Klansmen were next-door neighbors, noted in Sexton's FBI file obtained by the author through a Freedom of Information Act request, it would not be surprising if Milteer met with Sexton, as well. Source: New Years greeting card from Robert Shelton, Paul O. Peters Papers, Special Collections, Wooster College Library, Wooster, Ohio

Man in the hat standing in Dealey Plaza next to "Milteer" (left). The middle photo is of Melvin Sexton from the holiday photo, with the hat superimposed by the author. The photo on the far right is the same one of Sexton without the hat.

Willie Somersett reported a meeting of Milteer with Robert Shelton, the national Klan leader, on September 14, 1963, in Alabama, to the FBI. Since Melvin Sexton was also a high-ranking Klansman and Shelton's next-door neighbor it's likely that he was at the meeting, and that Sexton and Milteer knew each other.[411] That fact further increases the likelihood that the figure in the photo standing to the right of "Milteer" was Melvin Sexton.

The HSCA determined, in their investigation of the Martin Luther King, Jr. murder, that William Potter Gale of California was at a meeting, of an undisclosed nature, in Birmingham, Alabama, on September 14, 1963—which is likely the same meeting attended by Shelton and Milteer. Gale, a notorious anti-Semite and racist like Milteer, was also an associate of California extremist Wesley Swift, a member of the far-right Christian Defense League. Milteer was close to Swift and visited him often in California. He also knew Gale, and both were members of a "far-right hardcore underground," as will be discussed in later chapters.[412] Gale's travel across the country to the September 14, 1963, Birmingham meeting suggests that it was of major importance to the segregationist underground.[413]

The Milteer Affair and the House Select Committee On Assassinations Investigation

In 1977, the HSCA approached their investigation into the Milteer matter with the position that, if it could be reasonably demonstrated that the individual purported to be Milteer in the Dealey Plaza photo was not actually Milteer, then the entire affair could be discarded and given no further deliberation by the Committee. The investigators were apparently not persuaded by Somersett's conviction of Milteer's involvement (or the other evidence presented thus far in this work). The HSCA's rationale was one of the great mistakes of the twentieth century and a travesty of justice. The Committee called upon acclaimed anthropologist Dr. Clyde Snow to determine whether or not the photo of the figure in Dealey Plaza was Joseph Adams Milteer. (Dr. Snow was renowned for, among other things, determining that skeletal remains found buried in Brazil were those of notorious Nazi death camp physician Josef Mengele.) The Committee provided digitally enhanced photos of the subject that resembled Milteer in Dealey Plaza, which were captured not only in the Altgens still photo but also in movies taken by bystanders Bell, Nix, and Muchmore. The Altgens 35mm photo was of the highest quality, and was chosen for analysis.

The exact location from which Altgens took the photo could not be determined, but it was known that he was standing somewhere within the intersection of Houston and Main Street. The photo depicts the president's limousine passing the Dal-Tex building on Houston Street, just before the vehicle turned south on to Elm Street in front of the Texas School Book Depository. Dr. Snow set out to determine whether or not the Milteer look-alike was the same height as Milteer. The Committee provided Snow with a photo of Milteer marked with his height as sixty-four inches, or 5'4". Of the height given, Snow stated, "The only available height record on Milteer gives his stature as 64 inches," which was a colossal error of fact. FBI and Secret Service documents—overlooked by the Committee but found by the author—noted heights for Milteer of 5'8", 5'7", 5'6" and 5'5", facts that invalidate Snow's entire analysis.

Dr. Snow decided that he would use the two street signs to "Milteer's" left as measuring poles. The Dallas Service Department furnished information that, in 1963, the sign would have had dimensions of twelve by eighteen inches and that "city regulations specified that the lowest edge be set at eighty inches above the sidewalk." (The actual signs had been removed, but concrete patches where they once stood still remained, and do so today.) An analysis as important as this one should not have relied solely on the Dallas Street Department information. To begin with, there is no evidence that the signs were erected in 1963, or according to 1963 regulations. The signs may have been erected when the Records Building was constructed in 1956. Moreover, it is difficult to believe that a city worker in 1963 or at any time could be relied upon to set the height of the sign at precisely eighty inches. More likely, that height was intended as a guideline—and poles cannot reasonably be expected to represent accurate measuring sticks as assumed in this study. Thus, Dr. Snow's use of the sign pole as an accurate measuring stick should not have been the basis for his conclusion, but—unfortunately—it was. Using simple mathematics, Snow determined that the motorcade spectator was 5'10" tall. He also noted that errors as much as two inches, plus or minus, may occur in police and medical records (It's worth noting that various Warren Commission documents provide *seven* different heights for Lee Harvey Oswald. Reports of a person's height are notoriously inaccurate). Thus, although Milteer's height was assumed to be 5'4", factoring in error, he could have been actually as tall as 5'6", still too short to be the figure in the Dealey Plaza photo—who was calculated with the aid of the street signs to be 5'10." Snow concluded from his weak analysis, in strong terms, "the motorcade suspect could not have been Joseph Milteer." However, given the height of Milteer as 5'8"—which was noted by the Secret Service but unknown to Dr. Snow—and factoring in as much as a two-inch error, Milteer could have been the same height as the Dealey Plaza subject. Regardless of Milteer's actual height, Snow's method is deeply flawed and can not be relied on.

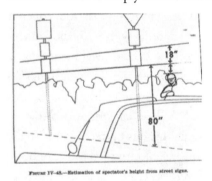

Figure IV-48.—Estimation of spectator's height from street signs.

The HSCA study of the "Milteer" figure's height based on the height of the street sign poles. Source: HSCA, Volume V

Dr. Snow employed a second independent method to determine whether or not the motorcade spectator was Milteer. Again, Snow depended upon the assumed height of 5'4" with no knowledge or consideration of the conflicting heights given in FBI and Secret Service documents of 5'8", 5'7", 5'6" and 5'5" which, as in the first analysis, dooms this one. The Milteer look-alike's height was compared to the height of twenty-seven spectators around him. Using national height averages based on gender, Snow concluded, "the odds are less than a million to one that the spectator was as short as 64 inches—Joseph Milteer's reported stature." The House Committee failed to ask anyone who knew Milteer about his height, including SA Don Adams, the FBI agent who observed Milteer on numerous occasions before the assassination and interrogated him five days later.[414, 415] The author, on the other hand, asked Dr. Edward Fields, who knew Milteer from National States' Rights Party meetings, his opinion on whether or not the motorcade spectator resembled Milteer. Fields declined to answer.[416]

Dr. Snow made the additional claim that the motorcade spectator was partially bald, while Milteer had a full head of hair, which he felt raised further doubts that the subject was Milteer. However, in the photos of Milteer found in his home, his hair was white. The grainy nature of the Altgens photo, and the lack of contrast between his white forehead skin and white hair may explain the perception of a receding hairline and Dr. Snow's claim the subject was balding, unlike Milteer. However, Milteer possessed a distinct characteristic growth pattern to his hair—the right-sided plume of hair—that was discovered by the author in photos that date back to 1921 The plume is present in the Dealey Plaza subject, something not noted heretofore, and further suggests the subject was, indeed, Milteer.

The author asked retired CIA photo analyst Dino A. Brugioni his opinion of Dr. Snow's HSCA analysis. Brugioni is famed for his 1962 discovery of Cuban missile silos in CIA aerial photos—a discovery which led to the Cuban missile crisis and placed the U.S. on the brink of nuclear war with the Soviet Union. He told the author he had doubts about Snow's study of the photo. Brugioni wondered why the HSCA didn't make a national call for others in the motorcade photo to come forward in order to use their actual heights as measuring sticks. Brugioni suggested to the author that the technique of photo superimposition would be a useful way of determining if Milteer was the motorcade spectator, a technique which was not available in 1977. Brugioni used the technique to prove that a 1971 photo purported to be of a soldier missing in Laos during the Vietnam War was not actually that soldier.[417, 418]

An accurate way of determining the motorcade spectator's height—a technique not used by Dr. Snow—would be to use Mark Bell's movie of the motorcade suspect, which was taken from a similar perspective as Altgens's photograph. The advantage of the Bell movie, unlike the Altgens photo, is that the exact location where Bell stood and shot the film is known. Bell can be seen in the Jay Skagg photo taken that day, standing on a six-foot concrete structure in Dealey Plaza. Bell was 5'11" to 6' tall and was shooting with a Kodak Brownie 8mm movie camera while using its eyepiece. Using a person of known height standing in the spectator's position and shooting the photo from Bell's concrete perch—which stands to-day—a precise measurement of height can be made by using the known width of the County Record Building's windows (visible in a larger photo) behind "Milteer" as a measuring stick.[419]

The HSCA's colossal failure to identify the additional heights on record in FBI and Secret Service documents indicating a taller Milteer than the height furnished to Dr. Snow—and Dr. Snow's fallacy of the sign post-as-measuring-rod were crucial in slamming the door on the most compelling evidence in existence of a conspiracy behind the assassination of President Kennedy. Snow's analysis, studded with impressive-looking, complicated mathe-matical equations—likely beyond the understanding of any members of the HSCA—was so compelling to them that they declined to consider additional related evidence in the Milteer case. The author met with the Assassinations Record Review Board in 1996 to urge them to pursue the Milteer evidence further. They, too, found the Snow analysis so persuasive they did not see the need to pursue the matter further.[420]

Bill Barry of the *Miami News* interviewed Willie Somersett in 1967 (the only person outside law enforcement to do so) and provided further evidence that Milteer was, in fact, in Dealey Plaza during the assassination. Somersett told him that Milteer admitted being in Dallas on the day of the assassination and also admitted to watching the event. Unfortunate-ly, Barry did not report the revelation in the *Miami News,* but rather in a somewhat obscure assassination journal. Moreover, by the time of Barry's revelation, there were few interested in the Milteer matter. Amazingly, Somersett revealed to Barry that Milteer had told him that he had been in Dealey Plaza *ten years before* Dan Christensen of *Miami Magazine* identified a Milteer look-alike in the Altgens photo. Somersett told Barry,

> About 10:30 I got a phone call, and I heard the operator tell the man to put the money in [the pay phone] and then the man [Milteer] said, "Hey! Well I'm down here in jackrabbit country." It was Joe. He was in Texas. He didn't answer me directly. He just said, "Well you won't be seeing your friend Kennedy down there in Miami no more." And then he just hung up, didn't say another word. I didn't know what to make of it, until just about two hours later exactly. It came over the radio that the president has been shot in Dallas. The sonofabitch went down there to see it happen. I was madder than hell, because we gave that tape to the Secret Service and the FBI, and they didn't do anything. They let the president get killed.

Somersett further recounted that Milteer was joyous about the murder the next day when he drove with Milteer to South Carolina. Somersett was reluctant to press Milteer on the subject because Milteer was carrying a .38 handgun and was afraid that Milteer might shoot him. Milteer stated that Dallas police officer J. D. Tippit—who was allegedly murdered by Oswald—Ted Jackman, and Dallas Klan leader R. E. Davis were involved, and that shots were fired from three directions. Somersett's allegation that Tippit was involved in the shooting of the president is astounding (Tippit will be discussed at length in Chapter Sixteen). Somersett stated that Milteer had gone to Dallas on Thursday, the day before the assassination. Milteer wrote the November 18, 1963, alibi letter (mentioned in the last chapter), and had his common-law wife mail it to make it look like he was still in Georgia at the time of the assassination. Somersett reported that Milteer left Dallas the day after the assassination, taking three connecting flights home to avoid detection. Milteer had just been home for a few minutes on Saturday, November 23rd, when he set off to meet Willie Somersett at the Jacksonville train station.

According to Bill Barry, Somersett recounted his interaction with Milteer in Jacksonville that day:

> He was beat, but he was so happy, it didn't seem to affect him. Somewhere in there, I took a chance and asked him, "Did you go down there to kill him?" And he says, "Hell no. I didn't go to kill him. But I didn't mind seeing him killed." And then he says, after thinking about it, "You ask too many damned questions. Just forget about it." So I shut up.

On March 18, 1967, just after it was revealed that the New Orleans district attorney's office was investigating the Kennedy assassination—and not long after Barry's story on the Milteer affair broke—Somersett called Barry and told him that a car drove up beside him and two men got out and stated that they would kill him if he wrote any more about the affair in his union newsletter.[421]

The FBI and the Whereabouts of Milteer During the Assassination

Milteer resided in Quitman in Brooks County, Georgia—one of nine counties covered by the FBI's Regional Agency based in nearby Thomasville. The Regional Agency office was strategically located in Thomasville in the busy transportation corridor between Florida and Georgia so that it could monitor violations of interstate commerce law. Special Agents Royal A. Mc-Graw and Donald Adams—who was added to the Regional Agency in 1963 after a brief stint in the Atlanta office—manned the Thomasville operation. Adams told the author that veteran agent McGraw was a tall, Protestant, Southern Democrat and former marine from Americus, Georgia. SA Donald Adams, in stark contrast to McGraw, was a rookie agent, a Republican, a Roman Catholic, and a transplant from the northern industrial city of Akron, Ohio. McGraw was a taskmaster and the relationship between the two was strictly professional. Adams had wanted to join the FBI since he was a boy. Adams graduated from the FBI academy in 1962 at age thirty-two. He met Director J. Edgar Hoover in Washington D. C. and called it one of the greatest days in his life.

Adams told the author that at about 5:30 p.m. on November 13, 1963, SAC John McMahon of the Atlanta office called Adams at his home and told him he had an urgent assignment for him. Adams was told of an informant's information that a plot to assassinate the president had been discussed at an Indianapolis, Indiana, meeting (the Constitution Party meeting on October 18–20, 1963). The informant had related that four people privately discussed plans to shoot President Kennedy during an upcoming trip to Miami, Florida. The would-be assassin was a WWII sniper and was prepared to sacrifice his life in the operation. The sniper planned to take a position in a palm tree and shoot the president as he motorcaded up Collins Avenue in a convertible from Homestead Air Force Base en route to the Kennedy family home in Palm Beach. In the event the Miami plot failed, a back-up plan was in place that involved renting an office across Lafayette Park behind the White House and assassinating President Kennedy as he strolled outside, using a high-caliber weapon with a scope on a tripod. Adams was told to do a "work up" on Milteer as soon as possible, to gather all the essential information on the suspect he could, and deliver the information to Atlanta.

Adams called the chief of the Quitman Police that night and the two met the next day. The police chief was quite familiar with Milteer and pointed out Milteer's Quitman home. Next, they traveled to Valdosta to meet with the police chief there, and gathered more background information on Milteer. On November 15, they went to the home of Mrs. C. C. Cofield (Milteer's common-law wife), in Valdosta, where they found Milteer's vehicle and recorded the license plates. A fingerprint card for Milteer—taken in a 1955 suspicion of burglary investigation— was located in the basement of the Valdosta Police Department. On Saturday November 16, 1963, after learning that Milteer often distibuted hate literature on the streets of downtown Quitman, Adams put on casual work clothes to visit Milteer under-cover. Adams approached Milteer and engaged him in casual conversation. Milteer made it clear that he hated the president, as well as Negroes and northerners. Adams attempted, but was unable, to surreptitiously photograph Milteer. When speaking with the author, Adams still had his FBI diary from 1963, and was able to recount accurately times and dates relevant to his Milteer investigation.

On November 22, 1963, Thomasville agents Adams and McGraw were traveling in their FBI vehicle just after lunch when a "Code 30" (a command to immediately report to the Thomasville Highway Patrol Office) came over the radio. At the office, they were given instructions to proceed to the Federal Agriculture Building, which had a Teletype. When he arrived at the Agriculture Building, Adams was asked for identification and was then taken to the Teletype room, where he received the message that the president had been killed. He was instructed to call the SAC in Atlanta, who ordered him to locate Milteer immediately. Adams traveled to both homes which Milteer spent time at in Valdosta and Quitman. Unable to find Milteer, Adams feared that somehow he may have bungled his work-up on Milteer in the prior week. His fears, however, were short lived. Not long after the assassination, Lee Harvey Oswald was captured and, within hours, Director Hoover declared that Oswald was the lone assassin and was a known Communist. Adams was greatly relieved, but over the following days he drove to both places Milteer had stayed, three times a day, but had no luck finding him. By then, though, Adams related, the urgency was gone since the alleged killer, Lee Harvey Oswald, had been captured.

On November 27, 1963, SA Adams observed Milteer's Volkswagen bus at the home of Mrs. Cofield, and presumed he was there. Adams left and called Agent Kenneth Williams of the Valdosta FBI Regional Agency for back up. When the two arrived at Mrs. Cofield's, Milteer and the Volkswagen bus were gone. The agents confronted Mrs. Cofield, and she told them that Milteer had just left and was headed north up the main highway to Atlanta. In hot pursuit, the agents pulled Milteer over fifty miles north of Valdosta. Milteer was searched, and his vehicle towed. Milteer, a diabetic, was given permission to take his dinner, which he had in a paper bag with him. Milteer was taken to the FBI office and interrogated. During the questioning, Milteer interrupted and stated that he knew the FBI was tape recording him, which they denied. At that point, Adams heard a whirring sound coming from Milteer's dinner sack. He was surprised to discover a tape recorder in the sack, recording the questioning. Adams was struck by Milteer's brazenness.

During the questioning, Milteer admitted that he had attended the Congress of Freedom meeting in New Orleans in April 1963 and the Constitution Party meeting in October 1963, but denied hearing anyone in his presence discuss an assassination plot. He also admitted to have been in Dallas in June of 1963 to persuade former FBI agent—and J. Edgar Hoover assistant—Dan Smoot, author of the far right *Dan Smoot Report*, to run as vice president on the Constitution Party ticket. (In the 1950s Smoot wrote a newsletter for wealthy oilman H. L. Hunt.) Director Hoover must have been disturbed upon learning of Milteer's association with a former high-ranking member of his FBI staff. A formal report of the detention and interrogation of Milteer on November 27, 1963, signed by Special Agents Adams and Williams and dated December 1, 1963, was dictated on an FD 302 FBI form. The report was sent to the FBI Director and Atlanta SAC in the early morning of November 28, 1963.[422]

After questioning, Milteer was released. Willie Somersett called Milteer after he was released, and reported to a Miami police detective that Milteer was "all fogged up, and could not understand why the FBI would question him and how it came about." Somersett told Detective Kay, "These people [the FBI] are going to get me killed by such actions." The FBI's interview with Milteer served not only to silence Milteer, but also to put Somersett's life in jeopardy.[423]

In spite of Adams's report to Atlanta indicating that Milteer was nowhere to be found on the day of the assassination, the Atlanta SAC sent a Teletype to the FBI in Washington, Dallas, and Birmingham, dated November 22, 5:43 p.m., stating that they had determined the whereabouts of Milteer—as well as J. B. Stoner and Melvin Bruce—and advised the Secret Service of that fact.[424] (Stoner was the prime suspect in the 1958 Atlanta Temple bombing and knew Milteer from the National States' Rights Party. Melvin Bruce was a member of Commander Rockwell's American Nazi Party, and had been arrested at the insurrection at Ole Miss on October 1, 1962, led by General Walker.[425]) Agent Harding sent the information regarding Milteer's whereabouts to the Secret Service on November 25, 1963.

The chief of the Atlanta Secret Service, SAIC A. B. Wentz noted the FBI's information in his report on November 27, 1963. FBI Agent Charles Harding contacted their agent (whose name was redacted) at Thomasville, who immediately ascertained that J. A. Milteer was in Quitman at the time of the assassination.[426] The Secret Service noted in a November 14, 1963, report that they were unable to obtain a photograph of Milteer, although they were trying to do so. In the memorandum from the Secret Service, it was noted that Atlanta FBI Agent Harding pledged to request photos from Thomasville Agent Royal McGraw who, he stated, had done the initial investigation on Milteer, a claim contrary to what Agent Adams told the author. Interestingly, yet another height for Milteer was given (5'6") in a Secret Service pre-assassination work-up report.[427]

Another Teletype went out on November 26, 1963, from the FBI SAC Atlanta at 6:27 p.m., that read:

J.A. MILTEER RESIDE QUITMAN GA
INVESTIGATION HAS INDICATED MILTEER
WAS IN QUITMAN ON NOV. TWENTYTWO,
SIXTYTHREE

The FBI Teletype is obviously directly contrary to both SA Donald Adams's findings that Milteer was not at home on the day of the assassination and the abundance of evidence presented that he was, in fact, in Dallas. In the FBI's efforts to vouch for Milteer's presence on the day of the assassination, they took evidence and statements from different dates, offices, and agents and combined them to make them appear as if they were all derived from the investigation that led to the November 27, 1963, questioning and report on Milteer. The Atlanta FBI office claimed (as mentioned above) that Agent Royal McGraw did the initial investigation. The problem with that claim is that there is no primary documentation originating from McGraw in the entire voluminous FBI files on Milteer. To the contrary, the November 27, 1963, FD 302, which was signed by Agents Williams and Adams, is clear evidence that they led the investigation, not McGraw—a fact supported by the diary kept by Adams and recounted to the author. Adams's FD 302—a report of an interview—is the only document in the Milteer Freedom of Information Act FBI file that would have any standing in a court of law. All other accounts of the Milteer affair, which are noted above and were passed on to the Secret Service, were hearsay compositions from Atlanta SAC Harding, consisting of questionable evidence of uncertain origin.

The physical description of Milteer provided presents another problem. The early Teletype message gave a description of Milteer as follows: "5'4";" "Heavy waisted;" "small round shoulders;" and "Is short legged, most of his weight from the waist upwards." That description was made before SA Adams's interrogation of Milteer on November 27, 1963. The writing and phrasing did not belong to Adams—who told the author that the wording used was so peculiar and foreign to him that he was sure it was not his. That description may have originated with the Miami FBI. According to the Miami FBI report to the director on December 3, 1963, they gave the same physical description of Milteer as being 5'4", including the peculiar phrase "Is short legged, most of his weight from the waist upwards."

A third problem with the evidence is the origin and date of the photo of Milteer attached to the January 22, 1964, summary, which was supposedly from SA Royal McGraw. The office and person who took the photo were not identified. In a November 14, 1963, report, the Atlanta FBI SAC notified the Secret Service and told them that they planned to call SA Royal McGraw of the Thomasville office and request that he take a photo of Milteer.[428] However, on January 14, 1964, the Atlanta SAC reported to the Secret Service that they did not have a photo of Milteer, which contradicts the date of November 27, 1963, which is written on the back of the photo.[429] Yet the photo of Milteer attached to the January 22, 1964, report was said to be taken by "FBI Agents" (plural) on November 27, 1963, which suggests attribution to SAs Adams and Williams—and not to McGraw, as implied. Adams told the author that neither he nor Williams took photos of Milteer on November 27, 1963. It's highly unlikely that McGraw photographed Milteer on the same day Adams questioned him, especially without telling Adams about it. The SAC from Miami stated on December 3, 1963 that that

The FBI photo of Milteer. Identifying information on the back notes Milteer's height as 5'5", contrary to the height of 5'4" given in the summary report. The photo was dated November 27, 1963, the date of his interrogation by SA Williams and SA Adams. SA Donald Adams denied taking any photos of Milteer. Adams told the author the handwriting was not his, which was verified by the author. Source: FBI file on Joseph Milteer

they had a photo of Milteer which had been taken at Christmas 1943 and that it was a good likeness of him. The conflicting evidence as to the origin of the Milteer photo suggests it was from another investigation at another time—or may even be the 1943 Christmas photo mentioned by the Miami office.

In composing the FBI's final report—which affirmed Milteer's presence at home on the day of the murder—the FBI stretched the evidence. The FBI employed the dubious claim that SA Royal McGraw did the initial investigation of Milteer, and they may have borrowed the peculiar description of Milteer from the Miami FBI, which definitely did not not come from SA Adams.

On December 1, 1963, the Atlanta office of the FBI summarized the Milteer investigation and noted Milteer's denial of involvement in the assassination in a November 27, 1963, interview. The post-assassination meeting of Milteer, Somersett, and individuals of the Carolina Klan was mentioned—along with Milteer's plan to blame the murder on the Jews. Somersett's information that Milteer agreed to murder an associate of Martin Luther King, Jr. in Atlanta—and a Negro male student at Morehouse College who was a member of the Student Non-Violent Coordinating Committee—was mentioned in the summary. The back-up plot to murder the president from a building behind the White House was also noted.[430]

On January 22, 1964, the Atlanta FBI completed another summary report of the Milteer affair that was sent to the Secret Service and the Justice Department. The report stated that it was prepared by Agent Royal McGraw of the Atlanta office, which represents another discrepancy since McGraw was from the Thomasville office. The report appears to be a composite of various pieces of information. Nonetheless, the Atlanta summary closed the door on the Milteer investigation, which at the time had become seemingly irrelevant to the investigation of the president's death after the capture of Communist Lee Harvey Oswald. After receiving the January report, an agent of the Secret Service noted, "In view of the contents of this report I see no reason for additional investigation."[431]

On April 8, 1964, the Atlanta SAC stated in a report to the director that, since there had been no activity on the part of Milteer, that the case was closed. The January 22, 1964, FBI summary of the Milteer matter was forwarded to the Warren Commission, but there is no evidence that they were actually aware of it or gave it any consideration.[432] The summary was not reproduced in the twenty-six volumes of the Warren Commission evidence. There is also no evidence the Warren Commission knew of or received the transcript of Milteer's taped foreknowledge of the assassination.

As time passed, SA Donald Adams became satisfied with the FBI and Warren Commission's finding of Oswald as the lone assassin and gave the Milteer matter little thought until three decades later. He came across a book about the Kennedy assassination which had the picture of the Milteer look-alike in the Altgens photo and was stunned. Adams was further shocked to learn—in 1994—of the existence of the Somersett-Milteer tape wherein Milteer gave a detailed description of the Dallas murder before it happened—the FBI had never told him about it.[433, 434]

There are scattered bits of evidence in the FBI's records that they investigated Milteer for other unstated reasons in 1962. No primary documentation for the 1962 investigation was present in the FBI documents from the Freedom of Information Act Request, and the name of the investigating agent was not given. According to an FBI Field Office statement on September 24, 1962, an unidentified female informant told them that she knew Milteer personally, and it was rumored that Milteer had resided in California and in Washington where he had concessions around military bases. The document noted that the authorities, on September 24, 1962, found no police identification records for Milteer, but also noted that Milteer had been arrested and fingerprinted for suspicion of burglary on January 29, 1955. Interestingly, within the same documentation, was a document dated November 27, 1963—the date that Agents Adams and Williams detained Milteer—that noted that Milteer had traded in his 1963 Volkswagen for a 1964 model the day before.

On May 19, 1962, an informant sent a hate pamphlet —apparently one of Milteer's— urging the public to attend a white supremacy rally in Macon, Georgia, on May 20, 1962, to the Atlanta FBI. On July 17, 1962, the informant stated the rally was poorly attended. On September 24, 1962, an informant told the FBI that he or she had known Milteer for ten years. The scattered informants' reports mentioned above are evidence that Milteer was of interest to the FBI in connection with matters other than the assassination. The FBI's interest in Milteer in 1962 may have resulted from suspicions that Milteer was involved in the wave of racial violence that was sweeping the South, including Milteer's alleged involvement in the bombing of a Negro man and wife in Chattanooga (which was alluded to by Willie Somersett, and noted in the prior chapter). The 1962 documentation is clear evidence that the FBI had already done a work-up on Milteer before Agent Adams was assigned to the investigation on November 13, 1963, and, in fact, one of the 1962 informants who had known Milteer for years may have been the source of the 1943 Christmas photo of him. SA Royal McGraw may also have been involved in the 1962 investigation, without Adam's knowledge, since he had not yet been assigned to the office.[435]

Either SA Donald Adams or the Atlanta FBI office lied about Milteer's whereabouts on the day of the assassination. The Dealey Plaza photo, Willie Somersett's statement that Milteer called him from Texas on the day of the murder, Milteer's admission that he saw Kennedy killed, Milteer's behavior immediately after the murder, and an abundance of additional evidence to be presented later in this work all suggest the Atlanta FBI office was lying. The false claim from the Atlanta office that Milteer was at home during the assassination closed the books on the FBI investigation. In turn, it led the Secret Service to close their investigation on the matter, as well. The Warren Commission did not receive any information on Milteer until their investigation was closed—and they never considered it. The author asked former SA Adams if he thought the Atlanta office of the FBI was "covering their ass" when they affirmed Milteer's presence at home during the assassination. Adams replied, "Of course they were."

Former Miami Intelligence Detective Everett Kay, who played a major role in the investigation of Milteer, never wavered in his conviction that Milteer was involved in a con-spiracy that led to the death of a president. Of the findings of the Warren Commission, Kay told the author, "I didn't put much credence in that . . . I always thought it was a hate group." Kay spoke to investigators of the Assassination Records Review Board that was established in 1992, and told the author, "They didn't seem like they were overly interested in what I had to say."[436]

Reporter Bill Barry called Dallas, in 1963, "the Southern hate capital of Dixie," which was a widely held view.[437] Unfortunately, some members of the Secret Service didn't see it that way. The chief council of the HSCA, G. Robert Blakey, found that the Protective Research Service (PRS) of the Secret Service made no effort to pass on the Milteer threat to Dallas Secret Service Advance Agent Winston G. Lawson, or Dallas FBI Agent-in-Charge Forrest Sorrels. PRS Special Agent-in-Charge Robert L. Buck explained to Blakey that the "threat by a right-wing extremist was not thought to be relevant to security in Dallas."[438]

Joseph A. Milteer and Ned Touchstone

The author discovered documentation, not uncovered by the FBI or Miami law enforcement investigation, that adds another twist to the Milteer affair: the personal papers of Ned Touch-stone at Louisiana State University Shreveport—revealed here for the first time.[439]

Touchstone was from Shreveport, Louisiana, and—like Milteer—was a Klansman and a member of the Citizens' Council. He was the leader of the local chapter of the John Birch Society and his sentiments were notoriously anti-African American and anti-Jewish. Touchstone published the outwardly racist monthly newspaper of the Louisiana Citizens' Council, the *Councilor*, and was on the state Board of Directors of the Citizens' Council along with Leander Perez and several associates of Guy Banister (as will be detailed in later chapters).

Touchstone wrote in the February 17, 1969, edition of the *Councilor* that he planned to reveal the "Top Gun" suspect identified during the district attorney of New Orleans's in-vestigation of the Kennedy assassination that was taking place at the time. Dr. Edward Fields of the National States' Rights Party read the *Councilor* story and erroneously concluded that the "Top Gun" whom Touchstone planned to name was Milteer. On February 6, 1969, Fields wrote to Milteer to warn him, and included what appears to be a printed supplement to his NSRP *Thunderbolt* newspaper. Fields stated in the supplement that, on January 2, 1969, New Orleans D.A. Jim Garrison met in Washington, D.C., with "Jew Mark Lane, [and] the Jew Bernard Fensterwald" to form a "National Committee to Investigate Assassinations." Fields stated that the "ADL Jew" Richard Gerstein, district attorney of Dade County (Florida), was planning to implicate members of the NSRP based on the information of William Somersett. Milteer's name was not mentioned in the story. Fields wrote a letter to Milteer on February 6, 1969, and stated: "We have just learned from positive sources that the man Somersett is going to put the finger on and charge as 'Top Gun' in the Jim Garrison investigation is—YOU!" Fields advised Milteer that if Garrison issued a subpoena for him that he should call attorney

J. B. Stoner right away. Fields also suggested that Milteer contact Touchstone at the *Councilor*.

On February 9, 1969, Milteer wrote to Ned Touchstone and began by saying that he was a reader of the *Councilor* and that he once visited Touchstone to ask his cooperation in an organization Milteer was forming called the American Eagles. Milteer enclosed Fields's letter to him and wrote, "Now as you can readily see, it appears that I am 'Top Gun' suspect from a leak that has come about and Dr. Fields has so informed me. I ask you faithfully and diligently and most carefully look into this matter fully and consider all angles before naming a RIGHT WING PATRIOT to such a diabolical plot as this. I am a RIGHT WING man, have been a RIGHT WING man and intend to be a RIGHT WING man the rest of my live long days." On February 12, 1969, Ned Touchstone, in a joint letter to Fields and Milteer, wrote, "The name of the top gun suspect is not Milteer. This name begins with an 'S.'"

The whole affair was a hoax. In later editions of the *Councilor*, Touchstone blamed the assassination on prominent Jewish individuals. It is clear Fields knew all about Willie Somersett's allegations about Milteer, although Milteer's name was never revealed by the press. Fields and Milteer knew each other from the NSRP. It will be recalled from the last chapter that Milteer conveyed the impression of the far right's involvement in the assassination to the South Carolina Klansmen he visited two days after the assassination. He may have conveyed the same sentiment to Fields. Milteer explained to the South Carolina Klansmen that the next step was to take care of the Jews, and he may have relayed the same plan to Fields. In the first edition of Field's newspaper, the *Thunderbolt*, to come out after the assassination, the headline boldly read "JEWS INVOLVED IN ASSASSINATION."[440]

On March 2, 1999, the author wrote a letter to Dr. Fields about the Milteer affair and asked him if he could identify the motorcade suspect in Dealey Plaza as Milteer. Dr. Fields replied in May of 1999, stating that he met Milteer at meetings [of the NSRP] but did not know Milteer personally. He said that Somersett was a life-long FBI informant. Fields did not respond to the question of whether or not the motorcade spectator was Milteer. Fields ended by stating that he would pass the letter along to J. B. Stoner for any comment he might wish to make. The author never heard from Stoner.[441] A letter found in Milteer's home after his death suggests that Milteer knew J. B. Stoner and Edward Fields well.[442]

Milteer's letter to Touchstone, pleading with Touchstone not to identify him as the "Top Gun," may reflect consciousness of guilt on Milteer's part for his ties to the assassination.

Conclusions

The evidence that Milteer was not in his home in Georgia, but rather in Dealey Plaza, during the assassination is substantial. The photographic evidence suggests Milteer could well be the motorcade subject, and certainly does not exclude him (as claimed by the HSCA analysis). If the man standing next to the Milteer look-alike is Klansman Melvin Sexton, then there is little doubt Milteer is in the photo. Modern computerized facial recognition technology may be useful in that regard today, though it not available when the HSCA completed their study.

The revelation, in a 1967 interview with William Somersett, that Milteer admitted to him that he watched the killing is strong evidence that he was, in fact, there. Milteer's dead-on prediction of the bloody events in Dealey Plaza, his own record of violence, and the compelling evidence that he was in Dealey Plaza would defy any explanation other than that he was part of the conspiracy.

At best, the FBI completely mishandled the case. The evidence is compelling that the FBI lied about Milteer being at home during the murder. The FBI decision to send SA Donald Adams to question Milteer five days after the assassination only served to silence him and may have been intentional, since Milteer had already revealed substantial pieces of the assassination conspiracy to Somersett. Had the FBI left him alone, it is likely he would have revealed more to Somersett—and a complete picture of the conspiracy probably would have emerged.

CHAPTER SIX

JOSEPH A. MILTEER AND THE CONGRESS OF FREEDOM, NEW ORLEANS, 1963

*I will put my head on a chopping block there will be some people
killed this time next year, and it will be in high places.*
— *Willie Somersett*

Joseph A. Milteer was part of what Willie Somersett called "the hardcore underground," a national group of far-right extremists. As noted in chapter four, Milteer traveled extensively across the nation beginning at least in 1958, networking with members of far-right groups and individuals in the Citizens' Council, Minutemen, National States' Rights Party, John Birch Society, American Nazi Party, Ku Klux Klan, and others. (Guy Banister, whom multiple witnesses saw in the presence of Lee Harvey Oswald, also had ties to all of those groups.)

In 1963, the hardcore underground met in three open national meetings of proponents of the ultra right, the Congress of Freedom, We the People, and the Constitution Party of America. Milteer was present at all three of the groups' national conventions, and Willie Somersett informed on two of the meetings for the FBI. The directors and membership of the Congress of Freedom, We the People, and the Constitution Party overlapped considerably with the John Birch Society, the Liberty Lobby, and the Christian Crusade. The differences among the three groups were primarily regional, but also varied in their emphasis of particular issues. For example, all the organizations were anti-Communist but We the People had an anti-federal tax bent, while the Constitution Party was focused on forging a far-right political party. Milteer made it clear that the Constitution Party was a front for the hardcore underground.

The Congress of Freedom held their yearly public conference on April 4, 5, and 6, 1963, at the Fontainebleau Hotel in New Orleans. Milteer attended with Somersett. Members of the Constitution Party also met informally at the same time in what Milteer called a "bob tail" meeting. At the meeting of the Congress of Freedom, plans for assassination of a large number of prominent political figures in government, business, and industry who were considered pro-Communist were revealed. Somersett reported the broad-based assassination plots to the FBI.[443] However, the FBI never told the Warren Commission about them. The FBI documents on the plots were available to the HSCA, but it is not clear if they were aware of them. Astonishingly, the assassination plots were not mentioned in the HSCA report on their investigation of Milteer, or in the accompanying volumes of evidence.

A month before the COF meeting, in March 1963, Lee Harvey Oswald was living on Neely Street in Dallas with his wife and daughter and working for the photographic firm of Jaggars-Chiles-Stovall. During that time, he purchased the mail order Italian-made rifle that later would become the assassination weapon. He corresponded with the Socialist Workers Party, the Communist Party of America, and the Fair Play for Cuba Committee, which further enhanced his appearance as a Communist. He ordered his wife Marina to apply for a visa to return to the Soviet Union, which drew the attention of the Dallas FBI. Efforts to return his wife Marina and their daughter to the U.S.S.R. were hampered when the Soviet Embassy informed them the paperwork could take up to half a year. At the end of March, the infamous backyard photos that pictured Oswald holding his rifle in one hand and copies of the *Militant* and the *Worker* newspapers (from two opposing Socialist/Communist groups) in the other were taken by Marina. On April 10, 1963, Oswald allegedly shot at General Walker and missed. Walker, like Oswald, was an associate of Guy Banister and it does not make sense that Oswald actually tried to kill him. (Alternatively, the shooting may have been an aborted phony stunt that will be thoroughly detailed later.) On April 24, 1963, Oswald left Texas for New Orleans by bus, leaving his wife and daughter behind with Ruth Paine, a generous woman who opened her home to the struggling Oswalds. Oswald stayed with his aunt, Lillian Murett, in New Orleans.[444] He was not in New Orleans during the Congress of Freedom meeting and had nothing to do with it—he was on a completely separate mission and track.

Descriptions of the yearly meetings of the COF in the 1950s chronicle the activities and concerns of the radical right of the era, as well as the individuals involved in the movement. A review of the yearly Congress of Freedom meetings is instructive in understanding the evolution of the hardcore underground and the motives of men like Milteer, Banister and other members of the movement. The Congress of Freedom was organized in 1952, in sympathy and support of the anti-Communist inquisitions of Senator Joseph McCarthy. The group had a decidedly anti-Semitic and anti-African American bent.[445] The pervasive attitude among the radical right in the 1950s was a disdain for President Roosevelt's New Deal, as well as for President Truman's Fair Deal, both of which were felt to be Socialistic. The far right felt that the civil rights position of the Fair Deal represented an assault on the sacred Southern institution of segregation.[446]

On October 1, 2, and 3, 1953, the Congress of Freedom meeting was held in Omaha, Nebraska. A headline describing the meeting read "DISSENTIENCE: MILITANT AMERICANS GATHER FOR CONGRESS OF FREEDOM." Archibald Roosevelt, the only living son of the late President Theodore Roosevelt, served as its General Chairman.[447] The 1954 meeting of the Congress of Freedom was also held in Omaha, Nebraska and the national press covered the event. General Bonner Fellers, General Douglas MacArthur's chief of psychological warfare, was a speaker.[448] Fellers was also the head of the group For America.[449]

The 1955 meeting of the COF was held in San Francisco and, among other things, denounced Presidents Eisenhower, Truman, and Roosevelt—and Chief Justice Earl Warren. Merwin K. Hart, Westbrook Pegler, Myron Fagan, Dr. A. G. Blazey, George Montgomery, and Robert LeFevre all addressed the meeting. A message from Dan Smoot—an associate of Milteer who worked for H. L. Hunt's *Facts Forum*—was read at the convention. Myron Fagan, a well-known anti-Semite and racist called for the impeachment of Earl Warren after the 1954 Supreme Court decision against segregation. Willis Carto named Lieutenant General George Stratemeyer and Lieutenant General Albert C. Wedemeyer as COF sponsors.[450] (Retired generals George Stratemeyer and Albert C. Wedemeyer were former aids to General MacArthur and close associates of H. L. Hunt.[451]) Columnist Westbrook Pegler attended and called for an "armed resistance movement." Joseph Zack Kornfeder, a "former Communist," was at the meeting and stated that the United Nations was a child of the New Deal and Communism. ("Ex-Communists" made a nice living exposing citizens as Communists in the inquisitions held by Senator McCarthy, Senator Eastland and others, especially those tied to the civil rights movement.) Wesley Swift, an anti-Semitic follower of Gerald L. K. Smith, and an associate of Milteer attended the meeting.[452] As we shall see, Swift was involved in the broad-based assassination plots revealed at the Congress of Freedom.[453]

In 1956, the Congress of Freedom met in Dallas, Texas, and Mary Cain attended.[454] The 1957 meeting of the Congress of Freedom was organized by Mary Cain, and was held in Biloxi, Mississippi. Outspoken racist Reverend R. Carter Pittman spoke at the meeting, and told of a letter he wrote to President Eisenhower that claimed, dubiously, "the bombing of Negro churches . . . fits the pattern of the Communist conspiracy."[455]

The Congress of Freedom met in Kansas City on April 17, 18 and 19, 1958. Mary Cain, R. Carter Pittman, Willis Stone, D. B. Lewis, Dan Smoot, General Bonner Fellers, and George Thomas were speakers.[456, 457]

In 1959, Senator James O. Eastland was invited by Mary Cain to address the Congress of Freedom in Colorado Springs, but due to campaign conflicts Eastland politely declined, in a letter reflecting their close relationship. (Cain, a newspaper editor from Summit, Mississippi, had worked for Eastland's campaigns in the past.)[458] Eastland was close to Guy Banister, Leander Perez, and other members of the hardcore underground that will be detailed later.

In 1960, the ninth annual meeting of the COF was held in Columbus, Ohio, on April 6–10 and was hosted by Ohio farmer Clifford J. Simpson. Milteer attended and tape recorded the meeting. Dr. Revilo Oliver, Mary Cain, Opal Tanner White, Robert Welch, Reverend T. Robert Ingram, George S. Montgomery, and Glenn O. Young were featured speakers. Other high-ranking members of the radical right in attendance, also Milteer associates, were Reverend Kenneth Goff, a professed "former Communist," and Billy James Hargis. The COF encouraged the public "to insist that Communists be driven from our government" and to join the COF.[459] Opal Tanner White was the assistant to the notorious anti-Semite,

Gerald L. K. Smith, who was present along with Leander Perez at Louisiana governor Huey Long's side when he was assassinated in 1935. Smith's blatant anti-Semitic message, published in his magazine *The Cross and Flag* made him somewhat of a public relations liability to the far right. (Guy Banister subscribed to the paper and kept reams of it in his office.[460]) Opal Tanner White attended various meetings of the radical right in Smith's place and, at the end of the day, mailed handwritten reports to him.[461] J. B. Stoner attended the 1960 COF meeting and spoke twice, but refrained from making his usual anti-Jewish and anti-FBI remarks, the FBI learned from an informant at the event.[462]

Billy James Hargis, another associates of Guy Banister, who was identified by Somersett as a fundraiser for the hardcore underground was the principal speaker at the 1961 Congress in Omaha.[463] Milteer taped the meeting and George Montgomery and representatives of the Liberty Lobby were in attendance.[464] A flier promoting the meeting was found in Milteer's home. The anti-Communist propaganda films *Operation Abolition* and *Communism on the Map* were shown for those in attendance.[465]

In 1961, the Congress of Freedom was held April 13–16 in Washington, D.C. Notable speakers at the meeting were General Pedro del Valle, General Bonner Fellers, Revilo Oliver, Mary Davison, Kenneth Goff, and George Montgomery. A senator and three congressmen were other notable attendees.[466]

The 1962, the Congress of Freedom was held In Houston, Texas, at the Rice Hotel, on March 28–31. Speakers included Chairman Arthur G. Blazey, Mary Davison, General Pedro del Valle, Ken Ryker, and George Montgomery. The flier implored the membership "to fight to rescue our nation from its traitors!" Robert Morris of Dallas, Texas, was presented the Congress of Freedom Award for outstanding service.[467] Morris was chief counsel to Senator Eastland's Senate Internal Security Subcommittee, an anti-Communist inquisitory body functioning much like Senator McCarthy's. Guy Banister assisted Morris in Senator Eastland's investigation of integrationists in New Orleans in 1956. Later, Morris would come to General Walker's aid when he was incarcerated at Springfield Federal Mental Hospital on the orders of Robert Kennedy, after he was arrested on charges of insurrection after he led a riot at Ole Miss in October 1962 (a later chapter is devoted to the incident). Joe Newbrough, who worked for Guy Banister in the Newman Building, was given a Congress of Freedom Award in 1974.[468]

(General Walker and Billy James Hargis were on a national speaking tour called Operation Midnight Ride—criticizing President Kennedy and warning Americans of the internal threat of Communism in the U.S.—at the time of the 1963 COF meeting, and did not attend. Their tour ran from February 27, 1963, until April 3, 1963, ending in Los Angeles. Walker returned to his Dallas home from the speaking tour on April 8, 1963, and was allegedly shot at by Lee Harvey Oswald on April 10, 1963.[469] Walker planned to speak at the Congress of Freedom meeting on April 11, 1964, in Birmingham, Alabama, however, he cancelled to attend the funeral of General Douglas MacArthur.[470])

The 1963 Congress of Freedom Assassination Plots

While attending the April 1963 meeting of the COF in New Orleans, with Milteer, Willie Somersett learned about a plot to assassinate members of the Council on Foreign Relations, left-wing politicians, and prominent citizens, and reported it to the Miami FBI. There were no known plots to kill President Kennedy revealed at the meeting. The Congress of Freedom meeting, also referred to as a "coalition of patriotic groups," was held in conjunction with the Council for Statehood, which was headed by Mary Davison of Palm Beach, Florida. A merger of the two organizations into one group was to be discussed during the meeting.[471] The Council for Statehood, formed in December 1962, was an outgrowth of another Davison group, the Freemen. The new organization was "to take an active part in segregation" and operate as an "action group." The group was designed to be able to call on outsiders to taken any necessary local action, leaving the local membership free of suspicions. Chapters of the Council for Statehood were organized in thirty-six states and a secret fund was amassed through membership fees and contributions. Publicly they would not advocate violence but, privately, they would "arrange acts if considered necessary." Their goal was to eliminate the Council on Foreign Relations (CFR) through legislation, if possible, but, if not, through assassination.[472] "Eskimos" was the code word they used for Jews. They advocated "knocking off the Eskimos with carbines." Both the Congress of Freedom and the Council for Statehood were equally active in the plot to assassinate members of the CFR, although neither was described as the prime mover behind them.[473]

The policies of the Kennedy administration were not merely considered objectionable to the radical right—they were considered treasonous. They were particularly disturbed with President Kennedy's civil rights initiatives, his disarmament program, his compromise with the Soviet Union, and his failure to overthrow Castro in Cuba. Mary Cain, an active organizer of the Congress of Freedom for many years, set the tone for the upcoming 1963 meeting of the group when she wrote in the February 14, 1963, *Summit Sun*, "Suffice to say that if you are sick to death of Kennedy and his whole villainous outfit and want something to change you'll find it at the Congress of Freedom." Cain described the meeting as "Three full days of association with 'the hardcore of Patriotic Americans'—People who glory at speaking out for God and Country."[474] The New Orleans *Times–Picayune* noted those behind the convention were "The Hard Core of Patriotic Americans."[475] Somersett, thus, was not alone in describing the group as "hardcore." Woody Kearns, a close friend of Milteer, attended the Congress of Freedom and represented the Citizens for Arrest of Traitors, along with attorney Millard Grubbs.[476] (Grubbs was the president of the Citizens' Council of Kentucky in 1958. He operated the National Law Enforcement Agency, an outgrowth of the Citizens' Council, that was comprised of retired members of the military and law enforcement. The purpose of the group was summed up in Grubbs's statement, "It was President Lincoln who said: 'We shall not overthrow the Constitution, but will overthrow the traitors who subvert it'." Grubbs planned to place the top traitors in the U.S. under citizens' arrest.[477])

Theodore "Ted" Jackman from Greenville, South Carolina, was flown in from California for the 1963 meeting and advocated violence in his speech. (Others from California attended the meeting but were not identified by Somersett.) Jackman told the audience about an operation devised by the Kennedy administration, Khrushchev, and Castro, which was supposedly being set up in Georgia by a Communist-subverted element of the U.S. Army, dubbed "Water Moccasin Guerilla Warfare." Jackman planned to fight the operation stating, "We will meet the army head-on and destroy them." Somersett identified Jackman as "one of the toughest killers."

After the assassination, Somersett told law enforcement that Ted Jackman was one of the Dealey Plaza riflemen.[478] Grady Bartlett, a friend of Milteer from California, sent Milteer a copy of a speech Jackman had made in Menlo Park, California, prior to the COF meeting. After listening to the tape, Milteer wrote Bartlett, convinced by Jackman's speech that, "I am of the opinion that we are not going to lose our great Country, we have already lost it. It makes me want to 'Have gun, will travel.' Want to join with me?"[479] Milteer wrote a letter to Jackman on December 20, 1964, and stated he understood he had some dynamite or TNT, and Milteer asked him for some.[480] Jackman's name appeared on the national roster of the John Birch Society's American Opinion Speakers Bureau, where he was identified as "Reverend Jackman." (Others listed on the speakers' roster were Courtney associate Hilaire du Berrier, John Rousselot, Banister associate Edward Hunter, and Hargis associate Fernando Penabaz.[481]) Somersett estimated that 75 to 90 percent of the top leadership at the COF meeting were members of the John Birch Society. He reported, "Any action by the Congress of Freedom regarding assassination would have the sanction of the John Birch Society."

Somersett told Miami Police Detective Lockhart Gracey, on April 10, 1963, that the New Orleans meeting had taken on an ominous tone. There was "a great deal [of talk] about political assassinations" that he had never detected in similar meetings in the past. The drinking and "hell-raising" that Somersett was accustomed to seeing at other meetings was conspicuously absent at the 1963 Congress of Freedom meeting. Somersett stated, "None of these people were sitting at the bars drinking or out chasing women." He stated, "They were there strictly on business . . . ." Another difference from meetings in past years was that this was the first time the group had ever met in New Orleans, which Somersett emphasized and found significant.

Somersett provided information in Miami, before the COF meeting, that members of the hardcore underground from the "Miami zone" had established—or were establishing— nuclei of individuals in coordination with various zones throughout the United States for assassinations. The "Miami zone" was likely under the influence of Mary Davison's Council for Statehood. The Miami FBI learned that Davison and the Council for Statehood had met weekly beginning in November of 1962 in South Florida, and that they planned to eliminate—by force if necessary—all Jewish people in government and business positions, and all Jews who were Communists.[482] Somersett learned at Council for Statehood meeting that a high-ranking inner circle, which had access to large amounts of money, would name the time and place for assassinations to begin. Somersett did not know who belonged to the inner circle. He felt Mary Davison likely belonged, and suspected Arthur Bohn, John Thurmond, and Thomas Williams, as well. Somersett thought it was significant that those four did not stay at the Fontainebleau where the COF meeting was held, but rather at the Plaza Hotel nearby. Somersett reported that Bohn and Davison had targeted Paul Epstein of the Miami Anti-Defamation League for assassination, and would give the order when the time came. Somersett noted that Davison had the power to order a murder and someone would carry it out.[483] Somersett also reported that Ted Jackman was part of the "high command" of the Council for Statehood.[484]

The first phase of the hardcore underground's program to take back the country from those perceived as Communists was to inform the citizenry and members of the United States Congress about the pro-Communist policies of the Eisenhower and Kennedy administrations. Members of the Congress of Freedom and others on the radical right claimed that President Kennedy had planned to place the government of the United States under the control of the United Nations in some capacity, under sponsorship of the Council of Foreign Relations. The far right coined the slogan, "Get the U.N. out of the U.S. and the U.S. out of the U.N.," reflecting their antipathy toward the organization. FBI Director Hoover popularized the idea that the United Nations, headquartered in Manhattan, was a "Trojan horse" filled with Communists, there to further the Communist agenda in the United States.

Phase two of the hardcore underground program disclosed at the COF meeting was to begin the assassinations of both individuals and groups of people. Individuals selected for assassination were prioritized. One of the "first choices" for assassination was Averill Harriman, President Kennedy's ambassador at large. Wealthy Jews in the financial industry, including those from the firms of Kuhn and Loeb, Lehman Brothers, Goldman Sachs, and others were priorities for elimination. The second choices for assassination were leaders of major American corporations, including Jews and non-Jews. Leaders in prominent U.S. corporations—including General Electric, Kroger, and Boeing Aircraft, to name a few—were targeted. The individuals named as second choices for assassination were chosen because they were related in some capacity to the Business Advisory Council. The far right believed the Business Advisory Council was an underground, hidden force in government, whose members were the real rulers of America. The third choice for assassination was the whole membership of the Council of Foreign Relations (CFR)—an academic, public policy think tank—to which President Kennedy belonged. The fourth choice for assassination were members of the International Bilderberger.

The targeted individuals' names appeared in a book distributed at the COF meeting, which had been written by Mary Davison, called the *Secret Government*. Davison's book was the first of at least three claiming the Council on Foreign Relations secretly ruled the country.[485] Books by Kent Courtney and Dan Smoot made the same claims. (Smoot, a friend of Milteer, was on the Board of Directors of the Congress of Freedom at one time.[486]) Davison hand marked the names of those of highest priority for assassination listed in her book and distributed copies at the COF meeting.

Davison, whom Willie Somersett knew well, spoke on the subject of the "Secret Government" on the first night of the COF meeting. Later, in an attempt to curry favor and to learn more about her operation, Somersett wrote a front-page story in his union newspaper praising her and her speech at the COF. In his article, Somersett also inflated the number of people attending the COF meeting to 2,000 to "open the gate" with Davison, when in fact only 700 attended.[487] (The only copy of Davison's book ever found by the author was in the papers of Willie Rainach, a close Banister associate.[488])

According to Miami FBI documents, "The Dixie Klan, which is described as an off-shoot of the hard core membership of the KKK, John Birch Society, White Citizens' Council, and other groups is pushing hard for assassinations."[489] (Milteer, as it will be recalled, was in the Dixie Klan with Jack Brown, who attempted to murder Martin Luther King, Jr.)

Lockhart Gracey, Jr, of the Miami police, asked Somersett, when he debriefed him after the Congress of Freedom meeting, "Do you believe they are going to kill all of these people?" Somersett replied, "I do I definitely do. As sure as we are sitting here, next year some of them will be killed . . . I will put my head on a chopping block there will be some people killed this time next year, and it will be in high places . . . I think when the time comes, from military leaders that they have in there with the information that they are getting, they are contemplating on starting before that certain stage. Whenever the high command gives the orders to kill people, that's when it's going to happen." Somersett stated that the military in the high command were several admirals and ex-generals; "This is supposed to be headed and directed by military men from the top." Somersett stated that General del Valle was involved in a big way.[490]

Somersett revealed to the Miami FBI that General Walker, General Clyde Watts, Major Archibald Roberts, and General Pedro del Valle were former high-ranking members of the armed forces who secretly belonged to the Council for Statehood and the Congress of Freedom.[491] They were also called the "military high command," and planned to obtain photographs and background information on possible victims for assassination. Somersett's revelation is stunning, considering that General Walker and his attorney, General Clyde Watts, both appeared before the Warren Commission, who had no idea they belonged to these murder-minded groups which were plotting assassinations. The FBI failed to inform the Commission. Striking is the fact that General Walker had a direct tie to Lee Harvey Oswald, who supposedly tried to shoot him. Further, Oswald admitted attending a speech Walker gave in Dallas on October 23, 1963. (The military high command of the Congress of Freedom will be discussed at length in the next chapter.) Clyde Watts, another significant figure, came to Walker's aide when allegations surfaced that Jack Ruby, Oswald's murderer, visited Walker's home on three occasions accompanied by members of the John Birch Society. Those events will be detailed at length in Chapter Seventeen.

The fact that Milteer knew both General Walker and his aide Robert Surrey, two Warren Commission witnesses, escaped the HSCA. Milteer jotted their names and addresses on a Colorado John Birch Society application postcard.[492] (The card was found among items taken from Milteer's home after his death and kept in a probate court storage room.) As we shall see later, Milteer visited the two in Dallas in June of 1964. In all, Milteer made five visits to Dallas between June 1963 and June 1964, of which, three trips were before the assassination—including the one he made on November 22. Milteer also visited the Colorado extremist Kenneth Goff and knew him well.[493]

Milteer jotted the names and addresses of General Walker and Robert Surrey on a Colorado JBS membership postcard. Source: Brooks County Probate Court

The author reviewed three separate versions of Milteer's FBI file, each slightly different from the others. Through a Freedom of Information Act (FOIA) request the author obtained the first Milteer files from the FBI in the 1990s. It bore writer Dan Christensen's name on it and appears to be a copy of the information received from Christensen's original FOIA request from around 1977. The author obtained a second FOIA request file prepared by the FBI for another assassination researcher in the 1990s. The third is the Milteer file placed online in the 2000s by the FBI in their electronic reading room prompted by the many FOIA requests. None of the three Milteer files, nor any documents in the National Archives, mentions Walker as a part of the military high command of the Council for Statehood or Congress of Freedom, as was revealed by Willie Somersett. The revelation that Walker was in the high command of this murder-plotting group was found in a separate FBI file on the Council for Statehood obtained from the FBI. The HSCA was unaware of it, but the Council for Statehood FBI file was at their disposal, and could have added to their information if they had done their due diligence and requested it.[494]

Guy Banister and the Congress of Freedom

Guy Banister attended the 1963 Congress of Freedom meeting, which is a stunning revelation, reported here for the first time. Banister's presence at the meeting was not mentioned in the Milteer FBI documents, or in the extensive HSCA documents on Milteer in the National Archives. The author found the document referring to Banister's attendance at the meeting in the FBI files of Mary Davison's far-right Council for Statehood, obtained from the FBI through a Freedom of Information Act request.

Here we have Guy Banister, who was seen by numerous individuals with the president's presumed assassin, Lee Harvey Oswald, in attendance at a meeting where political assassinations were plotted—along with Joseph A. Milteer, who knew of the plot to murder the president in advance and than watched it happen. Not to mention the fact that Banister's close friend, General Edwin Walker, secretly belonged to the murder-plotting group. Had the HSCA known about Banister's presence at the meeting, they surely would have given the Milteer and Banister evidence more consideration. Milteer tape recorded the COF meeting on seven reels, and sold copies as he had done before at meetings all over the country.[495] Willie Somersett obtained a copy of that recording, and handed it over to the Miami FBI. The FBI listened to the taped COF speech of Austin T. Flett in which Flett was heard pointing Banister out to the crowd. He told the audience that Banister was a close friend and also the former Special Agent in Charge of the Chicago FBI. He asked Banister to stand and take a bow. The FBI noted that Banister did not speak at the meeting. A memo reporting on the meeting was sent to FBI Director J. Edgar Hoover.

This revelation is yet another example of the indispensable evidence provided by Willie Somersett and the dismal failure of the investigatory bodies to act on it.

The tape recordings have been reviewed by the Miami Office and results set forth in enclosed letterhead memorandum. It is noted none of the recordings related to any secret or closed door meetings.

For the information of the Bureau, it is pointed out that AUSTIN T. FLETT of Chicago, Ill., who was scheduled to address the Session at 3:30 PM, 4/5/63, introduced GUY BANASTER as a close friend and former Agent in Charge of the FBI, Chicago. Prior to his speech, FLETT asked BANASTER to stand and take a bow. It is noted BANASTER did not make any statement and did not address the Session.

The Miami FBI documents identifying Guy Banister at the 1963 Congress of Freedom meeting. Source: FBI file on Council for Statehood

Austin T. Flett was an insurance broker from Chicago and an executive with United States Cold Storage. It is not known how Flett and Banister became close friends, but it may have been when Banister was the Chicago FBI director, or at prior meetings of the COF or other right-wing groups. Somersett reported that Flett—whom he believed to be in the "high command" of the group—gave one of the most outspoken speeches at the convention: in his speech he stated that the U.S. was ruled by a Communist dictator. Flett told the audience about his testimony before the Senate Committee on Foreign Relations in 1956 and 1957 and the Senate Committee on Internal Security (the Eastland Committee) in 1958. He stated that high government officials who were "part of the Communist conspiracy to take over the United States" suppressed much of the information he told the committees. Flett stated that he had not paid his federal income taxes since 1955 because he felt the IRS collected taxes to use them to overthrow the U.S. government. Flett predicted, "Our children will belong to the Communist Party" and would later be "put in a trade or put to work." Flett concluded, "We can win this fight by exposing the conspiracy . . . which will result in a mass protest in the use of public funds to overthrow and destroy our country."[496]

Kent Courtney and the Congress of Freedom

Kent Courtney was also present at the 1963 Congress of Freedom but played no part in the planning or promotion of the meeting.[497] The FBI reported that Courtney attended as a leader of the States' Rights Party in New Orleans.[498] As noted in chapter three, Courtney was a close associate of Guy Banister and was allegedly seen on multiple occasions with Lee Harvey Oswald. A letter from Guy Banister to the local leader of the New Orleans post of the American Legion—strenuously urging him not to invite Congressman T. Hale Boggs to speak at a Legion function—was found by the author in Courtney's papers. Enclosed with the letter was a detailed dossier citing Boggs's "pro-Communist" positions in Congress, which he based in part on Courtney's Conservative Society of America Congressional Voter Index. Banister stated in the letter: "the critical situation now threatening America—a situation created by Communist-Socialist infiltration and supervision working within America as well as Bolshevik aggression abroad . . . requires immediate attention." The letter exemplifies Banister's worldview that the threat of Communism was everywhere.[499]

Guy Banister's letter to Willie Rainach on April 26, 1960, applying for a position with the Lousiana Sovereingty Commission, also documents his move from the Balter Building to the Newman Building at 537 Lafayette Street. The front of the same building bore the address 544 Camp Street, which was also the address stamped on one of Oswald's handouts. Source: Rainach Papers, Noel Memorial Library, Louisiana State University Shreveport

As noted in the prior chapters, Courtney and Banister both served on the American Legion Un-American Activities Committee. That committee inspired legionnaire and State Representative James Pfister to establish the Louisiana Un-American Activities Committee, LUAC in the state legislature, and Pfister, Courtney, Banister, and Leander Perez joined forces in 1958 to defeat the Communist threat as noted in the first two chapters. Banister became chief investigator for LUAC in 1960. Perez was the mastermind behind the 1962 Communist Control Act, under which any person or group associated with a Communist like Lee Harvey Oswald faced decades of imprisonment. The law was designed to effectively outlaw civil rights organizations—particularly Banister's long-time nemesis the Southern Conference Education Fund. As we will see, Lee Harvey Oswald infiltrated three so-called Communist-front groups with direct ties to the Southern Conference Education Fund. The plan conceived by Perez was to demonstrate that a Communist from the Soviet Union had infiltrated the SCEF providing the basis to prosecute and destroy the organization under the Communist Control Act. Oswald was involved with Banister in LUAC's pursuit of the SCEF, but not in the assassination plotting at the Congress of Freedom, nor the later plotting to kill the president that Willie Somersett reported to the FBI in October 1963. Oswald did not figure into the president's assassination plan until after President Kennedy's trip to Texas was confirmed on September 20, 1963. Accordingly, all of Oswald's posturing as a Communist prior to that point was done solely to further LUAC's pursuit of the SCEF and the three so-called Communist front groups Oswald infiltrated in the summer of 1963.

Kent Courtney was well connected with the national far right and tape recorded interviews with scores of prominent members for his far-right radio program, including a number of individuals who were members of the hardcore underground alluded to in the Milteer-Somersett informant documents.[500]

Revilo Oliver and the Warren Commission

Revilo Oliver was the keynote speaker at the 1963 Congress of Freedom meeting. Oliver served on the national council of the John Birch Society, and was one of the most trusted advisors to Robert Welch, the Society's leader, when it was founded in 1958. *The Jewish Voice* out of California called Revilo Oliver Robert Welch's "chief theoretician," noting that Oliver spoke around the country attacking blacks and Jews, while Welch sat in the audience listening.[501]

Oliver proclaimed, in his speech at the Congress of Freedom, "the gang in Washington has become so bold or reckless that it scarcely takes the trouble to devise even the flimsiest pretext to cover treason."[502] (It may be interesting to note that Joseph Milteer tape recorded speeches by Oliver at a convention in 1961—and several other times—and they likely knew each other well.[503, 504] And, in reference to Oliver, William Somersett stated, "he was one of the main ones advocating, of course, violence."[505])

After the Kennedy assassination, Oliver wrote a two-part article published in the February and March 1964 issues of the John Birch Society's monthly magazine *American Opinion*, cleverly titled to emphasize Oswald's professed ties to Marxism, "Marxsmanship in Dallas." The two magazine covers featured portraits of General Douglas MacArthur and Senator Strom Thurmond, icons of the far right. In the article, Oliver postulated three possible motives for Oswald killing the president. He suggested that Kennedy, in secret, was a Communist. One possibility, Oliver wrote, was that Kennedy was righting his leftist ways and "turning American," thus becoming a liability to the Communists. In another scenario, he stated that Oswald's Communist faction was at odds with Kennedy's implied pro-Communist faction. Lastly, he stated the murder might have been done by the Communists so they could pin it on the far right.

Oliver, originally from Texas, was a Nazi sympathizer who stated at the 1966 "God, Family and Country" rally that the "vaporizing of Jews" was a "beatified vision."[506] Oliver taught classic languages at the University of Illinois; one professor who knew him told the author, "He looked strange, he even walked strange. He made his classwork so difficult for non-white students that they either flunked out or dropped out. He delighted in inviting Jewish faculty members to his home and surreptitiously serving them pork dishes."[507]

The Warren Commission was unaware of the Milteer story, his accurate prediction about the assassination, or the talk of broad-based assassination plots divulged at the Congress of Freedom. Remarkably—and for unclear reasons—they asked Oliver, the Congress of Freedom keynote speaker, to testify before the Commission about his published allegations about the assassination. Oliver testified on September 9, 1964, at a time when the Commission's deliberations were over and fifteen volumes of evidence had already been printed. Oliver was one of the few to testify before the Commission with an attorney present (as did General Walker and Dallas Nazi Robert Surrey—all three men were associates of Joseph A. Milteer). During his testimony, Oliver was asked by Commission counsel Albert E. Jenner, Jr. to explain his charges that Oswald was part of a Soviet-Communist plot, that with the help of the

CIA was responsible for the assassination of President Kennedy. They asked him for the basis of his claim that Secretary of Defense Robert McNamara knew of the plot and had ordered the U.S. Army to rehearse for the funeral more than a week in advance. They questioned him about his claim that Oswald stole radar codes and other secrets and handed them over to the Soviets. They pointed out to Oliver that his claim that Oswald never repaid the State Department money given to him to pay for his return from the Soviet Union was incorrect. (The Commission had determined that Oswald had repaid them the money and, therefore, it was not evidence that he was working for the U.S. government as claimed.)

Oliver was further asked what he meant when he wrote, "On his arrival in this country Oswald took up his duties as an agent of the Conspiracy, spying on anti-Communist Cuban refugees, serving as an agitator for 'Fair Play for Cuba' and participating in some of the many forms of subversion that flourish openly in defiance of the law through the connivance of the Attorney General, Robert F. Kennedy." Referring to a speech Bringuier gave at Billy James Hargis's Christian Crusade meeting, Oliver explained that he had personally heard the account of Oswald infiltrating the anti-Communist Cubans from Carlos Bringuier in Tulsa, Oklahoma (Bringuier was the anti-Castro Cuban that Oswald engaged in a fight and later debated on the subject of Castro's Cuba on a radio program in New Orleans).[508] Bringuier also participated in a post-assassination speaking tour that also featured General Walker, Billy James Hargis, and Kent Courtney at a stop at the Third Annual Christian Crusade Anti-Communist Leadership School in Shreveport, Louisiana, in February 1964.[509] (Evidence presented previously revealed that Walker, Hargis, and Oliver were associates of Joseph Milteer. Bringuier, Courtney, and Walker all had ties to Lee Harvey Oswald. Oliver was on the National Advisory Council of Hargis's Christian Crusade.[510])

Willie Somersett reported that Hargis raised funds for the hardcore underground during his speaking tours, and that Milteer recorded Hargis's speeches. All that can be heard on the tape of one speech is Hargis exhorting the audience to make donations to fill an ice cream bucket which was being passed around.[511] In 1960, Hargis made some factually incorrect statements in a speech he made, after which he wrote Milteer and asked him to delete the incorrect remarks from the tape.[512] Hargis was also a close associate of Kent Courtney, who spoke in prior years at his Christian Crusade meetings.

Oliver told the Warren Commission that newspaper features reprinted by the American Eagle Publishing Company were a source for Oliver's story. The Commission told him they were aware Robert Surrey was the president of the publishing company. (Surrey told the Commission he was president of the publishing company in his own testimony. The Commission had called him to testify to explain the "Wanted for Treason" poster featuring mug shot-type photos of President Kennedy that he printed and distributed before the assassination. The Commission was aware that he was an aide to General Walker. More importantly, they were not aware that he was the secretary-treasurer of the Dallas John Birch Society and head of the Dallas American Nazi Party.) Oliver told them other sources for his article in *American Opinion* included a Liberty Lobby article, written by Willis Carto, and articles from

Frank Capell's far-right newsletter *The Herald of Freedom*. (Capell, as we shall see, was part of the hardcore underground.)

In addition, Oliver told the Warren Commission, "I also heard from the publisher of the *Independent American* of an attempt by Oswald to obtain employment on that newspaper." Oliver elaborated, stating that Kent Courtney, the publisher, had told him personally that Oswald applied for a job at his newspaper. (It's plausible that Oliver told them the story to provide Courtney with an alibi in case the Commission had learned that Oswald and Courtney were seen together).[513] An assassination researcher who read Oliver's testimony contacted Courtney in 1986 and asked him if Oswald had visited him at his printing office. Courtney denied the claim, but stated he seemed to remember one of his printers raising that possibility.[514]

Oliver wrote that Oswald was ordered by the Soviets to murder General Walker, whom he talked to personally about the shooting. He cited the *Councilor* as a source of some of his information—the same publication Walker was pictured on the front page of alongside *Councilor* publisher Ned Touchstone, on the day of the assassination—attesting to the fact that Walker was not in Dallas on the day of the murder. Nearly all of Oliver's sources were either associates of General Walker or Joseph Milteer, a fact clearly not appreciated by the Commission.[515]

The 1963 Congress of Freedom and George Soule

In 1963, the Congress of Freedom was held in New Orleans and hosted by George Soule, a past president of the Congress of Freedom. Soule was the third-generation owner and headmaster of the venerable New Orleans institution Soule College, a business school located on Jackson Avenue in the Garden District. Soule was a close associate of Guy Banister, who had taken courses at the school in the past.[516, 517] Soule hosted Medford Evans in March 1960 to give an address on Communism to students and faculty at the college.[518] (As we shall see later, Evans was friend of Guy Banister and General Walker.)

In May 1960, Soule College hosted Milton M. Lory of the American Coalition of Patriotic Societies, who gave an anti-Communism speech.[519] On December 17, 1962, the New Orleans Branch of Women for Constitutional Government met at Soule College and adopted the position of "Defeat of Communism."[520] (Delphine Roberts, Guy Banister's secretary, was president of the New Orleans affiliate of the Women for Constitutional Government.[521])

Soule was the head of the New Orleans John Birch Society and hosted its founder, Robert Welch, at a meeting at the Jerusalem Temple—a Shriner's Hall on St. Charles Street at Lee Circle, not far from Guy Banister's 531 Lafayette/544 Camp Street office—on November 18, 1961; the two were pictured together in the *Times-Picayune*. Soule was also a member of the International House.[522] Banister's close friend Kent Courtney was the State Coordinator for the John Birch Society and had been closely associated with Welch before the inception of the group in 1958.[523]

New Orleans D.A. Jim Garrison was aware that Soule hosted the 1963 Congress of

Freedom meeting and probably learned of the affair from Miami district attorney Richard Gerstein. How much Garrison knew of the meeting and assassination talk is not known. There is little in Garrison's files about the meeting, but it is certain Garrison was aware of the Milteer-Somersett tape. Garrison attempted, but was unable, to get a list of those attending the meeting from the Fontainebleau Hotel where the conference was held. In a February 6, 1967, memorandum to Garrison, investigator James L. Alcock stated, "A tactful approach to MR. SOULE should be devised. With the right entrée, MR. SOULE might provide us with a list of those who attended the convention as well as the background material on the organization and its personnel." It's not known if Soule was questioned.[524] On August 21, 1968, investigator James Alcock interviewed William Somersett.[525] Ironically, Garrison received an award from the Congress of Freedom that same year.[526]

George Soule was critical of President Kennedy in an editorial he wrote—published on June 18, 1963—that stated, "The actions taken by President Kennedy at the University of Alabama and the earlier invasion by the defenseless State of Mississippi should warn you that he is fast turning our great country into a police state if it is not already one."[527]

In a number of letters to Senator Allen Ellender, Soule's wife toed the harsh John Birch Society line. In one letter, she was critical of President Kennedy's proposal for peaceful cooperation with the Soviets on some space projects, citing it as an example of "the treason that so boldly takes place every day."[528]

George Soule served as the Continuity Chairman of the New Orleans Indignation Committee, Inc. The "National Indignation" was founded in 1961 in Dallas, Texas, in protest of the Kennedy administration's policy of selling obsolete U.S. Air Force jets to the Soviet bloc country of Yugoslavia. Guy Banister's name was on the letterhead of the organization, along with four of his close associates: George Soule, P. Cameron Terry, Hubert Badeaux, and F. Jerry Brown. (Soule and Terry attended the COF meeting and likely also knew Milteer.[529]) Soule hosted notorious anti-Semite Richard Cotton as a speaker at Soule College in October 1964 under the auspices of the New Orleans National Indignation Committee.[530]

George Soule was a committee member of For America, which hosted Tom Anderson at a rally at the Jerusalem Temple in New Orleans on October 2, 1962. (Bonner Fellers, a former member of General Douglas MacArthur's staff in World War II, founded For America.[531]) Anderson, like Oliver, was on the council of the John Birch Society from its inception. He was a close

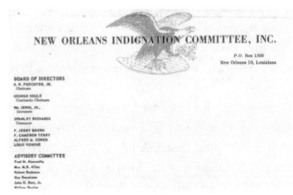

Guy Banister and four of his close associates, George Soule, Hubert Badeaux, F. Jerry Brown, and P. Cameron Terry were on the masthead of the New Orleans Indignation Committee, Inc., circa 1961. Source: deLesseps Morrison Papers, New Orleans Public Library

associate of General Walker. (Evidence will be presented in Chapter Nineteen that Anderson was an accessory after the fact in the assassination conspiracy, if not before.)

Soule was also an ally of Leander Perez. When the New Orleans Catholic Diocese abolished segregation in the Catholic schools, Soule joined Perez in the white-only private school movement. Soule was present with Perez at the groundbreaking of a private white school in the Ninth Ward on August 6, 1961, while a group of onlookers sang "Dixie."[532]

Soule hosted Billy James Hargis, who spoke at the Jerusalem Temple on October 25, 1963. In his speech, Hargis stated, "We must clean house in Washington and restore constitutional government."[533] Mary Brengel, who worked as a secretary for Guy Banister in October and November of 1963, told the author she saw Hargis at Banister's 531 Lafayette/544 Camp Street office at the time of her employment, which corresponds with the date of the Jerusalem Temple speech, and places Banister and Hargis together twenty-seven days prior to the assassination. Brengel had previously worked as an assistant editor for Kent Courtney's *Independent American* newspaper, as well as H. L. Hunt's *Life Lines* in Dallas. She met General Walker through Kent Courtney on two occasions.[534] (Milteer also knew Hargis, and told Willie Somersett that Hargis raised money for the hardcore underground.[535])

George Soule was the local leader of the States' Rights Party and belonged to the Anglican Orthodox Church of North America.[536] He was an associate of Ed Butler, General Walker and Kent Courtney. Ed Butler, a close Banister associate as noted in Chapter One, arranged a radio debate on August 17, 1963, between Carlos Bringuier and Lee Harvey Oswald during which Oswald proclaimed that he was a Marxist and a member of Fair Play for Cuba Committee. Interestingly, Oswald established—during the debate—that he was aware that a congressional subcommittee had held hearings on the FPCC, but did not establish a direct link between the FPCC and Communism. Instead, Oswald provided the link between the FPCC and Communism during the debate, when he professed that he was a Marxist and belonged to the FPCC, which was the entire purpose of creating a phony FPCC chapter in New Orleans, as we shall see. The committee mentioned by Oswald was Senator Eastland's Senate Internal Security Subcommittee. (Banister assisted Eastland and his committee when he conducted a raid on the home of integrationist—and alleged Communist—Hunter Pitts O'Dell in 1956.)

Soule was a member of the American Institute for Freedom Project, a group formed to combat Communism in South America—and an apparent offshoot of the Information Council of the Americas (INCA) founded in 1960 by Ed Butler. A July 27, 1961, meeting was attended by George Soule, Guy Banister, B. B. Deutsch of the Military Order of World Wars, Dr. Alton Ochsner, and Ed Butler of INCA. Garrison's files indicate that Butler and Ochsner were people of interest in the assassination for the D.A. During Garrison's investigation, rumors circulated that there might be an imminent arrest of an unnamed prominent New Orleans physician, thought to be Ochsner.[537] In a 1968 document, Garrison stated that Ed Butler was "currently working for Nazi types in California." (Butler worked for far-right-wing Patrick Frawley of California in 1968.) Garrison thought there was some significance to the proximity of Butler's home at 1901 Jefferson Street and Kent Courtney's operations on the 7800 block of Green Street in New Orleans, but did not elaborate.[538]

P. Cameron Terry and the New Orleans Citizens' Council

Willie Somersett identified P. Cameron Terry, who served with Banister and Soule on the New Orleans National Indignation Committee, as the representative of the New Orleans Citizens' Council at the 1963 Congress of Freedom. Somersett had met Terry in 1960 when he was asked to go to New Orleans on behalf of the FBI to inform on the activities of the segregationists during the integration of the schools, and subsequently joined the Citizens' Council of New Orleans. Somersett told the FBI that he saw Terry in the Balter Building at the time. Leander Perez, the Citizens' Council, and Guy Banister all had offices in the Balter Building at the time.[539]

The HSCA contacted Kent Courtney and asked him if he knew the whereabouts of Guy Banister's girlfriend, Delphine Roberts. Courtney suggested that Cameron Terry would be a good person to ask and suggested the two knew each other. Raymond Broshears told HSCA investigators that Courtney was involved in the assassination—as we will see later— but apparently did not take him seriously.[540] The HSCA subpoenaed Courtney, but never called him to testify.[541]

Joseph Milteer was associated with New Orleans Citizens' Council president Dr. Emmett Irwin, a bachelor, surgeon and azalea fancier. A letter addressed to Milteer bearing a return address of Irwin's was found among Milteer's belongings after his death, linking Milteer to the Citizens' Council of New Orleans.[542] George Soule was heavily involved with the Citizens' Council and spoke at a Greater New Orleans Citizens' Council meeting with Emmet Irwin and others on January 11, 1961.[543] Soule also appeared on stage at the New Orleans Mass Citizens' Council meeting on May 13, 1964, with George Singelmann, Ned Touchstone, and Emmet Irwin. The meeting was held four days prior to the tenth anniversary of the *Brown* decision, which they referred to as "Black Monday."[544]

The FBI and the Aftermath of the Congress of Freedom Meeting

The FBI interviewed Mary Davison, the leader of the Council for Statehood, on May 9, 1963, in connection with the murder plots discussed at the Congress of Freedom meeting and revealed by Somersett. She told them had she never advocated violence, and she knew of no one in her group who advocated assassination.[545] The FBI interviewed others from the Council for Statehood (their names were redacted) and they, too, denied plotting assassination. One unidentified individual whose name was redacted said there were many in the Council who were concerned about the FBI's suspicion that they were planning to overthrow the government or engage in acts of violence to accomplish their purposes. John Lanier, the only other name not redacted, gave similar denials to the FBI on June 21, 1963.[546]

Two hundred—or nearly all—of the names of the membership of Council for Statehood included in the FBI documents on the organization obtained by the author were redacted by the FBI. Three of the members, names redacted, were from New Orleans, and several were from the Dallas area. A wealthy industrialist from Houston, name withheld, backed the Council. The names Admiral John Crommelin and the Louisiana Sovereignty Commission under John H. Deere were revealed. The names of seven members of the board of directors were redacted. A future release of those names by the FBI could be of momentous historical significance.[547]

Thanks to Willie Somersett, the FBI's questioning of the plotters put an end to the broad-based assassination plots. However, the built-up fervor for assassination remained and, in October 1963, the FBI learned that Milteer attended the Constitution Party meeting and plots to kill President Kennedy by the hardcore underground were discussed.

The House Select Committee on Assassination and the Milteer Evidence

The HSCA limited their investigation of the Milteer affair and apparently failed to consider any of the voluminous intelligence on Milteer beyond the taped prediction of the assassination and the Dealey Plaza photo. Astonishingly—and defying any clear explanation—the HSCA failed to mention a word about the Congress of Freedom assassination plots in their report or its volumes of supporting evidence. The omission is stupefying, given that the HSCA was specifically charged by Congress to investigate assassinations, including President Kennedy's and Martin Luther King, Jr.'s.

Nor did the HSCA report mention that Milteer was known for extreme violence or that he consorted with some of the most violent individuals in the South, including Jack Brown—who had attempted to assassinate Martin Luther King, Jr.

Worse yet, they failed to assess and report the FBI's information that Milteer attended a meeting of the Constitution Party in October 1963 where plans to assassinate President Kennedy were discussed. It is hard to imagine a sinister reason for those gross failures of the HSCA on the Milteer matter. Poor scholarship and sloppy work were more likely the primary contributing factors. Whatever the reason for the oversight, it was a colossal failure for the cause of history and justice.

Conclusions

Joseph A Milteer and Willie Somersett attended the April 1963 Congress of Freedom meeting in New Orleans where assassinations of prominent individuals in government and industry were discussed. The evidence was kept from the Warren Commission and, for unfathomable reasons, was not deliberated upon or reported by the HSCA. The FBI never told the Warren Commission of the murderous plots discussed at the COF meeting that Clyde Watts and Revilo Oliver attended (Watts and Oliver ironically appeared before the hearings of the Warren Commission for completely unrelated reasons).

Remarkably, Milteer was an associate of two other Warren Commission witnesses, General Walker and Robert Surrey. Guy Banister and Kent Courtney—who had ties to the president's presumed assassin—as suggested in the first two chapters, attended the meeting with Joseph A. Milteer, who had foreknowledge of the president's assassination. The HSCA's failure to note Guy Banister's presence at the meeting, documented by the FBI, was a phenomenal mistake. Had they known about it, they might have undertaken a more diligent investigation of the Banister and Milteer evidence that, as we shall see, reveals the true nature of the far-right conspiracy in the death of President Kennedy.

The presence of Guy Banister, the former high-ranking FBI Special Agent in Charge, at the treasonous Congress of Freedom meeting may have been the reason the FBI never gave the Milteer and COF documents to the Warren Commission in a timely fashion to enable them to deliberate on them. The fact that Lee Harvey Oswald had contact with several anti-Castro Cubans who were FBI informers and associates of Guy Banister may have also been factors.

CHAPTER SEVEN

THE CONSTITUTION PARTY MEETING, INDIANAPOLIS, OCTOBER 1963

At the Indiana Convention is where they did the most talking about
knocking the president off.

— *William Somersett*

Joseph A. Milteer attended the Constitution Party meeting in Indianapolis, Indiana, on October 18–20, 1963, at the Marott Hotel (not "Marriott") where plans to kill President Kennedy were discussed. Somersett told the FBI that he believed that if he attended the Indianapolis meeting that it would solidify his position with Milteer and other leaders in the party. Lee McCloud of Atlanta drove with Milteer to the event and they shared Room 220 in the hotel. The plot to assassinate a large number of individuals which had been discussed at the Congress of Freedom had narrowed to talk of killing President Kennedy, just over a month after the *Dallas Times Herald* announced, on September 13, 1963, that Kennedy planned to visit Dallas in November.[548] (Shortly after that announcement, Lee Harvey Oswald left New Orleans for Mexico City—on either September 24 or 25—and afterwards relocated to Dallas.[549]) Somersett stated, "At the Indiana Convention is where they did the most talking about knocking the president off."[550]

Milteer unexpectedly paid a visit to Somersett's apartment in Miami on October 10, 1963, and showed him pamphlets he had prepared for the upcoming Constitution Party meeting. One urged ending the "the three K's"—the "Kennedy, Khrushchev, King Dictatorship." Milteer planned to take the pamphlets around the country to trusted individuals in the far right and encourage them to attend the Constitution Party meeting. He told Somersett the party was a cover for the hardcore underground. At the meeting, a board of directors was to be picked to direct an "underground army" in their respective areas. Milteer stated, "Next year there is to be a lot of killing and it may be necessary to go right into the State Department and place several traitors under citizen's arrest."[551]

Prior to the Constitution Party meeting, Milteer traveled to Chattanooga, Tennessee, and met with Jack Brown, who the Secret Service felt was a "dangerous man from the bombing standpoint."[552] (As noted in Chapter Five, Brown followed Martin Luther King, Jr., hoping to assassinate him.) Next, Milteer traveled to Louisville, Kentucky, then on to Provo and Salt Lake, Utah, to meet with Ezra Taft Benson, a Mormon.[553] Milteer had opened a bank account in Provo according to a June 2, 1962, letter found in his home.[554] He traveled to Denver to meet with Kenneth Goff, but missed him. Milteer made stops in Amarillo, Fort Worth, Grand Prairie, and Dallas, Texas. In Dallas, he "met a patriot who led a march on the Texas capitol in Austin" who planned to attend the Constitution Party meeting.[555] (Twenty people led by Booker T. Bonner of the Indignant White Citizens' Council led a march that began at the Stephen F. Austin Hotel in the Texas capitol on August 28, 1963. One marcher arrived with a placard stating, "Integration is communism." General Walker attended with an unidentified male in his thirties "to see what was going on." The Indignant White Citizens' Council was profiled by the FBI as a threat to the president on his trip to Dallas.[556]) The October Dallas visit was one of six documented visits Milteer made to the city between June 1963 and June 1964, including three before the assassination.[557] From Dallas, Milteer drove to Shreveport, Louisiana, and was successful in getting the editor of the *Shreveport Journal*, George Shannon, to announce the upcoming Constitution Party meeting in the newspaper.

Milteer drove his Volkswagen bus to the Indianapolis meeting adorned with signs promoting Strom Thurmond for president, reminiscent of Commander Rockwell's Hate Bus. Milteer spoke freely to the press, which rankled national spokesmen Curtis B. Dall, who was the designated party spokesman.[558] (Interestingly, the editor of the *Indianapolis Star* was M. Stanford Evans, son of Medford Evans, a close associate of General Walker, Guy Banister, and Kent Courtney.) Dall read a letter from the Louisiana Committee on Free Electors supporting the Constitution Party, signed by Senator Harold Montgomery, state chairman, and George W. Connor, Fourth District chairman in the state legislature.[559] (Guy Banister and Kent Courtney were very involved with the Free Elector movement, which will be discussed in detail in a later chapter.)

Milteer told Somersett that Millard Grubbs from Louisville, Kentucky, was a leader in the Constitution Party and attended the convention. Grubbs was a constitutional lawyer who headed an organization called "Citizens For Arrest of Traitors." Indiana State Chairman of the Constitution Party Arthur Blazey, who was present at the 1963 Congress of Freedom meeting, also attended. General Pedro del Valle was the main speaker.[560]

On the first evening of the Constitution Party meeting on October 18, 1963, approximately thirty individuals who were not satisfied with the Constitution Party met on the third floor, Room A, at the Marott. Milteer was one of them and suggested the formation of a "hardcore underground" to prevent a Communist takeover of the United States. Kenneth Goff from Colorado—who headed an organization known as "Soldiers of the Cross"—spoke against President Kennedy, as did Milteer at the same meeting, where Jack Brown and Stanley Popsisil were in attendance. Later on the first night of the meeting, Milteer, Somersett, Lee McCloud, and Earl Linder met in Room 222 of the Marott. They tried to prevent Atlanta, Georgia, Klan leader James Venable from speaking at the meeting and advocating Strom Thurmond for president. They felt a Klan endorsement would hurt a possible Thurmond bid for the presidency.[561]

At the meeting, Lee McCloud told Milteer that the U.S. government was spending $10,000 to protect a member of the integrationist group the Student Non-Violent Coordinating Committee (SNCC) in Atlanta. Martin Luther King, Jr. and Communist Party leader Gus Hall purportedly had visited the group. Milteer commented that he could kill the SNCC member by Tuesday, but that he would have to be certain of his identity first. (This is one example of why Willie Somersett called Milteer one of the most violent-minded men he had known—and another good reason the HSCA should have scrutinized the FBI documents at their disposal that reported his intent to murder.)

At 10:00 p.m. on the second night of the meeting, a woman from West Palm Beach, Florida, whose name was redacted in the FBI document, spoke against the Council for Foreign Relations and President Kennedy. Undoubtedly, the woman was Mary Davison, a leader of the Council for Statehood and the hardcore underground.[562]

History of the Constitution Party

Individuals who were well-known leaders of the national far right of the 1950s and 1960s had dominated the Constitution Party since its inception. Many were associated with Joseph A. Milteer and a number of those individuals, particularly General Pedro del Valle, are important in the assassination story.

The Constitution Party was founded in 1950. Robert Welch, R. Carter Pittman, and Ken Goff were contributing writers to its newspaper.[563] In 1952, the Constitution Party supported General Douglas MacArthur for president.[564] At the national meeting on August 28, 1956, the party drafted Virginia's T. Coleman Andrews and California's Thomas H. Werdel to run on their presidential ticket. At that time, the Constitution Party was organized in fifteen states.[565] Milteer was a Georgia delegate for T. Coleman Andrew's campaign and he was provided with pictures and platform sheets by Andrew's campaign organization.[566] Bonner Fellers and John U. Barr, who was a protégé of Leander Perez and served with Guy Banister on the New Orleans National Indignation Committee in 1961, were other notables involved with Andrew's campaign.[567]

The 1957 meeting of the Constitution Party was held in Fresno, California, and featured J. Bracken Lee, a former governor of Utah.[568] Mary Cain was the national vice chairman.[569] William Gale was elected the California state chairman of the party.[570] In 1960, the Constitution Party of Texas held a state convention. Tom Anderson, who was on the founding national council of the John Birch Society, was the featured speaker.[571] Pedro Del Valle, Olga Butterworth, and John C. Williams were in attendance.[572]

Curtis B. Dall was the chairman of the National Committee of the Constitution Party at the Washington meeting held on April 11–12, 1961. He announced that he wrote a letter of encouragement to General Walker after the "Military Muzzling" hearings in Washington, praising him because he had "drawn the line" for the American people.[573] (Walker had been censured by the Kennedy administration for stating in a speech that President Truman was "pink" or pro-Communist.) Benjamin Freedman, Revilo Oliver, Ken Goff, Pedro del Valle, and Billy James Hargis were among the speakers. Milteer attended and sold tape recordings of the speeches.[574] The Congress of Freedom was held in Washington on April 13–15, 1961, just after the Constitution Party meeting. The two organizations worked closely together and the dates were chosen to accommodate attendance at both meetings.[575]

In 1962, the Constitution Party was held in Dallas. A leader of the group, Edward Burgess of Houston, anticipated that General Walker would attend but it's not known if he did.[576] Dan Smoot contributed money to the Constitution Party, stating that the party's thirteen-point platform was "the only existing political platform to [his] knowledge that makes sense."[577] Billy James Hargis was the National Chaplain of the Constitution Party in 1962.[578]

In 1964, the Constitution Party met on July 23–25 in Houston, Texas, and Milteer planned to attend.[579] Throughout the 1960s and early 1970s, Milteer and the same extremist associates from the earlier years dominated the Constitution Party.[580]

Milteer (right) is pictured in the 1971 *Constitution–News Review* on July 31, 1971, in the only known photo of Milteer outside of the law enforcement files. Source: Mary Cain Papers, Mississippi Department of Archives and History

On October 21–23, 1971, the Constitution Party meeting was held in Springfield, Illinois. Milteer was the National Chairman of the National Association of Constitution and Affiliated Parties and Groups. Milteer was the "man in charge" and master of ceremonies of the meeting.[581] Congressman John Rarick, a protégé of Leander Perez who hailed from St. Francisville, Louisiana, was a guest speaker. (Rarick was a judge in Clinton, Louisiana, where Lee Harvey Oswald was seen in a voter registration line organized by the Congress of Racial Equality in 1963. Rarick admitted seeing Oswald and that remarkable event will be detailed in Chapter Twenty-one.[582]) Notables at the 1971 party meeting included Revilo Oliver, Dan Smoot, Curtis Dall, General del Valle, Dean Manion, and Tom Anderson.[583] Groups invited to attend were Americans for America, the Christian Nationalist Crusade, Committee of the States, the Congress of Freedom (headed by Brigadier General Richard B. Moran), Defenders of the American Constitution Inc. (headed by General Pedro del Valle), Liberty Lobby (headed by Colonel Curtis B. Dall), and the Soldiers of the Cross (headed by Kenneth Goff).[584] The fact that he was overseeing a meeting of so many important people and organizations demonstrates that Milteer held a significant position among the national radical right in the 1950s, '60s and '70s.

Wally and Olga Butterworth

Herbert Wallace "Wally" Butterworth and his sister Olga attended the 1963 Constitution Party meeting and discussed—in the presence of William Somersett—the feasibility of assassinating President Kennedy. According to Somersett, they did not dwell on specifics but rather speculated on various methods and the need to accomplish it.[585] Milteer knew the two well. Olga Butterworth was secretary of the National Committee of the Constitution Party.

Arthur Blazey who attended the Congress of Freedom earlier in the year was the event planner.[586] (Olga may have been at the COF meeting. A letter which she sent to Milteer noted she planned to attend.[587]) Somersett heard Wally Butterworth "criticizing President Kennedy and the way he was operating the government." According to Somersett, Wally encouraged everyone to gather guns, and advocated killing the president. Olga, who lived in Wallingford, Pennsylvania, stated at the meeting she "felt like doing what the Buddhists do and getting a bomb and tying it to herself for the purpose of blowing herself up and everyone around her and killing President Kennedy." Wally was a subject of interest to the Secret Service and they were fully aware of his call for the killing of the president before the assassination. The Secret Service noted that Wally, "Makes up a lot of hate propaganda and tapes urging the people to arm themselves and kill the president and take over the government."[588]

Wally Butterworth was a disc jockey and in 1950, and traveled the country playing rare recordings featuring the voices of Caruso, Melba, and Tetrazzini from his extensive record collection to packed audiences, according to an article in *Newsweek* magazine.[589, 590] Earlier in his life, he had tried a career as an opera singer. When his career in television declined, he blamed it on the Jews, whom he claimed dominated the industry. In 1961, he published the *Fiery Cross* for Robert Shelton's Klan.[591] Butterworth was the public relations director for Shelton's United Klans of America in 1962.[592] Butterworth once wrote for Conde McGinley's magazine *Common Sense* and credited McGinley for teaching him everything he knew about the "Jew-Communist conspiracy." In 1962, he moved into the Stone Mountain, Georgia, home of Klan leader James Venable, and he recorded albums consisting of racial and anti-Semitic propaganda promoted by the National States' Rights Party and *Common Sense* magazine.[593] One album paid a "glowing tribute to Mr. H. L. Hunt."[594] Butterworth was an officer in James Venable's Klan and was a cofounder, along with Venable, of the Defensive Legion of Registered Americans, Inc., a group that stood for states' rights and segregation.[595]

Wally Butterworth invited close Banister associate Leander Perez to speak at a Defensive Legion of Registered Americans, Inc. meeting on July 4, 1962, that was scheduled to coincide with an NAACP meeting. The meeting was advertised on radio, in the press, and in handbills.

Butterworth also once sponsored a speaking engagement by Mary Davison who, as has been noted, was principal in the broad-based assassination plots revealed at the Congress of Freedom. She, at one time, spent an entire week with Butterworth.[596] Obviously, Butterworth was close to the same group of national extremists as Milteer.[597]

Just prior to the Constitution Party meeting in late August and September 1963, Butterworth embarked on a three-week trip north from his home in Atlanta. On the trip, he visited close Milteer associate and assassination co-conspirator—as will be shown in the next chapter—General del Valle at his home in Annapolis, Maryland. In a letter, Butterworth discussed how Kennedy's executive orders were traitorous, and he praised General del Valle. He ominously wrote, "things are cooking with Pete [Pedro] del Valle & we'll soon advise you."[598] Butterworth's trip may have been related to the plot to kill the president.

Butterworth corresponded with Vic Knight of Key Records in Los Angeles, a John Birch Society member. Key Records recorded many of the propaganda records for members of the far right wing, including General Walker, Dan Smoot, Billy James Hargis, Fred Schwartz, Birch leaders Tom Anderson, Granville Knight, W. Cleon Skousen, and "former Communist" Karl Prussian. Knight reproduced the tape recording of Lee Harvey Oswald's debate with Ed Butler on a record for Billy James Hargis. Strangely, Hargis substituted Butler's voice in the debate with his own.[599] After the assassination, the Secret Service learned of a Butterworth recording of his views on the president's murder. In it, Butterworth blamed the murder on the "Jewish-Communist conspiracy." The Secret Service passed on a transcript of the recording to the Warren Commission.[600]

Following the assassination, Butterworth called for citizens to arm themselves for the Communist takeover of the U.S. and, in 1965, Butterworth offered for sale, for 250 dollars, a package consisting of a shotgun, a carbine, a repeating rifle, a hand gun, and a walkie talkie for families who wanted to join paramilitary "Shooting Clubs" set up at the county level. General del Valle and Admiral Crommelin approved the weapons assortment.[601]

Woody Kearns

W. J. "Woody" Kearns of St. Albans, West Virginia, was the Kanawa County Chairman of the West Virginia Constitution Party and was, perhaps, Milteer's best friend. Their wives were close friends, and they were frequent overnight guests at each other's homes.[602] Kearns was present with Milteer at the October 1963 Constitution Party. There were dozens of carbon copies of letters exchanged between Kearns and Milteer among the large number of letters found at Milteer's house after his death.

During the Constitution Party meeting, Kearns was in a hotel room with General Pedro del Valle where it is suggested that he learned about the plan to assassinate the president that culminated in the Dallas murder. (That evidence, found in a cryptic letter from Kearns to del Valle, will be presented in the next chapter.)

Milteer and Kearns often wrote cryptically or with caution to each other. For example, in one note on July 11, 1964, Milteer wrote, "The Col. in W. Va. will contact you possibly the 26th and or 27th. His phone is monitored & put on tape. If you wish to call him talk cryptic that will be all right. He thinks we should work out on our own key words for further thoughts for future use & do it by personal contact. He is reluctant to do anything pertaining to our field of interest over the phone until we get a code into operation."[603] In another letter, Milteer advised Kearns, "As time unfolds you will also learn many things that just now you do not present them. And it may come to a complete surprise to you. I sincerely hope such does not happen, but as from one friend to another, keep your eyes and ears open and your mouth shut. One can learn much in this manner."[604]

In another example of the cryptic nature of their correspondence, Kearns wrote to Milteer in 1970 and stated that Roy Harris, Dr. Snook, Dr. Hughes, Gale, and Newby are "Key Men." Kearns discussed operating at a low level and of not taking any definite position until he met with "Bill." He stated, "I believe Frank C. is doing some hard thinking. He is a shrewd politician and knows which side of his bread is buttered." ("Frank C." may be a reference to Frank Capell, a close associate of Pedro del Valle. Capell and del Valle exchanged ominous-sounding letters and had a meeting prior to the assassination, as we shall see in the next chapter.)[605]

Kearns, like Milteer, was armed to the hilt and inclined to violence. Kearns, in many letters with Milteer, discussed ways to machine and alter weapons.[606] In a 1967 letter, Kearns boasted about a weapon he invented that he called the "Home Guard" that would "scare the hell out of the Internal Enemy." He stated there was a large reserve of weapons in hiding, sufficient to carry on a civil war, known only to those involved. Kearns mentioned General del Valle's *Alert* newsletter and sent a copy to Milteer.[607] Del Valle's *Alert* warned the far right about events taking place that might signal a Communist takeover and the need for action. In one letter, Kearns wrote Milteer "Nothing slow about you I must say. Thanks for carrying out the mission. This is one mode that will stump the enemy."[608]

William Gale and Wesley Swift

Upon returning to Miami from the Constitution Party meeting, Willie Somersett reported on the activities of Californians Colonel William Potter Gale, U.S. Army retired, and his colleague Dr. Wesley A. Swift, to the Miami Intelligence Unit. He did not explicitly say that either man was at the party meeting but he suggested it. Gale had been a significant force in he Constitution Party since at least 1956—Milteer mentioned Swift often in conversation with Somersett. Milteer stated that Swift was a great man and that "he had already predicted that Kennedy would be killed, before he got out of office."[609, 610] Somersett learned at the Constitution Party meeting that Swift and Gale were planning to visit Florida in an attempt to "stir up people down here, probably on the lower east coast." Somersett also reported from the meeting that Colonel Gale and Wesley Swift were going to start a "Hate Campaign" soon on the east coast.[611, 612]

In the documents reviewed by the author, Somersett did not say that Gale or Swift were involved in the discussion about assassinating President Kennedy that took place at the meeting. Nonetheless, the FBI set out to establish the whereabouts of Gale and Swift after the assassination and reportedly determined that the two men were at their homes during the murder.[613, 614] Gale was interviewed by the FBI on November 16, 1963, and—among other things—stated oddly that he had access to secret and confidential documents of the hearings of the House Committee on Un-American Activities. Milteer was close to Gale; he subscribed to Gale's *Posse Comitatus* newsletter, and two addresses for Gale were found in Milteer's home after his death.[615]

The FBI learned that, months prior to the October 1963 Constitution Party meeting, Gale and Swift were a part of a broad-based assassination plot that—in all likelihood—was the same as the one that was divulged at the Congress of Freedom meeting in April 1963. It's not known if Swift or Gale attended the COF meeting. In April and June 1963, a member of the Gale-Swift group, George Harding, Jr., told the FBI of a plan by their group to assassinate 300 public officials in high positions in government and industry. Harding's cousin, James Shoup from Lancaster, California—who was a student minister in the church and a leader in the group—had introduced Harding to Swift's church. Eight men were to be assigned to each of the 300 targets, and the assassinations were to be carried out simultaneously, if possible. Harding was told that he might be tapped as one of the assassins and was warned that if he did any talking, his ex-wife and children would be harmed. Harding attended one more meeting and told the group he had obtained a job out of town and had to move—an obvious ploy to dissociate himself from the group. He relocated to Reno, Nevada, and was there during the assassination.

The FBI furnished Harding's information of the Gale/Swift plot to the Warren Commission, although it did not appear in the twenty-six Commission volumes and was not made readily available to the public. The timing of the FBI investigation into Gale's group, regarding their musing on assassinations in April–May 1963, corresponds with the April date of the 1963 COF meeting in New Orleans and strongly suggests the California plot and the COF plot to assassinate a large number of individuals were one and the same.[616] The names of those involved with assassination plots were furnished to the Los Angeles FBI, but were redacted in the FBI documents and are known only to the FBI. However, it's known that the FBI was interested in Gale just ten days before the assassination.

On November 12, 1963, the Miami FBI learned that Gale had been working underground and though his location was unknown, reports speculated that he was in California and in the South.[617] During the subsequent decades, Gale and his group were involved in various acts of violence, killing, and arrests that were chronicled in his biography *Committee of the States*.[618]

The FBI learned also learned from George Harding, Jr. that, according to separate FBI documents, on April 9, 1963—three days after the Congress of Freedom meeting in New Orleans—Swift was involved in the same plot as Gale's group. Additionally, it was noted that members of sixteen different groups "planned to kill 300 persons who ran the government, industry, social and religious life, in a mass assassination; that there were people ready to take over the running of the country armed and ready to enforce the change in leadership."[619] Again, on June 5, 1963, the FBI learned from an informant that Swift was contemplating violence against the Jews in conjunction with Gale.[620]

Willie Somersett and Joseph Milteer were aware that Swift had prophesized the assassination of President Kennedy in 1960. Moreover, members of Swift's church notified the FBI on several occasions that Swift stated in 1960 that Kennedy would not finish his term in office. On the first Sunday of January 1963, when he gave his annual prophecy, Swift proclaimed that something would happen to President Kennedy. An informant told the FBI that he heard Swift say on a tape recording six weeks before the assassination "Kennedy was entering a critical period." In yet another account, a church attendee told the FBI that based on astrology Swift told the congregation that "something drastic would happen to the president of the U.S."[621]

Somersett believed the conspiracy to kill President Kennedy probably had its origins in California—suggesting Gale's and Swift's possible involvement—as well as New Orleans and Miami.[622] Milteer told Somersett, "There is a good underground in Texas and California." Somersett gathered from Milteer that, "this conspiracy originated in New Orleans, probably some in Miami, and different parts of the country, probably in California . . . I am pretty sure California had a lot to do with it, because he mentioned Dr. Swift very often, what a great man he was and that he'd [the president] already be killed before he got out of office."[623]

The HSCA investigation of the Martin Luther King, Jr. murder revealed that Gale was at a meeting in Birmingham, Alabama, on September 14, 1963, which is likely the same meeting attended by Joseph Milteer as reported by Willie Somersett, noted in Chapter Three. Also at the meeting were Klan Leader Robert Shelton and his associate Melvin Sexton (who bears a strong resemblance to the man standing next to Milteer in Dealey Plaza).[624]

According to Somersett, Milteer returned to his home in Valdosta, Georgia, on December 31, 1963, after making a trip to the West Coast where he was in contact with Wesley Swift in the vicinity of Los Angeles. Milteer recounted to Somersett that the meeting was very profitable and "plans are being set for real action in 1964." During his trip to and from the West Coast, Milteer traveled through several cities in Texas, including Dallas and Houston. On his return trip, he made stops in Jackson, Mississippi, and Montgomery, Alabama. Milteer had planned a future meeting to be held somewhere in the central U.S., apparently for the underground.[625] Unknown to the FBI or HSCA, a receipt from a Dallas auto repair shop, dated December 27, 1963, was found in Milteer's home after his death.[626] He likely made the stop on his way to visit Swift in California. As previously noted, Milteer is known to have made six trips to Dallas between June 1963 and June 1964.

A receipt for maintenance service at a Dallas auto repair, dated December 27, 1963, documents Milteer's fifth trip to the city since June 1963. The receipt was found in Milteer's home after his death and was apparently overlooked by HSCA investigators. Source: Brooks County Probate Court

On July 7, 1965, and again on February 5, 1969, FBI Director J. Edgar Hoover notified the Secret Service (in accordance with their presidential protection agreement) that Swift represented a threat to the president based on subversive, ultra-racist and Fascist criteria and on a propensity toward violence.

Given their close ties to Joseph Milteer and their involvement in assassination planning, the lives and times of Gale and Swift merit further scrutiny. Most of what follows on Swift and Gale was obtained through the FBI files—not part of the HSCA investigation—on the two, obtained through the Freedom of Information Act.

According to those files, Reverend Wesley Swift specialized in prophecy: in 1948, he told a group that the Russians were planning to bomb Los Angeles; he predicted a Russian invasion and a Negro uprising; in 1949, Swift created his theory of British Israelism and, in 1950, he organized a group of gun-owning sportsmen to fight against an impending Communist uprising. He attended one of the earliest Congress of Freedom meetings in San Francisco and, in 1956, Swift traveled to Washington, D.C., to meet with Senators Eastland, McCarthy, and Jenner. (Guy Banister worked with Senator Eastland's committee, also in 1956.) The FBI suspected Swift was receiving intelligence from an undisclosed U.S. Army Intelligence Officer in Washington, D.C. Swift reportedly was bequeathed an annual annuity from automaker and anti-Semite Henry Ford, and was included in his will upon his death. (Ford wrote the conspiratorial and anti-Semitic, widely circulated work *The International Jew*. Ford included the book *The Protocols of the Learned Elders of Zion*—a discredited book that promoted a Jewish conspiracy—in the glove compartments of his new cars.)

Swift was a member of the White Citizens' Council; in 1958, he spoke before the Citizens' Council of Tulsa, Oklahoma. In 1958, the FBI interviewed Swift in regards to bombings in the South and learned that Swift had organized a "Black Shirt fully armed Fascist-like organization" that he intended to merge with Gerald L. K. Smith's America First Party. In August 1960, Swift met with Senator Ellender, of Louisiana, and other southern senators in Washington D.C.; that same year, he also met with Commander George Lincoln Rockwell in Virginia (the FBI suspected that Swift was funding Rockwell's operation). In September 1962, Swift was initiated into the Jacksonville, Florida, KKK. Swift spoke at many meetings of the National States' Rights Party and advocated the impeachment of President Kennedy.[627] In 1963, Swift was second in command and Klud (chaplain) of a Klan organization known as Christian Knights of the Invisible Empire, in Lancaster, California, whose members wore hoods and robes.[628] In June 1964, Lincoln Rockwell met with Swift and discussed a merger of the Christian Defense League with the American Nazi Party. Milteer listened to tapes of Swift's sermons and once stated he would gladly join Swift's church if one were convenient.[629] Swift's extremist affiliations are very similar to those of Guy Banister and Joseph Milteer.

Swift was a former Ku Klux Klan rifle instructor—he was said to have had one of the largest gun collections in California and maintained a rifle range. Swift became the legal representative for Gerald L. K. Smith.[630]

Swift also had ties to Senator Joseph McCarthy's office in Washington. In 1951, Anna M. Rosenberg was appointed Assistant Secretary in charge of manpower to Secretary of Defense George C. Marshall. The move drew the ire of the radical right since she was Jewish, a long-time friend of President Roosevelt, and a proponent of the Truman Fair Deal. The far-right propaganda machine immediately started up and accused her of belonging to the Communist organization the John Reed Club in the 1930s. Swift proclaimed that Rosenberg "was not only a Jewess but an alien from Budapest with Socialistic ideas . . . with a well-known anti-Christian and pro-Communist record." Anna Rosenberg fought the charges and stated she was not *that* Anna Rosenberg of the John Reed Club, denying the accusations. Joining the fray was wealthy pro-Arab and renegade, renounced Jew, Benjamin Freedman, who had a secret plan to block Rosenberg's Senate nomination. Swift appeared in Washington and presented two memoranda to members of Congress in support of the Communist allegations against Rosenberg, both signed by Benjamin H. Freedman. Interestingly, Senator Richard Russell, who would later sit on the Warren Commission, was on the Senate Armed Services Committee in charge of the hearings. Freedman produced a witness, a "former Communist," to testify and affirm the allegations. During the hearings, it came out that Freedman recruited his witness through a well-known anti-Semite and former member of the German-American Bund, and that Senator McCarthy's office was involved in the scheme with Freedman and Swift. After probing the witness, the Senate committee learned that Freedman had admitted that his original written statement to the Committee was taken in the office of Congressman Rankin, an anti-Semite from Mississippi who was involved with Swift. Freedman also testi-fied and his convoluted and conflicting claims were thoroughly discredited and resulted in a total collapse of the case. During the hearings, Gerald L. K. Smith, who was in Washington with Swift, was seen circulating a copy of Freedman's original statement in the Senate office building. Swift declared that even if Rosenberg was not a Communist, the fact that she was a Jew should prohibit her from serving in the government. Senator Joseph McCarthy, who was eager to continue exposing the Communist menace, had initiated the hearings against Rosenberg.[631]

The Swift-Rosenberg case illustrates how members of the far right operated in con-junction with the witch hunts of McCarthy's committee and other similar inquisitorial bodies. "Former Communists" often testified in the congressional hearings against leftists and—we shall later see—Lee Harvey Oswald was destined to fill a similar role in the Ban-ister operation. Guy Banister and his associates Leander Perez, Kent Courtney, and Hubert Badeaux also contributed to similar congressional committees. The congressional inquisitors invariably relied upon the radical right to gather fodder for their investigations, as they did in the Rosenberg case.

Colonel William Potter Gale was a self-described "Army brat." His father fought with Teddy Roosevelt's Rough Riders at San Juan Hill. Gale, himself, joined the army in 1945 and was promoted to lieutenant colonel. Gale served on the staff of General Douglas MacArthur in World War II as an infantry officer and general staff corpsman trained in logistics, one of many former MacArthur military staffers involved with the Congress of Freedom or the Con-stitution Party.[632] Later, Gale served under generals Stratemeyer and Wedemeyer in Germany, who were also members of MacArthur's staff and close associates of General Pedro del Valle. (It should be recalled that generals Stratemeyer and Wedemeyer were involved in the COF in the 1950s.) Subsequently, Gale worked under General Bonner Fellers in Australia. Gale retired from the army in 1950, at age thirty-three, to become an Episcopal minister.

Gale was an advocate of the notorious anti-Semite Gerald L. K. Smith and a former bodyguard. He was an associate of retired Admiral John Crommelin who, as we shall see later, was involved in a similar broad-based assassination plot in his Alabama operation. In 1956— the same year he was introduced to Wesley Swift—Gale was the Constitution Party's write-in candidate for California governor. Gale and Swift were proponents of the Christian Identity movement in California—"identity" was a term coined by Gale—rooted in the belief that the identity of the true Chosen People of God was not the Jewish people, but rather Anglo-Saxons, and that Jesus was not a Jew.[633]

Gale was close to Milteer's colleague General Pedro del Valle as letters found in del Valle's papers attest. On December 1, 1977, apparently still preparing for a Communist takeover of America, Gale wrote del Valle and told him he had established a 100-acre national headquarters in the Sierra Nevada Mountains with a radio station with worldwide capabilities.[634]

Gale headed an organization formed in 1968 known as the Committee of the States; author Cheri Seymour wrote a biography of Gale by the same title.[635] Gale formed a group known as *Posse Comitatus* that believed no government agency above the county level had any authority, in which he took the roll of second in command to Swift.[636]

Gale claimed to have built the Constitution Party using his military mind and organizational skills, but he eventually parted ways with the Constitution Party and organized the Christian Defense League with Christian Identity minister S. J. Capt. Gale likened the CDL to the Anti-Defamation League (ADL) and NAACP, but as a white Christian advocacy group. Later, Richard G. Butler became the president of the CDL while Gale, Swift, and Reverend Bertrand Comparet served on its board. (In the 1970s, Butler formed the neo-Nazi group the Aryan Nation in Idaho.) The eastern regional director of the CDL was Admiral John Crommelin. Gale assigned a member of his group, Bill Fowler, to deliver the message of Christian Identity to the Glendale, California, American Nazi Party. (Fowler later moved into the Florida home of Oren Potito, with whom Joseph Milteer and General Walker were associated.)[637]

Gale also operated a Minutemen-type hardcore militia known as the California Rangers, formed in the 1960s, which recruited its members from the more militant members of his church, the Christian Defense League, and the Ku Klux Klan.[638, 639] Oren Potito was president of Swift's Church of Jesus Christ–Christian's "Eastern Conference" in St. Petersburg, Florida. Potito's church organized guerilla warfare units and Milteer was a member of Potito's American Rangers, a group which was part of Gale's militia.[640] Milteer often signed his letters "26," a reference to his Ranger or Minuteman militia-type involvement that identified members by number, rather than name, for anonymity. Of Potito, Milteer stated in a letter, "I wonder if Potito is an FBI agent? He cusses greatly at home. This, to me is not in keeping with the position he holds as a Minister." Milteer was strongly religious, often praising Jesus Christ and invoking scripture in his correspondence.[641]

Milteer often made cryptic references in his letters, at times referring to individuals by the cities they lived in. He referred to Gale as "Glendale," as well as del Valle by "Annapolis" and Admiral Crommelin as "Wetumpka" in his letters. "Phoenix" was not an obvious reference to any one person but may be a reference to Milteer's friends Art and Kay Westerman of Phoenix. It appears that these individuals were key members of the hardcore underground in 1966.[642] Kearns's notation of "the Florida man" seems a likely reference to Oren Potito. In correspondence between Kearns and Milteer in 1965, Kearns felt his calls were being monitored and suggested they develop a formal secret code system.[643]

In January 1964, the FBI learned that Gale was the founder of the group known as the Army of the American Kingdom of Evangelists, or AWAKE. Gale announced that there would be a group within AWAKE called the "Inner Den," which would be the most militant members of his Christian Knights of the Invisible Empire who would commit acts of violence.[644] Gale's group was aligned with General del Valle's Defenders of the American Constitution, Inc. and members were required to subscribe to his newsletter, *Task Force*. William Gale was described as friendly to both General Walker and to Commander George Lincoln Rockwell (Gale stayed at Walker's home in July 1963).[645, 646] Gale met with Rockwell on June 10, 1964, to discuss a merger of their two groups.[647]

General Walker and Colonel Gale

General Walker was in Mississippi during the integration crisis at Ole Miss in September of 1962 and was a guest of Governor Ross Barnett in the governor's mansion. Walker put out the clarion call for 10,000 patriots from every state to come to Oxford, Mississippi, to oppose President Kennedy's U.S. Marshal-enforced integration mandate to enroll the first black student ever, James Meredith, in the University of Mississippi (Ole Miss). Louisiana State Representative William Rainach, who advised Barnett in the governor's mansion during the crisis negotiations with President Kennedy, contacted his close friend William Gale and requested his presence at the University. Gale was supposed to meet with General Walker at Ole Miss, but was arrested carrying weapons before the meeting could take place. Rainach's close ties to Gale are reflected in the letters between the two men, which were found in Rainach's personal papers. Gale made numerous trips to Rainach's Homer, Louisiana, home and was often an overnight guest. (Homer is in northern Louisiana and was not far from the Mississippi home of Governor Barnett.)[648, 649] Rainach was also a close associate of Guy Banister as reflected in their correspondence.[650] It will be recalled that Guy Banister, Leander Perez, and Hubert Badeaux testified before the Rainach-led Louisiana Joint Legislature Committee on Subversion in Racial Unrest. The conclusion drawn from that hearing was that the integration movement was Communist-backed. Wesley Swift also planned to come to General Walker's aid at Ole Miss, and the FBI learned that Swift was in charge of a large group of armed Minutemen who were supposed to leave Los Angeles for Oxford, Mississippi, on about September 28, 1962, but it is not known if the delegation ever arrived at Ole Miss.[651]

Gale was close to Walker's former aide-de-camp, Major Archibald Roberts, U.S. Army, retired.[652] Roberts served in the army with Walker in Germany, and wrote his anti-Communist pro-blue program that eventually led to Walker's censure by the Kennedy administration. Roberts was the military liaison of Mary Davison's Council for Statehood that plotted the assassination of prominent figures in government and industry at the New Orleans Congress of Freedom meeting, as was discussed previously. The Miami FBI learned that Roberts was at a January 15, 1963, meeting of the Council for Statehood and, in a report, stated "It was learned that ARTHUR [sic] ROBERTS of the United States Army, stationed at Fort Collins, Colorado, is the person that sets up the military underground for this national organization. ROBERTS is reportedly a close friend of General EDWIN WALKER." According to Willie Somersett, the Council wanted as many military people as possible to join their organization "in order that they would have access to military arms and would be in a position to take over the government." They complained that the "United States is presently being taken over by President KENNEDY." Somersett noted that Roberts was supposed to attend another Council for Statehood meeting, but couldn't make it. An organizer from an undisclosed group from California attended the meeting.[653, 654]

Kenneth Goff

According to Willie Somersett, Milteer's friend, Kenneth Goff—an "ex-Communist" and minister—was critical of President Kennedy in his speech at the 1963 Constitution Party meeting. Somersett described Goff as "heading an organization fighting Kennedy and the Communists and the Jews, and the negroes [sic]." Goff accused the leadership of the Constitution Party of having sold out to the left wing. Milteer spoke next, urging people to back Strom Thurmond for president and calling for the formation of a hardcore underground to prevent the Communist takeover of the U.S.[655]

Goff was allegedly a member of the Communist Party from May 1936 to October 1939. In 1939, he voluntarily appeared before Congress's Dies Committee and gave 300 pages of testimony about his work in the Communist Party. He was a board member on the American Youth Congress, along with heavyweight boxing champion Gene Tunney. He eventually exposed the organization as a Communist front, causing its demise. Like other Communists, he operated under an alias, John Keats. (Similarly, Lee Harvey Oswald operated under the alias Alek Hidell.) After "leaving" the Communist Party he was instrumental in the removal of over 169 Communists from federal payrolls and authored a number of books.[656] In a signed affidavit, Goff claimed that, when he was with the Communist Party, they discussed how fluoridation was used in the water supply of Russian prison camps as a tranquilizer. Goff claimed that the Communists plotted to fluoridate U.S. water in order to induce a state of docility in the country to facilitate Communist takeover.[657] The members of the radical right gained fame and profit testifying before the Dies- and Joseph McCarthy-type Communist inquisitions against leftists. Like Goff, Lee Harvey Oswald had terrific credentials for a career as an "ex-Communist" witness. He would have been a tremendous witness against integrationists in both Congress's and the State of Louisiana's Communist-hunting committees that Guy Banister was involved with.

Kenneth Goff was a subject of FBI interest and they learned that he spoke to the National States' Rights Party on January 7, 1963. The FBI suspected that Goff was a member of the group Vigilantes for a Free America.[658] He wrote an article in Gerald Winrod's newsletter, *The Defender* and rallied against godless Communism and its one-world, "one-family of man" ideology.[659] After the assassination of President Kennedy, Goff was critical of Attorney General Robert Kennedy's failure to make every Communist register as an agent of a foreign government as suggested by the Nixon-McCarran bill. He argued that President Kennedy would have lived if Lee Harvey Oswald had been forced to register under the bill. Goff was also critical of Robert Kennedy for not outlawing the Fair Play for Cuba Committee and for Kennedy's actions in the integration crisis at the University of Mississippi in 1962. (General Walker was arrested on orders of Attorney General Robert Kennedy for leading an insurrection at the university.) Goff, as did many on the far right, referred to Jack Ruby as "Rubinstein" and implied he was an agent of the Kremlin. Goff once claimed that when he was a Communist he had known Ruby.[660] Goff argued that the Communists killed Kennedy in order to blame it on the right wing.[661] Many, including Presidents Truman and Eisenhower—who rightfully expressed skepticism of the authenticity of the claims of "former Communists" like Goff—considered Goff's claims suspicious. It's hard to believe Goff subscribed to Communism's embrace of all races and creeds before he became a fanatical racist and anti-Semite. Goff was described as "a notorious professional anti-Semite" and was an associate of Gerald L. K. Smith in 1946.

Goff is known to have spoken before a Boston chapter of the John Birch Society.[662] In 1963, Goff was on the board of Liberty Lobby with notables including General Stratemeyer, Billy James Hargis, and Tom Anderson.[663] Goff debated Communist Party leader Gus Hall on January 10, 1964.[664]

Goff was the leader of a hate group called Soldiers of the Cross, a para-military arm of his church, and hosted Revilo Oliver as speaker at his youth camp in 1963.[665] Cadets at the 1964 Soldiers of the Cross summer camp in Colorado wore air force-style uniforms and were schooled in Christianity and the menace of Communism; self-defense and rifle shooting were also taught.[666] Milteer attended the camp on August 17–24, 1964.[667] The theme of the meeting was "survival" and Milteer was displeased when a speaker told the crowd they were stupid to think they could accomplish their goals with rifles, side arms, and gasoline bombs.[668] Wally Butterworth was involved with taking applications for Soldiers of the Cross in 1966.[669]

In 1964, Goff's school enrolled fifteen students for a seven-month course in which students were given .30 caliber rifles and 100 rounds of ammunition, and were taught bomb-making and how to survive in the hills in the event of a Communist takeover. An informant told the FBI that Goff had an arsenal of weapons at his camp that "would knock your eyes out."[670] A concerned citizen contacted the FBI and told them that the true purpose Goff's operation was to destroy the government and the churches. He told the FBI that Goff taught his students that Jesus was not of Jewish parentage and that Eleanor Roosevelt and President Eisenhower were Communists. Goff distributed thousands of rounds of ammunition to his followers in an effort to save the government from imminent takeover by the Jews. Goff's school was reportedly underwritten by wealthy individuals.[671] Goff's camp operated similarly, in some ways, to the camp north of Lake Pontchartrain that David Ferrie and Lee Harvey Oswald allegedly were involved with.

An unnamed individual who knew Goff told the FBI that he felt Goff represented a great threat to the country. Following the assassination, Goff denounced the murdered President Kennedy as a traitor. The informant was convinced that if President Johnson were to come to Denver, that Goff was unstable enough to assassinate him.[672] On June 4, 1965, the FBI director notified the Secret Service and placed Goff under the presidential protection agreement as a threat to the life of President Johnson.[673]

Goff was a notoriously violent man. In 1965, he met an exotic dancer at a show when he was preaching in Los Angeles and proceeded to follow her around the country lavishing her with gifts. She later accompanied him on his speaking engagements in the U.S. and in Europe as his mistress. However, one day, the dancer discovered Goff drinking with a pregnant woman in a bar and they began to argue, at which point Goff took off his prosthetic leg and beat both women. (Goff claimed to have lost the leg when Communists tossed him under a train.) He had beaten his mistress on a prior occasion which had been documented in a police report. The dancer told police that Goff was in the practice of contacting "Skid Row" women—dope addicts—then befriending them and taking them to his Soldiers of the Cross school, where he would supply them with cough medicine containing large amounts of codeine. He then took them on speaking tours throughout the country.[674] A police complaint was filed by another woman, saying she feared for her life, who gave birth to a child by Goff.[675]

Goff was elected cochairman to a group of fifty people who formed an organization seeking a congressional investigation of Dr. Martin Luther King, Jr. General Edwin Walker was a planned speaker for the group's March 8, 1966, meeting in St. Louis.[676]

Goff was a friend of Robert DePugh and spoke before Minutemen Patriotic Party meetings across the country; in turn, DePugh visited Goff's Soldiers of the Cross camp. In 1966, DePugh made Goff a full partner in the Minutemen. When DePugh became incarcerated in late 1967 for violations of the Federal Firearms Act, Goff took a more active role in DePugh's group. FBI informant Jerry Brooks testified against DePugh in the trial and, after the trial Brooks, told the FBI on August 17, 1967, that he was forcibly taken by members of DePugh's Minutemen to Gale's Soldiers of the Cross camp near Evergreen, Colorado. At the camp, Brooks met Goff, who told him he could not leave the camp. Brooks learned that the Minutemen had a secret cabin—located at an elevation of 14,000 feet on a nearby mountain—that was supposed to serve as the future headquarters where DePugh would keep his files and lead the revolution. The files consisted of lists of known or suspected Communists whom he had marked for assassination. Brooks told the FBI that Roy Frankhouser was at the camp with Goff and DePugh. (It will be recalled that Nazi Dan Burros committed suicide at Frankhouser's home when it was revealed that he was a Jew, and that Burros's name and address appeared in Lee Harvey Oswald's notebook.) As talk of bombing and murder circulated in the camp, Brooks managed to escape to FBI protective custody.[677]

Goff spoke at DePugh's Patriotic Party convention on July 4, 1967, and stated that the CIA employed Oswald to kill President Kennedy, as well as using Jack Ruby to kill Oswald—a tale often circulated by the radical right.[678, 679] DePugh told the author that Goff died when a car hit him as he stepped off a curb in Chicago in 1972—a death which DePugh felt was suspicious.[680]

James Venable

Willie Somersett revealed James Venable was a speaker at the 1963 Constitution Party meeting. Venable was the Imperial Wizard of the National Knights of the Ku Klux Klan and shared office space with attorney J. B. Stoner of the National States' Rights Party (NSRP), across the street from the Fulton County Courthouse in Atlanta, Georgia.[681] Venable held a national meeting of the Dixie Klans, Knights of the Ku Klux Klan on January 12 and 13, 1963, at which he read a letter he had written to General Walker for a "job well done" for his part in the insurrection at the University of Mississippi.[682] Robert Shelton's United Klans of America split from Venable's National Knights in 1963. Venable defended J. B. Stoner and five others in the NSRP who had been indicted in the infamous 1958 Atlanta temple bombing.[683] (It's not known whether Venable was involved in the assassination plotting that took place at the meeting.)

Interviewed in the 1970s, an aged Venable told author Patsy Sims that Lee Harvey Oswald had approached him in his Atlanta law office before the assassination—an alleged meeting Sims had first heard about from another Klansman. Venable told her he was positive the man was Lee Harvey Oswald. Oswald allegedly stated he was going to Chicago and wanted the names of right-wing leaders there. Venable refused to provide Sims with the name of the Chicago-area Grand Dragon. Venable held annual Klan rallies on his Stone Mountain property and, in 1962, invited Leander Perez to speak.[684] At one time, Venable's family owned the entire mountain where the faces of the heroes of the confederacy, Robert E. Lee, Jefferson Davis, and Stonewall Jackson, were carved on and he had once served as the town's mayor.[685]

On October 23, 1963, after the Constitution Party meeting was over, an article titled "Constitutionalists Develop Split" appeared in the *Indianapolis Star*. The article quoted Curtis B. Dall, National Chairman of the Constitution Party, who stated that the representatives at the meeting supported Barry Goldwater for president. The article additionally noted that a move was made to kick Milteer out of the party for falsely claiming that he was the regional chairman for the State of Georgia and, in that position, favored Strom Thurmond's candidacy, contrary to the party position. Milteer became disillusioned with the Constitution Party and planned to form his own party that he called the Constitutional American Parties. His new group was to be a front for a hardcore underground, formed to engage in violence, as needed, in combating integration.[686] However, in 1964, he put aside his differences and was formally appointed chairman of the Constitution Party of Georgia by National Chairman Bert Ellis of Houston, Texas.[687]

When FBI SA Donald Adams questioned Milteer about his activities, five days after the assassination, Milteer admitted traveling to the National Convention of the Constitution Party with Lee McCloud of Atlanta, Georgia, and William Somersett of Miami, Florida. Milteer stated that Curtis B. Dall, former son-in-law of the late President Franklin D. Roosevelt, invited him to the meeting.[688] (Dall had married and divorced FDR's daughter before FDR assumed the presidency. He wrote a book claiming to know that "shadowy forces" exploited FDR. Dall was a member of the Christian Crusade National Advisory Board and was chairman of the Liberty Lobby Board of Policy.[689]) Milteer told the FBI agent that he was a non-dues-paying member of the party and also belonged to the White Citizens' Council and the Congress of Freedom. Milteer emphatically denied making threats to assassinate the president or ever hearing anyone make such threats.[690]

Conclusions

Thirty-five days before the assassination of President Kennedy, a consortium of the most violent-minded, far-right political extremists in America gathered at the Constitution Party meeting in Indianapolis on October 18, 1963, and there was talk of killing the president. The festive mood of similar past meetings was absent. Mary Davison attended and was a principal in the broad-based assassination plots at the Congress of Freedom meeting in April 1963, which were revealed to the FBI by Willie Somersett.

Kenneth Goff and Wesley Swift also were present at the Constitution Party meeting; two different informants told the FBI about Goff and Swift's involvement in similar plots. Swift and Goff headed Minutemen-related militias primed for insurrection. Swift had ties to Senator Joseph McCarthy's Communist witch hunts in the early 1950s and "prophesized" the death of President Kennedy. Kenneth Goff attended the meeting and was a professed "former Communist." Goff ran a militia camp in Colorado that taught students military maneuvers, bomb making, religion, and anti-Communism. His underground militia was prepared for insurrection against the government of the United States. It was not until after President Johnson assumed the presidency that the FBI identified Swift and Goff as dangers to the life of the president and notified the Secret Service of the threat. Jack Brown, whom the Secret Service felt was a dangerous man "from the bombing standpoint," was also in attendence at Indianapolis; Brown had tried to assassinate Martin Luther King, Jr. Wally Butterworth called for the murder of President Kennedy at the meeting. Also at the meeting, Joseph Milteer readily agreed to murder a black Morehouse College student involved in the integration movement.

If there existed any group of individuals in America with the motive, means, and opportunity to assassinate President Kennedy it was this one, and the FBI knew all about it—yet the Warren Commission heard not a word of it. The House Select Committee on Assassinations had at their disposal the FBI documents that served as the basis for this chapter, yet no mention of this murderous cabal appeared in their report or volumes of supporting evidence. Three weeks after the Constitution Party meeting, Joseph Milteer told Willie Somersett in a tape-recoded conversation that the president would be killed by a high-powered rifle that could be broken down, from an office building—and that someone would be picked right away to throw authorities off. In addition to Milteer's dead-on accurate prediction and his almost certain presence in Dealey Plaza at the time of the murder, evidence presented in the next chapter will further show that the threats against the president made at the Constitution Party meeting were directly related to the Dallas murder.

CHAPTER EIGHT

LIEUTENANT GENERAL PEDRO DEL VALLE AND THE
FORMER MILITARY MEN IN THE HARDCORE UNDERGROUND

The hand of God directed the bullet that killed President Kennedy.
— Pedro del Valle

Willie Somersett made it clear to the FBI that he learned at the Congress of Freedom meeting that former high-ranking members of the armed forces secretly belonged to the organization and headed up the broad-based assassination plots revealed at the meeting. Specifically, he stated that retired general Pedro del Valle was involved "in a big way."

Somersett told Miami Police Detective Lockhart Gracey, "the army officers are using their own strategy of training how things will be done. This is supposed to be headed and directed by military men from the top."[691] The Miami FBI learned from an informant, probably Somersett, that Davison's Florida group had acquired carbines and a target practice site for the purposes of "knocking off the 'eskimoes'," a code name for Jews.[692] Somersett also identified Major Arch Roberts, U.S. Army retired, as the individual "put out of the army and as another of the men heading up the military operation for Mary Davison. Roberts made a speech at a Daughters of the American Revolution meeting on April 19, 1962, supporting General Walker after he had been relieved of his command by the Kennedy administration. Afterward, the army reprimanded Roberts for making "improper remarks," and he was removed from active duty on April 19, 1962.[693] Mary Davison later sponsored Roberts at a speech in Palm Beach on May 1, 1963. Pamphlets handed out in advance noted the tile of his speech was "Why your soldier son serves under the command of a Soviet Communist." In his speech, he said he doubted that President Kennedy was the Supreme Commander, claiming instead that he was a Soviet Communist.[694]

Willie Somersett reported on a meeting of Mary Davison's Council for Statehood in Florida on January 15, 1963. The plot to assassinate a large number of individuals was discussed, including members of the Council on Foreign Relations—the same plot promoted at the Congress of Freedom meeting. At the Florida meeting it was revealed that General Pedro del Valle, Major Archibald Roberts, and generals Clyde Watts and Edwin Walker were part of the military underground that would lead the takeover of the U.S. government.[695][696] Del Valle was on the advisory committee of the Congress of Freedom.[697] Surprisingly, General Walker's name was redacted in the FBI documents in both Milteer's FBI file and the voluminous records on Milteer in the National Archives which were at the disposal of the HSCA. However, Walker's name was found un-redacted in documents received after a Freedom of Information Act request by the author on the Council for Statehood.[698] Also surprising is the fact that Somersett never mentioned Walker's name elsewhere.

Lieutenant General del Valle, U.S.M.C. retired, was the principal speaker at the 1963 Constitution Party meeting.[699] In his speech, del Valle stated that the invisible government managed both political parties and that the Council on Foreign Relations had chosen the top government officials for years. He stated that international bankers wanted the debt ceiling raised so they could reap further interest

> The source advised that according to statements by MARY DAVISON, THOMAS WILLIAMS and other unrecalled individuals, the membership within the COF contains high-ranking members of the Armed Forces, who secretly belong to the organization.
>
> some of the high-ranking officers include General EDWIN WALKER, retired, (first name unknown) ROBERTS, and General DE VALL (phonetic).

Willie Somersett named the members of the military high command that secretly belonged to the Congress of Freedom in this document from the FBI files on the Council for Statehood. It was the only time Walker was mentioned in the FBI's files. (General Walker's name was redacted in the same document found in Milteer's FBI file obtained under the Freedom of Information Act.) Source: FBI FOIA, Council for Statehood MM157-739

profits. Marxists controlled the U.N., he claimed.[700] Dr. Blazey described del Valle as "one who has not retired from the battle to serve this country from such enemies as the United Nations and current administration collaborators who want to strip our Republic of all defense arms and resources in order to subject our people to one-world tyranny." Del Valle was close to Joseph Milteer as archival correspondence between the two—taken from over a period of many years—shows. Milteer visited del Valle at his Annapolis home on at least

Pedro del Valle as a brigadier general (left). Right photo: General Clyde Watts (left) and General Walker (middle) secretly belonged to the Congress of Freedom and were two of the organization's military advisors. Robert Morris (right) was Walker's attorney and worked with Guy Banister in New Orleans in 1956 investigating the alleged Communist ties to the integration movement. Source: USMC public relations photo (left); Corbis (right)

one occasion.[701] Somersett learned from Milteer at the Congress of Freedom that del Valle received confidential information through his association with members of the different branches of the armed forces, "probably the War Department and the Pentagon."[702]

Pedro del Valle was born in San Juan, Puerto Rico, and boasted of his pure Castilian bloodline. Known to his friends as "Pete," Del Valle served thirty-three years in the U.S. Marines and fought in the Pacific theater under General Douglas MacArthur, who was named commander of the Army of the Far East by President Roosevelt. Like MacArthur, del Valle was critical of President Harry Truman, who appointed MacArthur commander of United Nations forces in Korea in 1951, but relieved him of his command when he urged opening up a second front in the war. The FBI learned that, in the period of 1950 to 1952, del Valle wrote a letter to President Truman calling him a traitor for the way he conducted the Korean War. Following the incident, attempts were made by the Marine Corps to bring del Valle off the retirement list and give him a general court martial.

Like Joseph Milteer and Guy Banister, del Valle had ties to the John Birch Society, Citizens' Council, National States' Rights Party, Congress of Freedom, and American Nazi Party. He was a part owner of the anti-Semitic tabloid *Common Sense*.[703] The FBI investigated del Valle and learned that he belonged to the White Citizens' Council of the District of Columbia, and that Nazi George Lincoln Rockwell had contacted him on two occasions. Del Valle served as Vice President of International Telephone and Telegraph in retirement, and was a candidate for the Maryland Republican gubernatorial nomination in 1958.

In the 1950s, del Valle claimed that the Joint Chiefs of Staff asked him to write a plan to help combat worldwide Communism. He claimed, suspiciously, that his plan was then handed over to the CIA, who offered him a job on orders of Anna Rosenberg. (It will be recalled that Wesley Swift was involved in a failed effort to block Rosenberg's appointment as an assistant to General Marshall, claiming she was a Communist.) Del Valle further claimed the CIA set up a meeting with him, believing that he was at odds with General MacArthur (although he wasn't), and wanted to send him to Tokyo to "pull the rug out from under MacArthur." Del Valle refused—he admired the defiant MacArthur and wanted no part of undermining him. He implied that Anna Rosenberg, a Communist, set up the whole affair to discredit MacArthur.

In 1954, del Valle spoke at a meeting and stated that miscegenation was the aim of the enemy, an "invisible" world organization.[704] In 1955, del Valle began publishing the monthly bulletin *Task Force*, an openly anti-Semitic, four-page newsletter of his organization The Defenders of the American Constitution. Del Valle also periodically printed another brief newsletter, *Alert* that would notify readers of any impending Communist takeover.[705]

In 1959, Robert Welch of the John Birch Society wrote to del Valle. Although Welch disagreed with del Valle's harshest generalizations about the Jews, Welch more diplomatically stated, "too large a percentage of Jews are Communists, and too large a percentage of Communists are Jews."[706] Del Valle attended a meeting of the JBS with Welch in 1959, and recommended a lawyer who would be willing to head up a movement to impeach Earl Warren, a favorite JBS aim.[707] Del Valle served on Liberty Lobby's Board of Policy in 1962, alongside other important figures in this work, including Billy James Hargis, Tom Anderson, General Stratemeyer, Curtis Dall, Mary Cain, and Kenneth Goff.[708]

Seeds of Conspiracy, 1961

It was not long after President Kennedy assumed office in 1961 that the radical right expressed alarm at his policies and began plotting a plan of action. On September 13, 1961, del Valle wrote to Robert Welch of the John Birch Society and stated, "The time has come for action, Treason sits enthroned in the seats of Power, and treason will soon land us in the Red One Worlder's Paradise unless we take steps to prevent it, and do it now and with decisiveness." Del Valle urged the creation of an armed resistance force.[709] Nationally syndicated columnist Drew Pearson discovered information in 1961 that the radical right bitterly disdained the president and were planning action. His November 21, 1961, column warned of a "movement inside the armed forces and reservists not unlike in the French army which tried to topple President de Gaulle." Pearson noted that del Valle "has already come close to urging armed insurrection" and was threatening armed resistance if the traitors were not voted out. Pearson cited Arch Roberts and General Walker as troublemakers and noted that Hilaire du Berrier, a Kent Courtney and Walker associate, had supported the French Army's insurrection against President de Gaulle. Pearson stated that Senator Strom Thurmond had documents smuggled to him including "military plans of the highest magnitude." Some of the documents were traced to General Arthur Trudeau, the army's research chief, who was about to retire, with close ties to Colonel Philip J. Corso, a purveyor of disinformation regarding the Kennedy assassination—as will be discussed later.[710]

According to an informant in the National States' Rights Party, del Valle wrote the group a letter in 1961 stating, "when a free people find their elected servants following a destructive course of action regarding the Constitution, the people must take effective action to restore same by taking the matter into their own hands and forcing the traitors out of power."[711]

The FBI reported that in del Valle's *Alert* No. 5, dated August 9, 1963, he stated that there was a one-world international plot to take over the U.S. and make it a province of the U.N. Del Valle once again urged the formation of powerful armed resistance groups.[712] An informant told the FBI that del Valle, sometime before the assassination of President Kennedy, paid a visit to two individuals involved in right-wing activities in the New Jersey area for the purpose of forming an "army" of armed citizens numbering 500,000 which could save the country. Del Valle contended that even if Goldwater won the 1964 Presidential election, Kennedy, while still in office, would be blackmailed into surrendering the country to the Soviet Union.[713]

In 1964, an informant and former member of the armed forces was invited to a luncheon meeting in Washington by a man whose name was concealed by the FBI but who was described as a scholar, author, and authority on the Panama Canal. Del Valle and two other unnamed men were present. During the luncheon the group displayed extreme right-wing attitudes, were anti-Semitic, and sympathetic to the John Birch Society. They insinuated that Presidents Eisenhower and Kennedy were Communists. Del Valle stated that there was a need to establish contact with responsible military commanders, so "when the time comes" they would act correctly. The group expressed their admiration for Major General Edwin Walker, while condemning Alabama governor George Wallace for backing down and allowing President Kennedy's forced integration of the University of Alabama. The group also spoke with approval of the American Nazi Party and its leader George Lincoln Rockwell. Remarking on the Kennedy assassination, del Valle stated, "The hand of God directed the bullet that killed President Kennedy."

After the meeting, del Valle gave the informant a large number of reprinted journal articles, which included excerpts from the *Congressional Record*, the *Protocols of the Learned Elders of Zion*, *The Rockwell Report* of the American Nazi Party, *The Paul Revere Associated Yeoman's*, *P.R.A.Y.*, and *Roosevelt's Communist Manifesto*. A Christian Crusade pamphlet praising Francisco Franco, with a preface from General Willoughby, was included as well—in addition to a two-page typed letter that spelled out del Valle's strategy. He stated that the Patriots were at war with the Communists, the Council on Foreign Relations, and the U.N., but the Patriots had an advantage over the Communists since they believed in an afterlife and were not afraid of dying for the cause. He also believed that prisoners of war should be taken and interrogated. The informant recounted that del Valle's newsletter, *Task Force*, carried the "true word." One person at the meeting said that when the time came, the man to watch for was General del Valle—and he nodded in agreement.

In *Alert* No. 11, dated January 30, 1964, del Valle claimed that *Life* magazine was interviewing members of the far right and planning an attack on anti-Communists. The attack, he stated, was part of a 1960, Moscow-directed mandate to liquidate the opposition. Del Valle claimed that the most vicious aims of the planned *Life* article would be an attempt to blame the assassination of President Kennedy on the right. Del Valle contended that, had Oswald successfully escaped law enforcement, the assassination would have been pinned on the far right.[714]

The Correspondence of General Pedro del Valle: A Chronicle of Conspiracy

Incredibly, in the 1970s, an archivist from the University of Oregon set out to obtain the personal papers and correspondence of leading right-wing figures and was successful in obtaining Pedro del Valle's personal papers, among others. The letters in the papers—reproduced in part here—with additional evidence that will be presented later, reveal the genesis and overall organizational structure of the conspiracy that led to the death of President Kennedy. The letters revealed here, for the first time, are summarized or reproduced, below.

On June 18, 1962, del Valle wrote a letter, responding to General Walker on the subject of "insurgency." Walker and General del Valle always referred to each other by their formal active army titles; Lieutenant General del Valle and Major General Walker. Both made religious references in their letters. Walker had written a widely circulated pamphlet entitled "What Does Counterinsurgency Mean," which characterized the "Patriots" like Walker as the insurgency and the military under President Kennedy as the counterinsurgency. Del Valle was familiar with the pamphlet from another source and he was impressed, ordering additional copies. The remainder of the letter is reproduced below and is the first piece of evidence of a concerted effort of a group of disaffected radical right-wing former military men to consider acts of violence.[715] Because of its tremendous importance and for authenticity, the author

I hope you will find time to read this letter and the enclosures. We have a formula, a plan of action, the very last hope before we resort to violence. It is therefore of the utmost importance that you, and several other retired officers who are informed, keep in touch, for the time is exceedingly short. I am sending copies to Stratemeyer, Wedemeyer, Bonner Fellers, General McArthur, and various and sundry other flag and general officers whom I absolutely trust. They, too, will be alerted to keep in touch, and some day we might even hold a conference to map out our possible future actions.
With God's help we can and must win.

Sincerely,

P. A. del Valle,
Lieut. General U.S.M.C. (Ret)
President, D.A.C.

Source: Pedro del Valle Papers, Special Collections, University of Oregon Library

chose to include the pertinent part of the letter below rather than transcribe it.[716])

Not long before del Valle wrote the letter, Walker was publicly warning his followers about the threat the Kennedy administration posed to the country. Walker gave a speech on May 3, 1962, before the Dallas National Indignation Convention and alleged that President Kennedy had issued orders to the military reserve in every state that they were to receive counterinsurgency training "to put down opposition in any area—social, political, economic—to administration policy." Walker added that the counterinsurgency plan was part of a plot to put U.S. forces under U.N. command.[717] In another statement that spring, Walker said, "There is no doubt that in the present situation we are in dire peril, with grave threats to life and property." Walker then alluded to the advantages of an underground resistance movement and cited the effectiveness of the underground that fought Communism in Europe.[718] Del Valle and Walker were clearly on the same page in their belief that the Kennedy administration posed a dire threat to the nation.

General Walker replied to del Valle's letter on June 21, 1962—he had already been in touch with other retired far-right high-ranking military men.[719] Walker told del Valle that there was an urgent need for a "strategy conference," and wrote that General Wood would definitely attend, but aging generals Stratemeyer and Wedemeyer would not attend due to health problems. Walker proposed that the meeting take place in a secluded area of Dallas that he would arrange, and asked for del Valle's consideration of the matter. The only public statement to be made about the meeting, Walker wrote, was to say that it was for the purpose of "the training of military men serving our armed forces under the U.N." The bizarre statement was meant to put the military on alert that he was wise to the purported plot of President Kennedy to place the U.S. military under the U.N., a common story being repeated by the far right. Walker also mentioned in the letter that he had recently been in touch with Senator Strom Thurmond. On January 18, 1963, General Walker wrote General Robert E. Wood and thanked him for appearing with him in his support at a conference attended by Senator John Tower. Walker posed this ominous question to Wood: "Is it too late and what can be done?"[720]

On June 25, 1962, del Valle wrote Walker and stated, "Regarding the strategy conference, it is very important that you and I exchange ideas as to whom we can rely upon," and he requested a list of trusted individuals from Walker. Del Valle proposed Wedemeyer, Willoughby, MacArthur, Vice Admiral Sharp (U.S. Navy retired), Captain Miles Duval (U.S. Navy retired), and Rear Admiral Stevenson (whom Walker had met before at lunch), as men who could be relied on as shown below.

On September 15, 1962, del Valle wrote to conservative Texas congressman Dale Alford and complained that Adam Yarmolinsky, an aide to Kennedy's secretary of defense, introduced seventy-five new Jewish appointees into the "Kennedy ménage."[721] Yarmolinsky was a target of smears from del Valle's friend Frank Capell, a print propagandist for the far right.[722]

> Wedemeyer I know personally and believe he is sound. Same goes for Willoughby. Of course MacArthur. Of the Navy I am certain only of Vice Admiral Sharp, USN(Ret), but he is old and cannot get away from tending a very sick wife. Then there is Capt. Miles DuVal, USN(Ret) in whom I have perfect confidence, and, of course Rear Admiral (M.C) Stevenson of Virginia, whom you met at lunch. I regret to say I cannot mention many marines, but I believe Major General Robert Blake USMC(Ret) of San Francisco, Calif. is sufficiently informed to be of some help. If we could get MacArthur it would solve a lot of problems. I was under his command only a short time during World War II, when the 1st Marine Division went to Australia after the Guadalcanal business. I was then a brigadier,

Source: Pedro del Valle Papers, Special Collections, University of Oregon Library

On September 20, 1962, Walker wrote a letter to del Valle and explained he was supposed to hear from Admiral Crommelin, but had not, suggesting that Walker and del Valle were expecting to attend a meeting planned by Crommelin. (Crommelin, as will be detailed later, was close to a number of individuals associated with Milteer and the hardcore underground.) Walker proposed that all senior officers "in this cause"—a number he put at between ten and twenty—meet in Tennessee or Texas for no fewer than four days. He proposed a press release stating the group was considering service under the U.N. as he had before in a prior letter to del Valle. Walker preferred that the conference last a week and include "top cause civilians" for a half day to brief them "first and further on their beliefs and capability." In the letter, Walker said that he wrote to General MacArthur and asked him to attend the meeting. According to Walker, MacArthur replied, "The issue would have to be left to younger people than he." Walker remarked that he was sure that he could cover all expenses for those attending the proposed meeting, except perhaps travel expenses, though he did not mention where the money would come from. (Walker was unemployed, which suggests he had significant financial backing behind him.)

On September 22, 1962, del Valle wrote to Walker and stated he had not heard from Admiral Crommelin and had expected to receive the names and pictures "of all our enemies within" from him.[723] (It will be recalled from the Chapter Six that Somersett learned at the Congress of Freedom meeting that the "military high command" had planned to obtain photographs and background information on possible targets for assassination.) The del Valle letter indicates the process of obtaining the information on the enemies began more than six months beforehand. A likely source of the names and pictures was del Valle's friend Frank Capell, who claimed to have compiled the names of a million U.S. Communists. In his book *Treason is the Reason*, Capell published a short biography of hundreds of alleged U.S. Communists, at times accompanied by their pictures.[724] (According to an investigator for Jim Garrison, Guy Banister had a copy of Capell's *Herald of Freedom* in what remained of his files.)[725] Del Valle told Walker the meeting of the former military men, which had been proposed previously, would have to be postponed because of his work, family matters, and a planned trip to Spain. Del Valle also told Walker that World War III was on the horizon. Del Valle cited the purported jailing of forty anti-Jewish patriots by President Roosevelt in World

War II in telling Walker that they might meet the same fate and "we shall all land in jail." He stated that Kennedy's disarmament policy was a "piece of treason." Del Valle closed the letter by saying that Jackman would send Walker any names he might wish.[726] (It will be recalled that Theodore "Ted" Jackman was a violent associate of Joseph Milteer and Somersett stated that Jackman had been involved with the actual shooting of President Kennedy.) Jackman was at the April 1963 Congress of Freedom and was in the "high command" of the hardcore underground. At the meeting, he advocated violence and armed resistance. Milteer wrote a letter to Jackman requesting dynamite or TNT, as was noted in Chapter Five.[727]

While del Valle attended to his personal business in September 1962, with the meeting of the retired military officers postponed, General Walker traveled to Mississippi to aid Governor Barnett in his fight against President Kennedy's forced integration of the University of Mississippi. Walker put out the call for 10,000 people from every state to join him at Ole Miss. On the evening of September 30, 1962, Walker led the riot that left two dead and dozens of U.S. Marshals injured. He was arrested and sent to the federal mental hospital at Springfield, Missouri, on the orders of Attorney General Robert Kennedy. Del Valle's letter to Walker on September 22, 1962, warning him that "we shall all land in jail" proved prophetic. Walker was in the national spotlight for the second time for his open defiance of the president. (The first time was when he was pictured on the cover of *Newsweek* magazine in December 1961 after the Kennedy administration relieved him of his command for insinuating that President Truman was pro-Communist.) General Clyde Watts, secretary for del Valle's Defenders of the American Constitution, and a long-time friend and attorney for Walker, worked for Walker's release from prison.[728] Walker spent much of the end of 1962 dealing with his legal troubles with the federal government, until an all-white Southern jury acquitted him.

In a six-page prepared speech that followed the October 1962 Cuban Missile Crisis, which was given at a meeting apparently sponsored by Frank Capell—whom he called a "good friend"—del Valle charged Truman and Eisenhower with treason, blamed Kennedy for the Communist takeover of Cuba, and called Kennedy's advisors Zionists. He stated that when Kennedy allowed the Soviets to place nuclear weapons in Cuba it was an act of "TREASON."[729]

Unfortunately, there is a gap in del Valle's correspondence from September 22, 1962, until March 12, 1963. There are no letters to document whether the strategy meeting of former military personnel and leaders of the civilian far right took place as proposed. There were, however, a number of public meetings of the far right that took place during the nearly six-month gap in del Valle's letters. The 1962 Constitution Party meeting was held in Dallas in December 1962. Unfortunately, the author was unable to learn more about it. The meeting, held in Walker's hometown, would have been the perfect place to continue the plotting mentioned in the letters exchanged between del Valle and Walker. Walker was supposed to attend the meeting, but it is not known if he did.[730] It's not known if Dallasite and Milteer associate Dan Smoot, a known contributor to the Constitution Party in the past, attended, either.[731]

Billy James Hargis, who raised money for the hardcore underground and was an associate of Guy Banister, Milteer, and General Walker, was the National Chaplain of the Constitution Party in 1962.[732] Hargis, along with Kent Courtney, Tom Anderson, Robert Morris, John Rousselot, General Willoughby and Hilaire du Berrier, among other important individuals in this story, did appear at public meetings of the far right during the gap in the del Valle correspondence.[733] The meetings afforded the far right the opportunity to further develop the plans discussed in the del Valle and Walker correspondence.

On February 14, 1963, General Walker and Billy James Hargis announced a national speaking tour, named Operation Midnight Ride, that would begin on February 27, 1963, in Miami, Florida, followed by stops in over a dozen cities across the country before ending in Los Angeles on April 3. 1963. Like Paul Revere, the two men set out to alert their countrymen to the dire threat posed to the country—in this case by President Kennedy's policies. Kent Courtney traveled to Miami to be with Walker at the opening of the tour. After his final speech in Los Angeles on April 3, 1963, Walker's whereabouts are not known until he arrived home on April 8, 1963.

On April 10, 1963, someone fired a rifle shot through General Walker's den window, where he was allegedly working on his taxes. The culprit was never found, but Lee Harvey Oswald told his wife that he was responsible—a detail which was divulged after the Kennedy assassination. Walker said he suspected the Communists were out to kill him, which prompted him to initiate another speaking tour called "Operation Alert," to warn the country of the peril of Communism. The tour was to take place in nearly a dozen cities, ending in Baton Rouge on May 27 and in New Orleans (interestingly) on May 28, 1963. The incident presents a paradox: Why would Lee Harvey Oswald, who—as noted in Chapters One and Two—was seen on multiple occasions with Guy Banister and Kent Courtney, shoot at Walker who likewise was close to Banister and Courtney? An entire chapter in this book is devoted to the speaking tour and the shooting.

During the time of the extensive Walker-Hargis tour, a public far right meeting, billed as a "Strategy Seminar" of the Anti-Communist Liaison, took place on April 26–27, 1963, at the Washington Hotel. (The meeting may have been related to the "strategy conference" Walker proposed in his letter to Pedro del Valle on June 21, 1962.) General Willoughby, one of del Valle's "trusted men" spoke on psychological warfare. General Bonner Fellers, another one of his "trusted men," and retired general Claire Chenault attended.[734]

The del Valle correspondence resumed March 12, 1963, when he wrote a letter to Mary Davison, a principal in the broad-based assassination plots later revealed at the Congress of Freedom meeting in April. He told her that, for years, he had lobbied members of Congress to begin impeachment proceedings against federal officials who had violated their oaths of office. Del Valle told her that the legal approach was too slow and the "enemy" was moving too fast, writing: "Perhaps your approach may produce the needed action, and, as far as I am able, I will lend a hand." More than likely the "approach" of Davison's that del Valle referred to was the ambitious plot to assassinate members of the Council of Foreign Relations and others, which had originated in the Council for Statehood meetings in December and January of 1962 and had been revealed at the Congress of Freedom meeting in New Orleans on April 4, 5, and 6, 1963. Del Valle concluded the letter ominously as follows:

```
          State sovereignty can only be rescued by the states themselves.
If the state governments are also in the grip of the terror induced by the
Invisible government, then there is nothing left but violence and bloodshed.
And that, of course, will be our lot whether we resist or whether we sur-
render without a fight. The advantage of the former lies in the satisfac-
tion men feel when they know they are on the side of Christ against the
anti-Christ which is, whoever his disguise, our ever present enemy.
          So I wish your project well, and, within my limitations, will
try to help.                    Yours in Christ,    P.A. del Valle
```

Source: Pedro del Valle Papers, Special Collections, University of Oregon Library

On June 22, 1963, del Valle wrote to radio and print media propagandist Richard Cotton, an anti-Semite who published the *Conservative Point of View* and thanked him for sending his mailing list to del Valle so he could send Cotton's subscribers copies of his own newsletter *Alert*.

On July 2, 1963, del Valle wrote Wickliffe "Wick" Vernard, a leader in the Constitution Party, and stated that he had been in touch with a worldwide Christian movement headquartered in Madrid, Spain, "whose objectives are in accord with yours." The Madrid group agreed to meet Vernard. Vernard's representatives were to pose as tourists, and the meeting would take place at a quiet hotel. Del Valle assured Vernard that his Madrid contacts would offer collaboration and a scheme of action. The letter is filled with cryptic references suggesting a secret operation that may have been related to an assassination plot.[735]

In a personal letter to the editor of *American Challenge* on July 8, 1963, del Valle distilled his case against the Federal Government citing three examples. He stated first that the validity of the Fourteenth Amendment could not be sustained in any honorable court of law; he felt the states had the legal right to abrogate the Fourteenth amendment, as well as the Supreme Court *Brown* decision. Second, he stated that the Supreme Court did not have the legal powers under the Constitution to uphold the *Brown* decision—a decision that he felt was responsible for the "Black Insurrection." Third, he stated that President Kennedy's Treaty of Disarmament surrendered the sovereignty of the United States to the United Nations, which exceeded the power of any federal agency and was treasonous. Del Valle pledged to fight to the death rather than surrender the rights of the states.[736]

On July 24, 1963, in a letter to West Wuichet of Escondido, California, del Valle stated that the organizational effort was underway. Del Valle wrote that the country had been set up "into 4 zones of action" precisely reflecting Somersett's information and language from the Congress of Freedom that geographic command "zones" for the underground were being set up. Del Valle wrote that a headquarters was set up, as well as a communications network. Del Valle told Wuichet that he wanted to "discreetly" help and that he should contact Colonel William P. Gale. The FBI learned soon after the Congress of Freedom meeting that Gale was also involved in plotting assassinations—the same as those discussed at the Congress of Freedom. The FBI sent the documents related to Gale's plot to the Warren Commission, where they were apparently not taken into consideration. Thus, Gale is established as another member of del Valle's group of former military men involved in a broad-based assassination plot. Del Valle said in the letter, "We organize . . . to fight in any way necessary against a Red take-over."[737] William Gale had once served under generals Bonner Fellers, Charles Willoughby, and Albert Wedemeyer, all "trusted men" in del Valle's group.[738]

On September 6, 1963, Wally Butterworth wrote to "Eunice and Vic" and told them that Kennedy's executive orders were traitorous. He had just returned from a visit to del Valle's home and praised him, calling him the right arm of General MacArthur at Guadalcanal. He reported that del Valle had walked out of his church two weeks earlier when the Catholic leadership announced plans to integrate the church. Butterworth ominously wrote, "things are cooking with Pete del Valle & we'll soon advise you." He further wrote, "I have laid out plans for defense–food–Walkie Talkies–Medicines–Codes etc. God help us! If we do not have them. Now you see where I've been. I go next week."[739] On September 13, 1963, President Kennedy's trip to Dallas was announced.

On September 19, 1963, del Valle wrote Frank Capell at his Staten Island, New York, address and spoke of an imminent meeting to take place with Capell and should include Colonel McKeon in the vicinity of Boundbrook, New Jersey.[740]

On September 25, Lee Harvey Oswald departed New Orleans for Houston, Texas, by bus. On September 26, he reportedly departed by bus to Mexico City, Mexico.[741]

On September 26, 1963, Frank Capell wrote del Valle and mentioned that he had given anti-Communist speeches to two groups. He told del Valle cryptically that one group was about ready "to proceed." There is a gap in del Valle's correspondence until November 19, 1963, when he wrote to Nazi George Lincoln Rockwell, referring to him as "Commander." Del Valle accepted an invitation by Rockwell to speak to his "young Patriots" along with John Crommelin and "confer on the subject of a united effort."

On November 22, 1963, President Kennedy was assassinated. On November 27, 1963, del Valle wrote to Frank Capell and expressed his views on the assassination: "We are entering the last stages of the 'take-over.' It is always heralded by assassination of an important official. In this case, however, the victim was their man, only he failed to an extent rendering his election in 1964 doubtful. The double slaying is accounted for by the necessity to seal the lips of agent #1. In the news photo Oswald has a look of fear and recognition of agent #2: Rubenstein. The hired press still tries hard to pin this on the Right-wing! Johnson and his Yiddish lady may seem a bit better team to the Invisibles. It remains to be seen how the mighty Kennedy tribe takes the liquidation of their head man. We are all in God's hands."

Del Valle toed the same far-fetched line as Revilo Oliver (and others on the far right including Joseph Milteer) in his Warren Commission testimony, which suggests the conspirators had coordinated their rationalizations of the murder in advance. The often-repeated storyline was that Kennedy was no longer doing enough for the Communists, and that a Communist took him out as a result. Invariably the far right called Jack Ruby, "Rubinstein," as did del Valle and Revilo Oliver.[742]

After the assassination, Milteer circulated a Thanksgiving Day, November 28, 1963, form letter calling Jack Ruby "Rubenstein" and asking his readers to think of the significance of that name. He stated that an admitted pro-Castro had committed the crime and added, "the Right Wing Group had nothing what-so-ever to do with this awful, dastardly act." He ended the letter stating, "Thanksgiving Day is such a wonderful day—We should make every day Thanksgiving Day."[743] At a 1965 Christian Crusade Convention, General Walker remarked, regarding the Oswald-Ruby affair, "that Ruby's name was Rubenstein and they can't change that no matter how often they refer to him as Ruby."[744] The far right again claimed that since Karl Marx—the founder of Communism—was Jewish, that Communism was a Jewish plot. Therefore, they rationalized, the murder of the president had been a Jewish-Communist plot.

Pedro del Valle and the Post-Assassination Period

After the Kennedy assassination, del Valle continued his murderous plotting against the U.S. government until his death. A review of a large amount of correspondence through 1979 revealed del Valle was involved with radicals across the country, including Minutemen leader Robert DePugh, Clyde Watts, William Gale, Kenneth Goff, Commander Rockwell, and others. A few of the more significant letters are summarized here (the remainder are summarized in the endnote). The letters make it clear that del Valle and his cadre of extremists advocated assassination, bombings, and insurrection against the federal government. There are two letters to H. S. Riecke of New Orleans who published a newsletter for the Paul Revere Associated Yeoman's, *P.R.A.Y.*, that mentioned that the group was a part of del Valle's underground that provided Riecke's operation with funding. One letter suggested that Riecke coordinate his efforts with Jim Venable and Wally Butterworth, who were in attendance at the Constitution Party meeting in 1963.[745] Del Valle recommended H. S. Riecke to represent the State of Louisiana during the 1965 Constitution Party meeting.[746] In 1965, the FBI learned that Riecke was a member of Robert DePugh's Minutemen and was assigned number 41529.[747] Guy Banister had one of Riecke's "Wake Up Americans" newsletters in his surviving files. Riecke reported in the newsletter that he was collaborating with generals Charles Willoughby and Pedro del Valle.[748]

On December 9, 1964, close del Valle friend Frank Capell wrote to General Willoughby and told him he had been to a recent meeting of anti-Communists representing different parts of the country and that plans had been made for closer relationships between the groups. Willoughby was told he would have access to a confidential intelligence service that would periodically send him intelligence reports and anticipated actions, including reports from former military and naval officers in various parts of the country. Attached to each report would be the name "Frank," regardless of where it was mailed from, but they would otherwise be unidentifiable. In turn, "Frank" would pass anything that Willoughby desired to the anti-Communist groups. Periodic meetings of many national leaders "under the tightest of security" were planned. Attached to the letter was Frank Capell's *Herald of Freedom* business card.[749]

On September 1, 1966, del Valle wrote affectionately to Commander Rockwell and whole-heartedly agreed with his "march on the niggers" planned for Chicago. On March

11, 1967, del Valle wrote to Louisiana congressman John Rarick and praised him for his work. Rarick had had the distinction of observing Lee Harvey Oswald in a voter registration drive among members of the Congress of Racial Equality in September 1963 in Clinton, Louisiana, where Rarick served as a district judge.[750] (An entire chapter later in this book is devoted to Oswald's appearance in Clinton and the role of Rarick in the incident.) On July 30, 1972, Olga Butterworth wrote to del Valle and told him that she had written a letter to Congressman Rarick advising him to stay out of the congressional dining room, suggesting that someone might try to poison him. In another letter in the collection, in August 1967, del Valle wrote to William Gale and discussed volunteer militias and the feasibility of having helicopters "armed with M.C.'s, rockets and hand grenades to quell urban rioting."

On December 15, 1970, del Valle wrote to Butterworth and stated he advocated the bombing of synagogues. He wrote, "We must stop talking and begin counter measures of violence against the revolutionaries who have publicly stated . . . taking over in the name of Satan. . . . We should avoid assassinations for the time being . . . but kidnappings and bombings of people and places with key importance to the revolution we must commence at once. Kidnapping a dozen or so of the most powerful Jews, bombing of synagogues, and the United Nations, the Council of Foreign Relations headquarters, etc., would soon put the fear of God into them. But this must be carefully planned and executed. It will not be easy, but must be done."[751]

On August 28, 1973, friends and colleagues of General del Valle gathered in Washington to celebrate his eightieth birthday and the twentieth anniversary of his group the Defenders of the American Constitution. Among them was Josephine P. Beaty, the widow of John Beaty, who wrote the anti-Semitic book, *Iron Curtain Over America*—a favorite of del Valle and the right wing. Frank Capell, Mary Davison, General William C. Lemly, Mrs. John Rarick, Wickliffe Vernard, and General Clyde J. Watts were in attendance.[752] (General Lemly was close to Wally Butterworth and described himself as a hardcore "Bircher." Lemly had known del Valle since 1923. In 1965, Lemly attended Carl McIntire's Cape May retreat where General Walker once spoke.[753])

On February 10, 1975, del Valle wrote to Olga Butterworth and explained that he did not join the American Party because: "This thing can not be cured by Politics of any kind . . . and it follows paragraph 2 of the Declaration, which calls for the people to take things into their own hands."

On May 3, 1976, del Valle wrote that it was it was no longer possible to restore the Constitution by Constitutional means. He wrote, "there is only one sure way to toss these traitors out, namely by a military coup d'etat, which beats the traitor's leader and seizes control by force." On March 11, 1975, del Valle wrote to Colonel M. P. McKeon and told him he had been to a West Coast meeting of Liberty Lobby with a lot of patriots, including John Rarick, General Clyde Watts, Ned Touchstone, Colonel Dall, Courtney Smith, and Willis Carto. Del Valle stated that the Republic was wrecked and the only way out was "through the Joint Chiefs," suggesting that a junta was the answer.

General del Valle and Woody Kearns: Evidence of Conspiracy

Milteer's close friend Woody Kearns wrote del Valle on October 30, 1976, and reminisced about the Constitution Party meeting held at the Marott in 1963 (where assassinating the president was discussed). The letter is reproduced here:

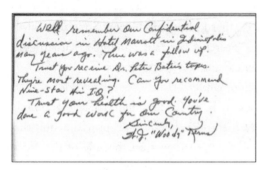

Part of a letter from W. J. "Woody" Kearns to Pedro del Valle dated October 30, 1976, found in the papers of Pedro del Valle. The letter suggests cryptically that the assassination was discussed at the 1963 Constitution Party meeting in Indianapolis, Indiana, at the Marott Hotel and was indeed accomplished. Source: Pedro del Valle Papers, Special Collections, University of Oregon Library

The letter suggests that Kearns was cryptically reminding del Valle that he was present when plans for killing of the president were discussed at the Constitution Party at the Marott Hotel and were later carried out. Talk of "knocking off the President"—as you'll remember that Somersett noted—was the only notable event at the 1963 Constitution Party meeting that would seem to merit the remarks in the letter, written thirteen years later. The closing with "You've done a good work for our Country" suggests that perhaps Kearns was paying tribute to the single most important accomplishment in the career of a political extremist nearing the end of his life: the assassination of President Kennedy. Del Valle died on April 28, 1978.

The Former Military Staff of General Douglas MacArthur and the Hardcore Underground

The correspondence between General del Valle and General Walker named four former high-ranking military men of particular interest, among ten to twenty others, as people they could rely on and confer with at proposed strategy meetings to deal with the perceived dire peril they felt the country faced under the Kennedy administration. All four generals—Charles Willoughby, George Stratemeyer, Albert C. Wedemeyer, and Bonner Fellers—formerly served under the dissident General MacArthur in World War II. They were all well-known national far-right political activists from the post-war period into the 1960s. It's not known if any of them had a direct tie to the assassination; however, they may have planned, encouraged, or sanctioned the operation, which would make them accessories.

General Charles Willoughby is the most significant, since there is intriguing evidence he may have been involved in the assassination conspiracy. Willoughby was also close to other key figures in the assassination story, Kent Courtney, Billy James Hargis, and others, as we shall see. Generals Wedemeyer and Stratemeyer are noteworthy because del Valle discussed involving them in his strategy plans with General Walker, and because they were closely aligned with wealthy oilman H. L. Hunt of Dallas, Texas, and multiple other key figures important in this story. (Joseph Milteer paid a visit to the Hunt organization in Dallas, which has never been revealed before, and will be discussed later.) Hunt had ties to Guy Banister and General Walker, as well as to General MacArthur—all of whom are people of tremendous significance that will be discussed in Chapter Eleven. Bonner Fellers is the fourth general from MacArthur's staff mentioned by del Valle and is also of interest here because of his close ties to members of the national far right. Author Joseph W. Bendersky noted in his book *The Jewish Threat* that generals Charles Willoughby, Bonner Fellers, and George Stratemeyer were known in the aftermath of World War II as the "Secret Americans," a clique that struggled against the "Jewish forces that undermined America" and the West.[754]

General Douglas MacArthur was the commander of the U.S. Army Forces in the Far East in World War II under President Roosevelt. In 1950, President Truman appointed MacArthur head of the U.N. forces in the Korean conflict; his forces captured Seoul, then invaded North Korea, which led Chinese forces to enter the war on the side of the North Koreans. MacArthur had assured President Truman that the Chinese would not intervene in the war and—if they did—they would be slaughtered. However, MacArthur greatly under-estimated the numbers of Chinese already in Korea by ten-fold, based on faulty intelligence gathered by his intelligence chief, General Charles Willoughby. Confident that the Chinese would not intervene, MacArthur promised the soldiers of the Twenty-fourth Division that they would be home for Christmas. However, in reality, a land war against the Chinese was un-winnable since the Chinese had a nearly inexhaustible supply of soldiers. When MacArthur received advanced knowledge of a Truman plan to open peace negotiations with the Chinese, he acted on his own and called for unconditional surrender from the Chinese—which they would never have found acceptable. MacArthur had often acted on his own and had been reminded that he was not to release any statements regarding foreign or military policy without Department of Army clearance—a policy he called "muzzling." With support of the Joint Chiefs and the Department of State, President Truman relieved MacArthur of his command.[755]   Ten years passed before another U.S. Army general, Edwin A. Walker, was relieved of his command, in this case by President Kennedy. FBI documents on both MacArthur and Walker suggest they were mentally unstable.[756] The April 15, 1951, issue of *Common Sense*, the anti-Semitic magazine later promoted by Joseph Milteer, declared in headlines that MacArthur was the victim of the "Invisible Government."[757] Just how great a threat President Truman felt MacArthur posed was not revealed until 2003 when a 1947 diary belonging to President Truman was discovered. In the diary, Truman wrote of a dramatic offer he made to General Dwight Eisenhower to serve as Eisenhower's Vice President on the 1948 Democratic ticket if it appeared that General MacArthur was heading for the Republican Presidential nomination.[758] It was also a factor in Truman's decision not to seek re-election in 1952.

Upon returning to the U.S., MacArthur was given a hero's welcome. H. L. Hunt and Clint Murchison chartered an Eastern Airline jet and brought him to Texas; MacArthur then went on a national speaking tour and bitterly criticized President Truman. (After General Walker was relieved of his command, he also went on a national speaking tour and was critical of President Kennedy.) MacArthur echoed the sentiment of the far right when he stated: "If this nation is ever destroyed, it will be from within, not from without"—from U.S. leaders under Marxist philosophy.[759]   Hunt worked behind the scenes testing the waters for a MacArthur presidency. Hunt sent MacArthur detailed state polling estimates and joined him at the 1952 Republican Convention.[760] In a similar fashion, Hunt backed General Walker in his bid for governor of Texas in 1962, which he hoped would be a springboard to the presidency and the defeat of President Kennedy in 1964, as we shall see.

Major General Charles Willoughby

Major General Charles Willoughby, U.S. Army (retired), served under MacArthur as his Chief of Intelligence in both World War II and the Korean conflict. Willoughby was generally regarded as a right-wing extremist and racist. He was an admirer of both Benito Mussolini and Francisco Franco.[761] Willoughby was anti-Jewish and also expressed disdain for those from the "Orient" and the "Tropics."[762] After the Korean War, Willoughby found his way to a far-right-wing, Fascist intelligence network known as the International Committee for Defense of the Christian Culture that was financially backed by Lamar and Nelson Bunker Hunt (sons of H. L. Hunt), as well as Billy James Hargis.[763] On October 8, 1963, Willough- by spoke before the group.[764] Willoughby's publication, the *Foreign Intelligence Digest* was an offshoot of the group. Willoughby was a supporter of the Anti-Bolshevik Bloc of Nations, and its founder, pro-Nazi Jaroslaw Stetzko, was listed on the letterhead of Willoughby's *Foreign Intelligence Digest*.[765, 766]

Willoughby's ties to the radical right wing are extensive.[767] He served on the board of Billy James Hargis's Christian Crusade. Willie Somersett cited Hargis as being a fundraiser for the hardcore underground, and Hargis met with George Soule and Guy Banister in 1963, as was noted in Chapter One. Hargis published Willoughby's *Foreign Intelligence Digest*—which was odd for a religious organization—as a part of his *Weekly Crusader* newsletter. On April 16, 1961, Hargis and Willoughby spoke at a "Save America Rally."[768] In late 1961, Willoughby permitted Robert Welch of the John Birch Society to hold a secret meeting in his Washing- ton, D.C., home.[769] On March 21, 1962, Hargis held an invitation-only "secretive meeting" in Washington, D.C. John Rousselot, Bonner Fellers, Ed Hunter, Ben Gitlow, Charles Wil- loughby, Frank McGehee, and Arthur Blazey were in attendance.[770] At the August 3–5, 1962, Christian Crusade meeting in Tulsa, Oklahoma, Willoughby spoke with Carl Prussian (an "ex-Communist"), John Rousselot, Martin Dies, and General Campbell.[771] On April 26–27, 1963, a strategy seminar of the Anti-Communist Liaison took place at the Washington Ho- tel, as previously noted, where Willoughby, Bonner Fellers, Archibald Roberts, and Claire Chenault were speakers.[772] Willoughby worked for H. L. Hunt in the 1950s and, at one point, Willoughby proposed inserting Hunt's *Life Lines* newsletter into the *Weekly Crusader* bulletin along with the *Foreign Intelligence Report*, but Hunt declined.[773]

Willoughby was a board member of Young Americans for Freedom—a group that Larrie Schmidt operated in Dallas.[774] Willoughby met with Schmidt on more than one oc- casion.[775] The Warren Commission took an interest in Schmidt, who was the force behind the infamous "Welcome Mr. President" advertisement that was critical of President Kennedy and appeared in the *Dallas Morning News* on the morning of the president's murder. The ad was paid for by Nelson Bunker Hunt and promoted by the Dallas John Birch Society. Willoughby was on the Board of Advisors of Major Archibald Roberts's Committee to Restore the Constitution, along with Pedro del Valle. Roberts and del Valle were both in the military "high command" of the murder-plotting Council for Statehood.[776] Importantly, Willoughby was on the board of Kent Courtney's Conservative Society of America. As previously noted, on several occasions Courtney was allegedly observed in the company of Lee Harvey Oswald in 1963, and was a close associate of Guy Banister.[777]

Willoughby was a close associate of Benjamin Mandel, research director for Senator Eastland's Senate Internal Security Subcommittee (SISS).[778] Willoughby was also close to Robert Morris, a former counsel to Eastland's SISS, and contributed money to Morris's failed 1958 Senate campaign.[779] Willoughby testified before the House Un-American Activities Committee and furnished them with intelligence on foreign matters.[780]

Guy Banister and Robert Morris worked together aiding Senator Eastland's SISS 1956 investigation of Communism in the integration movement in New Orleans. Robert Morris screened applicants for the Dallas Minutemen directed by General Walker and H. L. Hunt, which will be discussed later. As in the case of Wesley Swift, far-right extremists like Willoughby and Banister were often involved in the congressional inquisitions against leftists and integrationists accused of being Communists.

An anonymous source claimed Charles Willoughby was involved in the Kennedy assassination. After Dick Russell wrote an article about a professor's theory on the "Manchurian Candidate" and the Kennedy assassination in *The Village Voice* in 1975, he received a letter from an anonymous source telling him that if he wanted to solve the Kennedy assassination that he would have to look into an individual named Tscheppe-Weidenbach, a famous American general. The source, who stated he spoke fluent Mandarin Chinese, reported that prior to the death of Tscheppe-Weidenbach [on October 25, 1972] that he had spent several days with him. The note—all in capital letters—which the source stated was written in a Toronto, Canada, hotel was published in the assassination book *The Man Who Knew Too Much* in 1998, and appeared as follows:

> YOUR CANADIAN COMPUTERS RESEARCHING THE AS-
> SASSINATION OF JOHN KENNEDY DEVELOPED LEADS
> TO A MAN NAMED TSCHEPPE-WEIDENBACH BORN IN
> 1892 IN HEIDELBERG, GERMANY AS HAVING MASTER-
> MINDED THE ASSASSINATION WITH THE APPROVAL.
> "THE" MAN WHO COULD DO NO WRONG IN AMERI-
> CAN HISTORY?"
> YOUR GEN [EASY RESEARCH] MIGHT WELL PROVIDE A
> LEAD TO THE CLEVER MIND FROM HEIDELBERG.

Russell later discovered by chance, while he was doing research on General MacArthur, that the individual referred to as Tscheppe-Weidenbach was General Charles Willoughby, a German immigrant who changed his name before he came to America in 1910, at age eighteen.[781] This information means that the claim made in the cryptic note suggests that General Willoughby masterminded the assassination with the approval of General MacArthur. The correspondence between General Walker and General Pedro del Valle, mentioning Willoughby and MacArthur, suggests there may be some credence to the anonymous allegation of Willoughby's role in the assassination.

Willoughby was close to Gerhard Frey, editor of the *Deutsch National Zeitung*, a newspaper in Munich, Germany.[782] Frey and General Walker were friends from Walker's military service in Germany. Frey's far-right newspaper contacted General Walker for an interview after the Kennedy assassination, and his publication was the first to report that Lee Harvey Oswald had made an assassination attempt on General Walker in April of 1963. However, it was not revealed by Marina Oswald that Lee Harvey was involved in the Walker shooting until *after* the German paper reported the story. This means that Walker told the German paper that Oswald was involved—something he could not have known unless he was somehow involved in the episode with Oswald. As we shall see, the incident was a phony shoot-and-miss stunt to further Oswald's persona as a Communist and a threat to America and anti-Communists like Walker.

At the same time as the Walker shooting incident, the Guy Banister operation was building a case against several leftist organizations connected to the integration movement that Oswald later infiltrated in the summer of 1963 for the purpose of outlawing them under the harsh Communist Control Act. The Act, created and put forth by close Banister associates, proclaimed that Communists (like Oswald) were a clear and present danger to the people of Louisiana and, for that reason, warranted the stringent measures called for by the legislation. As we have discussed, under the Communist Control Act, anyone in a leftist group associated with someone like Lee Harvey Oswald could face thirty years in prison, and it was anticipated that the law would effectively abolish the integration movement in the South.

General Albert C. Wedemeyer

General Albert C. Wedemeyer, mentioned by del Valle in his letters to Walker, also served under General MacArthur. He was an ardent anti-Semite and voiced the opinion that the Jews and the Communists drove the U.S. into World War II.[783] General Wedemeyer appeared on the cover of *Time* magazine on June 4, 1945. He had extensive ties to the radical right.[784] Wedemeyer also had ties to H. L. Hunt and General Walker. Wedemeyer was on the Advisory Board of H. L. Hunt's radio and television show *Life Lines*.[785] On November 14, 1961, General Walker spoke at the Miami, Florida, National Indignation Rally with General Wedemeyer and General Arleigh Burke.[786] Wedemeyer published a newsletter and a book called the *Wedemeyer Reports*.[787] He also served on the board of the National Strategy Committee of another well-known far-right organization, the American Security Council, along with Patrick J.

Frawley, Robert Morris, and Robert E. Wood. Benjamin Gitlow, an advisor to the committee and "former Communist," once testified with Guy Banister in 1957 during the hearings in the state legislature on Subversion on Racial Unrest in the Louisiana, as we shall see later.[788, 789] General Robert E. Wood was mentioned in the June 21, 1962, letter sent by Walker to del Valle, noting that Wood had planned to attend their strategy conference. Robert Morris, was on the same committee.

Patrick Frawley was the owner of Schick Safety Razor Company and the Eversharp Corporation in Los Angeles, California; Dr. Alton Ochsner served on the board of Eversharp. Dan Campbell, who worked for Guy Banister, told the author that Alton Oschner was a close associate of Guy Banister, as was noted in Chapter One. Frawley, who made rare public appearances, once appeared on H. L. Hunt's radio program *Life Lines*.[790]

Ed Butler, who served under Oschner at the Information Council of America in New Orleans was also a Banister associate, and along with Carlos Bringuier debated Lee Harvey Oswald—who admitted over the radio that he was a Marxist. Frawley was impressed with a movie Butler made called "Hitler In Havana," and offered him a job after Kennedy's assassination. Butler accepted and moved to Los Angeles. The *New York Times* called Butler's movie, "the crudest form of propaganda."

Lieutenant General George E. Stratemeyer

Lieutenant General George E. Stratemeyer was the World War II Chief of Air Staff and Far East Air Forces commander under MacArthur in the first year of the Korean War.[791] He appeared before the Senate Internal Security Subcommittee and testified on the failure of the Korean War, stating, "We were not permitted to win." He further explained, "something is going on, has been going on since World War I ended . . . There is some hidden force . . . or something that is influencing our people." Later, Stratemeyer would find the answer to his concerns in the book *The Iron Curtain Over America* by John Beaty, a former G2 officer in Washington from 1941 to 1947, and expressed his gratitude to Beaty in a letter. In the book—one of the most vicious anti-Semitic works of the time—Beaty blamed America's problems on "Judaized Khazars" and secret "Forces." Beaty felt the Holocaust was a fantastic hoax. Beaty created a scandal when he included Stratemeyer's praise of the book in its promotional materials. When the Anti-Defamation League asked Stratemeyer to repudiate the book, he was offended and refused—and actively promoted it, instead. General Wood and Wedemeyer praised Stratemeyer for his stand. General del Valle called Beaty's book a "magnificent book."[792] H. L. Hunt's security chief, Paul Rothermel, told the author that generals Wedemeyer and Stratemeyer "were near and dear to my boss's heart."[793]

Brigadier General Bonner Fellers

Bonner Fellers was another member of MacArthur's staff that comprised a group, which was referred to in *The Jewish Threat*, as the "Secret Americans" after World War II. He had extensive ties to the national radical right.[794] Fellers was affiliated with America First, the isolationist movement that strove to keep the U.S. out of World War II. He worked for the 1948 MacArthur For America movement, and later formed the group For America that was a reemergence of the forces in America First.[795] As noted in Chapter Two, Fellers spoke at a For America meeting headed by Banister associate George Soule in New Orleans; he also presented at a meeting of New Orleans Discussion Unlimited, a group Guy Banister's secretary Delphine Roberts was involved with. In 1956, For America endorsed a nationwide Free Elector movement, which had been proposed by the New Orleans-based Federation for Constitutional Government, a segregationist group that was led by Banister colleague Leander Perez and J. Evetts Haley.[796] General Wedemeyer, General Stratemeyer, Admiral Ben Moreel, and J. Evetts Haley served on the Federation's National Policy Committee.[797] Fellers wrote articles for the anti-Semitic magazine *Common Sense*, which was promoted by Joseph Milteer, as did General del Valle, Wally Butterworth, and Kenneth Goff.[798]

The Shickshinny Knights

The Shickshinny Knights of the Order of St. John of Jerusalem were a far-right-wing group that had its headquarters in Shickshinny, Pennsylvania. The group was a Catholic organization that claimed to be the real Knights of Malta. Its grand marshal was Charles Pichel, who corresponded with Ernst Hanfstaengl, who was once an aide to Adolf Hitler. Members of the order worked with Liberty Lobby and Lyndon LaRouche's libertarian group.[799] Generals Charles Willoughby, Pedro del Valle, Bonner Fellers, and Lemuel Shepard, and colonels Phillip Corso and Benjamin F. von Stahl were members of the Armed Services Committee of the Shickshinny Knights.[800, 801] Bonner Fellers and Russell Maguire, the editor of *American Mercury*, sponsored Willoughby for membership.[802] Sir Barry Edward Domvile, an admiral in the British Royal Navy and a Nazi sympathizer, was another member of the Shickshinny Knights.[803, 804]

Frank Capell and Philip Corso are two other noteworthy members of the Shickshinny Knights.[805] It will be recalled the Revilo Oliver, in his far-fetched testimony before the Warren Commission on the assassination, credited three individuals in the hardcore underground as sources of his theories: General Walker, Kent Courtney, and Frank Capell. Capell was the source for Oliver's assertion that Marina Oswald was the adopted daughter of a colonel in Soviet military intelligence, as well as a number of other false claims.[806] Capell was a far-right propagandist who published *The Herald of Freedom* in Zarephath, New Jersey, about which he noted, "This publication has supplied documentation on organizations whose activities are against the best interests of our country." Capell stated that he supplied information on suspected Communists to congressmen, senators, and individual patriotic Americans. Capell claimed to have intelligence sources across the U.S. and in many countries. He called the *Herald of Freedom* "essentially a national news service and private intelligence agency whose contacts were former military and naval officers, [and] former government investigators . . . ." In his book *Treason is the Reason (847 Reasons for Investigating the State Department)*, Capell named and published short biographies, at times with photos, of individuals he considered to be security risks in government and, particularly, in the State Department. In the book, Capell thanked all of the former armed forces officers who assisted him in his work, stating, "They shall remain nameless, lest conspiracy take retaliatory measures against them."[807] Capell was also associated with General Willoughby's *Foreign Intelligence Digest* and, as noted earlier, Capell was also close to General del Valle and met with him before the assassination.[808] After the Kennedy assassination, del Valle sent Capell a written account of his own concocted theory of the meaning of the assassination, which may have served as a template for other similar far-right theories on the event.

Lieutenant Colonel Philip J. Corso, like Capell, was a member of the Shickshinny Knights and was a major source of disinformation about the assassination. Corso spoke before Congress on "military muzzling" after General Walker was drummed out of the army by the Kennedy administration. He had a long career in army intelligence before retiring and going to work for Senator Strom Thurmond. Corso was one of the first to spread the rumors that Oswald had been working as a paid informant for the FBI.[809]

According to an investigation by the FBI, Corso was connected with U.S. Army Intelligence for over twenty years, and for years furnished the FBI with information on alleged subversive activities. In 1955, Corso provided evidence he had accumulated on "Fabian Socialists" in policy-making positions in the U.S. government to General Arthur Trudeau. Trudeau, after being relieved of his position as an assistant chief of staff of G-2 in the Military Intelligence Corps in August 1955, presented Capell's evidence in September 1955 to the FBI and other government agencies; the FBI found the allegations unsubstantiated. Trudeau was relieved of his duties as a result of charges by CIA Director Allen Dulles that his activities had been prejudicial to U.S. intelligence activities. In May 1961, Trudeau, working as chief of army research and development, tried to revive his allegations of Fabian Socialists working in the government through Corso. Corso went before the Senate Internal Security Subcommittee and said that the Fabian Socialists in the Kennedy White House staff included W. W. Rostow, McGeorge Bundy, Arthur Schlesinger, Jr., and J. B. Wiesner. The FBI determined that the Corso/Trudeau allegation was the type of allegation that had gotten Trudeau in trouble in the 1950s with the Dulles family. The FBI concluded, "Trudeau has a fetish about security and intelligence work and cannot keep his fingers out of that area." The FBI determined that the purpose of Capell's accusation was to smear the Kennedy administration. They also found that Corso had appeared before Senator Eastland's Senate Internal Security Subcommittee on May 13, 1961; April 15, 1961; and April 3, 1962.[810] Frank Capell noted that the Dies Committee had determined that Arthur Schlesinger, an advisor to President Kennedy, was affiliated with a number of Communist-front organizations. Capell cited a statement from John Rousselot, claiming that Schlesinger planned to turn the people of the U.S. over to a "monolithic Socialist Fascist-Marxist type of tyranny." Trudeau's basis for the smears of members of President Kennedy's White House staff likely emanated from Frank Capell, as they are named as security risks in his book, *Treason is the Reason*.[811] Columnist Drew Pearson identified Trudeau as a top military official who smuggled documents to Strom Thurmond in 1961.[812]

In February of 1964, the FBI learned from an official and reliable source that a rumor had been passed along to high government officials that Lee Harvey Oswald had been an FBI informant and was being paid $200 a month. When interviewed by the FBI, Philip Corso admitted to being the source of the rumor and claimed his source was a CIA friend—whom he refused to identify—who "had no facts whatsoever." According to the FBI, the CIA had characterized Corso "as a parasite who never produced any intelligence through his own efforts but has profited from information provided by dedicated Government agents and investigators." J. Edgar Hoover concluded, "Corso is a rat." On February 10, 1964, Hoover met with Senator Eastland to discuss the Oswald-FBI allegation.[813]

On February 22, 1964, the Warren Commission was informed by Dallas County Attorney General Bill Alexander that Lee Harvey Oswald had been an undercover agent for the FBI since 1962 and was receiving payment of $200 a month. Gerald Ford, who served on the Warren Commission, said, when he learned of the rumor, "he could not recall a meeting more tense and more hushed" than when the Commission met in an emergency session to discuss the allegation. The story was carried in the *New York Times* and in the press across the country. No hard proof for the allegation was offered; the rumor was one and the same as that propagated by Shickshinny Knight Philip Corso, as the FBI would later determine.[814]

On July 17, 1965, Charles Pichel wrote to General Walker from Shickshinny, Pennsylvania, and told him that Walker had been accepted into the Knights of Malta as a member of the Military Affairs Committee because of his patriotic work. He was "qualified by blood and career."[815]

Rear Admiral John G. Crommelin

Rear Admiral John G. Crommelin, another close Milteer associate, was mentioned in the 1962 plotting correspondence between generals del Valle and Walker, which suggests he was another member of the military high command of the hardcore underground. The FBI learned that Crommelin was a member of the Council for Statehood that was involved with the broad-based assassination plots revealed at the Congress of Freedom meeting in 1963. Crommelin's name was brought up at the Constitution Party meeting, but it is not known if he was there. Wally Butterworth, who called for the murder of President Kennedy at the meeting, moved in to Crommelin's home in 1964. Crommelin had ties to many of the same groups as Milteer and Guy Banister, including the Klan, Citizens' Council, and National States' Rights Party, and Gerald L. K. Smith's anti-Semitic organization.[816]

Crommelin, from Wetumpka, Alabama, hailed from a distinguished navy family. In 1950, he was involved in a dispute with the navy and leaked confidential materials to the press to support his position. As a result, he was forced to resign from the navy with the rank of Rear Admiral.[817] A source told the FBI another factor in his forced resignation was his "Wildman talk" about the Jews and "other undesirables" that he claimed undermined the country.

After the navy, he embarked on a new career as a violence-advocating hate monger. In 1954, he participated in the "Committee of Ten Million Americans for Senator McCarthy" that circulated petitions in support of the senator in response to the threat of his censure in the U.S. Senate. In 1955, Crommelin joined the Northern Alabama Citizens' Council. The following year, he appeared on Birmingham television in a paid political broadcast and stated that "Marxist Jewry" controlled the federal government. Gerald L. K. Smith hosted Crommelin in a speech in Los Angeles on April 11, 1957, on the "hidden force." On September 16, 1957, the FBI noted that Crommelin was on the board of strategy that correlated the work of all the groups that fought integration. At a December 1958 Klan meeting, the FBI learned that Crommelin was involved with a group whose aim was "getting rid of the Jews" and blowing up every synagogue in the country.

Crommelin wrote a letter to J. Edgar Hoover on November 1, 1958, and gave his view on Communism, stating, "Some call it Marxism, and I call it Judaism. The center of Communism was in New York, not in Moscow." Hoover was well aware of Crommelin and often left hand-written comments about him in the margins of his FBI file documents. An informant told the FBI, in December 1958, that Crommelin declared that violence was "necessary in the movement."[818] In 1958, Crommelin formed the Defend America Fund to provide for legal expenses for members of the National States' Rights Party accused of bombing the Atlanta Temple.[819] Crommelin ran for governor of Alabama in 1958 under an openly anti-Communist, anti-Zionist platform.[820] In 1960, he was chosen as the National States' Rights Party candidate for president of the United States.[821] In 1962, Crommelin ran for the U.S. Senate and Milteer's friend, Oren Potito, was his campaign manager.[822] In 1959, Crommelin became closely associated with Robert Shelton of the Klan. Crommelin belonged to the American Association for Justice, Inc., which had been set up to help defend members of the far right. The board of directors of the association included Crommelin, General Pedro del Valle, and General Clyde Watts (General Walker's friend and attorney).[823]

On August 1, 1962, he traveled to Oxford, Mississippi, to join the opposition to the integration of the University of Mississippi. When he arrived, highway patrol and army units prevented his entrance to the city. On April 23, 1963, Crommelin and twenty others picketed Attorney General Robert Kennedy's visit to Governor George Wallace to discuss the integration crisis at the University of Alabama. On March 26, 1963, at a meeting of his Minuteman-type outfit, the Alabama Militia Volunteers, Crommelin said he was personally not competent to lead land forces and suggested William Gale or "some marine General," likely referring to Pedro del Valle, as possible candidates.

On June 4, 1963, Crommelin revealed at a meeting that he had a "special plan" but did not elaborate. Two days later, on June 6, 1963, the FBI learned that William Gale was trying to raise money to fund the assassination of three hundred people of Jewish faith.[824] An informant told the FBI that he, the informant, attended a secret meeting prior to September 15, 1963, in Birmingham, Alabama, attended by Gale, Noah "Jeff" Cardin, of Dade County Florida, Sidney Barnes, and Crommelin before the bombing of the Sixteenth Street Baptist Church in Birmingham. At that meeting, Crommelin discussed possible "action" with Barnes.[825] The FBI learned who attended the secret meeting from three apparently different sources. (As was noted before, Willie Somersett told the FBI that Milteer attended a meeting with Robert Shelton of the Klan on the night before the bombing.) In a separate report on the murder of Martin Luther King, Jr., FBI documents revealed that Melvin Sexton and William Gale also attended the meeting.[826] It is not clear if the FBI put together the three separate reports indicating that Milteer, Crommelin, Sexton, DePugh, and Gale all attended the same secret meeting in Alabama on the eve of the Birmingham bombing. The nature of the secret meeting is not known, but is highly suspicious since Milteer, Gale, and Crommelin all were tied to plots involving violence.

On November 13, 1963, Crommelin visited Wesley Swift at a strategy conference that discussed mass violence by "inner dens" of the Christian Knights of the Invisible Empire. The FBI learned that mass violence would occur all across the U.S. at some unspecified times and places in the future. George Lincoln Rockwell told the FBI in a separate report, on March 7, 1964, that Crommelin, Gale, and del Valle planned to forcibly overthrow the government. Rockwell learned about the plot from Ed Fields of the National States' Rights Party while at a meeting of the group in Louisville, Kentucky, on March 1, 1964. The FBI questioned Fields, who refused to give them any information. According to a March 17, 1964, memo, an informant told the FBI that Crommelin expressed interest in obtaining rifles, incendiary bombs, and hand grenades for the formation of a citizens combat unit and possible conspiracy to commit mass violence.[827]

Crommelin was on the screening committee of the 1965 Constitution Party and represented the State of Alabama. Joseph Milteer, Pedro del Valle, and Oren Potito represented their respective states the same year.[828] It is apparent that Crommelin was an integral part of this violence-oriented far-right clique.

Conclusions

Grave discontent with the Kennedy administration was abundantly evident among the radical right in 1961. General Pedro Del Valle, reflecting the prevailing feeling among the radical right, was particularly troubled by the *Brown* decision that outlawed segregation in the schools—as well as President Kennedy's civil rights initiatives. He felt that President Kennedy's handling of the Cuban situation and his disarmament policies were treasonous. He was certain that Kennedy had intended to hand over the United States to the United Nations.

The remarkable correspondence between generals Walker and del Valle revealed that time had run out for a non-violent remedy. By September 1962, the two discussed gathering the names and photos of their enemies, suggesting the plot to assassinate a large number of individuals in leading positions in business and government (revealed at a Council for Statehood meeting in December 1962) was already underway. They discussed plans to involve a number of former high-ranking military men in the plotting. By March 1963, del Valle indicated there was no recourse but "bloodshed and violence." The broad-based assassination plots discussed at the Congress of Freedom in April 1963 narrowed to talk of killing the president after the FBI questioned the principals in the early plots. A letter written years later from Milteer's best friend, Woody Kearns, to del Valle suggests del Valle told Kearns at the Constitution Party meeting about the plot that led to the Dallas murder. Philip Corso's claim that Lee Harvey Oswald was a paid FBI informant was one of many examples of the disinformation campaign propagated by the radical right.

Sufficient evidence is lacking to discern who among the former military officers mentioned in Walker and del Valle's plans may or may have not been involved in the assassination, or those who were accessories by virtue of knowing about the plot, participating in the planning of it, or encouraging it. Beyond generals del Valle and Walker, who are obvious suspects, the added suspicion of General Willoughby is merited by an intriguing anonymous letter accusing him of involvement in the assassination, along with his extensive ties to others important in the case. General Walker stands out above the rest of the military men. Walker lived in Dallas, the site of the murder, and was close to Milteer—who precisely predicted the assassination—as well as Guy Banister and Kent Courtney, who were seen on multiple occasions with Lee Harvey Oswald. Walker had a direct tie to Lee Harvey Oswald in the shooting incident at Walker's home. Walker had a personal vendetta against the Kennedy's after he was relieved of his command by the president and later arrested by Attorney General Robert Kennedy for leading an insurrection against the United States at the University of Mississippi.

CHAPTER NINE

OSWALD IN NEW ORLEANS AND THE JIM GARRISON CASE

*Oswald's professed Marxist sympathies were just a cover for his real
activities. Oswald would have been more at home with* Mein Kampf
than Das Kapital.

— *Jim Garrison*[829]

The FBI's superficial investigation for the Warren Commission of Lee Harvey Oswald's activities in New Orleans in the summer of 1963 was perhaps due, at least in part, to the fact that former FBI Special Agent Guy Banister was a close friend of New Orleans FBI agent Regis Kennedy. The HSCA, which pointed out the Warren Commission's deficiencies in the development of the New Orleans evidence, did not perform much better. New Orleans district attorney Jim Garrison, on the other hand, uncovered a wealth of information on Lee Harvey Oswald and the Banister operation. Garrison's discovery of Oswald's ties to Guy Banister, David Ferrie, and the office at 544 Camp Street are essential pieces of the assassination story. Unfortunately, as Garrison's investigation became public in 1967, it quickly derailed and ultimately ended in complete disgrace. Lee Harvey Oswald's activities in New Orleans—and particularly those discovered by the Garrison investigation—will be presented in this chapter.

At the age of twenty-four, Lee Harvey Oswald departed Texas for New Orleans, the city of his birth, on April 24, 1963. Oswald, while in Texas, had tried and failed to obtain a visa to send his wife back to the Soviet Union, due to the mire of Soviet Embassy bureaucracy. Oswald left behind his wife, Marina, and daughter, June, at the home of Ruth Paine, their gracious liberal friend, in Fort Worth, Texas. His departure from Texas followed the unsolved March 10, 1963, Walker shooting incident. (After the Kennedy assassination, Oswald's wife told the FBI that her husband told her he shot at Walker.) Also in March 1963, Oswald had enhanced his credentials as a dangerous Communist by having his wife take a photo of him holding the alleged assassination rifle and two newspapers of opposing leftist ideologies, *The Worker* and the *Militant*.

In New Orleans, he stayed with his aunt, Lillian Murret. On May 9, 1963, he landed a job as an equipment oiler at the William B. Reily Coffee Company. William B. Reily, in contrast to Oswald's professed pro-Castro sympathies, was a major supporter of anti-Castro Cubans in New Orleans. Oswald rented an apartment on Magazine Street, where his family would later rejoin him. At Reily Coffee, Oswald was repeatedly warned about his poor work performance. On numerous occasions during his employment, Oswald was seen in the waiting room of Adrian Alba's nearby Crescent City Garage, thumbing through gun magazines—including the *American Rifleman*, published by the conservative National Rifle Association. Oswald purchased his Manlicher Carcano rifle, the alleged assassination weapon, through the mail from a Chicago gun dealer advertising in the magazine.[830] A witness reportedly told Garrison that Adrian Alba was a member of the far-right paramilitary Minutemen—like Guy Banister.[831]

Sometime in May 1963, Oswald visited the office of attorney Dean Andrews in the company of several never-identified homosexual men. On other occasions, he sought Andrews's counsel on upgrading his Marine Corps discharge and other matters. Also in May 1963, Oswald ordered 1,000 copies of his self-designed handbills promoting his one-person chapter of the pro-Castro Fair Play for Cuba group from Jones Printing Company, which was across the street from Reily Coffee. Oswald had written to FPCC director V. T. Lee in New York, and had told him he was interested in forming a New Orleans chapter of FPCC, but had been discouraged by Lee. He also ordered some of the "basic pamphlets" from Lee. Oswald passed the handbills out on June 16, 1963, at the Dumaine Street wharf off the French Quarter, where the USS *Wasp* was docked, a good place to attract publicity. When the ship's commander saw him, he called the Harbor Police, who told Oswald to leave. On July 19, 1963, Oswald was fired from Reily Coffee.[832]

In early August, at the same time that he was promoting Castro's Communist Cuba, Oswald allegedly visited the clothing store of Carlos Bringuier, a Cuban-exile member of an anti-Castro group in New Orleans. Bringuier, as noted in Chapter One, knew Guy Banister, a fact pointed out by the Garrison investigation. Bringuier had visited the infamous 544 Camp Street office building that housed Banister's operation, and whose address was stamped on one of Oswald's handbills. According to Bringuier, Oswald offered to train anti-Castro fighters in guerrilla warfare, and gave Bringuier his *Marine Guidebook*. (Bringuier claimed Oswald was trying to infiltrate his group as a Communist.) However, a Garrison investigator found an eyewitness who was present during the meeting between Oswald and Bringuier who provided credible evidence that the encounter with Oswald occurred in May and not August, suggesting Bringuier was lying about his relationship with Oswald. The fact that Bringuier and Oswald knew Banister and both were at the Newman Building at 544 Camp Street creates more problems for Bringuier's story.

The nature of the relationship between Oswald and Bringuier became more suspect when—four days after the two purportedly met in Bringuier's store—Bringuier and another Cuban encountered Oswald passing out Fair Play for Cuba handbills in front of the old Trade Mart at 124 Camp Street in the central business district on August 9, 1963. A scuffle followed and Bringuier and Oswald landed in jail. Evidence will be presented that the whole affair was a phony collaboration between Oswald and Bringuier. Oswald wrote FPCC director V. T. Lee on August 1, 1963, *before* the incident occurred, stating that there had been a fight. Police Lieutenant Martello questioned the incident stating, "He [Oswald] seemed to have them set up to create an incident."

The author will present new evidence that, after the altercation, Bringuier sought out Kent Courtney for his advice in getting an attorney after the phony fight. It will be recalled that Courtney was one of Revilo Oliver's sources for his article *Marxsmanship in Dallas*, which was the subject of his Warren Commission testimony, wherein he blamed Kennedy's assassination on the CIA.

John Martin, a Minnesota Minuteman who served under General Walker in 1960 in Germany, filmed the Oswald-Bringuier fight after having traveled to Dallas to film the bullet holes in Walker's home. The filming defies any reasonable explanation other than that Walker knew about Oswald and his planned fight with Bringuier before the rest of the world, contrary to his Commission testimony. Given the fact that Walker and Kent Courtney were close, the allegation presented in Chapter Two that Courtney and Oswald were working together, and that Bringuier sought out Kent Courtney after the incident, it's likely Courtney told Walker about the planned scuffle between Oswald and Bringuier. (The film will be discussed in greater detail in Chapter Fifteen.)

Further promoting his image as a pro-Castro leftist, Oswald visited the newspaper office of New Orleans *States–Item* reporter David Chandler and told Chandler he would like him to do a story about his arrest, and about him personally. Chandler told Oswald that this was unlikely since they were not sympathetic to his cause.[833] A consistent characteristic of Oswald's activities in New Orleans was that he flaunted or advertised his purported Communist sympathies.

Bern Rotman, the Senior News Editor for station WDSU, was in contact with Oswald during his radio interview and gave Oswald a short tour of the studio. A short time later, Oswald called Rotman and told him he was going to picket again. Oswald asked him what date he'd like him to picket and Rotman responded that he did not want Oswald to picket. Oswald told Rotman that if he did picket he was going to call the newsroom and make them aware of it.[834] Aware of Oswald's public promotion of FPCC, on August 17, 1963, William Stuckey (a WDSU radio station director), paid a visit to Lee Harvey Oswald at his apartment. Realizing that leftists were a rare commodity in New Orleans, Stuckey claimed he wanted Oswald to appear on his radio show for what he called "the sheer novelty value" of the event. After learning of their meeting, Carlos Bringuier supposedly became upset that Stuckey provided Oswald with a forum for his pro-Communist agenda and suggested that Stuckey and WDSU arrange a true debate between the two. Stuckey agreed, and for good measure invited far right winger Ed Butler, another close associate of Guy Banister. During the August 17, 1963, debate, which was tape recorded for posterity, Oswald proclaimed himself a Marxist. (Evidence that has already been presented, along with additional evidence, will demonstrate that the Oswald-Butler-Bringuier debate was another phony scheme to document through his own words that Oswald was a Marxist.) Ed Butler's link to the hardcore underground in New Orleans and California will be detailed later in this work.[835, 836]

The greatest significance of the Fair Play for Cuba Committee saga, beyond the enhancement of Oswald's image as pro-Communist, was the fact that the group shared key board members with the integrationist group the Southern Conference Education Fund, long a nemesis of Guy Banister.

Oswald infiltrated a second leftist organization in New Orleans in the summer of 1963, the New Orleans Committee for Peaceful Alternatives (NOCPA), which, like FPCC, had direct ties to the Southern Conference Education Fund (an entire chapter will be dedicated to the incident). In early September 1963, Lee Harvey Oswald was observed standing in a voter registration line organized by the civil rights group Congress of Racial Equality (CORE), in Clinton, Louisiana. (Clay Shaw and David Ferrie allegedly accompanied him to the town and those events will be detailed in Chapter Twenty-one.) CORE, a leftist integration group, like FPCC and NOCPA also had direct ties to Southern Conference Education Fund and were, like SCEF, specific targets of the Banister operation-inspired Communist Control Act.

While Oswald was making a public spectacle of himself infiltrating the three leftist groups, the Louisiana Committee on Un-American Activities had been planning a raid on the New Orleans offices of SCEF, for violation of the Communist Control Act (Banister was an investigator for the committee). Using the materials confiscated in the raid, hearings were planned to show the Communist influence in SCEF, and the three related groups Oswald which had infiltrated: FPCC, NOCPA and CORE.

The Communist Control Act was written by Banister associate Leander Perez and enacted into law by another close Banister associate, Representative James Pfister, in the state legislature at the same time as Oswald's return from the Soviet Union in June 1962. The barbaric law provided for the penalty of decades of imprisonment for anyone in a leftist or integrationist group—like SCEF, FPCC, NOCPA, and CORE—who associated with a Communist like Lee Harvey Oswald. (The subsequent raid on SCEF under the Communist Control Act was not an incident covered by Jim Garrison or any other investigation, and will be dealt with at length in later chapters.) The brief overview of the seminal Communist Control Act and any related events is presented here since it is the primary and overriding force that, though never revealed before, shaped all of Oswald's activities in New Orleans in the summer of 1963. None of his associations with the various leftist groups had anything to do with the plotting revealed by Joseph Milteer or with the Kennedy assassination. Rather, Oswald and his "adversaries" were on a separate plot track in New Orleans.

On September 17, 1963, Oswald applied for a tourist card at the New Orleans Mexican Consulate, just after the president's trip to Dallas was tentatively announced on September 13, 1963. On September 23, 1963, Ruth Paine arrived in New Orleans to pick up Marina Oswald and drive her back to Irving, Texas, with her two children. The next day, Lee Harvey Oswald waited for his Texas Employment Commission check, but was unable to collect and cash it until the next morning, September 25th. He then departed New Orleans by bus for Mexico City. While there, he reportedly argued with personnel at the Cuban and Soviet Embassies while demanding entrance visas to the two Communist countries. When the visas were refused, Oswald created a hostile, disruptive scene that left a lasting impression on the embassy staff. The president's trip to Dallas was formally announced in the newspaper on September 26.[837]

Three Versions of the Jim Garrison Case

"The Jim Garrison Case" can be viewed in three different ways, each with common elements but important distinct differences.

The first was Garrison's case against Clay Shaw, whom he charged with conspiracy to murder the president of the United States, with co-conspirators David Ferrie and Lee Harvey Oswald (Ferrie and Oswald were dead by then). Garrison's evidence to support the charge against Shaw was poor; Shaw was acquitted, and Garrison was thoroughly discredited. The alleged involvement of the CIA which Garrison touted was not brought up during the Shaw trial, nor was any evidence of Oswald's all-important association with Guy Banister or other New Orleans far right wingers mentioned during the proceedings. It is entirely possible that Clay Shaw may have been set up as a straw man to deflect attention away from the significant evidence of Oswald's ties to the Banister operation.

The second version of Garrison's case was presented in his *Playboy* magazine interview in June 1967, and later in Garrison's 1979 book on the case, *On the Trail of Assassins*. In the published accounts, Garrison publicly proclaimed that U.S. government intelligence was responsible for the assassination because of Kennedy's desire to break away from the established Cold War policies.[838, 839] Those government agencies named in Garrison's claims included the Office of Naval Intelligence, the CIA, the FBI, and the Secret Service, along with—or in cooperation with—the National Aeronautics and Space Administration. Garrison's evidence to support the claim of government intelligence involvement was weak. The problem with his broad-based, multi-agency plot was that it was so complex that it was unlikely to have been feasible. As a result, Garrison later narrowed the assassination conspiracy to the involvement of former employees of the CIA—who were opposed to the Communist regime of Fidel Castro in Cuba—but not CIA officials. Garrison failed to prove that any of the proposed key members of the plot were affiliated with the government or the CIA—or that the CIA was involved in the assassination in any way.

A third version of the Garrison case, unlike the other two—in that this one was genuine and revealing—is his case as divulged in the actual New Orleans district attorney's investigative files, which are not widely available to the public. Those files reveal practically no evidence of a U.S. government conspiracy in the assassination. Instead, the files are rife with evidence of a far-right-wing operation involving Lee Harvey Oswald and a New Orleans hardcore underground consisting of members of the Citizens' Council, Klan, John Birch Society, National States' Rights Party, American Nazi Party, and Minutemen. Garrison, in spite of his publicly pronounced CIA allegations, fittingly and correctly—at least early on—referred to the conspirators as "master-racist authors of the assassination."[840] Garrison also stated that the assassins were a group of "Fanatical anti-Communists—people who could be described as neo-Nazi."[841] Garrison's investigation established that Lee Harvey Oswald was working with Guy Banister at his Camp and Lafayette Street office, and this claim was substantiated by an abundance of credible evidence. (The connection between the hardcore elements in New Orleans, Joseph Milteer's underground, and the high command in its leadership will be detailed in the next chapter.) Garrison's district attorney files were not publicly seen until after the investigation, when the widow of one of Garrison's investigators, William Wood, made them available to researchers.[842] During the HSCA investigation from 1977 to 1979, Garrison supplied copies of some of his files to the committee; they later became public through the National Archives in the 1980s.

In 1994, a year after the death of Jim Garrison, the author accompanied a group of assassination writers and researchers to New Orleans to view and copy Jim Garrison's personal copies of his copies of the district attorney's JFK files, courtesy of his son Lyon Garrison.[843] The files contained evidence of a far-right conspiracy that has never been revealed before.

Garrison, Part I: The Clay Shaw Trial

In public, Clay Shaw was a prominent New Orleans businessman and, in 1963, director of the International Trade Mart, and, in his private life, a promiscuous homosexual. He used the alias "Clay Bertrand" in the course of his double life in the French Quarter gay scene.

On November 25, 1963, New Orleans attorney Dean Andrews, while in the hospital, contacted the New Orleans FBI and Secret Service and told them that Lee Harvey Oswald consulted him three or four times in the summer of 1963 for legal advice on his marine discharge and his wife's immigration status. Andrews's first encounter with Oswald was when he came to his office with approximately five "gay kids"—the police, in a weekend scoop operation, had picked up the young men wearing women's clothing. Twice, Oswald was at the office with a gay young man thought to be of Mexican extraction. Andrews stated that "Clay Bertrand" had sent gay kids to him in the past to parole or obtain bond for them. He also assumed "Bertrand" had sent Oswald and these "gay kids" to him. "Bertrand" guaranteed bail bond payment for the gay kids who couldn't make bail. The day after the Kennedy assassination, "Bertrand" allegedly called Andrews while he was in the hospital and asked him to represent Oswald, the alleged assassin, in Dallas. Andrews told "Bertrand" that he was ill and could not do it, but told "Bertrand" he would find someone who could, which became unnecessary when Oswald was killed the next day. "Bertrand" said that he would visit Andrews in the hospital later that day, but never did.

New Orleans FBI Special Agent Regis Kennedy interviewed Andrews in the hospital. Kennedy was a close friend of Guy Banister and a regular visitor to Banister's Camp and Lafayette Street office, as well as to the office of Friends of Democratic Cuba when it was located in the Balter Building. Allegedly, the FBI investigators made attempts to locate "Clay Bertrand" but were not successful. Remarkably, Kennedy attempted to convince Andrews that "Clay Bertrand" was "a figment of his imagination." Kennedy told Andrews that the "Clay Bertrand" lead was not solid, and that he was going to close the book on the case. Andrews told the Warren Commission that, after he talked to the FBI, his office had been rifled.[844]

Andrews testified before the Warren Commission and told them he had met "Bertrand" two years earlier, and had run into him six weeks prior to his testimony before the Commission. "Bertrand" supposedly ran away when the second encounter occurred. Andrews reported to the FBI just after the assassination that "Bertrand" was 6'1" tall and had brown hair. Later, in 1964, he stated that "Bertrand" was 5'8" and had sandy hair. When the marked discrepancy was pointed out, Andrews stated that both times when he saw "Bertrand," he was sitting down.[845] The Commission quickly lost interest in Andrews's story.

Garrison's investigators interviewed Prentis Davis, Jr., a private investigator for Andrews, in 1967, and Davis told them that Andrews's clients were "either homosexuals, pimps, prostitutes or huslers [sic] from Bourbon Street." Davis had also seen Oswald at the office in the company of the "kids," some of whom he thought were Cuban. Davis confirmed that Andrews's office was broken into and his files were searched after Andrews got out of the hospital.[846] When Garrison interviewed Andrews on March 2, 1967, Andrews stated that "Bertrand" called him on the occasion Oswald visited the office and told him, "I'll personally handle the fee." Andrews stated that the homosexuals he had represented knew "Bertrand's" phone number and called it from the office.[847]

Early during the Garrison investigation, Bob Scott of WNAC Radio in Boston interviewed Dean Andrews. Andrews told him he didn't want to get involved because he "liked to live," stating: "If a guy can put a hole in the president, he can just step on me like an ant . . . ." Andrews repeated several more times that he was afraid for his life.[848] On April 12, 1967, State Police Sergeant John J. Buccola ran into Andrews—whom he knew—and urged him to avoid perjury charges by disclosing "Clay Bertrand's" true identity. Andrews replied that he would rather spend five years in jail, because that was better than being dead.[849] In 1966, Garrison sent investigators out on to the streets and into the gay clubs—where a large number of witnesses were located who identified Clay Shaw as "Clay Bertrand." Garrison's chief investigator Lou Ivon told the author that there was overwhelming evidence that Shaw was "Bertrand."[850]

In early 1967, Garrison invited Andrews to lunch. Garrison had known Andrews since they had both attended Tulane Law School. Garrison had a frank conversation with a nervous Andrews and asked him to reveal the identity of "Clay Bertrand." Andrews refused, stating that if he did it would be "good bye" and that he'd get a bullet in the head. Andrews was later called by Garrison as a witness in the Clay Shaw trial, and when asked if Bertrand was Shaw, Andrews replied, "I can't say he is and I can't see he ain't," after which Garrison successfully charged and convicted Andrews of perjury.

Despite Andrews's reluctance to tell the truth, Garrison had other convincing evidence to support that "Bertrand" was Shaw. A hostess at a the VIP lounge of Eastern Airlines testified that she saw Clay Shaw sign the guest book as "Clay Bertrand."[851] When Shaw was arrested and booked on charges of conspiracy in the assassination of President Kennedy, he was asked routinely if he used any aliases. Shaw allegedly replied, "Clay Bertrand."[852]

Other witnesses identified Shaw in the company of Lee Harvey Oswald. Vernon Bundy was shooting heroin when he witnessed Shaw hand Oswald an envelope of cash at the Lake Pontchartrain sea wall. In spite of Bundy's known drug addiction, his testimony was found to be quite credible.[853] Several town officials and citizens in Clinton, Louisiana, testified that Oswald was there with David Ferrie and Shaw in the late summer of 1963, and that the two waited in a car while Oswald stood in a black voter registration line. Garrison used the Clinton witnesses to establish an Oswald-Ferrie-Shaw link, which will be extensively detailed in Chapter Twenty-one.

The establishment of a relationship between Oswald and Shaw, through the allegations of Dean Andrews and others, was far from the proof that Garrison would need to demonstrate that the two conspired to kill the president. That changed when Perry Russo, a young insurance man from Baton Rouge—formerly of New Orleans—showed up at the D.A.'s office on February 24, 1967, just eight days after the news of Garrison's investigation was reported in the papers. (Russo claimed he wrote a letter to Garrison immediately after the story broke, but Garrison never received it.)

Russo, suspiciously, was a friend and admirer of David Ferrie in the summer of 1963. Russo had first met Ferrie in 1960 when the family of a CAP cadet whom Russo coached on an athletic team approached Russo to "break Ferrie's hold on their son."[854] Russo told the author that, when he first met Ferrie and heard him charismatically speaking amongst a group of his friends, he thought, "Man, he's really got something."[855] After Ferrie's death, Russo stated that he had heard Ferrie threaten President Kennedy, saying "We are going to get him" and "It won't be long." Russo told Garrison that Ferrie was "obsessed with Kennedy."[856] Russo recounted that he attended a party at David Ferrie's apartment and "Leon" Oswald and Clay Shaw were in attendance. He claimed Ferrie and Shaw discussed assassinating the president and how it could be done by a triangulation of fire. Oswald reportedly stood in the adjacent dining room during the discussion and cleaned his rifle. Imitating Ferrie, Russo, with a flair for the dramatic, reenacted the scene in Ferrie's apartment for the author in 1994, after Russo gained access to the then-vacant apartment. Russo paced back and forth in Ferrie's former living room with the thumb, index finger, and little finger of his hand extended and raised, repeating the phrase "triangulation of fire" as he gestured.[857]

Russo's claims, however, were fraught with problems. In his first news interview, with the *Baton Rouge Times*—before his call to Garrison on February 24, 1963—he failed to mention anything about Oswald, "Bertrand," or an assassination plot. Further, Russo waited over three years to tell law enforcement that he overheard Shaw and Ferrie discussing the assassination of the president in Oswald's presence. Moreover, in early news reports on Russo's revelations, he referred to David Ferrie as a Marxist, which was far from the truth—and Russo should have known better as Ferrie's friend. Just the opposite, Ferrie was a fanatical anti-Communist.[858, 859] In another interview, Russo stated that Ferrie supposedly told him Castro "was not a bad guy."[860]

On February 24, 1967, Russo was again interviewed by the news media and mentioned nothing at all about Oswald, "Bertrand," or Shaw. In an interview later that same night, Russo stated that he never knew Oswald and had not heard of him until after the assassination. When Russo was interviewed by Andrew Sciambra of the D.A.'s office the next day, Russo told him that Ferrie was obsessed with the idea of assassinating President Kennedy. Russo was shown a picture of Clay Shaw and did not identify him as the man with Oswald and Ferrie discussing assassination. Russo mentioned that Ferrie had a roommate, whose name he couldn't remember, whom he had seen on a few occasions. He said the roommate had dirty blonde hair and a husky beard, and appeared to be a typical beatnik who was extremely dirty. His hair and beard were unkempt and he wore a dirty T-shirt with "cruddy tennis shoes and no socks." Russo was shown a photo of Oswald and asked if it was the same person as Ferrie's roommate. He hesitated, because the photo showed that Oswald was not "cruddy" and did not have a beard. Sciambra then drew a beard on Oswald's picture and Russo identified him as Ferrie's dirty, bearded roommate.

On May 27th, Russo was given intravenous Sodium Pentothal, the so-called "truth serum"—which he chose rather than a lie detector test—and was again interrogated by the D.A.'s office. He was shown several pictures of Oswald with beards drawn on them and he identified them as Ferrie's roommate. Russo also, for the first time, identified "Clay Bertrand" as the man at Ferrie's apartment when the assassination discussion took place. On February 28th, Russo had positively identified Shaw, while observing him outside Shaw's apartment as the man he knew as "Bertrand."

On March 1, Shaw was arrested based on Russo's statements. Russo was later hypnotized and interrogated, but at no time claimed that he saw Shaw (or "Bertrand") at Ferrie's apartment. Russo's statements under hypnosis were marred with inconsistency. Some investigators felt that the hypnosis was actually used to plant false recollections into Russo's mind.[861] A Yale University Law professor later examined the transcripts of Russo's interrogation under hypnosis and concluded that the hypnotist led Russo to his responses by the nature of his questions and that the "record does not distinguish between truth and fantasy."[862, 863]

Shaw was tried and acquitted of conspiracy. Although Garrison was successful in convincing the jury of the inherent flaws of the Warren Commission's findings, he produced no motive for Shaw's alleged involvement in a plot to assassinate the president—and none was discerned by the jury.

Russo had a change of heart thirty years after the assassination, when he was essentially immune from prosecution, and told the truth—that Oswald was a far right winger, not a Marxist, and would never have been at the home of another far-right-wing fanatic, David Ferrie, if he weren't. Russo stated of Oswald: "He comes to New Orleans. He comes in and joins a group, when he is supposed to be a left-wing Marxist—he isn't. He's a right-wing Fascist. This is the real Oswald. He is not left wing. I don't care what the Warren Commission says. It was dead wrong. He was in the wrong house to be a left-wing Marxist because you're dealing with rabid right-wing Fascists that were violent in their desire to overthrow Fidel."[864]

The question remains as to why Russo went out of his way to frame a seemingly innocent man in Clay Shaw, based on the questionable witness account that he kept to himself for three years following the assassination. It's possible that Russo implicated Shaw to steer the investigation away from the true conspirators. That theory suggests that Russo set Shaw up on behalf of the conspirators. Russo, like his friend David Ferrie, was a gay far right winger. Russo may have attempted to steer the investigation toward David Ferrie who was now dead, and Clay Shaw (who had no obvious connection to the hardcore underground), and away from those who were involved in the assassination or with Oswald. Shaw may have been made the fall guy because he brought attention to himself, and perhaps the New Orleans conspirators, by contacting Dean Andrews to represent Oswald when he was charged in the president's murder. By doing so, he opened up the possibility of tying the "gay kids"—whose legal bills were paid for by Shaw/"Bertrand"—to David Ferrie and, in turn, to the Banister operation. Secondly, Shaw was reportedly one-eighth African-American—an "Octoroon" in the jargon of the time—which may have made him expendable to the hardcore racists in the far-right underground of New Orleans.[865]

It's possible that Ed Butler, who debated Oswald on the radio, was the one who actually influenced Russo to implicate Shaw. (Butler, as it will be recalled, had ties to Guy Banister and George Soule of the Congress of Freedom.) At the time of the Garrison investigation, Butler was working for Patrick Frawley in California—whose connections to the American Security Council and Pedro del Valle's friend Frank Capell have been noted.

The author spent a day with the cordial Russo in 1994. At the conclusion of the interview Russo was asked to jot down something with his signature as evidence of our interview. Russo wrote, "To Jeff, Razor's Edge will find the truth. Perry."[866] Russo died a year later.

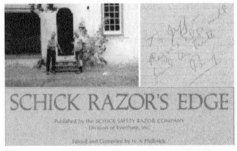

Because Butler ended up working for Patrick Frawley at Eversharp Corporation—who published an anti-Communist newsletter called the *Razor's Edge*—the cryptic note may have intended to tip the author off, thirty-one years after the murder, and implicate Ed Butler in either the assassination conspiracy or the Shaw affair. The evidence strongly suggests that Butler plotted with Lee Harvey Oswald in the phony radio debate (which will be detailed later) in the summer of 1963. At the time of Oswald's presence in New Orleans, Butler was a frequent visitor to the office of Guy Banister, as was David Ferrie during the period of his friendship with Perry Russo. It may be that Butler, who was about the same age as Russo, and was in New Orleans in 1963, persuaded Russo to implicate Ferrie and

(Top left) The author (left) in 1994 with Perry Russo (right) in front of David Ferrie's 1963 apartment. Source: Author's collection. Perry Russo inscribed a note to the author (top right), "To Jeff – Razor's Edge will find the truth. –Perry." Note that Razor's Edge is capitalized. Herbert A. Philbrick wrote the Schick Razor's Edge newsletter (bottom) for Patrick Frawley. Frawley hired Butler after the assassination. Source: Letterhead from the Herbert A. Philbrick Papers, Library of Congress

Shaw to move the investigation away from the real conspirators on the far right.

Interestingly, Herbert Philbrick wrote the newsletter *Schick Razor's Edge* for Patrick Frawley's Schick Razor Corporation; Butler began working for Frawley after the assassination. (As noted in the last chapter, Frawley was impressed with Butler's cheap anti-Castro propaganda movie "Hitler in Havana" and hired him.) Philbrick kept a file on Butler, his organization INCA, and his debate with Lee Harvey Oswald in his papers, which are now in the Library of Congress. It's likely the two knew each other. After the assassination, Philbrick was quick to point out—in detail—the Communist link to Fair Play for Cuba Committee.[867] Philbrick was on the faculty of the Fred Schwarz Greater New Orleans School of Anti-Communism in 1961.[868] Guy Banister was on the advisory committee of the school at the same time, as was noted in Chapter One.

Philbrick infiltrated Communist groups for the FBI. At age twenty-five, he joined a Boston-area youth group, and he allegedly later learned that the Communists controlled the group, or so the story goes. Philbrick told the FBI, and they encouraged him to play along as an informant. He supposedly rose to the top of the Communist Party leadership in America. He became a public figure in 1949, when he became a government witness in the trial of eleven leaders of the Communist Party, known as "the Communist Party 11," who were indicted for violations of the Smith Act—which made it unlawful to advocate overthrowing the government. He testified before a number of House and Senate investigative bodies regarding Communists and their activities in the United States between 1949 and 1967. He published an account of his work infiltrating the Communist Party in his book *I Led 3 Lives: Citizen, "Communist," Counterspy*. A television program was produced, which was based loosely on the book and ran from 1953 to 1956—it was Lee Harvey Oswald's favorite show, which he watched with his mother.[869]

The storylines were often far-fetched. In one episode entitled "Assassination," a congressman gave a television address claiming that Communists had infiltrated a youth camp. In response, leaders of Philbrick's Communist cell ordered him and a "comrade" to go to the camp and destroy the papers proving the Communist infiltration of the camp. The congressman just happened to be vacationing near the youth camp, and the FBI told Philbrick to keep his "comrade" away from him, fearing he might try to kill him. When Philbrick and his comrade arrived at the youth camp, they found the files had been rifled through and assumed the Communist connection to the camp had been discovered by the authorities. The "comrade" then declared there was only one thing to do but to assassinate the congressman with a high-powered rifle. Philbrick had no chance to notify the FBI and was forced to act on his own. He dropped a lit cigarette in the forest, starting a fire and attracting the forest ranger and, effectively, thwarting the assassination. Thus, Philbrick's television fairy tale propagated the myth that Communists were prepared to murder for their cause.[870]

However, Philbrick reported to the Subversive Activities Control Board that he never told J. Edgar Hoover about any Communists engaging in acts of violence involving arms. He nonetheless depicted Communists as murderers on his TV show. One TV critic called the show "corny melodrama" that showed Philbrick "walking up and down streets looking furtively over his shoulder and momentarily expecting to be done in by the Reds."[871] The script of each episode was more fantastic than the last, but nonetheless it served to heighten the Red Scare of the era. In 1956, the show aired in Great Britain and the first show featured Philbrick's improbable account of how he prevented a railway strike. The British public found the subsequent three programs so preposterous that they prompted letters and phone calls of protest, and the British Broadcasting Company dropped the series. British viewers considered it bad entertainment and were not sympathetic to a "stool pigeon" in Philbrick who incited workers to violence, then betrayed them.[872]

Philbrick helped the national far right in their effort to promote and embellish the role of Communism in the Kennedy assassination. On December 11, 1963, John Birch Society Council member Clarence Manion wrote Philbrick and asked him: "How can we prove that Oswald was 'under discipline'?" Philbrick responded, "Just keep clobbering away at his affiliations with the Fair Play For Cuba Gang and the Committee to Secure Justice . . . We just publicize all of the names of all of the FPCC people and say: watch for those rats to come out of their holes disguised under another name."[873] ("Party discipline" referred to the purported Communist Party-indoctrinated readiness of its adherents to murder traitors of the party as needed.[874])

Philbrick kept a listing of the extensive Communist-front affiliations of Reverend George Paine, a resident of his home state of Massachusetts. Reverend Paine was the father of Michael Paine, whose wife Ruth was the kind woman who took Marina Oswald into her home while Lee Harvey was unemployed in Texas.[875] Philbrick and Earl Lively of the Dallas John Birch Society wrote an unpublished manuscript, entitled *The Strange Death of President Kennedy* that promoted the Communist angle. They wrote, "killers Castro, Khrushchev, the comrats and their assorted fellow travelers were in this right up to their Red necks."[876] Philbrick served on the Advisory Board of the American Committee to Free Cuba, Inc., in 1963, along with Kent Courtney, John Rousselot, and a number of other prominent members of the far right. General Walker's close aide, Robert Surrey, was also on the board.[877]

The chronology of Oswald's life in relation to his favorite TV show and other events is worth reviewing. The 1950 Joseph McCarthy Communist witch hunts were front-page news until 1953, when McCarthy fell into disrepute. From September 1952 to January 1954, Oswald and his mother were forced to live in New York City with his half-brother John Pic due to financial difficulties. It was during that time that the Philbrick show aired, depicting the anti-Communist, infiltrator-hero Herbert Philbrick undermining the nations' enemies—the Communist Party USA. While enrolled in the New York City schools, Oswald was frequently truant, a fact that the Warren Commission maintained established Oswald's early emotional instability. However, school counselors learned the true reason for his school absence: Oswald did not want to attend schools with African Americans, a normal response from a white child brought up in the segregated South. Oswald would later tell United Press International reporter Aline Mosely in Moscow, "I was brought up like every Southern boy, to hate the Negroes.[878] In 1955, while the Philbrick show was still airing, Oswald joined a unit of the Civil Air Patrol led by the fanatically anti-Communist David Ferrie who his cadets called "spell binding." In October 1956, at the age of seventeen, Oswald joined the marines—who were ostensibly protecting the U.S. from the Communists in the Soviet Union and around the world. Herbert Philbrick's television show may have eventually inspired—and served as a guide for—Oswald's infiltration of at least three leftist groups in the summer of 1963 as a phony Communist, as we shall see later.

Kent Courtney, Carlos Bringuier, and the Shaw Case

The author uncovered a tape recording—among the personal papers of Kent Courtney—of a private conversation Courtney had with Carlos Bringuier after Jim Garrison questioned Bringuier on February 17, 1967, before the district attorney's case became public. Courtney had the peculiar habit of tape recording his phone conversations, as well as discussions with individuals in his office. On the tape, Bringuier confided in Courtney that Garrison asked him questions about a "well-known conservative" who was unnamed—but was undoubtedly Guy Banister. In response to that, Courtney inquired, "Oh yeah, anybody I know?" Bringuier responded, again saying only that he was a "well-known conservative." The two discussed the fight between Oswald and Bringuier, and how, afterward, Bringuier sought Courtney's help in finding an attorney, but the name of the suggested attorney was not audible on the tape. Bringuier then stated that he had heard that Theodore Brent, Clay Shaw's predecessor as director of the International Trade Center—and also a homosexual—had left Shaw, upon his death, a $100,000 legal defense fund to aid homosexuals with legal problems. Courtney stated that he had heard the same thing.[879]

Although speculative, the allegation of the "homosexual defense fund" offers an alternative motive for Shaw/"Bertrand" paying Dean Andrews's fees for his legal help for Oswald and the "gay kids" who accompanied him—and also asking Andrews to defend Oswald after the assassination. Garrison had good evidence that David Ferrie and Oswald were in contact with each other in 1963, and also that Shaw and Ferrie, both homosexuals, knew each other. It may be that Oswald was a recipient of Shaw's largesse and benefitted from the homosexual defense fund as a favor to David Ferrie, or because Shaw concluded, by Oswald's association with Ferrie, that he, too, was a homosexual. Shaw's attempt to find legal representation for Oswald after the assassination, thus, may have been an innocent act of generosity to help out one of David Ferrie's friends by using the defense fund.

Clay Shaw and the Far Right

Jim Garrison contended that Clay Shaw was an agent involved in a CIA plot to kill the president, but he failed to disclose Shaw's ties to the far right. His CIA case got a boost when an Italian newspaper, *Paese Sera*, reported on March 4, 1967, that Shaw was on the Board of Directors of an Italian Trade Mart affiliate called Permindex, which was a subsidiary of Centro Mondo Comerciale, or CMC. CMC was pegged as the organization that was a "creature of the CIA" set up as a cover for transfer of CIA funds into Italy for "illegal political-espionage activities." Members of CMC reportedly were European Fascists and supporters of the para-military far right. Shaw admitted his connection to CMC but minimized his role, stating that he accepted the position "in exchange for two New Orleans-Rome airline tickets."[880]

Jim Garrison obtained a copy of a translated edition of the Soviet daily *Pravda* from March 7, 1967, that stated the "U.S. Central Information Agency" [sic] had used the ser-vices of Shaw, which further bolstered Garrison's flimsy case of CIA involvement in the as-sassination. More telling, they also noted that the aim of CMC was to finance "intolerant anti-Communist groups." Shaw's duties were said to include establishment of contacts with extreme rightist groups in Rome, including neo-Fascist organizations. CMC had close rela-tionships to a number of Fascists, including a relative of Adolf Hitler's banker Hjalmar von Schacht.[881] Shaw's address book contained a preponderance of far-right contacts including, the names of several Fascists of European extraction, including Herman Bochelman (who ad-mired the Nazi Waffen-SS) and John DeCourcy (who was imprisoned in England for Fascist sedition).[882] One source told Garrison that Shaw was in touch with all of the radical-right groups and white supremacists.[883]

The allegation of a relationship between the CIA and CMC remains unproven. Nev-ertheless, even if it is true, the evidence falls far short of proof of a CIA conspiracy involving Clay Shaw and Lee Harvey Oswald in the death of President Kennedy. The Fascists behind CMC were of the same familiar political stripe as those in the anti-Bolshevik Bloc of Nations whose members included such native Fascists as General Charles Willoughby, H. L. Hunt, Billy James Hargis, Hilaire du Berrier, Harold Lord Varney, and others associated with Gen-eral Edwin A. Walker.

Garrison was somewhat redeemed when, in 1979, CIA Chief Richard Helms ad-mitted to the House Select Committee on Assassinations that Shaw, as an international busi-nessman, was a part-time contact in the Domestic Contact Division of the CIA.[884] However, the HSCA determined that, in the period of 1959 to 1963, as many as 25,000 Americans annually provided information to the CIA's Domestic Contact Division on a nonclandestine basis after returning from trips abroad.[885] It has not been shown that Shaw's ties to the CIA were any more special than those of the legions of other patriotic Americans who served a similar role.

FBI Agent Regis Kennedy, who interviewed Dean Andrews after the assassination and tried to convince him that his Oswald-"Clay Bertrand" allegation was a figment of his imagination, may have tipped off Garrison to Shaw's connection to the CIA. According to one witness, Betty Parott, Kennedy was a frequent visitor to Banister's anti-Castro group Friends of Democratic Cuba while it was located in the Balter Building before it relocated to the building bearing the infamous 544 Camp/431 Lafayette Street addresses. Regis Kennedy told Parott that Shaw was a former CIA agent who did some work for the agency in Italy over a five-year span.[886] Garrison interviewed Regis Kennedy in 1967 and Kennedy admitted when asked that he had been in Banister's office, but denied seeing Lee Harvey Oswald (or

Jack Ruby) there.[887] Of course, Kennedy may have been trying to steer Garrison to Shaw and the CIA—and away from former FBI SAC Banister.

The CMC allegation was not the only evidence linking Clay Shaw to the far right. Garrison determined that Shaw had flown to San Francisco and spoken before a luncheon meeting of the San Francisco World Trade Center on the day of the assassination.[888, 889] One of Garrison's investigators, William Turner, interviewed a witness who stated that Shaw had visited some of his co-workers, who were cliquish and extremely right wing in their political views, at a San Francisco Bay-area virus laboratory on the day before or day of the assassination. They were described as anti-Semitic and said to have openly used the term "dirty Jews." The coworkers often talked about a "super race" theory and Nazism. The witness, Thomas C. Brietner—a Jew and refugee from a concentration camp—reported that Shaw engaged the leader of the "clique" in an earnest conversation for a period of time.[890] Another source told Garrison that Shaw was involved with a shipment of weapons from the West Coast.[891] In yet another Garrison file, Shaw was reported to have been in the vicinity of Clinton, Louisiana, before the assassination, "getting up the Klan."[892] (Shaw's alleged trip to Clinton, Louisiana, in September 1963 will be discussed in Chapter Twenty-one.)

Writer Harold Weisberg, who joined Garrison's investigation, interviewed Dean Andrews and asked him what happened to Banister's files. According to Weisberg's notes, Andrews drawled in response, "Evuh heah uh d' 'T'underbolt'? It's in A'gustuh, Gawgiah. Try theah." The *Thunderbolt* was the newspaper of the National States' Rights Party, which Milteer, Banister, and many others described in the prior chapters had ties to. Andrews's response suggests he was aware that Banister had ties to the radical right.[893]

Clay Shaw, Lloyd Cobb, and Alvin Cobb

Clay Shaw's relationship with Lloyd Cobb was another important tie to the far right. Shaw served under Cobb, who was president of the New Orleans International Trade Mart. His brother, Alvin Cobb, was one of Guy Banister's two closest friends. (The other was George Singelmann, who was the assistant to Leander Perez.)[894] Lloyd was called to testify at the Shaw trial, in which he vouched for Shaw's presence in New Orleans in September of 1963, when Shaw was alleged to have been in Clinton, Louisiana, during a civil rights registration drive with Lee Harvey Oswald. In his testimony Lloyd, gratuitously volunteered that if Shaw had taken part in any civil right efforts, he would have objected to it.[895]

There is not a lot known about Lloyd Cobb, other than that he was a well-to-do attorney. Alberto Fowler who knew Lloyd Cobb, Ed Butler, and Clay Shaw described Lloyd: "Cobb is extremely conservative, but anti-establishment. Cobb believes there is a secret government (liberal) running U.S. and other governments (a secret power structure). Cobb is a Goldwater man." The statement suggests Lloyd subscribed to the far-right belief of a "secret government" as described in the writings of Mary Davison, Kent Courtney, and Dan Smoot.[896]

Lloyd Cobb may have been an associate of Henry S. Riecke, who (as noted in the prior chapter) operated an extremist organization in New Orleans called the Paul Revere Associated Yeomen, and received funding from General Pedro del Valle. On December 27, 1963, Riecke wrote a letter to Leander Perez and Willie Rainach.

In the letter, Riecke praised the printing of a photograph in the most recent issue of the *Councilor*, which showed liberal Louisiana congressman Hale Boggs giving a clenched fist salute, which was alleged to be a Communist salute. Lee Harvey Oswald was pictured giving a similar salute, which Revilo Oliver—in his Warren Commission testimony—described as the Communist signal for "mission accomplished." After implying that Boggs was a Communist, Riecke urged patriotic organizations, "our own Paul Reveres, the Citizens' Councils," to back a well-known candidate like Lloyd Cobb to run against Boggs in the 1964 congressional election. He further remarked that the "Nat W. Knights" could defeat Boggs with the proper backing.[897] Although he did not disclose a name, Riecke may have been referring to Lloyd's brother Alvin, who was the leader of a Klan group called "Knights of the White Christians."[898]

Del Valle wrote Riecke, in 1964, and recommended that he coordinate his efforts with Klan leader Jim Venable of Georgia and Wally Butterworth, both of whom were in attendance at the October 1963 Constitution Party meeting with Joseph Milteer, where discussion of murdering the president took place.[899] Del Valle recommended Riecke to represent the State of Louisiana during the 1965 Constitution Party meeting.[900] John F. Rau, Jr., who received the same letter sent from del Valle to Riecke, served as the legal counsel for the Parents and Friends of Catholic Schools, Inc. (Jack Helm, a Klansman-associate of David Ferrie and Guy Banister, was president of the segregationist organization.)[901, 902] Riecke, a fanatical anti-Communist, praised the John Birch Society and also wrote to its leader, Robert Welch. Riecke attended the May 23, 1961, luncheon given by the Christian Anti-Communist Crusade—another organization that Banister and Herbert Philbrick were involved with.[903]

Banister kept a file on Lloyd Cobb, but its contents are unknown.[904] Garrison listed some of the names of Banister's file headings in his 1979 book, claiming they related to government intelligence. (They did not.) He conveniently failed to mention names like Lloyd Cobb in the files.[905] Among the Warren Commission papers of Louisiana congressman Hale Boggs, is a phone message he received from Banister's close associate George Singelmann. The note stated only that the phone call regarded Leander Perez and Lloyd Cobb, but nothing more. Mention of the three names on a single phone message slip is intriguing, since Perez and Singelmann ran the New Orleans Citizens' Council out of the Balter Building at the same time that Banister had an office in the building. The note suggests a relationship among the three, who together may have been keeping tabs on the deliberations of the Warren Commission through Boggs, who served on the Commission.[906]

The author also found evidence of a likely relationship between Lloyd Cobb and mob leader Carlos Marcello, whom Banister and Ferrie worked for. Lloyd owned a potato farm in West Feliciana Parish. When one of his farm hands died, Marcello's wife and children attended the funeral.[907]

Alvin Cobb was head of the Knights of the White Camellia, the Knights of the White

Christians, and the Robert E. Lee Patriots. The FBI also had identified him as, at some point, being the Exalted Cyclops for the United Klans of America in New Orleans (the National United Klans received its corporate charter in Atlanta, Georgia, in 1961). The FBI opened a file on Alvin during World War II, because he would call or write them and urge them to investigate certain individuals simply by virtue of the fact that they were Germans or of German extraction.[908] In 1957, the FBI described Alvin as a "self-styled detective for 25 years" and also a public notary and real estate broker.

Alvin ran for mayor in the 1950 election as a Dixiecrat candidate urging white supremacy. On June 14, 1955, Cobb ran an advertisement in the *Times–Picayune* under the headline "Knights of the White Christians" and urged citizens to protect segregation and the traditions of the South, which led to an FBI investigation. Sources described him as a "negro [sic] hater," a "shady character" and a "nut." In 1956, Alvin gave a speech and called the NAACP the "National Association for Advancement of the Communist Party."[909]

He sent a telegram to FBI Director J. Edgar Hoover on September 27, 1964, objecting to a news report about Hoover. Alvin complained to Hoover about the "tyrannical rule of the Kennedy pro-Communist dictatorship" and "The dictatorial rule of the Justice Dept. by the Irish Fabian Roman Robert Kennedy." On June 16, 1965, Alvin appeared before the Joint Legislative Committee on Un-American Activities for the State of Louisiana, and was questioned by council Jack N. Rogers on his activities in the Knights of the White Camellia. (As will be recalled Guy Banister, who died in June 1964, had been LUAC's chief investigator.) The Klan group was named on the attorney general's list of subversive organizations. Rogers stated that all the members had completely gone underground and detailed a romantic history of the group dating back to the Reconstruction.

Interestingly enough, of the four distinct Klan organizations in Louisiana which were described, the largest was The Original Knights of the Ku Klux Klan, headed by the Imperial Wizard identified as "a man named Davis from Dallas, Texas."[910] "Davis" appears to be Roy Elonza "R. E." Davis. Willie Somersett named Dallas Klan leader R. E. Davis as one of the actual triggermen in the assassination of the president. Davis became the subject of a Secret Service investigation, based on Somersett's allegations in connection with the assassination.[911] In response to the author's Freedom of Information Act request, the Secret Service stated they had destroyed their records on Davis.

Roy Elonza Davis was a member of the Dallas Indignant White Citizens' Council, which was described as "an extremist organization composed of people opposing integration of the races." The organization was formed on July 20, 1963, in Grand Prairie, Texas, by Bobbie Savelle Joiner. Joiner, along with friends and family members, was demonstrating at the Dallas Trade Mart where the president was scheduled to speak after the motorcade, when the assassination occurred. Afterward, they were arrested for suspicion of conspiracy and trespassing, and, later, released. Robert Hatfield, a member of the Indignant White Citizens' Council—as well as the John Birch Society and "General Walker's group"—had been previously arrested during a demonstration against U.N. Ambassador Adlai Stevenson in October 1963.[912] (As we shall see later, General Walker's group was behind the disruption of Stevenson's speech in October 1963.)

On July 28, 1965, an unnamed member of the Joint Legislative Committee on Un-American Activities for the State of Louisiana contacted the FBI and advised them that Alvin Cobb told him that Alvin's organization, the Robert. E. Lee Patriots, was planning to organize "suicide squads for the purpose of taking care of the Communist leaders of this country." When asked who his targets were, Alvin named President Johnson, Vice President Hubert Humphrey, Attorney General Nicholas Katzenbach, and members of the Supreme Court. The informant told the FBI that Alvin "could be extremely dangerous." Alvin was interviewed by the FBI and stated that he was not an advocate of violence or the assassination of President Johnson, but that he wanted to prevent "the further take over by niggers and Communists."

The FBI had also interviewed Alvin in connection with the bombing of the First Unitarian Church in New Orleans in 1965.[913] Cecilia Pizzo, who knew both Guy Banister and Delphine Roberts, referred to Alvin as New Orleans' number one "Kon Artist."[914, 915] On September 30, 1965, FBI Director J. Edgar Hoover—pursuant to the presidential protection agreement between the FBI and the Secret Service—placed Alvin Cobb on a list of individuals felt to be a potential threat to the president's life based on conduct or statements indicating a propensity for violence.[916]

On May 8, 1965, Alvin joined Banister associates George Singelmann and Jack Helm at a segregation rally at Bogalusa, Louisiana, along with Ned Touchstone and John Rarick.[917] Rarick had been Jim Garrison's law school classmate. He was also the leader of the St. Francisville Klan; four members of Rarick's Klan outfit testified during the Clay Shaw trial that they had seen Shaw with David Ferrie and Lee Harvey Oswald in Clinton, Louisiana, in the summer of 1963. Evidence to be presented in Chapter Twenty-one will show that they lied in their testimony and were, in fact, a part of the hardcore underground.

The evidence suggests that Alvin Cobb and, likely, Lloyd Cobb were both involved in the Banister operation to some degree.

Garrison, Part II: The Written Accounts of the Garrison Case

The Garrison case—as presented to the media in the form of interviews with Garrison, the *Playboy* interview, and his 1979 book on the case—tells a different story than the one presented to the jury in the Clay Shaw trial. Two allegations not brought up at the trial, but put forth by Garrison, were that government intelligence agencies were behind the assassination, and, importantly, that Lee Harvey Oswald was associated with Guy Banister.

Jim Garrison granted an extensive interview to *Playboy* magazine in mid-June 1967, three months after the first story of his investigation broke, which was published in the October 1967 issue. In the interview, Garrison claimed that the Kennedy assassination was carried out by former employees of the Central Intelligence Agency, but that no high-ranking officials of the CIA were involved. Later, he clarified that it was former employees of the CIA and the *paramilitary right.* In other accounts—and later in his 1979 book—Garrison dropped the paramilitary right from the scenario.

Garrison claimed from the onset of his investigation that Lee Harvey Oswald was not a Communist at all, but was an informant for the government and aided anti-Castro Cubans. The claim that Oswald was not a Communist was well founded, but he never proved that Oswald was working for the government.[918]

Guy Banister's status, as a former director of the Chicago FBI is well known. However, Garrison's claim that Banister worked with the Office of Naval Intelligence (ONI), during World War II is completely unsubstantiated.[919] Joseph Oster, who was a partner in Banister's detective agency in the 1950s, told the author that Banister was never in the military, and FBI records reflect continuing FBI service during the war.[920] In fact, the evidence shows Banister was not in the ONI, but that his close friend Guy Johnson—one of Clay Shaw's first attorneys—was.

In 1960, Banister learned from a confidential informant that approximately 100 Jeeps, weapons carriers, and trucks had been shipped to Cuba through the port of New Orleans over a few months and invoiced at the Port of New Orleans as "agriculture equipment." (The vehicles were actually military surplus that had been completely refurbished.) Maurice Gatlin hired Banister to investigate the matter. Banister wrote a report on his investigation in unmistakable FBI style on a Guy Banister and Associates letterhead, entitled, "Fidel Castro—Purchase of War Supplies." He sent copies to Senator Allen Ellender and Senator James O. Eastland. The story made the front page of the New Orleans *Times–Picayune* on October 1, 1960, which noted that through Ellender's intercession that the Commerce Department had put a hold on the Jeep shipments.[921] Prior to the story, Banister wrote to his friend Guy Johnson on August 31, 1960, and sent him a report of his investigation. In turn, Johnson sent Banister's letter and his investigative report to the Office of Naval Intelligence. The ONI noted that Johnson had been a Naval Reserve officer with the Naval Intelligence during World War II. The ONI also noted Banister's FBI background, but there is no reference to him ever being in the ONI. The ONI took a dig at Maurice Gatlin, calling him "an attorney with a very plush office and not many clients," and stating that he was apparently not held in very high esteem by local attorneys.[922] The Banister Jeep incident is important for two reasons: it refutes Garrison's claim that Banister served in the ONI, and it may explain what has been called the "Bolton Ford" incident.

Only months after Banister's investigation into the Jeep exports to Cuba, two men claiming to represent the Friends of Democratic Cuba entered the Bolton Ford dealership on January 20, 1961—three months prior to the Bay of Pigs operation. One man was a large Latin, the other a young Anglo-Saxon who identified himself as "Oswald." They said they wanted to buy ten Ford pickup trucks, but never returned to complete the deal. (Oddly enough, Lee Harvey Oswald was in the Soviet Union at the time.)[923] After Kennedy's assassination, the incident was reported to the FBI. The meaning of the Bolton Ford incident is not clear, but it may have been an attempt to show that a known Communist (in this case the fake "Lee

Harvey Oswald") could purchase vehicles intended for Cuba without difficulty. Ross Banister was fully aware of his brother's 1960 investigation of the Jeep shipments to Cuba. He told the HSCA that the reason that Oswald used the 544 Camp Street address on his pamphlets was to embarrass Banister over his well-publicized campaign that halted the Jeep shipments. The problem with Ross Banister's allegation was that Oswald was in the Soviet Union in 1960, and likely knew nothing about the Jeep incident.[924]

There is no credible evidence that Banister had ties to the CIA—neither Garrison nor the HSCA established a Banister tie to the CIA. Garrison's claim that Banister's "work in New Orleans with Cuban guerillas had to be CIA" is not substantiated, and is not proof of a CIA relationship. Garrison stated that the Bolton Ford incident "smelled of CIA."[925] The evidence presented earlier, however, suggests the Bolton Ford incident was not CIA related, but may have been the work of two fanatic anti-Communist crusaders: Maurice Gatlin and Guy Banister.

William Wood, who was formerly with the CIA, worked as an investigator for Garrison's assassination investigation under the pseudonym "Bill Boxley." After getting clearance from the CIA, he disclosed his former ties to the CIA to Garrison. While with the CIA, Wood had trained foreign agents overseas for more than a year, then taught classes in Washington, D.C., on the case histories of the CIA before leaving the CIA in 1953. Wood had a drinking problem in the CIA, but left on his own accord and became an editor for the *Houston Tribune*.

While researching a story on the Garrison case for the newspaper, Wood was hired as an investigator for Garrison after passing a lie detector test. Garrison told Wood he did not want to go to trial with the Clay Shaw case because he felt that he essentially had no case. Wood was suspicious of the motives of some of Garrison's investigative staff, including Harold Weisberg. He felt that Weisberg might have convinced Garrison that he was still a CIA agent, which led to his being fired later. He feared that Garrison was using him as a "cat's paw," or dupe. Wood interviewed William Martin, who worked in the International Trade Mart, who told him that Shaw might have been a part of the old Gehlen-CIA apparatus, but there is no evidence to substantiate the claim whatsoever. (Reinhard Gehlen was the Nazi German Intelligence Chief during WWII and was in charge of the eastern front. After the war, the U.S. recruited him to set up a spy ring directed against the Communist Soviet Union.)

Wood wrote a summary of various aspects of the Garrison investigation. He noted that Banister's files indicated he was running an intelligence operation directed against leftists and integrationists. Garrison asked Wood his opinion as to whether or not Banister worked for the CIA. Wood cited a report that indicated he did not. Wood noted that, according to a report in the remnants of Guy Banister's files, the statement was made by Banister: "It appears that WE may have cut across a CIA operation here and great care must be taken not to expose it." Wood concluded logically that the CIA did not employ Banister, because if he were a CIA agent he would not have made that statement. Wood stated that if Banister was a CIA agent and had written anything at all, he would not have identified the agency or included names of the operating personnel as he did.[926] Banister's brother Ross told the HSCA that his brother never mentioned the CIA, but did tell him that Clay Shaw was getting paid one hundred dollars a month as a CIA informant.[927]

Garrison was correct that the Banister operation had an air about it of an intelligence operation, but not the kind he claimed "smelled of CIA." Banister and his friend Guy Johnson, who was formerly employed by the Office of Navel Intelligence, were considered for another kind of intelligence-gathering operation, but not for the U.S. Government. In 1960, James Pfister of the new Legislative Committee on Un-American Activities set out to inform the citizens of Louisiana that there were subversive influences from leftists and integrationists operating in the state. The committee interviewed private investigators for a position with the committee—including Banister and Johnson. Banister got the job.[928]

Carlos Bringuier

Carlos Bringuier is a suspect figure in the events surrounding Oswald's adventures in New Orleans in the summer of 1963, especially because he knew Guy Banister and had ties to the anti-Castro Cubans at the 544 Camp Street address in Banister's office building. Garrison deserves credit for raising suspicions about Bringuier and tying him to Banister. Unfortunately, the Warren Commission and HSCA had no misgivings whatsoever about Bringuier.

In 1961, Bringuier left Cuba—where he had been trained as a lawyer—and opened a clothing store in October 1962 in New Orleans. Bringuier later testified before the Warren Commission that Oswald visited his store on August 5, 1963, while Bringuier was talking to a teenager named Philip Geraci about distributing literature critical of Castro. Oswald reportedly joined the conversation and agreed with Bringuier's views that were also unfavorable of Communism. Oswald told him that he had been in the Marine Corps and was trained in guerilla warfare. Oswald allegedly offered to train anti-Castro Cubans—and even fight against Castro himself. The next day, Oswald returned to the store and left his copy of the *Marine Guidebook*. Bringuier told the FBI that he was not acquainted with Geraci and that since Geraci and Oswald entered the store around the same time he thought they were together.[929]

When Oswald had returned to Texas from the Soviet Union in June 1962, he had joined—or attempted to join by mail—a number of Communist or leftist organizations, including the Communist Party USA; the Socialist Workers Party; the Fair Play for Cuba Committee; and others. In New Orleans, he informed the Communist Party of his activities in the FPCC—a group critical of the U.S. policy toward the Castro government—and submitted his membership cards from his phony chapter to various party officials. Oswald informed the Communist Party, on November 1, 1963, that he had moved back to Texas and attended a lecture by General Walker, as well as a meeting of the American Civil Liberties Union. When Oswald traveled to Mexico City in September 1963, he showed Cuban embassy officials his FPCC membership card. While in New Orleans, from April to September 1963, Oswald engaged in activities purportedly on the behalf of the FPCC. In April 1963, he received a membership card for the FPCC, but the FPCC felt there were far too few members in New Orleans to grant Oswald a chapter, and he was advised not to open an office but, rather, to maintain a post office box instead. Later, Oswald told them he had been evicted from the office he had opened. The Warren Commission later determined that Oswald's FPCC was entirely fictitious and that there were no other members. The national office of FPCC did not write Oswald again after May 29, 1963.[930]

Oswald distributed printed FPCC handbills on at least three occasions in the central business district, or in the French Quarter at the Dumaine Street wharf. On August 9, 1963, Bringuier learned that an individual who later turned out to be Oswald was demonstrating at the 700 block of Canal Street with a "Viva Fidel" and "Hands Off Cuba" sign. Bringuier claimed that he felt Oswald had double crossed him, before realizing that Oswald was actually a pro-Castro Communist agent trying to "infiltrate" his organization. After arguing, Bringuier threw a punch at Oswald, who blocked it with his arms and then allegedly urged Bringuier to try and hit him again. Dropping his arms, he allegedly said, "OK, Carlos, if you want to hit me go ahead." A scuffle followed, and they were taken to jail. The Warren Commission determined that one of the pieces of Oswald's literature was stamped with address 544 Camp Street.[931, 932]

On August 12, 1963, Oswald pled guilty in court for the disturbance. Bringuier gratuitously told the Warren Commission that the courtroom was segregated into white and "colored" sections and that Oswald sat in the colored section, which was unheard of in 1963. Bringuier was angered, because he felt Oswald was trying to curry the favor of the "colored people" or he was trying—provocatively—to demonstrate FPCC's solidarity with blacks. (The anti-Castro Cuban exiles who left Cuba were almost exclusively white and from Spanish descent, whereas those who remained were largely people of color.)

Oswald distributing an FPCC handbill in New Orleans. Perhaps the biggest contribution made by Garrison was the discovery that the 544 Camp address stamped on Oswald's literature was the front entrance address of the building on Camp and Lafayette that housed Guy Banister's operation. Source: Warren Commission

In the days before Oswald sat in the "colored section" of the court, the newspapers reported that white members of the civil rights group the Congress of Racial Equality (CORE) in Clinton, Louisiana, threatened to integrate the black section of the courthouse. Guy Banister had direct ties to the segregationist Clinton town officials who were trying their best to disrupt CORE's voter registration drive for blacks. It would not be surprising if Oswald was imitating the CORE workers when he sat in the black section of the New Orleans courthouse. As we shall see later, three weeks after he sat in the colored section of the court after his fight with Bringuier, Oswald infiltrated the CORE voter registration line in Clinton, Louisiana, in another Banister scheme against the left. On August 21, 1963, Oswald debated Bringuier on radio station WDSU, along with Ed Butler, Oswald's last New Orleans publicity stunt.[933]

Jim Garrison also deserves credit for raising suspicions about Carlos Quiroga, another associate of Guy Banister and visitor to the 544 Camp Street office. The Warren Commission and HSCA had no suspicions about Quiroga. However, on August 16, 1963, Oswald was again distributing pro-Castro literature and Carlos Quiroga allegedly brought Bringuier one of Oswald's pamphlets. Bringuier suggested that Quiroga visit Lee Harvey Oswald at his Magazine Street apartment to check him out. Quiroga allegedly met with Oswald for about an hour to determine his motives—at which point he discovered Oswald spoke Russian and had a Russian wife—and Oswald gave Quiroga an application to his FPCC chapter.[934] Quiroga later failed a lie detector test given by Garrison. Then, when asked if he knew that Lee Harvey Oswald was not a real Communist and that his FPCC activity was a cover, Quiroga pled the Fifth Amendment. When asked if he had knowledge of a conspiracy in the assassination of President Kennedy, he again took the Fifth.[935] Garrison interviewed Quiroga extensively during his investigation and repeatedly asked Quiroga: "Would you be surprised if I told you that Oswald was not a Communist at all?" In the interrogation of Quiroga, Garrison also revealed that he had information showing that Oswald had been seen in the presence of Sergio Arcacha Smith in the summer of 1963, and had visited the training camp across Lake Pontchartrain.[936]

As has been discussed, the fact that Oswald had been seen in the company of fanatical anti-Communists Guy Banister and David Ferrie—and was also alleged to have been with nationally known anti-Communist, Kent Courtney in the summer of 1963—suggests that Oswald was not actually a Communist, but was merely posing as one. The Oswald-Bringuier incidents are more evidence that Oswald was not a genuine Communist.

Oswald and his supporting cast of Butler and Bringuier—all Banister associates—committed a number of blunders while acting out their staged productions. The Warren Commission determined that Oswald was pro-Castro and a genuine Marxist who was exposed by Bringuier and Butler while trying to infiltrate an anti-Castro group.

The problem with the official account of the FPCC saga begins with Bringuier's account of meeting Oswald in his store. Harold Weisberg interviewed Philip Geraci III, a gay teenager, who was in Bringuier's store when Oswald allegedly offered his assistance to the anti-Castro cause. Weisberg told the author that, while working as an investigator for Jim Garrison, he had interviewed Geraci. Geraci told Weisberg that it was May 1963—not August as Bringuier claimed—when he saw Oswald at the store. Geraci had gone to the store to sell Bringuier fifty-cent Cuban war bonds in support of the anti-Castro effort. Garrison possessed a receipt for Geraci's war bonds, dated in May, which—according to Weisberg—was proof that Bringuier lied about Oswald being in his store in August. Weisberg contended that he gave Garrison a tape-recorded interview that "could have nailed Bringuier," but Garrison ignored what Weisberg considered an airtight case. For that, and other reasons, Weisberg grew to despise Garrison. When the author asked Weisberg why he never publicly disclosed the truth of the Geraci story, he replied that he grew close to the Geraci family and did not want to risk disclosing young Phillip Geraci's homosexuality.[937]

Another major problem with the Bringuier-Oswald saga is that Oswald wrote to the national director of the FPCC, V. T. Lee, on August 1, 1963, and told him some Cubans had attacked him and the police were involved *before* the attack actually took place on August 9th. The letter is another example that the Oswald-FPCC activity was a charade with Bringuier playing a knowing part.

Bringuier's presence on the Billy James Hargis Christian Crusade speaking tour in early 1964 with General Walker, General Willoughby, and Kent Courtney (as noted in the last chapter) raises further significant suspicions about him. Of course, the fact that Oswald was associated with six anti-Castro Cubans who had direct ties to the 544 Camp office and/or Guy Banister, as detailed in Chapter One, leaves no doubt that Oswald was working with the Cubans to further the objectives of the Banister operation.

Lee Harvey Oswald's August 1, 1963, letter to V. T. Lee, the national director for Fair Play for Cuba. The "attack" (truly a fight with Carlos Bringuier) and subsequent police intervention did not occur until August 9, 1963, suggesting that the whole affair was a phony set up. Source: Warren Commission, XX, 524

Oswald's radio debate with Carlos Bringuier and Ed Butler on August 17, 1963, was another phony scheme that further shows Oswald was only pretending to be a Communist. The Oswald-Bringuier fight was contrived and designed to set the stage for the radio debate and to bring Ed Butler into the picture. During the debate, Butler got Oswald to admit he was a Marxist and, after the Kennedy assassination, Butler played back the tape-recorded admission for news reporters. The day after the assassination, Butler flew to Washington and delivered the taped debate and Marxist admission to Senator Eastland's committee. He told the committee that Oswald had a tremendous capacity to repeat rote Communist propaganda.[938] Interestingly, Carlos Bringuier immediately issued a press release urging a congressional investigation of Oswald after their altercation.[939] The statement suggests that Bringuier may have been aware that "Operation Tip Top" (which will be discussed later) and state and congressional investigations of Communist activities in New Orleans had already been in the works. The Oswald and Bringuier incidents were obviously contrived to serve as evidence that the New Orleans FPCC had been infiltrated by a Soviet Communist and that the organization was in violation of the Communist Control Act created by key members of the Banister operation.

Further evidence that the Oswald-Bringuier-Butler radio debate was contrived—as a part of Banister's larger anti-Communist agenda—was Butler's scheme to train anti-Communists as phony Communists, which is revealed here for the first time. According to an obscure congressional committee record—unknown to the Warren Commission—Ed Butler testified before the Subcommittee on International Organizations and Movements of the Committee of Foreign Affairs of the House of Representatives on September 11, 1963, about his "Conflict

Managers" scheme to fight Communism. He planned to train individuals—whom he referred to as "Conflict Managers"—to impersonate Communists, speak their jargon, and infiltrate Communist groups. He explained that the conflict managers' "sole business is destruction of the Communist Party . . . ." He did not describe his plan further, but Oswald's impersonation of a Communist followed Butler's plan precisely. Butler told the congressional committee: "We have been privately counseling certain individuals and organizations with whom we have established contact throughout the hemisphere on specific 'how to' methods for counteracting the party and destroying it in individual cases." The evidence suggests Oswald was one of those "privately counseled" individuals. Butler stated that a conflict manager should become "adept at phrasing and remembering his statements according to the party line."[940]

During the debate with Butler and Bringuier on Cuban-American relations, Oswald's phrasing sounded scripted as would be expected from one of Butler's conflict managers. Furthermore, Oswald's use of the Spanish word *gusano* (or "worm") in his letter to V. T. Lee describing his imaginary fight with the anti-Castro Cubans—that had not yet happened—is another example. As noted in Chapter One, the American Consular officials in the Soviet Union detected similar phenomena and felt Oswald "was following a pattern of behavior in which he had been tutored by a person or persons unknown . . . seemed to be using words he had learned, but did not fully understand. In short, it seemed to me there was a possibility that he had been in contact with others before or during his Marine Corps tour who had guided him and encouraged him in his actions."[941]

It's worth noting that all of the theater surrounding the FPCC saga, culminating in the radio debate and Butler's appearance before the congressional committee, occurred *before* there was any public confirmation of Kennedy's intention to visit Dallas in November 1963. Given his involvement with Oswald, Butler would have been foolish to testify before Congress about his scheme to create phony Communists if he knew Oswald was destined to become the alleged assassin of the president. The FPCC theatrics were not related to the assassination, but nonetheless were used to support the Warren Commission's belief that Oswald was an authentic Communist. Fortunately, for Butler, his presentation before Congress went undiscovered until found by happenstance by the author.

Bringuier spoke with Ed Butler on the subject of Communist methods in Argentina, which took place at an INCA meeting on November 19, 1963, at the International House. He told the audience that one tactic used by Communists in Argentina was for two Communists to stand on a street corner with one defending Capitalism, the other Communism. When the crowd grew big enough, the pro-Capitalist would concede that the pro-Communist was right. Usually a few plants in the crowd would also side with the pro-Communist. Bringuier, demonstrating that he was aware of Butler's scheme to train phony Communists, concluded his speech by saying, "The Communists need trouble so they manufacture it with agents who specialize as 'Conflict Managers'."[942]

Ed Butler was a constant visitor to the Camp and Lafayette office of Guy Banister in the building at 544 Camp Street at the time of the Bringuier confrontation that set the stage for the Oswald-Butler debate.[943] Banister's widow later told Garrison that she saw FPCC leaflets at her late husband's office.[944] As noted in Chapter One, FPCC propaganda was also found at David Ferrie's house and in the 544 Camp Street second-floor office, suggesting that the FPCC affair was concocted, since Oswald was the only know source of FPCC propaganda in New Orleans. Garrison was aware of the Butler-Banister relationship, but never apparently interviewed Butler—who was in Los Angeles during Garrison's investigation—nor was Butler called as a witness. Garrison did, however, note the Butler-Banister relationship in the secret Grand Jury proceedings and in his files. Instead of investigating Butler, who had ties to dominant figures in the far right—most notably Dr. Alton Oschner and Patrick Frawley—Garrison focused his case on Lee Harvey Oswald and David Ferrie (who were dead) and on the seemingly hapless homosexual, Clay Shaw, and others of no significant standing. Ed Butler, like Kent Courtney, whom Garrison had some evidence against, seemed untouchable.

Garrison kept his investigative files on Ed Butler under the heading of "Radical Right Wing." He knew Butler was once a member of the John Birch Society and that his organization INCA enjoyed the support of the White Citizens' Council. Butler was ultimately asked to leave the Free Voice of Latin America, according to William R. Klein who knew him, because, "This young man's ultra right wing views were not only embarrassing but in my opinion, dangerous. He could think of nothing but the danger of some kind of globe encircling Communist conspiracy . . . ."[945]

Butler voluntarily provided to the CIA information that he received through his organizations INCA and Free Voice of Latin America on leftist radio studios, transmitters, and their locations in South America. Garrison was apparently not aware of Butler's voluntary assistance to the CIA.[946] (There is no evidence that Butler's involvement with Oswald in 1963 was part of a CIA plot.)

A number of Garrison's other investigative files revealed Garrison's suspicion of Butler, which he never revealed in his interviews or in the written accounts of his investigation. Garrison noted, "Butler is now working for Schick (razor blades) on West Coast—Schick is right wing nut."[947] Garrison apparently considered charging Butler and Bringuier as conspirators engaged in "image-creating" in reference to Oswald's Communist persona.[948]

Gordon Novel

Gordon Novel became a subject of Garrison's investigation in 1967, when Garrison learned that, in 1961, Novel—along with Guy Banister (whom he had known since he was very young) and David Ferrie—stole munitions from the Schlumberger Company bunker in Houma, Louisiana. The munitions were allegedly taken to Guy Banister's office, and then shipped to anti-Castro Cubans in Miami. Garrison implied that it was a CIA operation, but provided no supporting evidence. The problem with the claim is that, if it were a CIA operation, they would not have needed to commit a burglary and risk arrest to obtain munitions as the CIA could obtain any weapons they might need legally.[949] Further, Novel's ex-wife Marlene Mancuso stated clearly, when interviewed by Garrison, that the Houma bunker burglary of munitions did not involve the U.S. government.[950] The evidence that Gordon Novel was involved with the CIA was created and self-proclaimed by Novel—and he actively promoted the fabricated relationship.

When Garrison subpoenaed Novel, he skipped town and ended up in Langley, Virginia—home of the CIA—where he supposedly took a polygraph administered by a CIA man. There was no evidence he did; his alleged travel to Langley was another ploy. When Novel was finally arrested outside of Columbus, Ohio, on an extradition warrant issued by the D.A.'s office, Garrison called the Houma bunker burglary "the most patriotic burglary in history" and claimed it was done for the CIA invasion of Cuba.[951] The CIA was questioned by the United States Justice Department in 1967, according to documents which were kept secret at the time, and denied any CIA involvement in the bunker burglary—or with Gordon Novel.

When Novel moved out of his apartment to avoid arrest by Garrison, he left a letter he had written in pencil to a "Mr. Weiss"—an apparent imaginary CIA official—in the kitchen under a dish mat where the next tenants could not miss it, and the letter was turned over to the *Times–Picayune.* Novel's planted note stated that his subpoena by Garrison might have been related to his purported "Top Secret" activities with "Operation Double Check" in Miami, in 1961. He stated that the FBI had interviewed him about his activities in Double Check, and he also denied the connection. He suggested in the "Mr. Weiss" note that the "Defense Intelligence Agency" be contacted to take counter measures against Garrison.[952] The letter was hoax. The operation of Double Check was publicly known and did not reflect any unique knowledge on the part of Novel. Operation Double Check had been revealed in a 1964 book published by Random House entitled *The Invisible Government.* The book revealed that Double Check was a CIA front in Miami that recruited pilots for anti-Castro operations. Novel's attorney, in response to the letter that Novel left to be discovered, also stated that Novel worked with the CIA. Novel himself clarified the matter stating he was a CIA intermediary[953]

There is no credible evidence that Novel had any ties to the CIA. To the contrary, he was a radical right winger like his colleagues Guy Banister and David Ferrie. The author interviewed the widow of Vincent Bonomo—who knew both Gordon Novel and David Ferrie well. Bonomo was a well-known boxer, who had a relatively successful career on the national scene. Commenting on Ferrie and Novel, Bonomo's widow told the author, "The part I don't get is this thing about Ferrie and Novel being in the CIA. I knew them well and they were just scum and bottom feeders." Tragically, a jealous male friend murdered Vincent Bonomo in his wife's presence and, suspiciously—before police arrived—Ferrie and Novel seemingly appeared out of nowhere and removed a large cache of armaments from the trunk of the victim's car and left with them.[954] According to one source, Novel had put thoughts in the murderer's mind to kill Bonomo.[955] Ferrie reportedly later told one of his former CAP cadets that he was working with the FBI on Bonomo's murder, but the cadet didn't believe him.[956] After Bonomo's death, Ferrie showed up at the D.A.'s office claiming he was Mrs. Bonomo's attorney.[957]

Garrison had other clues to Novel's true character. He was in possession of state police documents that indicted that Novel was a member of the Stormtroopers in Jefferson Parish in the 1950s. Later, Novel was allegedly part of a Corvette theft ring where the engines of the cars were removed and the chassis dumped into the Mississippi River.[958] As a minor, Novel reportedly tried to derail a train, and threw rocks at cars.[959]

Jack Ruby, who murdered Oswald after the assassination, was a strip club owner. Tommy Cox—who had lived with one of Ruby's strippers, claimed to have seen Novel in Dallas shortly before and after the assassination, at the Champion poolroom.[960] Reporter and John Birch Society member Early Lively claimed that, in 1963, he was approached in Dallas by Novel and Larrie Schmidt and asked to contribute to an anti-Castro fund. (Schmidt, it will be recalled, was the prime mover in the infamous "Welcome Mr. Kennedy to Dallas" ad in the newspaper on the morning of the assassination.)[961]

Another witness stated that Novel was an associate of Edgar Eugene Bradley (who will be discussed later in this chapter), one of Garrison's California suspects—who reportedly took his orders from William Potter Gale, an associate of Joseph Milteer.[962] Novel was also associated with Ed Butler.[963] Butler's cousin, Rancier Ehrlinger (was involved in a drag strip operation with Novel in Hammond, Louisiana), also verified the Novel-Butler relationship.[964]

Novel was charged, in 1976, with conspiracy to bomb the Federation of Churches building in New Orleans on Mardi Gras after losing the option to purchase the property, where he had intended to build a hotel office complex. The man Novel paid to do the bombing backed out and called the Bureau of Alcohol, Tobacco, and Firearms because he didn't want to hurt anybody during the holiday. There were two mistrials. During the second trial, Novel failed to cooperate with the defense and was ordered to undergo mental competency tests. Jim Garrison was Novel's chief counsel in the initial proceedings, which was quite odd considering Garrison's interest in Novel during his investigation of the murder of President Kennedy. A January 27, 1979, *Times–Picayune* story noted that Novel told the court that he was involved with the cover-up of the assassination of President Kennedy. Eventually, Novel was sentenced to three years in jail on conspiracy to commit arson.[965, 966]

Finally, Novel allegedly appeared in video news footage protesting the government's actions during the 1993 Bureau of Alcohol, Tobacco, and Firearms siege of the Branch Davidian compound in Waco, Texas, that housed a radical religious sect whose member had murdered four agents.[967]

There is no evidence that Novel ever worked with or for the CIA—his ties to the CIA were entirely self-proclaimed. Not surprisingly, it was in fact the aim of the radical right to place the blame for the assassination on the CIA, which began with Revilo Oliver in his Warren Commission testimony and was later promoted by others. The theory, simple and elastic, was difficult to disprove and served to deflect suspicion from the far right. The evidence suggests that Novel was not a government operative but rather was an alleged former Nazi, car thief, arsonist, and member of Banister's far-right operation.

Garrison, William Gaudet, and the CIA Claims

In support of his CIA theory, Garrison further stated that a CIA agent accompanied Oswald to Mexico City in September of 1963. The claim, which involves William Gaudet—an elderly New Orleans publisher of a Latin American newsletter called *Latin American Reports*—was false. Gaudet did, in fact, provide information obtained in the course of his travels to the CIA. He purchased a tourist card for entrance into Mexico on September 17, 1963, numbered 824084. Oswald purchased the next tourist card in sequence after Gaudet, numbered 824085 on the same day. Remarkably, Gaudet told author Anthony Summers that he had seen Oswald in the past in the company of Guy Banister, as well as during his FPCC pamphleting, but stated he did not recall seeing Oswald getting a tourist card. More importantly, though, he did not accompany Oswald—since Gaudet flew to Mexico City while Oswald supposedly took a bus. Gaudet however did feel the tourist card affair was more than mere coincidence: He suggested that the plotters might have had a reason for having Oswald purchase the tourist card *after* him, but didn't elaborate.[968] It's possible Oswald was told to follow Gaudet and purchase his card after Gaudet to give the appearance of a relationship to the CIA. The HSCA did determine from CIA records that Gaudet was a source for the New Orleans CIA Domestic Contact Division and provided information on political and economic conditions in Latin America—but was not involved in clandestine activities. The HSCA concluded that there was no evidence that Oswald had contact with Gaudet on behalf of the CIA.[969]

Other spurious claims came out of the Garrison investigation in an attempt to show that Oswald was involved in the CIA. Garrison stated that Oswald was schooled in Russian in the marines as proof he was recruited by the CIA. The claim is false. There is absolutely no evidence that the marines schooled Oswald in Russian.[970] Oswald did take a Russian proficiency test in the marines, but scored poorly. Moreover, when he arrived in Minsk, in 1959, his co-worker laughed at his poor Russian speaking ability. His future wife thought from his speech that he was from Estonia, whose language is derived from an entirely different base.[971]

Garrison investigator William Turner, writing in *Ramparts* magazine, stated that George de Mohrenschildt may have been Oswald's CIA "baby sitter." Garrison cited the claim as another example of Oswald's ties to the CIA.[972] However, there is no evidence that de Mohrenschildt ever worked for the CIA. In fact, the records of the Office of Strategic Services (OSS), the precursor of the CIA during WWII, indicated that they rejected de Mohrenschildt's attempt to find employment with them when they suspected that he was a Nazi sympathizer during World War II. The HSCA concluded that there was no evidence that de Mohrenschildt had ever been an American intelligence agent.[973]

De Mohrenschildt was a member of the Dallas White Russian community. His anti-Bolshevist, or anti-Communist, group befriended Oswald upon his return to Dallas from the Soviet Union. Oswald's close relationship with the White Russians raises more doubts about his claim to be an authentic Communist.

Trying to find any CIA ties at all, the author asked Garrison's investigator William Turner what he felt was the evidence for a Banister-CIA tie. Turner responded that Banister had coordinated a Bay of Pigs diversionary strike.[974] The claim seems unlikely, since Banister had no military experience and there is no other corroborating evidence to support it.

Kerry Thornley

Kerry Thornley was in the marines with Oswald and was stationed at El Toro marine base in Santa Anita, California, in 1959. The Warren Commission questioned a number of marines who served with Oswald and all denied that he had any Communist sympathies—including those who had known him the longest. Kerry Thornley was the one exception, stating that Oswald did show an interest in Communism.[975] Thornley wrote a book about a character based on Oswald in 1961—after he learned of Oswald's 1959 defection to the Soviet Union—entitled *Idle Warrior*, yet he denied having in any contact with Oswald in 1963 when they both resided in New Orleans.

Not surprisingly, Thornley stated he "accidentally" met Guy Banister in 1961 and discussed the book he was writing based on Oswald, who was in the Soviet Union at the time. Thornley met David Ferrie in 1962 and claimed his contact with him was also "accidental" and that no significant conversation transpired. In September 1963, Thornley visited Mexico City—the same month as Oswald—allegedly as a tourist.[976] Interestingly, Thomas Beckham, a regular at Banister's office, told the HSCA that Kerry Thornley was part of Banister's cell, along with Lee Harvey Oswald.[977]

According to Phil Boatright, Kerry Thornley applied for a job with Kent Courtney to work on his far-right paper the *Independent American*.[978] Boatright, a widely published poet, had worked for Courtney from August to October of 1962. Boatright knew Thornley, and told Garrison investigator Harold Weisberg that Thornley's views were in sympathy with Courtney's, although Courtney turned him down for the job supposedly because he didn't have a college degree. Boatwright stated that Thornley had a "very, very strong dislike for President Kennedy." When Boatright was asked if he thought Thornley had any ties to the CIA, he responded that Thornley "would not associate himself with the government because he felt the government were a bunch of Socialists."[979] Thornley told Garrison, in his Grand Jury testimony in the Clay Shaw trial, that he had worked for Kent Courtney for two days in 1961 stuffing envelopes. Garrison told the Grand Jury that Lee Harvey Oswald had also worked for Kent Courtney, but did not elaborate.[980]

Courtney denied knowing or employing Thornley, when asked by one of Garrison's investigators.[981] However, it will be recalled that Marguerite Oswald telephoned Kent Courtney after the Warren Commission's findings were published and asked Courtney if her son had worked for him.

Thornley told the Warren Commission that he was unaware that Oswald was in New Orleans at the same time he was in 1963. However, contrary to his denial, one witness—who was deemed highly reliable by Jim Garrison—saw Thornley with Oswald at the Bourbon House shortly after Thornley's return from Mexico City. Others also stated they saw the pair together including an unidentified "Negro chemistry professor."[982, 983, 984] Moreover, after viewing a photo of Thornley, neighbors of the Oswalds confirmed he had visited their Magazine Street apartment and another witness stated he saw Thornley a number of times at Oswald's apartment.[985]

Bernard Goldsmith, a left winger who knew Thornley, reported that he was "a right winger and so set in his political beliefs that he, Goldsmith, made an agreement not to talk politics." Goldsmith stated that Thornley was far right and that in every conversation and discussion of politics he was an "arch conservative." Goldsmith could not recall if Thornley knew Kent Courtney or Carlos Bringuier. Thornley had told Goldsmith that he had known Oswald and that he was not a Communist. On the night of the assassination, Goldsmith heard Thornley say, "Have you heard the good news?"[986] On the night of the assassination, Thornley remarked to Allen Campbell, who had worked for Guy Banister, "It could not have happened to a nicer guy."[987] Thornley was an active participant in a Friday evening discussion group with Goldsmith, a group also attended by William Cuthbert Brady and Ross Buckley who were founders of Citizens for a Free Cuba. Goldsmith described Brady as dangerous and a "radical extremist, violent segregationist and somewhat gay."[988, 989]

In May 1963, a person who identified himself as "Osborne" placed an order for the printing of Oswald's Fair Play for Cuba handbills at Jones Printing. The FBI showed a photo of Lee Harvey Oswald to the employees and none recognized Oswald as the person who picked up the handbills.[990] Assassination writer Harold Weisberg, who worked for Jim Garrison, told the author that he took a standard police mug shot identification book, with a picture of Kerry Thornley included, to Jones Printing. Weisberg asked employees if they recognized anyone at all in the book as the person who picked up the FPCC pamphlets. The employees readily picked out the picture of Kerry Thornley.[991] Garrison also claimed that Thornley had been impersonating Oswald.[992] However, Phil Boatright, who knew Thornley well, stated that they didn't look alike.[993]

Peter Deageano told the D.A.'s office that he saw Oswald handing out FPCC leaflets on Canal Street and recognized him as the same person he had seen eating at the Bourbon House a few days before. Oswald was with Kerry Thornley and Jean Hack at the Bourbon House, who introduced Deageano to Oswald.[994]

Thornley departed New Orleans shortly after the Kennedy assassination and became a doorman at an Arlington, Virginia, apartment house. After his Warren Commission testimony, he headed west to attend a college described by Garrison as a "rather unique institution of Ayn Rand orientation."[995]

Harold Weisberg was a steadfast advocate of the CIA's involvement in the assassination—a theory presented in a number of books he had written. He was suspicious of Colonel Robert Castorr of Dallas, whom he called an "Intelligence officer." Castorr was a close associate of General Walker, and they worked together stirring up resentment against President Kennedy in the Dallas Cuban community. Later, Castorr moved to Arlington, Virginia—not far from Weisberg's home in Frederick, Maryland. Weisberg told the author that the two later became friends. On one occasion, Castorr invited Weisberg to dine with him at the Army-Navy Club in Washington and praised Weisberg, calling him "America's greatest patriot." Castorr did not tell Weisberg what he meant by the statement. One reason he may have praised Weisberg was because he steered the readers of his assassination books away from right-wing extremists like Castorr and his friend, General Walker, and toward his theories of government intelligence involvement.[996, 997]

In the mid-1970s, long after Garrison's investigation ended, Thornley sent Garrison a fifty-page affidavit of evidence he had uncovered in New Orleans of "Nazi activity" in connection with the president's murder, in an effort to exonerate himself. (The affidavit was not located by the author.)[998] Garrison had Nazism in mind when he asked Thornley during the secret Grand Jury session if he knew Tommy Baumler, Baragona, and Louis P. Davis (who were all identified as Nazi supporters in Chapter Three). Along the same line, Garrison also asked Thornley if he knew Jack Helm, who has been identified in prior chapters as a Klan leader and associate of both Guy Banister and David Ferrie. He also asked him about Larrie Schmidt, the Dallas right winger and associate of generals Willoughby and—as will be shown later—Walker.[999] Obviously Garrison was well aware that Thornley was a radical right winger and attempted to tie him further to extremist associates of Guy Banister in his questioning.

Thomas Beckham

Thomas "Tommy" Beckham was a teenager when he began hanging out at Guy Banister's office. Beckham was a singer when he met Banister associate Jack Martin who was interested in promoting his records. Beckham became acquainted with the Cuban underground through Martin, who offered to help Beckham become ordained in the Old Catholic Church that he and David Ferrie belonged to. During Garrison's investigation, Beckham was subpoenaed to testify before the Grand Jury. Beckham claimed, "I was advised on what not to say, if I knew what was best for me. And I did—I wanted to live."[1000] After the subpoena, Beckham fled to Iowa, but agreed to testify if offered immunity from prosecution, which was granted.[1001, 1002]

On February 15, 1968, Beckham testified before the Orleans Parish Grand Jury in proceedings that were secret and made public many years later. Beckham testified that he ran errands, picked up office supplies, and helped on domestic cases for Guy Banister as a favor—but was occasionally paid a few dollars. One time, Beckham said that Banister asked him to pay a visit to Bluford Balter and inquire as to the availability of office space in the Balter Building for a Cuban group. (It will be recalled that Balter had rented space to Banister in the past, as well as to Leander Perez and the Citizens' Council, and his property was a center for activity of the American Nazi Party.) As he approached Balter, Balter pulled a gun and said, "Don't move, back away." Beckham "thought the man was nuts." Balter, like Roswell Thompson and Gordon Novel, were the kind of violence-inclined men who surrounded Banister.

Garrison and others on the D.A.'s staff repeatedly asserted, as if it was established fact, that, Guy Banister and David Ferrie were doing work for the CIA and wanted Beckham to confirm it. Garrison stated in the secret courtroom proceedings: "Are you aware that in 1962 or '63 he [Banister] was doing work for the Central Intelligence Agency for the U.S.

government?" Beckham repeatedly denied knowing of a Banister-CIA connection. Garrison further asked, "Are you aware that David Ferrie who was a priest in the Old Orthodox Church that was connected to the CIA?" Beckham replied, "No." Frustrated, Beckham told Garrison, "Mr. Garrison, why are you trying to make me out to be a CIA agent or something, I'm not." Garrison replied, "You are lying. Now when you come back I want no more lies. You are dismissed now, come back in an hour but no more lies because the name of that is perjury."[1003]

Beckham was accompanied to the Grand Jury proceeding by A. Roswell Thompson, who sat outside the courtroom during the secret deliberations. Garrison later mockingly referred to Thompson as Beckham's "lawyer," knowing full well he was not a lawyer.[1004]

As will be recalled from Chapter Three, Roswell Thompson was close to Guy Banister, and was a constant visitor at Banister's Camp and Lafayette Street office in 1963. Thompson ran for councilman-at-large on a ticket with Guy Banister on what was called the Conservative Political Organization, a far-right version of the mainstream Regular Democratic Organization. Thompson was a leader in the New Orleans National States' Rights Party and the Ku Klux Klan, and was the subject of an FBI "Racial Matters" investigation. He attended National States' Rights Party meetings at Holsum's cafeteria in 1967—a place allegedly frequented by Lee Harvey Oswald, and he spoke at a Nazi meeting with David Duke in 1973.

In 1978, with Roswell Thompson and other leaders in the New Orleans radical right wing deceased, Thomas Beckham drove to Washington and unexpectedly—and without subpoena—volunteered to testify before the HSCA. Beckham told the Committee that Roswell Thompson knew Jack Ruby and he had seen Ruby in New Orleans in 1962 or 1963 on two occasions. He also claimed that he saw Ruby with Clay Shaw. Beckham stated that Ruby said he was pulling for Roswell at the time he was running for office (perhaps a suggested reference to Roswell's bid for election on the ticket with Guy Banister). Beckham said he met Clay Shaw through G. Wray Gill, as well as through David Ferrie. (Gill was the attorney of New Orleans mob boss Carlos Marcello, and had an office in the Pere Marquette building. Banister and Ferrie both worked with Gill.) Beckham stated he knew Lee Harvey Oswald and had met him at a cafeteria and had become "good buddies." Of Oswald, Beckham stated, "I can't understand this Russia thing, because he was always 100% American he seemed like." He stated that Oswald was anti-Castro and that Oswald had said, "Karl Marx was a Jew."

Beckham told the Committee about a meeting he had attended in the Algiers section of New Orleans in 1963, with anti-Castro Cuban leader Sergio Arcacha Smith, along with Ferrie, Shaw, and Gill. He stated that "Charlie Marullo or Marello," who owned Jefferson Music and a motel, was at the meeting, (an apparent reference to Carlos Marcello or one of his sons). The attendees engaged in conversation concerning President Kennedy's alleged withdrawal of air support in the Bay of Pigs invasion and blamed him for its failure, stating, "he ought to be killed."

Beckham claimed he was asked by Ferrie to take some papers to Dallas about two weeks before the assassination. He picked the papers up at Gill's office and found Gill with Carlos Marcello, David Ferrie, Jack Martin, and Roswell Thompson. Beckham stated that the package contained photographs of streets, cars, and buildings, drawings, and a photo taken out a window. He also said there were neatly drawn maps and diagrams, but he did not know if they were taken in Dallas.[1005, 1006, 1007] Right after the assassination, Beckham was "scared to death." He tried to locate Banister, Shaw, Martin, Thompson, and Gill but they had all left town. He went to Thompson's house, where he found Anna Burglass—an ultra-right-wing friend of Thompson—who told him to get away from Roswell's house and stay away. Beckham left town and used several aliases to hide from Martin and the others.[1008]

The Committee asked Beckham if had told the Grand Jury in the Garrison case the same story he told the Committee. He said "no." When subpoenaed by Garrison, his friend Fred Crisman told Beckham "everything was going to be taken care of, that they had an 'in' in the district attorney's office, and that the investigation would be ran the opposite direction, so for me [Beckham] not to worry."[1009] Crisman told Beckham he was an "operative" and also a CIA agent.[1010] (Crisman reportedly knew Banister from his days in Chicago, not from New Orleans.[1011]) Beckham told the Committee that he had been coached by Roswell Thompson in his testimony to the New Orleans Grand Jury and admitted that he had committed perjury. Crisman had advised Beckham that it would be "unhealthy" for him to cooperate with Garrison.[1012] Beckham understood that if he cooperated with Garrison's investigation his life would be in danger.[1013]

At the time of the Grand Jury, Garrison recognized that Beckham was associated with the radical right wing without saying so, and demonstrated this knowledge by asking Beckham if he knew a number of extremists, including three of Joseph Milteer's associates: Billy James Hargis, Wesley Swift, and Colonel William Gale. (Gale and Swift also came up in Garrison's investigation of Californian Edgar Eugene Bradley in December 1967.)

Raymond Broshears, a close friend of David Ferrie, told Garrison—as we shall see in Chapter Nineteen—that Ferrie confided to him that Hargis and General Walker were involved in the assassination. (It will be recalled that William Somersett pegged Hargis as a fundraiser for Milteer's hardcore underground.) The FBI investigated Swift and Gale when they learned of their involvement in a plan to murder a large number of the members of the Council of Foreign Relations and prominent Jewish figures. The plot was similar—if not identical—to the plot revealed in the New Orleans April 1963 meeting of the Congress of Freedom.

Garrison asked Beckham if he knew Kent Courtney, William Duff, Dallas American Nazi Party leader Robert Surrey, Colonel Gale, Larrie Schmidt, and oilman Lester Logue. (Although it was not mentioned by Garrison, all of those men were associates of General Walker.) He was asked if Beckham knew Klansmen Jack Helm and Jules Ricco Kimble, as well as Nazi sympathizers Tommy Baumler, Wesley Swift and Louis P. Davis, but did not tell the jury they were Klansmen or Nazis (as was noted in Chapter Three). Beckham denied knowing any of the men.

Unfortunately, many of Garrison's files were destroyed. The author has not seen any Garrison files that identified Billy James Hargis, William Duff, Robert Surrey, Colonel Gale,

Larrie Schmidt, or Lester Logue as people of interest. As we shall see, however, they are all-important figures in the assassination story presented in this work. In the secret Grand Jury proceeding, during the cross examination of nearly every witness, the D.A.'s prosecutors repeatedly stated categorically—as if it were fact—that Lee Harvey Oswald, David Ferrie, and Guy Banister worked for the Central Intelligence Agency.[1014] At the same time the prosecutors also inquired as to Beckham's possible association with at least seven close associates of General Walker, who had no known ties to the CIA but was a high-ranking member of the Council of Statehood that had plotted assassination at the Congress of Freedom and at the Constitution Party meeting.

Since the Grand Jury proceedings were closed, the media was unaware that Garrison brought up the names of prominent figures in the national radical right. Garrison knew no one would ask him why he asked Beckham about an assortment of Klansmen, Nazis, and close associates of General Walker and Joseph Milteer who obviously were not tied to the CIA. Instead of directly charging Clay Shaw with conspiracy to murder the president, Garrison took a lot of credit for first convening a Grand Jury as an example of his fairness.[1015] In fact, it gave him a chance to probe witnesses in the realm of the radical right wing—but outside his CIA theory—without anyone knowing about it, since the Grand Jury transcripts would not be available to the public for many years after the trial.[1016]

Guy Banister, the anti-Castro Cubans, and the CIA

Garrison's best shot at convincing the world that the assassination was the result of a CIA or government plot was by connecting Guy Banister to anti-Castro Cuban Sergio Arcacha Smith in New Orleans, a member of the Cuban Revolutionary Council (CRC). The CIA backed the CRC, but their support waned after the Bay of Pigs operation—and was discontinued in May 1963. Garrison claimed that the paramilitary training camps north of Lake Pontchartrain were a further example of CIA involvement in the Banister operation. As noted in Chapter One, however, they were not CIA camps. Instead, camp participants included a dozen or so anti-Castro Cubans, members of the John Birch Society, Minutemen, and Nazis.

The California Suspects: Edgar Eugene Bradley, Stanley Drennan, and Clinton Wheat

On December 20, 1967, over a year into his investigation, New Orleans district attorney Jim Garrison issued an "at-large warrant" for Californian Edgar Eugene "Gene" Bradley, which was yet another surprising development in the case. Gene Bradley was the West Coast representative of nationally known, far-right minister Carl McIntire of Collingswood, New Jersey. According to a newspaper story, Garrison claimed he had evidence that Bradley had been in New Orleans and plotted with Shaw, Ferrie, and Oswald in the middle of September 1963. He also claimed Bradley was in Dallas during the murder. Ultimately, California governor Ronald Reagan blocked the extradition of Bradley from California to New Orleans, due to insufficient evidence showing that Bradley was in Dallas at the time of the assassination. Thereafter, the Bradley/California aspects of the case fizzled and Bradley was not further pursued.[1017] (Unfortunately, Garrison did not apparently know that Bradley was close to William Gale, an associate of Joseph Milteer, nor did he know about the broad-based assassination plot identified at the Congress of Freedom meeting, which both Gale and Milteer were a part of.)

Some, including Bradley himself, speculated that he was brought into the case due to mistaken identity. They charged that Garrison had confused Edgar Eugene (Gene) Bradley with Eugene Hale Brading (a.k.a. Jim Braden). The Warren Commission established that Jim Braden (not Gene Bradley, as charged by Garrison) was present in Dealey Plaza at the time of the assassination, and—due to Braden's suspicious actions—he was arrested and later released. Jim Braden, who was also from California, claimed his innocence, stating he was in Dallas on business with H. L. Hunt. (As will be shown later, Joseph Milteer paid a visit to Hunt Oil Company. Hunt and Jim Braden will be discussed in Chapter Eleven.) Therefore, remarkably, two out-of-towners tied to H. L. Hunt—Joseph Milteer and Jim Braden—were present in Dealey Plaza during the assassination. That startling fact has never been revealed before.

Jack Ruby also visited the office of H. L. Hunt before the assassination (as will be shown later, however, this may have been a coincidence). Unfortunately, Garrison dismissed both the Braden and Ruby visits to H. L. Hunt's office, calling them a "one shot deception gambit," or a decoy.[1018] Equally significant, news correspondent Peter Noyes later established that Jim Braden visited the office of David Ferrie and G. Wray Gill in the Pere Marquette Building in New Orleans. Evidence will be presented in a later chapter, suggesting that Milteer was at the same Ferrie/Gill office as Braden, which is further evidence of a far-right conspiracy.[1019]

Jim Garrison, however, did *not* charge Gene Bradley out of name confusion with Warren Commission witness Jim Braden. In fact, he had plenty of evidence against Bradley. According to several sources, principally Thomas Thornhill, Carol Aydelotte, and Margaret McLeigh, Gene Bradley was close to Colonel William Potter Gale, a colleague of Joseph Milteer. Garrison also learned that Bradley allegedly had tried to recruit a member of the American Nazi Party to shoot President Kennedy and had shown him a variety of assassination devices. Carol Aydelotte had known Bradley well through their participation in radical right-wing and John Birch Society activities.[1020] According to another source, Bradley tried to recruit Dennis Mower to assassinate President Kennedy when Kennedy was a presidential candidate in 1960. Mower was a former co-defendant with Robert DePugh, leader of the Minutemen, and a colleague of Colonel Gale, the right-hand man of Wesley Swift. Bradley reportedly had blueprints of the underground storm drain system in Dealey Plaza, from which shots at Kennedy could be taken. Aydelotte stated that one time, after she mentioned to Bradley that her husband had a .375 magnum rifle, Bradley tried to persuade him to use the rifle to assassinate President Kennedy.[1021] Aydelotte also alleged that, after Kennedy was elected, Bradley found a hotel room from where he could take a sniper shot at the president.[1022] Bradley admitted to one of Garrison's investigators that he had heard Colonel Gale speak when he was running for governor, but denied knowing him.[1023]

Bradley told Mrs. Wesley Bice that he had been in Dallas on the day of the assassination and that he had scheduled stops in Houston and Shreveport to meet with Ned Touchstone, after which he planned on meeting an unidentified wealthy man. (General Walker was with Ned Touchstone in Shreveport, Louisiana, on the day of the assassination at the time Bradley scheduled his visit with Touchstone.[1024]) Bradley stated that he stayed in a hotel halfway between Dealey Plaza and the Hotel Dallas during the murder, and that he left the next day. Officially, however, Bradley admitted traveling by bus only as far as El Paso, Texas, at the time of the assassination, and said that he was on business for Carl McIntire.[1025] (As will be shown later, McIntire was close with General Walker and was named by David Ferrie's confidant, Raymond Broshears, as a member of the assassination conspiracy.)

According to Bradley's neighbor, Bradley talked about Gordon Novel and Herbert Philbrick (the former communist and TV idol of Lee Harvey Oswald). At one time, Philbrick reportedly met with Bradley in an all-day meeting. A different Bradley neighbor described another meeting at Bradley's house with "the Colonel"—likely a reference to Gale. Bradley took his orders from the Colonel, who was described as a youngish, nice looking man—an apt description of Gale. With regards to the Colonel, Bradley's neighbor stated she heard him say, "He's the big shot I take all my orders from." Bradley's wife told neighbor Margaret McLeigh on the day of the assassination, "I've prayed every night, every night of my life that he'd [the president] be shot and killed." She stated, "You know Gene [Bradley] is right down there in it. He's right down in there. I'll be hearing from him any minute." When Bradley returned home from his alleged trip to El Paso on November 30, 1963, the neighbor asked him "Well, if I know you, you pulled the trigger." Embarrassed, he said, "Well, not exactly but I damn sure as well know who did." McLeigh rarely saw the Bradley's again. Bradley's son was overheard arguing with Bradley and told him he "shouldn't have done it" and "he was an innocent person" in reference to President Kennedy. Bradley responded that he "was evil and no good for the world." After the argument, it is said that Bradley beat his son with a strap and told him to never talk about it again.[1026, 1027]

An unnamed acquaintance of Gene Bradley accused him of delivering a death threat note to Robert Cline, a candidate for the Twenty-second Congressional District, according to a news story. Bradley reportedly "questioned Cline's ancestry." Bradley filed a slander suit against the acquaintance, and accused three former John Birch Society members of telling the FBI that he delivered the death threat. The acquaintance reported being told by Bradley's wife that, on the day of the assassination, he had just called her from Dallas. Later, Bradley admitted he was present in Dallas during the assassination.[1028] Another witness, Max Gonzales, stated in an affidavit that he had seen Bradley at the New Orleans Lakefront Airport with David Ferrie more than once between June and August 1963.[1029, 1030]

Loran Hall, who was engaged in anti-Castro guerilla activity and was an associate of General Walker, told Garrison that he had been at a meeting at Clinton Wheat's home in San Fernando, California. He claimed he heard Bradley discuss getting rid of Kennedy at that meeting, where William Gale and Dr. Stanley Drennan were also in attendance. Hall stated that "anti-Jewish and anti-Negro radicals" attended the gathering, where they discussed raising funds to equip guerillas with arms for an invasion of Cuba. Hall also reported that three attempts on his life had been made since his name surfaced in the Garrison investigation.[1031] Both Bradley and Gale admitted being at the meeting with Hall at the home of Clinton Wheat, but disagreed as to when they attended and what was discussed. When Gale learned his name had come up in the Garrison investigation, he accused Garrison and Hall of being agents of Castro's Cuba.[1032]

Roger Craig, a deputy sheriff in the Dallas County Sheriff's Department was in Dealey Plaza at the time of the assassination and told Garrison, in a signed affidavit, that he was on the steps of the Texas Book Depository and spoke to a man who represented himself as a Secret Service agent. When he later saw Bradley's picture in the newspaper during the Garrison investigation, Craig said that he was positive the man who called himself an agent was actually Bradley.[1033]

A friend of Bradley, Betty Helm, came forward and stated in a letter that she had known Bradley for more than twenty years. She said Bradley had arrived in Tulsa by bus on November 20, 1963, and had met her for dinner that evening.[1034] Garrison investigator Mark Lane obtained the letter and contacted Betty Helm. She told him that Bradley had asked her to sign an affidavit stating he was in Tulsa on November 21 and 22, 1963, but she had refused.[1035]

Bradley asked for an introduction to meet General Walker after a speech he gave at the Sports Arena in Los Angeles, shortly after Walker's release from Springfield Mental Hospital (after his arrest for leading an insurrection at Ole Miss in October 1962).[1036] Carol Aydelotte provided evidence that Bradley knew some unidentified associates of General Walker. She noted in a memo to Garrison that Bradley was close to Gale, leader of the paramilitary California Rangers, whom she described as "violent and revolutionary." Aydelotte noted that in 1962, when General Walker was arrested at the University of Mississippi, three Dallas men (from what she described as the hardcore right wing) traveled from Dallas and spent the night at Bradley's home, flying back to Dallas the next day.[1037]

The FBI was also familiar with Bradley. From 1958 to 1964 Bradley furnished to the FBI the names of people he considered to have Communist leanings—as well as members of the John Birch Society—who had professed far-right views, but whom he felt were actually members of the far left.[1038]

Bradley met with Madame Nhu, widow of assassinated Ngo Dinh Diem, the president of South Vietnam, a popular figure among the radical right, in the latter part of October 1963.[1039]

In 1991, Bradley met with Garrison who reportedly admitted he made a mistake by charging Bradley. In the 1991 meeting, Bradley claimed Garrison told him that they had both been set up.[1040]

Gene Bradley and Carl McIntire

Gene Bradley was in charge of six California radio stations owned by Reverend Carl McIntire, who had a national following. Bradley reportedly first met McIntire "down south," and McIntire had at least once been an overnight guest at Bradley's home.[1041] McIntire was on the Advisory Board of the Young Americans for Freedom with General Willoughby and other leaders of the radical right.[1042] He was close to Edgar Bundy, who had visited General Walker in Germany prior to his censure.[1043] McIntire was also a close associate of Senator Joseph McCarthy. At McIntire's invitation, Fredrick Schwartz emigrated from Australia in 1953 and founded the Christian Anti-Communist Crusade, which was later sponsored by Patrick Frawley of Schick Razor.[1044] Guy Banister was on the Advisory Committee of Schwartz' New Orleans Anti-Communism School in 1961 (as was noted earlier). McIntire operated Shelton College (a Bible school), as well as the Christian Admiral, a seaside religious retreat in Cape May, New Jersey. McIntire commissioned gold-framed oil portraits of leaders of the far right—including prominent members of the John Birch Society—to hang in the Gallery of Christian Patriots in the Christian Admiral.[1045] Dan Smoot, Billy James Hargis, and Frank McGehee were aligned with McIntire in 1963.[1046] On June 8–14, 1963, McIntire hosted Senator Strom Thurmond and Dr. Bob Jones at the Christian Admiral Leadership Conference.[1047] When Shelton College lost its state accreditation in 1969, McIntire enlisted the help of the notoriously racist governor of Georgia, Lester Maddox, who came to the college to lend his support. The National States' Rights Party Color Guard was present for his arrival.[1048]

McIntire published a newsletter entitled the *Christian Beacon*, and had a national radio show called the *Twentieth Century Reformation Hour* that aired on 305 stations in 1962. When the program was taken off his local radio airwaves, Joseph Milteer composed and circulated a pamphlet in protest.[1049]

McIntire was ardently anti-Catholic and anti-Kennedy, and rallied against what he called "Romanism"—the rule of the Pope. He also opposed Communism and liberalism.[1050] McIntire stated: "The Catholic Church is the harlot church and bride of the anti-Christ."[1051] In 1960, the Democratic National Committee (DNC) called McIntire an "anti-Catholic extremist." In response, McIntire demanded an apology from the DNC and its presidential candidate, Senator John F. Kennedy.[1052]

Garrison considered McIntire's church an "odd church" and postulated a connection to the "odd church" that David Ferrie, Jack Martin, and Thomas Beckham belonged to. McIntire alleged that Garrison's motive in accusing Bradley was to smear McIntire's religious organization. McIntire, responding to Garrison's charges against Bradley, claimed he was promoting the Communist line.[1053] McIntire was opposed to the National Council of Christian Churches (NCCC), and organized his own council, the American Council on Christian Churches (ACCC). Gene Bradley served on the Laymen's Commission of the ACCC, along with well-known far-right author John Stormer.[1054] The far right (including McIntire) believed that Communists had infiltrated the NCCC. McIntire organized a simultaneous rally set for December 23, 1963, in Philadelphia to oppose President Kennedy's proposed address before the NCCC on the same date in the city; General Walker was the planned speaker. The McIntire and Walker protest rally was cancelled after Kennedy was assassinated. Nationally syndicated columnist Drew Pearson had heard of McIntire's planned protest meeting and expressed his contempt for the hatred McIntire voiced toward the president in a December 9, 1963, column.[1055] General Walker later spoke at the Christian Admiral in 1965.[1056]

McIntire was well known to the FBI. After Kennedy's assassination, the FBI tried to locate McIntire for an interview, but he was out of town and unavailable until November 29, 1963. The FBI's interest in McIntire apparently stemmed from a radio broadcast denouncing Kennedy's planned speech before the NCCC on November 23. In the broadcast, McIntire made a statement relative to "something happening to prevent President Kennedy from attending the [NCCC] meeting." McIntire attempted to clarify his radio remarks to the FBI, stating that he hoped that Kennedy would realize his attendance at the NCCC meeting would be in conflict with the principles of separation of church and state—as he had pointed out to Kennedy in a letter he had sent him earlier.[1057]

On April 4, 1970, McIntire held the "March for Victory in Viet Nam" in Washington. He was joined by Louisiana congressman John Rarick—an important individual in the saga of Oswald's appearance in Clinton, Louisiana, which will be discussed in Chapter Twenty-one. Alabama governor George Wallace, and Senator Strom Thurmond sent letters of support. Georgia governor Lester Maddox also attended the rally.[1058] In 1968, General Pedro del Valle was the Honorary First Officer of McIntire's "Victory in Viet Nam Banquet Committee." Others serving on the committee were Mary Cain, Richard Cotton, Clarence Manion, General Richard Moran, Major Arch Robert, and General Stratemeyer. A press release issued by the Institute for American Democracy, Inc. aptly described the group as "a frightening mélange of old-time anti-Semites, retired right-wing Generals, John Birch Society and Liberty Lobby leaders and assorted other military and civilian personages . . . ."[1059] General Westmoreland hosted McIntire in Viet Nam in 1967; General Abrams hosted him in Viet Nam in 1970.[1060]

McIntire had more sinister ties to the Garrison case and its suspects beside his relationship with Bradley. Garrison failed to reveal publicly that he had reliable information that Guy Banister attended a McIntire speaking engagement at the Capitol House Hotel in Baton Rouge in 1963. A month later, another meeting took place at the Capitol House that featured General Walker and Billy James Hargis. George Ratliffe, a right-wing extremist, owned part of a Baton Rouge radio station that aired McIntire's propaganda. McIntire was also a friend of American Nazi Party members Comrade Randolf Brown and James Leahart. (It will be recalled from the Chapter Three that Guy Banister bailed Leahart out of jail after he was arrested in Commander Rockwell's Hate Bus incident.) Muncy Perkins alleged that he saw Lee Harvey Oswald with Leahart at the St. Charles street car terminal in New Orleans in the summer of 1963. Leahart wrote to Joseph Milteer in 1959. A member of law enforcement, Joe Cooper, made the report on McIntire and the Nazis in Baton Rouge. McIntire, Banister, Ratliffe, and Leahart were all mentioned in the same Garrison memorandum, and a relationship between the four was implied.[1061]

As will be shown in later chapters, McIntire formed a close friendship with General Walker beginning in 1961, as is reflected in a number of letters exchanged between the two. Walker met with McIntire at his Cape May retreat on August 20, 1963, which will be discussed in Chapter Fifteen. David Ferrie's close friend and confidant, Raymond Broshears, reported that Ferrie told him in 1967 that McIntire was part of the assassination conspiracy. (The allegation will be discussed at length in Chapter Nineteen.)

McIntire is yet another prominent member of the national radical right who is tied to Milteer's hardcore underground through Gale and Bradley, and he also apparently knew Guy Banister (since Banister attended a meeting with McIntire in Baton Rouge). Unfortunately, Garrison was unaware that Colonel Gale, a close associate of Gene Bradley, was a part of the broad-based assassination plots that surfaced during the Congress of Freedom meeting and also was a close associate of Joseph Milteer, who predicted the assassination in advance and was present in Dealey Plaza when it happened. The evidence suggests that Gene Bradley, along with Jim Braden and Joseph Milteer, was another member of the radical right present in Dealey Plaza during the murder.

Stanley L. Drennan

Stanley Drennan, a physician, was an associate of William Gale and was subpoenaed—along with Clinton Wheat—by Jim Garrison.[1062] According to Loran Hall, Drennan attended a meeting at the home of California Ku Klux Klan leader Clinton Wheat, along with Gene Bradley and Colonel Gale. Moreover, a Warren Commission document indicates that Drennan tried to recruit Captain Robert Kenneth Brown to "get rid of President Kennedy."

Captain Brown, from the School Brigade in Fort Benning, Georgia, "advised that he had been active in Cuban matters for several years and during the spring of 1963, in connection with anti-Castro activity, he was in contact with the National States' Rights Party in Los Angeles, California. In this connection he contacted Dr. Stanley L. Drennan . . . North Hollywood, California, who was active in the National States' Rights Party. Brown stated that once, while a guest in Drennan's home, Drennan stated in general conversation that he could not do it, but what the organization needed was a group of young men to get rid of Kennedy, the Cabinet, and all members of the Americans for Democratic Action and maybe ten thousand other people. Brown stated that he considered the remark as being 'crackpot'; however, as Drennan continued the conversation, he gained the impression that Drennan may have been propositioning him on the matter." The FBI reportedly interviewed Drennan on June 14, 1963, regarding the conversation.[1063, 1064] Drennan admitted meeting with the Secret Service, who accused him three different times of threatening the president and warned him he could be put away on mental charges.[1065] Interestingly enough, Brown had furnished information to the FBI in 1965 or 1966 of talk from right-wing militants of assassinating Miami district attorney Richard Gerstein because he was Jewish. Gerstein, it will be recalled, was a principal in the Miami police investigation of Joseph Milteer.[1066]

The author discovered a letter that Drennan wrote to Dean Clarence Manion, a prominent member of the John Birch Society, on July 20, 1963, wherein Drennan professed his outrage over the Secret Service's interrogation of him. Drennan wrote; "On Saturday June 10, 1963, John F. Kennedy visited Los Angeles, speaking at the Palladium at 9:30 a.m. Two of my acquaintances were awakened by the Treasury Dept. Secret Service Agents . . . I was only two miles from where the president was riding in an open convertible sitting high on the back of the seat. The climax of the Treasury Agents' questioning was why this writer (S.L.D.) was plotting the assassination of Mr. Kennedy." Drennan reported in the letter that a friend of his was also interviewed by the Secret Service on the matter. Drennan claimed that the Secret Service told him that anyone who contemplated violence would be considered mentally unbalanced and would end up in an institution. Drennan told the Secret Service agents, "the administration was not following our Constitution and was apparently plunging us into One World chaos and I intended, in my small way, to double and redouble my efforts to see such politicians defeated and relieved of governmental responsibilities."[1067]

Drennan wrote General Walker on January 15, 1962, and told him he had attended his January 11, 1962, Sports Arena speech. He told Walker, "We need you as our spokesman and our standard bearer, and with the wave of patriotic Americanism sweeping the country it may be possible, in fact I feel it is possible, we can reverse the stampede toward own burial."[1068]

George King, Jr., another associate of William Gale, was a member of the Christian Defense League, American Nazi Party, and John Birch Society. He was arrested after he was overheard discussing the possibility of assassinating the president, according to August 1963 FBI and Secret Service reports.[1069, 1070, 1071] King was also a member of Gale's California Rangers.[1072]

Woody Kearns was likely cryptically referring to Drennan in a 1965 letter to Joseph Milteer when he mentioned, "The doctor on the west coast." "The doctor," like Kearns, according to the letter, felt his phone calls were being monitored.[1073]

The Drennan affair is yet another instance where Garrison's professed investigation into a CIA or government intelligence conspiracy, was in reality a probe into the radical right wing connected to the National States' Rights Party, the John Birch Society and the Ku Klux Klan, among other extremist groups. Drennan's spring 1963 threat to kill the president, his Cabinet and many others, sounded similar to the broad-based plot discussed at the April 1963 Congress of Freedom meeting in New Orleans, which targeted members of government and industry. It was also similar to the plot discussed by Colonel William Potter Gale and Wesley Swift, Joseph Milteer's California colleagues.

Clinton Wheat

Garrison subpoenaed Clinton Wheat, an associate of William Gale, along with Stanley L. Drennan, on May 13, 1968.[1074] By the time of his subpoena, Wheat had already earned a place in a popular 1967 book about the far right entitled *The Farther Shores of Politics* by historian George Thayer. Thayer described Wheat as a member of he KKK closely tied to Gale and Swift's Christian Defense League, who carried a Colt .45 automatic in his belt in the small of his back.[1075] Wheat's Klan group was aligned with James Venable's Klan of Georgia. (Venable and his fellow Klansman Wally Butterworth were both at the Constitution Party meeting with Joseph Milteer in October of 1963 where plans to kill President Kennedy were discussed.)[1076] Garrison's subpoena alleged that, in 1963, Wheat and Drennan had participated in discussions in Wheat's home about assassinating President Kennedy. (Garrison had learned from a former FBI informant that Wheat held meetings of the Church of Jesus Christ Christian, the Christian Defense League, and the American Nazi Party at his Los Angeles home. At one meeting, Colonel Gale reportedly stated that the Jews supposedly killed during the Holocaust were actually in America. Wheat responded to the remark by saying that he had two gas chambers ready for them now.) The informant told Garrison that three top members of the group led by Wheat and Gale went to Montgomery, Alabama, in 1963, and one met with Governor George Wallace.[1077] A witness told the FBI that Wheat contacted him and told him he needed to borrow 400 dollars to take a trip to Dallas, Texas, during the fall of 1963.[1078]

Carol Aydelotte was certain she saw Gordon Novel, Guy Banister's colleague, visit Clinton Wheat along with Loran Hall. She correctly identified Novel from a photo shown to her by the district attorney's office.[1079]

In early 1968, Garrison learned of a possible threat to his life. According to an informant, Jack Knowles (a friend of Gene Bradley)—who was a Minuteman and member of the Los Angeles Police force—may have been involved in a plot to murder Garrison. The informant hoped to be subpoenaed by Garrison as a material witness. He provided names of others closely associated with the Minutemen, Gale, and Swift.[1080]

Conclusions

Jim Garrison's prosecution of Clay Shaw in the murder of President Kennedy was based primarily on the conflicting and unbelievable claims of Perry Russo, a right-wing friend of David Ferrie. While there was plausible evidence that Shaw knew Oswald, there was no evidence he was involved in the assassination conspiracy. The conspirators may have used Shaw as a scapegoat, since the investigation of Shaw revealed no direct ties to the Banister operation. The Garrison case, in reality, was an excursion into the world of the New Orleans radical right wing and Garrison knew it.

As credible evidence will show in Chapter Nineteen, David Ferrie—at the onset of Garrison's investigation—told him that prominent members of the far right, including H. L. Hunt, General Walker, Billy James Hargis, and Carl McIntire were involved in the assassination. Garrison's purported former CIA employee-suspects, Gordon Novel and Ed Butler, as well as the California suspects, were nothing more than right-wing extremists tied to one or more of the far-right organizations of the John Birch Society, Ku Klux Klan, Minutemen, National States' Rights Party, and Citizens' Council.

During his investigation, Garrison's life was threatened, making it unlikely that Garrison could have openly pursued a prosecution of the determined and murderous individuals in the hardcore underground and remain alive. On the other hand, Garrison was able to safely conduct a parallel investigation into an apocryphal CIA plot, which at the same time allowed him to investigate the radical-right under that guise. His attacks on the government, including the FBI and Warren Commission were often justified.

For his faults and deceptions, Garrison can be thanked for his investigation of Guy Banister and the 544 Camp Street story among other things, as well as for leaving his district attorney JFK assassination files to posterity. Garrison's investigative files were helpful in demonstrating that Ed Butler, Carlos Bringuier, and the five other Cubans who had contact with Oswald were working on the same side and in concert with Oswald as a part of a Banister operation, which unfortunately Garrison did not publicly reveal. There is no evidence those individuals were involved in the assassination; however, the fact that they knew Oswald was not who he claimed to be made them accessories.

The evidence Garrison uncovered on the West Coast branch of the same radical-right group connected to Joseph Milteer and the assassination is of tremendous importance. Gene Bradley, like Milteer, was a foot soldier representing nationally prominent members of the radical right, including William Gale and Carl McIntire. There is plausible evidence that Bradley, like Milteer, was also in Dallas—if not Dealey Plaza—during the assassination. Gale is directly tied to Milteer and the broad-based assassination plots noted in Chapter Eight, and McIntire had ties to Guy Banister.

If Garrison's evidence against Gale, Bradley, and McIntire had been combined with the evidence amassed by Willie Somersett for the FBI, a powerful case against the radical right could have been made. Unfortunately, the FBI concealed Somersett's information and Garrison concealed much of the evidence against McIntire, Bradley, Gale, and the other California suspects.

CHAPTER TEN

JOSEPH A. MILTEER AND THE HARDCORE UNDERGROUND OF NEW ORLEANS

*I have devoted a good deal of time to this question of Communist
infiltration. I remember when the Supreme Court handed down the
decision in March 1954. I could smell it...*
— Leander Perez

Joseph Milteer was associated with a number of New Orleans individuals connected with the Guy Banister operation that will be discussed in this chapter. All of them were leaders of the segregation effort who, like Leander Perez, felt that the Communists infiltrated the integration movement. In that context, as we shall see, the purported Communist persona of Lee Harvey Oswald and his infiltration into several leftist groups aligned with the integration movement makes perfect sense.

Joseph A. Milteer and Judge Leander H. Perez

Joseph Milteer was an associate of Judge Leander H. Perez, who was a close associate of Guy Banister. Banister's close friend George Singelmann was Perez's personal assistant. Moreover, Banister's detective agency and Perez's Citizens' Council had offices a floor apart in the infamous Balter Building, prior to Banister's move to the Newman Building in 1962. Like Banister, Perez saw Communist infiltration as the force behind the *Brown* decision that outlawed segregation in the public schools. Milteer tape recorded a Perez speech in Atlanta on February 2, 1961, which was discovered by HSCA investigators who apparently attached no significance to it.[1081] Four days after the Kennedy assassination, Willie Somersett alluded to Perez as a financial backer of the murder in a debriefing by Miami police, as follows: [1082]

Milteer traveled to New Orleans in late September or early October 1963 and wrote about it in

```
I don't know how to figure him out too much, because he seems to
know too much, and what he predicts comes true.

Q:  Where do you think this money would have come from?
A:  Well, there is no telling, you see, like he said, when he mentioned
    the name Leander H. Perez; this man was a judge down there.

Q:  Where was he a judge at?
A:  Plakman Parish, that is right outside of New Orleans. This man has
    taken a stand for States Rights against segregation, and he has been
    ex-communicated from the Catholic Church on the stand he has taken
    in New Orleans. Well, this Milteer seems to be a friend to him, or
    to know him very well, and several other people in the State of
    Louisiana and Texas. But he didn't go to work and give me all the
    names and addresses, but he give me all the
    people to understand that he knew them,
    and had associated with them.
```

Source: FBI file of Joseph Milteer

an October 3, 1963, letter to his friends in the Constitution Party, Joe Lightburn and Woody Kearns. (As was discussed in Chapter Seven, talk of killing the president took place at the October 18–20, 1963, Constitution Party meeting.) In the letter, Milteer related that he had just finished a 6,055-mile trip to promote the Constitution Party meeting. The people and places mentioned in the letter are of tremendous importance in the assassination story.

The trip included a stop in Chicago to attend a national meeting of a far-right group, We the People. He also visited Ezra Taft Benson—a Mormon elder and former member of President Eisenhower's cabinet—in Utah, where he gave an interview on the upcoming Constitution Party meeting that was published in the *Provo Herald*. (Suspiciously, Milteer had an account in a Provo bank under an assumed name.) Milteer traveled to Colorado where he had just missed Kenneth Goff, who also attended the Constitution Party meeting. He traveled to Fort Worth, Texas, and gave a newspaper interview on the upcoming meeting. He met with "another Patriot" (who was not named) in Grand Prairie, Texas, then stopped in Dallas but did not mention meeting with anybody there. (He had also been to Dallas in June or July of 1963.) He traveled to Shreveport and gave an interview regarding the upcoming Constitution Party meeting that was published in the *Shreveport Journal*. He then traveled to Alexandria, and then to New Orleans, Louisiana. Milteer stated: "There I missed seeing Judge Leander Perez, but left word with his secretary for him. I also saw a couple of young lawyers and maybe one of them will attend our [Constitution Party] meeting." He met with Mary Cain in Summit, Mississippi, then met with Citizens' Council leaders in Jackson, Mississippi.[1083]

Another letter, on May 5, 1964, from Milteer to "George" reflects his admiration for Leander Perez. Milteer wrote: "I am anxious to get something started where-in we people on the RIGHT can move out and take charge of matters in no uncertain ways. And we do need a Leader very badly. One other man that I wish to offer for your consideration and that is none other than Judge Leander Perez. As you recall he is known as the King of the Bayou Country who made a million or two or three on 6,500.00 annual pay. Of course a little sulfur and oil helped out a wee bit along with his tenacious ways."[1084] Like Milteer and Banister, Leander Perez had ties to the National States' Rights Party. He spoke at their meetings, held at the New Orleans Italian Hall on two occasions, and supported the group financially.[1085, 1086] A piece of paper with the address and phone number of the New Orleans Citizens' Council in the Balter Building, written in Milteer's handwriting, was found in Milteer's home after his death by HSCA investigators.[1087] Banister's close friend George Singelmann, Perez's personal assistant, manned the NOCC office. Banister moved

Top: Milteer jotted the Balter Building address of Judge Perez's Citizens' Council office on a piece of paper found by HSCA investigators after his death. Source: NARA, HSCA Box 51. Bottom: Guy Banister letterhead with the Balter Building address (and the Argonne Street address scribbled out). Source: Rainach Papers, Noel Memorial Library, Louisiana State University Shreveport

his detective agency from his home on 7059 Argonne Street to 434 Balter Building in the spring of 1958, before moving to the infamous Newman Building at 544 Camp/531 Lafayette Street.[1088]

The HSCA compiled a list of addresses found at Milteer's residence and, in addition to the Balter Building address, they also noted the address "General Walker 4011 Turtle Creek." The Warren Commission determined that Oswald fired a shot at General Walker at his Turtle Creek Street address in April 1963. As previously noted, Walker was a friend of Guy Banister and was also one of the military advisors to the Council of Statehood who plotted the assassination of leftist members of government and industry. General Walker and Leander Perez are significant figures in this story and their ties to Banister and Milteer will be detailed at length in this and later chapters.[1089]

Judge Leander H. Perez

Leander Henry Perez was born in Louisiana in 1891. He graduated from Tulane Law School in 1914, and served briefly as a district judge in Plaquemines Parish, where he was politically appointed after the sudden death of his predecessor. He was elected to another term, then left the bench. However, thereafter, Perez was referred to by most as "Judge" for the rest of his life. He served as the district attorney of Plaquemines and St. Bernard Parishes for forty years.

Plaquemines Parish, it should be noted, stands just below New Orleans on a stretch of high ground along the levies of the Mississippi River as it enters the Gulf of Mexico; the remaining 90 percent of the parish is swampland. Perez became wealthy subleasing parish-owned land that held rich oil and mineral rights—a practice regarded by most as illegal. By the 1920s, he was the undisputed boss of Plaquemines.

His biographer, Glen Jeansonne, estimated Perez's net worth at 100 million dollars. Perez ruled the government of the parish like a dictator; tongue-in-cheek, he described his own corrupt practice of buying votes as "the current Louisiana purchase." (He was the subject of a federal grand jury in 1950 for voter fraud.) Though he owned a home in Plaquemines, Perez spent most of his time in a stately residence on Newcomb Avenue in the uptown section of New Orleans. He controlled the printing of the local newspaper, *The Plaquemines Gazette*, and stories about him appeared in practically every edition.[1090, 1091] He was closely aligned with Huey Long when Long ran for Louisiana governor in 1928, and Perez was partly responsible for stopping the impeachment drive against Long in 1930. Perez was at Long's side when he was assassinated in front of the state capitol, where Gerald L. K. Smith was also present.[1092] (Smith, it will be recalled was a well-known anti-Semite who was closely aligned with Joseph Milteer and his inner circle in the California hardcore underground, Wesley Swift and Colonel William Gale.[1093])

Perez was a national figure and the titular head of the Southern fight to preserve segregation. After the 1954 *Brown* decision that outlawed segregation in the public schools, Perez and the Southern segregation movement adopted a strategy of tying integration to Communism in an attempt to ride the growing fears in the country about Communist infiltration.

(There were a few well-known black Communists, like W.E.B. DuBois and Paul Robison, but not many.) After World War II, tensions with the Communist Soviet Union rose. In 1948, Alger Hiss—an employee of the State Department—was called before the House Committee on Un-American Activities and was accused of spying for the Soviet Union; he was indicted for perjury. The public was further alarmed when Senator Joseph McCarthy gave a speech in 1950 announcing that the State Department was infested with 204 Communists. In 1950, the U.S. joined South Korea in the war against the Communist North Koreans who were supported by "Red China." In 1951, Julius and Ethel Rosenberg were convicted of passing atomic bomb secrets to the Soviet Union, which led to their eventual execution in 1953. Those and other events gave rise to what has become known as the "Red Scare."

In 1956, Senator Eastland conducted hearings in New Orleans to demonstrate the Soviet influence in the integration movement. The hearings featured the investigative police work of none other than Guy Banister and his right-hand man Hubert Badeaux. (Interestingly, that same year, Lee Harvey Oswald began to act like a Communist.) In 1957, the State of Louisiana held hearings to demonstrate that subversion was the basis for the state's racial unrest; Banister, Badeaux, and Perez were the star witnesses. In 1958, Banister appeared before the Arkansas State Legislature and testified that the Communists were behind the integration movement. Those events will be discussed in detail later.

Perez traced the resurgent integration movement "back to all of those Jews who were supposed to be cremated at Buchenwald and Dachau and weren't, and Roosevelt, [who] allowed two million of them illegal entry into our country." Perez testified before his friend Senator Eastland's Senate Committee on the Judiciary in 1959, and asserted that the civil rights movement had its origins in a 1930s plot of Soviet leader Joseph Stalin. He stated, "There is a hidden hand that moves in the whole matter of race relations in the United States" and the Zionist Jews were the "main driving force behind forced racial integration." Perez performed legal work for Senator Eastland's powerful Senate Judiciary Committee and Senate Internal Subversion Subcommittee (SISS), that was the bulwark for the preservation of segregation in the U.S. With Perez's help, Eastland, as head of the Senate Judiciary Committee, succeeded in defeating civil rights legislation in the Senate and halting its progress for years.[1094]

Perez's name was a household word in the Deep South in the 1950s and 60s. His staunch defense against integration and his racist tirades were widely covered in the national media. He considered President Kennedy a Communist for his progressive racial policies. Perez gave a speech September 25, 1960, urging the defeat of Kennedy at the polls because when Kennedy was a student in England he had studied under a Communist teacher.[1095]

Perez appeared on national television with CBS correspondent Dan Rather in September of 1963 in a segment entitled "Priest Politician" on the subject of integration of the Catholic schools. He appeared on other television shows with David Brinkley, David Suskind, and William F. Buckley, editor of the *National Review*. His personal friends were Strom Thurmond, Ross Barnett, Lester Maddox, and George Wallace—all of whom were legendary defenders of the Southern way of life. Of African-Americans, Perez said, "There's only two kinds of Nigras; bad ones are niggers and good ones are darkies." These views led Perez to segregate the Plaquemines's education system into white, black, and mulatto schools.[1096] Speaking on the subject of democracy, Perez stated, "I hate that word."[1097]

In 1948, Perez joined the States' Rights Democratic party, dubbed the Dixiecrats, that bolted from the Democratic Party because of President Harry S. Truman's civil rights platform, and the Federal Employment Practices Act, which was created to prevent discrimination in federally funded jobs, anti-lynching laws, and laws abolishing the poll tax. The Dixiecrats chose Strom Thurmond and Fielding Wright, staunch segregationists, for their presidential ticket. The Dixiecrat movement gave way to the National States' Rights Committee in 1949, with Perez serving as vice president. Senator Eastland, whom author Glen Jeansonne called Leander Perez's "ideological twin," credited Perez for personally defeating President Truman's 1949 civil rights bill. Perez dominated the proceedings of the Louisiana state legislature for most of his lifetime; he wrote half the bills passed and chose different legislators to introduce them.[1098] He was the prime mover behind the 1962 Communist Control Act—of critical importance in this story.[1099]

After his break with the Democratic Party in 1948, Perez never supported a Democratic presidential ticket again. He was a "Red baiter" early on, and readily called those he disagreed with "Communists." He despised the liberal congressman from New Orleans, Hale Boggs. When Boggs declared his intent to run for governor of Louisiana in 1952, Perez accused him—through a stand-in candidate—of having joined the leftist American Student Union during his days at Tulane University. Perez then claimed that Boggs was ineligible to run for governor because of that alleged Communist affiliation. Perez argued before the Louisiana State Legislature that Boggs was an advocate of world government and that he was as dangerous as Alger Hiss, who was accused of being in a Soviet spy in 1948. Boggs lost the primary and Perez's smear tactics led the newspapers to call Perez "the poor man's McCarthy."[1100, 1101]

In 1958, Perez sent Senator Eastland a list of Louisiana organizations that he felt were subversive. He requested bound volumes of all of the 1956 Communist investigations of the House Committee on Un-American Activities. He also requested the membership lists of the Louisiana American Civil Liberties Union, and the Southern Conference Education Fund (SCEF) in New Orleans.

Senator Eastland said he would use Leander Perez as a star witness during his hearings aimed at defeating President Eisenhower's civil rights bill in 1959. Eastland stated, "Judge Perez has been a tremendous help to me in opposing these bills in the Senate judiciary committee. He defeated the Truman omnibus bill when he showed that it was based on [Communist] Dictator Tito's 'all-racial' laws."[1102]

It is important to note that Lee Harvey Oswald had ties to both the ACLU and SCEF. Oswald purchased a membership to the ACLU by mail while in Dallas. However, it was not possible to join the SCEF, since they had no true "membership"—only subscribers to their newspaper and a board of directors. (Guy Banister was also a subscriber and an enemy of SCEF as will be shown later.) Oswald did the next best thing to joining SCEF by joining the Fair Play for Cuba Committee. Both groups shared alleged Communists Anne and Carl Braden as officers in their organizations. SCEF and the Bradens were targets of a number of congressional "subversive" investigations that included one conducted by Eastland's SISS committee.[1103]

After the *Brown* decision in 1954, Perez pledged at a testimonial dinner that he was dedicating the rest of his life to the principle of segregation of the races. By the mid 1950s, Perez left all of his business affairs to his two sons, so that he could devote his time to the preservation of segregation. With John U. Barr, Perez launched the Federation for Constitutional Government—formed to unite the Citizens' Council and the Georgia States' Rights Council into an effective movement against integration—on December 28, 1955. Barr served on the advisory committee of the New Orleans Indignation Committee in 1962, along with Guy Banister, Hubert Badeaux, Gus LaBarre, and others. (Directors of the National Indignation Committee included George Soule and P. Cameron Terry, who were present at the Congress of Freedom meeting in New Orleans in 1963 attended by Joseph Milteer and Willie Somersett.[1104])

Under Perez's direction, the Federation of Constitutional Government supported the "doctrine of interposition" that had been adopted by Virginia and made the *Brown* decision null and void. Senator Eastland was the prime mover behind the organization, and the attendees at the first meeting were pledged to secrecy. A printed speech from Senator Eastland was passed that stated, "Defeat means death, the death of Southern culture and our aspirations as an Anglo-Saxon people. . . . Generations of Southerners yet unborn . . . will have preserved for them their untainted racial heritage, their culture and the institutions of the Anglo-Saxon race." Roy V. Harris, William Simmons, Willie Rainach, W. Scott Wilkinson, and General Sumpter Lowry served on the advisory committee.[1105] James D. Johnson of Crosett, Arkansas—a leader in the Arkansas Citizens' Council and publisher of its newsletter—served on the executive committee. In 1957, Johnson goaded Governor Faubus of Arkansas into a confrontation with President Eisenhower in the Little Rock school integration crisis. In 1960, the FBI learned that Johnson had met two men implicated in the bombing of Little Rock's black Philander Smith College. (In the 1980s and '90s, he was an ardent foe of Arkansas then-governor Bill Clinton.)[1106] Joseph Milteer, it will come as no surprise, subscribed to the Federation newsletter.[1107]

J. Evetts Haley, a Canyon, Texas, self-described "cow puncher" served on the Federation board. Haley authored the book *A Texan Looks at Lyndon*, a broadside aimed at damaging Lyndon Johnson's run for the Presidency in 1964. The John Birch Society and the Republican Party both heavily promoted the book; nearly eight million copies were printed at the time—third in history to only the Bible and Dr. Spock's book on baby care.[1108] Robert Surrey, a Walker aide, Dallas Nazi and Warren Commission witness, initially planned to publish the book at his employer's publishing company. The company—the same one used by Surrey to produce the printing plates for the notorious "Wanted for Treason" posters circulated at the time of the assassination in Dallas—declined, fearing liability for Haley's wildly unsubstantiated claims. While Haley was writing the book, nationally syndicated columnist Jack Anderson alleged that Commander George Lincoln Rockwell was in the vicinity of Haley's remote ranch. Haley eventually ran for Texas governor in 1956 on a pro-segregation, states' rights platform, and was active in promoting General Walker's bid for governor of Texas in 1962.[1109, 1110]

Tom P. Brady, a Mississippi attorney and Citizens' Council leader; as well as W. Scott Wilkinson of Shreveport, Louisiana, served on the Federation's legal committee. Wilkinson later represented General Walker in his defamation suit against the national press, regarding accusations that Walker fostered the riots at Ole Miss in 1962.[1111]

The Louisiana State Citizens' Council was founded in 1956 with Willie Rainach, a close Banister associate, as its president. Perez infused money into the Council, and was also the prime mover behind the Greater New Orleans Citizens' Council in the Balter Building. Perez's personal aide George Singelmann, who oversaw the Council, was a former newspaperman who served at Perez's beck and call.[1112] Singelmann accompanied Perez everywhere and was called his "satchel man."[1113] The Greater New Orleans Citizens' Council claimed to have 50,000 members at its peak, but Perez consistently drew crowds of about 6,500 at Council rallies. In 1964, a fourteen-year-old named David Duke—America's most famous racist and anti-Semite in the twenty-first century—read the segregation literature in the Citizens' Council library in Singelmann's office.[1114]

Singelmann rose to national infamy when he initiated the "Freedom Rides North" or "Reverse Freedom Rides," in April of 1962. The "Reverse Freedom Rides," like Commander Rockwell's Nazi Hate Bus were born in response to the Southern incursion of CORE's integrationist "freedom riders" from the North. Singelmann offered one-way bus tickets to any African-American who wished to relocate to targeted, largely all-white areas in the North including Hyannis Port, Massachusetts—home of the Kennedy family compound. The bus ticket offers were posted in prisons and penitentiaries. President Kennedy called the operation "a rather cheap exercise."[1115]

Segregation was the paramount issue in the 1960 Louisiana governor's race. Guy Banister's friend, state senator Willie Rainach, entered the primary and ran against Jimmie Davis, who had served as governor from 1944 to 1948. Both were staunch segregationists and were close to Leander Perez—but Rainach had the more prodigious pro-segregationist credentials. In the wake of the *Brown* decision, Rainach had passed a resolution through the 1954 legislature creating the Joint Legislative Committee on Segregation, and became its first and only chairman.[1116] In 1958, Guy Banister and his close colleagues Leander Perez and Hubert Badeaux testified before the Joint Legislative Committee on Segregation as to the Communist influence in the integration movement. The Committee enlisted the help of a number of well-known "former Communists," veterans of the House Committee on Un-American Activities, and Eastland's Senate Internal Security Subcommittee witch hunts to support the claims that there were Communistic influences in integration.[1117] (Some critics of the hearings doubted if the "former Communists" were really ever Communists at all.)

Perez threw his support to Davis—who eventually won—because he did not believe Rainach had a chance of winning. A wounded Rainach eventually endorsed Davis; George Singelmann headed the Friends of Rainach for Davis Committee. The Joint Legislative Committee on Segregation was dissolved in 1960 and replaced with the infamous Sovereignty Commission. Leander Perez personally drafted the legislation that created the Sovereignty Commission and evidence (presented in Chapter One) strongly suggests Guy Banister and his secretary worked for the Commission. Willie Rainach was offered the director's position, but declined.[1118] Kent Courtney was another avid supporter and friend of Rainach in his bid for the governor's office.[1119] Interestingly, upon Banister's death the Sovereignty Commission acquired some of Banister's files.

Perez had created the Louisiana Sovereignty Commission to resist the court-mandated integration of the New Orleans Public Schools. When federal district court judge Skelly Wright enjoined the school board from operating segregated schools, and ordered integration to begin in 1960, Mississippi Supreme Court Justice Tom Brady telegraphed Governor Ross Barnett and stated: "If the battle of New Orleans was lost they would be fighting it in Mississippi." On November 14, 1960, McDonough School in New Orleans was integrated. That same night, 5,000 people gathered at a Citizens' Council meeting at the New Orleans Municipal Auditorium to hear Leander Perez and Willie Rainach speak. Perez implored the crowd, "Don't wait for your daughters to be raped by these Congolese."[1120]

Archbishop Joseph Rummel threatened Perez, Jack Ricau, and Una Galliot with excommunication on March 31, 1962, after Perez urged parents to remove their children from the integrated Catholic Schools.[1121] Perez's opposition to the Catholic archbishop's decree to integrate the New Orleans Catholic schools led to Perez's excommunication from the Catholic Church on April 16, 1962—which he blamed on the Communists and Jews. He stated: "I am a life-long Catholic and will continue to be so, regardless of Communistic infiltration and influence of the National Council of Churches and Jews upon our church leadership."[1122] Joseph Milteer's friend J. B. Stoner wrote to Perez after the excommunication, and pledged to work with Catholics against the Jews and the "race mixers." In 1961, at the national Citizens' Council meeting, Perez declared ominously that Southerners had no choice but to rise up in physical opposition to integration.[1123, 1124] Banister's secretary Delphine Roberts was also excommunicated for her part in opposing the Archbishop's decree.[1125]

Leander Perez attended the 1960 Democratic convention along with Willie Rainach. After the nomination, Perez stated that he was "1,001 percent" opposed to the Kennedy-Johnson presidential ticket. He called Kennedy "a stooge of Walter Reuther, a student of Moscow." (Reuther had attended the Stalin School in the 1930s.) Perez claimed, "Kennedy is the Henry Wallace of 1960" (referring to the presidential candidate of the 1948 Progressive Party who advocated the abolition of racial segregation). Perez called the 1960 Democratic platform "the Congolese Constitution."[1126]

Perez was the driving force behind the Free Electors movement, another anti-Kennedy contrivance. In 1960, there were 537 members of Congress and 537 Electoral College votes, with 269 required to obtain a majority in the House of Representatives. Theoretically, by withholding the electoral votes of the Southern congressmen, the required majority could not be obtained. The Southern congressmen would then bargain with the presidential candidates and award their votes to those who pledged opposition to integration.[1127] On August 4, 1960, Perez convened a Free Electors strategy meeting in New Orleans. The movement was defeated when the State Democratic Central Committee voted 51–48 to back Senator John F. Kennedy for president. In response, Perez loaned his support to the Louisiana States' Rights Party.[1128] In 1960, the steering committee for the States Rights' Party of Louisiana included Leander Perez, Kent Courtney, Delphine Roberts, Louis P. Davis, and Emmet Irwin.[1129] Kent Courtney became the States' Rights Party candidate for governor in 1960.[1130] Courtney admitted that he had a slim chance at winning the governorship, but he pledged that, if elected, he would not accept forced integration, stating: "If and when a Negro child or children attempt to enter any public school in the state of Louisiana, I will send state troopers to the school or schools and have them peacefully removed."[1131]

Dan Smoot spoke at a Free Electors meeting in New Orleans with Leander Perez and Willie Rainach on October 26, 1960, and stated: "Kennedy is a personification of the evil which American constitutionalists want to get out of Washington."[1132, 1133] (As was previously noted, Guy Banister's former partner Joseph Oster told the author that Banister and Smoot were friends.[1134] Joseph Milteer had known Smoot since at least 1959, and had visited him in June or July of 1963 in Dallas, Texas.) Perez warned the crowd that if President Kennedy were elected, Kennedy was going to integrate every public school and every area of community life.[1135]

In 1962, Perez organized the national Electoral Reform Committee. He enlisted the help of H. L. Hunt in the venture, who offered his advice. Hunt (as will be detailed in the next chapter) was yet another associate of both Milteer and General Walker.[1136]

By the spring of 1963, Perez felt certain that President Kennedy's reelection would bring desegregation to New Orleans and the South.[1137] However, President Kennedy did not wait until his next term and, on June 11, 1963, he proposed the sweeping Civil Rights Act, which called for the right of all Americans to be served in facilities that were open to the public—including hotels, restaurants, retail stores, and similar establishments. If Kennedy's Civil Rights Act passed, it would be the death knell for the white Southern way of life—the cause to which Leander Perez had dedicated his life. In response, Perez and Plaquemines Parish officials authorized the funding of a right-wing research group to submit proof that the pending 1964 Civil Rights Act was designed by the Communists for the purpose of stirring up racial strife.[1138]

In May 1963, Perez resurrected the unpledged elector scheme, which had become known as "the Perez plan" and introduced it into the legislature. Two hundred people gathered in Baton Rouge to create the Louisiana Committee of Free Electors and representatives from each congressional district were chosen. Guy Banister was chosen to represent the First

District; state senator Harold Montgomery, an outspoken racist, was elected chairman[1139]; and Cameron Terry, who was at the 1963 Congress of Freedom, was an Elector in Ward Two.[1140] (When the Baton Rouge hotels eventually became desegregated in 1964, Montgomery refused to stay at one and pitched a tent on the capitol grounds.[1141]) Kent Courtney promoted the "Perez plan" on his radio program, warning that—if the free electors were successful in keeping President Kennedy's name off the ballot—then Bobby Kennedy might send in U.S. Marshals to take over the elections.[1142]

The Free Electors met again on September 4, 1963, at the Capitol House Hotel in Baton Rouge. In attendance were Jack Ricau, Guy Banister, and General Walker, and governors Jimmie Davis and George Wallace. Ricau stated after the Capitol House meeting: "The dictatorial Kennedys fear the Free Electors more than anything else."[1143] (Around the same time, Lee Harvey Oswald was observed standing in a voter registration line organized by the Congress of Racial Equality, just north of Baton Rouge in Clinton, Louisiana.) A number of people reported to the FBI of talk at the Capitol House of assassinating the president, as will be discussed later. Clinton district judge John Rarick and attorney Richard van Buskirk (a friend of Guy Banister) had provided the legal research for the "Perez plan" during the summer session of the legislature that year.[1144]

The "Perez plan" was defeated in the state senate largely due to the efforts of liberal Louisiana AFL-CIO leader Victor Bussie.[1145] In 1965, Bussie hosted Vice President Hubert Humphrey at a Baton Rouge speaking engagement. Two armed Klansmen were in the audience preparing to assassinate Humphrey when the Secret Service, tipped off by an informant, arrested them.[1146] After the assassination of President Kennedy, Perez threw his support to a slate of electors pledged to George Wallace's presidential candidacy.[1147] On April 10, 1966, Perez debated Victor Bussie on WDSU radio's "Conversation Carte Blanche," the same station and program that hosted the Oswald-Butler-Bringuier debate in 1963.[1148]

One of Leander Perez's most treasured accomplishments was propelling Alabama governor George C. Wallace to national prominence.[1149] Perez was present on the podium at the inauguration as Wallace was sworn in as governor of Alabama. The ceremony was on the same spot—and with the same Bible used for the swearing in of Jefferson Davis, the president of the Confederacy in 1861. There, Wallace delivered his infamous defiant decree: "And I say segregation today, segregation tomorrow, segregation forever."[1150] Wallace entered the 1964 Democratic presidential primaries and did surprisingly well. It may be noted that Joseph Milteer claimed to know Governor Wallace well.[1151] According to a Milteer letter, he had worked hard to try to get Wallace to attend the October 1963 Constitution Party meeting.[1152]

Later, Perez and the segregationists also directed their efforts toward the defeat of Lyndon Johnson and the election of Barry Goldwater, whom they felt would support states' rights and the preservation of segregation as president. Jim Johnson—the latter-day foe of President Bill Clinton—traveled to Montgomery, Alabama, to convince Governor Wallace to withdraw from the campaign and lend his support to Goldwater. Perez greeted Goldwater's vice presidential running mate, William Miller, at the airport in Louisiana on his way to a banquet in 1964, and Perez was on the podium with Goldwater during his speech at the Sugar Bowl at Tulane University. Kent Courtney flew to Phoenix, Arizona, and told Goldwater that he would support his presidential bid. Courtney helped set up Goldwater's headquarters in San Francisco for the Republican National Convention in 1964.[1153] Goldwater later voted for—to the dismay of his supporters—the Voting Rights Act of 1965, which protected African Americans from the rampant Southern practice of disenfranchisement.

In 1965, Senator Eastland called Leander Perez before the Senate Judiciary Committee to join him in denouncing the Voting Rights Act. Perez testified that the Voting Rights Act was a Communist plan. Eastland told the Committee, "It is our women that we have to protect, and we are going to protect them, and if the people have to go underground, that's where they are going."[1154]

Upon Perez's death in 1969, governors John McKeithen of Louisiana and George Wallace of Alabama, Senators James O. Eastland and Allen Ellender, and Congressman F. Edward Hebert attended his funeral.[1155] A lengthy obituary appeared in the *New York Times*.[1156] In 1977, the Honorary Committee of the Judge Perez Memorial Association included Senator Eastland, Congressman Hebert, Governor Wallace, three former—and one current— Louisiana governors, and four retired justices of the Louisiana Supreme Court. At the 1977 dedication of a Judge Perez statue in Plaquemines Parish, George Singelmann invited Perez's longtime close friend Roy V. Harris to attend. (Harris was also a close friend of Joseph Milteer, as we shall see.)[1157]

Leander Perez and Guy Banister

As has been mentioned previously, Guy Banister was close to Leander Perez. Allen Campbell, who had worked for Banister, told the author that Perez was in Banister's office "all the time."[1158] Their relationship is critical, given the wealth of evidence presented that Lee Harvey Oswald and Guy Banister were working together—and Willie Somersett's revelation from information gleaned from Joseph Milteer that Leander Perez was a financial backer of the Kennedy assassination.

Banister's relationship with Perez began in 1956 when Banister assisted Senator Eastland in his search for Communists in the integration movement during the Senate Internal Security Subcommittee hearings held in New Orleans, which were given the provocative title *The Scope of Soviet Activity in the United States, 1956*. Following Banister's widely reported involvement in the hearings—which were broadcast on New Orleans television and which Lee Harvey Oswald may have watched—Perez offered his help to Banister in his further pursuits of the Communist menace. (The most important hearings will be discussed further at length.)

Banister was photographed with Perez at a 1961 Independence Day ceremony, wearing a trademark rose in his jacket lapel (see below).[1159] Banister spoke at the event, which was organized by his future secretary and love interest, Delphine Roberts. At the ceremony, Leander Perez was presented with a "patriotism award."[1160]

Guy Banister with Leander Perez at the Independence Day ceremony, 1961. (From left to right) Judge Oliver P. Schulingkamp, Guy Banister, Associate Justice Walter B. Hamlin of the Louisiana Supreme Court, and Leander Perez. Source: *The Plaquemines Gazette*, July 7, 1961; with permission

In 1961, a change in the city charter was sought that would allow Mayor deLesseps Morrison to run for a fifth term. Banister opposed Morrison and the charter change and—in another example of the working relationship between Banister and Perez—Banister conferred with Perez on the matter and determined that a majority of all registered voters would be needed to change the city charter, not a mere majority of the votes cast.

Banister spoke out about the matter while addressing a meeting of the Louisiana Un-American Activities Committee (LUAC), in Baton Rouge.[1161] (As was noted in Chapter One, Banister was the chief investigator for LUAC.) Banister's position on the charter was backed by Louis P. Davis, who was chairman of the Gentilly (a New Orleans suburb) Citizens' Council, as well as a personal friend and supporter of the Hate Bus visit to New Orleans in 1961 described in Chapter Three.[1162] Perez and his assistant George Singelmann both also served on the Gentilly Citizens' Council board.[1163]

Leander Perez and General Walker

General Walker frequently spoke at Citizens' Council meetings throughout the South and was an ardent supporter of the segregationist cause. Walker was ever present among the national leadership of the Citizens' Council, and was one of their most prized endorsers. Upon his return from Germany after President Kennedy relieved him of his command, General Walker's first major speech was to the Mississippi legislature, with Citizens' Council leader Mississippi governor Ross Barnett at his side on December 29, 1961.[1164]

Walker traveled from Dallas to New Orleans a few days before the Kennedy assassination and met with Leander Perez, Kent Courtney, and two employees of Guy Banister's detective agency. Hilaire du Berrier, a member of the board of Kent Courtney's Conservative Society of America stayed at Walker's Dallas home in his absence. While in New Orleans, Walker spoke at an event organized by Courtney three days before the assassination. Walker later met with Perez in his office. Walker attended a meeting at the Jung Hotel on the eve of the assassination with Joe Newbrough and Jack Martin, employees of Guy Banister's detective agency. An informant for the Louisiana State Police reported on the meeting.[1165] Walker departed New Orleans on the morning of the assassination and was on a Braniff Airlines flight to Shreveport during the murder.[1166]

The meeting of General Walker—one of the military advisors of the Council for Statehood who plotted assassinations—with Leander Perez (who reportedly funded the president's assassination) is of monumental significance in the assassination story. Walker and

Perez were both associates of Joseph Milteer (who knew of the murder plot in advance and was in Dealey Plaza when it happened). The incident is all the more crucial considering that Lee Harvey Oswald was allegedly seen multiple times with both Kent Courtney and Guy Banister—close associates of both Walker and Perez. Due to its significance, the incident will be taken up in detail later.

Leander Perez and Roy V. Harris

Roy V. Harris of Augusta, Georgia, was one of Leander Perez's closest friends. Like Perez, he too was a close associate of Joseph Milteer.[1167] Harris had agreed to help Milteer set up his new paramilitary organization (which he called "the U.S. Eagles") in 1968.[1168] Harris's gesture came after Milteer had traveled to visit General Pedro del Valle and gained his support for the group.[1169] Like Banister and Milteer, Harris was associated with the National States' Rights Party.[1170] Louisiana historian Glen Jeansonne described the relationship between Perez and Harris as follows: "They didn't have to correspond. They thought so much alike that they knew exactly what was on each other's mind." On March 24, 1956, Harris shared the podium with Perez and Willie Rainach at the New Orleans Municipal Auditorium.[1171]

Harris was an original founder of the Citizens' Council. He retained the name "Georgia States' Rights Council" in his home state, instead of "Citizens' Council" in deference to Georgia's early states' right movement. Senator Eastland addressed the Council in 1961 at Harris's invitation.[1172] In 1958, Harris conferred with Willie Rainach by letter about setting up a free electors campaign in Georgia.[1173]

Roy Harris was known as "Georgia's kingmaker" and "Mr. Segregation."[1174] He was 5' 4" in height and was described in a bowling analogy as "ten-pin shaped."[1175] As speaker of the Georgia House of Representatives and chief strategist for Georgia governor Eugene Talmadge, he was described as "the most powerful back-room man in Georgia politics." When Eugene Talmadge died, Harris led the successful campaign to elect his son Herman Talmadge to the governor's office and, in 1956, to the U.S. Senate.[1176] After Harris lost his office as speaker in 1946 he declared he would never run for political office again, stating: "I reached the conclusion that in order to carry on the fight for a segregated society . . . that I needed to get in the background and back somebody else and form a coalition . . . ."[1177] In March 1956, Harris addressed the New Orleans Citizens' Council and stated in the wake of the *Brown* decision, "Patience and moderation on the subject of the Supreme Court decisions destroying segregation in the public school systems means integration. . . . To resist and set aside the Supreme Court decision is our only salvation" and urged impeachment of the Court.[1178] With Talmadge's support, Harris was able to persuade the Georgia legislature to establish the Georgia Education Committee, in 1953, which—like Perez's Sovereignty Commission—was devoted to the preservation of segregation.

In 1957, Ed Friend worked for both Harris and the Sovereignty Commission and was sent to the Highlander Folk School in Monteagle, Tennessee, to photograph a meeting of national civil rights leaders. (Miles Horton and James A. Dombrowski had founded the Highlander Folk School—a rustic retreat located west of Chattanooga—in 1932, to train union leaders in the Congress of Industrial Organizations. Later, it became a training center for the civil rights movement and became an immediate target for Southern segregationists who saw it as a "cancerous growth.") In attendance at the 1957 meeting were civil rights legends Martin Luther King, Jr., Rosa Parks, Anne Braden, Aubrey Williams, and Myles Horton.[1179] At the meeting, the anthem of the civil rights movement was born. Based on a Negro spiritual and a union song, Zelphia Horton composed "We Shall Overcome." Popular folk singer—and a victim of a congressional Communist witch hunt—Pete Seeger was in attendance and sang and played the song on his banjo. After the meeting, Anne Braden drove Dr. King to the Louisville, Kentucky, airport for his return home. Anne Braden told the author that Dr. King was so pleased by the song he sang it all the way to the airport.[1180]

As the Georgia Sovereignty Commission's operative, Ed Friend traveled to Highlander with his wife and told Myles Horton that he was just passing by on vacation, was a freelance photographer, and wondered if he could take some pictures. The naïve participants at the Highlander meeting, which took place on Labor Day 1957, received Friend graciously, and he registered as a delegate. Friend took photos of the group that were released to the public with the intention of offending the Southern racists. One particularly provocative image showed black and white participants—male and female—performing choreographed physical interactions designed to ease the discomfort of open associations of the races, which were forbidden in Southern society.[1181] Friend also made a motion picture film that showed a black male adult (or older teen) swimming in a pond at Highlander with white male and female children—an unforgivable Southern offense.[1182]

Harris and Friend's pièce de résistance was a photo of Martin Luther King, Jr., seated behind a squatting Abner Berry—a member of the Central Committee of the Communist Party and writer for its paper, the *Daily Worker*. (It just so happens that Lee Harvey Oswald subscribed to the *Daily Worker*, as did many on the far right.) In the photo, below, Dr. King is labeled number one, Berry is number two, Aubrey Williams is number three, and Myles Horton is number four. Seated, as the fourth person to Dr. King's left, is Rosa Parks.

The text below the picture notes that Karl Prussian, a Herbert Philbrick-type counterspy for the FBI for twenty-two years, charged that King belonged to sixty Communist front organizations and was "encouraged and promoted by the Kennedys." Aubrey Williams was the president of SCEF located in New Orleans, the integrationist archenemy of the Eastland-Perez-Banister operation. Fair Play for Cuba Committee was a scion of SCEF. ("SCEF and the FPCC are just one big ball of wax," as Herbert Philbrick once told a friend.[1183]) Aubrey Williams had been appointed by President Franklin D. Roosevelt as the Assistant Relief Administrator and reported to Harry Hopkins, who created many of the projects in the New Deal Works Progress Administration—and Roosevelt's wife Eleanor once attended Highlander.[1184] The Highlander School had been under the watchful eye of J. Edgar Hoover and the FBI since the 1930s, when allegations of Communist activity were first reported.[1185]

The Highlander Folk School was dubbed a Communist Training School by the far right after Abner Berry (number two, squating on floor) inserted himself in front of Martin Luther King, Jr. (number one) while an agent of Roy V. Harris's Georgia Sovereignty Commission, Ed Friend, snapped the picture. Source: Ed Friend Papers, Special Collections, University of Georgia

Horton, who had welcomed Friend and Berry, stated that no one at the meeting knew them, but that Friend and Berry seemed to know each other. Berry did not tell Horton that he was a reporter for the *Daily Worker*, or that he was on the Central Committee of the Communist Party. As Friend was shooting a picture of Dr. King, Berry squatted down in front of the group, then jumped and inserted himself into the photo. Horton told him to get away, and suspected that Friend and Berry had conspired to produce the photo. Berry denied knowing Friend, then later admitted to having been used. Berry wrote a story in the *Daily Worker* favorable to Highlander naming those in attendance; he resigned from the Communist Party two months later. As a result of the photo, Highlander became known as the "Communist Training School."[1186] It would not be surprising if Berry was not an authentic Communist, but simply a plant who infiltrated the Communist Party and *Daily Worker* for the far right. Either way, the infamous so-called "Highlander Communist Training School" poster became the greatest propaganda piece ever produced by the segregationists.

The photo appeared everywhere in the South—from Klan literature, to mainstream Southern newspapers and roadside billboards. Harris stated: "I tell you, I think we published a million copies of that paper at state expense . . . And I'm tellin' you, you've got no idea how many of those things were reproduced all over this country and spread out." The photo prompted the *Birmingham News* to investigate Highlander and conclude that the master plan behind racial unrest was Soviet-inspired.[1187] The John Birch Society headquarters in Belmont, Massachusetts, reproduced the picture on a post card.[1188] A copy of the "Highlander Communist Training School" story was even found by HSCA investigators among Joseph Milteer's belongings after his death.[1189]

In 1962 and 1963, Leander Perez and George Singelmann—as well as Ned Touchstone of Shreveport—printed thousands of copies of the Highlander photo. Shortly before Martin Luther King, Jr.'s march across the Edmund Pettus Bridge in Selma, Alabama, en route to Montgomery on March 7, 1965—a day that became known as "bloody Sunday"—a billboard with the Highlander photo was erected near Montgomery under Ned Touchstone's supervision. Touchstone told reporters that King had viewed the billboard. Touchstone remarked, "we are in good shape in exposing King if the boys in New York don't decide to kill him. They may wish to make a martyr out of him. I certainly hope not."[1190]

Harris published the *Augusta Courier*, an openly racist and anti-Semitic weekly newspaper until it folded in 1974. Harris published the Highlander picture on the last page of the *Courier* and featured a two-line headline in bold upper case print. The first line was in fiery red ink, the second in black. In the headlines or bylines, Harris constantly complained about Communism, race mixing, Zionism and Federal Government misconduct.

After the Ed Friend photo was published, Highlander was investigated by the Tennessee Legislature, who recommended that local law enforcement keep it under surveillance. In 1960, Highlander was raided and Horton was charged and convicted with selling "intoxicating beverages"—cans of beer he sold at cost—and operating a school in violation of the state's segregation laws. The state then confiscated the Highlander property—in addition to Horton and his mother's nearby homes that were not connected to Highlander—and sold them at a public auction.

Anne Braden attended the 1957 meeting at Highlander but was not photographed. She and her husband Carl were leaders in SCEF whose predecessor, the Southern Conference of Human Welfare, was a target of a number of congressional investigations beginning with a 1948 probe by the House Committee on Un-American Activities (HUAC). More importantly, the Bradens were officers in Fair Play for Cuba Committee, a group that Lee Harvey Oswald infiltrated by establishing a phony chapter in 1963. HUAC subpoenaed Myles Horton, Aubrey Williams (who appeared in the Highlander photo), James Dombrowski (who was later head of SCEF in New Orleans), Virginia Durr, and others to testify before the Committee. HUAC concluded, "The Southern Conference for Human Welfare has further revealed itself as a Communist-front organization by its cooperation with other Communist-dominated front groups." They further stated: "They have placed themselves on record as favoring an independent Negro Soviet Republic in the Southern Black Belt . . ."[1191]

Lee Harvey Oswald reportedly viewed the Highlander photo and shuddered when he saw it at an alleged Klansman-owned barbershop when he traveled to Clinton, Louisiana, in September of 1963. The next day he (suspiciously) joined a group of African Americans in a Congress of Racial Equality voter registration line in Clinton, two hours from New Orleans. Like FPCC, CORE had direct ties to SCEF, whose supporters were participants at the Highlander meeting.

Roy Harris praised white students at the University of Georgia for rioting on January 11, 1961, in response to the attempt to desegregate the school.[1192] Although Georgia governor Jimmy Carter refused to reappoint Harris to the Board of Regents during his tenure in office from 1971 to 1975, an oil portrait of Roy Harris was paid for by the Georgia General Assembly in 1977 and hangs in the state capitol today.[1193]

Harris spoke with General Walker at the October 25–26, 1963, Annual Leadership Conference of the Citizens' Council of America in Jackson, Mississippi. Walker stated at that time that the Kennedys had liquidated the country and that Kennedy "liberalism" or "Socialism" was the definition of Communism. He told the audience that President Kennedy was the head of the anti-Christ movement. Walker concluded his speech portentously. Referring to President Kennedy, he stated, "It's interesting that the Communists killed first the people that helped them in their revolution. First! So we've got something to look forward to, ladies and gentleman." Walker was obviously suggesting that President Kennedy had helped the Communist cause—and that his segregationist audience could expect to look forward to the Communists killing Kennedy. Twenty-seven days after his remarks a Communist killed President Kennedy. Either Walker could see into the future, or he knew something others didn't. The press did not carry Walker's speech.[1194]

Willie Somersett and Leander Perez, 1960

In 1960, Federal Marshals were sent to New Orleans to monitor the court-ordered integration of the public schools. Willie Somersett was asked by the FBI to travel from his home in Miami to New Orleans "to determine if any potentially dangerous individuals who are members of the KKK or other organizations advocating violence were coming to New Orleans for the purpose of violence." He arrived in New Orleans on November 15, 1960. Arrangements were made for daily contact with a special agent in the New Orleans office of the FBI. Somersett was instructed to develop information regarding the activities of a member of the New Orleans National States' Rights Party (NSRP), whose name was redacted by the FBI (but may well have been James Ray Leahart, who was head of the New Orleans group). Somersett, who was working undercover and was well known in the NSRP, wired a message either to the NSRP member of the FBI's interest or another one (the FBI documents are not clear) and, three days later, received a personal letter from that contact, which served as a means of introduction to another unknown individual in the NSRP.

In connection with the matter, Somersett also provided a copy of the New Orleans edition of the *Thunderbolt*—without any redactions of the names in the paper—to an FBI informant in Birmingham. The paper revealed that Ray James Leahart wrote the feature story for the New Orleans edition of the *Thunderbolt*, and was also the secretary of the NSRP. (It's likely that Leahart was the person of the FBI's interest.) Leahart wrote a letter to Milteer in 1959, as was presented in Chapter Three. As also noted in Chapter Three, a citizen notified the FBI that he saw Lee Harvey Oswald with Ray Leahart in 1963.

The foregoing suggests Leahart was a subject of the FBI's interest in 1960, which was not revealed in the FBI documents received through a Freedom of Information Act request made by the author. If the FBI knew, as the author suspects, that Leahart was part of an extremist group, that information should have gone to the Warren Commission with the report of the sighting of Oswald with Leahart. It is also evidence of Somersett's long, valuable and dependable service to the FBI prior to revelations on Milteer's assassination foreknowledge.

Although heavily redacted—and without mention of Perez's name—Somersett appears to have provided information to the FBI on members of Perez's private schools project in St. Bernard Parish, the Citizens' Council, and other matters related to the Perez operation. Among other things, Somersett learned that the Louisiana State Legislature planned to meet with then President-elect Kennedy to determine his position on the federal takeover of the schools. If Kennedy was favorable to the integration plan, they planned to proceed with the

Free Elector scheme to throw the election into the House of Representatives. On November 15, 1960, Somersett attended the New Orleans Citizens' Council rally in the Municipal Auditorium, which raised $42,200 to resist the federal integration effort. He was told that the Citizens' Council planned to resort to violence, if needed, and could have 500,000 people help in the battle. He noted, "They would have to go down fighting in New Orleans or the Communist Party and the Negroes would take over." He added that the Council would go all the way and had backing from the governor and those in neighboring states. On November 28, 1960, Somersett visited the Citizens' Council office at 323 Balter Building, and was signed up as a member by an individual whose name was redacted by the FBI but was likely Banister's friend George Singelmann, who manned the office. The FBI concluded that the information provided by Somersett was very valuable and had helped avoid violence.[1195]

In 1962, the FBI monitored the Perez-led resistance to the integration of Catholic schools. They determined that Delphine Roberts, Guy Banister's secretary and paramour during the summer of 1963, was an ally of Perez. They identified and photographed Roberts picketing an integrated Catholic school, holding a placard denouncing the archbishop's decree to integrate the schools.[1196] In another demonstration, she carried a placard stating, "One Negro in a white school is too many."[1197] Roberts picketed as a member of "Save Our Nation" whose president was Una Galliot. Galliot was excommunicated from the Catholic Church—along with Leander Perez—by Archbishop Rummel, and regularly made headlines for her protests against the integration of the Catholic schools.[1198] John F. Rau, Jr. was the legal counsel for the Perez-backed Parents and Friends of Catholic Schools. Jack Helm, who was a Klan associate of David Ferrie, was president of the organization.[1199] Louis P. Davis was another ally of Perez in the organization—and a close Banister associate, as we shall see.[1200] Somersett's information revealed that key members of Banister's operation were heavily involved in Perez's segregation efforts in the Catholic schools. Somersett was thoroughly familiar with Perez when Milteer told him he was a financial backer of the assassination.

Jim Garrison and Leander Perez

Jim Garrison boasted in his book, *On the Trail of Assassins* that he had no major political backing when he won his bid for district attorney in 1962, which is not quite correct.[1201] Leander Perez and his family backed Garrison, and contributed $2,000 to his campaign—a tidy sum for a D.A. race at that time. With Perez's support no doubt came the support of the Klan and other far-right organizations that supported Perez. After his victory, Garrison thanked the Citizens' Council "and other organizations" for their support.[1202] Another source also confirmed that Garrison received considerable financial backing from Perez for the 1962 campaign. Garrison wrote a letter to Perez, in which he thanked him and offered his assistance to him and his sons any time they needed it.[1203]

Garrison had run in opposition to the incumbent D.A., Richard Dowling. In 1959, Richard Dowling was an ally of Perez's archenemy Governor Earl Long.[1204, 1205] During a campaign speech, Garrison insinuated that Richard Dowling was a member of a Communist organization.[1206]

During the D.A. contest, James Arthus, a Citizens' Council member and janitor at the infamous 544 Camp Street building, circulated scathing campaign pamphlets attacking Dowling.[1207, 1208] (Arthus, you'll remember, so despised President Kennedy that he put a dead pigeon in a shoebox and sent it to Kennedy with his correct name and return address. As a result, any time President Kennedy came near New Orleans the FBI or Secret Service would carefully observe him.[1209, 1210]) Arthus was ultimately arrested for circulating "obscene and libelous documents." He told authorities that George Singelmann was in charge of distributing 100,000 copies of the anti-Dowling documents; Singelmann denied the charges.[1211] D.A. Dowling subpoenaed Singelmann and searched the offices of the Citizens' Council in the Balter Building for the circulars, but none were found.[1212] Thus, Garrison was not only aided in his campaign by the Perez family, but also by Perez's personal aide, George Singelmann, and a janitor of the infamous 544 Camp Street building.

Garrison was supported in his 1969 bid for reelection by several attorneys on the radical right whose names are familiar ones in this story, including: G. Wray Gill, Sr., Guy Johnson, Cy Courtney (brother of Kent Courtney), and Thomas Baumler—who was discussed in the Nazi chapter. All were known (or at least likely, as in the case of Cy Courtney) associates of Guy Banister.[1213]

Attorneys Benjamin E. Smith and Bruce C. Walzer—two integrationists connected with SCEF and the bitter enemies of Banister, Senator Eastland, and Perez—supported Dowling in his re-election bid. SCEF shared board members with Fair Play for Cuba Committee and was the target of investigations by both HUAC and Senator Eastland's SISS. Banister's close friend Hubert Badeaux joined the New Orleans police raid on the offices of SCEF and Dowling supporters Smith and Walzer, in October 1963—while Singelmann and Perez stood outside and watched. Garrison was fully aware of the operation and it was his role to prosecute the men under the Communist Control Act. The boxes of seized materials were sent to Senator Eastland in Washington. (The SCEF raid will be discussed in detail in a later chapter.)

The author asked Garrison's chief investigator Lou Ivon whether or not Perez showed any interest in Garrison's subsequent assassination probe. He replied that Perez regularly contacted the D.A.'s office and kept tabs on the investigation.[1214]

Jim Garrison and the Citizens' Council

Jim Garrison attended several meetings of the Greater New Orleans Citizens' Council, including one on March 2, 1962—just days before the D.A. election. He was introduced from the stage to the crowd by council vice president C. E. Vetter. State senator Wellborn Jack spoke at the meeting and urged New Orleanians to picket President Kennedy during his 1962 visit to the Crescent City. Leander Perez also spoke, and was bitterly critical of the recent Diocese order to integrate the Catholic schools. George Singelmann took the stage and urged support for his "reverse freedom bus" scheme to counteract the effects of the Congress of Racial Equality's Freedom Rider's campaign.[1215]

While blatant racism and anti-Kennedy sentiment filled the hall, Jim Garrison sat there and took it all in.

Joseph Milteer and Emmet Irwin

Emmet Lee Irwin was the chairman of the Greater New Orleans Citizens' Council and was well aquatinted with several key Guy Banister associates.[1216] An envelope from Irwin, post-marked in 1959, addressed to "J. A. Milteer" was found in Milteer's home after his death, and attests to a relationship between the two men.[1217] Irwin spoke with Leander Perez and George Singelmann at the May 8, 1962, Citizens' Council meeting, and on a number of other occasions. Complaints against the Kennedy brothers and accusations of the Communist influence in the civil rights movement were constant themes at the meetings. One speaker at the May 1962 event complained that the NAACP had never been cited as a subversive organization, asking, "And why not? With good old Jack in the White House and Bobby across the street, how could they be cited?" He went on to say, "Communism is the driving force behind the integration movement."[1218]

A 1959 envelope addressed to "J. A. Milteer" from Emmet Irwin. Source: NARA HSCA, Box 51

Guy Banister's close friend Willie Rainach, as well as Milteer's two associates, Leander Perez and Emmet Irwin, were officers of the state Association of Citizens' Councils when it was incorporated on January 27, 1956. Later, Louis P. Davis, who was involved with the Hate Bus saga, became an officer of the Council.[1219, 1220]

Irwin told a Citizens' Council meeting, on February 14, 1956, that the NAACP was a part of the "Communist conspiracy."[1221] Irwin presided over a Citizens' Council mass segregation rally on March 20, 1956, at the New Orleans Municipal Auditorium, which included Roy V. Harris, Leander Perez, Willie Rainach, and Georgia State Attorney General Eugene Cook as speakers. Cook told the crowd of 8,000 that fifty-two high-ranking members of the NAACP were Communists.[1222] Irwin spoke with Kent Courtney, Rainach, Senator Eastland and Perez at a New Orleans Citizens' Council rally on November 18, 1957.[1223] On July 25, 1958, Courtney addressed another Council crowd of 8,000, with Irwin and others, and urged support of the Council.[1224] Irwin also attended meetings of the States' Rights Party of Louisiana, along with Courtney, John U. Barr, Louis P. Davis, Jack Rogers, and C. E. Vetter.[1225] (Both Rogers and Banister worked for the Louisiana Un-American Activities Committee, as was noted in Chapter One, and C. E. Vetter was listed on the masthead as a commissioner of the Sovereignty Commission in 1969, when the agency was abolished.[1226])

All three of Milteer's Citizens' Council associates—Perez, Harris, and Irwin—appeared together at a May 17, 1960, New Orleans Citizens' Council meeting, and were pictured in the *Times–Picayune*. At the meeting, Harris expressed his concern that the NAACP was stirring up trouble, saying, "We can stop them if we unite. . . . When mothers start teaching their kids to ostracize the niggers, they'll catch on and the kids will find a thousand ways to make them miserable."[1227]

Representing the D.A.'s office, Jim Garrison and Frank Klein attended a testimonial banquet hosted by Leander Perez on May 23, 1963, in honor of Emmet Irwin, which was held at the Fontainebleau Hotel.[1228, 1229] Several public officials were present, including Lieutenant Governor T. C. "Taddy" Aycock. Five days after the banquet, General Walker paid Aycock a visit in Baton Rouge.[1230] (Though he lived in Dallas, Walker was a frequent visitor to the state of Louisiana.)

Irwin wrote an editorial on July 1, 1963, and accused President Kennedy of violating the Constitution in the federal intervention in the racial crises in Mississippi and in Alabama.[1231]

A storeowner informed the FBI, on December 21, 1963, that one of his customers—a New Orleans Citizens' Council member named Walter Schneider—told him he was upset at President Kennedy's intervention in the racial crisis at the University of Mississippi. (General Walker had been arrested for leading the riots against the U.S. government during the September 1962 crisis.) The customer stated that he belonged to an organization that could just pull a name out and have a man killed, alluding to Kennedy. He said the organization had planned to kill Kennedy in March 1963 but couldn't get to him. After the assassination, Schneider called another store employee and boasted that he was a "good prognosticator." The FBI interviewed Schneider, who denied the accusations. Instead, he told the FBI he belonged to the Citizens' Council at 509 Delta Building and the American Legion Brunner Post 5518 on Magazine Street.[1232]

What makes the store owner's allegation compelling is the fact that the Citizens' Council office of Leander Perez and George Singelmann had moved from the Balter Building—and had been relocated in the Delta Building—at the time of the assassination. Kent Courtney and Guy Banister were members of the American Legion Un-American Activities Committee, and Courtney belonged to the Brunner Post, to which Schneider belonged. Although Banister was a special advisor to the Legion—not a member per se, since he had not served in the military—he addressed the Brunner Post in 1962.[1233]

Joseph Milteer and George W. Gill, Jr.

The business card of attorney George W. Gill, Jr.—the son of G. Wray Gill, Sr., who was also an attorney—was found in Milteer's home by HSCA staff.[1234] The office address is the same as his father's was in 1963. Because the card bears a post office ZIP code, rather than a zone—the U.S Post Office switched from zones to ZIP codes in July 1963—Gill, Jr.'s card can then be dated after July 1963.[1235]

The HSCA collected business cards and handwritten addresses of a number of individuals from Milteer's house after his death, including Gill's card and Milteer's card. Source: NARA HSCA, Boxes 49-51

After Milteer dropped in on Leander Perez's office in October 1963, just prior to the Constitution Party meeting, he met two young lawyers, who were not named in any of the documents the author found. One may have been George W. Gill, Jr., who worked out of his father's office—as did David Ferrie.

Milteer wrote his friend Woody Kearns on October 3, 1963, and described his New Orleans meeting: "I also saw a couple of young lawyers and maybe one of them will attend our meeting."[1236] G. Wray Gill, Sr. was an attorney for both David Ferrie and New Orleans Mafia boss Carlos Marcello. Gill, Sr. had represented Marcello since he had been subpoenaed to testify before the Kefauver Committee that was investigating organized crime in 1951—Gill's office had been located in the Balter Building at the time.[1237] Gill was also a friend of Guy Banister; both Banister and Gill flew to Florida to testify on behalf of David Ferrie in his dismissal hearings from Eastern Airlines.[1238]

By 1963, Gill, Jr. had practiced law for over ten years. A graduate of Louisiana State University, he had practiced in both state and federal courts "in about every conceivable civil litigation on the docket."[1239] After Banister employee Jack Martin told the press, just after the assassination, that David Ferrie was associated with Lee Harvey Oswald, Gill, Sr. learned of the matter.

Gill, Sr. was questioned by the FBI and told them that he had known Ferrie since 1961, when he represented him in a criminal matter in Jefferson Parish, and again in a grievance against Eastern Airlines following his dismissal from the company. Afterward, Ferrie worked for Gill, Sr. as an investigator and an all-around handyman. Gill, Sr. denied knowing of a relationship between Ferrie and Oswald. Gill, Sr. related that a TV station had contacted him on November 23, 1963 and told him of the allegation made by Jack Martin of the possible involvement of Ferrie in the assassination. Gill, Sr. then called W. Hardy Davis, who told him about Martin's allegations that Oswald—upon his arrest in Dallas—possessed a library card bearing Ferrie's name. (The library card never materialized, but Oswald's landlady told the FBI that Ferrie had come by Oswald's apartment and asked her about it.)

Martin told Davis that Ferrie had told him (Martin) that President Kennedy should be killed, and that Ferrie had outlined plans to accomplish it. Martin also had claimed Ferrie had known Oswald, and had trained him to use a scoped rifle—and had flown him to Dallas. Gill noted that Ferrie and Martin were once good friends, until Martin blamed Ferrie for the loss of a job involving work in a large territory for the Holy Apostolic Catholic Church of North America. Thereafter, he reportedly slandered Ferrie at every opportunity. Gill, Sr. vouched for Ferrie's whereabouts on the day of the assassination, stating that Ferrie had been with him in the courtroom during the deportation trial of Carlos Marcello.[1240] (In March 1962, Ferrie had entered into an agreement with Gill, Sr. that Gill, Sr. would represent him in his legal troubles over his dismissal for Eastern Airlines, in exchange for Ferrie's research and investigative work on other cases; he entered into a similar agreement with Guy Banister.)

By the fall of 1963, Ferrie and Banister had become actively involved in the defense investigation of federal charges against Carlos Marcello, the mob boss of New Orleans regarding a fraudulent birth certificate—an investigation which lasted through 1966. Ferrie had flown to Guatemala on behalf of Marcello and had stayed at Marcello's countryside estate, Churchill Farms, on the weekends of November 9 and 16, 1963—supposedly to work on his legal case.[1241] Delphine Roberts gave Gill, Sr. some of Banister's files after his death, according to Gill, Sr.'s widow.[1242] Carlos Marcello testified before the HSCA in an executive session and admitted knowing that Ferrie worked for his lawyer, G. Wray Gill, Sr., but stated that he was not close to him.[1243]

According to a Garrison investigator's interview, Clara Flournoy "Bootsie" Gay said that she had enlisted G. Wray Gill, Sr. to do some legal work for her in a civil case. She had visited the office on several occasions before the Kennedy assassination and observed David Ferrie, who had a desk in Gill, Sr.'s office and understood him to be an investigator for the law practice. The day after the assassination, Gay went to Gill, Sr.'s office and observed two females cleaning out Ferrie's desk. According to D.A. investigators: "She saw a chart or a sketch, and what caught her eye was the fact that this chart had ELM written on what appeared to be a street. There was also a building and on the street was a square with letters 'VIP' written in this square. Mrs. Gay stated that she remarked to the receptionist that this should be turned over to the FBI. The receptionist then picked it off the desk then threw it into the trashcan stating it was nothing." The investigator's memo concluded by stating: "She [Gay] appears to be the type of individual that likes to see justice prevail."[1244] Gay obviously suspected that the drawing referred to Elm Street in Dealey Plaza, where the president was shot.

Thomas Beckham, the former teenage singer who ran errands for Guy Banister, voluntarily—without subpoena or legal council—testified before the HSCA on May 24, 1978. Among other things, he told the committee that he had attended a meeting in the Algiers section of New Orleans with Sergio Arcacha Smith, and an individual whose name he pronounced phonetically as "Charlie Marullo" who obviously was Carlos Marcello. Also in attendance were Lucius Rabel, David Ferrie, and G. Wray Gill, Sr. Beckham testified that they talked about how President Kennedy ought to be killed because of the Bay of Pigs fiasco.[1245] As noted in Chapter Two, David Ferrie took Beckham to Gill's office, where Beckham was asked by Gill to go to Dallas and deliver a package of photos of streets and pictures taken from a window. Beckham took the package to Dallas and gave it to a man he had seen before in New Orleans—whom he only knew as "Howard."[1246] The delivery took place one or two weeks before the assassination.[1247]

G. Wray Gill, Sr. died in 1972. On October 20, 1977, HSCA investigators interviewed his son, George W. Gill, Jr., and asked about his father's activities. Gill, Jr. told them that the Marcello files were protected by attorney-client privilege and that he thought Ferrie took his files with him when he was fired in 1964.[1248, 1249]

Milteer is not the only individual who had been in Dealey Plaza during the murder, who had apparent ties to the Gill father-and-son law firm in the 1507 Pere Marquette building. Eugene Hale Brading (who also went by the name Jim Braden, as was discussed earlier) was in Dealey Plaza and, after the shooting, walked to the Dal-Tex Building adjacent to the Texas School Book Depository. There, an elevator operator noticed Brading acting suspiciously and called law enforcement. Brading was taken into custody by the Sheriff's department.

Throughout his questioning in detention, Brading lied and represented himself as "Jim Braden." (Brading had recently assumed the alias "Jim Braden" and had somehow managed to get a driver's license listed in that assumed name through the California department of motor vehicles.) He lied further, stating that he was in Dealey Plaza because he was at the nearby courthouse to speak to a parole officer, and that he had merely entered the Dal-Tex building to find a telephone. Brading/Braden told the Sheriff's department that he was an oil dealer from Beverly Hills, California, and had been staying at the Cabana Motel, Room 201. Satisfied with his story, the Sheriff's department released him.[1250]

The FBI visited "Braden" on January 29, 1964, and he further lied when he told them he was not familiar with Dallas—when he had, in fact, lived in Dallas at one time and had been arrested there by the Sheriff's department in 1952.[1251] Nonetheless, the FBI remained satisfied with his explanations.[1252]

Brading/Braden's lies were not exposed until years later when a Los Angeles television news anchor, Peter Noyes, investigated the matter and wrote about it in the 1973 book *Legacy of Doubt*. Noyes's investigation was spawned by information gathered from William Turner, the former FBI agent, and investigator for Jim Garrison, who was also from California. Later, when the HSCA took up the "Braden" matter, Brading/Braden was asked why he lied and did not reveal his real name. He replied, "They didn't ask me."[1253]

Laurence Meyers—a salesman from Chicago—was also staying at the Cabana Motel at the same time as Brading/Braden. Meyers, a married man, had been at the Carousel Club—a strip club owned by Jack Ruby—on the evening before the assassination with Jean West, whom he picked up at a party in Chicago; Jack Ruby had joined him at the table. Meyers had known Ruby for a year or two at the time, as he had frequented Ruby's club while on business. (Ruby was originally from Chicago, and in addition to their common Chicago origins, they were both Jews.) Ruby met Meyers that same night for a drink at the Cabana. The HSCA determined from Jim Garrison's investigation that, on November 24, 1963, David Ferrie telephoned Meyers's hotel room from Gill's office. Meyers had no explanation for the call. The HSCA was unable to draw any conclusions about the entire matter. It's possible that the phone records were in error, and the call was not made to Meyers's room. Nonetheless, a phone call from Ferrie to the Cabana in Texas—made on Gill's phone—just before the assassination, remains suspicious.[1254, 1255]

Peter Noyes used parole board records and other evidence to expose Brading/Braden. From the California attorney general's office, Noyes reportedly also learned that Lee Harvey Oswald may have been a right winger with ties to a paramilitary group. Noyes stated, without providing evidence, that Brading had ties to the oil mafia and far-right industrialists. In his research, Noyes discovered that Brading worked out of the 1701 Pere Marquette office of oil geologist Vernon Main, Jr., which was adjacent to the office of Gill and Ferrie in Room 1707. Noyes stated that Brading made several trips to New Orleans in the fall of 1963.[1256] Brading told the HSCA that he had lived in New Orleans for two or three months to tend to his oil interests in the city of Lafayette, but could not recall the time periods.[1257]

Brading/Braden was a life-long criminal with a rap sheet that had thirty-five entries and he changed his name to Braden legally around the time of the assassination. He had received permission from his parole officer to travel to Texas at the time of the murder, and arrived in Dallas via Houston on November 1, 1963. He checked in with a Dallas parole officer on November 21, 1963, whom he told that he planned to see Lamar Hunt and other oil speculators. He denied visiting Hunt Oil—or knowing H. L. Hunt—but admitted that his partner, Roger Bauman, had met with H. L. Hunt.[1258] Brading/Braden was asked by the HSCA about his parole record, pointing out that he listed the Pere Marquette building as his business address. Brading/Braden stated that that was simply the conclusion that Peter Noyes arrived at from his investigation. Brading/Braden reported that Noyes received parole records concerning a "Bradley" real estate transaction that were addressed to Jim Braden, 1705 Pere Marquette. Contradicting himself, Brading/Braden stated that Noyes got the number 1706 Pere Marquette building from parole records. Asked about the address of Vernon Main's office that he worked out of, Brading/Braden stated, "I think it was 1701." The HSCA asked Brading/Braden if he knew G. Wray Gill, Colonel Bluford Balter, David Ferrie, Carlos Marcello, and "Frank Delabor" (no doubt referring to "Frank de le Barre," as there are a large number of different spellings of the name) who operated the John Birch Society training camp north of Lake Pontchartrain, but he denied knowing any of them.

Interestingly, the HSCA asked Brading/Braden if he knew anything about a "Kill Squad" or the American Volunteer Group, and he clamed to have no knowledge of it, either.[1259] Gus D. LaBarre, uncle of Frank D. (de) LaBarre, had an office on the seventh floor of the Pere Marquette, as did G. Wray Gill and David Ferrie.[1260] Joseph Milteer, Pedro del Valle and other important people in this story were connected with the far right American Volunteer Group, which was reportedly backed by Nelson Bunker Hunt, as will be discussed in the next chapter.

Noyes also learned that prior to Brading/Braden's trip to Dallas, he had told the California parole board (as he later told the Dallas parole board) that he planned to meet with Lamar Hunt in Dallas. John Curington, an attorney and employee of the Hunt family, had an office adjacent to Nelson Bunker Hunt's—which enabled him to overhear people in the office. He told the FBI, in 1977, that an individual named "Braden" and a William Cies were in Nelson Bunker's office a couple of times in 1962–1963, although his recollection was vague.[1261] Hunt associate Paul Rothermel told Noyes that Brading/Braden had been in the office on the day before the Kennedy assassination.[1262]

Milteer and Brading/Braden have a number of things in common, things which are far too unique to be coincidence. Both men traveled from opposite ends of the country and ended up at the kill zone in Dealey Plaza at the time of the assassination for no good reason. Both had ties to New Orleans and the Gill/Ferrie office in the Pere Marquette building, which was also frequented by Oswald associates Ferrie and Banister. Both Brading/Braden and Milteer also had ties to the Hunt family. Brading/Braden stated on California and Dallas parole records that he planned on meeting with Lamar Hunt during his trip to Dallas. Stunningly—and never revealed before—Milteer had visited the Hunt Company in October 1963 (as we shall see in the next chapter), during his cross-county trip promoting the October 18–20 Constitution Party meeting where talk of assassinating the president was heard. (It should be noted that the Hunt family was a major backer of General Walker's extremist activities in Dallas.)

Evidence presented in prior chapters suggests two others from the radical right: Melvin Sexton and Gene Bradley were also present in Dealey Plaza during the murder. There is little doubt Joseph Milteer was there. The man beside him in the photo in Dealey Plaza bears a strong resemblance to national Klan treasurer Melvin Sexton. Credible evidence presented in the last chapter suggests that Gene Bradley was there, representing far-right minister Carl McIntire. It's unlikely they aided the murder, but their presence may have been as representatives of the leaders of the national right who were "honored" to witness the execution of their enemy.

G. Robert Blakey, who headed the HSCA, took a special interest in mob boss Carlos Marcello and his attorney G. Wray Gill, Sr. His committee concluded that the mafia had the "motive, means and opportunity" to kill President Kennedy. Attorney General Robert Kennedy's relentless pursuit of Marcello—and his ordered deportation to Guatemala in 1961 (in what Marcello called a kidnapping)—provided some of the motive. In September 1962, an informant for the FBI with mob ties allegedly heard Marcello say, "Don't worry about that Bobby son-of-a-bitch. He's going to be taken care of." He recited, further, the Sicilian curse: "*Livarsi na pietra di la scarpa*," which means "Take the stone out of my shoe." Marcello allegedly had a plan to have a "nut," who was detached from the mob, commit the murder of the president. He used the reasoning that if you cut off the head of the dog (John Kennedy) the tail will die with it (Robert Kennedy). (The FBI learned of the allegation in 1967, but did little to investigate it.[1263]) In the mid-1960s, Carlos Marcello was arrested with other organized crime figures Santos Trafficante and mob attorneys Jacob Wasserman and Frank Ragano. Allegations were made during the HSCA investigation that other major mob figures were involved in an assassination conspiracy.[1264]

Hubert Badeaux, Guy Banister's close friend who headed the New Orleans Police anti-subversion unit under Banister, was interviewed in 1992 and gave his opinion on the allegation that Carlos Marcello was involved in the assassination. He stated: "Anyone that told that story about Carlos swearing in Italian about getting a stone out of his shoe has seen *The Godfather* too many times. Carlos doesn't talk like that. He talks with 'dees, dems, and dose,' just like in Brooklyn." He noted that Marcello did not come from Italy, but from North Africa. Badeaux concluded, "That story does not fit Carlos Marcello. You have to know Marcello and know how he talks to understand how stupid that story is."[1265] (Evidence of Badeaux's close involvement in the Banister operation will be presented later, and, from that perspective, his absolution of Marcello from the assassination may have merit.)

Blakey's HSCA investigation of Jack Ruby determined that he was involved with prominent organized crime figures in the months and years before the assassination, and that those figures had a strong motive to assassinate the president. Blakey concluded that "the murder of Oswald had all of the earmarks of an organized-crime hit, an action to silence the assassin, so he could not reveal the conspiracy."[1266]

In fact, however, the murder of Oswald did not resemble an organized crime hit. Mob hit men are not martyrs; they do not kill in front of a national television audience in the middle of a police station. Blakey noted that Oswald's uncle, Dutz Murret, had some ties to organized crime. However, when asked what ties Oswald had to the mob, he conceded, "hardly any."[1267] The lack of evidence of any meaningful ties between Lee Harvey Oswald and organized crime, combined with Oswald's phony portrayal as a Communist, his ties to the radical right wing, and supposed shooting of General Walker—among the mountains of other evidence of Oswald's activities that have no conceivable relevance to the mob—critically undermine the theory of mafia involvement.

The author filed an Open Records request with the Louisiana State Police for records on Leander Perez's personal assistant George Singelmann, and was surprised to find that Singelmann had acted as a character witness in a case against Carlos Marcello. Singelmann, Banister's best friend and a Citizens' Council leader, was a prominent figure in the segregation effort and had no other known ties to the mafia.[1268] Given Leander Perez's tremendous power and influence on state and federal politicians, favorable testimony about Marcello's character by Perez's close aide may have significantly benefited Marcello's case. Through his connections with the segregationists, Carlos Marcello may well have had foreknowledge of a plot to kill the president—and he certainly had the motive.

However, the considerable amount of evidence presented herein of Oswald's ties to the far right wing and the segregationists was overlooked by the HSCA. Importantly, Carlos Marcello was a notorious racist and if he or the mob participated in—or supported—the assassination, it may have been on the basis of his solidarity with the New Orleans extremists who waged war against the Kennedys to preserve segregation. According to biographer John Davis, Marcello was a particularly vile racist who exploited poor young blacks in his early business affairs. He always referred to blacks with derogatory epithets and considered them subhuman. He despised Martin Luther King, Jr., and was a generous donor to segregationist organizations throughout the 1960s.[1269]

Jack Ruby and the Judge

Author Jim Marrs interviewed Nancy Powell and wrote an article about her that appeared in *The Continuing Inquiry* in 1977. Powell was a stripper at Jack Ruby's Carousel Club in Dallas in 1963, working under the stage name of Tammi True. Powell told Marrs about some of Jack Ruby's activities before the Kennedy assassination, including the following brief account. Marrs wrote:

> Tammi said prior to the assassination, "some big wheel in New Or-
> leans" was in Ruby's club. "I think it was maybe the district attorney
> or a judge or something," she said. Ruby made a big deal of the visit
> and told acquaintances that the D.A. had visited him. She said it

was about this time in the fall of 1963 that Ruby went to New Orleans and brought back the stripper Jada.[1270]

Marrs told the author he did not know the identity of the person described as the "big wheel," "judge," and "D.A." from New Orleans whom Powell was referring to.

The author contacted Powell, and she recalled the interview in general. Unfortunately, she had no recollection—some thirty-five years after the event—of the account of the mysterious visitor from New Orleans whatsoever. Interestingly, at the time of the interview, Powell was married to Wally Weston, who had been a manager and promoter at Ruby's Club in 1963.[1271]

It is obvious, however, that the three-sentence description aptly fits Leander Perez on all points. His moniker was the "Judge." Perez was a "big wheel"—a man of enormous financial wealth and a powerful force in local and national politics. He was the "D.A." of Plaquemines and St. Bernard Parishes, and was "from New Orleans."

The author asked Glen Jeansonne—who wrote Perez's biography *Leander Perez, Boss of the Delta*—if he thought the visitor to Jack Ruby's club was Leander Perez based on the Powell interview. Jeansonne replied, "Probably." However, Jeansonne—who grew up in New Rhoades, Louisiana, and attended one of Perez's speeches—never suspected Perez's involvement in the Kennedy assassination. He had done the research for his biography in Perez's office, not long after his death, using his personal papers under the watchful eyes of his sons Lea and Chalin Perez.[1272]

Joseph Milteer and the Davis Well Drilling Company

A piece of paper with the name "Davis Well Drilling Company" written on it was found in Milteer's home after his death.[1273] Although this is not conclusive evidence, it is possible that the company may have been owned by Louis P. "L. P." Davis of New Orleans. In any case, it would be surprising if he did not know Milteer, given his background and relationship with the far right. Davis was a member of the pipefitters union, perhaps related to the well-drilling business—a common enterprise in the New Orleans area;[1274] another source states that Davis was in the dredging business.[1275]

Davis was an original founding officer of the Louisiana Citizens' Council, along with Leander Perez and Emmet Irwin—both Milteer associates—and was a speaker at the second national convention of the Citizens' Council in Jackson, Mississippi, on October 10, 1956.[1276] Delphine Roberts and L. P. Davis were delegates to the Citizens' Council of America meeting on July 26–27, 1961, where Milteer's friend Roy V. Harris spoke at the Jung Hotel.[1277]

As will be recalled from Chapter Three, Davis was the primary force—along with Leander Perez and George Singelmann—responsible for bringing Commander Rockwell's Hate Bus to New Orleans. He was a close associate of Guy Banister, and was at his office frequently. Davis also had a close relationship with General Walker. One source told Garrison's investigators that Louis P. Davis "[owned] General Walker."[1278]

Thomas Baumler, who worked for Davis infiltrating leftist organizations—and was reportedly seen going in and out of Guy Banister's office—told one of Garrison's investigators that, "We have a society of seventy. We almost got control of it this time." Each person had to commit a murder to belong to this society.[1279] Baumler's "society of seventy" sounds similar to Milteer's hardcore underground, which also plotted murder.

L. P. Davis was reportedly also close to Jim Garrison. At one point early in his investigation—when Garrison was pointing to the radical right, before blaming the Kennedy assassination on government intelligence—Davis called Garrison and told him he was heading in the wrong direction and that the Communists were involved in the assassination.[1280]

Davis, like Banister, engaged in anti-subversion work. Garrison's investigators interviewed George Higganbotham—a friend of Davis—who stated that because of Garrison's friendship with Davis he refused to investigate Davis's anti-subversion work and "follow them to a conclusion." Garrison later wrote on the transcribed interview, which he had received from the investigator, "This is Louis P. Davis, a Minute man type, Associated with Roswell Thompson, who appeared with Thomas Beckham at his 1968 Grand Jury appearance. JG."[1281] Garrison later sent a copy of the interview to the HSCA in 1977, but deleted the part where Higganbotham said that Garrison and Davis were friends.[1282]

Davis supported Garrison's crackdown on vice in 1963 stating: "The People of New Orleans wisely chose a man with no alliance as district attorney, who can act freely in the interest of the people and not be suppressed by commitments to a political organization."[1283] As has been previously noted, Davis supported Garrison in his bid for reelection to the district attorney's office in 1969, along with G. Wray Gill and Kent Courtney's brother Cy. Garrison's friendship with Davis and his indebtedness to Leander Perez—who helped put him in office—may be reasons why Garrison changed course and blamed government intelligence for the assassination after initially placing the blame on the radical right.

Hubert Badeaux

Joseph Milteer traveled the country extensively, attending radical-right meetings—and tape recording them for sale—beginning in at least 1957. Some of the tape recordings were recovered by the HSCA when they entered Milteer's home after his death, in 1978.

The author was stunned to discover one tape labeled "Hubert Badeaux" and "Kenner Citizens' Council" sitting on a shelf in the audio department of the National Archives.[1284] Hubert Badeaux was another close associate of Guy Banister—something investigators for the Committee were unaware of—and is another example of their extremely poor performance in their investigation of both Banister and Milteer. The author assumed incorrectly that Milteer attended and recorded Badeaux's speech, and only later discovered from Milteer's probate court papers that Milteer's friend Grady Bartlett had actually recorded it and sent it to him. Bartlett, from the Los Angeles area, was closely aligned with Reverend Wesley Swift—who was involved in the same broad-based assassination plots revealed at the Congress of Freedom meeting noted in Chapter Six.[1285] Although the recording does not directly link Milteer to close Banister associate Hubert Badeaux as the author first thought, it importantly establishes a direct tie between Swift's extremist operation in California and Banister's work in New Orleans. (Willie Somersett made it clear that the assassination had its origins in Texas, New Orleans, and California.) Another tie between the Banister operation and Swift was the close friendship between Swift's associate, William Gale, and Banister's close friend Willie Rainach—Gale was a frequent visitor to Rainach's home and an overnight guest.[1286]

Sergeant Hubert Badeaux was the agent-in-charge of the New Orleans Police Division of Intelligence, a "subversion" investigative body, who served directly under Guy Banister beginning in 1955. A 1957 letter from Badeaux on a New Orleans Police letterhead lists "Chief Guy Banister" as assistant superintendent of police. In his position with the police force, Badeaux passed on "Communist affairs" intelligence to Willie Rainach. Correspondence between Badeaux and Rainach revealed that the two were close and had a working relationship with Senator James O. Eastland.[1287] Jim Garrison's chief investigator, Lou Ivon, volunteered to the author that Badeaux was one of Banister's closest associates. Ivon knew them both from his time on the police force.[1288]

Like Banister, Badeaux was a particularly vulgar racist. The only thing the author could discern on the poor-quality tape of Badeaux's speech, which was retrieved from Milteer's home, was: "and a nigger doesn't have a lick of sense." In 1955, Badeaux and Banister drew the attention of the press when Banister fired two black police officers on the recommendation of Sergeant Hubert Badeaux. Attorneys for the fired police officers raised questions about Banister's actions and asked him if he based the dismissal "predicated on the human mind of Sergeant Badeaux," implying a racial bias. Banister was asked if he was aware "that numerous complaints about brutality toward Negroes" had been made against Badeaux. Banister adamantly denied any wrongdoing in the matter.[1289]

In March 1956, Eastland's Senate Internal Security Subcommittee (SISS), investigated Herman Liveright, a New Orleans WDSU radio program director. Liveright refused to answer when asked if he was involved in the Communist Party in New Orleans or in New York City and, as a result, was fired by his employer.[1290] Afterward, Mayor Morrison directed Chief Guy Banister to investigate other subversive activity in the city.[1291] Banister and Morrison flew to Greenwood, Mississippi, to confer with Senator Eastland. Morrison stated later: "Mr. Banister has complete liaison with the [SISS] committee's staff which was the main object of out trip." All three were pictured on the front page of the newspaper standing next to an airplane.[1292] Days later, the SISS announced it would hold more hearings in New Orleans.

The SISS targeted Hunter Pitts "Jack" Odell, an African-American later affiliated with Martin Luther King, Jr. Odell's house was raided by Hubert Badeaux and, allegedly, an extensive collection of Communist literature was seized, according to Banister.[1293] Odell later was questioned in Washington before Eastland's committee (the hearings will be covered in detail in Chapter Twenty-two).[1294]

In an April 27, 1957, letter to Rainach, Badeaux boasted of expanding his counter-intelligence network "particularly in the direction of counter attacking the Red effort to use minority groups" and "liberal fronts." Badeaux stated further—on police letterhead—the following:

Source: Rainach Papers, Noel Memorial Library, Louisiana State University Shreveport

The letter was written right after Badeaux testified with Leander Perez and Guy Banister, on March 9, 1957, before Willie Rainach's state hearings, which were entitled "Subversion in Racial Unrest." Their testimony, Rainach stated, "establishes Communism as the prime cause of racial unrest in the United States . . ." He praised Banister for his investigation of Communism in New Orleans and the state of Louisiana, compiling extensive records on subversives and cooperating with the committee before and during its public hearings.[1295]

A number of circumstances favor that the "out-of-town person" referred to by Badeaux was Lee Harvey Oswald. Oswald had joined the marines at age seventeen and, on October 21, 1956, arrived at boot camp in San Diego, California. By the date of Badeaux's letter on April 27, 1957, Oswald was at the Naval Air Technical Training Center in Jacksonville, Florida, which made him an "out-of-towner." Upon his discharge from the marines in September 1959, Oswald—just before his twentieth birthday—was of the right age to infiltrate "into the University." In fact, evidence exists (as will be presented in Chapter Twenty) that after his service in the marines and return from the Soviet Union, Oswald infiltrated leftist groups on campus. His "grooming" actually appears to have started while he was in New Orleans in the period of 1955–56 while he was a cadet in the Civil Air Patrol under the direction of the fanatical anti-Communist Captain David Ferrie.

United Press International correspondent Aline Moscow interviewed Oswald in Moscow in 1959 and he told her that he started reading Communist books when he was fifteen years old.[1296] Thus, in the period of a year or so from 1955 to 1956, Oswald went from a boy in the Civil Air Patrol to being a soldier in the United States Marine Corps. Lee's older brother Robert recalled their mother telling him that, prior to Lee joining the marines, a man in a military-style uniform came to her home and urged her to let Lee join the marines. Robert speculated that it was Captain Ferrie in CAP garb. If someone other than Oswald was the person being groomed by Badeaux, they never publicly emerged in the way that Lee Harvey Oswald did. Oswald made numerous public displays—posing as a Communist in his radio debate and FPCC pamphleting. (As will be shown later, he infiltrated a leftist campus group called the New Orleans Committee for Peaceful Alternatives and also infiltrated the Congress of Racial Equality.)

William Wulf testified before the Warren Commission that Oswald's professed interest in Communism began in 1955, during the period of time he was in the Civil Air Patrol with Captain Ferrie (though others recalled a different year). Oswald contacted William Wulf around August or September of 1955 about joining the New Orleans Amateur Astronomy Club, an organization of high school students interested in astronomy and telescopes. Wulf, like Oswald, was sixteen years old at the time. Wulf was skeptical about Oswald joining, since the members of the group had an advanced, sophisticated knowledge of astronomy and their discussions, and he felt the discussions would be over Oswald's head. At the time, Oswald was working for Phisterer Dental Lab as a delivery boy, and had learned about the club from a co-worker. On Oswald's second meeting with Wulf, he started expounding the Communist doctrine and said he was highly interested in Communism. According to Wulf, Oswald "was looking for a Communist cell in town to join but he couldn't find any," to his dismay. Oswald told him "he couldn't find any that would show any interest in him as a Communist." When Wulf's father overheard the conversation he "politely put him [Oswald] out of the house." Wulf stated that Oswald was "a boy who would get violent over Communism, who, if you did not agree with his belief, he would argue with you violently over it." Wulf expressed the opinion that Oswald was "a self-made Communist. I don't think anybody got to him, if you want to put it that way. He just learned it on his own." Wulf noted, "He expressed the belief that he could be a good Communist, he could help the Communist Party out, if he could find the Communist Party to join it . . . ." Wulf stated further: "he definitely was looking for a Communist Party to join and he was very disgusted because he couldn't."[1297] The account of Oswald trying to find "a cell" sounds Herbert Philbrick-inspired and scripted. "Cell" was an FBI term, and not a term that the Communists would necessarily use. Perhaps self-conscious of the fact that he may be perceived as a false Communist, Oswald wrote in his 1959 diary, while in the Soviet Union, "I would never become a pseudo-professional Communist such as Herbert Philbrick or maCarthy [sic]."[1298]

Another point favoring Oswald as the one being "groomed" by Badeaux was the distinction he made between a Marxist and a Communist in his 1963 radio debate with Carlos Bringuier and Ed Butler. Hubert Badeaux made the same distinction years earlier. In the debate, Oswald was asked by the moderator, "Are you or have you been a Communist?" Oswald replied that he had already answered the question prior to the program. The moderator then asked, "Are you a Marxist?" Oswald replied, "Yes, I am a Marxist." At that point, Ed Butler—who, like Badeaux, "groomed" infiltrators in his "conflict managers" scheme—entered the questioning by asking, "What's the difference?" Oswald went on to explain the difference between Communism and Marxism.[1299]

In a January 1959 address to the Young Men's Business Club in New Orleans, speaking on his investigative activities, Badeaux stated, "Those people in New Orleans follow the philosophy of Marx and therefore are Marxists, but not Communists. Ideologically they were never Communists because they could not take the party discipline. . . . There are a number of such persons in New Orleans but they never had formal ties to the Communist Party."[1300] Thus, Badeaux and Oswald both made the same odd and esoteric distinction between Communism and Marxism for reasons not entirely clear, but perhaps, because there was no Communist Party presence in New Orleans.[1301]

If Oswald was genuinely interested in joining a Communist cell, as he had told William Wulf, he certainly wouldn't have found one attending CAP meetings directed by the rabid anti-Communist David Ferrie—or by joining the United States Marine Corps a little over a year after his conversation with Wulf.

Infiltrating leftist organizations was an activity Willie Rainach engaged in, as well. In 1960, he retained the services of Joe Vinson of Pendleton Detectives, Inc., in New Orleans, to investigate a white Tulane student, Lanny Goldfinch, who was suspected of traveling to Guatemala for Communist training. Vinson interviewed both Goldfinch and Hugh Murray—both of whom were reported to be card-carrying NAACP members.[1302, 1303]

Louis P. Davis was yet another associate of Guy Banister (and perhaps Milteer) who engaged in infiltrating leftist organizations. Thomas Baumler, as was discussed in Chapter Three, infiltrated liberal elements on college campuses and elsewhere in the employ of Louis P. Davis. Baumler eventually tried to obtain a position as an investigator for Jim Garrison during his assassination investigation.[1304] According to the minutes of the meeting of the board of directors of the Association of Citizens' Councils, on June 25, 1961, Davis had friends who infiltrated a number of organizations sponsoring integration. Davis claimed that, in practically every instance, the Zionists were behind integration groups, specifically in the NAACP and in CORE.[1305] The idea of infiltrating leftists groups was pervasive among the hardcore underground in New Orleans: four associates of Guy Banister, including Hubert Badeaux, Ed Butler, Willie Rainach, and Louis P. Davis, Jr. engaged in infiltrating leftist organizations as an integral part of their strategy to defeat the integration movement.

Badeaux appeared on the second *Citizens' Council Forum*, on May 6, 1957, and lectured on the subject of "Techniques on Communist Subversion." *Citizens' Council Forum* was a television program that featured prominent anti-Communists and segregationists—including Myers Lohman, General Walker, and others. Interestingly, on the same page of *The Citizens' Council* that reported Badeaux's television appearance appeared a letter to the editor from Byron De La Beckwith in praise of the Citizens' Councils, who was later convicted of the 1963 murder of NAACP leader Medgar Evers.[1306]

In a May 23, 1957, letter to Willie Rainach, Badeaux related that he attended a law enforcement conference in Jacksonville, Florida, that addressed a recent wave of bombings. He was provided a list of active Klansmen and he disclosed to Rainach that many were Citizens' Council leaders. Badeaux complained that he suspected Jews in the B'nai B'rith and other organizations, which he felt were primarily interested in subverting the Constitution, had provided the Klansmen's names. He suggested that perhaps the Jews themselves were responsible for the bombings. Badeaux stated, "I have no choice but to conclude that they [the Jews] are not only the root of the fight to promote integration but are the prime movers of the entire communistic movement." Again, Badeaux was reluctant to discuss his Jewish suspicions in writing and suggested they talk about it another time.[1307]

On November 29, 1957, Badeaux wrote Rainach and discussed his dismay at the lack of intelligence on two suspected Communists who worked at the *New Orleans Times–Pica-*

yune, Harold Rubin and John Foster. Badeaux suggested that Rainach ask Senator Eastland for his help in the matter.[1308] On March 8, 1958, Badeaux wrote Rainach and told him he was free to discretely use any surveillance information that Badeaux had gathered—including a confidential file on liberal professor Dr. Albert D'Orlando, who he called "a prime mover in the integration movement." Rainach stated he was "most anxious to neutralize his (D'Orlando's) influence," but despite his best efforts he had not been able to "get a break." Rainach anticipated that in about a week the House Un-American Activities Committee would expose D'Orlando. He noted that D'Orlando was a Unitarian minister quite popular in Protestant church circles and he had been a top-ranking Communist in Massachusetts. Badeaux revealed his ties to the House Committee on Un-American Activities in Washington when he noted that he had given D'Orlando's name to the Committee the previous year. Badeaux stated that HUAC had finally uncovered witnesses and were going to subpoena D'Orlando to appear before a hearing in Boston on March 21, 1958. Badeaux agreed to serve the HUAC subpoena to D'Orlando, stating, "I will do this with much gusto." He added, "I hope the bum gets out of line and gets cited for contempt." (HUAC was only vested with the power to find its subjects either guilty of contempt of Congress or perjury.) Badeaux closed his letter, stating, "D'Orlando has no idea I have been stalking him . . . ."[1309] After Badeaux served the summons on D'Orlando and he appeared before the House Un-American Activities Committee, FBI undercover agent Carroll H. Foster identified D'Orlando at the hearing as a member of the Communist Party.

Badeaux, at the time, was also the director of the South Louisiana Citizens' Council.[1310] In another letter to Rainach, on July 10, 1958, Badeaux mentioned an investigation he was conducting into the American Civil Liberties Union, another leftist organization that Lee Harvey Oswald had later joined. In his ACLU investigation, Badeaux utilized the help of a husband and wife who were former members of the Communist Party. Of the couple, Badeaux stated, "I cannot emphasize enough that they are quite valuable to me in the underground and I would go to some extremes in protecting them from exposure and harassment." Badeaux mentioned a book he was writing called *Communism in Louisiana*, noting "nearly every top Red sent to Louisiana has been either a nigger or a Jew."[1311]

When Willie Rainach ran for governor in the 1959 primary, Hubert Badeaux served as his coordinator in the First and Second Congressional districts, while Delphine Roberts served as the New Orleans parish coordinator. Cy Courtney, Kent's brother, ran on the Rainach ticket as lieutenant governor.[1312]

Badeaux told Rainach that the fourteenth and fifteenth wards in New Orleans were "kindly disposed" towards him because he had tracked down the notorious "'John the Baptist', a nigger who burglarized about a 1000 homes . . . ." Badeaux organized Rainach's campaign in Jefferson Parish as well, expecting to be appointed to the head of the state police if Rainach was elected governor.[1313]

According to a newspaper account, Badeaux investigated the St. Tammany Parish nudist colony for the New Orleans Police Department. On July 4, 1959, Badeaux wrote to

Rainach about his recent investigation into a nudist camp. "I feel better now that I can wear clothes again . . . ," he related. He concluded, "The international nudist movement was controlled by Marxists" and were "a direct outgrowth of the Marxist philosophy."[1314]

On April 28, 1961, Badeaux, Medford Evans, and Tom Anderson were listed as members of the Independent American Federation of State Parties. His association with two national figures—Anderson and Evans—places Badeaux among the elite in the national far right and with two men who were close to General Walker. (Medford Evans was at Walker's side during the Senate "muzzling hearings" after Walker's military censure by the Kennedy administration. Correspondence in the papers of Tom Anderson reflects that he and Walker were very close.[1315]) Evans acknowledged, years later in a John Birch Society publication, that he was also a friend of Guy Banister.[1316]

In October 1963, while Oswald was in Dallas, Badeaux was involved in the raid on the Southern Conference Education Fund in New Orleans, which was a result of SCEF violating the state Communist Control Act. Leander Perez and George Singelmann watched from outside the SCEF Perdido Street office. With purported SCEF "Communist" materials in hand, the Louisiana Un-American Activities Committee planned to investigate not only SCEF but also FPCC and CORE—two groups that were infiltrated by Lee Harvey Oswald. Badeaux delivered the confiscated files to Senator Eastland, who planned an SISS investigation of SCEF. A fierce legal battle between SCEF and Eastland followed, with Eastland ultimately losing when the Supreme Court ruled the seizure of their records unlawful. Not deterred, the Louisiana Un-American Activities Committee launched their own investigation into SCEF and was quick to point out, after the assassination, that Lee Harvey Oswald was associated with FPCC, which had direct ties to principals at SCEF.

According to CIA documents on the Garrison probe into the murder of President Kennedy, Badeaux had become an investigator for Garrison during his assassination investigation.[1317] On May 6, 1967, Gordon Novel, whom Garrison claimed was an employee of the CIA, contacted the FBI. Novel made a number of claims, some fantastic, about Garrison's investigation. Novel told the FBI that the basis for Garrison's allegations that the Central Intelligence Agency was involved in the Kennedy assassination plot came directly from Hubert Badeaux.[1318] The FBI passed Novel's allegations about Badeaux to the CIA. Additionally, Novel noted Badeaux's close ties to Guy Banister, and accused Badeaux of passing along information to Garrison regarding "the assassination camp run by Cubans in the area across Lake Pontchartrain . . . ."[1319] As was presented previously, the camps north of Lake Pontchartrain were run by far-right-wing extremists connected to the John Birch Society, Minutemen, Nazis, and a few anti-Castro Cubans. Badeaux was close to FDV de La Barre (also noted as LaBarre, F.D.V. Dela Barre and D. Barre), who owned the land where one of the camps operated. At a speech on May 25, 1962, Badeaux and de La Barre joined Stuart McClendon at the speaker's table at a Conservative Democratic Organization (CDO) event. (Guy Banister had run for councilman on the CDO ticket and McClendon accused President Kennedy of ignoring the Communist menace in Cuba and said, "And that is treason.")[1320]

Garrison's CIA theory behind the assassination was not only promoted by his own staff members Harold Weisberg, William Turner, and others, but was actively pitched to him by long-time close Banister associate Badeaux as well—who managed to find a place on Garrison's staff. The difference between the three staff members was that Turner and Weisberg believed in the CIA theory, while Badeaux more likely fabricated his CIA allegations to throw the investigation away from the radical right. It's inconceivable that Badeaux did not know all about Lee Harvey Oswald—specifically that he wasn't who he pretended to be—if not the entire assassination conspiracy. Garrison staff member Harold Weisberg doubted the truthfulness and dependability of Badeaux's investigative work for Garrison, because he was an anti-Communist fanatic and distributed literature describing Congressman (and member of the Warren Commission) Hale Boggs, as a Communist.[1321] Badeaux also tried to discredit Banister employee Jack Martin and the claims Martin made to the FBI and Secret Service that David Ferrie and Lee Harvey Oswald were closely associated—which are well corroborated by an abundance of other evidence (presented in Chapter Two). Badeaux told a writer, "Jack drank, took pills, and had a criminal record . . . He was goofy to begin with and lied all the time."[1322] Hubert Badeaux was a recipient of some of Banister's files upon his death, as were Cy and Kent Courtney.[1323]

Guy Banister and Joseph Milteer

Michael L. Kurtz, professor of history at Southeastern Louisiana University, was the first—in a 2006 book—to present two witnesses who reported seeing Guy Banister in the presence of Joseph Milteer and other right-wing elements in New Orleans.

"Richard Eberle," manager of the New Orleans Confederate Museum, told Kurtz that he knew Banister and saw him with Milteer on several occasions. On one occasion, according to "Eberle," Banister introduced him to Milteer and the three men joined in a discussion critical of President Kennedy. Another witness, Samuel Wilson—a prominent French Quarter architect—told Kurtz that he saw Banister and Milteer together at a popular French Quarter bar. Wilson had known Banister since the 1950s, and was aware of his extremist views. He recalled Banister and Milteer voicing criticism of Kennedy because he was "soft on Communism," and also because of his racial policies. Wilson also claimed to know Clay Shaw and claimed Shaw held similar radical views to Banister. He saw Shaw and Banister together, and he believed he saw Milteer with them once. Wilson also saw Banister, accompanied by Milteer, conversing with associates of Carlos Marcello.[1324]

The author attempted to locate these two witnesses to corroborate their claims, but unfortunately Samuel Wilson had died. The author located Bernard Eble, Jr. (the apparent correct name and spelling), son of Kurtz' witness "Richard Eberle," through the Confederate Museum, and Eble graciously asked his ninety-three-year-old father about a list of names provided by the author, including those of Guy Banister and Joseph Milteer; sadly his memory had faded. Of all the names presented, only the name Guy Banister was vaguely familiar.[1325]

Even without corroboration, the allegations of a Banister-Milteer relationship are extraordinary, but not surprising, given the abundance of evidence presented herein of Milteer's association with four individuals tied to Banister, as well as the fact that Banister and Milteer both attended the April 1963 Congress of Freedom meeting in New Orleans. Nor are the allegations surprising that Banister and Milteer were seen with associates of Carlos Marcello's organization, given the business card found at Milteer's home which had come from George W. Gill, Jr., son of Marcello's attorney G. Wray Gill, Sr., as was presented earlier in this chapter. Professor Kurtz's investigation of the New Orleans aspect of the assassination conspiracy and on Banister and Milteer are obviously remarkable and invaluable contributions to history.

Conclusions

Joseph A. Milteer was associated with four individuals who were associates of Guy Banister in New Orleans. They include: George Soule, Leander Perez, George W. Gill, Jr., and Ray James Leahart. (Louis P. Davis was possibly a fifth.) It's likely that Emmet Lee Irwin, who knew Milteer, was another associate of Banister in view of the active participation of Banister and Irwin in the Citizens' Council. Those associations—and the fact that Banister and Milteer both attended the Congress of Freedom meeting in April 1963—lend credibility to the allegations of two witnesses who claim they saw Banister and Milteer together.

Willie Somersett learned from Milteer that Leander Perez was a financial backer of the Kennedy assassination. That allegation, and the evidence that Perez and Banister were close associates, the fact that Banister was seen by multiple witnesses with Lee Harvey Oswald, the fact that Banister associated with a number of Milteer's colleagues in New Orleans, and the fact that Milteer knew of the assassination in advance—and was in Dealey Plaza at the time that it occurred—is evidence of conspiracy in the assassination of President Kennedy.

The conspiracy involved the radical right and other forces dedicated to preserving the Southern institution of segregation, as will be further shown in future chapters. Milteer's relationship with mutual friends Leander Perez and Roy V. Harris, national leaders in the movement to preserve segregation—as well as with General Walker—attests to Milteer's high position in the national far right.

Roy V. Harris was the genius behind the creation of the Highlander poster entitled "Martin Luther King at Communist Training School." After the *Brown* decision, the Southern segregationists' strategy was to tie the integration movement to Communism and the Red Scare. A major problem with the strategy was the lack of any significant involvement of Communism in the movement. To remedy that, the segregationists fabricated evidence of Communist involvement. Harris's operative Ed Friend collaborated with Abner Berry of the Communist Party—whom no one at Highlander knew—and inserted himself into the photo with Dr. King, establishing King's guilt by association.

Ex-Communists and false Communists were recruited by the state and congressional inquisitions to falsely accuse people in the integration movement of being Communists. As we shall see, that is precisely where Lee Harvey Oswald fit into the scheme.

The evidence presented favors Oswald as the person Hubert Badeaux, Banister's close colleague, "groomed" in 1956 to be like Hebert Philbrick and infiltrate leftist groups. Banister and his colleagues Badeaux, Ed Butler, Willie Rainach, and Louis P. Davis all engaged in infiltrating leftists groups. Banister and Badeaux joined Senator James O. Eastland in his 1956 hearings, which determined that there was Soviet influence behind the civil rights movement, all in the same year that Oswald began to act like a Communist—and three years before he left for the Soviet Union. Banister, Badeaux and Leander Perez testified in the state hearings on Subversion in Racial Unrest in 1957, and stated that the Communists were behind the integration movement. Badeaux also had a working relationship with the House Committee on Un-American Activities in 1958, another anti-subversion body.

The allegations suggesting that Badeaux fed Garrison misinformation to tie the assassination to the CIA is further evidence of the far right's efforts to divert attention from the far right to the CIA. Revilo Oliver, Milteer's colleague, was the first from the radical right to blame the CIA for the assassination in his testimony before the Warren Commission in 1964. Furthermore, Badeaux's claim to Garrison that the training camps north of Lake Pontchartrain were run by the CIA served to deflect attention from far-right organizations—primarily the John Birch Society and Minutemen elements at the camp.

The HSCA was keenly aware of the relationship between attorney G. Wray Gill, Sr. and his client, mobster Carlos Marcello—as well as with radicals Guy Banister and David Ferrie—when they concluded that organized crime was behind the assassination. Yet HSCA investigators involved with the investigation of Carlos Marcello, G. Wray Gill, Sr., and the New Orleans aspects of the case showed no knowledge of the existence of the business card of his son and law partner George W. Gill, Jr., which had been uncovered by investigators from Milteer's home. Nor did the HSCA staff investigating the Milteer allegations appear to appreciate the significance of the George W. Gill, Jr. card they found. It is a case of the left hand not knowing what the right hand was doing—and a monumental error of history. Milteer had no known ties to organized crime. If Marcello or the Gills were connected with the assassination conspiracy, it may have been related to their ties to the segregationists.

CHAPTER ELEVEN

JOSEPH A. MILTEER AND THE HARDCORE UNDERGROUND OF DALLAS, TEXAS

*These are unusual times . . . At present the polls indicate Kennedy will
still be a formidable candidate. . . . At stake is the entire future.*
— H. L. Hunt, June 11, 1963

Joseph A. Milteer made at least five trips to Texas within a period of a year, three prior to the Kennedy assassination, and two after. Evidence, which has been provided in earlier chapters, strongly suggests that Milteer was in Dallas—and Dealey Plaza—at the time of the assassination. This chapter will tie Milteer's Dallas associates directly to a far-right conspiracy in the murder of the president.

Milteer told FBI Special Agent Donald Adams, on November 27, 1963, when he was picked up and interrogated, that he had visited Dan Smoot in Dallas in June, and had tried to get him to run for Vice President on the Constitution Party ticket. Milteer failed to tell the FBI that he had also been in Dallas in early October 1963. As presented previously, Milteer wrote his friend Woody Kearns on October 3, 1963, and told him he had just finished a 6,055-mile cross-country trip promoting the upcoming Constitution Party meeting, and had met with individuals in Grand Prairie, Fort Worth, and Dallas, Texas, before calling on Leander Perez and two young lawyers in New Orleans. It's not known whom he may have met on his second known trip to Dallas. Milteer's third known trip to Dallas in 1963 was at the time of the assassination. Milteer called Willie Somersett on the morning of the assassination and told him that he was down in "jackrabbit country" and that he wouldn't see "his boy" (Kennedy) again. Later, when Somersett asked Milteer if he shot the president, he denied it, stating he didn't mind watching though. The FBI learned from Somersett that Milteer had been to Dallas on December 12, 1963; a car repair receipt found in Milteer's probate court records showed he was also in Dallas on December 29, 1963, on his fifth trip to the city. A letter found in Milteer's home after his death revealed he had also visited General Walker and Robert Surrey in Dallas in June 1964. Additionally, Milteer's correspondence in May 1965 mentions a seventh trip to Dallas, in which he wrote in a letter he had stopped at the offices of H. L. Hunt Oil Company in Dallas, as we shall see.

The FBI effectively kept all of the their files on Milteer from the Warren Commission. The HSCA, on the other hand, had all of the evidence of Milteer's seven visits to Dallas at their disposal—but showed no awareness of them, which was an enormous oversight. Had they not so readily dismissed the Milteer evidence, and done a modest amount of investigation, they might have discovered that three of the individuals Milteer met with in Dallas were associates of Guy Banister, as will be shown next.

Joseph A. Milteer and Dan Smoot

Joseph A. Milteer told the FBI that he visited Dan Smoot in Dallas in June of 1963 and that he had no other business in Dallas.[1326] The relationship between Milteer and Smoot dates back to at least 1960, when Smoot's name appeared on Milteer's Christmas card list.[1327] Smoot's name was also on a handwritten list of people who recieved pecans as a gift from Milteer (the list of pecan recipients included Wesley Swift,[1328] whom the FBI established was involved in a plot to assassinate a large number of individuals, similar, if not the same as those discussed at the Congress of Freedom meeting).

Smoot was a former FBI agent who began his career in Cleveland, Ohio, where he was a part of a special squad that investigated Communists. He later served in the Dallas office of the FBI, where he met H. L. Hunt, a billionaire oilman and radical right activist. Smoot claimed to have been an FBI "Administrative Assistant to the Director." He resigned from the FBI in 1951 and went on to work for H. L. Hunt's *Facts Forum*, which produced TV programs, a monthly magazine called *Facts Forum News*, and a free circulating library that offered the works by men on the far right such as Joseph McCarthy. Together, Hunt and Smoot produced a TV and radio program, a four-page paper radio script published three times a week, and a large, slick coffee table magazine similar in appearance to *Life* and *Look* magazines. The April and May 1955 *Facts Forum* magazine featured a two-part series on the Oppenheimer case, which was written by Paul Crouch.[1329] Crouch was a "former Communist" who testified about the alleged Communist ties of the Southern Conference Education Fund (SCEF) before Senator Eastland's Committee in 1954.[1330] (Crouch, like Herbert Philbrick, may have served as a model for Lee Harvey Oswald, and will be discussed a length later.)

Smoot admired Hunt, and was quoted as saying: "The H. L. Hunt that I knew was a gentleman, and a great man. I treasure the influence he had upon my life." Smoot left Hunt in 1955 to publish *Dan Smoot Speaks*—later called *The Dan Smoot Report*—a four-page weekly. In 1962, *The Dan Smoot Report* had a paid circulation of 30,000 to 40,000 readers. In the newsletter, he strongly defended General Walker after his arrest for leading the insurrection at Ole Miss. He received major financial backing for his TV and radio enterprises from D. B. Lewis, the California dog food manufacturer. (Upon his death, Lewis left a million dollars to Smoot's far-right operation. In addition, Lewis left a million dollars to the John Birch Society and a half million dollars to Robert Morris's Defenders of Liberty, a far-right version of the ACLU.)[1331, 1332] In 1957, Smoot's picture graced the cover of the retired FBI agent's magazine *Grapevine*.[1333] On October 26, 1960, he spoke at a States Rights and Free Electors dinner in

New Orleans, at the invitation of Leander Perez.[1334, 1335] Smoot, like Perez, was a racist and viewed racial integration as "an American tragedy" that he blamed on the Communists.[1336] He stated that the *Brown* decision "poisoned our constitution."[1337] Smoot saw Communism everywhere, and claimed, with regards to the Kennedy administration: "There is abundant evidence that the government of the United States, in the interests of 'world peace,' is actively plotting the surrender of our country to world Communist-Socialist control."[1338] Smoot despised democracy, stating that, "the contemporary ideal of democracy is evil" and "democracy by majority rule is evil that feeds on itself."[1339]

Smoot was affiliated with a number of far-right groups and was elected to the board of the Congress of Freedom in 1956. He was also affiliated with far-right groups such as We the People and For America.[1340] He spoke at Kent Courtney's New Party meeting in Chicago on October 23–24, 1959.[1341] Smoot was also a speaker on a Billy James Hargis Christian Crusade five-hour radio marathon, along with Carl McIntire, General Willoughby, and Senator Eastland whose importance in this work has been highlighted previously.[1342] Smoot's activity in the Dallas Minutemen will be discussed later.

Smoot hated President Kennedy and devoted a good deal of his newsletter to bitterly criticizing the Kennedy administration. He felt Kennedy was under the influence of the Communists. In the June 3, 1963, edition of *The Dan Smoot Report*, entitled "Planned Dictatorship," Smoot wrote, "President Kennedy, by Executive Orders which bypass Congress, has already created a body of 'laws' to transform our Republic into a dictatorship—at the discretion of the president."[1343] The October 28, 1963, edition of *The Dan Smoot Report* bore the headline of "Lawless Government," referring to Smoot's numerous claims that President Kennedy violated the Constitution, the authority of Congress, states' rights, and the rights of General Walker in Walker's October 1962 arrest for leading a riot at Ole Miss. The first sentence of the newsletter published just before Kennedy's assassination posed the question: "How much tyranny and lawless behavior on the part of their own government will the American people tolerate? Well let us see."[1344] The president was murdered twenty-four days later.

Smoot was close to retired general Clyde Watts, whom he called "a valued friend of mine."[1345] Watts (as will be recalled from Chapter Seven) was one of the military advisors to the Council of Statehood and the Congress of Freedom, along with Pedro del Valle, Edwin Walker, and Archibald Roberts. Watts was a speaker at the 1963 Congress of Freedom meeting where Willie Somersett learned of a plot to assassinate a large number of people in business and government, which would be directed by military advisors—which Somersett told the FBI. Watts was a close friend of General Walker and was his attorney during Walker's testimony before the Warren Commission in their investigation of Oswald's alleged shooting of Walker.

Smoot was scheduled to address the New England Rally for God, Country and Family to be held on November 23–25, 1963, but the rally was cancelled after the assassination. The annual event was closely aligned with the John Birch Society. Other planned speakers at the 1963 rally were Billy James Hargis, Tom Anderson, Kent Courtney, and John Rousselot, important figures in the assassination story as will be shown. Another Milteer associate, Ezra Taft Benson, was also scheduled to appear.[1346]

Guy Banister's former partner in Guy Banister and Associates, Joseph Oster, told the author that Banister and Smoot were friends.[1347] Banister featured a column by Smoot in the weekly newspaper he co-owned, which was called the *West Bank Herald*.[1348] Smoot was alive and well during the 1977 to 1979 HSCA investigation of the Kennedy assassination, but the Committee had no apparent interest in him. The facts that Smoot was a friend of Milteer and he lived in the city of the president's murder should have been reason enough to investigate him.

Smoot left 120 boxes of papers from his long career to Texas A&M University. He was a prolific public speaker and left a large volume of his prepared notes for the years of 1959 to 1975, but suspiciously purged every speech from 1963.[1349]

The fact that Smoot knew Milteer, Banister and at least two of the military advisors tied to the assassination plots discussed at the Congress of Freedom meeting (generals Walker and del Valle) raises significant suspicions about his role in, or knowledge of, the assassination.

Joseph A. Milteer and Robert A. Surrey

As noted in Chapter Six, Milteer jotted the names and addresses for Robert A. Surrey and General Walker on a Colorado John Birch Society membership application. A letter from Milteer, which was found in Milteer's home after his death confirms he personally knew the two men.

Milteer wrote to A. J. Porth on June 6, 1964, and told him of his meeting with Surrey and Walker in Dallas. Milteer wrote: "I stopped in Dallas and talked to Mr. R. A. Surrey, who is connected with the Johnston Printing Company, 2700 North Haskell in Dallas, Texas. Mr. Surrey and I were finishing our talk when the F. B. I. walked up and asked to speak to him. I had just given him some of my literature and he had it in his hands and then I bade ado and went my way."[1350] Porth, a well-known member of the radical right and a critic of the federal tax system, had attended the 1963 Congress of Freedom meeting.[1351] Milteer went on to say in the letter that he spoke to Surrey about a book Porth planned on writing; Milteer wrote that Surrey told him his company did book binding, and he suggested that he and Porth work something out. Milteer suggested that Porth present his writings in the format of *The Dan Smoot Report*, which Milteer felt made for easier reading. Milteer ended the letter with a postscript, stating that he enclosed Surrey's latest printed material. (Surrey co-owned, with General Walker, the American Eagle Printing Company that published Walker's far-right propaganda.) Surrey was called before the Warren Commission to testify about his role in producing—using Johnston Printing Company plates—the infamous "Wanted for Treason" posters that he circulated in Dallas before the assassination. The Warren Commission was unaware that Surrey was the head of the Dallas American Nazi Party. (Had they known about the Nazi link, they might have found Lee Harvey Oswald's notebook entry of the name Dan

Burros and the American Nazi Party of more interest.) Surrey was also the secretary treasurer of the Dallas John Birch Society.

This means that the HSCA had documents at their disposal that showed Milteer visited with two Warren Commission witnesses—including one who had an encounter with Oswald—but apparently overlooked them.

Robert Surrey printed the infamous Wanted for Treason poster circulated in Dallas before the Kennedy assassination. Surrey was the Secretary-Treasurer of the Dallas JBS, the head of the Dallas American Nazi Party, as well as the top aide to General Walker. Source: Warren Commission Exhibit, 996, XVIII, 646

Joseph A. Milteer and General Edwin A. Walker

Milteer also mentioned to Porth in the June 6, 1964, letter that after leaving Robert Surrey's residence, he called on General Walker. He wrote, "I left Mr. Surrey and went to call on Gen. Edwin A. Walker and we talked for about an hour. I left more literature with him and we exchanged different ideas of interest. One outstanding point brought out by Gen. Walker was a way and means to ruin and even destroy cars the niggers own. That is, ruin and destroy the motors so as to stop the niggers from riding. Just put a little destructive element in the crankcase when oil is added or changed that will cause the motor to 'freeze-up' and be of no more use, (With-in 50 or 100 miles or so.) [sic]" Milteer closed the letter saying, "this is our year to win and win we will with the help of a good and kind LORD and SAVIOUR JESUS CHRIST."[1352]

The relationship between Milteer and Walker—revealed by the author for the first time here—is of momentous historical significance. Anyone from Dallas who knew Milteer, whose presence in Dealey Plaza and his foreknowledge of the assassination inextricably ties him to the conspiracy in the death of President Kennedy, should also be a suspect in the assassination. This especially applies to a person like Walker who was close with Guy Banister, lived in the city of the president's murder, and had some kind of relationship with Lee Harvey Oswald (in this case, the Walker shooting incident). Moreover, as a former major general in the army, Walker had the tactical expertise to execute the murder. Further, it will be recalled that in the correspondence between Walker and General del Valle, beginning in 1962, it was strongly alluded to that there was a need and desire to overthrow the U.S. government. Also in 1962, Willie Somersett revealed that del Valle and Walker were the military advisors to the assassination plots of the Congress of Freedom and Council for Statehood. The initial Congress of Freedom plot to murder a large number of the members of the Council on Foreign Relations in the spring of 1963 gave way to a plot to kill the president, which was revealed in the October 1963 Constitution Party convention. A letter from Milteer's close friend Woody Kearns to General del Valle (presented in Chapter Eight) strongly suggests that del Valle was behind the plot that culminated in the murder of the president. Walker had a personal vendetta against President Kennedy for relieving him of his army command in Germany in 1961 and for ordering his arrest in the 1962 insurrection against the U.S. during the integration crisis at Ole Miss. He was also bitterly opposed to Kennedy's racial polices and his handling of the Cuba situation.

Joseph A. Milteer and the H. L. Hunt Oil Company

Suspicions about H. L. Hunt and his two sons' involvement in the Kennedy assassination have been raised before. The best accounts appear in the 1981 book by Harry Hurt, III, *Texas Rich*, and in Dick Russell's 1992 *The Man Who Knew Too Much*. Joseph Milteer's visit to the H. L. Hunt Company—revealed here for the first time—as well as other new evidence makes Hurt's and Russell's allegations compelling. In a letter to Woody Kearns, dated May 23, 1965, Milteer wrote, "I made a successful trip to Dallas, Texas, and called on H. L. Hunt Company and after another short trip I shall be in a position to make another report to you regarding."[1353]

What Milteer's "success" with Hunt Oil Company was, in regard to the "SURVIVAL meeting" (as Milteer typed it in a letter) is not clear, although the Hunts were prodigious contributors to the far right. Evidence presented in Chapter Seven that Milteer handled money for the national far right was suggested by his establishment of a bank account in Provo, Utah, under an assumed name. In another letter, Milteer wrote to Colonel Charles Askins from San Antonio, Texas, and stated he had just written Colonel Stahl regarding a "SURVIVAL meeting" to be held near Montgomery, Alabama, on October 8, 9, and 10 and wished to invite Askins too. The group planned on meeting at the Coliseum Motel before moving to an undisclosed meeting place. Milteer wrote that a barbeque dinner was planned, prepared by a white person that they could trust. Milteer stated, "every precaution has been taken for our welfare and the meeting will not be bugged. Nor will there be any intruders."[1354, 1355] The nature of the meeting was not discussed. Milteer expected that twenty to thirty individuals would attend and some were noted to have an interest in the Constitution Party.[1356] He stated that there would be no publicity. Milteer wrote a similar invitation to William Ferrasie of New Jersey.[1357] In another letter, Milteer wrote "George" and stated that the "SURVIVAL meeting" could not be held in Atlanta, due to fears that it would be bugged. He told him, "We are anxious to get matters started our way and get the show on the road."[1358]

The meaning of the "SURVIVAL meeting" remains a mystery, but given the distance the attendees were expected to travel, the meeting was evidently of great importance. Moreover, it was the first time Milteer spoke of attending a meeting where careful security measures were being taken. The meeting may have been in response to enormous blows suffered by the radical right to their segregationist cause as a result of recent civil rights legislation, specifically the enactment of the Civil Rights Act on July 7, 1964, the enactment of the Voting Rights Act on August 6, 1965, and the public outcry against the savage and unprovoked attacks by racist law enforcement officers against civil rights marchers crossing the Edmund Pettis Bridge in Selma, Alabama, on March 7, 1965.

H. L. Hunt

Haroldson Lafayette Hunt became wealthy in the oil business in the 1920s. He operated the Hunt Oil Company offices out of the Mercantile National Bank Building on Main Street in Dallas, with his sons Nelson Bunker and Lamar. Former FBI men Paul Rothermel and attorney John Curington served as their security directors and had offices nearby. Hunt became active in far-right-wing politics beginning in at least the 1950s. After General Douglas MacArthur was relieved of his command in Korea, Hunt and Clint Murchison picked him up and flew him to Dallas for a speech.[1359, 1360] Hunt was the main force behind the movement to elect MacArthur to the presidency.

A fanatical anti-Communist, Hunt was a friend and financial backer of Senator Joseph McCarthy.[1361] He first developed a relationship with McCarthy when McCarthy spoke to the American Legion in Dallas in 1954.[1362] Hunt's pastor was W. A. Criswell who, in 1960, started a movement to keep Catholic presidential contender John F. Kennedy out of the White House.[1363] Hunt printed 200,000 copies of a Criswell speech that claimed that the election of John F. Kennedy would represent the end of religious freedom and distributed them at the 1960 Democratic convention.[1364] The *New Republic*, in 1954, described Hunt's publication, *Life Lines*, by saying, "its net effect is to disseminate fear, suspicion and divisive propaganda."[1365] Hunt's principal advisor in the radio propaganda business was nationally syndicated far-right radio and print reporter Fulton Lewis.[1366] He started *Facts Forum* in 1951, which consisted of a fifteen-minute radio show and a newsletter.[1367] One editor of *Facts Forum* was Medford Evans, a friend of Guy Banister and General Walker.[1368, 1369] When Dan Smoot served as the commentator for the *Facts Forum* TV show, Hunt's wife and Albert Wedemeyer served on the advisory board.[1370] Hunt was a nationally known figure, and appeared on the CBS television program *60 Minutes* on April 1, 1969.[1371]

Interestingly, about three weeks prior to the Kennedy assassination, Jack Ruby attended the Texas Products Show in the Dallas Exhibit Hall, where H. L. H. Products—an H. L. Hunt-owned food company—displayed its products. Along with the food exhibits at the unattended booth, sample copies of *Life Lines* and *Facts Forum* radio show broadcast scripts were offered. Ruby picked up the literature and, when he read the scathing anti-Kennedy remarks, became incensed. He grabbed a bunch of copies and took them over to a friend exhibiting at another booth. Ruby told his friend Edward J. Pullman that he was going to send copies to the president, stating: "Nobody has any right to talk like this about our government." Pullman described Ruby as "all excited and red-face, livid." Ruby then put the *Life Lines* and scripts into his pocket and left the exhibit hall.[1372] After Ruby murdered Oswald on November 24, 1963, the propaganda was found in the trunk of his car near by. Perhaps Ruby left it for a purpose.

Like Dan Smoot, Hunt hated democracy, African Americans, and Jews. Hunt authored the book *Alpaca* about a fictional nation where citizens were accorded votes based on their income tax brackets.[1373] He wrote "the more taxes you pay, the more votes you get . . . [and] if you accept state aid because you are poor or sick, you can not vote at all."[1374] One of his employees described Hunt's attitude toward African Americans, by saying, "H. L. hated niggers. It pissed him off that they could cancel his vote."[1375] Hunt promoted the hate literature of notorious anti-Semites Joseph Kamp and John Beaty.[1376]

H. L. Hunt was close to many leaders of the national radical right, including a number of former military men. He was close to General Walker and felt Walker would make a good Texas governor in 1962, and U.S. president in 1964.[1377] He credited generals Robert E. Wood, Albert C. Wedemeyer, and Charles Willoughby as men who shaped his thinking. (All of those former military men were discussed as men who could be trusted in the plotting letters between generals del Valle and Walker, as presented in Chapter Eight.) Robert Welch, of the John Birch Society, and Billy James Hargis were two more of Hunt's influences.[1378] He promoted the books of Kenneth Goff, a friend of Milteer; as well as Bonner Fellers, General Pedro del Valle's trusted friend (as noted in Chapter Eight).[1379] H. L. Hunt consulted with prominent New Orleans physician Alton Ochsner, a pulmonary surgeon who also ran the Information Council of the Americas (INCA) with Ed Butler, a close associate of Guy Banister, in regards to his son Hassie's deteriorating schizophrenia.[1380]

According to Paul Rothermel, H. L. Hunt sent him to purchase the first copy of the Zapruder film immediately after the assassination.[1381] Rothermel confirmed the story in an interview with the author, in which he said, "For what I know it was the first copy and it was real clear."[1382] The FBI and Warren Commission were not aware of Rothermel's claim that Hunt purchased the original copy of the film, however Hunt was close to Claire Boothe Luce, the wife of *Life* magazine owner Henry Luce.[1383] (*Life* purchased the rights to the Zapruder film of the assassination and tucked it away in a vault.) The American public did not see Abe Zapruder's amateur video of the assassination until March 1975, a year after H. L. Hunt's death, when it was shown on the network television program "Good Night America." The violent backward movement of the president's head was consistent with a gunshot from the front—or grassy knoll area—and not from Oswald's position in the rear from the Texas School Book Depository. Shots from both the front and rear are evidence of conspiracy. The public outrage after seeing the film that cast doubt on the official story of one shooter from the rear, is part of what led to the establishment in Congress of the Church Committee, which initiated an investigation into aspects of the assassination. It is conceivable that Hunt persuaded Luce to purchase the film before anyone else did—to conceal it from the American public.

Paul Rothermel, a Hunt employee, advised the FBI in 1977: "by 1963 the Hunt family considered KENNEDY a tool of the Communists, so when President KENNEDY was assassinated the news was not unwelcome." He further stated, "The Hunt family was very concerned that they would be blamed for the assassination in some manner."[1384]

After the assassination, H. L. Hunt asked his employee John Curington to check out the security at the Dallas jail holding Lee Harvey Oswald. Curington assessed that there was no jail security whatsoever. While at the jail, Curington shared an elevator with Captain Will Fritz and Lee Harvey Oswald, which clearly showed that Oswald was vulnerable, even in a police station.[1385]

On July 11, 1963, H. L. Hunt wrote Louisiana Democratic governor Jimmie Davis and urged him to join with the state's Republicans and select the same slate of presidential electors in hopes of defeating President Kennedy's re-election. In essence, Hunt asked Davis to get behind Leander Perez's free elector scheme. The ominous letter, which warned of dire consequences, was written a month after President Kennedy proposed the Civil Rights Act, which would end segregation in the South—and the Southern way of life. Hunt wrote: "These are unusual times and I believe that party loyalty should be set aside in hopes of saving our freedom. The South can no longer depend on a coalition to safe guard against bad legislation. It is often said you cannot beat someone with no one and at present the polls indicate Kennedy will still be a formidable candidate . . . . At stake is the entire future. Dr. Edward Teller recently told me, and is probably right, that there is no chance to get the Kennedys out unless they are defeated in 1964 . . . . I am writing other outstanding Democrats and would prefer that my name not be mentioned as you discuss the best moves to save the nation with other prominent Democrats in the South."[1386]

Governors George Wallace (left) and Jimmie Davis (middle) with H. L. Hunt (right). The photo is undated but possibly was taken at the Free Electors meeting in Jackson, Mississippi, on June 17, 1963, and appears to have accompanied the letter (noted above) from Hunt to Davis. Source: Jimmie Davis Papers, Southeastern Louisiana University

Like Dan Smoot, Mary Davison, and Kent Courtney, Hunt believed a secret government ran the U.S. During the 1964 presidential race Hunt stated that the media had gone wild trying to advance the wishes of the "the eastern Establishment, the Big Money minority, the 'Invisible Government', the king makers or something equally sinister." Hunt was a fervent supporter of Barry Goldwater in the 1964 election, appearing at the Republican National Convention in San Francisco, where he rented an entire floor at a hotel for his delegation.[1387] Kent Courtney also attended the convention.[1388]

Lamar Hunt and Jack Ruby

Lamar Hunt, one of H. L. Hunt's sons, was best known as a pioneer in the early days of the American Football League and, later, for owning the Kansas City Chiefs in the National Football League. On the day before the Kennedy assassination, Jack Ruby drove Connie Trammel to the Hunt Oil Company office to see if she could get a job with Lamar. Trammel had met Ruby in April 1963 when she visited his nightclub, while staying at a hotel across the street in connection with the promotion of a boat show. She had been looking for employment in mid-November 1963, and had called Ruby to see if he had any job openings. He offered her a job as a stripper, but she declined. She later told the FBI that, around November 20, 1963, she called Ruby and told him she had talked to Lamar Hunt and made an appointment with him about a job opening. Trammel had read that Lamar had bought a bowling alley and was converting it into a teenage club; she hoped she could get a job in public relations for the club. Ruby picked Trammel up at her apartment and told her that he would also like to meet Hunt. Ruby drove to the Mercantile Bank and walked in with Trammel, but did not go up stairs with her. It was the last time she saw Ruby. Lamar did not offer her a job.[1389]

The FBI asked Jack Ruby about the incident after his arrest for the murder of Oswald. Ruby repeated Trammel's story and stated that while he was there he visited his attorney at the Mercantile Securities Building next door. Afterwards, he waited for Trammel to come down, and left when she didn't show up.[1390] After the arrest of Jack Ruby for the murder of Oswald, the FBI found Lamar Hunt's name in his notebook. On December 1, 1963, the FBI questioned Lamar and he denied ever knowing Ruby. He could think of no reason why his name was found in Ruby's notebook.[1391]

John Curington told the FBI, in 1977, that he had never seen Ruby in the offices of Hunt Oil but, to the best of his recollection, "the talk on the street" was that Ruby had been in Lamar's office on several occasions prior to the assassination, although he had no evidence to substantiate the rumors.[1392]

Like his father, Lamar Hunt was close to General Walker. According to a David Ferrie colleague, Raymond Broshears, it was Lamar who was instrumental in obtaining General Walker's release from the Springfield, Missouri, federal mental hospital after his arrest at Ole Miss.[1393]

The Hunts, Billy James Hargis, General Charles Willoughby and Others on the Far Right

H. L. Hunt was close to a number of the individuals who have been discussed in prior chapters as possible accessories to the assassination conspiracy. Evidence already presented has noted that H. L. Hunt was close to General Douglas MacArthur's aide General Charles Willoughby. Willoughby wrote the *Foreign Intelligence Digest* that was attached to Billy James Hargis's *Weekly Crusader* newsletter. (It will also be recalled from Chapter Eight that a cryptic letter received by author Dick Russell alleged that General Willoughby confessed on his deathbed to his involvement in the assassination.) Joseph Milteer reportedly told Willie Somersett that Willoughby colleague Billy James Hargis was a fundraiser for the hardcore underground. Hargis corresponded with Milteer about a tape recording he made of one of Hargis's speeches. According to a story in the *New York Times* in 1961, H. L. Hunt contributed to several of Hargis's projects.[1394]

After the assassination, Willoughby appeared on a speaking tour with Carlos Bringuier. In the ominous 1962 correspondence between General Walker and General del Valle, del Valle named Willoughby as a man he could trust in their dark ventures before resorting to violence (as noted in Chapter Eight). Willoughby served on the board of the Committee to Restore the Constitution, in 1970, along with three of the four military advisors of the Council of Statehood/Congress of Freedom: Clyde Watts, Pedro del Valle, and Archibald Roberts. Others on the Committee board included the prominent members of the Congress of Freedom meeting in New Orleans in April 1963: Mary Cain, Mary Davison, and Revilo Oliver.[1395] Willoughby had been a board member of Kent Courtney's Conservative Society of America since at least 1961.[1396]

Nelson Bunker Hunt (H. L. Hunt's other son) represented the state of Texas in the International Committee for Defense of Western Culture, an international Fascist-oriented group. Billy James Hargis represented the state of Oklahoma, and General Willoughby, the District of Columbia, in the organization, as was previously noted.

Willoughby's colleague, General Albert Wedemyer—who also served on MacArthur's staff—was close to H. L. Hunt. His name appears on Hunt's *Life Lines* newsletter as a contributor. Wedemeyer was another individual Pedro del Valle cited as a person he could depend on in his ominous correspondence with General Walker in 1962. Moreover, in 1966, Willoughby went to work for Nelson Bunker Hunt.[1397] Of the generals—Willoughby, Stratemeyer, and Wedemyer—Hunt employee Paul Rothermel told the author, "those men were very near and dear to my boss's heart."[1398]

H. L. Hunt and other wealthy oilmen, as well as D. B. Lewis (the wealthy California dog food producer), were financial contributors to Billy James Hargis's Christian Crusade.[1399] Like many of Hunt's associates, Hargis knew Guy Banister and was in his office in October 1963.[1400] Hargis called the Hunts "real people and close friends."[1401] On March 20, 1962, Billy James Hargis held a "secretive meeting" in Washington, D.C., called the Anti-Communist Liaison, which was by "invitation only." Those in attendance included John Rousselot, William Potter Gale, Bonner Fellers, Edward Hunter, Benjamin Gitlow, Charles Willoughby, and Frank McGehee—all significant figures who will be discussed further in this work.[1402] The gathering came at the suggestion of Hargis, at the We the People meeting in September 1961.[1403, 1404] Edward Hunter, as was discussed in Chapter One, was an associate of Banister. Gale was associated with Milteer, and was questioned by the FBI in the spring of 1963 about a plot to assassinate a large number of individuals—likely the same plot discussed at the 1963 Congress of Freedom meeting in New Orleans. Arthur Blazey, a prominent figure in the Congress of Freedom and Constitution Party, also attended the meeting. John Rousselot formed the League of Right Wing Organizations at the meeting.[1405] Evidence will be presented later implicating Rousselot in the assassination conspiracy. The Hunt family was instrumental in setting up this "secretive meeting" of the national radical right, along with D. B. Lewis, the financial supporter of Milteer's friend Dan Smoot.[1406, 1407]

George de Mohrenschildt, the White Russian émigré who befriended the Oswalds on their return from the Soviet Union, was interviewed extensively over the years and developed a close relationship with Dutch reporter Willem Oltmans. After de Mohrenschildt's suicide in 1977, just after an investigator from the HSCA came to Mohrenschildt's house to interview him, Oltmans held a news conference in Washington. He stated that de Mohrenschildt had strong ties to both Lee Harvey Oswald and H. L. Hunt. He later recanted his story.[1408]

According to Paul Rothermel, anti-Castro Cuban leader Sergio Arcacha Smith was a frequent visitor to the Hunt offices. Arcacha Smith was also close to Banister and had offices in the Balter Building and later at the 544 Camp/531 Lafayette Street building that housed the Banister operation. Arcacha Smith had allegedly departed New Orleans in 1962 for Texas. Rothermel described General Walker and Arcacha Smith as "pretty good friends."[1409] As was discussed in Chapter One, veteran assassination researcher Bud Fensterwald interviewed William Gaudet, a CIA domestic contact, who told him that he believed Arcacha Smith knew Oswald well. Gaudet was one of the many people who saw Oswald with Banister in 1963.

Hunt was close to Cuban exile leader Mario Garcia Kohley, Sr. and other Cuban exiles.[1410] Hunt stated that the failure of the U.S.-backed Bay of Pigs invasion was just as well because it was "just one Communist government trying to overthrow another," implying—like many in the radical right—that the U.S. government, as led by President Kennedy, was Communist influenced.[1411]

H. L. Hunt was also associated with Tom Anderson, another high-ranking leader of the national far right. At one time, Anderson tried to interest Hunt in taking over his failing *Farm and Ranch* magazine. (Strong evidence that Anderson was part of a far-right-wing cabal behind the assassination will be presented in a later chapter.) Hunt wrote to Anderson on June 9, 1958, and expressed his fears about a Communist world takeover saying, "I hope you will look into *Life Lines* very exhaustively. As far as I can tell, and it is the judgment of many astute people, *Life Lines* has the best chance of any organization to start a turning of the tide. Unless and until there is such a start I do not believe that any of the existing organizations can make any net progress toward saving the Free World."[1412]

H. L. Hunt and Leander Perez

H. L. Hunt and Leander Perez were associates, as well. In 1962, Perez organized the national Electoral Reform Committee. He enlisted the help of Hunt in the venture, who offered his advice.[1413]

The author asked Paul Rothermel if Hunt knew Perez. He replied, "Of course, he did. Most of Mr. Hunt's wells were in Plaquemines and Terrebonne Parishes. You couldn't do business in Plaquemines Parish without knowing Leander Perez."[1414] Like Perez, Hunt was a friend and supporter of Senator James Eastland and George Wallace.[1415]

Nelson Bunker Hunt

Nelson Bunker Hunt clearly was the Hunt who was most inclined to political extremism and violence. Paul Rothermel told the FBI that Nelson Bunker advocated violence and illegal measures to deal with the Communist threat and certain liberal world leaders. When Nelson Bunker confided his dark ideas to him, Rothermel told him he refused to get involved in any illegal schemes, after which Nelson Bunker no longer trusted him. Rothermel advised the FBI that Nelson Bunker's philosophy was that the real Communists were not in Moscow and Peking, but were located in Washington, D.C., and New York. He stated that Nelson Bunker learned from a German magazine, *Der Spiegel*, of an experimental Russian and East German gas gun that would kill a person, but would leave the impression that the victim had died of a heart attack. Nelson Bunker asked Rothermel to investigate the gas gun and find out if it had been used to eliminate certain conservative U.S. leaders. (The radical right rumored that Senator Joseph McCarthy—the Communist hunter and close Hunt family friend who died of cirrhosis of the liver—was actually murdered.) Nelson Bunker wanted the Hunt family to use the same gas gun to eliminate the Communists in the United States. Rothermel stated, "NELSON BUNKER HUNT would have been more inclined to have acted now on the basis of his conservative philosophy and thought about it later than any man in Dallas." Rothermel noted that Nelson Bunker's violence-prone statements came out of "bull sessions." Eventually, Rothermel had a falling out with the Hunts; he left the Hunt's employ in 1969 and, in 1971, signed an agreement with the Hunts not to publish a book about them. He told the FBI—in 1977—that Nelson Bunker probably still held a grudge and might arrange to have him killed someday.[1416]

On March 6, 1963, Nelson Bunker Hunt wrote to Clarence Manion and voiced his complaints about President Kennedy. He stated that Kennedy was planning to change the tax law, which would effectively prevent most of the American oil companies from entering into, or continuing in, foreign oil operations. He told Manion that the law effectively gave the free world's undiscovered oil reserves to the Communists by default. Hunt claimed further that the supporters of Medicare who attacked the medical profession for opposing Kennedy's proposed creation of Medicare, as well as the Kennedy's proposed oil tax changes, would constitute Socialism's "foot in the door." He felt those initiatives would be followed by further assaults on private industries until "Americans will suddenly awake to find they have Communism."[1417]

Nelson Bunker was close to the founder of the John Birch Society, Robert Welch, and "helped Welch quietly for many years." He eventually was placed on the John Birch Society National Council.[1418] In 1965, Welch wrote Nelson Bunker and stated he had hoped to visit him to secure more funding for a John Birch Society campaign against the civil rights movement. He asked Nelson Bunker for money to pay for full-page ads in a hundred or more newspapers throughout the country on December 9, 1965, to expose the "civil rights fraud."[1419] Nelson Bunker became part owner of the John Birch Society magazine *American Opinion* in 1965.[1420]

Nelson Bunker endorsed the radical ministry of Reverend Carl McIntire.[1421] It will be recalled that Guy Banister met with McIntire in 1963 at the Capitol House Hotel in Baton Rouge (this was noted in Chapter One). Other evidence presented strongly suggests that Gene Bradley, McIntire's west coast representative, also traveled to Dallas at the time of the assassination and may have been present in Dealey Plaza at the time of the murder. (As we will see later, McIntire was also a close associate of General Walker.)

Nelson Bunker was implicated in an illegal wiretapping scheme in 1970. James McCann, the wire tapper in the incident, had already been jailed on wiretapping charges and became a potential witness against Nelson Bunker. On January 1, 1974, Nelson Bunker urged close friend Senator James Eastland to inquire as to the possibility of parole for McCann. Jack

Anderson, in the *Washington Post*, reported that a letter was mailed to Nelson Bunker Hunt from Eastland, stating that contact with the parole board had been made. James McCann was asked under oath if Nelson Bunker slipped Eastland any cash in exchange. McCann replied, "If it was, it wasn't but $50,000 or $60,000. It was tiny compared to everything else." An attorney testified that Eastland received the money—and a cattle deal. The attorney noted it was "kind of unusual for a Mississippi senator to send a letter for a Texas wire tapper who he has never met."[1422]

Nelson Bunker Hunt, J. Evetts Haley, and Others in the Texas Hardcore Underground

J. Evetts Haley, a wealthy Texas rancher, merits scrutiny since he had ties to the Hunts—as well as three other Texas associates of Joseph Milteer: Dan Smoot, General Walker and Robert Surrey. Haley also had ties to Milteer and Banister associate Leander Perez. In addition, Haley's correspondence reflects a working relationship with General Pedro del Valle dating to 1956.[1423] Direct ties between Milteer and Haley have not been established, although Haley was associated with a large number of groups and individuals in the radical right, discussed throughout this work, as is detailed in his voluminous papers left to posterity. Those groups included the Congress of Freedom, the Constitution Party, We the People, and the Citizens' Council.

Haley's correspondence with Nelson Bunker Hunt provides a rare glimpse into the two men's far-right radicalism. Haley advocated violence in dealing with the civil rights movement. He admired Birmingham Commissioner of Public Safety Bull Connor, who thanked Haley for his support in 1959 and told him, in a letter, "I am going to do all in my power to preserve the Southern way of life."[1424] (Later, Connor became internationally infamous when he turned police dogs and fire hoses against non-violent black protesters in Birmingham in 1963.) In 1968, Haley wrote Nelson Bunker Hunt and H. L. Hunt and told them that he could not support George Wallace for president. Haley was critical of Wallace for not ordering his law enforcement officers to fire on the federal marshals sent by President Kennedy and Attorney General Robert Kennedy to enforce the integration of the University of Alabama—specifically Wallace's June 11, 1963, "stand at the schoolhouse door" incident where he ceremoniously blocked federal marshals from admitting two black students to the University of Alabama, then moved aside and admitted them based on a pre-arranged deal with the Kennedy administration.[1425]

Nelson Bunker Hunt wrote Haley on September 26, 1964, and told him he thought Haley should write a book on the "Warren Commission cover-up of the Communist-directed assassination of Kennedy." Nelson Bunker felt it was greatly needed since, "Various 'Lefty writers' have been turning out books intimating a 'Rightist Plot'."[1426]

Haley wrote to Nelson Bunker on February 19, 1965, and told him that Robert Morris had agreed to do what he could do for the cause—which was not described—"on a strictly personal basis." He noted further, "Our organization is helping with this." Haley asked Nelson Bunker to put a check in an envelope, so he could send it to Morris. Nelson Bunker admired Haley's activism and, on July 1, 1965, told him, "If there were 500 fellows like you in the U.S. the 'lefties' wouldn't have a chance."[1427]

(Morris was General Walker's attorney during his military censure and he also served as counsel to Eastland's Senate Internal Subversion Subcommittee and worked with Guy Banister in 1956, during Banister's investigation of the "Soviet influence" in the integration movement. As we shall see later, a member of the Minutemen told an FBI informant that Morris screened applicants for Walker's Minutemen groups in Dallas in 1963.[1428] The Bureau of Alcohol, Tobacco and Firearms determined General Walker and H. L. Hunt were the leaders of the Dallas Minuteman—which will be discussed in length later.)

Nelson Bunker Hunt was influential in mainstream national politics in the 1980s. He asked J. Evetts Haley to join the National Conservative Policy Advisory Council, which was a group dedicated to electing conservatives to Congress. Hunt boasted about how the group exposed the liberal records of prominent congressmen and helped to elect conservatives. Hunt stated that his group received confidential political briefings from members of President Reagan's cabinet and other political leaders in Washington. According to Hunt, Ronald Reagan called Hunt's Council "our best bet to stop the liberals from seizing total control of Congress," and listed as one of the benefits of joining the Council was a private meeting with President Reagan at the White House on February 22, 1983. Hunt urged Haley to join the group and said he would inform President Reagan of his planned attendance. Haley attended the event, called the "Second Annual Conservative Conference" and a private White House reception on February 22–23, 1983, and had his photo taken with President Reagan. One honored guest at the private meeting was Congressman John McCain of Arizona.[1429]

Haley's correspondence reveals a close relationship to others important in this work. As discussed in the prior chapter, Haley served on the board of the Federation for Constitutional Government in 1956, with Leander Perez. Senator Eastland was present for the first organizational meeting of the Federation on December 28–29, 1955, in Memphis, Tennessee. Eastland proclaimed that the Federation was set up to fight the Supreme Court, the C.I.O., the NAACP, and all groups "who are attempting our destruction."[1430] Jim Johnson was on the board of the Federation and, in later years, became the bitter foe of Bill Clinton when Clinton served as Arkansas governor and United States president.[1431] Correspondence between Haley and Jim Johnson reflect a close relationship.[1432]

Haley's letters reflect a cordial relationship with Leander Perez dating back to 1955, as well as Roy V. Harris in 1959—both Milteer associates.[1433, 1434] Haley met with Perez and Judge Tom P. Brady—both national Citizens' Council leaders—and other "distinguished citizens from Louisiana and Mississippi" at Perez's home on December 11, 1958, to discuss "tactics to employ between now and 1960."[1435] Haley was a member of Kent Courtney's Committee to form The Independent American Federation of State Parties, and attended an organizational meeting with Courtney on November 4, 1959, which included Medford Evans, and John U. Barr. The organization was part of Courtney's scheme to start a third, "new party."[1436] Haley possessed a copy of the Highlander Folk School "Communist Training

School" poster (which had been published by Roy V. Harris's *Augusta Courier*) in his papers. Haley made a "generous contribution" to the Citizens' Council Freedom Bus North program, a scheme hatched by Guy Banister and Leander Perez associate George Singelmann. [1437] Haley's correspondence reflects extensive ties to the earliest days of the Citizens' Council and its leadership. [1438]

As discussed in the last chapter, Haley initially planned to have Johnson Printing, where Robert Surrey was employed, publish his 1964 mass-produced smear of Lyndon Johnson, *A Texan Looks at Lyndon.* (Surrey, as will be recalled, was the head of the Dallas American Nazi Party, a Warren Commission witness, a Milteer associate, an aide to General Walker, and creator of the infamous "Wanted for Treason" poster distributed before the assassination.) The deal to have Haley's book published by Surrey's employer fell through because the book had not been cleared by a lawyer for questions of libel. Surrey got stuck with the bill for initial startup costs of $462. Surrey's wife wrote Haley, begging for his help in recouping the costs. She lamented, "Because of the Warren Report, and Bob's name being so prominently evident in it, the Jews have finally decided they've had enough of Bob Surrey and his open defiance of their plans." She noted that Bob Surrey was the one who located a printer for the people (who were not identifed) who wrote and distributed the "Treason leaflets"—and had gotten stuck with the majority of that bill as well. [1439]

In Surrey's June 14, 1964, Warren Commission testimony, the Commission told Surrey that they had planned to ask him about two incidents: the "Wanted for Treason" poster circulated before the assassination, and the Walker shooting. Surrey agreed to testify about the Walker shooting, but refused to testify about the "Wanted for Treason" poster, invoking his Fifth Amendment rights. He also took the Fifth when asked if General Walker was involved with the "Wanted for Treason" posters. [1440]

Haley was an early supporter of General Walker after he was relieved of his command by President Kennedy in 1961. An outraged Haley wrote to George Montgomery, an influential force among the radicals, commenting on the censure hearings, and told him: "I have been trying to formulate a letter in my mind to the president, telling him what sort of treason this is and that I do not intend to be bound by loyalty to any such individual as himself. This is complete betrayal." Montgomery agreed with Haley's sentiment and added ominously, "If the tide doesn't turn we are going to have a very bleak choice between drowning quietly and doing something more than talking." Montgomery had a longstanding relationship with the Congress of Freedom. Of Walker, Montgomery stated, "He is a figure on the horizon who will not be silenced by man or devils." [1441] When Walker moved to Dallas, Haley guaranteed the lease on Walker's Turtle Creek residence on January 9, 1962. [1442]

At the urging of H. L. Hunt, General Walker ran for governor of Texas in 1962. J. Evetts Haley, who had run for governor of Texas in 1956 on a segregation platform, ran Walker's campaign. Haley served on the Citizens' Committee for General Walker, which was headquartered in Chicago, and stayed with Walker when he spoke to the group at the Hotel Ambassador on February 9 and 10, 1962. [1443] Haley spoke with Walker at the May 2, 1962, National Indignation Rally in Dallas. [1444]

On September 24, 1962, Walker wrote to Haley and mentioned a case against Clyde Watts that had been withdrawn, but did not elaborate. (Watts spoke at the infamous 1963 Congress of Freedom meeting in New Orleans attended by Joseph Milteer and Guy Banister, and was a military advisor to the group.) For no stated reason, Walker finished the letter, "I am looking for a place to stir up more trouble. Keep a look out."[1445] A week later, in the early morning of October 1, 1962, Walker was arrested on the orders of Attorney General Robert Kennedy on a charge of insurrection against the U.S. government at Ole Miss. Haley was with Walker at the University, where two men were murdered during the Walker-led riots. Clearly, Walker intended, in advance, to cause trouble—and indicated that in his letter to Haley, who headed the Walker Defense Fund in December 1962.[1446]

Kennedy humiliated Walker and enraged the radical right when he had him imprisoned in a federal mental facility. Haley wrote a letter to Myers Lowman, an avid Communist hunter, on General Walker's stationery on October 28, 1962. Haley asked Lowman if two of the psychiatrists assigned to assist Dr. R. L. Stubblefield—who initially found Walker mentally unstable after his arrest—had any leftist affiliations.[1447]

Proud of his fame and his defiance of the Kennedys a year earlier at Ole Miss, on October 14, 1963 Walker wrote Haley and stated, "We started a good one. 10,000 fliers going all over Dallas. Hope you can come in for it. There may be some fun on the 24th. Also I plan to be in Jackson Miss on the 25th and 26th. Our mutual friend Sarah Hughes is sponsoring U.N. weeks & Adlai." He invited Haley to join him for "the fun." (He was facetious when he called Hughes, a supporter of Lyndon Johnson, a friend.) Walker was also critical of Republican Texas congressman, and future president, George H. W. Bush. He mentioned that the Soviets might have already taken over the White House.[1448] Walker's statement, "There may be some fun on the 24th," was a reference to the upcoming Dallas visit and speaking engagement on October 24, 1963, of Adlai Stevenson, President Kennedy's Ambassador to

General Walker organized the demonstration against President Kennedy's U.N. Ambassador, Adlai Stevenson, which led to Stevenson being spat on by one member of Walker's group, and struck with a placard by another, Cora Hendrickson. Source: Corbis

the United Nations. When Stevenson spoke in Dallas, he was heckled by a crowd of picketers, struck on the head with a placard, and spit on. Larrie Schmidt—who was behind the "Welcome Mr. Kennedy to Dallas" advertisement that appeared in the paper on the day of the assassination—protested with fourteen college students.[1449] One individual arrested during the Stevenson incident was Edward Hatfield, whom the FBI identified as a member of the "Edwin A. Walker Group." Cora Hendrickson, who struck Stevenson on the head with a placard, was also identified as a member of the Walker Group.[1450]

Neither the media, the White House, nor the Warren Commission were aware that Walker was behind the violence at Stevenson's speaking engagement, which received national attention. It was the third violent incident Walker was involved in after leading the riot at Ole Miss on September 30, 1962, and after the shooting incident at his home that in some way involved Lee Harvey Oswald in April 1963. Some worried that the Stevenson assault signaled danger ahead for President Kennedy's November visit to Dallas. This may have been suggested by the way Walker ended the letter to Haley, ominously stating that there were "good fights ahead."[1451]

On the evening before the Adlai Stevenson visit to Dallas, a group of students in the Young Republican Club of North Texas University attended the United States Day Rally at the Dallas Municipal Auditorium, which featured General Walker as its speaker. Walker had planned the speech to counter Stevenson's expected speech promoting the United Nations, a body Walker and the far right despised. The students had met previously at Walker's home and had planned demonstrations during President Kennedy's upcoming trip to Dallas. One of the students in attendance, William Drew Fitz announced that, during the upcoming visit of President Kennedy, "We will drag his dick into the dirt."[1452]

It should be noted that the Warren Commission was aware that Lee Harvey Oswald attended the Walker speech on the eve of the Stevenson visit, and that he notified Arnold Johnson of the Communist Party about it in a letter.[1453] Oswald implied to Johnson that he attended the speech to check out his anti-Communist adversaries. Johnson later noted that Oswald's attending the speech was not the kind of behavior that members of the Communist Party engaged in.

Haley served on Harold Lord Varney's Committee on Pan American Policy in 1963, along with generals Pedro del Valle, George Wedemeyer, Albert Stratemeyer, and Charles Willoughby, as well as Revilo Oliver—all of whom are identified in this work as members of the hardcore underground.[1454] Varney, who served on the board of Kent Courtney's Conservative Society of America, spoke in New Orleans two nights before the Kennedy assassination at a meeting sponsored by Kent Courtney. General Walker—it is important to note—attended the speech, which will be discussed further, later.

Haley was associated with most, if not nearly all, of the far-right groups and individuals of noted importance in this work, including the prominent leaders of the Citizens' Council, the John Birch Society, Congress of Freedom, and Constitution Party. He was closely aligned with most of the notable associates of Joseph Milteer, the former military men and associates of General Pedro del Valle, and many of the other central figures in this work, too numerous to list here. (Those groups and individuals are detailed in the endnote).[1455]

Nelson Bunker Hunt and the American Volunteer Group

Numerous sources tied Nelson Bunker Hunt to the far-right militia group called the American Volunteer Group (AVG). Earl Golz, a Dallas newspaper reporter, learned from his sources that Nelson Bunker had contributed money to the AVG to purchase armaments for the California group to fight the Communists. John Curington, a former Hunt employee, speculated that Nelson Bunker's dealings with Californian Jim Braden (a.k.a. Eugene Hale Brading)—who, as previously noted, was arrested in Dealey Plaza at the time of the assassination—were for the purposes of "financing certain conservative causes," which perhaps included the American Volunteer Group. Curington said he saw "checks and money going out into California."

During author Dick Russell's interview with Paul Rothermel in 1992, Rothermel related that Nelson Bunker told him some years before that he was forming a group known as the American Volunteer Group and intended to draw from the ranks of General Walker's cell in the John Birch Society in Dallas. One purpose of the group was to obtain a type of gas gun from Europe to kill people and make it look like a heart attack, a scheme noted earlier in the chapter. Reporter Peter Noyes learned through the California Attorney General's office that Jim Braden apparently worked for Nelson Bunker, and helped establish the AVG on the West Coast. Rothermel departed from the Hunt Oil Company in 1969, and wary of the Hunts, was astounded when author Peter Noyes called him and told him that he knew about the American Volunteer Group.[1456]

William Turner, the former FBI man, one of Garrison's investigators, and writer for *Ramparts* magazine, provided some insight into the AVG in his 1970 book *Power on the Right*. Turner described the divide in the paramilitary underground in California as follows: "At this stage it would appear that DePugh's protracted efforts to centralize control of California factions in the hands of his Minutemen are largely a failure. The picture is, to say the least, a jigsaw puzzle, made no less intricate by yet another piece, the American Volunteer Group."

Named after the official designation for General Claire Chennault's Flying Tigers, the AVG had been formed in 1967 by several private pilots in Borger, Texas, who installed a former Chennault aide as a figurehead. As it spread, the AVG took in a number of Dallas followers of General Edwin Walker and secured a financial angel in the scion of a wealthy oil family.[1457] William Turner told the author that he learned from Minuteman founder Robert DePugh that the "financial angel" of the American Volunteer Group was none other than Nelson Bunker Hunt.[1458]

Providing more evidence of Nelson Bunker's violent inclinations, Hunt employee John Curington told author Dick Russell that Nelson Bunker had a list of undesirable leaders that he felt should be killed, including liberal Senators J. William Fulbright and Jacob Javits of New York.[1459]

After Joseph Milteer's death, a slip of paper was found in his home with the name and address of the American Volunteer Group written on it. In a letter to Woody Kearns dated March 29, 1969, Milteer had mentioned he would like to talk with a number of individuals in order to get "the pulse of the nation and plan a course of action." The individuals named were Pedro del Valle, J. B. Stoner, A. J. Porth, and others, including "a fellow in Calif. with A.V.G."[1460] The slip of paper and the letter to Kearns tie Milteer to the Nelson Bunker Hunt-sponsored American Volunteer Group.

The author failed to find any reference to the AVG in many years of extensive research in far-right archives until a copy of the AVG newsletter was found in the papers of Kent Courtney.

None other than Milteer's friend, Pedro del Valle, is pictured above on the cover of the American Volunteer Groups' newsletter, published by the group alleged to be a "kill squad" funded by Nelson Bunker Hunt through Californian Jim Braden—who was present in Dealey Plaza during the murder.

The newsletter was titled the "American Volunteer Groups," and listed an address of Dana Point, California. The date of April 18, 1968, was stamped on the newsletter, and was probably the date Courtney received it. Along with the picture of General del Valle, who is noted as a member of the Strategic Advisory Council, are quotes from Thomas Jefferson and Patrick Henry. Retired Brigadier General Robert Scott, Jr. and Brigadier General William C. Lemly are pictured on the inside and denoted as members of the Military Advisory Council. The AVG National Chairman was Medrick G. "Bud" Johnson. Lieutenant Colonel John Howe is listed as co-chairman. Listed, but not pictured, are General Richard B. Moran and Colonel Harvey W. Mathews. An AVG convention to be held in Amarillo, Texas, on July 4th and 5th is mentioned. The newsletter mentions that Admiral Crommelin purchased television time to promote his run for Senate and to explain the AVG and its "Military Patriots."[1461] (FBI records on John Crommelin noted he was a member of the National Advisory Board of the American Volunteer Group in 1969.[1462]) As noted in Chapter Eight, Crommelin was an associate of Milteer and was involved in the same type of assassination plotting discussed at the Congress of Freedom meeting.

General Pedro del Valle pictured on the front page of the American Volunteer Groups' newsletter. Source: Courtney Papers, Special Collections, Northwestern State University of Louisiana

All of the retired military men listed in the AVG newsletter had extensive ties to the radical right. Brigadier General Richard Moran, retired, was from Kerrville, Texas, and had all the credentials of a high-ranking member of the radical right. FBI documents indicate he was "a close associate and friend of General Edwin A. Walker" and "He conducted JBS meetings in the area."[1463] Moran joined Mary Davison, George Soule, Revilo Oliver, and others on the board of the Congress of Freedom in 1967.[1464] He served on the boards of Liberty Lobby and the Christian Crusade.[1465] Moran spoke at Kent Courtney's Congress of Conservatives in 1965 along with General Walker, Harold Lord Varney, and Lester Maddox.[1466] He was a regional vice president of We the People in 1967. (It will be recalled that Joseph Milteer attended the 1963 We the People meeting whose president was Billy James Hargis.)[1467] In 1975, Moran was the vice president of the National Alliance to Keep and Bear Arms, a Minuteman organization out of Norborne, Missouri, in which Robert DePugh served as treasurer.[1468]

Brigadier General Robert Scott, Jr., U.S.A.F. retired, was a Georgia-born World

War II flying ace, and an original member of Claire Chennault's Flying Tigers—who were the original American Volunteer Group.[1469] Brigadier General William C. Lemly was on the Council of Advisors to Major Archibald Roberts's Committee to Restore the Constitution in 1972. (Others on that council included General Willoughby, Brigadier General Richard Moran, Revilo Oliver, John Rarick, Mary Cain, Admiral J. J. Clark, and Hilaire du Berrier.) Lemly was described as a strong John Birch Society member.[1470] Lemly served on the national Committee of American Friends of John Rarick in 1967, along with Tom Anderson, Pedro del Valle, Evetts Haley, Billy James Hargis, General Richard Moran, Major Arch Roberts, General Stratemeyer, and Edwin Walker.[1471]

H. L. Hunt and General Walker

H. L. Hunt revered and promoted General Edwin A. Walker, as he did General Douglas MacArthur. Both generals were relieved of their command for their outspoken differences with the civilian leadership of the nation. Walker, as we have discussed, was relieved of his command in Augsburg, Germany, in 1961, by President Kennedy after he implied that former President Truman and former First Lady Eleanor Roosevelt were "pink," or pro-Communist.

His rapid assent to the top of the national radical right culminated with his appearance on the cover of *Newsweek* magazine on December 4, 1961. On January 8, 1962, Hunt sent a letter to J. Evetts Haley and told him that he was wildly enthusiastic about the prospects of General Walker rising to the highest levels of power. Hunt told Haley about his strategy to get General Walker elected as the Republican governor of Texas. He felt Walker would then go to the 1964 Republican National Convention and easily win over liberal Nelson Rockefeller, whom Gallup Poll results at the time showed was favored over Barry Goldwater as the Republican nominee for president in 1964. Hunt did not feel Walker should run for governor as a Democrat because did not feel Walker could beat the incumbent, President Kennedy, in the 1964 presidential election primary, running against him within the same party.

Hunt formulated detailed plans as to when, where, and about what Walker would speak in his bid for high office. He stated, "If Walker is heard by many people making electrifying statements, he can in a few weeks time become a natural force toward saving the free world." Hunt told Haley that he believed that the mantle of Theodore Roosevelt and General MacArthur would fall on Walker's shoulders. Hunt felt a nationwide speaking trip by Walker in his campaign for governor of Texas would "practically assure him the presidential nomination in 1964."[1472]

Lee Harvey Oswald and "Mr. Hunt"

Warren Commission critic and newspaper publisher Penn Jones from Midlothian, Texas, received a piece of mail in 1976 from an unknown source in Mexico City. The mailing contained a letter that appeared to be handwritten by Lee Harvey Oswald to "Mr. Hunt," and was dated November 8, 1963. A typed letter from the anonymous source—in Spanish—accompanied the note and stated that a copy of the Oswald note had been sent to FBI director

Clarence Kelley late in 1974.

Of the letter, the source stated, "To my understanding it could have brought out the circumstances of the assassination of President Kennedy. Since Mr. Kelley hasn't responded to that letter, I've got the right to believe something bad might happen to me, and that is why I see myself obligated to keep away for a short time . . ."

The FBI denied receiving a copy of the letter.[1473, 1474]

Penn Jones passed the Oswald note to Earl Golz, a Dallas reporter who had been a steadfast researcher of the assassination. Golz showed the note to Paul Rothermel, who had left the Hunts' employ in 1969, and asked for his thoughts about it.

The FBI contacted Golz and set out to determine the authenticity of the note. Golz told the FBI that he received the letter from Jones approximately six months after the date on the Spanish transmittal letter of August 18, 1975. He sent out copies to Paul Rothermel and John Curington. Golz had tried to check out allegations of the Hunt family's possible involvement in the assassination in the past, but had never developed any solid leads. Golz told the FBI that he learned from his sources that the guns and arms recently found in California possibly belonged to the American Volunteer Group and that Nelson Bunker Hunt financed a lot of the weapons in the 1960s.[1475]

Lee Harvey Oswald letter to "Mr. Hunt." Source: JFK Exhibit F-506, HSCA IV, 337

The *Dallas Morning News* retained three handwriting experts to analyze the note and all three concluded that the signature was Oswald's. The HSCA handwriting experts, however, were not able to come to any firm conclusions. They could not confirm its authenticity, nor could they confirm it was a forgery. The HSCA expert, Mr. McNally, when asked by the HSCA staff, stated, "We are not able to accurately determine that it is specifically a forgery . . ." They noted that Oswald had misspelled "concerning" as "concerding" and left the "e" out in Harvey in the note—as he had done in other writings in the past.[1476]

Reporter Earl Golz pointed out that, around the time of the November 8, 1963, letter, Oswald was working in the Texas School Book Depository and told his wife Marina that he became interested in a new job. Oswald had been living apart from his family in a rooming house, but stayed with them on weekends. Marina testified before the Warren Commission (having no knowledge of the "Mr. Hunt" letter) on February 4, 1964, and was asked, "Did your husband come back to Irving from Dallas on November 8 (a Friday)?" She recalled he did not return to her residence on that Friday, as was the usual case, but rather came back on Saturday. Oswald had explained to her that he did not come on Friday because, "he wanted to visit another place—supposedly there was another job open, more interesting work."[1477]

The Hunts and Jim Braden

In connection with the "Dear Mr. Hunt" letter, the FBI interviewed former Hunt Oil employees Paul Rothermel and John Curington. The investigation sheds new light as to why Jim Braden, a.k.a. Eugene Hale Brading, of California, was in Dealey Plaza, like Milteer. Braden/ Brading was examined in Chapter Nine in the discussion of Garrison's suspect with a similar sounding name, Gene Bradley, a California representative of the far-right minster Carl McIntire, who likely was also in Dealey Plaza during the murder.

When Jim Braden, a felon, arrived in Dallas before the assassination he checked in with the Dallas probation department and told them he had traveled from California to meet with Nelson Bunker Hunt on business. It will be recalled, however, that Jim Braden exited an elevator in a building next to the Texas School Book Depository right after the murder. A building employee found him suspicious and notified the police, who took him in for questioning and let him go, satisfied with his responses.

Years later, reporter Peter Noyes discovered that Braden had an office near the law office of G. Wray Gill and his son Gordon W. Gill in the Pere Marquette Building in New Orleans. Both Guy Banister and David Ferrie did work for the Gills, and Gordon W. Gill's business card bearing the Pere Marquette address was found among Joseph Milteer's possessions after he died. It is beyond coincidence that Milteer and Braden—from opposite ends of the country—were both in Dealey Plaza at the time of the murder and both had ties to Hunt Oil, and to the office of the Gill law firm in New Orleans. This is evidence of conspiracy between the Hunts, Braden, and Milteer, which more evidence will bear out.

Former Hunt Oil employee John Curington told the FBI that Nelson Bunker Hunt had organized what he called a "kill squad" to eliminate certain liberal and Communist world leaders, naming Castro in Cuba, Sukarno in Indonesia, and Juan Bosch in the Dominican Republic. Curington told the FBI, in 1977, that Jim Braden was in Nelson Bunker Hunt's office in the period of 1962–63. Curington speculated that Hunt's relationship with Braden had to do with "financing certain conservative causes." Curington stated that H. L. Hunt believed that his radio program *Life Lines* would help destroy the Communist threat. However, Hunt was concerned that Nelson Bunker might go beyond his anti-Communist efforts and do something more violent to further his own goals.[1478]

Paul Rothermel told author Peter Noyes that he was sure Jim Braden, a.k.a. Eugene Brading, had dropped into the Hunts' office and visited both Lamar and Nelson Bunker Hunt. Braden told the Dallas probation officer on November 21, 1963, that "he planned to see Lamar Hunt and other oil speculators while here."[1479] According to a memo Rothermel kept on Braden, "James Braden was arrested on the day of the assassination. He was on parole for the State of California. He had been in both prior to and after the assassination to see us on an oil deal . . . ."[1480]

The FBI interviewed Nelson Bunker Hunt, who denied knowing Braden. He further accused Rothermel of stealing nine million dollars from the Hunts and forging the "Dear Mr. Hunt" letter.[1481] Neither H. L., Nelson Bunker, nor Lamar Hunt were called to testify before the Warren Commission.

Joseph Milteer and Jim Braden had several things in common. Both had business with one or more members of the Hunt family. Both traveled a long way to be in Dealey Plaza at the time of the assassination, for no good reason. Both had ties to the American Volunteer Group. Both had connections with the New Orleans law office of G. Wray Gill and his son Gordon W. Gill, Jr., who in turn worked with Guy Banister and David Ferrie. Those relationships defy any reasonable explanation other than the fact that the Hunts must have been involved, in some way, in the assassination of President Kennedy.

H. L. Hunt and the Garrison Case

Jim Garrison suspected that H. L. Hunt was involved in the assassination from the onset of his investigation. In the beginning of his investigation—while it was still secret—Garrison reportedly used the code words "Harry Blue" for H. L. Hunt and "Eddie Blue" or "True Blue" for Edwin Walker, according to the diary of Tom Bethell who worked for Garrison. In the same manner, he referred to Lee Harvey Oswald as "Patsy," David Ferrie as "Lindberg," and the overall investigation as the "Smith Case." The author has reviewed extensive files from Garrison's investigation, but has never viewed any Garrison documents that used the code words for Hunt or Walker, which suggests that Garrison may have purged them from his files. Just as Garrison abandoned his earlier claims that the radical right wing was behind the assassination, he also ended up abandoning his suspicions of Hunt and Walker—even distancing himself from them. According to Tom Bethell, an investigator for Garrison who kept a diary on the investigation noted, on October 3, 1967, "Garrison seems certain that General Walker and H. L. Hunt are involved in the assassination, although I am not clear on what evidence." Bethell stated further, "Walker's 'involvement' is supposed to have something to do with the fact that he was in New Orleans on the day of the assassination, and then traveled to Shreveport. H. L. Hunt also has a home in Shreveport. Movements to Shreveport—Cody, Walker, Bruce Ray Carlin to N.O. and back to Fort Worth, all seen as passing messages to avoid records of long distance phone calls—this is the way Garrison likes to speculate. He gets fairly far from reality at times like this, and regards it as completely obvious that there was such a wide spread and all-embracing conspiracy, no one else but him would ever have stumbled across it."[1482] As will be discussed in Chapter Nineteen, David Ferrie, according to a close friend, told Garrison at the onset of his investigation that H. L. Hunt and Walker were involved in the assassination.

Garrison declared, in the September 22, 1967, *Times–Picayune*—after his investigators had just returned from Texas—that the assassination was paid for by "a handful of oil-rich psychotic millionaires," also described as "Texas style" millionaires who were extreme conservatives. Garrison stated that John F. Kennedy was assassinated "by armed ultra-militant, para-military elements that were patriots in a psychotic sense." Garrison again aptly describes the hardcore underground of Joseph Milteer, stating, "The connecting link at every level of operation from the oil rich sponsors of the assassination down to the Dallas police department through Jack Ruby and including anti-Castro adventurers at the operating level were Minute Men [sic], Nazi-oriented. It was essentially a Nazi operation." Garrison later shifted course and blamed the murder on U.S. intelligence.

Paul Rothermel conducted his own investigation of the assassination, on behalf of the Hunts. He told the author: "My job was to keep my bosses' names out of the assassination books."[1483] In the fall of 1967, Rothermel informed H. L. Hunt that his investigation showed that "Garrison is referring to either you or Bunker as the wealthy oilman in his probe." Rothermel advised Hunt not to travel to New Orleans, because he might be arrested. As a result, Hunt cancelled his appointment with his friend, Louisiana senator Russell Long.

At some point, Rothermel got hold of a hand-drawn chart, which purportedly detailed Garrison's theory of the assassination. The chart consisted of a series of names, boxes, and circles connected by dotted lines and arrows. At the top of the chart was the name "H. L. Hunt" and, below that, the notation "screened three times by Rothermel." Directly below Hunt's name were lines pointing to the Dallas police, Jack Ruby, the FBI, Oswald, a Texas congressman, and several lesser-known New Orleans and Texas characters. The chart did not explain exactly what all the lines and boxes were supposed to mean. However, the implication was clear: Garrison and/or his investigators apparently believed H. L. Hunt had a hand in Kennedy's murder.[1484]

Rothermel told the author that the Hunts paid to fly one of Garrison's investigator, and assassination author, Harold Weisberg to Dallas from New Orleans to meet with Hunt.[1485] Weisberg told the author that he assured Hunt that he was not a suspect in the Garrison case. Weisberg told the author, years later, that he did not believe Hunt was involved. Weisberg felt the U.S. government was behind the assassination of President Kennedy.[1486] Jim Garrison agreed with Weisberg and wrote the forward for Weisberg's book, *Oswald in New Orleans: Case for Conspiracy with the CIA.*

On April 4, 1968, another of Garrison's investigators, William Wood (a.k.a. Bill Boxley), apologized to H. L. Hunt for the rumors that Garrison was investigating Hunt and gave him assurances that they did not feel he was involved in the assassination. Wood/Boxley explained that Garrison, "will prove the assassination was a plot by officials in the Federal Government and consisted of CIA, Secret Service, FBI, and one or two military men."[1487]

In 1968, the book *Farewell America* was written under the pseudonym James Hepburn and was reportedly published by French intelligence. The book implicated wealthy Texas oilmen and Hunt in the assassination. As a joke, Garrison's investigator Wood/Boxley, asked newspaper publisher and assassination researcher Penn Jones to print up a dust jacket for the book that stated that H. L. Hunt distributed the book "in the interest of free speech."[1488]

It is not known what evidence Garrison had against Hunt or why he did not pursue it. Although, pursuing a case against the murderous radicals behind the crime may not have been viewed as either feasible or survivable.

Guy Banister and the Hunt Oil Company

H. L. Hunt and Guy Banister were close associates according to Joseph Oster, which is information being revealed in this work for the first time. Oster was a young police officer in the mid-1950s, serving under Chief Guy Banister in the New Orleans Police Department. When

Banister was dismissed from the department, Oster joined him as a partner in the Guy Banister and Associates detective agency that operated out of Banister's home on Argonne Street, prior to moving to the Balter Building. Eventually, Oster left Banister's agency. Oster told the author, "He was always doing things that didn't bring any money into the office." Even so, Oster always remained respectful of Banister, whom he continued to call "the Chief." Oster was glad to help him out whenever he was asked.

The author interviewed Oster in 1999—when Oster was still practicing as a private investigator in Monroe, Louisiana, and was a respected polygraph operator. Oster's daughter staffed his New Orleans office.

In the mid-1960s Oster was employed by Governor McKeithen's office to investigate corrupt union practices that had the effect of driving industry out of the state of Louisiana. With this information in mind, on a lark, the author asked Oster if Banister knew H. L. Hunt. Oster replied, "Oh yes. We met with Hunt a number of times at the Petroleum Club [in Dallas.]" Oster went on to explain that the Hunt's oil operations in Louisiana were plagued by continuous thefts of drilling equipment and Hunt retained Banister and Oster to investigate the problem.

Banister discovered that the thieves were stealing the drilling equipment and selling it back to unsuspecting Hunt operators. Banister solved the problem by initiating a system of applying serial numbers to the drill collars. Upon Banister's death in 1964, Oster—then working for Harry Robert's Southern Research detective agency—took over the Hunt Oil contract. Oster showed the author letters—on Guy Banister and Associates stationery—that referred to the work Banister had done for Hunt. Oster stated that Banister also did security work for Sun Oil and Texas oilmen Clint Murchison and Sid Richardson.[1489]

The author interviewed Paul Rothermel in Richardson, Texas, in 2000, Hunt's former security chief who, at the time, was working part time as a judge. Rothermel readily confirmed that Guy Banister, Joe Oster, and Harry Robert's Southern Research all performed security work for Hunt Oil and knew H. L. Hunt well. As noted earlier, the author asked Rothermel if Hunt also knew Leander Perez. He replied, "Of course he did. Most of his wells were in Terrebonne and Plaquemines Parishes. You couldn't do business in Plaquemines Parish without knowing Leander Perez."[1490]

Author Dick Russell interviewed Rothermel and Rothermel alluded to knowing Banister, but no details were given.[1491] The author also asked Rothermel, a former FBI man, if he knew Banister and he stated that he did—not from the FBI but, rather, from his role in Hunt Oil security. Rothermel volunteered that "Guy Banister was 'the best shoulder weapon man in the FBI.'" He said that Banister was an expert marksman, as was Special Agent Foster of Boston. The two were considered the best shots in the Bureau. Rothermel agreed that Banister and H. L. Hunt were like-minded politically. He knew that Banister and General Walker were friends, and that Walker phoned and visited Hunt. He stated that he felt that Walker's actions at Ole Miss were a mistake and that the incident hurt him politically on the right. Rothermel did not believe Hunt was associated with Jack Ruby in the area of gambling. "They were not in the same league. H. L. was a high roller."

Rothermel traveled with Dan Smoot during his speaking engagement on behalf of *Facts Forum*. Rothermel originally set up *Life Lines* for Hunt, but he displeased Hunt because he wasn't right wing enough. Rothermel refused to tell the author how he obtained the first copy of the Zapruder film, but insisted that he did.[1492]

According to Joe Newbrough, who was a private investigator with Guy Banister from 1958 to 1964, an unnamed man who worked for H. L. Hunt was a frequent visitor to Guy Banister's office and once gave Banister some money to take to Governor McKeithen or Shelby Jackson in Baton Rouge for their campaigns.[1493] Garrsion investigator William Wood ("Bill Boxley") interviewed Rothermel who told him he knew Banister and that they had both left the FBI at the same time.[1494] According to another memo of a Wood/Boxley interview with him in 1967, Rothermel was greatly surprised and in apparent disbelief when he was told that Banister had died.[1495]

Rothermel provided some information about Austin's Barbeque, where police officer J. D. Tippit worked a part-time job. Very little is known about Tippit—who was allegedly murdered by Lee Harvey Oswald after the assassination—because the Warren Commission hardly investigated his background out of respect for him and his family. Warren Commission critic Sylvia Meagher aptly described Tippit as "unknown and unknowable."[1496] The Warren Commission documented that Tippit provided part-time security for Austin's Barbeque, which they noted was owned by a member of the John Birch Society. Importantly, Rothermel told the author that Austin's Barbeque was not only owned by a member of the John Birch Society, but also served as a meeting place for the group. Rothermel was asked to give a speech to the John Birch Society at Austin's about his experience as an FBI agent. He claimed the speech was not well received because he "was not right wing enough."[1497] Robert Surrey, General Walker and the Hunt's were all involved in the Dallas John Birch Society. If police officer J. D. Tippit was involved in the assassination conspiracy, as some have claimed, it may have been on the basis of a connection with the John Birch Society.

The Dallas Minutemen

Joseph A. Milteer and his key associates in Dallas and New Orleans belonged to the Minutemen. Frank Ellsworth of the Dallas Bureau of Alcohol, Tobacco and Firearms noted, in 1964, "An organization known as the Minutemen is the right wing group in Dallas most likely to have been associated with any effort to assassinate the president."[1498] He was also quoted as saying: "The Minutemen in Dallas are closely tied to General Walker and H. L. Hunt."[1499] As we shall see later, Robert Surrey, another Milteer associate, was also involved in the Minutemen. Robert Morris screened applicants to the Dallas Minuteman.

As was noted previously, Guy Banister and his colleagues Maurice Gatlin and Hugh Ward were also Minutemen. Jerry Brooks, who was a top-ranking associate of Robert DePugh's national Minutemen organization in Missouri worked out of Banister's office. Rich Lauchli, another top aide to DePugh, was involved in the paramilitary camps north of Lake

Pontchartrain. Lee Harvey Oswald frequented the waiting room of Minuteman Adrian Alba's garage while on break from his job at Reily Coffee.

According to author Harry Hurt, III, Paul Rothermel informed the Hunts, in a November 4, 1963, interoffice memo that there had been "unconfirmed reports of possible violence during the parade [Kennedy's motorcade]." The information was apparently derived from the FBI and the Dallas Police Department, who had informants placed in General Walker's group in Dallas and on the campus of North Texas University in Denton. Rothermel warned, "If an incident were to occur, the true story of who perpetrated it would never come out."[1500]

H. L. Hunt was disturbed by the repeated suggestions in the news that he was involved in the assassination. He complained especially about a United Press International report that quoted a Democratic Oregon senator as saying of Hunt: "If anybody is responsible, he is."[1501] He "has to bear a lot of the onus because of the fanatical broadcasts he sponsors." An editorial in the *New Republic* claimed that the *Life Lines* program that was broadcast on the day of the assassination was the kind of propaganda that an extremist might act upon.[1502]

Conclusions

Suspicions about the Hunt family's involvement in the assassination are not new but the evidence against them—prior to this work—has been far from sufficient to solidly establish their guilt. The new evidence—presented for the first time here—strongly suggests the involvement of the H. L. Hunt family in the conspiracy behind the assassination of President Kennedy.

The evidence for Joseph Milteer's involvement in the assassination conspiracy has been presented in prior chapters. In brief, Milteer had precise advanced knowledge of the assassination and was present in Dealey Plaza during the murder. Those circumstances, among others, defy any explanation other than that he must have been involved in some way. Milteer not only had a direct tie to one or more members of the Hunt family—as evidenced by his visit to Hunt Oil Company—he had also been an associate of close Hunt ally, and former employee, Dan Smoot since at least 1960.

The new evidence also establishes a relationship between General Walker, a close associate of both the Hunts and Milteer. Walker was the supposed near-shooting victim of Lee Harvey Oswald, as well as a Warren Commission witness. The evidence also ties Milteer to a second Dallas Warren Commission witness and close Walker aide, Robert Surrey, who was head of the Dallas American Nazi Party. All of Milteer's Dallas associates—H. L. Hunt, Walker, Smoot, and Surrey were members of the Minutemen, as were Guy Banister and several of his associates in New Orleans.

Of course, significant suspicions about General Walker have been raised throughout this work since the author uncovered and reported upon the ominous correspondence of generals Walker and Pedro del Valle. Their chronicle of conspiracy revealed plans for an insurrection that included the consideration of violence. The positions of generals del Valle and Walker as military advisors for the Council for Statehood and Congress of Freedom—groups that developed plans for widespread assassinations (plans which were later honed down to the assassination of the president)—have been presented. The case against General Walker is momentous and devastating to the official story and will be presented in the next chapters.

H. L. Hunt's lofty dream of toppling the Kennedy regime by propelling General Walker to the presidency in 1964 disintegrated when Walker was soundly defeated in the 1962 primaries for governor of Texas. As was noted earlier, Hunt held little hope that Kennedy could be defeated at the polls in 1964. As a consequence, he lamented, "At stake is the entire future"—a reference to Kennedy's plan to abolish the Southern institution of segregation. With Walker out of the picture as a viable political candidate capable of defeating Kennedy at the polls, Hunt's options "to save the country"—as he emphasized to Governor Jimmie Davis was a task which had to be done—were few and dire.

The case against the Hunt family is not established solely based on Milteer's appearance at Hunt Oil Company or Milteer's association with Hunt cronies Dan Smoot and General Walker. New evidence presented in the prior chapter demonstrated a relationship between Milteer and George Wray Gill, Jr., whose law office in the Pere Marquette Building was frequented by Oswald associates David Ferrie and Guy Banister. The Hunts had another associate, Jim Braden, who—like Milteer—was present in Dealey Plaza during the assassination and had ties to the Gill law office in New Orleans.

The fact that Braden and Milteer traveled from opposite ends of the country, were in Dealey Plaza during the murder for no good reason, and were associates of the Hunts suggests conspiracy. Moreover, evidence that Milteer and Braden had direct ties to the Hunts, as well the Gill law office in the Pere Marquette building in New Orleans, is compelling. The information suggesting that Nelson Bunker Hunt, Braden, and Milteer had ties to the American Volunteer Group is evidence, within reasonable historical certainty, that the three men were part of the assassination conspiracy. The evidence suggests that Braden served as Nelson Bunker Hunt's conduit for financing the American Volunteer Group. New evidence revealed for the first time shows General Pedro del Valle led the group that included individuals from General Walker's group. (It will be recalled that credible evidence, presented in Chapter Eight, showed that plans to assassinate the president were divulged by del Valle in a room at the Marott Hotel during the October 1963 Constitution Party meeting.) Importantly, the American Volunteer Group newsletter revealing del Valle's leadership role in the group was discovered in the personal papers of close Guy Banister associate Kent Courtney.

Additional evidence against H. L. Hunt was his strong association with numerous individuals suspected of involvement in the assassination conspiracy. H. L. Hunt was close to retired generals Charles Willoughby, Albert Wedemeyer, and George Stratemeyer, who—in their plotting correspondence—General del Valle advised General Walker were "trusted individuals" and could be relied upon.

Of the generals, Charles Willoughby deserves special scrutiny. An anonymous source sent author Dick Russell a letter alleging that Charles Willoughby confessed on his deathbed of his involvement in the Kennedy assassination. Furthermore, Willoughby was close with two other associates of Milteer and H. L. Hunt—General Walker and Billy James Hargis. Willoughby, Walker, and Hargis went on a cross-country speaking tour for the Christian Crusade after the assassination that also featured Oswald's purported adversary, Cuban Carlos Bringuier.

The fact that H. L. Hunt dispatched employee John Curington to check on the security of the Dallas jail housing Oswald raises the possibility that Hunt had done so to determine the feasibility of silencing Oswald in the jail.

Unfortunately, the evidence for Jim Garrison's claim of the Hunts' involvement in the assassination may no longer exist. However, the worries of H. L. Hunt, which were stirred by Garrison's investigation; the formation of his own investigation into Garrison's claims; meetings with Garrison's investigators; and Hunt's overall concern over getting his name in the assassination books suggests consciousness of guilt on the part of Hunt.

The establishment, made here for the first time, of the Hunts' relationship with Guy Banister, who had direct ties to Lee Harvey Oswald, leaves little doubt of the Hunts' involvement in the assassination.

CHAPTER TWELVE

GENERAL WALKER AND THE MILITARY MUZZLING, 1961

We are at war. You are infiltrated and your cause starts in every home,
church, school, street corner, and public gathering. Man your weapons
and attack! Our objective is to defeat the national pretenders and the
professional power-mad politicians, and the Reds in every land.
                                    — General Walker, December 12, 1961

Geneneral Walker's personal vendetta against President Kennedy began in 1961 after Walker was "muzzled" or censured for remarks made against a former president and first lady. The vendetta grew when Walker was arrested by order of Attorney General Robert Kennedy for leading a riot against U.S. Marshals during the integration crisis at Ole Miss in 1962. The correspondence between retired generals Edwin Walker and Pedro del Valle, which began in mid-1962 (as discussed in Chapter Eight), described their desire to promote insurrection against the administration, including the possible use of violence. By late 1962, Walker, del Valle and another retired general, Clyde Watts, along with former Walker aide Major Archibald Roberts, became military advisors to the Council for Statehood and the Congress of Freedom. In April 1963, at the Congress of Freedom, plans to assassinate a large number of people in the Council of Foreign Relations and other prominent figures were revealed, but after the FBI questioned the principals the plot was abandoned. Two months later, President Kennedy announced a sweeping civil rights bill that would end the white Southern way of life forevermore and the plot narrowed.

A plan to assassinate President Kennedy was revealed by Joseph Milteer's hardcore underground at the October 1963 Constitution Party meeting. Evidence tying General Pedro del Valle to the plot was discussed. A high-ranking member of the hardcore radical right, Milteer revealed the plotting to FBI informant Willie Somersett, who relayed the information to Miami police and the FBI. Milteer's ties to both the New Orleans and Dallas hardcore underground, which in turn had connections with Lee Harvey Oswald, were described in the last two chapters. Oswald's connections to Guy Banister and his New Orleans operation were extensive. Less extensive—but compelling—was Oswald's involvement in Texas with Walker in the shooting incident. Milteer was directly tied to General Walker in the last chapter, when it was revealed he had met with him in Dallas. Finally, Milteer was the man who had direct knowledge of the assassination plots revealed at the Congress of Freedom and Constitution Party meeting and had detailed foreknowledge—documented by Somersett's surreptitious tape recording—of how the assassination actually happened. Milteer's now-known ties to General Walker raise suspicions, to say the least, of the dissident general's involvement in the assassination. Anyone involved with Milteer and Oswald, if only in the context of being a supposed near-shooting victim of Oswald, as Walker was, surely is suspect. In the past chapters, evidence was presented that implicated the H. L. Hunt clan, who were close to Walker, in the assassination.

Evidence in the next chapters will further establish Walker's close ties to Guy Banister who, extensive evidence shows, was closely aligned with Lee Harvey Oswald in 1963. (The allegation that Kent Courtney and Lee Harvey Oswald were associated was presented in Chapter Three.) Courtney's ties to General Walker, presented in this chapter, raise further suspicions about the dissident retired general.

The Rise of General Walker

Edwin "Ted" Anderson Walker was born in Center Point, Texas. He graduated from the New Mexico Military Institute in 1927 and from West Point in 1931, ranking 219th in his class. He commanded a joint Canadian-American commando team in the Italian Campaign during World War II. During the Korean War, Walker rose to the rank of colonel and commanded an artillery unit.[1503, 1504] Walker stated that he first began to ponder the "internal Communist conspiracy" in 1945. After World War II, he was critical of the media's treatment of General George S. Patton for a statement he gave at a news conference on September 22, 1945. Patton said, with indifference towards the German Nazi Party, "Well this Nazi thing is just like a Democratic and Republican election fight . . . I don't know anything about parties."[1505]

Another event that changed Walker's thinking was President Harry S. Truman's removal of Major General Ovral A. Anderson from Korea in 1950. General Anderson stated, "give me the order to do it and I can break up Russia's five A-bomb nests in a week . . . And when I went up to Christ I think I can explain to him that I have saved civilization."[1506] While in Korea in 1953, Walker made a personal vow "to find out why the war terminated as it did under the circumstances and conditions in which it did."[1507] Like many on the far right, Walker was critical of the Korean War stalemate, which became known among the radical right as a "no win war."

After returning to the states from Korea, Walker visited meetings held by various anti-Communist groups which had sprung up at the beginning of the Cold War and were proliferating around the country.[1508] In 1955, Walker was assigned as senior advisor to the chief of staff of the Chinese National Army, Generalissimo Chiang Kai-Shek. Walker was critical of what he considered the United States's "uncertain policy" in the Pacific. Believing the U.S. was not doing enough to help in the fight against the Chinese Communists, Walker pointed to a group of medals on his uniform and remarked, "What good are they. The war is not over, it can never be won as long as subversion exists in America."[1509]

On September 24, 1957, President Eisenhower ordered U.S. troops to Little Rock, Arkansas, to ensure implementation of the court-ordered integration of Central High School. Walker had received a reserve assignment, in June 1957, as the commander of Arkansas Military District in Little Rock, and was placed in charge of the federal troops. The 2,000 men under his command were mainly office workers. Eisenhower federalized the Arkansas National Guard, and dispatched paratroopers from the 101st Airborne Division, swelling Walker's command to 12,000 troops. Governor Orval Faubus responded to the invasion of federal troops in Little Rock in a TV speech, stating: "We are now in occupied territory. In the name of God what's happening in America?" Many in the South and on the far right shared the sentiment.[1510]

Milteer's associates Emmet Irwin and Leander Perez—with Willie Rainach and the New Orleans Citizens' Council—invited Governor Faubus to address the Council on the plight of Little Rock on November 10, 1958. The event demonstrated the close-knit relationship between defiant Southern state officials and members of the Citizens' Council across the South.[1511] Senator Eastland said in response to the federal government's invasion of Little Rock, "This makes reconstruction II official. This is an attempt by the armed forces to destroy the social order of the South. Nothing like this was ever attempted in Russia."[1512]

In New Orleans, on October 14, 1957, Colonel Bluford Balter hosted members of the Little Rock Corporation, an organization created to raise funds for private white schools in New Orleans.[1513] Balter set up a special Little Rock booth on the corner of Canal and Elk Streets to raise money for private schools for Little Rock, with plans for a permanent office in the Balter building. (The offices of Guy Banister and the Citizens' Council offices were in the Balter Building at the time.)[1514]

Walker, a Southern racist who felt the Communists were behind the racial trouble, thoroughly opposed the Little Rock military operation. On August 4, 1959, he submitted his resignation as commander of the Arkansas Military District, which was refused. Instead, Walker was reassigned to the 24th Division in Heidelberg, Germany.[1515] Walker later told the FBI that he "led forces on the wrong side in the Little Rock incident and [was] happy to be on the other right side."[1516] In 1962, he gave his reason for resigning, stating, "In my opinion the fifth column conspiracy and influence in the United States minimize or nullify the effectiveness of my ideals and principles, military mission and objectives and the necessary American public spirit to support sons and soldiers. I have no further desire for military service at this time with this conspiracy and its influences on the home front."[1517]

General Edwin A. Walker (left) commanded the 101st Airborne division that was sent to Little Rock, Arkansas, to enforce President Eisenhower's desegregation order at Central High School. Source: Corbis

Following the 1954 *Brown* decision—and prior to the 1957 Little Rock incident—little progress had been made in the civil rights arena, in part due to the Supreme Court's vaguely defined time mandate for desegregation to proceed "with all deliberate speed." Both the civil rights movement and the organized mass resistance to desegregation in the Citizens' Council were reinvigorated by the Little Rock incident and their respective followings grew. The slogan "Brotherhood by Bayonet" was coined by the Citizens' Council in response to the troops in Little Rock, and appeared in their literature and on bumper stickers.

During his last years as commander of the Arkansas Military District, Walker made "hard hitting" remarks before civic groups in Arkansas about the continuing threat of Communism.[1518] Just before Walker's assignment to the 24th Infantry Division in Germany, he was given the highest conservative civilian award in the fall of 1959 by George Benson, head of the ultraconservative Harding College in Searcy, Arkansas, whom he had first met in 1957. Benson was one of the earliest nationally recognized leaders of the far right to be associated with Walker, before he achieved national fame in 1961. (Benson's college produced the popular far-right-wing propaganda film, "Communism on the Map.")

Prior to joining the John Birch Society in 1959, Walker had been a dedicated anti-Communist and spent 5,000 to 10,000 dollars of his own money "alerting people to the dangers of Russia." Walker asserted, "I joined in 1959 and handed them $1,000 which I could not afford. I was looking for a cause."[1519] Prior to 1961, he had participated in "Freedom Forums" and had sent a "personal emissary" to the Billy James Hargis Christian Crusade in Tulsa, Oklahoma.[1520, 1521]

Walker invited Edgar Bundy—a well-known national leader of the far right who conducted "counter subversive seminars"—to lecture to his troops in Germany. The seminars were built around Bundy's book *A Manual for Survival* that discussed the Communist techniques of infiltration and subversion. The manual recommended Carl McIntire's *Christian Beacon* and *The Dan Smoot Report*. Bundy had been ordained as a Baptist minister in Louisiana while serving in the air force. He served as an intelligence officer under General Claire Chennault in China during World War II.[1522, 1523] In the early 1950s, Bundy's research spawned an American Legion attack on the Girl Scouts for their supposed trafficking of subversive propaganda into Illinois.[1524] In 1956, Bundy was a major in the Air Force Reserve. Later, he headed a layman's group called the Church League of America in Wheaton, Illinois. He wrote the book *Collectivism in the Churches*, which Walker recommended to the study group of the wives of his troops. The book purported to expose "the alarming extent to which Communist propaganda has penetrated religious groups and institutions." Bundy kept files on between 400,000 and one million individuals, organizations and publications that he felt were related to the Communists or "fellow travelers." Complete sets of Communist literature, including the *Daily Worker* were collected. Files were also kept on liberal groups including the American Civil Liberties Union and Americans for Democratic Action. He boasted that few other files on Communism in the country were comparable to the Church League files.[1525, 1526, 1527] The massive files were kept in Wheaton, Illinois, in a steel and concrete vault rigged with alarms and electronic devices and guarded by five German Shepard's and their handlers.[1528] Bundy was a protégé of Carl McIntire and he kept close ties to McIntire's organization.[1529] After Bundy's death, Minutemen leader Robert DePugh told the author that he tried to acquire Bundy's files, but they eventually went to the John Birch Society headquarters in Belmont, Massachusetts.[1530]

Walker also recruited another notable anti-Communist, William Schlemm—associate editor of the John Birch Society magazine *American Opinion*—to address his troops.[1531] The army noted that Walker had been involved in right-wing causes for years, stating, "He is an eccentric, and is not openly violently anti-Communist but has been for years working at it with a passion, studying, lecturing, and reading all literature available on the subject."[1532]

As in other states in the South, provoked by the federal incursion at Little Rock, the Arkansas Legislature convened hearings on "alleged Communist subversion behind racial trouble in Arkansas." On December 15, 1958, the Arkansas State Legislative Council committee hearings began with the purpose to reveal that "communistic influences" were behind the racial unrest that centered on Little Rock's Central High School. The state attorney general testified at the hearings that the Southern Conference Education Fund (SCEF), the Highlander Folk School, and the NAACP—among other organizations—were subversive. J. B. Mathews, a former House on Un-American Activities (HUAC) investigator and professional former Communist witness, testified that five Arkansas colleges "have been successfully penetrated by Communists."[1533] Mathews had formerly worked for Senator Joseph McCarthy's committee, and testified on the penetration of Communist agents into schools involved with the SCEF, the organization which was the arch nemesis of Leander Perez, Guy Banister, and Hubert Badeaux. (The hearings mirrored those of Willie Rainach's Subversion in Racial Unrest hearings in Louisiana in 1957 that also featured Banister, Perez, and Badeaux as witnesses.) On the third day of the hearings, Banister testified and agreed that Communism was behind racial unrest in Arkansas, and listed the names of subversive people and organizations that were operating in the state.[1534, 1535]

Although Banister and Walker were both in Arkansas in 1959, and on the same side of the Little Rock issue, there is no evidence that they knew each other at that time. However, it's worth noting that on September 14, 1959, General Walker was in New Orleans to give a speech to reserve officers at the New Orleans City Hall at the same time Banister engaged in his anti-Communist operation. After being honored earlier that day at a dinner at Camp Leroy Johnson, Walker stated that the Communist objective was to centralize the government and take away individual rights, which he called "national suicide."[1536]

The Muzzling of General Walker

By 1961, U.S.-Soviet Cold War tensions were already running high when Soviet Premier Khrushchev heightened fears by predicting, on May 5, 1961, that Communism would gain control of the world one day without resorting to bayonets or rockets. He declared, "We do not need a war to achieve domination of our ideas, the most progressive Marxist-Leninist ideas." The Pentagon and Kennedy administration were concerned about a surge in the number of military officers making provocative, anti-Communist speeches at public forums, which they felt heightened the Cold War antagonism. As a result, the Pentagon ordered all planned military speeches to be screened in advance for inflammatory remarks. The censorship was extensive—the Defense Department reviewed 1,500 to 2,000 speeches during this period.[1537] President Kennedy called the censoring system "very valuable" and said he intended to continue it.[1538]

In one censored speech in February 1961, Army Brigadier General John W. White declared, "Victories on each of the battlefields of the Cold War is essential to survival of freedom." A Pentagon censor changed the word "victories" to "the defeat of Communist aggression," which is an example of how, at times, their censorship was petty. General Arthur Trudeau, who gave (on average) one speech a week, accounted for a goodly share of those that were reviewed by censors. (It will be recalled from Chapter Eight that Trudeau had smuggled "military plans of the highest magnitude" to Senator Strom Thurmond. Trudeau was tied to Philip Corso, who fabricated and spread rumors that Lee Harvey Oswald was a paid informant of the FBI. Corso, in his testimony before Senator Eastland's Senate Internal Subversion Subcommittee, smeared members of President Kennedy's cabinet, calling them Fabian Socialists.)[1539]

General Walker in Germany. Walker's 24th Division was the only division among NATO's troops to win Le Clerc matches for marksmanship two consecutive years in a row. Source: Edwin A. Walker Papers, Dolph Briscoe Center for American History, University of Texas at Austin

As commander of the 24th Infantry Division in Europe, Walker gained a reputation as a strict commander and rigid disciplinarian (some of his field training exercises became prototypes for those later used in Vietnam). Walker's 24th Division was the only division among NATO's troops to win Le Clerc matches for marksmanship two consecutive years in a row.[1540] Walker entered the "muzzling" maelstrom when the April 16, 1961, edition of *Overseas Weekly*—a German newspaper published for American servicemen—leveled several accusations against him. They reported that Walker had given a speech before two hundred parent-teacher association members at the American School at Augsburg, Germany, and had stated that President Truman, former first lady Eleanor Roosevelt, and former Secretary of State Dean Acheson were "definitely pink"—implying they were just a shade or so less than outright "Red Communists." Walker stated that renowned journalists Edward R. Morrow and Eric Sevareid, along with 60 percent of the American media, were Communist-controlled. The paper accused Walker of encouraging his men to read the literature of the John Birch Society and to vote for conservatives in the 1960 election.[1541] (Walker had had a prior run-in with *Overseas Weekly* when a reporter called Walker "crazy." As a result of that earlier incident Walker ordered the reporter off the base in 1960 for spreading rumors about his mental capacities.[1542])

General Walker rose to national fame when accusations about him were published in the April 1961, *Overseas Weekly* in Germany. Source: Richard B. Russell Papers. Richard B. Russell Library for Political Research and Studies, University of Georgia Libraries

Overseas Weekly was nicknamed *Oversexed Weekly* for its inclusion of photos of scantily dressed young women in provocative poses in its pages. General Walker said of the newspaper: "We have the Communists and we have the *Overseas Weekly*. Neither is God's blessing to the American people or their soldier sons overseas."[1543]

On October 15, 1960, Walker established an anti-Communist indoctrination program for his troops called the Pro-Blue program. Largely designed by his aide, Major Archibald Roberts, the program's purpose was to indoctrinate Walker's troops in far-right anti-Communism ideology. (The Pro-Blue program was so named because the free nations were depicted on the world map by the color blue, while the Communist countries were depicted in red.)[1544] Like Walker, General Pedro del Valle and General Clyde Watts, Roberts secretly became a military advisor to the Council for Statehood and Congress of Freedom in late 1962.

The army had previously warned Walker about remarks he had made in inflammatory speeches in August and October of 1960, and in March of 1961. After the *Overseas Weekly* article exposed Walker's charges that prominent Americans were "pink," on April 17, 1961, Secretary of Defense Robert McNamara relieved General Walker of his command, pending a four-week investigation. The Bay of Pigs invasion in Cuba occurred on the same day. Walker called on Senator John Tower of Texas for advice during the investigation. Tower in turn called Defense Secretary McNamara and urged him to give Walker a fair hearing. The hearing concluded that although there were some minor inaccuracies, the *Overseas Weekly* allegations against Walker were substantiated. They found that Walker did, in fact, make derogatory remarks against President Truman, former Secretary of State Dean Acheson, former first lady Eleanor Roosevelt, and newsmen Eric Sevareid and Edward R. Murrow as well as television news anchor Walter Cronkite. The army determined that Walker had directed his troops to voluntarily study works on anti-Communism similar to the directives of the John Birch Society, but not specifically the program of the John Birch Society.[1545]

Meanwhile, in Washington in April of 1961, Attorney General Robert F. Kennedy voiced concerns about the John Birch Society (JBS). In response, Representative John H. Rousselot of California identified himself as a member of the JBS and characterized the society as "basically a study group, not arm-waving people who run around harassing others." JBS leader Robert Welch sent a telegram to Senator James Eastland inviting him to investigate his organization.[1546] On April 14, 1961, the *Dallas Times Herald* noted that Robert Welch planned to speak to 1,000 John Birch Society members in Dallas. The meeting was closed to reporters, but Dallas Police Chief Jesse Curry was to attend as a non-uniformed observer. Joseph Grinnan (who with money from Nelson Bunker Hunt was largely responsible for purchasing the derogatory, black-bordered "Welcome Mr. President" ad printed in the *Dallas Morning News* on the day of the assassination) reserved the Baker Hotel for the engagement.[1547]

President Kennedy ordered an inquiry into the Walker case, stating in a news conference on April 22, 1961: "He will be given every opportunity, and those who have been critical of him will be given every opportunity to present their case. A final decision will then be made by Mr. McNamara . . . and I will then review it, without prejudice to General Walker."[1548] The army found Walker in violation of army regulations "by making speeches, inflammatory and derogatory remarks to past public officials, arranging for speakers who gave inflammatory speeches, quoting and recommending material which was in varying degrees nonfactual, biased and inflammatory in character under an assumed responsibility for prior psychological warfare prior to 15 October 1960." Walker's attempt to influence the vote of his men in the 1960 congressional elections—a violation of the criminal statutes of the Hatch Act—was the most serious charge that had been leveled against him. Walker had urged his men to check the ratings given to potential candidates in the conservatively biased index of Americans for Constitutional Action (ACA), which had been developed to counter the liberal Americans for Democratic Action and was headed by retired admiral Ben Moreel.[1549] Despite his violation of the Hatch Act, the army decided not to prosecute General Walker, opting for an oral admonishment instead, on the approval of President Kennedy. McNamera chose the lesser admonishment because of Walker's "brilliant combat record and sincerity in purpose in fighting Communism."[1550]

Walker's brother George wrote to the Christian Crusade on April 24, 1961, at the request of General Walker, and told them that his brother was being investigated in Germany and that the general wanted to get in touch with General Willoughby. George told them he had received a cable earlier in the week from his brother, who wanted it conveyed to Willoughby, that stated, "Water is deep, enemy is vicious, you are free to enter the fray, as you see fit."[1551]

The FBI followed the Walker affair with interest and, on May 4, 1961, they noted that the Senate Armed Services Committee were receiving fifteen to twenty-five telegrams a day from Shreveport and New York in support of Walker and critical of the committee.[1552] The conservative monthly magazine, the *National Review*, saw General Walker as being at war with the Kennedy administration. They wrote, "General Walker was hero-stuff or he is nothing, and he is a poor judge of human materials who mistakes him for anything else . . . Let us, then, not be dropping flowers on his grave, which has yet to be dug, but rather preparing ourselves to fight at his side, when at a time and place of his choosing, he next joins battle with the enemy."[1553] Walker's brother George wrote Phoebe Courtney on May 8, 1961, and thanked her for supporting his brother's fight against Communism and for Kent's recent radiobroadcast in his defense.[1554]

On May 20, 1961, Major Archibald Roberts, working at the U.S. Army Information Office in New York, wrote General Willoughby in Washington, D.C., and told him, "It would be very helpful to our campaign to enlist German professionals on the post to assist in the exposé of *Overseas Weekly*." Roberts told him that Fritz Cramer in Bonn, Germany—who published an anti-Communist newspaper—could help their cause and secure files on the publishers of *Overseas Weekly* and "help tie in the Commie technique of the operation." Roberts asked Willoughby, "Can we impose on your prestige to establish contact with this man, General?" Roberts concluded the letter saying, "All we're after is evidence that will enable us to destroy Marion Respach [an editor for the newspaper], smash *Overseas Weekly*, and expose the International Communist Conspiracy." On May 25, 1961, Walker wrote Roberts and thanked him for his great work. He told him, "I am worried about nothing."[1555]

General Walker's mother wrote a letter to her son in Germany on July 23, 1961, which was later discovered by the author in General Walker's personal papers. (Walker kept carbon copies of the volumes of letters he wrote. Even so, the Walker papers contain none of his plotting letters found in the papers of other members of the hardcore underground reported in this work. They were obviously purged from the forty boxes of papers he left to posterity.) In the letter, Mrs. Walker gave her son her blessing should he decide to resign. She stated that, on Friday, Mr. Courtney, from the *Independent American* had telephoned her other son, George, who lived with her in Center Point, Texas, and told them he wanted to visit with him and his mother. They agreed and met him at the airport on Saturday. Courtney had dinner with Mrs. Walker and George at their home. Courtney told her that after seeing General Walker's home and family that, "[h]e felt that Gen. Walker is the man the country needs to rally conservatives behind such a leader." He told her his plan was "to put Gen. Walker on a salary plus commission etc. for speaking engagements all over the country, to combat the election of liberals where ever they might be up for election and defeat them with conservatives. Courtney said one reason he came over here was to get George to introduce him to you by phone, that he and Gen. Willoughby planned to go to Germany to see you, next week."

The letter also mentioned that Courtney told her that General Willoughby was under contract with Billy James Hargis. Courtney told her that her son, General Walker, had been treated unfairly. She suggested to Courtney that he write out his proposition and send it to General Walker and he agreed. In the letter, Mrs. Walker cautioned her son to remain independent and to consider very seriously the prospect of giving up his distinguished career. She related that Courtney told her "time is of the essence, to take advantage of your publicity." She noted that Courtney's newspaper had the largest circulation of all conservative groups and wondered how many other organizations would want to use him to further their aims. Courtney showed her one of Walker's cards with the quote, "Though the heart is broken, the steel is tempered." Courtney used the quote in his speeches. She said Courtney spoke "about getting you publicity when you return to this country and not to let you slip back quietly to a sedentary life at home." Mrs. Walker finished the letter telling her son that she "hoped he was recovering from another heart break ridge" and when it was over there would be "satisfaction in your heart, for the intestinal fortitude to stand up for your ideals."[1556]

(In 1962, the FBI developed a psychiatric profile of Walker and noted, "Walker appears to be a 'mama's boy'; that is, he is dominated by his mother. Walker's brother George Walker, Jr., a graduate of Massachusetts Institute of Technology appears to be in competition for their mother's affections."[1557])

The letter is a stunning piece of historical evidence. It places Walker, while still in Germany, in the spheres of both General Willoughby and Kent Courtney. General Willoughby was a true American hero from World War II, a top aide to the iconic General Douglas MacArthur, and a noted author. Walker, as a fellow officer in World War II and Korea, had to be impressed with the prospect that Willoughby would fly overseas to see him. The German-born Willoughby, as will be recalled, was one of the "trusted men" formerly in the military that General Pedro del Valle told Walker could be relied upon in the plotting correspondence that took place in 1962.

It's not known whether or not Willoughby and Courtney accomplished their plan to fly to Germany and meet Walker. On September 15, 1961, Phoebe Courtney wrote Walker, now stateside, and thanked him for the recent two-day meeting with her and her husband in New York. She told him they had met with Strom Thurmond on August 22, 1961. Afterward, they met with Congressman John Rousselot.[1558] Kent Courtney met Walker again in October of 1961 in New York City.[1559]

The case against Willoughby, as presented in Chapter Eight, included a letter from an anonymous source stating that Willoughby was involved in the assassination conspiracy. Substantial evidence suggesting General del Valle's involvement in the assassination was also presented. Kent Courtney was closely associated with Guy Banister and his operation that included Lee Harvey Oswald. As has been shown, Walker later became a close associate of both Willoughby and Courtney. Had those relationships not been formed, the assassination would have never happened, as we know it.

In August of 1961, Senator Strom Thurmond's support for the practice of bringing outside anti-Communist speakers to indoctrinate troops spurred harsh debate in the Senate. Senator Albert Gore argued with Thurmond stating it was not the military's function to "give political instruction to the American People . . . on essentially domestic political matters."[1560] The sheer number of anti-Communist speeches given by members of the military, many to those on the far right, also alarmed liberal Senator J. William Fulbright. Fulbright addressed his concerns in the *Congressional Record* on August 2, 1961, in what became known as the "Fulbright Memorandum." Fulbright expressed his strong belief in the principle of military subordination to civilian control. He was critical of the practice of military personnel making use of "extremely radical right wing speakers and/or materials, with the probable net result of condemning foreign and domestic policies of the administration in the public mind."[1561] The far right, led by Senator Thurmond, regarded the Fulbright Memorandum as an appeasement of Communism. In an August 10, 1961, news conference, President Kennedy sided with Fulbright's concerns stating, "This [military subordination to civilian control] is an important protection for our country, and is an equally important protection for the military."[1562]

As support for Walker grew, Congressman Dale Alford, a democrat from Arkansas, hosted Walker at a luncheon on Capitol Hill attended by retired military men and other congressmen. An informal "Justice for Walker" committee was created in Congress and headed by Senators Robert Dole, Strom Thurmond and John Tower.[1563] On August 28, 1961, Walker addressed a confidential Executive Session of Senator Eastland's Senate Internal Security Subcommittee.[1564]

On November 4, 1961, Walker—through a statement issued through the office of Senator Strom Thurmond—resigned from the army. Walker declared in his statement of resignation that he was leaving the army to "find other means of serving my country in the time of her great need, in order to pursue the dedication of a life time. To do this, I must be free from the power of little men who, in the name of my country, punish loyal service to it." He added that Communism was the enemy and that "[w]e employ its agents in the teaching professions, allowing them to work on the fertile minds of our youth seeking a champion to pit against a scapegoat. They infest our entertainment media. They long ago have infiltrated our government so that a scheme of subversion can be traced through three decades."[1565] The army knew of Walker's zealous anti-Communist views for many years and disclosed that Walker had tried to resign on August 4, 1959, but was dissuaded. No attempt was made to discourage his resignation after the "muzzling" affair.[1566]

Later, when asked about his resignation from the army, Walker stated, "I was never fed up with the army. I was fed up with the Kennedys."[1567] Years later, he gave another explanation for resigning—he said that he felt that during his interval assignment to Hawaii, that the Kennedys were planning another undeclared "no win war" in Vietnam and didn't want to participate in a war "with the Kennedys at my rear." He believed that he was sent to Hawaii as "an insult from the Kennedys to muzzle me and then want me to fight the Communists."[1568] Walker's later-revealed homosexuality may have been another reason for his resignation from the army, which would perhaps afford him more opportunity to pursue that lifestyle.

After his resignation, Walker noted, "Patriotic groups have called me from all over the country. From California to Florida to Chicago to New York, they all have wished me well and hope I will join in causes that are going on."[1569] The *Dallas Morning News* wrote a laudatory editorial about Walker and stated his case was "bungled" and he was treated "shabbily." An accompanying editorial cartoon depicted a uniformed Walker lying face down in the dirt with a large bloody dagger held impaled in the dirt at his feet. The dagger was engraved with the Soviet hammer and sickle symbol, and the words "HOME FRONT PINKOS" inscribed on the knife sleeve.[1570]

Phoebe Courtney wrote General Walker on November 4, 1961, after she had just learned of his resignation and told him that she was thrilled and it was "just as if war had been declared on the Soviet Union!" She told him, "Someone once said that in time of crisis God always provides a leader for the people. I firmly believe this, Ted, and believe that you are the man!"[1571]

On December 14, 1961, Stanley Latham, vice president of Hunt Oil Company, wrote Walker and told him that none of the world's great military leaders were so magnificent as when Walker said, "I have no fear and I give no quarter," at his speech in Dallas on December 12, 1961. He added, "You stood as the last best hope to provide the leadership this nation must have to steer its course back toward survival."[1572] H. L. Hunt wrote Walker on January 6, 1962, and told him he had a "[l]egion of potential followers who would welcome you as a new type of Commander and Chief." Hunt recommended that he use material from *Life Lines* transcripts as the basis for his speeches.[1573]

Walker summed up the "muzzling" case by saying "I was framed in a den of inequity represented by coexistence, 'no win', collaborating, soft-on-Communism national policy. This is the hidden State Department policy being implemented by Mr. Rusk and being withheld from public view. It was the policy I ran into head on . . . I have found a new freedom, uncensored and unmuzzled among a host of dedicated, patriotic and militant Christians, willing to fight for the cause of freedom, sovereignty, constitutional government and independence."[1574]

The "muzzling" affair catapulted Walker to national fame with his picture appearing on the cover of the December 4, 1961, cover of *Newsweek* magazine. The radical right had found a new and defiant figurehead—a knight in shining armor to replace his predecessors, the fading General Douglas MacArthur and deceased Senator Joseph McCarthy. As in the case of both McCarthy and MacArthur before him, H. L. Hunt praised and promoted Walker. On December 3, 1961, Walker appeared on the ABC national television show "Issues and Answers."[1575]

In 1961, Kent Courtney and his wife Phoebe published the book *The Case of General Edwin A. Walker, The Muzzling of the Military Who Warn of the Communist Threat* and *How the Appeasers Propose to Substitute Surrender for Victory.* The book was more of a broadside against the Kennedy administration and less about the "muzzling" case of Walker. The Courtneys, who only took three weeks to write the book, contended that the "muzzling" stemmed from a Communist directive issued by Moscow in December 1960.[1576] Referring to the new darling of the radical right, the Courtneys commented on Walker: "He's the one. Just wait till he tastes blood and the little old ladies start pawing him." The book further demonstrates the early ties between Walker and Courtney—a prominent figure in the New Orleans far right.[1577] In 1962, *Life* magazine called Courtneys' book "silly" and noted that the proceeds from its sale bought him a new station wagon. On the other hand, JBS member Congressman John Rousselot reviewed the book and stated, "You are commended for a forthright and accurate account of the viciousness of the drive against anti-Communists in the military."[1578]

Outraged by the way Walker was treated, Senator Strom Thurmond, at the urging of Billy James Hargis and the Christian Crusade, the John Birch Society, and other right-wing groups, urged citizens to write their congressmen and demand support of a congressional hearing on Walker's "muzzling" case. In response, Congress received 147,000 letters in three days. Hargis, like H. L. Hunt, felt Walker was presidential material. Hargis called him a "hero" and "a great man." Hargis wrote with adoration that Walker, "is a great American and the kind of patriot that I pray God will give us in the White House. He stands with the Patrick Henrys, the Henry Clays, the Abe Lincolns. He is a champion of Americanism, a genuine statesman."[1579]

On January 24, 1962, Strom Thurmond began Senate hearings to investigate Pentagon troop indoctrination and the "muzzling" practices of the military in a special subcommittee of the Armed Services Committee with Senator John Stennis as chairman. Thurmond claimed the "muzzling" was an example of a U.S. "no win" policy that kept them from winning the Cold War. Thurmond charged that the Pentagon was "muzzling" military leaders because they spoke out against Communism.[1580, 1581] As the hearing began, President Kennedy and Joint Chief of Staff Chairman General Lyman Lemnitzer announced that they backed the Pentagon policy of censorship.[1582] President Kennedy refused to allow the military to testify in the hearings.[1583] Thurmond called Kennedy's refusal "one of the most dangerous acts" ever committed by a president.[1584] President Kennedy, fearing Walker would become a *"cause celebre,"* banned television cameras and photography at the meeting.[1585] (It's worth repeating that a marine roommate of Lee Harvey Oswald told the Warren Commission that Oswald had written to Strom Thurmond in 1956.[1586] The author was unable to find the letter from Oswald in Thurmond's papers.)[1587] On February 8, 1962, General Walker accused President Kennedy of "gagging" the Senate military censorship inquiry and not doing everything he could to stand firm against Communism. Walker stated the "gag" placed the country in "dire peril."

Meanwhile, embarking on his career as the voice of the far right, on February 10, 1962, Walker spoke in Chicago before 5,000 people and ripped the United Nations as a tool of tyranny. Walker told the audience that his speech marked the beginning of his campaign for governor of Texas.[1588] On February 22, 1962, U.N. Ambassador Adlai Stevenson criticized "our angry men of the right wing"—a clear reference to Walker and the controversial John Birch Society that he was affiliated with. Then, on March 1, 1962, former Vice President Richard Nixon urged Republicans to get out of the John Birch Society.[1589]

On April 4, 1962, General Walker was called as a witness before the special Armed Services Committee. Flanking Walker at the hearings were his advisors Clyde Watts and Medford Evans. A former general, Watts was an old school chum of Walker from the New Mexico Military Institute—and served as his attorney. Medford Evans was a close associate of Guy Banister.[1590] (Their relationship dates back to at least 1958 when they spoke together at an anti-Communist gathering.[1591])

Medford Evans is an important figure in this story, having close ties to Guy Banister, H. L. Hunt, Kent Courtney, and practically every prominent member of the far right presented thus far. Medford Evans and Leander Perez spoke together at the Citizens' Council of New Orleans in 1963. In his speech, Evans called segregation "Christian, scientific, American and legal."[1592] Evans spoke to students and faculty members at Soule College in 1960, and said that Communism may fail but may also destroy other forms of government in the world before its own death.[1593] George Soule, head of the college—yet another Banister colleague, and chairman of the infamous New Orleans Congress of Freedom meeting in 1963—introduced him. Evans was the secretary of the Louisiana States' Rights Party when Kent Courtney ran for governor under the party banner in 1960. (When Courtney ended his bid for governor on the States' Rights ticket, he threw the party's support to Willie Rainach, who was running in the Democratic primary with Kent's brother, Cy Courtney.)[1594]

Medford Evans spoke at a Citizens' Council meeting with General Walker and Raymond Butler. In his opening remarks, Butler declared, "Throughout the pages of history there is only one third class race which has been treated like a second class race and complained about it—and that race is the American Nigger." Evans followed and introduced General Walker by saying: "The most important individual in the United States is General Walker."[1595] Evans was a writer for H. L. Hunt's *Facts Forum* from 1955 to 1959,[1596] as well as a Citizens' Council and John Birch Society leader, who wrote for their publications.[1597] Evans interviewed Walker for an article that appeared in the *National Review* on December 16, 1961. Walker stated in the interview that he intended to continue public speaking and assisting "patriotic Americans—first, last and always." Walker went on to say that he felt the U.S.-backed invasion of Cuba was mishandled and the forces were prevented from using all the weapons at their disposal.

General Clyde Watts spoke at the April 1963 Congress of Freedom in New Orleans, which was attended by Joseph Milteer, Guy Banister, and Kent Courtney, flying to the meeting on his daughter's wedding day.[1598] Watts, who was part Cherokee Indian, shared the same extreme views as his school pal General Walker. Watts became an anti-Communist while in the army when, in 1944, it was his job to tell the Nationalist Chinese that the U.S. was supporting the Communist Chinese. It was that event that led him to launch his personal mission "to awaken the U.S. to the Communist threat." "The Communists study and understand us. We must become more aware of them," he stated.[1599] Watts wrote an article, which was reprinted in the *American Mercury*, entitled "Strategy for Survival." (Representative Walter H. Judd first published the article in the *Congressional Record* on May 15, 1961.) Watts began the article stating "WE ARE AT WAR . . . War to the hilt between Communism and capitalism is inevitable."[1600] Watts later became a board member of the American Association for Justice, Inc. based out of Tulsa, with Rear Admiral John G. Crommelin and General Pedro del Valle, both identified by the FBI as members of the hardcore underground who plotted assassination at the Congress of Freedom and Constitution Party in 1963. The organization was started to come to the defense of "patriots."[1601, 1602]

Like Walker, Watts saw Communists everywhere, even in the adolescent comic magazine *Mad*. On October 9, 1961, the FBI noted that *Mad* sued Watts for calling it "The most insidious Communist propaganda in America today." Watts cornered an assistant director of the FBI, Alan H. Belmont, at a speaking engagement and asked him if the FBI had any material on *Mad* that he could use in his court battle. Watts told Belmont that he planned to have ex-Communists Herbert Philbrick and Matt Cvetic testify in the suit.[1603] General Walker called *Mad* "subversive" in 1959, and claimed it contained hidden meanings. Walker stated *Mad* topped Harvard on his list of pet peeves.[1604]

In 1975, Watts rose to the National Council of the John Birch Society and board of Liberty Lobby.[1605] Watts's name appeared on the letterhead of the John Birch Society along with John Schmitz and former vice president Spiro Agnew in 1975.[1606] Agnew had resigned the vice presidency in disgrace, later pleading "no contest" to charges of bribery and money laundering in the state of Maryland in a negotiated settlement. Schmitz became the presidential candidate of the American Party in 1972, and pledged that if he won he would offer the position of secretary of state to Dan Smoot and the Department of Justice or secretary of defense position to Clyde Watts.[1607]

At the April 4, 1962, meeting of the Special Armed Services Committee, with Evans and Watts at his side, Walker told the committee in his more than seven hours of testimony that dark forces of "collaboration and collusion" with Communism imperiled the United States. He aimed his barbs particularly at Adam Yarmolinsky, an aide to Secretary of Defense Robert McNamara, stating, "His connections with Communism have certainly been close and his activities have aided Communism."[1608] The fact that Yarmolinsky was a Jew and the son of Russian immigrants fueled Walker's attack. Walker stated that Yarmolinsky's father, Abraham, had had Communist connections and his mother had belonged to many Communist fronts.[1609] The *Dallas Morning News*, in an editorial, agreed with Walker, stating, "Walker hit the nail on the head we believe, in his charges against Adam Yarmolinsky, one of Secretary McNamara's aides."[1610] (After the Kennedy assassination, Walker regularly told his audience that Jack Ruby was a Jew whose real name was Rubenstein in an effort to demonstrate a Jewish-Communist link between Ruby and Lee Harvey Oswald.)

Walker told the Special Armed Services Committee that he was critical of the CIA, stating that they tailored their intelligence estimates to fit the State Department's preconceived policies.[1611] Walker declared that he was "a scapegoat of an unwritten policy of collaboration and collusion with the international Communist conspiracy." Walker said he was a victim of a "No win" policy in the government.[1612] He further stated that President Kennedy had been "prosecutor and judge" by directing the investigation and approving the army findings and that Walker should receive an oral admonishment.[1613] He said that Kennedy's undersecretary of state, Walt Rostow, had been in control of the operating arm of the CIA and was part of the country's "control apparatus." Walker declined to name Rostow as a Communist—or the State Department as Communist-influenced—but instead said, "I reserve the right to call them something else—traitors."[1614]

Walker presented himself poorly at the two-day hearing, misinterpreting the facts, and at times rambling incoherently. His hands shook and he frequently stumbled over words. Walker made no attempt to hide his ties to the John Birch Society. He argued before the committee that the Communists concocted the whole case against him. After the hearing, the conservative *National Review* changed their tune and described Walker's testimony as "pitiful" and that Walker was "consigned to history's trash can."

Nazi Commander George Lincoln Rockwell attended the proceeding and was ejected for refusing to remove a swastika lapel pin. Walker took out his angst from the ordeal by punching a reporter in the eye after he was asked to comment on Rockwell's appearance at the hearing.[1615, 1616] The press reported in September 1961 that Walker was "crazy" and might have a brain tumor.[1617, 1618]

The radical right was already incensed due to the administration's failure in the Bay of Pigs invasion early in Kennedy's tenure in office, which they felt represented his unwillingness to stand up to the Communists in Cuba. They blamed the failure of the Bay of Pigs invasion on President Kennedy for calling off air support for the operation. The far right felt the failure was deliberate, as were the administration's actions against men like Walker who did stand up to the Communists. Kennedy, responding to the accusation, denied it and told reporters that no U.S. air cover had been planned for the invasion—a claim backed by one of the leaders of the invasion.[1619]

Dallas Morning News editor Ted Dealey exemplified the contempt many in the South and on the right had for President Kennedy when he insulted Kennedy to his face at a luncheon he attended at the White House with nineteen other Texas publishers on October 27, 1961. Dealey told Kennedy: "We need a man on horseback to lead this nation and many people in Texas think you are riding Caroline's tricycle. The general opinion here of the grass roots thinking in this country is that you and your administration are 'weak sisters'." Another newspaper publisher responded to Dealey, "Ted, you're leading the worst Fascist movement in the Southwest and you don't realize that nobody else is with you."[1620]

Walker was defeated, but not finished, after his first battle with the Kennedy administration. He found new platforms to wage his war against the Kennedys in the emergent National Indignation Committee, the John Birch Society, the Citizens' Council, the Christian Crusade, and other far right groups.

General Walker and the Texas Governor's Race

As noted in the last chapter, H. L. Hunt promoted Walker's bid for governor of Texas as a stepping stone to the White House with the hope that Walker would defeat President Kennedy in 1964. When Walker announced he was running for governor on February 2, 1962, Senators Tower and Thurmond tried hard to dissuade him. Walker stated, "This is why I am in this race, to put the full strength of the governor of Texas into the fight against the dictatorial power of the Kennedy Administration and its controls in Texas."[1621] Walker pledged a campaign against "professional liberals" and he said he believed President Kennedy fit into that category.[1622]

J. Evetts Haley ran Walker's campaign and accompanied him to a speech in San Angelo, Texas, on March 1, 1962.[1623] On May 3, 1962, Walker addressed a crowd of about 500 in Dallas and upped the tone of his criticism of President Kennedy. Walker accused the Kennedy administration "of leading the nation into a totalitarian state," and foresaw "an end to free elections in the United States under United Nations military control."[1624]

Minutemen leader Robert DePugh told the author that he visited Walker at his Dallas home during the primary campaign. Walker asked DePugh to have his men kidnap him in a publicity stunt, which DePugh refused. Walker had planned to blame the kidnapping on the Communist conspiracy, in an effort to help his campaign.[1625] (Walker's intention of faking a serious crime to further his political agenda will be reconsidered later in a discussion of Lee Harvey Oswald's purported shooting at Walker.) During the primary campaign, prominent Congress of Freedom leader George S. Montgomery of New York wrote General Douglas MacArthur and asked him if he would make a personal appearance with Walker during the primary. MacArthur sent his regrets.[1626] Walker finished last out of a field of six in the May 5, 1962, Democratic primary. John Connally was the winner and went on to become the governor, and was wounded with President Kennedy on November 22, 1963.[1627] H. L. Hunt blamed Walker for the loss, saying that Walker "was too unresponsive to my suggestions."[1628]

General Walker and the National Indignation Convention

In 1961, reserve National Guard pilot Harry Rickenbacker became upset when he observed the training of five or six Yugoslavian pilots at Perrin Air Force Base in Sherman, Texas. (Yugoslavia, at that time, was a member of the Soviet Communist bloc.) He sent a letter of protest to Senator John Tower on September 27, 1961, calling the training "treason." The letter was reprinted in the *Dallas Morning News* and drew outrage from the far right. Tower's protests over the pilot training spawned a new far-right-wing group, the National Indignation Convention (NIC) that was led by Frank McGehee, a member of the John Birch Society. The inaugural meeting of the NIC (also called the National Indignation Committee) was held in October 1961. A telephone malfunction prevented Senator Tower from addressing the meeting from Washington.[1629, 1630] The FBI determined the John Birch Society was the "prime mover" behind the NIC and that Frank McGehee was an associate of General Walker.[1631, 1632] The NIC eventually promoted Walker's candidacy for governor of Texas.[1633]

General Walker became a principal speaker for the National Indignation Committee, which provided him with a new forum for attacking the Kennedy administration. The administration's provision of jets and pilot training to the Soviet bloc nation of Yugoslavia provided additional "proof," as Walker and the radical right saw it, that the Kennedys were further aiding the Communist conspiracy. The coincidence of the rise of the NIC and General Walker allowed Walker to resign from the army on November 4, 1961 and take his fight against Kennedy and Communism to the cities of America through the NIC.

Other prominent members of the hardcore underground highlighted in this work joined him in the NIC. On October 7, 1961, Walker spoke at a Miami, Florida, National Indignation Convention meeting.[1634] Kent Courtney was the planned speaker at the Dallas National Indignation Committee meeting on October 17, 1961.[1635] Tom Anderson and J. Evetts Haley, close associates of the H. L. Hunt family, were the featured speakers at the National Indignation Committee meeting at the Dallas Auditorium. At the event, Haley quipped, "Tom Anderson has turned moderate. All he wants to do is impeach [Chief Justice Earl] Warren—I'm for hanging him." (Warren was despised for his role in the *Brown* decision that outlawed segregation in the public schools.) The event featured a ten-minute talk via phone hook-up by Eddie Rickenbacker. Sidney Latham, H. L. Hunt's attorney, interviewed Rickenbacker, who stated that the U.S. should quit training Yugoslavian pilots and fire those responsible for the policy.[1636]

On November 8, 1961, a suggestion was made to Robert Welch that General Walker be given an active role in the management of the John Birch Society. Welch responded that Walker had been an enthusiastic member of the JBS before he left for Germany. Welch saw two drawbacks in Walker: 1) As a high-ranking military man he felt Walker did not have the inclination or temperament to handle the multitude of details required to run the organization; and, 2) From reports Welch had received, Walker was a poor speaker, was poorly organized and had a propensity to ramble. Welch wanted Walker to become more active in the Society, but wanted it kept a secret.[1637]

On November 13, 1961, the NIC denied it was backing Walker as a presidential candidate in 1964.[1638] The next day, Walker spoke at the Miami, Florida, National Indignation Convention meeting in the first speech of a planned tour with retired generals Albert Wedemeyer and Arleigh Burke.[1639, 1640] On November 15, 1961, Kent Courtney and Frank McGehee were the principal speakers at the NIC meeting in Miami Beach.[1641]

On November 15, 1961, Robert Kennedy blasted the National Indignation Committee and the John Birch Society in an address to the Associated Press Editors Association in Dallas. He criticized the groups for irresponsible charges against the government, Supreme Court and the president. He chided the John Birch Society, stating: "The John Birch Society has been looking for Communists. And only found one—President Eisenhower." Kennedy was referring to the claim of Robert Welch, founder of the JBS, who wrote in the "Blue Book" of the society that President Eisenhower was a "conscience agent of the Communist conspiracy." Outside Kennedy's speech, NIC protestors circled the building.[1642]

On November 18, 1961, Walker was invited to speak at the National Indignation Convention meeting in Los Angeles at the Hollywood High School auditorium with Rear Admiral Chester Ward and Harry Rickenbacker. The group planned to march and picket President Kennedy's speech at the nearby Palladium.[1643] In the president's speech, alluding to the Walker case and the rise of far-right extremism, he said, "You and I and most Americans take a different view of our peril. We know that it comes from without, not from within. It must be met by quiet preparedness, not provocative speeches."[1644] The FBI took note of Walker's planned speech and was concerned about reports that a crowd of 2,000 of his followers might march to the Palladium. The White House and the Secret Service were also notified of Walker's appearance and proposed demonstration.[1645] Others on the far right, important in this work that spoke at NIC meetings included Revilo Oliver and Tom Anderson.[1646]

Contrary to the radical right, the country at large was happy with President Kennedy's performance in office, giving him a whopping 78 percent approval rating in December

1961.[1647] On December 12, 1961, Walker spoke in Dallas at the "Texans Welcome General Walker Day" rally—the first speech after his recent resignation—where Texas governor Coke Stevens was the master of ceremonies. Walker declared in combative terms, "I know there is an organization behind the enemy's desire to destroy our freedoms and our hopes. I am a target for destruction. I have no fear and I give no quarter. I have drawn the battle line, which has only two sides."[1648, 1649] (Walker often made the claim that he was a "target for destruction"—his prediction seemingly came true when on April 10, 1963, someone shot a rifle though a window of his study. The Warren Commission determined the shooter was Lee Harvey Oswald.) *Time* magazine covered Walker's speech and noted, "Walker was visibly nervous, with his shaking hands and had a real facility for misreading passages from his 90 minute speech." *Time* dubbed him the "misfit in mufti."[1650] One Washington reporter commented, "By the grace of God he may be the worst speaker in the United States."[1651] After the speech, Dallas mayor Earle Cabell presented Walker with an honorary citizen award and a Stetson hat.[1652]

On December 17, 1961, Senate Democratic leader Mike Mansfield warned that "extreme right wingers" pose a great threat to the security and welfare of the United States, referring to Walker.[1653]

The FBI learned that on, December 29, 1961, a member of the National States' Rights Party traveled to a General Walker speaking engagement in Jackson, Mississippi, in an attempt to interest him in running for president on the National States' Rights Party ticket.[1654, 1655]

On January 3, 1962, General Walker addressed the New Orleans National Indignation meeting by a phone hook-up.[1656] Walker again spoke by phone hook-up to the NIC of New Orleans at Soule College on January 20, 1962.[1657] Walker made a speech at an NIC meeting in Odessa, Texas, in January of 1962, and appealed for the destruction of the United Nations—the speech was carried by long distance telephone to numerous cities.[1658, 1659]

In a January 8, 1962, Chicago speech sponsored by retired general Robert E. Wood, Walker asserted that the presidential "gag" placed the nation in "dire peril."[1660] He added, "We are not only in dire peril, but that the course of national leadership has involved deception and misrepresentation."[1661] (As noted in Chapter Eight, General Wood was mentioned in the June 21, 1962, letter sent by Walker to General Pedro del Valle noting that Wood had planned to attend their strategy conference.)

On January 11, 1962, Walker addressed a crowd of over 14,000 at the Los Angeles Sports Arena. Walker claimed "that there were Communists in every phase of American life—but not necessarily in key or effectual positions."[1662] (It will be recalled that Edgar Eugene "Gene" Bradley, whom Jim Garrison attempted to subpoena as part of his assassination investigation, had hoped to meet Walker during the Los Angeles engagement.)

Walker's speech on January 20, 1962, in New Mexico, was broadcast to seventy NIC meetings in thirty-eight states.[1663] A pamphlet for the meeting promoted Walker's "American Eagle Crusade For Truth."[1664] In March of 1962, George Soule of the New Orleans

NIC announced that the organization had passed a resolution demanding that the United States withdraw from the United Nations and move the U.N. off of U.S. soil. He said the U.N. "stands today before the bar of a non-Marxist opinion."[1665] Walker made it clear in his speeches that he saw the Kennedy administration turning the country into a totalitarian state, furthering a pro-Communist agenda dedicated to promoting the integration of the races and appeasement of the Communists in Cuba, Yugoslavia, and around the globe.

The hardcore underground of New Orleans was well represented in the New Orleans National Indignation Convention. George Soule—who was the director of the Congress of Freedom meeting in April 1963 attended by Joseph Milteer—was chairman of the New Orleans NIC.[1666] General Walker addressed the New Orleans NIC by closed circuit TV at a meeting held at Soule College.[1667] P. Cameron Terry, who also attended the 1963 Congress of Freedom meeting, was listed on the stationery of the New Orleans NIC along with Guy Banister, Gus LaBarre, and Hubert Badeaux, all who were linked to a hardcore underground associated with Joseph A. Milteer in the prior chapters.[1668]

Some of Guy Banister's files survived and were obtained by Jim Garrison. Banister kept a file on the NIC, 14-59, that contained a few of their newsletters from 1962 and 1963 and a transcript for a program narrated by Frank McGehee on Communism.[1669]

By 1962, the NIC had held 200 conventions, mostly in the South. The NIC demanded that anybody having anything to do with the training of the Yugoslavian pilots be fired. They demanded the impeachment of President Kennedy and dismissal of his cabinet.[1670] In 1962, a resolution to stop training Communist pilots was introduced in the Senate by John Tower and in the House by Bruce Alger and John Rousselot. Rousselot left Congress in 1962 and became a coordinator for the John Birch Society in California and joined the leadership of the national far right. (Evidence linking Rousselot and General Walker to the conspiracy in the assassination of the president will be presented later.)

Eventually, plane sales to Yugoslavia and Communist pilot training quietly ended, as did the NIC.[1671] Sue Eastman, the sister of NIC founder Frank McGehee, eventually took over the operation and moved it to Norborne, Missouri, in a merger with Robert DePugh's Minutemen organization.[1672]

General Walker and the Citizens' Councils

In the midst of his "muzzling" travails and just after he gained national fame from appearing on the December 4, 1961, cover of *Newsweek,* Walker found another venue to further wage his war against the Kennedy administration in the form of the Citizens' Council. He became a celebrity in the Council and energized the cause of the segregationists. On December 29, 1961, Walker spoke before the legislature in Jackson, Mississippi, beside Governor Ross Barnett. Walker said, "Three decades of Potomac Pretenders—New Dealers, Fair Dealers, Red Herrings, Co-existence artists, and U.N. One-Worlders New Frontiersmen—have conspired in the liquidation of our Constitutional government by, for, and of the people. They are buying you and selling the nation." Walker declared, "We are at war. You are infiltrated and your cause starts in every home, church, school, street corner, and public gathering. Man your weapons and attack! Our objective is to defeat the national pretenders and the professional power-mad politicians, and the Reds in every land." Walker's speech was filmed and shown on television as a part of the Citizens' Council Forum, and the Citizens' Council produced and sold a long-playing record album of the speech.[1673]

On December 29, 1961, Walker spoke before a crowd of 5,000 at a Citizens' Council "Crusade for Truth" meeting at the Jackson City Auditorium. One hundred leading Mississippi patriots called "Friends of General Walker" sponsored the speech, where Governor Barnett was in attendance.[1674] Governor Barnett, Representative John Bell Williams and Jackson Mayor Allen Thompson, along with a crowd of fifty supporters, greeted Walker at the Jackson airport.[1675]

The Dallas equivalent of the segregationist Citizens' Council went by the name of the Indignant White Citizens' Council, so as not to be confused with the non-political civic group who had adopted the name "Citizens' Council" years before. According to intelligence gathered by the Dallas Police Department, Bobby Savelle Joiner of Grand Prairie, Texas, formed the organization on July 20, 1963. (It's worth noting that Joseph Milteer visited "a patriot" in Grand Prairie on his cross-country trip prior to the Constitution Party meeting, as was noted in Chapter Seven.) Fifteen individuals in the Indignant group were identified by name, of which seven members were arrested carrying anti-Kennedy placards at the Dallas Trade Mart on the day of the Kennedy assassination. (Kennedy had planned to speak at the Trade Mart after his motorcade procession through Dallas.) One member of the Council, Robert Edward Hatfield, had been arrested at the scene of Adlai Stevenson's October 1963 address on the United Nations at the Dallas Memorial Auditorium. Hatfield was also a member of the John Birch Society and "General Walker's group."[1676] Three in the Indignant White Citizens' Council were members of the Ku Klux Klan, including the Dallas leader, Roy Elonza "R.E." Davis. (Davis, according to Willie Somersett, was one of the shooters in Dealey Plaza.)[1677] Bill Baker notified the Dallas FBI that an acquaintance of his, Joseph Noble Adams, had made various statements indicating that the Indignant White Citizens' Council was responsible for the assassination of President Kennedy. On that tip, Adams was located by the FBI, but told them he was an alcoholic and was intoxicated when he made the remarks.[1678]

General Walker attended the National Leadership Conference of the Citizens' Council in Jackson, Mississippi, on October 25–26, 1963, as a delegate from Texas.[1679] Roy V. Harris, Milteer's friend, was present at that conference. It will be recalled from the last chapter that Walker made ominous remarks during his speech, suggesting that a Communist might kill President Kennedy. Walker asserted, "It's interesting that the Communists killed first the people that helped them in their revolution. First! So we've got something to look forward to, ladies and gentlemen."[1680]

The Citizens' Council had an ally in the John Birch Society. JBS director Robert Welch told an audience on April 19, 1961, in Shreveport, Louisiana, that the JBS was opposed to forced integration. He added that the Communists "heavily influenced all major decisions in our government since 1941."[1681] Billy James Hargis was also a friend of the Citizens' Council and spoke before the New Orleans group on June 22, 1961.[1682]

Bulletin 7277, the U.S. Program for General and Complete Disarmament in a Peaceful World

In September of 1961, the State Department created Bulletin 7277, entitled "The United States Program for General and Complete Disarmament in a Peaceful World." The four goals set forth were: the disbanding of all national armed forces; the elimination of national arsenals of all armaments including weapons of mass destruction; effective means for enforcement under the principle of the U.N.; and the establishment of an effective operation of an International Disarmament Organization to insure compliance during the planning stages of the comprehensive plan for complete universal disarmament.[1683] President Kennedy signed on to the idealistic and futuristic proposal in Bulletin 7277 on September 25, 1961.

Although not intended to do so, the language of the bulletin invited the paranoid radical right-wing view that President Kennedy desired to disarm the United States as part of a one-world United Nations initiative. The program for disarmament, as presented, may have been one of the biggest mistakes of the Kennedy administration: the radical right saw the proposal as proof of Kennedy's desire to surrender to the Communist agenda. In August of 1961, John McCloy, Kennedy's chief disarmament advisor and principal negotiator for the program, admitted that the prospects for total disarmament were remote, stating: "We can not have it (disarmament) until we have a means of settling international disputes. But the emergency is so great that we must explore every avenue." He also doubted that the United States would get anywhere in the upcoming nuclear test ban talks in Geneva due to the Soviet Union intransigence.[1684] (John McCloy, Secretary of State Dean Rusk, and President Kennedy were members of the Council on Foreign Relations, and McCloy served as chairman of the Council from 1954 to 1970. McCloy was specifically listed as a target of assassination in the April 1963 Congress of Freedom meeting in New Orleans, as was noted in Chapter Five.)

Walker and his top aide Robert Surrey set up the American Eagle Publishing Company, the propaganda machine that printed Walker's most widely circulated pamphlets entitled the *Victory Purge* and *What is Counter Insurgency?* (It will be recalled that Surrey prepared the printing plates for the infamous "Wanted for Treason" poster distributed in Dallas before the assassination.) The *Victory Purge* was a critique of Bulletin 7277 from the State Department. Walker stated that Bulletin 7277 provided for: 1) placing all armed forces under an international organization—the U.N.; 2) placing all weapons under an international organization; and, 3) building only those weapons necessary for the internal police of the U.S. Walker accused the Kennedy administration of planning to place the U.S. military under United Nations control.[1685]

If Walker had been correct in his interpretation of the disarmament proposal, then it would have been treasonous. However, treason was not the intent of the proposal—or the president. Walker's bitter criticism of the Kennedy administration's disarmament plan was a central topic at every one of his speeches.

The American Eagle Publishing Company also served as the mouthpiece for Walker's organization "Friends of Walker," which he ran with volunteers out of his home. Outside his home, Walker erected a billboard that displayed right wing messages that he periodically changed. The press dubbed the home "the fortress on Turtle Creek."[1686] Nearby on Turtle Creek Boulevard stood a statue of Robert E. Lee.[1687]

Robert Morris, Walker's friend who later served as his attorney, summed up Walker's feelings on Kennedy's disarmament proposal by stating: "Walker has been a military man, a battlefield hero and he feels it would be disastrous for the United States to dissolve the army he served all his life, as our present policy provides for the years ahead."[1688] Morris was so disturbed by the disarmament bulletin that he resigned from his position as president of the University of Dallas so he could devote his efforts to work against it.[1689] On August 19, 1963, Morris announced the formation of the Defenders of American Liberties, an organization designed to defend members of the far right.[1690] Morris's ties to Guy Banister date back to 1956, when the two worked together on Senator Eastland's investigation into the "Soviet influence" in the integration movement. Banister and Morris were united again when both were participants of the Greater New Orleans School of Anti-Communism held in October 1961, where Herbert Philbrick and Cleon Skousen were part of the faculty.[1691] Morris testified in 1962, before the Louisiana Un-American Activities Committee, LUAC, about Communist propaganda entering the Port of New Orleans.[1692] (Banister was the chief investigator for LUAC, as was noted in Chapter One.)

National leaders of the radical right wing shared Walker's critical view of Kennedy's disarmament plan and the U.N. Kent Courtney said, in view of an increasing international crisis and the military draft and call up of the reserves in response to the Cuban crisis, that "disarmament just doesn't make sense to me!"[1693] H. L. Hunt called the disarmament act "a law and not a rumor." Hunt asserted three weeks before the assassination that "if the law were put in effect there may be no Air Force Academy, no West Point, no Annapolis, no private firearms—no defense!"[1694] Congressman Bruce Alger of Dallas said Kennedy was "unilaterally disarming the United States in a number of ways . . . by following all of the points in disarmament document 7277 where the U.S. would turn over most of the military to the United Nations."[1695] Robert Morris summed up the far rights' feelings on the United Nations, "I simply say the U.N. is controlled by our enemies."[1696]

On May 5, 1962, Joseph Grinnan, Chairman of the Dallas Volunteers for Walker for Governor took out a half page ad in the *Dallas Morning News*, declaring: "STATE DEPART-MENT PLANS TOTAL U.S. SURRENDER TO THE UNITED NATIONS!" in reference to Bulletin 7277; endorsers of the ad included NIC leader Frank McGehee, Robert Surrey, Joseph Grinnan, and dozens of others.[1697] The Louisiana legislature also viewed State Department Bulletin 7277 on disarmament literally and with grave concern.

On May 22, 1963, the Louisiana state senate passed a House-approved resolution asking Congress to take note of the disarmament publication. They went on record against the U.S. turning its armaments over to any other nation or international body. The measure was sponsored by Senator Harold Montgomery, Leander Perez's colleague, who was a leader in the free electors movement. One opponent of the measure argued proponents were misinterpreting the publication.[1698]

Louisiana senator and staunch segregationist Allen Ellender, who was friendly to the radical right, viewed the nation's disarmament policies more reasonably. He wrote back to a constituent who feared the policy and told him that the Arms Control and Disarmament Agency "was not created for the purpose of disarming our country, but instead to seek ways and means of gradually obtaining agreements for world disarmament, in an effort to promote world peace and security."[1699]

The U.N. had long been despised by the far right, who were violently opposed to the admission of Communist nations to the organization. They felt the U.N. was a sanctuary for Communists on U.S. soil and often cited the Alger Hiss case as an example of the Communist influence in the U.N. Hiss served as the secretary-general of the United Nations Charter Conference in San Francisco in 1945, and was accused during the House Un-American Activities Committee hearings in 1948 of secretly being a Communist agent while in government service. (Hiss was later convicted of perjury—but not of espionage.) The far right dubbed the U.N. "the house that Hiss built." They likened the U.N. to a Trojan horse—a vehicle housing surreptitious Communist activity in the heart of New York City—which would lead to more conflicts such as the Korean War. The Korean War was a U.N. action, which in the U.S. was officially known as a "conflict," since the U.S. never declared war. The conflict was waged principally by the U.S., with the aid of U.N. forces from member nations. The failure to gain victory and the resultant stalemate was perceived by the far right as planned and Communist-U.N. directed.[1700]

Walker, Pedro del Valle, and others on the far right firmly believed that President Kennedy was preparing the U.S. for a takeover by the U.N.—and repeatedly made a point of discussing it. Seldom, if ever, did General Walker fail to mention the purported U.N. takeover of the U.S. in his speeches. That belief, as much as any other, was a key reason for their violent opposition to President Kennedy and his cabinet. The unfortunate, utopian wording of State Department publication Freedom from War, #7277 left such an interpretation plausible, although unintended.

Conclusions

General Walker's first battle with President Kennedy, the "military muzzling," began in April 1961—just months after Kennedy's inauguration—with Walker's admonishment and, later, his resignation. The "muzzling" saga culminated a year later in the Senate hearings in April 1962 held by right-wing senators who supported Walker.

Walker's disdain for the national media and the government, and his belief in an "internal conspiracy" dated back to just after the Second World War. Like generals MacArthur and Pedro del Valle, he was critical of President Truman's policy of stalemate in Korea.

Following Walker's reluctant command of the federal troops enforcing integration in Little Rock in 1957, he began to emerge amongst the ranks of prominent national leaders in the radical right wing, forging ties with George Benson and Edgar Bundy, and with Robert Welch in 1959 at the creation of the John Birch Society.

Walker rocketed to national fame in the period from April 1961 to April 1962 through the "muzzling" affair, culminating with his appearance on the cover of *Newsweek* magazine in December 1961. Kent Courtney and General Willoughby formed a liaison with Walker early in his muzzling travails, a seminal event in the assassination story. (Of course, Courtney was a close friend of Guy Banister who multiple witnesses saw with Lee Harvey Oswald in 1963, and an allegation that Willoughby was involved in the assassination conspiracy was presented in Chapter Eight.)

After resigning from the army, Walker found a ready-made, national platform—in the National Indignation Convention, John Birch Society, Citizens' Council, and other far-right-wing venues—to voice his disdain for President Kennedy's policies and to lengthen his shadow. He became a knight in shining armor who invigorated the radical right wing that had deteriorated in the wake of the Joseph McCarthy-era debacle.

He rapidly became acquainted and aligned with prominent far-right extremists across the country, including important figures in the assassination story such as Kent Courtney, and H. L. Hunt. A close associate of Guy Banister, as well as H. L. Hunt, Medford Evans came to Walker's aid during the Senate hearings. Clyde Watts—who would later be named to the secret high military command of the assassination-plotting Council of Statehood and Congress of Freedom—provided Walker with legal counsel. As will be discussed later, Watts also played a role in covering up evidence in an alleged and likely General Walker-Jack Ruby relationship.

Walker's hopes for high public office were dashed with his loss in the Texas governor's primary in the spring of 1962. However, in the end, Walker gathered a formidable national hardcore following and rose to a leadership position in the national far right. Walker became a prominent figure in the Citizens' Council and an ally in their fanatical war to maintain segregation in the South. One of his earliest speeches during his rising prominence was before the Mississippi legislature at the side of Governor Ross Barnett in December 1961. The alliance forged by these two leaders of the segregation movement and the far right would be a critical factor in the Walker-Barnett showdown with President Kennedy over his forced integration of the University of Mississippi in September 1962 (which will be detailed in the next chapter). Throughout the 1960s, Walker shared the dignitaries' table at the Citizens' Council meetings with prominent figures associated with Joseph Milteer, including Revilo Oliver, Leander Perez and Roy Harris.

President Kennedy's introduction of the Program for General and Complete Disarmament in a Peaceful World outlined in Bulletin 7277 was, by itself, reason enough for the radical right wing to declare war on his administration. (The far right, as noted in the Congress of Freedom chapter—Chapter Five—believed the Council on Foreign Relations was the "secret government" that ran the United States.) The idealistic plan, which proposed—at some time in the future—the placement of all of the world's armaments and armed forces under United Nations command, was considered an outright sign of treason and a handover of the United States to the United Nations. Unfortunately, the language of the program as presented in the Bulletin allowed for such an unintended interpretation.

Walker's opinion that Kennedy's disarmament plan was treasonous provided more than enough motive to plot insurrection and assassination. Adding to the motive were the "muzzling" affair and the president's policies, as well as events that occurred in the first year of his administration, including the failed Bay of Pigs invasion, the Berlin crisis, the confrontation with the Soviets in Germany, the Supreme Court's outlawing of school prayer, and proposals aimed at facilitating African American voting rights.

Walker's declaration, in December 1961: "We are at war . . . Man your weapons and attack! Our objective is to defeat the national pretenders and the professional power-mad politicians, and the Reds in every land"—would turn out to be more than idle rhetoric. Walker's threats of violence and insurrection against the government would materialize in incidents in 1962 and 1963 that will be described in the next two chapters.

CHAPTER THIRTEEN

GENERAL WALKER, 1962: THE ROAD TO INSURRECTION AT OLE MISS

*The South is armed for revolt. These white people will accept another
civil war knowing they are going to lose.*
– William Faulkner, 1956

Geneˌral Walker, although suffering defeats in the "muzzling" affair and in the Texas governor's race in the spring of 1962, remained steadfast and undeterred in his quest to save the country from the perceived-Communist menace and the Kennedys. The FBI took an interest in Walker's activities—but did not take a keen one until after his arrest in October 1962 at the insurrection at the campus of the University of Mississippi. The FBI received complaints about Walker's extremist tirades and followed newspaper stories on his speaking engagements. Unfortunately, as in the case of Joseph Milteer and informant Willie Somersett, there were no known informants who were very close to Walker or his group. Fortunately, there exists important inside—and implicating—documentation outside of the FBI in the personal papers of Walker's colleagues, General Pedro del Valle, J. Evetts Haley and Tom Anderson.

Practically every action taken to advance the rights of black Americans by civil rights leaders or the Kennedys was countered by an opposing action by the segregationists. For example, the American Nazi Party's Hate Bus and George Singelmann's Freedom Bus North countered the Congress of Racial Equality's Freedom Riders bus campaign in 1961. (Leander Perez and the Banister group were behind both of those segregationist's schemes.) The court-ordered desegregation of the University of Mississippi and resultant violent resistance by the segregationists—led by Walker—is another of many examples. Accordingly, significant events of the segregationists, integrationists, and actions of the Kennedys will be presented to illustrate the point. After General Walker resigned from the U.S. Army, he took command of a hardcore underground army engaged in fomenting a second Southern insurrection.

General Walker, 1962

General Walker expanded his propaganda machine in 1962 when he became the military editor of the national magazine, *American Mercury*. A group called the Legion for Survival of Freedom that had ties to Willis Carto and Liberty Lobby were the owners of the openly anti-Semitic magazine.[1701] The venerable H. L. Mencken was, much earlier, the editor of the magazine, which was once highly regarded. A sampling of contributing writers in Walker's time reads like a who's who of the radical right wing and includes Pedro del Valle, Tom Anderson, Harold Lord Varney, Medford Evans, Revilo Oliver, Carl McIntire, Edward Hunter, Kenneth Goff, Robert Welch, Hilaire du Berrier, and General Stratemeyer.[1702]

H. L. Hunt wrote Walker on January 6, 1962, and told him that if he ran for governor as a Democrat he would never attain an office higher than senator and would not make any worthwhile contribution toward saving freedom. Hunt felt that Walker's chances of becoming president in 1964 would be better as a Republican. He further suggested that Walker's staff use material found in *Life Lines* in his speeches.[1703]

Carl McIntire wrote Walker on January 22, 1962. He recalled that when they had met in Jackson, Walker told him, "I am a militant soldier and I am a militant Christian." McIntire asked Walker to speak at his church along with a 1,000-person choir, and offered to pay him whatever he asked. Delegations from different patriotic organizations were expected to attend.[1704] (As we shall see in Chapter Nineteen, a close associate of David Ferrie stated that McIntire was connected with the assassination conspiracy.)

On February 2, 1962, Walker entered the Texas gubernatorial primary and embarked on a cross-state, as well as national, speaking tour. On the same date, an informant told the FBI that he had spent considerable time talking to Walker and listening to his political philosophy and it was his personal opinion that Walker was mentally ill.[1705] The charge was made often.

Left: General Walker's speech in Dallas on December 12, 1961, was dubbed by an admirer as "Truly one of the greatest American speeches of all time." The speech was transcribed and distributed. Right: Walker's campaign flier for his bid for Texas governor. The first plank in his campaign platform was a pledge to defend state sovereignty. Source: Edwin A. Walker papers, Dolph Briscoe Center for American History, University of Texas at Austin

From January 29, 1962, to February 2, 1962, the Christian Crusade's National Anti-Communist Leadership School met in Tulsa, where General Walker delivered a special message to the group. Speakers included General Willoughby, Revilo Oliver, Myers Lohman, Edward Hunter, and Matt Cvetic—who worked for the FBI impersonating a Communist. Benjamin Gitlow and Barb Hartle, "former Communists" who testified against alleged Communists in the House and Senate Communist inquisitions, were also guest speakers.[1706] On February 3, 1962, Walker warned the crowd that the nation was "in dire peril."[1707]

On February 7, 1962, President Kennedy stated that the John Birch Society did not have a place in either the Democratic or Republican parties. However, he declined to comment on General Walker's candidacy for governor of Texas when asked.[1708]

On March 4, 1962, General Walker said in a campaign speech in Kerrville, Texas, that his campaign couldn't be conventional because he was a target of the Communist conspiracy.[1709] (Although it did not impact his campaign, his prophecy became realized when the self-professed Marxist, Lee Harvey Oswald tried to kill Walker in April 1963—or so the Warren Commission claimed.) Around the same time, he asked Minutemen leader Robert DePugh to kidnap him so he could blame it on the Communists and enhance his campaign for governor. (The incident will be described further later.)[1710]

When the Young Americans for Freedom (YAF) asked Walker to speak before them, Senator Tower tried to discourage them. Barry Goldwater gave the YAF, an ultimatum stating he would not attend the meeting if Walker were a speaker. They eventually withdrew Walker's invitation, but their snub of Walker drew harsh criticism from Phoebe Courtney in the *Independent American*.[1711, 1712] On March 7, 1962, the Young Americans for Freedom program, entitled "Rally for World Liberation from Communism" was broadcast on the radio without General Walker. Senators Barry Goldwater, Strom Thurmond and John Tower were speakers. A banner which was unfurled from the balcony declared "We Want Walker."[1713]

On March 13, 1962, Walker colleague Robert Morris, the former chief counsel for Eastland's Senate Internal Subversive Subcommittee, spoke before the Louisiana Un-American Activities Committee chaired by James Pfister and counsel Jack N. Rogers of the Louisiana legislature. (As was noted in Chapter One, Guy Banister was the chief investigator for the committee.) Morris told them that less literature was coming in from the Soviet Union because the Communists in the U.S. were publishing their own literature. "If you are looking for literature advocating the overthrow of the U.S. government," Morris declared, "you are looking for the wrong thing. The Communists are interested in the gradual encirclement of America." He also said, "Words are bullets. Selling the *Daily Worker* [the Communist Party newspaper] on the streets of New York is as important as manning machine guns at Stalingrad." Morris asserted that civil liberties must be forgotten when dealing with political propaganda.[1714] On May 22, 1962, Robert Morris planned to speak at the Orleans Club in New Orleans on the topic of "One, Two, Three—surrender."[1715]

Also on March 13, 1962, after a two-month intensive investigation, reporter Fletcher Knebel wrote an article for *Look* magazine on the national far right, entitled *Rightist Revival: who's on the Far Right?* He interviewed or wrote about a number of key members of the far right underground that are subjects in this work, including General Walker, Dan Smoot, H. L. Hunt, Robert Welch, Kent and Phoebe Courtney, Billy James Hargis, General Charles Willoughby, and Edward Hunter. The article concluded that the resurgence of the radical right by early 1962 was fueled largely by the failure of the U.S.-backed invasion of Cuba that occurred shortly after President Kennedy took office. In addition, he noted the far right's disappointment over the stalemate in the Korean conflict, the 1954 Communist partition of Indochina, the Soviet Union's bloody repression of the Hungarian revolt that left thousands dead in 1956, and Communist inroads in Laos, Vietnam, and the Congo.[1716] Struck by the fanaticism of the radical right that he witnessed, Knebel wrote the book *Seven Days in May* about a dissident general who attempted to assassinate the president, which was published in September 1962.[1717] General Walker reportedly inspired the book. An acclaimed Hollywood movie was also made and bore the same title.

Knebel had spent three days with Kent and Phoebe Courtney in December of 1961 gathering material for the book. After it had been released, Phoebe Courtney wrote to Walker on September 20, 1962, and told him to immediately get a copy of *Seven Days in May*, which she called "dynamic." She told him, "I am convinced the only reason Fletcher Knebel wrote it was because of you. Right-Wing generals put the Left-Wing in a quivering, quaking frenzy of fear." Referring to the dissident military men in Knebel's book, she told Walker it was "the part I believe you are destined to play in the future survival of this nation!"[1718]

On March 16, 1962, Walker spoke before a crowd of 4,000 in Houston and declared, "Now is the time for a change—a change in all echelons of administration that have not been assisting America and its future." Another speech was planned in Houston that week, but the "Win with Walker" committee declined to announce Walker's arrival plans "for security reasons." (Walker often claimed the Communists were out to get him.)[1719] On March 20, 1962, Walker spoke in Dallas and was critical of the Eisenhower and Kennedy administrations. Walker held up the State Department disarmament pamphlet and said it was a blueprint for putting American weapons and personnel in an international force under the United Nations. He said the plan was to "de-Americanize the American soldiers, then U.N.-ize them."[1720]

The March 1962 "Secretive Meeting" and Early Seeds of Insurrection

On March 20, 1962, Billy James Hargis, leader of the Christian Crusade, held a "secretive meeting" by invitation only in Washington, D.C. John Rousselot, Bonner Fellers, Edward Hunter, Benjamin Gitlow, General Charles Willoughby, Frank McGehee, and Arthur Blazey attended, as was noted in Chapter Eleven.[1721] The secretive meeting was suggested at the We the People meeting in September 5, 1961, by Billy James Hargis, who was president of the organization.[1722]

At the meeting, the League of Right Wing Organizations was organized by John Rousselot.[1723] Hargis refused to divulge to the press any of the names in the secret fraternity at the meeting but their identities were eventually discovered. Among their aims were pushes to outlaw the Communist Party and end the army practice of "muzzling." Interestingly, Hargis was also on the Advisory Board of the John Birch Society.[1724] Over one hundred people, representing seventy-five right-wing groups attended the "secretive meeting."[1725]

Edward Hunter told the crowd that a CBS television program entitled *Thunder on the Right* attacked the far right, adding that an article written by Mike Newberry also claimed that anti-Communist military generals were secretly plotting a revolution. Furthermore, according to Hunter, the article contended that General Walker had retired to lead the revolution and set up a Fascist dictatorship. The television program reportedly began by showing Minutemen engaged in war games on the bank of the Mississippi River. Then the television program immediately switched to footage of General Walker to convey the idea that he was the leader of the plot. Hunter objected to the premise of the show, stating that nothing could be further from the truth and that CBS was promoting the Communist line.[1726]

The allegations that the far right was planning a revolution are not at all far-fetched when the individuals at the "secretive meeting" are examined. Many of them had ties to the assassination conspiracy and/or the conspirators. Willie Somersett learned from Joseph Milteer that Hargis was raising funds to finance the hardcore underground. Milteer had been at the September 1961 We the People meeting, where Hargis spoke, and tape recorded him speaking at another meeting as noted previously. (Edward Hunter who spoke at the "secretive meeting" was an associate of Guy Banister, and will be discussed later.)

On June 1, 1962, Edward Hunter wrote to General Walker and told him there was an obvious need for guerilla training. As chairman of the Anti-Communist Liaison Hunter explained that the group did not have members, only "contacts," which is what Hunter also called Walker. Hunter asked Walker for the names of other potential "contacts" in his area. Walker responded to Hunter's letter on June 16, 1962, and told him about the disarmament plan to place U.S. soldiers under the U.N.[1727]

Pedro del Valle, in a letter to General Walker on June 18, 1962, wrote that Bonner Fellers—who attended the "secretive meeting"—was one of his "trusted men," referring to his "plan of action . . . before we resort to violence" which was referred to in Chapter Eight. Arthur Blazey, who attended the meeting, was also at the April 1963 Congress of Freedom meeting and the October 1963 Constitution Party meeting (attended by Milteer) where assassinations were discussed. Arthur Blazey, as noted before, described General del Valle as "one who has not retired from the battle to serve this country from such enemies as the United Nations and current administrator collaborators who want to strip our Republic of all defense arms and resources in order to subject our people to one-world tyranny." A California FBI informant, as we shall see, alleged that John Rousselot, who also attended the "secretive meeting" was a part of the assassination conspiracy.

Rumblings of insurrection began in 1961 (as was noted in Chapter Eight) and are worth repeating here. Just after Hargis suggested holding the March 1962 "secretive meeting" during the September 5, 1961, We the People meeting, nationally syndicated columnist Drew Pearson wrote in a November 21, 1961, column warning "of a movement inside the armed forces and reservists not unlike the French army which tried to topple President de Gaulle." He noted that Pedro del Valle "[had] already come close to urging armed insurrection," threatening armed resistance if the traitors were not voted out. Pearson cited Major Archibald Roberts and General Walker as troublemakers and noted that Hilaire du Berrier (a Kent Courtney and General Walker associate) had supported the French Army's insurrection against President de Gaulle. Pearson's sources are unknown but, as noted in Chapter Eight, Pedro del Valle wrote a letter to the National States' Rights Party in 1961, stating: "when a free people find their elected servants following a destructive course of action regarding the Constitution, the people must take effective action to restore same by taking the matter into their own hands and forcing the traitors out of power." On September 13, 1961, del Valle wrote to Robert Welch and stated, "The time has come for action, Treason sits enthroned in the seats of Power, and treason will soon land us in the Red One Worlder's Paradise unless we take steps to prevent it, and do it now and with decisiveness."[1728]

After the "secretive meeting," the far right continued to claim that the Kennedy administration was furthering the Communist agenda. In a February 8, 1962, column, Billy James Hargis stated that the president's disarmament policy was a major Kremlin goal.[1729] The Kennedys, on the other hand, continued to deny there was any significant threat from Communists within the country. On March 24, 1962, Attorney General Robert Kennedy characterized the American Communist Party as a "Political organization of no danger in the United States."[1730] On March 30, 1962, Walker spoke to the Press Club of Fort Worth and told reporters he could never support President Kennedy's reelection "unless he did a 100 percent reversal in the next two years."[1731]

The discontent of the far right led to sporadic acts of violence. On May 18, 1962, *The Jewish Voice* reported: "A fantastic terrorist plot involving the bombing of a local editor's home, the alleged planned assassination of prominent Jews here [in Miami] among them Dade County State Attorney Richard A. Gerstein, and police counterintelligence work in which undercover policemen deliberately planted simulated 'dynamite' sticks in front a synagogue, was revealed here this week in Criminal Court." The paper was referring to the bombing of the home of the editor of the *Miami Herald*. Willie Somersett came forth and identified the three men involved, who were accused of being in the Minutemen and having an interest in George Lincoln Rockwell's American Nazi Party.[1732]

Meanwhile, the segregationists lost ground on several fronts. On April 3, 1962, United States district court judge Skelly Wright ordered the desegregation of New Orleans schools in grades one through six, which was a huge defeat for Southern segregationists.[1733] In response to the crisis, Leander Perez traveled to Washington, D.C., to confer with Senator Eastland.[1734] On April 10, 1962, Robert Kennedy urged removing literacy tests that deprived thousands of black Americans of the right to vote in federal elections. He promoted the move at a subcommittee hearing on a bill that would make a sixth-grade education adequate to meet the literacy requirements to vote.[1735] The bill was met with stiff resistance by Southern segregationists, and the Senate voted to delay passage for the year.[1736] Along with President Kennedy's order banning racial discrimination in federally aided housing (on November 20, 1962, but first proposed in September of 1961), removal of the literacy test was a further encroachment on the Southern institution of segregation and was looked upon as further motive for insurrection.[1737]

On April 12, 1962, Walker told a crowd that he promised "more thunder on the right before the country goes down to defeat."[1738] On April 16, 1962, Leander Perez was ex-communicated from the Catholic Church in New Orleans after his bitter opposition to the diocese-ordered desegregation of Catholic schools.[1739] On the following day, Major Archibald Roberts gave an off-the-cuff speech to the Daughters of the American Revolution without the requisite Pentagon clearance.

The Pentagon had earlier refused to preapprove a written copy of the speech which Roberts had submitted. (Roberts it will be recalled, had been General Walker's aide in Germany.) In the speech, Roberts questioned the loyalty of Los Angeles Mayor Sam Yorty, claiming he had Communist ties in his background. Roberts claimed that assistant Secretary of State Williams had leftist leanings. He was also critical of *Overseas Weekly*. The army suspended Roberts on April 19, 1962, pending an investigation, which earned front-page headlines in the press. Roberts blamed the army's actions on his association and support for General Walker.[1740, 1741] Roberts later claimed that he had the materials to back up his leftist charges against Yorty and Williams and hoped he would be called to the "muzzling" hearings.[1742] Roberts, like generals Pedro del Valle, Clyde Watts, and Edwin Walker would become a member of what Willie Somersett called "the high military command" that plotted assassinations at the end of 1962 in the Council of Statehood/Congress of Freedom. On April 28, 1962, Roberts was stripped of his army commission and returned to civilian life.[1743] Walker and Roberts at some point in time had a falling out.[1744] Nonetheless, Roberts devoted much of his radical-right-wing energies to heading the Committee to Restore the Constitution, which he founded in Colorado. When the author contacted Roberts in 2000, he was either confused or did not wish to cooperate.[1745]

On April 22, 1962, Walker asked President Kennedy to turn over the Texas National Guard to the state, rather than place them under command of the United Nations—as he alleged was the president's aim. Walker stated: "I consider Kennedy's plan to place all armed forces under the United Nations to be a complete and final refutation of the Constitution of the United States."[1746]

On May 2, 1962, Senator James Eastland spoke in the Senate against the Kennedy administration's proposal that would allow those with only a sixth grade education to vote. He stated that the Supreme Court, in forty-six out of seventy recent decisions, had upheld "the position advocated by the Communist Party" or its sympathizers.[1747]

On May 3, 1962, General Walker spoke with J. Evetts Haley and Frank McGehee at a National Indignation Committee convention and said the Kennedy-Johnson administration was leading the country into a totalitarian state and that he saw an end to free elections in the U.S. under United Nations military control. He lost the primary in the governor's race the next day.[1748, 1749] Tom Anderson and J. Evetts Haley had been in Walker's election headquarters the day before the election. Afterwards, Anderson called the defeat quite a blow.[1750] After Walker's defeat in the governor's race, the number of public speaking engagements diminished.

The wife of Mississippi governor Ross Barnett attended the May 1962 meeting of the Women for Constitutional Government in Dallas, which welcomed visitors with "Indignant Women of America, Welcome to the Indignant City of South-Dallas." Mrs. Barnett was the center of attention after her husband's struggles with the federal government over segregation. General Walker entertained the group at his home; Frank McGehee had addressed the group earlier.[1751] Mrs. Barnett was a member of Mary Cain's Women for Constitutional Government. (Cain, as noted in prior chapters, was a principal in the Congress of Freedom and Constitution Party and served on the board of Liberty Lobby.)[1752]

On May 5, 1962, Robert Kennedy declared that the advancement of civil rights at home was "as important as the race to outer space . . . ."[1753]

In the June 6, 1962, issue of Billy James Hargis's *Weekly Crusader*, General Walker was quoted as saying that President Kennedy, Secretary of State Dean Rusk, and Defense Secretary Robert McNamara were "even worse than Communists." He called them part of the "hidden apparatus."[1754]

On June 13, 1962, Lee Harvey Oswald, along with his wife and daughter, returned to the United States and were assisted at the port in Hoboken, New Jersey, by Spas Raiken of the Travelers Aid Society. Raiken was the secretary-general of the American Friends of the Anti-Bolshevik Bloc of Nations—a fanatically anti-Communist, pro-Fascist, and pro-Nazi organization.[1755] General Charles Willoughby was closely associated with the organization. The Oswalds flew to Fort Worth, Texas, and stayed with Lee Harvey's brother Robert Oswald. Soon after their return Lee Harvey continued to adopt the posture of a Communist and wrote the Soviet Embassy in Washington to ask for Communist literature. He began corresponding with the Communist Party U.S.A. and the Socialist Workers Party and later subscribed to the *Worker*. During the same period of time, the Louisiana Legislature approved the Leander Perez-directed Communist Control Act that meant any leftist organization aligned with a Communist like Lee Harvey Oswald could face decades in jail and huge fines. James Pfister, who was the head of the Louisiana Un-American Activities Committee (LUAC), sponsored the act. Pfister and Guy Banister (who served as LUAC's chief investigator as noted in Chapter Nine) had worked together in the anti-Communist effort since 1958.

On June 19, 1962, Oswald called Peter Gregory, a petroleum engineer who was born in Siberia, and asked him for a letter attesting to his ability to read and speak Russian. On June 26, the FBI interviewed Oswald about his stay in the Soviet Union. In mid-August, Oswald and his family moved into a one-room apartment. His wife became acquainted with the openly-anti-Communist Russian community through Peter Gregory, and later met George de Mohrenschildt (whom the Office of Strategic Services felt was a Nazi sympathizer during World War II). During that period of time, Oswald began to beat his wife and she moved out of their apartment on two occasions. This means that, in Fort Worth in 1962, Oswald wrote away for Communist literature at the same time that he socialized with the anti-Communist Russian émigrés who were his only known friends.[1756]

On June 17, 1962, President Kennedy urged Congress to act to improve the lot of black Americans and adopt a limited civil rights bill that would facilitate black voter registration and extend the Civil Rights Commission.[1757] That same day, the Supreme Court ruled against school prayer and Bible reading in public schools. Both decisions particularly infuriated those in the Southern "Bible belt."[1758]

The dark, plotting letters between generals Walker and Pedro del Valle were presented in detail in Chapter Eight and will be briefly recounted here.

A June 18 letter from del Valle to Walker, the first in the existing correspondence between the two, was a reply to a letter Walker had sent del Valle, but Walker's first letter was not among del Valle's papers. In the letter, del Valle wrote, "We have a formula, a plan of action, the very last hope before we resort to violence. It is therefore of the utmost importance that you, and several other retired officers who are informed, keep in touch, for the time is exceedingly short. I am sending copies to Stratemeyer, Bonner Fellers, General MacArthur, and various and sundry other flag and general officers whom I absolutely trust."

On June 21, Walker wrote to del Valle and expressed the urgent need for a strategy conference and suggested a secluded place in Dallas. Walker stated that retired generals Willoughby and Stratemeyer could not come because of their health but retired general Robert Wood would definitely attend. On June 25, del Valle told Walker—with regards to the strategy conference—that it was important to determine who could be relied upon. He suggested Charles Willoughby and other former military men (who are of no known importance in this story but were noted in Chapter Eight). It should be mentioned that all of the aforementioned generals were associates of H. L. Hunt. Unfortunately, there is no record of the strategy meeting, or if one was held.

On July 4, 1962, Alabama governor George Wallace asserted that "the duty of the South [was to] repudiate the Washington dictators."[1759] The entire South had a stake in seeing that Ole Miss not be integrated.

On July 7, General Walker sent a telegram to the Governor's Conference in Hershey, Pennsylvania, stating that the government had offered the armed forces and all U.S. weapons to the U.N. and thereby abrogated the Constitution.[1760] On August 3–5, 1962, Walker spoke in Tulsa at the Fourth Annual National convention of the Christian Crusade, with John Rousselot, Billy James Hargis, and General Willoughby; "former Communist" Karl Prussian was also a speaker. Hargis presented Rousselot with the Statesman of the Year Award. (From August 19 to 26, the Christian Crusade's World's Fair Congress was held in Seattle at the time of the Seattle World's Fair. "Former Communist" Benjamin Gitlow was a speaker with Hargis.[1761] "Former Communists" like Prussian and Gitlow were favorite speakers at the public meetings of the far right, even though many "former Communists" were like Herbert Philbrick, who had impersonated Communists to inform on them.)

An informant told the FBI that, during a Minutemen meeting on July 28, 1962, Robert DePugh, the national leader of the organization, stated that he had been in Dallas a few weeks prior and had met Robert Welch, General Walker, Slobodan Draskovich, and Frank McGehee of the John Birch Society. The five men had tentatively agreed to form a combined organization known as "Citizens of the Republic." Their target was the American news media—they planned to force newspapers to print a petition they called "Redress of Grievances." According to DePugh, this was to "Open a crack in the high-Red wall of fact manipulating news media."[1762]

In August of 1962, Lee Harvey Oswald subscribed to the *Worker*, a publication of the Communist Party, U.S.A., and tried to initiate other dealings with the party—but they were not particularly responsive. He informed them of his activities in Fair Play for Cuba Committee.[1763]

On August 22, 1962, would-be assassins sprayed French President Charles de Gaulle's car with bullets. He was not injured.[1764]

As noted in our discussion of Walker's correspondence, on September 20, Walker wrote del Valle and told him he had not heard from Admiral Crommelin, who was expected to convene a meeting that Walker and del Valle would attend. Walker proposed that ten or twenty senior officers "in this cause" meet in Tennessee or Texas for at least four days, along with "top cause civilians," for a half day for briefings on "their beliefs and capabilities." Crommelin was a particularly insidious racist and was close to Joseph Milteer, and FBI documents noted that he was a party to the assassination plots that emerged at the 1963 Congress of Freedom.[1765] Walker agreed to pay for the expenses of the attendees, except for airfare. On September 22, 1962, del Valle replied to Walker, saying he expected to have "names and pictures . . . of all our enemies within." The clear implication is that the names and pictures of the enemies were of those targeted for assassination as later revealed at the 1963 Congress of Freedom meeting. Far-right-wing publisher Frank Capell, who worked out of Staten Island, New York, and was close to Pedro del Valle, may have been the individual who supplied "names and pictures" to del Valle. Capell published the names and biographies of people he considered were part of the Communist conspiracy, often accompanied by a photo.[1766]

Willie Somersett told the FBI—according to FBI documents dated March 12, 1963—that "[t]he inner group reportedly is in the process of obtaining photographs, addresses, and description of individual names within this report so that, on the day that the selection of the assassin had been made, all available pertinent information as to the habits and so forth of these individuals will be given and directed to the assassin who has been selected by the inner circle." The assassinations were to begin in 1963, when President Kennedy was expected to place the U.S. government under the United Nations. Members of the high command of the Council of Statehood were to pick the assassins from among their members, and also their targets.[1767]

Therefore, based on Walker's and del Valle's correspondence and the FBI reports from Somersett, it's likely that the ambitious assassination plots eventually revealed at the 1963 Congress of Freedom meeting originated as early as September 1962—and were masterminded by generals del Valle and Walker.

It will be recalled that del Valle told Walker the meeting with former military men would have to be postponed for personal reasons. He told Walker that Ted Jackman could get him the names of anyone he wished, suggesting at least that Walker was drawing up a list of those to be assassinated. Jackman was a violent associate of Joseph Milteer, who advocated armed resistance. (Willie Somersett noted that Jackman was one of the actual shooters in Dealey Plaza as was noted in Chapter Eight.) Jackman was at the 1963 Congress of Freedom meeting in New Orleans and spoke, telling attendees that there was a plot between the Kennedy administration, Khrushchev, and Castro to train guerillas as Communists to be used against the United States. Jackman said that when the guerilla activity commenced he would advocate fighting the U.S. Army, if needed.[1768] Somersett noted that Jackman, Mary Davison, and others constituted the "high command" of the Council for Statehood who—when the time came—would order the assassinations revealed at the Congress of Freedom meeting.[1769]

There is no existing correspondence between Walker and del Valle from the period from June 25 to September 20, 1962, which suggests the letters were removed from del Valle's personal papers, likely by del Valle himself. During that three-month period of sparse accounting of Walker's activities or whereabouts, it is reasonable to assume—based on the June and September 1962 correspondence between Walker and del Valle—that Walker was networking and organizing a cadre of former military men and civilians in a far-right-wing underground for the purpose of insurrection, or as del Valle put it, "a plan of action, the very last hope before we resort to violence." On August 15, 1962, for instance, Walker wrote to Medford Evans and told him he had just returned from speaking three days in New York and three in Boston. He met with Robert Welch and signed autographs for his staff.[1770] "The very last hope" may have left by September 1962, when Walker publicly surfaced from his three-month near absence, leaving only "violence" as a consideration. On September 13, 1962, Walker appeared at a meeting of Lampasas County (TX) ranchers, where he stated that President Kennedy was "a Boy Scout in outer space." J. Evetts Haley, a close associate of the Hunt family was present at the meeting.[1771]

In late 1962, Willie Somersett reported to the Miami police and the FBI that generals Pedro del Valle, Edwin Walker, and Clyde Watts, along with Major Archibald Roberts, were the military advisors or "high command" of the Council of Statehood that used the Congress of Freedom as a front group in 1963. In November, in Palm Beach Florida, the name Council for Statehood was officially adopted for the group. At that same time, Somersett revealed the group's ambitious plans to assassinate large numbers of individuals in the Council on Foreign Relations, Jewish figures, and individuals in business and industry. A high-ranking inner circle, which had access to large amounts of money, would name the time and place for assassinations to begin. In the Council for Statehood FBI documents, Walker's name appears but once: as a member of the Council for Statehood military advisors.[1772, 1773] The FBI referenced the existence of other documents relating to General Walker—which were not found in the documents obtained by the Freedom of Information Act—that the author has not seen.

The Walker-del Valle correspondence lends credence to the allegations made in late 1961 and early 1962 by Drew Pearson, Mike Newberry, and CBS television that the far right was contemplating a revolt against the government—and that Walker was going to lead it.

James Meredith and the Fifth Circuit U.S. Court of Appeals

The day after President Kennedy's inaugural address on January 20, 1961, James Meredith, an African American, sent a letter of request for an application for enrollment to the then all-white University of Mississippi, affectionately known as "Ole Miss," in Oxford, Mississippi. Meredith received an application, but when he was unable to fulfill the requirement of having five letters of recommendation from Ole Miss alumni, the University curtly responded that he would not be considered. Meredith relayed the rejection to the Civil Rights Division of the Justice Department under Attorney General Robert Kennedy, as well as to the local FBI. Meredith asked the NAACP for assistance and, on May 31, 1961, filed a suit in U.S. District Court in Meridian, Mississippi, claiming race discrimination. At about the same time, the Congress of Racial Equality's Freedom Buses rolled into Mississippi, further heightening racial tensions in the state. The matter was decided on December 12, 1961, and Judge Sidney Mize ruled that Meredith had not been denied admission because of his race.

After graduating from high school, James Meredith had enlisted in the air force in 1951, just after President Truman desegregated the U.S. Armed Forces in 1948. He was honorably discharged in 1960, and then registered at the all-black college Jackson State in Jackson, Mississippi, where he majored in political science. Meredith had discussed the idea of enrolling at Ole Miss with his friend, Mississippi NAACP leader Medgar Evers, who had encouraged him, which led to his initial dismissal.

On January 12, 1962, the U.S. Fifth Circuit Court of Appeals in New Orleans ruled that the requirement of having five letters of recommendations from Ole Miss alumni was unconstitutional. On February 3, 1962, the case was referred back to Judge Mize's Mississippi District court, and the case was reheard. Mize again ruled that Ole Miss was not racially segregated.

On June 25, 1962, Federal Judge John Minor Wisdom, of the Fifth Circuit Court of Appeals, ruled that Meredith was denied admission solely on the basis of his race. Fellow Fifth District judge Ben F. Cameron issued four injunctions to Wisdom's order. The matter went to the Supreme Court, where Justice Hugo Black—who was in charge of oversight of the Fifth District Court—vacated the injunctions on September 10, 1962, so that Meredith was legally free to register, at which time Judge Mize ordered Meredith's immediate admission to Ole Miss.[1774]

Less than a year later, on June 12, 1963, Meredith's friend in the NAACP, Medgar Evers, was murdered by a white segregationist.

Ross Barnett, Guardian of the White Southern Way of Life

Ross Barnett was sixty-two years old when he became governor of Mississippi in 1960, and the Meredith dilemma and the violence that followed fell directly on his shoulders. Barnett was a primitive, bitter racist like his fellow Mississippian and friend Senator James Eastland. Barnett's father had fought for the Confederacy in the Civil War, and his horse had been shot from beneath him at the battle of Shiloh. Later, after the siege of Vicksburg, he had walked back to his home.[1775]

Joseph Oster, Guy Banister's former partner in his detective agency in the 1950s, told the author that Barnett and Banister were friends.[1776] Barnett, like Banister, was a stalwart supporter of the Citizens' Council from its inception and owed his election to the governor's office to them. Barnett often used metaphors for war and violence in his speeches advocating the preservation of segregation. In 1961, Barnett and the Citizens' Councils braced for the possible invasion of federal troops to enforce the court-ordered integration of Ole Miss. (Barnett had a close relationship with many prominent figures in the Citizens' Council of Louisiana and other states.) While running for Mississippi governor, Barnett spoke with Banister and Perez crony Willie Rainach at a rally in Shreveport, Louisiana, on February 27, 1959.[1777] At a January 1960 South Carolina Citizens' Council meeting, Barnett declared "that continued separation of the races is vital if we are to preserve the greatness of America." Roy V. Harris, Milteer's friend, appeared with Barnett who promoted the free electors scheme.[1778] On January 4, 1960, Rainach was appointed an "Honorary Colonel" on Ross Barnett's staff, for helping with his 1960 gubernatorial campaign.[1779]

Ross Barnett quoted his friend Senator Eastland, saying that the civil rights plank in the 1960 Democratic Presidential platform "could have been written by the Communists in Moscow."[1780] Eastland denounced the civil rights plank in the platform, saying that it was worse than the acts of "the carpetbaggers who infested the South after the War Between the States." Barnett called the plank "repulsive" and "obnoxious."[1781] Barnett addressed the New Orleans Citizens' Council on March 7, 1960, and asserted, "To win this life-or-death fight, we must start with a total mobilization of all our resources." He touted the Mississippi Sovereignty Commission, whose duty it was to protect the state from "encroachment thereon by the Federal Government." He was encouraged that Louisiana was forming a Sovereignty Commission under the direction of Willie Rainach, a close Banister friend.[1782] The Mississippi Sovereignty Commission recommended Guy Banister as a source for intelligence on the civil rights movement, and Banister applied to work as an investigator for the Louisiana Sovereignty Commission. Barnett declared, "My friends, the only way we can win this fight is to defeat the enemy—destroy them before they destroy us. The left wing in this country must be utterly crushed, and that's just what we intend to do . . . ."[1783]

Governor Barnett urged the formation of a free electors campaign at a New Orleans Citizens' Council meeting on March 7, 1960, where Leander Perez introduced him. William Simmons of the Jackson (MI) Citizens' Council, a key advisor to Barnett, was also present.[1784] Barnett vowed to defend segregation in 1960, stating, "Nobody wants violence but red-blooded Southerners should not turn aside from a fight when such principles are involved—a fight to preserve what we know is right."[1785] He added, "Ross Barnett will rot in jail before he will let one Negro ever darken the sacred threshold of our white schools."[1786] He proclaimed further, "Friends I am a Mississippi segregationist—and proud of it. . . . We must separate the men from the boys! We must now identify the traitors in our midst! We must eliminate the cowards from our front lines! You did not elect me governor to bargain away your heritage in a smoke-filled hotel room!"[1787, 1788]

Kent Courtney is one of a number of individuals from New Orleans tied to Oswald and/or the Banister operation who were associates of Governor Barnett. On March 26, 1960, Courtney was in Jackson to discuss the states' rights movement with Governor Barnett.[1789] Courtney organized a "Solid South" rally in Jackson, Mississippi, on May 6–7, 1960, where

Dan Smoot and Tom Anderson were the planned speakers. Senator Lyndon Johnson was the principal target of the rally, due to his support of civil rights measures.[1790]

Ross Barnett spoke at a drive to organize the Southern states in "Southern Unity" in Jackson, Mississippi, in July 1960. He led Mississippi's defiance at the Democratic National Convention in 1960, and gave their electoral votes to Senator Harry F. Byrd, instead of John F. Kennedy. Barnett attacked Robert Kennedy for using federal marshals to protect the Freedom Riders in Montgomery, Alabama.[1791]

In December 1961, the Mississippi Citizens' Council in Jackson announced the formation of a Minutemen-type militia throughout the South to combat integration. Their purpose was to gather on short notice to protest against "any invasion of our institutions."[1792] Joseph Milteer, a Minutemen and Citizens' Council stalwart, mentioned a number of times in his correspondence that he made visits to Jackson, Mississippi, but unfortunately it is not known with whom he met.[1793]

The Coming Fury

Certain that the federal courts would order the admission of James Meredith to the University of Mississippi, Governor Barnett enlisted the aid of Citizens' Council leader William J. "Big Bill" Simmons who had long been an ally of Barnett's war against integration. Simmons's passion for the preservation of segregation in Mississippi, and his power to control politicians so that he could ensure tough measures to maintain the Southern institution made him the Mississippi equivalent to Leander Perez, who was a close associate of his. Author William Doyle, who wrote a riveting account of the Meredith-Ole Miss affair in his book *An American Insurrection,* said that Simmons was Barnett's "de facto secretary of war" and his senior advisor, strategist, and speechwriter. Simmons was a key participant in strategy conferences during the weeks before the Ole Miss riots, and also directed the Mississippi Highway Patrol during the riots.[1794] Simmons was Barnett's representative at Ole Miss and stayed nearby at the Alumni House during the crisis.[1795] Doyle wrote, "On the subject of race, it was Bill Simmons, not Ross Barnett, who ruled Mississippi."[1796]

Simmons also had early ties to the national far right; on December 4, 1960, Simmons was invited to address the American Coalition of Patriotic Societies in Washington. Also to appear on the program with Simmons were General Charles Willoughby and Revilo Oliver.[1797, 1798] Barnett had ties to Wally Butterworth, another important figure in the far right, who—as noted—was at the October 1963 Constitution Party meeting in Indianapolis with Joseph Milteer and Willie Somersett, where he spoke of plans to kill President Kennedy. Butterworth stated in a letter that he talked with Barnett in 1963 and received "a fine letter" from him."[1799]

The FBI had investigated William Simmons in 1942 and learned from a physician—who reportedly treated Simmons as a "psychopath"—that he was disgruntled with the U.S. and Great Britain because they failed to realize his potential as an intelligence officer. The FBI learned from another source, in 1955, that Simmons was close to Nazis in Europe, and had been discharged from the Navy as a security risk.[1800] Simmons frequently spoke at Greater New Orleans Citizens' Council meetings beginning in the 1950s, which proves his close ties to the New Orleans hardcore underground.[1801] When Hubert Badeaux was named a director of the South Louisiana Citizens' Council on January 5, 1960, Simmons and Willie Rainach were named as lifetime honorary members of the Council.[1802] (As has been noted, in 1956, Badeaux, serving under the authority of assistant superintendent of the New Orleans police Guy Banister, was grooming an individual to infiltrate leftist organizations—a person who fit the description of Lee Harvey Oswald.) Badeaux was also a featured speaker at a Citizens' Council meeting in Jackson.[1803]

Simmons predicted that President Kennedy would never dare risk enforcing the integration of Ole Miss, since surely the result would be insurrection, massacre, and occupation that would require tens of thousands of federal troops. Simmons reasoned that, if a bloody showdown ensued, the result would be the withdrawal of federal troops and a victory for segregation.[1804] He made a grave miscalculation.

On September 1, 1962, Walker wrote Kent Courtney and—in reference to the Mississippi situation—told him, "If Kennedy wins this one, it may be the critical issue of the century."[1805]

On September 13, 1962, as the showdown with the federal government over Meredith's admission to Ole Miss was looming, Barnett threw down the gauntlet in a statewide radio and TV address. Barnett declared, "I speak to you as your governor in a solemn hour in the history of our great state—in a solemn hour indeed in our nation's history. I speak to you now in the moment of our greatest crisis since the War Between the States. In the absence of Constitutional authority and without legislative action an ambitious Federal Government, employing naked and arbitrary power has decided to deny us the right of self-determination in the conduct of our Sovereign State. . . . We must either submit to the unlawful dictates of the Federal Government or stand up like men and tell them 'NEVER' . . . . No school will be integrated in Mississippi while I am governor!"[1806]

Leander Perez sent a telegram to Barnett, stating, "Congratulations on your patriotic, statesman-like declaration of interposition for the State of Mississippi against the ranks of the usurpers of ungranted federal power over your state university."[1807] The concept of interposition was a contrivance, with roots going back to Thomas Jefferson, that purported to exempt states from federal mandates which were objectionable to them. Later, a federal Judge in the Meredith case called the concept of interposition, *"Alice in Wonderland* stuff."[1808]

Guy Banister orchestrated the picketing by Citizens' Council members of the Fifth Circuit Court of Appeals from September 25 to October 2, 1962. New Orleans Police Captain Presley Trosclair observed Delphine Roberts on September 28, 1962, carrying a sign reading, "Gov. Barnett, do not agree to any face saving compromise with Kennedy Bros., Have that showdown. Interposition will work."[1809]

President Kennedy, expecting the possibility of trouble at Ole Miss, in accordance with federal law, had the U.S marshals at his disposal to enforce the court-ordered admission of James Meredith. Robert Kennedy had used the U.S. marshals before to protect the Freedom Riders, who were attacked by segregationists in Alabama in 1961 (as described in Chapter Three). Joseph A. Milteer's friend, Kenneth Adams, was behind the attack. Seeking to avoid confrontation, Attorney General Robert Kennedy called Governor Barnett on September 15, 1962, in an attempt to work out Meredith's planned enrollment. Barnett told Kennedy what he envisioned happening was that a small group of U.S. marshals would appear for Meredith's registration attempt. He would be refused, and the whole affair would continue in the courtroom.

On September 20, Meredith made his first attempt to register; a crowd of nearly 2,000 greeted him with chants of "Go home, nigger." Non-student segregationists were spotted among them. Meredith met face to face with Barnett—who had been recently made temporary university registrar—who refused his admission.[1810] Barnett read to Meredith the proclamation of interposition and told him that, under it, he refused the federal order to admit him.[1811] Meredith left, and a confrontation was avoided. In turn, the Fifth District Court found Governor Barnett in contempt.

That same day, according to an FBI memo, the FBI learned that Robert Surrey departed Dallas in General Walker's station wagon for Jackson, Mississippi. J. Evetts Haley departed Dallas with Walker's secretary at the same time. On September 21, 1963, while the FBI was keeping tabs on Walker, they learned from a source, "that it was common knowledge that the general opinion of individuals who knew Walker felt he was mentally deranged."[1812] Walker kept in touch with Haley during the week of September 24, 1962. The same memo reported that the FBI learned from a former Walker employee, Dave Boggs, that Walker got his financial backing from J. Evetts Haley, H. L. Hunt, and Clyde Watts.[1813] The groundwork was being laid for Walker's arrival at Ole Miss.

Joseph Milteer's associate, United Klans of American leader Robert Shelton, declared, "This could be another War Between the States." Shelton told his supporters that if the integration of Ole Miss were successful then the segregated schools of Alabama would be next. Shelton put the Klan on "standby alert" and told them to be prepared to man their weapons and travel to the university in Oxford.[1814]

Leander Perez was the principal speaker at the National Citizens' Council meeting in Montgomery, Alabama, on September 22, 1962, that was (suspiciously) closed to the public. Other speakers were Roy V. Harris, George Singelmann, and Robert Patterson of the Jackson, Mississippi, Citizens' Council. At the meeting, a resolution was adopted supporting Ross Barnett.[1815]

On September 24, 1962, Leander Perez appeared at the Barnett contempt hearing in the federal courthouse in New Orleans. He was greeted by a number of picketers carrying anti-integration signs and small flags along the Camp Street side of the old post office, as well as in the corridors.[1816] Video footage from the Mississippi State Archives shows Perez leaving the court proceedings with a look of disgust. The FBI learned that Guy Banister had organized the pickets. As usual, Delphine Roberts and others carried signs bitterly critical of President Kennedy.[1817]

On September 25, 1962, Governor Barnett told Robert Kennedy about a scheme he had concocted to save face. In a tape-recorded phone conversation, Barnett told the attorney general that he wanted all the marshals to pull their guns and point them at him. He would then step aside and allowed Meredith to register. Robert Kennedy at first agreed and told him he would send twenty or thirty armed marshals, and the head marshal would pull his gun. Barnett countered that only one gun would embarrass him in front of the anticipated surrounding crowd. In turn, Barnett gave his reassurances that the state police would prevent any violence.

Robert Kennedy decided his next move would be to register Meredith on September 25, 1962, in Jackson, at the state office building across from the governor's mansion—rather than in Oxford. As Meredith and the marshals attempted to register there, Governor Barnett headed across the street from the mansion to meet them with an entourage of aides, highway patrolmen, and legislators. In a moment of comic relief, Barnett surveyed Meredith and his all-white assemblage and asked, "Which one of you is Meredith?" Again, Meredith was refused admission. Barnett was served a summons for civil contempt by the Court of Appeals, but he refused to take it. Robert Kennedy called Barnett that night, after learning of Meredith's rejection, and sternly notified him that Meredith would attend classes at Ole Miss in the morning.[1818]

In New Orleans, Jackson Ricau told a South Louisiana Citizens' Council meeting, "what happens in Mississippi with regard to this issue will affect the solemn sovereignty of Louisiana and that of every other state."[1819]

Also on September 25, General Walker, while in Dallas, called for massive resistance if federal troops were sent to Mississippi. He declared: "Now is the time to be heard; 10,000 from every state in the Union." The Pentagon declined to comment on Walker's call. Referring to his role in enforcing integration at Little Rock in 1957 with the 101st Airborne, Walker stated, "The last time I was on the wrong side. This time I am on the right side and I will be there." When asked if he was suggesting that the volunteers going to Mississippi carry arms, he replied, "The administration has indicated it will do whatever is necessary to enforce this unconstitutional action. I have stated that whatever is necessary to oppose that enforcement and stand behind Governor Ross Barnett should be done." Regarding the possible deployment of federal troops, Walker asked, "Would they be under the United Nations flag?" That same evening, Guy Banister's close associate, Louis P. Davis sent Walker a telegram pledging "ten thousand from Louisiana alone under your command." Willie Rainach urged volunteers and Governor Jimmie Davis to go to Mississippi to protect Governor Barnett.[1820]

Barnett and his Citizens' Council advisors had already chosen General Walker to command the Southern Resistance Army to combat what they felt would be the inevitable use of force by the Kennedys used to enroll James Meredith into the University of Mississippi. Citizens' Council leader and Barnett's "secretary of war" William Simmons predicted that a bloody showdown would end the federal attempt to enroll Meredith. Governor Barnett's advisors in the Citizens' Council influenced and energized Simmons heavily—among them were key individuals in the Louisiana Citizens' Council tied to the Guy Banister operation. Barnett waffled on his plan of action during the crisis and "was in rebellion one moment and then again not, depending on whom he was talking to."[1821]

Revealed, here, for the first time, on September 26, 1962, General Walker wrote an audacious, threatening, letter to President Kennedy, a copy of which was found in the personal papers of his friend, Tom Anderson, by the author. In the open letter, Walker blasted Kennedy for his inaction in Cuba and for the crisis in Berlin with the Soviet Union. He accused Kennedy of assisting our enemies in Cuba and allowing a breach of the Monroe Doctrine. He criticized what he called the "centralized police state methods being used in Mississippi," which he felt were a collaborative effort with the current Soviet influence in Cuba. He accused Kennedy of being blackmailed by Cuba, and warned the president that if he did not take aggressive measures against Cuba then "a volatile and dangerous public opinion will reflect its angry mood toward losses to Communism throughout the entire world" and "such a mood could rebel in a repulsive repudiation" of his accommodation of the Communists.[1822] Walker's letter to the president, in some ways, resembles the warnings issued by the first Continental Congress in 1774 to King George III of England in the Declaration of Rights and Grievances that preceded the Revolutionary War. Walker's statement that "dangerous public opinion will reflect its angry mood" and that a rebellion could ensue was written just four days before he led the rebellion at Ole Miss—and the timing was not a coincidence. The infamous "Wanted for Treason" flier, printed by Walker's aide Robert Surrey, and the mocking "Welcome Mr. Kennedy to Dallas" newspaper ad sponsored by Walker associates Joseph Grinnan, Nelson Bunker Hunt, and Larrie Schmidt published on the morning of the assassination may have also served as Declarations of Grievances that preceded the president's murder on November 22, 1963.

On Wednesday, September 26, 1962, James Meredith was turned away from registering again, this time by a show of force—Klansmen from Louisiana and Alabama had joined the crowds.[1823] One observer noted, "There were many scary people around who had come to see the show, armed with hunting rifles, shotguns, hatchets and bricks." Citizens' Council leader William Simmons surveyed the situation. Ross Barnett called Robert Kennedy and begged him not to continue with the efforts to enroll Meredith. Kennedy told Barnett that if he did not comply with the federal order then a judge would issue orders for his arrest.[1824] Senator Eastland proclaimed that the next few days would determine if "a judicial tyranny as black and as hideous as any in history exists in the United States . . . ."[1825, 1826] Barnett pledged to keep his vow to go to jail rather than desegregate, noting that after the Civil War three Confederate governors were confined as prisoners in Georgia.[1827]

On September 26, 1962, Edward Fields of the National States' Rights Party, an associate of Joseph Milteer, sent a telegram to Barnett, telling him he was "ready to issue a call to our thousands of members to rendezvous" in Jackson. Fields added, "Let's show the entire world how far the white man will go to stay white." Kenneth Adams, Milteer's friend—and bomber of the Freedom Bus in Alabama—wired Barnett that several hundred Klansmen were on standby waiting for Barnett's call to protect the sovereign state of Mississippi.[1828] That day, General Walker announced by telephone on a Shreveport, Louisiana, radio program, "It is time to make a move . . . we have listened and we have been pushed around by the anti-Christ Supreme Court. It's time to rise. To make a stand beside Governor Ross Barnett at Jackson, Mississippi. He is showing the way. Now is the time to be heard. Ten thousand strong from every state in the nation. Rally to the cause of freedom . . . Bring your flag, your tent and your skillet." He added, "I have been on the other side in such situations in a place called Little Rock, and I was on the wrong side. This time I will be in Jackson, Mississippi, on the right side."[1829, 1830]

A few days after Walker's radio address, the Kennedy administration warned that Walker could be held in contempt of court if he interfered with the integration of Ole Miss.[1831] Walker called for a volunteer force to go to Mississippi "when and if the president of the United States commits or uses any troops, federal or state, in Mississippi." A legislative leader for Governor Barnett warned him that "[i]t was highly possible that a gun battle would erupt between federal authorities and state officials." General Walker was asked if he had talked to Governor Barnett about his plans, but only commented, "I've been talking to a lot of people in Mississippi." He added, "Lots of people are waiting for me, they're already going to Mississippi from California."[1832]

On Thursday, September 27, 1962, Barnett warned Robert Kennedy that "hot-headed" people might start shooting and that he needed time to disperse them. Barnett declared, "There is liable to be a hundred people killed here." The FBI learned that thousands of volunteers from across the county were prepared to join the insurrection. The climate became increasingly dangerous, and Kennedy called off the day's registration attempt while arranging for military support.[1833] Milteer associate Emmet Irwin of the New Orleans Citizens' Council wired President Kennedy urging him to avoid the "great blunder" of sending troops to enforce the integration of Ole Miss, noting that Eisenhower's action in 1957 at Little rock was "clearly illegal." Jackson Ricau of the South Louisiana Citizens' Council urged Governor Davis to send the Louisiana State Police to assist Governor Barnett.[1834]

On September 27, 1962, Phoebe Courtney wrote Walker and told him that she learned from the Cuban Student Directorate that underground sources in Cuba reported that the Russians were in Cuba and planned to build a long-range missile base.[1835]

On Friday, September 28, the Fifth Circuit Court of Appeals ordered Barnett to enroll Meredith by October 2 or face fines of $10,000 per day.[1836] Eleven Mississippi congressmen wired President Kennedy warning him, "The power to save human blood, even human life, is in you hands, Mr. President. A holocaust is in the making."[1837] Lieutenant Governor Johnston warned that if federal marshals tried to push through a cordon of state troopers at Ole Miss, "25 or 30 persons would have been killed." George Soule, a Milteer and Banister associate, acting as a representative of the New Orleans National Indignation Committee, telegraphed Robert Kennedy asking him to "call off all attempts to subdue Governor Ross Barnett and the state of Mississippi." Soule told the attorney general to tell his brother to blockade Cuba, instead. That night, General Walker noted growing support for his call for volunteers stating, "Thousands are already on their way here."[1838]

President Kennedy declared, "The federal government will see the order of the federal court presently outstanding will be maintained and enforced." He added, "Mr. Meredith will be registered." In response, Barnett ordered the "citizens" forces back on to the campus.[1839, 1840] A Los Angeles FBI informant told the bureau that one hundred armed fighters pledged to Walker had left for Oxford. Fifty volunteers from Orange County, California, were reported to have already left for Oxford on September 28. A telegraph was sent to Governor Barnett, urging him to "Hold fast and pray. We are in route to stand beside Gen. Edwin Walker in the defense of the sovereign state of Mississippi. Your fight is all America's fight."[1841] Louis P. Davis, who headed up the Gentilly Parish Citizens' Council outside of New Orleans, wired Walker, "You called for 10,000 volunteers nationwide for the Ole Miss to fight against federal Tyranny. Will pledge 10,000 from Louisiana alone, under your command . . . They will come from all over the state . . . I have been reliably informed that Mississippi already had 15,000 volunteers." Willie Rainach pledged 10,000 volunteers as well. (As noted in prior chapters, L. P. Davis was a close associate of Guy Banister and Leander Perez and was a key individual behind the scheme that brought George Lincoln Rockwell's hate bus to New Orleans in 1961. Rainach, as noted before, was also a close friend of Banister, Perez, and California para-military extremist William Potter Gale. Gale led the California contingent that traveled to Oxford.[1842] It will be recalled that Gale was a friend of Joseph Milteer and was party to the murderous plots discussed at the Congress of Freedom in 1963.) Florida, Georgia, and Alabama pledged contingents. The FBI had learned that six hundred Klansmen planned to converge on Oxford. The FBI picked up a ham radio message to all Minutemen and Rangers to stand by for further information on Ole Miss.[1843] (The Rangers were William Potter Gale's right-wing militia in California.)

Willie Rainach made many trips to visit Governor Barnett before the showdown at Ole Miss and served as an advisor to the governor on the matter. Three unnamed members of the board of directors of the Louisiana Citizens' Council flew to Jackson to confer with Barnett on the Friday following Barnett's first refusal to enroll Meredith. Charles Barnett, president of the Louisiana Citizens' Council, maintained a continuous liaison with the Mississippi Citizens' Council leaders, William Simmons, Bob Patterson, and Dick Morphew throughout the crisis. On the evening of the arrival of federal troops, George Singelmann worked across the street from the governor's mansion with the Citizens' Council. The next morning, Willie Rainach and Jack Ricau rushed to the scene.[1844] Five hundred armed men from the Florida Citizens' Council pledged to aid Ross Barnett on Monday October 1, 1962, if called by Ross Barnett.[1845] So many men showed up at Oxford (in Layfayette County) with arms, that one marshal commented, "It seems as if everyone in Lafayette County is going squirrel hunting tonight."[1846]

The Department of Justice determined that Willie Rainach and L. P. Davis, two close associates of Guy Banister and Leander Perez, met with Ross Barnett and Colonel Tom B.

Birdsong, head of the State Highway Patrol, on September 29, 1962, to plan "cooperative action."[1847, 1848] According to the FBI, a staff member of the Mississippi National Guard had heard that General Walker was also at the governor's mansion on the morning of September 29.[1849] The Justice Department determined that the token presence of the Mississippi Highway Patrol on the campus of Ole Miss gave President Kennedy and the small U.S. marshal contingent false assurances that they would be able to quell any civil disturbance. At the last minute, in a pre-mediated plan directed by the aforementioned members of the Perez-Banister operation, Ross Barnett and Birdsong pulled the Highway Patrol off campus as the rioting began, leaving the U.S. marshals tremendously outmanned and in grave danger. The Justice Department learned that General Walker and William Simmons were behind the preplanned scheme.[1850] Birdsong and Barnett were of like minds and were a perfect pairing to accomplish the deceptive operation. Birdsong, like Barnett, saw Communism behind the civil rights movement and in June 1961 stated in response to the Freedom Buses entering Mississippi that they were "directed, inspired and planned by known Communists."[1851]

On September 29, 1962, the FBI learned that Walker had a pledge from one hundred armed men from the Los Angeles area, possibly a Minutemen or similar group, gathering to go to Oxford to resist Federal troops. On the same day, the FBI reported they had interviewed Walker and asked him if he had called for a citizens' army to amass at Ole Miss. He specifically denied it.[1852]

On September 29, Walker himself landed by private plane in Jackson, flown by his friend James J. Allred, and held a press conference on the tarmac. (Allred was the son of former Texas governor James V. Allred. The FBI learned in April 1964 that Allred was working with Walker in smuggling guns to assist anti-Castro Cubans planning raids on Cuba.[1853]) Walker told the assembled media, "I am in Mississippi beside Governor Ross Barnett. I call for a national protest against the conspiracy from within. Rally to the cause of freedom . . . . There are thousands, possibly tens of thousands of people on their way to Mississippi from across the nation."[1854] Walker added that "thousands and possibly tens of thousands of people from Florida to California" were on their way to Jackson to support Ross Barnett, "in the position he had taken for states' rights."[1855] Walker stated in a separate news conference at the Sun and Sands Motel in Jackson that he had been in touch with the capitol but had not been in touch with Governor Barnett personally. He pledged to "stand with Governor Barnett shoulder to shoulder." Walker's claim of not being in touch with the governor is questionable. They knew each other well, as was noted in the last chapter, and Barnett had been taking advice and direction from in-state and out-of-state segregation leaders. Walker added, "This today is a disgrace to the nation in dire peril—a disgrace beyond the capacity of crucifixion by the anti-Christ conspirators of the supreme court in their denial of prayer and their betrayal of nation."[1856]

Kent Courtney called the Ole Miss situation, "as important of a constitutional crisis as ever faced this nation."[1857] Reacting to Walker's call for volunteers, Senator Wayne Morse stated that he believed Walker was willing to lead an armed rebellion against the American flag and "Such Fascist-minded ex-generals as Mr. Walker must be held to an accounting for such subversive activities against Democracy . . . people who seek to lead any contingent in to rebellion against the United States will have to be dealt with, with whatever forces necessary to maintain government by law in this country."[1858]

On September 29, with Robert Kennedy at his side, President Kennedy called Governor Barnett and urged an amicable solution and the avoidance of violence and death.[1859] That Saturday, a mass rally was held in Shreveport to support Governor Barnett. One hundred and fifty cars from Shreveport planned to meet up with sixty cars from Monroe, Louisiana, on Sunday and travel in a motorcade to Jackson. State Representative Wellborn Jack and Willie Rainach spoke to the group. Rainach said he had been in Jackson with Ross Barnett the day before and said Barnett that told him that "Large forces from other states might hamper our plan for Tuesday, but I will not reject them. I will be on hand to welcome them." Rainach expected to be in Oxford on October 2, when Meredith's attempt to register was anticipated.[1860]

On the night of Saturday September 29, to the cheers of a full stadium, Governor Barnett appeared at the Ole Miss football game in Jackson. He declared his love for the state, its customs and heritage.[1861] General Walker was also present at the stadium, but kept a low profile.[1862] Walker had driven from Jackson to Oxford that day and clandestinely checked in to the Mansel Motel under the name "John Waters."[1863] That night, President Kennedy federalized the state National Guard.[1864] Also on September 29, 1962, according to an FBI informant, Walker told members of his group to remain in Dallas until he gave the orders to leave.[1865]

On Sunday, September 30, Governor Barnett revised his secret scheme where he would agree to secretly admit Meredith but maintain a public posture of absolutely refusing to do so. He called Robert Kennedy and told him that he wanted Meredith and his escorts to go through two lines of Mississippi law enforcement officers with their guns drawn. The first line would consist of 175 to 200 highway patrolmen. The second would consist of seventy-five to one hundred deputies. Barnett would stand before the large contingent of law enforcement and read a proclamation in front of the world's media refusing to admit Meredith. In response, he proposed that Kennedy would then order the U.S. marshals to draw their guns and he would voluntarily step aside. Kennedy felt the plan was dangerous and told Barnett, "I think its silly going through this whole façade of your standing there, our people drawing guns . . . ." Kennedy added that the scheme might help Barnett politically, but would not help the people of Mississippi or the people of the U.S. He told Barnett that he had broken his word to the president when Barnett's representative told him he would register Meredith in Jackson while the segregationist protestors were in Oxford. Because of this deceit, Kennedy told Barnett that the president was going on TV that night to tell the American public of Barnett's secret agreement to throw in the towel and allow Meredith to register. Barnett was upset and begged him not to do it.[1866, 1867]

A rumor circulated in Jackson that the federal government might arrest Governor Barnett at the governor's mansion, which led hoards of sympathizers to surround the mansion to protect him.[1868] John Wright, chairman of the Jackson Citizens' Council, spoke to a large crowd that had gathered on the east side of the governor's mansion from the Council offices on the third floor of Plaza Building, across a side street from the mansion. At his urging, the crowd formed a circled around the entire block of the mansion to protect the governor from arrest by the federal authorities. The crowd stayed "on guard" for the rest of the night.[1869] The press reported again that Governor Barnett got much of his advice from radical pro-segregationists, including William J. Simmons, who stayed at the Alumni House in Oxford to counsel Barnett during the crisis. Simmons went so far as to suggest at an Oxford Citizens' Council meeting that city officials tear up the streets and build a moat around the campus.

Another close Milteer friend, Oren Potito, offered Governor Barnett the support of his men in the National States' Rights Party and his church, either "armed or unarmed." As Potito traveled to Ole Miss, eleven highway patrol cars stopped and searched his vehicle. Potito was turned over to federal marshals. They confiscated five high-power rifles and shotguns. He was accompanied by two men who said they were in town to attend a pro-segregationist rally and then planned to go fishing in Louisiana.[1870] (Walker later stayed with Potito at his home in St. Petersburg, Florida, in February 1963 while on his Operation Midnight Ride speaking tour with Billy James Hargis—which may have been when Walker first met Joseph A. Milteer. The Midnight Ride tour will be discussed later.)

Richard Lauchli, a high-ranking member of the Minutemen, brought a load of arms through Mississippi during the crisis at Ole Miss. Lauchli was connected with the right-wing training camp north of Lake Pontchartrain on the property of the McLaney's that was busted by the FBI, as was noted in Chapter Nine. Garrison claimed that the CIA ran the camp as a part of his assertion that government intelligence was behind the murder of the president.[1871]

Ned Touchstone, the *Councilor* editor, traveled from Shreveport to Jackson and stated, "Bobby Kennedy's going to find out they don't play touch football at Ole Miss." (The Kennedy's were known for playing touch football at family gatherings.)[1872] (Walker was in the air on a flight from New Orleans to visit Touchstone in Shreveport at the time of the assassination of President Kennedy. A photograph of Touchstone and Walker taken on the day of the assassination appeared in the *Councilor*, attesting to the fact the Walker was not in Dallas during the president's murder.[1873])

Police intercepted Ashland Burchwell, who worked for Walker's campaign for governor, carrying a small arsenal of arms on his way to join Walker in Mississippi. Burchwell had also served under Walker in the 24th Infantry Division in Germany.[1874] Two hundred cards were found in Burchwell's possession, which appeared to have numbers instead of names of members of a right-wing extremist group.[1875] (The Minutemen used numbers to identify members to maintain secrecy. Joseph Milteer was a part of a Minutemen-type group and had the designated number "23" that he would sometimes sign his letters with. The author asked Minutemen leader Robert DePugh if he knew Milteer, but DePugh remained silent and refused to answer.[1876]) Burchwell also had an address file containing the names of Dan Smoot, Robert Surrey, Joe Grinnan, and Johnston Printing Company. The FBI felt that the file cards were those of an organization that "may well be one whose aims and purposes are to overthrow the present form of government in this country due to activities of Walker at the University of Mississippi, where he was instrumental in inciting disobedience to Federal law."[1877] A former Walker employee told the FBI that the weapons that Burchwell was taking to Ole Miss belonged to General Walker.[1878] In another FBI report, it was reported that Burchwell told them that the Walker group was gathering equipment to resist the takeover of the United States by U.N. troops, which they felt was imminent.[1879] Johnston Printing Company was the firm Robert Surrey worked for and where he manufactured the printing plates for the infamous "Wanted for Treason" posters circulated in Dallas before the assassination. After Burchwell's arrest, Dallas attorney—and employee of H. L. Hunt—Tom Crouch was retained to defend him.[1880]

The FBI determined that Joseph Grinnan also had a carload of arms ready to assist General Walker at Ole Miss. (Grinnan, Nelson Bunker Hunt, and the John Birch Society were the financial donors behind the insulting "Welcome Mr. Kennedy to Dallas" advertisement that was bitterly critical of President Kennedy and was published in the *Dallas Morning News* on the day of the assassination.) The FBI noted Grinnan was a volunteer aide to General Walker.[1881]

Thus, three close associates of General Walker—Oren Potito, Robert Surrey, and Joseph Grinnan—each were separately caught taking weapons to Ole Miss. Two of the three, Surrey and Potito, were also known associates of Joseph Milteer. On October 4, 1962, an FBI informant stated that Walker had been obtaining arms for the last several months and had joined a rifle association.[1882]

A plane with 173 U.S. Marshals arrived in Oxford, and Deputy Attorney General Nicholas Katzenbach ordered them to be stationed around the Lyceum building on campus—which housed the registrar—in preparation for Meredith's enrollment the next day. A plane carrying Klan leader Robert Shelton was refused clearance to land by airport authorities.

On Sunday, September 30, General Walker arrived at Ole Miss and issued a statement: "As the forces of the New Frontier assemble to the north, let history be the witness to the courage and determination that calls us to Oxford to support a courageous governor. His lawful stand for state's sovereignty is supported by thousands of people beyond the state's borders now on the way to join you at Oxford."[1883] Walker stated he had been in touch with the capitol but had not talked to Governor Barnett directly. Walker adopted the position of being distant from Barnett, so as not to give the impression that they conspired together for the impending mayhem.[1884] (The Justice Department would later determine that Walker, Barnett, key advisors in the Citizens' Council, and the head of the state police all conspired in advance to bring about the insurrection at Ole Miss.)

As large numbers of protestors gathered at "The Circle" in front of the Lyceum to see the spectacle of the Federal Marshals—who were joined by Federal Bureau of Prison guards and the U.S. Border Patrol—surround the Lyceum, the riot began. The highway patrol, who for weeks had been blocking the marshals, were now—by Governor Barnett's agreement—supposed to help them. The marshals were pelted with rocks and debris. Tires were slashed and trucks burned. Newsmen were attacked and their equipment was destroyed. By 7:00 p.m., the campus was in full riot. Non-students began to outnumber students. At 7:35 p.m., an order came over the radio calling for the highway patrol to withdraw from the university, leaving the outnumbered marshals in peril.

Meanwhile, U.S. Marshals began tear-gassing the crowd after an initial period of restraint. At

8:00 p.m., President Kennedy addressed the nation on TV and announced that Meredith was now in residence on campus. Meredith, inside his dorm, was unaware of the pandemonium that was taking place.[1885] General Walker was in The Mansion restaurant in Oxford, eating dinner with a young aide, when President Kennedy appeared on the TV screen. Walker called the address "nauseating," turned off the TV, and headed for the campus.[1886] The Mississippi state Democratic leader called Kennedy's speech "the funeral oration" for Kennedy's chances of getting votes in the Southern states and predicted that no Southern politician would support the Democratic national party in the next election.[1887]

Bricks and spent tear gas canisters litter the ground in front of the Lyceum the day after the riot at Ole Miss. Source: Corbis

At 8:40 p.m., reporter Paul Guihard neared the campus with a photographer. The two split up and, not long after, Guihard was shot dead and his body was found next to a nearby dormitory. The FBI later determined that the fatal .38 Special bullet was fired from either a Smith and Wesson .38 or a .357 Magnum. From the coat jacket bullet entrance, the FBI determined he was shot from a distance of less than twelve inches, in the back, execution style—there were no witnesses and no suspects.[1888] Paul Guihard was a thirty-year-old New York-based reporter for a French news agency and a London paper, who wore a fiery red goatee and resembled a liberal Beatnik—a sight unseen in the South. Prior to the riot, he joked, "I'm going to pose as a Kentucky colonel and cover this thing with a mint julep in my hand."[1889, 1890] Guihard's physical appearance as an outsider may well have cost him his life. In his last story for the French press he wrote about a Jackson Citizens' Council speaker who declared, "America will not join Africa," and "a Negroid America will lose her greatness." Guihard stated, "It is in these moments when you feel there is a distance of a century between Washington and irredentists in the South. The Civil War has never ended."[1891]

Ray Gunter, who went to the campus as an observer, was struck in the head by a .38-caliber bullet from a Smith and Wesson-type revolver and was the second person to die at Ole Miss.[1892]

(One of the arrested men from Georgia roughly fit the description of Joseph Milteer. The FBI, in their investigation of Milteer before the Kennedy assassination, noted in their reports that Milteer was armed and dangerous and was known to carry a .38 revolver with him. Unfortunately, in the over 10,000 pages of FBI and other agency documents on Ole Miss that the author obtained through the Freedom of Information Act, the names of the arrested were redacted.[1893])

General Walker arrived on the campus at 8:43 p.m. on the thirtieth and was recognized by some students. He conferred with fifteen individuals, who appeared to be the leaders of the riot.[1894] He was asked if he would agree to lead them, and he did. Walker told them to keep rioting all night, and that more people were coming to join the cause. Walker attracted a crowd at the Confederate monument on The Circle in front of the Lyceum as he stood on the base of the monument and told the crowd that they had a right to protest and blamed the federal government for the bloodshed. Walker reenergized the rioters, who led repeated charges on the marshals. Later, when surrounded by newsmen, Walker toned down his inciting rhetoric.[1895]

The Associated Press described Walker's involvement after the marshals had scattered the rioters with tear gas: "For a time they scattered the troublemakers. Then General Walker led a charge of about 1,000 of the students against the marshals, still holding their positions around the red brick administration building. The students moved in on the marshals throwing bottles and rocks and bricks. The marshals fired more tear gas. The attackers backed up. Walker said his student force would regroup and charge again."[1896]

On October 2, the Associated Press again reported on Walker's involvement in the riots, writing, "Walker led students in charges that failed against the gas launching of U.S. Marshals during night long rioting on the university campus that cost the lives of two persons and injured 20 others."[1897]

Newsweek quoted Walker speaking from the Confederate monument, "Don't let up now. You may lose the battle but you will have to be heard . . . . . .You must be prepared for possible death. If you are not, go home now."[1898] A reporter from *The Evening Star* wrote, "It was a mob encouraged by Edwin A. Walker, discredited former Army major general who was seen during the night exhorting his 'troops' from atop the Confederate monument."[1899] Reverend Duncan Gray, who confronted Walker at Ole Miss, reported that Walker said to the students, "I compliment you on what you are doing. I have just come from a conference with a representative of your Governor. I was told to tell the students at Ole Miss they had been sold out."[1900]

The rioting escalated and armed men from Louisiana, Alabama, and elsewhere entered the campus. Snipers fired on the marshals with .22-caliber automatic rifles and shotguns. President Kennedy called Governor Barnett and urged him to stop the rioting. Barnett agreed to travel to the campus and restore order if Kennedy agreed to remove Meredith— Kennedy refused.

Time magazine called the riot the "gravest conflict between federal and state authority since the Civil War."[1901] The U.S. Marshals were running out of tear gas and were on the brink of defeat when, at 10:00 p.m., President Kennedy ordered the U.S. Army to crush the insurrection. Deputy Attorney General Nicholas Katzenbach ordered the National Guard from a nearby armory to encircle the Lyceum.[1902] Secretary of Defense Robert McNamara— who a year before had relieved Walker of his command in Germany—assured the president that the air force was prepared to mass airlift thousands of Army troops to Ole Miss by midnight. Thirty-one thousand federal troops arrived and occupied Oxford in the first week of October.[1903]

Just before midnight on September 30, Governor Barnett gave a radio address and pledged to never yield in the fight he was engaged in.[1904] Reinforcement National Guard troops from the nearby town of Pontotoc drove to Oxford. They were given the specific job of seizing General Walker, who had been warned by the Kennedys before the rioting not to interfere with Meredith's enrollment or he would face contempt charges, but he could not be found. The Army moved in by 5:00 the next morning.

President Kennedy reportedly had gone to bed at 5:30 a.m., assured that things had quieted down at Ole Miss—but when he awoke a few hours later he learned about the continuing violence. The president called Governor Barnett, who once again was worried that Kennedy would reveal Barnett's earlier agreement to secretly allow Meredith's admission. Kennedy implored Barnett to order the state police to help restore order. Afterward President Kennedy called the solicitor general of the United States, Archibald Cox, and inquired as to the legalities of arresting Governor Barnett. The president gave orders to seize Barnett if he flew into the Oxford airport from Jackson.[1905] By daybreak, the riot had been quashed and the Lyceum secured. Meredith was registered at 8:30 that morning in the Lyceum.

The FBI received a rumor that a cache of arms was being held at the Ole Miss fraternity of Trent Lott, Sigma Nu. (Years later, Lott served in the United States Senate from 1988 to 2007. In 2002, Lott attended a reception for Strom Thurmond, who was retiring from the Senate after forty-eight years. At Thurmond's side, Lott stated, "When Strom Thurmond ran for president [as a Dixiecrat on a platform of segregation], we voted for him. We're proud of it. And if the rest of the country had followed our lead, we wouldn't have had all these problems over the years, either.") Twenty-four weapons were removed from Sigma Nu.[1906, 1907]

Walker managed to return to his motel for a few hours of sleep, then reemerged on the town square of Oxford, encouraging the rioters who had moved there. One army officer recalled, "Walker walked right through our line. The crowd cheered him like a baseball hero after the home run that won the game, patting him on the back. They followed him out of the square like the Pied Piper."[1908] When an army officer asked Walker to move from the square, he refused, at which point several soldiers with rifles surrounded him and pointed their bayonets inches from him.[1909] J. Evetts Haley was with Walker at the time.[1910]

While the Justice Department was contemplating possible action against Walker, he got into a car with Haley and tried to leave town, but he was stopped at a checkpoint.[1911, 1912] The army was unsure of the legalities involved in their dealing with Walker, so a decision was made to "temporarily delay" rather than detain him at the checkpoint. One soldier very politely asked Walker—who was dressed in a white Stetson hat, coat, and tie—if Walker would accompany him to the Lyceum. Walker, surprised at his courtesy, agreed. Walker then insisted on being called "Mr. Walker," rather than "General Walker."[1913, 1914]

(White House correspondent Fletcher Knebel and Charles W. Bailey wrote the best-selling novel *Seven Days in May*, which was published in September 1962. The book is about a dissident army general who plotted assassination of the president and takeover of the U.S. General Walker and the active air force chief, Curtis Lemay—who told Knebel off the record of Kennedy's cowardice during the Bay of Pigs operation—were inspirations for the book. Lemay ran as segregationist George Wallace's vice-presidential running mate in the 1968 presidential election. John and Robert Kennedy got advance copies of the book in late summer of 1962. Knebel got the idea to write the book after his earlier *Look* magazine investigative article on members of the radical right, including General Walker and Kent Courtney, as was noted earlier. Knebel was struck by the hardline and extremist posture that the far right had adopted. President Kennedy was eager to see a movie made of the book, hoping to alert the nation to the specter of far-right treason. He contacted the producer of the Cold War movie thriller, *The Manchurian Candidate*, John Frankenheimer, and urged him to make the movie version of *Seven Days in May*, which was released to the public in 1964. General Walker's name was specifically mentioned in the movie as one of the troubling military voices of dissidence.)

As Robert Kennedy and President Kennedy learned of Walker's involvement on the night of the riot and were contemplating arresting him, the president remarked, "General Walker. Imagine that son of a bitch having been commander of a division up till last year." The president's remarks spurred advisor Ted Sorensen to wonder about of a military coup. He asked the president, "Have you read *Seven Days in May*?" He responded, "Yeah."[1915, 1916]

Walker was placed under arrest at the Lyceum at 11:30 a.m. on Monday morning, October 1, by U.S. Marshals under a warrant issued by the Justice Department.[1917] He was charged with insurrection against the United States and was flown to the U.S. medical center for federal prisons in Springfield, Missouri, where he arrived at 7:10 p.m.[1918] (The center was often used to determine the sanity of accused people in criminal cases.) Robert Kennedy stated that Walker would be offered bail like any other person.[1919]

Psychiatrist Dr. John H. DeTar, a Reno, Nevada, John Birch Society spokesman, stated that the temporary commitment of General Walker was a political imprisonment.[1920] Fred Schlafly, an attorney—and husband of well-known conservative writer Phyllis Schlafly—corresponded with Edgar Bundy and the two agreed on the need to help patriots like Walker, whom he called "America's first political prisoner." Schlafly also noted he had recently been in touch with Clyde Watts.[1921] Three carloads of Minutemen were sent to picket in Springfield on behalf of General Walker. (Later, at the October 13, 1962, Minutemen National Freedom Rally, a tape-recorded speech by Tom Anderson was played. At the meeting, three Minutemen hatched a scheme to assassinate liberal Arkansas senator William Fulbright; Robert DePugh claimed he dissuaded the men from the murder.[1922])

On October 3, 1962, the FBI received a letter from a citizen (or informant) stating that an individual—whose name was redacted by the FBI, but who was obviously Walker aide Robert Surrey—was an ardent member of the John Birch Society, operating as secretary and treasurer of the JBS at Walker's residence. According to the source, "I know that for the past two years [name redacted] has been contemplating an uprising and I know that he has ordered by mail numerous guns, rifles and averages buying one box of shells to avert suspicion. I am sure his arsenal could be found at his home at the above address." The source said the individual, likely Surrey, "corresponds with Robert Welch getting and giving advice." He said he wrote to church leaders and Rabbis who he felt were Communists. He said, "I believe you will find him associated with the mad hatter, former Gerald Edwin A. Walker." The source warned, "upon close investigation, you will uncover several arsenals in the homes of members in his organization." The source said Walker was doing much harm to the country and would like to see him out of Dallas. He stated that the individual (Surrey) could "very well be a dangerous individual with someone like former Gerald Edwin A. Walker as a leader."[1923] He stated that there were arsenals in the homes of Walker associates in the John Birch Society.[1924]

The Department of Justice, in investigating the conduct of the Mississippi State Highway Patrol, determined the following and released it in a memorandum:

It is evident from the Yarbrough-Katzenbach conference and from the monitoring of the State Police radio that the police were withdrawn intentionally and that the plan to withdraw the police in the middle of the rioting was formed at a high level before the violence even began. In view of the apparent complicity of Mississippi deputy sheriffs in the arrival and activities of General Walker and his supporters (see particularly the treatment of reporter Ledgers of the *Denver Post*) and in the light of the telephone calls made by Judge Moore and by William Simmons to outsiders, it seems reasonable to postulate that the State Government was party to a plan to create a riot and to do nothing about it. The degree in which we will be able to substantiate such complicity may be become more evident upon the completion the FBI investigation of the Citizens' Council's role in the Oxford Riot.[1925, 1926]

As the Justice Department memorandum succinctly described, the insurrection was a well-planned-out, pre-meditated conspiracy involving General Walker, Governor Barnett, and their directors and advisors in the Mississippi and Louisiana Citizens' Council. A private letter from J. Evetts Haley described his participation at a meeting with Governor Barnett in Jackson, Mississippi, on June 17, 1962, well in advance of the riot.[1927] Prominent members of the Louisiana Citizens' Council L. P. Davis, Jackson Ricau, Willie Rainach, and George Singelmann were all in Jackson conferring with Barnett just before the riots. All four were close associates of Guy Banister. Thus the Banister operation that spawned Lee Harvey Oswald was also a party to the conspiracy to commit rebellion against the U.S. government and the defiance of President Kennedy in 1962.

The Walker Imprisonment and the Aftermath

In prison, Walker stated that he was a political prisoner and gave the prison doctors only his name, rank, and serial number, "such as any American soldier would do if captured by the enemy." Clyde Watts, who represented Walker during the Senate "muzzling" hearings, led Walker's corps of attorneys. Watts stated, "He believes he is being held as a political prisoner. This can now happen to any person who disagrees with the government."[1928] Watts learned from the judge at Springfield that the order for the psychiatric exam was issued on the basis of testimony from Bureau of Prisons psychiatrist Charles E. Smith, who had not even seen Walker.

Robert Morris joined Watts on Walker's defense team; Morris called Walker's detention "a new evil introduced in the United States—detention of political prisoners" and "a sad hour for the United States if all of this is true."[1929]

Morris is an important figure, since he had ties to both General Walker and Guy Banister. Robert Morris was a part of Senator Eastland's Communist-hunting subcommittee in New Orleans in 1956—the group operated to preserve segregation in the South and its members included Guy Banister and Hubert Badeaux. Morris served as chief counsel for the Senate Judiciary Subcommittee on Internal Security (SISS) from 1951 to 1953 and again during Senator Eastland's chairmanship of the committee from 1956 to 1958. The *New York Times* described the committee as "far overreaching the House Committee on Un-American Activities, as it far outreaches Senator McCarthy..." Morris was described as "more McCarthyesque than the Senator himself" and did more damage than McCarthy.[1930] On March 21, 1956, New Orleans Mayor deLesseps Morrison ordered Guy Banister to conduct an investigation into subversive activities in the city. Morrison arranged a meeting with Banister and Eastland in Mississippi to discuss the SISS hearing in the city.[1931] As a result of Banister and Eastland's collaboration, Sergeant Hubert Badeaux raided the home of Hunter Pitts O'Dell, an African American and known member of the Communist Party. O'Dell was questioned before the SISS on April 12, 1956, by counsel Robert Morris. O'Dell took the Fifth and refused to say if he was a Communist. At that time, Leander Perez offered his assistance to Banister, and this appears to be the beginning of their close relationship. That same year, 1956, Lee Harvey Oswald began posing as a Communist and told William Wolfe at the Astronomy Club that he was trying to find a Communist cell to join. Oswald joined the marines in October 1956 and departed New Orleans. In early 1957, Sergeant Badeaux wrote a letter to Willie Rainach on the letterhead of Assistant Superintendent of Police Guy Banister and told Rainach he was grooming an outsider to infiltrate leftist groups (as noted in Chapter One). Oswald, by adopting the posture of a Communist in 1956—as well as his later actions—paralleled the activities of Eastland's Communist-hunting SISS, as we shall see later. In December 1962, Robert Morris announced the formation of the Defenders of American Liberties, in Dallas—a sort of ACLU for the far right. Morris was considering taking the case of a Chicago man who came to Dallas claiming he had eluded Communist assassins all the way there. The man told Morris about an individual who could save the world if he could just get him out of a mental institution.[1932] Interestingly, Morris had been close to General Charles Willoughby since at least 1956[1933] and he was invited by Robert Welch to join the Council of the John Birch Society in 1962, after he was relieved from his position as president of the University of Dallas for his extremist activities.[1934]

In the aftermath of Ole Miss, Morris urged Senator Eastland to investigate Walker's confinement at the psychiatric facility.[1935] Curtis Dall, chairman of the Board of Policy of Liberty Lobby—and an associate of Joseph Milteer in the Constitution Party in 1963—solicited donations for the Walker defense fund.[1936]

The most serious charge made against Walker was seditious conspiracy, which carried a maximum fine of $20,000 and twenty years in jail. He was also charged with inciting to rebellion, which carried a maximum fine of $10,000 and ten years in jail. The third and fourth charges against him were assaulting a federal officer and conspiracy to hinder officials in the performance of duty, which carried lesser fines and jail time.[1937]

After Walker's arrest, aide Robert Surrey slipped a statement to a reporter containing a message to Governor Barnett, which read, "Mr. Walker hoped his efforts were in your behalf for freedom everywhere. Do nothing based on my status that is not in support of your own objectives."[1938]

On October 7, Walker was released from Springfield on $50,000 bond after six days in a maximum-security prison cell.[1939] He flew back to Dallas—where two to three hundred supporters greeted him—on a private plane with his mother, J. Evetts Haley, and Clyde Watts.[1940] (On November 8, Walker submitted to a court-ordered psychiatric exam at Parkland Hospital. The examining psychiatrist, Dr. Robert Stubblefield concluded that Walker was "currently functioning at a superior level."[1941])

On October 8, 1962, Robert Welch sent out letters to members of the John Birch Society Council and noted that three individuals, including Medford Evans, J. Evetts Haley and a third unnamed person, guided Walker in the Ole Miss incident. (The letters were private and discovered by the author.) Welch felt their advice "left much to be desired." Welch stated he did not approve of the unnamed person and noted that Walker refused "to pay any attention to those who have tried to caution him about this source, and it is one we do not trust at all, even as to good intentions." Welch also noted: "There is, in our opinion, danger of some very serious embarrassment to a lot of good Conservatives and even to the conservative cause in general if Walker continues to listen to that advice, or takes any overt actions based on it, or even merely gets himself definitely associated with this source." Notwithstanding, Welch felt Walker was innocent of the charges of insurrection at Ole Miss, and was critical of his detention at the Springfield mental facility.[1942] The identity of the unnamed source is anyone's guess. However, Walker's aide, Robert Surrey—who was head of the Dallas John Birch Society—is a good bet since he could have been particularly embarrassing to Welch if his ties to the American Nazi Party became well known.[1943]

The New Orleans Citizens' Council held an emergency meeting on October 10, 1962. Mississippi state senator John McLauren told the crowd that federal marshals deliberately incited the Ole Miss riots to crush resistance to the admission of James Meredith. He said marshals shot gas in the dorms to get the students to come out and fight. "This might be the act which will remove them [the Kennedys] from office," he declared, adding, "[he] must be stopped in 1964, for if he should be re-elected, we will have reached a point of no return." Leander Perez was present and warned the audience "conditions will get worse." Emmet Irwin and Louis W. Hollis, the executive director of the Citizens' Council of America, were also present.[1944]

On October 13, 1962, Tom Anderson spoke at a "Dallas Freedom Rally" with Frank

McGehee. Anderson attacked Kennedy's disarmament plans and claimed he planned to seize personal firearms. He told the crowd, "The time to buy firearms is when it becomes unlawful to have them."[1945]

On October 22, 1962, President Kennedy announced a naval blockade of Cuba after discovering the presence of Soviet nuclear missile sites in what has become known as the "Cuban Missile Crisis."[1946] The new crisis effectively turned the nation's attention away from the Ole Miss crisis. The United States and the Soviet Union teetered on the brink of thermonuclear war, until the Soviets agreed to withdraw their missiles. President Kennedy directed John J. McCloy, chairman of the Council on Foreign Relations, to ensure Soviet compliance.[1947] Walker, commenting on the president's action in Cuba, stated, "An equally forceful action to that in Mississippi would have solved the Cuban problem years ago."[1948]

Melvin Bruce, a member of the American Nazi Party, who was arrested at Ole Miss, spoke before the New Orleans Citizens' Council with Milteer associate Emmett Irwin. He told them his experience at Ole Miss was the "most terrifying experience" of his life."[1949, 1950] The marshals found a rifle—a Mauser with seven-point ammunition—with him and a sticker on the rifle that read, "This is a Republic, not a Democracy. Let's keep it that way," which was a John Birch Society slogan.[1951]

In the aftermath of the riots, a crude, anonymous two-page newsletter called the *Rebel Underground* surfaced on the campus of Ole Miss. The newsletter claimed that actions taken against a student for violent demonstrations toward Meredith were "an example of a Soviet type government." They wrote, "his 'crime' [the student's] was that he was accused of yelling 'nigger' at a coon the likes of which have been called and are called niggers in this area for centuries." The existence of a resistance group called the "Brick and Bottle Minute Men" with chapters in other Southern states was noted in the newsletter. The newsletter referred to General Walker and Melvin Bruce as "our good and honorable friends."[1952] (Later, in January 1963, the *Rebel Underground* called for the impeachment, removal and execution of President Kennedy.[1953])

Tom Anderson spoke in New Orleans on October 30, 1962, with National Indignation Committee founder Frank McGehee in a *For America* rally sponsored by George Soule. Anderson lashed out at Kennedy's disarmament act, calling it "suicide, slavery, treason," and stating it provided for a program of "One, Two, Three, Surrender."[1954]

On November 12, 1962, Louisiana state representative Wellborn Jack told the Greater Citizens' Council of New Orleans that he was in Oxford when Meredith was registered. He told the audience that he heard from individuals—but could not recall their names—that James Meredith would be killed, and dared the FBI to ask him about it.[1955]

On November 15, 16, and 17, 1962, Walker spoke along with Clyde Watts at a Blockade Cuba Rally in Chicago.[1956]

In November 1962, the Miami FBI learned that Mary Davison and the Council for Statehood was meeting weekly in South Florida and planned to eliminate—by force if necessary—all Jewish people in government and business positions and all Jews who were Communists.[1957] At the meeting, a high-ranking inner circle, which had access to large amounts of money, would name the time and place for the assassinations to begin. (Willie Somersett reported on another meeting of Mary Davison's Council of Statehood on January 15, 1963, where it was revealed that Major Archibald Roberts and generals Pedro del Valle, Clyde Watts, and Edwin Walker were part of the military underground that would lead the takeover of the U.S. government.[1958, 1959])

On December 7, 1962, Walker visited the Mississippi House of Representatives and got a standing ovation from its members who voted 101–10 to let him speak. Walker told the body that the planned reorganization of the National Guard and reserves was part of the State Department's plan to put the armed forces under control of the U.N.[1960] On the same day, Governor Barnett charged that the U.S. was planning to make Mississippi a "permanently occupied territory."[1961]

On December 9, 1962, *News Latin America* reported that the Kennedy administration had adopted a "Hands Off" Cuba policy that ordered commentators broadcasting radio programs to Cuba to refrain from making disparaging remarks. The paper reported that the Kennedy administration informed the Cuban Student Revolutionary Directorate they would not tolerate any further excursions into Cuba.[1962] On December 21, 1962, President Kennedy signed a pact with Cuban leader Fidel Castro for a $53 million ransom paid to Cuba for the release of 1,113 men who were captured in the Bay of Pigs fiasco. The radical right widely criticized the action.[1963]

Then, on January 21, 1963, an all-white federal grand jury in Oxford, supportive of Walker's efforts at Oxford to maintain segregation, failed to indict Walker and—a few hours later—a U.S. Attorney asked that the charges be dismissed. Burns Tatum of the Ole Miss police testified at the proceeding that he had heard Walker tell the students during the riot, "Stand by your governor. Charge!"[1964] Radio Executive John King, Jr., testified that, after Walker's speech, he heard Walker say, "You're doing all right—riot. You are getting news all over the country. Now, you've got casualties."[1965] Had the case gone to trial, noted criminal attorney Percy Foreman planned to join the defense. (Foreman later would defend James Earl Ray, the convicted assassin of Martin Luther King, Jr.)[1966]

Walker's arrest and confinement by the federal government on the orders of Attorney General Kennedy appeared to be legally questionable and particularly vindictive. Robert Kennedy had a history of humiliating and heavy-handed actions against his enemies, as in the cases of Carlos Marcello, Jimmie Hoffa, and others, which left them deeply resentful. (When Marcello made a routine visit to the Immigration and Naturalization office in New Orleans in 1961—as was required of him as an alien—Kennedy ordered agents to handcuff him, put him on a waiting government plane, and deport him to Guatemala. They refused to let him call his attorney, or his family, and he was taken with only the clothes he had on and the money in his pockets in what Marcello called a kidnapping; Kennedy's actions were arguably illegal.[1967] David Ferrie, Lee Harvey Oswald's Civil Air Patrol leader, flew to Guatemala and brought Marcello back to New Orleans.[1968]) *The Chicago Daily Tribune* was critical of Robert

Kennedy's humiliating treatment of Walker, writing, "whatever their views on Walker, the people will watch such developments very closely. The present administration seems to have all too great an attachment to the procedure of railroading people into psychiatric wards." They cited the U.S. government's fraud case against Billie Sol Estes and the seizing of Estes's secretary from his office and sending her directly to a mental institution, where she stayed for twelve days before being found mentally sound.[1969]

Walker had never personally undergone a psychiatric evaluation by anyone prior to his incarceration at the Springfield mental facility. Instead, the Bureau of Prisons psychiatric assessment, performed by Dr. Charles Smith, served as the basis for his placement in a psychiatric facility. The assessment was entirely made upon the Associated Press's accounts of his behavior and was of questionable legality. The placement of Walker in maximum security appeared excessive, and Dr. Smith later defended his actions when called as a witness by the government, saying he based his opinion on army medical records and testimony given during the Senate "muzzling" hearings.[1970] The American Medical Association received volumes of letters from physicians and medical societies charging Smith with unethical conduct. The AMA, however, absolved Dr. Smith of unethical conduct, stating that he did not violate ethical confidence and did not make a medical diagnosis but, rather, gave "an impression or an opinion" in regard to Walker's mental condition. Smith stated in an affidavit in regard to Walker, "some of his reported behavior reflects sensitivity and essentially unpredictable and seemingly bizarre outbursts of the type often observed in individuals suffering with paranoid mental disorder."[1971] Congressman John J. Rooney of New York stated more bluntly, "It's high time to see to it that Walker is committed to a lunatic asylum. Or, if he is proved sane, he ought to be jailed."[1972]

Robert Kennedy's handling of Walker's arrest backfired on him and had the unintended effect of further increasing Walker's stature among the radical right.[1973] Robert Kennedy defended the arrest and transport of Walker to the Springfield psychiatric facility, implausibly saying the "action was for the protection of General Walker."

Clyde Watts gave his opinion on the legality of the Walker arrest in the September 1965 *American Mercury*. Watts asserted, in essence, that since Ole Miss was not under marshal law, the military had no authority to arrest Walker.

Walker sued the Associated Press for libel for writing that he "led the charges" at Ole Miss. The suits were brought by Shreveport attorney Scott Wilkinson, who served on the board of the Federation for Constitutional Government in 1956, along with Leander Perez and J. Evetts Halley. Walker won two of the suits, which were then appealed all the way up to the Supreme Court—where they were overturned in favor of the Associated Press. Ironically, Earl Warren—a target of bitter criticism by Walker and the John Birch Society over the years—was the chief justice involved in the case. Walker claimed Warren—who was despised by segregationists and the far right for presiding over the 1954 *Brown* decision and others—should have removed himself from the case based on conflict of interest.[1974]

James Meredith remained enrolled at Ole Miss and attended classes daily under careful guard. He was constantly threatened. The FBI learned through an informant that the United Klans of America planned to keep a low profile, then later hang Meredith from the campus gates.[1975]

Meanwhile, in New Orleans, Delphine Roberts picketed with a sign reading, "Kennedy is responsible for lives lost, bloodshed in Mississippi. Kennedy is helping Khrushchev and Castro."[1976]

In the end, two innocent people (Paul Guihard and Ray Gunter) died; 166 U.S. Marshals and forty-eight soldiers were injured; and thirty U.S. Marshals were wounded by gunfire. An estimated 375 civilians were injured, while seventy-five people who had traveled to Ole Miss from places such as Georgia and California were taken prisoner. Many more non-students than students were arrested, but none were ever convicted.[1977] Each side blamed the other: Senator Eastland blamed the bloodshed largely on the Fifth Circuit Court of Appeals, and the marshals for inciting the riot, and planned a complete investigation. The Justice Department defended the marshals' actions and said that white segregationists harassed the marshals before they undertook appropriate anti-riot measures.[1978]

On July 23, 1963, the army withdrew from Oxford and, on August 18, 1963, Meredith graduated from Ole Miss.[1979] Mississippi State Sovereignty Commission member Horace Harnad, Jr. captured the Southern sentiment surrounding Ole Miss, stating, "It was the final battle. It was the last stand for states' rights in the big scale. Since then they've taken the balance of what sovereignty we had left."[1980]

President Kennedy commented on the rise of the radical right and General Walker, often referred to as a man on horseback, saying: "The discordant voices of extremism are heard once again in the land. Men who are unwilling to face up to the danger from without are convinced that the real danger comes from within. They look suspiciously at their neighbors and their leaders. They call for a man on horseback because they do not trust the people. They find treason in our finest churches, in our highest court and even in the treatment of our water. Let us not heed these councils of fear and suspicion. Let us concentrate more on keeping enemy bombers and missiles away from our shores, and concentrate less on keeping neighbors away from our shelters, let us devote less energy to organized armed bands of civilian guerillas that are more likely to supply local vigilantes than national vigilance. Let our patriotism be reflected in the creation of confidence rather than crusades of suspicion."[1981, 1982]

Despite the two deaths and scores of injuries, Walker showed no remorse over the Ole Miss affair. Billy James Hargis quoted Walker as saying, "It was a comedy watching the students derive ways and means of protesting."[1983] An informant told the FBI, "Walker glories in his experiences at Oxford."[1984] After Walker's release from Springfield, he told reporters ominously, "I was safer in the prison cell than John F. Kennedy in the White House."[1985]

Conclusions

By 1962, it was clear that General Walker was an angry soldier looking for a fight. His rise to national fame and the development of a dedicated following of segregationists, Klansmen,

Minutemen, and others on the far-right fringe made him all the more a dangerous man. There were four seminal events that occurred in 1962 that indicated General Walker was intent in acting against the federal government and the Kennedys and was prepared to resort to violence in doing so.

In late 1961 and early 1962, media sources reported on rumors that the national radical right was preparing for rebellion against the federal government and pointed directly at generals Walker and Pedro del Valle as the troublemakers behind it. Billy James Hargis's March 1962 "secretive meeting" of members of the national right wing—who were alarmed by the actions of President Kennedy in the military muzzling, the Bay of Pigs fiasco, and the disarmament act—was attended by a majority of individuals who have been or will be tied to the conspiracy to assassinate President Kennedy.

The second event was the collaboration between generals Walker and del Valle, which was reflected in their correspondence beginning in June 1962 and revealed a strategic plan was in the making that would include former military men, top civilians on the far right, and the use of violence, if needed, to save the country—which they felt to be in dire peril. By September 1962, generals Walker and del Valle emerged as the architects of the broad-based assassination plots targeting members of the Council of Foreign Relations, prominent Jewish figures, and leaders of business and industry—the third critical event in the Walker story. The plots were revealed by FBI informant Willie Somersett, first in late 1962 and again at the New Orleans Congress of Freedom meeting in 1963, and further indicate Walker's propensity for the use of violence against the governing establishment. The FBI knew all about the plots thanks to Willie Somersett, but kept them from the Warren Commission.

The fourth seminal event was the September 30, 1962, Walker-led rebellion at Ole Miss that left two dead and scores bloodied and battered. Federal courts ordered James Meredith admitted to the University of Mississippi and the president and attorney general were intent on seeing the order obeyed. By September 1962, the ultimate showdown between the insurrectionists in the segregation movement and the federal government was nearing. The Justice Department determined that Governor Barnett, General Walker, and key members of the Louisiana Citizens' Council tied to the Guy Banister-Leander Perez operation—as well as William Simmons and members of the Mississippi Citizens' Council—collaborated with the highway patrol to foment the bloody rebellion. Sparse accounting of Walker's whereabouts in June, July, and August 1962 may be attributable to his conspiring with Governor Barnett and segregation leaders to combat the integration of Ole Miss. General Walker's September 26, 1962, letter to President Kennedy served as an ominous Declaration of Rights and Grievances that preceded his leading the riots at Ole Miss on September 30. Governor Barnett enjoyed a close relationship with those from New Orleans who were a part of the Guy Banister operation that included Leander Perez, Willie Rainach, Kent Courtney, L. P. Davis, Jack Ricau and Hubert Badeaux. Many of those individuals were also associates of Joseph Milteer, as well as General Walker, and several were also in Jackson or Oxford advising Barnett.

Walker was acquitted of serious felony charges by the Southern white establishment, which was virtually the rule in all crimes committed by whites in that era of segregation in the South. Had justice prevailed, Walker would have spent many years in a federal prison. While there is no known evidence that the far right was plotting to kill the president as early as 1962, it is clear that General Walker was more than ready to shed blood for his cause—and that he felt justified in doing it.

CHAPTER FOURTEEN

THE WALKER-HARGIS NATIONAL SPEAKING TOUR AND THE WALKER SHOOTING INCIDENT, SPRING 1963

If I had the Kennedys here I would line them up and shoot them.
— General Walker

General Walker began 1963 without a stage or forum to warn the country of the dangers of Communism and the Kennedys. As the National Indignation Committee lost steam and his run for governor ended, his public speaking engagements declined. That changed when he teamed up with far-right evangelist Billy James Hargis and embarked on a national speaking tour. After the first leg of the tour ended in April 1963, someone fired a rifle at Walker, narrowly missing him while he was reportedly working at his desk at home. Walker blamed the shooting on a Communist and claimed it reenergized him and he went out on another speaking tour shortly after. (The Warren Commission later concluded that Lee Harvey Oswald was the perpetrator of this shooting, based on the testimony of Oswald's wife.) The speaking tour and related shooting incident merit scrutiny in this chapter particularly in light of the fact that Walker and Hargis were both associates of Joseph Milteer, who is inextricably tied to the assassination conspiracy; as well as Guy Banister, who had direct ties to Lee Harvey Oswald. Important events of 1963, in addition to the speaking tour and the shooting incident, will be chronicled.

Early 1963

Billy James Hargis began the year speaking at the New England Rally for God and Country on January 6, 1963. John Rousselot, Edward Hunter, Tom Anderson, Kent Courtney (all important figures in this work), and Joseph Mlot-Mroz were present. The annual New England Rally was not officially affiliated with the John Birch Society, however seventeen of the twenty-four speakers were John Birch Society members.[1986, 1987, 1988, 1989] Joseph Mlot-Mroz was a perennial anti-Jewish crusader who stated that the Jews invented Communism to wipe out Christianity. He felt the Jews should be destroyed "like cockroaches."[1990]

On January 21 and 22, the FBI noted that Gary Patrick Hemming, an anti-Castro adventurer, met with General Walker and discussed the international situation. Hemming was married to a Cuban actress, who had once been imprisoned in Castro's Cuba. The experience led Hemming to become violently anti-Castro.[1991] On February 3, 1963, Hemming wrote in a letter, "Spent some time with General Edwin Walker both of those days. Appears he plans to involve his element in the Cuban fight. Contacted money people in Dallas to finance lectures and travel for the leaders of the raider groups, i.e. Alpha 66, D.R.E. [Cuban Student Directorate], Cardenas Raiders, and Major Vidalis Raiders." Hemming stated that his organization was financing D.R.E. lectures in Denver, and—with any money they raised—hoped to take their anti-Castro films and message to Texas and California.[1992] Hemming's liaison with Walker is the first indication that Walker, like his New Orleans counterpart Guy Banister, was involved with the anti-Castro Cubans and their efforts to overthrow Castro's Communist regime.

On February 8, 1963, Alabama governor George Wallace gave his inaugural speech, proclaiming: "Segregation now, segregation tomorrow, segregation forever." Leander Perez was on the stage with him.[1993]

On February 11, 1963, Henry Hill, in a letter to the director of the Citizens' Council of Louisiana, R. B. Mahoney, proposed the formation of a "Patriotic National Army" made up of divisions that he called the General Pedro del Valle Corps, the Stratemeyer Corps, the MacArthur Corps, and the Walker Corps. Hill asserted, "The only way to get rid of the despots and Brigands was through combat."[1994]

On February 11–15, 1963, Billy James Hargis held the second Anti-Communist Leadership School in Tulsa, Oklahoma. Notable speakers were General Bonner Fellers, Carl McIntire, General Albert Wedemeyer, Hilaire du Berrier, and Dan Smoot—all important figures in this work.[1995]

On February 14, 1963, General Walker addressed students at Southern Methodist University and blasted the United Nations.[1996]

On February 17, 1963, Marina Oswald wrote to the Soviet embassy and told them she wanted to return to the Soviet Union and that her husband was not going with her. She was later informed, in March, that it would take five to six months to process her application.[1997]

February 1963 also marked the beginning of the General Walker and Billy James Hargis national speaking tour dubbed "Operation Midnight Ride."

Billy James Hargis

Walker's speaking partner, Billy James Hargis—an associate of Guy Banister and Joseph Milteer—was known as a "ball and jump" radio evangelist. At the peak of his Christian Crusade's empire, he spread his anti-Communist and pro-segregationist propaganda on 500 radio stations and 250 television stations. He gained international fame in 1953 when he released 100,000 balloons, containing quotes from the Bible, across the Iron Curtain into Communist Eastern Europe, "to succor the spiritually starved captives of Communism."[1998]

Hargis was a close personal friend of Senator Joseph McCarthy and the two were photographed together in 1955.[1999] He once even wrote a speech for McCarthy. During the 1956 presidential campaign, Hargis attempted to link the Democratic ticket of Adlai Stevenson and Estes Kefauver to Communism, which prompted an investigation by Senator Albert Gore's subcommittee on Privileges and Elections in 1957. Hargis teamed up with General Charles Willoughby, in 1957, to "lend military authority to Christian Conscience Crusade lectures, appearances, television and radio."[2000]

Famed reporter Mike Wallace interviewed Hargis in 1957 on television station WABD in New York.[2001] Hargis's claim that the Communists had infiltrated the National Council on Churches somehow found its way into the air force training manual. The matter was investigated, and the manual was later withdrawn. Hargis sponsored an all-night, anti-Red radio crusade on April 18 and 24, 1958, which featured Carl McIntire, Senator James Eastland, Senator Barry Goldwater, Martin Dies, J. B. Mathews, and General Willoughby.[2002] Hargis was a very close friend of John Birch Society leader Robert Welch and had supported the society since it was formed in 1958.[2003] In 1959, Kent Courtney wrote an article for Hargis's *Christian Crusade* magazine that was critical of U.S. foreign aid and taxation policies.[2004]

As we have learned, Hargis was an avowed segregationist. In 1960, the FBI investigated reports from two men who told an informant that they suspected Hargis was involved in bombings in Little Rock, Arkansas. They interviewed Hargis about the bombings, and the FBI ultimately arrested three men associated with Hargis—but not Hargis, himself—for bombing the historically black Philander Smith College in Little Rock.[2005] Hargis published a widely circulated pamphlet entitled "Unmasking the Deceiver" that "unmasked" the alleged Communist associations of the Highlander Folk School that Martin Luther King, Jr. had attended in 1957.[2006]

In 1960, Hargis attended the Congress of Freedom meeting in Columbus, Ohio, along with Revilo Oliver and Kenneth Goff. The FBI noted that Hargis, at the time, was head of the Constitutional Party of Indiana, which took a stand against presidential hopefuls Hubert Humphrey and John F. Kennedy.[2007] In 1961, he acquired the Communist files of fanatical anti-Semite, Allen Zoll.[2008] Joseph Milteer, at an unknown time, recorded one of Hargis's speaking engagements and Hargis can be heard on the recording soliciting contributions from the audience.[2009] (According to a letter found in Milteer's home, he recorded a speech by Hargis in 1960, even though Hargis did not personally know Milteer at the time). Hargis asked George Thomas—director of the Congress of Freedom—to contact the man taping at the meeting (Milteer) and ask him to delete one incorrect statement made in the speech. Thomas forwarded the request to Milteer.[2010]

Willie Somersett reported that Hargis raised funds for the hardcore underground.[2011] As we shall see, Hargis and Milteer both attended the We the People meeting in Chicago in September 1963. Then, in late October 1963, Hargis visited with Guy Banister at his Camp and Lafayette Street office (where, at various times, numerous individuals saw Lee Harvey Oswald).[2012]

Operation Midnight Ride, February-March 1963

The Walker-Hargis speaking tour was named "Operation Midnight Ride" after Paul Revere's 1775 patriotic midnight ride to warn of the advancing British Redcoats. General Walker fancied himself as a modern-day Paul Revere, who was setting out to warn the country of the advancing "Red Communists."

During a typical appearance, Billy James Hargis spoke first, warning the audience of the external—or international—threat of Communism, while Walker spoke for the last hour on the internal—or domestic—threat of Communism. The "internal Communist threat" was a euphemism loosely used by the far right to describe their enemies: known Communists, liberals on campuses and in the churches, integrationists, organized labor, and ban-the-bomb groups. Walker's other speech targets were the United Nations and the United States Departemnt of Defense. The tour included twenty-seven cities in seventeen states, beginning in Miami, Florida, and ending five weeks later in Los Angeles, California.[2013, 2014]

The real reason for the speaking tour, besides fundraising for the hardcore underground, was to muster a militant citizen hardcore underground following across the country, as was discussed in Chapter Eight. Later, in 1964, the FBI investigated allegations that Walker had been raising an army for insurrection and will be discussed later. Further evidence that Walker was networking and raising a far-right underground army is an FBI report that noted that during the period from March 1963 through 1965, Walker was "considered a very important person" within the militant, far-right California Minutemen, "and apparently was an advisor" in California, Texas, and Iowa. (The Minutemen were gearing up for an anticipated Communist takeover of the U.S.) He was personally acquainted with, and in contact with, numerous important men in the organization, even before he spoke in California in March 1963 as a part of the Operation Midnight Ride tour.[2015]

On February 23, 1962, Walker departed Dallas for Florida. On February 24, 1963, a source told the FBI that Walker was visiting Oren Potito (a close associate of Joseph Milteer) in St. Petersburg and staying with him until March 1, 1963. Potito was an organizer for the white supremacist, openly anti-Semitic National States' Rights Party.[2016, 2017] The FBI obtained the membership file cards from the Dallas National States' Rights Party, and Walker's name and address was found on one of them.[2018] Potito's home apparently served as a base for Walker while speaking on the Operation Midnight Ride tour in three Florida cities. Walker's week-long stay with Potito, who was closely aligned with and lived in the same region as Milteer, may have been when Milteer first established his well-documented association with Walker.

The first engagement of the Operation Midnight Ride tour was in Miami on February 27, 1963. Kent Courtney traveled from New Orleans to attend the event and cover it in his newspaper. Courtney referred to the tour as "country saving." (Courtney also attended the March 4 rally in Tampa.) Walker repeated his charges that President Kennedy planned to put the U.S. military under U.N. control.[2019] On March 1, Walker and Hargis spoke in Palm Beach where during a preceding press conference, a reporter accused Walker of leading the riots at Ole Miss. Hargis interceded and called the assertion "unfair and unjust," telling the reporter that it was not only untrue, it was un-American. The reporter responded, "Mr. Hargis, I was in Oxford. I saw him lead the student riots."[2020]

On March 1, the FBI learned from Legat (the FBI Europe office), Bonn, West Germany, that Walker had been corresponding and sending circulars to various European Fascists, calling for worldwide action against Jews. (This is not surprising in light of Walker's involvement in the high military command behind the plots to assassinate leading Jewish figures and others, which was revealed at the Council for Statehood meeting in late 1962 and reiterated at the Congress of Freedom meeting in April 1963.)[2021] At the same time, on March 1, Walker and Hargis were speaking at the George Washington Hotel in West Palm Beach to a crowd of one thousand.[2022]

On March 4, Dallas FBI Agent James Hosty reopened the case on Marina Oswald. He noted that she could not speak English.[2023]

On March 6, 1963, the Operation Midnight Ride tour stopped at Jacksonville, Florida,[2024] followed by stops in Atlanta and Knoxville. The tour continued on and Walker and Hargis spoke at the Montgomery, Alabama, City Auditorium on March 9. During his speech in Montgomery, Walker referred to the Kennedy family as "the Kennedy dynasty and dictatorship" repeatedly.[2025] The radical right reasoned that if the three Kennedy brothers served eight years each as president, they would monopolize the office until 1984, hence the term "Kennedy dynasty."

On March 10, while General Walker was on tour, Lee Harvey Oswald took a number of photographs of Walker's Dallas home from different vantage points. The photos were discovered after the assassination, and gave the impression that Oswald had been staking out the residence in preparation to shoot Walker. The photos would have no value in accomplishing the murder of Walker, but would merely serve to incriminate Oswald—which was his whole point of taking them, as we shall see later. Had the whole gambit played out, Walker would have been able to prove what he often claimed—that the Communists were out to get him and the real threat of Communism was from within.

On March 12, 1963, Oswald purchased the Manlicher-Carcano rifle that the Warren Commission determined was used in the murder of the president and likely was also used in the Walker shooting incident.

Also on March 12, 1963, Walker spoke with Hargis at a Greenville, South Carolina, rally sponsored by Bob Jones University, and asserted, "I resigned the service to be free, I refuse to lead soldiers under the United Nations flag." He added, "I am hoping to see Kennedy out of the White House in 1964." Walker stated that the Bay of Pigs invasion had been intended to fail and that President Kennedy wanted to destroy the Constitution.[2026]

Tom Anderson presided over Walker's tour stop in Nashville, Tennessee, on March 13. General Walker challenged President Kennedy "to take one division of airborne troops from Fort Bragg, N.C., and liquidate the scourge" in Cuba. Walker told the crowd that Anderson had made seventy-six speeches in the last year but that the Kennedy-controlled press did not report them. In addition to the one-dollar admission, in Nashville, Hargis passed around a collection plate as he usually did. A handbill promoting an upcoming John Roussel-ot speech in Nashville on May 17 was also distributed.[2027] As will later be seen, Anderson was an important Walker confidant; the allegations that Anderson and Rousselot were involved in the assassination conspiracy will be discussed later.

On March 14, 1963, the Dallas FBI determined that Lee Harvey Oswald had con-tacted the Communist Party U.S.A. newspaper, *The Daily Worker*.[2028] On that same day, Walker and Hargis spoke in Phoenix, Arizona, at the Shrine Temple Auditorium.[2029]

On March 19, Myers Lowman of the Circuit Riders sponsored the tour in Cincinna-ti,[2030] which was followed by a stop in St. Louis hosted by Dr. J. Hess.[2031] That day, Pedro del Valle wrote Walker and told him that he was doing a great job on the tour and that he believed he could be elected president in 1964.[2032]

On March 25, 1963, Medford Evans—who was at General Walker's side during Walker's Senate muzzling-hearing testimony—was the featured speaker at the New Orle-ans Citizens' Council meeting with George Singelmann and Leander Perez.[2033] (Evans was a friend of Guy Banister's and had worked for H. L. Hunt in the 1950s as was previously noted.) On March 26, Walker and Hargis spoke in Denver and were picketed by Fair Play for Cuba Committee and the Socialist Labor Party.[2034] (Oswald had corresponded with both of those leftist groups.) On March 27, General Clyde Watts was the tour chairman for the Oklahoma City stop.[2035]

On March 29, 1963, Oswald contacted the Fair Play for Cuba Committee in New York and told them that he wanted to form a chapter of FPCC in New Orleans.[2036] The incident suggests that Oswald had planned on leaving Dallas for New Orleans at that time, before the Walker shooting incident on April 10. It also suggests the Banister operation likely directed the FPCC contact, since they were intimately involved in the FPCC saga in New Orleans that unfolded out of the building at 544 Camp Street.

While Oswald was in Dallas, apparently preparing for the staged shooting, Kent Courtney, had access to generals Walker and Clyde Watts, both of whom were closely tied to the shooting incident and its aftermath. Courtney was with General Walker at the Florida speeches on February 27 and March 4. (Later, Courtney and Guy Banister were in attendance when Walker's close associate, Clyde Watts spoke at the infamous April 5, 1963, Congress of Freedom meeting. The encounters of Walker and Watts with members of the New Orleans operation behind Oswald—Courtney and Banister—provided them with the opportunity to offer input into the Walker shooting incident that took place on April 10, 1963.)

The April 1 tour stop in San Diego was presided over by famed FBI counterspy Karl Prussion, who, like Herbert Philbrick, made a living speaking on the Communist menace and testifying before state and congressional committees.[2037]

On April 2, 1963, the Kennedy administration sent a draft of a four-point bill aimed at speeding up black voter registration.[2038] Southerners became incensed by President Kenne-dy's increasing advocacy of African American rights.

Dan Smoot's financial angel, D. B. Lewis, presided over the tour stop on April 3, in

Los Angeles.[2039] Walker and Hargis spoke to their largest audience—4,500 people—to end the tour. California congressman John Rousselot, who later became a John Birch Society co-ordinator, presented Walker with a plaque proclaiming him the "greatest living American."[2040] (Allegations of Rousselot's involvement in the Kennedy assassination conspiracy will be presented later.) As has been noted, the California stop heralded the documented beginning of Walker's relationship with the California Minutemen—which included Milteer's friend, Colonel William Potter Gale. Also on April 3, 1963, Kent Courtney wrote to Walker and suggested he let members of the armed forces know that President Kennedy "is proceeding on a conscious, calculated plan to disarm the United States."[2041]

Interestingly, Walker's whereabouts from April 4 to 8 are unknown, but it is known that, at dusk on April 8th, he arrived back home in Dallas from the tour and was visited by Robert Surrey.[2042]

During the period of April 6–24, 1963, the Warren Commission determined that Lee Harvey Oswald might have distributed Fair Play for Cuba materials in Dallas.[2043]

Operation Midnight Ride was a success; in the end Walker and Hargis spoke before nearly 40,000 people. The sale of literature and collections from the audience likely earned them a tidy sum.[2044, 2045]

General Walker (left), with Billy James Hargis (middle), showed the press the U.S. State Department pamphlet on disarmament and said it indicated that the U.S. was soft on Russian Communism. The two spoke at the March 19th Operation Midnight Ride tour stop in St. Louis hosted by J. Hess, M.D. (right). Source: Corbis

On April 4, 5, and 6, 1963, the Congress of Freedom met in New Orleans, just after the first leg of the Operation Midnight Ride tour came to an end. Willie Somersett informed the FBI that members at the meeting were plotting to assassinate large numbers of prominent Jewish figures, members of the Council on Foreign Relations, and others in business and industry (as described in Chapter Six). Notables in attendance at the meeting were Joseph Milteer, General Clyde Watts, Kent Courtney, and Guy Banister. After the meeting, the FBI interrogated prominent members of the Council for Statehood and they denied involvement in any assassination plots. The plots were abandoned as the FBI's interrogation served to place the principals involved on notice and alerting them that they had an informant in their midst. The FBI interviewed informants who attended Operation Midnight Ride speeches as a part of their investigation into "Racial Matters," not because of Walker's role in the high military command of the Council for Statehood that plotted assassinations. (Some in the FBI knew about the plotting in late 1962, long before the Midnight Ride tour began.)

On April 10, just after his return from Operation Midnight Ride, someone shot at General Walker and missed. Walker was quick to blame it on a Communist, and the Warren

Commission eventually determined it was Lee Harvey Oswald. Two weeks later, on April 24, 1963, Ruth Paine drove Oswald to the bus station, where he left for New Orleans without his family. (The shooting incident will be discussed at length following the next section, which details the second leg of the Walker speaking tour—following the shooting.)

Walker and Hargis used the shooting for publicity during the next leg of their speaking tour, even pointing out that a Communist did the shooting—but without bringing Lee Harvey Oswald into the picture. On May 17, 1963, a writer for Hargis's *Weekly Crusader* wrote a first-page story entitled "Edwin Walker: The Target and the Man." The writer said that Walker was "designated for the first organized public assassination of a prominent figure in the memory of millions of Americans." The article cited an interview where Walker stated the gunman may have come from outside Texas, and that he had been marked for destruction by the Communist apparatus as early as the 1950s. He added that if he had been permanently detained at the Springfield mental facility after his arrest at Ole Miss, it would have served the same purpose as the shooting. Walker claimed that the Soviet paper *Pravda* had identified him as a target in the early spring of 1961, when a Communist dossier pointed him out as an "ultra," a term the Soviets used to describe the radical right. (Oswald was in the Soviet Union at that time.) Walker said he did not just become a target of the Communist conspiracy on April 10, 1963, but had been one since he learned of the Communist influence behind integration at Little Rock. General Walker supposedly telephoned Hargis before the press reported the shooting incident and told him, "Billy, let's make another tour immediately. This attempt to kill me has only made me determined to speed up our anti-Communist activities. This proves that the front line in the fight against Communism is at home."[2046] Walker told the press, "The shooting here is going to speed me up. You know I said when I came back home that the front lines were right here at home—Dallas."[2047] Of course, there was no *public* inkling that Oswald, a self-proclaimed Marxist, was involved in the shooting at the time Walker alluded that a Communist tried to kill him.

On April 12, 1963, Carl McIntire sent Walker a telegram after he learned about the shooting, stating, "Deeply grateful for God's providence that spared you." Walker wrote McIntire one week later, thanking him for the message, and told him, "Swastika posters appeared on stores of 9 Jewish merchants yesterday. We expect a shooting on the other side or near miss that kills an innocent child. The script is always the same. The blame must be shifted to our side."[2048] (The allegation that McIntire was involved in the assassination conspiracy will be presented in Chapter Nineteen.)

On April 16, 1963, Kent Courtney sent Walker a copy of the radio edition of *The Independent American* newspaper, reporting the facts about the recent assassination attempt on him "as you [Walker] gave them to us." Walker told him he had no personal enemies and that "the only people who would like to see him out of the way are the Communists . . . . This is proof that there is a Communist threat from within our nation." Courtney added, "Now the Communist Reds are shooting at the patriotic Americans."[2049]

The Walker Shooting Incident, April 10, 1963

Someone shot at General Walker while he was working near a window at his home on April 10, 1963, just after his return from the first leg of the his speaking tour. Based on Marina Oswald's testimony, her husband was unquestionably involved in some way. The fact that General Walker was close to both Guy Banister and Kent Courtney—whose operation was closely aligned with Lee Harvey Oswald—is enough evidence to conclude that Oswald was not actually trying to kill General Walker. The shooting served other purposes, as we shall see, that were also unrelated to the assassination of the president.

Aside from Walker's and Oswald's mutual associations with the Banister operation, there are telling clues which can be found in a close examination of the Warren Commission evidence in the Walker shooting incident that also strongly suggest the entire affair was phony. Oswald took pictures around General Walker's house on March 10, 1963, indicating the plan for Oswald's involvement in the Walker shooting incident began at least a month before it happened. The Warren Commission determined Lee Harvey Oswald did the shooting with the Manlicher-Carcano rifle he purchased by mail order on March 12, 1963. Oswald instructed his wife to take pictures of him holding the rifle in his back yard, which served to produce more incriminating evidence against him.

The pictures show a menacing Oswald, dressed in black, wearing a holstered .38 pistol and holding his rifle in one hand. In the other hand he held copies of both the Communist Party U.S.A. newspaper, *The Worker*, and the Socialist Workers Party newspaper, *The Militant*, which didn't make sense.[2050] The ideologies of the Communist Party and Socialist Workers Party were conflicting, and the groups were at odds with one another. For someone to actually have both papers would be as incongruous as a person holding copies of literature from both the Republican Party and the Democratic Party. Walker, like many on the far right, subscribed to *The Worker*.[2051]

Marina Oswald took this picture of her husband before the Walker shooting incident. Oswald is holding the Kennedy assassination weapon and two newspapers of conflicting ideologies. Source: Warren Commission

General Walker returned home to Dallas from the Operation Midnight Ride tour on Monday, April 8th. While he was allegedly filling out his income taxes, sitting at a desk by an open window, on Wednesday April 10th, he claimed he heard what sounded like a firecracker. He saw a hole in the wall just to his left and his arm allegedly bled from the bullet's flying debris. Walker then claimed he ran upstairs, grabbed his pistol, and looked around the premises. At about 9:10 p.m., he notified the police by phone. The police immediately arrived, with reporters not far behind. When asked whom he thought had shot at him, Walker replied that it was someone from the "other side" who was a lousy shot. He added, "The Kennedys say there's no internal threat to our freedom." When everyone left, Walker returned to filling out his income taxes.[2052] Walker implied a Communist had shot at him and he also took the occasion to gratuitously complain about the Kennedys, who, he felt, ignored the Communist threat at home (the "internal threat").

The early city edition of the *Dallas Morning News* on Friday April 12, 1963, covered the Walker story and reported that a gunman with a high-powered rifle took a shot at Walker through a rear window while he was working at his desk at 9:30 at night. According to the newspaper story, Walker was raking slivers out of his hair and right sleeve when reporters got there. He said he had returned home on Monday (April 8) from the coast-to-coast Operation Midnight Ride speaking tour. On Monday night, two days before the shooting, one of his assistants supposedly noted a late-model car parked without lights in the alley behind Walker's house. The car remained there for thirty minutes while one of the occupants walked up to the back door to look in, then left. When Walker was asked if he had any idea who shot at him, the paper reported that he had said, "There are plenty of people on the other side. You don't have to go overseas to earn a Purple Heart." Deciphered, Walker implied that he didn't have to fight the Communists overseas to get wounded by one at home. He added, "I've been saying the front was right here at home."[2053] Communists were few in Dallas in 1963, yet Walker had apparently already surmised correctly that a Communist was involved right after it happened.

The FBI determined there were seven known Communists in Dallas and they were members of a cell. They had an informant in the cell and received excellent intelligence from him—he'd never heard of Oswald.

The Friday, April 12, evening edition of the *Dallas Morning News* reported that a Walker aide told police that he saw *two* men in a late-model car behind Walker's home on Saturday night studying the back of the house. In this second account, the aide—who turned out to be Milteer associate Robert Surrey—moved the date back two days from his first account. Surrey said the men left in a dark purple or brown Ford that had no license plates. According to the news story, the police felt the shot was fired from the alley at a distance of thirty-five to forty yards, where there was a clear view. They felt the shot was taken where a fresh wood chip on a lattice-type fence was found. Walker declared that the sniper's attempt only succeeded in convincing him that his anti-Communist speaking campaign needed intensifying.[2054]

As we shall see, the phony shooting incident served, in part, to energize the next leg of the Walker-Hargis speaking tour. More importantly, as the evidence will show later, it was part of the New Orleans operation to demonstrate that Oswald—who later in 1963 infiltrated several groups tied to the integration effort—was not only a Communist, but also a dangerous one. The introduction to the text of the Louisiana Communist Control Act— which was the brainchild of Leander Perez—stated that Communists represented a "clear and present danger" to the people of Louisiana. The plan of the Banister operation was to use the Communist Control Act and Oswald to destroy several liberal organizations, including Fair Play for Cuba Committee, that were tied to the integration effort. (A detailed discussion of that important subject will be provided later.)

According to the Dallas police, in a December 31, 1963, report prepared for the FBI after the Kennedy assassination, Walker—contrary to his earlier claim—told them he had no idea who fired the shot at him. Robert Surrey, repeating his story in more detail, told the police he noticed a white male sitting in a 1963 dark green or purple Ford without license plates parked at the rear of Walker's house. He saw two men get out of the car and walk around Walker's house. The police report noted, "The complainant [Walker] did not seem to be disturbed about the incident." Surrey told the Warren Commission that, two nights before the shooting, he saw two men around the house peeking in windows. The story, yet again, differed from the original. Moreover, Walker, when speaking to the Warren Commission, claimed he gave the information about the men walking around his house to the police *before* the shooting, which is not corroborated by Dallas Police reports.[2055]

Kirk Coleman, a fourteen-year-old next-door neighbor, heard the shot fired on April 10th. He told the police that the suspects were in several cars that were on the church parking lot adjacent to Walker's house. He said that he went over to a fence and looked out to the church parking lot and saw an unknown white male speed down the driveway with the door open in either a 1949 or 1950 light green Ford. The man was described as middle-sized, with long black hair. Coleman said that he then noticed an individual in a black 1958 Chevrolet with the door open that appeared to be someone putting something on the car floorboards. The man got in the car and left, but did not appear to be in a hurry. Coleman was initially standing in the doorway, which led from his bedroom to the outside of his house, and which the FBI estimated was fourteen feet from the fence behind Walker's home—or a two-second walk away. Coleman stated the man in the Ford looked back at him. The area was well illuminated by floodlights from the church. He described the man in the Ford as white, nineteen or twenty years old, about 5'10" tall and weighing about 130 pounds. He had dark, bushy hair and a thin face with a large nose, and was "real skinny." He described the other man in the Chevrolet as a white male, about 6'1" and 200 pounds. When questioned after the Kennedy assassination, Coleman told the FBI that neither man resembled Lee Harvey Oswald, who did not have a car and did not drive.[2056]

Based on Coleman's information, one of the men who left the scene knew there was an eyewitness. The man could not know how much of the incident Coleman had witnessed. For all he knew, Coleman saw the shooter and, perhaps, recognized the fleeing men as men he had seen before with Walker or his aide. If the purpose of the shooting was to demonstrate that Oswald, the Communist, was out to kill Walker—and represented the internal Communist threat that Walker often talked about—then if someone other than Oswald did the shooting (or there was other conflicting evidence), the gambit was exposed.

Commenting on a newspaper report about Kirk Coleman's story that appeared after the assassination, Dallas Police Lieutenant L. E. Cunningham—who had led the original investigation of the shooting in April—expressed his skepticism about the supposed attempt on Walker's life. He stated, "This was a method used by General Walker to gain additional publicity . . . Walker will exploit current news releases to the fullest to gain maximum publicity . . . ."[2057] Walker was all about publicity and self-promotion. One FBI informant who knew Walker described him as "being very much an egotist who would do almost anything for publicity."[2058, 2059] The police's skepticism combined with the existence of an eyewitness, Kirk Coleman, compromised the lone-gunman scheme and it was never fully played out, as will be shown.

After the Kennedy assassination, Marina Oswald reported that a month before the shooting incident her husband had been writing in a notebook that he kept hidden in his room. He showed her several pictures he had taken of General Walker's house. She said that the notebook contained descriptions of the various distances to the house and the locations of the windows. (The photos and notebook plans were completely superfluous information for someone wanting to shoot General Walker, which was a simple proposition.) She said Oswald returned from the shooting without his rifle, and said he buried it far from where police dogs could pick up its scent. The story of police dogs and burying the rifle seems far-fetched. More believable is Kirk Coleman's eyewitness account that suggests an unidentified man, not Oswald, placed the rifle on the floorboards of his car and left with it.

Marina further reported that, three days later, Oswald brought the rifle back and, an hour later, burned his notebook. Marina told the Warren Commission that she surmised the notebook had contained Oswald's plans for the shooting. When asked why he kept the incriminating evidence in the notebook, she replied, "I am guessing he did it to appear to be a brave man in case he was arrested, but that is my supposition."[2060] Marina told the Secret Service that her husband read in the newspaper about the boy who saw three people leave the scene in a car. He told her the Americans always think they need to use a car to get away from the scene of a crime, but that he used his feet, then took a bus home. [2061, 2062]

Warren Commission counsel Wesley Liebler was not entirely imperceptive, sensing the possibility that there was something phony about the shooting incident, when he posed the following questions to Marina:

> Mr. Liebler: Did it seem strange to you at the time, Marina, that Lee did make these careful plans, take pictures, and write it up in a notebook, and then when he went out to shoot at General Walker he left all that incriminating evidence right in the house so that if he had ever been stopped and questioned and if that notebook had been found, it would have clearly indicated that he was the one that shot at General Walker?
>
> Mrs. Oswald: He was such a person that nothing seemed peculiar to me . . .
>
> Mr. Liebler: Did you ever have the feeling that he really wanted to be caught in connection with the Walker affair?
>
> Mrs. Oswald: I don't know how to answer that—Maybe yes and may be no. I couldn't read his mind.[2063]

It was not the only time Oswald wanted publicity and expected to get arrested. For example, in August 1963, in New Orleans, Oswald got into a half-hearted fight with anti-Castro Cuban Carlos Bringuier while passing out Fair Play for Cuba literature. Since the fight occurred in front of a police officer, arrest was expected. He spent the night in jail and his wife stated that, afterward, he was pleased with the incident. Oswald had notified the New York head of FPCC that he had been in a fight days before the actual fight occurred, which is proof that it was phony. Marina Oswald told the Warren Commission, "I think that Lee engaged in this activity primarily of the purposes of self-advertising. He wanted to be arrested. I think he wanted to get into the newspapers so that he would be known."[2064] (The Bringuier "fight" and Oswald's arrest and another incident where Oswald expected to get arrested will be detailed later.)

The backyard photos of Oswald and his rifle served to advertise that he was a militant Communist and would, if the scheme had been carried out, have captured police interest in him as a suspect in the shooting incident. The fact that Oswald was a phony Communist— and that the shooting incident was bogus, as the evidence will continue to show—leaves no other obvious reasons for the photos to be taken. Oswald even told his wife the purpose of the menacing backyard photos was to send them to a newspaper or *The Militant.* He also wanted to save a copy for his daughter June. Perhaps Oswald envisioned himself, one day, as a Herbert Philbrick-type patriotic Communist infiltrator and wanted to keep a souvenir of his work for his daughter.[2065]

Staff members of *The Militant,* after the Kennedy assassination, recalled receiving the photos.[2066] Had they actually published the photos, as perhaps Oswald hoped—there being no other good reason for sending them—the outcome could have been spectacular. After alerting the police to *The Militant* photo and Oswald as a suspect, a search of his possessions would have revealed the rifle, the incriminating notebook, and photos of Walker's home. The case against Oswald would have been airtight and Walker would have had the dramatic evidence he needed to show that the domestic Communists were a clear and present danger to the country and were out to get anti-Communists like him. Oswald might have agreed to the scheme, knowing that Walker would refuse to press charges against him—perhaps instead blaming the Kennedys for the shooting, as he actually did, for their inaction against the Communist menace. Having someone else do the shooting might also have made Oswald more comfortable about getting involved in the scheme.

FBI Director J. Edgar Hoover provided his analysis of the Walker shooting incident to the Warren Commission: "It is pointed out the two automobiles and the two individuals described in the interviews with [Name redacted] have not been identified. It appears only logical these two individuals are (1) either accomplices of the individual shooting at General Walker; (2) are witnesses to the shooting who are reluctant to divulge their identity, or (3) they are associates of General Walker."[2067]

Operation Alert, May 1963

After the shooting, Walker and Hargis decided to begin another, smaller, speaking tour called Operation Alert. The tour was to last thirteen days, beginning on May 15, in Salt Lake City, followed by stops in Seattle, Portland, Minneapolis, Little Rock, Memphis, and Baton Rouge, ending on May 28, interestingly, in New Orleans. (*Alert* was also the title of General Pedro del Valle's newsletter that warned his readers of the imminent Communist threat.)

During the same period, the Kennedy administration contemplated action against the segregationists and the segregationists, in turn, contemplated action against the Kennedy administration. On April 17, 1963, the U.S. Civil Rights Commission recommended that President Kennedy cut off federal funds to Mississippi because of the racial disorder in the state. Senator Eastland called the proposal, "the most libel that has ever been leveled against a state in this union."[2068] The following day, the Mississippi State Sovereignty Commission met in closed session and discussed allocating state funds to carry out Governor Barnett's anti-Kennedy free elector plan. Barnett had already met in Montgomery with representatives from six or seven other states to discuss a unified Southern states' free electors scheme.[2069]

On April 24, 1963, in a story that illustrates the wanton violence that occurred in the South for the cause of segregation, Walter Moore was shot and killed at close range on Highway 11 in Attalla, Alabama. Moore was a white mailman from Baltimore who was on a one-man walking campaign for racial equality that began in Chattanooga and was to end in Mississippi. Moore was wearing a provocative sign that read on one side "Eat at Joe's, both black and white" and on the other side "Equal rights for all—Mississippi or bust."[2070] President Kennedy expressed shock at what he called "the assassination of a citizen on a public road."[2071]

On that same day, Robert Kennedy traveled to Montgomery, Alabama—the cradle of the old Confederacy—to pay a courtesy call on Governor George Wallace. He gave an interview at a local TV station where two state troopers refused to shake his hand. He met with Wallace the next day.[2072]

One week later, on May 1, 1963, the infamous race riots broke out in Birmingham, Alabama. Firemen and police officers used fire hoses and German Shepherd attack dogs on the black protestors. The horrific scene was shown around the world and caused widespread outcry.

On May 2, Kent Courtney held a meeting of the Conservative Party of America in Des Moines, Iowa. Courtney said, "The Communists haven't gained power by convincing the masses but by convincing people in key positions."[2073]

On May 3, the unpledged electors bill was introduced into the Louisiana Legislature in an attempt to deprive President Kennedy of the state's Electoral College votes for the 1964 election.[2074] A free elector rally was held at Capitol House Hotel on May 10, 1963, in Baton Rouge. Guy Banister was named as a representative to the First District in the electors campaign.[2075] The Sovereignty Commission backed the electors.[2076]

On May 8, George Singelmann, Guy Banister's close associate, was scheduled to present a film about the desegregation of the Washington, D.C., public schools at a Lakeview Citizens' Council meeting.[2077] (The film was shown around the South and selectively depicted unflattering views of African-American students in the integrated schools.)

On May 9, 1963, Carl McIntire spoke at the Shreveport Municipal Auditorium.[2078] (As noted previously, Banister attended a speech by McIntire at the Capitol House Hotel in Baton Rouge.) Allegations that McIntire's west coast representative, Gene Bradley, was a part of the assassination conspiracy surfaced during the Garrison investigation (as was noted in Chapter Nine).

Also on May 9, 1963, Lee Harvey Oswald rented an apartment at 4907 Magazine Street in New Orleans. The following day, he took a job as a machine oiler at Reily Coffee Company. Oswald often ducked out of work and went next door to read gun magazines at a service garage waiting room. The manager of the garage, Adrian Alba, like Guy Banister, was in the Minutemen.[2079]

On May 18 and 19, Robert Welch was scheduled to conduct a two-day Dallas John Birch Society chapter meeting at 4508 Lakeside Drive.[2080] The FBI identified Robert Surrey, and his wife Mary, as the Dallas chapter's leaders.

Jackson Ricau, a Banister colleague, spoke at a South Louisiana Citizens' Council meeting on May 20, 1963, and commented on the recent racial tensions in Birmingham. He stated: "With the exception of Little Rock and Oxford never since the dark days of Reconstruction has this nation witnessed the likes of what is happening in Birmingham."[2081] On May 21, 1963, the anti-Kennedy Unpledged Electors Bill was introduced to the Louisiana House of Representatives.[2082]

On May 24, Hargis and Walker spoke in Little Rock. During his speech, Walker said he heard that the White House had been blackmailed by the Catholic Church to cut the air support for the Bay of Pigs operation.[2083]

On May 26, 1963, Walker and Hargis spoke in Shreveport, where Walker's speech was entitled "Choices before us—U.S. or U.N.?"[2084] Later that evening, they spoke at the Capitol House Hotel in Baton Rouge.[2085] Hargis spoke for the first hour, criticizing liberals. Walker spoke for the last hour, criticizing the NAACP and the United Nations, calling the latter "the biggest spy and propaganda building ever built."[2086]

The next day, Walker and Hargis spoke before a crowd of one thousand people in Baton Rouge as part of Operation Alert. Walker stated, "Its harder every day to tell the difference between Kennedyism and Communism." Walker said the front of the Cold War ran "through Havana, the United Nations and the White House." Hargis said "three of the rankest Communists in the United States and two carloads of race agitators" had recently invaded Baton Rouge—a reference to the volunteers working for the Congress of Racial Equality's voter registration initiative. Walker earlier had appeared at the state senate, where he walked down the aisle to pay his respects to Lieutenant Governor C. C. Aycock. Senator Wendell Harris told the Senate, Walker "will be remembered most from Oxford," and asked the Senate to give Walker "a vote of thanks and confidence." They applauded Walker as he walked down the Senate aisle with the sergeant at arms.[2087]

On May 28, 1963, Walker and Hargis visited New Orleans to conclude the Operation Alert tour. Hargis, again getting more mileage out of the unsolved Walker shooting incident, told the press that the tour was prompted by a shot fired at Walker on April 10, 1963. Hargis said, "Before the news ever reached the public General Walker called me and said, 'Billy, let's make another tour immediately.'"[2088] (Lee Harvey Oswald was in New Orleans at the time of the New Orleans tour stop.)

The significant accomplishment of the Operation Midnight Ride and Operation Alert tours was that it gave Walker and Hargis a public platform to rail against the Kennedys and an opportunity to network and rally citizens to their cause across the country. It put them in direct contact with leading members of the far right: Oren Potito, Kent Courtney, Myers Lowman, D. B. Lewis, Clyde Watts, John Rousselot, Bob Jones, and Tom Anderson. The tour, which included sales of literature, was a source of funding for Walker's operation. FBI informant Willie Somersett stated that Hargis was using his speaking engagements to raise funds for the hardcore underground. Importantly, the tour and related shooting incident brought Lee Harvey Oswald—the one essential constant in the assassination story—into Walker's sphere. After the tour, letters of praise and financial contributions poured into Walker's Turtle Creek Boulevard residence and headquarters.[2089]

William "Scottie" Duff

General Walker's secretary, Julia Knecht, was interviewed on April 12, 1963, and said she believed William Duff was a possible suspect in the Walker shooting incident. William "Scottie" Duff was a volunteer/employee of General Walker, who acted as Walker's valet and chauffeur. According to the FBI, Duff was suspected of the shooting primarily because he was a "con man."[2090] No one alleged that Duff was a Communist and, as a Walker admirer and volunteer/employee, he was probably just the opposite.

Knecht told the police that Walker's neighbor had a dog that "barked at anything and everything." However, she noted that the dog did not bark at the suspects on the night of the shooting, adding that the dog was very sick for two days after the shooting.[2091] One implication of Knecht's story was that someone poisoned the dog so it would not bark at the shooter. In fact, the dog's owner believed someone had given her dog something to drug or poison him to quiet him.[2092]

Walker aide Robert Surrey told the police that a large floodlight in the back of Walker's house was out on the night of the shooting, which is odd considering Surrey said he had seen strangers around the property looking into windows days earlier. Surrey told the police that William Duff had arrived at Walker's home in December 1962, and had offered to help his organization in exchange for a place to stay. He reported that Duff became lazy about his duties and, on March 10, 1963, his luggage was moved into the hall and he was asked to leave. Surrey said that Duff was not truthful about his whereabouts before arriving in Dallas.

General Clyde Watts became involved in the Duff affair. Watts, who was in the high military command of the assassination-plotting Council for Statehood, later became Walker's attorney during his Warren Commission testimony about the shooting incident. Watts also testified and elaborated on Knecht's suspicions. Watts said that he and Knecht suspected Duff because Knecht received an anonymous phone call from a woman whose daughter was dating Duff. The woman claimed her daughter told her that Duff was involved in the shooting and bragged about it. Watts said he was unable to identify the anonymous woman caller. General Walker interjected, stating that Watts got the story wrong. Walker insisted that the mother who called Knecht was upset with Duff, but that she never said Duff admitted he was involved in the attack.[2093]

On June 6, 1963, Walker told Dallas police a different story, saying that a lady called his secretary and told her that she had heard from Charles Holloway, whom Duff roomed with after he ended his stay at Walker's, saying that Duff had shot at Walker. The police interviewed Holloway and he said Duff never told him he shot at Walker. The police were unable to identify the lady that Walker alleged had called his secretary. The police concluded that "Bill Duff did not have anything to do with the assault on General Walker."

The police interviewed Peggy Marie Whitley, who had previously been engaged to Duff, but broke it off, on April 16, 1963. She had not seen him since April 6. She stated he had come to her place in various vehicles including a 1963 Ford, but the police report did not list a color. The inference was that one of Duff's cars could have been the 1963 dark green or purple Ford that Robert Surrey claimed to have seen on the night of the shooting. However, none of Duff's cars came close to meeting the description of the suspects' cars—a 1949 or 1950 light green Ford and a black 1958 Chevrolet—as provided by Kirk Coleman.

Police also interviewed Walker again on April 16, and Walker told them that Duff came back to his house on April 13 and told him he had been in Phoenix, Arizona, when he heard about the shooting. Walker gave the police phone numbers for two friends of Duff who had been interested in raising money for Walker's cause. He told police that there might have been a tie between the shooting and the individuals who had recently painted swastikas on businesses and residences owned by prominent Dallas Jewish citizens. (There is no indication that the police were aware that Robert Surrey, Walker's top aide, was the head of the Dallas American Nazi Party. Had they been aware of that fact, they might have found Walker's claim about the individuals behind the swastika-painting affair strange.)

On April 18, the police arrested, jailed, and then released William Duff, pending investigation. They noted that Duff made his money "sponging and mooching money from friends" and that he engaged in "bumming off friends and obtained money under false pretenses."

Dallas police detective Ira Van Cleave, who investigated the shooting, received a curious letter from Miami, Florida, dated April 22, 1963, that read as follows:

Dear Mr. Van Cleave,

I BELIEVE THAT CASTRO'S COMMUNIST SECRET AGENTS (RED ARMY SECURITY OFFICES) WHO HAD BEEN TRAINED IN SILENT MURDER, ARSONISM, TERRORISM, SABOTAGE, REVOLUTIONARY WARFARE BY HIGHLY COMPETENT SOVIET 'K.E.B.' [sic] INSTRUCTORS AT THE 'KUCHINO SCHOOL IN MOSCOW, RUSSIA', THEY FIRED THE ASSASIN'S [sic] BULLET THAT WANTED TO KILL FORMER U.S. ARMY GENERAL MR. WALKER. CASTRO'S RED SECRET AGENTS THEY OPERATE FROM THE CUBAN EMBASSY.

Mari Murais, who claimed to be a former officer with the Cuban federal police, signed the letter. It's not clear if the intent of the letter was to try to implicate Lee Harvey Oswald—who had returned from the Soviet Union less than a year before—in the shooting. The letter, like Walker, blamed the shooting incident on a Communist. It's not known if the FBI questioned "Mr. Murais," who, like Oswald, was a poor speller.

On June 6, 1963, Bill Keester and Cliff Roberts, two private detectives from Oklahoma City, who were in the employ of General Clyde Watts, contacted the Dallas police. (As we shall see later, one of the detectives, like Watts, was a racist and a Kennedy hater.) Watts had recently hosted Walker and Hargis at the March 27 Operation Midnight Ride speech in Oklahoma City. The convergence of Walker, Watts, and Hargis at the meeting afforded them the opportunity to plan the staging of the shooting incident. On April 4, 5, and 6—days before the April 10 shooting incident—Watts was at the murder-plotting Congress of Freedom meeting in New Orleans attended by Joseph Milteer, Guy Banister, George Soule, and Kent Courtney. Watts, in his testimony to the Warren Commission, told them that Walker's secretary, Julia Knecht, called him and said she suspected that William Duff was involved in the shooting.

Cliff Roberts, one Watts's hired detectives—who had formerly worked for the Oklahoma State Narcotics Bureau—told police he had come to Dallas in the later part of May 1963 and rented an apartment in the same building Duff lived in to get close to him. (It should be noted that Watts went to the extraordinary expense of sending detectives, one full time, from Oklahoma to Dallas when—if the investigation had not been bogus—local detectives could have done the job for far cheaper.) Roberts told police that he engaged in casual conversation with Duff about General Walker and then, he said, he told Duff that someone should kill Walker. Duff told him he would do it if the price were right. Roberts told Duff that he knew a party that would pay to have the job done. Roberts then called his partner William Keester, who came to Dallas and met with Duff.

Keester told Duff he had the money to pay for killing Walker, and the three planned how it was to be done. Roberts made a surreptitious tape recording of the plans and gave it to the police. However—apparently without the knowledge of the two detectives—Duff had already reported the affair to FBI agent James Hosty, which is evidence of Duff's innocence.

The Dallas police gave Duff a lie detector test on June 12, 1963, and they concluded that Duff had no knowledge of the identity of the assailant who fired a shot at Walker. However, they were of the opinion that Duff would have taken the $5,000 offered by Watts's detectives. Duff, on the other hand, told police that the reason he engaged the detectives in the scheme was to attempt to determine who was behind the April shooting at Walker's home.

On December 31, 1963, the Dallas police performed another lie detector test on Duff. Duff denied having a grudge with Walker, owning a rifle, shooting him, or knowing who did. The police determined that Duff was telling the truth. There were no other suspects.[2094] The matter rested until the Warren Commission looked into it.

The Warren Commission and the Walker Shooting

On December 3, 1963, after the Kennedy assassination and the murder of her husband, Marina Oswald revealed for the first time to the FBI that her husband had told her he had shot at Walker with his rifle. She stated that she was afraid to report it to the police at the time. She reported that, on April 5, Oswald wrapped up his rifle in a raincoat and told her he was going for target practice. He boarded a bus with the rifle, but did not return with it. She told the police that her husband also left a note for her on the night of the shooting, explaining to her what she should do if he was captured by police.

After the Kennedy assassination, the bullet fragments from Walker's house were tested. They matched the physical characteristic of the bullets used in the Kennedy assassination, however the bullet was too mangled to conclude with certainty that it was fired from Oswald's rifle. The FBI announced, on December 6, 1963, that Oswald had attempted to kill General Walker, and the news was reported in the newspapers the next day. They based their conclusion on Marina's revelations and the discovery of Walker's name and phone number, LA 1-4115, in Oswald's notebook, which they felt were connected to the murder attempt.[2095] However, a man who seeks to assassinate another has no need to write the name of his victim in his notebook. When one saves Walker's telephone number it is to phone him. Unfortunately, the FBI did not suspect that Oswald might have had the information because the two were working together.

Marina Oswald testified before the Warren Commission that, on March 10, 1963, Oswald traveled across town by bus and photographed the alley behind Walker's Turtle Creek Boulevard home. He told Marina that he made measurements around the house and collected schedules of buses that serviced the area. On March 12, he ordered the rifle that the Warren Commission determined was the assassination weapon by mail. The rifle arrived on March 25, and Oswald showed it to a fellow employee at work. On March 31, he asked Marina to take pictures of him in their backyard, posed holding the rifle in his right hand and holding copies of the Communist Party U.S.A. newspaper, *The Worker,* and the Socialist Workers

Party paper, *The Militant* in his left. (It may be interesting to note that the issue of *The Worker* which Oswald was holding featured a story on General Walker referring to him as the "American Fuehrer.")[2096] As was noted earlier, the Socialist Workers Party promoted Trotskyism, as opposed to the Communist Party's Stalinism. (Leon Trotsky had split from Stalin and was expelled from the Communist Party and Soviet agents assassinated him in 1940.) Therefore, it doesn't make sense that Oswald, an avowed Marxist, would subscribe to the newspaper of the opposing Communist organization and flaunt it.

Later, Oswald asked Marina to inscribe one of the photos to his friend George de Mohrenschildt in Russian with the words "The Hunter of Fascism. Ha, Ha, Ha." Gerald Ford, who served on the Warren Commission, called de Mohrenschildt "a conservative anti-Communist type," which is an understatement.[2097] The OSS, the precursor to the CIA, suspected that de Mohrenschildt had been a Nazi collaborator during World War II. Marina Oswald told investigators that de Mohrenschildt came by their apartment a few days after the Walker shooting incident and remarked in a joking manner to the effect, "How is it that you missed General Walker?"[2098] Oswald and de Mohrenschildt had a good laugh over the shooting and the photo.

The facetiously inscribed photo, and de Mohrenschildt's joking remark, suggest he was privy to the phony plot. De Mohrenschildt and his wife left Dallas for Haiti on June 1, 1963, where they resided at the time of the assassination. De Mohrenschildt committed suicide on the day he was supposed to give an interview with an HSCA staff member at his home.

Secret Service agent Forrest Sorrels interviewed Marina Oswald on December 26, 1963 and she stated that Oswald left the house after dinner on the day of the shooting. When Oswald failed to return by 10:00 or 10:30 p.m., she went to his room and found a note instructing her what to do if he was arrested, along with a post office key.

Oswald returned home very late on the night of the Walker shooting, and appeared pale and very nervous. Marina stated that he told her "he had shot at General Walker." She stated, "And he told me not to ask any questions." Oswald was not sure whether or not he had hit Walker. He instructed Marina to "[s]end any information as to what has happened to me to the Embassy and include newspaper clippings (should there be anything about me in the newspapers). I believe that the embassy will come quickly to your assistance on learning everything."

Oswald's comments on the Soviet Embassy may have been intended to convey that he had a working relationship with the Soviet government—something that would serve to further embellish his credentials as a genuine Communist. It's doubtful, however, that the Soviet Embassy would inflame Cold War tensions and go out of their way to help the wife of the man who tried to kill a former high-ranking general in the U.S. Army. The comments also indicate that Oswald expected he might get his picture in the newspaper. If the newspaper learned that a Communist—seen in a photo posing with the rifle used in the Walker shooting and two Communist newspapers—had a cozy relationship with the Soviet Embassy, it would make for sensational news.

Oswald further told his wife that the bills were paid, and that she should dispose of his clothes but not his personal papers if he were arrested. He wrote, "If I am alive and taken prisoner, the city jail is located at the end of the bridge through which we always passed on going to the city."

When he supposedly learned from the newspaper that the shot missed Walker, he said that he "was very sorry that he had not hit him." Oswald told his wife that he had planned the shooting for two months. Three days later, he showed her a notebook containing photographs of General Walker's home taken days before the shooting, and a map of the area where the house was located. Oswald told her he had buried his rifle near the scene.[2099]

One of the four photos Oswald took of Walker's residence was of a parked 1957 Chevy at the rear of the house. The picture, published by the Warren Commission, showed that the rear license plate had been cut out. Marina insisted that the license plate was not cut out in the original photo.

Years later, Dallas police chief Jesse Curry wrote a memoir on the Kennedy assassination and pictured an assortment of Oswald's belongings including the Chevy photo. The photo in Curry's book clearly shows that the license plate was not cut out, although the numbers could not be discerned. The incident strongly suggests that someone in authority cut out the license plate, altering evidence—perhaps someone who was part of the conspiracy.[2100]

Killing Walker with a high-powered rifle and scope—at a distance of 105 to 120 feet with a clear view—should have been easy. The Warren Commission concluded that two of three shots fired by Oswald hit the president—who was in a moving vehicle that was emerging from under the canopy of a tree. The first hit the president's upper back at a distance of between 176.9 and 190.8 feet, and the third struck his skull at 265.3 feet. Oswald's failure to strike Walker—a stationary target—at less than half the distant of the fatal shot to the president further adds doubts about the allegations that Oswald truly attempted to kill General Walker.[2101]

William Duff and the Walker-Ruby Allegation

In the course of Secret Service interviews about the Walker affair and the assassination, William Duff was also asked if he knew Jack Ruby, the man who murdered Lee Harvey Oswald. Duff was interviewed on January 24, 1964, while Duff was in the army, and said he was positive that he had never seen Ruby. He told the FBI he had seen many photographs of Ruby, but was certain he had never seen him before the murder.[2102]

On April 8, 1964, William Duff told Secret Service agent James R. Cantrell, in an interview while he was in the army at Fort Sill, Oklahoma—and again in several subsequent phone calls—that he had seen Ruby at the Walker residence. He told Cantrell that Ruby visited the Walker residence about once a month during the period of December 1962 through March 1963, while Duff was employed there. Each time Ruby visited, he was in the company of two unidentified white males and arrived in a Ford car.[2103] Explaining his initial denial of knowing Ruby, Duff said that when he was first interviewed by the Secret Service in January, he had been recovering from double hernia surgery in an army hospital, and that he was more concerned with his surgery than about telling the FBI that he had seen Ruby at Walker's residence a number of times.

Duff told them that Ruby was called "Jack" at the Walker residence. He said one of Ruby's associates was a member of the John Birch Society. Duff even volunteered to take a lie detector test.[2104] Duff stated that Ruby and his two companions met on each occasion in Walker's living room behind French doors. Duff said that it was possible that others in the Walker household might have also seen Ruby but he doubted they would admit it, out of loyalty to General Walker.[2105]

Duff called Agent Cantrell on May 20, 1964, and told him that Cliff Roberts—who had offered him $10,000 to kill General Walker—had been following him in Lawton, Oklahoma. As noted earlier, Roberts—who formerly worked for the Oklahoma State Narcotics Bureau—left that job to form a private detective agency and was retained by General Watts to entrap Duff after the Walker shooting incident. Duff told Agent Cantrell that Roberts, who now worked for the State Crime Bureau, had falsely told his wife that there were several outstanding warrants against Duff. Duff implored Agent Cantrell to call his wife and assure her that he had no outstanding warrants against him. Agent Cantrell called Mrs. Duff and she told him that her husband had vital information concerning the assassination of President Kennedy, namely that he had seen Ruby at Walker's home. William Duff insisted he was telling the truth and volunteered to take a lie detector test, but wanted to wait until after his June 1 discharge from the army. Cantrell contacted detective Roberts, who told him that Duff had been examined by an army psychiatrist and was diagnosed as a pathological liar, in an attempt to undermine Duff's credibility. The Secret Service apparently did nothing to verify Roberts's allegation.

According to the Secret Service, "[Duff] had failed to supply this information concerning an alleged association between Jack Ruby and General Walker in prior interviews by the Secret Service and the FBI out of fear of General Walker." On Agent Cantrell's second interview with Duff, on May 25, 1964, he "gave Duff the opportunity to correct this story," if it was not the truth. Duff stood by his allegation and again volunteered to take a polygraph test.[2106] Duff added that "he felt that he knew too much of Walker's operation and of the persons visiting his residence, intimating that Walker was diverting funds collected for the John Birch Society for personal use at the Highland Park Bank, Dallas, Texas."[2107] Duff had good reason to be afraid of Walker.

If the Warren Commission had taken Duff's allegation about Ruby and Walker seriously, Walker would have had to have been looked upon as a suspect in the assassination. If the Commission were aware of the allegation that Duff, Walker's employee, had been seen in the company of Lee Harvey Oswald at a restaurant (as will be presented shortly), they would have had even more reason to be suspicious of Walker. Walker's publicly known hatred for the president, the Walker shooting incident involving Lee Harvey Oswald, and that allegation that Jack Ruby visited Walker's house are circumstances that would defy any reasonable explanation other than that of Walker being involved in some way. Walker was a powerful man and would not have allowed himself to be implicated in the assassination if he could help it.

In June of 1964, Duff once again denied seeing Ruby at General Walker's, after he had first denied knowing Ruby in January 1964, then later, in May 1964, admitted to seeing Ruby at Walker's home. Duff had lost his credibility.

However, there were very good reasons for Duff's inconsistent allegations. The final denial came after he reported that General Watts's detective, Cliff Roberts, had been tailing him in Oklahoma in May 1964 and scaring his wife, alleging outstanding warrants for his arrest. Duff made it clear, in no uncertain terms, that he feared Walker. He felt that he knew too much of Walker's operation and of the people visiting his residence, and also that that he knew Walker was diverting funds collected for the John Birch Society for personal use. Duff may have known a lot more about the Walker operation that placed him in grave jeopardy. (Evidence that he knew Lee Harvey Oswald, likely through the Walker operation, will be presented next.) Since Duff was living in Walker's home in December 1962—when Willie Somersett had reported that generals Walker and Watts were in the military high command behind the broad-based assassination plots later discussed at the Congress of Freedom meeting—he may have been privileged to the information. Had he relayed that information to the Secret Service, history's view of the assassination of President Kennedy might have changed forever.

On June 12, 1964, Duff's wife told the FBI that she had finally secured Duff's phone number (they had recently divorced) and called to remind him to contact Secret Service agent Cantrell to arrange the lie detector test that he had earlier agreed upon. According to Mrs. Duff, her ex-husband told her, "You notify Cantrell and I'll be gone." Mrs. Duff judged by his statement that Duff had no intention of pursuing the matter in which he alleged that Jack Ruby had visited Walker's house.

On June 16, the FBI interviewed Duff and he denied that he ever saw Ruby at Walker's. In fact, he went to extremes in this denial—too much so to be believed. He told the FBI that he was not sure if the man he saw at Walker's was Ruby, based on news photos of Ruby after he murdered Oswald. He waffled further, stating, he "would not swear definitely," had "doubt in his mind," and was "not sure" that it was Ruby. Duff said he had no basis for associating Walker with Ruby. He said the view of the man he thought was Ruby was a profile, and was a view of the man's back only. Incredulously, he gave a description of the man that he originally believed to be Ruby as having "graying white hair" and being "very thin." (Every person in the world who followed the assassination knew that Ruby was just the opposite of the man Duff described. Ruby had dark brown hair without a single gray hair, which appeared jet black in the black-and-white media of the day. Ruby was pudgy and round-faced—hardly "very thin.") Duff's claim that he really saw a skinny man with graying white hair and later believed him to be Ruby is not credible. He also, at this time, claimed there was only one man—instead of two—with the man he erroneously thought was Jack Ruby. His earlier claim that one of "Ruby's" companions was in the John Birch Society was not mentioned. He now claimed the single companion of the man was of Italian or Mexican descent, while Anglo-Saxons dominated the xenophobic John Birch Society.[2108]

The Background of William Duff

During their research, the Secret Service compiled a brief biographic sketch of Duff. William McEwan Duff was born in Scotland and served in the British Army. He moved to California in 1957, and served in the U.S. Air Force. He moved to Dallas in November of 1962, following a girl he hoped to marry and also looking for work. One day, Duff passed by Walker's home and recognized the house that he had heard about in the news by the American and Texan flags flying on the front lawn. He stopped by and asked Walker for a job. He was hired as a chauffer in December. In return, meals, cigarette money, and a room were provided. He worked as a chauffer and handyman from about November 1962 until March or April 1963, according to Duff. Duff told the FBI that he heard Walker say, "If I had the Kennedys here I would line them up and shoot them." He told the FBI that another employee, Bob Sutton, also heard Walker make the statement. (He meant Bob Surrey. It's not clear if the mistake was Duff's or the FBI's—or if they asked Surrey/Sutton about Duff's allegation.) There is no evidence that the FBI took Duff's allegation seriously.

Duff stated that he quit his job with Walker after a disagreement with a woman employee who became very demanding of him, ordering him to make coffee, tea, and perform other menial chores that were not a part of his job duties. Duff and Walker had made an agreement that, when Walker was out of town, Duff was free to do as he cared. Duff finally had had enough of the demanding woman and left Walker's employ. Duff worked at another job in Dallas until he left for Oklahoma in August 1963 to pursue a job for truck drivers for which he had seen an ad posted in a newspaper. When he got to Oklahoma he found out that, since he didn't own a truck, he was not a candidate for the job. He decided to join the U.S. Army in August of 1963, and was sent to Fort Polk, Louisiana, for basic training—which is where he was at the time of the assassination. Duff said he had not heard from Walker after he left his employ. On December 20, 1963, he arrived at Fort Sill, Oklahoma, where the FBI interviewed him on January 24, 1963, as noted earlier, where he originally denied knowing Jack Ruby. He told them he saw many visitors, some of them "queer people" who came to Walker's residence, and he was sure none was Oswald—and that he had never seen Jack Ruby.[2109, 2110, 2111, 2112]

Lee Harvey Oswald and William Duff

According to a December 14, 1963, FBI report, restaurant owner Joe Loria advised the Dallas FBI that he saw William Duff—whom he described as a former resident of General Walker's home—on one occasion in his restaurant in the company of Lee Harvey Oswald. The sighting occurred seven to eight months prior to the date of Loria's FBI interview. Duff left Walker's home on March 10, 1963, before the April 10 shooting incident, which places

Loria's sighting of the two towards the end of Duff's employ with Walker. Loria knew Duff well, but he did not know Oswald.[2113, 2114] Loria recognized Oswald from pictures after the Kennedy assassination.[2115] On January 24, 1964, the FBI interviewed William Duff and he simply denied knowing Oswald—and the matter was given no further consideration.[2116, 2117]

After the Kennedy assassination, the FBI received a lot of claims from citizens saying that they had seen someone at some time with Lee Harvey Oswald. Most turned out to be cases of mistaken identity, which perhaps is why the FBI so easily dismissed Loria's claim. However, placing Oswald with Duff is a whole different matter, since both were subjects of interest in the assassination investigation and had ties to General Walker, which greatly increases the likelihood that the sighting was genuine. It is possible that the FBI agent who received the information from Loria and dismissed it may have known nothing of the investigation of Duff in connection to the shooting incident. Likewise, those investigating Duff and the shooting incident may not have known about the Loria allegation.

Duff worked for Walker, an Oswald "near-victim" and a Warren Commission witness, which alone merited intensive FBI scrutiny of the Duff affair. However, as in the Milteer and New Orleans investigations, the FBI's investigation into the Duff-Oswald allegations was a colossal failure. Of course, some at the FBI knew Walker was in the military high command connected with the assassination plots revealed at the Congress of Freedom meeting, because Willie Somersett had told them. The FBI essentially concealed that information from the Warren Commission, removing it from the equation. Although not appreciated by the FBI, the evidence presented here overwhelmingly also suggests that Walker and Oswald were working together. If Joe Loria's sighting was genuine—and there is no reason to believe it was not—then Duff and Oswald most likely met in connection with their mutual ties to General Walker. The sighting of Oswald with Duff was so unique that the statistical odds that it was anything but authentic are remote.

Duff's denial of knowing Oswald is understandable. No one would want to admit having been at a restaurant with the future murderer of both a president and a Dallas police officer. Duff was likely in the precarious position of being able to tie Oswald to the Walker operation, as well as to Ruby. As a result, Walker would have been exposed, something he and the resurgent national radical right and segregation movement could not afford. Crossing General Walker—the leader of an army of violent-minded radicals like Joseph Milteer—was a life-threatening proposition. The evidence suggests someone had gotten to Duff, causing him to back off his claim that he had seen Ruby on several occasions with a member of the John Birch Society at Walker's. Duff admitted to law enforcement that some of his statements, as we shall see, were made out of fear of General Walker, because of Duff's knowledge of the Walker operation. The FBI, who showed little interest in Duff, failed to have him elaborate on those fears.

General Watts Finds Duff a New Job and Housing

After steadfastly contending that William Duff tried to kill his close friend and client, Clyde

Watts did the unimaginable: he found Duff a job and housing in Oklahoma. Of course, it was not until after Duff told the FBI that Jack Ruby was at Walker's house on several occasions, among other things. On June 23, 1964, in Oklahoma City, the FBI interviewed Duff, who told them he had been discharged from the army for failing to notify them that he had also served in the air force; they discharged him for "failure to adapt." He had been divorced from his wife and moved to Oklahoma City on June 2, 1964. A week before moving to Oklahoma, he had visited General Watts, whom he had met before, when Watts had visited Walker's home. Watts found Duff temporary employment in Oklahoma City with the Paul T. Blakeny Company, which distributed and repaired lawn mowers. Duff was given temporary living quarters with Marion Osborne, a retired friend of Watts, who managed the company. Duff anticipated that Watts would find him employment as a heavy equipment operator.[2118]

The FBI's interview of Watts's private detective, William Keester, fills in some of the details of their investigation of Duff and the shooting. Keester told the FBI that Walker told him that he thought the Black Muslims—a fourth possible suspect in the shooting in addition to a Communist, the Nazi vandals, and Duff—might have been involved with the Walker shooting. Keester said he befriended Duff, who agreed that he would shoot Walker for $5,000, if he were supplied with a passport out of the country, a car, a driver, and a rifle. He told them Duff drove around Walker's house with the two detectives searching for an assassination perch. After Keester surreptitiously tape recorded Duff's agreement to shoot General Walker, Keester and Cliff Roberts consulted with Walker and Watts, who told them to take their evidence to the Dallas police. However, unbeknown to Keester, that same day, Duff beat him at his game and had gone to the FBI and told them about the scheme. Keester said that he felt Duff had no intention of killing Walker, but would have taken the money.[2119]

Clyde Watts took a keen interest in the Warren Commission investigation of the Walker shooting incident, as well he should have. The breach of the Walker operation by William Duff meant there might be other breaches in the fabricated shooting story, which could spell big trouble for Walker. On January 4, 1964, the Warren Commission received a letter from Watts, serving as Walker's attorney, requesting a transcript of all pertinent information on the allegations of Marina Oswald about her husband's confession to the attempted murder of General Walker. The request was purportedly made in the interest of Walker's safety. He told the Commission about his two private detectives' investigation of Duff, and furnished the information to the Commission because he felt there might be a possible link between Oswald and Duff.[2120] On June 27, 1964, Watts turned over several .30-caliber rifle shells to the FBI, which had been obtained from Duff's apartment by his detectives in the spring of 1963 without Duff's knowledge—keeping one for himself. There were no cartridges recovered from the scene at Walker's house, and they did not find a weapon at Duff's residence. One of Watts's detectives suggested the shells may actually have been souvenirs from Duff's military career.[2121]

A friend of Jim Garrison who was a writer, only identified as "S," provided the D.A. with information on the Watts-Duff affair and pointed out the folly of Watts providing Duff with a job. In 1967, the unidentified writer interviewed Clyde Watts, and disclosed the conversation to Garrison during his investigation of the assassination in a letter, as follows:

> Why, I asked did you after both you and Walker thought Duff to be
> such a bum that Walker fired him and you both still think he tried
> to kill Walker, why did you find work for him? "I felt sorry for the
> man." That's a quote world. Anyone wants it can use it, did you ever
> hear such pure horse shit? Here is a man (Watts) as mean and tough
> and right-winged as they come, who just through the goodness of
> his heart finds employment for a man who had only gotten through
> linking Ruby to Walker! HA! At any rate, Watts said he put Duff to
> work with a family by the name of "Butrum" in Okla City (Butrum
> I think). This is a right-wing multi-millionaire group.

Garrison learned from the writer "S" that Keester and Roberts were former Oklahoma police detectives, who had been fired for drunkenness and shooting out streetlights. He interviewed William Keester and stated, in a handwritten note, that Keester was, "very right wing. Hated the Kennedys, negroes [sic], etc. Was convinced Duff shot at Walker." Roberts talked to Ruby in the summer of 1963, and said Ruby was "100% behind gen. [sic] Walker and thought Cuba should be blown out of the ocean." (The writer probably meant Blakeny of the Paul T. Blakeny Company, instead of "Butrum.")[2122] An FBI interview with Keester provides corroborating evidence for the unknown writer's report to Garrison regarding Ruby and Keester. The FBI noted in their report on Keester: "[Keester's] acquaintanceship with Jack Ruby, pre-dating the investigation, had been established through contacts with the Dallas police Department and several visits to the night club operated by Ruby."[2123] The fact that Keester knew Ruby before the assassination is striking and, unfortunately, is not further explained. The author found no evidence that anyone asked Ruby about Roberts's claims regarding whether or not he knew Roberts, had been to General Walker's home, was a Walker supporter, or agreed with Walker's violent opposition to Castro's Cuba.

The Secret Service bought the story of Watts's detectives—two men who tried to unscrupulously entrap Duff by offering him money to shoot Walker, who lied to Duff's wife about outstanding warrants, who followed him in May 1964, who took rifle casings from his home, and who accused Duff of being a pathological liar. Further diminishing detective Keester's credibility was the fact that he, like Walker and Watts, was a Kennedy hater and far-right racist. The only logical reason Watts would provide Duff with housing and employment was to ensure his silence about what he had seen and heard at the Walker residence. Generals Watts's and Walker's roles as military advisors to the Council for Statehood, which plotted large-scale assassinations beginning in late 1962, were known to some in the FBI and should have been factored into their investigation of Duff, but their dealings with Clyde Watts and the shooting incident were not.

Duff and the "Queer People" Allegation

Duff held other threatening trump cards against General Walker. The first was his allegation that he had heard Walker remark that he would shoot the Kennedys. The second was his potential ability to tie Walker to Oswald; the third was his potential ability to tie Walker to Ruby—which would make Walker a prime suspect in the assassination. The fourth was the alleged knowledge that Walker was diverting funds, collected for the John Birch Society, for his own personal use—which could create problems with Walker's supporters. The fifth was the possibility that he knew about the roles Walker and Watts held as military advisors to the murder-plotting Council for Statehood. (Duff lived with Walker at the time in late 1962 when Willie Somersett told the FBI about the broad-based assassination plots.) Sixth, was the fact that he likely knew—or suspected—that Walker was a homosexual, which—if that fact had been exposed—would have been the end of him. Together, those trump cards explain General Watts's intensive efforts to implicate Duff in the Walker shooting incident, entrap him in an attempt to murder Walker, and offer him a job and housing in Oklahoma where Watts could keep his eyes on him and ensure his silence.

Duff's report to the FBI that "queer people" visited Walker's residence suggests that Duff knew about Walker's closeted homosexuality.[2124] Duff was an outsider in the Walker operation; in the course of the investigation of Duff, it was noted that General Walker and his volunteer workers were cautious that Duff neither saw correspondence nor overheard conversation of a business nature.[2125] Nonetheless, he lived in the house and they could not hide everything from him.

Walker's homosexuality was not publicly revealed until he was arrested on June 23, 1976, by the Dallas Park Department for public lewdness. He reportedly had made sexual advances to a plainclothes policemen. Walker responded to the charges in his unique way, saying, "It's more of the same, but with some further clarification of poses and setups of mutual interest which can be worked both ways. That's all I've got to say." On March 16, 1977, a Dallas Park Patrol officer arrested Walker in a public men's room on his second charge of public lewdness.[2126, 2127]

In the mid-1970s, the homosexuality of Walker's speaking partner Billy James Hargis's was revealed when four male students from his private religious school came forward and reported Hargis had had sexual relations with them. Hargis had threatened to blacklist the youths if they talked. Ironically, Hargis published the bestselling book, *Is the School House the Proper Place to Teach Raw Sex?* Hargis justified his homosexual encounters by citing the Old Testament friendship between David and Jonathan.[2128]

The author asked Minutemen leader Robert DePugh about the homosexuality that existed in the leadership ranks of the far right. DePugh replied, "There were a lot of them," and a discussion ensued about California Minutemen leader Troy Houghton and Walker's old friend Major Edgar Bundy.[2129] Mainstream America had absolutely no tolerance for homosexuality in 1963. Exposure of a public figure's homosexuality meant a certain end of the exposed person's career, family, and friends. It would have been the end of Walker's career role as a key leader of the anti-Communist and Southern segregation movements. It also would have humiliated a lot of public figures in those movements who had grown close to him, such as Ross Barnett, Leander Perez, H. L. Hunt, George Wallace, and many others who tied the South's fortunes to him. Walker, Watts, and the organizations they led could not afford to allow that to happen.

Duff may have known a lot more about the people behind the assassination then his off-and-on allegations of a Walker-Ruby connection. According to a Jim Garrison document included with the letter from "S," Jim Standard, a reporter for the *Daily Oklahoman,* met a man in Oklahoma City—perhaps Duff—who, trembling all over, told him that Ruby knew about the assassination ahead of time. Standard refused to give Garrison the name of his source.[2130]

The *Deutsch National-Zeitung und Soldatan-Zeitung*

On November 29, 1963, the *Deutsch National-Zeitung und Soldatan-Zeitung*, an extreme-right German newspaper, published the first mention of Oswald's involvement in the Walker shooting. The problem is that it was before anyone else suspected Oswald's involvement—and that it was four days *before* Marina Oswald first revealed her husband's involvement to the FBI. There is no way anyone else could have known about it—unless they had inside knowledge of the incident. In addition, the German newspaper peddled the story that Attorney General Robert Kennedy had interfered with the arrest of Oswald by law enforcement after the Walker shooting incident, which is clearly unsubstantiated. They added that had Robert Kennedy not interfered, Oswald would have been imprisoned and would not have been able to murder the president. The story was a pure propaganda piece aimed at confirming the far right's claim that Robert Kennedy's soft stand on Communism resulted in his own brother's murder. Walker and the far right wing had constantly repeated the same tale after the assassination. Billy James Hargis, for example, in 1962 had demanded that Robert Kennedy enforce the Supreme Court's ruling that required Communist Party members to register. Kennedy never did.[2131]

On February 14, 1964, the FBI translated the *National Zeitung's* front-page article about the shooting incident that was entitled "The Strange Case of Oswald." An Iron Cross—a military decoration given out in Nazi Germany—separated the words "National" and "Zeitung." Also published on the front page was a transcript of two telephone interviews, done twenty-four hours apart in a question-and-answer format, between General Walker and the German journalists. Hasso Thorsten (spelled "Thorsteau" in the Warren Commission documents) conducted the first interview. The "exclusive interview" story began with the headline "Kennedy's Death Did Not Come As A Surprise." An unkind accompanying editorial piece called the dead president's accomplishments "fiascos," "sterile successes," and policies that ran counter to the interests of Germany and the world. The FBI translator noted that the paper was a publication of the extreme right and included articles in every edition about Dr. Goebbels, whom they called—in an understatement—a "violent anti-Communist."[2132] Joseph Goebbels had been one of Adolf Hitler's closest associates, and was Reich Minister of

Propaganda in Nazi Germany from 1933 to 1945. He was a fanatic anti-Communist and anti-Semite and was responsible for orchestrating violence on Kristallnacht, as well as pogroms against the Jews.

The word *Zeitung* was symbolically divided through the letter "e" by the black bar at the far right border that symbolized the Berlin wall, which separated West Germany from Communist East Germany. Source: Richard Russell Papers, University of Georgia

Walker provided an account of his activities in the days preceding the German newspaper interview in his Warren Commission testimony. He told them that he gave a speech in Hattiesburg, Mississippi, on November 18 or 19 and then went to New Orleans for two or three days and was on an airplane halfway to Shreveport when the pilot announced the president had been assassinated. He stayed at the Hotel Shreve on November 22 and 23, and returned to Dallas thereafter. He was entering his house when he learned that Lee Harvey Oswald had been shot.[2133] Ned Touchstone (editor of the *Councilor*) attended the Shreveport speeches and a photo of Walker with Touchstone on the day of the assassination was published in the *Councilor* and attests that Walker was not in Dallas during the assassination.[2134] Touchstone reported in a story in the *Councilor* that he asked Walker, "General is it possible that the same rifle which killed Kennedy fired the bullet intended for you?" Walker answered, "I can't say that and you can't say that. Let's wait to see if someone on the other side will mention the possibility."[2135]

The first German newspaper interview took place while Walker was at the Hotel Shreve on Saturday, November 23, the day after the assassination. Walker was in a jovial mood and, at the onset of the interview, expressed astonishment at the German newspaper's finding him. They even knew his room number, which caused Walker to laugh. As the interview began, Walker demonstrated that he either had a short memory or lied when he told them he had just left Dallas ten hours before—in fact, he had left Dallas at least four to six days earlier. Walker next told the reporter he was going to be on *Meet the Press* at 10 o'clock. Walker asked the reporter for his German telephone number to verify the origin of the call. After he received it, Walker laughed again and said, "Okay! Let's have it."

The two discussed Walker's idea that Kennedy's assassin was not an ultra rightist as many first believed, but was part of a Marxist plot. Walker was asked if the murder came as a surprise and he said "no" and blamed it on the Communists. Walker discussed the U.N. and Barry Goldwater, whom he called the recognized leader of the conservative movement. While Walker was on the phone, word came to him that Oswald, from his Dallas prison cell, had just asked for New York lawyer John Abt to defend him. Walker told the reporter, correctly, that, "Mr. Abt is an American Jew who defends all big Communist cases." The reporter responded, "How come you have one of them in your now 'Promised Land?'" The interview ended with Walker saying, "Give my regards to my German friends, especially Gerhard Frey," a remark whose significance was apparently not fully comprehended by the Warren Commission. Gerhard Frey was the editor of the paper and not only was he a friend of Walker but—

unknown to the Warren Commission—he was also a friend of General Charles Willoughby, as we shall see later. Frey and Willoughby were members of the far-right Anti-Bolshevik Bloc of Nations. (The evidence against Willoughby in the assassination conspiracy was presented in Chapter Eight.) With all the newspapers in Texas, in the U.S.—and the world—it would seem unlikely that it was a coincidence that an obscure extreme right-wing German newspaper would be able to locate Walker's room and phone number in his Shreveport hotel room without some inside help. The Walker shooting incident was not brought up in the published transcripts of either this or the next interview Walker gave.

A second interview occurred twenty-four hours later when Walker telephoned the *National Zeitung* on Sunday, November 24th, from Dallas—the same day that Ruby murdered Oswald. The text of the second interview which the FBI translated from the newspaper melds in with the first with only a line separating them, giving the appearance of one interview. The name of the reporter in the second interview was not given. Walker told the reporter that—now that Oswald had been shot— "carefully planned lies will sweep the world" after a Marxist was assassinated in police custody. Walker told the reporter, "Mark my words. The second slayer is one Rubenstein who, among other things, is a gangster from Chicago and has a record of convictions on charges of disturbing the peace and illegal possession of arms." Walker digressed, pointing out a supposed Jewish connection by emphasizing Ruby's Jewish background and calling him Rubenstein.[2136] (Ruby had legally changed his name from Rubenstein in 1947.[2137]) Walker's knowledge that Ruby was a Jew—only hours after the world first learned about him—raises suspicions. The transcript of the second interview is less than a page long, consisting of six brief exchanges between the two, with no concluding pleasantries as in the first, which suggests the remainder of the interview was not disclosed in the newspaper.[2138]

An FBI source told them that *National Zeitung* reporter Helmut Muench conducted the second interview, and that Walker told him about the April shooting incident at that time, which was not mentioned in the transcript obtained by the FBI. According to Muench, in the follow-up interview with the FBI source, Walker stated he believed Oswald was the one who shot at him. Muench passed the information on to Dr. Gerhard Frey, the editor of the paper, who included it in a March 29, 1964, article. Muench was of the opinion that it was Frey who, on his own initiative, inserted the tale about Robert Kennedy stopping the investigation after the Walker shooting incident. A second source confirmed for the FBI that Frey was the one who embellished the part about Robert Kennedy.[2139]

The FBI interviewed Muench directly and he told them that Walker told him in his transatlantic telephone call that he believed Oswald was the man who made the attempt on his life. Muench gave the information to Gerhard Frey, who he believed—like his fellow reporter Thorsten—embellished the part about Robert Kennedy blocking the arrest of Oswald for the shooting.[2140] Although, later, Walker flatly denied saying or knowing that Oswald was involved in the shooting incident in his Warren Commission testimony. Reporter Muench had no obvious reason to lie when he said that Walker told him that Oswald was involved in the shooting. Walker, on the other hand, had plenty of reasons to deny it. To keep his story straight, he couldn't honestly admit to knowing about it when Marina Oswald, the sole corroborating witness, had not yet come forward and implicated her husband.

Warren Commission counsel Wesley Liebler cross-examined General Walker and asked him if he knew, or ever talked to, Helmut Muench. Walker denied any contact with Muench. Walker did, however, admit to seeing a copy of the November 29 *National Zeitung* article. Walker noted the article stated that it was known before the assassination that Oswald shot at Walker and—had proper action been taken at that time—the president's murder would not have happened. He admitted that someone called him on a transatlantic call, but said he did not recall the name. Walker claimed, instead, that he did not know where the German newspaper got their information on Oswald and the shooting. Liebler apprised Walker that, accompanying the article, was a transcript of Hasso Thorsten's interview of Walker. Walker admitted that Thorsten called him on the morning of November 23, 1963, while he was in Shreveport, and again sometime later to verify some of the facts.

Liebler then asked Walker if it was on that occasion that he had told the newspaper reporter that Oswald had attacked him. Walker replied that he did not give the reporter all of the information, or the part about Oswald attacking him, and said he had no way of knowing at that time that Oswald had attacked him—and still didn't as of his testimony to the Warren Commission on July 23, 1964. Walker insisted that he did not say that Oswald shot at him before the assassination and that he knew nothing about Oswald's involvement in the case, and denied saying he did during his November 23 interview with the German reporter. Walker said he was surprised at the German article. He said the newspaper published two articles: one based on his interview and another that the reporter fashioned on his own.

Libeler noted that the article claimed Oswald had shot at Walker and that this was known before the Kennedy assassination, implying that the information came from Walker. Walker again denied it. Liebler pointed out that, on November 29, the German newspaper was the first to claim Oswald attacked Walker. The fact that Oswald's involvement in the shooting incident was not revealed to the public until December 3, 1963, when Marina Oswald told authorities that Oswald admitted he was involved in the shooting, was again noted. Liebler, unfortunately, admitted he was puzzled about the matter of how the German newspaper knew about Oswald's connection to the shooting before anybody else did. Walker suggested that it was just a guess. Liebler helped out his witness and agreed with Walker, adding that perhaps the article was based on speculation—or that the newspaper was predated from information they received after the public knew about Oswald's involvement.

Liebler apparently did not entertain the notion that maybe it was Walker, or a confederate, who told Gerhard Frey that Oswald was involved, in an effort to make Walker appear as a near victim of Oswald. That would also serve to remove any suspicions that might arise that Walker was involved in the assassination. Liebler, in fact, had no evidence that the newspaper was predated, as he surmised and ultimately concluded. To the contrary, the FBI learned from a confidential source that the paper had not been printed after Marina

Oswald's revelation of Oswald and the Walker shooting incident on December 3. The FBI source learned from Gerhard Frey himself that the actual printing of the *National Zeitung* was *postdated*, not predated, and took place on November 25 and 26, with the date of November 29 printed on the paper.[2141]

The Warren Commission got it wrong again. The story unequivocally was written before Marina Oswald implicated her husband.

General Walker and Gerhard Frey

Gerhard Frey likely found out that Oswald was involved in the Walker shooting incident either before—or shortly after—the Kennedy assassination from General Walker since the two had been friends when Walker was in Germany. No other person or paper at home or abroad surmised it. Having Frey leak the story in his paper, an ocean away, may have seemed like a good idea, rather than having a Walker associate leak it in a publication at home and arouse suspicions. Walker made a mistake, though, and probably did not expect the FBI to know that Frey was a friend of his. He probably could not have anticipated that Marina Oswald would come forth and implicate her husband, leaving the Warren Commission to wonder how the *National Zeitung* knew before Marina's revelation.

General Walker had immersed himself in far-right ideology during his tenure as Commander of the 24th Infantry Division in Augsburg, Germany, from 1959 to 1961. His assignment in Germany afforded him the opportunity to forge relationships with members of the European far right, like Gerhard Frey. As noted, a month before the shooting incident, the FBI learned on March 1, 1963, from Legat, Bonn, West Germany, that Walker had been corresponding and sending circulars to various European Fascists calling for worldwide action against Jews. His references to Jews, John Abt, and Jack "Rubenstein" in his interview in the *National Zeitung*, smacked of anti-Semitism and seemed to please the reporters of the German newspaper.[2142]

Gerhard Frey also had ties to General Charles Willoughby. The author found a personal letter written (in German) in 1965 from German-born Charles Willoughby (a.k.a. Tscheppe-Weidenbach) to Gerhard Frey among Willoughby's personal papers, attesting to the fact that the two were friends.[2143]

It was not the detective work of the FBI that led to their discovery of the *National Zeitung* article. The FBI first learned of the article when General Pedro del Valle's friend, Frank Capell, brought it to their attention.[2144, 2145] Capell, as will be recalled from Chapter Eight, was a far-right print propagandist. (His book *Treason is the Reason* blacklisted supposed Communists. Descriptions of their backgrounds were given, sometimes accompanied by a photo. As was pointed out before, Capell's book may have served to identify the targets of the ambitious assassination plots divulged at the Congress of Freedom meeting in 1963.) Capell was part of General del Valle's covert network, as evidenced in their September 1963 correspondence noted in Chapter Eight. Three days after the Kennedy assassination, del Valle coldly wrote to Capell, "The hand of God directed the bullet that killed Kennedy." Interestingly, Capell was also a friend of General Willoughby. In a letter, noted in Chapter Eight, Capell told Willoughby that he planned to provide Willoughby with intelligence reports, presumably on the covert actions of the hardcore underground. It's also possible that Charles Willoughby tipped off his friend Gerhard Frey of the *National Zeitung* to Oswald's involvement in the Walker shooting incident. It was then left to Frank Capell to bring the news article to the attention of the FBI.

It was not only the *National Zeitung* and Frank Capell who initially wanted the world to know that Oswald tried to kill General Walker. Atlanta Attorney John A. Dunaway sent a copy of the German newspaper, complete with a translation of the story, to Senator Richard Russell of Georgia on December 16, 1963. Dunaway told Russell, who served on the Warren Commission, that he represented General Walker—and asked Russell for evidence, if any existed, that Robert Kennedy cut short the investigation into the Walker shooting right after it happened. Russell thanked him and pledged to send him details of the investigation when they became available.[2146]

Revilo Oliver (who Willie Somersett told the FBI was one of the individuals who advocated violence at the Congress of Freedom meeting, and who spoke at the infamous 1963 Congress of Freedom meeting), weighed in with the Warren Commission on the Walker shooting incident. In his testimony about the claims made in his article "Marxsmanship in Dallas," Oliver stated he talked to Walker and he told him that the bullet would have struck him if, at the last moment, Walker had not turned his head. Oliver also noted that Frank Capell provided him with a copy of the *National Zeitung* story, and that Capell was his research consultant.[2147]

John Curington, a former H. L. Hunt employee, provided more evidence for Walker's involvement in the phony shooting incident. Curington, in an interview with author Dick Russell (not the same as Senator Richard Russell), told Russell that he had run cross Oswald before the assassination and he was known in different circles to be an extremist. Curington related that General Walker was a pretty good friend of H. L. Hunt. Curington and Hunt visited Walker's home before the assassination and Walker had told them that Oswald had come up in his investigation of the shooting.[2148]

The Schmidt Brothers, Oswald, and the Walker Shooting Incident

On December 29, 1977, Earl Golz, the reporter for the *Dallas Morning News* who covered Kennedy's assassination from the beginning, wrote to General Walker in response to materials that Walker had sent to Golz and Speaker of the House Tip O'Neill, perhaps relative to the HSCA investigation that began in 1976 and concluded in 1978. (Although O'Neill did not serve on the HSCA.) The letter is as follows:

> Dear Mr. Walker,
>
> I received a copy of the material you sent to Tip O'Neill and others. It may open some eyes and I hope it does. I am especially interested

in Marina's message on the back of the photograph which you say was dated five days before the shot fired at you by her husband.

A friend of Larry [sic] Schmidt's recently told me that Larry and his brother, who he says was then associated with you, had accompanied Oswald in the brother's car to the scene of the shooting. Larry Schmidt supposedly has protected himself since that time by placing written accounts of this story in safe deposit boxes around the country.

I also wonder if you know there is any truth to the story that Delessips [sic] Morrison had a hand in forcing you to retire as an army general in West Germany. If his name rings a bell as an agent of JFK in such a mission, this may open some new doors. Morrison was reactivated into the military as a favor to JFK, I was told, in an effort to get you in the Blue Book controversy. He was killed in an airplane explosion over Mexico about four months after the assassination.

Yours Truly,

Earl Golz

For unknown reasons, Walker wrote in longhand on the back of the letter and explained why he wrote to Golz. He stated that he had sent Golz a copy of one of Golz's news articles and wrote his thoughts about it on it. He also sent a copy to Speaker Tip O'Neill to pass to "the committee," presumably the HSCA. Walker's response to the allegations about the Schmidt brothers, if any, is not known. Golz's letter appears to reflect a cordial and collaborative relationship with Walker and indicates little suspicion about him or the Schmidt-Oswald story.[2149] Like virtually everyone else who has looked into the case, Golz probably viewed Walker as a near-victim of Oswald, not a confederate. Golz did not seem overly concerned about the allegation, and perhaps dismissed it altogether. Instead, he showed interest in Walker's own research into the assassination and what he might learn from Walker. The fact that a citizen (Golz's "friend") came fourth with information that, if true, was evidence of a conspiracy involving Oswald, Walker, and the Schmidt brothers—and gave it to a reputable reporter of a major newspaper at the same Congress was investigating the assassination—makes the allegation compelling. The source may have expected that Golz would have made the claim public or passed it on to the HSCA, which was his duty. He apparently did not. Golz had, however, communicated with the HSCA about reporting on the Dallas murder including discussing the "Dear Mr. Hunt" letter that appeared to be in Lee Harvey Oswald's handwriting that surfaced years after the assassination (noted in Chapter Eleven).[2150]

As we have discussed, Larrie Schmidt is a familiar name in the Dallas story. He was the mastermind behind the derogatory "Welcome Mr. Kennedy" ad placed in the Dallas newspaper on the morning of the assassination, and was called before the Warren Commission to explain it. In 1961, while he was in the army in Munich, Germany, Larrie Schmidt started an ultraconservative organization, called Conservatism–USA (CUSA), with a cadre of fellow soldiers. Their plan on return to the U.S. was to dominate the conservative movement. Upon leaving the army, he decided to relocate to Dallas in 1962, where he joined the Dallas John Birch Society.[2151]

A week after Schmidt's arrival in Dallas, he obtained a full-time paid job with Frank McGehee of the National Indignation Committee, which folded shortly after.[2152] He landed a job with a Dallas ad agency that handled the campaigns of conservatives, including Robert Morris—an associate of Guy Banister and an attorney for Walker. Morris asked Schmidt to speak to a group at his home. Schmidt greatly impressed Morris when he argued that while the government was sending soldiers aboard to combat Communism, they were not doing enough to fight it at home. The performance landed Schmidt the position of director of the Southwestern section of the Young Americans for Freedom—a group tied to General Willoughby.

Schmidt's brother Bob also moved to Texas and became General Walker's aide-de-camp. Larrie led a group of fourteen that picketed the Adlai Stevenson speech in Dallas in October 1963. Larrie became friends with Joe Grinnan, a coordinator for the Dallas JBS, in the fall. He asked William Burley and Bernard Weissman, his army mates in CUSA, to join him in Dallas. They arrived in November 1963. Schmidt conceived of the derogatory "Welcome, Mr. Kennedy" ad and persuaded Weissman to allow him to use his name on it. Joe Grinnan raised money for the ad from members of the JBS, including Nelson Bunker Hunt. Larrie was in a car with Grinnan when he learned about the assassination.[2153]

Bernard Weissman, a Jew, testified before the Warren Commission about the ad and his relationship with Larrie Schmidt. He told them that, one time, Schmidt tried to get him to change his name and religion since, as a Jew, he might not be received well by the far right. Schmidt wrote to Weissman, who was in New York, and told him on October 1, 1963, that his brother Bob had become a fulltime paid employee for General Walker and that plans and strategy were being formulated for Adlai Stevenson's visit to Dallas for a U.N. Day Speech in October. Weissman was worried that the association of Schmidt's brother with Walker might give their group a "black eye."[2154] Schmidt told Weissman to watch the newspapers for news about the huge demonstrations being planned for Stevenson's visit, stating: "Plans already made, strategy being carried out."[2155] Afterward, Larrie Schmidt called Weissman and told him about his protest of Adlai Stevenson's speech and about the one picket who struck Stevenson. Schmidt was pleased with the demonstration that he had organized with students from the University of Dallas and told Weissman "We made it." He wrote Weissman, "I am a hero to the right" and a "fearless spokesman and leader of the right wing." He stated, "what I worked so hard for in one year—and nearly failed—finally came through one incident in one night." He told Weissman to get to Dallas to take advantage of the publicity. On October 29, 1963, Larrie Schmidt wrote Weissman, "Kennedy is scheduled in Dallas on November 24. All big things are happening now."[2156]

Weissman described Larrie's brother Bob as a moron who drank too much and was happy to receive the $35 per week, with room and board, that Walker paid him to work as a fulltime chauffer and aide.[2157]

The *Dallas Times Herald* on October 27, 1963, identified Larrie Schmidt as the leader of the fourteen-student demonstration against Stevenson. Schmidt denied involvement with the protester who spit on Stevenson, as well as with another who hit him on the head with a placard. (Those assailants were members of Walker's group, as we shall see in the next chapter.)[2158] After the demonstration and news story, Schmidt got threatening phone calls and death threats.[2159]

Either Larrie or Bob Schmidt told Weissman about the anti-Kennedy "Wanted for Treason" handbills that were circulated before the assassination. Weissman saw a copy in the back of Walker's station wagon when it was being driven by Bob Schmidt. Weissman did not know whether Walker or his close aide Robert Surrey was behind them.[2160] (As will be shown in the next chapter, Robert Surrey printed the handbills, which depicted a mug shot-type image of President Kennedy accompanied by comments that were bitterly critical of him.) Surrey was later called before the Warren Commission to explain the handbill.

On November 2, 1962, Larrie Schmidt wrote Weissman, "Arrangements are being made for me to meet the heads of the Dallas John Birch, General Walker, and H. L. Hunt, Texas oil millionaire."[2161] On June 13, 1963, Schmidt wrote to Weissman, "Warren Carroll, our only other recruit to CUSA, is already a PhD and two MS's. Warren is a scriptwriter for Lifeline, the H. L. Hunt television and radio series. Hunt is the millionaire oilman . . . Warren is 32, former CIA man. Don't worry, he has been checked out. Hunt checked him out."[2162, 2163]

Bradford J. Angers, a former army security agent and private investigator, related a similar story about the Schmidt brothers and Oswald to author Dick Russell, who published the account in his 1992 book *The Man Who Knew Too Much*. Angers was an electronic surveillance equipment manufacturer who was briefly employed by H. L. Hunt in 1963 until Hunt ordered him to relocate to Washington to work on the "Lifeline" radio project, an order which Angers refused. Several weeks after the assassination, Hunt called Angers and told him he was sending over a man and ordered Angers to put him to work. Angers refused to disclose the name of the individual. By Angers's description, Russell was certain Angers was talking about Larrie Schmidt. Angers said the man "patterned himself after Joseph Goebbels." Angers and the man "talked about how Goebbels used symbolic logic to build the Nazi empire." Angers got him a job in advertising at an Austin radio station owned by the first lady, Lady Bird Johnson. The FBI paid a visit to Angers and asked him how much he knew about the man that he had gotten a job for at Johnson's radio station. The FBI told Angers about CUSA and the "Welcome Mr. Kennedy" ad. Angers tried to call the man, but he had disappeared.

Then the man's housekeeper called Angers and told him that the man needed medical care and money. Angers visited the man at his apartment and he had bandages on his face and splints on his arm. His wife's leg was in a cast. He said he had been in an accident in Denton

County. Angers called the Denton county sheriff, who told him there had been no accidents near the county, but that one of his men had picked up a man and a woman who had been beaten and thrown out of a car. Angers confronted the man with the sheriff's story. The man told him that he and his wife had been picked up by the Secret Service, who told them that if they mentioned "any relationship with the Kennedy assassination or the Hunts, they'd be dead." Angers said that, before the assassination, the man's brother had gotten close to Walker and had eventually become his chauffer, purportedly to infiltrate Walker's organization. The man said that neither he nor his brother could stand Walker. As the story goes, the brother also got close to Oswald, who was also trying to get close to Walker. Oswald and the two brothers allegedly got drunk and talked about shooting Walker. Oswald told them he had a rifle and that they should do it. They drove to Walker's and Oswald got down on the embankment of a creek. Walker was pacing in front of the front window. They saw his shadow on the back wall and shot at it. They then jumped in the car and took off. (It was determined by the Dallas police that the shooting took place from an alley in the rear of the house, not from a creek embankment.)

Russell re-interviewed General Walker in 1992, and Walker said he remembered Larrie Schmidt and his brother Bob. He told Russell that Schmidt wanted to take over the National Indignation Committee, the Young Americans for Freedom, and Walker's group. Walker was not sure when he took Bob Schmidt on to his staff but he thought it was probably before he went on the speaking tour with Billy James Hargis in early 1963 (the tour began on February 27, 1963). Robert Surrey had brought the Schmidts to Walker. Walker said Bob ran errands in Walker's station wagon, picking up people at the airport and literature at the printer. He said Larrie hung around "just being a nuisance." Eventually, Walker ran Larrie Schmidt out of his house and told him to never set foot in it again.

Russell asked Walker if the Schmidt brothers could have gotten together with Oswald to shoot at him. Walker told Russell that several people who investigated the shooting told him that the three were possibly involved.[2164]

Jack Ruby, General Walker, and the John Birch Society

Just before the president's murder, Jack Ruby left three clues that pointed in the direction of the Hunts and the John Birch Society as culprits in the assassination. Later, Ruby also alluded, in his Warren Commission testimony, that General Walker and the John Birch Society were involved in the assassination, which lends credibility to William Duff's claim that he saw Ruby in the company of a member of the John Birch Society at Walker's house in 1962 and 1963.

Ruby was placing the weekend ad for his striptease nightclub at the *Dallas Morning News* advertising department on the morning of the assassination, when he overheard incoming phone calls from citizens complaining about the paper's printing of the insulting "Welcome Mr. Kennedy to Dallas" full-page advertisement. As we know, the ad, composed by Larrie Schmidt, appeared in the morning edition of the paper on the day of the president's visit to the city. Ruby saw the ad before the assassination and, at first glance, thought it was a nice welcome. He was further delighted to see the name of a Jew, Bernard Weissman, attached to the advertisement. He thought President Kennedy had been a good friend of the Jews and that, in turn, a Jew was welcoming him to Dallas. Also in the ad was the post office box number 1792. Ruby's feelings changed after he read it in full and realized its insulting content. The next day, after the murder, he told a friend that the black border surrounding the ad represented "mourning" and that whoever put the ad out "Must have known that the president was going to be killed."[2165] Ruby realized that the gratuitous use of Weissman's obviously Jewish name on the ad was an attempt to link Jews to the assassination.

By all accounts, Ruby was genuinely and deeply grieved over Kennedy's death. At 4:00 a.m. on the morning of November 23, the day after the assassination, Ruby drove to his apartment and rousted his roommate, George Senator, out of bed. They proceeded to Ruby's nightclub, where Ruby picked up his employee Larry Crafard, who had a Polaroid camera, and drove to a billboard urging the impeachment of Earl Warren. Ruby said he couldn't understand why anyone would want to impeach Earl Warren. (The billboard was the work of the John Birch Society, although no mention of the society was made on the billboard.) Nonetheless, Ruby perceptively proclaimed, "This must be the work of the John Birch Society or the Communist Party." The billboard invited the public to write to post office box 1757, Dallas, for more information on the impeachment effort.

When he first saw the "Welcome, Mr. Kennedy" ad, Ruby thought, astutely, that it bore a similar post office box number as the "Impeach Earl Warren" billboard that he had recalled seeing. He took the unusual step of driving to the billboard at 4:00 a.m. in an attempt to connect the two. Three Polaroid pictures of the billboard were taken for what Ruby claimed would be a "scoop." Ruby never specified what his scoop was, but the clear implication was that Ruby sensed that those behind the "Welcome Mr. Kennedy" ad, as well as those behind the "Impeach Earl Warren" billboard, were behind the assassination. As the evidence in this work will show, he was quite correct.

Another clue—in addition to the ad and the billboard—that Ruby left behind pointing toward the conspirators was the copy of H. L. Hunt's *Life Lines* radio script that he had picked up about three weeks prior at the Texas Products Show (and then had bitterly complained about its anti-Kennedy content, as was described in Chapter Eleven). He became "all excited and red-face, livid" at the time and "planned to send a copy to President Kennedy," a friend noted. Ruby added, "Nobody has any right to talk like this about our government."[2166] Ruby showed the *Life Lines* script to a friend on the evening of the assassination as he was complaining about the anti-Kennedy ad and the "Impeach Earl Warren" billboard. While discussing the *Life Lines* script, Ruby told his friend that there was a group of "Radicals" in Dallas who hated President Kennedy and Ruby indicated that he felt they were partially responsible for the assassination. (The Warren Commission noted that the *Life Lines* script was entitled "Heroism" and was from a "conservative radio program." However, they failed to mention that it was critical of the Kennedy administration.)[2167]

The incident suggests that Ruby was subtly pointing at H. L. Hunt, the Walker camp, and the John Birch Society as the ones behind the assassination when no one else did. On the contrary, the FBI director announced on the day of the assassination that the culprit was a Communist—just the opposite of the Hunts, Walker, and the John Birch society. The *Life Lines* radio transcript was found in the trunk of Ruby's car after he murdered Oswald. Ruby's notebook was found to contain the Boston address of John Birch Society leader Robert Welch's chief aide, Thomas Hall. In addition, the phone records of Ruby's brother Earl—who lived in Detroit—contained the phone number of the Welch Candy Company that was founded by Robert Welch. Neither the Warren Commission nor anybody else has attempted to provide any other reasonable explanation for attention paid by Ruby to the "Welcome" ad, impeachment billboard, or Hunt radio script since they were so incongruent with the official story that a lone Communist assassin committed the murder. Ruby's apparent inside knowledge of the assassination conspiracy may well be explained by his dealings with General Walker and the John Birch Society—as asserted by William Duff. (An entire chapter will be devoted to the Ruby affair, and the question of whether or not the General Walker operation compelled Jack Ruby to silence Lee Harvey Oswald will be explored.)

Beyond the subtle clues left by Jack Ruby, he was more pointed in his testimony before Chief Justice Earl Warren and his staff in his June 1964 Warren Commission testimony. In his testimony, Ruby appeared to be a desperate man afraid for his life. He repeatedly told Warren he was afraid for his family's lives and the lives of the Jewish people. He repeatedly begged to be taken to Washington, stating that he could not tell his story in Dallas. Exhorted by Sheriff Decker to "be a man and tell the truth," Ruby confessed the following to an obtuse Chief Justice Warren:

> Mr. Ruby: There is an organization here, Chief Justice Warren, if it takes my life at this moment to say it, and Bill Decker said be a man and say it, there is a John Birch Society right now in activity, and Edwin Walker is one of the top men of the organization—take it for what it is worth, Chief Justice Warren.
> Unfortunately for me, for me giving the people the opportunity to get in power, because of the act I committed, has put a lot of people in jeopardy with their lives.
> Don't register with you does it?
>
> Chief Justice Warren: No, I don't understand that.

Ruby made further references to the John Birch Society, as well as other significant revelations in his testimony that eluded the Warren Commission, HSCA investigation, assassination scholars, and other writers. The Ruby affair and his all-important Warren Commission testimony will be detailed in another chapter.[2168]

The Warren Commission's conclusions on the Walker shooting incident were reported under the provocative heading, *"PRIOR ATTEMPT TO KILL, The attempt on the Life of Maj. General Edwin A. Walker."* They concluded that Oswald not only killed the president, but that he had also tried to kill Walker. In the end, the Commission's analysis of the Walker Shooting incident was exculpatory for Walker, and damning for Oswald. The Warren Commission concluded in a section of their report entitled "Speculations" that: "In their investigation of the attack on General Walker, the Dallas police uncovered no suspect and planned no arrests." They ignored the fact that William Duff was a suspect in the case—and was arrested.

The John Martin Home Movie

John Martin, a Minuteman from Minnesota who served under General Walker in Germany, filmed a home movie that begins with a view out the window of an airplane, and then cuts to General Walker's home in Dallas. Next, the film abruptly cuts to locations in New Orleans, including iconic Lafayette Park and scenes of Audubon Park, culminating with a view of several police cars on Canal Street, and ending with a shot of Oswald's FPCC leaflets strewn on the sidewall. (The film—as available today from the Sixth Floor Assassination Museum in Dallas—has apparently been altered and is of extremely poor quality. Faces are difficult to make out. The author could not find out information from Martin, because Martin donated the film with the stipulation that no one contacts him.)

In 1968, Martin, for unknown reasons, gave the film to assassination writer Harold Weisberg, and Paul Schoener, who were lecturing together at the University of Minnesota. Schoener recalled that Martin was a Minuteman from who served under Walker in Germany and had moved away from the far right. Schoener remembered that the film showed the bullet holes in Walker's window, as well as footage taken inside Walker's home of a bullet hole in the wall. Schoener's copy was apparently different from the one available today, and showed Oswald being taken away by police after his fight with Carlos Bringuier, ending with a view of the discarded FPCC pamphlets. Weisberg and Schoener were intensely interested in the identities of the people surrounding Oswald while he was leafleting. Focusing on the second part of the film—Oswald's leafleting in New Orleans—they ignored the first part of the film that showed the bullet holes in Walker's Dallas home, and did not appreciate its significance. The FBI obtained a cache of discarded Minutemen membership cards, one listing a John L. Martin, age 17, from Minnesota. If the card is accurate, John L. Martin was too young to have served under Walker. However, there is no evidence the John L. Martin listed on the cards is the same Martin that made the home movie.[185]

The most likely explanation for the film is that General Walker directed Martin to film both the Dallas and New Orleans scenes tied to Oswald—which means that it is evidence Walker knew in advance about Oswald, and his planned phony fight with Bringuier, contrary to his Warren Commission testimony that he knew nothing of Oswald before the assassination.

It will be recalled from Chapter Nine that, after Bringuier's arrest for his fight with

Oswald, he met with Kent Courtney and asked him for advice on retaining an attorney. As noted, Courtney first became acquainted with Walker in 1961, wrote a book about him, and traveled to Miami in February 1963 to attend two Walker speaking engagements. After the Walker shooting, Walker called Courtney and told him about it.

As will also be shown later, Walker traveled to New Orleans and met with Kent Courtney, Leander Perez, and two employees of Guy Banister just days before the assassination. It's likely that Courtney and Walker collaborated with Oswald and others in the Banister operation in the staging of the phony fight with Bringuier.

Conclusions

General Walker and Lee Harvey Oswald both had ties to the Guy Banister operation that included Kent Courtney, as was noted in the first two chapters. Clearly, with those ties, Oswald was not trying to kill General Walker—they were working on the same side. Kent Courtney was with Walker on two separate occasions before the shooting, and may have had a hand in the planning. It also made little sense that Oswald would want to kill both Walker and the president, since they were diametrically opposed enemies. It therefore follows that Oswald was not trying to kill General Walker and that the shooting incident was bogus. The Walker shooting incident was, in part, a phony attempted publicity stunt to promote the Walker-Hargis speaking tour. Even Dallas Police Detective L. E. Cunningham, who investigated the incident, suspected it was a publicity stunt. It was not the first time Walker had plotted faking a serious crime for publicity. A year earlier, he had asked Minutemen leader Robert DePugh to kidnap him so he could blame it on the Communists and gain publicity for his run for governor.

The Walker shooting incident had nowhere the impact it might have if Oswald had been caught and the incriminating evidence he left behind found. Had the photos of Walker's house, the notebook describing the plot, and the menacing backyard photos of Oswald posed as a militant Communist been discovered in Oswald's apartment after the shooting it would have had a spectacular effect. Walker would have had his proof that the Communist threat was from within and that it was the real threat to America and to anti-Communists like him. All of that evidence Oswald left behind after the shooting incident—superfluous in terms of committing the act—even raised the suspicions of Warren Commission counsel Wesley Liebler.

The incident was witnessed in part by a neighbor, Kirk Coleman, standing fourteen feet away—and one of the men leaving the scene knew it. Since they could not have known how much Coleman had seen that might expose the incident as bogus, the presumptive plot to blame it on a willing Oswald was abandoned. If the plot had been carried to fruition, it would have embellished Oswald's credentials of not only being a Communist trained in the Soviet Union, but a dangerous one. (As will be shown later, the Leander Perez-inspired Communist Control Act that was created and passed in the state legislature by another close associate of Guy Banister, James Pfister, was designed to outlaw any leftist group tied to the integration moment that associated with Oswald. As will also be shown later, Oswald had infiltrated at least three leftist groups—two that will be presented for the first time in this work—that were targets of the Communist Control Act.)

Aside from the evidence that Walker and Oswald had ties to the Banister operation, there were significant clues in the Warren Commission's evidence that suggested the Walker shooting incident was a sham. Not least of which is the fact that none of the men seen leaving the scene resembled Oswald. The facts that the back door light was burned out and the neighbor's barking dog suddenly fell ill were all too convenient. The accounts of Walker and his aide, Robert Surrey, were inconsistent—and claims made by Watts and Walker that Duff told his roommate and his wife he shot at Walker were false.

General Watts went to great length and expense to try to entrap Duff in an assassination attempt on Walker. After Duff asserted that he saw Jack Ruby at Walker's on three occasions—and at one time with a member of the John Birch Society—General Watts persuaded Duff to relocate to Oklahoma and provided him housing and a job, even though he steadfastly claimed that Watts tried to kill his friend and client General Walker. Watts's detective, Cliff Roberts, tailed Duff in his car. Coercion and intimidation were used on Duff to keep him silent about what he heard and saw at Walker's house. Duff's admitted fear of General Walker was the reason he recanted his statement that he had seen Ruby at Walker's home. If Duff hadn't retracted the allegation, Walker would have been a prime suspect in the Kennedy assassination. Duff lived with Walker during the time that Walker was plotting with General del Valle, and also while generals Walker, Watts, and del Valle were involved in the Council for Statehood assassination plots. Duff was potentially in the position to have known about them, further making him an extreme liability for generals Walker and Watts.

The allegation that Larrie Schmidt and his brother Bob, two associates of General Walker, drove Oswald to the shooting incident gains credibility due to the fact that it was reported to a reputable reporter for the *Dallas Morning News* who had been working with the HSCA, which was investigating both the assassination and the shooting incident.

The claim by *National Zeitung* that Oswald shot at General Walker—reported before any other person or paper suspected it and before Mariana Oswald confirmed his involvement—further suggests that Walker was involved in the incident. Although he denied blaming the shooting on Oswald, Walker had been a friend of the editor since his time in Germany and gave an interview with the paper two days after the murder. The chances that the paper learned about it in any other way are remote.

Jack Ruby left behind several subtle clues pointing toward H. L. Hunt and the John Birch Society in the Kennedy assassination. He went out in the middle of the night after the assassination and photographed a John Birch Society bulletin board for no reason that the Warren Commission could discern. A copy of H. L. Hunt's *Life Lines* radio transcript that was bitterly critical of President Kennedy was discovered in the trunk of his car after he murdered Oswald. Ruby was more pointed in testimony before Chief Justice Earl Warren when he alluded to Walker and the John Birch Society as forces behind the murder. Unfortunately,

Warren failed to comprehend what he was saying. Ruby's Warren Commission testimony lends credence to William Duff's claim that he saw Ruby at General Walker's home with a member of the John Birch Society.

The John Martin film of the bullet holes in Walker's home and the Oswald-Bringuier fight provide further evidence that Walker was involved in the Oswald affair with the New Orleans operation, likely through his liaison with Kent Courtney. Walker had to know the Bringuier-Oswald fight was pre-planned (Kent Courtney likely told him), and directed Martin to travel to New Orleans to film it.

CHAPTER FIFTEEN

GENERAL WALKER, 1963: EVIDENCE OF CONSPIRACY

*I have seen this country being sold out, lock, stock and barrel by a bunch
of sophisticated professors, Harvard liberals who are at a loss as where
to go and what to do, and I can assure you they are going to pay for
it one way or another. . . . It's interesting that the Communists killed
the first people that helped them in their revolution. First! So we've got
something to look forward to, ladies and gentlemen.*
— General Walker, October 25, 1963

After the Walker shooting incident, Lee Harvey Oswald left for New Orleans, where
he began publicly flaunting his Communist persona. While, at the same time, numerous individuals saw him in the presence of fanatical anti-Communists, including
Guy Banister, David Ferrie, and a number of anti-Castro Cubans who operated out of the
office building at 544 Camp Street.

During that same period of time, in the second half of 1963, General Walker maintained a much lower profile. The activities of Oswald, Walker, the Banister operation, and
the Kennedys will be chronicled in this chapter from the period of time following the Walker
shooting incident up to the assassination of the president on November 22, 1963.

The Road to Dealey Plaza

The FBI learned, on April 24, 1963, that General Walker and Robert Surrey planned to travel
to New York City where Walker was to address the National Society of New England Women. The FBI noted that Walker and Surrey were closely associated in the period from April
24, 1963, to October 1964, and that Surrey accompanied Walker on trips. They noted that
Surrey's wife, Mary, was a long-time volunteer for Walker, and had been the founder of the
John Birch Society in Dallas. The FBI also reported that Robert Surrey accompanied Walker
to Oxford prior to the Ole Miss riots.[2169]

On April 24, 1963, Ruth Paine drove Lee Harvey Oswald to the bus station in
Dallas, where he left for New Orleans.[2170] Also on April 24, 1963, the *Dallas Times Herald*
announced that President Kennedy planned to make a trip to Texas that year.[2171]

On May 12, 1963, shots were fired at the homes of two African Americans in Anniston, Alabama. Joseph Milteer's friend Kenneth Adams was arrested and found guilty of the crime.[2172]

On May 29, 1963, the free electors bill was passed in the Louisiana House of Representatives and was sent to the state senate. The bill was designed to deprive President Kennedy of Louisiana's Electoral College votes in the 1964 election.[2173]

On June 1, 1963, the John Birch Society held a recruiting meeting in New York City that featured Robert Welch, Revilo Oliver, and Tom Anderson—all close Walker associates.[2174]

On Monday June 3, 1963, President Kennedy formulated a special message that he planned to send to Congress the following week asking for strong new civil rights legislation. The proposed legislation would allow the attorney general to file suits against schools that were segregated and forbid racial discrimination in businesses.[2175]

On June 4, 1963, Senator Estes Kefauver, a Democrat from Tennessee, ordered a U.S. Senate inquiry into the free electors activity in five states and proposed a constitutional amendment that would change the electoral system.[2176] The press noted that Willie Rainach and Leander Perez, both Banister colleagues, worked behind the scenes in the free electors movement. Perez stood at the Louisiana senate rail during the proceedings and was on the floor at recess "wheedling, cajoling and threatening" opponents of the measure.[2177]

On June 2, 1963, Billy James Hargis held the Christian Crusade's Anti-Communist Seminar featuring Revilo Oliver and Edward Hunter as speakers.[2178]

On June 6, 1963, the Free Electors bill was defeated in the Louisiana state senate in an 18–20 vote.[2179]

On June 10, 1963, Lee Harvey Oswald wrote to *The Worker*, the newspaper of the Communist Party U.S.A., and notified them that he had organized a chapter of Fair Play for Cuba Committee in New Orleans, and requested literature from them.[2180] The Warren Commission later established that the chapter was a sham and did not exist. Senator Eastland, a Banister colleague, held ongoing hearings on FPCC and concluded it was a Communist-backed organization.

General Walker and the Minutemen Assassination Teams

On June 10, 1963, the FBI interviewed Gerald L. Beasley, Jr., M.D., of Duncan, Oklahoma, a member of the John Birch Society. Dr. Beasley contacted the FBI with information he had about General Walker. Dr. Beasley told the FBI that a salesman for a Houston pharmaceutical company, Charles Elkins from Oklahoma City, had paid a visit to his office.

Elkins noticed some literature posted on Beasley's wall that indicated he was also a "strong conservative." The two discussed conservative politics, and Elkins told him his job as a salesman enabled him to make contacts in the four-state area for the Minutemen organization. Elkins told him that his Minutemen organization was under the direction of General Walker. Elkins's job was to find dependable men in different communities to head up local

Minutemen organizations. Elkins told Dr. Beasley that the Minutemen had contacts in the military through whom they were able to obtain the latest weapons, including rifles, grenades, and explosives. Dr. Beasley asked the Minutemen organizer why the groups were armed, and Elkins explained that the local Minutemen groups were actually "assassination squads." He explained that local assassination squads would go into action and attempt to assassinate all known Communists, if the country headed into a dictatorship.

Elkins encouraged Dr. Beasley to head up a local Minutemen group. Elkins told him that Robert Morris would check on his reliability and someone would contact him when everything checked out favorably. Dr. Beasley told the FBI that, because he was a strong conservative, he had made a lot of enemies. His concern was that Elkins might be one of them and had perhaps had a tape recorder in his briefcase and taped their discussion to use against him in some way.[2181]

Dr. Beasley's statement about General Walker heading up Minutemen assassination squads fits with the reports by Willie Somersett that Walker was a part of the "military high command" behind the broad-based assassination plots of the Council of Statehood (reported in Chapter Six) and his plotting with General del Valle (noted in Chapter Eight). The Bureau of Alcohol, Tobacco and Firearms also established that General Walker and H. L. Hunt were the leaders of the Dallas Minutemen, noting, "An organization known as the Minutemen is the right-wing group in Dallas most likely to have been associated with any effort to assassinate the president."[2182]

A California informant reported that Colonel William Potter Gale and his militia were connected to assassination plots similar to the Council for Statehood/Congress of Freedom plots. In Gale's case, the FBI learned additionally of the plan to organize six-man assassination teams to commit the murder of designated individuals—which appears very similar to General Walker's assassination teams that Dr. Beasley told the FBI about.

As in the case of the other FBI evidence of the radical right's involvement in the Kennedy assassination, there is no evidence the FBI told the Warren Commission about Dr. Beasley's allegation about General Walker's Minutemen assassination teams. It would have made for interesting questioning during Walker's testimony to the Warren Commission about the shooting incident at his home. Importantly, the allegation places Robert Morris in the organization that planned to resort to assassination if needed. Morris, a Dallas resident and a close associate of Walker, had managed to be left out of the various other reports of violent plotting on the part of the radical right wing. Morris was one of Walker's attorneys, along with Clyde Watts, during Walker's incarceration after the Ole Miss insurrection. While chief counsel for Senator Eastland's Senate Internal Security Subcommittee (SISS) Morris worked with Guy Banister and Hubert Badeaux during the 1956 SISS inquisition on subversion in New Orleans. The SISS hearings were held at the same time that Lee Harvey Oswald first began posing as a Communist—the same period when Hubert Badeaux began grooming an individual to infiltrate leftist organizations, as was noted in Chapter One.

On June 11, 1963, the Citizens' Council of New Orleans and George Singelmann,

Banister's close friend, were sued by thirteen faculty members of the Louisiana State University of New Orleans after Singelmann made remarks about them that held them in "disrepute, ridicule and contempt" on a TV show on "Americanism."[2183]

That same day, President Kennedy federalized the 18,000 troops in the Alabama National Guard to enforce the admission of African Americans Vivian Moore and James Hood to the University of Alabama. Governor Wallace blocked the entrance to the school in what became infamously known as the "stand in the schoolhouse doorway." With one hundred soldiers in full battle dress standing a block away, Wallace finally stepped aside and admitted the students.[2184]

The Response of the Segregationists to the Civil Rights Act of 1963

June 11, 1963, also was the day President Kennedy announced plans to introduce a sweeping civil rights bill, which was designed to end discrimination in jobs, voting, schools, and access to restaurants, hotels, and other accommodations. President Kennedy announced the bill before a national television audience and poignantly noted that: "The Negro baby born in America today, regardless of the section of the nation in which he is born, has about one-half as much chance of completing high school as a white baby born in the same place on the same day; one-third as much chance of completing college; one-third as much chance of becoming a professional man; twice as much chance of becoming unemployed; about one-seventh as much chance of earning $10,000 a year; a life expectancy which is seven years shorter; and the prospects of earning only half as much."

The May 14, 1954, Supreme Court decision in *Brown v. Board of Education* was the beginning of the end of segregation; President Kennedy's Civil Rights Act would be its final demise. After *Brown*, the Southern states adopted laws that maintained separation of the races. Partially due to the vague mandate of *Brown* that called for desegregation of public schools "with all deliberate speed," the South remained, for the most part, solidly segregated. That would all change with President Kennedy's proposed Civil Rights Act. All of the South's Jim Crow laws, the lynching, burning, bombing, rallies and rhetoric of the segregationists directed at maintaining the bulwark of segregation would be for naught. However, the major obstacle for the Civil Rights Act passage would be getting it through Senator Eastland's Senate Judiciary Committee, where, in the past, civil rights initiatives had been stalled or defeated.

Georgia senator Richard Russell, who was later appointed to the Warren Commission, said in response to Kennedy's proposal that he saw the nation declining into a "banana republic." Eighteen Southern senators held a strategy meeting and planned a "slow-down" campaign against the legislation.[2185] A second Civil War was threatened. Walker wrote an open letter to the "Congressmen and Legislators of the United 50 States." He told them that the "(Civil) Police Rights Bill" was illegal and unlawful, destroyed the government of the fifty states and "inherently provides for an 'Internal Police Force'."[2186]

On June 12, 1963, Mississippi NAACP leader Medgar Evers, a friend of James Meredith, was assassinated.[2187] Willie Somersett told the FBI that the murder was in retaliation for

President Kennedy's National Guard-enforced integration of the University of Alabama.[2188] The *Dallas Morning News* reported later that unnamed law enforcement officials working on the murder confirmed that the shooter was an expert marksman. The *News* stated, "There is growing belief that the sniper might have been a red agent, intent on stirring bloody rioting." "I hate to bring Communism into it," said one Jackson, Mississippi, attorney, "but this thing was quite likely red inspired."[2189] (Contrary to supposition, Byron De La Beckwith was arrested for the murder on June 23, 1963.[2190] Beckwith was a Klansman, Citizens' Council member, and a friend of Willie Rainach.[2191])

It was standard practice during the civil rights period to blame bombings, murders, and other hate crimes against blacks on the Communists. The FBI obtained a letter on July 8, 1963, addressed to the president of the United States from the Citizens' Council of American, Atlanta, Georgia. It said ominously, "The execution of one of your unlawful agitators, Medgar Evers, is only the beginning of events such as you have never anticipated . . . This is not so much a threat as it is a solemn promise to defend our way of life by whatever means becomes necessary . . . Because you continue on your road of attempted conquest of this country, we urge you to consider the consequences."[2192]

On June 13, the press reported that the U.S.S. *Wasp*, an aircraft carrier with a crew of 2,800, would be docking at the Dumaine Street wharf in New Orleans. The ship would be open to the general public from June 14 to 19, and would remain until June 20. Accompanying the carrier were two destroyers and a submarine.[2193]

On June 14, 1963, Ed Butler, a Banister colleague and Lee Harvey Oswald's future debating foe, addressed the Conference on Cold War Education in Tampa, Florida, on the topic of "The Way to Win—How to Create a Conflict Corporation Cartel." He asserted that a global conflict cartel of anti-Communist organizations to mount a worldwide "brain war" could be formed as a way of combating Communism.[2194] (On August 21, 1963, Oswald engaged in a "debate" with Butler and Carlos Bringuier and admitted he was a Marxist. The debate was bogus because all three men were associated with Guy Banister's anti-Communist operation that worked out of the building at 544 Camp Street.)

June 14, 1963, also marked General Walker's speech in San Francisco in which he asserted, "I could take the 82nd Airborne Division and take it [Cuba] back."[2195] He declared that the main issue in the 1964 election would be "U.S. or U.N.," in reference to his belief that President Kennedy was in the process of placing the U.S. under U.N. control through the disarmament plan outlined in Bulletin 7751. He said the Cuban crisis was a hoax, accomplished under the guidance of the U.N. He claimed there were traitors in the State Department and that both political parties were cooperating with the Communists.[2196]

On June 15, 1963, Oswald checked out the books *The Huey Long Murder Case* by Herman B. Deutsch, and *Portrait of a President* by William Manchester, from the New Orleans Public Library.[2197]

On June 16, 1963, Lee Harvey Oswald handed out Fair Play Cuba Committee leaflets in front of the *Wasp*. The fanfare and press coverage of the *Wasp*'s heralded visit to the city afforded Oswald the opportunity to share the limelight.

On June 17, 1963, Medford Evans, another Banister associate, wrote Walker and told him he enjoyed his recent visit to Walker's home. Evans wrote in code—in a similar fashion to that of Joseph Milteer—referring repeatedly to "a person in Nashville" and "the man." Evans told Walker that he wondered if the 30-30 rifle used to kill Medgar Evers was the same caliber as the one fired at Walker, and suggested somebody should make a ballistics comparison. He ended the letter stating, "Of course Kennedy is responsible for both shots."[2198] Evans was suggesting that the man who killed Evers might have also tried to kill Walker, which is a far-fetched conclusion. Walker paid a visit to Byron De La Beckwith, the man accused of killing Evers, who had the same radical background as Walker, as we shall see.

On June 17, 1963, an organizational meeting of the free electors was held in Jackson, Mississippi. George Wallace, Jim Johnson, and Leander Perez addressed the meeting and Tom Anderson was the main speaker.[2199] J. Evetts Haley, Willie Rainach, Roy Harris, and William Simmons were all present. Barnett said, "The South, by working together, will hold the balance of power in selecting the next President of the Untied States." Perez declared, "We've not lost the fight [for segregation] in Louisiana."[2200]

On June 18, 1963, Clyde Watts and Tom Anderson served on the advisory committee of the newly formed Freedom of Speech for Civil Servants founded by George W. Prechter. The group aimed to insure the rights of civil servants to engage in patriotic activities without being construed as engaging in political activities, which was prohibited.[2201]

General Walker planned a "strategy seminar" for June 19 and 20, in Dallas, on the subject of "Sovereignty—U.S. or U.N., U.N. Peace Force; Govt. vs. people" according to Walker's handwritten notes from his personal papers. The seminar was to take place "midnight to midnight." The meeting was "Top Secret," and those who were chosen to attend had to accept the committee requirements with respect to "all security identifications, classifications, and public or private statements and releases." Those expected to attend included "Hargis, Walker, Smoot, Welch, Oliver, Anderson, Benson, Courtney, McIntire, Hunter, Bundy, [and] Mathews." Nothing more is known about the top-secret meeting.[2202]

On June 19, 1963, Oswald, a notoriously poor worker, was fired from Reily Coffee.[2203] He had a habit of leaving work and going next door to the service garage to read gun magazines in the waiting room of owner, Adrian Alba, who was in the Minutemen.

That same day, President Kennedy revealed his proposed civil rights bill, the most sweeping of its kind since Reconstruction.[2204] Threats of civil war and bloodshed, thinly veiled as predictions, followed.

On June 20, 1963, Ross Barnett pushed the free electors plan in an appearance in New Orleans.[2205]

On June 24, 1963, Lee Harvey Oswald applied for a passport in New Orleans and stated he was a photographer and wanted to visit England, France, Germany, Russia, Poland, Finland, and Italy.[2206] Later, he reportedly told his wife he was unhappy and that he wanted to return to the Soviet Union with her. Marina wrote to the Soviet Embassy and asked for permission for her and her daughter to return to the Soviet Union. In another letter to the embassy, Oswald told them to consider the cases separately, indicating he did not want to go with her. Marina Oswald told the Warren Commission Lee had a basic desire to go to Cuba and even discussed hijacking an airplane.[2207]

On July 4, 1963, General Walker addressed a non-political picnic group and said that the people were fed up with Bobby Kennedy. He scolded the press for encouraging the Black Muslim Negro movement.[2208]

On July 9, 1963, Louisiana States' Rights leaders—along with George Shannon, head of the Louisiana free electors movement—stated in a meeting at the Capitol House Hotel in Baton Rouge that the South must defeat the Kennedy administration in 1964 or suffer dire consequences. Members of the John Birch Society, the Citizens' Council, and other groups were present. Leander Perez protégé John Rarick delivered a special message for the youth in attendance.[2209]

On July 12, 1963, Mississippi governor Ross Barnett, testifying before the Senate Commerce Committee in Washington, accused the president of "sowing seeds of hate." He threatened that if the civil rights proposals were enacted "the nation could reap a bloody harvest." He added, "If you think 500,000 Negroes marching in Washington is something, pass the legislation and you'll find out what one hundred million angry white Americans will do." Barnett showed the audience the 1957 Highlander Folk School photo of Martin Luther King, Jr. (contrived by Joseph Milteer's friend Roy Harris) as proof that Communism was behind racial strife.[2210] On July 14, Governor George Wallace of Alabama testified before the Senate Commerce Committee that the president's handling of the racial problem rendered the country "a nation torn by strife and turmoil on the brink of civil war." Wallace cited—as proof that the civil rights movement was Communist-inspired—the evidence uncovered in Senator Eastland's SISS hearing on the Southern Conference Education Fund in New Orleans.[2211] President Kennedy responded to the Barnett and Wallace accusations and stated that the top civil rights leaders were not Communists or Communist-controlled.[2212] Nonetheless, the Louisiana segregationists were set to prove that integration was Communist inspired.

The plans to prove their charge had been in the works since June 1962, the same time Oswald had returned from the Soviet Union, when the Communist Control Act was enacted. Under the law, the brainchild of Leander Perez, an elaborate plan to raid the headquarters of the New Orleans integration group, Southern Conference Education Fund (SCEF), and charge the officers with sedition under the Act, was formulated. The officers in SCEF faced decades in jail if convicted. The SCEF raid took place on October 4, 1963. As will be shown later, Lee Harvey Oswald had infiltrated three groups affiliated with SCEF; any one of the members of those groups that were shown to be associated with a Communist like Lee Harvey Oswald, were liable to be arrested under the Act and face lengthy prison terms. The Act—and the raid—involved people closely aligned with Guy Banister's operation, as will be shown later.

On July 20, 1963, Tom Anderson told a John Birch Society seminar in Houston,

Texas, that he would support Barry Goldwater for president in 1964 and Strom Thurmond as vice president. Anderson declared darkly that, "The country will be saved from the grassroots . . . by rebellious patriots." General Walker attended the meeting as an observer. Long-time Congress of Freedom leader George Montgomery, of New York, was a speaker.[2213]

On July 26, 1963, Robert Kennedy sent a statement to the Senate Commerce Committee that asserted that the government had no evidence that any of the top civil rights leaders, including Martin Luther King, Jr., were Communists or Communist controlled.[2214]

On July 27, 1963, Oswald gave a lecture to his cousin's seminary class in Mobile, Alabama, and was critical of the Soviet Union.[2215] That same day, Delphine Roberts, Guy Banister's love interest and secretary, urged "Congress to demand the removal of the Kennedy brothers and impeachment against both be begun immediately."[2216]

On July 31, 1963, Frank Voelker of the Louisiana Sovereignty Commission agreed to contribute $150,000 to a nationwide movement to fight Kennedy's civil rights bill. A group composed of Southern segregationists, called the Coordinating Committee for Fundamental Freedoms, was formed—with offices in Washington—to defeat the measure. The group met with gubernatorial candidates and top segregationists, including Leander Perez.[2217]

The Fifth Annual National Convention of the Christian Crusade was held August 2–4, 1963, in Oklahoma City. Featured speakers included General Walker, Tom Anderson, General Richard Moran, Bob Jones, Robert Welch, and Billy James Hargis.[2218] It will be recalled from Chapter Eleven that General Moran was a part of Pedro del Valle and Nelson Bunker Hunt's American Volunteer Group—the so-called "kill squad." Speaking at the meeting on August 3, 1963, General Walker launched a tirade against the Kennedy administration, stating that it was a "Socialist-Democrat administration headed to a world Socialist republic." He called Kennedy's civil rights proposal "a new name for Communism." He added, "To adjudicate social rights is only within the capability of a police state." He said the solution to the racial problem was "to get a new president. We've had too many Kennedys and Eisenhowers."[2219] On August 4, 1963, Walker stated that President Kennedy was not overtly Communist "because the people of the United States are not Communists and it wouldn't be smart. Castro was not overt until he had complete control of Cuba." Walker devoted much of his speech to criticizing the U.N.[2220] Walker stated that the Communists were behind "all racial disorder, all racial riots, in all disorder, and breakdown, all riots." Walker dominated the convention and blasted the "contemptuous Kennedy brothers and sadistic Harvard associates." Walker was a far more adroit speaker in front of sympathetic crowds—unlike in his performance at the Senate hearings—and had become a big draw. Walker called the current racial unrest a "triumph for Communism," adding, "The best thing for niggers, for their own good, is to be separated."[2221] Walker called Martin Luther King, Jr.'s upcoming March on Washington "Mr. Kennedy's march, led by the administration against the Congress."[2222] Walker called Walter W. Rostow, Kennedy's national security advisor, a traitor. Of the Supreme Court, he asserted, "These turncoats deserve your pity" and said they were a tool of the Communist conspiracy. There were some at the convention who were uncomfortable with

Walker's crass remarks about blacks and his assertion that the last four presidents were Communists. The three-day convention raised $18,000 for the Crusade Against Communism.[2223] Luis V. Manrara of Miami, Florida, who was president of The Truth About Cuba Committee, was a speaker. JBS leader Robert Welch reportedly gave such a long, rambling, and dull speech on the evils of government that a few people, including Walker, got tired and left.[2224]

On August 1, 1963, Oswald wrote V. T. Lee, the national director of the Fair Play for Cuba Committee in New York, and falsely told him he had rented an office in New Orleans for FPCC but, he implied, it was promptly closed under political pressure. Oswald blamed the lack of support for his chapter on the attack on him by Carlos Bringuier and his associates. The "attack" however, did not occur until eight days *after* he wrote the letter to V. T. Lee and is more evidence that the later "fight" with Bringuier was pre-planned and phony.[2225] (Moreover, Oswald and Bringuier were both associates of Guy Banister suggesting they were working on the same side.)

On August 2, 1963, Walker and Hargis spoke at a Christian Crusade meeting in Oklahoma City. The FBI informant at the meeting remarked, "It's hard to imagine I had attended a meeting in Oklahoma City. I thought I was in a lunatic asylum."[2226]

On August 5, 1963, the *Dallas Morning News* reported that General Walker stated that the Siege of Stalingrad (twenty years earlier) was a farce and was exaggerated by the Communists for propaganda purposes.[2227] Walker's historical revisionist remarks reflect his pro-Nazi and anti-Communist sentiment. According to most history books, the Nazi siege of Stalingrad in World War II was horrific and left over a million Nazi and Russian soldiers dead.

On August 5, 1963, Carlos Bringuier would later claim, Oswald entered his Decatur Street store and purportedly offered to train anti-Castro forces.[2228] (Evidence that Bringuier lied about the date that Oswald visited his store was presented in Chapter Nine and is one of several examples that demonstrates that the Oswald-Bringuier antagonistic relationship was phony.)

On August 5 the Nuclear Test Ban Treaty, prohibiting all the testing of nuclear weapons except underground, was signed by the Soviet Union, Britain, and the United States in Moscow.

The FBI reported that in General del Valle's publication, *Alert* No. 5—the August 9, 1963, issue—he wrote there was a one-world international plot to take over the U.S. and make it a province of the U.N. Del Valle urged, once again, the formation of powerful armed resistance groups. An informant told the FBI that, at some point before the assassination, General del Valle paid a visit to two individuals involved in right-wing activities in the New Jersey area for the purpose of forming an "army" of armed citizens—numbering 500,000—to save the country. General del Valle contended that even if Senator Barry Goldwater won the 1964 presidential election, that Kennedy, while still president (before Goldwater's inauguration), would be blackmailed into surrendering the country to the Soviet Union.[2229]

On August 9, while Oswald was distributing Fair Play for Cuba Committee leaflets, Carlos Bringuier and two other Cubans approached him.[2230] The incident was detailed in

Chapter Nine and will be briefly recalled here. The skirmish that ensued was—as we have shown—phony and planned in advance. (Oswald notified the FPCC in New York about the fight *before* it happened.) The two were arrested and Bringuier consulted Walker's friend, Kent Courtney, and asked him to recommend an attorney. During the court proceedings, Oswald sat in the Negro section in the segregated courtroom, a disingenuous performance to dramatize the supposed-Communist solidarity with the Negro plight. White volunteers for the Congress of Racial Equality had threatened to do the same thing in a Clinton, Louisiana, courthouse, days earlier. (Guy Banister was also an associate of Richard Van Buskirk, the Clinton town attorney who claimed that CORE had Communists in its ranks. Banister kept tabs on CORE's activities and had a news clipping about Van Buskirk and CORE in his files. He may have known about CORE's attempt to integrate the Clinton courthouse, since it was reported in the New Orleans newspapers before Oswald integrated the black section of the New Orleans courthouse.) The Oswald-Bringuier "fight" was another instance of their phony relationship. Oswald's pamphlets and the booklet by Corliss Lamont that he passed out, entitled, "The Crime Against Cuba"—which was confiscated during his arrest—bore the address of 544 Camp Street.[2231] The FBI, in a cursory investigation after the assassination, found no evidence that Oswald rented an office at 544 Camp Street.[2232]

David Chandler, a reporter for the *New Orleans States–Item*, told the FBI that a couple of days after the Bringuier fight Oswald came to his office at the newspaper and told him Bringuier was training guerillas for future fighting in Cuba. Oswald told him he would like the newspaper to do a story on his (Oswald's) arrest and on him personally. Chandler told him that not many were in sympathy with FPCC and the paper would not do the story.[2233] The incident is one of many which Marina Oswald claimed represented Oswald "advertising" his Communist persona.

On August 10, 1963, George Wallace addressed the Shreveport Citizens' Council. W. Scott Wilkinson was chairman of the steering committee for Wallace's appearance and Willie Rainach was co-chair.[2234] General Walker led a caravan of Texans from Dallas to the meeting.[2235] The crowd cheered as Wallace declared, "I've had enough of Kennedy." General Walker was introduced to the audience while an organist played "The Eyes of Texas."[2236] In 1959, Wilkinson had represented the state of Louisiana along with Leander Perez, and had testified before the Senate Judiciary hearings in Washington in opposition to a civil rights bill.[2237] W. Scott Wilkinson was among those on the advisory committee for the founding meeting of the Senator Eastland-inspired Federation for Constitutional Government in 1956, with Leander Perez and Roy Harris.[2238] Wilkinson would later represent Walker in his libel suit against the press for their comments against him at Ole Miss. Walker spent a great deal of time in Louisiana in 1963 with men like Perez and Harris who were associated with Joseph Milteer.

Walker gave speeches on successive days in New York, Connecticut, and Massachusetts, from August 12 to August 19, 1963. On August 20, 1963, he was scheduled to meet with Carl McIntire at the Christian Admiral Hotel in Cape May, New Jersey.[2239] (Evidence for

McIntire's involvement in the assassination conspiracy will be detailed in Chapter Nineteen.)

On August 13, 1963, Wickliffe Vernard of Houston wrote Walker and mentioned that he had paid one thousand dollars for the appointment of Billy James Hargis as the National Chaplain of the Constitution Party, Milteer's group. He told Walker that Pedro del Valle was the greatest living Christian in America, and that he was laying plans for "Christianity in action, to save the last bastion of Christianity on the face of the earth." Vernard also stated that the country would be saved by "Ballots or Bullets."[2240]

Also on August 13, the *Times–Picayune* reported that Lee Harvey Oswald was ordered to pay a $10 fine for disturbing the peace while distributing Fair Play for Cuba Committee leaflets. On that same day, Oswald wrote to Arnold Johnson of the Communist Party U.S.A. and thanked him for some literature he had received and gave him an honorary membership card to his Fair Play for Cuba Committee chapter.[2241]

On August 14, 1963, Bob Joiner, who was head of the Grand Prairie Indignant White Citizens' Council, planned to send members to Austin, Texas, and Washington, D.C., to counter-demonstrate against the March on Washington being led by Martin Luther King, Jr.[2242]

On August 16, 1963, Oswald distributed FPCC leaflets in front of the International Trade Mart, and the demonstration was filmed and shown on the evening news.[2243] The incident is one of many where Oswald made a public spectacle of himself—something his wife called "advertising."

On August 17, 1963, Southern governors convened in White Sulphur Springs, West Virginia, for their annual conference. Governor Wallace (AL) said he planned to introduce a resolution to denounce the use of federal troops to enforce desegregation. Governor Barnett (MS) stated, "If anyone tries to bring up anything about discrimination in housing or matters like that they'll have the fight of their lives on their hands." Wallace and Barnett warned their fellow governors, "This is a serious hour in our nation."[2244] The remarks were directed at President Kennedy's Civil Rights Act.

On August 17, 1963, Oswald wrote a letter to FPCC chairman V. T. Lee and told him that, as a result of his fifteen-minute appearance on a WDSU-TV show called "Latin Listening Focus," he was flooded with people interested in joining his FPCC chapter. In reality, the TV appearance never happened and was a complete fabrication—Oswald had, in fact, appeared for less than five minutes on a radio program called "Latin Listening Post" on the 17th. The only response he got for his appearance on the radio was a call from an associate of Carlos Bringuier.[2245] Also on August 17, 1963, Oswald was briefly interviewed about the Fair Play for Cuba Committee on WDSU *radio*.[2246]

On August 19, 1963, General Walker spoke in Boston, where he discussed the nuclear test ban, and said, "This will be the 51st broken treaty. Six senators in Moscow were intimidating the Senate."[2247]

In a Gallup poll on August 20, 1963, President Kennedy held a 70 percent to 26 percent lead over Barry Goldwater, as presumptive presidential candidates in the 1964 election, in the New England and the Middle Atlantic states.[2248]

On August 21, 1963, Oswald "debated" Ed Butler and Carlos Bringuier on WDSU radio and revealed that he was a Marxist. They posed as enemies, but were not. As noted in Chapter Nine, Butler was a radical right winger and close associate of Guy Banister; Bringuier was an associate of Banister, as well. The relationship of Oswald, Butler, and Bringuier to Banister is evidence that the radio debate was also bogus, like the Walker shooting incident. Evidence was previously presented that, before the debate—and revealed for the first time in this work—Butler had testified before the U.S. Congress and his remarks were printed in the *Congressional Record*. Butler told them of a scheme to train "conflict managers" to pose as Communists, infiltrate their organizations, and learn their catchphrases and manner of communicating. It would not be surprising if Butler had something to do with Oswald posing as a Communist. The day after the Kennedy assassination, Ed Butler flew to Washington D.C., to present the tape recording of the "debate" to Senator Eastland's committee. (As you will remember, Eastland was an associate of Banister and Leander Perez.) William Stuckey, who worked at the radio station, bragged when he told the Warren Commission about it, "I think we finished him [Oswald] on that program . . . because we had publicly linked the Fair Play for Cuba Committee with a fellow who lived in Russia for three years and who was an admitted Marxist."[2249] Under the Communist Control Act that was created by Leander Perez and James Pfister, two close associates of Guy Banister, any person or organization linked to a communist like Lee Harvey, faced decades in jail and huge fines. Carl and Anne Braden, officers in the integrationist Southern Council Education Fund in New Orleans, and long the targets of segregationists, were also officers in FPCC.

General Walker and the March on Washington

The FBI was concerned that General Walker might attend the historic March on Washington on August 28, 1963, where Martin Luther King, Jr. was to give his now-famous "I Have a Dream" speech. Their worry was that Walker might start another riot, like at Ole Miss.

When Walker was asked if he planned to attend the march, he replied, "I will go where the spirit moves me. Wait and see." The FBI had the definite impression that Walker planned to attend the march, based in part on the announcement by Commander George Lincoln Rockwell that a "prominent figure of national renown that took part in the riots of the University of Mississippi" would join the American Nazi Party in a counter-demonstration.[2250] The FBI took note of a press report in which Walker urged resistance to the march in a speech in Avon, Connecticut. Walker had told the press that there would be opposition in the streets of Washington. He would not say if he was involved with the opposition, but stated that he had "friends all over the nation and people were rallying behind United States Senator Strom Thurmond." Walker added that the "[t]hree main problems" facing the country were the nuclear test ban treaty, the Kennedy administration's civil rights program, and the March on Washington. Robert Shelton, Imperial Wizard of the United Klans of America Inc., was listed among the "hate groups" and their members that planned to attend the march, in addition to Walker and Rockwell.[2251] Shelton, like Walker, was an associate of Joseph Milteer. (It will be recalled that Milteer met with Shelton on September 14, 1963, on the eve of the murderous Sixteenth Street Baptist Church bombing in Birmingham, Alabama.)[2252]

President Kennedy was not going to repeat the mistakes that were made at Ole Miss. He would not be short on military manpower during the March on Washington. When it was anticipated that Walker might lead another insurrection, the president ordered 4,000 combat troops and one marine battalion to be on alert status, and 25,000 combat-ready troops to be available on the outskirts of Washington. In addition, 2,850 uniformed police officers and 2,000 marshals were to be present.[2253] President Kennedy was on a "war footing" with the Southern insurrectionists and General Walker, as was evidenced by the massive military presence assembled for the March on Washington. Kennedy would no longer tolerate the defiance of Southern governors backed by the civilian brigades armed with bricks and bottles, squirrels rifles, and small arms, as he had at Ole Miss. By the time of the March on Washington, attempts to save segregation by armed resistance were too late.

The Southern rebels were running out of options for stopping President Kennedy and his plans to end "the Southern way of life." On August 28th, Walker was in Austin, Texas, with Bob Joiner of Grand Prairie, Texas, who led a handful of men and boys on a march on the state capitol in protest of Martin Luther King, Jr.'s march. Accompanying Walker was Robert Surrey, who said that he and Walker had just finished a two-week tour of the Northeast where they found "immense support for states rights."[2254] The FBI noted that Walker gave a speech in Avon, Connecticut, and another in Boston around the time of the march. His other whereabouts on his trip to the Northeast are not known.

August 28, 1963, also marked the day Lee Harvey Oswald wrote to the Communist Party U.S.A., told them he had lived in the Soviet Union, and asked their opinion as to whether he should stay above ground or go underground to fight for progressive causes. On September 19, 1963, Arnold Johnson of the Communist Party advised Oswald that he should stay "in the back ground, not underground."[2255]

On August 29, 1963, President Kennedy met with leaders of the March on Washington in the White House. The group included Whitney Young of the National Urban League, Dr. Martin Luther King, Jr., John Lewis from the Student Nonviolent Coordinating Committee (and a former Freedom Rider), Rabbi Joachim Prinz from the American Jewish Congress, Dr. Eugene Carson Blake from the National Council of Churches, AFL-CIO vice president A. Philip Randolph, Walter Reuther from the United Auto Workers, and Roy Wilkins who was the NAACP executive secretary. The radical right despised all of those men and organizations. Kennedy stated that the march advanced "the cause of 20 million Negroes" and all mankind.[2256]

Governor Ross Barnett wrote an article for the September 1963 John Birch Society publication *American Opinion* entitled "The Rape of our Constitution and Civil Rights." He made a derogatory reference to the senators who accompanied the secretary of state to Moscow to sign the Nuclear Test Ban Treaty.[2257]

On August 31, 1963, Lee Harvey Oswald wrote to *The Worker*, notifying them that he planned to relocate his family.[2258]

Also on August 31, 1963, wanted posters—very similar to the "Wanted for Treason" poster that accused President Kennedy of treason, which were designed and circulated by Robert Surrey before the assassination—were found glued on the walls of downtown Dallas businesses. The posters, also likely the work of Surrey, read, "Wanted for Murder—Khrushchev", and featured front- and side-view, mug shot-type photos of Soviet Premier Nikita Khrushchev. Below the photos they called Khrushchev, "an extremely vicious criminal who should under no circumstances be trusted." The Minutemen were noted as the posters' sponsor. The posters were an attack on Kennedy's recent signing of the Nuclear Test Ban Treaty with the Soviets. The Dallas police, according to the newspaper article on the poster, stated that the Minutemen in Dallas were defunct—in spite of the fact they had identified Robert Surrey as a member of the Minutemen after the Ole Miss riots less than a year earlier.[2259]

On September 1, 1963, Oswald wrote to the Communist Party U.S.A. and told them he was going to relocate to the Baltimore or Washington area in October and wanted to know how to contact the Communist Party there.[2260] At the time, there were no definite plans for a presidential trip to the South. As noted by Willie Somersett, the original plans to assassinate the president involved shooting him as he strolled the rear grounds of the White House.

Governor Ross Barnett (MS) told a crowd at a free electors fundraiser in Monroe, Louisiana, on September 3, 1963, "John Kennedy must be defeated in 1964 if this nation is to be saved."[2261] Barnett told the audience, "We at this hour are one short step from dictatorship in America." George Shannon, editor of the *Shreveport Journal* told the crowd, "If the American people secede the dictators out of Washington the man who deserves most of the credit will be Governor Ross Barnett," whom he called "a giant among men." Barnett stated that if the South could withhold between fifty and sixty electoral votes in 1964, the elections would be deadlocked and "all [presidential] candidates will come crawling to the South on their knees." Earlier in the year, Barnett had persuaded the Mississippi legislature to pass a law practically guaranteeing that Mississippi's seven electoral votes would be free and unpledged.[2262] Willie Rainach attended the September event, as did John McKeithen—the Public Service Commissioner and future Louisiana governor.[2263] Jim Garrison had given McKeithen a glowing endorsement in his bid for governor in 1963.[2264]

Senator James O. Eastland and the Fair Play
for Cuba Committee Inquisition, September 1963

In Washington, D.C., on September 4, 1963, J. G. Sourwine, counsel to Senator Eastland's Senate Internal Security Subcommittee, questioned witnesses from the Fair Play for Cuba Committee in hearings entitled "Castro's Network in the United States." He concluded that Fair Play for Cuba Committee was sponsored by Communists.[2265] (Kent Courtney was an associate of Sourwine and at one time traveled to Washington to confer with him.[2266])

FPCC leader V. T. Lee, the man whom Oswald had been corresponding with, took the Fifth Amendment in response to every question—including whether or not he was a member of the Communist Party in the United States or in Cuba. Nonetheless, V. T. Lee's testimony filled fifty-two pages of the hearing's report.[2267]

At the same time, Senator Eastland—a long-time associate of Leander Perez, Guy Banister and Hubert Badeaux—was conducting his inquisition of FPCC, Lee Harvey Oswald was posing as the leader of what the Warren Commission determined was a non-existent FPCC chapter in New Orleans. Oswald handed out FPCC leaflets at one point that bore the address of 544 Camp Street, the building that housed the office of Guy Banister, and Banister's secretary later admitted that she had seen the pamphlets in the building, along with Oswald's placards.

Guy Banister and General Walker at the Capitol House Hotel, Baton Rouge, September 4, 1963

During the month of September, 1963, General Walker settled into a protracted stay in the state of Louisiana, appearing at anti-Kennedy and segregationist meetings on the 4th and 5th, as well as very possibly on the 6th, 7th, 14th, and 16th, as will be discussed next. It was during the latter part of Walker's September Louisiana sojourn that plans for President Kennedy to visit Dallas were announced. The allegations were presented (in Chapter Two) that Lee Harvey Oswald was seen on numerous occasions in Baton Rouge with Kent Courtney, a backer of the free electors movement, in the summer of 1963, and may have been connected to the anti-Kennedy free electors meetings held in the city on September 4, 6, and 7.

The Louisiana free electors campaign held a meeting at the Capitol House Hotel in Baton Rouge on Tuesday, September 4, 1963. The meeting proceeds were to be used to finance Senator Harold Montgomery's free elector committee initiative.[2268] Montgomery was a dedicated racist and sat at the head table with Leander Perez and his wife, Hollis Metcalf, and George Shannon. (Metcalf served on the Louisiana Committee for Free Electors with Guy Banister, Harold Montgomery, Stuart McClendon, and George Shannon.)[2269]

George Shannon, editor of the *Shreveport Journal* introduced Mississippi lieutenant governor Paul Johnston, a leader of the free electors movement, who—standing in for Governor George Wallace of Alabama—told the crowd that unless President Kennedy was defeated in 1964 they'd "seen [their] last free elections."[2270]

Governor Wallace was initially scheduled to speak, but cancelled due to another desegregation crisis in Alabama. Wallace called up hundreds of state troopers and was preparing to defy a federal order calling for integration of three of Birmingham's public schools. Attempts by black students to enter white public schools were blocked by a Wallace decree. The home of Arthur Shores, a black civil rights leader, was bombed for the second time. Another black man, John L. Coley, was shot and killed with three bullets to the head. Blacks in Birmingham rioted in response. In Washington, Attorney General Robert Kennedy met with top Justice Department officials to deal with the crisis.

Wallace addressed the electors meeting by phone. Wallace and Johnston urged the

South to unite to free itself from the dictatorship of the Kennedy administration. Wallace pledged that Bible reading in the public schools would continue, regardless of the Supreme Court decision that prohibited it. Leander Perez spoke, saying "if a slate of free electors is pitted against a slate of Kennedy electors in Louisiana, Kennedy won't have a ghost of a chance of winning this state. Our country is truly sick, when we see military might such as was used by Eisenhower in Little Rock and by Kennedy in Birmingham and Oxford." Another speaker proclaimed, "John Kennedy must be defeated in 1964 if this nation is to be saved." Four hundred people attended the meeting, including a delegation from Houston.[2271]

Joe Cooper, a Baton Rouge police officer who infiltrated the Klan and other far right groups, saw Guy Banister at the meeting with General Walker and attorney Richard Van Buskirk.[2272] Cooper did not give a date of the sighting, and Walker and Banister's presence could have been on a day other than September 4. However, that day seems likely, given Walker's long stay and frequent appearances in Louisiana around the same time. It's not surprising that Walker, who had developed close ties to the Louisiana segregationists, was at the meeting. Guy Banister had previously been named as a representative to the First District Free Elector Rally held at Capitol House on May 10, 1963, and his presence at the meeting was not unexpected.[2273] The Garrison memo about the event is the first written report of the Banister-Walker relationship. The author discovered four witnesses who affirmed that Walker and Banister were close, which include Garrison investigators William Turner and Lou Ivon; Joseph Oster, Banister's former business partner; and H. L. Hunt employee Paul Rothermel.[2274]

The September 4 Capitol House meeting, attended by the triumvirate of General Walker, Guy Banister, and Leander Perez, is of tremendous historical significance. Here we have Banister, who not only was seen by eleven witnesses with Lee Harvey Oswald, but who was also present at the plotting during the 1963 Congress of Freedom meeting, and has also been tied directly to Joseph Milteer. Evidence in Chapter Nine showed that Hubert Badeaux and Guy Banister were the likely "groomers" of Oswald as a phony Communist in 1956 and 1957.

Also present at the Capitol House meeting was Leander Perez, whom Willie Somersett identified as a financier of the Kennedy assassination. A Milteer personal letter established a direct Perez-Milteer relationship. The evidence of a Walker-Banister relationship is also evidence that Oswald would not have tried to kill Walker during the Walker shooting.

Taking the following facts together, there is abundant evidence to support the involvement of General Walker in the assassination conspiracy:

The fact that Joseph Milteer, who predicted the assassination in advance and was present in Dealey Plaza when it happened (and was at the Congress of Freedom meeting where the broad-based assassination plots were discussed in April 1963, which was attended by Clyde Watts, Guy Banister, and Kent Courtney) inextricably ties him to the assassination conspiracy.

The fact that Walker was a military advisor to the murder-plotting Congress of Freedom/Council for Statehood and that Walker and Banister were each associated with Milteer, is further evidence against him. Walker's plotting correspondence with General Pedro del Valle who advocated violence and who—as the evidence revealed in Chapter Eight suggests—revealed that the assassination of President Kennedy was in the planning is more evidence of conspiracy involving Walker.

The fact Walker was close with Billy James Hargis, who Willie Somersett reported was raising funds for the hardcore underground, as well as Leander Perez, is more evidence against him. Walker was closely tied to the H. L. Hunt clan, and evidence for their involvement in the assassination conspiracy was presented in Chapter Eleven.

Substantially more evidence against Walker will be presented in the next section.

The presence of Richard Van Buskirk with Walker and Banister at the meeting is of tremendous significance in its own right. Van Buskirk was an attorney in the town of Clinton, Louisiana, thirty minutes from Baton Rouge. His best friend was Clinton judge John Rarick, who was a member of the board of directors of the state Citizens' Council with Leander Perez, Kent Courtney, and George Singelmann, who were all close associates of Guy Banister. John Rarick was a protégé of Leander Perez, who backed him for his successful bid for Congress in 1966. Rarick and Van Buskirk helped write the legislation at the state capitol for the Free Elector bill. When the bill failed, the funds raised for it at the all-important September 4 Capitol House Hotel meeting were donated to John Rarick's congressional campaign.[2275] Rarick was also a friend of General Walker, and they appeared together at Fourth of July segregation rallies in both 1964 and 1965, which will be discussed later. Not coincidentally, Lee Harvey Oswald was seen by a large number of people from the Clinton area while he was standing in line with a number of African Americans who came out to register to vote at the encouragement of the Congress of Racial Equality at or around the time of the September 4th Capitol House meeting.

In an upcoming chapter, the entire Rarick-Van Buskirk-Oswald affair in Clinton will be explored in detail. In brief, Oswald was attempting to infiltrate the Congress of Racial Equality (CORE) in an effort to taint it as a Communist front. Walker associates Van Buskirk and Rarick, who also happened to be Klansmen, were part of the plot. Under the Leander Perez-inspired Communist Control Act, anyone in CORE associated with a Communist like Lee Harvey Oswald was liable to spend decades in jail and face huge fines. The law could have had the effect of putting the civil rights effort out of business.

On September 5, 1963, the New Orleans Citizens' Council held a mass meeting that featured Leander Perez.[2276] That same day, General Walker was scheduled to speak at a Citizens' Council mobilization rally in Shreveport, Louisiana.[2277] On September 6 and 7, 1963, Leander Perez was present as the free electors met again to discuss strategy prior to the upcoming Democratic Central Committee meeting. A resolution was prepared that would permit "the nomination of free and unpledged presidential electors in no way bound to support the nominees of the national Democratic Party. Particularly if such a nominee is a Kennedy in 1964."[2278] Since Walker was in Baton Rouge on the 4th, and Shreveport on the 5th, it would not be surprising if he was present again at another free electors meeting where Leander Perez was present on September 6 or 7.

On September 6, Senator Barry Goldwater called for postponing the Nuclear Test Ban Treaty that the radical right called appeasement.[2279]

On September 7, 1963, the Louisiana Democratic State Central Committee voted 53–42 to set a democratic primary for presidential free electors in July 1964. The plan, developed and submitted to the legislature by Leander Perez, would result in withholding the state's ten electoral votes from President Kennedy. Perez stated that the resolution was not a free elector measure, but rather favored a slate pledged to a favored candidate: "some fine upstanding, Southern or Western Democrat." The scheme was modified to avoid a direct reference to "free electors" since a proposal by that name had already been rejected after intense debate. Some of those supporting Perez's resolution bitterly attacked President Kennedy and his administration. There was no guarantee of passing the measure in 1964, since a new central committee would be in place then.[2280, 2281, 2282] (By 1964, only forty of the elected officials behind the free "unpledged or independent" electors scheme were reelected to Democratic State Central Committee. Fifty-three were needed for continued control of the party. By 1964, the death of President Kennedy apparently dampened enthusiasm for the scheme, and the bill was defeated.[2283])

Also on September 7, 1963, General Walker filed a two-million-dollar slander suit against Hodding Carter, the prize-wining editor of the *Greenville–Delta Times*, for a speech he made a month after the Ole Miss riot—which, Walker claimed, defamed his good name. Carter responded to the suit by stating: "General Walker has been exposed for once and for all for what he is, a seditious psychopath."[2284]

After Governor George Wallace defiantly threatened to send state troopers to close Alabama schools rather than integrate them, President Kennedy warned Wallace, on September 9, 1963, that he would send federal troops to counter the move.[2285] The next day, Kennedy federalized the Alabama National Guard to enforce the integration orders. Wallace backed down, avoiding another military confrontation and, as the press noted, he was left standing as a general without an army.[2286]

On September 10, Walker filed a libel suit against the Associated Press. W. Scott Wilkinson of Shreveport, a close associate of Leander Perez, and a Citizens' Council leader, represented him.[2287]

On September 12, 1963, there was an unconfirmed report that the president planned to visit Dallas.[2288] That date marks a watershed division in the history of the Kennedy assassination. From September 12 onward, the activities of Oswald, Walker, and others were largely related to the impending trip of the president to Dallas. There is little evidence that the activities of Walker, Oswald, and others central to the assassination story were part of an assassination plot before September 12. Oswald's portrayal as a Communist, as we shall see later, was initially done solely to taint several leftist organizations as being Communist-backed. After mid-September, however, plans for Oswald appear to have changed.

On September 14, 1963, Walker addressed a crowd of a thousand people in Monroe,

Louisiana, at an event sponsored by the Citizens' Council. He said he favored the independent elector movement. Walker stated that Strom Thurmond, a man he called "the greatest patriot in the Senate" would be the best choice for president. He called Kennedy's Nuclear Test Ban Treaty a step closer to a Soviet takeover.[2289] He called "The Kennedy-Rockefeller party" a single machine and "a conspiracy."[2290]

On September 14, 1963, Joseph Milteer met with Robert Shelton, the leader of the United Klans of America, in Tuscaloosa, Alabama, as was noted in Chapter Four; Shelton told Milteer he did not advocate violence. (Rather than actually having a genuine aversion to violence, it is more likely that Shelton wisely feared that the FBI might pick up on it if he promoted it.) It will be recalled from that chapter that Melvin Sexton, who was the Klan secretary and Shelton's next-door neighbor, bears a strong resemblance to the man seen wearing a hat and standing next to Milteer in Dealey Plaza during the assassination. It's reasonable to suspect, therefore, that Sexton was at the Milteer-Shelton meeting.

On September 15, 1963, Klansman Robert E. Lee Chambliss—also known as "Dynamite Bobby"—from Gardendale, Alabama, bombed the Sixteenth Street Baptist Church in Birmingham, Alabama. The church had been used as a meeting place for civil rights leaders including Martin Luther King, Jr., Ralph Abernathy, and Fred Shuttleworth—none of whom were in attendance at the time of the bombing. Four young girls attending Sunday school, Denise McNair (11), Addie Mae Collins (14), Carole Robertson (14) and Cynthia Wesley (14), were killed. The bombing occurred after tensions grew when the Southern Christian Leadership Conference (SCLC) and the Congress of Racial Equality (CORE) became involved in a campaign to register African Americans to vote in Birmingham. When Chambliss was arrested, a box containing 122 sticks of dynamite was found in his possession. A jury found Chambliss not guilty of murder, but found him guilty of possession of dynamite without a permit. He was sentenced to six months in jail and fined one hundred dollars. Only a week before the bombing, Governor Wallace had told the *New York Times* that to stop integration Alabama needed a "few first-class funerals." Martin Luther King, Jr. wired Wallace and told him that, "the blood of four little children . . . is on your hands. Your irresponsible and misguided actions have created in Birmingham and Alabama the atmosphere that has induced continued violence and now murder."[2291] It was the fourth bombing since September 4, 1963, when the Kennedy-Wallace desegregation crisis came to a head and forced Governor Wallace to cancel his appearance at the Capitol House meeting attended by Guy Banister and General Walker.

On the evening of September 16, 1963, General Walker addressed a crowd of 500 people in Alexandria, Louisiana, at an event sponsored by the Friends of Walker.[2292] The Alexandria mayor proclaimed the day "Edwin A. Walker Day." Walker stated, "I hope you know why I resigned from military service. I resigned because I don't like the Kennedys. I don't like the Eisenhowers either, they're just as bad and a disgrace to the nation. Eisenhower is a snake in the grass." Walker said he had gone to Ole Miss to see the first use of United States troops by the United Nations. (Walker's belief that the U.S. was being secretly turned over to the

United Nations was a constant theme in his speeches.) He added, "It looks very much like to me that the president is leading a military dictatorship." Walker advised that the only way to get any reliable information was to read the Dan Smoot Report, the Christian Crusade and John Birch Society literature.[2293] He also called President Kennedy "a disgrace to the nation."[2294] Walker said that the disunity caused by racial strife "in the face of the enemy is surely treason." He added that the "Leadership in the Negro effort which is appealing to Moscow is sinister and seditious." He predicted Soviet Premier Khrushchev would remove missiles from Cuba just prior to the 1964 election to aid President Kennedy's bid for a second term.[2295]

On September 17, 1963, Lee Harvey Oswald applied for a fifteen-day Mexican tourist card at the New Orleans Mexican consulate.[2296] Oswald's plan to visit the Soviet and Cuban embassies in Mexico that September may have been in response to the recent rumor of a presidential visit to Dallas. The trip would further enhance the Communist persona of Oswald, the future murderer of the president, and lay the murder on the laps of the Cuban's and Soviet's.

President Kennedy met with Martin Luther King, Jr. and six other black civil rights leaders in Washington on September 17, 1962, to discuss the racial situation in Birmingham, Alabama. They urged him to send federal troops to Birmingham and cut federal funding to the state.[2297]

On September 19, 1963, the Louisiana Citizens' Council presented Mayor Victor Schiro with a four-point program for preserving racial peace.[2298] The proposal countered Mayor Schiro's proposal of the formation of a biracial committee to smooth racial tensions. Guy Banister advised his friend Willie Rainach that he was against the mayor's proposed committee.[2299]

We the People Meeting, September 21, 1963

Billy James Hargis, Kent Courtney, Tom Anderson, and Robert Welch were the featured speakers at the Ninth National Constitution Day convention of the far-right group, We the People meeting on September 21, 1963, in Chicago.

Joseph Milteer attended the meeting but, unfortunately, Willie Somersett apparently did not.[2300] Milteer had been associated with We the People since 1958.[2301] The willing Somersett certainly would have been there had the FBI felt it important. However, the dust had settled on the FBI's investigation of the April 1963 Congress of Freedom assassination plots after principals denied any involvement in them to the FBI. Tom Anderson, a trustee and director-at-large of the group, told the 250 delegates present that the Kennedy administration—through the Nuclear Test Ban Treaty—was guaranteeing that Russia "will stay ahead where it is ahead and we will stay behind where we are behind." He predicted that the Soviet Union would take over the United States by 1973. He said, "We have to start worrying about the real pink army within instead of the Red army without."

Robert Welch of the JBS was presented the We the People Patriot Leader Award.[2302] Harry T. Everingham, chairman of the group, stated, "The prime purpose of the convention is to find the most effective ways and means to end the New Frontier in November, 1964. This is the last-ditch fight to save America from Socialism."[2303] Everingham, in a personal letter to Clarence Manion inviting him to the meeting, told him, "When we consider how far and fast the Kennedys and their A.D.A. aides are taking us militarily, economically, etc., we know we have very little time left to awaken the American people."[2304]

We the People was comprised of individuals in the John Birch Society, Congress of Freedom, and other far-right-wing organizations. The group's aims differed slightly from the rest in that it had its focus on repealing the federal income tax. We the People letterheads from 1966, 1969, and 1970, list a familiar group of officers, including: Tom Anderson, J. Evetts Haley, General Clyde Watts, Curtis Dall, and General Richard Moran.[2305, 2306] General Pedro del Valle was affiliated with the group in 1956.[2307, 2308] General del Valle and We the People's chairman Harry Everingham were on the policy board of Liberty Lobby in 1960.[2309]

The FBI noted, in a 1961 report on We the People leader Harry Everingham, that he "believes that the Communist takeover in the U.S. is well along and that there are many who are working with the Communists to accomplish this."[2310] Everingham, another prominent member of the national far right, spoke with Bonner Fellers, Revilo Oliver, and Senator James O. Eastland (all important figures in this work) at an all-night Billy James Hargis radio marathon in April 1960.[2311] Hargis, an associate of Walker, Banister, and Milteer, was the president-emeritus of We the People.[2312] In his speech at the marathon, Hargis attacked liberals, integration, and Senator Hubert Humphrey.[2313] Tom Anderson was a featured speaker at a 1961 We the People meeting and was bitterly critical of the Kennedy administration.[2314] We the People held mock "Citizens' Hearings" on April 20, 1963, in order "to tell the American people" how the Communists work from within and what could be done about it. "Testifying" at the hearings were Harry Everingham, senators Strom Thurmond and James O. Eastland, Billy James Hargis, and Ronald Reagan.[2315] Kent Courtney once interviewed Everingham for his *Independent American* newspaper.[2316]

The 1963 We the People meeting is important, since the speakers were all associated with General Walker and evidence has been—or will be—presented that shows most were a part of the Kennedy assassination conspiracy. Since Milteer was also there, having an informant (such as Somersett) at the meeting that took place two months before that assassination certainly might have been productive. The FBI had no evidence at that time to connect Hargis, Anderson, or Courtney to any assassination plots. General accounts of the meeting were reported in the newspapers, but there is no information of any possible conspiratorial activities of the group. The meeting is also important, since it took place less than a month before Somersett first learned of the far-right-wing plot to assassinate President Kennedy on October 18, 1963.[2317]

Meanwhile, on September 23, Marina Oswald and her daughter departed New Orleans for Ruth Paine's home in Fort Worth.[2318] On September 24, 1963, Lee Harvey Oswald left his New Orleans Magazine Street apartment for Mexico City, owing rent.[2319]

On September 24, 1963, the U.S. Senate ratified the Nuclear Test Ban Treaty by an

80–19 vote.[2320] The treaty was widely criticized by the radical right as a sellout to the Soviets.

On September 25, the *Dallas Morning News* said it could now confirm the September 12 report that President Kennedy was planning a visit to Texas in the near future. The report gave no date of the visit, but did say Kennedy planned to visit the cities of Dallas, Fort Worth, San Antonio, and Houston.[2321]

On September 26, the *Dallas Morning News* confirmed exclusively that President Kennedy would visit Texas on November 21 and 22. There had been speculation about a visit for some time, but the final decision had just been reached.

Also on September 26, 1963, Frank Capell wrote General del Valle and mentioned that he had given anti-Communist speeches to two groups. He mentioned cryptically that one group was about ready "to proceed."[2322]

Oswald in Mexico City

According to the Warren Commission, Lee Harvey Oswald left New Orleans for Mexico City (traveling via Houston), probably around noon on September 25, arrived on the 27th, and stayed until October 3, 1963. Traveling on the bus to Mexico City, Oswald told witnesses he had hoped to meet Fidel Castro after he arrived.

In Mexico City, Oswald made three visits to the Cuban embassy and one to the Soviet embassy. Representing himself as the head of the New Orleans branch of the Fair Play for Cuba Committee, he requested a visa from the Cuban embassy and said he wanted to be accepted as a friend of the Cuban revolution. He told the embassy that his request for a transit visa to the Soviet Union was based on his prior stay there, his work permit for the country, and several unidentified letters in the Russian language that he brought with him. He wrote on his application that he was a member of the Communist Party (although it was untrue—he never was).[2323]

Sylvia Duran took Oswald's application at the embassy. She told the House Select Committee on Assassinations (HSCA) that Oswald's large assortment of papers attesting to his Communist affiliations, stay in Russia, and marriage to a Russian was peculiar, coming from a citizen of America where Communism was not well-looked upon. She said, "It was strange . . . I mean crossing the border with all his paper, it was not logical . . . I mean if you're really Communist . . . you go with just nothing, just your passport, that's all. And there was something I didn't like . . . ." She was suspicions of Oswald's documents and discussed it with the embassy consul, Eusebio Azcue. Never before had anyone come to the embassy with a pile of papers like Oswald's, and it worried the embassy consul, as well. Oswald's ostentatious display of papers is consistent with what Marina Oswald called his penchant for "advertising." Oswald took an application with him and left the embassy. He filled it out, had some photos of himself made, and returned the next day with them. He then visited the Soviet embassy a few blocks away.

On his third visit to the Cuban embassy, they told him that they would not grant a visa to Cuba unless he had also procured a visa from the Soviets. Duran, trying to accommodate Oswald, phoned the Soviet embassy and they told her it would take three to four months to process his request. Upon learning this news at the Cuban embassy, Oswald became insistent and hostile. When Duran was unable to make him understand the problem, she went to Consul Azcue for help. Azcue came and explained all of the requirements, becoming very angry with the obstinate Oswald, who turned red and appeared desperate. The two argued. Oswald's shouting and crying could be heard from the street. Azcue told Oswald, "You're no friend of the revolution" and told him to go away or he was going to kick him out. He opened the door and told him to go. Oswald slammed the door behind him.[2324] On his return home, Marina noted he was disappointed and discouraged at his failure to reach Cuba.[2325]

The Warren Commission concluded that Oswald's desire to go to Cuba and to return to the Soviet Union "may well have been Oswald's last escape hatch, his last gambit to extricate himself from the mediocrity and defeat which plagued him through most of his life." The Warren Commission frequently and gratuitously rendered amateurish psychological opinions as to Oswald's motives, portraying him as a disillusioned and troubled loser. To the contrary, as the evidence in this work will show, Oswald went to embellish his Communist credentials for his future roles infiltrating leftist groups—or to suggest he was a Cuban or Soviet agent after he was identified as the assassin of the president. The August 24, 1963, trip to Mexico happened twelve days after an unconfirmed report of the president's trip to Dallas was announced on August 12. It's hard to say if Oswald had been figured in to a Dallas assassination plot in that short period of time and, hence, if the trip was related to the Kennedy assassination. Nonetheless, after the assassination, his visit to the Cuban and Soviet embassies was cited as evidence by the radical right and others that Oswald was a Cuban or Soviet agent. The Warren Commission and the HSCA, however, concluded he was not.

President Fidel Castro quickly saw through Oswald's Mexico City visit as a subterfuge. He astutely told the Cuban people, by radio, "In the eyes of the world it is clear that the reactionaries of the United States wanted our country to be the victim of their criminal designs even at the price of assassinating the president of the United States." He added that the "Intellectual authors of the crime sent Oswald to Mexico to seek a visa to Cuba en route to Russia. How strange, why go to Mexico to request a visa to Russia by way of Cuba? Ideal to make the American people believe the assassin had been an agent of Cuba and the Soviet Union." Castro continued, "Why did (Oswald) become annoyed when the Cuban consulate denied him the visa? No friend of Cuba does that." Castro stated that those involved wanted Oswald eliminated to keep him from talking.[2326]

The HSCA interviewed President Castro and asked him his opinion as to whether there might have been Cuban involvement in the assassination. Castro replied, "That would have been the most perfect pretext for the United States to invade our country which is what I have tried to prevent for all of these years in every possible sense."[2327] After the assassination, the Soviet Union turned over its file on Oswald to the U.S. The documents revealed that the Soviets felt Oswald was more of a crackpot, rather than a Communist. They did not feel he was a serious Communist or supporter of the Soviet Union, despite his avowed Marxist beliefs.[2328]

The Sylvia Odio Incident

On September 26 or 27, 1963, two anti-Castro Cuban men and an American (later identified as Lee Harvey Oswald) allegedly showed up at the Dallas apartment of Cuban exile Sylvia Odio. (Despite the fact that the dates of the Odio incident overlap with the days Oswald was thought to been in Mexico City, the HSCA concluded that Oswald was involved in both incidents around the same time.)

Odio had emigrated from Cuba in 1960 and moved to Dallas in 1963. Her parents, once of great wealth, were imprisoned in Castro's Cuba. Left by her husband to raise four children alone, Sylvia Odio was nearly destitute. Like her parents, she was a dedicated member of the Cuban Revolutionary Junta or JURE that was more to the left than other anti-Castro groups. She helped with the group's business affairs, including raising funds to fight Castro. She described the two Cubans who visited her in September 1963 as greasy and uneducated. Her sister Annie opened the door with the safety chain in place and Sylvia joined her. Sylvia said the taller man identified himself by his war name as Leopoldo. The other Cuban, she thought, might have been identified as Angelo or Angel. The third, an American, was introduced to Sylvia, as Leon Oswald—who, she was told, was very much interested in the anti-Cuban cause. Leopoldo told her the three had just driven from New Orleans and were about to leave on a trip. The two Cubans claimed also to be members of JURE and to have known her father when they were in Cuba.

They asked Sylvia, who was well educated, to translate a Spanish letter into English so they could use it to solicit funds from businesses to purchase armaments for the anti-Castro cause. Sylvia had done similar work before on behalf of JURE, but she told them she did not have the time for it and could not do it. The next day, Leopoldo telephoned her and told her that it was his idea to introduce the American into the underground because "he is great, kind of nuts." He said the American had been in the Marine Corps and was an excellent shot. He stated that the American (Oswald) told him that, "Cubans don't have any guts because President Kennedy should have been assassinated after the Bay of Pigs, and some Cubans should have done that, because he was the one who was holding the freedom of the Cubans actually." After the assassination, Odio claimed the American who accompanied the two Cubans was Lee Harvey Oswald. Her sister Annie, who had not heard the American introduced in the hallway as "Leon Oswald," nonetheless also identified him (from pictures in the media) as Lee Harvey Oswald.

After hearing about the assassination at her job—but not yet having seen a picture of Oswald—Sylvia Odio feared that the man she knew as Leon Oswald might have been involved. Work was suspended for the day and, while Sylvia was in the parking lot—distraught over the murder—she passed out. (She had a history of emotional problems and passing out.) Annie met her at the hospital and both were sure, from pictures of Lee Harvey Oswald shown on TV after the assassination, that Lee Harvey Oswald was the same individual who visited Sylvia's apartment and was introduced as "Leon Oswald."

The Odio sisters' allegation presented a massive problem for the Warren Commission. The basis for most of their deductions about Oswald and the assassination was predicated on the assumption that Oswald was a genuine Communist. The allegation of Oswald being with two anti-Communist, anti-Castro Cubans called that position into doubt. The FBI persuaded Warren Commission investigators that the man could not have been Lee Harvey Oswald, based on the visit dates of September 26 and 27 (as given by Sylvia Odio) because he was reported to be on his way to Mexico at that time. The Commission requested the FBI to investigate the matter further, but they were unable to finish by the time of the Warren Commission's publication in September of 1964. Warren Commission counsel Wesley Liebler lamented, "There are problems. Odio may well be right. The Commission will look bad if it turns out that she is." On August 23, 1964, as time was running out and the Commission's deadline was approaching, chief counsel J. Lee Rankin wrote to J. Edgar Hoover to say, "It is a matter of some importance to the Commission that Mrs. Odio's allegation either be proved or disproved." Rankin asked the FBI to determine the identities of the three men by asking members of the anti-Castro Cuban groups in Dallas about them.

In a report dated September 26, 1964—three days before the final Warren Commission Report was presented to President Johnson—the FBI, belatedly, told them about an interview they had had with Loran Eugene Hall, who claimed he was in Dallas in September 1963 with two men who fit the description of the men who visited Odio's apartment. He claimed one of his companions, William Seymour, looked like Oswald. (In reality, he did not.) Hall told them Oswald was not one of the men. (The FBI noted what they considered was some phonetic similarity between the names Loran Hall and Leon Oswald.)

The Bakersfield, California, resident agency of the FBI had located Hall in Kernville, California, and Hall told them he was involved in anti-Castro activities in Dallas, soliciting funds at the time. (The HSCA was not able to determine the circumstances leading up to the FBI interview of Hall.) Within a week of Hall's allegation, the other two men, Lawrence Howard and William Seymour, whom Hall alleged were with him, denied it. Hall retracted his story about meeting Sylvia Odio in September. The damage had been done, however. Portions of the FBI's investigation—which was inconclusive in supporting the Warren Commission's contention that Mrs. Odio was mistaken—were not sent to Commission counsel Rankin until November 9, at a time when the final report had already been completed. Nonetheless, the Commission—knowing Hall's story was an admitted fabrication—concluded: "While the FBI had not completed its investigation into this matter at the time the report went to press, the Commission has concluded that Lee Harvey Oswald was not at Mrs. Odio's apartment in September 1963." In so concluding, the Commission committed another blunder of historic magnitude.

The HSCA was not satisfied with the Commission's conclusion and reinvestigated the matter. They interviewed Sylvia Odio, members of her family, and her psychiatrist at the time. Psychiatrist Dr. Burton Einspruch told them that Sylvia had told him of the meeting shortly after it occurred and *before* the assassination. The HSCA concluded that "Silvia Odio's testimony is essentially credible," and the HSCA "was inclined to believe Mrs. Odio."[2329, 2330]

Sylvia Odio's allegations are compelling for several reasons. "Leopoldo" told Odio that the three had just traveled from New Orleans. In fact, Oswald had traveled from New Orleans to Houston on that day, and could have stopped in Dallas at the time and visited Odio. Also, the Cubans correctly and uniquely identified Oswald as a marine. Moreover, the alleged remark made by "Leon Oswald"—that the Cubans should have killed Kennedy—was consistent with someone who had been involved with violent Kennedy haters such as Guy Banister and General Walker.

The HSCA concluded: "Oswald, judging from the evidence developed by both the Warren Commission and this committee, had to have access to private transportation to get to Dallas from New Orleans a situation that indicates possible conspiratorial involvement."[2331]

Loran Eugene Hall

The fabrication of one man, Loran Eugene Hall, scuttled what the Warren Commission might have developed from the Sylvia Odio allegation—that Oswald was not really a Communist. The meaning of the murky Odio allegation becomes abundantly clear by mention of the simple fact that Loran Hall was an associate of General Walker and a member of the radical right. Documentation of Hall's connections to the Walker operation was available to the HSCA. However, since Walker was never a suspect in the assassination, Hall's ties to Walker had no relevance. In the end, it was Sylvia Odio, rather than Loran Hall, who was essentially called a liar by the Warren Commission.

The HSCA, however, reinvestigated Odio's allegations and believed her. They investigated Hall as well, but failed to understand the significance of the Odio visit. Grasping at straws, the HSCA, strangely, raised the possibility that Oswald—an authentic Communist—wanted it to appear that he had an association with the left-of-center Cuban Revolutionary Junta, JURE, (and was at odds with the far-right anti-Castro groups) in order to implicate the JURE in the Kennedy assassination by association.

In many crimes, the attempt to cover up or corrupt the evidence—in this case by Loran Hall—is often more revealing than the evidence itself, and so it is in the Sylvia Odio saga. The exploits of Hall were well documented by the FBI and CIA long before the Odio incident and are well known to assassination scholars. Hall fought with Castro before the revolution, then switched sides. The reason he lied about visiting Sylvia Odio was because she was correct that Oswald was at her apartment with two anti-Communists—a circumstance that destroys the Warren Commission's conclusion that Oswald was an authentic Communist. The evidence suggesting he was an anti-Communist with possible Cuban confederates points the finger of guilt in the direction of the radical right wing and the anti-Communists.

The monumental significance of Loran Hall and his lies, not reported before, is that he was an associate of General Edwin Walker, H. L. Hunt and Dan Smoot, who were associates of Joseph Milteer and Guy Banister. Hall was acquainted with Colonel William Potter Gale—another Milteer associate—who the FBI knew was involved in the Congress of Freedom plots calling for the assassination of prominent figures in the Council of Foreign Relations, among others.

Walker admitted knowing Hall in a June 24, 1963 letter he wrote to Bob Love, who served on the national council of the John Birch Society. Walker told Love that "Lorenzo" Hall was in a group of five men who had come to see him. He mentioned that he, himself, would have no dealings with Hall. He told Love that any assistance to the Cuban fighters should go to the main Headquarters of Alpha 66.[2332]

The FBI had compiled considerable information on Loran Hall from an informant before the Kennedy assassination. They learned that Hall had married a woman from Kansas and had served in the U.S. Armed Forces. In 1959, the Cuban police in Havana had detained him. Hall claimed to have trained a group of men in Cuba to invade Nicaragua. Hall was felt to be of low moral character, appeared to have a criminal background, and was not liked by other soldiers of fortune.[2333] Hall and his two companions, William Seymour and Lawrence Howard, who he alleged were with him at Sylvia Odio's before he recanted the story, were soldiers of fortune in a group called Interpen. All three had been arrested on No Name Key, Florida, in December 1962, as part of President Kennedy's crackdown on anti-Castro operations—a policy which was the result of an agreement Kennedy had made with Khrushchev and Castro to stop militants from invading Cuba, and which the anti-Castro forces considered a "betrayal."[2334]

An informant told the FBI, on March 10, 1963, that Hall had been in Miami for the last three months and had associated with Gary Patrick Hemming, an anti-Castro adventurer. Hemming told the FBI that he first met Hall in Cuba in 1959. While Hall was in Miami, he proposed invading Haiti. Hemming met Hall again in January 1963, in Los Angeles. Hall accompanied Hemming on a trip from Miami to California in February 1963, according to the FBI.[2335] The two stopped in Dallas on January 21 or 22, and paid a visit to General Walker. Walker told Hall and Hemming of his travails in the muzzling affair and of his unfair treatment at Ole Miss. He told them he planned to involve his group in the anti-Castro fight. While in Dallas, Hemming contacted wealthy people in Dallas to solicit contributions for the Cuban cause.[2336, 2337]

Hall and William Seymour were en route from California to Miami in the summer of 1963 with Garand rifles which had been converted into automatic weapons. The money for the weapons had been raised in California. An FBI informant said Hall's loose connections to Cuban revolutionary activities were a gimmick he used to obtain money for his living expenses. His practice was to contact local chapters of the John Birch Society, claiming he and his companions were anti-Communist freedom fighters, and ask the JBS for money to carry on their work. They were arrested in Dallas for possession of narcotics (that supposedly were to be used for the wounded in proposed military actions in Cuba). In October 1963, Hall visited Dallas, for the purposes of soliciting donations, with William Seymour who, he claimed, was the man thought to be "Leon Oswald" at Sylvia Odio's apartment. They received a donation from Lester Logue, an oil geologist and friend of General Walker.

On October 30, 1963, Hall was arrested by U.S. Customs—while on a highway in the Florida Keys—for transporting a boat, a quantity of arms, munitions, explosives and supplies to be used in the anti-Castro effort but was not prosecuted. The boat was to be used by the Frente Revolucionario anti-Communists for raids on Cuba. Hall was last seen in Miami in November 1963, with Lawrence Howard—the third man that Hall falsely told the FBI accompanied him to Sylvia Odio's apartment.[2338]

New Orleans district attorney Jim Garrison took an interest in Loran Hall during his 1967 investigation of the Kennedy assassination. As was noted in the Chapter Nine, Garrison's files were full of information on the radical right and anti-Castro Cubans. Garrison subpoenaed Hall for his probe.[2339]

Steven J. Burton, a reporter for KHJ news in Los Angeles, interviewed Hall on December of 1967 and tape recorded it. Burton asked Hall about his arrest in Dallas. Hall said that the purpose of his visit to Dallas was to raise funds for the purchase of weapons, and that during the course of his visit he was arrested for possession of narcotics. Hall told Burton he got thrown into jail and a lawyer friend got him out. Hall admitted to knowing many conservatives in Dallas including H. L. Hunt, Lester Logue, and a man named Paterson or Peterson. Hall noted that he originally fought with Fidel Castro in Cuba, became disgusted, and then fought against him. He denied any connection to the CIA.[2340]

Garrison's investigators interviewed Lawrence Howard on January 25, 1968, and Howard called Hall a liar and blamed him for bringing him into the Odio affair. Howard admitted being in Dallas with Hall in October 1963, and mentioned meeting Lester Logue for an hour. Howard admitted knowing Colonel William Potter Gale, a California associate of Joseph Milteer.[2341]

A Garrison memo from July 17, 1968, contained an interview of Captain Robert Kenneth Brown, who had been involved with the Cuban affairs since the 1950s. In 1967, Brown was employed by *Life* magazine to research the Kennedy assassination and the Garrison case. In 1960--63 he spent much of his time in and around Miami involved in anti-Castro adventures. Brown first met Loran Hall in 1959 and, when interviewed, called Hall a pathological liar. Brown ran into him again in 1963, when Hall was "operating with the Birchers." Brown had interviewed Lester Logue and found out Logue was one of ten people who threw a party for General Walker when he returned to Dallas, presumably after the 1961 muzzling affair.[2342]

A citizen from Waco, Texas, who knew Loran Hall, wrote to Jim Garrison on June 18, 1967, and told Garrison that Hall had been in Dallas in May or June 1963 to raise money for an invasion of Cuba. Hall allegedly told Garrison that President Kennedy was a traitor to the cause of Cuban liberty. Hall further told him that he had been in contact with a wealthy Dallas oilman interested in the anti-Castro cause. Hall returned to Dallas the week of September 23 to 28, and again in October. The informing citizen, whose name was deleted by Garrison, correlates with the FBI's notes of the dates of Hall's visits to Dallas and suggests an additional fourth Hall visit to Dallas that year.[2343]

Hall admitted to Garrison's investigator that he knew Edgar Eugene (Gene) Bradley, and claimed he heard a casual discussion of "getting rid of Kennedy" at a meeting attended by

Bradley and "anti-Jewish and anti-Negro radicals." Bradley, as pointed out in Chapter Nine, was a member of the California hardcore underground associated with William Potter Gale, a Walker and Milteer associate. Strong evidence was presented in Chapter Nine that Bradley was in Dallas at the time of the murder.[2344] In an interview with Lawrence Howard, which was conducted by Steven Burton for Garrison, Howard stated he also knew Gene Bradley, whom he called a "man of action."[2345] Bradley was Reverend Carl McIntire's west coast representative. (McIntire befriended General Walker and the two became close early after Walker's return from Germany, as was noted previously.) That relationship makes the compelling allegation that Bradley traveled to Dallas from California at the time of the assassination, and was involved in the conspiracy, all the more likely.

The HSCA interviewed Loran Hall on August 20, 1977. Hall told a similar story as the one he had told Garrison investigators. He told them that he went around to see a lot of people in the conservative movement in Los Angeles, including John Rousselot and Dick Hathcock. He also told them that, in January 1963, they called on Robert Morris (Walker's attorney) who gave them the names of Lester Logue and a man named Paterson. Logue gave Hall money to repair his car at a dealership. A salesman took Hall and Hemming over to see General Walker, whereupon Hemming told Walker of his plan to start an anti-Communist mercenary army. Walker gave them verbal encouragement. They then left for New Orleans, where they called on Frank Bartes and Larry Labord. In Jacksonville, they left a phone message with mob boss Santos Trafficante.

After reaching Miami, Hall went back to Dallas to see Lester Logue. Logue told him he wanted to get a former member of the Cuban government together with people with "big money" to start a government in exile. Hall returned to Miami and met with John Martino. Hall made another trip to Dallas in June 1963 and stayed with Wally Yeats, who wanted Hall to introduce him to H. L. Hunt, General Walker, and Dan Smoot. Yeats wanted to form a conservative group in Dallas to oppose blacks and Jews "when they take over the country." A mimeograph machine and stacks of anti-Kennedy, anti-Black, anti-Jewish, and other "anti-" material was in Yeats's garage. During the June visit to Dallas, Hall met with Lester Logue, wealthy "men in suits" and "a guy associated with H. L. Hunt." Hall claimed that he was offered a large sum of money at the meeting by an unidentified member at the meeting, to "blow Kennedy's ass off." Hall refused. Logue said he didn't want to hear that kind of talk in his office. Hall did not feel the man who made the threat was involved in the assassination.

The circumstances surrounding how the FBI found their way to Hall during the Warren Commission investigation is not known. What is certain is that Hall was associated with General Walker, Dan Smoot, H. L Hunt and Colonel William Potter Gale, who, in turn, were all associated with Joseph Milteer. Hall's relationship to those men defies any other explanation than that his false claim of being at Sylvia Odio's was given at the direction of the Walker operation in order to quash what has long been considered the most significant piece of evidence discovered by the Warren Commission—the Odio incident—of a conspiracy in the assassination of President Kennedy. It is, however, not evidence of Hall's involvement in the assassination. Oswald's persona as a Communist, amplified by the Warren Commission, was a key element in deflecting suspicion from the radical right wing and was jeopardized by Sylvia Odio's claim of Oswald being in the company of two anti-Communists. The Warren Commission concluded in their section titled "Motive" that "His [Oswald's] commitment to Marxism and Communist papers appear to have been another important factor in his motivation [for the assassination]."[2346] If Oswald were not a Communist, as the Odio incident suggests, then the Commission and the radical right would have had a major problem.

Oswald had other reported ties to anti-Communist Cubans. Buddy Walther of the Dallas County Sheriff's Department told the Secret Service on November 23, 1963 that he had information on Oswald that "for the past few months at a house at 3128 Harlendale some Cubans had been having meetings on weekends and were possibly connected to the 'Freedom for Cuba Party' of which Oswald was a member. I don't know what action the secret service has taken but I learned today that sometime between seven days before the president was shot and the day after he was shot these Cubans moved from this house. My informant stated the subject Oswald had been to this house before." Author Dick Russell compiled information that a member of the anti-Castro Alpha 66 rented the Harlendale house and was noted to be violently anti-President Kennedy.[2347]

The Odio incident, the Harlendale Avenue house incident, and Oswald's contact with six anti-Communist Cubans (noted in Chapter One—including Carlos Bringuier with whom he engaged in a phony fight and a radio debate) suggest that Oswald was working with the anti-Communist Cubans.

Resuming the chronicle of events leading up to the assassination, we find that, on September 30, 1963, the Civil Rights Commission urged penalizing states that refused to grant black voting rights by slashing their membership in the House of Representatives. Richard Russell, a senator from Georgia and future Warren Commission member, led the fight against the proposal. That same day, Texas governor John Connally asked President Kennedy for a meeting to discuss his upcoming trip to Dallas.[2348]

On October 2, 1963, the White House announced that they would defeat the Communists in Vietnam by 1965.[2349]

On October 3, 1963, Lee Harvey Oswald returned to Dallas from New Orleans and stayed at the YMCA. He began searching for work, and spent the weekend with his wife and daughter at Ruth Paine's home in Irving, Texas, outside of Dallas. He then settled into a rooming house on North Beckley in the Oak Cliff section of Dallas, which was operated by Gladys Johnson, where he registered under the pseudonym O. H. Lee.[2350]

On October 3, 1963, a Gallup Poll found, for the first time, that 52 percent of Americans were more concerned about racial problems than international problems, Russia, or the threats of war or unemployment.[2351]

On October 4, 1963, the Louisiana State Police—in conjunction with the New Orleans Police and members of the Louisiana Un-American Activities Committee (LUAC)—raided the headquarters of the Southern Conference Education Fund (SCEF), a leading integration group. Guy Banister was an investigator for LUAC, which was operated by two of his longtime colleagues, James Pfister and Jack Rogers (as was noted in Chapter One). SCEF's officers were arrested under the state's Communist Control Act (the brainchild of Leander Perez, which was introduced into law in the legislature by Representative James Pfister). (Two SCEF officers who were not in town during the arrests, Anne and Carl Braden—past targets of congressional anti-Communist inquisitions—were also officers in Fair Play for Cuba Committee.) A huge cache of the group's records was seized.

Both the LUAC and Senator Eastland's committee planned on investigating the group, as well as Fair Play for Cuba Committee, the Congress of Racial Equality, and the New Orleans Committee for Peaceful Alternatives. Lee Harvey Oswald had infiltrated all three of those groups. However, SCEF had no membership, so infiltrating its affiliated groups was the next best thing. The association of Oswald, a purported Communist, with all three of those groups, put the officers of those groups at risk of facing thirty years in prison and paying massive fines under the Communist Control Act. If the Act and the subsequent arrests were successful, the Louisiana segregationists expected other states to adopt similar legislation in hopes of putting the civil rights movement in the South out of business. (An entire chapter will be devoted to the subject.)

On October 5, 1963, a day after the raid on SCEF and the arrest of the three officers with alleged Communist connections, attorney Richard Van Buskirk, in the small hamlet of Clinton, Louisiana, stated that at least one Communist infiltrator was on the scene during the Congress of Racial Equality's black voter registration drive to promote trouble in the town, although he declined to identify the infiltrator. He said CORE had been cited more than 400 times with Communist-front activities.[2352] Not coincidentally, in the weeks prior to Van Buskirk's claim that there was a Communist in town, Lee Harvey Oswald had been in Clinton, standing on a sidewalk among blacks registering to vote in a CORE voter drive. Dozens of people later recalled seeing him there. One man even claimed he had seen Oswald going to a CORE meeting. Van Buskirk, himself, had been seen in the company of Guy Banister and General Walker at the free electors meeting at the Capitol House Hotel in Baton Rouge on September 4, 1963, as noted previously.

On October 8, 1963, General Willoughby spoke to the International Committee for the Defense of the Christian Culture, an H. L. Hunt-backed group.[2353] As will be recalled from Chapter Twelve, Willoughby had planned to travel to Germany in 1961 with Kent Courtney, during Walker's early muzzling troubles, to recruit him as a man on horseback and defiant figurehead of the radical right.

On October 10, 1963, the CIA notified the FBI that Lee Harvey Oswald had visited the Soviet embassy in Mexico City.[2354]

On October 11, Austin Flett, who attended the 1963 Congress of Freedom meeting in New Orleans, wrote to President Kennedy and stated, "certain of your political advisors have led you unknowingly into very deep water, where it may be impossible to save yourself from political suicide as it would appear from these exhibits that the president of the United States has provided political and financial aid and comfort to persons that are guilty of internal subversion . . . widespread prosecutions under Title 18, United States Criminal Code, are in order."[2355]

On October 13, 1963, General Walker attended a meeting of the Student Revolutionary Directorate (DRE), which had been advertised in the paper. An organizer of the meeting provided the FBI with a list of names of the thirty people who attended. General Walker was on the list. The organizer, on the other hand, was relatively certain that Lee Harvey Oswald was not there.[2356]

On October 14, Ruth Paine, who graciously hosted Marina Oswald and her daughter in her home while Lee stayed at a rooming house, told her neighbor that Lee Harvey Oswald needed a job. The neighbor said that her brother, Buell "Wesley" Frazier, who lived with her, worked at the Texas School Book Depository. She suggested he apply for a job there. Paine telephoned the depository superintendent, Roy Truly, and he told her that Oswald should come in for a job interview.[2357]

That same day, George Soule—the host of the infamous Congress of Freedom meeting attended by Joseph Milteer, Guy Banister, and Kent Courtney—wrote a "reader's editorial" for the *Shreveport Journal*. Soule was critical of Kennedy's disarmament proposal, his failure to uphold the Monroe Doctrine in Cuba and failure of the Bay of Pigs invasion, his civil rights initiatives, and his alleged plan to subjugate the U.S. under the United Nations. He concluded that Kennedy "was not qualified for high office," was "destroying our great Republic," and was "whittling away our personal freedom and national independence."[2358]

On October 16, Lee Harvey Oswald began work at the Texas School Book Depository, continuing to visit his wife and daughter on weekends at Ruth Paine's home in Fort Worth.[2359]

On October 18 through 20, 1963, Joseph Milteer, Willie Somersett, and General Pedro del Valle attended the Constitution Party meeting at the Marott Hotel in Indianapolis, about which Willie Somersett reported to the FBI that the meeting "is where they did the most talking about knocking the president off" (as was noted in Chapter Seven). Wally Butterworth also attended that meeting, and was a subject of interest to the Secret Service. They were fully aware of his endorsement of assassinating the president at the meeting.[2360] General del Valle was the probable source that there was a plot in the works—the actual plot that resulted in the killing of the president, as was presented in Chapters Seven and Eight. It was noted in Chapter Eight that Butterworth was close to del Valle and met him at his Annapolis home just prior to the Constitution Party meeting.

On October 20, 1963, Marina Oswald gave birth to her second child with Lee Harvey, Audrey Marina Rachel Oswald. (It will be recalled that Lee objected to naming her Rachel because it sounded too Jewish.)[2361]

On October 21, the *Jackson Daily News* reported on the Constitution Party meeting and identified Joseph Milteer and Pedro del Valle by name as having attended.[2362] Milteer noted in his correspondence that he had visited editors of a number of newspapers to promote the meeting and it can be assumed that he was the probable source of the news report.

Walker and the Adlai Stevenson Incident, October 24, 1963

On October 24, 1963, Adlai Stevenson, the United States ambassador to the United Nations, was spat on and hit with a placard in Dallas after addressing a United Nations Day rally at the Municipal Auditorium. General Walker's group was behind the ugly Stevenson protest. (It will be recalled from Chapter Eleven that Walker wrote his friend J. Evetts Haley before the visit and told him they had planned "some fun" for Stevenson's visit.) Robert Edward Hatfield, a member of Walker's group, was arrested for assault in the spitting incident.[2363]

Adlai Stevenson had been the Democratic nominee for president in 1952 and 1956 and lost both elections to Dwight D. Eisenhower. President Kennedy appointed him the ambassador to the United Nations.

In anticipation of Stevenson's appearance in Dallas, Walker rented the Dallas Municipal Auditorium on October 23, 1963, the evening before Stevenson's speech. The Walker-led "U.S. Day Committee" program was held to counter Stevenson's planned speech on "U.N. Day." Walker explained the purpose of the meeting, stating at a press conference, "We stand for a United States and free nations and not a free United Nations." A right-wing group persuaded Texas governor John Connally to declare October 23 "U.S. Day." (He also declared the next day "U.N. Day," which drew bitter criticism from Walker.) Bumper stickers were printed, stating, "U.S. Day or United Nations Day—There Must Be a Choice."

Many shared Walker's anti-U.N. sentiment, including Congressman Bruce Alger, who introduced a bill in Congress to withdraw the U.S. from the U.N. The Texas legislature passed a bill that made it a crime to display a U.N. flag.[2364, 2365] Many of the 1,200 people who attended the U.S. Day rally, were members of the John Birch Society, the National Indignation Convention, and the Minutemen, according to the press who covered the meeting. The meeting began with the reading of sympathetic messages from Joseph Milteer's friend, Dan Smoot. Messages from Banister associate Robert Morris and Senator Strom Thurmond were read.

"Adlai's coming to sell his hogwash," Walker declared, "and here's what is sponsoring him in Dallas." Walker then recited a list of organizations promoting Stevenson's appearance. Walker blasted the Kennedys and the Cuba situation and then turned his attention to Stevenson and the U.N. Walker told the crowd, "I'll tell you who started the U.N. It was Alger Hiss and that crowd." (Alger Hiss had served as the secretary-general of the United Nations Charter Conference in 1945. Hiss was later accused of being a Soviet spy in 1948 and convicted of perjury in connection with the case in 1950.) The crowd, reacting to Walker's bitter criticism of the Kennedy administration, was whipped into a near frenzy, setting the stage for the confrontation to come with Adlai Stevenson the next day.[2366] "Tonight we stand on a battleground identified on this stage as U.S. Day—the symbol of our sovereignty." Referring to Stevenson, he added, "Tomorrow night there will stand here a symbol to the Communist conspiracy and its United Nations." (Lee Harvey Oswald wrote a letter to the Communist Party and told them he had attended Walker's U.S. Day speech. The Communist Party thought Oswald's attendance at the far-right meeting was peculiar, something a Communist would not do.)[2367]

Stevenson arrived for his speech at 8:00 p.m. the next day, October 24, and had no reason to expect anything but a friendly crowd. By 7:45, protesters carrying anti-U.N. placards had begun to gather around the auditorium. Inside, Walker supporters and others opposed to Stevenson joined the audience, carrying Confederate and American flags and noisemakers. Dallas department store owner Stanley Marcus introduced Stevenson to the crowd. As Stevenson spoke, the protestors began making noise and disrupting the speech. A large banner which had been secretly hidden in the auditorium was unfurled, displaying the message: "Get the U.S. out of the U.N. and the U.N. out of the U.S." One man screamed, "Kennedy will get his reward in hell."[2368]

Frank McGehee, a Walker associate who was the head of the National Indignation Convention, stood on the floor and tried to get Stevenson's attention. Stevenson, responding to the intrusion, told the crowd, "I don't have to come here from Illinois to teach Texans manners." McGehee persisted, and Stevenson told the crowd he would "give the man equal time when [he was] through," drawing laughs from the crowd. As police escorted McGehee out a side door, Stevenson remarked, "For my part, I believe in the forgiveness of sin and the redemption of ignorance."[2369]

Among the crowd were Stevenson supporters, who at times gave Stevenson standing ovations. A member of the clergy repeatedly told the protesters there was "No excuse for bad manners." Another supporter compared the disruption to the scene of the Munich Beer Hall Putsch. Stevenson commented on Walker's previous night's U.S. Day rally, saying, "I understand some of these fearful groups are trying to establish a U.S. Day—at least in Dallas—in competition with U.N. Day. This is the first time the U.S. and the U.N. are rivals."

When the meeting ended, a shaken Stevenson left the building with a police escort, muttering, "Animals . . . Animals!" Outside, Stevenson decided to approach one screaming woman, Cora Frederickson—a member off General Walker's John Birch Society chapter as well as a member of the Indignant Citizens' Council—who had been present at Walker's speech the night before.[2370] As Stevenson attempted to address her concerns, she banged him on the head with a sign which said, "If you seek peace, ask Jesus."[2371, 2372] He asked the woman what the problem was. She replied, "If you don't know what's wrong I don't know why. Everyone else does."[2373] Later, when she was asked why she struck Stevenson with the placard, Fredrickson stated, "I was pushed by a Negro."[2374]

Robert Edward Hatfield, a follower of Walker, spit on Stevenson as police tried to hustle him away to safety. As Stevenson sought refuge inside a waiting car, the crowd started rocking the vehicle. The driver gunned it, and they made their escape. Wiping the spit off his face, Stevenson commented, "Are these human beings or are these animals?"[2375] Dallas Mayor Earle Cabell condemned the Stevenson protestors, whom he called "radicals" and "a cancer on the body politic." Aptly pointing out the differences between the far-right protestors and conservatives, Cabell said, "These are not conservatives. They are radicals." He added, "We have an opportunity to redeem ourselves when the president pays us a visit next month."[2376]

General Walker denied having anything to do with the disruption—which is contrary to fact. A letter written by Walker to his friend J. Evetts Haley (discovered by the author and noted in Chapter Eleven) indicated that Walker had planned the disruption, calling it having "a little fun." The anti-U.N. placards carried by the disruptive protestors were seen and reported by students who were at Walker's residence the day *before* the Stevenson speech. When asked if he had attended the Stevenson speech, Walker stated, "I didn't have to be there, I had done enough against him." He added, "Adlai got what was coming to him."[2377] Walker gloried in the violence he fomented, again, as at Ole Miss, where his supporters had killed two men and wounded dozens of others.

After reading about the sordid Stevenson episode, President Kennedy instructed his special assistant, Arthur Schlesinger, Jr., to call Stevenson and express his sympathy. Stevenson told Schlesinger, "But, you know, there was something very ugly and frightening about the atmosphere." Stevenson said he had later talked with Dallas civic leaders and they wondered whether President Kennedy should keep his plans to visit Dallas on November 22. Vice President Johnson called Stanley Marcus, who was a first-hand witness to the ugly Stevenson reception, to discuss the president's November trip arrangements. Marcus told the vice president, "Try to get the president to cancel his plans."[2378]

Three days after the Stevenson incident, the press reported that Walker flew the American flag outside his house upside down, because he was dismayed that the mayor had apologized to Stevenson for the ugly incident. Walker denied the allegation, explaining the upside-down flag was a signal for a ship in distress, referring to the Cuban and Vietnam situations.[2379] Unfortunately, the press, the public, and the president were unaware of the fact that Walker was clearly behind the violent, sordid incident.

Billy James Hargis's October pre-Assassination Speaking Tour, October 1963

Walker's colleague Billy James Hargis spoke in Memphis, Tennessee, on October 22, and in Jackson, Mississippi, on October 24, before embarking on a seventeen-city speaking tour in Louisiana and Texas. He referred to the speaking tour as hitting the "sawdust trail" to bring "decadent America to her knees before God for her salvation."[2380, 2381] Hargis spoke at the Jerusalem Temple in New Orleans at 1127 Saint Charles Street, on October 25, 1963. He was pictured in the newspaper with Congress of Freedom leader George Soule at a press conference in Soule's office. Hargis declared, "We must clean house in Washington and restore constitutional government."[2382]

The author interviewed Mary Brengel, one of Guy Banister's secretaries at the time of Hargis's visit to the city, in 1996. She recalled that Hargis visited Guy Banister's office in the fall of 1963.[2383] Brengel knew Banister, as well as his girlfriend Delphine Roberts, well. She told the author that Delphine Roberts told her Lee Harvey Oswald had been at Banister's office. Brengel's sighting of Hargis at Banister's office is not surprising, given that Hargis was closely associated with several of Banister's colleagues including General Walker, Kent Courtney, and George Soule.

On Saturday, October 26, Hargis spoke in Baton Rouge under the theme "America, Back to God and Americanism." He made appeals for contributions to the Christian Crusade and asked them to begin at $500. Hargis said that unless the country wrested the reins of government from the liberals in the 1964 election, the U.S. would be sold out to Socialism. The press reported that Hargis planned to visit fifty cities as part of his fall tour.[2384] On Sunday, October 27, 1963, Hargis planned to speak in Shreveport at the Ark-La Music Center.[2385] It is worth noting that exactly one month prior to the assassination, beginning on October 22, 1963, Billy James Hargis spoke in three cities in Louisiana: New Orleans, Baton Rouge, and Shreveport as a part of his "Southern Tour." Walker, like Hargis, frequently traveled to Louisiana before the Kennedy assassination, where Oswald and Banister operated.

Hargis continued with a "Texas Tour," stopping in thirteen cities from November 3 to 17, 1963. According to Hargis, the tour's goal was to educate citizens on the moral aspects of the fight against godless Communism. The tour ended, suspiciously, just five days before the assassination, with stops on November 16, in Fort Worth, and on November 17, in Dallas, where Lee Harvey Oswald resided.[2386]

Joseph Milteer told Willie Somersett that Hargis raised funds for the hardcore underground during his speaking engagements. Hargis, as we know, was a Milteer associate who had ties to the assassination conspiracy, as well as to Guy Banister and General Walker, who had ties to Lee Harvey Oswald. The presence of Hargis at Banister's office a month before and his stop in Dallas—just days before the assassination—raises further suspicions about him.

The FBI noted that Mary Surrey, wife of Walker's top aide Robert, was one of the founders of the Dallas John Birch Society and the Volunteers for Walker. Surrey's fifteen-year-old daughter, Karen, presented Madame Ngo Dinh Nhu—considered to be the first lady of Vietnam—with a bouquet of roses on her visit to Dallas on October 23, 1963. She toured the U.S. to try to mend relations with President Kennedy after making inflammatory remarks about his administration. Her husband, Ngo Dinh Nhu, and brother-in-law, President Ngo Dinh Diem, were assassinated shortly after her visit to Dallas, in a coup d'état on November 2, 1963.[2387]

On October 25, 1963, Lee Harvey Oswald and Michael Paine attended an American Civil Liberties Union meeting at Southern Methodist University. Paine stated that Oswald told the ACLU that President Kennedy was doing fairly well in the civil rights struggle.[2388] The ACLU was another organization that Senator Eastland and the far right felt was pro-Communist. Oswald joined the ACLU for a nominal fee and the act was another example, on paper only, of Oswald aligning himself with the left. Raymond Krystinic attended the ACLU meeting that Oswald and Paine attended. After the assassination, Krystinic went to the FBI and told them that the meeting was the day after the Stevenson incident. He said that Oswald jumped to his feet and interjected himself into the discussion by stating that General Walker was responsible for the trouble at the Stevenson meeting, and stated emphatically that General Walker was both anti-Semitic and anti-Catholic. Afterward, Krystinic and Oswald engaged in a heated discussion, and Oswald told Krystinic that he was a Marxist. Krystinic asked Oswald if he was a Communist, to which Oswald replied, "All right, if you want to call me that, that is what I am, I am a Communist."[2389]

General Walker at the National Citizens' Council Meeting, October 26, 1963

On October 26, 1963, General Walker spoke at the National Citizens' Council of America meeting at the Robert E. Lee Hotel in Jackson, Mississippi. A crowd of Citizens' Council leaders and 120 delegates from sixteen states were present. Governor Ross Barnett of Mississippi and Roy V. Harris were also featured and promoted the free electors scheme. Harris presided over the meeting, and it would not be surprising if Milteer were there. Barnett accused President Kennedy of using civil rights issues to get votes. He added, "Bobby Kennedy is a liability to the nation and Jack Kennedy is a liability to the free world."[2390] Mississippi lieutenant governor Paul Johnston told the crowd he pledged to "fight fire with fire" to preserve racial integrity. Harris stated that Martin Luther King, Jr. needed the civil rights violence to raise money for his own use. He added that Mississippi "[was] the only lily white state left." Johnston urged expanding the Sovereignty Commission. Other speakers at the two-day meeting included William Simmons, Louis W. Hollis, and Banister associate Medford Evans.[2391] (Billy James Hargis was in Jackson at the same time giving a speech at another venue as noted earlier.) If Leander Perez was at the October National Citizens' Council meeting, as expected, it would represent—as we shall see—one of at least three meetings he attended with General Walker just prior to the assassination.

A transcript of an ominous speech that Walker delivered at the national meeting was found by the author and is revealed here for the first time. Walker delivered the most scathing, threatening speech on the president he had ever given. He asserted, "Mr. Kennedy is no longer backed by a whole constitution. He is out on a limb. His administration is on the rocks . . . I personally hope their temporary tour is about over." Walker claimed that the State Department was thoroughly infiltrated with Communists. Walker stated, "The best definition I can find for Communism is 'Kennedy Liberalism'. . ." He called the president "the greatest leader of the anti-Christ movement" and "a liability to the free world." Walker said Kennedy's actions at Ole Miss would "go down in history as the biggest failure and mistake Kennedy ever made."

The transcript of Walker's speech concludes ominously. He stated, "I saw plenty in Mississippi. I saw plenty in military service. I have seen this country being sold out, lock, stock and barrel by a bunch of sophisticated professors, Harvard liberals who are at a loss as where to go and what to do, and I can assure you they are going to pay for it one way or another. Because I've seen the Communist hangman's noose coming tighter and tighter on every one of them. It's interesting that the Communists killed the first people that helped them in their revolution. First! So we've got something to look forward to, ladies and gentlemen."[2392]

In his speech, with November 22 nearing, Walker did more than ramp up the rhetoric against the Kennedys. He predicted that the Harvard liberals—a direct reference to the president and an oft-made Walker remark—were going to pay for the biggest mistake of their lives (the federal intervention and the arrest of Walker at Ole Miss). General Walker, according to an aide, "thought Harvard was the bad place, the factory where they made Communists. He was sure death on Harvard."[2393] (It should be noted that, by the time of

Walker's speech, FBI informant Willie Somersett had already learned from Milteer—sixteen days earlier at the October 10, 1963, Constitution Party meeting—that the assassination of President Kennedy was being planned.)

John, Robert, and Edward Kennedy were all Harvard graduates and the White House liberally recruited from the elite university. Deciphered, then, Walker predicted in his speech's last sentences, that the hangman's noose was tightening on the president and that the audience could look forward to the Communists killing President Kennedy, who helped the Communists in their revolution. The Communist reference suggests that Oswald—as the Communist hangman—was already figured into the scheme to kill the president (the one who helped the Communists), at the time of the October 26 speech.

(Willie Rainach, Guy Banister's close friend, preserved the transcript of Walker's speech in his personal papers. Rainach committed suicide on January 26, 1978, during the same period of time that the HSCA and FBI investigators descended upon Louisiana to reinvestigate the president's murder. Rainach's personal papers, unlike those of every other collection of papers from other members of the hardcore radical right, appear unexpurgated. His widow donated them to Louisiana State University Shreveport after his death.)

Walker wrote General Richard B. Moran on October 28, 1963, and told him, "The national publicity about Adlai's treatment here in Dallas is a good thing for our side and we're doing our best to keep the thing going as long as possible. This is worth two million dollars in publicity across the country."[2394]

On October 29, 1963, John Rousselot, the former Republican congressman from California, who had become the western district governor of the John Birch Society, gave a speech on disarmament to the John Birch Society in Dallas. When asked, Rousselot—a close Walker associate—said that he was not convinced that President Eisenhower was as dedicated an agent of the Communist conspiracy as Robert Welch, JBS director, had claimed. Rousselot did, however, admit, "many of the acts of Eisenhower border on treason."[2395] The compelling allegation that Rousselot was involved in the Kennedy assassination conspiracy will be presented later. His visit to Dallas just three weeks before the assassination, like Hargis's visit, is noteworthy.

Also on October 29, 1963, General Walker paid a weekend visit to the jail cell of Byron De La Beckwith, who was on trial for the murder of Mississippi NAACP leader (and mentor to James Meredith) Medgar Evers. Walker wished Beckwith and his family well.[2396, 2397] General Walker's visit to Beckwith is consistent with his known advocacy for violence in the name of the segregationist cause. (In 1964, two all-white juries were unable to come to a consensus and Beckwith went free. Decades later, he was retried and found guilty. He died in prison in 2001.)

In October 1963, President Kennedy's approval rating dropped from 57 percent favorable to its lowest point in his presidency—a drop which was attributed to his handling of racial issues. After his announcement of the civil rights bill, his approval in the South plummeted. Many of those polled felt Kennedy was pushing integration too fast.[2398]

On October 29, 1963, Supreme Court Justice Earl Warren, who presided over the court's 1954 *Brown* decision outlawing segregation in the public schools, was leaving a testimonial dinner on his behalf given by the New York Bar Association, when demonstrators hurled leaflets and placards at him.[2399] The radical right and the segregationists hated Warren, as the demonstration attested. Later, in his testimony to the Warren Commission, Jack Ruby told Warren that his life was in danger. Ruby also told Warren that his own life was in danger, implying both their lives were endangered by the same element that hated Warren.[2400]

In a letter postmarked November 1, 1963, Oswald informed the Communist Party that he had moved to Dallas and had attended General Walker's U.S. Day speech, as well as a meeting of the American Civil Liberties Union. Oswald asked the opinion of the Communist Party for their general views of the ACLU and "to what degree, if any, [he] should try to heighten its progressive tendencies."[2401] A written reply from the Communist Party showing approval of the ACLU would have been something the ACLU detractors behind Oswald would have found valuable. It's not known if they answered Oswald's letter.

Also on November 1, 1963, Oswald rented a post office box in the Annex Building in Dealey Plaza, which he claimed on the application would be used for the Fair Play for Cuba Committee and the American Civil Liberties Union. The claim was another charade, since Oswald was not a representative of either group.[2402]

On November 1 and 5, 1963, FBI agent James Hosty paid visits to the Paine household, where Oswald's family stayed.[2403]

On November 8, 1963, at the John Birch Society's American Opinion Forum in Dallas, speaker Westbrook Pegler engaged in a general attack on President Kennedy.[2404]

In a letter dated November 9, 1963, Oswald wrote the Soviet Embassy and told them of his meeting in Mexico City with "Comrade Kostin" at the Soviet Embassy. He described his visit, and made a number of inaccurate comments about it. He also told them that the FBI had visited him on November 1 and warned him about engaging in FPCC activities—which was another lie. In a draft of the letter to the embassy, Oswald had indicated that he did not use his real name in obtaining his visa—another lie.[2405] Oswald's repeated lying in his correspondence with the Communist Party, *The Worker*, and V. T. Lee of FPCC regarding his appearances at the Soviet and Cuban Embassies is more evidence to suggest that his entire represented persona was disingenuous "advertising."

Also on November 9, 1963, Willie Somersett surreptitiously tape recorded his conversation with Joseph Milteer in Somersett's Miami apartment. Milteer told Somersett that the assassination of President Kennedy was "in the works." Milteer told Somersett that the assassination would take place from an office building and with a high-powered rifle that could be broken down into pieces, and that someone would be taken into custody to throw off the public. (Milteer may have learned of the plot from one of his known Dallas associates, General Walker, Robert Surrey, Dan Smoot, or one of the H. L. Hunt clan.)

On November 11, 1963, the *Dallas Morning News* reported that a motorcade through Dallas would be unlikely, due to the president's tight schedule. The next day, they reported he would in fact ride in a motorcade through downtown Dallas. The motorcade was expected to travel west on Main Street before turning north after driving through the triple overpass en route to a luncheon at the Dallas Trade Mart off the Stemmons freeway.[2406]

On November 11, 1963, a citizen notified the FBI that he was an engineer on a ship docked in Baton Rouge and stayed at the Heidelberg Hotel next door to the Capitol House Hotel. On November 10, 1963, he went to the Capitol House to purchase some reading material and heard four well-dressed men—who seemed to be politicians or businessmen—speaking at the nearby coffee counter. He distinctly heard one state, "If we can't put a man in by ballot, we'll get rid of this one with a 30-30 [rifle]." One of the four men, according to the report, was wearing a Stetson hat. The FBI interviewed employees of the hotel who had worked on those days, and none recalled seeing Lee Harvey Oswald there or hearing those remarks being made. The employees pointed out that the weekend of November 9–12, 1963, immediately followed the Democratic primary for governor. They noted that state Senator A. O. Rapellet was registered at the hotel on November 12, 1963, and wore a Stetson hat. State Senator Cecil Blair also wore a Stetson hat, but was not registered at the hotel.[2407] Both Rapellet and Blair were involved in the free electors movement.[2408]

On November 18, 1963, General Walker attended a speech by Alabama governor George Wallace in Dallas. Walker pointed out that, in contrast to the enthusiastic response to Wallace's appearance, sales of tickets to the president's $100/plate reception, planned for Kennedy's November 22 visit, were not selling well. News footage of Wallace's speech was taken by Dallas television station KRLD at the request of CBS national news. After getting several shots of Walker, the cameraman remarked, "I got to thinking that Walker being a national figure . . . I'd better get some more footage of him." In response to the cameraman moving closer, Walker got up from his table and said, "I'm tired of this. I've had enough. Get out." When the cameraman said, "One more time," Walker grabbed the man's camera and shoved him into the lap of a woman, then into the aisle. Walker turned to Governor Wallace and said, "Excuse me."[2409]

On November 18, 1963, President Kennedy spoke in Miami. The Secret Service cancelled his motorcade to the event after they learned that there was a plan to have a sniper in a tree assassinate him, according to what Joseph Milteer had told Willie Somersett. Based on that information, the president was flown by helicopter to the engagement instead.[2410] As was mentioned previously, the Dallas Secret Service was not told about the Miami assassination plot.

On November 19, Walker gave a speech to the National Defense Council of the Daughters of the American Revolution, in Hattiesburg, Mississippi. He was critical of the U.N., as usual. Walker stated, "The best definition I know of Communism with regard to our national policy of internal affairs is Kennedy liberalism." He added, "The attitude in Dallas toward the insolvency of the Kennedy administration is exemplified in the opposition of Adlai Stevenson." He said the U.N. "has now extended activities into a declaration of integration."[2411]

Also on November 19, 1963, Carlos Bringuier, Oswald's radio debate opponent, spoke at a meeting at the International House of the Information Council of America (INCA), the anti-Communist organization run by Guy Banister's associate Ed Butler. Bringuier described how the Communists used "plants" disguised as Capitalists in debates and how the Communists manufactured agents who specialize as "conflict mangers"—a term coined by Butler, who was in attendance.[2412]

On November 19, 1963, General Pedro del Valle wrote to George Lincoln Rockwell, referring to him as "Commander." In the letter, del Valle accepted an invitation by Rockwell to speak to his "young Patriots," along with John Crommelin and "confer on the subject of a united effort."[2413]

On Thursday November 21, the day before the assassination, Oswald spent the night with his wife. He had been staying at a rooming house in the Oak Cliff section of Dallas, and he usually spent weekends with his wife and children at Ruth Paine's home in Fort Worth. Never before had he stayed the night with Marina at the Paine house on a weekday. The next morning, on the day of the assassination, he took off his wedding ring and left it on the bedroom dresser, something he had not done before. He left her with $170, likely all the money the family had.[2414]

Walker in New Orleans, November 20–22, 1963: Prelude to Assassination

General Walker had left Dallas for New Orleans days before the assassination. On the evening of the assassination, a citizen, Ken Elliot, told the FBI that he heard that General Walker had been visiting New Orleans for the past few days and that Walker was a close associate of radio announcer Charles Ray—a rabid segregationist and an advocate of Nazi leader George Lincoln Rockwell. Elliot told them that he heard that Rockwell was also supposed to have been in New Orleans at the same time.[2415]

On November 20, Harold Lord Varney spoke before the Woman's auxiliary of Chamber of Commerce at the Roosevelt Hotel in New Orleans and urged the U.S. to overthrow Cuba.

Kent Courtney was present at the speech and recorded it. Walker was in the audience, and spoke briefly against the United Nations, asserting that the U.S.—under U.N. control—would mandate all the states to legislate and promote integration. He claimed the U.N. controlled the U.S., and that the U.N. was responsible for the November 2, 1963, assassination of Vietnamese president Ngo Dinh Diem and the failure of the Bay of Pigs operation. He expressed sympathy for Madame Nhu, stating, "The bloodshed of her kin is on the hands of the Kennedys." He called the Kennedys "tools of the U.N." Walker said the Monroe Doctrine was a thing of the past, because of the signing of the U.N. charter.[2416]

J. Evetts Haley had introduced Varney to Walker at his Walker's home in 1962.[2417] Varney wrote to Walker on October 2, 1962, telling him it had been a pleasure to meet him in Dallas and to hear his viewpoints. He told Walker that his arrest at Ole Miss should serve as a rallying point for the anti-Communists.[2418] Harold Lord Varney, who wrote for the openly anti-Semitic *American Mercury*, had admitted just prior to World War II that he was a Nazi and was sympathetic to the German Nazi regime.[2419] Varney and Pedro del Valle corresponded—on November 13, 1963, and November 20, 1963—about the need to clear Communism out of Cuba, by force if necessary.

The fact that Varney was in communication with del Valle nine days before the assassination, and was with General Walker three days before, suggests that Varney may have been another high-ranking member of the far right tied to the assassination conspiracy.[2420] Varney published *Pan American Reports*, which was affiliated with the International Committee of the Defense of the Christian Culture, and backed by Lamar and Nelson Bunker Hunt. Varney was also on the Board of Directors of Kent Courtney's Conservative Society of America.[2421]

No one had more motive, means and opportunity to commit the murder of President Kennedy than General Walker. Walker's motives to murder the president have been presented throughout this work. He felt Kennedy was destroying the nation though his proposed Civil Rights Act that would abolish segregation. His policies toward the U.N., Cuba, the Soviet Union, and disarmament were major factors in Walker's dislike for him. On a personal level, Walker had a vendetta against Kennedy for relieving him of his command of the 24th Infantry Division in Augsburg, Germany. The president's sanctioning of his arrest for insurrection against the government of the United States at Ole Miss—and confinement of him to a federal mental facility—was another factor. As a military man and a Dallasite, Walker also had the means and opportunity to execute the murder through a loyal, murderous following composed of men like Joseph Milteer.

General Walker, Joseph Newbrough, Jack Martin, and Leander Perez: The "Mysterious" Pre-Assassination Meetings in New Orleans

The evidence of a relationship between General Walker and Leander Perez, who Joseph Milteer revealed was a financier of the assassination, is extensive. Walker was a constant figure at national Citizens' Council meetings with Perez and other associates of Milteer. Walker was with Guy Banister at the September 4, 1963, free elector meeting at the Capitol House in Baton Rouge, while Perez was also in attendance. As will be discussed here, Walker met with Perez on November 20, 1963, in New Orleans—just two days before the assassination—which is further evidence of conspiracy in the assassination of President Kennedy.

The relationship between Milteer and Perez was presented in Chapter Ten and will briefly be recapped here. Milteer told Willie Somersett that Perez helped to finance the assassination. Milteer paid a visit to Perez's office in New Orleans in late September or early October 1963.

An informant for the Louisiana State Police, "S.A. –B-4951" (also identified as "B.G.") reported that Walker held four meetings in New Orleans over a two-day period prior to the assassination. He told the state police that General Walker met with Leander Perez at Perez's office for at least four hours, two days before the assassination. Later that same day, several individuals, who were not identified, attended a meeting with Walker in the National

Bank of Commerce building. Later on that day, Walker met with several unidentified people at the Jung Hotel. A fourth "confidential" meeting of unidentified individuals with General Walker was held at the Jung Hotel on the eve of the assassination. Walker was a guest at the Jung Hotel, which was located on Canal Street and was close to where Lee Harvey Oswald had passed out Fair Play for Cuba Committee pamphlets that summer.

Louisiana historian Romney Stubbs discovered a complete and unredacted copy of the informant's memo about Walker and Perez at Tulane University in the personal papers of Congressman Hale Boggs, and provided a copy to the author. This memo is revealed in its unredacted state for the first time in this work. The state police obviously felt the Perez-Walker meeting was of some significance in relationship to the assassination, since they sent a copy of the informant's report to Louisiana congressman Hale Boggs, who served on the Warren Commission. Boggs sent a copy of the informant's report to Warren Commission chief counsel Lee Rankin on May 15, 1964, at Rankin's request.

Joseph Samuel Newbrough, Jr., Guy Banister's employee in his detective agency at the building a 544 Camp Street, was mentioned in the original report about Walker and Perez. However, for unexplained reasons, Newbrough's name was deleted in the first paragraph of the copy Boggs sent to Rankin. Furthermore, the entire third paragraph, and a postscript that mentioned Joe Newbrough and Jack Martin (another Banister employee) were deleted.[2422] The full, unaltered text of the memo is presented as follows:

> From S.A.–B-4951
> Louisiana State Police
> Subject General Edwin A. Walker
> Report of his activities in New Orleans
>
> On November 20th, 1963, at about 11:00 a.m., I informed Mr. Frank Manning of the Attorney General's office of a mysterious meeting the above subject had in Judge Leander Perez's office in the National American Bank Building. Later there was also a meeting at the National Bank of Commerce in the National Bank of Commerce Garage Building. While I was not in the meeting room proper but noticed several of the people that were in attendance there, I noted that especially one, Joseph Newbrough was there. Shortly after that, about 1:30 p.m., Mr. Manning asked me to see if I could find out what was going on. I then went to the vicinity of Mr. George Singleman's [sic] office at 3:00 p.m. and while waiting in Mr. Singleman's [sic] office, I heard a telephone conversation, evidently from Judge Leander Perez that General Walker was still in his office in private conference. I later learned that General Walker was having some kind of meeting at the Jung Hotel. They had a

confidential meeting in a small room at the Jung Hotel where General Walker met with about 35 conservative political leaders. Most of these people were from the immediate vicinity of New Orleans. I was unable to gain an entrance to this meeting. I did not leave the hotel lobby until about 2:00 a.m. and then noticed General Walker in the lobby. He went upstairs about 2:00 a.m., 11/21/63.

On Thursday, 11/21/63, at approximately 8:00 p.m, General Walker had another meeting and had approximately 90 members. I talked to General Walker for quite some time making his acquaintance and did not leave the hotel until 1:00 a.m. but I was unable to learn of anything of any importance. There was evidently no further activity on the general's part. I was unable to learn at what time the general left the city.

I understand Mr. Joe Newbrough was recently convicted of a Federal offense involving use of the mails to defraud; that Mr. Newbrough was also in the marines and was an expert in jujitsuism. Mr. Newbrough was also very friendly with one Jack Martin. Mr. Jack Martin is the man who filed the petition with the State Central Committee in an endeavor to disqualify Mr. Gremmillion as a candidate for Attorney General on the grounds that he had been convicted on Federal grounds and so forth and so forth. We know that this was done by Mr. Martin on the instructions of Mr. Leander Perez. Mr. Martin's correct name is Edward Stewart Suggs. He was born in Arizona and he is about 44 years old. He appears to have a long criminal record and is wanted for murder somewhere around Dallas or San Antonio. I am not yet aware of the full disposition of these murder charges.

Respectfully submitted,
B.G. S.A.–B-4951

P.S Joe Newbrough is considered to be a very dangerous individual. His record is available from the FBI. Jack Martin has been missing from the city, however, I understand he was seen a couple of days ago and that he had grown a Van Dyke. He is also a dangerous psychopath. He has a long record in mental institution [sic]. His record is also available to the FBI.

Respectfully,
FHM

The three initials signed below the postscript, "FHM," stand for Frank Manning, the head of the state police. Five of the names mentioned in the informant's memo—Walker, Perez, Singelmann, Newbrough and Martin—were close associates of Guy Banister, whom numerous witnesses saw with Lee Harvey Oswald in the summer of 1963. Leander Perez was close to Guy Banister and their relationship goes back to 1956, when Perez offered his aid to Banister in connection with Senator Eastland's probe into alleged Communist activities in New Orleans. George Singelmann was Perez's personal assistant, ran the Citizens' Council initially out of the Balter Building, and was considered Guy Banister's best friend. Joe Newbrough and Jack Martin both were private investigators who worked out of Banister's office at the infamous Newman Building at 531 Lafayette Street/544 Camp Street. (One batch of Oswald's Fair Play for Cuba leaflets bore the address 544 Camp Street.) Jack Martin is the person who, while feuding with David Ferrie at the time of the Kennedy assassination, went to the media and told them that Ferrie had been Oswald's Civil Air Patrol Captain, had taught him how to shoot a rifle, and had suspiciously driven to Texas after the assassination. (The district attorney's office, the FBI, and the Secret Service later interviewed Martin and he denied the earlier accusations he made to the media about Ferrie and Oswald. The matter was not pursued further.) The informant's memo sheds some light on Martin's actions, noting that he was "missing from the city" after the assassination and grew "a Van Dyke." The actions suggest he grew a beard as a disguise, afraid for his life after he ill-advisedly revealed the Ferrie-Oswald relationship to the media out of a personal grudge he had with Ferrie. After all, drawing attention to Ferrie risked drawing attention to Banister, whom he worked for.

Informant "B.G." is probably Bob Guzman, an associate of Guy Banister, who once worked for Banister and was a known state police informant. Banister's secretary, Mary Brengel, told investigators that Guzman was Guy Banister's gun expert, and that the two men would sit around the office handling rifles and discussing the merits of one over another.[2423] One of Garrison's investigators interviewed Guzman for unrelated reasons and Guzman told the investigator that he was not an investigator for Guy Banister but did do intelligence work for Frank Manning of the state police. There is no evidence that Garrison, or his investigators, were aware of the mysterious Walker-Perez meeting. However, Garrison knew that Walker was in town before the assassination, which is the reason he suspected Walker was behind the assassination, as he expressed once in a meeting with his staff.[2424] Guzman told the D.A.'s office that he knew Banister and had seen Ferrie "about twice" but had never talked to him.[2425] Guzman was a smalltime contractor and a one-time house detective for the Holiday Inn on Royal Street according to Joe Newbrough, who mentioned Guzman in a completely unrelated HSCA interview in 1978.[2426, 2427]

Frank Manning was a Special Investigator for state Attorney General Jack P. F. Gremillion. Jack Martin, working for Leander Perez, attempted to get Gremillion disqualified in his bid for the attorney general. Perez's animosity toward Gremillion may stem from the fact that, in 1960, Gremillion was a Democratic Party loyalist and was an elector pledged to the Kennedy-Johnson ticket. As a result of the rift between Gremillion and Perez, Frank Manning sent his undercover informant, "B.G.," to spy on Perez on November 20 and 21—just before the assassination. Thus, as a result of the hostilities between Perez and Gremillion, the "mysterious" Walker-Perez meeting was discovered. Martin, in 1966, complained to the FBI that Manning was showing his rap sheet to his personal friends and telling them he had a murder case revived against him in Texas. According to the FBI memo on the matter, Manning had been to Guy Banister's office, where Banister cautioned Manning that he had better be careful because he was misusing information obtained from the FBI.[2428]

A letter sent to Louisiana congressman Allen Ellender in 1960 revealed that Manning,—like most white citizens in New Orleans—was a staunch segregationist. Manning congratulated Ellender on his fight against integration. He wrote, "I do believe that the kind of integration sponsored by the NAACP would be the beginning of the end of our nation."[2429]

The HSCA showed no awareness of the mysterious Walker-Perez meeting. They interviewed Joe Newbrough in connection with his employment with Guy Banister. Newbrough told them he was a private detective employed by Banister from 1958 to 1964. As noted in Chapters Nine and Ten, Newbrough stated that he had heard that Lee Harvey Oswald had rented the second or third floor at 544 Camp Street building. Newbrough claimed he was with Banister at the time of the assassination, installing a bug for a client. Newbrough gratuitously added that he thought Oswald was a CIA agent.[2430]

It's unfortunate that the names of Jack Martin and Joe Newbrough were removed from the copy of the state police report sent to Warren Commission counsel Lee Rankin by Boggs. Had that not happened, an astute Commission staff person might have recognized Jack Martin as the man the FBI interviewed on December 25, 1963, who told them that he provided television station WWL in New Orleans with information about David Ferrie's Civil Air Patrol. In the television interview, Martin told them he had seen a picture of Lee Harvey Oswald in a Civil Air Patrol photo in Ferrie's home and that Ferrie had taught Oswald how to shoot a rifle. He also said, during the TV interview, that he had seen Fair Play for Cuba Committee literature in Ferrie's home. Later, Martin recanted the story when questioned by the FBI—at the same time he was laying low and growing a beard—apparently afraid for his life, as was mentioned, above.[2431] Unfortunately, the HSCA concluded that there was not enough evidence to establish a relationship between Ferrie and Oswald—in the CAP or elsewhere. Author Gus Russo produced irrefutable evidence of their relationship when he found a photograph of Oswald and Ferrie at a CAP outing—a photo that was shown on a November 20, 1994, Public Broadcasting Service television documentary. Moreover, the HSCA was not aware of a Border Patrol agent's sighting of Oswald with Ferrie, going in and out of Guy Banister's office on multiple occasions, as was noted in Chapter One.

Conclusions

In 1963, President Kennedy intensified his efforts in the civil rights field—to the chagrin of the Southern segregationists. He pushed for black voter rights and used force to integrate the Alabama schools, narrowly avoiding a confrontation with Governor Wallace. The segregationists fought back with bombings, burnings, and murders—most notable among them the infamous Birmingham riots, the church bombing murders of four back girls, and the assassination of NAACP leader, Medgar Evers.

Leander Perez, described as a financier of the Kennedy assassination by Milteer, was the mastermind behind the segregationists' free electors scheme designed to defeat President Kennedy at the polls by depriving him of the South's Electoral College votes. General Walker endorsed the free electors scheme and was seen in the presence of Guy Banister at a free electors meeting at the Capitol House Hotel, which was also attended by Perez. Perez was also behind the Communist Control Act, under which opponents planned to prove that the civil rights movement was Communist-infiltrated, then prosecute the movement's leaders for sedition under it and put them away in prison for decades. Several Louisiana leaders in the Southern Conference Education Fund were arrested under the act in an October 1964 raid led by close associates of Guy Banister. Those arrested were also affiliated with three other leftist groups that Lee Harvey Oswald just happened to have infiltrated in the summer of 1963. President Kennedy had had enough of the violence and the contrived state laws of the segregationists and, on June 11, 1963, proposed the sweeping Civil Rights Act that would end segregation once and for all—in response to which southern leaders threatened another Civil War.

During the same time, Lee Harvey Oswald made a spectacle of himself, posing as a Communist in the summer of 1963 in New Orleans, and managed to get coverage on television, on the radio, and in the press. His wife told the Warren Commission he was "advertising" as he had also done around the Walker shooting incident and others. Oswald again made a spectacle of himself at the Cuban Embassy in Mexico City. The embassy staff felt Oswald's appearance there was bizarre. While Oswald was flaunting his Communist credentials, eleven witnesses saw him with Guy Banister—a fanatical anti-Communist, who was an investigator for the Louisiana Un-American Committee, which later organized the raid on the Southern Conference Education Fund. The sightings of Oswald with Banister and David Ferrie—another fanatical anti-Communist—are evidence that Oswald was a false Communist.

After the Walker shooting incident, General Walker continued his intensive attacks on President Kennedy, accusing him of being pro-Communist. Walker railed against Kennedy's policies on integration, Castro in Cuba, and disarmament. He was certain, as were his friend Kent Courtney and others on the far right, that President Kennedy was going to place the U.S. military under U.N. command. Walker was behind the vicious attacks against President Kennedy's U.N. ambassador, Adlai Stevenson, in Dallas in October 1963. Unfortunately, neither the press nor President Kennedy were aware that Walker was behind the sordid affair, which so disturbed some close to the president that they urged him not to go to Dallas in November. President Kennedy was wary of the violent and erratic Walker and sent a massive military force to protect those attending the historic March on Washington, spurred by rumors that Walker planned to lead another insurrection as he had at Ole Miss. Some in the FBI knew that Walker was a military advisor to the Council for Statehood/Congress of Freedom's broad-based assassination plots, but did not inform the Warren Commission. The FBI had credible information from a citizen that Walker's Minutemen teams were really assassination squads. The FBI knew from Willie Somersett that the radical right talked about assassinating the president in October 1963, at the Constitution Party meeting attended by Joseph Milteer and Pedro del Valle, two close associates of General Walker. In October 1963, Walker spoke at a meeting of Citizens' Councils leaders and told them that they could look forward to a Communist killing the president. The remarks suggest that Oswald had already been figured into the scheme at that time. The FBI knew that Milteer told Willie Somersett— on November 11, 1963—that the assassination was in the works, explaining how it would happen in accurate detail.

The allegation that Lee Harvey Oswald visited Cuban émigré Sylvia Odio with two anti-Castro Cubans came dangerously close to revealing the fact that Oswald was not a Communist at all—something that would have created a mammoth problem for the Warren Commission. Anti-Castro adventurer Loran Hall saved the day when he came forth and told the FBI that he and two companions visited Odio—not Oswald and the other two Cubans she described. It was either unknown or unappreciated by any investigators that Hall was an associate of General Walker and had been to his home. Hall also was an associate of H. L. Hunt, Dan Smoot, and William Potter Gale, all of whom were members of Milteer's hardcore underground. After the Warren Commission published their findings and declared that Oswald was a genuine Communist, Hall admitted he had lied about his own visit to Odio.

General Walker came full circle when he returned to New Orleans and the company of Banister associate Kent Courtney two days before the Kennedy assassination. In 1961, as noted in Chapter Twelve, Courtney and General Charles Willoughby had planned to travel to Germany to meet with Walker—while the army and the Kennedy administration were deliberating whether or not to relieve Walker of his command—when they had planned to offer Walker the paid position of the standard bearer of the radical right. While in New Orleans, Walker also met in secret with Leander Perez, an associate of Joseph Milteer. Of course, Perez was also close to Guy Banister.

Moreover, Walker met with Joe Newbrough, who worked out of Banister's office at the building at 544 Camp Street. A U.S. Border Patrol agent saw Lee Harvey Oswald going in and out of Banister's office on multiple occasions. There is no way to reconcile Walker's visit to New Orleans and contact with Kent Courtney, Leander Perez, and an employee of Guy Banister's office, frequented by Lee Harvey Oswald, other than to conclude that it is evidence of conspiracy involving General Walker in the death of President Kennedy.

Chapter Sixteen

The Assassination of President Kennedy, November 22, 1963

We don't have any proof that Oswald fired the rifle, and never did.
Nobody's yet been able to put him in that building
with a gun in his hand.
— Dallas Police Chief Jesse Curry

D allas civic leaders were concerned about the atmosphere of extremism in the city that had become evident during the violent Adlai Stevenson episode on October 28, 1963. They were anxious to avoid another ugly display during President Kennedy's planned visit to the city on Friday, November 22, 1963. Mayor Earle Cabell felt that Dallas needed to "redeem itself." The Dallas chief of police pledged that he would not permit the mayhem that had occurred during Stevenson's visit just twenty-five days earlier. The *Dallas Morning News* warned, "Another incident similar to the Stevenson one could deal Dallas a deadly blow on the national level, particularly from the political standpoint."[2432]

As early as October 3, 1963, Senator J. William Fulbright told the president, "Dallas is a very dangerous place. I wouldn't go there. Don't *you* go there."[2433] Dallas department store owner Stanley Marcus urged Vice President Johnson to persuade the president to cancel his visit. Byron Skelton, the Democratic Committeeman from Texas, had a bad feeling. He wrote to Attorney General Robert Kennedy and cited General Walker's statement that, "Kennedy is a liability to the free world," and told him, "Frankly, I am worried about President Kennedy's proposed trip to Dallas. . . . A man who would make this kind of statement is capable of doing harm to the president." Skelton asked that cancellation of the Dallas leg of the trip be given "earnest consideration." He added that he would "feel better if the president's itinerary did not include Dallas." Two days later, Skelton wrote to Vice President Johnson's right-hand man, Walter Jenkins, and expressed his concerns about the climate of the city. Going even further, he flew to Washington the next week and discussed his fears with the head of the Democratic National Committee and told him it wasn't safe—and that the trip should be cancelled.[2434]

The FBI and the Dallas Police Department heard rumors that Walker's group was planning an incident during the president's visit. On the morning of November 22, the host of H. L. Hunt's radio program, *Life Lines*, told his audience that the Kennedy administration intended to outlaw the right to own and bear arms.[2435] Several associates of General Walker, including Nelson Bunker Hunt and members of the John Birch Society, took out a full-page ad in the *Dallas Morning News* mocking the president, entitled "Welcome Mr. Kennedy to Dallas" then included a list of the far-right grievances against him. Billy James Hargis defended the "Welcome" ad, saying, "The ad was a factual presentation of the case of conservatism against President Kennedy and his Administration."[2436] General Walker's aide—and Dallas Nazi leader—Robert Surrey printed and circulated the infamous "Wanted for Treason" flier that resembled a wanted poster for President Kennedy, listing what were considered the president's crimes against the American people. Braced for a far-right incident during the president's visit, it came as a complete surprise to many people when a Communist was charged with the murder.

Lee Harvey Oswald and the Assassination

Lee Harvey Oswald left behind so much incriminating evidence against himself on the day of the assassination that the case against him was a prosecutor's dream. That is not to say that it was without problems. Nonetheless, in all likelihood—if Oswald had not been murdered—then, based on a mountain of evidence, he would have been found guilty of capital murder and executed in the Texas electric chair.

The investigating bodies never ventured to explain why Oswald left behind so much incriminating evidence in the Kennedy murder, when he could have easily done better. For example, he could have purchased another cheap rifle that could not have been traced to him, but didn't. Had he done that, it would have been hard to pin the murder on him. The implicit assumption, it seems, was that Oswald was inept. Further, he was inept on two occasions, since he also left significant evidence behind in his purported attempt to assassinate General Walker. (There are striking similarities in the way Oswald left obvious incriminating evidence against himself in both the Walker and the Kennedy shootings.) He also apparently expected to get caught in both cases. The difference in the two incidents was that the Walker shooting was a shoot-and-miss gambit. In the Walker case, Oswald may not have actually done the shooting, if the testimony of the neighbor boy who saw another man leave the scene—apparently with a rifle that he placed on the floorboards of his car—is correct. Oswald may not have done the shooting in the president's murder, either. As Dallas Police Chief Jesse Curry pointed out, "We don't have any proof that Oswald fired the rifle, and never did. Nobody's yet been able to put him in that building with a gun in his hand."[2437]

Oswald, perhaps under the spell of General Walker and others, may have thought he was involving himself in another shoot-and-miss scheme in Dallas, where no one would get hurt and the punishment against him would be nominal, in comparison to the political capital gained. Under a shoot-and-miss scenario in the Kennedy case, Walker would have been able to pointedly demonstrate to the president that, indeed, native Communists were a threat to the country. Under that scenario, ways could have been devised to manipulate the evidence so that Oswald would have gotten off the hook—or so he could have been led to believe. Also under that scenario, Oswald's credentials as a Communist would have been made known, something desirable to him. Close examination of Oswald's behavior—and the evidence he left behind—strongly favors that Oswald believed he was getting involved, in some way, in another shoot-and-miss operation. In fact, there is good evidence to suggest that Oswald was not directly involved in the assassination of the president—and that he did not do the shooting, nor did he know that the murder was going to happen.

The investigating bodies never considered, as has been demonstrated in this work, that everything Oswald engaged in—as a purported Communist—was phony, staged, and deliberate. They never considered that Oswald might be a phony Communist in the case of the president's murder, as will be shown. As pointed out earlier, there was a large amount of evidence that would have incriminated Oswald in that phony Walker shoot-and-miss incident, had it been carried to fruition and not witnessed by a neighbor. (Examples of this evidence include the note to Marina on how to proceed if he were arrested, the notebook with various measurements of distances around Walker's home, photos of Walker's home, and the backyard photos of Oswald in a Marxist pose with his rifle.) The contrived evidence was superfluous for the purpose of shooting Walker, but was vital if Oswald wanted to get charged in the incident. Warren Commission counsel Wesley Liebler, if only for a moment, sensed something funny about Oswald leaving all that incriminating evidence behind, which led him to ask Marina, "Did it seem strange to you at the time, Marina, that Lee did make these careful plans, take pictures, and write it up in a notebook, and then when he went out to shoot at General Walker he left all that incriminating evidence right in the house so that if he had ever been stopped and questioned and if that notebook had been found, it would have clearly indicated that he was the one that shot at General Walker?" Liebler did not, unfortunately, have the same suspicions about the evidence left behind in the president's shooting.

Lee Harvey Oswald's initial behavior on the day of—and around the time of—the assassination was consistent with that of a man who believed he was playing a part in a phony shoot-and-miss gambit and is inconsistent with the behavior of a man who intended to shoot the president and get away with it, as will be shown. Right after the assassination, his behavior abruptly changed and became that of a man who had been duped, a victim of a classic "bait and switch" scheme, with his life and liberty left in jeopardy.

Oswald expected to be arrested after the assassination, just as he had in the Walker shooting incident. He left his wedding band at home, along with enough money to support his family for weeks. He told both his co-worker Wesley Frazier and his wife that he did not plan on returning to Ruth Paine's that night, as would have been expected on a weekend. Oswald was, in fact, guilty of *something* that day, but the evidence will show he had not intended to become a martyr. Oswald ran for his life when he discerned from those around him that the president had been shot.

One scenario fully explains Oswald's odd behavior. Suppose Oswald was led to believe that the president was to be shot at and deliberately missed. He might have been assured that the shoot-and-miss would be from a dissimilar rifle with bullets and casings that could not be traced to his own rifle, or a similar scheme. Another individual, he might have been told, would do the shooting, assuring Oswald that he could not be identified as the shooter. In turn, Oswald would agree to be the patsy, go to jail, and expect to be released in a few days for lack of ballistic evidence. This scenario fits Oswald's known behavior.

In the end, however, Oswald was framed to take the blame and—as Joseph Milteer put it—throw the public off, as we shall see. It is also worth noting that the barrels of both Oswald's pistol and rifle had been rechambered or drilled out. Although this is speculation, it is conceivable that he was led to believe that the rechambering of the barrels would make the bullets untraceable. The lead bullets from his pistol were, in fact, untraceable, but not those from his rifle.

Oswald committed several acts which an adept, rational assassin would not have. Oswald advertised the rifle by carrying it to the Texas School Book Depository in a rifle-sized, self-fashioned, paper package—in front of coworker Wesley Frazier—when he didn't have to, which provided the Commission with key evidence of Oswald's guilt. After the shooting, he did not immediately flee the scene. When he did, Oswald did not choose the safest and most direct route for escape. He did not provide himself with sufficient funds to sustain an escape, although he could have. There would have been no other particular reason to immediately suspect Oswald in the shooting without Frazier's sighting of the suggestive paper package, since it would have taken some time to trace the presumed murder weapon to its owner. (In fact, the rifle was not traced to "A. Hidell," Oswald's alias, until 4:00 a.m. the next morning.) In the proposed shoot-and-miss scenario, a timely arrest of Oswald would have been desirable and it could have been facilitated, as Oswald expected, by Frazier surmising that Oswald had actually carried a rifle in the paper sack (which he was told by Oswald contained curtain rods) and so notified authorities after the shooting.

Oswald could have brought his rifle into the Book Depository at any time. He unnecessarily chose to bring it on the morning of the assassination in a long, self-fashioned paper package, which was witnessed by a coworker and was used to tie him to the murder rifle. Source: Warren Commission Exhibit 142, XVI, 513

Oswald deliberately left his own traceable rifle on the sixth floor for it to be discovered and traced to him, which was yet another critical act that supports the postulated shoot-and-miss scenario. Not only did he leave his rifle behind, he facilitated the tracing of the rifle to himself by carrying the draft registration identification card he had forged—in the name of "A. J. Hidell"—in his wallet at the time of his arrest. (The rifle had been purchased in the mail before the Walker shooting incident from Klein's Sporting Goods in Chicago in the name of "A. Hidell.") Had Oswald not been carrying the identification card with the name A. J. Hidell on it, authorities may not have connected the rifle to Oswald for days. In addition to transporting the rifle by carrying it in the long brown paper bag and carrying the A. J. Hidell identification card, Oswald performed a third act that served to tie the rifle to him. He needlessly left his clipboard—a unique homemade affair that was unmistakably Oswald's—near where the rifle was stashed, when he could have left it any-where in the cavernous Book Depository. (A Book Depository employee found the clipboard many days later.)

In a hypothetical shoot-and-miss scenario, Oswald would have lingered in the Book Depository (which he actually did), exposing himself to arrest while the actual shooter—who would have deliberately missed the president, as Oswald would have been led to believe—would have slipped down the rear stairway and out the back door. The rifle would have been traced to Oswald with the help of Frazier (which is what actually happened). Under the hy-pothetical scheme, Oswald would have expected to be charged with attempted murder, but would have maintained his innocence.

Alternatively, Oswald might have been led to believe that the shooter would shoot into the horizon where the bullets would never be recovered.

In reality, after Oswald was apprehended, he asked for famed New York Commu-nist-defending attorney John Abt, which was part of the act. As has been shown—and will be detailed further later—Oswald was no Communist and had no need for a Communist-de-fending lawyer. General Walker knew all about John Abt and called him, "an American Jew who defends all big Communist cases," as was noted in Chapter Fourteen. Oswald's asking for Abt is suggestive of another ploy to advertise he was a Communist—and also fits well into the hypothetical shoot-and-miss scheme that Oswald appeared to be following. Under a shoot-and-miss scenario, Oswald would have expected to become known internationally. All his Communist credentials—including his stay in Russia, his Russian wife, his visit to the Cuban and Soviet Union embassies in Mexico City, his FPCC activities, and other Commu-nist acts would have been made known—which is something that actually happened. Under the shoot-and-miss scenario, he could have expected confinement for a number of days in jail until the ballistics tests came back—indicating the bullets did not come from his rifle—and he would have had to have been let go for lack of evidence. The world would have been dumbfounded when they learned there was no case against Oswald.

Nonetheless, under the hypothetical scenario, it would have been expected that wide-spread suspicion would remain that a Communist was in some way involved in an attempt to assassinate the president. The radical right wing would then have had the opportunity to use Oswald as a propaganda tool, supporting their contention that the real Communist threat came from within.

There were several distinct phases of Oswald's behavior: 1) after the murder, he was complacent; 2) as he left Dealey Plaza he was frantic; 3) on the night of the murder, he denied murdering anyone and insisted he was a patsy; 4) the next day, he resumed his play-acting as a Communist when he asked for attorney John Abt. He assured his family everything would be all right. At that time, he may have believed he would somehow be exonerated—perhaps holding the belief that the ballistics testing would fail to tie the fatal bullets to his rifle. (Unfortunately, he was murdered the next day—a day before the ballistics came back that showed the bullets came from Oswald's rifle. If the ballistics results had come back before Oswald was murdered, there is no telling how he might have acted. Knowing the game was over, he might have revealed the masterminds behind the murder to save his life.)

The shoot-and-miss hypothesis will be put to the test as the evidence is laid out and Lee Harvey Oswald's actual actions on the day of the assassination are described.

Lee Harvey Oswald and the Texas School Book Depository

On October 14, 1963, Ruth Paine learned from a neighbor, Linnie Mae Randall, that her brother, nineteen-year-old Wesley Frazier (who was staying with her), had recently started a job at the Texas School Book Depository. Marina Oswald was expecting her second child and was living at the Ruth Paine's when Ruth took it upon to herself to call the Book Depository and inquire about a job for Oswald. She telephoned the building superintendent, Roy Truly, and told him that Oswald was desperately in need of a job in order to support his expectant wife and child. Truly told her to send Oswald over to fill out an application. (Truly was under the favorable, although incorrect, impression, that Oswald had recently been discharged from the marines.) Oswald was offered the job of "order filler" and he reported to work on the morning of October 16.

The Texas School Book Depository was a seven-story building in downtown Dallas— which faced due south at the corner of Elm and Houston Streets—where they warehoused and sold school textbooks. As an order filler, Oswald was required to pick up a customer's order on the first floor, gather the requested textbooks from stock—principally from the fifth, sixth, and seventh floors, and take them to the shipping department for packaging. (The so-called "sniper's nest," where the shooting occurred, was in the far southeast corner of the Book Depository's sixth floor. Stacked boxes of books surrounded the area, forming a "nest.")

The Book Depository was eighty-four by eighty-four feet square. There were no partitions on the sixth floor, only stacks of boxed books and support pillars. The stairway and elevators were in the rear west corner, diagonally across from the sniper's nest. Next to the stairs were two freight elevators that operated side by side in the same shaft. The Depository had fifteen employees, including a superintendent, foreman, shipping clerk, and clerical staff, and six order fillers. Oswald was paid minimum wage, but he was a good worker who was quiet and kept to himself.[2438] Sixty-five individuals, including those connected to the publishing companies who did business there, had access to the Book Depository.[2439] The FBI determined that seventy-three people were known to be in the Book Depository at some time on November 22.[2440] It was not a secure building, however, and with all of the people who had access to the Depository, a stranger could easily have entered and not been noticed.

While Marina Oswald was living without charge at Ruth Paine's home in Fort Worth, Oswald moved into a tiny room in an inexpensive rooming house in the Oak Cliff section of Dallas on October 14, which he rented under the alias of "O. H. Lee." The arrangement worked well for all of them. Oswald could do what he pleased without anyone knowing about it. Ruth was separated from her husband and benefited from Marina's company, and the situation also afforded her the opportunity to learn the Russian language from Marina. Oswald told his wife that the arrangement made sense, since they were saving money by not renting an apartment—and since his rooming house was much closer to his job in Dallas.[2441]

Since he was a neighbor of Ruth Paine, Wesley Frazier routinely drove Oswald to the Paine home on Friday afternoons after work and picked him up on Monday morning to start the work week. On the other days, Oswald would take the city bus from his rooming house to and from work. On November 16, Oswald told Frazier that he would not need a ride to Ruth Paine's that weekend because he planned to take a driver's license test in Dallas—a story which was a fabrication.[2442] Marina told Lee that the Paines were having a birthday party for one of their children on November 16 and 17, and it was better if Lee did not visit her that weekend.[2443] On November 17, Marina and Ruth decided to call Oswald at his rooming house. They were told there was no one there named Lee Harvey Oswald. Oswald called his wife the next day and she was furious about his use of an alias. Oswald explained he did not want his landlady to read anything that might appear about him in the paper, nor did he want the FBI to know his whereabouts. Marina was irate, stating, "After all, when will all your foolishness come to an end? All of these comedies. First one thing and then another. And now this fictitious name." Lee called her several times that Monday, November 18, and she hung up on him each time.[2444]

On Thursday morning, November 21, the day before the assassination, while at work, Oswald asked Frazier if he would drop him at Ruth Paine's after work, so he could pick up some curtain rods for his rooming house. That was the first time Frazier ever took Oswald to Ruth Paine's other than on Friday.[2445] Oswald's arrival at Ruth Paine's after work that Thursday was completely unexpected. He told his wife that he was lonely, especially since he had not stayed with her the prior weekend. She told the FBI "He wanted to make peace with me." Lee was upset that she would not speak to him. He tried very hard to please her. He spent quite a bit of time putting away the children's diapers and playing with the children on the street. Lee suggested to her that they rent an apartment together in Dallas. She told him it would be better to continue to live apart to save money. She asked him to buy her a washing machine for the babies' diapers, and he agreed.

That night before the assassination, Oswald went to bed before his wife retired. She did not speak to him in bed, although she felt he was still awake. The next morning, the day of the assassination, he left for work before anyone else arose. He left his wedding ring in a cup on his dresser—for the first time in their married life—and $170 in a wallet in one of the dresser drawers. He took $13.87 with him to the Depository.[2446] If Oswald expected to kill the president and escape, he did not take sufficient funds to do so, even though he could have.

Rather than wait for Wesley Frazier to stop at Ruth Paine's home to pick him up in his car, Oswald walked the half block to Frazier's sister's home with a long package in hand. There, Oswald placed the long paper package across the back seat of his car. Oswald then walked over to a window and saw Frazier and his sister eating breakfast. Frazier joined Oswald outside and, as they walked to the car, Frazier noticed the package in the back seat and was told it contained the curtain rods that Oswald had told him about the day before. Later, both Frazier and his sister—who also saw the paper sack through her window while Oswald was walking to Frazier's car—would be adamant that the package Oswald had that morning at her home was too short to contain the assassination rifle, even if it were broken down. They both described how Oswald had held one end of the sack cupped in his hand, with the other end tucked under his armpit. That could not have been done if Oswald's disassembled rifle was in the paper package because the rifle was too long. The Warren Commission nonetheless determined the paper sack did, in fact, contain the assassination rifle.

Linnie Mae Randle, who rented Oswald a room in her house, testified to the Commission that Oswald dressed in a white T-shirt and brown or tan shirt with a gray jacket when he returned to her house after the president's assassination. Frazier testified that Oswald wore a gray flannel wool jacket. Fibers inside the paper sack were later found to be consistent with those of the blanket Oswald had kept the rifle wrapped in while it was stored in the Ruth Paine's garage, and this fact was presented as evidence that Oswald did actually carry the rifle into the Depository in the paper sack.[2447] The Fraziers, the Commission determined, were mistaken about seeing the package tucked under Oswald's armpit.

In the past, upon arrival to work at the Book Depository, Frazier and Oswald had always walked in together from the rear parking lot. That did not happen on the morning of the assassination. Instead, Oswald walked fifty feet ahead of Frazier, with his long paper sack in hand, as he entered the Book Depository from the rear. Oswald earlier told Frazier, ominously, that he would not need a ride to Ruth Paine's that evening after work, as he usually did on Fridays.[2448]

No one noticed anything unusual about Oswald that morning. He went about his job, clipboard in hand, filling book orders on different floors—including the sixth floor, where the shooting took place. Charles Douglas Givens, a fellow emplyee, saw Oswald filing orders at 8:30 a.m., wearing a greenish shirt. At 11:45 a.m., Givens saw Oswald again, while he was standing at the elevator gate on the fifth floor as Givens was descending by elevator from the sixth floor for lunch. Several other employees were on the two elevators racing each other to the ground from the sixth floor and saw Oswald as well. When Givens got downstairs, he discovered he had left his cigarettes and jacket up on the west end of the sixth floor, where he had been laying flooring earlier. He got a drink of water and used the men's room, then went back to the sixth floor to retrieve his cigarettes and jacket. There, he saw Lee Harvey Oswald coming from the area of the sniper's nest with his clipboard at 11:55 a.m.—thirty-five minutes before the shooting took place. Givens asked Oswald if he was coming to lunch, to which Oswald replied, "No sir." Oswald asked Givens to close the elevator gate for him when he went down, which was necessary should Oswald need to summon it up to the sixth floor.

Oswald was not seen again until after the assassination and his whereabouts in the Book Depository after Givens last saw him at 11:55 a.m. are completely unknown.[2449]

Meanwhile, another employee, Bonnie Ray Williams, ate lunch adjacent to the sniper's nest on the sixth floor where Williams had been working that day. He left behind the remnants of his chicken lunch and a Dr. Pepper, and joined his coworkers on the fifth floor at approximately 12:20 p.m.—or about ten minutes before the assassination. He did not see Oswald on the sixth floor during the entire time he ate his lunch. If Oswald—or anyone else—was on the sixth floor, he was hiding.[2450]

The Shooting

The Hertz billboard atop the Texas School Book Depository, overlooking Dealey Plaza, showed 12:30 p.m. when the first shot rang out. The limousine had just passed the Depository, heading west, when the president was first struck by a bullet from the rear, where the Book Depository stood, as the Warren Commission determined.

Patrolman Marrion Baker was riding his motorcycle next to the last press car in the presidential motorcade, heading north on Houston Street directly toward the Book Depository, when he heard rifle shots. He was a block behind the president, about sixty to eighty feet north of Main Street on Houston, near the area where Joseph Milteer was standing and watching the procession. Baker recognized at once that what he heard were heard rifle shots, since he had just gotten back from a deer-hunting trip, so the sound was familiar to him. He saw pigeons fly up from the roof of the Book Depository and he immediately thought the shots came from the roof of the Depository or from the building just to the east. He revved up his motorcycle and rode 180 to 200 feet to the corner of Houston and Elm Street, where he parked his motorcycle and ran to the Book Depository's front entrance stairs, pushing his way through the hysterical crowd. He heard a woman screaming, "Oh, they have shot that man, they have shot that man."

Baker set out for the Depository roof. He was joined by building manager Roy Truly as they entered the lobby and Baker asked him where the stairs were. Truly told him that he would take him to the elevators in the west (rear) of the Depository. Truly pushed the buttons to bring the elevators down and called for them twice, but was unable to get them, so he took the stairs and Baker followed him.

On the second floor, through the small glass window of a vestibule door adjoining the lunchroom, Baker caught a glimpse of Lee Harvey Oswald walking away from him. With his revolver drawn and pointed at Oswald, he told him, "Come here." Oswald walked toward him. Truly, climbing the stairs in front of Baker, initially did not see Oswald and was on his way up the stairs to the third floor when he heard voices and noticed that officer Baker was not behind him. Truly vouched for Oswald as an employee, and the two resumed their run up the stairs to the roof—Baker did not see Oswald again until after his arrest. The two made it to the roof, where they searched and found nothing. By the time Baker and Truly were on their way back down, other police officers had entered the building.

Baker and Truly later told the Warren Commission that, when they saw Oswald, he had nothing in his hands. Officer Baker said there was nothing about Oswald that made him suspicious, and that Baker was simply doing his duty by talking to Truly about him. The

Warren Commission asked Baker about Oswald's appearance when he encountered him less than two minutes after Oswald presumably had shot the president, wiped the rifle free of fingerprints, stashed it behind boxes, and ran downstairs—four stories—into the lunchroom. Baker told them "He didn't appear that to me [to be out of breath]. He appeared normal you know." They asked, "Was he calm and collected? He answered, "Yes sir. He never did say a word or nothing. In fact, he didn't change his expression one bit." Baker asserted that Oswald didn't flinch at the drawn gun, held three feet away.[2451] Roy Truly corroborated Baker's description of Oswald, saying, "I didn't see him panting like he had been running or anything." Truly added, "He didn't seem to be excited or overly afraid or anything. He might have been a bit startled . . . but I can not recall any change in expression of any kind on his face."[2452]

The Secret Service later timed a simulation of Oswald's presumed departure from the sixth floor sniper's nest, including running to the opposite side of the building, wiping fingerprints from the rifle, stashing the rifle, and the going down four flights of stairs to the second-floor lunchroom. They found it took one minute and thirteen seconds in one trial. They simulated Marrion Baker's run into the Book Depository from the time of the first shot until he encountered Oswald in the lunchroom and determined it took one minute and fifteen seconds to accomplish in one trial, one minute and thirty seconds in a second trial. Thus, they reasonably determined that Oswald had enough time to perform the shooting and make it to the second-floor lunchroom where Baker found him.[2453]

What the Commission also demonstrated—without saying so—was that someone other than Oswald could have done the shooting, stashed the rifle, and run down to the first floor and out the back door without having been seen by either Marrion Baker, Roy Truly, or anyone else. Baker's and Truly's description of a cool and collected Oswald less than seventy-five seconds after he supposedly blasted away the president's head, wiped down the rifle, stashed it, and descended four flights of stairs is remarkable. It is not, of course, remarkable if he did *not* do the shooting and did *not* run down the steps from the sixth floor—or if he believed it was another shoot-and-miss gambit like the one that occurred in the Walker shooting incident. In those cases, he would have had little to worry about. Oswald's calm demeanor was the first instance of several strange and remarkable behaviors on the part of the presumed assassin following the shooting with more to follow.

After Oswald's encounter with officer Baker, he got off the direct path of escape to the stairwell, and instead went the opposite way—into the lunchroom—not something one would expect of a man who had just mortally wounded the president. Having gotten safely by Officer Baker, Oswald could have slipped down the rear stairs to the first floor rear door and left the building, but didn't. As more law enforcement officers began to approach the building, Oswald chose to buy a Coke in the lunchroom rather than escape—another piece of strange and remarkable behavior. Jeraldean Reid, a clerical supervisor at the Book Depository, witnessed Oswald with the Coke. Reid told the Warren Commission that she had eaten lunch in the second-floor lunchroom at 12:00. She went outside early to watch the president's motorcade. She was standing with Roy Truly when the shots rang out. She went back into the building to a large office in front of—and connected to—the second-floor lunchroom. She saw Oswald enter the office from the rear door an estimated two minutes after the rifle shots—and just after Oswald's encounter with officer Baker. In her testimony to the Warren Commission, Reid told them that she remarked to Oswald, "Oh, the president [has] been shot, but maybe they didn't hit him." Oswald mumbled something and kept walking. "He was very calm," she stated. "He had gotten a coke and was holding it in his hands and I guess the reason it impressed me seeing him in there I thought it was a little strange that one of the warehouse boys would be up in the office at the time, not that he had done anything wrong. The only time I had seen him in the office was to come and get change and he already had his coke in his hand." She was asked if Oswald was moving very fast. She responded, "No; because he was moving at a very slow pace, I never did see him moving fast at any time."

Thus, it was a calm Oswald who took the time to buy a Coke and dawdle in the office—after having a gun pointed at him by a police officer, with more police on the way—which was more unusual behavior for someone who supposedly had just murdered the president of the United States. At that point, Oswald had the opportunity to either leave by way of the front stairway leading to the front door, as law enforcement was descending upon the building, or—more safely—down the rear stairs and out the back door. He again declined to take the safest route for escape as a rational assassin would: the back door. He instead chose to go out the front. Reid saw him exiting the door from the office toward the front stairway with his full bottle of Coke, wearing a T-shirt and no jacket. The Warren Commission determined that Oswald exited the building down the front stairs and out the front door of the Book Depository.[2454, 2455]

National Broadcasting Company newsman Robert MacNeil got out of the motorcade press car after the shooting and ran up to the Book Depository. He asked a young man—an apparent employee of the Depository—where he could find a phone. The man directed him to the phone inside the Depository. Phone records from the Book Depository note that a call was, in fact, made to NBC in New York at 12:34 p.m. When asked later, MacNeil could not positively identify the helpful man as Lee Harvey Oswald. Considering that the helpful young man must have been an employee to know the location of the Depository phone, and the fact that the whereabouts of the other employees were known, the man was probably Oswald. In fact, Oswald stated, after his arrest, that he had come down the front steps of the Depository and had been stopped by a man asking for a phone. Since the man was wearing identification, Oswald assumed he was a Secret Service agent, but the man may have been newsman Robert MacNeil wearing his press credentials. Oswald's courteous assistance to a newsman—who he thought was a Secret Service agent—was also unusual behavior for the presumed presidential assassin, especially because this caused a further delay in his escape. At that point, it suggests that Oswald still may not have fully realized that the president had been hit.[2456]

At some point between his presumed encounter with Robert MacNeil in front of the depository and his boarding of a city bus just a few blocks away, Oswald's behavior changed dramatically. He transformed from the calm and collected man who dawdled in the lunchroom, sipped a Coke in the office after having a confrontation with a pistol-pointing police officer, and graciously assisted a reporter, into a frantic man who was running for his life.

The Commission determined that, after leaving the Depository at approximately 12:33 p.m., Oswald walked seven blocks east on Elm Street, to the corner of Elm and Murray, where he boarded a city bus heading back in the direction of the Book Depository on its way toward his rooming house in Oak Cliff. Remarkably, someone on that bus actually knew Oswald—an event which defies the odds and is a fortuitous accident of history.

Mary Bledsoe—who, on October 7, had briefly rented a room to Oswald—was on the bus, and recognized him. The day Oswald took the room, he brought in a container of milk and asked if he could put it in the refrigerator. His room did not entitle him to kitchen privileges, and the incident disturbed Bledsoe. After a week at her home, and after some other petty incidents, she decided she didn't like him and asked him to leave.

When asked about seeing Oswald on the bus, she described him as looking "like a maniac." He was dirty, with a hole in the right elbow of the sleeve of his brown shirt, which was undone. He did not have a jacket on. She said, "he looked so bad in the face, and his face was so distorted." She heard the bus driver say, "Well the president has been shot." She began to discuss the shooting with others on the bus. Bus traffic had slowed to a crawl because of the turmoil in Dealey Plaza, and Oswald got off after a brief ride. If Oswald had not known—or was not sure—the president had been shot after standing amid the pandemonium in front to the Book Depository, the bus driver let him know it. A once calm and collected Oswald turned abruptly into a "maniac" with a distorted face. When Oswald was arrested, he was wearing a brown/burgundy sport shirt with a hole in the right sleeve at the elbow. During her testimony, Bledsoe identified Oswald's shirt as being the same as the one he had on during the bus ride.

Oswald next walked to the Greyhound Bus station and got into a cab that took him near his North Beckley Street rooming house in Oak Cliff. As Oswald seated himself in the front seat of the cab, an old lady asked the driver to call a cab for her. Oswald offered his cab to the lady, but she declined. During the estimated six-minute cab ride, the driver noted police cars and sirens everywhere. The cab driver dropped Oswald off a few minutes' walk away from his room at 1026 North Beckley Avenue. When later questioned, the cab driver identified the shirt taken from Oswald at his arrest as the same one his passenger wore.

The employee records of the Texas School Book Depository did not have Oswald's North Beckley Avenue address, only the address of Ruth Paine's house. Only Ruth Paine and Marina had the rooming house address—unless a conspirator also had it. Having been let off near—but not at—his rooming house, suggests Oswald was exercising caution when returning to his room, perhaps fearing someone might be trying to find him there. Reconstructing Oswald's travels, the Commission determined that Oswald would have arrived at his rooming house at about 1:00 p.m. And, in fact, Earlene Roberts, Oswald's housekeeper, testified that Oswald, whom she knew as O. H. Lee, arrived at the house about 1:00 p.m. She was watching the televised news of the shooting when she saw Oswald enter and remarked, "Oh, you are in a hurry." Oswald did not respond. She described his pace as, "All but running." He entered the house in shirtsleeves but, as he left, he was zipping up a jacket. A few seconds later, she saw him standing at a bus shelter near the house. During her testimony, she was shown the shirt taken from Oswald at the time of his arrest and she said it looked like the one he had been wearing.

During the estimated three to four minutes Oswald was in his room, a police car pulled up in front of the house, according to Roberts, parked and honked the horn "tit tit." The fact that the police showed up at the same time Oswald was there is beyond coincidence. They were not there to investigate Oswald and the assassination. If they had been, they would have gone into the house and investigated.

Earlene Roberts had worked for some of the Dallas police and they would sometimes stop by in car 170, honk the horn, and deliver a message to her from their wives. But the car was not number 170 and she paid no attention to who was in it. She first told the FBI it was number 207 and later said it was number 107. She said it was a black car with two uniformed policemen in it, and that she saw it drive off. (As we will see, there may have been only one officer.) The car was not there for a social visit. Every police unit in Dallas was on high alert after the assassination that had taken place thirty minutes earlier. The tooting of the horn, as described, was not a proper police procedure, but is generally regarded as a signal between familiar parties that means, "we are here" or "come out." The fact that a police car happened to pull up to Oswald's rooming house—whose address was unknown to anyone but Marina and Mrs. Paine—during the very short time Oswald was there, adds more suspicion. Neither the police department nor the Book Depository had Oswald's address, yet the officer(s) in that car apparently did. The Warren Commission determined that there was no record of a police car in the area at that time. The incident raises high suspicions that the police visit was part of the assassination conspiracy.

Oswald was next seen about nine-tenths of a mile away from his rooming house

J. D. Tippit's police car, number ten, at the scene of his murder. Earlene Roberts thought the car that came to the house while Oswald was briefly there bore the number 107 or 207. She thought there were two officers in the car, but she may have mistaken the spare uniform seen in the back seat for a second officer. Source: Warren Commission, Exhibit 789

at the corner of Tenth Street and Patton Avenue, moments before the murder of police officer J. D. Tippit. A bystander used Tippit's radio to alert the police to his murder, which was recorded on a police headquarter's tape at about 1:16 p.m. A reconstruction demonstrated that if he had left his rooming house at 1:00 at a brisk pace, Oswald would have reached the murder scene in fifteen minutes—in time to commit Tippit's murder.[2457]

Was it J. D. Tippit—whom the Warren Commission determined was murdered by Oswald—who drove up to Oswald's rooming house and tooted his horn? It could have been, as Tippit was on patrol in Oak Cliff. While Earlene Roberts thought there were two officers in the car, they ordinarily carried only one. Photos of Tippit's police vehicle shown after his shooting show a spare police uniform hanging in the rear window that Roberts may have mistaken for another police officer. Although Roberts provided two different car numbers, she stated that the number on the visiting police car was not the number on Tippit's car. One of Robert's guesses as to the number of the police car she saw—107—was close to number ten, Tippit's car, and she did identify the car as having been the same type and color as Tippit's.

The Murder of J. D. Tippit

The Warren Commission determined that Oswald murdered police officer J. D. Tippit as Tippit tried to apprehend him. J. D. Tippit had joined the Dallas Police Department in 1952 and had a reputation of being "a very fine, dedicated officer." Some have claimed that the initials "J. D." stood for Jefferson Davis, the Mississippi senator who became president of the Confederacy in 1861. Others claim J. D. stood for nothing in particular.[2458] (Southerners were—and some still are—proud of their Confederate heritage, as was the case with the parents of Lee Harvey Oswald, who named him after General Robert E. Lee.)

Tippit patrolled District Seventy-eight, the Oak Cliff section of Dallas—solo—in a police car with "No. 10" displayed prominently on each side. President Kennedy was assassinated at 12:30 p.m. At 12:45, the police dispatcher ordered officer number seventy-eight, Tippit, to move into the central Oak Cliff area. At 12:54, Tippit radioed in that he was at Lancaster and Eighth. He was told to be alert for any emergency.

The Warren Commission decided that Tippit must have heard the radio description of the suspect, broadcast at 12:45 p.m., as being a "white male, approximately 30, slender build, height 5 foot 10 inches, weight 165 pounds," and, based on the description, would have suspected Oswald as he walked down the street. The description was so general that the Warren Commission's claim is questionable. It's also questionable that anyone would believe that the man who had just murdered the president would be out in public on foot. The Commission did not believe Oswald and Tippit knew each other. However, it's worth pointing out that Willie Somersett reported that—according to Joseph Milteer—J. D. Tippit was a part of the assassination conspiracy, as has been noted. Somersett's claims about the assassination have never been shown to be incorrect.

Tippit was about eight blocks from where he had last reported his location to the dispatcher when he encountered a man who was likely Lee Harvey Oswald. He was a hundred feet past the intersection of Tenth and Patton when he stopped a man walking and called him over to his car. The man reportedly approached the car and exchanged words with Tippit through the right (passenger-side) front or vent window. Tippit got out of the car to walk around to the front. As he reached the left (driver-side) front wheel, the man pulled out a revolver and fired several shots, killing Tippit instantly.

The man started back to Patton Avenue, ejecting the gun's empty cartridges before reloading. Tippit had apparently reached for his gun, which was found outside of his holster under his body. At least twelve people saw the man with the revolver in the vicinity of the crime. Six identified the man as Lee Harvey Oswald in a police lineup. Three others subsequently identified Oswald from a photograph. Two felt Oswald resembled the man they saw. Three saw the two men, heard the shots and saw Tippit fall.

William Scoggins, a cab driver, said he saw Tippit, heard the shots, and saw him fall over. He heard the shooter mutter, "Poor dumb cop" or "Poor damn cop" as the man ran past his cab. He later identified Oswald in a lineup as the man involved in the incident. Domingo Benavides saw a man standing on the left side of the police car, heard shots fired, and saw Tippit fall. He used Tippit's radio to call in the murder at 1:16 p.m. He could not identify the man who fired the shots. He noticed that Tippit had his gun in hand and had fallen on it.

Helen Markham witnessed the shooting. She saw a young man come to the right window of the car. As he talked, he leaned on the ledge of the right window. She saw the man step back as the policemen "calmly opened the door" and very slowly got out and walked to the front of the car. She saw the man pull a gun, heard three shots, and saw the officer fall to the ground. She described the gunman as "30, 5'8," black hair, slender." There were significant problems with Markham's accounts. She identified Oswald in a lineup.[2459]

The Capture of Lee Harvey Oswald

At 1:22 p.m., Dallas police radioed a description of Tippit's murderer as a male, thirty, five-foot-eight, black hair, slender, wearing a white jacket, white shirt, and slacks. After the shooting, two men saw the gunman run to the rear of a service station on Jefferson Boulevard, where a light-colored jacket was found in the parking lot, which was later identified by Marina Oswald as belonging to her husband. Witness accounts on the color of the jacket varied, but it is clear that when Oswald left the rooming house he had on a zipper jacket that he did not have on when he had arrived.

At 1:24 p.m., the police radio reported that the suspect was running west on Jefferson. The Texas Theater was about eight blocks from the Tippit murder scene in the direction he was running. Nearby was a shoe store. The store owner had heard about the murders of the president and a police officer and heard the sirens in the area. A man, whom the Commission would later determine was Oswald, entered the lobby of the shoe store. He had on a T-shirt, outer shirt, and no jacket. The storeowner thought he looked funny and scared. His hair was messed up. He looked like he had been running. The cashier of the nearby Texas Theater saw a man duck into the theater. She heard the sirens and walked to the curb to see what was going on. The suspicious shoe store owner had followed the suspect and was told by the cashier that the man entered the theater without paying for a ticket. The cashier called the police.

At 1:45 p.m., the police radio dispatcher stated that they had information on a suspect in the Texas Theater on Jefferson. Patrol cars carrying at least fifteen officers converged on the theater and entered from the front and rear. The shoe store owner pointed out Oswald to the police. Patrolman N. M. McDonald approached Oswald and told him to get on his feet with his hands up. As he began to search Oswald's waist for a gun, McDonald heard Oswald say, "Well, it's all over now." Oswald then punched McDonald in the left eye with his right fist and drew his gun with his left hand. A struggle ensued and what sounded like the snap of the hammer was heard. (Most of the officers present said they heard the click of the hammer from Oswald's revolver. The Warren Commission determined that Oswald tried to shoot the officer but the handgun misfired.[2460]) Oswald was subdued, handcuffed, and taken to the police station.

While in the police car, Oswald said, "I don't know why you are treating me like this. The only thing I have done is carry a pistol in a movie." Officer Hill replied, "you have done a lot more, you have killed a policeman." Oswald responded, "You can only fry for that."[2461] When Oswald was arrested, the gun he carried was found to be a Smith and Wesson .38 revolver. Four cartridges were found in the bushes near where Tippet had been shot, and the cartridges were determined to be from Oswald's pistol to the exclusion of all others. The bullets fired from the pistol were slightly smaller than the rechambered barrel, causing an erratic passage through the barrel, which left inconsistent markings on the lead. The bullets could have been fired by Oswald's pistol, but the bullet evidence was inconclusive. The Warren Commission found that Oswald had purchased the revolver by mail order from a Los Angeles company using the name A. J. Hidell, on January 28, 1963. He wore the same pistol in a holster in the infamous backyard photos.[2462]

The Interrogation of Lee Harvey Oswald

Will Fritz, head of the Dallas police homicide and robbery division, interrogated Oswald on the third floor of the Records Building adjacent to the Dallas Police Department, beginning at 2:25 p.m. on November 22. Intermittently, FBI and Secret Service agents joined him. He kept no notes during the approximately twelve hours of questioning, which took place over the forty-eight-hour period of Oswald's captivity before his murder. Oswald repeatedly lied during the interrogation, and made factually correct statements at other times. Throughout the questioning, Oswald maintained his persona as a leftist. Oswald carried identification in the name of Lee Harvey Oswald, as well as A. J. Hidell.

Lee Harvey Oswald helped investigators tie the assassination rifle to him by carrying phony identification (right) in the name of Alek James Hidell. Since Oswald purchased the rifle by mail from Klein's Sporting Goods in Chicago, in the name of A. Hidell (left), they would have had a tougher time tracing it to Oswald had he not unnecessarily carried the Hidell picture identification card to work. Source: Warren Commission

Oswald told Fritz about his upbringing and his service in the marines. Oswald said he was having a cheese sandwich and a Coke with other employees when the shooting happened, and that he left work because there was so much excitement that he did not think there would be any work that day. He denied owning a rifle. He said that, after he left, he caught a bus to his rooming house, changed his clothes, got his gun, and went to the movies. When told about the cab driver's statement to the police (that he had carried Oswald from the bus station to within blocks of his home), Oswald later admitted to taking a cab. Oswald said the only thing he had done wrong was striking the police officer in the movie theater. After that he maintained his charade as a Communist. When asked if he belonged to the Communist Party, he denied having a card but gratuitously offered that he belonged to the Fair Play for Cuba Committee and paid $25.00 in dues to the ACLU. He told them, "I am a Marxist but not a Leninist-Marxist."[2463] He said he was in favor of the Cuban revolution. Oswald asked for New York attorney John Abt, noting that Abt had defended people in violation of the Smith Act—which was well known at the time. FBI agent James Hosty, who had contacted Oswald in the past in regard to his stay in the Soviet Union, broke in the interrogation and asked him about Russia and Mexico City. Oswald became angry, threw a tantrum, and beat on the desk. He denied being in Mexico City, but admitted having lived in Russia.

Oswald was arraigned by a judge for the murder of J. D. Tippit at 7:10 p.m. On further questioning, Oswald was sarcastic, irritable, and impudent. He denied carrying curtain rods—or any long package—to work. He denied reloading his gun after shooting Tippit. He told the interrogators that he picked up the name A. J. Hidell in New Orleans, but did not want to talk about it. He said he was having lunch with Depository employees Junior and another boy when the president was shot. He said he purchased his pistol six to seven months earlier in Fort Worth, which was untrue. When asked what he thought about President Kennedy, he gave no comment other than he thought Kennedy had a nice family. He denied killing the president, adding that there would be a new president in a few days and people would forget about it.[2464] Late Friday night, after an impromptu news, conference Oswald shouted to reporters, "I'm just a patsy," which may indicate he was beginning to lose his resolve.

Police officers brought the backyard photos of Oswald posing with the rifle and gun—that they had found in Ruth Paine's garage—back to the jail and showed them to him on Saturday afternoon. Oswald claimed the photos were fakes and that someone had taken pictures of his face and put it on a different body. He denied living on Neely Street where the photos were taken, which was another lie. Saturday afternoon he reassured his wife that everything would be fine. When his brother Robert told him, on Saturday afternoon, that the police had his pistol and rifle and that he had been charged with shooting the president and Tippit, Lee told him, "Don't believe all this so-called evidence."[2465]

Officer Fritz told the Warren Commission that he did not ask Oswald about the Walker shooting incident. The Commission asked Fritz for his overall impression of Oswald. He stated, "He acted like a person who was prepared for what he was doing."[2466] Fritz was asked if Oswald was afraid, and he responded, "No, sir; I don't believe he was at all." Fritz added that he did not think Oswald was a nut and that he had above-average intelligence.[2467]

On Sunday, November 24, Joseph Milteer remarked to Willie Somersett that Oswald had not said anything and he would not say anything, as was noted in Chapter Four.

Willie Somersett and J. D. Tippit

Was J. D. Tippit involved in the assassination conspiracy? Willie Somersett said he was. Somersett told Miami police intelligence that Tippit, Theodore "Ted" Jackman, and R. E. Davis were the actual shooters of the president. Somersett did not elaborate, and nothing more is known about the allegation.

Dealing with an allegation like Somersett's—from a single source, without any other witness corroboration—is problematic. However, Somersett has never been shown to have given false or misleading information before. What's more, anyone who had advance knowledge of the plot to kill President Kennedy (and, later, Martin Luther King, Jr.), as Somersett did, deserves to be taken very seriously. What strengthens Somersett's allegation is that Jackman and Davis, the other two named gunmen, were associates of General Walker. A letter from General del Valle to General Walker (noted in Chapter Eight) recommended Jackman to General Walker as a man who could provide him with pictures and names of individuals—presumably those who were targeted in the Congress of Freedom assassination plots.

It's worth noting that Somersett never implicated Walker in the Kennedy assassination. He identified Walker only as a military leader of the hardcore underground. Nor did Somersett identify Jackman and Davis as associates of General Walker. However, the author made the connection from documents unrelated to Somersett.

Further strengthening Somersett's claim about Jackman as a shooter is the fact that Jackman spoke at the infamous 1963 Congress of Freedom meeting in New Orleans, where the broad-based assassination plots targeting members of the Council of Foreign Relations, Jews, and others took place. Walker's close friend, Clyde Watts, was also a speaker at that meeting. Guy Banister, Joseph Milteer, and Kent Courtney were three other Walker associates who were present at the Congress of Freedom meeting.

Milteer's friend Grady Bartlett had tape recorded a Menlo Park, California, speech given by Jackman in 1963 and mentioned it in a letter to Milteer. In the letter, he told Milteer that Strom Thurmond would be a good choice to run on the Constitution Party ticket for president, with John Rousselot as his vice president. Rousselot was also a friend of General Walker's, and credible allegations that he was involved in the assassination conspiracy will be presented later.[2468, 2469] Jackman and Milteer shared the same taste for violence and the use of explosives. On December 20, 1964, Milteer wrote Jackman a letter, stating, "I have been advised you have something working new that is dynamite, (TNT) (Atomic) or whatever is stronger. How about sending me something so that I can learn first hand of what you have? Thanks for your kindness."[2470]

In May 1965, the FBI learned from Jimmy Burden, from Halton City, Texas, that an individual named George Hale was an apparent associate of both General Walker and Ted Jackman. Hale invited Burden to his home, where he berated Negroes and Jews—whom he called "the plague of the world." Hale told his guest of a map prepared by Ted Jackman that showed the location of caves in Oklahoma that held storehouses of food to be used when the end of the world came—presumably when the takeover by the aforementioned Negroes and

Jews began. Hale showed Burden a list of phone numbers, including General Walker's.[2471]

As we shall see later, the FBI had numerous reports that Walker was forming an "army of insurrection" after the assassination. As a result, FBI director J. Edgar Hoover repeatedly sent notices to the Secret Service under the presidential protection agreement notifying them that General Walker was a threat to the life of President Johnson.

Ted Jackman was a member of the John Birch Society's *American Opinion* speakers' bureau in 1962.[2472] General Walker had a flier in his personal papers advertising an anti-Communist speech by Jackman, complete with his photo. The flier was on photographic paper, perhaps suggesting it was a template for duplication.[2473] Given Jackman's association with the Constitution Party plots, as well as with Milteer, Walker, and Del Valle, Somersett's allegation that Jackman was one of the shooters of the president deserves to be taken seriously.

A picture of Theodore "Ted" Jackman on a flier on photographic paper was found in Walker's personal papers. Willie Somersett named Theodore Jackman, an associate of General Walker, as one of the Dealey Plaza gunmen. Source: Edwin A. Walker Papers, Dolph Briscoe Center for American History, University of Texas at Austin

Roy Elonza "R. E." Davis was another individual named by Somersett as a shooter. Somersett also mentioned Davis in connection with the Constitution Party plots and Milteer's November 9, 1963, statements that the assassination of President Kennedy was in the works before the murder happened. Somersett later identified Davis as a shooter after the assassination.[2474]

In 1961, the New Orleans *Times–Picayune* reported that R. E. Davis was the national Imperial Wizard of the Original Knights of the Ku Klux Klan and was organizing in Shreveport and northwestern Louisiana. Davis said he had more than 1,000 men in the Shreveport area. He stated that blacks "are turning the white man's government into a mongrel government" and that the Klan "is not going to let them do it regardless of what this statement may imply."[2475, 2476] Davis was also a member of the Dallas Indignant White Citizens' Council—which was described as "an extremist organization composed of people opposing integration of the races" and was formed on July 20, 1963, in Grand Prairie, Texas, by Bobbie Savelle Joiner. (Joiner, along with friends and family members, demonstrated at the Dallas Trade Mart, where the president was scheduled to speak after the motorcade through Dealey Plaza. They were arrested for suspicion of conspiracy and trespassing and later released.) Robert Hatfield, another member of the Indignant White Citizens' Council, as well as the John Birch Society and "General Walker's group," had been previously arrested for spitting on U.N. Ambassador Adlai Stevenson in October 1963.[2477, 2478] As was noted in the last chapter, while President Kennedy was bracing for a possible Walker-led riot during Martin Luther King, Jr.'s March on Washington, General Walker and Robert Surrey instead joined Bobbie Savelle Joiner's protest march in Austin, Texas, against the March on Washington. Cora Fredrickson, a member of the Walker group and General Walker's John Birch Society chapter, was a member of the Dallas Indignant White Citizens' Council, like

Davis and Joiner.[2479] It will also be recalled from the last chapter that Fredrickson struck Adlai Stevenson with a placard during his October visit to the city.

On June 16, 1965, one of Guy Banister's best friends, Alvin Cobb, appeared before the Joint Legislative Committee on Un-American Activities for the State of Louisiana and was questioned by council Jack N. Rogers on his activities in the Knights of the White Camellia, a Klan organization which appeared on the attorney general's list of subversive organizations. (Banister had been an investigator for the Committee.) Rogers stated that all the members had completely gone underground. Interestingly enough, of the four distinct Klan organizations in Louisiana, the largest was the Original Knights of the Ku Klux Klan, which was headed by the Imperial Wizard, who was identified as "a man named Davis from Dallas, Texas."[2480] Davis appears to be one and the same as R. E. Davis.

Davis was a subject of a Secret Service investigation, based on Somersett's allegations. When the author requested documents from the Secret Service on their investigation of Davis, pursuant to the Freedom of Information Act, they responded that the documents had been destroyed.[2481] The author independently established that Davis was the Imperial Dragon (national leader) of the Dallas Ku Klux Klan. An article in the Klan newsletter *The Fiery Cross*, written by Davis—who was also the editor—noted that he was an avid deer hunter.[2482] (Davis died on August 8, 1966, at Oak Cliff Medical and Surgical Hospital, of natural causes at the age of seventy-six. His death certificate lists his occupation as a minister.[2483])

The Dallas police had the names of Dallas Ku Klux Klan members, including Davis, and had investigated them to see if they planned anything embarrassing during President Kennedy's visit.[2484] It's impossible to know what roles, if any, the three men named by Somersett—Tippit, Jackman, and Davis—had in the shooting. Davis may have been too old to shoot Oswald's rifle, scamper down the rear stairs, and go out the back door of the Book Depository. Tippit may have been more useful somewhere other than the Book Depository. That leaves Jackman, who in the end may have been the murderer of President Kennedy.

The Warren Commission never had the opportunity to examine the Secret Service's investigation of R. E. Davis, which stemmed from Somersett's informing on Milteer and the hardcore underground. Of course, the Warren Commission did not have the voluminous files on Milteer and the radical right's plan to kill the president. The HSCA had access to them, but did not review them or did not appreciate what they contained. Taken together, with the suspicion that it was Tippit that tooted his horn at Oswald's rooming house—when he had no legitimate reason to be there—his unlikely encounter with Oswald, and his murder, there is good reason to suspect that J. D. Tippit was involved in some way in the assassination conspiracy.

Early Warren Commission critic and author Sylvia Meagher aptly described J. D. Tippit as "unknown and unknowable."[2485] Tippit was considered a hero who gave his life in pursuit of the president's assassin. There was a tremendous national outpouring of sympathy for his widow and children, and they received one hundred thousand dollars in donations from the public in the weeks following the assassination. Accordingly, the Warren Commission treated the Tippit matter with kid gloves, authorizing a "limited" investigation. What little the Commission reported about him was that he moonlighted on weekends at Austin's Barbeque in Dallas. Tippit worked on Friday and Saturday nights from 10 p.m. to 2 a.m. for three years before the assassination, keeping an eye out for teen-age troublemakers who frequented the establishment. The Warren Commission noted that Tippit's employer, Austin Cook, was a member of the John Birch Society, but Cook told investigators that he never discussed politics with Tippit.[2486]

The author interviewed Paul Rothermel, H. L. Hunt's security chief, and Rothermel stated that he gave a speech to the John Birch Society at Austin's Barbeque, where they held their meetings. Rothermel felt the speech did not go well, because the crowd did not feel he was "right-winged enough."[2487] More significant than working for a member of the John Birch Society was the fact that Tippit worked at the place where the Dallas John Birch Society held their meetings—a fact not noted by the Commission, which is revealed for the first time by the author from the interview with Rothermel. General Walker was Dallas's best-known John Birch Society member. As had been noted, Walker aide Robert Surrey and Surrey's wife Mary founded the Dallas John Birch Society chapter. Tippit's part-time work at Austin's, where the John Birch Society held their meetings, afforded him the opportunity to associate with Walker and members of his group during Walker's two-and-one-half-year rise to power, following his 1961 return from Germany.

It's pure speculation as to what Tippit's motives were for stopping Oswald. Perhaps he thought Oswald might be the assassin. It doesn't seem reasonable that anyone would suspect that the man—who had forty-five minutes earlier shot the president—would be walking around the streets of Dallas. Oswald was an ordinary-looking man. The description of the president's assassin given on the police radio was ordinary and could have applied to a large section of the general population.

Perhaps Tippit was part of the conspiracy, and wanted to assure Oswald that the killing of the president was a mistake, an accident, or the renegade action of one of the conspirators. Perhaps he wanted to persuade Oswald to go along with getting arrested and to continue with the original scheme, at the same time assuring him he would be exonerated. Perhaps Tippit wanted to kill him to silence him.

The Dealey Plaza Witnesses

Several witnesses saw a man with a rifle at the farthest east window of the Texas School Book Depository. None identified him as Lee Harvey Oswald. As we have discussed, the Warren Commission determined that that was the location from which the shooting took place and dubbed it "the sniper's nest."

Sixteen-year-old Amos Euins was standing in front of the Book Depository and saw what looked like a pipe extending out the window. He heard four shots. The only feature of the man in the window—where he saw the pipe-like object—that he could discern, was a bald spot on his head. Euins told motorcycle police officer D. V. Harkness, who stood just west of the Depository, what he saw. The officer told him to get on the back of his motorcycle, and they rode up to the front of the Book Depository. Harkness radioed in a call for men to surround the Depository. While Euins was waiting to give his statement about what he had witnessed, he overheard a construction worker—who had been behind the Depository—tell the police he saw a man with a bald spot on his head run out the back.[2488] (Oswald did not have a bald spot on his head.)

Harkness placed Euins in Inspector J. Herbert Sawyer's car parked in front of the Book Depository, so he could question him later. Sawyer had checked the perimeter of the building, and then stood at the front of the Depository, where information from witnesses and other officers was funneled to him. It's not clear whom the construction worker gave the information to, Sawyer or Harkness. In the chaos of the moment, Sawyer and Harkness could not recall all of the names or witnesses they talked to. Euins told the Commission, "Another man told him he had seen a man run out the back." Euins did not know who the man was. He told them, "He was a construction man working back there. . . . He said the man—he said he had kind of a bald spot on his head. And he said the man come back there." It is not clear if Euins was in the car, or at the front of the Depository with Harkness, when he overheard the construction worker's account.[2489]

Robert Jackson, staff photographer for the *Dallas Times Herald*, told officials that he saw a rifle, but could not identify the person with it. He heard three shots.[2490]

Arnold Rowland and his wife arrived in Dealey Plaza early to watch the motorcade. Rowland raised the subject of the recent violence encountered by Adlai Stevenson and talked to his wife about security measures taken for the president. At 12:15 or 12:20 p.m., Rowland observed a man standing ten to fifteen feet back from a Book Depository window holding a rifle—which appeared to be a .306 rifle with a telescopic sight—in the southwest corner of the Book Depository nearest the overpass and opposite the sniper's nest. He remarked to his wife that the man with the rifle must have been a Secret Service agent. The man held the rifle diagonally across his chest, in the "port arms" position, as the military called it. Rowland described the man as a slender white male with dark hair with "a light colored shirt, open at the neck." He saw the man momentarily and then he seemed to disappear in the shadows of the sixth floor of the Book Depository. Fifteen minutes later, the motorcade passed and Rowland heard the shots. He did not look up at the Book Depository. Rowland told the FBI that he was too far away to identify the man, and could not say whether he was Lee Harvey Oswald.[2491]

James Crawford, a deputy district clerk for Dallas County, watched the parade from the southeast corner of Houston and Elm. After hearing three shots, he saw a movement in the southeastern window of the Book Depository, the only window that was open on the sixth floor. He saw a very light-colored, indistinct figure. He told a coworker standing with him that if the sounds were shots, they came from that window.[2492]

Howard Brennan was sitting on a concrete railing directly across from the Book Depository, 120 feet from the sixth-floor window, when he saw a man come and go, a couple of times, in the southeasternmost sixth-floor window. He heard a backfire or firecracker, looked up and saw the same man fire the last shot, withdraw the weapon, and disappear. Brennan said he heard two shots. The Warren Commission determined Brennan's description most probably led to the radio alert sent to police cars at approximately 12:45 p.m., which described the suspect as "white, slender, weighing about 165 pounds, about 5'10" tall, and in his early thirties." (Lee Harvey Oswald was twenty-four years old, 5'9" tall, and weighed 136 to 150 pounds.) The man in the window was wearing "light-colored clothes, more of a khaki color." Brennan was called to view a lineup of suspects at the police department that included Lee Harvey Oswald. In spite of seeing a picture of Oswald on television, he could not pick Oswald out in the lineup.[2493, 2494]

Ronald Fischer and Robert Edwards were standing near Brennan during the shooting. Just before the motorcade arrived, Edwards pointed out a man in the Depository window to Fisher. "Look at that guy there in the window," he told him. Fisher said the man wore a light-colored, open-neck shirt, either a sport shirt or T-shirt, had brown hair, was slender, and appeared to between twenty-two and twenty-four years old, and was looking at the triple underpass. After seeing a picture of Oswald, Fisher was not sure the man he had seen was Oswald, but said it could have been. Edwards described the man as average-sized, possibly thin, with light brown hair, wearing a light-colored sports shirt. Neither man saw a weapon.[2495]

Carolyn Walther was standing on the east side of Houston Street about fifty or sixty feet from the south curb of Elm Street. She saw a man on the fourth or fifth floor of the Depository at the southeasternmost window, leaning out the window with a rifle. The barrel was short and the stock seemed large and round, giving her the impression it was a machine gun. The man was wearing a white shirt and had blonde or light brown hair. She saw a second man standing in the window next to him, wearing a brown suit coat, but could not see his face. She was positive the window was not as high as the sixth floor. After the president passed by, she walked away and heard four or more shots. She did not see were they came from.[2496]

The six aforementioned witnesses, who saw a man in the upper floor window of the Book Depository, all described him as wearing a white or light-colored shirt, while Lee Harvey Oswald was wearing a dark burgundy plaid shirt on the day of the assassination. Perhaps he took it off for the shooting and put it back on after. Or perhaps another man, dressed in a white or light-colored shirt, did the shooting.[2497]

James Worrell, Jr. was a nineteen-year-old high school senior who cut class to see the president. He was standing four to five feet in front of the Book Depository, in the area of Elm and Houston, when he heard a shot and looked up and saw six inches of a rifle sticking out of the easternmost fifth-floor or sixth-floor window, the area of the sniper's nest. The next day, he saw a plea from law enforcement in the newspaper for any witnesses to the shooting to come forth and give their account to the Dallas police. Worrell told them that, after the first shot, he looked up and saw the rifle fire during the second and third shots. Each gave off a little flash of fire and smoke. He became frightened and figured the safest place to go was the rear of the Depository. He stated that, after the fourth shot, he ran north up Houston toward the rear of Depository. He crossed Houston at an angle and rested for three minutes to catch his breath and saw a man "bustling out of this [back] door." The man was running the whole time Worrell saw him. He identified the man as 5'7" to 5'10," in his late twenties or early thirties, weighing 155 to 165, with black or brunette hair. Worrell said he did not see the man's face, but saw him only in profile. He wore a dark-colored sport jacket. On a second interview, Worrell told the FBI the man resembled Lee Harvey Oswald—although it could not have been Oswald, since it was established that he went out the front door. Later, in his testimony to the Warren Commission, Worrell said he could not identify the man as Lee Harvey Oswald since he only saw him in profile.[2498]

The FBI tested the assassination rifle and noted it did give off a small amount of smoke and an orange flame during firing, but the flame was only visible in a dark or darkened room, not in daylight. They did not simulate the rifle firing from the Book Depository and look for a flame in the setting of the overcast conditions on the day of the assassination, or from Worrell's position in front of the Depository.[2499]

James Romack was eating lunch on the Missouri, Kansas, and Texas railroad dock, facing Houston Street and the rear of the Book Depository, when he heard the shots. He did not come forth and share his observations with law enforcement until March 6, 1964, after he read about James Worrell's Warren Commission testimony in the *Dallas Times Herald* about the man "bustling out" the back door of the Book Depository after the shooting. At that time, Romack telephoned the FBI and said that he was in a position to observe the back door the whole time and Worrell's story couldn't be true.[2500] Romack told the Warren Commission that he was 100-125 yards behind the northeast rear corner of the Book Depository, eating lunch and "piddling around" the loading dock, when he heard three shots, high up, which—as a hunter—he recognized as rifle shots. Immediately, he saw a policeman running north up Houston toward him to see if anyone was running out the back of the building then the officer left. The Commission corroborated the sighting of the police officer and identified him as Charles Barnett. Sensing something was wrong, Barnett stated he immediately watched the rear of the Depository from the time of the shots and said no one left the building.

Unlike Worrell's fresh account, which was given within twenty-four hours of the shooting, Romack's recollection was three and a half months old. Romack could not have known, in the ninety seconds after he heard the first shot, that the president was shot and the assassin was in the building in front of him. Therefore, it is unlikely that he was carefully looking to see if an assassin was exiting the rear of the Book Depository. Was he watching the rear door after the first shots or was he still eating lunch, piddling around, or preoccupied with the later pandemonium going on at the intersection of Houston and Elm visible from his position?

The Shots

The number—and direction—of the shots fired in Dealey Plaza is a matter of tremendous controversy and an attempt to iron out that contentious problem will not be made here.

Scores of books have been written, which have been critical of the Warren Commission and HSCA conclusions about the shots which were fired. Few, if any, agree exactly on the number and the direction of the shots, and they all illustrate the human limits on determining the exact nature of a complex event. The Warren Commission interviewed 171 people who were present in Dealey Plaza. Seventy said they did not know where the shots came from. Forty-six said they came from the Book Depository. Twenty said they came from the grassy knoll. Twenty-nine said they came from somewhere other than the Book Depository or grassy knoll.[2501]

The Warren Commission determined that three shots were fired. The first shot struck the president from above and behind, indicating it came from the direction the Book Depository. The bullet entered the president in his right back, near the base of his neck, and exited his throat. According to Secret Service agent Roy Kellerman, after the first shot, he saw the president's arms lurch up and he heard him say, "My God, I am hit." Another shot—which was also determined to be from above and behind the president—was fired and tore the president's head open. The Warren Commission determined this bullet entered the right rear of the president's head and exited from the right temple of the head, leaving a large wound. The third shot missed.

Afterward, Mrs. Kennedy cradled her mortally wounded husband and said, "Oh. My God, they have shot my husband." Blood and tissue was splattered on the seats. Mrs. Kennedy crawled on the trunk of the limousine and attempted to retrieve a fragment of the president's skull. Governor Connally, sitting in a jump seat in front of the president, insisted he heard the first shot and was hit in the back by the second shot. He exclaimed in the limousine, "Oh no, no, no. My God they are going to kill us all," as the Secret Service rushed them off on the four-mile journey to Parkland Hospital.

The Wounds

At Parkland Hospital, the president was taken into trauma room number one. A massive head wound, with a sizable portion of tissue missing, was discovered with what initially appeared to be a bullet entrance wound in the throat. A tracheotomy was done to assist the president's breathing through the bullet hole, which altered the medical evidence of the shooting. The president's back was not examined at the hospital, and they missed the back wound (which was found at autopsy). Dr. William Clark examined the president's head, and other than the large gaping wound, found no bullet holes. At 1:00 p.m., the president was pronounced dead.

Governor Connally was taken to trauma room number two, where he was found to have an entrance wound in the left rear thorax, a shattered rib, and a large sucking wound in the front of his chest. According to the Warren Commission, the same bullet, upon exiting his chest, fractured Connally's right wrist and entered his left thigh about five inches above the knee. Connally was taken to surgery and survived.

A "nearly pristine" bullet was found on the stretcher of Governor Connally. It was determined that the pristine bullet was fired from above and from the rear of the president, entered his posterior neck and exited his throat, then entered Connally's chest, fractured a rib, and entered his wrist, where it fractured the bone and then entered his thigh, from which it fell out onto his gurney. Small bullet fragments were found in Connally's wrist.

Critics have held that it was impossible for the pristine bullet to cause the wounds to the president and the wounds (including bone fractures) to Connally—leaving behind both fragments and a nearly completely intact bullet. Critics have mockingly called the single bullet theory, the "magic bullet theory."

The president's body was flown to Washington, D.C., where an autopsy was done at Bethesda Naval Medical Center. A six-by-fifteen millimeter wound was found an inch to the right and slightly above his external occipital protrusion (or just above the hairline at the base of the skull). A second head wound measured five inches at its greatest width, but was difficult to measure because of multiple crisscross fractures radiating from the large wound.

A portion of the president's skull which was recovered from the Elm Street grassy median was brought in for examination. Thirty to forty tiny lead fragments were found in a line along the bullet's path. Two small, irregularly shaped fragments were recovered from the head. A second wound, determined to be an entrance from the first shot, was found in his right upper back. The doctors who completed the autopsy concluded that the second bullet exited through the throat wound. The autopsy was poorly conducted, however, and was rife with uncertainties and inconsistencies that will not be discussed here. X-rays and photographs were taken at the autopsy, but were not used by the doctors who performed the autopsy—or by the Warren Commission—to make their determinations. There was a fear that any such evidence might find its way to the public and would result in an invasion of privacy.[2502]

The Zapruder film of the assassination was kept from the public until March 1976, when it was first shown on television. The film appeared to show that the president was struck in the side of the skull, which moved him backward and to the left, suggesting a frontal shot, which was contrary to the Warren Commission's assertion that he was shot from the rear (from Oswald's position). Growing public skepticism about the Warren Commission's findings led to the formation of government panels in 1968 and 1975 that reviewed the autopsy, photos, and x-rays. The panels drew the same conclusions as the Warren Commission. There were significant and troubling discrepancies among the reports of what the Parkland Hospital doctors saw, the findings of the autopsy doctors, and, later, the HSCA forensic panel.

The House Select Committee on Assassinations, in 1978, assembled a medical panel to review the medical evidence. The panel determined that only two bullets struck the president. The first entered the back and exited the throat. The second entered the lower back of the head and exited the front side of the head to the right. The HSCA panel found a semicircular beveled defect in the skull to be certain evidence of a bullet entrance wound in the back of the head. They decided that the wound was actually four inches higher, in the cowlick in the upper back of the head, rather than lower down in the occipital protuberance where the autopsy doctors saw it. The HSCA panel gave their differing opinion solely based on the x-rays and photos of the autopsy. They found no evidence that any bullet entered from the front of Kennedy. They concluded that the nerve damage from the shot which hit his head—not a frontal or grassy knoll shot—caused the neck muscles to tighten up, resulting in the backward motion of the head seen on the Zapruder film. The HSCA also validated the single bullet theory that one bullet caused both Kennedy's throat wound and all the wounds of Governor Connally.

The claim that the jerking backward of the head represented a neuromuscular reflex due to the rear head entrance of the bullet was contrived. A similar neuromuscular reaction has never been reported elsewhere in the chronicles of medicine. Newton's third law of motion is inviolate and dictates that the head should have moved forward—not backward as was the case—from a shot from the rear to the back of the head. In the end, however, the unsupported theory of a neuromuscular reaction trumped the laws of physics.[2503]

There are significant problems with the determination of the location of the bullet hole in the head. A bullet hole is a 360-degree round, vacuous area in the bone or scalp of the head. None was found either at autopsy or on x-rays of the president. What the Warren Commission incorrectly called a "bullet hole" was a small, slightly semicircular defect along the irregular fracture margin of skull bone. Its semicircular shape and beveling were the only features of the defect that led to the conclusion it was part of a bullet hole. Those features can also be produced by the way a bone happens to fracture. The irregular area was beveled, or "shelved," inward. At best, the defect could have represented less than half a bullet hole. The rest of the purported hole was never identified elsewhere in the skull bone x-rays. Gunshot wounds to the head (although not from high-powered rifles) are common in the U.S. None of the investigating bodies have ever demonstrated a semicircular defect along the margin of a skull fracture line from a bullet in any other murder case. It is one-of-a-kind evidence, without precedent, and cannot be relied on to represent an actual bullet entrance wound.

The HSCA analyzed a tape recording of a radio transmission from the microphone of one of the police motorcycle escorts of the shooting in Dealey Plaza. The Warren Commission did not know the tape existed. Acoustic experts determined the first, second, and fourth shots came from the Book Depository. The third—according to these experts—came from the grassy knoll, located to the front right of the president. The HSCA determined, however, that the third shot missed the president. Based on the shot analysis, they concluded there were two gunmen and, therefore, there was a conspiracy in the murder of President Kennedy.

The problem with the acoustics analysis was that it was a one-of-a-kind examination, with no statistical degree of accuracy and no track record.[2504] The forensic and autopsy evidence does not exclude either a head shot from the front or the involvement of two or more shooters.

Conclusions

The president had ample warning that Dallas was a dangerous place for him to visit. Unfortunately, as noted, the Dallas Secret Service were not apprised of Joseph Milteer's information that a hardcore underground existed, which was intent on killing the president—and that a plot to shoot him from a tall building with a high-powered rifle was in the works. Dallas authorities were not aware of the information that there had been a plan to shoot the president from a palm tree on an earlier visit to Miami on November 18, 1963.

The evidence suggests that Lee Harvey Oswald expected to get arrested on the day of the assassination, a fact which was not appreciated by the official investigations, and it was not something new for him. He had also expected to get arrested after the phony April 1963 Walker shooting incident and was, in fact, arrested after the phony "fight" in New Orleans in August with Carlos Bringuier. Walker and Bringuier, like Oswald, both had ties to Guy Banister, a fanatical anti-Communist. Oswald left his wedding ring behind in a cup, along with 170 dollars—likely their entire savings—for his wife on the morning of the assassination, which is also evidence that suggests he expected to get arrested that day.

The behavior of Lee Harvey Oswald around the time of the assassination was consistent with a willing man who believed he was engaging in a phony shoot-and-miss scheme similar to the one he had participated in with General Walker earlier in the year. Oswald was aware of two violence-related stunts contrived by General Walker, including both the Walker shooting incident and the assault of Adlai Stevenson. Being asked to take part in another one, during the president's visits to Dallas, would not have seemed strange to him.

Acting was not new for Oswald. He had acted the part of a Communist at age sixteen, during his sojourn to the Soviet Union, in the Walker shooting incident, during his leafleting exploits in New Orleans on behalf of his non-existent chapter of Fair Play for Cuba, and at the Cuban and Soviet Embassies. Oswald left behind a large amount of self-incriminating evidence on the day of the assassination—so much so that it appears deliberate—just as he had in the Walker shooting incident. Oswald unnecessarily advertised his rifle by carrying the rifle-sized paper package to work—in front of coworker Wesley Frazier—on the morning of the assassination, when he could have made other arrangements. He facilitated the tracing of the rifle to him, bought under the alias A. Hidell, by needlessly carrying the A. J. Hidell identification card that allowed for the identification of Oswald as the assassination rifle's owner. He committed a number of acts which an adept, rational assassin would not have done. He lingered in the Texas School Book Depository, instead of immediately fleeing the scene, risking arrest from officer Marrion Baker. Given a second chance for flight, he decided to drink a Coke, instead. When he did decide to leave, he chose to walk out the front door, on to Dealey Plaza, into the mass of parade watchers and law enforcement. At some point, when it became apparent to everyone in Dealey Plaza—as well as the driver of the bus Oswald left the Depository on—that the president had been shot, Oswald's demeanor turned from calm and collected to frantic. He then displayed the behavior of a man running for his life, something he apparently had not anticipated, since he had not provided himself with the funds to sustain flight when he could have.

The visit of the police car to Oswald's rooming house at the same time he was there—when no one besides his wife and Ruth Paine knew its address—is beyond coincidence and suggests the officer involved was part of the assassination conspiracy. The encounter between

J. D. Tippit and Oswald shortly afterward suggests it was Tippit who visited Oswald's rooming house and that Tippit was part of the conspiracy. Since Tippit's gun was drawn when he
was killed, it is possible it was his intention to kill Oswald—first at his rooming house and
then shortly after when he found him walking down the street. The fact that Tippit worked
for a member of the John Birch Society, at the restaurant where they held their meetings,
adds more suspicion. Willie Somersett's claim that Tippit was involved in the assassination
conspiracy makes it all the more likely.

While under arrest, Oswald was arrogant and displayed a sense of invincibility, suggesting he may have felt he would be exonerated. Although he was not actually a Communist,
Oswald kept up with the charade of acting like one when he asked for famed Communist
defender, John Abt. Affecting an association with Abt was better for advancing his image as a
Communist than for establishing his innocence. If Oswald had been assured and was confident that another rifle would be used in the shooting incident and the ballistics of the bullets
that were fired would fail to match his rifle, then he would have had no worries. Unfortunately for Oswald, that never happened. He was murdered the day before the FBI determined, on
Monday, November 25, that the bullets matched his rifle. Under that scenario, had he lived
to learn that the bullets matched his rifle, he would have realized that he had been used as a
patsy and was a dead duck. He'd have had no reason to continue to play the game and spare
the others who set him up.

No one saw Oswald do the shooting. Six witnesses who saw a man with a rifle in the
Book Depository said the mystery man was wearing a white or light-colored shirt. Oswald
wore a dark burgundy shirt over a T-shirt on the day of the assassination, and was arrested in
the same clothing. Very serious consideration must be given to Willie Somersett's allegation
that J. D. Tippit, Ted Jackman and R. E. Davis were the actual shooters of the president.
Tippit's ties to the Dallas John Birch Society, whose most celebrated Dallas leader was General Walker, afforded him a connection to Walker. Both Jackman and Davis were members
of Walker's group, as identified by evidence independent of the information obtained from
Willie Somersett.

There were two reports that a man left the Book Depository via the back door right
after the shooting. One witness saw a man bustling out, who kept running. However, within
a few hours after the shooting, investigators felt they had their man, and they knew he left
the building from the front entrance. The man who left through the back door was never
identified.

Although there is no direct evidence to show that Oswald thought he was getting
involved in a harmless shoot-and-miss gambit, it is the only scenario that has been proposed
that explains his peculiar behavior. He was neither inept nor a martyr. As fictional detective
Sherlock Holmes famously asserted, "Once you eliminate the impossible, whatever remains,
no matter how improbable, must be the truth." Considering Oswald's involvement in a shoot-
and-miss scheme in the Walker shooting incident, it is hardly improbable to suggest that he
thought he was participating in a similar operation during the president's visit.

In 1967, the probate attorney for Jack Ruby's estate, Alan Adelson, asked Sheriff Bill Decker for a tour of the sixth floor of the Book Depository. Decker pointed out the location where the rifle was found, "right in the open," and the site of Oswald's nearby clipboard. The attorney remarked, "It sure seemed as if he wanted to be discovered, leaving his clipboard and his rifle so close together."[2505]

The point of marshaling evidence that suggests that Oswald did not do the shooting is not to restore his virtue. If he was anything close to being like those people he associated with (as were noted in the first three chapters), he had no virtue. Moreover, he was capable of murder. He likely murdered J. D. Tippit, and tried to murder Officer MacDonald in the Texas movie theater. The point is to make sense of a complex set of evidence that suggests that Oswald was connected with the conspirators, but not directly and knowingly with the conspiracy to kill the president. The ingenious plotters got Oswald to plant self-incriminating evidence that he thought was for another purpose—a shoot-and-miss gambit—so the far right could lay the murder on the far left. The grisly plot necessitated that the plotters eliminate one of their own—Oswald—which is what happened. Perhaps that was to be accomplished in the Book Depository by Officer Marrion Baker, although that would have been unlikely. It is more likely the deed was to be done by Officer J. D. Tippit and, ultimately, by Jack Ruby. Generals send their men in battle on missions to advance the war, fully knowing they will probably never come back. That may be have been the case here.

The theory presented cannot be proved or disapproved with absolute certainty and the controversy is likely to persist. However, this theory best fits the evidence when other theories do not. In the grand scheme of the assassination of President Kennedy, it is far more important to identify the masterminds of the plot than to name the triggermen. Few remember the names of the pilots who flew the planes into the World Trade Center, the ground at Shanksville, Pennsylvania, or into the Pentagon. Most know that Islamic terrorists were behind the plot and that Osama Bin Laden was the mastermind. In the Kennedy case, an abundance of the evidence presented converges on General Walker as the mastermind of the murder that involved a consortium of far-right extremists, including segregationists, members of the Minutemen, and the John Birch Society.

CHAPTER SEVENTEEN

JACK RUBY

There is an organization here, Chief Justice Warren, if it takes my life at this moment to say it, and Bill Decker said be a man and say it, there is a John Birch Society right now in activity, and Edwin Walker is one of the top men of the organization—take it for what it is worth, Chief Justice Warren.

— Jack Ruby

Jack Ruby shot Lee Harvey Oswald at 11:21 a.m. on Sunday, November 24, 1963, in the basement of the Dallas Police Department, less than forty-eight hours after the assassination of President Kennedy. The murder was shown live on television while Oswald was being transferred from Dallas police custody to the county jail to await trial. There was immediate speculation that Ruby acted on behalf of a conspiracy group that committed the murders of both President Kennedy and Oswald.

Both the Warren Commission and the House Select Committee on Assassinations found no evidence that Jack Ruby was a part of a conspiracy to assassinate the president. The Warren Commission also found no evidence that Jack Ruby was part of a conspiracy to kill Lee Harvey Oswald. To the contrary, the HSCA concluded that Jack Ruby likely acted as part of an organized crime conspiracy to murder Oswald.

G. Robert Blakey, who headed the HSCA, believed that Ruby understood how the mafia worked and that he had no choice but to carry out the order given to him to kill Oswald. The HSCA based their conclusions solely on Ruby's extensive ties to organized crime figures—ties that were not uncovered in the Warren Commission investigation. The problem with the HSCA findings was they had absolutely no direct or proximate evidence that anyone from organized crime ordered Ruby to kill Oswald. Ruby's ties to organized crime alone were enough for the HSCA to conclude that he silenced Oswald on their behalf—a case of guilt by association. The HSCA determined that most of Ruby's mob ties were related to his business dealings with the mafia-controlled union that his entertainers belonged to. Further weakening the HSCA theory that the mob was involved was the lack of any evidence to tie Oswald, the essential constant in the assassination, to organized crime.

Ruby never directly said who was behind the murder of the president, though he knew who was behind it—as we shall see—and he repeatedly alluded to those involved. Ruby left behind a number of clues and symbolic pieces of evidence that pointed toward those behind the assassination conspiracy. Unfortunately, they were unappreciated or ignored by the official government investigations.

The Life and Times of Jack Ruby

Jack Ruby was born Jacob Rubinstein in Chicago in 1911. His parents were Jewish immigrants from Poland, which at the time was under the rule of Czarist Russia. He was one of eight children in a household where Yiddish was the primary language spoken.[2506] As a boy, Ruby was a troublemaker who ended up spending time in a foster home. He legally changed his name from Jacob Rubenstein on December 30, 1947, at a time when anti-Semitism was widespread in the United States. He followed his brother, who changed his name to Ruby after a former employer advised him that using his Jewish name on company orders was detrimental to the business.[2507]

Ruby left Chicago to join his sister, Eva Grant, in Dallas after she started a nightclub in 1947, and, once there, he helped her operate it. In 1963, Ruby operated the Carousel Club, a striptease club, on Main Street in Dallas, as well as the Vegas Club, a rock and roll club. In June 1963, facing stiff competition from other strip clubs, he traveled to New Orleans to hire a high-profile stripper named Jada.

Ruby's finances were chaotic, and he was in debt with the Internal Revenue Service at the time of the Kennedy assassination. Although many of Ruby's employees had a favorable attitude toward him, others reported that he became physically violent with them at times. Ruby, not uncommonly, fought with disruptive club patrons. Before the assassination, he had numerous prior arrests for suspicion of carrying a concealed weapon, as well as liquor, dance hall, and traffic violations.

According to Dallas Police Chief Jesse Curry, Ruby was acquainted with twenty-five to fifty Dallas police officers on a force of 1,200. Besides extending courtesies at his club to police officers, he was known to have attended the funeral of one and held a benefit for the widow of another. Some officers worked for him, and others were his personal friends. One of his strippers even married a Dallas police officer. One former employee, Nancy Perrin Rich, told the Warren Commission, "I don't think there is a cop in Dallas that doesn't know Jack Ruby. He practically lived at the station, they lived at his place. Even the lowest patrolman on the beat."[2508]

Ruby, although not a particularly devout Jew, always attended services on the Jewish high holy days. He was sensitive about being Jewish and got into fights with those making disparaging remarks about Jews. While in Chicago, Ruby often disrupted rallies of the pro-Nazi German-American Bund and frequently "busted heads." Ruby was inducted into the U.S. Army Air Force in 1943 and those who knew him described him as extremely sensitive about hearing insulting remarks about Jews. He attacked a sergeant for calling him a "Jew bastard."

After returning from the war in 1946, Ruby's brother found him covered in blood after getting in a fight with someone who called him a dirty Jew.[2509] Ruby did not tolerate comedians in his club telling jokes about Jews or African Americans, and once yelled at the master of ceremonies at his club for telling racial jokes.[2510]

Jack Ruby and Organized Crime

The Warren Commission determined there was no significant link between Jack Ruby and organized crime. Conversely, author and newsman Seth Kantor noted that Ruby's links to the mob dated back to 1947 in Chicago—and were maintained up until the assassination. Ruby was involved in professional card games and horseracing and was friendly with a number of professional gamblers. In the months before the assassination, Ruby was in contact with a number of characters tied to the mob with criminal records. Phone records for Ruby indicated he made several phone calls to underworld figures. However, there was no evidence that the calls were related to the assassination.

Kantor uncovered evidence that Ruby visited mob boss Santos Trafficante in a Havana jail in 1959. The HSCA investigated Kantor's allegation, but doubted the visit occurred. In 1959, Ruby did, however, travel to Cuba for eight days at the expense of professional gambler Lewis McWillie, an associate of mob figure Meyer Lansky. At the time, McWillie oversaw the gambling casino in the Tropicana Hotel in Havana. Ruby had known him since about 1950, when McWillie operated a nightclub in Dallas. McWillie was staunchly anti-Castro.

The HSCA noted that Ruby traveled to Cuba five times in 1959. According to Ruby's lawyer, Melvin Belli, Ruby tried to make a deal with the Castro regime to sell them Jeeps shortly after Castro's overthrow of dictator Fulgencio Batista. At the time, many considered Castro a hero, and he enjoyed a warm reception during a visit to the United States. The favorable attitude toward Castro changed when it became known that he was a Communist.

Ruby contacted McWillie a number of times in Las Vegas in 1963. Kantor established that Ruby also had dealings with associates of Teamster boss Jimmy Hoffa. Phone records indicate that Ruby had called Nofio Pecora, a lieutenant of New Orleans mob boss, Carlos Marcello, a Banister associate, but Pecora denied getting a call from Ruby. Ruby knew Marcello associate Joseph Civello, who headed up organized crime activities in Dallas. Ruby worked with the American Guild of Variety Artists representative, James Henry Doland—who reportedly was an associate of Carlos Marcello, Nofio Pecora, and Santos Trafficante—on nightclub labor matters.[2511] The HSCA felt, by and large, that the phone calls made before the assassination to lower mob-connected elements were related to Ruby's ongoing labor disputes with the American Guild of Variety Artists, his strippers' union, in regard to what he considered were the unfair practices of his competitors in the hiring of exotic performers. The HSCA investigation determined that Ruby was not a member of organized crime, but had direct and indirect contacts with underworld figures that were connected to the most powerful leaders in the Cosa Nostra.[2512]

The HSCA concluded that New Orleans mob figure Marcello had the motive, means and opportunity to commit the assassination, but they could not find any direct evidence of his involvement.[2513] They concluded, "The committee believes, on the basis of the evidence available to it, that the national syndicate of organized crime, as a group, was not involved in the assassination of President Kennedy, but that the available evidence does not preclude the possibility that individual members may have been involved."[2514] Outside of the mafia, they found no evidence any other group was involved in the assassination.

The HSCA determined that Oswald's uncle, Dutz Murret, was a minor underworld gambling figure in New Orleans.[2515] That was as close as they got to tying Oswald to organized crime. Lack of any other evidence linking Oswald to organized crime further critically undermines the HSCA theory that the mob was behind the assassination. If Ruby had significant connections with the mafia, he could have settled his dispute with the strippers' union with a phone call. Dallas Police Captain Jack Reville, who worked on the vice squad, told the HSCA that Jack Ruby was volatile, a buffoon, and a liar who liked the limelight. He stated, "If Jack Ruby was a member of organized crime, then the personnel director of organized crime should be replaced."[2516]

As was pointed out in Chapter Nine, Marcello was an associate of two men close to Lee Harvey Oswald: Guy Banister and David Ferrie. In addition, Joseph Milteer had in his possession a business card from George W. Gill, the son of Marcello's attorney, G. Wray Gill. Also as was discussed in Chapter Nine, if Marcello—who was also a fanatical racist—was involved in the assassination, it may have been on the basis of an association with far-right extremists Banister, Ferrie, possibly Milteer, and their cause, rather than in the interests of organized crime.

The Jack Ruby Timeline

The Warren Commission set out to document, as precisely as possible, Ruby's activities before the assassination and up until the murder of Oswald to determine if there was any evidence of his involvement in the assassination conspiracy.

On Thursday, November 21, 1963, on the eve of the assassination, Ruby performed his usual duties operating the Carousel Club and the Vegas Club. Earlier that day, he took a young woman friend to visit Lamar Hunt in hopes of finding a job (as was noted in Chapter Eleven).[2517]

On the morning of the assassination, Ruby visited the *Dallas Morning News* advertising department to compose his weekend nightclub ads. While there, Ruby overheard the incoming phone calls to the paper from its readers complaining about the insulting "Welcome Mr. Kennedy to Dallas," full-page advertisement that appeared in the paper's morning edition. The ad was bitterly critical of the president. Ruby was at the newspaper when the assassination occurred blocks away.[2518, 2519] Ruby saw the ad and at first glance thought it was a nice, welcoming piece. He was further delighted to see the name of a fellow Jew, Bernard Weissman, attached to the advertisement. He thought President Kennedy had been a good friend of the Jews and, in turn, a Jew was welcoming him to Dallas. His feelings changed when he read its derogatory content. Attached to the ad was the Dallas post office box number 1792.[2520] Ruby grew incensed. He noted that Weissman did not spell his name quite like a Jew and, if he was a Jew, he should be ashamed of himself.[2521] Ruby felt the apparent Jewish sponsorship of the ad was done on purpose to insult both the president and Jews. The John Birch Society and General Walker's friends, Nelson Bunker Hunt and Joseph Grinnan had financed the ad, as was later determined by the Warren Commission. Grinnan, an independent oil operator, solicited funds for the ad. (Grinnan was questioned about the ad after the assassination and he requested a delay because he wanted to consult with his lawyer, Robert Morris.)[2522, 2523]

Morris also screened applicants who applied to join Walker's Minutemen group. Morris, as has been noted, was an associate of Guy Banister and represented General Walker after his incarceration for inciting the riot at Ole Miss. The Dallas Police had identified Grinnan in October 1962 as a member of the Dallas Minutemen, along with (Milteer associates) Dan Smoot and Robert Surrey. H. L. Hunt and General Walker were the leaders of the group.[2524, 2525, 2526] The FBI determined that Joseph Grinnan had his car loaded with arms, ready to assist General Walker at Ole Miss, and was a volunteer aide to General Walker.[2527]

Other contributors to the ad were H. R. "Bum" Bright, an oilman and friend of H. L. Hunt, and Edgar Crissey. Bright refused to tell the FBI who the person was who solicited funds from him. (Bright is better known for purchasing the Dallas Cowboys football franchise in 1984.)

Larrie Schmidt, whose brother at one time served as a chauffer for General Walker, convinced Bernard Weissman to permit his name to be used as a sponsor. Bernard Weissman was a new arrival in Dallas and a former army friend of Schmidt. As was noted in Chapter Fourteen, Schmidt and his brother were accused of driving Lee Harvey Oswald to Walker's home for the shooting incident. Schmidt later became active in Young Americans for Freedom along with General Charles Willoughby, one of General Pedro del Valle's "trusted men."

On December 1, 1963, an informant told the FBI that he visited his aunt, the secretary for Edgar Crissey (spelled "Crissie" by the FBI), in the hospital, where she had undergone a minor operation. The aunt told her nephew, the informant, that Crissey was active in the John Birch Society. She also told him that, as Crissey's secretary, she handled correspondence that indicated that he had ordered large quantities of guns, which were reportedly stored somewhere around the Turtle Creek area, where Walker lived and operated his extremist group. She told her nephew that the John Birch Society had "enough guns to start a war." She noted that Crissey carried a pistol on him, sometimes two.[2528] There is no evidence that the FBI or the Warren Commission interviewed Crissey's secretary about the allegations. Thus, at least three of the four men—but likely all four—who sponsored the ad that Ruby was so distraught and obsessed with, were directly tied to General Walker and his extremist effort. Another citizen wrote an anonymous letter to the FBI on October 2, 1962, and told them that Crissey was an ardent member of the John Birch Society and an associate of Walker.[2529]

The day after the assassination, Ruby told a friend that the printed black border surrounding the "Welcome Mr. Kennedy" ad represented "mourning," and that whoever put the ad out, "Must have known that the president was going to be killed."[2530] Ruby's room-mate, George Senator, told the FBI, "He said he couldn't understand anything of this nature appearing in the paper." Ruby regarded the black border around the "Welcome" ad as "a sign of death."[2531]

The ad featured a list of grievances by the far right against the president in a similar fashion to a letter written by General Walker to the president before the insurrection at Ole Miss. Ruby perceptively surmised that the ad was the work of those who knew the assassination was in the works. Ruby never explicitly stated that the advertisement was the work of the John Birch Society and he made that quite clear to his lawyer, Joe Tonahill, after the murder of Oswald. Ruby thought the "1792" post office box number on the "Welcome Mr. Kennedy" ad might have been the same as the one written on a billboard calling for the impeachment of Earl Warren, sponsored by the John Birch Society. It is somewhat remarkable that Ruby was familiar enough with the small, poster-sized "Impeach Earl Warren" billboard—on a building adjacent to the Stemmons freeway—that he remembered that the post office box number was similar or the same as that given in the newspaper ad.

After the assassination, Ruby vowed he would not open his clubs that night out of respect. Ruby changed the original format of his ad, adding a black border around the an-nouncement that he was closing his clubs. Later, he drove around to his competitors to see if they had the decency to do the same.

Veteran reporter Seth Kantor, who knew Ruby well, saw Ruby at Parkland Hospital, where the mortally wounded president was taken right after the assassination. The Warren Commission did not believe Kantor's story about Ruby at Parkland, a reputable newsman, who was covering the president's visit as a Washington correspondent for the Scripps Howard Newspaper Alliance.[2532] Kantor had no known reason to lie. Ruby's presence at the hospital and frequent visits to the jail where Oswald was held showed Ruby's preoccupation with the events surrounding the assassination. Kantor had known Ruby since the start of the Kennedy administration, when he had been a reporter for the *Dallas Times Herald* newspaper. Ruby later wrote Kantor a long personal letter from jail. (Years later, after reading Kantor's book about the Warren Commission, Burt Griffin—who played a major role in the investigation and writing of the Warren Commission account on Ruby—conceded that Kantor did see Ruby at Parkland Hospital.) Kantor was present at the jail when Ruby murdered Oswald.[2533]

At 2:10 p.m. on the afternoon of the assassination, Ruby told one of his employees he was closing the club. He was noted to be "half sobbing."[2534] By all accounts, Ruby was genuinely grieved by the president's murder. According to his roommate, George Senator, he talked about the tragedy of Mrs. Kennedy and the children over and over. Many people saw Ruby crying, including the nightclub custodian.[2535] Ruby's Carousel employee Larry Crafard told the Warren Commission that Ruby was affected by the assassination more than others, and acted like it was a death in his own family.[2536]

After 6:00 p.m., Ruby went to his sister Eva Grant's apartment, where he threw up.[2537] At 9:30 p.m., Ruby attended a memorial service at Shearith Israel Synagogue.[2538] At about 10:00 p.m., Ruby went to a delicatessen and had ten or twelve "real good sandwiches" made up. Then he called Detective Sims in homicide and told him he was bringing the sandwiches over. Sims told him they were fine, and were wrapping things up for the night.[2539]

At 11:15 p.m. on the evening of the assassination, Ruby entered the police station without difficulty and he greeted a few of the officers he knew. He saw officers escorting Oswald to the assembly room where they were going to give a news conference. Oswald passed two to three feet away from Ruby.[2540] Ruby posed as a reporter during the impromptu news conference. The police brought Oswald out of his cell to show reporters that he was not being mistreated. A photograph documents Ruby's presence at the news conference. When District Attorney Henry Wade reported that Oswald was connected with the Free Cuba Committee, Ruby spoke out and told him the correct name of the group was "Fair Play Cuba." It was unusual for the politically naive Ruby to make the fine distinction between the names Free Cuba Committee and Fair Play Cuba. (Ruby later said he heard the name of the group on the radio.)[2541, 2542] As Oswald was led away from the news conference, he yelled out, "I'm just a patsy."

At 1:30 a.m. Saturday morning, Oswald was arraigned for the murder of the president.[2543]

Ruby next stopped at the *Dallas Times Herald* building after the news conference and talked to his friend, Roy Pryor, a printer and former emcee at one of his clubs. Pryor told the FBI later that Ruby seemed pleased that he managed to get an ad, which he referred to as a memorial, in the paper, announcing that his clubs would be closed over the weekend.

Jack Ruby (left), wearing eyeglasses, posed as a reporter at the Dallas Police Department news conference on the night of the assassination, standing just a few feet away from Lee Harvey Oswald as he passed by. Source: Corbis. Jack Ruby mug shot (right) after his arrest for the murder of Oswald. Source: Warren Commission

Ruby took the sandwiches to the newsroom at radio station KLIF at 2:00 a.m. on November 23. Newscaster Glenn Duncan recalled that Ruby "seemed pleased in the sense that he was being in on something that was important to everyone." He felt that Ruby was happy. Ruby told him about his encounter with Oswald and explained that he did not know about the impromptu press conference and was accidently caught up in the commotion. He conveyed to Duncan that his attendance there was not by design.[2544, 2545, 2546] Ruby brought with him his copy of H. L. Hunt's *Life Lines* radio script that was critical of President Kennedy, which he had picked up weeks earlier at the Texas Products show. He showed it to a radio employee, Russ Knight, who was also a friend of his. He told Knight that there was a group of "radicals" in Dallas who hated President Kennedy and indicated that he felt they were partially responsible for the assassination.[2547] Ruby also discussed the "Welcome Mr. Kennedy" advertisement with Bernard Weissman's name attached to it. He talked about the editorial that his friend at the radio station had written on the Adlai Stevenson incident, another product of associates of General Walker. Edward Pullman, a friend of Ruby, recalled how he bitterly complained about *Life Lines'* anti-Kennedy comments when he first picked it up at the Texas Products Show, noted in Chapter Eleven. Ruby became "all excited and red-face, livid" when he first saw it and planned to send a copy to President Kennedy. He added, "Nobody has any right to talk like this about our government."[2548] Ruby was aware H. L. Hunt published it.[2549] The Warren Commission pointed out that one radio script was entitled "Heroism" and was from a "conservative radio program." However, they failed to note that its content was also critical of the Kennedy administration.[2550] H.L. Hunt was an associate of Joseph Milteer, Guy Banister and General Walker and the case against him in the assassination conspiracy was presented in Chapter Eleven. Ruby suspected radicals and those behind the "Welcome Mr. Kennedy" ad were behind the assassination. If Ruby wanted to find out if any information had turned up suggesting that those behind H. L. Hunt's *Life Lines* might have been connected to the assassination, then the radio KLIF newsroom was a good place to go. Ruby's discussion of the Adlai Stevenson incident at the radio station, along with the ad and radio script—three products of associates of General Walker—were subjects that completely preoccupied him after the assassination. It is not known if he discussed the "Impeach Earl Warren" billboard at the radio station as well, although it was a fourth product of Walker's group that Ruby was preoccupied with, as we shall see next.

The "Welcome Mr. Kennedy" ad and two issues of *Life Lines*, program 31 (dated June 18, 1963) and program 131 (dated September 17, 1963), were found in Ruby's car trunk after he murdered Oswald.[2551] The Polaroid photos that Ruby took of the "Impeach Earl Warren" billboard were found in his pocket. Did Ruby leave behind the ad and transcript in his car, and the photo in his pocket, purposely to point law enforcement toward the

Three pieces of evidence were left in Jack Ruby's car or on his person after he shot Oswald. The ad (left) and the *Life Lines* radio scripts (right) consumed Ruby, but no one investigating the case knew why. The ad and *Life Lines* radio script were found in the trunk of Ruby's car near the jail where he murdered Oswald. The billboard Polaroid camera photos (one of which is shown in the middle) were found in his pants pocket at the time of the murder. H.L. Hunt or General Walker's group sponsored all three. Source: Warren Commission

conspirators? The Warren Commission and the HSCA treated Ruby's preoccupation with the "Impeach Earl Warren" billboard, the "Welcome Mr. Kennedy" ad and the *Life Lines* radio scripts with little interest. Assassination writers also glossed over the incidents.

The "Impeach Earl Warren" Billboard

Ruby decided to investigate the "Welcome Mr. Kennedy" ad, which he suspected might be the work of the conspirators, as well as the "Impeach Earl Warren" billboard. He suspected that the ad and billboard used identical post office box numbers and, therefore, were produced by the same individuals. He set out on Saturday morning (November 23) at 4:00 a.m., to find out.

Ruby drove to his apartment and rousted his roommate, George Senator, out of bed. Ruby and his roommate proceeded to his nightclub, where he picked up employee Larry Crafard and a Polaroid camera and drove to a billboard that read "Impeach Earl Warren" to see if it bore the same post office box number as the "Welcome Mr. Kennedy" ad. The billboard was not a typical large highway billboard. According to Crafard, it was a three feet by three feet poster, affixed five to six feet up on the side of a building.[2552] (Ruby discovered that the billboard displayed the post office box number 1757, which, although similar, was not the same as the post office box number (1792) displayed in the "Welcome Mr. Kennedy" ad.)

The billboard invited the public to write for more information on the Warren impeachment effort at post office box 1757, according to Ruby. Crafard described the billboard as a "hate ad," and noted that it bore a Massachusetts address.[2553]

The visit to the billboard was extraordinary and, heretofore, has never been explained. One assassination writer, commenting on Ruby's early morning enigmatic action, wrote, "It is unclear what motivated Ruby to photograph the billboard. We only know that he went out of his way to do it."[2554] Ruby told George Senator, "I can't understand why they want to impeach Earl Warren. . . . This must be the work of the John Birch Society or the Communist Party." Ruby later called his friend at the radio station and asked him to explain the meaning of the billboard.[2555]

Ruby's suspicions were correct. The John Birch Society, in fact, sponsored the Dallas billboard. The JBS despised Earl Warren because of his role as Chief Justice in the 1954 *Brown* decision that eventually led to the abolition of racial segregation in public schools. Warren was also often accused of endorsing court decisions considered favorable to the Communists. The JBS purchased "Impeach Earl Warren" billboards across the nation, but they were concentrated in the South. Eventually, the John Birch Society's effort to impeach Supreme Court Chief Justice Earl Warren became one of their most publicized efforts.

Ruby testified before the Warren Commission that New Bedford (or some city of similar name in Massachusetts) appeared on the billboard. At his trial for the murder of Oswald, he wrote down the address of "Beltham," Massachusetts, on a piece of paper for his attorneys, as follows: "Wrote down impeach, EARL WARREN, WRITE TO BELTHAM, BOX 1757 MASS." Ruby likely meant "Belmont," not Beltham or New Bedford. (The national headquarters of the John Birch Society was in Belmont, Massachusetts, home of founder Robert Welch.)

However, a photo in the 1962 John Birch Society *White Book*, located by the author, shows another, much larger billboard with the address clearly shown as post office box 1757,

Dallas, Texas. It would be improbable that one "Impeach Earl Warren" billboard bore a Massachusetts post office box 1757, and another the Dallas post office box 1757. Ruby's sister Eva Grant saw the Polaroid photos of the billboard and stated, like Larry Crafard, that they bore a Massachusetts address. Nothing more than "Save Our Republic, Impeach Earl Warren, for information write BOX 1757" can be seen on Ruby's photo of the billboard in the National Archives. The designers of the billboard probably assumed that the reader would understand they were being invited to write to a Dallas post office address.

Warren Commission staff counsels Leon Hubert and Burt Griffin went out to look at the billboard. They described it as a small, green metal sign that was not particularly conspicuous and could only be seen from one direction from the Central Expressway. It appeared to be commercially printed and mass-produced. The notation "Post Office Box 1757" had been hand painted on the sign. At the bottom of the sign, in small blue letters, was the name and address of "Mr. Hill," which is not visible on Ruby's photos. The bottom portion of the sign was partially obliterated and it was not possible to read the first name or the complete address—or whether or not Hill's telephone number was on the sign.

It should be noted that the sign Hubert and Griffin inspected was not the original. The original had been painted over or otherwise disturbed after Oswald was killed and this was a new poster, but it was identical to the old one, according to the Secret Service. The original sign that Ruby and Crafard saw probably had the Belmont address at the bottom with Mr. Hill's name.

The poster also had stickers on it that said, "Serve America—Join the John Birch Society."[2556] Jack Ruby had the telephone number and address of Robert Welch's personal assistant, Thomas Hill, in Belmont, Massachusetts, written on an envelope in his notebook, which was found after the murder of Oswald.[2557] He probably copied them from the sign.

To the author's knowledge, the FBI never sought to find out who rented post office box 1757, at the time that the address was printed on the billboard (which was most likely a Dallas post office box). Unfortunately, Ruby's claim that it was a Massachusetts post office box 1757 on the billboard, not a Dallas address, may have had the effect—intended or not—of steering investigators away from the Dallas John Birch Society (which was dominated by General Walker and his group) and toward the Massachusetts operation.

The secretary-treasurer of the Dallas John Birch Society was Robert Surrey, Walker's top aide. Surrey's wife Mary was the head of the Dallas chapter and a Walker volunteer. The Surreys are the ones who, most likely, rented the billboard and the Dallas post office box. If so, the Warren Commission was unaware of it and Surrey was, unfortunately, not asked any questions about the post office box or the billboard during his testimony before the Warren Commission. Surrey was called to testify before the Commission because he published the provocative and insulting "Wanted for Treason" poster, which featured pictures of President Kennedy in a "mug shot" format, and was circulated just before the assassination. Thus the billboard—like the "Welcome Mr. Kennedy" ad—was most likely another product of an associate of General Walker.

(As it turns out, three of General Walker's organizations had post office boxes at the zone 21 post office: the Walker Defense Fund, the American Eagle Publishing Company, and the Friends of General Walker. Johnston Printing—where Walker's aide Robert Surrey worked and where he printed the plates for the "Wanted for Treason" posters—also had a post office box there.[2558])

In an abstract, symbolic way, Ruby's leaving the billboard Polaroid photos on his person when he was arrested—and the "Welcome Mr. Kennedy" ad in the trunk of his car, found near the jail after his arrest—served to point the blame in the direction of General Walker. The further significance of the billboard affair was that Ruby knew that the John Birch Society was behind it, even though the society's name was not attached to it. He suspected the ad and billboard were connected and that those behind them had known that the assassination was going to occur.

After taking the Polaroid pictures of the billboard, Ruby and his companions traveled to the post office to further investigate the post office box number on the "Welcome Mr. Kennedy" ad. Ruby approached the night post office worker and asked, "How does it happen that they have given a box to a person placing an ad of that sort in the newspaper?"[2559] Ruby located post office box 1792 rented by the sponsors of the ad and found it full of mail.[2560] There is no evidence he looked for box 1757.[2561] He may not have, since after seeing the billboard he apparently was under the impression it was a Massachusetts post office box.

After leaving the post office, Ruby and Senator went to the Southland Hotel coffee shop and Ruby reread the "Welcome Mr. Kennedy" ad with Weissman's name on it, which he found in a newspaper laying on the counter. Ruby told Senator that he had earlier checked the phone book to see if Bernard Weissman's name was listed. It wasn't, which made him think that Weissman's name might have been made up. Senator remarked on Ruby's feelings on the ad and the billboard, stating, "He was very, very disturbed over both of these." The way Ruby looked and sounded was different than anything that Senator had ever observed. He recalled that Ruby was deeply hurt over he assassination. Senator observed that Ruby had a "far away, unnatural look," cried, and kept repeating what a tragedy it was. Senator noted, "It didn't look like the normal look like I have known him. . . . The thing was getting at him."[2562]

Ruby's attorney Joe Tonahill, like everyone else, missed the significance of Ruby's fixation with the ad and the billboard. Tonahill did not appreciate that Ruby felt those behind the billboard and ad were behind the assassination. Tonahill wanted to bring up the subject of Ruby and his two associates going to the billboard at 4:00 a.m. during Ruby's lie detector examination after his arrest, because he thought it would demonstrate that Ruby was one hundred percent American, showing that his actions meant he thought the billboard was un-American. However, months after the murders, Ruby denied saying the John Birch Society was behind the ad. While in jail, Ruby told his attorney, "Don't mention anything about that—we're in a bad spot down here because of that. I didn't refer to the John Birch—with reference to that [ad]." Ruby's comments suggest perhaps someone was pressuring him to stop connecting the John Birch Society to the ad.[2563]

The Polaroid pictures were taken for what Ruby claimed would be a "scoop." Senator told author Seth Kantor that Ruby thought he was onto something big.[2564] Ruby never specified what his scoop was, but the implication is clear. Additionally, Ruby said the special purpose for the photos was to give them to radio newsman Gordon McClendon, so that McClendon could run an editorial on them. Ruby praised McClendon, the reporter who delivered the editorial critical of the ugly Adlai Stevenson incident.[2565]

After his visit to the billboard and post office, Ruby returned to his apartment. He woke at 11:30 a.m., and was seen on the third floor of the Dallas police department at 12:00 noon.[2566] At 2:30 p.m., Ruby was seen outside the county jail.[2567]

A friend of Ruby, Frank Bellocchio, testified at his trial for the murder of Oswald that Ruby was still upset about the "Impeach Earl Warren" sign and "was not coherent" when Bellocchio saw him at a bar that afternoon. Ruby told him he had a "scoop" and planned on turning over the billboard pictures to the FBI.[2568] Eva Grant corroborated Bellocchio's account, and testified that Ruby planned on taking the photos to the FBI on Monday morning.[2569]

Oswald's wife Marina and his mother Marguerite went to the jail on Saturday, November 23, to visit him. They had not been permitted to visit him the day before. Oswald told Marina not to worry and that everything would turn out okay.[2570]

At 4:00 p.m., Ruby called radio station KLIF and told them Oswald was going to be transferred to the county jail.[2571] The transfer was later cancelled. At 9:00 p.m. Saturday evening, Little Lynn/Karen Bennett (one of Ruby's employees) called Ruby and told him she had not been paid because the club was closed and she needed money to pay her rent.[2572]

In the early morning hours of Sunday, November 24, Dallas police lieutenant Billy Grammer was working in the police communications room when he received a phone call warning him that Oswald was going to be killed in the basement of the police department and that the police needed to change their plans. Grammer immediately recognized the voice as Jack Ruby's, although the caller did not identify himself.[2573] If Ruby was being compelled to kill Oswald—by General Walker, the John Birch Society, or anyone else—tipping off the police might have relieved him of his burden. If Ruby, in fact, made the phone call, it suggests that he did not murder Oswald of his own volition as the Warren Commission concluded—and may mean that he was compelled to commit the murder. Ruby later denied making the call.

The Murder of Lee Harvey Oswald

On Sunday, November 24, Ruby awoke at 9:00 a.m. and watched television. Little Lynn/Karen Bennett called Ruby again about her paycheck—this time from her home, thirty-five miles away in Fort Worth, at 10:18 a.m. The call came eighteen minutes after Oswald was supposed have been moved from the Police headquarters to the county jail as announced. Ruby dressed and put a money roll containing over two thousand dollars in one pants pocket and the .38 revolver that he usually carried in the other. At 11:00 a.m., he left his apartment with his beloved dachshund, Sheba, and drove toward the downtown jail taking a route which took him past the assassination site, rather than the more direct route down Commerce Street.

He drove downtown, passing the Texas School Book Depository, to the nearby Western Union Telegraph, to wire twenty-five dollars to Little Lynn/Karen Bennett. From there, he could see crowds gathering at the nearby police station. Ruby completed the money transfer at 11:17 a.m., according to the time that was printed on the money order receipt given to Ruby, which was later found in his pocket. Lee Harvey Oswald had just minutes before Ruby would walk the short distance from the Western Union storefront to the Dallas jail and shoot him.

Leaving his cherished dog in the car, Ruby walked 350 feet down Main Street to the police station, which took approximately three and a half minutes. Ruby entered the police station from the front ramp to the basement, and took a position among the reporters and televisions crews. At 11:20 a.m., Oswald appeared in the basement, flanked by two policemen, while reporters shouted questions.

Ruby, a squat figure in a business suit and felt hat, leaped out of the crowd of reporters and fired a single shot into Oswald's abdomen. The exact time of the shooting was recorded as 11:21 a.m. Oswald sustained massive internal injuries, and succumbed to them at 1:07 p.m. in an operating room at Parkland Hospital, across from the room where the president had died.

Chief of Police Jesse Curry had told reporters on Saturday night that Oswald would not be moved before 10:00 a.m. on Sunday. The move was delayed by the postal inspector's late visit Sunday morning to advise the police on the matter of Oswald's post office box. Had the postal inspector's meeting not delayed the transfer, Ruby would have missed the opportunity to kill him altogether. The slightest delay en route to Western Union—or in the processing of the money order—would have caused Ruby to miss Oswald's transfer. Even if Ruby was tipped off about the delay from someone inside the jail, allowing for the perfect timing of his arrival at the jail, he was still cutting it close.

Ruby's timing, on the one hand, can be viewed as perfect—with no time to spare— suggesting that someone had tipped him off about the delayed transfer. On the other hand, it may also be viewed as sloppy and haphazard, since the announced plan had been to move Oswald over an hour earlier. Perhaps the timing reflects indecisiveness or reluctance as to whether he would commit the deed.

After the shooting, Ruby was taken into custody and was reminded of his Constitutional right to remain silent. He was transferred to the Dallas County Jail, under the custody of the sheriff's department. Secret Service agent Forrest Sorrels interviewed Ruby after the shooting. Ruby told Sorrels he did it for the sake of Mrs. Kennedy—and that he wanted to show that Jews had guts.[2574] Police officer Don Archer said Ruby told him, "I intended to shoot him three times." Officer Patrick T. Dean testified before the Commission, "he said when he noticed the sarcastic sneer on Oswald's face [on Friday night], that's the first time that he thought he would kill him."

Ruby allegedly explained that because Oswald had killed the president and J. D. Tippit he didn't see any point in putting Mrs. Kennedy through a lengthy trial. Ruby told officer Dean, as he did the Secret Service, that he wanted to kill Oswald, "because he wanted to let the world know that Jews do have guts." During Ruby's trial for the shooting, Ruby's lawyer, Melvin Belli, considered Officer Dean's testimony to be the most damaging evidence of premeditation. Dean also testified that Ruby told him that when he left Western Union and saw the crowds at the jail, he hoped he would see Oswald. Officer Jim Levealle, who had been handcuffed to Oswald when he was shot, testified that, one minute after Ruby shot Oswald, Ruby said, "I hope the SOB dies."[2575]

Meanwhile, Joseph Milteer was in South Carolina with Willie Somersett, as was noted in Chapter Four. He was overjoyed by the president's murder. He told Somersett on both the night before—and the morning of—the murder of Oswald that the Jews killed Kennedy and it was now time to focus on killing the Jews. When he heard the news that Oswald had been shot, he remarked, "That makes everything perfect now, the Jews killed Kennedy and the Jews killed Oswald. Now we have no worry."

FBI director J. Edgar Hoover wrote a memorandum to presidential aide Walter Jenkins, hours after Oswald's death, saying: "The thing I am most concerned about, and so is Mr. Katzenbach, is having something issued so we can convince the public that Oswald is the real assassin."[2576] United Press International wrote, on December 3—before the Warren Commission convened—that the FBI was about to send a report to the White House indicating Oswald was the lone and unaided assassin, a story which Hoover himself had leaked to the press.[2577]

The Trial of Jack Ruby

After the shooting, there was widespread suspicion that both Jack Ruby and Lee Harvey Oswald were involved in the conspiracy. Various allegations of a Ruby-Oswald relationship emerged, although none were substantiated.

Prosecutors had even a better case against Ruby than they had had against Oswald, since the whole world saw him shoot Oswald. Even so, there was a concern that, perhaps, jurors would be sympathetic to Ruby. Newspaper surveys taken after the murder found nearly half of those polled felt Ruby should serve no sentence at all.[2578] On the other hand, a jury could not overlook the fact that Ruby had murdered a defenseless, shackled man in cold blood. The trial proceedings add a few more insights into the Jack Ruby story.

Ruby's legal team, led by Ralph Paul, considered an insanity defense. However, co-counsel Tom Howard did not think Ruby was insane nor did Howard feel he could convince a jury of it. Howard's strategy was to get a conviction for murder without malice, which carried a maximum five-year sentence. The Ruby family wanted high-profile attorney Melvin Belli, and he joined the team *pro bono*, in exchange for the opportunity to write a book about the trial. Belli had great respect for Texas attorney Joe Tonahill, and brought him in on the case. Attorney Phil Burleson was added as well. District Attorney Henry Wade headed the prosecution, and was joined by Bill Alexander.[2579]

The trial began on March 4, 1964, in the midst of the Warren Commission investigation. Ruby's roommate, George Senator, testified, and provided a few more details about the billboard affair. According to Senator, Ruby awoke him at 3:00 a.m. the morning after the assassination. He recalled, "[Ruby] was very excited . . . He asked me if I had seen this ad in the paper. He was crying out loud and saying what a terrible thing to happen to the president . . . to Mrs. Kennedy and the children. He had a look on his face like I'd never seen before—like he was out in space."[2580] Ruby wanted to know the identity of the holder of the post office box of the Impeach Earl Warren billboard and the "Welcome Mr. Kennedy" ad. According to Senator, "He thought the John Birch Society or the Communist Party or a combination of both were behind the billboard and ad."[2581]

According to the testimony of Arnold C. Gadosh, a printer at the *Dallas Morning News* who talked to Ruby during his visit to the paper, Ruby insisted that since the ad was signed "Bernard Weissman" (obviously a Jewish name), that, "the son of a bitch is trying to put the blame on the Jews!"[2582] Ruby told his civil attorney, Stanley Kaufman, that the black border on the ad meant mourning.

Kaufman gave the following account: "He seemed to be alarmed about a number of things. He had told me he took some pictures of a sign, 'Impeach Earl Warren.' He told me he had noted in this full-page ad that was taken in the Dallas *News*, it had a great big black border around it, which indicated to him that this was a mourning thing, and whoever put that ad in must have known the president was going to be killed."[2583]

The most damaging trial testimony came from the law enforcement officers who were with Ruby in the immediate aftermath of the Oswald murder.

The defense sought to exonerate Ruby on the dubious grounds that he shot Oswald as a manifestation of a rare form of epilepsy, although Ruby told attorney Belli that he wanted to take the stand and tell the jury that he did it for Jackie and the kids, and forego an epilepsy or blackout defense.[2584] Even so, Ruby's defense team brought in a number of psychiatrists who testified that Ruby suffered from psychomotor epilepsy, based on electroencephalogram tracings. As a witness for the defense, Dr. Roy Shafer testified that Ruby had organic brain damage, most likely psychomotor epilepsy. The prosecution countered with their psychiatrists. One psychiatrist said Ruby called Oswald a "vicious animal."[2585]

On March 14, 1964, the jury was not persuaded by the neuropsychiatric defense. They determined that Ruby had planned to kill Oswald three days in advance of the shooting. They found Ruby guilty of murder with malice and recommended the death penalty after two hours and nineteen minutes of deliberation. Lead attorney Melvin Belli was fired. In Detroit, Ruby's brother Earl retained attorney Sol Dann for the appeal. Percy Foreman, who later represented James Earl Ray, the convicted assassin of Martin Luther King, Jr., briefly served on the defense team.

Ruby's mental state deteriorated after he was sentenced to death. The family requested a sanity hearing on April 27, 1964. In 1966, the verdict was overturned on appeal and a new trial was granted.

The Warren Commission Testimony of Jack Ruby

Jack Ruby testified before the Warren Commission on June 6, 1964, at the Dallas County Jail. Commission members Chief Justice Earl Warren and Gerald Ford were present. A number of Commission counsel, Ruby's attorney Joe Tonahill, Secret Service agent Elmer W. Moore, the sheriff and deputies of Dallas County, and others were present. Ruby's testimony was a mere formality.

The Commission had already concluded that he was innocent of any conspiracy and had acted alone. The Associated Press had already reported, on March 29, 1964, that the Warren Commission found no evidence that the Kennedy assassination was anything but the irrational act of one individual, Oswald—and the Commission, at that time, felt that most of the information was in.[2586] That news from the Commission must have been tremendously comforting to General Walker and General Clyde Watts, who would not testify before the Commission until July 23, 1964—as well as Robert Surrey, who did not testify until June 16, 1964.[2587]

Ruby's Warren Commission testimony was taken more than six months after the assassination, and more than two months after his guilty verdict. The Commission did not actively seek out Ruby's testimony—it was a step taken to avoid prejudice or interference with Ruby's appeal of his murder conviction. They did so reluctantly at the pleading of his sister, Eva Grant.

By the time of his testimony, the Commission had already established that Ruby did not know either Oswald or J. D. Tippit, and that he was not a Communist. They also had determined that Ruby's trip to Cuba in 1959 was completely unrelated to Oswald's attempt to get a visa to Cuba at the embassy in Mexico City. Ruby's testimony before the Commission was more of a token procedure than a quest for the truth.

In a quirk of fate, Ruby found himself testifying before Earl Warren—the subject of the John Birch Society billboard that Ruby was so obsessed with on the night of the assassination. Ruby's very first remark in his testimony was a request to take a lie detector test. Warren agreed to arrange one, but did not recommend it. Ruby said he wanted to tell the truth at his trial, but his lawyer reminded him that in doing so he would be "speaking of a premeditated crime." Ruby must have already sensed that his testimony was a mere formality when he asked Earl Warren, "Am I boring you?"

In several pages of testimony, Ruby described his activities on the days before the murder of Oswald, then suddenly surprised Warren when he requested to go to Washington, as follows:

> Mr. Ruby: Is there any way to get me to Washington?
> Chief Justice Warren: I beg your pardon?
> Mr. Ruby: Is there any way of you getting me to Washington?
> Chief Justice Warren: I don't know of any. I will be glad to talk to
> your counsel about what the situation is, Mr. Ruby, when
> we get an opportunity to talk.

> Mr. Ruby: I don't think I will get a fair representation with my
> counsel, Joe Tonahill. I don't think so. I would like to re-
> quest that I go to Washington and you take all the tests that
> I have to take. It is very important.

Ruby mentioned his dissatisfaction with his attorneys for their failure to arrange a lie detector test, and a discussion with Warren ensued. The subject again returned to transporting him to Washington.

> Mr. Ruby: I would like to request that I go to Washington and take
> all the tests that I have to take. It is very important.

Next, Ruby resumed his story about taking sandwiches to the radio station where he said he remained until 2:00 a.m. Ruby discussed the "Welcome Mr. Kennedy" advertisement with Bernard Weissman's name attached, and the editorial on the Adlai Stevenson incident by his friend at the radio station. Ruby related how he left and drove to the *Times Herald* building. Ruby then suddenly changed his stream of thought again.

> Mr. Ruby: Gentlemen unless you get me back to Washington, you
> can't get a fair shake out of me. If you understand my way
> of talking you have to bring me to Washington to get the
> tests. . . . Unless you can get me to Washington, and I am
> not a crackpot, I have all my senses—I don't want to evade
> any crime I am guilty of.[2588]

Ruby argued with his lawyer on the subject of premeditation and other issues during his testimony. He told Warren it was too bad they did not get him back to Washington six months earlier. Warren explained that the delay in getting Ruby's testimony was because the Commission did not want to interfere with or prejudice his murder trial. Sheriff Decker interjected that Ruby had requested to be able to tell him his story but he had refused to listen, since that would have made him a material witness.

Ruby discussed the details of his whereabouts on the night of the assassination, stating that he ran into one of his employees, Kathy Kay, who was out with a Dallas police officer whom she apparently was having an affair with. The officer expressed to Ruby that Oswald should be cut to ribbons, inch by inch. While Ruby was telling the story to Warren, Ruby's attorney, Joe Tonahill, passed him a note. On it, he had written that the officer's statement "started Jack off." Ruby read the note to Warren, and expressed his contempt for his attorney for suggesting he admit to getting "started off." If Ruby had been "started off" the day before the murder of Oswald—as his own lawyer had just stated—it would lend support for premeditation on Ruby's part. Ruby felt his own attorney was working against him. Ruby berated

Tonahill, who defended himself, stating that a psychiatrist had told him that that may have been what set Ruby off.

Following the argument, Ruby asked Sheriff Decker and other members of law enforcement to leave the room. Ruby resumed his plea to go to Washington.

> Mr. Ruby: Boys, I am in a tough spot, I tell you that. . . . But this isn't the place for me to tell what I want to tell . . . Chief Warren, your life is in danger in this city, do you know that?

Warren denied knowing that his own life was in danger during his stay in Dallas. Ruby stated, "It has something to do with you, Chief Warren." Ruby's statement was a reference to the hatred many Southerners and the far right had for Warren. (The far right wing often spoke of Warren in threatening terms, and it will be recalled that Walker's friend and financial supporter, J. Evetts Haley, in a speech to the National Indignation Committee, said he would do more than impeach Warren; he'd hang him.[2589])

Ruby made yet another plea to go to Washington, stating that he had 'problems,' but Warren again denied the request.

After the request was again rejected, Ruby continued, telling Warren that he had read in the newspaper about the safety precautions taken for Warren during his visit to Dallas and the remarks made by crackpots about Warren.

Warren then changed the subject and asked Ruby if he had known Oswald before the shooting. Ruby responded, saying he wanted to document his answer of "no" on the lie detector, and changed the subject back to wanting to go to Washington. Throughout his testimony, Ruby repeatedly asked Warren if he appeared rational and "sober," and if he "sounded as if [he had] made sense." He wanted Warren's affirmation of his sanity. Ruby continued and related that his life was threatened and he was not safe in Dallas.

> Mr. Ruby: Gentlemen, my life is in danger here. Not with my guilty plea of execution. Do I sound sober enough to you as I say this? . . . I may not live tomorrow to give any further testimony. The reason why I add this to this, since you assure me that I have been speaking sense by then, I might be speaking sense by following what I have said, and the only thing I want to get out to the public, and I can't say it here, is with authenticity, with sincerity of the truth of everything and why my act was committed, but it can't be said here. It can be said; it's got to be said amongst people of the highest authority that would give me the benefit of the doubt. And following that immediately give me a lie detector test after I do make the statement. Chairman War-

> ren, if you felt that your life was in danger at the moment,
> how would you feel? Wouldn't you be reluctant to go on
> speaking, even though you request me to do so?
>
> Chief Justice Warren: . . . If you think anything that I am asking
> you is endangering you in any way or form, I want you to
> feel absolutely free to say that the interview is over.
>
> Mr. Ruby: What happens then? I didn't accomplish anything.[2590]

Warren missed Ruby's point. Warren acted as if Ruby was concerned about saying something that may jeopardize the appeal of his murder conviction. He wasn't. Warren told him he realized he was in a "delicate situation" with his murder appeal, and had Ruby not volunteered to testify before the Commission, Warren said to Ruby: "I wouldn't have bothered you. Because I know you do have this case that is not yet finished, and I wouldn't want to jeopardize your position by trying to insist that you testify."

Ruby, however, made it clear that he was not afraid of jeopardizing the appeal of his murder conviction, but rather he was afraid of a force he has yet to name, but would shortly. Whoever Ruby was afraid of, he appears to imply that Warren is in jeopardy from the same force, as well as his family—and the Jewish people. Warren was obtuse and instead encouraged Ruby to exercise his right not to incriminate himself and not say anything further. However, it was not Warren's place to tell Ruby to stop talking. Warren did not represent him. Ruby had his own counsel present. It was Warren's job to find the truth, which he failed at miserably.

Ruby's assertion that he could not tell his secret while in the Dallas County Jail may reflect his awareness that, just as it was easy enough to kill Oswald at the police department, someone could do the same to him at the county jail. Ruby recognized his paramount place of importance in the assassination story, but didn't feel Warren—who treated him as just another witness—did.

Warren asserted, "We have taken the testimony of 200 to 300 people, I would imagine, here in Dallas without going to Washington." Ruby responded, "Yes; but those people aren't Jack Ruby." Warren did not feel Ruby was involved in any conspiracy and, by implication, that Ruby's story was of questionable relevance to the assassination of the president.

Ruby tried to make his case about the danger he faced as follows:

> Mr. Ruby: I tell you, gentlemen, my whole family is in jeopardy. My
> sisters, as to their lives. . . . Naturally, I am a far gone con-
> clusion. My sisters Eva, Eileen, and Mary, I lost my sisters.
>
> My brothers Sam, Earl, Hyman, and myself naturally—my in-laws,
> Harold Kaminsky, Marge Ruby, the wife of Earl, and Phyl-
> lis, the wife of Sam Ruby, they are in jeopardy of loss of
> their lives. Yet they have, just because they are blood related
> to myself—does that sound serious enough to you, Chief
> justice Warren?

Warren agreed it sounded serious, and Ruby eventually repeated his reason for shooting Oswald:

> Mr. Ruby: . . . And I have never had the chance to tell that, to back it up, to prove it.
>
> Consequently, right at this moment I am being victimized as part of a plot in the world's worst tragedy and crime at this moment. . . . At this moment, Lee Harvey Oswald isn't guilty of committing the crime of assassinating President Kennedy. Jack Ruby is. How can I fight that, Chief Justice Warren?
>
> Chief Justice Warren: Well now, I want to say, Mr. Ruby, that as far as the Commission is concerned, there is no implication of that in what we are doing.[2591]

Finally Ruby decided, after talking to Sheriff Bill Decker, "to be a man" and come out and name names, "if it [took] his life to say it." "To be man" in Yiddish—"to be a *mentsh*"—has a special meaning of "Nothing less than character, rectitude, dignity, a sense of what is right, responsible, decorous."[2592] Ruby knew that what he was about to say could cost him his life and he took the risk.

> Mr. Ruby: All right, there is a certain organization here—
>
> Chief Justice Warren: That I can assure you.
>
> Mr. Ruby: There is an organization here, Chief Justice Warren, if it takes my life at this moment to say it, and Bill Decker said be a man and say it, there is a John Birch Society right now in activity, and Edwin Walker is one of the top men of the organization—take it for what it is worth, Chief Justice Warren. Unfortunately for me, for me giving the people the opportunity to get in power, because of the act I committed, has put a lot of people in jeopardy with their lives. Don't register with you does it?
>
> Chief Justice Warren: No, I don't understand that.
>
> Mr. Ruby: Would you rather I just delete what I said and just pretend that nothing is going on?[2593]

Justice Warren told Ruby he did not want him to delete anything. Ruby might have hoped that the Warren Commission had discovered evidence of a possible conspiracy involving General Walker and the John Birch Society that they had not yet publicly revealed. If so, Ruby may have been trying to lead Warren's line of questioning into the direction of Walker and the Birch Society. At this point, however, Ruby gave up on the imperceptive Warren, who showed no further interest in the matter and asked no follow-up questions to draw Ruby out. Unfortunately, neither Warren nor his Commission had any suspicions about Walker or the JBS whatsoever.

Ruby then abruptly changed the subject and told Warren how he was gripped with emotion over the assassination—so much so that he killed Oswald to spare Mrs. Kennedy from having to testify at Oswald's murder trial. He told Warren the steps he had taken leading up to the Oswald shooting.

Ruby changed the subject again to his visit to Cuba in 1959 and his relationship with gambler Louis McWillie. Ruby denied trying to send Jeeps to Cuba. At one point, the stenographer paused to change the paper on the machine. Ruby turned to Warren Commission counsel Arlen Specter, a Jew, and asked him, "Are you a Yid [Yiddish]? They're cutting off the legs and arms of Jewish children." Although Specter had been sent to the proceeding because Ruby had requested that a member of the Jewish faith from the Commission be present during his testimony, he did not answer Ruby, because the stenographer had finished putting the paper into the machine and he didn't want his response on record.[2594]

Ruby abruptly changed the subject again, this time pointing the finger at the John Birch Society.

> Mr. Ruby: How can I prove my authenticity of what I have stated here today?
>
> Chief Justice Warren: Well, you have testified under oath and I don't even know that there is anything to disprove what you have said.
>
> Mr. Ruby: No; because I will say this. You don't know if there is anything to disprove, but at this moment, there is a certain organization in this area that has been indoctrinated, that I am the one that was in the plot to assassinate our president.
>
> Chief Justice Warren: Would you tell us what that is?
>
> Mr. Ruby: The John Birch Society.
>
> Chief Justice Warren: Can you tell us what basis you have for that, Mr. Ruby?
>
> Mr. Ruby: Just a feeling of it. Mr. Warren, you don't recall when I— Friday night after leaving the *Times Herald*, I went to my apartment and very impatiently awakened George Senator. As a matter of fact, used the words, as I state, "You have to get up, George. I want you to go with me."[2595]

Ruby again was trying to get Warren to understand the symbolism of the billboard. Ruby had access to the daily news in his jail cell. He was deeply disturbed that, after the assassination, General Walker and the John Birch Society had heavily promoted the idea that Ruby and Oswald had plotted the assassination as a part of a Jewish-Communist conspiracy (as we shall see shortly).

Ruby next related going to his club with Senator to pick up the Polaroid camera, and explained that he had stopped at the post office to check on Bernard Weissman's post office box, which was listed on the "Welcome Mr. Kennedy" ad.

Ruby continued his testimony about the billboard:

> Mr. Ruby: . . . I recall seeing a sign on a certain billboard "Impeach Earl Warren." You have heard something about that?
> Chief Justice Warren: I read something in the paper, yes; that is all.
> Mr. Ruby: It came from New Bedford, or Massachusetts; I don't recall what the town was. And there was a similar number to that, but I thought at the time it would be the same number of 1792 but it was 1757. That is the reason I went down there to take the Polaroid picture of it, because of that remaining in the city at that time. What happened to the picture, I don't know. . . .

Warren showed no interest in the billboard matter, in spite of the fact that no one had provided any explanation as to why Ruby was so obsessed about it. There was never an inquiry into who had purchased the billboard. Warren was poorly prepared for his examination of Ruby. He should have read the FBI's interviews with Larry Crafard and George Senator on the subject of the billboard in advance. Instead, what he knew about it came from a newspaper. The billboard could have provided a clue as to who was behind the assassination, but Warren did not pick up on it—even after Ruby repeatedly broached the subject. (Ruby will bring up the billboard again, as we shall see.)

Ruby was asked if he knew Bernard Weissman, and he said he did not. He stated that he went to the post office and asked them who held the post office box listed in the "Welcome Mr. Kennedy" ad, but they refused to give the information out. Warren Commission counsel Lee Rankin changed the subject and asked Ruby if he had known Officer Tippit. Ruby denied it. Rankin asked him about a story that he had heard, which alleged that Ruby had been seen sitting with Bernard Weissman, J. D. Tippit, and an unnamed rich oilman, together at the Carousel Club shortly before the assassination. Ruby asked Rankin the name of the rich oilman, but Rankin could not recall it. Ruby changed the subject abruptly to the photo of the "Impeach Earl Warren" billboard and said he took it to another club the following day, where an individual who saw it became very emotional. The testimony again turned to the allegation that Ruby had been seen with Weissman, Tippit, and the rich oilman at the Carousel. Ruby replied, "No, I am as innocent regarding any conspiracy as any of you gentlemen in the room, and I don't want anything to be run over lightly."[2596]

Ruby explained why he killed Oswald stating, "Being of the Jewish faith, I wanted to show my love for my president and his lovely wife."[2597] Congressman Ford interjected and asked him about his trip to Cuba. Then the Chief Justice resumed:

> Chief Justice Warren: Congressman [Ford] do you have anything
>   further?
> Mr. Ruby: You can get more out of me. Let's not break up too soon.[2598]

It's clear that Ruby had more information to give and, under the right circumstances, was prepared to give it. Warren declined to "get more out of Ruby," completely missing any opportunity he might have had to learn Ruby's secret.

Congressman Ford asked more questions about Ruby's trip to Cuba. The dialogue changed to questions about Ruby's allegation that his family was being threatened. Ruby asserted that he had been falsely accused of being part of a conspiracy to silence Oswald. Ruby then stated that the John Birch Society had put forth falsehoods that he was part of the conspiracy to kill the president.

> Mr. Ruby: . . . Now it is the most fantastic story you have ever
>   heard in a lifetime. I did something out of the goodness of
>   my heart. Unfortunately, Chief Earl Warren had you been
>   around five or six months ago, I know your hands were tied,
>   you couldn't do it, and immediately the president would
>   have gotten hold of my true story, or whatever would have
>   been said about me, a certain organization wouldn't have so
>   completely formed now, so powerfully, to use me because
>   I am of the Jewish extraction, Jewish faith, to commit the
>   most dastardly crime that has ever been committed. . . .
> Chief Justice Warren: Well, I don't quite get the significance of it, Mr.
>   Ruby. I know what you feel about the John Birch Society.
> Mr. Ruby: Very powerful.
> Chief Justice Warren: I think it is powerful, yes I do. Of course, I
>   don't have all the information that you feel you have on
>   that subject.
> Mr. Ruby: Unfortunately you don't have, because it's too late. . . .

Ruby continued on the subject of the persecution of the Jews and repeatedly stated that the Jewish people were being exterminated.

> Mr. Ruby: I want to say this to you. The Jewish people are being
>   exterminated at this moment. Consequently a whole new

form of government is going to take over this country, and I know I won't live to see you another time. Do I sound sort of screwy in telling you these things? . . . But it is a very serious situation. I guess it's too late to stop it, isn't it?

Getting no insightful response from Warren, Ruby abruptly changed the subject and asked again to be taken to Washington. Congressman Ford continued the examination.

> Representative Ford: Are there any questions that ought to be asked to help clarify the situation that you described?
>
> Mr. Ruby: There is only one thing. If you don't take me back to Washington tonight to give me a chance to prove to the president that I am not guilty, then you will see the most tragic thing that will ever happen. And if you don't have the power to take me back, I won't be around to prove my innocence or guilt . . . Maybe something can be saved, something can be done. What have you got to answer to that, Chief Justice Warren?
>
> Chief Justice Warren: Well I don't know what can be done, Mr. Ruby, because I don't know what you anticipate we will encounter.
>
> Representative Ford: Is there anything more you can tell us if you went back to Washington?
>
> Mr. Ruby: Yes; are you sincere in wanting to take me back?
>
> Representative Ford: We are most interested in all the information you have.
>
> Mr. Ruby: All I know is maybe something can be saved. Because right now, I want to tell you this, I am used as a scapegoat, and there is no greater weapon that you can use to create some falsehood about someone of the Jewish faith, especially at the terrible heinous crime such as the killing of President Kennedy. Now maybe something can be saved. It may not be too late, whatever happens, if our president, Lyndon Johnson, knew the truth from me. But if I am eliminated, there won't be any way of knowing. . . .
>
> Mr. Tonahill: Who do you think is going to eliminate you, Jack?
>
> Mr. Ruby: I have been used for a purpose, and there will be certain tragic occurrences happening if you don't take my testimony and somehow vindicate me so my people don't suffer because of what I have done. . . . You have lost me though.

> You have lost me, Chief Justice Warren.
>
> Chief Justice Warren: Lost you in what sense?
>
> Mr. Ruby: I won't be around for you to question me again.

Ruby again begged for a lie detector test to verify his story. He again expressed concern for the safety of his people because of lies told about him.

> Mr. Ruby: You have a lost cause, Earl Warren. You don't stand a chance.
> They feel about you like they do about me, Chief Justice War-
> ren. . . . But you are the only one who can save me. I think
> you can.[2599]

Ruby repeated that all he wanted to do was to tell the truth. At the end of his testimony, Ruby concluded that it was now too late, they wouldn't see him again, and he had lost his family. Ruby again told Warren he did not feel he believed his testimony. Ruby was granted his wish to undergo a lie detector test, but not in Washington. The HSCA concluded the lie detector had numerous procedural errors during the test and, consequently, they were unable to interpret the exam. The HSCA noted, "It is emphasized by the panel, however, that no opinion could be rendered on the validity of this examination or the reliability of the result for the numerous reasons discussed in this report."[2600]

The Warren Commission's examination of Jack Ruby, a key figure in the assassination story, was awful. Ruby had a secret to divulge, but clearly felt he could not do it safely in Dallas. He alluded to General Walker and the John Birch Society as the forces that had something to do with the assassination. He hinted that he had been used to silence Oswald because he was a Jew. He was deeply disturbed that the John Birch Society was promoting the notion that he, a Jew, was involved in the assassination of the president—and that Walker and the radical right were promoting the idea that the assassination was just one more example of a purported Jewish-Communist plot that they believed undermined America..

The accusation that he was a part of the conspiracy to assassinate the president particularly disturbed Ruby. General Walker and the far right heavily promoted the charge and also claimed that Ruby and Oswald were part of a Communist cell.

General Walker and Billy James Hargis attended the Third Annual Anti-Communist Leadership School Christian Crusade meeting in Shreveport from February 17 to 21, 1964, according to the FBI. (Kent Courtney, Carlos Bringuier, and Captain Kenneth Ryker were some of the other speakers at the meeting. Bringuier's speech was entitled "Oswald: Castro's agent in the United States."[2601]) Reverend Frederick Fowler, from Duluth, Minnesota, told the FBI that he was in a private meeting in Walker's room when Walker stated that Oswald shot and deliberately missed him as part of a pre-arranged plan by the Communists. The meeting also included Fernando Penabaz, an anti-Castro Cuban and a friend and biographer of Billy James Hargis. Penabaz told the FBI that Walker told him, "if he [Walker] a conservative, were also shot at, this would make his shooting and that of President Kennedy appear as the work of a crank." (Walker seemed to imply that Oswald wanted both shootings to appear as the work of a crank to disguise the fact they were the work of a Communist.) This means that Walker had spun a new version of the tale of the of April shoot-and-miss incident. Walker also told Fowler that Oswald and Ruby were two of six members of a Communist cell active in Dallas and were both part of the conspiracy to kill the president.

Penabaz told Fowler that he had heard that President Kennedy and Soviet Premier Khrushchev had an agreement to eliminate Castro. Castro had heard about it, decided to eliminate Kennedy, and paid Oswald ten thousand dollars to do it during his visit to the Cuban Embassy in Mexico City. As the story goes, Oswald was then supposed to have been near Ruby's apartment just after the shooting of the president (he actually was), where a Cuban would identify him by the color of his jacket and take him to Cuba. The scheme supposedly failed when Oswald wore the wrong color jacket. Ruby was allegedly part of the Cuban plot and supposedly shot Oswald for failing to follow the escape plan.

Reverend Fowler stated to the FBI that the Penabaz tale was published in the *New York Times* and the *National Review*. The FBI questioned Penabaz, and he said he had heard about the Cuban who was going to take Oswald back to Cuba from another Cuban in Miami. He said, however, that it was just a rumor or conjecture—not fact. He denied making many of the statements attributed to him. Penabaz stated that Billy James Hargis was also at the meeting where the statements were made.[2602] Penabaz was a member of the John Birch Society's American Opinion speaker's bureau in 1962.[2603]

The FBI learned that the *Dallas Times Herald* carried a UPI release entitled "Walker Claims Communist Cell Active in Dallas." The article was based on a Walker radio address on February 12, 1964. The FBI interviewed Walker, in the presence of one of his attorneys, Joe Mathews, and found that Walker was "rambling, incoherent, and could furnish no information of substance." The FBI concluded: "In view of Walker's apparent inability to respond rationally to questions, no further contact with him is contemplated."[2604] Even so, on February 20, 1964, the FBI interviewed Walker again. After answering some of their questions, Walker told them he wanted to speak with his attorney, Clyde Watts, before answering any more.[2605]

The FBI reported, on April 17, 1964, that they had learned from a source that Walker's friend Ned Touchstone had been investigating the New Orleans aspects of the assassination and had claimed in the *Councilor* that "Oswald and Rubenstein" were connected in employment matters. The source said Touchstone obtained this information when he visited General Walker in Dallas in December 1963.[2606]

It should be recalled that the radical right, including General Walker, universally referred to Ruby as "Rubenstein." Walker claimed that "Rubenstein knew Oswald" at the 1964 Congress of Conservatives meeting with Kent Courtney.[2607] The Minutemen newsletter *On Target* referred to Ruby as Rubenstein.[2608] Revilo Oliver referred to Ruby as "Rubenstein" in his testimony to the Warren Commission—as did Billy James Hargis in his Christian Crusade publications, in an effort to promote the so-called Jewish-Communist conspiracy.

Ruby, the Nazis, and the Persecution of the Jews

The consensus opinion of the examining psychiatrists was that Jack Ruby suffered from the mental illness of paranoid psychosis. However, Ruby's purported paranoia was unusual, since it was focused on a singular, encapsulated belief—valid or not—and was not global. He believed that the forces behind the assassination were killing members of his family, and of the Jewish faith.

Ruby also made a few half-hearted suicide gestures in jail, which were thought to be further evidence of his mental illness. He once rammed his head into the plaster wall of his jail cell. Another time, he tried to hang himself with his trousers. Once, he tried to electrocute himself by jumping up and sticking his finger into the overhead light socket. Some felt the actions were ploys to substantiate an insanity defense.[2609] Ruby believed his involvement in the assassination story brought shame on the Jewish people.[2610] Considering that Ruby was a man sentenced to die in the electric chair, who believed his family and the Jewish people were being murdered as a result of his involvement, his suicide gestures were understandable.

Dr. William Beavers saw Ruby eight or nine times and further diagnosed him with the condition of psychotic depression with auditory hallucinations. He noted that Ruby's delusion was that his family was being mutilated and that there was a pogrom against the Jews. Interestingly, he opined that although Ruby was delusional he was otherwise sound.[2611] Ruby's family and attorneys weighed in on Ruby's preoccupation with the persecution of the Jews and the question of his sanity. His sister, Eva Grant, testified that Jack told that her twenty-five million Jews had been slaughtered on the floor below his jail cell. When Ruby heard airplanes go by, he told his sister that they were dropping bombs on the Jews.[2612] Earl Ruby testified that Jack read books on the Jewish persecution and "went to lectures on it, the synagogue, that had movies of killing of the Jews in Germany. . . ."[2613] Ruby's lawyer, Phil Burleson, told Earl that Jack was "off his rocker" and ". . . has got himself involved with all the Jews all over the world and doesn't know what he is talking about." Earl Ruby insisted, on the other hand, "[his] brother did know what he was talking about, it was Burleson who didn't understand. Because in order to understand—it's a Jewish problem—and most Jews would understand it."[2614] Attorney Melvin Belli told Earl Ruby, "I have a patient, not a client."[2615] For nearly three years after Ruby murdered Oswald, he was locked in a jail cell without windows under around-the-clock surveillance. He repeated over and over that the Jews were being killed because of his crime. He felt that the guards, at one point, were pumping mustard gas into his cell.[2616]

Warren Commission counsel Burt Griffin, serving under Leon Hubert, was largely responsible for the Warren Commission investigation into the Jack Ruby aspects of the case and offered his opinion on the question of Ruby's sanity. Griffin had a falling out with Dallas authorities and was not invited to be present during Ruby's testimony. Years later, Griffin opined, "I would have treated this thing as possibly the efforts of a serious man, rather than a crazy man."[2617]

Sol Dann, the legal advisor to the Ruby family, insisted that Jack Ruby did not get

0

a fair trial because of the "vicious attitude in Dallas, towards Catholics, Jews, and Negroes." In a letter to Hobart Taylor, Jr., the assistant general council to the president, written on June 16, 1964, Dann asked him if the Warren Commission, still in deliberation, had found any connections between the Ku Klux Klan or John Birch Society and Oswald or the murders. He wanted to know if the judge, the four prosecutors, or any of the jurors or witnesses for the prosecution were members of the Ku Klux Klan or John Birch Society. Dann took an interest in the billboard, when no one besides Ruby had, and went out and took his own picture of it.[2618]

The Nazis also obsessed Ruby. In a January 31, 1966, letter composed in jail, Ruby wrote "So you must believe me . . . there is only one kind of people that would do such a thing, that would have to be the nazi's [sic], and that is who is in power in this country right now . . . There is only one kind of people that would go to such extremes, and that would be the Master Race. . . ."[2619] During his incarceration, Ruby jotted the words "nazi's" and "negroes" with his doodlings. In a letter, Ruby wrote of his fear of Nazis and Germans. Author Seth Kantor noted that Ruby did not equate Oswald with the Communists but, rather, with the Nazis. Ruby indicated in the letter that he did not kill Oswald to avenge the Kennedy murder but to avenge the death of Jews in the gas chamber.[2620]

Perhaps Ruby knew more about Oswald than anyone realized. (In Chapter Three, Oswald's ties to the Nazi-oriented Banister operation in New Orleans were described in depth.) The credible allegation that Oswald was seen with New Orleans American Nazi Party leader, Ray Leahart, was presented earlier. Guy Banister bailed Leahart out of jail after he was arrested in the 1961 Hate Bus incident, which was orchestrated by Nazi Commander George Lincoln Rockwell. Leahart, in turn, was an associate of Joseph Milteer (another relationship documented in Chapter Three). Oswald had the address of the Secretary of the American Nazi Party, Dan Burros, in the notebook that was examined by the Warren Commission, and evidence was also presented in Chapter Three which suggests Oswald may very well have known Burros.

Ruby was not entirely delusional if he had sound, rational reasons to believe there was a campaign against the Jews and his family. If Ruby had visited General Walker on three occasions—as Walker employee William Duff credibly alleged—then he may have known Walker's top aide, Robert Surrey, who was head of the Dallas American Nazi Party and secretary-treasurer of the Dallas John Birch Society. Walker and Surrey were both rabid anti-Semites. If Ruby knew they were involved in the assassination conspiracy, then he would have had sufficient reason to believe there was a campaign underway against the Jews. As was revealed at the Congress of Freedom meeting in the spring of 1963, Walker was a military advisor to the plot to kill a large number of prominent Jewish figures and others, in what amounted to a planned pogrom—the very thing Ruby feared. In his testimony before the Warren Commission, Ruby directly alluded to the largely anti-Semitic John Birch Society and its most militant member, General Walker, as the powerful force that had used him because he was a Jew. It will be recalled from Chapter Six that Birch Society council member, Revilo Oliver, called the vaporizing of Jews a "beatified vision." On March 1, 1963, the FBI learned from

Legat, Bonn, West Germany (the FBI Europe office), that Walker had been corresponding and sending circulars to various European Fascists, calling for worldwide action against Jews (as was noted in Chapter Fourteen).

There is no direct evidence that anyone compelled Ruby to kill Lee Harvey Oswald. However, Ruby implied that someone did, and alluded to Walker, the John Birch Society, the Minutemen, and the Nazis. General Walker was not present in Dallas for at least four days preceding the assassination and was not in a direct position to compel Ruby to kill Oswald. If Walker gave the order for Ruby to kill Oswald, then the person in Dallas most likely in charge of carrying it out was Robert Surrey, his top aide. If so, then perhaps Ruby knew that Surrey was the leader of the Dallas American Nazi Party—or perhaps Surrey made a point of telling him. Surrey, no doubt, owned a Nazi military uniform and a swastika arm ban, as did his fellow American Nazi Party comrades, Ray Leahart and Dan Burros (pictured in Chapter Three).

Robert Surrey was also a Minuteman, as we shall see—a fact that Ruby may also have been aware of from his past dealings. Ruby may have known Surrey initially only as a Minuteman and not a Nazi. He may have been referring to Surrey as the Nazi who framed him in the following quote from a Ruby jail letter:

> They are going to come out with a story that it was the Minutemen
> that killed the Jews, don't believe it, they are using that to cover up
> for the Nazis. . . . Oh the way I fucked up this world who would ever
> dream that the mother fucker was a Nazi and found me the perfect
> setup for a frame. . . . I was used to silence Oswald. I walked into
> a trap the moment I walked down that ramp Sunday morning.[2621]

Surrey perfectly fit the description of the person Ruby thought was a member of the Minutemen, but was really a Nazi—and found him the perfect setup for a frame.

Not long before Ruby died (in 1967), according to an article in the *London Sunday Times*, he told psychiatrist Werner Teuter that the assassination was "an act of overthrowing the government" and that he knew "who had President Kennedy killed." He added: "I am doomed. I do not want to die. But I am not insane. I was framed to kill Oswald."[2622] It was the second time that Ruby suggested he was compelled by a frame-up to kill Oswald. Ruby claimed to know who was behind the assassination, which he noted was an act of overthrowing the government.

Previously, the FBI had investigated reports that Walker was engaged in conspiring to overthrow the U.S. government, as will be detailed in the next chapter. As a result, the FBI notified the Secret Service, in 1964, that Walker was a threat to the life of President Johnson. Ruby's claim that those behind the assassination were engaging in the act of an overthrow of the government fits exactly the known activities of General Walker and his group.

On June 1, 1964, Ruby's attorney, Sol Dann—following Ruby's guilty verdict—

wrote a brief entitled "Why Ruby Shot Oswald (The '6 million' plus)." In it, Dann placed the blame on anti-Semitism and added Ruby to the millions of victims killed in the holocaust. One section, entitled "Texas Hot-bed of Anti-Semitism," appeared as follows: "Vicious Anti-Semites like Rockwell and Gerald L. K. Smith are openly and primarily supported by Mr. Hunt, one of the wealthiest oil men in Texas. (Such men often exert their influence over courts). The headquarters of many of these Anti-Semitic organizations are in Texas, from where a large part of Anti-Semitic literature emanates. (See files and records of B'nai B'rith Anti-Defamation League). Ruby was repeatedly reminded by the Nazi Rockwell that what happened to Jews in Germany could also happen here in America. This affected <u>non</u>-observing as well as observing 'Jews.'"[2623]

Dann was insightful. As noted in prior chapters, General Walker had corresponded with Gerald L. K. Smith. Guy Banister subscribed to Smith's literature. Men tied to Smith (Colonel William Potter Gale and Wesley Swift) were privileged to the plots to kill prominent Jews revealed at the Congress of Freedom meeting. (Oswald's ties to men in Rockwell's American Nazi Party are well documented in Chapter Three.) "Mr. Hunt" (no doubt H. L. Hunt, an associate of General Walker and Guy Banister) was correctly identified as a financial angel for the far right, including General Walker. It will be recalled from Chapter Eleven that H. L. Hunt's employee, John Curington, stated that Hunt sent him to the Dallas jail on Saturday, November 23, to check on the security and found it nonexistent. The incident suggests that Hunt may have had a hand in planning the execution of Oswald.

The John Birch Society

William Duff's allegation that he had seen Jack Ruby at General Walker's home several times in 1962 and 1963—at least once with a member of the John Birch Society—was discussed in Chapter Fourteen. Evidence will be presented later in this chapter that Ruby may have had dealings with the John Birch Society involving the illegal procurement of guns.

Jack Ruby was close to his brother Earl, who operated Cobo Cleaners—a dry cleaning operation in Detroit, Michigan. They often discussed business matters with each other. In one instance, Jack was interested in manufacturing a balancing board novelty called a twist board. Jack consulted with Earl in November 1963 and discussed where to buy the bearings and how to have them manufactured and sold. After analyzing the prospective enterprise, Earl told Jack that it wouldn't be profitable and, thus, discouraged him.[2624]

Phone records from Cobo Cleaners showed that a long distance call was placed on May 1, 1963, to the James O. Welch Company, phone number 491-2500, 810 Main Street. Earl denied making the call, and suggested that perhaps his brother Hyman might have placed the call for business reasons.[2625, 2626] Robert Welch's brother James owned the James O. Welch Company—a candy manufacturer located in the Boston, Massachusetts, area.

Robert Welch had been the vice president in charge of sales for his brother's company until 1956, when he left the business "to put his whole life into the fight against Communism." He founded the John Birch Society in 1958.[2627] Like H. L. Hunt, Welch despised democracy and decried it as "merely a deceptive phrase, a weapon of demagoguery, and a perennial fraud," and claimed that it was "the worst of all forms of government."[2628] The meaning of the phone record suggesting that Earl Ruby placed a called to the James O. Welch Company is unknown. It is only mentioned in the context of Jack Ruby's intense interest in the John Birch Society billboard following the assassination, and the allegations that Jack Ruby was seen at General Walker's home with members of the JBS.

Jack Ruby had the telephone number and address of Thomas Hill—on an envelope in his notebook when it was found by the FBI in the trunk of his car after the murder of Oswald that he apparently copied from the "Impeach Earl Warren" billboard.[2629] What the FBI did not acknowledge was that Thomas Hill was the director of Field Activities for the John Birch Society in Belmont, Massachusetts—and the long-time staff assistant to Robert Welch, head of the Society.[2630] The author has reviewed volumes of John Birch Society letterheads, correspondence, and literature in the personal papers of John Birch leaders Clarence Manion, Tom Anderson, and Granville Knight, and the Society's address was always given as "The John Birch Society, Belmont 78, Massachusetts."[2631] Therefore, the post office box number given on the "Impeach Earl Warren" billboard must have been a Dallas address, and not a Massachusetts's address as Ruby apparently believed.[2632, 2633]

Nelson Bunker Hunt, Robert Welch, John Rousselot—all close associates of General Walker—and others, owned one of the John Birch Society's magazines, *American Opinion*. Revilo Oliver, who addressed the infamous Congress of Freedom meeting in 1963, was an associate editor of the magazine.[2634] Dallas was a John Birch Society stronghold in 1963 and General Walker was its most famous member. Robert Welch visited Dallas often and conducted a two-day John Birch Society Dallas chapter meeting in Dallas on May 18 and 19, 1963.[2635] Welch was close to General Walker, frequently sharing the speaker's platform with him. The twenty-eight-member council of the John Birch Society contained some familiar names. Welch is listed as the founder on a November 1963 JBS letterhead. Members of the council listed included: Revilo Oliver, Thomas Anderson, Clarence Manion, and Slobodan Draskovich. (Draskovich was an ardent anti-Semite and initially refused to serve on the council because it included a far-right-wing Jew, Alfred Kohlberg.)[2636]

Guy Banister had ties to Robert Welch's office in Belmont, Massachusetts. D. A. Waite, Ph.D., an assistant to Robert Welch, wrote to Banister on August 14, 1963. Waite told Banister that Welch had given him the June MMM (Members Monthly Messages), which Banister had sent to him for a reply. Waite told Banister that Welch wanted more detailed information on his investigation of the Saturn Plant in New Orleans, "especially on any result such as the identification and possibly the discharge of JBS members." Welch replied he would keep it confidential, if necessary, or would use it if he could do so effectively.[2637] Guy Banister had a folder in his files entitled, "U.S. Government Interference With John Birch Society, 14–62."[2638] (The letter and file folder were obtained during the Garrison investigation.) The John Birch Society had a research department and kept files on those people it felt were subversives. They urged JBS members to submit MMM reports on subversives to the

Belmont office.[2639]

The John Birch Society promoted the theory that the president was killed as the result of a Communist conspiracy. After the assassination, the JBS executive council proclaimed, in a published statement, that: "The President of the United States had been murdered by a Marxist-Communist within the United States. It has been pointed out by the Hon. Martin Dies, since the assassination, that 'Lee Harvey Oswald was a Communist,' and when a Communist commits murder he is acting under orders."[2640]

R. W. Thomas of Waco, Texas, notified the FBI on November 29, 1963, that a fellow salesman and active member of the John Birch Society, John W. Johnson, had not reported to work on November 21 and November 22. When Johnson returned to work on November 23, he told Thomas that he was glad the president had been killed. He said that President Kennedy would "mow us over"—meaning members of the John Birch Society—if he got the chance. Thomas argued with Johnson and said he hoped they hanged Oswald. Johnson retorted that Oswald did not kill the president. The FBI made an appointment to question Johnson, but he failed to appear.[2641]

Paul V. Carroll appeared at the El Paso FBI office on the day of the Kennedy assassination and told the FBI that there had been a conspiracy in 1961 and 1962 by the John Birch Society and the American Nazi Party to gain control of the United States. Despite the fact the Carroll was under the care of a psychiatrist, J. Edgar Hoover ordered the matter to be "pressed vigorously" and without delay.[2642]

The Warren Commission took some, but not much, interest in Robert Welch and the John Birch Society. When they asked FBI Director Hoover about the JBS, Hoover responded to Warren Commission counsel J. Lee Rankin on February 7, 1964, stating, "*American Opinion*, the John Birch Society, and Welch have not been investigated by this Bureau." Hoover told Rankin, however, that the FBI had been sent sixteen stickers containing the statement "Communism Killed Kennedy," that were available from the *American Opinion*, Belmont, Massachusetts.[2643]

Jack Ruby, the John Birch Society, and the Minutemen

The mutual interests of Jack Ruby, General Walker, the John Birch Society, and the Minutemen were their involvement in the illegal procurement of large quantities of armaments. In Walker's case, it was to arm both the anti-Castro Cubans as well as an underground militia which could overthrow the government of the United States, as we shall see in greater detail in the next chapter. Ruby, as was noted by both the Warren Commission and HSCA, was suspected of running guns for the anti-Castro effort.

Nancy Perrin Rich, a twenty-seven-year-old former employee of Jack Ruby, testified to the Warren Commission on June 2, 1964, that Ruby was involved in an arms deal for the anti-Castro effort. Perrin Rich had been married to Robert Perrin—a bodyguard for the syndicate—who died in New Orleans in August 1962, of suicide by arsenic ingestion; she later remarried.[2644] Perrin had been a professional soldier in Spain as Francisco Franco was coming into power. He was a gunrunner for Franco in the late 1930s and early 1940s.

The couple had been living in Belmont, Massachusetts, before Perrin Rich's husband left her. Belmont was—as we have discussed—the home of Robert Welch and the John Birch Society, but it is not known if the Perrins were associated with the organization. Perrin Rich traveled to Texas to try to find her estranged husband in May 1962. She took a job as a bartender at Jack Ruby's Carousel Club in 1962 for two months, beginning in May or June 1962, and she reunited with her husband. She testified to the Warren Commission that Ruby got rough with her at the Carousel Club, because he felt she was not cleaning the glasses well enough and was not pushing drinks on the customers. She was outraged and quit on the spot.

Perrin Rich and her husband attended a meeting with a colonel or "light colonel," who was described as a member of the air force or, more likely, the army. She testified that Dave Cherry was also present at the meeting. Cherry, a bartender, had approached her husband with a proposition. He and the colonel wanted Perrin, who knew the island of Cuba well, to pilot a boat to bring Cuban refugees out of Cuba to Miami. The colonel agreed to pay Perrin ten thousand dollars. Another meeting took place five or six days later, with more people attending. The group consisted of a uniformed colonel, described as balding, age forty to fifty; an older, mannish woman; a man who looked like a prizefighter; and a couple of other men who sat in the corner of the meeting room, one of whom had a dark complexion. The group's plan was to move anti-Castro Cubans off the island—and Enfield rifles and military supplies onto it—in the summer of 1962. The colonel stated that they had been taking small arms and explosives off of a U.S. military base for the previous three months. Perrin Rich knew the operation was illegal and was not sanctioned by the federal government. She and her husband understood that it was a high-stakes mission and agreed to do it for twenty-five thousand dollars.

Perrin Rich learned that those present at the meeting were expecting a delivery of money to be used to purchase rifles from Mexico. There had been a hitch, however, and the delivery of the money had been delayed. Later, there was a knock on the door and Jack Ruby entered. Perrin Rich had the shock of her life. She recalled, "And you could have knocked me over with a feather" when she saw Ruby.[2645] The group seemed short of funds until Ruby arrived and saved the day. At the time, the Perrins were going by the assumed names of Jack and Nancy Starr, and both Ruby and Dave Cherry knew that those were not their real names. During the meeting, Ruby and Perrin Rich glared at each other. Ruby had a bulge in his breast pocket, something Perrin Rich had been accustomed to seeing while she was employed at the Carousel Club. When Ruby left the meeting, the pocket bulge was gone. It was her impression that Ruby was there to the deliver money, which he had kept in his pocket. Ruby met with the colonel in another room. Ruby left after ten minutes and everyone was happy. She believed the two men in the room, whom she described as looking pugnacious and Cuban, now had the finances they needed to travel to Mexico to buy guns.

The Perrins were told that it was up to the bigwigs in the group to decide whether or not they would pay them the twenty-five thousand dollars to carry out the Cuban mission. Three to four days later, they attended another meeting at the same apartment. The twenty-five thousand dollars requested by the Perrins for the mission was refused and fifteen thousand dollars was offered instead. The whole thing was postponed. After another meeting, the Perrins told them that they did not want anything to do with the operation, and Perrin Rich left Dallas two weeks later.[2646] Perrin Rich was known for providing reliable evidence. The Sacramento, California, district attorney commended her for her undercover work on an abortion case on October 23, 1963, which was noted by the Warren Commission. While she lived in Massachusetts, Perrin Rich had also worked as an undercover police informant.[2647]

Newsman Seth Kantor put together more evidence that Ruby was involved in gun running. Although it was not made public, Kantor learned that the Warren Commission suspected Ruby had been to Cuba in 1963.[2648] Ruby reportedly attended three meetings, in Dallas in 1961, in connection with the sale of arms to anti-Castro Cubans, according to an informant named Edward Brunner. After Ruby's arrest for the murder of Oswald, Ruby anticipated using Brunner as one of his attorneys.[2649] Ruby was also involved with Thomas Eli Davis, III—who ran guns into Cuba—and he hoped to do business with Davis on a regular basis. The CIA was aware that Davis was involved in gun running and training anti-Castro Cubans at a secret camp in Florida. At the time of the assassination, Davis was jailed in Algiers, where he was charged with running guns for the secret army insurgency that was attempting to assassinate French Premiere Charles de Gaulle.[2650] An informant told the FBI, on November 29, 1963, that Ruby, using the name Rubenstein, had been active in arranging illegal flights of weapons from Miami to the Castro organization in Cuba in the 1950s. He said that he was sure Ruby and Rubenstein were the same man after seeing photos of Ruby after the assassination.[2651] Warren Commission counsel Burt Griffin told Seth Kantor that he was suspicious that Ruby was involved in a significant way with Cuban affairs.[2652]

Wally Weston, a master of ceremonies at Ruby's nightclub, recalled having a conversation with Ruby at the jail where Ruby mentioned things about Cuba, guns, and New Orleans that particularly shook Weston up. Weston noted that the conversation took place during the period just before Ruby died when he was rapidly losing weight. According to Weston, Ruby told him, "now they're going to find out about Cuba, they're going to find out about my trip to Cuba, they're going to find out about the guns, find out about New Orleans, find out about everything." After Ruby confided his concerns about Cuba, guns, and New Orleans, Weston was afraid to visit him again.[2653]

Guy Banister and David Ferrie were also involved in the Cuban effort and the procurement of arms, but in New Orleans. It will be recalled from Chapter One that witnesses reported that they saw caches of military weapons at Guy Banister's New Orleans office, and that Banister and Ferrie had stolen weapons from the Schlumberger bunker outside of New Orleans. As was noted in Chapter Ten, one of Ruby's strippers recalled an incident where Ruby became very excited while expecting a visit from a man described as a big wheel, district attorney and judge from New Orleans, who fit the description of Leander Perez. Ruby and Perez couldn't have been any more dissimilar. Perez was a Southern racist and anti-Semite.

Ruby was a Northern Jew. If Leander Perez were the mysterious visitor to Ruby's club, it would not have been for social or political reasons but, conceivably, might have been related to acquiring guns—an activity Perez's close associates Guy Banister and General Walker had engaged in. If so, it may have been the activities involving Perez and the New Orleans hardcore underground that Ruby was alluding to when he revealed his fear to Wally Weston that "they're going to find out about my trip to Cuba, they're going to find out about the guns, find out about New Orleans, find out about everything."

The FBI learned of another plot to illegally procure weapons from the U.S. military for anti-Castro efforts that appears remarkably similar to the arms deal Ruby was involved in, as alleged by Nancy Perrin Rich. The operation differed from the one involving Ruby in that arms were being procured for both the anti-Castro effort and the far-right Minutemen and John Birch Society. The Minutemen were arming to the hilt and it may have been difficult to distinguish between the arming of the Minutemen and the arming of the anti-Castro Cubans.

The FBI obtained information that John Thomas Masen might have been involved in an insurrection plot under the direction of General Walker. They learned that, in October 1963, Masen was in contact with an army captain at Fort Hood, Texas, and he was trying to find someone interested in selling military armaments for a large-scale Caribbean exercise. Masen contacted the captain on several occasions, inquiring as to where certain firearms could be purchased. Some of Masen's inquiries concerned the possible purchase and resale of firearms and ammunition to a group that planned to attack Cuba. On November 20, 1963, Masen was arrested by the Alcohol and Tobacco Tax Unit (ATTU) in Dallas, for violation of the Federal Firearms Act—and was accused of selling parts, which could be used to convert an M-1 semi-automatic carbine into a M-2 fully automatic carbine. Masen pleaded guilty to the charges. Masen told the ATTU agents that he had strong right-wing beliefs and inclinations. He said there was a small "elite group" of patriots in the Dallas area who were arming for the defense of the country, inasmuch as they felt the government was being infiltrated by Communists. He told the FBI that the fear of a Communist takeover was fostered by propaganda put out by General Walker's American Eagle Publishing Company. The ATTU determined that Masen was a member of the Minutemen—or strongly sympathetic to them—and might be selling firearms to members. The Irving, Texas, police department noted, in a December 4, 1963, report, that John Thomas Masen had been in touch with the Minutemen, the John Birch Society, and various Cuban counter-revolutionary agents.[2654] On February 11, 1964, a police officer from Irving, Texas, contacted the FBI and reported that Masen had told him that: "Minutemen and Birchers in Dallas had contacted him for the purposes of buying ammunition."[2655]

The Dallas Police Department Criminal Intelligence Section determined, in October 1962, that Robert Surrey, Dan Smoot, Medford Evans, Bob Hatfield, Joe Grinnan, Julia Knecht (Walker's secretary), and others, were members of the Minutemen.[2656] As has been noted previously, Smoot and Surrey were friends of Joseph Milteer, and Smoot was also close to H. L. Hunt and General Walker. Evans was an associate of Hunt and Guy Banister. Hatfield was the member of Walker's group who spit on Adlai Stevenson. And it will be recalled that Grinnan was the Dallas John Birch Society leader who contributed money to the "Welcome Mr. Kennedy" ad.

In addition to William Duff's allegation that he saw Jack Ruby at the home of General Walker (the leader of the Dallas Minutemen) on three occasions, there was another report that tied Ruby to the Minutemen. According to a 1967 report from the investigation of Jim Garrison, two members of the Dallas Minutemen, Ronnie A. Wisk and Harold L. Helm, were issued permanent pass cards numbered 238 and 239 to Jack Ruby's Carousel Club. Wisk was reported to have been at a Minutemen Patriotic Party meeting at 3510 Greenville Avenue, Dallas, where a plot to assassinate Dallas department store owner Stanley Marcus was discussed.[2657] A flier announcing a speech in Dallas by Minutemen founder Robert DePugh, located by the author, bore the same Greenville Avenue address, which was the headquarters of The Patriotic Party, the political arm of the Minutemen—which lends credibility to the findings of Garrison.[2658]

The FBI uncovered information in 1964 that a group in Fort Worth, whom they felt was aligned with the Minutemen, was organized to fight against what they believed was the government selling out to the Communists. General Walker reportedly acted as an advisor to the group, which was collecting firearms and ammunition to take action against various Negro leaders in the Fort Worth area in the event of a "Negro uprising."[2659]

The press reported that the Minutemen were responsible for "Wanted for Murder—Khrushchev" posters, which were plastered on downtown Dallas business windows on August 31, 1963, and featured mug shot-style photos of Soviet premier Nikita Khrushchev. The name "Minutemen" was stamped at the bottom of the posters. The posters were critical of President Kennedy's nuclear test ban treaty with the Soviet Union and Britain. Jack Reville, head of the Intelligence Bureau of the Dallas police, told a reporter that he knew of no Minutemen organization in Dallas.[2660] The Khrushchev poster was so similar to the "Wanted for Treason" poster with the mug shot-like photos of Kennedy distributed around Dallas just prior to the assassination by Robert Surrey, a member of the Minutemen, that he must have also been behind the Khrushchev posters. (Surrey was close to Dudley Daugherty, a member of a prominent Texas oil family. According to a Jim Garrison memo, the Daughertys owned a large tract of land in Beeville, Texas, where Minutemen training may have occurred.)[2661]

Jerry Milton Brooks was an original member of Robert DePugh's Minutemen. He joined in 1960, through founding member Richard Lauchli. Brooks began working for DePugh in 1962, in Kansas City. Disillusioned, he left in 1965 and took with him files that contained three-by-five cards containing information on Minutemen members. He was the principal witness against DePugh during the trial in which he was convicted on federal weapons charges. Brooks revealed the names of 150 to 200 Minutemen from around the country, which he had found in the stolen files, and handed them over to a Jackson County, Missouri, Grand Jury during DePugh's trial.[2662] Brooks worked out of Guy Banister's office in New Orleans sometime before the assassination, and traveled the country for the Cuban exile cause.

Robert DePugh told the author that he did not personally know Banister, but that he knew about him through Brooks and was familiar with his work in the Anti-Communist League of the Caribbean.[2663]

Laird Wilcox, who accumulated a massive collection of far-right-wing materials (that are housed at the University of Kansas today), interviewed Brooks and tape recorded the meeting. Wilcox deemed Brooks, "totally reliable."[2664] The transcription of the tape is terrible, and the name of nearly every Minutemen member identified was misspelled. There are significant gaps in the transcript, probably from the poor quality of the tape recording. Brooks explained on the tape that the mission of the Minutemen was to "overthrow the government by violence and force." He stated, "After you take the five phases of training, you find that they want to overthrow the government by force and violence and do away with half of the people of the United States. And they are prone to violence and nearly every member carries a gun on his person or in his car or truck." He noted that the Minutemen infiltrated Communist and leftist groups and kept the names of their members on file. The role of the John Birch Society, according to Brooks, was to "furnish more guns for the Minutemen." Several members of the John Birch Society council were members of the Minutemen. Brooks named Walker as a member and heavy contributor to the Minutemen. Dan Smoot, transcribed incorrectly as "Dan Sleet," was named as a "member of Minutemen, contributory member to do [sic] with the violence." Smoot, as has been noted, was close to General Walker and had been an associate of Joseph Milteer since at least 1960. Brooks stated that most members of the Minutemen were John Birch Society members, as well.

Brooks identified a man named "Whiteman," possibly with first name of "Joe," who reportedly worked with Kent Courtney as a State Coordinator for the Minutemen in Louisiana.[2665] Another close Banister associate, Maurice Gatlin, misspelled as "Murray Lambert" of the New Orleans "Communist Committee in the Caribbean Area [sic]" at room 1635 Claiborne Towers, was named as a Minutemen member. (The same address appears on a letter Gatlin wrote to Senator Ellender and confirms that the individual named was Gatlin, not "Lambert.")[2666] As was previously noted, Gatlin was a close working associate of Guy Banister. Brooks also noted that the California Rangers, Colonel William Potter Gale's outfit, were Minutemen. Gale was involved with the broad-based assassination plots revealed at the Congress of Freedom meeting in 1963 and was a friend of Joseph Milteer. Gale was also a frequent visitor to the home of Willie Rainach.

General Walker's activities in the procurement of weapons for the Cuban effort, as well as for the hardcore underground, were also well documented by the FBI. The FBI learned from an individual sympathetic to Walker that he might be engaged in gun smuggling to aid the exile raids in Cuba.[2667] On October 3, 1962, the FBI received a letter from either a citizen or informant, stating that an individual (name redacted by the FBI, but who was obviously Walker aide Robert Surrey) was a fervent member of the John Birch Society and operated as secretary and treasurer at Walker's residence. (The information about Surrey and the John Birch Society is supported by other FBI documents, noted earlier.) The source stated that the member (Surrey) wrote to members of the clergy and Jewish rabbis and called them "Communists and paranoids." According to the source, "I know that for the past two years [Surrey] has been contemplating an uprising and I know that he has ordered by mail numerous guns, rifles and averages buying one box of shells to avert suspicion. I am sure his arsenal could be found at his home at the above address." The source said the individual (Surrey), "corresponds with Robert Welch getting and giving advice." He said, "I believe you will find him associated with the mad hatter, former General Edwin A. Walker." The source warned, "Upon close investigation, you will uncover several arsenals in the homes of members in his organization." The source went on to say that Walker was doing much harm to the country and would like to see Walker out of Dallas. He stated that the man we can assume to be Surrey was a rabid follower of Robert Welch and the John Birch Society and "he could very well be a dangerous individual with someone like former General Edwin A. Walker as a leader."[2668] The source also told the FBI that there were arsenals of arms in the homes of associates of General Walker.[2669]

As discussed in the last chapter, the FBI learned from another source on June 10, 1964, that the Minutemen squadrons were actually "assassination squads" that were under the direction of General Walker and Robert Morris. The source alleged, "the Minutemen organization had contacts in the military whereby they obtained the latest weapons, i.e. rifles, grenades, explosives, etc."[2670] The Minutemen activity appears very similar to the activity that Jack Ruby was involved in in 1962, as alleged by Nancy Perrin Rich.

Bureau of Alcohol Tobacco and Firearms agent Frank Ellsworth told Warren Commission counsel Burt Griffin, on April 13, 1964, that General Walker and H. L. Hunt were leaders of the Minutemen in Dallas. Ellsworth stated, "At the time of the assassination of the president, there was almost no information available to the Government concerning the activities of Dallas Cubans and other groups in illegal arms." Ellsworth noted that, "An organization known as the Minute Men [sic] is the Right-Wing [sic] group in Dallas most likely to have been associated with any effort to assassinate the president."[2671] The Warren Commission, on the other hand, concluded that a lone Communist killed the president and gave no weight to the Bureau of Alcohol Tobacco and Firearms's assessment. The FBI put together information that H. L. Hunt and Walker were well known among the Minutemen. According to an FBI source, cyanide capsules were tested on cattle at Walker's ranch to determine their effect.[2672, 2673] An informant told the ATTU that, in the period around September 1963, he saw a stash of arms at Walker's farm.[2674]

The Joseph Milteer Timeline: November 22, 23, and 24, 1963

Joseph Milteer's activities around the time of the Kennedy assassination were documented by Willie Somersett and relayed to the Miami police and the FBI on November 26, 1963. They were described in Chapter Five and will be briefly recapped here because of their relevance to the Jack Ruby story.

Milteer and Somersett attended both the April 1963 Congress of Freedom meeting and the October 1963 Constitution Party meeting where assassinations were plotted. The broad-based plot was transformed to a plot to assassinate President Kennedy, which was revealed at the October Constitution Party meeting. On November 9, 1963, Somersett tape recorded Milteer's remarks that the assassination of President Kennedy was in the works, and that it would be accomplished with a high-powered rifle, from an office building, with a weapon that could be broken down—and that someone would be picked up right away to throw off law enforcement. He was correct on all counts.

On the morning of the assassination, Milteer phoned Somersett from Texas (or "jack rabbit country") and told him, "I guess you won't be seeing your boy again." The Altgens photo, among other evidence, documented Milteer's presence in Dealey Plaza, standing on Houston Street, at the time of the assassination.

The next day, Saturday the 23rd, Milteer met Somersett at the Jacksonville, Florida, train station, and the two set off in Milteer's car to meet Klan members in South Carolina. While riding with Milteer, Somersett observed that Milteer was jubilant over the assassination. Milteer told Somersett, "Everything ran true to form. I guess you thought I was kidding you when I said he would be killed from a window with a high-powered rifle." When asked by Somersett whether he was guessing or not, Milteer stated. "I don't do any guessing."

In another account of his Saturday meeting with Milteer, Somersett noted that Milteer was happy, shook Somersett's hand, and said, "Well I told you so, it happened like I told you didn't it? It happened from a window with a high-power rifle." Somersett replied "I don't know if you were guessing or not, but you hit it on the head pretty good." At that point, Milteer said he did not want to talk about the assassination because the next step was for the underground to work on the Jews. Somersett stated, "This Milteer says he doesn't want too much talk about Kennedy any more, now he is alleging he was against the Jews, and their associates," and "The underground is going to work on the Jews." Milteer told Somersett that propaganda would be put out to prove that the Jews murdered President Kennedy.

The pair arrived at the Wade Hampton Hotel in Columbia, South Carolina, around midnight Saturday, November 23.

About 9:00 a.m. Sunday morning, Milteer—having just finished making a long-distance phone call—told Somersett, "Oswald [has] not said anything and he will not say anything." Somersett responded, "Why do you think that?" He replied, "Well, he will just not say anything, and nobody has any worry." Milteer went on to say, "The right wing [has] no worry whatsoever, because there [will] never be nothing to get out, because it was a small job, and very few people knew anything about it." Milteer was correct. Oswald did not say anything about the conspiracy.

Sunday morning, the 24th, before the murder of Oswald, Milteer told Somersett that the patriots within the far-right underground had no worries of being exposed because Oswald had infiltrated the Communist-linked Fair Play for Cuba Committee and the assassination would be laid in the laps of the Communists. Milteer was correct again. He elaborated that the far-right patriots had infiltrated the FPCC to lay the assassination not only in the laps of the Communists, but also Castro. Somersett was confused about Oswald's relationship with FPCC and the patriot underground's infiltration of the FPCC and asked Milteer about it several times. Milteer replied, "Let it go just like it is." Milteer noted that both Oswald and the far-right patriots had infiltrated the FPCC, suggesting they were one and the same.

As a veteran FBI informant, Somersett kept careful records of the dates and times of the events he informed on. At 10:20 a.m. Eastern Standard Time, Milteer and Somersett met with the Carolina Klansmen at their hotel. (A minute later, Jack Ruby shot Oswald, which they would not know until later.) A general discussion followed, and Milteer told the group that the right-wing underground had no worries in regard to the assassination. Milteer cautioned them that they should not "give the impression to our people that we had infiltrated this pro-Castro organization." (Milteer's statement that "our people" infiltrated the pro-Castro organization seems to imply an admission that Oswald, who infiltrated the Fair Play for Cuba Committee, was one of "our people.")

Milteer told the Klan leaders that the purpose of the meeting was to get their help circulating a proposed pamphlet to blame the assassination on the Jews. He stated that what was important "was to get out a pamphlet laying the murder of Kennedy at the foot of the Jews." Milteer then wrote out his proposed pamphlet on a piece of hotel stationery: "Notice to all Christians—The Zionist Jews killed Christ 2,000 years ago and on November 22, 1963 the Jews killed President Kennedy—You Jews killed the president. Now we are going to kill you. —The International Underground." (On November 26, 1963, Somersett received the finished version of Milteer's pamphlet by air mail. It read: "It now becomes the solemn duty of every true red-blooded American to seek, find, expel, drive out from our country every traitor be he Zionist Jew, Communist, or what have you. – International Underground") Milteer added, "We the Christian people must push the Jews from the continental United States. Unless they did get out, that we would kill them . . ."

At the time of the meeting, the Klansmen were shocked and dismayed over the assassination, saying that it would not have been so bad if it were Martin Luther King, Jr. who was killed. Milteer responded, saying King was just one of Kennedy's race agitators and was not important, since if they did kill King, the Jews would just set up another race agitator. He added, "There's still time to get him." (Remarkably, if Somersett's accounts are accurate, Milteer's talk about blaming the assassination on the Jews took place before it was known that Jack Ruby had killed Oswald.)

Milteer, Somersett, and the Klansmen drove to the Anchor Restaurant and found it completely filled by a group of "church people." Just outside the restaurant, one Klansman ran into a friend, who told him Oswald had just been shot. The group then rode to the Piggy Park Drive-in and the slaying of Oswald was confirmed on the car radio on the way. Milteer reacted to news of Oswald being shot, saying, "That makes everything perfect now, the Jews killed Kennedy and the Jews killed Oswald. Now we have no worry."

Milteer told Somersett that the Miami plot to kill the president had failed because someone had called the FBI. Afterward, Milteer said, "Everybody kept quiet and waited for Texas."

When asked by the Miami police for his opinion of Milteer and his revelations,

Somersett told them, "I am satisfied that this man beyond doubt knew that this was going to happen, and from the impression I got from him this conspiracy originated in New Orleans, probably some in Miami and different parts of the country, probably in California." He added that the groundwork for the assassination had been laid in five or six different states.

Milteer's statements were tantamount to calling for a pogrom against the Jews—which was the oft-repeated fear of Jack Ruby. The blaming of the assassination on the Jews by Milteer on the Saturday and Sunday *before* Ruby shot Oswald suggests he knew Ruby was going to murder Oswald. The fact that Ruby was a Jew also gave the conspirators the secondary gain of blaming the assassination conspiracy on the Jews. There were no other Jews remotely connected to the assassination story and there would have been no reason to blame the assassination on the Jews without Ruby.

It's not known who apparently told Milteer that a Jew was going to be involved, but a good guess would be that it was one of his friends, either Robert Surrey or General Walker. That could have happened during the Sunday morning long-distance call that Milteer made from the Wade Hampton Hotel.

Ruby's Motive for Murder

Ruby claimed he murdered Oswald to save Mrs. Kennedy from the additional anguish of having to testify at Oswald's trial. That may have been sufficient motive for an ordinary citizen to commit the murder, but Ruby cannot be considered an ordinary citizen since there is good evidence to suggest that he knew who the conspirators were.

Ruby, of course, claimed he was used and framed. William Duff's allegation that he saw Ruby at General Walker's home on several occasions—along with Ruby's statements to Chief Justice Earl Warren alluding to Walker and the John Birch Society—suggests that if anyone compelled Ruby to shoot Oswald, it was General Walker or someone in his operation. Ruby also repeatedly claimed that his family was going be eliminated by some element. If the conspirators told him they would murder his family if he did not kill Oswald, then that alone was sufficient reason for him to commit the murder. With a sympathetic jury and a little luck, he might have figured he would get off altogether (or serve a modest prison sentence)—a small price to pay to save his family. Walker and his violent-minded followers, like Joseph Milteer, easily had the capability and the anti-Semitic inclination to eliminate Ruby's family, if not attempt a pogrom against the Jews.

Ruby also claimed twice, both in a letter from jail and in a statement to psychiatrist Werner Teuter, that he had been framed for the murder. Since Ruby actually did commit the murder, he most likely meant that rather than being framed that he was set up, forced or coerced into it by holding something over him. Far too little is known about Ruby to know, with any certainty, the specifics of what might have been held over him. Although it is purely speculative, it is possible that a threat by the conspirators to divulge Ruby's illegal gunrunning activities could have served as a major inducement for Ruby to kill Oswald. If the conspirators carefully documented Ruby's gunrunning activities before the assassination in order to hold it over his head later to compel him to kill Oswald, then that would constitute the evidence against Ruby that he referred to as a "frame-up" (more likely meaning a set-up). A conviction for gunrunning, theft of armaments from a U.S. military base, and illegally exporting them to Cuba in violation of U.S. law would have landed Ruby in jail for perhaps the rest of his life. That may explain his statement in jail to Wally Weston that, "now they're going to find out about Cuba, they're going to find out about my trip to Cuba, they're going to find out about the guns, find out about New Orleans, find out about everything." On the other hand, a conviction for manslaughter for the murder of Oswald might have earned him a jail sentence of five years or less. Given the choice of a short jail sentence for the murder of Oswald or a life sentence for gunrunning, the decision by Ruby to kill Oswald—a man many felt deserved to die—would have been an easy one under that circumstances.

Jack Ruby never directly said who was behind the assassination. He was often ambiguous and he used allusion and symbols that pointed in the conspirators' direction. If both Oswald and Ruby had the ability to divulge the identity of the conspirators, it would do no good for Ruby to silence Oswald and take his place in jail. The liability for the conspirators would remain. However, it would be far better for the conspirators to have Ruby alive and in jail rather than Oswald. Oswald faced certain death in the electric chair for the murder of the president—even though he likely did not commit it—and the murder of a police officer, whom he may have killed in self defense. However deeply Oswald was committed to the hardcore underground and the conspirators, when he realized he would die for a murder he did not commit—and that he had been double-crossed by those whom he was loyal to—he was bound to talk sooner or later. He would have had little to lose by talking and, perhaps, a lot to gain. Ruby, on the other hand, had a strong inducement to remain silent, including what he believed were threats against his life, his family, and the Jewish people.

General Walker's Warning: Ruby Might Talk

On October 5, 1966, the Texas Court of Criminal Appeals granted Jack Ruby a new trial, citing the fact that Ruby's statements to the police shortly after the shooting should not have been admissible. The death sentence was reversed, and the venue was changed to Wichita Falls, Texas. When the sheriff of Wichita Falls arrived to transfer Ruby, he noticed that Ruby was ill and refused to move him. Ruby was taken to Parkland Hospital on December 19, 1966, and was diagnosed with pneumonia. Shortly after that, it was determined that Ruby had cancer in both lungs.

On December 28, 1966, nine days after Jack Ruby entered the hospital, General Walker wrote to Billy James Hargis and expressed his fear that Ruby might talk, and then Walker issued a warning. The information was buried in the third paragraph of a letter following a trivial discourse about a briefcase Hargis had given him, his regrets that he could not attend a function with Hargis and his family, and his libel law suit. The letter was discovered by the author and revealed here for the first time. Walker wrote:

Another peculiarity—with de Mohrenschildt returning to Dallas from Haiti as Rubenstein is allegedly dying with cancer (and might talk)—de M. made a front-page spread; and our informant produced his address and whom he is staying with—not good.

A warning. When Rubenstein leaves the hospital in a box (the only way he will come out), there is no further "block" to returning the blame on the right wing. The books and press will gradually pick it up again. RFK must have it—it must be done, as insurance and assurance—an RFK political necessity.

The letter concluded with seven unrelated paragraphs about the business matters of the Christian Crusade.[2675]

The letter and comments are extraordinary. Walker is not completely sure Ruby is dying of cancer, deeming it only an allegation. History regards Walker as a near victim of the president's assassin, not a confederate. As such, Walker has no need to be concerned about George de Mohrenschildt, the Russian who had an early relationship with Oswald—and may have known that he was not the true Communist the Warren Commission concluded he was. De Mohrenschildt suspected Oswald was involved in the Walker shooting incident from the beginning and asked him how it was that Oswald had missed him. In turn, Oswald gave de Mohrenschildt the photo, taken before the shooting, of him standing in the backyard holding his pistol and rifle, and the Communist newspapers, which was inscribed with the words, "The Hunter of Fascism. Ha, Ha, Ha." The inscribed comments suggest that Oswald was letting his friend know that the shooting was a hoax. If so, Walker had plenty to worry about regarding de Mohrenschildt and what he might say on his recent return to Dallas. Otherwise, as Oswald's near victim, Walker would have had no need to take the extraordinary step of using an informer to determine where de Mohrenschildt resided and with whom. De Mohrenschildt's return and interview in the newspaper was, as he put it in his letter to Hargis, "not good" for Walker.

Walker's worry and warning that Ruby might talk is astonishing. It is inconceivable that Walker meant anything else in the message to Hargis other than that he would murder Ruby before he allowed him to leave the hospital (and presumably leave Dallas for Wichita Falls for his re-trial, where Walker had no power). As long as Ruby was in Dallas, the comment suggests, Walker could block him from talking. With Ruby out of the Dallas County Jail, and on his way to the change of venue for re-trial in Wichita Falls (which was scheduled for February 1967), then the block on his talking was off. Only a guilty man makes the type of remark Walker made to Hargis. (As we shall see in the next chapter, during the Clay Shaw trial, Walker relayed his concerns about Marguerite Oswald in another letter, and had informers watching her very closely. He embedded the remarks, similarly, in an otherwise ordinary letter to another close associate.)

As was noted earlier, Ruby indicated to the Warren Commission and others that he was under pressure in jail—"blocked"—not to talk about the John Birch Society, as was further reflected in a comment made to his lawyer while in jail: "Don't mention anything about that—we're in a bad spot down here [in jail] because of that. I didn't refer to the John Birch—with reference to that [ad]."

During the same period of time as Walker's letter to Hargis, Ruby's brothers—speaking in Yiddish so the guard could not understand what they were saying—tried to get a tape-recorded confession from Jack at the hospital. Ruby still denied being part of any conspiracy. He died suddenly on January 3, 1967, not from cancer, but from a massive blood clot in his lungs. He owed 40,000 dollars to the IRS.[2676, 2677, 2678]

A year later, Robert Kennedy announced his plan to run for president. Close Kennedy associate and writer/comedian Mort Sahl told the author that Kennedy told him that if he were elected he planned to reopen the investigation into the assassination of his brother.[2679]

Conclusions

Jack Ruby knew who was behind the killing of the president, but stopped short of specifically identifying the killers. Instead, he alluded to General Walker and the John Birch Society in his testimony before the Warren Commission. Ruby left behind a number of symbolic clues as to who was behind the assassination in the form of the photos of the "Impeach Earl Warren" billboard, the "Welcome Mr. Kennedy" ad, and H. L. Hunt's *Life Lines* radio scripts. Unfortunately, no one paid any attention to that evidence, even though all three symbolic clues were products of General Walker or the H. L. Hunt clan (the case for their involvement in the assassination has been made in the preceding chapters). At the same time that he was obsessing over those three pieces of information, Ruby also brought up the Adlai Stevenson incident, a fourth product of the Walker operation.

In the near forty-eight-hour period between the murder of the president and the murder of Oswald, Ruby was concerned with nothing but those four products of the Walker operation. Six months later, during his examination before the Warren Commission, the "Impeach Earl Warren" billboard and the "Welcome Mr. Kennedy" ad dominated his testimony. Then, after mustering up the courage—"acting like a man" while claiming it could cost him his life—he uttered General Walker's name to a clueless Earl Warren.

The Warren Commission's examination of Jack Ruby, the most important witness in the most notorious murder of the twentieth century, was nothing short of terrible. The debacle was all the worse, considering it was done by no less than the Chief Justice of the Supreme Court, Earl Warren, and a future United States President, Gerald Ford. Ruby made it abundantly clear that he had a secret to tell, but could not tell it in the county jail for fear of his life. (After all, Ruby knew better than anyone that a person could be easily eliminated in the custody of Dallas law enforcement.) He repeatedly begged to be taken to Washington to tell his secret. Warren's refusal to take him to Washington was a colossal error of history.

Ruby's fear of a pogrom against the Jews had a rational basis, assuming that he knew (or suspected) that Walker had plotted against the Jews, or if Ruby knew and had dealings with Robert Surrey, the leader of the Dallas American Nazi Party that openly called for the extermination of the Jews.

There was abundant evidence presented that both Ruby and General Walker's group were engaged in the illegal procurement of weapons from the U.S. military for the anti-Castro Cuban cause, and, perhaps, for the Minutemen. (William Somersett never used the word Minutemen, but rather described the same group as a hardcore underground.) A mutual interest in procuring weapons would explain Ruby's visit to Walker's home with a man from the John Birch Society in 1962 and 1963, and adds credibility to William Duff's allegations of a Ruby-Walker tie.

Ruby's claim that the assassination was committed in conjunction with a plan to overthrow the government was partially corroborated in this chapter. Walker, the John Birch Society, and the Minutemen were armed to the hilt and planning insurrection, as we shall see in the next chapter.

Once again, the inside information provided by informant Willie Somersett was invaluable in understanding the assassination and the Ruby affair. Joseph Milteer's repeated claim that Jews were behind the assassination—made before Ruby arrived on the scene, if Somersett is correct—suggests that Ruby had been figured into the conspiracy with the secondary gain of blaming the president's assassination on a Jewish-Communist conspiracy (just as Ruby feared).

Walker's worry about Jack Ruby talking when he was taken from jail to the hospital, and Walker's vow that Ruby would not leave the hospital alive, are compelling evidence of Walker's involvement in the assassination conspiracy. These pieces of information confirm what Ruby was alluding to when he named Walker in his Warren Commission testimony. The information also adds further credence to William Duff's claims that he saw Jack Ruby at Walker's home on three separate occasions.

CHAPTER EIGHTEEN

THE AFTERMATH

Those Birchite bastards ought to be happy.
– Congressman Hale Boggs, upon hearing of the assassination

Years after the Kennedy assassination, Deputy Attorney General Nicholas Katzenbach was asked by the HSCA to describe the immediate problems the government had in the aftermath of the event. Katzenbach told them of the concerns that were related to the question of Oswald's visit to Russia, his marriage to a Russian, his visit to Mexico City, and any possible connection between Oswald and Ruby. On the question of conspiracy, Katzenbach was concerned as to whether a foreign power was involved, or whether it was a left-wing or right-wing conspiracy. He also had concerns as to whether the right wing was trying to put the conspiracy on the left, and vice versa. Katzenbach at least considered that the right wing might have tried to lay the conspiracy at the feet of the left, which was the case (as we shall see further in this chapter). In the end, he, like J. Edgar Hoover, felt it was the best thing for the country to convince the people that Oswald acted alone, and not on behalf of the Communists or the far right, while the radical right vigorously promoted the idea that the Communists were behind the assassination.

The FBI had reports suggesting that General Walker and his group were arming for insurrection following the October 1, 1962, Walker-led insurrection at Ole Miss. In 1964 and 1965, more evidence came forth that suggested Walker was, in fact, planning an insurrection, especially if President Johnson was elected in 1964. In fact, a Klansman in Meridian, Mississippi, told the FBI that Walker had 100,000 followers storing ammunition and weapons in case Lyndon Johnson was elected president.[2680] Concerned about Walker, the FBI repeatedly notified the Secret Service that they felt General Walker was a threat to the life of President Johnson, as we shall see.

Walker's activities in the aftermath of the assassination lend credence to Jack Ruby's repeated claims that the assassination conspiracy was part of a plan to overthrow the government of the United States. Walker's post-assassination activities and those of others on the far right will be chronicled in this chapter.

The Walker Alibi and the Assassination Propaganda Machine

As was noted in Chapter Fifteen, General Walker was in New Orleans and attended a speech by Harold Lord Varney, a board member of Kent Courtney's Conservative Society of America, two days before the Kennedy assassination. He also met with Leander Perez, a Guy Banister employee, and a group of unidentified citizens. After the mysterious Perez-Walker meetings and Jung Hotel meetings, Walker left New Orleans on November 22.

Walker was on an airplane from New Orleans to Shreveport with an unidentified friend when he heard the news that the president had been shot. Walker left his seat and approached a stewardess. According to Walker, "The stewardess wrote the names of the flight crew, numbers and times at my request, which was in anticipation of such infamy."[2681] It's not clear what he meant, though he documented that he was not in Dallas during the murder. After landing, Walker stayed in Shreveport for two days before returning to Dallas on Sunday, the day Oswald was shot and killed.[2682, 2683]

A meeting between Walker and Klansman Ned Touchstone at the Citizens' Council newspaper, the *Councilor,* also attests to Walker's absence from Dallas at the time of he assassination and his presence in Shreveport.[2684] On Saturday, November 23, he addressed a Citizens' Council meeting organized by Ned Touchstone. (The FBI were suspicious about some Louisiana Klansmen and ordered their agents in New Orleans to ascertain the whereabouts of a number of them on the day of the assassination, including Touchstone.)[2685]

While Walker was in Shreveport, miraculously, an obscure Nazi-oriented German newspaper, *The National Zeitung*, located him and interviewed him (as was described in Chapter Fourteen). The paper learned before anyone else that, supposedly, Oswald had fired at Walker. Walker told them Oswald shot at him, according to the German reporter—although Walker publicly denied it. As the evidence which has been presented suggests, Walker and Oswald were confederates in the phony shoot-and-miss ploy. *The National Zeitung*'s knowledge of Oswald's involvement in the shooting incident was a clue that the incident was phony, which the Warren Commission failed to realize.

(Walker, when asked years later denied foreknowledge of the Kennedy assassination. He also said he had nothing to do with the "Welcome Mr. Kennedy" advertisement or "Wanted for Treason" posters which were circulated before the assassination.[2686] Nonetheless, as documented in the last chapter, he was close with the men who were behind the ad and the poster. At least three of the four—but probably all of the financial backers of the "Welcome Mr. Kennedy ad"—were associates of Walker, and Walker's right-hand man, Robert Surrey, produced the "Wanted for Treason" posters.)

On December 2, 1963, Phoebe Courtney wrote Walker and stated, "Ever since they caught Oswald I have had this recurrent thought: Do you think it was Oswald that tried to shoot you?"[2687]

In December of 1963, the John Birch Society purchased full-page newspaper advertisements across the country, at a cost of $35,000, declaring that Oswald's involvement in the assassination proved it was a Communist plot and that the John Birch Society had been justified in their crusade to warn the American public about the Communist threat.[2688] On December 2, 1963, Walker met with twenty-three newspaper, radio, and television representatives at a scheduled news conference at the Baker Hotel in Dallas. He blamed the assassination on the internal Communist conspiracy.[2689] At the February 17–21, 1964, Christian Crusade meeting in Shreveport, Walker stated the assassination of the president arose out of an agreement between Kennedy and Khrushchev to eliminate Castro.

Herbert Philbrick, writing on the stationery of the America Committee to Free Cuba, stated after the assassination: "The obituary of President Kennedy was written in 1961 by a member of a pro-Castro organization calling itself Fair Play for Cuba Committee." Philbrick cited Eastland's 1961 committee hearing on "Castro's Network Inside the United States, Fair Play for Cuba Committee." The American Committee to Free Cuba included Kent Courtney, Herbert Philbrick, J. B. Mathews, John H. Rousselot, Walter Knott, and W. Cleon Skousen. Philbrick blamed the Secret Service for placing the right wing under surveillance, but not the extreme left.[2690] Herbert Philbrick (Lee Harvey Oswald's boyhood hero who posed as a Communist for the FBI) and Earl Lively of Dallas planned on collaborating on a book on the assassination of President Kennedy.[2691] (An FBI memo noted that General Walker was a friend of Lively.[2692])

Hilaire du Berrier informed the FBI that he had been staying at Walker's home at the time of the assassination, and that Walker was not in Dallas at the time. He told them that a man driving a blue Mercury ran up to the lawn and threw Walker's American flag to the ground. (Walker's habit of flying the American, Texas, and Confederate flags in front of his house was well known in Dallas. In fact, William Duff first recognized Walker's house from the flags while driving by it after reading about them in the paper.) Du Berrier told the FBI he read a story about Oswald in two publications that reported that a man resembling Oswald got out of 1958 or 1959 blue Mercury, entered a gun store, and asked about having a telescopic sight mounted on his rifle.

Du Berrier contended that the car that "Oswald" arrived in at the gun shop was the same as that of the man (not Oswald) who tore down Walker's flag on the day of the assassination.[2693] Du Berrier's gratuitous reporting of the alleged individual who drove to Walker's house and knocked down his flag served two purposes. First, it served to notify the FBI, in writing, that Walker was not in Dallas during the assassination. Second, du Berrier implied that Oswald had an ally in the man involved with the gun shop and flag incident who had animosity toward Walker, like Oswald. Du Berrier's tale was an implausible attempt to make sense of something that made no sense, i.e. why would Oswald want to kill both Kennedy and Walker, two diametrically opposed enemies?

(Revilo Oliver, who advocated violence at the infamous 1963 New Orleans Congress of Freedom meeting, offered a similar non-sensical explanation in his testimony to the Warren Commission as to why Oswald would shoot both the president and General Walker. He explained to the Commission, as he had in his convoluted article *Marxsmanship in Dallas* (which was published by the John Birch Society), that Oswald shot the president because the president was leaning away from Communism and turning American.)

Hilaire du Berrier was a prominent member of the national far right. He was a board member of Kent Courtney's Conservative Society of America, and was on the board of advisors of Major Archibald Roberts's Committee to Restore the Constitution, along with Charles Willoughby, Pedro del Valle, Mary Cain, Mary Davison, Richard B. Moran, and Revilo Oliver, in 1970.[2694] Du Berrier was present at the March, 1962, "secretive" meeting of far right wingers in Washington that included a majority of the national right wing that have been (or will be) implicated in the assassination conspiracy. Du Berrier was listed on the roster of the American Opinion speaker's bureau with Ted Jackman and John Rousselot, who were both associates of Walker.

Meanwhile, in New Orleans on the day of the assassination, Carlos Bringuier and Ed Butler—the two Banister associates who "debated" Oswald on the radio—were pictured in the New Orleans *Times Picayune* newspaper. They were photographed holding a picture of Oswald, Oswald's *Marine Guidebook* with his name inscribed on it, and a Fair Play for Cuba Committee leaflet with his Magazine Street home address stamped on it. (Wisely, they did not display the leaflet bearing the 544 Camp Street address. If they had, it might have led the press to Guy Banister's office building.)

Butler and Bringuier recounted to reporters stories of Oswald's stay in the Soviet Union and his admission, during the radio debate, that he was a Marxist. Butler claimed he had acquired newspaper stories about Oswald's activities before the assassination through a third party in Washington. Suspiciously, he did not identify the third party who supposedly gathered stories on Oswald before the assassination when no one else was paying any attention to him. (Of course, Butler did not need a source in Washington. Banister could have told him—and probably did tell him—all he wanted to know about Oswald.)

The *Times Picayune* newspaper article described how Oswald plunked his passport on the U.S. embassy desk in Moscow in late 1959 in a rebuke of the U.S. and a show of solidarity with the Soviet Union.[2695] Thus, Bringuier (a Guy Banister and Kent Courtney associate), along with Butler (who was constantly in the Guy Banister office) were the first to tell the media and the world that the man who supposedly killed the president was a Communist with direct ties to the Soviet Union.

Butler, as was noted in Chapter Ten, was considered a violent individual who was once a member of the John Birch Society. He called the FBI and told them he was scheduled to appear before Eastland's Senate Judiciary Committee on Sunday, November 23, 1964, and was concerned for the safety of his wife and children. (Presumably because the Communists might retaliate against him for revealing to the world that Oswald was a Communist.)[2696] He flew to Washington, D.C., and, on Sunday—while Oswald was drawing his last breaths—Butler addressed an emergency session of Senator Eastland's Senate Internal Security Committee. Eastland, perhaps wisely, did not attend. (It's not known how Eastland's committee learned about Butler or why they dispatched him to Washington the day after the assassination, but one of Eastland's associates, Leander Perez or Guy Banister, could have arranged it. Butler presented the Eastland committee with a tape recording of the radio "debate" with Oswald and Oswald's declaration that he was in Russia and was a Marxist. Eastland's committee wasted no time in promulgating the "Communists killed the president" line after hearing from Butler in Washington. (It will be recalled that, in 1956, Guy Banister and Hubert Badeaux worked together in New Orleans with Senator Eastland's committee to expose Communism in the city and in the civil rights movement. Walker's close associate, Robert Morris, was the committee's counsel, and Perez offered his assistance to Banister's Communist investigations. The 1956 collaboration of Eastland, Banister, Badeaux, and Perez appears to be the nascence of the underground intelligence network organized to fight integration. It was also in 1956 that Oswald began playing a Communist and that Hubert Badeaux announced in a personal letter that he was grooming an individual to infiltrate the left.)

Leander Perez was quoted in the *Times Picayune*, saying that the assassination was "a shocking horrible crime—and a crime against the nation." Perez stated emphatically "that it would have been impossible for any decent white conservative Southerner to have done such a thing." He said it was important that Oswald be caught, otherwise the South would have been accused.[2697] Perez said Oswald was "a Castro agent and a confessed Marxist of Communism, just the opposite of members of the White Citizens' Council and John Birchers who are anti-Communists."[2698]

On November 23 and 24, 1963, the annual New England Rally for God and Country was to be held in Boston. The planned speakers were Tom Anderson and John Rousselot.[2699] (The case against Anderson and Rousselot—both associates of General Walker—as accessories in the assassination conspiracy, will be made in the next chapter.) The New England Rally, although not officially a John Birch Society-sponsored event, was nonetheless operated and attended predominantly by JBS members. Both Kent and Phoebe Courtney were separately en route by airplane to the New England Rally on the day of the assassination, which leaves no question as to their whereabouts. Courtney learned of the assassination during a layover in Summit, New Jersey, and returned to New Orleans when the rally was cancelled.[2700] The official program and list of others to speak at the 1963 rally, found in Walker's personal papers, was to have included Courtney, Billy James Hargis, Myers Lowman, Ezra Taft Benson, Frank McGehee, and Edward Hunter.[2701]

Like the Courtneys and General Walker, Billy James Hargis was in flight during the assassination, attesting to the fact that he also was not in Dallas during the murder. Hargis had flown from Tulsa to San Diego on the morning of the assassination to conduct a radio marathon. (Although, scheduled to be at the New England Rally, he apparently changed his plans.) He had to change planes in Los Angeles and was flying over the ocean when the pilot announced that the president had been assassinated. He cancelled and returned to Tulsa the same day. Later, Hargis claimed outrage when he heard news reports blaming the murder on the far right. Hargis was quick to point out in his paper, the *Weekly Crusader* that Oswald had shot at General Walker. He referred to Ruby as "Rubenstein," as expected, never once calling him Ruby.[2702]

On November 27, 1963, General del Valle wrote to right-wing publisher Frank Capell and expressed his views on the assassination, as was noted in Chapter Eight:

> We are entering the last stages of the "take-over." It is always heralded by assassination of an important official. In this case, however, the victim was their man, only he failed to an extent rendering his election in 1964 doubtful. The double slaying is accounted for by the necessity to seal the lips of agent # 1. In the news photo Oswald has a look of fear and recognition of agent #2—Rubenstein. The hired press still tries hard to pin this on the Right-wing! Johnson and his Yiddish lady may seem a bit better team to the Invisibles. It remains to be seen how the mighty Kennedy tribe takes the liquidation of their head man. We are all in God's hands.

Like everyone else connected with the far-right conspiracy, del Valle referred to Ruby as "Rubenstein." He, like Revilo Oliver and Hilaire du Berrier, insinuated implausibly that the president was initially pro-Communist and his later movement away from the left was the reason that he was eliminated. Walker's attorney Robert Morris and Congressman Martin Dies (who led some of the Communist witch hunts) were quick to point out that Oswald was a Marxist and devotee of Fidel Castro.[2703] Morris told the press that he had observed the motorcade from his window of his Main Street, Dallas, office, five blocks from the assassination, which accounts for his whereabouts during the assassination.[2704]

Kerry Thornley served in the marines with Lee Harvey Oswald. Thornley, as was noted in Chapter Nine, was a radical right winger associated with Banister and Courtney. Kerry Thornley told reporters, on November 27, that Oswald had told him "Communism was the best religion."[2705] Thornley was the only marine associate of Oswald to claim Oswald had Communist leanings. All of the others interviewed by the Warren Commission vehemently denied that Oswald had expressed any pro-Communist sentiment.

Also on November 27, 1963, the Louisiana Joint Legislative Committee on Un-American Activities declared there was a clear-cut connection between the Fair Play for Cuba Committee and the Southern Conference Education Fund, the New Orleans integration group—Anne and Carl Braden served on the board of both organizations.[2706] As has been discussed, Oswald could not join SCEF—long a target of Southern segregationists and congressional committees including Senator Eastland's—because they had no membership, but joining the Fair Play for Cuba Committee was the next best thing.

Billy James Hargis was also quick to tie the Fair Play for Cuba Committee to the Southern Christian Education Fund in his publication, the *Weekly Crusader*. Hargis claimed that Norman Redlich, special assistant to the Warren Commission's chief counsel, J. Lee Rankin, was a leftist. He cited Redlich for signing a petition for clemency for Carl Braden of SCEF, and for signing petitions to abolish the House Committee on Un-American Activities.

Redlich was a member of the Emergency Civil Liberties Union, which was considered to be subversive by Eastland's SISS. Hargis alleged that the Emergency Civil Liberties Union had ties to the Fair Play for Cuba Committee.[2707]

The Greater New Orleans Citizens' Council blamed the Communists, not only for the death of the president, but also for the civil rights movement and racial turmoil that had rocked the South. Leander Perez and other associates of Guy Banister dominated the Council. They issued a statement to the press on the assassination: "Our Citizens' Council leaders have consistently warned of the grave threat of Communism and its fronts who threaten the safety of every individual, and who thrust its many communities into a condition of anarchy. We stressed the nature of Communist or subversive domination of the NAACP, CORE and MARTIN LUTHER KING'S activities against peace and good order and to stir up racial strife and hatred throughout the land. Now, from absolute evidence laid bare to all of us, a Marxist-Communist, devoted to Cuba's Castro, has shed the blood of the president of the United States by cold-blooded assassination. In turn, the Communist assassin violated his party rule by being caught, and then his lips were sealed by liquidation, the Communist way."[2708]

General Walker and Robert Welch issued a joint statement saying that the fact that a Communist committed the assassination vindicated their beliefs that the danger of Communism came from within. Billy James Hargis proclaimed in his *Christian Crusade* magazine that the assassination was a "coldly planned, diabolical act of the trained and dedicated Communist—exactly the sinister type of attack we have long feared and against which we have warned incessantly."[2709]

On November 26, 1963, Stanley Goland of Illinois notified the FBI that he had been listening to Reverend Carl McIntire's radio program sometime before the assassination, when McIntire brought up the fact that President Kennedy was supposed to speak at the November 23, 1963, meeting of the National Council of Churches in Philadelphia that McIntire called "Communist-infiltrated." McIntire suggested holding a protest meeting nearby, featuring General Walker as the main speaker. Golan recalled, later, that McIntire mentioned that perhaps something would happen to the president that would prevent him from speaking. Goland wondered if this was a chance premonition, or if McIntire knew Kennedy was going to be assassinated.[2710] McIntire, like nearly all of the far right, referred to Jack Ruby as "Jack Rubenstein."[2711] As has been noted, McIntire became a close ally of Walker, shortly after his return from Germany. Guy Banister attended a meeting that McIntire held at the Capitol House Hotel in Baton Rouge in 1963, as has also been noted. On November 4, 1964, Carl McIntire wrote a letter to Joseph Milteer thanking him for his effort to get his (McIntire's) broadcasts back on the air in Quitman, Georgia.[2712] (In Chapter Nineteen, it will be shown that a confidant of David Ferrie claimed McIntire was involved in the assassination conspiracy.)

In a speech in Shreveport, General Walker claimed Oswald was working for a Communist cell in Dallas, as was noted in the last chapter.[2713] The FBI countered Walker's claim in a February 14, 1964, memo, stating that there were seven Communist Party members in the

Dallas territory. The FBI had an informant in the Dallas Communist Party that could identify every member and Oswald was not one of them.[2714]

Dan Smoot wrote in his newsletter that the "Communists felt they could get along better with President Kennedy than with any other American who might become president." He added, "the international Communist conspiracy instigated the assassination . . . to make a martyr of him, calculating that the ensuing turmoil would halt the rising tide of conservatism and silence critics of the new frontier policies which Communists are clearly on record as approving." Smoot's tale as to the motive behind the assassination was as implausible as those of his colleagues, Joseph Milteer, General Walker, Hilaire du Berrier, Revilo Oliver, and Pedro del Valle. The similarity of their far-fetched declarations suggests there may have been a coordinated post-assassination propaganda effort.

The far right blamed the assassination on the president and his brother Robert because of their lax stand on Communism. Edward Hunter, a national figure in the far right and an associate of Guy Banister, stated: "President Kennedy was deluded by the line that Communism is not a menace here in America. He paid for this illusion with his life."[2715] Kent Courtney asserted, "It is now tragic that his [Robert Kennedy's] coddling of Communists within this nation has resulted in his own brother falling victim to a Communist assassin's bullet . . . ."[2716]

On November 30, 1963, Leo Sauvage, a correspondent for the Paris newspaper *Le Figaro*, visited General Walker's home, which he recognized by the three flags flying in front of it. (A week earlier, Walker had flown them upside down as a sign of distress for the city's apologizing for the shameful treatment of Adlai Stevenson. However, after the assassination, they were right-side-up, again.) Walker told Sauvage that the foreign press had come to interview him, but, he noted, "No American reporters dared to come and ask my views." When Walker told him that all who were right of center shared the American concept of an orderly constitutional government, Sauvage interrupted and asked him if that included the Klan, who were also right of center. Walker became incensed and told the reporter that the Klan was a "movement that supports the principles of constitutional government." Coldly glaring at Sauvage, Walker called him an "out-and-out leftist, a Socialist." The reporter continued, asking Walker his opinion on the formation of the Warren Commission, which had just been announced. Walker responded by saying that if the Commission followed the line of *Pravda*, blaming the assassination on right-wing extremists, then it would be a distortion of reality. He added, "It's obvious that Oswald was a Marxist Communist and that Rubenstein is connected with the underworld." Sauvage observed that the General seemed like he was not speaking to him but dictating lines and keeping an eye on his notebook to make sure he was voicing his words verbatim. When asked if he really felt the Warren Commission might follow the line of *Pravda*, Walker stopped the interview.

As Sauvage headed out the front door, Walker called him back and summoned him to his study in the rear of the house, where Walker showed him the bullet hole in the window sash and in the wall. Walker then told him about the shooting that had occurred in April while he was at his desk doing his income taxes. The reporter asked him about what the police knew. Walker responded, "The Dallas police . . . It's a mistake to think that Dallas is a conservative town." Walker told him, "Dallas is under the control of liberals, don't forget it. They bow down before the U.N. and apologize to Adlai Stevenson. Look at them . . . Not one of the city officials goes around today without a bodyguard, at city expense. But me—did you see anyone on guard near here, when there are so many Oswalds running around loose?" Walker shook his head bitterly, pointed to the hole in the wall, and said, "The police came, stuck their noses here and there, and that was all. . . . They could have found the man who tried to kill me if they really wanted to find him." The allegation that Oswald shot at Walker surfaced a few days after Sauvage's interview with Walker. Thus, Walker surmised that one of the "Oswalds" of the world did the shooting, and got away with it, because of, implausibly, a liberal Dallas Police Department.[2717] (It should be recalled that Walker's statement was made before Marina Oswald revealed her husband's role in the shooting.)

In December of 1963, Herbert Philbrick, Oswald's boyhood hero, weighed in on the assassination. He stated that Senator Eastland had exposed FPCC as Castro-backed in his hearings, and that they were behind Oswald and the shooting of the president. Philbrick wrote, portraying Oswald as a Fidel Castro agent, that the shots fired by Oswald from his "revolution rifle" were "noble noises of the Fidelistas" directed at a "cruel aggressor, bent on mayhem."[2718] Philbrick had not yet learned what Robert Oswald later told the Warren Commission: that Lee admired him and his TV series that glorified anti-Communists that infiltrated Communist organizations.

On December 5, 1963, the Washington, D.C., offices of *Life Lines* received an anonymous letter that threatened the lives of the officials at the paper, General Walker, and others.[2719] The FBI received another anonymous letter that stated that Walker was the brains behind Oswald—and threatened to kill Walker within six months.[2720] The Dallas Police Department notified the FBI that Walker had received a phone call from someone in Louisiana threatening to kill him, and accusing him of paying to have President Kennedy shot.[2721] General Walker cancelled his plans to speak at the Garden City Hotel in New Jersey on December 9, 1963, for "security reasons." The sponsors, the John Birch Society and Long Island Friends of General Walker, received three threatening phone calls.[2722]

On December 29, 1963, Milteer again visited Dallas, documented by a car repair receipt, which was later found in Joseph Milteer's probate court property.[2723]

After Revilo Oliver published his piece "Marxsmanship in Dallas," which concluded that the Communists killed JFK because he was forsaking the Communists and was now "turning American," a citizen, Irvin Golden, wrote to Oliver on February 12, 1964. Golden told Oliver that his article was a "foul piece of filth" and that the president was murdered "on orders by the Birch Bastards led by that perverted moron Edwin A. Walker." Oliver sent a copy of the letter to Walker.[2724]

On March 9, 1964, Marcus R. Brown wrote to Guy Banister and said that Jerry Brooks had told him that Banister had documentation available showing that Chief Justice

Earl Warren was at one time a Communist—or affiliated with a Communist front organization. Brown enclosed ten dollars and asked Banister to furnish him with any evidence he might have.[2725] (Brooks was a high-ranking member of the Minutemen and was associated with Banister from 1961 to 1964: at one point he even worked out of Banister's office.[2726])

The radical right fervently supported Arizona senator Barry Goldwater's 1964 candidacy for president. Ned Touchstone photographed Leander Perez with Goldwater at a campaign speech in Baton Rouge. Kent Courtney flew to Phoenix, Arizona, and pledged his support for Goldwater. Courtney set up headquarters in San Francisco for the July 13 to 16, 1964, Republican convention at the Cow Palace.[2727] Courtney announced at a pre-convention meeting, on July 11, 1964, that, "General Walker telephoned to say he was delighted with Goldwater's strong statement" before the Republican Party platform committee. Tom Anderson also spoke at the meeting.[2728] Courtney produced 4,000 Goldwater placards that were paraded around the lobbies and entrances of the hotels where the delegates were staying. Courtney boasted that members of "the dirty squad" circulated 97,000 copies of the *Socialist Views of Nelson Rockefeller*, Goldwater's liberal Republican opponent, in California and Oregon. In his acceptance speech at the convention, Senator Goldwater recited the famous words, "extremism in the defense of liberty is no vice and . . . moderation in the pursuit of justice is no virtue." The far right who supported him must have been pleased by the remarks. The speech was written by Karl Hess, Goldwater's chief speechwriter—and a member of the Anti-Communist Liaison headed by Edward Hunter, an associate of Guy Banister. Hess was also the former editor of the anti-Semitic *American Mercury*, where General Walker later became the military editor.

General Walker was spotted at the Jack Tar Hotel in San Francisco, where the Texas Republican delegation was headquartered.[2729] H. L. Hunt, who donated $3,000 to Goldwater's campaign, stayed in a room not far from Goldwater's.[2730] Robert Welch raised $2,000 for Goldwater, whom he considered his friend.[2731]

Reports of anti-Semitism among Goldwater supporters and Walker and his associates may have contributed to Jack Ruby's fear about the prosecution of the Jews. Walker was a close friend of James Oviatt, who was an avid California supporter of Barry Goldwater and the John Birch Society. Far-right, anti-U.N. literature was distributed at the Los Angeles Republican headquarters where Oviatt's wife worked for the Goldwater campaign.[2732] Oviatt reportedly sent out "bales of anti-Jewish literature."[2733] Oviatt rented office space in the Oviatt Building to Joseph Milteer's friends, Wesley Swift and William Potter Gale. He was a member of Gale's Christian Defense League.[2734] *The Jewish Voice* tied General Walker to Oviatt's attack on Jews in 1963 and the distribution of hundreds of copies of an anti-Semitic work entitled the "Israel Cohen Hoax."[2735] Dr. Walter Becher, an old German Nazi, attended the Republican convention and wrote a glowing piece on Goldwater in the *Deutsch National-Zeitung*. Becher made frequent trips to visit political leaders on the far right in the 1950s, including Senator Joseph McCarthy and William Jenner, and was reportedly the liaison between neo-Nazi groups in West Germany and the U.S. (It will be recalled that the *National Zeitung's* editor, Gerhard Frey, was a friend of General Walker's and was the first to report that Oswald shot at Walker.)[2736]

The Left Blames the Right

Liberal Louisiana congressman Hale Boggs, after the assassination and prior to his appointment to the Warren Commission, declared, "Those Birchite bastards ought to be happy."[2737] Earl Warren (a Republican who was considered a leftist by the far right), prior to his appointment to what would become the Warren Commission, stated that the assassination "was a result of hatred and bitterness that has been injected into the life of our nation."[2738]

A retired teacher from Indiana wrote to the FBI director on the day of the assassination saying, "You need no advice of that I am certain but I do suggest the most likely suspect is the demoniacal beast General Walker. I suggest he be taken into custody." She added she didn't believe Walker did the shooting, because she felt he lacked the courage to do it.[2739] Judge Sarah Hughes, who swore Lyndon Johnson in as president after the murder, stated that Dallas was "a city of hate, the only city in which the president could have been shot."[2740]

TASS, the Soviet News agency, hit the nail on the head when they blamed the assassination on "racists, the Ku Klux Klan and the Birchists." They added that the murder was "a new link in the chain of crimes committed by Southern racists and extremists." They stated it was clear that those behind the murder were trying to implicate the Communist Party in the murder. They added, "All the world knows their vile methods; murder from around the corner, bombing of Negro churches, unpunished assassinations of fighters for civil rights."[2741] The Soviets felt Oswald was a crackpot and not a serious Communist or supporter of the Soviet Union, and turned over their files on him to the U.S.[2742] Fidel Castro told the people of Cuba, in a radio address, that Oswald's visit to the Cuban Embassy in Mexico City had been for the purpose of laying the assassination in the lap of Cuba.[2743]

Florida governor Leroy Collins said the assassination was fostered by "Dixie battle cries, which incite the sick souls to violence." He said the "climate of violence has been created by 'the rabble-rousers' call to 'stand up and fight' for segregation and states' rights.'" He asked Southerners how long they would tolerate the death of black children (referring to the Birmingham church bombing), and the assassination of prominent civil rights leaders (referring to Medgar Evers's death and the president's murder).[2744]

General Walker and the Post-Assassination Insurrection Plot

Jack Ruby claimed repeatedly that those behind the assassination were planning to take over the country. The Warren Commission didn't ask the FBI if they had any information about any person or group planning a take over of the country which would corroborate Ruby's claim. Had they asked—and had the FBI responded in earnest—they would have learned that the FBI possessed extensive documentation of allegations that General Walker was plotting to take over the country.

As has been discussed previously, General Walker led an insurrection against the U.S.

government at Ole Miss in 1962. He was acquitted of all charges by an all-white Southern jury, and gloried in the affair. Shortly after, the FBI learned that he and his right-hand man, Robert Surrey, were arming to the hilt and preparing for another insurrection. In fact, the FBI learned in its investigation of Walker, in the aftermath of the Ole Miss insurrection, that followers of General Walker were gathering armaments and ammunition "for the imminent take over of the United States."[2745] On October 4, 1962, four days after the Ole Miss insurrection, an informant told the FBI that all of Walker's local followers had been obtaining arms for the past several months and had joined a rifle association as a means of covering for the excessive acquisition of firearms.[2746] An agent from the Bureau of Alcohol, Tobacco, and Firearms reported that General Walker and H. L. Hunt headed the Dallas Minutemen.

A citizen told the FBI that Walker's Minutemen organization was formed to create an insurrection if a Communist takeover occurred. He called Walker's Minutemen group an assassination squad. Walker's attorney Robert Morris and Milteer's friend Dan Smoot were a part of the Dallas Minutemen. On August 28, 1963, an informant told the FBI that Walker "considered himself as the leader of all groups against integration."[2747]

In 1964 and 1965, the FBI put together substantially more evidence that Walker was planning an insurrection against the U.S. government. The FBI determined that Walker's group was "gathering arms and ammunition" to resist an impending Communist takeover.[2748] On January 7, 1964, Walker wrote to W. R. Owens of the Freedom Fighters of America and told him he was working on a program of concerted action that he felt was absolutely necessary for survival. Walker said he would be in contact with him soon "with exact plans for future action." The letter was discovered in Walker's personal papers and corroborates the FBI's concerns.[2749] On May 4, 1964, the FBI labeled the "Edwin A. Walker Group" an extremist group. They noted that William Duff was affiliated with the group, as well as Frank McGehee and Robert Hatfield (a member of the Indignant White Citizens' Council).[2750] Walker had not yet testified before the Warren Commission when his group was labeled as extremist. Even so, the Warren Commission showed no awareness of the FBI reports on Walker's extremism or any of his activities beyond those related to the Walker shooting incident.

In the spring of 1964, Carlos Bringuier went on tour in California with Billy James Hargis. Bringuier asked the general manager of the Christian Crusade if he would ask General Walker for a copy of the "Assassination story," which Walker had published and Bringuier had seen while attending the Christian Crusade Leadership School in Shreveport. Bringuier was said to be "very, very impressed with this and was a great admirer of [Walker]."[2751]

On May 8, 1964, Walker was the overnight guest of Countess Rosalind Wood Guardibassi in Beverly Farms, Massachusetts. Guardibassi was described as an eccentric and liked to associate with people she considered "intellectuals," and Walker had spoken at Beverly Farms in the past. He addressed a group of about 100 attendees at the Padanaram Fire Station, where he got into a shoving match with a reporter. The Countess called the local police and asked them to station a uniformed policeman at her home during Walker's stay. The police notified the FBI of the event.[2752] Nationally syndicated columnist Jack Anderson called Countess Guardibassi "a notorious contributor to hate causes."[2753] (Guardibassi was an heiress to a woolens fortune and donated money to far-right causes including the anti-Semitic organization of Gerald L. K. Smith and the National States' Rights Party.[2754])

On May 18, 1964, Walker addressed a segregation rally in Little Rock, which was sponsored by the Capitol Citizens' Council.[2755] On August 7–9, 1964, Walker and Hargis—as well as Robert Welch and Major Pedro Diaz Lanz—spoke at the Christian Crusade Sixth Annual Convention, which was held in Dallas, Texas. Dan Smoot appeared at the convention, and was named "Christian Crusade Radio Commentator of the Year." The Christian Crusade "Guardian of Freedom Award" was given to Carlos Bringuier.[2756]

On July 23, 1964, Walker, in anticipation of appearing before the Warren Commission, typed out a list of questions he wanted to ask the Commission. One was, "Why do you not release your muzzling of Kirk Coleman?" On the paper, he listed Coleman's address and phone number.[2757] What Kirk Coleman, Walker's young neighbor, might have seen and heard the night of the shooting incident seemed to bother Walker.

An informant told the FBI on September 30, 1964, that a Mississippi Klansman told him that Walker was in charge of 100,000 men in several southern and western states, and was going to lead an insurrection in December 1964 or early 1965 if Lyndon Johnson was elected president in November 1964. The informant advised the FBI that Walker and his followers had been storing ammunition for a period of time. His 100,000 followers were said to be from Texas, Arizona, Oklahoma, Louisiana, Mississippi, and New Mexico. (The FBI contacted several of their informants in various cities, but none had heard of the plot.) The informant told the FBI about Patrick H. Harrington of Shreveport, who was in the marine reserves, and who was an admirer of General Walker and personally knew him. Harrington referred to President Kennedy derogatorily and said the present government had gone completely Socialist. He was a strong follower of the John Birch Society and said, "If the president is re-elected there very easily could be violence." Another individual, Robert Raabe, told the informant that he was a great admirer of General Walker and concurred with Harrington's beliefs. Raabe stated, "This is a year of violence."

An informant for the Austin Police Department said, on December 3, 1964, that Dr. James Lassiter told him he had spent $1,000 for firearms and ammunitions. Lassiter told the informant there would be a "shake up" in January and a heavy run on firearms, possibly during the inauguration of President Johnson.[2758] According to another FBI report, General Walker would lead an insurrection plot with the participation of the Ku Klux Klan from Mississippi and Alabama, if President Johnson were reelected. If martial law were invoked, Walker's followers planned a revolution in the later part of December 1964 or in January 1965 according to another informant.[2759, 2760]

On November 6, 1964, Robert Welch appeared on the national television show *Meet the Press*. The moderator opened the discussion mentioning that the Democratic platform for 1964 had condemned the John Birch Society, along with the Ku Klux Klan and Communist Party, for "extreme tactics." A recent Gallup Poll had shown that only eight percent of the

American people had a favorable opinion of the John Birch Society. Welch countered, saying that the criticism was the result of a politically motivated smear campaign.[2761]

On November 7, 1964, Brigadier General Richard B. Moran wrote to Walker and told him, "I am convinced we have no other chance to win by ballot. It seems to me that we will have to knit ourselves into a small, dedicated, <u>action</u> group now." He suggested that Walker and Pedro del Valle, along with men like Billy James Hargis, Carl McIntire, and Dean Manion, should lead the operation."[2762]

The FBI determined, on November 16, 1964, that a Fort Worth Minutemen group was more closely tied to General Walker than Robert DePugh's organization in Missouri. The FBI also referred to Walker's Minutemen group as the "American underground." An informant told them that Walker and his movement maintained stores of ammunition at an undisclosed location.[2763]

On November 19, 1964, the FBI learned that General Walker had spoken before the Americans for the Preservation of the White Race in Brookhaven, Mississippi. In his speech, Walker was critical of Martin Luther King, Jr. and talked about the recent allegation that Walker Jenkins, a key advisor to President Johnson, was a homosexual and had sent flowers to another man. Walker stated "that it was most surprising and fantastic to me that men sent flowers to each other. I never heard of this before." J. Edgar Hoover wrote in the margin of the FBI report, "Walker is 'nuts'."[2764]

On November 23, 1964, the press reported that George Lincoln Rockwell had been in Dallas for a five-day visit. Rockwell stated that an American Nazi Party headquarters was "extensively remodeled and armed" in the Oak Cliff section of Dallas. Rockwell said he had two hundred supporters in Dallas and that "They are coming over to us because of the unjust blame heaped on Dallas . . . for the Communist murder of President Kennedy last year."[2765]

On December 16, 1964, the Dallas FBI learned of a possible attempt by the Minutemen to raid the Northeast Texas Armory.[2766]

The FBI investigation of the Walker insurrection case was captioned as "THE ALLEGED KLAN PARTICIPATION IN INSURRECTION PLOT, RACIAL MATTERS" and the information originated from sources in Birmingham, Alabama. It appears that the information they received, in numerous reports, that Walker was involved in planning an insurrection against the government, had been discounted by the FBI, because their main focus was curbing the violence of the Ku Klux Klan—which they were investigating under the subject of "RACIAL MATTERS."[2767] (The FBI had intensified their "Racial Matters" investigation following the bombing and murder of the four children at the Sixteenth Street Baptist Church in Birmingham on September 15, 1963.)

Walker, 1965

On March 26, 1965, an informant told the FBI that Walker was in touch with the Original Knights of the Ku Klux Klan and had asked them to reorganize into a new group that the informant thought sounded like the "Volunteers of America," or "VAAV," or something similar, but he could not recall the exact name of the organization. The Klansman told the FBI that the Klan was a thing of the past. All men in the "Volunteers" were to have high-powered rifles. The organization planned to organize along military lines, led by a commander-in-chief, a chief of staff, and five generals in charge of various departments such as propaganda, and medicine. The informant heard that there were 2,000 men in New Orleans prepared to join the group, which he felt was an exaggerated number.[2768] The American Royal Eagles were organized at a meeting in Bossier City, Louisiana, on May 9, 1965, and were described as a replacement for the Klan to fight Communism. Walker was reported to have jurisdiction over the organization, but his name was not to be openly connected with it. According to the FBI, the group was formerly known as the Volunteers of America.[2769]

The informant—or the FBI—may have erred and may have meant the "American Volunteer Group" (AVG), Nelson Bunker Hunt's alleged "kill squad," which included General del Valle. The group and their operation, described by the informant, and del Valle's AVG were similar, if not the same. The Volunteers of America, on the other hand, is a well-known charitable group, and it's not likely the ex-Klan group went by that name.

On April 21, 1965, an informant told the FBI that Delbert Ray admitted that he was a member of the John Birch Society and was a friend of General Walker. Ray told the informant he possessed dynamite. Ray said that there was an underground movement in Dallas associated with General Walker that maintained a cache of ammunition. The purpose of the underground was to save the country if the Communists took over.[2770]

An informant told the FBI in April or May of 1965 that Richard Cotton was promoting the Minutemen on his radio show and was working underground to purchase guns and ammunition for the group. The informant alleged that Cotton had been involved in a plot to kill Martin Luther King, Jr. during King's recent visit to California. Cotton was reported as being very anti-Negro and anti-Semitic. He was a friend of Joseph Milteer (and corresponded with him as was noted in Chapter Seven).[2771] He was also a friend of General Pedro del Valle,[2772] and was close to Milteer associates William Potter Gale, Wesley Swift, and Herbert Wallace Butterworth.[2773]

In June 1965, Walker appeared at a "We the White People" rally at the State Capitol Building in Baton Rouge, which was hosted by the Louisiana Citizens' Council.[2774] Walker also spoke at the United Conservatives Rally of the United Klans of America on July 4, 1965, in Baton Rouge.[2775] On August 10, 1965, Walker told a Long Beach, California, crowd that there was a "Red Plot" aimed at "you, the white race—just ninety miles from Florida."[2776]

General Walker anticipated collecting a large sum of money on November 29, 1965, in his libel suit against the United Press International, who claimed he fomented the riot at Ole Miss. (He ultimately did not prevail.) Walker pledged financial support to overthrow the government of Costa Rica when he collected his award. A meeting was being arranged for Walker to meet with deposed Dominican general Elias Wessin y Wessin in Miami, in 1965.[2777]

General Walker spoke in Atlanta on September 13, 1965, and told a cheering crowd,

"There will be a KKK in the USA longer than there will be an LBJ."[2778]

Walker met with the Imperial Wizard of the Ku Klux Klan in Shreveport, Louisiana, in October 1965, and was offered the position of Grand Dragon of the United Klans of America for the State of Texas.[2779]

Walker was behind an organization called the Western American Security Police (WASP) and, in October and December of 1965, met with WASP members in Houston. The group "was anti-Communist and had only a secondary interest in opposing Negroes and Jews."[2780]

General Walker and the Threat to President Johnson

From May 3, 1965, to October 2, 1965, FBI Director J. Edgar Hoover notified the Secret Service in writing—six separate times under the presidential protection agreement between the FBI and Secret Service—that General Edwin A. Walker constituted a threat to the life of President Johnson. Walker was placed in the category of "Subversives, ultra rightists, racists and Fascists who meet one or more of the following criteria: Prior acts or conduct or statements indicating a propensity for violence and antipathy toward good order and government." Hoover sent Presidential Protection notices, citing Walker as a threat, to the Secret Service four separate times in May 1965, alone, perhaps believing that an attempt to assassinate President Johnson was imminent and feeling that, if that happened, the Secret Service—not Hoover's FBI—would be at fault.[2781]

General Walker and the Later Years

Lyndon Johnson won the 1964 presidential election, defeating Barry Goldwater in a landslide. Walker never led an insurrection, perhaps having been rendered ineffective by the FBI and their informants, who had thoroughly infiltrated his organization.

After the Kennedy assassination, Walker made fewer speeches and garnered less media attention.[2782] His interrogation by the Warren Commission and investigation by the FBI and Secret Service (who deemed him a threat to the life of President Johnson) likely had something to do with his assuming of a lower profile.

After 1965, FBI documents on Walker, which were obtained by the author through the Freedom of Information Act, were sparse. Walker may have been more cautious and left the plotting to others to save the country from the Communists that he saw everywhere. Perhaps his sexual proclivities hurt his standing as the leader of the hardcore underground. Walker remained highly regarded among the leadership of the Citizens' Council, however, and he was frequently pictured in their monthly magazine *The Citizen* among the Council leaders throughout the 1960s. When Robert Kennedy was invited to speak at Ole Miss Law School on March 18, 1966, Walker planned to counter the event and speak in the evening at the nearby Oxford Courthouse, at an event sponsored by the Citizens' Council of America.[2783]

Michael Rayes wrote Walker on May 26, 1966, and told him about the "Survival Program for the ultra conservative community." He named Robert Welch, Admiral Ben

Moreel, General Charles Willoughby, Clarence Manion, Reverend Wayne Poucher, Billy James Hargis, General William Campbell, Dan Smoot, H. L. Hunt, D. B. Lewis, Charles S. Jones, and Walker, himself, as "the hard core upon which our future rests by virtue of their position of influence, and the capacity for immediate action." Rayes stated that Hunt, Lewis, and Jones would be prevailed upon for the necessary supplies and weapons to be stored in the San Louis Valley before March 10, 1966. He said that Hunt was the man to convince, since he had the capacity to supply them and at the same time he would be saving his vast empire. Rayes, using Bible prophesy, told Walker the blackest period would be from 1966 to 1969. During that period, he predicted, the government would fall. Russian agents would first take over the missile bases, then invade. He said the patriots alone would survive in the sanctuary of the provisional government in Salida, Colorado. Rayes's four-page letter at times appeared irrational. However, given the references to people who are important in this work, the mention of the "Survival" program by name, and the inclusion of a sanctuary in Colorado that may be the same as Kenneth Goff's anti-Communist paramilitary operation in Colorado attended by Joseph Milteer, Rayes appears to be a part of what Milteer referred to as the "Survival" operation described in the letter about his meeting with H. L. Hunt, which was noted in Chapter Eleven.[2784]

General del Valle wrote Walker on May 13, 1966, and told Walker that he would share "his million and a half with all who work for His victory."[2785] D. B. Lewis may have been del Valle's financial angel. As has been noted, Lewis, the wealthy dog food producer, left millions to others on the far right—including Dan Smoot—after his death.

In 1967, Patrick Frawley added Robert Morris, Walker's attorney who screened applicants to Walker's Minutemen group, to the Technicolor board, the motion picture film company that Frawley owned.[2786] It will be recalled from Chapter Nine that Ed Butler (the associate of Guy Banister who, with Carlos Bringuier, "debated" Lee Harvey Oswald on the radio) went to work for Patrick Frawley after the assassination.

On January 16, 1968, Walker was in Jackson, Mississippi, to attend the inauguration of Governor John Bell Williams.[2787]

In 1968, the radical right's dream of a viable, ultraconservative, national third party came to fruition through the formation of the American Independent Party (AIP). Walker and Dan Smoot spoke at the AIP Convention in Dallas in March 1968, and the group nominated George Wallace for president. Kent Courtney was a key organizer for the Wallace campaign, and Leander Perez was the Louisiana state coordinator for the Wallace effort. Another Milteer friend, Roy V. Harris, was the Georgia campaign organizer. Bard Logan, who was a member of the Constitution Party and John Birch Society, was the Texas organizer of his campaign.[2788] The hardcore underground and the John Birch Society were major supporters of George Wallace's campaign. Wallace and the AIP made a respectable showing in the race for President in 1968, winning 13.5 percent of the popular vote and 46 electoral college votes.

In July of 1970, Walker, Tom Anderson, and Clyde Watts were named to the board of regents of Billy James Hargis's new college, the American Christian College. Watts later became the general counsel of Pedro del Valle's Defenders of the Constitution in 1971.[2789] In 1972, Walker grew a beard, moustache and long hair.[2790]

In 1975, the CIA noted in a security file on General Walker that he operated a twenty-four-hour phone message called "The Dallas Weekly Message." In his January 12, 1975, message, the CIA noted that Walker accused Henry Kissinger of controlling both the KGB and the CIA.[2791]

Walker was arrested for the second time for soliciting sex from a park ranger in a men's room on March 16, 1977.[2792]

In 1978, when he moved out of his Turtle Creek Boulevard home, Walker removed the window that was struck by a bullet in the 1963 shooting incident. He contacted the FBI and showed them the window, because he did not want anyone to say he had "faked" the window.[2793] The HSCA was re-investigating the assassination at the time, and perhaps he thought they might feel removing the window was suspicious.

In 1982, during President Reagan's term in office, the U.S. Army quietly reinstated Walker in rank, pay, and benefits of $45,120 per year.[2794]

While the left was blaming the right, and the right was blaming the left for the assassination, its clear that many in the government were resolute in not wanting the blame anyone but Lee Harvey Oswald. It may seem puzzling after considering the evidence documented in this work that no one ever suspected General Walker or—in any meaningful way—the segregationists and radical right of involvement in the Kennedy assassination. Perhaps it had to do with the thinking of people like Nicholas Katzenbach and J. Edgar Hoover in the Justice Department, who felt that it was imperative for the good of the country that the people be convinced that Lee Harvey Oswald had acted alone and not as the result of either a far-left Communist plot or a far-right plot. (Deputy Attorney General Nicholas Katzenbach, serving under Attorney General Robert Kennedy, wrote a memo three days after the assassination, as was mentioned previously, to Bill Moyers (a special White House assistant to Lyndon Johnson) stating that the public must be satisfied that Oswald was the assassin and that he did not have confederates who are still at large. Katzenbach urged that any claims that this was a Communist conspiracy or a right-wing conspiracy to blame the Communists be cut off. However, Katzenbach recognized that "the facts on Oswald seemed about too pat—too obvious [Marxist, Cuban, Russian wife, etc.]")[2795]

The FBI had volumes of documents—principally from Willie Somersett—of a far-right plot to assassinate a large number of people in the Council of Foreign Relations, in high offices, and prominent Jews, all of which was disclosed at the Congress of Freedom meeting. Further, the FBI had evidence that generals Edwin Walker and Clyde Watts, both Warren Commission witnesses, were military advisors to the plotters. The FBI knew that the broad-based assassination plots had evolved to a plot to kill the president during the October 1963 Constitution Party meeting. The FBI also knew that, on November 9, 1963, Joseph Milteer told Willie Somersett that the assassination of President Kennedy was in the works; that it would be accomplished by a high-powered rifle that could be broken down; and that someone would be picked up right away to throw the public off. Milteer was correct on all counts, yet the Warren Commission never heard his tape-recorded remarks and never saw the volumes of documents on the far-right plotting. The HSCA had many of the documents and heard the tape recording, but foolishly cut short any meaningful investigation, based on a sophistical photo analysis of the man in Dealey Plaza—which evidence presented in Chapter Five strongly suggests was Joseph Milteer. The failure of the Warren Commission and the HSCA to deliberate on or properly evaluate the volumes of evidence of a far-right plot was a tragedy and a colossal error of history.

Walker died on October 31, 1993. A blue ribbon was found among his personal papers that draped his casket at his funeral that read, "Edwin Walker—Patriot."

Conclusions

Jack Ruby repeatedly stated that those behind the Kennedy assassination were planning to take over the county. It's unlikely that he was referring to anyone other than General Walker.

The FBI compiled a large amount of information that Walker was planning insurrection. The allegations that Walker thought he could muster a citizens' army of 100,000 for insurrection in 1964 and 1965 is close to the number he felt would support him at the insurrection at Ole Miss in 1962 when he called for "10,000 strong from every state" to join him. The FBI documents that the author has reviewed and cited in this work, which were obtained under a Freedom of Information Act request, were heavily redacted and probably represent only a partial representation of those in existence at the FBI and National Archives. Less than a year after the Warren Commission concluded both that Lee Harvey Oswald acted alone and that he was not a part of any conspiracy, the FBI repeatedly notified the Secret Service that they felt General Walker represented a threat to the life of President Johnson.

An abundance of evidence was presented—and it is probably not a coincidence—that the members of the conspiracy let it be known where they were at the time of the assassination; that is: not in Dallas. There also appears to have been a coordinated propaganda effort on the part of the far right to lay the assassination at the feet of the Communists. The far right universally referred to Jack Ruby as "Rubenstein" as a ploy to tie the assassination to the Jews, as Jack Ruby feared. Despite the far-right propaganda campaign, few in the general public believed the assassination was a Communist or Jewish plot.

The mountain of evidence revealed by Willie Somersett in the Joseph Milteer affair, as well as the plotting activities of General Walker and his followers, was never meaningfully deliberated on by any investigation, which was a colossal error of history. More evidence against General Walker will be presented in the next chapter.

CHAPTER NINETEEN

INSIDERS AND INFORMANTS

Maybe we need some killings, Senator.
I believe there was treason afoot in the Cuban fiasco,
I believe in killing traitors. How about you?
— *Thomas Jefferson Anderson*

onspiracies often have leaks, a fact conspiracy critics cite as evidence against conspiracy in President Kennedy's assassination. However, people have talked, but no one in power took them seriously.

Joseph Milteer, a friend of General Walker, talked, but the Warren Commission never heard about it, and conspiracy writers were not persuaded by the Milteer story. Jack Ruby alluded to General Walker and the John Birch Society, but that information was ignored. The six major books on Ruby make no mention of Ruby's comments about General Walker.[2796]

The allegations of two other individuals who have informed on, or had inside knowledge of the Walker-led conspiracy in the assassination of President Kennedy, will be presented in this chapter. General Walker and his friend Tom Anderson, a conspiracy insider, slipped up in 1969 and left behind a piece of incriminating evidence that will be presented. The "prediction" of the president's murder by one darling of the John Birch Society and the disinformation apparatus of Liberty Lobby, a John Birch Society-dominated lobby group that placed the blame on the CIA, will be discussed, as well.

Thomas Jefferson Anderson and General Walker: Evidence of Conspiracy

Thomas Jefferson Anderson was born a "super patriot." He was one of the leading figures of the John Birch Society, Liberty Lobby, and other far-right-wing groups that emerged in the mid-to-late-1950s. He was called the loudest voice of the so-called "Rigid Right." He was a close friend of General Walker and Billy James Hargis and a frequent speaker at the same far-right venues as his friends Walker, Hargis, Courtney, and many others, and his name was mentioned in many of the prior chapters.

While searching through Anderson's—undoubtedly purged—papers at the University of Oregon, the author discovered a letter written to him by General Walker, dated January

15, 1969, which is reproduced in the "Documents" section at the back of this book. The letter was written three weeks before Jim Garrison's trial of Clay Shaw for his involvement in the assassination of President Kennedy that began on February 6, 1969, and culminated with a not guilty verdict on March 1, 1969. When Anderson filed the letter to Walker away in his papers he put it in his "George Wallace" file. He probably did so accidentally and did not realize that he was preserving a telling admission from Walker concerning Lee Harvey Oswald's mother, Marguerite Oswald.

The letter begins with Walker offering his thoughts on "the *Pueblo* incident," a pressing issue of the day. The North Koreans commandeered the USS *Pueblo* in 1968, claiming it had strayed into their territorial waters. Somewhat in line with his halting public speaking habits, Walker—in his writing—would often completely change the subject after one or a few sentences. Wedged in between his wandering thoughts were two brief revealing sentences about "Mrs. M. Oswald," which refer to Oswald's mother, Marguerite, and not his widow, Marina.

(All through the Garrison investigation and trial of Clay Shaw for conspiracy in the Kennedy assassination, Marguerite Oswald was a vocal proponent of her son's innocence and publicly proposed various theories about his place in the story of the assassination. To the contrary, Marina Oswald withdrew from public life. She remarried, becoming Marina Porter, and busied herself taking care of the two children she had with Lee. In essence, Marina accepted the Warren Commission's conclusions on the assassination, while Marguerite Oswald did not.)

Walker packed his thoughts so tightly in the letter to Tom Anderson that he neglected to place them in separate paragraphs. He separated them by drawing little breaks between the sentences. Walker, in his haste, wrote two pertinent and remarkable sentences: "Mrs. M. Oswald should never be underestimated. We watch her moves closely."

Why would anyone fear Marguerite Oswald, a pitiable figure and the mother of a murdered son? In disbelief of the Commission's findings, Marguerite told Warren Commission Counsel Lee Rankin, "So if you want to call it speculation, call it speculation. I don't care what you call it. But I am not satisfied in my mind that things are according to Hoyle. And I believe that my son is innocent." She called the Warren Commission findings, "lies, and lies, lies."[2797] She pointed out the implausibility of Oswald's failure to immediately flee the Book Depository, if he were the real assassin, choosing to dawdle and drink a Coke instead. Walker worried about Marguerite in 1969, because she openly stated that her son had been framed and she was actively looking for the truth and, if she found the truth, it would lead directly to General Walker. Walker was watching her closely—and she suspected she was being watched. However, it is not at all clear that Marguerite knew that it was General Walker who had framed her son. She may have known, but she made a lot of vague, conflicting statements and accusations.

Marguerite Oswald had sent a telegram to the FBI almost three years earlier—on June 26, 1966—and told them she had found many errors and discrepancies in the Warren

Commission's published findings after examining it for the past two and one-half years. She alleged that her phone was being tapped, that *she was being watched constantly*, and that someone had canceled her TV appearances—which had been earning her a living. She thought the Dallas Police were watching her. Since Walker was watching her moves closely in 1969, he may have been doing the same in 1966.

The FBI felt that Marguerite Oswald was unstable and advised the Secret Service that she would be in New Orleans during Vice President Hubert Humprey's visit to the city on July 18, 1966.[2798] They thought this tragic, elderly lady could be a threat to the life of Humphrey.

On August 24, 1967, one of Garrison's investigators, Tom Bethell, interviewed Marguerite Oswald and she steadfastly defended her son's innocence. Marguerite showed no interest in the New Orleans district attorney's assassination investigation, other than to say that she should be at the Clay Shaw trial fighting for her son. She was reluctant to tell them anything and appeared only willing to talk in exchange for payment. Bethell asked her if she possessed a letter from the State Department requesting her permission to enlist her son as an agent of the government. (The question was in line with Garrison's claim that the government was behind the assassination and had recruited her son as an agent.) She did not respond.

Bethell noted a brass scroll hanging on her living room wall, which stated, "My son—Lee Harvey Oswald, even after his death has done more for his country than any other living human being." She told Bethell that she had spent a great deal of money on her own investigation, including expenditures for phone bills that ran as high as five hundred dollars per month. She said that, as a result, she was down to her last $329. As a part of her campaign, she made two hundred TV appearances. She made the unexplained remark to Bethell: "I hold all the cards, I am the Mother. You've got to bring the family into this." She told the investigator she did not want to reveal all of her information and would perhaps bring it out in a book. She said that, in order to keep going, she was going to have to sell two more letters from her son. She noted she had not been in contact with Marina Oswald since December 1963.[2799]

Marguerite admitted that she was suspicious of a number of people connected to the assassination. They were far flung, and included "the negroes and the jews [sic]," Officer Marrion Baker, J. Edgar Hoover, Wesley Frazier, the Kennedys, Governor and Mrs. Connally, and Hale Boggs. In her Warren Commission testimony on February 10, 1964, Marguerite said that she suspected that her son was an agent, possibly of the State Department. She believed that Marina Oswald, Ruth Paine, the Secret Service, and high-ranking government officials were part of the conspiracy.[2800] It's conceivable that she may have suspected her son was an agent for General Walker (who was, once, a high-ranking government official) while both served concurrently in the military in the 1950s. She may have believed her son was still covertly working for him when they were both out of the military at the time of the assassination.

Marguerite, as was mentioned, also suspected the Jews; she told the FBI that someone told her that all the Jews in Dallas were rallying to the cause to free Jack Ruby. She told them that, in August 1963, she had worked as a nurse for a wealthy Jewish family in Fort Worth attending to a newborn grandson. She attended a "circumcision party" and was sure one person in attendance was Jack Ruby. One of her theories was that the Jews hired Ruby to kill her son.[2801]

During Tom Bethell's interview for Jim Garrison, Marguerite Oswald displayed "an unmistakable prejudice against Jews and Negroes, and speculated as to why Negroes have not been implicated as suspects."[2802] Marguerite's attitude toward Jews and blacks leaves little doubt as to the atmosphere where young Lee Harvey Oswald developed his worldview. The anti-Semitism in the Oswald household lends further credence to the author's claims, in Chapter Three, that Oswald may have known Dan Burros (secretary of the American Nazi Party, whose address was found in Oswald's notebook), and that he also was a likely associate of the head of the New Orleans's American Nazi Party, Ray Leahart.

Jean Stafford interviewed Marguerite Oswald for her 1965 book, *A Mother in History*. Marguerite remained evasive and guarded throughout the interviews, offering no significant revelations. She told Stafford, "I can absolutely prove my son innocent. I can do it any time I want by going to Washington, D.C., with some pictures, but I won't do it that way. I want to get my story before the public, so young and old all over the world will know the truth." She further told Stafford, "I know who framed my son and *he* knows I know who framed my son." She refused to say who *he* was or if *he* was in Texas. Marguerite wondered, "Did Chief Justice Warren have to whitewash something the public don't know about? . . . Who *used* my son? This is the question I must find the answer to." She explained to Stafford that the last time she was very close to Lee was in 1956, just before he joined the military. After that, their relationship was just correspondence. She felt that, at age sixteen, Lee was being trained as a government agent. She felt he was an agent who died for his country. (The evidence has been presented, with more to come, that Oswald was likely recruited out of David Ferrie's Civil Air Patrol unit as an agent for the radical right, probably by Hubert Badeaux working under Guy Banister of the New Orleans Police Intelligence Unit, not the U.S. government.) Marguerite said she was responsible for two presidents, but did not comment on her politics.[2803] (The author asked Mark Lane, Marguerite's attorney at one time, what her politics were. Lane responded, "She didn't have any politics."[2804])

Marguerite Oswald wrote a letter to the White House on January 20, 1969—five days after Walker's letter to Anderson expressing his worries about her—asking for someone to see and speak to her personally. Marguerite apparently had something pressing on her mind that she did not disclose in the letter. Was this letter, in effect, her plan to deliver on her statement to author Jean Stafford that she could prove Lee was innocent by going to Washington? We may never know. Perhaps Walker knew about her plans to contact the White House and that's what worried him and prompted him to watch her very closely. Marguerite may have been correct that her phone was wiretapped. Walker's close friend, Nelson Bunker Hunt, was implicated in illegal wiretapping a year later, and that wiretapping could have easily been a tool at Walker's disposal.[2805] Marguerite's White House request was referred to William

Ruckelshaus, the assistant attorney general, who told her that he first wanted some idea as to what she would like to discuss to determine if a personal conference would be beneficial.[2806] It is not known what transpired after he contacted her.

On the other hand, Walker had no worries about the impending trial of Clay Shaw. Garrison's staff had been thoroughly infiltrated with members of the hardcore underground, including Hubert Badeaux. As has been noted in prior chapters, Leander Perez regularly called Garrison to keep tabs on the investigation. One Garrison investigator, Pershing Gervais, stole Garrison's master file and gave it to the defense. Garrison had no plans to implicate Walker, H. L. Hunt, or anyone actually involved in the conspiracy. Nonetheless, Walker was rightfully worried about the enigmatic Marguerite Oswald.

The two sentences in Walker's letter to Tom Anderson relating his worries about Marguerite Oswald were simple, but nevertheless telling. They suggest consciousness of guilt on Walker's part—and worry of exposure. It also is evidence that Anderson was involved in some way in the conspiracy—certainly as an accessory after the fact. Based on the evidence to be presented next on Anderson, it is likely he was also an accessory *before* the fact.

At the same time that Walker was worried about Marguerite Oswald, on the eve of the Clay Shaw trial, he was also worried about his friend Ned Touchstone reporting on the trial, the assassination, and the Walker shooting incident. Touchstone was constantly writing stories in the *Councilor* about the assassination, blaming it on the Communist conspiracy, Jewish bankers, and others. General Walker wrote a letter to Touchstone, who was also the *Councilor* editor, on February 1, 1969—two weeks after his letter to Anderson—conveying his fears about Marguerite Oswald:

> Dear Ned,
>
> I note your letter and its reference to CIA vs. foe of Marxism. We cannot worry—nor should we certainly I don't—who they are found legitimately and correctly guilty of this deed against the president. I cannot think of anything more destructive and devastating than the assassination of the president.
>
> Any conviction in this case would have to be legitimate—in my confirmed opinion—with the powers of the pros and cons that have transpired. It is just too big to conclude with anything that is not lawful and legal.
>
> We should be glad to see it in the law and legal channels for the first time, and hence leave it to Garrison, who has put it there—and recognize that he is the court.
>
> I do not agree with, nor do I desire my name in anything to influence anything or anybody with respect to this trial—the court or the people. Please do not use any references to me.
>
> I have studied your view and would certainty not give readers

a trail that may not be that of the court and the environment that the court has developed. Let the law take its course. We must and we should want to.

Definitely, Ned, I did not tie Oswald or the gun to April 10, in any way or from anybody's conversation until I saw the German paper here—which was dated Nov. 29th.

I was awakened Saturday at 7:30 a.m. by the call from Germany; but the caller gave no such clue—only saying that he called because he knew of me in Germany. No one was present in the room.

Please respect my wishes and desires as stated.

Sincerely,

"Ted"
Edwin Walker

It is clear Walker was sensitive about Touchstone's writing about the assassination in the *Councilor*. He was especially sensitive about the implication that he had told the German newspaper, before Marina Oswald confirmed it, that Oswald was involved in the shooting incident. (Obviously, the only way he could have known Oswald was involved in the shooting incident is if he and Oswald were in on it together.) Walker looked forward to Garrison pinning the assassination on the government, on the dead David Ferrie, and on a hapless businessman (Clay Shaw)—and doing it in a court of law.

Shaw was found not guilty of conspiring to assassinate the president, and the trial was felt by many to be a sham and a disgrace. Nonetheless, Garrison's blaming of the assassination on the government and the CIA had contributed, to a large degree, to the vast predominance of assassination theories directed at government intelligence—and away from the radical right wing. For that, Walker must have been extremely grateful.

General Walker was with Touchstone in Shreveport on the day of the assassination. The text and tone of Walker's letter suggests that Touchstone was probably not a party to the assassination conspiracy.

The question remains: Who among Walker's close political associates were apprised of the assassination plot? Certainly Revilo Oliver, Robert Morris, J. Evetts Haley, and Dan Smoot, are obvious suspects. Walker was probably smart enough to keep the plot hidden from people like the headline-grabbing, outspoken Klansman, Ned Touchstone, who were targeted by FBI informants.

Walker also may not have been pleased by Touchstone's early exposure of David Ferrie in the *Councilor*. The headline of the March 14, 1964, edition was "The Madcap Aviator of Orleans." The source of the information was not disclosed. Touchstone correctly described the "Aviator," in detail, as a former airline pilot with many fake diplomas—but did not mention Ferrie's name. The *Councilor* later published a photo of David Ferrie, and they noted the "aviator" had a record of contributing to the delinquency of minors, some of whom he taught the rudiments of aircraft use in warfare. The paper claimed that Ferrie flew to Laredo shortly before Oswald showed up in Mexico City. It went on to say that he owned a rifle supposed to be identical to Oswald's, was involved in anti-Castro activities, and misrepresented himself as an attorney. The story was factual about Ferrie on all accounts. It is not clear, however, why Touchstone would want to expose Ferrie. The accusations that Ferrie knew Oswald had already been reported after the assassination and had been dismissed as inconsequential by the FBI, Secret Service, and New Orleans district attorney. Perhaps Touchstone really didn't know who was behind the assassination.[2807] In 1967, Touchstone wrote about Ferrie again and claimed he was the "Birmingham Bomber."[2808]

The Life and Times of Tom Anderson

Tom Anderson, a member of General Walker's close inner circle, entered the publishing business after he got a big break from a "rich and roaring Conservative" who helped him buy *Farm and Ranch* magazine.[2809] General Walker's close friend and backer, J. Evetts Haley, invested in *Farm and Ranch* magazine in 1964 years after Anderson bought it, when it began to falter. At the time, Haley was in the process of writing his broadside on Lyndon Johnson, later titled *A Texan Looks at Lyndon*, and considered publishing it in the John Birch Society *American Opinion* magazine.[2810] When the circulation of Anderson's magazine dropped, Anderson asked Nelson Bunker Hunt to invest in it.[2811] Along with the agriculture topics covered in the magazine, Anderson dedicated one page to his "pun-and-parable" editorial column called "Straight Talk" that toed the radical far-right-wing line against Communism and integration. The column was popular in his magazine and was syndicated in newspapers—primarily in the South.

Bob Hatfield, a part of the Walker group (who was arrested for spitting on Adlai Stevenson), wrote to Robert Welch of the John Birch Society on October 25, 1963, telling Welch to remove him from the membership rolls of the JBS temporarily, so he (Hatfield) would not be connected to the JBS during his trial for assaulting Stevenson. Instead, Welch, who obviously did not like Hatfield, permanently barred Hatfield from the JBS. (Hatfield was found guilty of aggravated assault on a police officer during the incident. Hatfield admitted calling Stevenson a traitor and said to him, "How do you like this?" before spitting on him.) The following year, on June 3, 1964, Hatfield sent a letter to General Walker, Tom Anderson, Revilo Oliver, Joe Grinnan, Ned Touchstone, and Charles Ray to notify them that he was resigning as a member and chapter leader of the JBS because of the "vicious campaign" against him. The letter reveals that the men who received copies of Hatfield's letter—including Anderson—were part of the inner circle of the Walker operation.[2812]

Anderson was a popular and prolific speaker. He was called the "barefoot wit" of the John Birch Society.[2813] He was a clever and entertaining speaker who was likened to Will Rogers, and was sought out from venues ranging from local Rotary Clubs, to the national forums of the Citizens' Council, National Indignation Conference, the Free Electors, and practically every other far-right forum of the time. He was a close friend of Billy James Hargis and spoke at Christian Crusade meetings. Particularly relevant to this work is his involvement in the same groups Joseph Milteer was associated with, including the Constitution Party and We the People. Anderson spoke at the September 22, 1963, meeting of We the People, which was attended by Milteer.

The far right wing had fallen into disarray with the 1954 censure of Joseph McCarthy in the Senate for his reckless Communist witch hunts and the disarray continued after his death in 1957. The John Birch Society was born to reinvigorate the far right and put a fresh face on it. On September 23, 1958, Anderson was invited by Robert Welch to attend the December 8–9, 1958, "off the record" founding meeting of the John Birch Society, and later served on its council. The landmark meeting was held in Indianapolis and twelve people—whose identities were not revealed—were expected to attend.[2814]

In advance of the 1958 meeting, Welch sent Anderson "an extremely confidential manuscript," which was later identified and openly published as *The Politician*. The book was critical of President Eisenhower, whom he called a "dedicated conscious agent of the Communist conspiracy." (In 1952, the radical right's first choice for president had been General Douglas MacArthur. When MacArthur declined to run, they threw their support to Republican senator Robert A. Taft, an ardent critic of the New Deal. Dwight D. Eisenhower, the beloved hero of World War II, defeated Taft in the Republican primary. The far right grew to despise Eisenhower for his moderate policy making. Even so, Eisenhower was reelected in 1956.)

Although its not known if Kent Courtney was at the founding meeting of the JBS—he was not on the JBS council—he was in contact with Welch during the John Birch Society founding. Welch telephoned Courtney before the 1958 Indianapolis meeting and they discussed it. (We know this because Courtney had the peculiar habit of tape recording his phone calls and the recording has been preserved at Northwestern State University of Louisiana.)

A huge repository of Anderson's personal papers is held at the University of Wyoming. The collection was obviously purged, and it is devoid of practically anything from 1963, or any personal letters to friends and colleagues. Marginal notes in his writings indicate he kept some documents filed in a safe. A very small portion of his papers was sent to the University of Oregon archives. A small collection of correspondence from 1963 was among the papers sent to Oregon, and the letters are more insightful and of a more personal nature. They reveal that he was an unapologetic anti-Semite and racist.

Anderson felt the U.S. was dragged into World War II, saying in one of his letters, "It was the wrong war at the wrong time against the wrong enemy. All we did was save the Russians from Hitler." He added, "I was all for going into Russia right after Germany surrendered." General MacArthur shared the same sentiment. Anderson stated that presidents Roosevelt, Truman, Eisenhower, and Kennedy were guilty of willful action against the United States. He stated in an interview, "Where does one-worldism end and treason begin?" Anderson further stated, "Why not hold treason trials? Perfect site: Hyde Park. It's close enough to Hyannis Port, the State Department, Independence and Gettysburg." (The hometowns of the four presidents he despised.) He called Herbert Hoover the "last moral president." He claimed every administration since had been willfully selling the country out to Socialism.[2815] Anderson was even critical of Kennedy after his murder. He compared the power of President Kennedy to Hitler, saying, "What can one man [Kennedy] do? One man, Adolf Hitler, cast the deciding vote in a beer hall putsch that set the world on fire."[2816]

Anderson believed it was imperative to elect Goldwater to the presidency in 1964, "to stop what he considered a slide toward utter Socialism." To that end, Anderson, General Walker, H. L. Hunt and Kent Courtney all attended the June 1964 Republican National Convention and supported Goldwater. Anderson asserted that the cause of American conservatism was hurt by the Kennedy assassination, claiming that if Kennedy had still been alive, Barry Goldwater would have defeated him handily. Anderson averaged two speeches per week up until the assassination. Afterwards, he cut back.[2817]

The Tom Anderson Pre-Assassination Chronology

The activities of Tom Anderson paralleled those of General Walker—and those of so many of the individuals presented throughout this book—and will be chronicled here. They provide a historical glimpse into the mindset and motives of the far-right leaders behind the assassination. Anderson's attacks on President Kennedy were often couched in violent terms, as we shall see.

On October 14, 1958, Anderson wrote to H. L. Hunt, suggesting they merge Hunt's *Facts Forum* and *Farm and Ranch* magazine.

On July 29, 1959, Kent Courtney wrote Anderson and mentioned their recent personal visit together. Anderson helped Courtney work on forming the New Party, which Courtney called, "a turning point in the history of our Republic."[2818] Anderson and J. Evetts Haley joined Courtney at an October 25, 1959, Chicago rally for the New Party, which was also attended by Revilo Oliver, Kent Courtney, Medford Evans, Dan Smoot, and J. Bracken Lee.[2819] On April 6, 1960, Kent Courtney, Tom Anderson, William M. Shaw, and Medford Evans spoke in a States' Rights meeting in Shreveport.[2820] (Shaw was a close collaborator in Willie Rainach's campaign to preserve segregation.) Anderson spoke with Courtney at a Solid South Rally to back the free electors movement in Little Rock, Arkansas, on June 6–7, 1960, also attended by former FBI counterspy Matt Cvetic.[2821]

In an October 31, 1960, letter from Liberty Lobby's Willis Carto, Anderson was asked to be on the Liberty Lobby Policy Board with Taylor Caldwell, Pedro del Valle, Harry Everingham, and General George Stratemeyer.

Tom Anderson was named as a possible vice-presidential candidate for Kent Courtney's New Party at a meeting in Chicago on April 13, 1961. The evidence presented in this work raises suspicions that the cadre of men assembled in the early days of Courtney's New Party were involved in the assassination conspiracy. In a June 27, 1961, letter to Courtney, Anderson told him that he conferred with people across the country that agreed that there was a need to "make some effort to get together in a common front." Anderson added, "Evidently the leader has not yet arisen who can at the same time unite a large portion of the conservative movement behind him. This is a chicken and egg proposition, I guess, but rather than wait on that leader to arise and unite us we might as well try to unite ourselves." Not long after Anderson expressed his thoughts to Courtney, they found their leader in General Walker. On July 13, 1961, Anderson invited Courtney to a meeting to unite conservatives under a common front.[2822]

On August 4–6, 1961, Anderson spoke with Robert Welch at Billy James Hargis's Christian Crusade Third Annual Christ Summit Conference.[2823]

On September 16, 1961, Anderson told a meeting of We the People that the Kennedy administration sought power even greater than the power possessed by Soviet Premier Nikita Khrushchev.[2824] At the meeting, Billy James Hargis moved to form a fraternity of anti-Communists and to meet in January in Washington. Among their goals was to outlaw the Communist Party and the muzzling of military men (the latter of which was obviously in response to General Walker's muzzling).[2825]

On March 28, 1962, Stuart McClendon of New Orleans wrote Anderson and invited him to speak in his hometown to protest President Kennedy's visit to the Nashville Wharf. It will be recalled from Chapter Ten that Hubert Badeaux was McClendon's campaign manager in his bid to unseat Hale Boggs in Congress.[2826]

Emmett Irwin of the New Orleans Citizens' Council, who had corresponded with Milteer, invited Anderson to speak at the Municipal Auditorium on March 30, 1962.[2827]

In 1962, Anderson read an article in the paper about the Senate investigation of William Wieland, a mid-level State Department official under John Foster Dulles. Wieland was blamed for Batista's downfall and Castro's rise in Cuba. Wieland described Castro incorrectly as a moderate, when he was, instead, a Communist. Congress investigated Wieland in 1961 and 1962—and he was a target of the Cubans and the far right, who called him a Communist and a traitor—but President Kennedy defended him. The whole Communist takeover of Cuba was, in essence, blamed on Wieland and the State Department. The radical right believed, following the accusations of Senator Joseph McCarthy, that the State Department was overrun with Communists. Wieland ultimately resigned in disgrace. Senator Olin Johnston was on the committee that investigated Wieland. According to the newspaper, Johnston said that if Wieland's testimony were released, it would infuriate the anti-Castro elements and that "there might be some killings." Anderson wrote to Johnston on January 5, 1962, and remarked on Wieland and the Cuba situation, "Maybe we need some killings, Senator. I believe there was treason afoot in the Cuban fiasco, I believe in killing traitors. How about you?" Anderson said the American people were "in peril" because of "subversion in our ranks." Anderson expressed contempt for Kennedy's "New Frontier viewpoint" and ended his letter to Johnston ominously: "There is a grassroots rebellion growing, Senator, which I earnestly hope will sweep out of office, through elections as well as impeachment trials, those responsible for out present plight."[2828]

On April 30, 1962, Ted Jackman wrote Anderson and discussed the Disarmament Act and invited Anderson to join him on a world tour to bring the American public "a better understanding of just what our government is doing around the world."[2829] (Joseph Milteer told Willie Somersett that Jackman was one of the shooters in Dealey Plaza.)

On May 10, 1962, Anderson wrote to a friend that Walker's defeat in the governor's race was quite a blow and that Anderson felt sorry for him. Anderson told his friend he had been at Walker's headquarters the day before the election with J. Evetts Haley.[2830]

On June 13, 1962, Anderson wrote to Sam Marcello (no known relationship to New Orleans mob boss Carlos Marcello) who had disapproved of Anderson's criticism of the president in one of his columns. Anderson responded to Marcello: "The Kennedy crowd stole the election and he is morally unfit to serve, as everybody who really knows the score is aware of . . . I hope I am wrong, but I think it is far too late for the kid glove approach. I think we are facing Socialism, insolvency, and surrender . . ."[2831]

On June 17, 1962, Anderson spoke at the Free Electors meeting in Jackson, Mississippi, with Jim Johnson, Ross Barnett, and Leander Perez.[2832]

On September 4, 5, and 6, 1962, Anderson spoke with Kent Courtney, Colonel Laurence Bunker, Harry Everingham, and Walter Knott in Los Angeles to promote The Liberty Amendment.[2833]

On September 26, 1962—three days before he led the riots at Ole Miss—General Walker wrote a threatening, open letter of grievances to President Kennedy, and he sent a copy of it to his friend, Tom Anderson.[2834] After the Walker-led insurrection on September 30, 1962, Anderson called the people of Mississippi "conquered people after the federal take over at Ole Miss," and he sided with Ross Barnett and General Walker. Anderson believed that the "goal of the Negro is not to be Negro, but to intermarry" and become a "tan race."[2835] Anderson was in Mississippi after the riots and was one of the first to talk to Walker upon his release from the Springfield mental facility. Robert Welch expressed his gratitude to Anderson for conveying Walker's first words to him after his release.[2836]

On October 5, 1962, Kent Courtney invited Anderson to the Cuban Liberation Rally in Chicago, which was to take place on November 17, 1963. John Rousselot also accepted an invitation to speak, along with a "mystery Cuban Freedom fighter." They planned to invite General Walker, if he could make it, when he was bailed out of the Springfield federal mental facility.[2837]

On October 13, 1962, Anderson spoke at a "Dallas Freedom Rally" with Frank McGehee of the National Indignation Committee. Anderson attacked Kennedy's disarmament plans and his alleged plan to seize personal firearms, stating: "The time to buy firearms is when it becomes unlawful to have them."[2838]

Anderson spoke in New Orleans on October 30, 1962, again with National Indignation Convention founder Frank McGehee at a *For America* rally presented by George Soule of the New Orleans *For America* chapter. Anderson called Kennedy's disarmament act, "suicide, slavery, treason," stating it provided for a program of "One, Two, Three, Surrender."[2839] The rally placed Anderson with Guy Banister's associate George Soule, who had presided over the Congress of Freedom meeting where Willie Somersett learned of the assassination plots described in Chapter Six. By 1963, Tom Anderson had twice been the recipient of the Congress of Freedom's Liberty award.[2840]

On January 6, 1963, Anderson spoke at the New England Rally for God and Country with Billy James Hargis, Kent Courtney, Ezra Taft Benson and John Rousselot; seventeen of the twenty-three speakers were members of the John Birch Society.[2841, 2842, 2843] It will be recalled that Joseph Milteer had met with Benson in Utah, just prior to the October 1963 Constitution Party meeting where talk of killing the president took place.

On January 11, 1963, Anderson spoke to the Louisiana Press Association's convention in New Orleans. Anderson warned, "If we are taken over by the Communists, it won't be they who did it. It will be the people who are idealists in many cases, who can't realize that the only one-world brotherhood in our time is a slave state."[2844]

Anderson presided over the Walker-Hargis Midnight Ride tour stop in Nashville, Tennessee, on March 13, 1963. At that tour stop, General Walker challenged President Kennedy "to take one division of airborne troops from Fort Bragg, N.C. and liquidate the scourge" in Cuba. Walker told the crowd that Anderson had made seventy-six speeches in the past year, but that the Kennedy-controlled press did not mention any of them. (At the same meeting, Hargis passed around a collection plate and handbills promoting an upcoming John Rousselot speech in Nashville on May 17.)[2845]

On April 18, 1963, Tom Anderson spoke with Herbert Philbrick, Lee Harvey Oswald's boyhood hero, at a meeting of the board of America's Future.

On May 8, 1963, Anderson and John Martino spoke in Dade County, Florida, at an event sponsored by Norbert Garrity of the Committee to Warn of the Arrival of Communist Merchandise on the Local Business Scene.[2846] Martino was an anti-Castro adventurer who had at one time been imprisoned in Cuba. (On December 12, 1963, the press reported on a speech by Martino in Birmingham, Alabama, where he claimed Lee Harvey Oswald had been active in the Miami area and was known to have passed checks drawn on the account of Fair Play for Cuba Committee.[2847] Martino was, obviously, yet another on the far right engaging in disinformation about Oswald and the assassination.)

On May 23, 1963, Tom Anderson spoke in Jackson, Mississippi. Anderson told the crowd, "I grew up wanting to fight the Civil War over. I saw *The Birth of a Nation* four times and every time I expected the South to win."[2848] (The 1915 silent film portrayed white supremacy and the Ku Klux Klan in a noble light.)

On June 1, 1963, the John Birch Society held a recruiting meeting in New York City that featured Robert Welch, Revilo Oliver—and Tom Anderson.[2849]

On June 17, 1963, an organizational meeting of the Free Electors was held in Jackson, Mississippi, and Anderson was the main speaker. George Wallace, Jim Johnson, and Leander Perez also addressed the meeting.[2850]

On July 20, 1963, Anderson told a John Birch Society seminar in Houston, Texas (which General Walker attended as an observer), that he would support Barry Goldwater for president in 1964, and Strom Thurmond as vice president. Anderson declared that, "The country will be saved from the grassroots . . . by rebellious patriots."[2851]

On August 20, 1963, Dr. Stanley L. Drennan wrote to Anderson and told him of a recent encounter with the Secret Service. He related that when President Kennedy spoke at the Palladium in San Francisco on June 10, 1963, Secret Service agents questioned two of Drennan's friends about him. (Other allegations about Drennan's threat to the life of President Kennedy were noted in Chapter Nine.) Drennan wrote in his letter to Anderson that "these people were twenty miles East of my dwelling, while I was only two miles from my dwelling where the president was riding in an open convertible sitting high on the back of the seat. The climax of the Treasury Agent's questioning was why this writer (S.L.D.) was plotting the assassination of Mr. Kennedy." In the letter, Drennan claimed that the Treasury Agents told him that anyone who would contemplate violence would end up in an institution. Drennan told the agents that Kennedy "was plunging us into One World chaos," and that Drennan intended to try and defeat him.[2852] Anderson replied to Drennan's letter and told him Drennan was "under the scrutiny of some of the field Gestapo of the Kennedy Oligarchy." Referring to Kennedy, Anderson wrote: "He should, as did Lincoln, go to the theater and relax."[2853]

On September 22, 1963, Anderson spoke at a We the People luncheon (attended by Joseph Milteer) and predicted that the Soviet Union would take over the United States by 1973. (He was the national chairman of the group.) Anderson implied that President Kennedy did not want to get ahead of the Soviet Union. Anderson stated that the nuclear test ban was just one of the many guarantees the Kennedy administration gave the Soviet Union so that that they would stay ahead of the United States. He said, "We have to stop worrying about the real pink army within instead of the Red army without."[2854]

On November 22, 1963, Dr. Curtis Caine of Jackson, Mississippi, wrote Anderson and said, "Some time ago you, Tom, suggested there would be less treason and treachery in America if there were a few 'neck-tying' parties for spies and traitors." Caine made a point of saying to Anderson that the letter was composed before the assassination.[2855]

Before the assassination, Key Record Company produced a record featuring a speech by Anderson, which was bitterly critical of President Kennedy, called "Bipartisan Treason." On November 27, 1963, Key owner Vic Knight—a Californian who produced long-playing record albums featuring members of the far right—wrote to Anderson and told him that he had edited and remastered the record after the assassination, "deleting all references that could be considered in bad taste with respect to the late occupant of the White House." He removed entirely a joke about President Kennedy's daughter, but was able to preserve a line about a diaper. Knight explained to Anderson that he was concerned it would hurt recruitment efforts of those who might consider the record "a personal assault on a dead man." He added that it was the best thing for the interests of the John Birch Society. (After the assassination, Knight also produced a record of the New Orleans Oswald-Butler "debate" wherein Oswald proclaimed he was a Marxist. In the new release, Billy James Hargis's voice, bizarrely, was substituted for

Butler's to give the effect of Hargis debating Oswald.)[2856]

On December 6, 1963, William Voit, an officer of the Arizona JBS wrote to Anderson, stating, "The reaction out here to 'the situation' has apparently been milder with a couple exceptions." "The situation" he referred to was obviously the assassination. He disclosed that the Phoenix JBS bookstore was "shot up" after the assassination, stating, "If anybody had been in the store, we would have suffered a decrease in membership in Phoenix." He noted, "John Rousselot is going ahead with his talks and not canceling and hasn't had a bad reaction." Voit wrote, "What we really need is a new record giving the straight scoop on 'the situation' including Earl Warren's participation, what we can expect from LBJ and why the conservatives must not relax or be discouraged now more than ever." Voit was calling for a far-right propaganda effort in response to the assassination.[2857]

Anderson (and the rest of the hardcore underground) did not fold their operation after November 22, 1963. He remained active in the radical right for over the next decade.[2858]

The Clairvoyant Taylor Caldwell

Taylor Caldwell was a world-famous novelist who seemingly predicted the assassination of President Kennedy in advance. She published dozens of books—many of them best sellers. She was close to so many in the radical right who were suspected of involvement in the assassination conspiracy, that she may have learned of a plan to kill the president; her prediction may not have been a spiritual revelation at all. Although many people thought "Taylor Caldwell" was a man, her real name was Janet Rebak. Few probably knew she was a fervent radical right winger and fanatical anti-Communist. There is no doubt that she was held in high esteem by Robert Welch. Caldwell's picture graced the cover of the JBS magazine *American Opinion*, an honor which was reserved for luminaries of the far right like Joseph McCarthy, Douglas MacArthur, and Strom Thurmond.[2859]

Caldwell's friendship with Tom Anderson goes back at least to 1958, when she wrote to him and told him his publication was extremely interesting and informative. In the letter, she stated she belonged to practically every patriotic organization in the United States and specifically praised Liberty Lobby.[2860] She wrote for the John Birch Society's *American Opinion* and the anti-Semitic *American Mercury*.

In an October 31, 1960, letter, Willis Carto, founder of Liberty Lobby, asked Tom Anderson to be on the Liberty Lobby Policy Board with Caldwell, Pedro del Valle, Harry Everingham, and General George Stratemeyer.[2861] Later, Billy James Hargis and Tom Brady of the Mississippi Citizens' Council also served on the board.[2862]

In 1960, Caldwell was on the board of governors of the Federation of Conservatives with Harold Lord Varney. Kent Courtney—who was also a board member—was with General Walker and Varney in New Orleans days before the Kennedy assassination.[2863]

The FBI file on Caldwell also noted that she was associated with two other Texas friends of General Walker: J. Evetts Haley and Dan Smoot.[2864] On February 23, 1962, the FBI received information that Caldwell and Billy James Hargis were behind a program called

"Congress Calling from Washington."[2865] She also served on the national advisory panel of Young Americans for Freedom.

Caldwell wrote a story for the October 31, 1963, edition of the conservative Catholic paper *The Wanderer* (published in St. Paul, Minnesota), and stated that she "sensed" President Kennedy's life was in danger. An analysis of the article revealed that she more than "sensed" the president's life was in danger. She probably knew the murder plot was in the works and understood, at least in part, how it was going to be done. Caldwell set out her story with an implausible tale that mimicked those told by Revilo Oliver and Pedro del Valle after the assassination. She made the same silly claim as Oliver and del Valle, saying that President Kennedy was moving away from his pro-Communist position and becoming "more American," thus becoming a target for assassination by the Communists. She claimed in her article, written three weeks before the assassination, that "[t]he 'tone' of the liberal periodicals . . . is wrathful against our president." She stated that the liberals (or pro-Communists) expected Kennedy to set up a "sort of crypto-Communist dictatorship" and had been disappointed when he hadn't done so. She suggested that, as a result, the president was "possibly in personal jeopardy and might be assassinated." Next, she alluded to one of the liberals (or pro-Communist people) who fit the description of Lee Harvey Oswald. She noted, "Then there are 'agents provocateurs' who would just love such an 'incident'." (Writers—as well as Jim Garrison—often referred to Oswald as an "agent provocateur.") Caldwell noted that, in a recent visit to Duluth, Minnesota, President Kennedy was under heavy guard by the military and law enforcement, in addition to the Secret Service.

The whole story was far fetched. Her claim that the liberals or pro-Communists expected Kennedy to set up a "sort of crypto-Communist dictatorship" is completely unsubstantiated and nonsensical. Later, she wrote a letter to the FBI about her prediction and they noted, "Her letter suggests a rather weird explanation of the presidential assassination." (She had long corresponded with the FBI and, in 1958, told them about a man she knew "who attempted to convert [her] to the Communist viewpoint.") Nonetheless, her prediction was correct and a Communist—or someone posing as a Communist in Lee Harvey Oswald— was presumed to be the president's assassin by the Warren Commission. Even though Caldwell's rationale was silly, her clairvoyance was nonetheless extraordinary—if that's what it was. However, there is good reason to believe that she was *not* clairvoyant but, rather, she knew that a plot to kill the president was in the works, and that Lee Harvey Oswald—likely her described agent provocateur "who would just love such an 'incident'"—was figured into it by the time of her October 31 article.

The fact that Caldwell's article appeared in an obscure right-wing publication aligned with Robert Morris, and that Morris was close to Walker, Guy Banister, Charles Willoughby, and others who have been (or will be) implicated in the assassination, raises the distinct possibility that she knew about the assassination (and how it was to be done).[2866]

Although the FBI was aware of Caldwell's prediction and kept a file on her, they thought little of it. What no one knew was that the conservative Catholic weekly, *The Wan-*

derer, which carried the prescient article, was aligned with Dallasite Robert Morris—a close associate of the top conspirator in the assassination, General Walker. (Morris, as has been presented, was Walker's friend and attorney, and represented Walker after his arrest for insurrection against the U.S. government at Ole Miss.) *The Wanderer* had been published under the name *Der Wanderer* from 1867 to 1956, because it had a predominantly German Catholic audience. Robert Morris had a regular front-page column titled "Around the World" in which he espoused his far-right beliefs. Schick Safety Razor was a major advertiser, and Medford Evans's son, Stanton Evans, advertised his far-right book *The Fringe on Top*, which was published by the Wanderer Press. Strom Thurmond was a contributing writer.[2867] Revilo Oliver and Tom Anderson also wrote for the paper.[2868] General Walker attended The First Wanderer Forum with his mother in St. Paul, Minnesota, on June 11–12, 1965, where the topic was the decline of the "Western Christian Civilization."[2869]

At the time Caldwell wrote her article (October 31, 1963), plans for the assassination of President Kennedy were indeed already in the works, and they had been revealed at the October 18–19 Constitution Party meeting in Indianapolis. Evidence was presented in Chapter Seven that General Walker's close associate Pedro del Valle was behind it. On October 25, 1963, Walker proclaimed at the Jackson Citizens' Council meeting: "I have seen this country being sold out, lock, stock and barrel by a bunch of sophisticated professors, Harvard liberals who are at a loss as where to go and what to do, and I can assure you they are going to pay for it one way or another. Because I've seen the Communist hangman's noose coming tighter and tighter on everyone of them. It's interesting that the Communists killed the first people that helped them in their revolution. First! So we've got something to look forward to, ladies and gentlemen." As discussed, Walker's statement suggests Oswald with his phony communist credentials had already been figured into the assassination. The scenario Walker presented was similar to Caldwell's.

The fact that Caldwell's article appeared in an obscure right wing publication aligned with Robert Morris, and that Morris was close to General Walker, Guy Banister, Charles Willoughby and others who have been or will be implicated in the assassination, raises the distinct possibility that she knew about the assassination in advance and how it was to be done.[2870] Morris was close to Revilo Oliver and Major Archibald Robert as well.[2871] Morris, as noted in Chapter Fifteen, screened applicants for Walker's Minutemen groups that, as a citizen informed the FBI, were really "assassination squads."

In addition to General Walker's October 25, 1963, speech to the Citizens' Council, when he hinted that a Communist might kill the president, Joseph Milteer reported to Willie Somersett (on November 9, 1963) exactly what was to happen to the president in Dallas. Their remarks, together with Taylor Caldwell's October 31, 1963, "sensing" that an agent provocateur would kill the president suggest that the plans to murder President Kennedy in Dallas were set in October 1963 and that Oswald had been figured into it by that time.

A December 14, 1963, letter from Caldwell to the FBI in her FBI file adds more detail to her prediction in *The Wanderer*. Embellishing further, she claimed that the FBI and Secret Service had been ordered to watch conservatives before the assassination and not known Communists like Lee Harvey Oswald. She said she wrote to President Kennedy in August 1963 and told him his life was in jeopardy from a "Liberal/Leftist/Communist Combine." She claimed she received a warm reply from the president, noting that he seemed amused and unalarmed. She claimed she was not satisfied with his response, and that's why she decided to publish her warning in *The Wanderer*.

Caldwell wrote a letter to the editor of the New York *Daily News* on December 18, 1963, and told them that it was her conviction that President Johnson faced the same fate as President Kennedy at the hands of "liberal Communists." She told the *Daily News* that, in late August, she had sent a letter to President Kennedy warning him "[t]he liberal Communists would attempt to take his life." She said that after reading articles by prominent leftists, she sent Kennedy "another rather desperate warning." She said her good friend Senator Joseph McCarthy—who died in 1957—had predicted Kennedy's death in the event he would assume the presidency. McCarthy allegedly wrote her a letter saying: "The people will never know the terrible power of the Communists and their fellow-travelers until a president is assassinated." Caldwell reportedly told McCarthy, "Mr. Kennedy might make a fine president." In response to the possibility of Kennedy being president, she reported that, "Joe said in horror, 'my God no, the Communists would kill him.'"[2872] The FBI noted that Caldwell told them that—prior to Kennedy's death—she saw his funeral on a television set that was not turned on.[2873]

Next, Caldwell's power of prophecy was directed toward President Johnson. On December 19, 1963, the United Press International reported that Caldwell stated that President Johnson "is in mortal danger" and gave a few more details on her earlier prediction of Kennedy's murder.

The FBI also felt, like Caldwell, that President Johnson might meet the same fate as President Kennedy. Only they thought it might come from General Walker, not a Communist, and notified the Secret Service on six separate occasions that Walker was a threat to the life of Johnson, as was noted in the last chapter.

Taylor Caldwell's knack for predicting assassinations didn't stop with the president's. Prior to Robert Kennedy's assassination—which occurred just after midnight on June 5, 1968—Caldwell wrote a letter to the FBI and told them that "something terrible is going to happen." They took her seriously and, on the day before Robert Kennedy's murder, a special agent of the FBI telephoned her to discuss her letter. She reportedly told the agent a bizarre and confusing story. (There appears to be something missing in the story and it is not clear to the author what Caldwell was saying. With that in mind, the basic story will be recounted—but an attempt to make complete sense of it will be limited.)

When they spoke on June 4, Caldwell told the FBI agent that she had gone outside her home (which was near Buffalo, New York) to plant flowers, when a "Negro teenager" rode up on his motor bike and asked her if she knew Donald Jackson. Believing incorrectly he was referring to a prominent black educational fundraiser that she knew by the same name, she told him that she did. The teen replied, "Did you tell the Secret Service what our friend in

New York wanted to tell them?" Her reply perplexed the teen when she said, "You mean about the Negro woman?" The teen replied that she had things mixed up. Then she told him, "I told the FBI." The teenaged boy, whom she had never seen before, rode away. She told the FBI that she was completely startled when the teen referred to "our friend in New York" and assumed it was the Negro businessman in New York City who had written to her that "something terrible is going to happen." (As a famous author, Caldwell received a large volume of letters from people.) She told the FBI that perhaps the murder of Robert Kennedy was what her Negro friend in New York City was alluding to when he wrote her that a "something terrible [was] about to happen." In her letter to the FBI, she told them an unknown Negro woman gave her the warning.

Trying to reconcile her statements, she told the FBI that perhaps what the Negro businessman had been trying to tell her was that the Negro woman was involved in the predicted terrible incident, but not necessarily as the victim. It is not entirely clear to the author what Caldwell was talking about in regards to the Negro teen, Negro woman, and Negro businessman from New York City. It is not clear if the FBI was really interested in untangling her claims, either. In other dealings with her she was referred to as "eccentric" and "weird," and that she often "intermingled fact with fiction." Caldwell concluded that she felt Senator Kennedy's death was more than just a coincidence and she was "not a believer in coincidence" and that there must definitely have been some connection between the information she had previously received and Senator Kennedy's death.

The June 7, 1968, FBI report of their interview with Caldwell was forwarded to the office in charge of the investigation of the assassination of Martin Luther King, Jr., under the three titles of "Alleged Plot in New York City New York to Harm or Kill a Prominent Woman," "Assassination of President John Fitzgerald Kennedy, Dallas, Texas, November 22, 1963" and "POOR PEOPLES CAMPAIGN." The author did not research the contemporaneous social-political events that took place in New York City in 1968. It appears that Caldwell was trying to link the individuals plotting to kill a prominent black woman to the murder of Senator Kennedy. New York City was a center for both civil rights and Communist Party activity. It may be the case that Caldwell was trying to link blacks and Communists to the murder of Senator Kennedy. Further investigation is needed, but is beyond the scope of this work.[2874]

Liberty Lobby and the Assassination Disinformation Machine

Three individuals with ties to Liberty Lobby (whose board of directors included Tom Anderson and Taylor Caldwell), Mark Lane, Victor Marchetti, and Fetcher Prouty, significantly advanced the widespread beliefs of conspiracy theorists that the CIA or some other shadowy secret government forces were behind the assassination of President Kennedy.

Liberty Lobby was conceived in 1955 and launched in 1961 by Willis Carto, a Nazi sympathizer and friend of Ned Touchstone, for the purpose of lobbying Congress on behalf of radical-right-wing causes. Carto wrote an introduction to Francis Yockey's book *Imperium*, containing a dedication in the introduction to Adolf Hitler. Carto was also an organizer of the

John Birch Society in 1959 and a director of the Congress of Freedom.[2875, 2876] Robert Welch, cognizant of the difficulties that Carto's ties to Nazism presented for the JBS, confided in Tom Anderson in a letter that "Carto is a man who can not be loved."[2877] Carto had a friend in San Francisco who was engaged in the business of taking pictures of people on the street and handing them a ticket to purchase the photos from him. He kept photos of interracial couples and sent them to Touchstone to publish in the *Councilor* to inflame its segregationist readers. Carto told Touchstone, "I can have him shoot all sorts of things. How about a male fairy and a nigger? Or a lesbian nigger with a White female?" Touchstone replied that he would be grateful to have the pictures.[2878] (The author met Carto in 2004. A slight, gracefully aged man, Carto was charismatic and affable. His wife Elizabeth retained her striking beauty in advanced age. Her blue eyes and German accent conjured images of Eva Braun.[2879])

An inspection of the board of Liberty Lobby showed a considerable overlap with those of the John Birch Society, Christian Crusade, Congress of Freedom, We the People, National Indignation Committee, and other far-right groups. In 1961 and 1962, the Liberty Lobby board of directors included Tom Anderson, Taylor Caldwell, Billy James Hargis, Pedro del Valle, Harry Everingham, General Richard Moran, General Albert Wedemeyer, Frank McGehee, Kenneth Goff and Mary Cain. Curtis Dall was the chairman of the board of Liberty Lobby in 1962.[2880, 2881] As was noted in Chapter Seven, Joseph Milteer told the FBI, following the Kennedy assassination, that Curtis Dall—who was the national chairman of the Constitution Party—had invited Milteer to the October Constitution Party meeting where a plot to kill the president was discussed. Dall was also a director-at-large for We the People. Liberty Lobby board members Kenneth Goff and Pedro del Valle were known associates of Milteer, and board members Tom Anderson and Billy James Hargis were featured speakers at the Chicago We the People meeting on September 21, 1963, which was attended by Milteer. Kent Courtney and Robert Welch also spoke at the We the People meeting. Generals Pedro del Valle and Richard Moran, another Liberty Lobby board member, were part of the American Volunteer Group—Nelson Bunker Hunt's so-called "Kill Squad." Liberty Lobby was infused throughout with individuals who were either a part of the assassination conspiracy or were connected to Milteer or General Walker.

In 1978, the HSCA investigation of the Kennedy assassination was under way. Liberty Lobby published an article in their weekly newspaper, *The Spotlight*, on August 14, 1978, entitled "C.I.A. to Nail Hunt for Kennedy Killing." Victor Marchetti, a former deputy director for the CIA, wrote the article. The articled claimed that CIA officer E. Howard Hunt was going to admit that he was involved in the conspiracy to kill President Kennedy during the concurrent HSCA investigation. Hunt sued Liberty Lobby and *The Spotlight* for libel, and a federal jury awarded him $650,000 in damages.[2882] (E. Howard Hunt is better known for working in the Nixon White house and for his role as "a plumber" in the Watergate break-in and burglary.) *The Spotlight*, according to one liberal watchdog group, "not only railed against 'dual-loyalist' Jews in government, but also ha[d] praised the Nazi skinhead movement and reported favorably on the 'spirit' of the Nazi Waffen-SS during World War II."[2883] After the libel verdict, Liberty Lobby retained early Warren Commission critic Mark Lane, of all people, to appeal the case, and they won. (Lane is probably the best-known critic of the Warren Commission and published the bestseller *Rush to Judgment* in 1966. Lane would later claim that the U.S. government had a hand in the Kennedy and King assassinations, as well as the 1978 Jonestown massacre in Guyana.)

After the libel suit and appeal, Willis Carto subsequently created the anti-Semitic Institute for Historical Review that promoted the theory that the Holocaust was a hoax perpetrated by the Jews for the benefit of the state of Israel. *Public Eye* (the newsletter of Political Research Associates) described Mark Lane's history with Liberty Lobby as follows: "But Lane is also an active apologist for the Institute for Historical Review and Willis Carto. Writing in his book *Plausible Denial,* Lane contends that 'I have never heard an anti-Semitic expression' from Carto. Lane uses his Jewish background and past leftist credentials to divert attention from Carto's role as the leading purveyor of racist, anti-Jewish and pro-Nazi literature in the U.S. Lane describes in *Plausible Denial* how he was recruited into the Carto network through the late Haviv Schieber, who Lane describes in glowing terms as a Jewish activist fighting for peace in the Middle East."

Former CIA executive Victor Marchetti, who wrote the E. Howard Hunt story for Liberty Lobby, loaned credibility to Jim Garrison's unsubstantiated claim that the CIA was behind the assassination when he implied that Jim Garrison's chief assassination suspects—David Ferrie and Clay Shaw—had worked for the CIA. In 1975 Marchetti made the claim that in 1969 CIA Director Richard Helms privately admitted Clay Shaw and David Ferrie worked for the CIA. Marchetti had served as Executive Assistant to the Deputy Director of the CIA at the time. Marchetti claimed that during the course of several high-level CIA staff meetings in January and February 1969 that Helms disclosed that David Ferrie, and Clay Shaw and at least one of Garrison's anti-Castro suspects had worked for the CIA. The disclosures allegedly came while the trial of Clay Shaw was underway. Marchetti claimed that Helms repeatedly expressed worry over Garrison's prosecution of Clay Shaw and instructed the CIA General Counsel and Helm's Deputy to "do all we can do to help Shaw." As noted in Chapter Nine, Clay Shaw was an inconsequential Domestic Contact officer connected to the CIA in the 1950's. Thousands of patriotic, citizen volunteers, especially those engaged in international commerce like Shaw, provided information to the CIA. They were not employees or agents. There is no proof that David Ferrie was connected to the CIA.

In a 1975 interview with national television news anchor Dan Rather, Marchetti was asked if Oswald was in some way connected to the CIA. Marchetti replied, "They could very well have dealt with him [Oswald] without CIA Director McCone ever being informed. I think that CIA knows more about the circumstances surrounding the Kennedy assassination that has not yet been made public about their relationships with Oswald." He said he did not believe the CIA as an institution was involved but he could not rule out the involvement of individuals acting on their own or remotely connected to the CIA in some capacity.

Marchetti resigned from the CIA in 1969 and wrote a book critical of the agency called *The Rope Dancer*. In 1973, he published another book, *The CIA and the Cult of Intelligence*. In 1989, Marchetti gave a speech at a meeting of Liberty Lobby's Institute for Historical Review.[2884] According to Political Research Associates' *Public Eye*, Marchetti co-published *Zionist Watch*, which was endorsed in direct mail appeals on Liberty Lobby stationery by the secretary of Liberty Lobby's board of directors, Lois Petersen.[2885] Marchetti never provided a shred of verifiable evidence to support any of his claims about David Ferrie, Clay Shaw, or any others that suggested a CIA tie to the Kennedy assassination. Marchetti's tie to Liberty Lobby suggests disinformation was the motive for his insinuations and perhaps was yet another conscious attempt to steer the public debate over the assassination away from the radical right.

Colonel L. Fletcher Prouty, U.S.A.F. retired, was a third individual tied to Liberty Lobby who promoted the claim that U.S. government intelligence operatives were behind the assassination. Prouty met with Jim Garrison years after the assassination and the trial of Clay Shaw. Their meeting—and what Prouty had to say to Garrison—was loosely depicted in the movie *JFK*. As the story goes, Prouty, or a Prouty-type composite figure, provided the military hardware to military intelligence for black operations and assassinations, and various other devices for destabilizing foreign governments. The Prouty character claimed that the U.S. had set up bases for invasion of Cuba in 1962 after the failed Bay of Pigs operation. President Kennedy's refusal to invade incensed the forces involved in the Bay of Pigs Operation. According to the movie, in 1963, the Prouty character claimed that he was working on a Kennedy-directed plan to remove all forces from Vietnam by 1965, drawing the ire of some in the military. He further claimed that it was his routine duty to provide additional protection for Kennedy's upcoming trip to Texas. Prouty allegedly later learned that the additional forces at Fort Sam Houston in San Antonio were told to "stand down" on the day of the assassination. He stated that the action was "the best indication of a massive plot in Dallas." He claimed that government "black ops" were the ones behind the withdrawal of security. He also claimed that Army Intelligence had a file on Lee Harvey Oswald that they destroyed. Finally, the character noted that Kennedy promised to splinter the CIA into a "thousand pieces." Thus, the Prouty character provided further motive for the CIA, Special Ops, Army Intelligence or other murky figures in the government (he was not discriminate) with sufficient motives to kill the president.[2886] Perhaps bolstered by Prouty's tale, Jim Garrison went on after the failed Shaw trial to promote a "the-government-did-it" story in his book *On the Trail of Assassins* in 1989.

In 1973, Prouty published the book *The Secret Team: The CIA and its Allies in Control of the United States and the World*, which was critical of the CIA. In his book, Prouty argued that the CIA's clandestine activities needlessly prolonged the Vietnam War. Liberty Lobby's Institute for Historic Review republished the book under its own imprint, Noontide Press. (At the time, Noontide Press was the largest distributor of pro-Nazi, anti-Jewish, white supremacist literature in the United States. Noontide Press also distributed *Auschwitz: Truth or Lie—An Eyewitness Report*, *Hitler At My Side*, and *For Fear of the Jews*.)[2887] Prouty's allegations, like Victor Marchetti's, lacked any corroborating evidence.

There is no evidence to tie Willis Carto's attorney, Mark Lane, to the active purveying of disinformation to affect a cover-up. He was a lawyer earning a living, and—as is often the case—represented an unsavory client. However, the distinct possibility is raised that Liberty Lobby used Lane as a tool to create disinformation and point the finger at the CIA and the government—and away from the radical right—in the plot to kill the president. Prouty and Marchetti, on the other hand, may well have been deliberate participants in the Liberty Lobby disinformation effort.

The Raymond Broshears Story

Raymond Broshears was acquainted with David Ferrie in New Orleans during three periods in his life: 1961–2, 1963, and 1965. They also talked by phone once in 1967. Ferrie was Lee Harvey Oswald's Civil Air Patrol squadron leader in 1955 and 1956. A U.S Border Patrol agent saw Ferrie and Lee Harvey Oswald entering Guy Banister's office on multiple occasions in the summer of 1963 as noted in Chapter Two. Jim Garrison, in 1967, and the HSCA, in 1977, each investigated Broshears. In the HSCA interview of Broshears, the interviewers noted he was an overt homosexual like Ferrie, and a self-styled priest.

Broshears and Ferrie were both involved in the offbeat Orthodox Old Catholic Church of North America in New Orleans. Guy Banister employees Jack Martin and Joe Newbrough were also involved in the church. Animosity between Ferrie and Martin, generated by a dispute about the church, prompted Martin to go to the press on the day of the Kennedy assassination and tell them that Ferrie had taught Lee Harvey Oswald to shoot a rifle, and that he had seen a picture of Oswald in Ferrie's apartment. D.A. Jim Garrison's office, the FBI, and the Secret Service interviewed Martin due to the allegations he made in the press and, unfortunately, dismissed them as baseless. According to Broshears, Ferrie told him that when the FBI investigated him (Ferrie) after the assassination they berated him for being a homosexual and a freak. (The failure by both the FBI and Secret Service to take Martin's allegations about Ferrie seriously is yet another example of the momentous failures of those agencies in the investigation of the assassination.)

Jim Garrison and Raymond Broshears

Stephen Jaffe, a California-based investigator for Jim Garrison, interviewed Raymond Broshears on July 27, 1968. He noted that Broshears had made a television appearance on *The Stan Borman Show* in Los Angeles. Broshears told Jaffe that he came back to New Orleans in 1965 from East St. Louis, where he had worked for the Congress of Racial Equality (CORE). Broshears told Jaffe that after going to Bogalusa, Louisiana, he was stopped by the Louisiana State Police and "was beat up"—something that happened commonly to civil rights workers. He went to New Orleans to escape his undisclosed problems and registered at a hotel under an assumed name. He explained how he first met Ferrie at a gay bar named "Dixie's," and later ran into him at a French Quarter bar called "Lafitte's in Exile." The two became friends.

Broshears related that Ferrie had told him Kent Courtney was involved in the assassination.[2888] Broshears referred to Courtney as a "financier in New Orleans." Jim Garrison wrote in the margin of the interview notes next to the sentence naming Courtney: "Does not check out as being involved in any way. JG." (The allegation that, in 1963, Courtney was seen on several occasions in the company of Lee Harvey Oswald was presented in Chapter Two. Courtney was close to General Walker and Guy Banister, as well as nearly every other radical-right-wing leader mentioned in this work. He was the state leader of the John Birch Society, was present at the infamous Congress of Freedom meeting in April of 1963, and was a close associate of Robert Welch. Even so, Courtney, prior to this work, has never been connected with the assassination conspiracy.) Broshears's mention of Courtney's name to Garrison strongly suggests that Broshears indeed knew something about the New Orleans end of the assassination conspiracy. Garrison may well have known Courtney from his support of the Citizens' Council and their rallies that he frequently attended. Prior to this, in 1962, Courtney had been on the state board of the Citizens' Council with Banister colleagues George Singelmann, Leander Perez, Willie Rainach, and an up-and-comer in the segregation and anti-Communist movement, John Rarick.[2889]

Broshears told Jaffe that Rich Lauchli from Illinois—a high-ranking member of Robert DePugh's Minutemen—was a conspirator in the president's murder. Jim Garrison discovered information that Lauchli was present at a training camp outside of Lacombe (on the north side of Lake Pontchartrain) that David Ferrie attended in 1963. Carlos Quiroga, a friend of Carlos Bringuier who visited Lee Harvey Oswald's apartment in the summer of 1963 (supposedly to determine if he was pro- or anti-Castro), told Garrison that Lauchli was at the training camp. A large amount of dynamite and bomb casings were seized at the camp, which was on the property of William J. McLaney, in August of 1963.[2890, 2891, 2892]

Garrison investigators compiled evidence from one of Guy Banister's student spies that Rich Lauchli had possible ties to Banister.[2893] The allegation is not surprising, since Jerry Brooks, a close associate of Minutemen leader Robert DePugh, spent time working with Banister at his office. (DePugh told the author that he and Lauchli engaged in a cross-country trip collecting armaments for the Cuban effort.[2894]) Lauchli had been arrested in 1959 for the theft of twenty-three bazookas from the government. He also brought a load of arms through Mississippi during the integration crisis at Ole Miss to aid General Walker.[2895] Lauchli was sentenced to two and a half years in federal prison in 1965 for the illegal manufacture, sale, and shipping of guns, including one hundred submachine guns and .50-caliber mortars.[2896] Ferrie's mention of Lauchli and Courtney to Broshears suggests further that Ferrie had in-depth knowledge of the assassination conspiracy and he was not just guessing.

Ferrie also told Broshears that liberal Louisiana congressman, and member of the Warren Commission, Hale Boggs—who was despised by the radical right—was one of the "names in relationship to the assassination of President Kennedy." (It is not at all clear what he meant.) Broshears also named Clay Shaw as a member of the assassination conspiracy and said Shaw was financially responsible for Boggs remaining in Congress. In response to allegations that Boggs was a name in the assassination, Garrison wrote in the margin, the "reference to Hale Boggs in this connection is but one example that [Ferrie] is too <u>haywire</u> to add up to ever being a source of <u>evidence</u>." Ferrie may have been suggesting that, because the Warren Commission had failed to identify the true conspirators, he considered Boggs to be an accessory after the fact. The implication, perhaps, was that Shaw somehow had a hand in compelling Boggs—in his position on the Warren Commission—to reach the erroneous conclusion that Oswald acted alone. The author found an apparent phone message on a piece of paper among Boggs's personal papers, indicating that Leander Perez, George Singelmann, and Lloyd Cobb (Shaw's boss at the International Trade Mart) had called Boggs's congressional office at an unknown point in time.[2897]

Broshears claimed that Ferrie stayed with him at his hotel room in New Orleans when Broshears arrived in 1965, and that two men forced their way in and threatened Ferrie. Ferrie claimed, in 1965—before Garrison's investigation began—that they were from the D.A.'s office. Ferrie was in a deep state of depression in 1965, and the only time he would confess to Broshears about the assassination was when he took pills and drank to excess. Ferrie confided in Broshears that he had been flying private planes to Guatemala, Costa Rica, and British Honduras for little pay. Broshears felt that Ferrie had been forced to work for "this organization" and never liked it, but was "hooked into it." Ferrie also confided to Broshears that he was working for "a group of people who wanted to take over the United States." He told Broshears that he was flying guns and ammunition. Ferrie also admitted his own involvement in the assassination conspiracy to Broshears.[2898]

The D.A.'s office interviewed Broshears again in August 1968 in New Orleans. Broshears repeated his story of working for the Congress of Racal Equality, being stopped by Louisiana State Troopers, and arriving in New Orleans in 1965. He told the D.A.'s office he was arrested for conspiring against the life of President Johnson (as he also explained later in more detail to the HSCA as we shall see). Broshears told them he really didn't threaten Johnson's life, but that in the past he had met some people who claimed they wanted Johnson dead. He said he had met a boy in "National City" who had a passionate desire to kill Johnson. The FBI reportedly had in their possession letters from Broshears that included threatening remarks about Johnson. Ferrie supposedly learned from Clay Shaw (who Broshears noted was also called "Bert" or "Clara") that the FBI was planning the imminent arrest of Broshears, at which time Ferrie told him to hide. Broshears sought sanctuary at a Veterans Hospital, telling the staff that he was suicidal, as a pretense, and was admitted.

Broshears was asked what Ferrie told him about the assassination. Broshears told the D.A.'s office what he later also told the HSCA. He said Oswald did not do the shooting, and that it was Ferrie's job to fly two assassins out of the country to South Africa via Central America. Broshears thought what Ferrie told him next was a "cock and bull story." He said Ferrie was "trying to tie Hale Boggs, a congressman here in Louisiana, trying to tie him in with Billy James Hargus [sic] and General Walker and H. Lemar [sic] Hunt and this guy in New Jersey [Reverend Carl] McIntyre [sic]. He said it's part of the great, great white, Anglo-Saxon protestant plot to take over the country to keep their man in and I couldn't buy it. I really couldn't buy it then and I still have a hard—well, I'm not having as hard a time buying it, I'll be honest with you. I am not having as hard a time buying it now as I did then." He again explained further that Clay Shaw kept Boggs in office and suggested Boggs had done what he was told to do with regards to his deliberations on the Warren Commission. Broshears then told them he had been detained by the Secret Service in 1966 and was told by them that David Ferrie had committed suicide. (Ferrie did not die until 1967.)[2899]

The author requested documents on Broshears from the Secret Service through the Freedom of Information Act. The Secret Service confirmed that they did investigate Broshears for threatening Johnson on September 6, 1965, and they determined he was "not dangerous." They reported that Broshears sent Johnson a note stating, "Mr. Johnson you are to die at 3PM EDT." They also investigated him for threatening President-elect Ronald Reagan on January 13, 1981, and again determined he was not dangerous, even though Broshears told them he had experience with firearms and grenades.[2900]

Carl McIntire's relationship with Walker began shortly after his return from Germany in 1961. Walker wrote an article for McIntire's *Christian Beacon* newspaper on December 28, 1961. On January 22, 1962, McIntire wrote Walker and told Walker he was prepared to marshal the resources of his extensive church organization and thirty to forty patriotic organizations to sponsor a speech by Walker on March 31, 1962. On April 12, 1963, two days after the Walker shooting incident, McIntire sent Walker a telegram stating: "Deeply grateful for God's providence which spared you, we pray for your continued safety and that you may be even more greatly used from now on in the Battle for Freedom. With high admiration and appreciation, Carl McIntire."[2901] On August 20, 1963, Walker was scheduled to meet with McIntire at the Christian Admiral in Cape May, New Jersey. It is not known if the meeting took place.[2902]

Billy James Hargis was an early protégé of McIntire. McIntire gave Hargis's career an early boost when he named him to head up the Bible Balloon Project. (The project sent bible tracts by balloon from free countries in Europe to the Communist countries behind the Iron Curtain in the 1950s.[2903]) Tom Anderson spoke at McIntire's Cape May retreat in the summer of 1963.[2904] Guy Banister attended a meeting with McIntire at the Capitol House in 1963, as was noted in Chapter Nine. Evidence also was presented in Chapter Nine that Carl McIntire's West Coast representative, Edgar Eugene "Gene" Bradley, was in Dallas during the murder of the president. Loran Hall, an associate of General Walker, alleged that he heard Bradley talk of killing the president in California.

It's clear Ferrie knew who the core individuals were in the assassination conspiracy from what he told Broshears. Those names were not pulled from thin air. The fact that Broshears did not believe the charges Ferrie made against those he named, lends the allegations all the more credibility.

Broshears reiterated to Jaffe that Ferrie had told him of a connection with Kent Courtney to the assassination. Broshears also mentioned Rich Lauchli again, whom Broshears had met once in Illinois. Broshears knew what he was talking about, because Lauchli (who owned Loxco Machine Company) was indeed a gunsmith and Minuteman from Collinsville, Illinois.

When asked if David Ferrie ever told him he worked for the CIA, Broshears told Jaffe he "mentioned the Agency, that is what he worked for. . . . He never used the words Central Intelligence." Broshears identified one of the assassins as "Carlos," a Cuban exile. Confused in the matter, he later told the HSCA that one of the assassins was named "Garcia." Broshears said that Ferrie told him that Kennedy was selling out the country to the Communists. Broshears said he did not feel Ferrie thought he (Ferrie) was part of the actual assassination plot. Ferrie said he was forced to do a job for fear of being blackmailed by a sex film that he and a sixteen-year-old boy appeared in and going to prison for the rest of his life. (Broshears's claim comports with the report from another source, which was noted in Chapter Two, that Ferrie had pornographic photographs of boys he used as a threat to keep them in line.) Broshears thought Clay Shaw might have been blackmailing Ferrie. When Broshears first met Clay Shaw, Ferrie had a hard time trying to convince Shaw that Broshears was not a Communist— as Shaw accused him of being when he learned he was working for the Congress of Racial Equality in Bogalusa. At one point, Ferrie told Broshears that he loved Lee Harvey Oswald and had some of his possessions including a hunter's hat with the initials "L.H." or the name "Lee" on it.[2905]

Raymond Broshears and the House Select Committee on Assassinations

Raymond Broshears told the House Select Committee on Assassinations (HSCA), in 1978, that—due to his relationship with Ferrie—he feared for his life, and that he was, "living in a continual state of fear." Broshears was not keen about being interviewed in his apartment in San Francisco. He agreed to it only because he did not want to be subpoenaed for an interview in Washington.

Broshears told the HSCA that he first met Ferrie in New Orleans in late 1961 or early 1962, while passing out the Christian Crusade literature of Billy James Hargis on the streets of the French Quarter. Broshears claimed he was not a homosexual at the time, and did not know that Ferrie was one. Broshears explained that, at the time, he was a vehement anti-Communist and an evangelist. He felt the Christian Crusade literature was the best of its kind in the religious, anti-Communist movement. He passed a copy of the literature to Ferrie, who was intrigued by it and wanted to talk further about it at a nearby bar.

Ferrie praised Broshears for his anti-Communist work. Broshears told him of others doing similar work and mentioned Robert DePugh, head of the Minutemen, as another who was greatly concerned about the rising Communist tide in America. Broshears said he had connections with DePugh's Norborne, Missouri, operation. Ferrie introduced Broshears to the Orthodox Old Catholic Church of North America and they became friends on both a political and religious basis. Ferrie and Broshears discussed the Cuban situation, which they felt had deteriorated during Kennedy's early tenure, as well as the subject of Communism. Ferrie discussed the anti-Castro Cuban activity that was taking place in New Orleans.

During his interview with the HSCA, Broshears stated that Ferrie was extremely angry with President Kennedy for selling out the country to the Communists. In their discussion, the two men agreed that Kennedy was not telling the truth to the media about Cuba. At the same time Kennedy was publicly taking a hard line against Russia and Cuba, the fact remained that the Russians were still in Cuba, as Ferrie and Broshears saw it. The two believed that Kennedy was engaged in secret negotiations with the Russians that kept them from overtaking the U.S. Naval installation in Guantanamo Bay, Cuba. According to Broshears, Ferrie never mentioned anything about CIA involvement with the anti-Castro groups.

He did note that Ferrie was a pilot and flew private planes to various places such as Mexico and the Caribbean. In 1965, Ferrie had told him he was engaged in gun running and flying supplies to anti-Castro forces. (Broshears's account suggests that Ferrie was in a similar line of business as Jack Ruby and General Walker.) Ferrie told Broshears he worked for New Orleans mob boss Carlo Marcello and flew "supplies" for him. As was noted in Chapter Nine, if Marcello was involved in the assassination it may have been because of his support of segregation—not the interests of the mafia.

One time in 1963, Broshears was at Ferrie's Louisiana Parkway apartment, when a man came by that Broshears would later recognize as Lee Harvey Oswald. He described Oswald as a nice-looking young man who was very sexy looking, but extremely nervous. Oswald spoke softly and Broshears didn't hear what he said. Ferrie became very upset and told Oswald that he shouldn't have come to his house, that he had no business there, and he was not supposed to be there. (If it is true that Oswald was at Ferrie's apartment, then it's likely that Ferrie did not want Oswald to risk blowing his Communist cover by appearing at the residence of the fanatically anti-Communist Ferrie.) Ferrie did not introduce Oswald to Broshears. Broshears estimated that Oswald's visit lasted between three and ten minutes, while an associate waited outside in a car for him. Broshears estimated Oswald was fifteen or sixteen feet away when he saw him. Ferrie never mentioned Oswald by name to Broshears, and the only thing Ferrie said to Broshears about Oswald after the visit was that it wasn't any of Broshears's business and that the man (whom he later found out was Oswald) was into something he couldn't handle and he was going to get himself hurt. Ferrie said he was a screwed-up, mixed-up guy that he had dealings with and he didn't like it.[2906, 2907]

The only other time Broshears saw Oswald was when he was with Ferrie at the office of Guy Banister and his partner Hugh Ward, also in 1963. (Former FBI agent and Garrison investigator William Turner interviewed high-ranking Minuteman Jerry Brooks, and he identified both Banister and Ward as Minutemen. Brooks was associated with Banister from 1961 to 1964 and worked at his office.[2908] As was noted in prior chapters, Banister's office was in the Newman building that had the entrances at both 537 Lafayette Street and 544 Camp Street.) Hugh Ward's name was seldom, if ever, mentioned in newspaper accounts of the Garrison investigation and Broshears's mention of the name affirms that he knew something about the Banister operation, lending further credibility to the claim that he saw Oswald there, as many others did.

The third period of Broshears's acquaintance with Ferrie was in 1965, when Ferrie was very ill, extremely depressed, and had begun to open up about the assassination. At the same time, Broshears had his own troubles. He was being investigated in connection to a plot by the Minutemen to assassinate President Johnson. Both having been suspects in assassination plots, Broshears and Ferrie now had something else in common. Ferrie told Broshears about his trip from New Orleans to Galveston, which had taken place on the afternoon of the Kennedy assassination. (It will be recalled that Ferrie was in the federal courtroom for the trial of Carlos Marcello when the assassination took place.)

Broshears said Ferrie told him that he (Ferrie) was supposed to pick up three men involved in the assassination and fly them from Galveston to Capetown, South Africa, which did not have an extradition treaty with the U.S. Broshears recalled that Ferrie told him that one of the men had a two-part Cuban name that included the name Garcia. The other two were not Cubans. The men never showed up, and Ferrie later learned that they had flown out on another plane. Ferrie didn't tell Broshears who hired him to fly the three men out, but Broshears was under the impression it was Carlos Marcello or Sergio Arcacha Smith. (Smith, as was noted in Chapter Eleven, was close to Guy Banister in New Orleans as well as H. L. Hunt in Dallas.) Ferrie told Broshears, in 1965, that there were three men involved in the Kennedy shooting—and he was very specific about that. Broshears could not say, however, whether there were three separate shooters, as opposed to one doing the shooting and the other two helping in some way.

Broshears told the HSCA that Ferrie made it "very, very clear" to him that Ferrie could have been prosecuted as a part of the Kennedy assassination conspiracy. If that had happened, Ferrie told him in 1965, he would have killed himself. (Ferrie's opinion on this course of action later changed.)

Ferrie allegedly told Broshears that Oswald did not shoot the president. Ferrie went on to adamantly point out that he knew Oswald was a poor shooter. Ferrie told him that Oswald could not hit a cow twenty-five feet away with a double-barreled shotgun. He said other people were following Oswald and other men shot the president and used or set Oswald up. Ferrie also told Broshears that Oswald was, nonetheless, guilty of being involved in the assassination conspiracy, which was a death penalty offense. Ferrie told him that the poor job done in investigating the assassination proved there was a government cover-up, and that there were Communists in the government.

Ferrie did not provide Broshears with any information on Jack Ruby. The only thing Ferrie discussed with him is how upset he was that the Dallas police allowed Oswald to be killed. He said Oswald's life "wasn't worth a plug nickel," and he was set up. Ferrie did not tell Broshears the details of how Oswald was set up. When the HSCA asked Broshears about it, he repeated that Ferrie told him Oswald was a dupe, a decoy. Ferrie had told Broshears that Oswald was in over his head and didn't know what he was doing. In Broshears's own mind, he understood exactly what Ferrie meant about Oswald being a decoy and did not question Ferrie about it.

During Ferrie's 1965 confession to Broshears, he told Broshears that Jim Garrison, the FBI, and someone with a Spanish-sounding name was harassing him. Ferrie said the man was someone he once flew for and who wanted to kill him and shut him up. (Garrison had investigated Ferrie right after the Kennedy assassination, based on the newspaper account of the accusation made by Jack Martin about Ferrie's ties to Lee Harvey Oswald.) Ferrie's early exposure to, and possible involvement with Oswald was a tremendous liability to the conspirators. Ferrie had reason to be afraid for his life.[2909, 2910] It's conceivable the man with the Spanish-sounding name that he was referring to was Leander Perez. Jack Martin told Garrison investigators that Ferrie was trying to determine "the possibility of negro [sic] blood in the family line of Leander Perez." It's also conceivable that Ferrie wanted to blackmail Perez, a white supremacist, to ensure his own safety.[2911, 2912]

Broshears said Ferrie told the truth about the assassination to four other people, including Garrison. He said Ferrie told the truth to an unidentified woman and a minister in the Orthodox Old Catholic Church of North America, which both Ferrie and Broshears were involved in. He was not sure if the third person was "Bob Martin" or another man. He could not remember the name of the fourth person who was a familiar name in the Garrison case, but only recalled his name later when it came up in the news in connection with *Playboy* magazine. (He may well be referring to Gordon Novel, who sued *Playboy* for their mention of his name in their published interview with Garrison in 1967.)

The last time Broshears heard from Ferrie was on February 14, 1967, Broshears's birthday, when Ferrie telephoned him in San Francisco. At the time, Ferrie was the primary subject of Jim Garrison's investigation into the Kennedy assassination. Ferrie told Broshears that, to certain people, he was more valuable dead than alive because of what he did. Ferrie told Broshears that he was afraid that the CIA and Garrison investigator Andrew Sciambra were going to kill him. Broshears told him he didn't want to hear anything about the CIA because, in 1967, Broshears was hearing the "Central Intelligence this, the CIA that, and it was getting a bit old, you know." (He was referring to Garrison's claims—and those of a wave of conspiracy writers—of CIA involvement.)

Contrary to what had happened two years earlier (in 1965), when Garrison implicated Ferrie in the assassination and allegedly offered him immunity in 1967, Ferrie told Broshears he was not suicidal—and that he wanted Broshears to know that he would never take his own life. (Garrison reportedly offered Ferrie immunity because his role in the assassination was only that of a getaway pilot.) Eight days after Ferrie called Broshears, he was found dead in his apartment from a ruptured brain aneurysm on February 22, 1967. Because Ferrie had told him that he would not commit suicide as a result of his exposure in the Garrison case, Broshears believed his death was murder and not a suicide or the result of natural causes (as was officially determined).

Broshears elaborated to the HSCA that he had gotten involved with some people, who wanted to assassinate President Johnson (which he said he did not know at the time). Broshears said he wrote and said some very stupid things and was carried off by the Secret Service. When asked the identity of the people involved in the Johnson plot he replied, "some people," only identifying them as anti-Communist people who believed Johnson was just as corrupt as Kennedy. Broshears was uncomfortable talking about the men involved, but admitted that two of them were members of the Minutemen. (As was noted it the last chapter, the FBI had received numerous reports that General Walker and his Minutemen group were making contingency plans to murder President Johnson. As a result, the FBI notified the Secret Service that they felt Walker was a threat to Johnson's life.)

Broshears was bothered when the investigators told him his name was mentioned in the book *Cover-up*, stating that he had never given an interview to anybody. He was troubled at several points during the HSCA interview, believing his cooperation might get him into trouble with the assassination conspirators. Broshears told the HSCA that, in 1968, Garrison's investigators took him back to New Orleans from California, and put him up at the Fontainebleau Hotel on Canal Street. After returning from Garrison's office, he had found his room ransacked. He had just come into the room and turned off the lights when two gunshots were fired through the window.

Broshears told the HSCA that, during Garrison's interrogation: "I wasn't going to tell those sons-of-bitches nothing especially after the very first day we're there my room is ransacked, and then later on, two bullets in the window the next day, I mean, are you out of your mind?" Broshears wrote his congressman and told him he thought the pending HSCA investigation was a waste of taxpayer money because he was sure they were going "to do a white-wash on the cover-up."[2913, 2914]

Hal Verb, who was a reporter for the *Berkeley Barb* in the 1960s, knew Broshears quite well and wrote several articles about him. Verb told the author that Broshears became a prominent gay leader in the San Francisco Bay area after the Garrison affair. According to Verb, Broshears was a flamboyant type and knew how to promote himself. Verb found Broshears constantly lying to him and contradicting himself and making outlandish claims. Broshears said once that Ferrie took the backyard photos of Oswald holding his rifle and two Communist newspapers when, in fact, Oswald's wife took the photos. Verb was an early, well-known Warren Commission critic and had equally harsh comments about assassination theorists, stating: "90% of the articles in this area got it all wrong."[2915] Broshears later explained to the HSCA that he incessantly told lies about the assassination for fear of his life. As long as he told foolish stories, he figured the conspirators would not harm him.

Time magazine featured a story on Broshears in 1973, describing how Broshears had started a vigilante group in San Francisco called the Lavender Panthers. Their function was to protect gays from violence in the same way that the Black Panthers protected blacks. On one occasion, when some teenagers stopped outside of a gay bar and started pushing the homosexuals around, Broshears and some friends "took pool cues and started flailing ass." The aim of the Lavender Panthers, according to Broshears, was "to strike terror in the hearts of all those young punks who have been beating up [his] faggots." Broshears himself had once been severely beaten outside his gay mission center.[2916] Broshears displayed the kind of militancy one would expect of someone who had been involved with the Minutemen.

The Harry Dean Story

The story of Harry Dean—another person directly associated with members of the assassination conspiracy—began with a United Press International story written by W. R. Morris on November 26, 1966, that reported that Marguerite Oswald told him that a former FBI man had put yellow chrysanthemums on her son's grave on November 24, 1966. A card placed with the flowers was inscribed, "He left all the world confused." The FBI located the florist who placed the flowers and were told that Harry Dean, a thirty-eight-year-old resident of California, had sent them. The FBI investigated the story and noted that Dean had sent the flowers because he thought Oswald had nothing to do with the killing of President Kennedy. Dean told the press he was a former undercover man for the FBI and had used the code name "Junior"—which was written on the card with the flowers.[2917] Although Dean was not mentioned by name in the UPI press release, the UPI item represents the first public emergence of a small part of the Harry Dean story.

After W. R. Morris wrote the UPI story, Dean read it and contacted Morris, and the two began collaborating. Morris and Dean developed a relationship with Marguerite Oswald. Morris was supposed to write a book with her until they had a falling out. Instead, Morris wrote part of a book and two monographs on the Harry Dean story, which will be detailed here.

Harry Dean and the FBI

According to FBI documents, Harry Dean allegedly infiltrated the Covina, California, branch of the John Birch Society and, as a result, claimed to have learned that General Walker engineered the actual shooting of the president. He claimed another high ranking JBS member, John Rousselot, raised funds for the assassination and organized other aspects of the crime. It should be noted that, according to the FBI documents, Dean had a history of mental illness, criminality, and misrepresenting his relationship with the FBI—and there is no concrete evidence showing that Dean reported his claims to authorities, although he said he did. After Harry Dean met writer and reporter W. R. Morris in 1966, in the wake of the UPI story, a variety of claims were made—some factual and important, and some not. The fact that he named Walker as a conspirator, however, lends credibility to his claims against Rousselot.

Records from the FBI show clearly that Dean contacted them regularly and furnished them with information about the Chicago Fair Play for Cuba Committee. He did so strictly on a volunteer basis, and the FBI did not solicit his information. FBI documents make it abundantly clear that Dean was never an agent of the FBI, nor was he, formally, an FBI informant. FBI documents trace Dean's career as a volunteer informant for the Chicago FBI to December 7, 1960, when he told them he had met a man named Ed Swabeck in Cuba the past summer. According to FBI reports, Swabeck invited Dean to attend a meeting of Fair Play for Cuba Committee in Chicago. Dean also met Dr. Juan A. Orta, who was a Secretary to Prime Minister Castro, while in Cuba. Dean told the FBI that Orta told him he had a friend who was a former Cuban Consulate representative in Chicago.

Dean had supported Castro before anyone knew Castro was a Communist, but he had a change of heart when Castro's Communist ideology was revealed, at which point Dean became a volunteer informant working against the pro-Castro forces. Dean called the Chicago office of the FBI and told them he had been elected to be the recording secretary of the Chicago chapter of FPCC. He also gave them information about Cuban nationals in the "26th of July Movement" (Castro's movement).

The FBI noted that Dean had a checkered past. He had skipped town after police in Indiana had charged him with passing bad checks. He was committed as a mental patient in Canada in 1941, and then was sentenced to one year in prison for breaking and entering. Detroit police arrested him one time for disturbing a religious meeting, and arrested him twice for using indecent and obscene language. He went AWOL from Fort Knox in Kentucky in 1949. His real name was thought to be Gordon Hunt, although it was suspected that he used a variety of aliases. Dean told the author that his mistreatment by the British-Canadians growing up as an American in Canada—and the resentment that followed—had led to his mischief-laden past. He admits in his manuscript, *Crossroads,* detailing his FPCC adventures that he had committed almost every act that was considered amoral, stating he was often a "misguided missile."

FBI documents show that Dean called the FBI on several occasions in 1961 and furnished more information concerning Cuban nationals connected with the 26th of July Movement. On June 7, 1961, the FBI told him, "[The] office did not desire his assistance." The Chicago FBI stated they "never considered him a PSI or informant by this office." Dean defined his status in another way for the author, stating that he served in "low-level U.S. Intelligence" and "low-level U.S. Intelligence cooperation"—which may be more accurate than his statements that he was an *agent* for U.S intelligence.

FBI documents show that FBI headquarters requested information on Dean from the Chicago FBI on the day of the Kennedy assassination, but that no reason was given for the request. The action partially corroborates Dean's claim that he notified them in September 1963 that there was talk of killing the president—something that neither Dean nor the FBI actually felt was going to happen. On January 28, 1964, the Los Angeles FBI office furnished the Chicago FBI information about their contacts with Dean.[2918] The content of the Los Angeles information is unknown. As we will see shortly, the FBI did investigate Dean in regards to his possible involvement in the assassination and cleared him. It is not known if Dean made any allegations about Walker or Rousselot while in contact with the FBI.

On December 10, 1963, the FBI contacted Dean at his home in California and he produced a receipt indicating that he had joined the FPCC in Chicago in 1960, and that he was a member of the 26th of July Movement, and had had connections with the group as early as 1958. He told the FBI that he traveled to Cuba in June 1960 and, on his return, joined the Chicago Fair Play for Cuba Committee. Thereafter, he furnished information on both groups to the FBI as a patriotic volunteer. The FBI reported that his name appeared on the Senate subcommittee report on the Chicago hearings of FPCC in Chicago on July 12–14,

1961. They reported that Dean had considerable anti-Communist literature in his home. The author checked the record of Senator Eastland's Senate Internal Security Subcommittee hearing on FPCC and verified that Dean's name does appear in them.

The FBI had in their possession a letter from Senator James O. Eastland to Harry Dean, dated April 3, 1964. The letter read, "Dear Mr. Dean, Thanks for your wire of April 2, confirming your telephone conversation with me on the evening of April 1. The committee contemplates holding hearings in California on Fair Play for Cuba Committee and you will definitely be given an opportunity to testify . . . Sincerely, James O. Eastland."[2919] Dean told the author he never heard from Eastland again after the letter was sent. This makes sense, because Oswald's ties to FPCC in the wake of the assassination brought about the organization's demise, which would have made further hearings unnecessary.

The Fair Play for Cuba Committee had debuted only a few years earlier, on April 6, 1960, with a full-page ad taken out in the *New York Times*. On April 29, 1960, Eastland's Senate Internal Subversion Subcommittee interrogated officials of the national FPCC. On December 2, 1961, and in April, May, June, and October of 1962, Eastland held hearings on FPCC. The House Committee on Un-American Activities investigated the Los Angeles FPCC and published its findings in a report entitled: "Communist and Trotskyist Activity within the Greater Los Angeles Chapter of Fair Play for Cuba." American Trotskyite groups, principally the Socialist Workers Party, were aligned with the ideology of Marx, Engels, and Lenin, as interpreted by Leon Trotsky. The Socialist Workers Party was an archrival of the Stalinist-led Communist Party USA and their bitter differences culminated in the assassination of Leon Trotsky in 1940. The congressional committees determined that FPCC was funded by the Cuban Government and was a Trotskyist front. Lee Harvey Oswald, of course, pretended he was a follower of Leon Trotsky, which may be why there were reports of him referred to as "Leon" Oswald at times, and why he insisted he was a Marxist rather than a Communist.

Dean, like many others, was among a large number of individuals—from the 1940s to 1960s—who volunteered to serve their country by infiltrating Communist organizations. These false Communists later became stool pigeons for the congressional witch hunts like those of the House Committee on Un-American Activities, Senator McCarthy's and Senator Eastland's committees. As the evidence presented in the next chapter will show, Oswald adopted phony Communist credentials for the purpose of infiltrating and informing on Communists groups, like Harry Dean did.

Harry Dean and *The Joe Pyne Show*

Harry Dean appeared on television with Marguerite Oswald on *The Joe Pyne Show*, on January 9, 1965, in Los Angeles. He told Marguerite that he was doing the same work for the FBI that Lee Harvey Oswald had been doing. Again, Dean misunderstood Oswald's role in the FPCC saga.[2920] It is not known what else Dean said on the program. Prior to his appearance on the show, the show's producer contacted the CIA. The CIA noted that *The Joe Pyne Show* was a local Los Angeles Saturday evening program that attracted "do-gooders, missionaries, repentant sinners, con men," and others. While making an appearance, the CIA reported, "the guest is cajoled, abused, thanked, or just tolerated by Pyne and the viewing public." The producer called the CIA to let them know that Dean had been an active pro-Castroite since 1959 and had helped solicit money and arms.[2921] Pyne was a pioneer in the crass, tasteless, physically confrontational genre of interview shows made popular later in the twentieth century by the likes of Morton Downey, Jr., and Jerry Springer that followed him.

Dean told the author that he and Marguerite talked on the phone before and after the TV show. Dean believed his public association with her forced the FBI to sever ties with him—which was a relief for Dean. Dean told the author that he conversed with Marguerite in "guarded generalities." She never outwardly told Dean that she suspected General Walker—or anyone else.

Harry Dean and Jim Garrison

According to documents from Jim Garrison's investigation, Harry Dean telephoned him during Garrison's late 1960s investigation and told him that he and Lee Harvey Oswald were involved in FPCC at the same time. Dean believed the differences between his involvement in the FPCC and Oswald's was that Oswald was not apparently in as deep as Dean—and he was in a chapter in a different part of the country.

Dean made a lot of statements about Oswald and FPCC that appear in the realm of supposition and opinion. Dean had no direct personal knowledge of Oswald and his FPCC involvement. He, therefore, could not have known that Oswald was apparently "less deep" in FPCC, as he claimed. In many of Dean's statements, he mixed what he actually knew with information from other sources. As a result, what he *professed* to know often appeared to be more than what he *actually* knew. Compounding this troublesome habit was his 1966 collaboration with writer W. R. Morris, who was far guiltier of embellishing and conflating outside information.

Dean assumed that because he had infiltrated the FPCC in order to inform on them to the FBI, Oswald had the same motive (which was not the case). Dean told Garrison that while he was in the Chicago FPCC, working for the FBI, he "blew the whistle" on his fellow members during a hearing on the organization. The FBI then "cut Dean off," and he traveled to California in 1961 for a senate hearing.

During the assassination investigation, Dean told Garrison that, in 1962, he moved to California and joined up with anti-Castro forces that talked about doing away with Castro. He said he had bought into the right-wing line and hated Castro—and still did. He told Garrison that he found himself in the circles of the political right, and said he discovered a lot of things he agreed with—and some that horrified him. Dean said he went along with the political right because he hated Castro and favored getting rid of him. Dean was embarrassed about his working for Castro in Cuba before it was known Castro was a Communist. Dean thought getting rid of Castro was a great idea, and got caught up in the Americanism and patriotism of it all.

Dean wrote in *Crosstrails* that there were individuals who donated heavily to the anti-Castro cause, further noting that the John Birch Society was behind the anti-Castro effort and touted the slogan "Cuba Free in '63." Dean reported that donations went to Lawrence Howard and Loran Hall. The "number-three man" was Guy Gabaldon, a subject of Garrison's investigation. Dean said those three men associated with assassination planners and revealed there had been a plot to shoot Kennedy in Mexico City in 1962. (President Kennedy did, in fact, travel to Mexico City on June 29–30, 1962, and was pictured on the July 13, 1962, cover of *Life* magazine standing in an open limousine in a parade through the city.) Dean told the author that Gabaldon told him about the operation in late 1962, and that the plot did not involve Walker or Rousselot (to Dean's knowledge).

According to Garrison documents, Dean said he went with Guy Gabaldon to the office of John Rousselot and Sam Moreno, in 1963, to get $10,000 for the Kennedy assassination plot. Gabaldon didn't get the money, but talked with Rousselot for four hours. Dean told Garrison, "Mr. Hunt and a lot of big shots that I agreed with, they can do these things and they will." Garrison asked Dean what he thought of General Walker and, since he knew him, if it was true that he might be involved. Then Garrison mentioned the Walker shooting incident. Dean didn't answer the question but, instead, jumped to the subject of the Walker shooting incident and said that he didn't think Oswald had shot at Walker. Garrison's original question regarding the involvement of Walker was not answered. Nonetheless, the asking of the question is further evidence that Garrison suspected Walker might be involved. In the brief transcript of Dean's phone call to Garrison, claims of Rousselot and Walker's involvement in the Dallas plot were not revealed.[2922]

The HSCA interviewed Dean on May 23, 1977, and Dean told them he had been an FBI informant in Chicago in 1961. He told them that when he left Chicago, he became an FBI informant in Covina, California. He said that while at meetings in 1962 and 1963, Loran Hall talked about how much he had been offered to kill President Kennedy. General Walker, Lawrence Howard, and Guy Gabaldon were also at those meetings. Hall stated that they would frame a Communist for the murder.[2923]

Harry Dean and W. R. Morris

W. R. Morris, who wrote the original story about Dean sending flowers to Oswald's grave, was an accomplished writer. Morris was the author of the best-selling book *The Twelfth of August*, the authorized biography of Sheriff Buford Pusser of *Walking Tall* fame.

During the Garrison investigation, Morris was invited to New Orleans and was a houseguest of Jim Garrison. Morris told the author that it was apparent to him that Garrison was a phony and had no interest in the Harry Dean story. He further told the author: "The D.A. took a special interest in me after learning I had a book contract with Marguerite Oswald." Morris was with Garrison when he first inspected Ferrie's apartment after Ferrie's death in 1967. He claimed that Garrison's case against Clay Shaw was outrageous and that Garrison had covered up a lot of concrete evidence.[2924]

In 1975, Morris published a monograph called *The Men Behind the Guns*. In the monograph, Morris stated that Dean claimed to have had "marble-hard proof" that John Rousselot (a former California congressman from the Twenty-sixth District) and General Walker had engineered the murder of President Kennedy. At the time, Rousselot was the western director of the John Birch Society. Dean claimed to have been working with the CIA and FBI, according to Morris. Dean claimed that Walker and Rousselot convinced some John Birch Society members that Kennedy was a Communist and should be eliminated for letting the U.S. "fall into Red hands." Dean said General Walker was obsessed with hatred for the Kennedy brothers and had a "personal grudge to settle." Dean claimed Robert Kennedy had Walker arrested after Ole Miss, had his clothes stripped off him, and had him sent to the Springfield facility as a mental patient. Dean said the leaders of the John Birch Society were "smooth talkers" able to brainwash their followers into believing President Kennedy was Communist and, therefore, into believing that killing him was not a crime. Dean claimed he told the FBI about Walker, Rousselot and the talk of killing Kennedy, but they ignored him. Dean said that stories about the CIA and Mafia masterminding the assassination were like children's fairy tales, entertaining but not factual. Dean maintained, like Raymond Broshears, that Oswald was not actually involved in the shooting. He said that Walker had met regularly with two sharpshooters to plan the shooting. He said Rousselot's role was to raise money for the operation. Walker's role was grooming the gunmen. He said Oswald was an innocent man and each year he sent flowers to his grave. (It should be noted that Morris's claims about Dean are corroborated by FBI documents, by a manuscript written by Dean, and the author's interviews with Dean.)

Morris also claimed to have gathered information on the assassination from another "agent" of either the FBI or CIA who would not permit him to use his name. Morris claimed his life was threatened many times and that he once received a phone threat from Eugene Hale Braden, the suspicious California man associated with Nelson Bunker Hunt who was arrested in Dealey Plaza after the shooting.

According to Morris, he and Dean were flown to New York to appear on NBC's late-night show, *Tomorrow*, with host Tom Snyder on June 9, 1975. The show was taped, but Morris claimed it was "too explosive" to air. However, a transcript of the show survived and was published by Morris. Dean was disguised by a mask and called "Mr. X." Dean had obvious trouble articulating his thoughts during the taping, perhaps due to stage fright or due to the serious nature of the accusation he was making about the assassination conspiracy. As a result, Morris often interjected and gave his own explanations. At one point, Dean expressed disagreement with Morris. As the show began, Snyder described Dean/Agent X as acting for both the FBI and CIA in the 1960s. Snyder described Morris as a reporter who had spent his lifetime writing, mostly in the South. Morris told Snyder that he had signed a contract with Marguerite Oswald to write a book about her son and the assassination. Morris explained how he came to write the story about the man who sent flowers to Oswald's grave. Dean, in the disguise of "Mr. X," told Snyder that Oswald was an agent doing his same job, infiltrating FPCC. He told Snyder that the John Birch Society was involved in the killing of the president. Snyder repeatedly asked why Dean didn't stop the plot. He replied that he told the FBI, but they "kicked it upstairs" to let a higher authority handle it. Dean said it was his superior's job to handle the information, not his. Snyder told Dean that he didn't accept the explanation. Morris explained to Snyder that part of the problem was that the John Birch Society exerted influence in the government. (Up to this point, claims by Morris are corroborated by Dean's own accounts. It's worth noting, however, that Dean never had any formal relationship with the CIA or FBI.)

While on *Tomorrow*, Morris named Eladio del Valle and Loran Hall as the assassins—something Dean never claimed. Morris may have "borrowed" the allegation of Eladio del Valle's involvement from Jim Garrison, who made the same claim. (As we shall see later, Dean told the author that Morris often lied and embellished the story.) According to Morris, Dean named the John Birch Society as being involved, but did not feel that Robert Welch was involved with the planning. Dean told him that John Rousselot had gathered money for a plot to assassinate the president in Mexico City. Snyder had trouble understanding what Dean was saying through his mask and Morris interjected to say that rumors about CIA and mafia involvement were just smoke screens. He asserted, "The people who actually carried out the execution of Mr. John F. Kennedy were the John Birch Society." Morris said that, for reasons he could not understand, the conspirators continually called Kennedy a Communist.

Dean went on to describe a military man from the Pro-Blue program who retired because of the Kennedys and refused his retirement pay. (Snyder guessed correctly that he was referring to General Walker.) Dean displayed a thorough knowledge of Walker's history. He said Walker had framed Oswald. Morris then stated that General Walker knew Oswald before the assassination and that the Walker shooting incident was a hoax. Still trying to draw Dean out, Snyder asked him why he had not revealed the information to authorities. Dean responded that it was because he had once posed as a Communist and the conspirators would use that against him if he talked. The show ended there, and was never aired.[2925]

After the show, Dean and Morris had a falling out. Dean told the author that Morris told him at the Snyder show, "We can make a fortune by doing a JFK book that will be bigger than *JAWS* (a movie) or you can continue to scratch out a living with the chickens in California. As for me I am looking down that long green road." Dean wasn't interested in working on a book with Morris. Dean told the author that, at first, he admired Morris's interest and investigation into the assassination. But, later, Dean called him an angry and desperate person. (Dean had not discovered Morris's writings on him until 1999.)

In 1985, Morris told the story again in the book *Alias Oswald*, which was coauthored by R. B. Cutler. The book was nearly all the work of Cutler, with Morris's contribution limited to a retelling of the *Tomorrow* show interview of Dean and Morris. In this version of that story—which wandered far from the original accounts—Lee Harvey Oswald was a CIA co-worker and friend of "CIA agent" Harry Dean, who infiltrated the assassination conspiracy. (Morris completely fabricated the claim of the two working together—Dean and Oswald were in different parts of the country in the years prior to the assassination.) Harry Dean, as the retold story goes, did not reveal the plot because he was afraid of retaliation but when writing the book he wanted "to unload his solitary burden." Morris removed the names Walker and Rousselot from the transcription of the *Tomorrow* show published in *Alias Oswald*, and replaced them with the pseudonyms "Crawley" for Walker, and "Duvernier" for Rousselot. (Morris told the author that at some point Rousselot threatened him with a lawsuit, which is probably why he used the pseudonyms for Walker and Rousselot in *Alias Oswald*, which was the most widely published account of the Harry Dean story.)

Morris explained in *Alias Oswald* that he felt the best way to reveal Oswald's supposed CIA status was for him and Dean to appear on a national TV show. Morris arranged the *Tomorrow* show appearance and was flown to New York with Harry Dean to tell their story. According to the book, following the TV interview, Dean and Morris surmised that Oswald was a hero who tried to save the president's life.[2926]

R. B. Cutler, who co-authored *Alias Oswald* with Morris, wrote in the book that a man known as A. J. Hidell, who could pass as Oswald's twin, was the man arrested and killed in Dallas, not Oswald. The book was another work that promoted the far-fetched notion of "two Oswalds" involved in an elaborate government intelligence scheme. The "two Oswalds" theme remains a popular concept among assassination writers. After Morris's death, Cathy Meadows, his widow, told the author that Morris regretted his collaboration with Cutler.[2927] (Walker had a copy of Morris's *The Men Behind the Guns* and *Alias Oswald* in his personal papers—the only assassination-related books found by the author among his papers.[2928])

In 1994, during a resurgence of national interest in the assassination, Morris self-published his last work, a twenty-four-page monograph entitled *The Secret Papers of Harry Dean, Former FBI-CIA Agent* by means of a home typewriter and copier. Morris told the author, in 1996, that he and Dean had had a falling out some years prior and he had not heard from Dean again. In the monograph, Morris went over the top in what appears to be a fabrication of many aspects of the Harry Dean story, amalgamated with some of the more popular and wilder conspiracy theories. In this version, Morris makes a number of fantastic claims, among them a claim that Dean knew Oswald in New Orleans and that the two were together at a secret assassination camp in Mexico. According to Morris's tale, told in the first person (purportedly by Dean), Castro and Dean were good friends. The story went downhill from there. "Dean" supposedly planned to assassinate Castro in Cuba, using a baseball rigged with explosives. The rest is farcical and not worth recounting here.[2929]

Dean told the author that Morris made it all up and "sanitarily placed his words in my mouth." He felt that Morris was vindictive after he had refused to cooperate on a book. Dean felt Morris was using him. Dean said that he laughed when he read *The Secret Papers of Harry Dean* in 1999. He stated, "Morris created a super-patriot idiot agent from his imagination." He saw Morris's effort as "totally sad."[2930]

Harry Dean and the *Between the Lines* Interview

Harry Dean gave an exclusive interview to *Between the Lines* (published by Valley Publications) on March 8, 1977, and provided more details. Dean stated that, in 1963 and 1964, the John Birch Society had a heavily armed network of citizen soldiers ready to take the streets if Lee Harvey Oswald was not found guilty of the Kennedy murder during the government's investigation. Dean alleged that threats were made against President Johnson and Earl Warren through intelligence sources and agents of the conspirators in order to ensure Oswald would be found guilty.

Dean claimed that he was an undercover operative for the JBS in Covina, California, outside of Los Angeles, from 1962 to 1964. He said there were three plans of action in regards to the plot to kill President Kennedy. The first was the 1962 plan to assassinate him in Mexico City, which was called off. The second was the Dallas murder. The third contemplated plan of action was retaliation if the murder was not successfully pinned on Oswald.

Dean claimed that the Covina JBS chapter was connected to the Drive Against Communist Aggression (DACA) and anti-Castro groups interested in invading Cuba. Guy Gabaldon was the Mexican director and Ray Fleishman was the American director. Dave Robbins, who had a close relationship with Gabaldon, was a high-ranking member of the Flour Corporation. (J. Robert Flour was a known close personal ally of John Rousselot.) Dean recalled a specific meeting when Walker came to town where Walker, Rousselot, Loran Hall, Lawrence Howard, and Gabaldon made plans to frame Lee Harvey Oswald—who they thought was a Communist—as the assassin. Dean witnessed Walker, Rousselot and a different combination of men planning the assassination. The story in *Between the Lines* ended there.[2931, 2932, 2933]

Dean's claim that Walker discussed that he was going to use Oswald fits the evidence presented in Chapter Sixteen on both the assassination and Oswald's peculiar behavior on the day of the murder. It was one of two claims made by Dean saying that he had heard of plans before the assassination to use Oswald in some capacity. The first was by Gabaldon posing as a CIA agent to Oswald, as was discussed earlier, to persuade him to visit the Cuban and Soviet Embassies in Mexico City and, the second, to use him as the fall guy in the assassination. Walker had to know that Oswald was not a genuine Communist, but might have told others that he was. After all, Walker's loyal followers might have found it disturbing if they knew that Walker had framed one of his own men (Oswald)—and was responsible for his murder. The reality that Oswald was not a genuine Communist, and the reason for Oswald's long journey, from the early days of his playing a Communist in 1956 through his odyssey in Russia and beyond, was not something that those outside of the central core of the conspiracy, like Dean, needed to know. Willie Somersett appeared confused as to how Oswald, a supposed Communist, was part of the far-right murder plot. Perhaps Joseph Milteer did not know that Oswald was impersonating a Communist, either.

Dean's claims about Lawrence Howard and Loran Hall being parties to the assassination plots fits with other evidence about the men. It will be recalled that when the Warren Commission investigated the allegation of Sylvia Odio (saying that two men came to her Dallas apartment door with a man that she later identified as Lee Harvey Oswald), the Commission asked the FBI to find the men. The FBI found Hall, who lied and told them he was there with Howard and William Seymour, who supposedly looked like Oswald (but didn't). The Warren Commission was satisfied that Odio was mistaken and Oswald had not been there. They closed their case, but found out, later (after the publication of the Warren Commission findings), that Hall had lied. What makes Dean's allegation about General Walker plotting with Hall plausible, as noted in Chapter Sixteen and prior chapters, is the fact that Hall was associated with Walker, Dan Smoot, H. L. Hunt and Colonel William Potter Gale, who in turn were all associated with Joseph Milteer. Hall's relationship with Walker, Hunt, Smoot, and Gale defies any explanation other than the fact that Hall's false claim about being at Sylvia Odio's apartment was made at the direction of the Walker operation in order to quash the Odio allegation, an allegation that has long been considered by some as the most compelling piece of evidence uncovered by the Warren Commission of a conspiracy in the assassination of President Kennedy. If the Warren Commission had established that Oswald was at Odio's with two anti-Castro Cubans, they would have had to consider that Oswald was actually a phony Communist, and the entire Warren Commission premise of Oswald as a lone Communist gunman might have unraveled.

A Jim Garrison interview of Loran Hall on May 6, 1968, partly corroborates some of Dean's claims. Hall told Garrison that he met with General Walker, attended fundraising meetings for the anti-Castro effort, and gave the proceeds over to Jose Norman, a Cuban, who turned them over to John Rousselot of the John Birch Society.[2934]

There is no other known information on Rousselot to corroborate his involvement in the assassination outside of Dean's allegation. There is, however, an abundance of circumstantial evidence that makes his involvement likely. The HSCA interview of Loran Hall on August 20, 1977, further linked Rousselot to Hall. Hall told them that he went around to see a lot of people in the conservative movement in Los Angeles, including John Rousselot, in 1963. (That evidence would not have been available to Harry Dean, thus adding credibility to Dean's story.) Furthermore, Hall admitted he had heard talk of killing the president at Southern California JBS meetings. (Rousselot, of course, was closely associated with other prominent members of the far right involved in the conspiracy, including General Walker, Billy James Hargis, and Tom Anderson. The life and times of John Rousselot and his high-ranking status in the JBS and national far right will be examined in greater detail later.)

In 1977, then-Congressman John Rousselot wrote the FBI and attached the newsletter story about Dean in *Between the Lines* (which named Rousselot) and told them he had been threatened concerning the matters mentioned in the newsletter. Rousselot, at that time had been reelected to Congress, serving from 1970 to 1983. Rousselot wanted to know if Harry Dean, as mentioned in the newsletter, was a "former operative" for the FBI who was given the mission to infiltrate the John Birch Society. In the memo from the FBI on the matter, it was noted that the FBI had investigated Dean in connection with the assassination and that he was cleared of any involvement. (The author has not seen those records.) The FBI noted that Dean had never been an informant for the FBI, but did furnish information to them on a voluntary basis in the early 1960s. They determined he was unreliable and was a former mental patient, and that his assistance was no longer desired by the FBI, in June 1961. The FBI could not reveal information on Dean to Rousselot under the Privacy Act of 1974, but they extended a courtesy to him, because he was a member of Congress. The FBI replied to Rousselot's inquiry and told him that Dean's claim in the newsletter that he had been an undercover operative of the FBI who was given the mission to infiltrate the John Birch Society was false. The FBI encouraged Rousselot to forward any threats against him to them for investigation. They noted in their internal memo that Rousselot had told them he had no intention of filing any complaints on the alleged threats.

The Harry Dean Manuscript and Interview

The author located Harry Dean and corresponded with him on a regular basis between 2009 and 2012. He graciously supplied a copy of a self-published manuscript telling his story, which was entitled *Crosstrails: A Memoirography and other writings*. He also provided the author with pictures of him in Cuba, a picture of the inside of the San Marino JBS headquarters, a Christmas card from Marguerite Oswald, and other ephemera. Dean's manuscript, at times, was difficult to follow; he admitted no one would publish his manuscript as written and he suffered from a limited education, having dropped out of school at age fourteen. Correspondence with him was challenging, as well. However, careful review of all the sources on Dean's allegation—clarified by Dean after persistent questioning by the author—when carefully sorted out, present a consistent, earnest, and compelling story about those behind the assassination.

The Dean manuscript begins with a biographical sketch. He was raised in Blenheim, Ontario, Canada. At age fifteen, he learned for the first time that he was an American citizen—his father was American, having been born in the U.S., then moving to Canada; his mother was Canadian. He developed a deep hatred for "the arrogantly crude British" and the "mostly oppressive social system" of "British-Canada" and their anti-American attitude. In the 1940s, he worked on the Great Lakes in the Merchant Marines. He ended up in the Michigan States Troops, a volunteer defense force, which he abandoned in 1945. Somehow, he ended up in a British-Canada prison camp for two years. He enlisted in the U.S. Army Air Force in 1945. He was court-martialed, and later cleared, after an incident with the Mexican police while on leave. The FBI, as was pointed out above, knew about his checkered past.

Dean became an ultrapatriotic American partly as a result of the abuse he suffered while growing up from the British Canadians who hated Americans. He was moved by the grandeur of the U.S. Constitution. He called Vladimir Lenin, the father of the Bolshevik revolution, "a disgusting old Communist." He readily admits he was fully in support of the John Birch Society and Minutemen philosophy. In 1962, Dean enlisted in the Minutemen in the Southern California district and was given the number 28515. Dean stated that the Minutemen plan "was to eliminate such as suspected Communists, leftist and social persons in positions of power during the 1960s as advocated by our national Minutemen leadership. This was just one rib in the umbrella in the national rebellion, by we brainwashed 'patriots'."

Dean's interest in Cuba began in 1957–58, when he watched a pro-Cuban revolution demonstration in Chicago. He supported the Cuban revolution and the overthrow of the "murderous tyranny" of Batista as a humanitarian act. He became an active member of Castro's 26th of July Movement for two years, but felt betrayed when Castro later admitted he was a Communist. His hatred of Castro increased over the years due to the unjust treatment he gave to those who helped him overthrow Batista (Castro threw some in prison and executed others). Dean felt the U.S. Communist Party exploited the Cuban problem to advance their position.

In his monograph, Dean claimed "Internal Security Intelligence" assigned him to infiltrate the Chicago Fair Play for Cuba Committee (FPCC), which he called a Communist front, to blow the whistle on them and the 26th of July Movement. He stated that, in June 1961, Senator Eastland's Committee subpoenaed him to testify at a hearing on FPCC and the 26th of July Movement that he had joined under cover. (Dean is listed as the secretary of the Chicago FPCC in the hearings of SISS on July 13 and 14, 1961.) Dean reproduced, in part, a letter from James Eastland on Judiciary Committee stationery, dated April 3, 1964, but the text was completely removed. It seems that nothing developed after his brief phone call with Eastland. When Lee Harvey Oswald was identified as a member of FPCC after the assassination, the entire FPCC operation folded.

Dean told the author he was elected secretary of the Chicago FPCC, which is confirmed by congressional records, as mentioned above. (Richard Criley and John Rosen, both Communist Party members, founded the Chicago chapter.) Dean passed information about FPCC to the Chicago FBI. The FBI, as noted, stated that Dean was not an informant as he claimed, and asked him not to contact them.

In his manuscript, Dean reproduced a letter, dated November 4, 1959, from Dr. Juan Orta in Havana, who was the executive director of the prime minister's office. Orta thanked him for his "selfless efforts in behalf of Dr. Castro and the Revolutionary Government." As a result of his work with FPCC and the 26th of July Movement, the Cuban Consular in Chicago gave Dean a letter of introduction to Castro. Dean, maintaining the posture of pro-Castroite, traveled to Cuba under assignment of "Internal Security," which he did without problems due to his position in the 26th of July Movement in June 1960. His assignment, as he related it, was to spot certain areas along the Cuban coast, get pictures, and determine the anti-Castro feeling of the population. Dean's contact with Castro was brief. The two merely shook hands in the hallway adjacent to the prime minister's office. Dean was harshly interrogated by Cuban G2 intelligence and was cleared to visit any section on the island nation. Dean claims he was debriefed by "Central Intelligence" and his "usual Internal Security contact agents." He said that he was asked during the debriefing if the Cuban people would rise up against Castro if the U.S. invaded Cuba, and he told them they would not. He claims he intervened and got Cuban authorities to spare the lives of three U.S. anti-Cuban raiders who had become lost in Havana harbor.

Dean left Chicago and the FPCC and relocated to Los Angeles, at which point he got in touch with Ed Swabeck, a member of the Socialist Workers Party, who was also a Chicago FPCC member who, coincidently, had also moved to Los Angeles and joined the local FPCC. Dean did not feel it would be safe for him to join the Los Angeles FPCC after he was mentioned in the transcripts of Eastland's Chicago FPCC hearings. Dean claims that the Los Angeles FBI gave him the phone number of Swabeck, whom he telephoned. Swabeck told Dean that Cuban G2/DG1 agent Francisco Vega was illegally in the country. (Dean knew Vega, having encountered him in Havana.) The FBI arrested Vega on Dean's information, according to Dean.

In his monograph, Dean asserted that, "The John Birch Society was an invention and extension of the Latter Day Saints [LDS], Mormon." He called the JBS "the Vanguard of the LDS." He stated that the JBS infrastructure was an exact miniature of the LDS church, designed to serve as its political arm. The LDS-JBS goal, according to Dean, was to create an opposition to the liberalism in the Democratic and Republican Parties "via initial infiltrations, seizure and use the Republican Party apparatus to serve the LDS/JBS 5-year plan to take over the U.S. *en toto*." Their plan was to commandeer the title of Conservatism, infiltrate the Democratic Party, and neutralize liberalism. He stated that Ezra Taft Benson, president of the LDS church, was in the forefront of the attack on President Eisenhower and the branding of President Kennedy and Earl Warren as "com-symps" (Communist sympathizers). The LDS, he said, poured millions of dollars into devising propaganda to spread the fear that the U.S. government might actually be under Communist influence and direction. The JBS tied the policies of the Kennedy administration with the plans of the Communists. Dean admitted in his transcript that he agreed with and aided them. Dean produced a news photo dated September 24, 1963, of JBS leader Robert Welch at a JBS dinner with Ezra Taft Benson. Dean said that Reed A. Benson, Dan Smoot, and W. Cleon Skousen were other leaders of the LDS. The LDS's first "five-year plan" was to usurp the power of the government through the use of the JBS action arm, and implementation of the "final solution" was considered urgent, based on the increasing fear that Kennedy might get reelected in 1964.

Dean told the author that he was well acquainted with national leaders of the radical right who passed through Southern California. Dean told the author that he knew "Welch, Reagan, Smoot, Knott, and endless other sponsors of the movement." He had met Smoot several times in Los Angeles and called him a convincing, serious person who was both an LDS member and a JBS member. Walter Knott was another far-right associate of John Rousselot. Dean met Cleon Skousen at the San Marino JBS office and at Knott's farm. He said Skousen was part of the assassination conspiracy. Dean was at a meeting in Pasadena attended by Welch, Ezra Taft Benson, Rousselot, and the mother of John Birch. He also talked to Welch one time in Birch headquarters in San Marino. Dean was aware of Billy James Hargis and told the author that most of his far-right associates paid more attention to Walker than Hargis. He went on to tell the author that he was a "totally faithful member and follower of their philosophy" until the assassination.[2935, 2936]

Cleon Skousen, a former FBI agent, may have known Guy Banister, since he was a member of the faculty of the Greater New Orleans School of Anti-Communism held in October 1961, along with Banister, Robert Morris and Herbert Philbrick.[2937] On September 16, 1963, Skousen planned to speak at an annual meeting of the Louisiana Television and Radio Broadcasting Association in New Orleans, which had been arranged by Robert E. Tracy, commander of the American Legion's Committee on Un-American Activities.[2938] (As has been noted, Banister and Kent Courtney were also involved in the American Legion's Committee on Un-American Activities.)

Dean associated with Carl Guy "Gabby" Gabaldon, a "cruel ex-Marine hero of Saipan," who, he stated, was in contact with the principals and financiers of the plot to murder the president. Guy Gabaldon, in league with some rightist Mexican federal police, was set to shoot the president in Mexico City in June 1962, but the plan was aborted at the last minute.

Dean claimed that he learned that after Oswald was identified as a member of FPCC in his radio debate with Ed Butler and Carlos Bringuier, Oswald's name was broadcast throughout the rightist circuit. General Walker selected Oswald as the fall guy after that radio debate. Dean and his associates found the idea of framing a Communist humorous.

In August 1963, Dean and Gabaldon met with former U.S. congressman John Rousselot, the western director of the JBS, at his San Marino office. Gabaldon picked up ten thousand dollars from a San Gabriel bank from Rousselot, and Dean claimed some of the funds were later given to Oswald. Dean also claimed in his monograph that Gabaldon, posing as a CIA agent, enlisted Oswald in a phony plot at the Cuban and Soviet embassies in Mexico City. Gabaldon allegedly dispatched Lawrence Howard and Loran Hall, also posing as CIA agents, to pick Oswald up in late September in New Orleans and take him to Gabladon's Mexico City office. Oswald received funds and instructions during the trip, then awaited instructions from another fake CIA contact. Gabaldon returned from Mexico in September 1963 and he and Dean readied a supply of medical drugs and supplies, which had been gathered from several LDS doctors throughout Southern California. Some of the drugs were slated for Gabaldon's JBS front operation, Drive Against Communist Aggression, to aid Cuban rebels. Skousen and Rousselot organized the effort, which was not a CIA operation, and some members of the group were arrested. Dean claimed that the timing of the Mexico City visit was not related to the September 13 newspaper announcement of Kennedy's visit to Dallas. The plotters had long known, through their sources in Washington, that the trip was going to take place before it was publicly announced.

The author asked Dean to clarify his remarks about Oswald and Gabaldon and Dean replied, "The money received by Oswald from Gabaldon motivated him to secretly and patriotically follow directions intended to use him and his past in the FPCC, pro-Communist, pro-Castro strike by Walker's rifle men in Texas." He stated that Oswald, whom Dean believed was a genuine Communist, was ripe for Gabaldon's phoney CIA recruitment claim.

After the assassination, Dean discussed, in a limited and guarded way, with Gabaldon, Hall, and Howard, the danger they faced if the conspiracy was exposed.

Dean wrote in his manuscript that the ultraconservative forces that began to organize in 1958 absorbed the anti-Castro movement. They created the American Committee to Free Cuba, Inc., a JBS front that was organized for the LDS by Skousen and Rousselot.[2939, 2940] The letterhead of the American Committee to Free Cuba included Kent Courtney, Rousselot, Walter Knott, Herbert Philbrick, J. B. Mathews, and Skousen.[2941] Loran Hall and Lawrence Howard served in the operation. Among the ultraconservative forces were "assassin-minded persons" who would seize control of the U.S. government if given the word. Dean wrote that the news of the plot against the president was skillfully spread down the line from "leading activist death designers." The idea of removing Kennedy, whom they perceived as a Communist, elated the radical followers. A false story was spread that assassins were secretely inside the Dallas Trade Mart where the president was to speak after the motorcade which took him through Dealey Plaza. (Members of Walker's group were, in fact, at the Trade Mart, and arrests were made. Perhaps the scheme was used to draw security away from the motorcade route.) Dean wrote that "Extremist veteran riflemen" under Walker's command were involved the Kennedy assassination and that "Armed Walker forces" were persuaded by "nationwide, brilliantly subversive propaganda that reached an almost high 'spiritual' cause."

Dean knew Walker personally and had met him in Southern California in Pasadena, Whittier, and Los Angeles. Dean sent the author a photo that, he said, was of Walker speaking in Pasadena. Dean admitted that, although he was closely connected to the individuals involved, and was getting bits and pieces of confusing information, he failed to detect a clearer picture of the real and subtler plot to kill the president. Dean claimed that he reported his scarce details to his contacts in the FBI in September 1963. Dean repeatedly referred to the assassination as an attempt at a permanent takeover of the U.S. government. Jack Ruby also stated that those behind the assassination were part of a plot to take over the U.S.

Dean and the ultraconservatives were aware that Jack Ruby alluded to the JBS and Walker in his testimony before the Warren Commission. In response, Dean stated that the "upper layer of our network leadership" quickly branded Ruby a Communist and a lifelong brutal gangster. Dean wrote in his manuscript that, "Every smokescreening effort was brought into action to offset his testimony about the secret works of General Walker and the national intrigues of the conspiracy vanguard (JBS)." Dean stated that Ruby was never a Communist, "But he shook the foundations of the 'very powerful' select few in the LDS Rocky Mountain fortress, Utah, and their (JBS) apolitical-political headquarters in Boston, with a clearly brave truth, about these who mislead the innocent."

Dean noted that "Jefferson Davis Tippit" worked weekends for a Dallas restaurant owned by another JBS member. He stated, "There was no mystery about Tippit's connections." He stated that when the death of J. D. Tippit was reported, all of the JBS members were quickly informed about it. He quoted a JBS special bulletin: "We were ready to step into that picture and ask our members for the support for Tippit's family . . . but it might be harmful for us to do so." (As was noted in Chapter Eleven, Paul Rothermel, who worked for H. L. Hunt, told the author that the Dallas John Birch Society held meetings at Austin's Barbeque, the restaurant where Tippit worked part time.)

Dean reproduced a letter in his manuscript that he claimed he wrote to FBI Director J. Edgar Hoover on November 19, 1963—three days before the assassination. The letter is heavily redacted, and it's difficult to make sense of it. It is probably not the original, but he likely obtained the copy sent to the FBI when he requested the FBI send him the file they kept on him through the Freedom of Information Act. In the letter, he told Hoover that he had given information to the Chicago FBI office on FPCC in 1960. He mentioned a "present assignment" with the Los Angeles office. He stated that, in June 1961, Eastland's Committee subpoenaed him for a hearing on FPCC and the 26th of July Movement that he had joined "under cover." He told them his exposure in the Eastland hearings limited his effectiveness. He felt his life was in danger in Chicago, apparently from the anti-Communists who learned of his work in the leftist groups, and he moved to Los Angeles. His fear of the anti-Communists was the apparent reason he wrote Hoover. There is nothing in the unredacted portion of the letter to suggest he was tipping Hoover off to the assassination plot. Dean claimed that, after Hoover received the letter, he dispatched FBI Agent Wes Grapp and two other agents from Washington "to urge [Dean's] continued silence on the day the president and Oswald were buried." Dean told the author that it was Grapp, of the Los Angeles FBI office, who arranged a personal meeting with Dean to discuss the JFK plot in September of 1963. Dean met Grapp prior to writing to Hoover, and drove him around and showed him places of interest in the anti-Castro and anti-JFK efforts. Neither Dean, nor the FBI agent, really believed that the murder plot would materialize. Despite knowing about the aborted 1962 plot to kill Kennedy in Mexico, Dean still didn't believe the assassination was going to happen.

Dean also reproduced in *Crosstrails*, in part (the text is redacted), a letter to him from General Walker dated April 22, 1963. Dean recalled for the author that it likely was a fund-raising note, one of several he received from "Friends of General Walker."

Dean printed a quote in his manuscript, purportedly from Robert Welch, boasting to his followers about the success of the assassination: "And we take tremendous encouragement from the one huge victory we have won over the Communists. We have become very much a part of the cast, therefore, in the final act of this gory performance. And I mean that last statement quite literally."

Dean told the author that the assassination cabal represented the "New Americanist scheme" and new power over the U.S. government. It was the culmination of the five-year plan from 1958 to 1963 to take over the government. Dean said he had favored it all, except for the assassination.

For over fifty years following the assassination Dean lived in a state of fear. He repeatedly stated that he felt he was endangered, and "a dead man on furlough" because he was "a low level spy that talked." He repeatedly told the author that what he was saying could cost him his life. Dean's involvement with the FPCC was well known to his far-right associates, he told the author. He always considered the possibility that they might develop a scheme to use his leftist connections in a way that might harm him. When Dean first wrote his manuscript in 1990, several of his anti-JFK associates were still living, including Hall, Howard, and Rousselot. He was also aware that Rousselot had contacted the Justice Department about him. Dean told the author that he feared a backlash from conspirators but forged ahead and distributed the manuscript worldwide, to the best of his financial ability.[2942, 2943]

What makes Harry Dean's story particularly compelling is the mention of Ezra Taft Benson's involvement in financing and backing the assassination. Unknown to Dean was the fact that Benson was an associate of Joseph Milteer, the Walker colleague who predicted the assassination in precise detail and was standing in Dealey Plaza when the murder took place. Benson was not mentioned in any of W. R. Morris's accounts of Dean's story, Dean's two television appearances, Dean's FBI, HSCA, or Garrison interviews, or his *Between the Lines* interview. The author was unaware of Dean's allegations about Benson until he was furnished, by Dean, with a rare copy of his 1990 self-printed monograph *Crosstrails*, in 2009.

It will be recalled that, before Milteer attended the Constitution Party meeting in Indianapolis in October 1963 (where talk of killing the president first emerged), he had embarked on a cross-country trip to promote the meeting noted in Chapter Seven. He traveled to Provo, then Salt Lake City, Utah, and met with Ezra Taft Benson.[2944] A letter dated June 2, 1962, found in Milteer's home after his death, indicated he had opened a bank account in Provo. Another letter indicated that Milteer deposited $10,000 in his account with the Utah Savings and Loan on August 2, 1962.[2945] His bank account passbook, which was hidden in a pile of letters in a closet, was made out to Samuel Steven Story and Mrs. C. C. Cofield, his common-law wife, and the account bore Cofield's Valdosta, Georgia, address. When the bank account was opened on July 31, 1963, five thousand dollars was deposited. Deposits of five thousand dollars and two thousand dollars followed on August 20 and September 24, respectively, before the account was closed abruptly on January 31, 1964, and all twelve thousand dollars were withdrawn. A letter to the bank, signed by Story, was in Milteer's handwriting, thus confirming that Story was his alias. Milteer had no legitimate reason to have a bank account in Utah—two thousand miles from his home—or any legitimate need to have another account in an assumed name. Milteer was a trusted soldier in the radical right, so much so that he was told, in precise detail, how the assassination would come about. With his free time and financial independence, he traveled the country on a regular basis contacting leaders of the radical right, which made him an excellent candidate as a courier for the funds which were used to finance the hardcore underground.

Ezra Taft Benson was expected to speak at the We the People convention in Chicago on September 22, 1962, with Billy James Hargis.[2946] Tom Anderson had been invited by John Rousselot to be the master of ceremonies for a testimonial to Robert Welch held at the Hollywood Palladium on September 23, 1963.[2947] Benson was the main speaker at the Palladium, and told the group that he had warned the State Department, two years before Castro took power, that Castro was a Communist, but the State Department had ignored him. Benson said he was not a member of the John Birch Society, but that he agreed with most of their principles.[2948]

UTAH SAVINGS
and Loan Association

Joseph Milteer opened a bank account at the Utah Savings and Loan Association in 1962. Source: Brooks County Probate Court

John H. Rousselot

John Rousselot, a Southern California Republican, served in Congress from 1961 to 1963. Ronald Reagan campaigned for Rousselot in his losing bid for reelection in 1962.[2949] (Robert Welch claimed that the JBS "in large part" helped elect Reagan governor of California in 1967.[2950]) While in Congress, Rousselot published the "Beliefs and Principles of the John Birch Society" in the *Congressional Record*, and a reprint was widely distributed.[2951] Rousselot had many of the same credentials which were held by many on the far right who were suspected of involvement in the assassination conspiracy, and they will be chronicled here.

In April 1961, Attorney General Robert F. Kennedy expressed concerns about the John Birch Society. In response, Representative Rousselot identified himself as a member of the JBS, and characterized the society as "basically a study group, not arm-waving people who run around harassing others." When some were calling the JBS a subversive, secret society, John Birch Society leader Robert Welch sent a telegram to Senator Eastland inviting him to investigate the organization.[2952]

On August 22, 1961, Phoebe and Kent Courtney met with Rousselot in Washington, after first meeting with Senator Strom Thurmond.[2953] On November 19, 1961, President Kennedy spoke at the Palladium in Los Angeles and commented on the "discordant voices of extremism"—a reference to the JBS. John Rousselot responded and criticized Kennedy for his remarks.[2954] On December 3, 1961, in a speech in California, Rousselot called President Kennedy a "Fabian Socialist President" and said the time was ripe to send the marines into Cuba.[2955]

In 1962, a resolution to stop training Communist pilots was introduced in the Senate by John Tower and in the House by Bruce Alger and John Rousselot. At the same time, the National Indignation Committee demanded that anybody having anything to do with the training of the Yugoslavian pilots at the center of the controversy be fired. They demanded the impeachment of President Kennedy and the dismissal of his cabinet. Rousselot later spoke at a meeting of the group, whose members included Guy Banister, Kent Courtney, and General Walker.[2956]

When Kent and Phoebe Courtney came to the defense of General Walker in the book *The Case of General Edwin A. Walker*, in 1961, John Rousselot reviewed it and stated, "You are commended for a forthright and accurate account of the viciousness of the drive against anti-Communists in the military."[2957]

Rousselot was a friend of conservative syndicated columnist Max Rafferty, who, in

1962, sponsored Project Alert with Joe Craig. At one of their meetings, a speaker called for the hanging of Chief Justice Warren.[2958] In Walker's long, rambling, 1961 resignation speech from the military, he quoted Rafferty in reference to the Communist menace in the U.S.[2959]

On March 20, 1962, Billy James Hargis held a "secretive meeting" by invitation only in Washington, D.C. John Rousselot and General Charles Willoughby were among the national leaders of the radical right who attended.[2960] The secretive meeting was suggested at the We the People meeting on September 5, 1961, by Billy James Hargis who was president of the organization.[2961] John Rousselot organized The League of Right Wing Organizations at the meeting.[2962]

On August 3–5, 1962, General Walker spoke at the Fourth Annual National Convention of the Christian Crusade with John Rousselot, Billy James Hargis, and General Willoughby. During the convention, Hargis presented Rousselot with the "Statesman of the Year Award."[2963] On November 17, 1962, Kent Courtney sponsored the Cuban Liberation Rally, where "Johnny Rousselot" was the featured speaker. General Walker and Tom Anderson were invited to the Cuban Liberation Rally, and a member of the Cuban underground (whose name was not disclosed) was expected to attend.[2964] In 1963, Rousselot was listed as a member of the Christian Crusade Board of Advisors and Trustees, along with Tom Anderson, Revilo Oliver, General Willoughby, General Stratemeyer, and Harold Lord Varney.[2965] On January 6, 1963, Billy James Hargis spoke at the New England Rally for God and Country. John Rousselot, Tom Anderson, and Kent Courtney were present.[2966, 2967, 2968, 2969]

On February 23, 1963, the press reported that Robert Gaston, an advocate of "militant conservatism," had been elected to the presidency of the California Young Republicans, with open John Birch Society support. The event prompted the outgoing president of the Republican assembly to assert that the John Birch Society's aim was the eventual takeover of the Republican Party. He said, "I think it is the closest thing we've had to a Fascist party in America. Somewhere, somehow, they'll find a man on horseback."[2970]

John Rousselot spoke at a Pasadena Birch Society Rally on February 23, 1963, with Tom Anderson and Revilo Oliver; Robert Montgomery, Robert Love, and Slobodan Draskovich, all JBS Council members, also spoke. Anderson urged the crowd: "Don't ever give up your firearms. The time to buy a gun is the time when it becomes unlawful to have arms."[2971]

As has been discussed, Tom Anderson hosted the Walker-Hargis Midnight Ride tour stop in Nashville, Tennessee, on March 13, 1963. A handbill promoting an upcoming John Rousselot speech in Nashville on May 17 was distributed at that time.[2972] Walker and Hargis ended their tour with a stop in Los Angeles on April 3, 1963. Congressmen John Rousselot presented Walker at the tour stop with a plaque proclaiming him the "greatest living American."[2973]

On September 23, 1963, the John Birch Society held a "Robert Welch Testimonial Dinner" at the Hollywood Palladium, which was organized by Rousselot. Tom Anderson was the master of ceremonies, and Ezra Taft Benson was invited to speak.[2974]

On October 29, 1963, Rousselot gave a speech on disarmament to the John Birch

Society in Dallas.[2975] The visit, three weeks before the Kennedy assassination, would have afforded him the opportunity to become actively involved in the assassination planning. It provided him with the chance to confer with Dallasites involved in the assassination, including the H. L. Hunt clan, Dan Smoot, Robert Surrey, and General Walker. Rousselot then spoke at a John Birch Society meeting in Houston, Texas, on October 30, 1963, on the subject of "Disarmament—Blueprint for Surrender."[2976] Billy James Hargis spoke in Dallas on November 16, 1963, a visit which afforded Hargis, like Rousselot, the opportunity to participate in the Dallas planning in the weeks before the assassination.

Rousselot had other ties to those linked to the conspiracy, as well. Reverend Theodore (Ted) Jackman, a friend of Joseph Milteer, was on the American Opinion Speakers Bureau along with Rousselot, Tom Anderson, Harold Lord Varney, and Revilo Oliver.[2977] As has been noted, Milteer told Willie Somersett that Jackman was one of the actual shooters of the president. On May 5, 1963, Milteer thanked his friend Grady Bartlett for sending him a recording of a speech by Ted Jackman in Menlo Park, California.[2978]

Rousselot, Nelson Bunker Hunt, Robert Welch and Thomas N. Hill (of Gloucester, Massachusetts) were listed as the owners for the Birch Society's magazine, *American Opinion*, in 1965. Hill was a field director for the JBS, while Revilo Oliver was an associate editor of the magazine. The name "Thomas Hill," it will be recalled, was written by Jack Ruby on an envelope that was found in the trunk of his car, when it was found parked near the Dallas jail where Ruby murdered Oswald.[2979]

Following his defeat for reelection in 1962, Rousselot served nearly two years as the JBS's Western States "Governor," and established a public relations department to further its growth. Rousselot was chosen by Robert Welch, himself, to head the campaign. Rousselot worked out of an office in San Marino, California, but spent considerable time in Belmont, Massachusetts. By 1965, he was considered perhaps the number two leader of the JBS, next to Welch.[2980] Rousselot also served with Barry Goldwater on the National Advisory Board of Young Americans for Freedom.[2981]

In 1965, Representative Gerald Ford and other leaders of the Republican Party denounced the efforts of the John Birch Society to take over the party. In response, Rousselot called Ford a member of "one of the most highly active left-wing groups in the Country—the DeBilderberger [sic] group—which meets clandestinely."[2982] The exchange illustrates the stark difference between a respectable moderate conservative like Ford and a radical like Rousselot.

Rousselot, like General Walker, despised the United Nations, stating, in 1965: "The U.N. was originally designed and planned by key Communist sympathizers, and today the organization is controlled and administrated by the Communists."[2983]

The press reported, on October 29, 1965, that John Rousselot announced that the Dallas John Birch Society ranked tenth in the U.S. in membership and activity strength. He claimed there were fifty chapters in Dallas, consisting of ten to fifty members each.[2984]

In 1966, California State Controller Alan Cranston made public a twenty-six-page report on the John Birch Society that called the JBS an attraction for bigots and racists. Rousselot responded: "Its pure poppycock—it's obvious that Cranston is a secret, card carrying agent for the Anti-Defamation League." Ronald Reagan, whom the *Jewish Voice* called a "bird of a feather" and close friend of Rousselot, responded to the report saying that he wanted to know what the facts in the matter were. California Democratic governor Edmund G. Brown criticized Reagan—who was running for governor in 1966—and the Republican Party for not disavowing the John Birch Society. Brown declared, "The John Birch Society is an issue in this election. . . . And my opponent has made it an issue by his repeated refusal to disavow the support of that secret political society, whose aims are extremist and authoritarian."[2985]

In September 1966, Rousselot boasted that the tragic race riots in the Hough neighborhood of Cleveland, Ohio, had noticeably swelled the local JBS membership.[2986]

Jewish War Veterans protested against California TV station KKTV in 1967 when Rousselot sat in for the host of the *Louis Lomax* show in Lomax's absence. A spokesman for the veterans stated: "It's tragic that a man whose boss, Robert Welch, says the last three presidents were part of the plot to deliver the United States into the hands of the Communists should be given a free hand on the airwaves."[2987]

Joseph Milteer openly admired Rousselot. Milteer wrote a letter to Grady Bartlett, dated May 10, 1963, and told him he thought that Strom Thurmond and John Rousselot would be good candidates for president and vice president, respectively, in the 1964 election.[2988]

With Rousselot's close ties to so many people who have been implicated in the assassination conspiracy, Harry Dean's allegation that Rousselot was involved in the plot to assassinate the president is not surprising.

Conclusions

General Walker's letter to Tom Anderson, in which he refers to his surveillance of Marguerite Oswald, defies any logical explanation other than it being an expression of the consciousness of his guilt in the murder of the president—and fear of exposure by her. Confiding his concerns about Marguerite Oswald to Tom Anderson makes Anderson an accessory after the fact. Anderson's high position in the radical right, and his association with so many others tied in this work to the assassination, makes him a suspect *before* the fact.

Anderson's calls for "killing traitors" and "neck tying parties" reflected a visceral, violent hatred of his enemies. Walker, in the letter, admitted watching Marguerite Oswald's moves closely on the eve of the Clay Shaw trial. Oswald knew she was being watched, and accused many people and said many things. One thing she said was: "I know who framed my son and *he* knows I know who framed my son." It's entirely possible that she had General Walker in mind. She was confident her son was framed—which the evidence in this work also suggests—and she knew the events in Dealey Plaza had been contrived.

Just prior to the Clay Shaw trial, when Walker was watching Marguerite Oswald's moves very closely, she was imploring someone from the White House to meet with her. Her contact with the White House may have prompted Walker to express his concerns about her in the letter to Tom Anderson, which was written at about the same time. Like Earl Warren's refusal to take Jack Ruby back to Washington, the White House's refusal to accommodate Marguerite Oswald in Washington, so she could tell her secret, was another massive blunder of history. (It will be recalled from Chapter Seventeen that Walker also suspiciously placed George de Mohrenschildt under surveillance in 1966, and feared Jack Ruby might talk.)

Taylor Caldwell was the strange authoress who supposedly predicted Kennedy's death by a Communist in advance in *The Wanderer*. If it were not for the facts that she was a darling of the John Birch Society, board member of Liberty Lobby, and associate of so many people tied to General Walker (and a large number of others tied to the assassination), we might chalk her prediction up to good guessing. However, the fact that Dallasite Robert Morris, one of Walker's closest associates, was a major contributor to *The Wanderer* makes Caldwell's "prediction" highly suspicious. Caldwell's prediction of the death of President Kennedy and her later prediction of the death of his brother Robert are tremendously disturbing. Caldwell may have been part of the larger disinformation machine of Liberty Lobby. Serving on the board of that radical-right and anti-Semitic operation with Caldwell were Joseph Milteer's friends Pedro del Valle, Curtis Dall, and Kenneth Goff, as well as Tom Anderson and Billy James Hargis (both of whom were tied to Walker and the assassination conspiracy). Mark Lane, Victor Marchetti, and Fletcher Prouty all contributed to Liberty Lobby's disinformation effort to blame the assassination on the CIA or some shadowy government forces and to steer the blame away from the radical right. They did so either as paid representatives, as in the case of attorney Mark Lane, or for more sinister reasons, as in the cases of Marchetti and Prouty.

The allegations of Raymond Broshears and Harry Dean both displayed unique knowledge of the conspiracy, which they could not have gotten anywhere other than from those who were involved. Each man named General Walker as a member of the conspiracy, when no one else did in the most investigated and written-about murder in history. Broshears named "H. Lemar [sic] Hunt", meaning either H. L. Hunt or Lamar Hunt. Dean alluded to a "Mr. Hunt's" involvement. As the evidence against the Hunts showed in Chapter Eleven, Broshears and Dean were correct. Broshears named Kent Courtney and Billy James Hargis, two men with ties to Guy Banister, as conspirators, and the case against them has been presented throughout this work. Broshears named Reverend Carl McIntire, a Kennedy hater, who was an associate of General Walker, Tom Anderson, and Guy Banister. Evidence was presented in prior chapters that suggested that McIntire's west coast representative, Edgar Eugene Bradley, talked of killing the president and was in Dallas during the murder. Broshears named high-ranking Minuteman Rich Lauchli who, as Carlos Bringuier's friend Carlos Quiroga told Jim Garrison, was at the Cuban and radical-right-wing training camp north of Lake Pontchartrain. That accusation links Lauchli to the hardcore underground of New Orleans and makes Broshears's allegation against Lauchli credible.

Broshears's allegation that he saw Oswald at David Ferrie's apartment and also at Guy Banister's office is persuasive given the fact that he also mentioned seeing Hugh Ward with Banister. Both Broshears and Dean stated unequivocally that Oswald did not do the shooting in Dealey Plaza and that he was set up, which the evidence in Chapter Sixteen well supports. Broshears noted that Oswald was tied to the conspirators, but was tricked and did not do the shooting. Dean was told that Oswald was framed. Dean claimed that the motive for killing Kennedy was the conspirators' belief that Kennedy was pro-Communist and turning over the country to the Reds, which was consistent with Walker's oft-stated position. Ferrie's allegation to Broshears that the president was killed by "a group of people who wanted to take over the U.S." is corroborated throughout these pages. Finally, Harry Dean named John Rousselot as a conspirator. The fact he was close to General Walker and the mountain of circumstantial evidence presented herein makes that allegation credible.

CHAPTER TWENTY

LEE HARVEY OSWALD ON CAMPUS

It was also my duty to develop and supervise those people called inform-
ers. To be more specific, we might say they were the counter spies sent
in to report on the activities of the party members. That was part of my
duties throughout the nearly seventeen years I served as Special Agent
in Charge.[2989]

– Guy Banister

Guy Banister had an intense interest in investigating leftists on college campuses and among integrationist groups, and employed people to infiltrate them. He used the information his spies gathered to aid the many inquisitions he worked with or testi-fied before, which were aimed at destroying the integration movement.

In 1956, Banister and Hubert Badeaux assisted Senator Eastland's Senate Internal Security Subcommittee (SISS) investigation of alleged Communism in the integration move-ment. General Walker's close friend Robert Morris was Eastland's special council during the proceeding. After the hearings, Leander Perez vowed to assist Banister in his anti-subversive efforts.

In early 1957, Badeaux, as a sergeant in the New Orleans Police Intelligence Divi-sion under Guy Banister, who was the Assistant Superintendent of the New Orleans Police Department, confided that he had been grooming an individual to infiltrate the universities. Evidence was presented in Chapter One and will be expanded upon in Chapter Twenty-two that favored Lee Harvey Oswald as the individual whom Badeaux was grooming.

Also in 1957, Banister, Perez, and Badeaux testified before hearings in the Louisiana state legislature entitled "Subversion in Racial Unrest," which concluded that Communists were behind the racial unrest. Then, in 1958, Banister testified before the Arkansas legislature that Communists were behind racial turmoil. That same year, Banister, Kent Courtney, and Perez teamed up with James Pfister and Jack Rogers of the American Legion's Un-American Activities Committee to voice opposition to a New Orleans student's plan to attend the Com-munist-sponsored World Youth Festival in Vienna. Banister became an advisor to the Legion's Un-American Activities Committee, and, in 1960, subsequently became a special investigator for the Louisiana Un-American Activities Committee, which was also staffed by Rogers and Pfister, who had become a state representative by that time. Banister, around the same time, began to work for the Sovereignty Commission, the state-sanctioned group that spied on the integration movement.

In May 1962, just prior to Oswald's return from the Soviet Union the following month, Pfister introduced the Communist Control Act, which was the invention of Leander Perez, into the state legislature. The law was passed and called for penalties of decades in jail and tens of thousands of dollars in fines if any person or group associated with a known Communist. The law was aimed at destroying the integration movement, first in Louisiana, with hopes that it would later be adopted across the segregated South. That same month, Senator Eastland sent two members of his staff to assist with the lengthy planning of the raid on the New Orleans offices of the Southern Conference Education Fund (SCEF), Louisiana's leading integration-advocacy group, and longtime nemesis of Eastland and Banister. Eastland joined forces with the Louisiana Un-American Activities Committee, as well as the state and local police, to plan the raid that took place on October 4, 1963. Close Banister colleagues Leander Perez and George Singelmann were seen by a news reporter watching the raid, which had been kept a secret. Three SCEF officers, James Dombrowski, Benjamin E. Smith, and Bruce Walzer, were arrested during the raid and were indicted under the Communist Control Act.

A primary focus of this chapter will be on Bruce Walzer, who was also the leader of the leftist New Orleans Committee for Peaceful Alternatives (NOCPA). Evidence will be presented that Lee Harvey Oswald infiltrated the group as an operative of the Banister operation. Anti-Castro Cuban Carlos Bringuier (a close Banister associate), Kent Courtney, and others in the Banister operation were also involved in the NOCPA intrigue, as will be shown. A review of Banister's interest in campus leftist activities and his use of student informants at Tulane University will be presented, as well.

Jerry Milton Brooks, Reluctant False Communist

The FBI report on Guy Banister and Jerry Milton Brooks, a radical right winger and top figure in the national Minutemen operation, exposes the Banister operation and his *modus operandi* of producing phony Communists. Brooks worked out of Banister's office in 1961, although the details of the arrangement are scarce. Minutemen leader Robert DePugh told the author that Brooks often called him from Banister's office and told him about Banister's work with the Anti-Communist Crusade of the Caribbean, but DePugh denied knowing Banister personally.[2990]

On March 27, 1961, Brooks called the FBI and told them that he had been in touch with Banister and Maurice Gatlin. He told the FBI that Banister and Gatlin had insisted that he write to the Communist Party headquarters in New York on March 16, 1961. He also telephoned the Communist Party headquarters and talked to the secretary. At the insistence of Banister and Gatlin, he asked about membership into the Communist Party and also subscribed to several of their publications. The report concluded with the FBI expressing the feeling that Brooks was unbalanced.[2991]

Lee Harvey Oswald did the same things Brooks was asked to do, beginning upon his return from the Soviet Union in 1962. Oswald corresponded with the Communist Party, Socialist Workers Party and other far-left organizations, and subscribed to their literature. When the New York headquarters of the far-left Fair Play for Cuba Committee refused to sanction a New Orleans chapter, as Oswald requested, he fabricated his own chapter and made himself the director (something the Warren Commission called a "product of his imagination"). The Brooks episode is more evidence suggesting Lee Harvey Oswald was a right winger and false Communist who was groomed in 1956 by the Banister operation while in the Civil Air Patrol unit of the fanatical, anti-Communist, David Ferrie, as was described in Chapter One.

Brooks may have ended up in New Orleans during a "ninety-nine-dollar" bus ticket cross-country tour (probably a ticket for unlimited bus travel) that Minutemen leader Robert DePugh sent him on. Brooks, from East St. Louis, joined the Minutemen in 1961 through Richard Lauchli, and defected four years later. (He worked with Lauchli up until October 4, 1962.) It will be recalled from prior chapters that Lauchli was present at the training camps north of Lake Pontchartrain, which have been tied to the Banister operation. And, as was noted in the last chapter, Raymond Broshears, Ferrie's confidant, named Lauchli as a member of the assassination conspiracy. Next to DePugh, Brooks was the most widely known Minuteman in the Greater St. Louis area from 1962 through 1964, describing himself as a member of the group's "counter-intelligence" unit.

According to J. Harry Jones, Jr., a reporter for the *Kansas City Star* and author of *The Minutemen* published in 1968, Jerry Brooks spied on Communists for the Minutemen. At first, Jones considered the Minutemen "a miniscule bunch of crackpots with a windy leader," but after the Kennedy assassination he began to take a closer look at the organization. Jones noted that the Minutemen organization, in the March 15, 1963, issue of their newsletter, *On Target*, openly threatened a Texas congressman and nineteen of his colleagues. The newsletter warned them of their possible fate, stating: "Crosshairs are on the back of you necks," after they voted to abolish the House Committee on Un-American Activities.

DePugh sent Brooks on his ninety-nine-dollar cross-country bus trip to visit people the Minutemen considered Communists and learn about them. Later, they sent these people intimidating letters conveying bits of information that Brooks had gleaned from their operations in an attempt to give them the impression that the Minutemen were watching them. During his travels, Brooks even paid a visit to Communist Party Chairwoman Elizabeth Gurley Flynn.

DePugh reportedly tried to groom two young women in the principles of anti-Communism, with the aim of using them to sexually seduce high-ranking members of the government who were felt to be pro-Communist. The women tired of the indoctrination, however, and when they tried to leave DePugh pulled a gun on them and held them against their will. The women eventually escaped and notified the police, who raided DePugh's home and found large caches of weapons and explosives. After the incident, Jerry Brooks defected from the organization, absconding with the files of the Minutemen membership, and went to the

FBI and Bureau of Alcohol Tobacco and Firearms Unit, telling them all about DePugh and handing over the files.

In 1966, following DePugh's arrest on federal weapons charges, Brooks walked into the newsroom of the *Kansas City Star* and told them that he had quit the group and was ready to talk. He told them of various plots for planned violence and assassinations, and of weapons caches. Brooks told a grand jury that DePugh discussed putting cyanide in the United Nations building and assassinating Senator William Fulbright. More charges were brought against DePugh and he was convicted of the federal weapons charges, serving time in prison from 1970 to 1973.[2992]

The author told DePugh about his suspicions that General Walker and H. L. Hunt were behind the assassination. DePugh made no comment other than to say that, immediately after the assassination, the FBI descended upon his home and asked him about it. DePugh speculated that the FBI had tapped his phone and heard him comment to a friend who called him about the murder, "It couldn't have happened to a nicer guy."[2993]

The New Orleans Council for Peaceful Alternatives

The author uncovered evidence that Lee Harvey Oswald infiltrated the New Orleans Committee for Peaceful Alternatives (NOCPA), a liberal, "ban the bomb" group at Tulane University, which was dedicated to curbing nuclear proliferation. Like Fair Play for Cuba Committee, NOCPA officers were integration leaders with ties to the Southern Conference Education Fund (SCEF). Oswald's infiltration of NOCPA, like FPCC, was the next best thing to infiltrating SCEF (which could not be infiltrated because it had no membership).

NOCPA was founded in the wake of the October 1962 Cuban Missile Crisis that brought the U.S. and Soviet Union to the brink of nuclear war. NOCPA initially considered merging with the national group The Committee for a SANE Nuclear Policy (commonly know as "SANE"), but did not. SANE had been founded in 1957 by Coretta Scott King, Albert Schweitzer, and Dr. Benjamin Spock in response to the nuclear arms buildup during the Eisenhower administration. Eleanor Roosevelt and a number of Hollywood's elite supported the organization. Acclaimed author Stephen Ambrose, who at the time was a faculty member at the University of New Orleans, was a member of NOCPA. Senator James Eastland claimed NOCPA was subversive, as he did the other groups Oswald had affected an association with, citing the "HUAC Report on the Committee on Peaceful Alternatives."[2994]

The New Orleans office of the FBI was aware that some of the members of NOCPA were integrationists connected to SCEF, CORE, and the freedom rides. On September 13, 1963, the New Orleans FBI wrote to Director J. Edgar Hoover and noted, in a memo: "The activities of this group should be followed, particularly in view of the racial problem in the area." Hoover directed the office to investigate NOCPA and determine whether or not they were a subversive or Communist-infiltrated organization. The New Orleans FBI indicated that they had an established informant in place, NO 1213-S, who had attended two meetings of NOCPA, and that they would use him to cover any further activities of the group.[2995, 2996]

Guy Banister and Special Agent Regis Kennedy of the New Orleans FBI were close friends and it would not be surprising if they shared information on groups like NOCPA.[2997] Jack Martin, a Banister employee, identified Kennedy as a frequent visitor to Banister's office.[2998] Kennedy was reportedly also seen in 1961 in meetings of anti-Castro Cubans.[2999] The HSCA determined there was malfeasance on the part of Kennedy in his FBI investigation of the Carlos Marcello affair, which Banister and David Ferrie were involved in. The HSCA noted that the FBI's "limited work on the Carlos Marcello case may have been attributable to a disturbing attitude on the part of the senior agent who supervised the case, Regis Kennedy."[3000] Kennedy had investigated the 544 Camp Street address on Oswald's pamphlets for the FBI and determined, after talking to Banister, that neither FPCC nor Oswald occupied the office at 544 Camp. Based on Kennedy's report, the Warren Commission had concluded, "Neither the Fair Play for Cuba Committee nor Lee Harvey Oswald ever maintained an office at that address."[3001] According to Jack Martin, Kennedy was protecting Banister.[3002]

Bruce Walzer, an attorney for SCEF, was the chairman of NOCPA and a victim of the collaborative efforts of Senator Eastland's committee, LUAC, the state police, and others in the raid on SCEF offices on October 4, 1963. It's no surprise that SCEF, and Walzer by extension, were being investigated in his role in NOCPA in advance of the SCEF raid. Comprised largely of students and faculty from Tulane University, Dillard University, and the University of New Orleans, NOCPA held some of their meetings at the nearby historically black Dillard University. Both the New Orleans Police Intelligence Division and the FBI investigated NOCPA extensively. Police intelligence shared their investigations with the FBI, which determined that some in NOCPA had past ties to the Communist Party or Communist-front organizations. Much, if not most, of what is contained in the FBI files on NOCPA apparently was derived from New Orleans police reports.

Lieutenant Francis Martello, deputy commander of the Intelligence Division of the New Orleans police in 1962 and 1963, testified before the Warren Commission about the interrogation of Lee Harvey Oswald after his arrest for fighting with Carlos Bringuier on August 9, 1963. Garrison's investigation had determined that Martello was Banister's right-hand man on the Intelligence squad and remained his New Orleans Police contact after Banister left the police department.[3003]

Martello told the Warren Commission that, in the course of his duties in the Intelligence Division, he investigated Tulane professor Dr. Leonard Reissman and said he appeared to be at the center of Communist-front activity in New Orleans and at Tulane, in organizations such as NOCPA and FPCC. Martello noted that Reissman had conducted meetings of NOCPA and led two or three demonstrations in the city. (Oswald may have participated in at least one NOCPA demonstration, as will be presented later.) Martello told the Commission that Dr. Reissman was close to SCEF leaders James Dombrowski, Bruce Walzer, and Benjamin E. Smith—all targets of LUAC, the state and local police, and Eastland's joint raid on SCEF in October of 1963. SCEF's attorneys Walzer and Smith were NOCPA members, which explains why Martello and Oswald (as will be seen) were interested in the organization.

Martello further claimed that Walzer traveled to Mexico City frequently to obtain funds from Castro's government for NOCPA. (It's not known if NOCPA actually received funding from Castro's government. FPCC was in fact, funded by Castro's government.)

Martello claimed that Reissman, like Dombrowski, was active in the integration movement.[3004] FPCC pamphlets were allegedly found on the ground near Reissman's home on Pine Street, according to Martello, prior to the time of Oswald's scuffle with Bringuier. Someone, who was not identified, allegedly told Martello that the FPCC pamphlets had "blown out of Reissman's car." Oswald told Martello, after his arrest for the scuffle, that FPCC held meetings on Pine Street. Martello asked Oswald if the meetings were held at Reissman's, but Oswald refused to answer. Even so, Martello judged by Oswald's expression that there was a possible connection.[3005]

Captain James Arnold was present as an observer at Martello's interview of Oswald and said Oswald did not give a verbal answer but that he also gathered from the expression on his face, and by the words uttered at the time, that Oswald knew (or was acquainted with) Reissman. Arnold noted that Martello attempted to pursue the matter further but Oswald refused to discuss it.[3006] Clearly, Martello was trying to tie Reissman to the leftist organizations, and Oswald, in a roundabout way, appears to have tried to link Reissman to FPCC. If it could have been shown that Oswald had collaborated with Reissman and attended a meeting at his home, then Reissman would have been in big trouble under the Communist Control Act.

The day after his arrest, Oswald furnished FBI Agent John Quigley with a copy of Corliss Lamont's tract called "The Crime Against Cuba," that bore the address 544 Camp Street.[3007] Lamont, at the time of Oswald's arrest, was under investigation by the Senate Permanent Investigations Subcommittee and was identified as one of the "four prides" of the Communist Party based on the testimony of "ex-Communist" Louis Bundez, a prominent figure in the national far right.[3008] Other "basic pamphlets" by Lamont listed on the tract in Oswald's possession were entitled, "To End Nuclear Bomb Tests" and "A Peace Program for the USA"—both of which were clearly in line with the ideology of NOCPA.[3009]

According to Martello, Dr. Reissman's name appeared on the FBI's subversives list.[3010] Martello also claimed James Dombrowski visited another Tulane professor and neighbor of Reissman, Forrest E. LaViolette, who he had heard possessed literature on FPCC.[3011, 3012, 3013] Guy Banister obtained the mailing list for the SCEF publication *Southern Patriot*, which was stamped with "Caddo Parish Sheriff's Dept." from whom Banister apparently received it. Jim Garrison obtained some of Banister's files during his assassination investigation, which included the publication's mailing list, filed as number 50–41. Notables on the list were Benjamin E. Smith, described as an SCEF attorney and member of NOCPA; Dr. F. E. LaViolette of the Tulane History Department; and Reverend Albert D'Orlando. Banister subscribed under the suspect title "Guy Banister Associated Industries" at his 531 Lafayette Street address. The front entrance of Banister's office building bore the address 544 Camp Street, the same address Oswald stamped on some of his leaflets and a Corliss Lamont tract. Jack Ricau, a close associate of both Banister and Leander Perez in the Citizens' Council was also listed as a *Southern Patriot* subscriber.[3014] The files suggest that Banister was actively investigating LaViolette, as were Martello and the Caddo Parish Sheriff's Department, possibly because LaViolette was on the advisory committee to SCEF at the time Dombrowski served as a director, according to SCEF documents.[3015]

In the earliest accounts, Martello was more definitive about an Oswald-Reissman relationship. He told the Secret Service, on November 30, 1963, that he asked Oswald if he was acquainted with Dr. Reissman and "Oswald replied he was." He was asked if meetings of FPCC were held on Pine Street and Oswald replied in the affirmative. Oswald was asked if he knew James A. Dombrowski (Guy Banister's long-time nemesis) and "he avoided the question and never did answer it." Martello pointed out to the Secret Service that Bruce Walzer appeared before Eastland's committee in 1956 as Dombrowski's attorney. (Banister had been involved in the proceedings.) He told them that Dombrowski was allegedly identified by Paul Crouch as the top Communist leader in the South along with Myles Horton of the Highlander Folk School.[3016] The mention of the names of Crouch and Dombrowski showed that Martello was well versed on Eastland's investigations. In fact, Eastland's hearings were the reason the New Orleans Police Intelligence Division was expanded under Guy Banister, which resulted in Martello's subsequent involvement.

Lieutenant Martello worked closely with the Secret Service monitoring racist groups prior to President Kennedy's trip to New Orleans on May 4, 1962. Martello placed Delphine Roberts, Banister's future secretary and love interest, under observation and identified her as head of the Catholic Laymen For Segregation. She was observed picketing with a group on April 30, 1962, with a sign saying, "GET ALL SOCIALISTS OUT OF U.S. GOVT INCLUDING JOHN F. KENNEDY, ADLAI STEVENSON, HALE BOGGS . . . ALBERT GORE . . ." and a host of other names. Another sign read, "IS PRESIDENT KENNEDY PLANNING TO USE N.O. AS THE PLACE FROM WHICH TO ISSUE THE 2ND EMANCIPATION PROCLAMATION, HE PROMISED RACIST AGITATOR MARTIN LUTHER KING WHEN THIS SOCIALIST AGENT VISITED THE 'BLACK' HOUSE?"[3017]

In 1996, the author interviewed Hugh Murray, a leftist student activist at Tulane in the 1960s, and NOCPA was discussed. After the interview, Murray contacted several former members of NOCPA and none recalled that Reissman or LaViolette were involved in the organization.[3018, 3019, 3020] Murray's name had been on the mailing list of *Southern Patriot*, SCEF's newsletter, which had been found in one of Guy Banister's files obtained by Jim Garrison.[3021] Murray told the author that he met Banister one time while he was dating Banister's daughter.[3022, 3023]

Reissman was interviewed by the FBI shortly after the Kennedy assassination and told them he had no connection with Oswald or any leftist organization.[3024] However, according to Oswald's aunt, Lillian Murret, Oswald told her he knew Tulane professor Reissman and had been to his home.[3025, 3026, 3027, 3028] Murret was under the impression that Oswald came into contact with Reissman through Ruth Paine while she visited New Orleans.[3029] Murret told the FBI that either Oswald visited Reissman's home or Reissman visited Oswald's. Murret learned that Reissman's daughter had been to Russia, a fact alone sufficient to raise police suspicions that the Reissmans were Communists and worthy of surveillance by the Intelligence Division.[3030] Richard Steele, the man Oswald paid to hand out FPCC leaflets with him at the time of the Bringuier fray, told the Warren Commission that he got the impression from Oswald that FPCC was connected with Tulane.[3031]

When Marina Oswald departed Ruth Paine's home in Texas for New Orleans, Paine wrote to fellow Quaker and New Orleans resident Ruth Kloepfer, whose name she found in a Quaker directory, and asked her to look in on Marina and her family as a courtesy. Paine was worried that Oswald might be abusing Marina and trying to send her back to the U.S.S.R.[3032] Kloepfer was a member of NOCPA, and visited the Oswalds in August of 1963 to check on them. The significance of the fact that Kloepfer happened to be a member of NOCPA and visited the Oswalds is not known. As a Quaker and a pacifist, the connection may be incidental and entirely unrelated, as will be seen, to Oswald's likely infiltration of NOCPA. Whether or not Oswald actually knew Reissman, he and Lieutenant Martello nonetheless tied Reissman to FPCC—and, in turn, SCEF—through his purported association with James Dombrowski, Bruce Walzer, and Benjamin E. Smith. If Oswald was tied to Reissman, a leftist with alleged associates in SCEF, then it might be inferred that Oswald was tied to SCEF as well.

SCEF was raided on October 4, 1963, and key members of the Banister operation were involved. After the raid, Banister colleagues and Louisiana Un-American Activities leaders James Pfister and Jack N. Rogers announced they confiscated evidence in the raid that proved that SCEF was Communist-affiliated. The leaders of SCEF were arrested under the Communist Control Act based on the alleged raid evidence—which was never disclosed. If Pfister and Rogers had evidence that the arrested SCEF officers collaborated with a Communist, then under the law they faced decades in prison. Later LUAC announced they also planned to investigate FPCC and CORE, as we shall see in Chapter Twenty-two.

Three individuals, William W. Barker, Jr., Vereen Alexander, and Brian Ampolsk, in separate accounts, reported that Lee Harvey Oswald associated with people who, as FBI records indicate, were members of—or attended meetings of—NOCPA, which is revealed for the first time in this work. A fourth witness, a member of the state police, saw a photo of Oswald marching in a parade on Canal Street, no doubt in the NOCPA parade. A fifth source, Carlos Bringuier, insinuated that Oswald knew a member of NOCPA, Donald Savery, and was connected with NOCPA, but Bringuier provided no basis for his statement, as we shall see. Oswald told his aunt, Lillian Murret, and police officer Frances Martello that he was at a meeting at Professor Reissman's home, whom the police connected to both NOCPA and FPCC. Oswald was also allegedly seen among NOCPA members Professor Leonard Krimmerman, Alfred Pecoraro, John D. Bass, and Edwin Clark as will be presented later.

A source told the FBI that NOCPA met at Dillard University on January 10, 1963, and that fifty people attended the meeting. Bylaws for the organization were adopted during the meeting and Benjamin E. Smith addressed the crowd. The FBI noted that Smith was a law partner of Bruce Walzer, an officer in the leftist National Lawyers Guild and a board member of SCEF. They characterized Smith as "a sympathizer of Communist Cuba and Castro." (Smith and Walzer were registered as agents of a foreign government because of their legal work on behalf of the Cuban government.)

Another meeting of NOCPA was held at Dillard University on March 7, at which Bruce Walzer presided and a fifty-mile hike for peace was proposed. More than sixty people attended the March meeting, including notables Stephen Ambrose, Donald F. Savery, Mr. and Mrs. Kloepfer, and Edwin Clark. One person expressed her belief that Castro would save Cuba from its dictatorial past. The FBI noted that, according to a source, the father of one person in attendance, Brain Ampolsk, provided the FBI with a letter that his son had received from the Young Peoples Socialist League (YPSL) that began, "Dear Comrade-To-Be Ampolsk." (It should be noted that Oswald had requested literature from the YPSL in 1956 during the time he was in the Civil Air Patrol under David Ferrie, a fanatical anti-Communist. He wanted to know if there were a branch in the New Orleans area, saying, "I am a Marxist and have been studying Socialist principles for well over fifteen months" in a letter.[3033, 3034]) Brian Ampolsk admitted he met Oswald one or two days before he was arrested for handing out FPCC leaflets. Ampolsk didn't agree with Oswald's pro-Castro position and described him as a member of the "fanatic fringe." He was unimpressed with Oswald, and felt he was not a sincere Marxist."[3035]

On April 17, 1963, NOCPA held a meeting attended by forty people at the Newcombe Art Building Auditorium. Speakers for the event were critical of the Civil Defense program. One speaker expressed pity for Cuba. The members planned to carry signs saying "Human Race Before the Arms Race" and pass out leaflets at the next demonstration. Then, on April 21, 1963, NOCPA members gathered to hold a demonstration in Jackson Square, but rescheduled it when they were told they needed a permit. Notables Ruth Ann Kloepfer, Leonard Krimmerman, Alfred Pecoraro, Benjamin E. Smith, and Bruce Walzer were present according to the FBI. Professor Krimmerman acted as the spokesman for the group prior to the arrival of Chairman Walzer. Fifteen people associated with Kent Courtney were also present. Courtney told the police that if NOCPA demonstrated then his group would counter-demonstrate. Carlos Bringuier was present and got into an argument with NOCPA member Donald Savery, as we will see later. (Like Oswald's token altercation with Bringuier in August 1963, Bringuier's confrontation with Savery may have been contrived for secondary gain.)

On April 22, 1963, NOCPA applied for a permit for a parade to be held on April 28, which would run from Audubon Park, adjacent to the Tulane campus, to Jackson Avenue. The permit was denied for lack of timely filing. The New Orleans Police Intelligence Division advised the FBI that NOCPA again applied for an application from the city to march in a parade on St. Charles Street from Audubon Park on Friday May 3, 1963. (Lee Harvey Oswald had been in New Orleans at the time, just a short while after having departed Dallas by bus on April 24, 1963.) Police showed up on May third, but no one from NOCPA was there. Even so, a "right-wing or conservative group" of people arrived to parade in opposition.

On Sunday May 5, 1963, thirty-six members of NOCPA showed up with picket signs. Bruce Walzer addressed the group and gave them the directions of the parade route. At that point, the police stopped Walzer and asked him for his parade permit. Walzer showed him the parade permit with the May 3 date on it, not at first realizing the permit did not have the proper May 5 date. In a loud voice, he accused the police of tampering with the date. They reached a compromise to allow two members of NOCPA to walk the parade route on the sidewalk. A college professor and a pastor proceeded with the march, and the others disbanded. The names of five members of NOCPA were identified in the FBI report, including Walzer, John D. Bass, Georg Iggers, and Alfred Pecoraro. (As will be seen later, Oswald was reportedly seen at a party with Pecoraro and Bass in the summer of 1963, as well as with Edwin Clark—who was in the subsequent NOCPA parade held on May 20.)

Clark was a member of the Congress for Racial Equality that—as will be shown in the next chapter—Oswald infiltrated in September of 1963. The police identified NOCPA as "an interracial group." Police recognized Banister colleague Festus Brown and Joseph Graffia (an associate of Delphine Roberts) in the group demonstrating against NOCPA as members of the "right-wing or conservative group." (When the FBI observed Roberts picketing against the integration of a Catholic School, Graffia provided the signs for the picketers out of his pickup truck.)[3036]

NOCPA obtained another parade permit from City Hall for May 20, 1963. The parade began on Pine Street (a street just off the Tulane campus) and St. Charles, and was led by Bruce Walzer. The names of the members of NOCPA were identified by the police Intelligence Division who noted: "this is an interracial group, but the persons recognized were all white people." Sixteen were identified by name, address, and occupation. Three were associated with the Congress of Racial Equality, two were identified as members of the Socialist Party USA, and one was identified as "wearing a beard." They held signs reading: "Human Race Before The Arms Race," "World Peace Through The UN," and other slogans.[3037] Leonard Krimmerman, who was associated with the University of New Orleans, and Donald Savery were also present at the march. (In a separate allegation Oswald was reportedly seen with Krimmerman at his university office, which means that at least three individuals from NOCPA were seen with Oswald, as will be discussed later.)

The police also identified members of the right-wing opposition appearing on May 20 and noted that they were affiliated with "Americans on Guard" (AOG). Mary Helen Brengel was the Chairman Pro-Tem of AOG and also served as Guy Banister's Secretary from October to December 14, 1963. Brengel stated that, on the day Banister died (Saturday June 6, 1964), she was waiting for Delphine Roberts and Guy Banister to counter-demonstrate against "the Peaceniks" (no doubt referring to NOCPA). She wrote, "We were going to picket the peace marchers . . . we were all going to meet at Audubon Park." When Roberts and Banister didn't arrive, she called Banister's home and there was no answer.[3038]

The author interviewed Brengel in 1996 before becoming aware of the NOCPA affair. She offered a rare glimpse into the Banister operation. Brengel was a member of the radical right and a lifetime John Birch Society member. She did not care for President Kennedy, but she "did not approve of anyone taking his life." After Jim Garrison compiled evidence made public in 1967 suggesting that Banister was involved with Oswald and the assassination, it was her belief Banister that he was. Brengel related that Banister had been preparing a car for an apparent trip and was not in the office on the day of the assassination. She felt Banister's alleged pistol-whipping of Jack Martin for stealing files was fabricated to attest to his presence in New Orleans on the day of the assassination.

Brengel, initially a writer in Dallas for H. L. Hunt's *Facts Forum News*, left for New Orleans when the publication folded and she subsequently became the assistant editor of Kent and Phoebe Courtney's newspaper, *The Independent American*. When the Courtneys separated on September 23, 1963, Phoebe Courtney took the operation to Colorado and Brengel was out of work. Guy Banister offered her the use of his office while she was looking for work. She was asked to voluntarily do filing work for him, and in exchange, if business picked up, he would pay her if he could. (Brengel felt the main reason Banister brought her in was to assure his wife in their failing marriage that there was no extramarital activity going on at the office with Delphine Roberts, his paramour.) Brengel's job was to clip articles on subversives out of the quasi-Nazi National States' Rights Party newspaper, the *Thunderbolt*, and Gerald L. K. Smith's monthly paper *The Cross and Flag*. The two papers were the largest anti-Semitic and anti-black publications in the country at the time—she considered them trash. Brengel stated there was an air of secrecy in the office and she had no access to the locked files, which were guarded by Roberts. The files, according to Brengel, contained "identification of all known Communists, integrationists and Cuban exiles." They also included "facts and identification of persons involved in the present political picture at this time."[3039]

Brengel further said that she did not recall seeing Lee Harvey Oswald at Banister's office. She said Roberts told her that Oswald had been at the office several times while she was there, but that she did not recall seeing him because he was "just another face in the crowd." (At the time, Banister's detective agency had won a contract to provide security on the waterfront and there were a lot of young men coming to the office applying for jobs and it was one of the few paying contracts that the office handled.) Brengel left on December 14, 1963, with Banister owing her 1,700 dollars.[3040]

Louise Decker, who worked for Banister for a few months in 1961, stated her job also consisted of mostly clipping articles on the "racial problems throughout the country and articles on Communism. Banister was a fanatic on these two subjects."[3041]

Brengel told the author that she knew General Walker and met him several times in New Orleans through the Courtneys, but did not see him at the Banister office. She said Phoebe Courtney was principally responsible for writing the book *The Case of General Edwin A. Walker* in 1961. Brengel volunteered to the author that Billy James Hargis had been at Banister's office in the autumn of 1963.[3042] As we know, Walker and Courtney were close; it will be recalled that Courtney and General Willoughby planned to visit Walker in Germany when his muzzling troubles had just begun in 1961. Moreover, Courtney traveled to Miami to attend the first speech on Walker's Midnight Ride tour that preceded the Walker shooting incident.

Brengel told Garrison investigators that Banister formed a group of former FBI men, including New Orleans FBI Special Agent Regis Kennedy, that applied for the contract to provide security to the Mississippi Test Sight. Banister was the head of the New Orleans retired FBI Association.[3043] Kennedy, as has been noted, was responsible for investigating much of Oswald's activity in New Orleans after the assassination, which is likely the reason the FBI uncovered so little pertinent evidence about Oswald's New Orleans activities.

Banister had a history of protesting for far-right causes prior to his involvement with AOG and the NOCPA affair. An informant for the FBI identified Banister demonstrating with a group outside the Federal Courthouse during the deliberations of the Fifth U.S. Court of Appeals on the admission of James Meredith to the University of Mississippi in 1962. Banister was also with Delphine Roberts when the police threatened to arrest her for protesting on Canal Street.

A *Times–Picayune* story, printed on May 20, 1963, reported that the Americans on Guard planned to picket the NOCPA march. The paper quoted Mary Brengel as saying that the first activity of the newly formed AOG was to counter the projects of NOCPA. She said her group planned to meet at Pine Street and St. Charles. One member of AOG, identified by the FBI as Festus Jerry Brown, was present at both the May 5 and May 20 marches. Joseph Graffia was another individual present at both the May 5 and May 20 marches.[3044, 3045, 3046, 3047, 3048] Kent Courtney was among the AOG counter-demonstrators, as well. A news article on Courtney noted that he was the head of the American Legion Americanism Committee, representing thirty posts. At one time, Courtney objected to a lecturer's appearance at the LSU Law School because Courtney claimed he was associated with several pro-Communist groups.[3049]

Anthony Peres was present at the May 20, 1963, NOCPA march with Kent Courtney, whom the FBI identified as the National Chairman of the Conservative Society of America. Peter J. Cavallo, Jr., a realtor, was present at the march and was a member of AOG. Alfred B. Joy, who was also present, was a John Birch Society member and was known to have a number of signs on his car, including one saying "Outlaw Communism." A member of Young Americans for Freedom was present, as well. The men told the police that their group had taken up positions along the parade route to express their opposition to NOCPA. They held placards captioned "Dis-armament Is Suicide" and "Co-existence Means No Existence."

A source advised the FBI that NOCPA met at St. Augustine High School, which was described as "a school for colored children," on May 27, 1963. Thirty-seven people attended. The source noted that one third of those in attendance were black and one half were white females. Bruce Walzer presided over the meeting and Father Berrigan, described as one of the intellectuals in the liberal branch of the Catholic Church, spoke on the immorality of nuclear armament. Alfred Pecoraro was also present. FBI informant NO 1213-S was ordered to attend the meeting to determine the dates of future demonstrations and the effect of the marches on their membership.

NOCPA next obtained a permit, signed by Bruce Walzer and Benjamin E. Smith, for a parade to take place on Canal Street on June 8, 1963, at 2:00 p.m. This was the only NOCPA parade known to have taken place on Canal Street—which is important, as we will see, because Lee Harvey Oswald was alleged to have been in a Canal Street parade and photographed in the summer of 1963. Seventeen people started the parade down Canal to Ramparts Street, then turned around and walked back on Canal Street and disbanded in front of the Casa Roca clothing store at 107 Decatur Street. Although it was not noted in the FBI memo, Casa Roca was Carlos Bringuier's store (where Oswald showed up one day, supposedly in August, and offered his assistance in training anti-Castro forces).

A number of members of AOG, including Anthony Peres and Joseph Graffia countered the NOCPA pickets. As will be seen later, Kent Courtney photographed the parade. One member of the NOCPA group was identified as "colored." The FBI identified several of the marchers as having extensive past ties to Communist organizations, Communist fronts, the ACLU, and the National Lawyers Guild. Bruce Walzer, Donald Savery, Leonard J. Krimmerman, and Alfred Pecoraro were among the marchers. Another NOCPA member present was Dr. Georg Iggers, who, as noted by the FBI's records, had given a Race Relations Day address at a church in Little Rock, Arkansas, in 1956. He was a member of the NAACP and the ACLU. The FBI, in their report on the NOCPA parades and on NOCPA members Donald Savery and Benjamin E. Smith, included an appendix on SCEF that noted that they had been found to be a Communist or Communist-influenced group by the 1947 HUAC hearings.

The police observed a Cuban, believed to be the owner of the Casa Roca store on Decatur Street, marching twenty feet behind the NOCPA parades with a sign depicting Cuba enchained in the grip of Communism. The police did not identify him by name but he was, of course, Carlos Bringuier, the owner of Casa Roca.[3050] (Bringuier and Donald Savery had engaged in an argument over Castro and Cuba at the April 21, 1963, demonstration by NOCPA at Jackson Square, which will be described later.) It's not clear why the NOCPA parade ended at Casa Roca, just off Canal, but perhaps it was done to antagonize Bringuier for his anti-Castro views.[3051, 3052, 3053, 3054, 3055, 3056] On June 11, 1963, the *States–Item* printed a letter from Kent Courtney with a heading reflecting his views on disarmament, entitled "Warning About Coexistence."[3057]

After the assassination, on November 25, 1963, Carlos Bringuier met with the FBI and told them about his supposed meeting with Oswald at Casa Roca on August 5, 1963. Oswald reportedly returned the next day and left his *Marine Guidebook*, and Bringuier mentioned that young Phillip Geraci had been present. (Geraci was supposedly there to sell him Cuban War Bonds.) Bringuier told the FBI of the August 9, 1963, fistfight with Oswald on Canal Street and their arrests. Surprisingly, he told the FBI that Donald Savery might have been an associate of Oswald because Savery was connected with NOCPA, but he provided no rationale for his claim. Bringuier said he met with Savery at a pro-Castro rally at Jackson

Square, but gratuitously offered that he did not see Oswald. Bringuier added that Bruce Walzer, who had recently been arrested in the October 1963 raid on SCEF, was the organizer for NOCPA.[3058] Bringuier, it appears, was trying to steer the FBI into an investigation of a possible link between Oswald and NOCPA.

In addition to Bringuier's insinuation of an Oswald-NOCPA tie, three other witnesses described seeing Lee Harvey Oswald with members of NOCPA. William W. Barker, Jr., who was employed by the Louisiana National Guard at Lakefront Airport, contacted New Orleans FBI Agent James R. Riordan on November 25, 1963. He told Riordan that, after seeing Oswald's photograph in connection with the assassination, he was fairly certain the he had seen Oswald come out of the office of "Subject KRIMMERMAN." Barker went on to tell the FBI that Krimmerman was a professor of Symbolic Logic at Louisiana State University in New Orleans in May or June, the last spring semester while he was a student there. Barker told the FBI that Krimmerman had frequently invited Barker to meetings or seminars at Tulane University. Barker refused to attend, however, because he had suspected Krimmerman of being anti-American because he always managed to bring Marxist theory into his lectures. Barker told the FBI that Krimmerman also distributed literature he considered "detrimental to the United States," which he would immediately destroy.[3059] Krimmerman, as has been noted, was a member of NOCPA—which was not mentioned in the FBI report of Barker's allegation. The FBI did not apparently crosscheck their files, which noted that Krimmerman was present at most of the NOCPA assemblies. The author found no evidence that the FBI questioned Krimmerman about his alleged association with Oswald. The FBI, in fact, showed no awareness that two other people saw Oswald with members of NOCPA in addition to Bringuier's insinuation that NOCPA member Donald Savery may have known Oswald.

In 1958, Festus Brown, Guy Banister, James Pfister, Kent Courtney, Douglas Caddy, and Medford Evans organized a conference to warn students about the threat of Communism.[3060] Brown, a member of the American Legion, recommended Banister, Guy Johnson, Jack N. Rogers, and George Shultz of the Caddo Parish Sheriff's Office as candidates for the position of Chief Investigator of the Louisiana Un-American Activities Committee in 1960.[3061] Interestingly, Brown spoke with General Walker, John Rarick, and Ned Touchstone at a Fourth of July rally in Baton Rouge in 1965.[3062, 3063]

Jim Garrison interviewed Brown on February 5, 1967, at a time when his investigation of the Kennedy assassination had not yet been made public. Garrison showed no awareness that Brown counter-demonstrated against NOCPA. Brown told him that he had met Banister for the first time when Banister was a speaker at an American Legion luncheon. He also met Banister during the congressional hearings on subversive activities. Brown told Garrison that Banister offered his services to Brown in connection with the American Legion's Americanism and counter-subversive activities. Brown called on Banister for his help to better understand Communism when Banister had offices in the Balter Building. (It will be recalled that Leander Perez and the Citizens' Council had offices above Banister at the Balter Building at the time. Perez's Balter Building address was found in Joseph Milteer's home.) Brown told

Garrison that he had visited Banister at his office on Lafayette Street and it is known that on two occasions Banister spoke to the American Legion on the world Communist conspiracy. Banister also served on the American Legion State Committee on Un-American Activities, which Brown chaired. Brown denied seeing Lee Harvey Oswald at Banister's office and, when asked if he knew any people that were employed by Banister, he told Garrison that he knew that Delphine Roberts and Mary Brengel had worked at the Lafayette Street office.[3064] (Banister's secretary, Mary Brengel, told Garrison that Festus Brown, who went by the name "Jerry," kept a watch on Banister's office and files on the evening of his death.[3065])

Delphine Roberts went to Banister's residence with Ivan Nitschke, Banister's close friend and a former FBI man, after Banister's death. She told Nitschke that she was worried about Banister's files because Banister told her they would "hurt an awful lot of big name people." Banister told her to take possession of the files if "something happens to me."[3066]

Banister's brother, Ross, was interviewed by the D.A.'s office and told the D.A. that Festus Brown "was either a client or investigator for [Banister]. Mr. Brown was closely related to him in some phase of his work."[3067] Festus Brown served as an officer on the New Orleans Indignation Committee, Inc. with Guy Banister and Hubert Badeaux in 1962.[3068]

In March 1963, television station WYES in New Orleans announced plans to televise a series on Communism to feature prominent members of the John Birch Society, including Clifton Ganus, and W. Cleon Skousen, which was to be shown throughout the public school system. The liberals demanded and received airtime to respond. Two members of NOCPA, Stephen Ambrose and Leonard Krimmerman, along with known integrationists from Loyola University, represented the left's view on Communism.[3069] George Singelmann, Leander Perez's aide, Citizens' Council director, and close friend of Guy Banister, was critical of the liberals' presentation on Communism and was sued for $455,000 by professor Leonard Krimmerman and the others involved for libel. They claimed Singelmann stated that they betrayed their teaching professions, were disloyal traitors, and should be investigated by the FBI. It's apparent that NOCPA was an object of Leander Perez's interest in view of the attack of his close aide Singelmann on the two NOCPA members who gave the television speech.[3070]

Vereen Alexander was another witness who saw Lee Harvey Oswald with individuals who were members of NOCPA. At the time, Alexander was a student at Newcombe College, the women's division of Tulane University. Alexander was from a prominent political family—her grandfather was the chief justice of the Louisiana Supreme Court. Alexander published a liberal newspaper called *The Reed*. In the summer of 1963, she met weekly with a group to discuss politics at the University Center. On May 23, 1963, a discussion ensued on the recent attempted assassination of French president Charles de Gaulle. Four individuals in the group had strong Marxist and pro-Cuban feelings.

In the summer of 1963, Alexander attended a party at an apartment near Slogan's bar on Magazine Street in New Orleans, with individuals identified to the FBI as Bass, Al Pecoraro, Ed Clark, Hampton, Patty Hahn, and Ben Hogan. The FBI memo from agent Donald Adams noted, "Miss Alexander had the strong belief that Lee Harvey Oswald was also possibly present at this party. She stated that Pecoraro was a leader or a member of a local Socialist group in New Orleans." Alexander did not mention NOCPA anywhere in her FBI interview.[3071] It is not known whether or not she knew that Bass, Clark, and Pecoraro, whom she identified at the party attended by Oswald, were members of NOCPA and participated in the parades and demonstrations previously mentioned.[3072]

Coincidentally, at the time of the assassination, Alexander had relocated to Thomasville, Georgia, and, on November 24, 1963, reported her sighting of Oswald at the party to regional FBI office Special Agent Donald Adams, at his home. Adams, it will be recalled, investigated Joseph Milteer before and after the assassination and took him into custody on December 27, 1963. When Alexander went to speak to Adams, he and his family were glued to the TV screen watching the ongoing coverage of the Kennedy assassination. His wife, Jeanette, answered the door and, in the course of her conversation with Alexander, let out a scream. Adams jumped up from his seat and rushed to see what was the matter. Adams, at first, thought Alexander was reaching for a weapon. He grabbed her and pushed her up against the wall and gave the purse to his wife, who searched it and found no gun. When things settled down, Alexander said that, earlier in the year, she had been at a meeting on campus in an upstairs lounge around a table with a number of people and was positive Oswald was one of them. She explained that the discussion that night had centered on the attempted assassination of Charles de Gaulle, and that a question was asked at the table about how one would go about assassinating the U.S. president.[3073] After Alexander's meeting with Adams, the New Orleans FBI investigated Alexander's claims further.

After the assassination, the FBI interviewed Professor Robert Reinders and asked him about Hogan, whom Vereen Alexander had said was at the party Oswald allegedly attended.[3074] The FBI had previously identified Reinders as the executive secretary of NOCPA.[3075] The author interviewed Reinders, who stated that he was a member of NOCPA and participated in the marches. He said he was also a member of the ACLU. Reinders said that the thing that struck him most when he first learned about Oswald was that no one on the left in the close-knit liberal community of New Orleans knew him.[3076]

The FBI interviewed Alfred Pecoraro on November 27, 1963. He told them that the last meeting of NOCPA was in June 1963 and recounted that he was the publicity chairman for NOCPA and that he was a member of a Socialist study group that met regularly throughout the city. He told them he was acquainted with William Clark, John Bass, Bill Hogan, Robert Hoffman, and David Hoffman. He denied ever seeing Oswald.[3077] The FBI interviewed David Hoffman and he also denied ever seeing or knowing Oswald.[3078] They interviewed Patty Hahn on December 2, 1963, and she told them that during the latter part of April or first week in May of 1963, while she was enrolled at Tulane, she attended at social gathering at David Hoffman's home at 10 Roberts Street, and she was certain that no one named Lee Harvey Oswald attended. She said there were no more than twenty-five to thirty people at the party and she knew them all either by name or sight.[3079]

Lieutenant John R. Knight of the Louisiana State Police prepared a forty-one-page report on Lee Harvey Oswald's activities for the Warren Commission, revealing another sighting of Oswald in an unidentified Canal Street parade—most likely the June 8, 1963, NOCPA demonstration. Knight's completed investigation was presented to State Police Superintendent Thomas Burbank and Governor Jimmie Davis in the form of a booklet. It was believed Burbank personally took it to Washington for the Warren Commission. (Burbank, as we shall see, was an associate of Guy Banister.) Andrew Sciambra, who was an assistant New Orleans district attorney, and an investigator for Jim Garrison's assassination probe in 1969, questioned Lieutenant Knight about the booklet, and noted that Knight seemed very truthful. Knight told him he had not made any copies of the report, nor did Major John R. Thomas make or have any copies. Thomas, who had worked for the Sovereignty Commission that Guy Banister was associated with, told Knight that he had simply handed the report over to Superintendent Burbank. Sciambra asked Knight to look over the report and to tell him what was missing. Knight noted that the information about Oswald's educational background was present and had also been published in the Warren Commission. He told them that what the report was missing were "many photographs of LEE HARVEY OSWALD at different stages of his residency down here." For example, Knight said he had a photograph of Oswald *marching down Canal Street with a group of people*, which was included in the booklet. He also said he had several pictures of Oswald in front of the International Trade Mart, and also some taken when he was arrested on Canal Street. Knight said he had gotten these pictures from the editor of the photography department at the *Times–Picayune* and that many of the pictures had never appeared in the newspaper or on television. He said that the omitted pictures had made up about half the original report. Lieutenant Knight promised to check with Major Thomas to see if he had a copy of the report (which, as we know, he did not).[3080] The booklet, as appears in Volume XXII of the Warren Commission, contained only thirty-four pages, not the original forty-one, and the only pictures of Oswald included in it were his arrest mug shot after the Bringuier fight and a school photo.[3081] There were no pictures in the Warren Commission report of Oswald in the Canal Street parade or leafleting at the International Trade Mart.[3082]

The HSCA interviewed State Police Major Ray Thomas in 1978. The HSCA were unaware that he had helped prepare the booklet sent to the Warren Commission—or that they were missing the photos of Oswald in the Canal Street parade. Thomas told them he was assigned to the Louisiana State Sovereignty Commission in 1960–61. He said his duties were to check out people who might cause violence during the period of integration in the state, as well as subversive elements, and this was the reason that the Sovereignty Commission obtained Guy Banister's files after his death. Thomas said he was later ordered to burn Banister's files, as well as other files that were not a part of any criminal investigation. He said he did not know what happened to the Sovereignty Commission files but that he believed they were destroyed.

State police officer Major Russell Willie told the HSCA, in 1978, that they purchased about five file cabinets, which were about half full of manila folders and three-by-five cards, in 1964 or 1965 from Mary Banister, for five hundred dollars. Willie told the HSCA that the state police cooperated with the Sovereignty Commission and Senator Eastland's committee. He noted that Banister had files on SCEF, a group that had been formerly affiliated with the Communist Party, reflecting his obvious knowledge of the findings of the Eastland committee.[3083] The HSCA also interviewed Major Joseph Cambre of the state police, who had been assigned to the Sovereignty Commission, and who obtained Banister's files with Major Willie. Cambre had also participated in the October 1963 raid on SCEF. He noted that Banister kept extensive files on SCEF, and that he also had a file on FPCC and a transcript of Oswald's radio debate. Willie recalled that FPCC had an address on Camp Street and said he was surprised to learn that 544 Camp Street was the same address of the building that Guy Banister had his office in.[3084]

Banister's brother, Ross, told the HSCA, in 1978, that he had hired Major Willie to work for him as an investigator after he retired from the state police.[3085] Ross Banister stated that Guy told him he had seen Oswald handing out FPCC literature. Ross offered the theory that Oswald used the 544 Camp Street address on his pamphlets in an attempt to embarrass his brother.[3086] Jim Garrison's office had interviewed Ross Banister on February 1, 1967, before his assassination investigation became public. (At the time, Garrison's assassination investigations of Oswald were disguised in his files as the "Smith Investigation," to keep it secret.) Ross Banister told investigators that Colonel Burbank of the state police might have some material, which his brother Guy was working on. As has been noted, the photos of Oswald in the Canal Street Parade went missing while they were in Burbank's hands on the way to the Warren Commission and the reason is now obvious: if Burbank had allowed the photo of Oswald in the NOCPA parade to go to the Warren Commission, further investigation might have revealed Oswald was working for Guy Banister's operation, which had ties to the state police. Ross Banister said that around September 12, 1964, Major Willie talked to him about getting Guy Banister's files. Garrison's investigator felt that Ross Banister was "rather hesitant and skeptical about revealing everything that he may [have known] or [had] access to."[3087]

In the author's review of an extensive collection of New Orleans district attorney memos from Garrison's assassination investigation—including those obtained from Garrison's son, Lyon—there was no indication that Garrison knew anything about the NOCPA parade on Canal Street that took place in 1963. The author's careful review of the New Orleans newspapers in 1963 found no other Canal Street parades, with the exception of Mardi Gras. The Warren Commission and the HSCA showed no insight into the SCEF and NOCPA affairs, or into the Banister operation, Sovereignty Commission, Eastland committee, LUAC, and the South's war on integration. Lieutenant Knight's report suggests that Oswald was in the NOCPA parade and that either Superintendent Thomas Burbank or Major John Thomas, both Banister associates, deliberately destroyed the photos. It is clear that Guy and Ross Banister had a cozy relationship with Colonel Burbank and the state police, which could explain why the photos of Oswald were purged from Lieutenant Knight's report before it reached the Warren Commission. The state police were working alongside the Banister operation in the war against integration, as was demonstrated by their collaboration with the Eastland committee, LUAC, and the notorious racists in the hardcore underground who encouraged them. There is no evidence that members of Louisiana state and local law enforcement had anything to do with the Kennedy assassination. However, it is likely that some of them knew Oswald was not who he was made out to be. That alone makes them accessories, which provides them with the incentive to conceal Oswald's involvement with the Banister operation after the assassination.

The realization that there are missing photographs raises a question as to why anyone would want to conceal photos showing Oswald in NOCPA, especially if they would just further confirm that Oswald was a leftist, as he publicly proclaimed—and as he wanted to be seen. The answer is, unlike Oswald's other public displays of his Communist persona, every NOCPA demonstration had counter-demonstrators from the Banister operation present—and was duly noted in the FBI reports, newspapers, and photographs. Banister's friend Kent Courtney and his secretary, Mary Helen Brengel, and others on the far right were a big part of the NOCPA story, so suspicions of collusion might have been cast upon them if Oswald's participation in NOCPA had been investigated. As we will see, members of Americans on Guard (AOG) appear in three of the thirteen existing photos of the Audubon Park NOCPA parade, yet the Warren Commission, the HSCA, and Jim Garrison each failed to investigate the NOCPA affair. As was the case in the other instances, Oswald's public posturing as a leftist during the NOCPA incident was independent of, and bore no direct relationship to, the Kennedy assassination. However, his false portrayal of a leftist, in this and other instances, made him an ideal patsy for the Walker forces to frame for the assassination.

After the assassination, the New Orleans police interviewed Sam Newman, the owner of the building at 544 Camp Street, the address that appeared on Oswald's leaflets that he handed out on the day of his August 9, 1963, arrest. Newman told the police that he knew nothing about Oswald or FPCC. Newman told them he had leased the office to the Cuban Revolutionary Council (CRC) fifteen months prior to the assassination and, after five months, had put them out for failure to pay the rent. Newman added, "Guy Banister was well acquainted with this organization," although the report failed to note that Guy Banister's office was on the ground floor of 544 Camp Street.[3088]

After the assassination the Secret Service investigated the 544 Camp Street address. They interviewed Cuban Arnesto Rodriquez, who told them that the CRC, headed by Sergio Arcacha Smith, occupied room six on the second floor of 544 Camp Street. The Secret Service interviewed Manuel Gil, who told them that he had been a member of the CRC and confirmed that they occupied the office at 544 Camp Street in 1961 and 1962. Gil gratuitously offered that Corliss Lamont, the author of Oswald's booklet "The Crime Against Cuba," which was stamped with the 544 Camp Street address, was a notorious Communist. Gil told the Secret Service that, at the time of the December 12, 1963, interview, Gil was working for Ed Butler of INCA.[3089] (Butler, as was noted in Chapter Nine, was a friend of Banister and a constant visitor to his office.) Suspiciously, Gil arranged the debate between Oswald and Bringuier.[3090]

In another interview building owner Sam Newman said Banister talked him into renting the office at 544 Camp Street to Cubans Sergio Arcacha Smith and Carlos Quiroga for the last three months in 1961, but they never paid rent and after they were kicked out of the offices they hung around Banister's office.[3091] He said Banister was very close to the Cubans from the 544 Camp Street office and that he saw them with Banister every time he visited Banister's office. Newman also said he saw Ferrie at both the 544 Camp Street office and at Banister's office downstairs.[3092] Banister's jilted widow, Mary Banister, said she saw FPCC pamphlets in Banister's office when she went there after his death.[3093] Ivan Nitschke recalled that one time, in Banister's office, he saw placards with slogans on them. He could not recall what they said, but stated, "It didn't make sense to him how Guy got tied up to those signs." (He didn't understand what a far right winger was doing with left-wing FPCC or NOCPA placards.)[3094] The FPCC pamphlets and the placards at Banister's office building suggest further that Banister was behind Oswald's FPCC and NOCPA sagas.

Bringuier's friend, Carlos Quiroga, whom Banister talked into renting space at 544 Camp Street, played Oswald's game, as well. On August 16, 1963, Quiroga brought Bringuier one of the leaflets Oswald had been passing out. Bringuier suggested he go to Oswald's house posing as someone who was pro-Castro and check him out, or so he claimed. Quiroga did, and Oswald gave him an application for his FPCC chapter.[3095] Quiroga later failed a lie detector test given by Garrison and, during his Grand Jury testimony for the Clay Shaw trial, pled the Fifth Amendment when asked if he knew that Oswald was not a real Communist and that the FPCC activity was a cover. When asked if he had knowledge of a conspiracy in the assassination of President Kennedy, he again took the Fifth.[3096] Garrison interviewed Quiroga extensively during his investigation and repeatedly asked Quiroga, "Would you be surprised if I told you that Oswald was not a Communist at all?" Garrison revealed that Oswald was seen in the presence of Sergio Arcacha Smith, whom Banister talked Sam Newman into renting space to at 544 Camp Street in the summer of 1963, and who had visited the training camp across Lake Pontchartrain.[3097]

As a part of his assassination investigation, Jim Garrison questioned Carlos Bringuier on February 14, 1967, just before his investigation was revealed to the press on February 17. According to Bringuier, Garrison told him that he knew that "conservative New Orleanians" had brought Oswald to New Orleans. This departs from Garrison's dubious public claims that the CIA directed Oswald and instead reveals what he privately believed. The author discovered a tape recording of a meeting between Bringuier and Kent Courtney, following Garrison's interrogation of Bringuier, in Courtney's papers in the Northwestern Louisiana University archives. On the tape, Bringuier told Courtney that Garrison told him Oswald was working for a "well-known conservative," who was not named. To that, Courtney responded, "Oh yeah, anyone I know?" Bringuier did not name the individual, but he was likely referring to Guy Banister, whom Garrison was extensively investigating at the time. (Garrison showed little or no interest in other New Orleans conservatives, including Leander Perez, Kent Courtney, and Ed Butler.) Additionally, Bringuier mentioned his arrest after the scuffle with Oswald and noted he had gone to Courtney for advice on getting an attorney. Courtney had provided him with the name of an attorney, but the author, due to the sound quality of the tape recording, could not discern it.[3098]

In response to Garrison's questioning him about the "conservative New Orleanians," an indignant Carlos Bringuier wrote a memorandum to Garrison on February 20, 1967, entitled, "Possible Reason Why Lee Harvey Oswald Contacted me on August 5th, 1963 [at Casa Roca]." Bringuier implied in the memorandum that Garrison ought to be investigating leftists in New Orleans and not conservatives. Bringuier stated that Oswald could have received orders from Castro's government through FPCC to infiltrate anti-Castro organizations like his. The second reason he surmised Oswald contacted him at Casa Roca had to do with NOCPA. Bringuier wrote in his memorandum that, on a Sunday in the spring of 1963, he had gone to Jackson Square for the NOCPA demonstration. (Bringuier did not furnish a date of the Jackson Square demonstration but, as noted previously, it was on April 21, 1963.) Bringuier met Donald Savery whom he noted was a Quaker and a pacifist with NOCPA. He claimed he gained Savery's sympathy by claiming he was pro-Castro and was invited by Savery for coffee at Café Du Monde. Bringuier claimed Savery told him that the Communists would take over the United States by revolution because 75 percent of the American people have a robot mentality. Bringuier stated further in his memo that, some weeks later, NOCPA held a march on Canal Street, a half block from where he worked. (This is the same parade that Lieutenant Knight said Oswald was seen and photographed in.) Bringuier noted he joined the marchers, but with an anti-Communist placard. Bringuier noted that Bruce Walzer and Donald Savery were there. (As has been noted, the Canal Street parade that went to Ramparts Street and back down Canal Street ending up at Bringuier's store near Decatur and Canal was on June 8, 1963. Sixteen members of NOCPA were in it.) Savery told Bringuier that he would not have bought him coffee if he had known that Bringuier was an anti-Communist. Bringuier wrote, "This means that members of the New Orleans Council for Peaceful Alternatives knew that I was an anti-Castro Cuban and even they knew where I was working, all of this just *a few weeks* before Oswald came to my place of business asking if this was the office of the Cuban exile headquarters." Bringuier noted in the memo that Ruth Kloepfer, like Savery, was a Quaker and had visited Oswald's home. Bringuier cited Lt. Martello's testimony to the Warren Commission stating that he believed Leonard Reissman was tied to FPCC and NOCPA. At the end of his memorandum, Bringuier recommended that Garrison interview Donald Savery and Bruce Walzer, noting they were members of SCEF, as well as Dr. Reissman, Dr. LaViolette, and Ruth Kloepfer.[3099]

Two striking observations emerge from Bringuier's memorandum. The first is his admission that he misrepresented himself as a pro-Castro Cuban to NOCPA's Donald Savery, just the opposite of what he actually was. By his actions, Bringuier, as a member of the far right, was in essence infiltrating—or at least ingratiating himself with—a leftist member of NOCPA. We now have an instance where Bringuier was acting just like Lee Harvey Oswald, when Oswald allegedly misrepresented himself as anti-Castro at Bringuier's store. Bringuier was playing Oswald's game. Bringuier's known ties to Guy Banister, as well as to Kent Court-ney (who was with Bringuier at the NOCPA parade) suggest that he, like Oswald, was playing the game under their direction.

The second point that stands out in the memorandum is Bringuier's two-part state-ment: "This means that members of the New Orleans Council for Peaceful Alternatives knew that I was an anti-Castro Cuban and even they knew where I was working, all of this just *a few weeks* before Oswald came to my place of business asking if this was the office of the Cuban exile headquarters." Bringuier's timing of events appears way off. Breaking the sentence down, he states that it became known to NOCPA's Donald Savery that Bringuier was anti-Castro sometime between the April 21 Jackson Square demonstration and the June 8, 1963, Canal Street Parade, or therefore, sometime possibly in May. The second part of Bringuier's state-ment indicates that Oswald came to his store a few weeks *after* the periods of April 21 to June 8—after the point in time that Savery knew Bringuier was anti-Castro. By this account, Bringuier placed the alleged visit by Oswald nowhere near August 5, the officially recognized date of Oswald's visit, but rather to around May.

As was discussed in Chapter Nine, there is further reason to suspect that Bringuier was lying about the August date of Oswald's appearance. Philip Geraci was a witness to the Oswald-Bringuier meeting and his account may reconcile the conflict in dates. Geraci, a teen-ager, was present when Oswald entered Casa Roca and was sure it happened in May and not on August 5 as Bringuier claimed, because, at the time, he was selling illegal fifty-cent Cuban War Bonds for Bringuier that had a dated receipt for May. Geraci revealed the May date of the meeting to Garrison investigator Harold Weisberg. Bringuier admitted that Geraci was at his store with the Cuban War Bonds. Bringuier stated in his book *Red Friday* that Oswald pulled a few dollars out to purchase the War Bonds and contribute to the anti-Cuban cause. Bringuier wrote that he told Oswald that Geraci could not sell him the Cuban War Bonds because the city had stopped him since he had no permit.[3100]

Harold Weisberg wrote about the conflict in dates of the Oswald visit given by Gera-ci and Bringuier, but did so cryptically without giving names in his book *Never Again*. Weis-berg provided the names to the author, however, and they have been inserted into Weisberg's text in brackets, as follows: "Garrison could have nailed the Warren Commission witness [Bringuier] who was important in pinning the phony 'red' label on Oswald. Garrison ignored the airtight, documented case I gave him [Geraci's May Cuban War Bond receipt]. He could have exposed the related kidnapping of a Warren Commission witness [Geraci] by another Warren Commission witness [New Orleans Police Vice Squad officer Fred S. Sullivan], who was in one police force, assisted by a member of another police force [Jefferson Parish police officer Sargeant Bourne]."

Weisberg stated that on the day David Ferrie died (February 22, 1967), Geraci was kidnapped and taken into hiding outside of Garrison's jurisdiction by the two aforemen-tioned police officers who testified before the Warren Commission. Weisberg took a taped admission he obtained from Geraci (in front of his attorney) about the kidnapping by the two police officers to Garrison. According to Geraci, the officers questioned him for two weeks but Geraci never understood what it was they were trying to get from him. Weisberg stated that Geraci had ignored three of Garrison's grand jury subpoenas. Weisberg added that Geraci and Vance Blalock were members of the Civil Air Patrol. Asked why he did not reveal any names in his books, he told the author that he did so to protect the fact that then-young Phillip Geraci was a homosexual. Weisberg's priorities in protecting Geraci's reputation over establishing the truth in the assassination are perplexing.[3101, 3102, 3103, 3104]

Ordinarily, Weisberg's accusations of a law enforcement cover-up of the facts regarding the Oswald and Bringuier store meeting would invite skepticism. However, the Oswald-Bringuier theatrics were related to a far larger, critically important operation of the Banister and Southern intelligence apparatus which had been set up to preserve the institution of segregation, as we shall see, related to the Communist Control Act, created by three close Banister colleagues. The apparatus involved Senator Eastland's committee, LUAC, the Banister operation, and members of the New Orleans Police and state police who all assisted the various investigations and conducted the raid on SCEF on October 4, 1963. All those groups had a lot to lose if it was revealed that the phony scheme involving Oswald and Bringuier was tied to Banister's operation. It would not be surprising if some in law enforcement knew that Oswald's and Bringuier's performances were for the cause of segregation and the radical right—unrelated to the Kennedy assassination—and had a vested interest in seeing that the whole affair never came to light. The state police assigned to work with the Sovereignty Commission who obtained Banister's files after his death, along with members of the hardcore underground, destroyed the files, according to the HSCA interviews of the officers.[3105] Both Banister and the state police were investigating integrationists.

Bruce Walzer, Benjamin E. Smith (who had ties to NOCPA) and James Dombrowski (who headed SCEF) were going to be the first to be prosecuted under the Communist Control Act after the October 4, 1963, raid on SCEF. Any evidence uncovered that demonstrated that they had a relationship with a Communist like Lee Harvey Oswald would have placed them in grave danger. If convicted under the Act, they faced ten to thirty years in prison and fines of ten to thirty thousand dollars. Most of Banister's files, obtained by the Louisiana Sovereignty Commission along with all the Sovereignty Commission files and the files of Louisiana Un-American Activities Committee (which Banister worked for) mysteriously disappeared from the state's holdings at some unknown time.

The mental lapse on Bringuier's part in his memorandum that placed the Oswald visit to around May adds credence to Geraci's claim that Oswald came to Casa Roca in May and that Bringuier was lying about the August 5 date. Bringuier may have moved the date of Oswald's visit to August 5 to place it close to the August 9 scuffle. That allowed Bringuier to claim that Oswald's purported August 5 visit to his store, during which he misrepresented himself as pro-Castro, was the spark for the fight four days later. Bringuier's portrayal of Oswald's foil was as false and as ridden with inconsistencies as Oswald's portrayal of a Communist.

In his FBI interview on November 25, 1963, Bringuier told them how Oswald entered his French Quarter clothing store and offered to assist him in anti-Castro Cuban matters. In the course of his interviews, the FBI noted he gratuitously told them, "Another individual that might be an associate of Oswald because he is connected with the New Orleans Committee for Peaceful Alternatives is Donald Savery, who lives on Alta Street in Metairie. He stated he met this individual when pro-Castros were having a rally in Jackson Square, but he did not see Oswald at this rally."

The FBI Files indicate that the New Orleans police already were aware that Savery lived at 1033 Alta Street. No one asked Bringuier if Oswald was at the NOCPA rally. No assassination investigative body, including the Warren Commission, the Garrison investigation, or the HSCA investigated NOCPA, much less ever considered that Oswald was a part of it. Nonetheless, Bringuier was trying his best to link Oswald to NOCPA, without coming out and saying that he knew Oswald was involved in NOCPA, or—as the evidence presented shows—that Oswald had infiltrated NOCPA. Bringuier may have been expecting the FBI to connect Oswald to NOCPA after the assassination and was paving the way for it.

Bringuier further told the FBI, "Bruce Walzer, New Orleans attorney, who was recently arrested by the local police in connection with a raid on the Southern Conference Educational Fund, was the New Orleans organizer for the Committee for Peaceful Alternatives."[3106] Bringuier was so eager to link Savery to NOCPA—and to Oswald—that he went through the trouble of finding out where Savery lived and relayed the address to the FBI. As a final touch, he linked NOCPA to SCEF through Bruce Walzer. It was just another ploy to link NOCPA, like FPCC and SCEF, to the supposed-Communist Oswald as a useful way to bring down NOCPA at future hearings by Eastland's committee, HUAC, or LUAC, and prosecuting their leaders under the Communist Control Act. At the time of the Kennedy assassination, Walzer was already under indictment under the Act, although the evidence against him has never been revealed. (The case of Walzer, Smith, and Dombrowski was taken up to the Supreme Court, as we shall see in Chapter Twenty-two, and the Communist Control Act was ruled unconstitutional.)

Oswald and Bringuier were two actors or agents provocateurs, playing good guy/bad guy roles in a theatrical production directed by the leaders of the New Orleans hardcore underground and the Guy Banister operation. The theatrics, unfolded in three acts, were the NOCPA parade, the Oswald-Bringuier "fight," and the WDSU radio "debate." Oswald played the role of the bad-guy Communist. Bringuier portrayed the good-guy anti-Communist. While it's unlikely that Bringuier had anything to do with the assassination, he certainly knew Oswald was not who he claimed to be, which alone makes him an accessory to the murder.

Ernesto Rodriquez, Jr. was another anti-Castro Cuban who showed an interest in NOCPA. Rodriquez was an FBI informer on Cuban matters. The FBI asked him if he knew anything about NOCPA, according to a February 2, 1963, FBI memo. Rodriquez told them he did not know about NOCPA, but offered to attend a meeting. Rodriquez, a member of

Crusade to Free Cuba, which had its office is 544 Camp Street in 1962, knew Guy Banister. He claimed that Oswald approached him in 1963 and inquired about taking Spanish classes at his St. Charles Street language school, as was noted in Chapter One.[3107] Investigators for Jim Garrison, for reasons unknown, asked Rodriquez if he knew Benjamin Smith or Bruce Walzer. Rodriquez told them that he knew Walzer because his wife had worked for Walzer. Rodriquez's wife would have been a highly prized asset if she worked for Walzer to spy on SCEF for Banister. They also asked him if he knew of any connection between Walzer, Smith, and FPCC.[3108]

A Pattern Analysis of Four Incidents with Carlos Bringuier

Carlos Bringuier was involved in four incidents from 1963 that demonstrate an unmistakable pattern that is worth reviewing. The first was Bringuier's April 21 altercation with Donald Savery. The second was the June 8 NOCPA parade that Bringuier and Courtney counter-demonstrated at. The third was Bringuier's August 9 scuffle with Lee Harvey Oswald while Oswald was handing out leaflets. The fourth was Oswald's debate with Bringuier and Ed Butler on August 21.

Table 1.

Date	April 21, 1963	June 8, 1963	August 9, 1963	August 21, 1963
Event	Oswald-Bringuier-Savery at Café du Monde	NOCPA Canal Street Parade	Oswald-Bringuier Fight	Oswald-Bringuier WDSU Radio Debate
Oswald involved?	No	Yes	Yes	Yes
Bringuier involved?	Yes	Yes	Yes	Yes
Courtney or Butler involved?	Courtney	Courtney	Courtney	Butler

Guy Banister's secretary-to-be, Mary Helen Brengel, headed up Americans on Guard, which was formally organized to counteract NOCPA. Close associates of Banister, Kent Courtney, and Festus Brown were publicly identified with AOG and were present at the counter-demonstrations against NOCPA. Courtney was also present at the April 21 NOCPA parade when Bringuier had coffee with Donald Savery and again at the June 8 NOCPA Canal Street parade. Courtney came into the picture again in relation to the Bringuier-Oswald fight. (As has been presented, Bringuier came to Courtney for advice on legal representation after the scuffle with Oswald and the related arrest.) Oswald's FPCC pamphlets and the booklets that he passed out during the day of the third incident, the Bringuier-Oswald scuffle, bore the 544 Camp Street address for the first—and only—time. As was noted in Chapter One, a U.S. Border Patrol agent saw Lee Harvey Oswald and David Ferrie coming and going repeatedly from the entrance of Guy Banister's office in the same building.

More evidence of Bringuier's collaboration with the Banister operation was the fourth incident (his third with Oswald), the August 21 radio debate with Oswald and Ed Butler. As was noted in Chapter Nine, Ed Butler was a constant fixture at Banister's office, a former member of the John Birch Society, and was felt to be potentially dangerous. New Orleans police investigated the address of 544 Camp Street found on Oswald's leaflets after his fray with Bringuier. Although they failed to note that Guy Banister's office was on the ground floor at that address, they did find that 544 Camp Street was once the address of the Cuban Revolutionary Council. Manuel Gil worked out of the 544 Camp Street office and, at the time of the Kennedy assassination, he was working for Ed Butler. In other words, through Courtney and Butler, the Banister operation was tied to all four of Bringuier's public demonstrations.

Kent Courtney is owed a debt of gratitude for his peculiar habit of tape recording his conversations and leaving them to posterity, which was first discovered by the author. Courtney left tape recordings from a 1958 phone conversation with Robert Welch, where they alluded to the founding of the John Birch Society, in his personal papers. The intimate call attests to Courtney's high-ranking place in the national far right. In another taped conversation, from 1967, between Courtney and Bringuier (which occurred after Jim Garrison interrogated Bringuier), it was revealed that Bringuier came to Courtney for advice on legal counsel after his scuffle with Oswald.

Even as remarkable, Courtney tape recorded a meeting with Jerry Ray, the brother of James Earl Ray, who was convicted for the 1968 murder of Martin Luther King, Jr. The taping was done while the two were walking in Lafayette Square. Jerry Ray explained to Courtney that a rich, unidentified industrialist in New Orleans employed James Earl Ray between August 1967 and March 1968, before King's assassination. Jerry Ray brought up the fact that Courtney had exposed King's Communist background on Labor Day in 1967. A nervous Courtney kept asking Ray what he wanted from him. Ray told him he wanted to know if Courtney knew a good lawyer in Nashville to represent his brother.[3109] It's not clear what the meeting between Ray and Courtney was about, but it may be that Ray believed that Courtney knew the identity of the wealthy industrialist from New Orleans who allegedly employed James Earl Ray prior to the murder of King. (It's worth noting that Willie Somersett was told in advance that both Kennedy and King were going to be murdered and reported it to law enforcement. It would not be surprising if the same hardcore underground elements were involved in both cases.)

After the Kennedy assassination, Bringuier fancied himself as one of Lee Harvey Oswald's victims, as did General Walker, and Bringuier joined the core conspirators on a speaking tour. On February 10–14, 1964, Bringuier was a featured speaker at the Third Annual Christian Crusade Anti-Communist Leadership School with General Walker, Kent Courtney, Myers Lowman, Kenneth Ryker, and Fernando Penabaz.[3110] (Bringuier also went on a speaking tour with Billy James Hargis to eighteen cities in May 1964, all but four in Texas.[3111, 3112])

The *Councilor* NOCPA Photos

The openly racist newsletter of the Louisiana Citizens' Council, the *Councilor*, on July 23, 1963, featured photos taken by members of Americans on Guard of a NOCPA parade at

Audubon Park. The photos were discovered by the author and are presented here for the first time. The photos were captioned, "Let's take a look at the New Orleans Committee for Peaceful Alternatives," and "Pictures taken by Americans on Guard, a patriotic organization." The paper noted that NOCPA members were campaigning for liberal causes "including race-mixing and disarmament." The paper added: "These pictures show a number of faces already familiar to Conservatives," indicating that the "Conservatives" had placed NOCPA members under surveillance in connection with other liberal activities.

Ned Touchstone, a friend of General Walker, was the editor of the *Councilor*. Walker was in flight, heading for Touchstone's home in Shreveport, when the Kennedy assassination occurred. Citizens' Council records in Touchstone's papers note that the state board of directors of the Citizens' Council included, at various times, Leander Perez, Kent Courtney, and George Singelmann—all of whom were close associates of Guy Banister.

Thirteen photos of the NOCPA demonstration at Audubon Park were featured on the front page of the *Councilor*. More than forty people were pictured, including two individuals from AOG who were taking pictures of the demonstrators and appeared in three of the photographs. There was at least one African American mingling with the NOCPA demonstrators, which was taboo in the South in 1963.

Lee Harvey Oswald, shown in the top two photographs passing out FPCC leaflets, would have fit seamlessly into the NOCPA demonstration at Audubon Park shown in the bottom three photographs that appeared in the *Councilor*. The individual in the left lower photo bears a resemblance to Lee Harvey Oswald. Source: Top two photos are from the Warren Commission; bottom three photos are from the Special Collections, Louisiana Tech University

The author sent a copy of the *Councilor* carrying the above photos to Hugh Murray, a leftist activist at Tulane who was nearly expelled in 1960 for participating in New Orleans's first lunch counter sit-in at Woolworth's on Canal Street and was also a friend of some of the members of NOCPA. He was able to identify Al Pecoraro, Ed Clark, a CORE activist, Ruth Ann Kloepfer, and Georg and Wilma Iggers in the *Councilor* photos (all of whom had been identified by the FBI as members of NOCPA). He identified Connie Bradford—of Newcombe College—whom he knew as a Congress of Racial Equality member, in the photo.[3113,3114] Ruth Ann Kloepfer, daughter of Ruth Elizabeth Kloepfer, recalled to Murray that she was one of the NOCPA members who led the march that in front of Tulane University. She recounted that the counter-demonstrators repeatedly snapped pictures of them, apparently to rattle them—so many, in fact, that she thought the cameras might have been empty. However, neither Ruth Ann Kloepfer nor her parents were involved in the Canal Street march.[3115, 3116]

Murray's friend Clark Rowley told Murray that he was paid by Kent Courtney to spy on the New Orleans left in 1963.[3117] The author interviewed Rowley who stated that he had been interested in journalism while at Tulane but they had discontinued their journalism school. In the summer of 1963, he shopped around, looking for a summer job related to journalism, and was offered a job doing research for Kent Courtney. Rowley was apolitical, but recalled researching Pearl Harbor and copying the Republican Party's platform at the library for Courtney. Courtney showed Rowley the pictures he had taken of the NOCPA parade and asked Rowley to identify the participants. Rowley obliged and wrote their names on the pictures. Courtney told Rowley that the peace signs the demonstrators were carrying represented broken crosses, and were symbols of the anti-Christ and Communism.[3118]

Murray set out years later to determine if the allegation made by Lieutenant Martello to the Warren Commission that Professor Reissman was in NOCPA was true. He contacted another Tulane professor from the time, Robert Reinders, who told Murray he did not believe Reissman was involved in NOCPA. Murray interviewed Dr. Reissman's wife, and she incidentally told him that her husband, although liberal, did not know James Dombrowski.[3119]

During the author's interview with Professor Reinders, who attended an Audubon Park NOCPA march, Reinders recalled one instance, while he was working part time at the New Orleans Public Library, when Guy Banister came in looking for a picture of Congressman Hale Boggs with a clenched fist.[3120] The author later discovered that the *Councilor* showed pictures of Lee Harvey Oswald, Nikita Khrushchev, Hubert Humphrey, and Hale Boggs each displaying clenched fists, which the *Councilor* called the "Communist salute." The far right despised the relatively liberal Boggs and saw him as soft on Communism. The *Councilor* noted that Revilo Oliver furnished the Warren Commission with the picture of Boggs giving the "Communist salute" while he was s student at Tulane. The picture was reportedly placed in the permanent record during his testimony to the Warren Commission—on a day when Boggs was absent from the proceedings.[3121] Perhaps Banister furnished the Boggs photo he had obtained from the library to Oliver and the *Councilor*.

Kent Courtney wrote a letter to JBS leader Robert Welch on December 30, 1963, and told Welch that he had a photo from the *States–Item* from November 23, 1963, showing Oswald giving "a rather unusual salute." Courtney said it was "a hand sign of the members of he Soviet army when they wish to indicate that the mission has been accomplished." He sent copies of the letter to Robert Morris, General Walker, and Dan Smoot.[3122]

The weight of evidence strongly suggests that Lee Harvey Oswald infiltrated NOCPA. Three witnesses claim they saw Oswald with NOCPA members. In addition, Carlos Bringuier did his best to tie Oswald to NOCPA because he likely knew Oswald had infiltrated the group and that fact would eventually become public. Lieutenant Knight of the Louisiana State Police saw photos of Oswald in what most certainly was the NOCPA Canal Street parade. The photos were destroyed before they were sent in a booklet to the Warren Commission, likely by someone in the state police who was connected to the Guy Banister operation. Kent Courtney's association with both NOCPA and Bringuier was a liability to Courtney and the Banister operation after the assassination. Linking Oswald to NOCPA after the murder would not have been desirable, since it might have brought Courtney into the picture. (It will be recalled from Chapter Two that Marguerite Oswald accused Kent Courtney of having a working relationship with her son and told Courtney in a phone call. The allegation that Oswald was seen on numerous occasions with Courtney in the summer of 1963 was also presented in Chapter Two.)

Guy Banister and the Infiltration of the Campus Left

Communists were few and far between in Louisiana and the Deep South. The college campuses in Louisiana, on the other hand, had a ready supply of leftists, fellow travelers, Communist fronters, and integrationists to occupy the attention of Senator Eastland's Committee, the Louisiana Un-American Activities Committee, the Sovereignty Commissions, and the American Legion Un-American Activities Committee. Guy Banister collaborated with all those groups, which were part of a "Southern intelligence apparatus" that existed to preserve the sacred Southern institution of segregation. A substantial part of the Banister operation involved surveillance of the campus left. Sergeant Hubert Badeaux, while heading up the Intelligence Division under Police Assistant Superintendent Guy Banister wrote Willie Rainach in 1957 and told him he was grooming an individual to infiltrate the universities. That individual fit the description of Oswald who publicly emerged as a Communist in New Orleans in the summer of 1963.

On July 30, 1958, Guy Banister wrote to Senator F. E. Cole, who headed up the state special committee to investigate the colleges and universities, which was known as the Cole Committee. The Cole Committee was charged with investigating un-American activities and/or affiliations with Communist-front organization at Louisiana State University and other schools in the state. Banister appeared before the committee and offered his services as an investigator "at a very cheap price." Cole told Banister that he had no money to offer him a job. Banister wrote his friend Willie Rainach and told him about the Cole Committee's inability to pay an investigator. Rainach sympathized, telling him, "I am all too familiar with the frustration you feel in fighting a battle against Communism with one, or both, hands tied by financial and political restrictions."[3123]

In 1958, Banister, Kent Courtney, James Pfister, Douglas Caddy, and Medford Evans spoke at a seminar to alert college students to the dangers of attending the Communist-sponsored World Youth Festival.[3124]

In 1959, the South Louisiana Citizens' Council sent Guy Banister his membership card with an accompanying letter, which is more evidence of an intelligence apparatus that was principally interested in investigating integration. Hubert Badeaux was the first vice president of the council. Jackson Ricau, another Banister associate, was the executive director. A folder was included with the membership card that reportedly contained, "conclusive proof that racial integration is a part of the Communist conspiracy." Noting that the council's intelligence apparatus was at work, the letter stated, "We are conducting a searching and determined investigation of the disastrous desegregation of City Park. We are laying the groundwork for definite action to be taken." The newsletter noted that the council had obtained five hundred signatures protesting "the burial of a Negro in St. Patrick Cemetery."[3125] As was noted in Chapter One, Banister collaborated with Ricau in writing the Citizens' Council newsletter, and the subject matter was often derived from his files.

Contrary to claims by Jim Garrison and some assassination writers, the evidence is overwhelming that Guy Banister's files and life's work in his intelligence operation were for the cause of segregation and anti-Communism, two causes which are often viewed as synonymous. Some of Banister's investigative files survived and were obtained by Garrison. In a "Memorandum for the File" written by Banister, he noted that, on December 15, 1961, he received a telephone call from Edward Hunter of Arlington, Virginia, who told him he had been in New Orleans checking up on propaganda coming into the United States from Communist sources and wanted Banister's help. (Hunter was a prominent figure in the national radical right, which was not noted by Garrison in the memo.)

Hunter told Banister that he was intensely interested in learning what kind of literature a student, walking around in the college libraries, would pick up and read. Hunter was working on a book and he wanted to conduct an experiment and get a brief description of the kind of pamphlet or booklet a student would pick up, and when. He wanted to know about "the activities of a typical student and particularly a thumbnail sketch, very short, of the particular booklet." Hunter told Banister he had been at the Customs Office making inquires about Communist literature. He told Banister that the Customs Office employed a former White Russian who had fought in the Russian White Army during the Bolshevik revolution and was employed to translate the Communist literature coming through the office. Banister noted in his memorandum on Hunter, that, because of an order by President Kennedy, the translator was left sitting around doing nothing. Banister likened the event to Kennedy's muzzling of the military.

Jim Garrison wrote in the margin of the Banister memorandum, with a line drawn to Hunter's name, "Probably an agent," which was in line with Garrison's contrived theory that Banister and Oswald were involved with government intelligence. However, Garrison had no evidence that Hunter was an agent.

Hunter, for his part, was a well-known national figure in the radical right, and testified before HUAC on March 13, 1958, on "Communist Psychological War (Brain Washing)." During the Korean conflict, the North Korean Communists paraded captured U.S. soldiers before cameras where they renounced their loyalty to the United States. Hunter had first coined the term "brainwashing" to describe the technique used by the North Koreans on the prisoners. He testified before HUAC and told them, "The Communist inquisitors in the POW camps depended first of all on a screening process to provide them with the men most likely to succumb to brainwashing. They picked the ones they figured would be most useful to them . . . . They have based their technique primarily on the complete abandonment of morality." HUAC counsel Richard Arens, who in 1954 was counsel for Senator Eastland's committee investigating SCEF, performed the questioning of Hunter.[3126, 3127]

In response to Hunter's inquiry, Banister wrote to Tulane student Haywood H. Hillyer, III, of New Orleans, on October 26, 1962, in a "Personal and Confidential" letter and told him that Hunter wanted him to conduct surveillance on students at the Tulane library. He told Hillyer that Hunter was "interested in ascertaining an opinion as to the use made of foreign propaganda coming into the country from Communist sources. It is recalled that a considerable amount of this propaganda has been placed on tables in the library used by students of Tulane University. He is intensely interested in what a student walking around the library would pick up and read." Banister asked Hillyer to write a brief description of the pamphlet or booklet picked up by each student and the date the contact was made. He told Hillyer to maintain surveillance over the pro-Communist propaganda in the library and determine the number of students who studied it, the extent they studied it, and, if possible, to identify the students and their majors. Banister told him that Hunter planned to write a story about it in the *Liberator*.[3128]

There is evidence that Lee Harvey Oswald placed his FPCC pamphlets in the Tulane library. Harold Alderman, a Tulane graduate student, was given one of Oswald's FPCC pamphlets by his friend Hugh Murray, who recalled it had been handed out, possibly at the Tulane library. Alderman kept the pamphlet and reported it to the FBI after the assassination. The pamphlet bore the name "A. J. Hidell" and Oswald's post office box.[3129]

Edward Hunter's place among the national radical right wing and those implicated as accessories to the Kennedy assassination has been described throughout this work and will be recapped here. From January 29 to February 2, 1962, the Christian Crusade's National Anti-Communist Leadership School met in Tulsa. General Walker delivered a special message to the group and the event's other speakers included Edward Hunter, General Willoughby, Revilo Oliver, Myers Lohman, and Matt Cvetic, who had impersonated a Communist for the FBI. Benjamin Gitlow and Barb Hartle, "former Communists," who testified against alleged Communists in the House and Senate Communist inquisitions, were guest speakers.[3130]

On March 20, 1962, Billy James Hargis held a "secretive meeting" by invitation only in Washington, D.C., which had first been suggested by Hargis on September 5, 1961.[3131] Edward Hunter, John Rousselot, Bonner Fellers, Benjamin Gitlow, General Charles Willoughby, Frank McGehee, and Arthur Blazey attended.[3132] Rousselot organized the League of Right Wing Organizations at the meeting.[3133] Hargis refused to disclose to the press any of the names in the secret fraternity at the meeting, but their identities were eventually discovered. Among their aims were outlawing the Communist Party and ending the army practice of "muzzling."[3134] Edward Hunter was one more national figure on the far right whom Guy Banister knew and worked with—a group that also included nationally recognized far-right stalwarts Kent Courtney, Billy James Hargis, General Walker, Medford Evans, and H. L. Hunt.

Banister's December 21, 1961, "Memorandum for file" demonstrated that Banister was well acquainted with Hunter, three months before the sinister "secretive meeting" prompted by the rising discontent with the Kennedy administration. As was noted previously,

Edward Hunter stated in a speech at the "secretive meeting" that CBS and Mike Newberry both contended that anti-Communist military generals were secretly plotting a revolution. (The correspondence between General Walker and General Pedro del Valle from 1962, noted in Chapter Eight, demonstrated that their allegations were substantiated.) Furthermore, it was noted by Hunter that General Walker had retired to lead the revolution and set up a Fascist dictatorship.[3135] After the assassination, Hunter, like others on the far right, blamed the president for his own death, stating: "President Kennedy was deluded by the line that Communism is not a menace here in America. He paid for this illusion with his life."[3136]

Hunter was a friend of Walker. He inscribed a copy of his book *Brain-washing in Red China: the Calculated Destruction of Men's Minds* to Walker on January 27, 1962, during Walker's muzzling travails. Hunter wrote in the inscription, "To Gen. Edward A. Walker, — See p. 317 for your case—before it happened!" During the Korean conflict, American prisoners of war collaborated with the Communists. In response, the U.S. Armed Forces developed a code of conduct for POWs to resist Communist indoctrination in captivity. Hunter claimed the code was shelved by sinister elements in the government. He wrote in his book that the code to "restore American stamina and to teach our forces to understand the wiles of Communism had been sabotaged." On page 317 of his book, he claimed that efforts by members of the military to teach the dangers of Communism had been brazenly suppressed.[3137]

Hunter wrote an article in the November 1964 *Citizen*, the monthly magazine of the Citizens' Council of America. In the article, Hunter argued that Goldwater's defeat by Lyndon Johnson in the presidential election—which was attributed to sabotage by murky elements among the opposition—had a silver lining: it galvanized grassroots anti-Communists.[3138]

Banister employed another student, George Higganbotham, as an investigator from 1960 to 1961 and provided him with false credentials and a cover for infiltrating Communist groups under the code name "Dale." Higganbotham told Garrison investigators that, for some time, Banister and Kent Courtney worked together closely. Higganbotham stated, "He was kidding Banister about sharing a building with people passing out leaflets on the street, a reference to Oswald and another young man he paid to join him, and Banister said, 'Cool it . . . one of them is one of mine.'" Higganbotham suggested to Jim Garrison that he follow up on the possibility of a connection between Minuteman Rich Lauchli and Banister, because he had heard a rumor that the FBI caught Lauchli selling arms to Latin America. At the time of the interview, Higganbotham had been arraigned for marijuana possession and was represented by George Wray Gill, Jr. (whose business card was found in the home of Joseph Milteer, as was noted in Chapter Nine).[3139] It will be recalled from Chapter Nineteen that Raymond Broshears named Rich Lauchli, who was a high-ranking member of the Minutemen, as a conspirator in the murder of the president.

Tommy Baumler worked for Louis P. Davis, a close New Orleans friend of General Walker who came to Walker's aid during the Ole Miss crisis. Baumler was interviewed by Jim Garrison's office and he told the investigators that Banister had used him for many years to penetrate "liberal elements on college campuses and elsewhere in order to determine where the Communists were." Garrison's office concluded that Baumler and Higganbotham "appeared to have been undercover agents for Banister on campus."[3140]

On January 5, 1959, Guy Banister wrote to his friend Guy Johnson in a "Personal and Confidential Letter" about an informant he was recruiting, Wilfred A. Bergeron, Jr., who was attending Tulane University. Banister wrote: "We have discussed the advisability as well as the feasibility of establishing certain channels of information and it's possible that the above named individual will qualify." Banister noted that Bergeron was married and had served in the air force with an atomic clearance. He told Johnson that after he had verified Bergeron's reliability, he would set him up to work for him and pass along any information he produced to Johnson. At the time, Johnson was working for the law firm of Racivitch, Johnson, Wegmann and Mouledoux. (William Wegmann replaced Guy Johnson as counsel for Clay Shaw during his indictment as a co-conspirator in the Kennedy assassination.)[3141]

Another example of Banister utilizing young men to obtain intelligence on integrationists is the case of Allen Campbell. Banister file number 10–58, dated August 27, 1959, noted that Allen Campbell, a young former marine who worked for Banister, had surreptitiously entered James Dombrowski's SCEF office on Perdido Street.[3142] Campbell told the author that he observed Oswald at Banister's office in the summer of 1963. He explained to the author that he worked for Banister because he wanted to learn about Communism.[3143]

Banister spied on Tulane students who were involved in the civil rights movement and the historic lunch counter sit-ins on Canal Street using a "Confidential Informant." On November 23, 1960, Guy Banister wrote a "Memorandum for file, By: Guy Banister; Re: Annette Horsch, Subversive activities" as follows:

> On November 7, 1960 Confidential Informant T-01, who has furnished reliable information in the past, advised that the above named subject is a student at Tulane University probably Newcombe College, and that she was involved in the sit-in demonstration in New Orleans, and it is believed that she has been arrested for this. She received a letter from her mother in Houston advising that her father, because of her activities may lose his job. Her mother directs her not to write anymore.
>
> Informant advised that she was in tears in the cafeteria and it is believed her picture appeared in the newspapers.
>
> As a result by the pressure put upon her family, she is sending a through letter to the Congress of Racial Equality resigning from that organization. However, she will not resign, but will be the editor of their local newspaper the first issue of which is due out on November 7, 1960.[3144]

On February 2, 1961, Cuban exile Sergio Arcacha Smith told the FBI that he gave Banister the names of members of the Friends of Democratic Cuba, Inc., and a list of Cubans attending Louisiana State University in Baton Rouge so that Banister could check out the backgrounds of the members.[3145]

William Boxley, an investigator for Jim Garrison, recalled he saw a Banister file relating to a library employee at Loyola University in New Orleans, who had been hired by Banister to ascertain the identity of students checking out pro-Communist books.[3146]

Banister also hired William B. Martin, a law student at Tulane, to determine the political sympathies of Cuban and other foreign students at Tulane and to see if any pro-Castro students infiltrated the Friends of Democratic Cuba.[3147]

Michael Kurtz was a student at the University of New Orleans in 1963. He later became a professor of history at Southeastern Louisiana State University. Kurtz wrote about two visits Lee Harvey Oswald made, with Banister, to the University of New Orleans in which they engaged students "on heated discussions of federal racial policies." During the discussions, Oswald attacked the Kennedy administration's civil rights policies. Kurtz reported that Oswald and David Ferrie frequented the Napoleon House in the French Quarter, a popular college hangout in 1963. There, they debated Kennedy's foreign policies with students. Kurtz reported that Oswald and Ferrie were also seen in Baton Rouge where they openly denounced Kennedy's policies. Kurtz discovered another witness who saw Oswald with Ferrie and numerous Cubans dressed in military clothing engaging in military maneuvers while carrying automatic weapons. Kurtz noted that Oswald met with a prominent leader of the Citizens' Council, who was not named in writing (although he confided in a letter to the author that the individual was Kent Courtney). Kurtz concluded that "Oswald's public image as a pro-Castro Marxist was a facade masking the anti-Castro and anti-Communist agitator beneath."[3148] Kurtz wrote to Congressman Louis Stokes in 1978 during the HSCA deliberations on the assassination, and told him about the people he had interviewed who knew Oswald. Kurtz told Stokes that he had evidence that cast doubt on Oswald's claim he was a Marxist, and offered his service to the HSCA.[3149] Kurtz appeared before the Assassination Records Review Board (ARRB) in 1996 and repeated his account and told the board that he personally had seen Oswald with Guy Banister on two occasions discussing Kennedy's civil rights policies. Kurtz recommended that the ARRB pursue FBI files on Leander Perez and the Citizens' Council, but provided no basis for the recommendation.[3150] (As has been shown in this book, Kurtz's suspicions about Perez were well founded.) Kurtz's accounts, little known or appreciated among students of the assassination, comports completely with the objective findings reported throughout this work. Unfortunately, neither the HSCA nor the ARRB gave Kurtz's allegations any significant consideration. Hardly any of the foregoing accounts of Banister's intelligence operation against leftist and integrationists on campus have been reported before this work.

Conclusions

Jerry Brooks, the Minuteman radical, exposed the Banister operation when he complained to the FBI that Guy Banister insisted that he join the Communist Party, then call the New York office and subscribe to their literature. Lee Harvey Oswald also contacted the Communist Party and subscribed to their literature. Numerous witnesses saw Oswald with Banister, a fanatical anti-Communist. Banister was undoubtedly in the business of manufacturing false Communists.

The evidence presented strongly suggests that Oswald infiltrated the New Orleans Committee for Peaceful Alternatives, which had ties to SCEF and the integration movement, for the Banister operation. There were two witness reports of Oswald with two different people identified by the FBI as NOCPA members or having attended a NOCPA meeting. Another witness saw Oswald at a party with several NOCPA members. Yet another, Lieutenant Knight of the state police, saw a photo of Oswald marching in a Canal Street parade—most certainly the NOCPA parade. The photos disappeared in the hands of Banister associates, before they reached the Warren Commission. Kent Courtney, Banister's close associate, counter-demonstrated against the NOCPA parade with Carlos Bringuier, who later played the part of Oswald's foil in the August 9 "fight" and the subsequent radio "debate." Mary Brengel headed up Americans on Guard, a group that Guy Banister belonged to, with Kent Courtney, for the purpose of protesting against NOCPA. In September and October of 1963, Brengel worked as Guy Banister's secretary.

The NOCPA incident varied significantly from the other incidents Bringuier and Oswald participated in. Unlike the others, the NOCPA affair directly involved members of the Banister and Courtney operation and they were publicly identified in photos, newspapers, police, and FBI documents demonstrating against NOCPA. If the Warren Commission had linked the Banister operation, Courtney, and Bringuier to NOCPA—as well as Oswald—it may have raised suspicions of collusion. The open presence of members of Banister's operation, in conjunction with NOCPA demonstrators, explains why the photos of Oswald in the Canal Street NOCPA parade vanished from the report delivered by the state police to the Warren Commission. Oswald's infiltration of NOCPA had nothing to do with the assassination. If it had, the Banister operation likely would have been more careful.

The NOCPA affair provided significant revelations about Carlos Bringuier. Bringuier did his best to tie Oswald to NOCPA and SCEF after the assassination, although his efforts against a campus "ban the bomb" group were a little off target for an anti-Castro crusader. The Banister operation primarily opposed NOCPA because it was also an integrationist group tied to SCEF and CORE, as well as FPCC. (SCEF and integration was distinctly an American and Southern problem, which should have been of no particular interest to an anti-Castro Cuban.) Bringuier's repeated protests against NOCPA and SCEF suggest a direct link to the Banister-Courtney operation. Moreover, the four incidents Bringuier engaged in during the summer of 1963 were orchestrated by the Banister operation. Courtney's presence with Bringuier during the NOCPA counter-demonstration and Bringuier's visit to Courtney, seeking advice on legal counsel after the Oswald scuffle, strongly suggest Courtney was directing Bringuier as a false adversary to Oswald. In the same manner, Courtney and Banister were directing Oswald as a false Communist. The Banister operation was behind the scenes in the fourth incident, the Oswald-Bringuier radio debate, as well. Not revealed prior to this work it has now been shown that Ed Butler, who was a part of the debate, was a close associate of Guy Banister. A pattern analysis of the four incidents with which Bringuier was involved during the summer of 1963 clearly reveals that he, like Oswald, was an actor and agent of the Guy Banister operation.

Investigating and infiltrating leftists on campus was not an aberration for Banister. Rather, it appears to have been a primary objective of his investigative apparatus. Numerous examples of Banister hiring college students to spy on campus were presented. After Banister's participation in the 1956 Eastland hearings—not coincidentally the year Oswald began to behave as a Communist—his Intelligence Division chief, Hubert Badeaux, began to groom an individual to infiltrate the universities. Evidence was presented earlier that favored the conclusion that the individual was likely Lee Harvey Oswald. In 1963, Oswald emerged as an infiltrator on the campuses of the University of New Orleans and Tulane for the Banister .operation.

The most popular assassination conspiracy theories maintain that the CIA, anti-Castro Cubans, or the mafia were involved in the assassination. It would be difficult to conceive of a plausible reason for Oswald's consorting with the campus peaceniks in the context of a CIA, anti-Castro Cuban, or mafia assassination plot. Banister developed student spies to gather intelligence on integrationist and leftist groups in his roles with the Eastland committee, the Sovereignty Commission, and the Louisiana Un-American Activities Committee. Those agencies, with the state and local police, raided SCEF headquarters on October 4, 1963, and arrested the leaders under the Communist Control Act that had been enacted by key Banister associates. Those arrested SCEF leaders were also connected to NOCPA and CORE. Under the law, they faced decades in prison. The goal was to put the integration movement out of business, as we shall see in the next chapters.

CHAPTER TWENTY-ONE

LEE HARVEY OSWALD AND THE CONGRESS OF RACIAL EQUALITY

The CORE organization has been infiltrated by left wingers through-
out the history of its existence . . . and at least one individual who is a
member of a Communist-front organization is working with CORE
in East Feliciana Parish.

– R. G. Van Buskirk

Lee Harvey Oswald traveled to the small town of Clinton, Louisiana, in East Feliciana Parish, in late August or early September 1963, during a time of explosive racial tensions. He was observed by a large number of townspeople as he stood in a line of black residents attempting to register to vote in a drive organized by the Congress of Racial Equality (CORE). Others, including the parish's voter registrar, described having direct contact with Oswald.

Many Louisianans and the hardcore underground saw CORE, a leading civil rights group, like the New Orleans Committee for Peaceful Alternatives, Fair Play for Cuba Committee and the other leftist organizations that Oswald managed to align himself with, as a pro-integration, Communist-front group. Senator James Eastland cited all of the groups as subversive. Eastland published his investigation of CORE, as he had done with FPCC, in the *Congressional Record*, in an article entitled "Activities of CORE, 'Freedom Riders' in the Southern States" in 1961. Eastland stated that CORE had "followed the pattern set by Communist agitators the world over."[3151] Eastland called one CORE rider in 1961 Mississippi "a Communist agitator and organizer of the most dangerous kind."[3152] As will be seen in this chapter, which relies on a completely separate pool of evidence than the other chapters, Oswald's involvement with the CORE black voter registration drive was another event contrived by the hardcore segregationists in the Louisiana underground to paint CORE as Red-infiltrated.

The directors—and many of the cast of false witnesses—in the Clinton theatrical production were embittered segregationists and Klansmen tied to Guy Banister, Leander Perez, or General Walker. The Warren Commission did not know about or investigate Oswald's visit to Clinton. The incident came to light in New Orleans district attorney Jim Garrison's

1967 investigation. Garrison, as well as the HSCA in 1978, failed to recognize that Oswald's presence there was part of a pattern of behavior. Oswald associated with leftist groups as a part of the segregationist and radical right-wing strategy to prove that those groups were Communist-influenced, in effect trying to undermine them.

Oswald in Clinton, an Overview

Clinton, Louisiana, located 130 miles north of New Orleans—about a three-hour drive—is the seat of East Feliciana Parish. The rich alluvial soils of the Mississippi River basin made Clinton a thriving agricultural city early on. Wealthy cotton planters once supported Clinton as a center for culture and learning and left a number of historic structures behind, including the magnificent antebellum Clinton courthouse—one of the best examples of Greek revival architect in the South—which played a part in the Clinton incident. The courthouse is near the center of the small town, which is comprised of a city block of business establishments on both sides of the main street. The voter registrar's office was situated near the middle of the block in the Kline building.

In its heyday, Clinton was one of the legal centers of the South.[3153] Hollywood took note of Clinton's southern charm and chose it as the site to shoot a number of movies including 1958's acclaimed *The Long Hot Summer*, which was adapted from a novel by Mississippi native and Nobel Prize winner William Faulkner. Clinton, Louisiana, was one of the jewels of the Deep South in 1963—in many ways like Oxford, Mississippi. However, like the integration of Ole Miss at Oxford, many saw the public demonstrations in Clinton by African Americans in their quest for equality as a stain on the fabric of this quaint bastion of white supremacy.

While in Clinton, Oswald made a public spectacle of himself standing in the voter registration line and mixing with the town African Americans, an act which was forbidden in the segregated South—much like the spectacle of his FPCC demonstrations on the streets of New Orleans with the Cubans. Seemingly all of Clinton took note of the performance. It would not be surprising if the segregationist planners behind Oswald's actions photographed his presence in the CORE registration and, perhaps, at a CORE meeting house to later present as evidence of CORE's association with a known Communist. (Recall the intensive photographing of the NOCPA demonstrations by Kent Courtney and company, as was noted in the last chapter.)

If Oswald had done all the things that the eyewitnesses claimed he did (falsely as we shall see), it would have required a three-day visit to Clinton. The few hotels in the area in 1963 were located in Baton Rouge, about a thirty-minute drive away. More likely than Oswald making a six-hour round-trip drive to and from New Orleans each day, he probably spent the night in the area. On or around the time of Oswald's sojourn to Clinton, Leander Perez, Guy Banister, General Walker, and two Clinton principals in the Oswald-in-Clinton saga, John Rarick and Richard Van Buskirk, were attending the Free Electors meeting at the Capitol House Hotel in Baton Rouge on Tuesday, September 4, 1963. (As was noted in

Chapter Fifteen, General Walker had settled into the state of Louisiana at that time and made a number of appearances from September 4 through September 16, 1963.)[3154]

Lee Harvey Oswald, David Ferrie, and Clay Shaw in Clinton

Multiple witnesses identified Lee Harvey Oswald arriving in Clinton in a black Cadillac driven by someone identified as Clay Shaw, accompanied by David Ferrie. While much of the Clinton story was fabricated by the white Clinton witnesses associated with the Banister, Walker, and Perez operation, as will be seen, the actual identification of Ferrie, and possibly Shaw, with Oswald was likely factual and not a fabrication. The fact that several credible black witnesses, in addition to some whites, identified the three men as being there together suggests that they in fact were. The black witnesses were the bitter enemies of the white Clinton plotters behind Oswald's visit, and would not have schemed with them to place Oswald in Clinton with Ferrie and Shaw if those men had not really been there. While some have questioned whether or not Shaw was one of the men described by witnesses, there is little doubt that Ferrie, Oswald's former Civil Air Patrol captain, was with him. Ferrie's freakish appearance, with painted-on eyebrows and a self-fashioned, glued-on wig, made him unforgettable. Guy Banister and Clay Shaw, however, were both gray-haired men of somewhat similar appearance and age, which means that Banister, rather than Shaw, may have been the other man who accompanied Oswald to Clinton. (It will be recalled from Chapter One that an agent of the Border Patrol saw Oswald and Ferrie coming and going from Banister's office on multiple occasions.)

Jim Garrison sent investigators to Clinton in 1967 and reportedly found nothing fishy about the incident. He concluded, as did the HSCA later, that Oswald was in Clinton for the sole purpose of finding a job at a nearby state mental hospital. They were not concerned with the fact that Clinton was a long way from New Orleans where there were far more job opportunities. The white Clinton witnesses concocted the job story to cover for Oswald's attempted infiltration of CORE, as will be shown. Garrison's sole purpose in obtaining the Clinton witnesses' testimony linking Oswald to Ferrie and Shaw was to use it as key evidence in his far-fetched case against Shaw for conspiring with Oswald and Ferrie to murder President Kennedy. The Clinton witnesses' testimony corroborated Perry Russo's dubious testimony that he, Russo, was present at a meeting with Shaw, Ferrie and Oswald where the assassination was discussed (which was noted in Chapter Nine). The Clinton witnesses and Russo's testimony were the substantial elements of "proof" which Garrison offered in his failed prosecution of Shaw for conspiracy in the murder of President Kennedy. Investigator Bill Boxley warned Garrison that the jury might not find the white Clinton witnesses credible—if they knew the witnesses were all members of the local Ku Klux Klan—when they linked Shaw to Oswald. Garrison had them testify anyway.[3155]

The jury in the Shaw case found the Clinton witnesses (false witnesses as we shall see) credible, as did the HSCA later. They never found out about their Klan connections and other suspicious ties.

The White Clinton Witnesses and the Concocted Cover Story

No one connected with either Oswald's appearance in Clinton or the assassination had anything to gain by having his visit there be publicized, and that is the likely reason the Warren Commission never learned about the incident. Had the FBI closely investigated the Clinton incident in 1963, and discovered that Oswald had been participating in a segregationist plot, it may have caused an unraveling of the entire assassination story. While Oswald's connections to numerous leftist or Communist organizations had the appearance of legitimacy, his presence in Clinton—so far from his home, standing among blacks in a CORE voter registration line (an instance of racial mixing that was taboo in the Deep South)—was more problematic for the plotters to explain.

When the story of his visit to Clinton finally got out years later, a clever, plausible story to explain Oswald's appearance in Clinton was contrived by the three Klan witnesses and others involved. As their story—which has become history's accepted innocent story—goes, Lee Harvey Oswald showed up one late afternoon or early evening at the barbershop of Edwin Lea McGehee in adjacent Jackson, Louisiana, in late August or early September 1963. He reportedly told the barber he was at the shop to get information as to how to get a job at a nearby state mental institute, the largest employer in the area. McGehee recommended that he see State Representative Reeves Morgan for help that evening and sent Oswald to Morgan's home. Allegedly, when Oswald arrived at Morgan's home they talked about what it would take for him to get a job at the state mental hospital. As the story goes, Morgan told him that preferences for a job would go to residents of the area and registered voters. Taking a cue from the state representative, the next day Oswald proceeded to Clinton to register to vote. Voter registrar Henry Earl Palmer then, allegedly, told Oswald in his office that since he didn't live in the area he could not register. (Most people would have known that.) Palmer then purportedly told Oswald that he did not need to be registered to apply for the mental facility job. The town marshal, John Manchester, came forward and stated that he, too, had seen Oswald and his companions at the voter registrar's office. Oswald, the next day, supposedly traveled to the state mental facility in nearby Jackson and applied for a job, which would have meant spending a third day in the area. (It might be interesting to note that a later search for Oswald's supposed job application was not fruitful.)

Incredibly, missing from Jim Garrison's publicized investigative findings of the Clinton incident, as well as those of the HSCA investigation ten years later, is the fact that all four of these "witnesses" (the barber, the state representative, the registrar, and the marshal) were members of the particularly violent local Ku Klux Klan. Moreover, the two leaders of the Klan, attorneys John Rarick and Richard Van Buskirk, were associates of Leander Perez, who has been tied repeatedly to the assassination in this work. Rarick held the title of Exalted Cyclops (Klavern leader) at some time, and registrar Palmer held the same position in 1964. Remarkably, two of the Klansmen, registrar Palmer and attorney Van Buskirk, were associates of Guy Banister. Finally—and importantly—two of the Klansmen associated with the four who crafted the Oswald-in-Clinton alibi, Van Buskirk and Rarick, were associates of General Walker.

The Clinton Klan Witnesses, the FBI, Free Electors and the CORE Injunction

Three of the four Clinton Klan witnesses had demonstrated their antipathy toward African Americans and CORE workers before Oswald arrived on the scene. Registrar Henry Earl Palmer had a record as a perennially bad actor in his war against black voters that went back years. The FBI knew before Oswald's arrival in Clinton that two of the white Clinton witnesses were racial troublemakers. The author discovered—although it was apparently unknown to Garrison or the HSCA—that both registrar Palmer and State Representative Morgan, had been investigated by the FBI on complaints that they had deprived black residents of their civil rights for their participation in recent CORE activities prior to Oswald's arrival. During Oswald's visit, a third white witness, town marshal Manchester, tried to run a black pedestrian off the road. He then arrested him, according to CORE archives, for obstructing the highway.

An important backstory in the events surrounding Oswald's visit to Clinton, was Leander Perez's concurrent, ongoing struggle to pass a modified Free Electors bill, which he had created, in the state legislature. The bill, as mentioned previously in Chapter Ten, was aimed at depriving President Kennedy of Louisiana's electoral votes in a legal effort to oust him from office by 1964.[3156] The legislation for the Free Electors bill pending in the state legislature at the time of Oswald's visit was co-written by Perez, Clinton judge John Rarick, and Clinton attorney Richard Van Buskirk. At about the same time that Oswald was in Clinton, Van Buskirk was present in the company of Guy Banister and General Walker at the nearby Capitol House Hotel in Baton Rouge at a Free Electors fundraiser (attended by Perez) on September 4, 1963.

Rarick, it is important to know, was a protégé of Perez and, in 1962, served with him on the state board of directors of the Louisiana Citizens' Council with notable Guy Banister colleague George Singelmann and state Klan leader Jack Helm. General Walker's friend Ned Touchstone served on the board with Rarick and Perez. At one time, the State Citizens' Council of Louisiana board included Banister colleagues Kent Courtney and Anthony Graffia, as well, who it will be recalled were the principals counter-demonstrating against the peace marchers from the New Orleans Committee for Peaceful Alternatives, as was described in the last chapter. Neither the Garrison investigation nor the HSCA showed any awareness of the Free Electors meeting going on around the time of Oswald's visit—or of its notable participants.[3157]

Also important in understanding Oswald's appearance in Clinton was the ongoing battle for the right of CORE to organize and demonstrate, which brought CORE attorneys to Judge John Rarick's courtroom in the picturesque Clinton courthouse. Clinton town counsel Richard Van Buskirk had argued in court, on behalf of the town of Clinton, for an injunction against CORE to bar them from picketing. His close friend, and fellow Klansman, Judge Rarick granted the injunction on August 28. At the next injunction hearing on September 30, after Oswald's visit, town counsel Van Buskirk declared in Rarick's courtroom: "At least one individual who is a member of a Communist-front organization is working with CORE in East Feliciana Parish." Van Buskirk never revealed who the individual was, but Oswald fit the description. Van Buskirk also may have had in mind CORE workers Edward Vickery or Martin Lesser when he suggested more that than one Communist may have been involved. The court fight and injunction between the Klan legal team of Rarick and Van Buskirk and the CORE attorneys wore on for months after Oswald's visit.

Around the time Oswald's arrival in Clinton, the *Dallas Morning News* reported, in an unconfirmed story, that the president planned to visit Dallas.

The Warren Commission documented the dates that Oswald cashed his unemployment checks, took out books at the library, and checked in at the unemployment bureau, which helps to establish his whereabouts on any particular day. It is known with certainty that the voter registrar's office in Clinton was open on Thursdays, Fridays, and Saturdays (for a half day). The hospital employment office was not open on Saturday. Given that, if Oswald did all the things that were claimed of him, it would require a three-day—Wednesday, Thursday, and Friday—visit to Clinton. Based on the Warren Commission timetable, Oswald cashed his unemployment check on September 6 making a September 4, 5, 6 visit difficult, which means that the only three days that would allow a three-day visit while the registrar's office was open was September 11, 12, and 13. However, it's likely the Clinton witnesses were lying, which makes it entirely possible that Oswald visited in prior weeks. Since Banister, Walker, Perez, and—presumably—Rarick, were at the Free Electors meeting on September 4 in nearby Baton Rouge, it's possible that Oswald visited Clinton on September 5, directly in conjunction with the Capitol House meeting.

The reason why it is important to set the days of Oswald's visit to Clinton is to establish that it occurred in the interval between the August 28 injunction hearing and the next immediate hearing on September 30, when Van Buskirk declared that a member of a Communist-front organization was working with CORE in East Feliciana Parish. Oswald slipped away from Clinton just days after he arrived as, apparently, a place for him was found in a new and evolving bigger scheme in Dallas. Clinton town attorney Van Buskirk never produced his promised Communist, and the gambit may have been aborted due to Oswald's departure for a place in the upcoming Dallas events.

On September 17, 1963, Oswald applied for a fifteen-day Mexican tourist card at the New Orleans Mexican consulate.[3158] Oswald's actions suggest a change of course in response to the recent report of a presidential visit to Dallas. On September 24, 1963, Oswald moved out of his New Orleans Magazine Street apartment and left for Mexico City.[3159] He arrived in Mexico City on the 27th and stayed until October 3, 1963, then relocated to the Dallas area.

The FBI identified both town marshal Manchester and registrar Palmer as members of the Ku Klux Klan in Clinton in 1964. Palmer was identified as Exalted Cyclops in August 1964.[3160] A 1966 FBI memo noted that a confidential source told the FBI that town marshal Manchester was a member of the Clinton Unit of the Original Knights of the Ku Klux Klan, or OKKKK, which was originally organized in Shreveport, Louisiana, in December 1960. The FBI interviewed him in a racial matters investigation and he would neither admit nor deny belonging to the Klan.[3161] According to another FBI memo, other members of the OK-

KKK included Bubba Thompson, a state police officer, as well as the sheriff of Union Parish. The FBI's source could not recall the name of another state police officer in the OKKKK who was reportedly assigned to nearby St. Francisville, but the FBI also identified the sheriff of East Feliciana Parish as a known OKKKK member in 1964.[3162] Prior to the author's obtaining FBI documentation of Palmer's and Manchester's Klan affiliation, the former district attorney for East Feliciana Parish at the time, Richard Kilbourne, told the author that all of the Clinton witnesses, McGehee, Morgan, Manchester, and Palmer, as well as Judge Rarick and Clinton town counsel Van Buskirk were members of a particularly violent Klan chapter.[3163] Congressman Jimmie Morrison identified Judge Rarick as the Exalted Cyclops of the East Feliciana Klan, a position also at one time held by registrar Henry Earl Palmer.[3164]

There are also allegations that Clay Shaw had ties to the Klan. Ed Dwyer of St. Francisville, near Clinton, told Garrison that he knew that Lloyd Cobb, Shaw's boss at the International Trade Center, owned a farm in St. Francisville and that Shaw had been there, and had been to Clinton many times. Dwyer told investigators that Shaw had some connection with the Klan in St. Francisville and that Shaw may have provided them with money.[3165] As was noted in Chapter Nine, Mrs. Carlos Marcello and her children attended the funeral of one of Lloyd Cobb's hands at his Marydale Farm on December 3, 1965, when Cobb was present.[3166, 3167]

Oswald's True Motive in Clinton; Eastland and the Communist Control Act

Senator Eastland and his chief investigator J. G. Sourwine, along with the Louisiana Committee on Un-American Activities, and state and local police, orchestrated a raid on SCEF headquarters in New Orleans on October 4, 1963, which was planned starting in 1962. Later, LUAC announced, as part of the SCEF investigation, that they also planned to investigate CORE. (The raid was a landmark event in the Kennedy assassination story and will be described in detail in Chapter Twenty-three.) Sourwine admitted in court papers that the aim of Eastland's committee was not only to investigate SCEF, but also the New Orleans "Fair Play for Cuba Committee and other Communist-front groups." That startling admission was tantamount to saying they planned on investigating Lee Harvey Oswald, since he was the only member of the New Orleans chapter of Fair Play for Cuba Committee, a group the Warren Commission called "a product of his imagination."

As Oswald returned from the Soviet Union in June 1962, the Louisiana legislature enacted the Communist Control Act. The new law was declared crucial by the sponsor because of the clear and present danger posed by Soviet-directed influence, funding, and calls for violence in the civil rights movement. In their investigations, Eastland and the New Orleans segregationists behind the Communist Control Act would not have had to look hard to find their predicted Communist from the Soviet Union who had infiltrated the various Communist-front and civil rights organizations. Lee Harvey Oswald had made a public spectacle of himself and his Communist connections on the streets of New Orleans passing out FPCC leaflets, by his likely participation in a NOCPA parade, and in front of the voter registrar's office in Clinton, as well as in the radio debate with Ed Butler and Carlos Bringuier, where he declared that he was a Marxist. It will be recalled from Chapter One that a member of the Immigration and Naturalization Service reported that Oswald pretended that he only spoke Russian after his arrest in the Bringuier fight, an action which served to let the New Orleans police—some of whom would later assist in the raid on SCEF under the Communist Control Act—know that he might be a Communist. Oswald's background would validate the critical need for the Communist Control Act, which would then effectively abolish the civil rights movement in the South by the Draconian penalties it called for.

All of the groups Oswald affected an association with—FPCC, NOCPA, and CORE—had two characteristics in common: Senator Eastland declared them all Communist-front organizations, and they all had ties to SCEF. SCEF had been providing legal assistance to CORE's voter registration efforts and, in April of 1962, Bruce Walzer and Ben Smith of SCEF defended CORE in a case that involved the integration of the Tulane University student cafeteria. That same month, Smith defended CORE Chairman Ronnie Moore who had been charged with illegally using a loud speaker at a rally at Southern University in Baton Rouge.[3168] Walzer was an officer in NOCPA, as was discussed in the last chapter. SCEF officers Carl and Anne Braden were officers in the Los Angeles Fair Play for Cuba Committee. During the SCEF raid, the membership list of NOCPA was seized from Walzer's home, suggesting that they planned to investigate that group, as well.

Clinton town counsel Richard Van Buskirk's announcement on September 30, 1963, that there was a member of a Communist-front group in Clinton coincides with the raid on SCEF offices on October 4, 1963, and suggests Oswald's appearance in Clinton was timed to be incorporated into the overall scheme of the Louisiana segregationists' and Eastland's war on SCEF and the civil rights movement.

The conclusion by Jim Garrison and the HSCA that Oswald had innocently traveled to Clinton simply to find a job missed the mark. Oswald's contact with known Klansmen whose leaders were linked to Leander Perez, Guy Banister, and General Walker in the tiny hamlet of Clinton, in the hinterlands of Louisiana, far from Oswald's home, suggests a conspiracy related to the SCEF raid. Although the incident had nothing to do with the Kennedy assassination, the fact that the small town of Clinton's white witnesses knew that Oswald was not who he pretended to be—and that they covered up his true purposes—makes the Clinton witnesses accessories to the murder of the president, after the fact. A more detailed, sourced account of the Clinton saga follows.

The Black Clinton Witnesses

CORE organizer Corrie Collins was one of the first five witnesses to testify at Clay Shaw's trial in connection to the Kennedy assassination on February 6 and 7, 1969.[3169]

Corrie Collins was a black mailhandler and was the head of CORE in Clinton. He conducted the black registration drive during August and September of 1963. He testified he was outside the voter registrar's building in August or early September when he saw a late-model black Cadillac pull up and saw Oswald get out of the rear seat and join the line waiting to register to vote. Collins later identified Clay Shaw as the man that was behind the wheel of the Cadillac, and David Ferrie as a passenger in the car. He stated that the Cadillac was parked near the registrar's office from about 9:30 a.m. to 3:30 p.m. He saw town marshal John Manchester approach the car and talk with the driver. After the Kennedy assassination, Collins recognized Oswald as the man who had been standing in the voter registration line with Shaw and Ferrie, as he later identified them. He testified that he told a state policeman about Oswald's presence there after the assassination, but that he was never questioned by the FBI. When asked why he did not tell the FBI about Oswald, he replied, "No one asked me. . . . I felt if they wanted to know they'd asked me."

The FBI noted that, in September 1963, local officials were attempting to have Collins placed under an injunction prohibiting the actions of CORE. Clinton authorities had arrested Collins on several occasions.[3170, 3171, 3172] Collins estimated Oswald's visit was in late August or early September. He had the impression at the time that the men in the black Cadillac were from the FBI. He estimated there were twenty to twenty-five people in line with Oswald. He identified Estes Morgan, a white man, standing in line at same time.[3173]

William Dunn, Sr. was a black man working with CORE trying to register voters. He testified in the Shaw trial, on February 7, 1969, that he saw the Cadillac in late August or early September. He identified Shaw and Oswald. He stated that Oswald stood in line until at least 2:00 to 2:30 p.m. He, too, had the impression at the time that the man he later identified as Clay Shaw was with the FBI.[3174]

State Police Lieutenant Francis Fruge stated that one of the most believable witnesses was Andrew H. Dunn, a black man who was found dead in jail before he could testify.[3175] According to Dunn's handwritten affidavit, he was sitting in front of Wright's barbershop across the street from the voter registrar's office, he believed on a Wednesday, and saw the men in the black Cadillac.[3176]

Henry Burnell Clark, a black man, recognized David Ferrie from a photo as one of the men that was in Clinton by his "unusual hair." He noted, "It was bushy and stood up all directions on his head like he had been out on a drunk all night." Looking at a photo, he identified Clay Shaw as the driver of the Cadillac.[3177]

Lee McGehee, Barber

Edwin Lea (referred to as "Lee" in most documents) McGehee testified before the Grand Jury in the 1969 Clay Shaw trial that a man, whom he would later identify as Lee Harvey Oswald, came alone to his barbershop in Jackson, a town thirteen or fourteen miles from Clinton, in late August or early September, but not after September 15. He said he saw a man whom he could not identify get out of an old, battered car in front of his shop, with a woman in the front and a bassinet in the back. While McGehee gave him a haircut, Oswald asked about a job at the state hospital. McGehee referred him to State Representative Reeves Morgan for advice on obtaining the hospital job.[3178] (It is not clear where McGehee was going with the story of the old car, woman and bassinet. Oswald did not drive.)

In another account, McGehee stated that Oswald entered his shop just before closing and sat down without giving his name. Oswald purportedly told McGehee that he was from New Orleans and wanted to know about East Feliciana Hospital. McGehee told him it was a mental hospital. His impression was that Oswald had just been out of work and drove straight up to Jackson and stopped at his barbershop, his first stop in town. McGehee commented in his testimony that a barbershop was a good place to get information. Oswald reportedly said he needed a job right away but did not know any politicians in New Orleans. McGehee told him that Reeves Morgan was the state representative and might be able to help him. He told Oswald, the only person he ever sent to Morgan, how to get to Morgan's house. McGehee supposedly then told Oswald it would help him if he first registered to vote with Henry Earl Palmer. (There could not have been a worse time to register, with all the racial turmoil going on around the voter registrar's office.) He noted in his testimony that Oswald did not need a haircut and was neat and nice. Oswald thanked him and left.

McGehee said that his wife worked at the hospital and that there were a lot of Cubans in the area and at the hospital. McGehee added that, in the old car he noticed on the street, there was a bassinet in the back and a woman in the front, whom he guessed was in her 20s. McGehee said he remembered Oswald continually staring at the picture of Martin Luther King, Jr. at the so-called Communist training school, which McGehee had hanging on the wall. He said Oswald was shaken by it, but did not comment on it. (It will be recalled from Chapter Ten that the famous, contrived Highlander School photo of King with Communist Abner Berry, who inserted himself into it, was the segregationist's much-touted proof of the Communist conspiracy in the civil rights movement. It was glimpse of where McGehee stood on the issue of race.)

Later on, McGehee stated that Representative Morgan never told him that Oswald took his advice and visited his home and McGehee recounted that he never talked to the FBI. When he was asked why he did not notify the FBI and waited five years to mention Oswald's visit to Clinton, McGehee replied, "No one approached me."[3179, 3180]

McGehee's claim that Morgan did not tell him about Oswald's visit with him is improbable because the two men were close friends, something which the investigators did not know. The chances are remote that the two men, McGehee and Morgan, who were very close—as documented in an August 2, 1963, newspaper article—did not discuss with each other their individual encounters with the twentieth century's most notorious alleged assassin, and suggests McGehee was lying. When the state legislature asked Morgan to designate a successor, in case a calamity would occur and wipe out the government in the Cold War era, he named McGehee, the barber, as his replacement.[3181] Even though McGehee and Morgan were so closely connected, the impression gained from the investigations led by both Garrison and the HSCA was that the white Clinton witnesses had no particular prior relationship to each other, which was hardly the case.

McGehee's relationship with John Rarick, the judge who issued the injunction against

CORE, is another example of the cronyism of the major players in the Clinton saga, which is not apparent from the investigations of the affair. The author asked McGehee where he got the Highlander School poster, and McGehee replied, "John Rarick came by one day with a stack of them."[3182] (The *Councilor* sold the photos inexpensively and in large quantities.[3183])

Another example that the Clinton witnesses, in this case Representative Morgan and Registrar Palmer were friends before Oswald seemingly randomly visited with them was gleaned from the local newspaper. The federal government and local officials launched an investigation into a $25,000 no-bid contract Palmer and Morgan entered into together with East Louisiana State Hospital to provide milk to the institution.[3184] It's hardly coincidental that when Palmer retired as Clinton voter registrar, he was succeeded by Jackson barber Mc-Gehee, who held that position when the author interviewed McGehee again in 1996.[3185]

The author also interviewed Mary Cobb Block, the daughter of Lloyd Cobb, Clay Shaw's boss at the International Trade Mart. Cobb had owned a farm near the hospital in Jackson. She scoffed at the notion put forth by McGehee that there were a lot of Cubans in the area.[3186] More likely, McGehee had fabricated the idea of a lot of Cubans in the area to add to the intrigue, suggesting a Cuban angle to Oswald's visit to Clinton. When all is said and done, there is no particular reason to believe anything McGehee said; especially since McGehee was a Klansman like the others. Oswald likely never even went into his barbershop. His story, as we shall see, was part of a coordinated cover, with his fellow Klan witnesses, to disguise Oswald's actual pro-segregationist reason for standing in the CORE voter line by concocting the phony job search story. The real purpose of Oswald's appearance among he CORE workers, consistent with his prior behavior, was to paint CORE as Communist-affiliated.

The greater significance of the Clinton story is that multiple reliable witnesses placed Oswald and David Ferrie together in Clinton in 1963, as well as New Orleans. Overwhelming evidence of a relationship between Oswald and Ferrie was presented in Chapter Two and Oswald's association with Ferrie is further evidence that Oswald was a false Communist, and, like Ferrie, a member of the radical right and fanatical anti-Communist.

Reeves Morgan, State Representative

Two of Garrison's investigators, Andrew Sciambra and Lieutenant Francis Fruge, interviewed Reeves Morgan in 1967. Fruge, a member of the Louisiana State Police, had been assigned to the Garrison case. He had previously worked for the nefarious anti-civil rights state spy agency, the Sovereignty Commission, which is reason enough to wonder why he went to work with Garrison. It is possible that Fruge may have found his way onto Garrison's staff as a Sovereignty Commission spy to make sure Oswald's actual reasons for being in Clinton were not discovered.[3187]

Morgan told the investigators that he was a member of the House of Representatives for East Feliciana Parish. He told investigators that, on a day in the later part of August, around dark, a man he later identified as Lee Harvey Oswald arrived at his home. Oswald indicated that he knew there was a job opening in the electrical department of the hospital and that he wanted the job. According to Morgan, Oswald did not tell Morgan that Lee Mc-Gehee had directed Oswald to his home. Instead, Oswald said he had relatives in Clinton. Morgan allegedly told Oswald that he needed to meet Civil Service requirements and fill out an application to get a job. Morgan said he would see if there was a job opening, but if there were he would have to try and get it for one of his constituents first.

Morgan's daughter Mary, a college student, was also in the house, and after the assassination she recalled the man's visit. She recalled there was a woman in the automobile waiting for him.[3188] In another account, Morgan's daughter said she did not pay much attention to the incident, as it was common for a lot of people to drop in at her Dad's house. She said, however, that she noticed a dark car outside, and she saw a woman in the car.[3189]

Reeves Morgan testified at the conspiracy trial of Clay Shaw that Oswald came to his home in late August or early September and talked to him for twenty to twenty-five minutes. He said he recognized Oswald's picture after the assassination, at which point he allegedly contacted the FBI and they "thanked him," but told him they already knew that Oswald had been in the vicinity of Jackson and never sent anyone to talk to him.[3190] In January 1968, when the FBI heard that Morgan had alleged Oswald was in Clinton and Jackson and that he had furnished the information to the FBI sometime after the assassination, they checked their records and found no evidence that Morgan contacted them.[3191]

Morgan recalled that Aline Woodside, who worked in the personnel department of the hospital, told him that she had seen Oswald's application at some time after the assassination in the personnel file but she did not know what became of it. It is extremely odd that she saw this historical document—filled out by the world's most infamous assassin—and did not set it aside for preservation and evidence for the FBI. The author is not aware of any investigative interviews with Woodside.[3192]

Bobbie Dedon was a receptionist at East Feliciana Hospital at the time and said she definitely saw Oswald and talked to him at the hospital. She said Oswald came to her and asked her how to get to the personnel office.[3193] Another employee, Maxine Kemp Drane told Garrison that she came across Oswald's application after the assassination filed as "Oswald, Harvey." She said she tried to find it for Jim Garrison, but it had disappeared.[3194]

It's possible that Oswald had planned to stay in Clinton and was actually looking for a job at the hospital at the same time he was trying to infiltrate CORE. Oswald had been unemployed for a couple of months (since July). If he wrote on the application that he had been working with CORE and their leaders, it would have placed CORE at risk of prosecution under the Communist Control Act which, like Oswald, was a product of the Banister operation. On the other hand, the claims of Bobbie Dedon and Maxine Kemp Drane that Oswald was at the hospital may have been fabricated and part of the cover-up, and would explain why his job application could not be found. Also troubling is the fact that Oswald's electrical training was limited to his work in a radio manufacturing plant in Minsk, in the Soviet Union—hardly qualifying him to work on medical electronics or building electrical systems.

As a curious aside, Thomas Williams, who was a close friend of Maxine Kemp Drane's husband Billy, volunteered to Garrison investigators that Billy told him that he was offered $25,000 to fly a dangerous mission that he later felt had to do with the JFK assassination. The individual who approached Kemp was initially said to have been a congressman, although Kemp later denied that the individual was a congressman.[3195]

Williams told the author that he owned a store across from the voter registrar, and he is certain that he, too, saw Oswald in the registration line. Williams told the author that he could not recall the congressman he told Garrison investigators about but recalled that he was from Texas.[3196]

Henry Earl Palmer, Voter Registrar

Voter registrar Henry Earl Palmer told Garrison investigators that he talked to Lee Harvey Oswald in his office some time between September 1 and October 15, 1963. He felt strongly it was the first week of October, possibly the 6th or 7th. (He revised the date to late August or early September in a later account.) He said there was a long line of "colored" people with Oswald. He said another white man, Estes Morgan, was in line with him. Palmer said that he saw two of Oswald's companions in a Cadillac parked in front of Cochran's drug store. He recalled one man had "heavy eyebrows." He identified David Ferrie from a picture shown to him by Garrison's investigators. He felt a photo of Clay Shaw appeared similar to the man he had seen in Clinton, but was not sure.

Palmer told the investigators that, at one point, he came out of his office and told some official near the Cadillac to do a registration check on the vehicle. This "official" could have been the town marshal, a state trooper, or Judge John Rarick, who, Palmer noted, "may have been with him at the time."[3197] Many years later, in an interview, Rarick admitted that he, too, had seen Oswald in the voter line.[3198] As it turns out, town marshal John Manchester testified that he was the one who checked the car registration and purportedly found out it was registered to the International Trade Mart, where Clay Shaw worked. Palmer asked Manchester what the men were doing in town. Manchester told him, laughing, that the driver told him, "Selling bananas." (The crude remark was obviously a derogatory reference to African Americans.)

Palmer claimed that Oswald told him he had been living with a doctor in Jackson at the hospital for six months, but Palmer could not remember the doctor's name. (Someone was incorrect here. Oswald had been living continuously in New Orleans.) Palmer said Oswald told him that he was at the registrar's office to register so that he could get a job at the hospital. Palmer told him that he did not need to register to get the job and Oswald left the registrar's office between 4:00 and 4:15 p.m.[3199] (That time frame probably would not have allowed for Oswald to visit the hospital employment office on the same day and would have required him to stay for a third day in the Clinton-Jackson area if the witnesses' stories are believed.)

In another account, Palmer stated that Oswald was one of two white men in the long registration line of Negroes. When Oswald's turn came up, he showed Palmer his U.S.

Navy identification card and told him he was seeking a job at the hospital. Palmer allegedly talked to him for about fifteen to twenty minutes and told him he did not need to be a registered voter to get a job, but it would be helpful if he either knew the mayor of Jackson, a state representative, or the business manager of the hospital. Palmer said Oswald told him he was residing with an individual in Jackson with a Spanish surname which Palmer could not recall.[3200] Palmer noted his office hours were 8:00 a.m. to 4:30 p.m. on Thursday and Friday and a half day on Saturday.[3201]

When Garrison arrested Clay Shaw in 1967 and his photo appeared in the papers, Palmer said he did not recognize him as the man in the Cadillac. Later, however, he said that the news photo bore a resemblance to the driver of the Cadillac.[3202]

Seven months after his first 1968 interview with Garrison investigators, Palmer told them that town marshal Manchester had recently told him that right around the time he saw the black Cadillac in Clinton he remembered "seeing a boy who fit Oswald's description coming out of a CORE meeting in Clinton." When he left the CORE meeting, Manchester reportedly followed him and "the car went in the direction of Jackson, Louisiana."[3203] (The Clinton CORE meetings were held in the homes of local African Americans. Oswald's visit to the home of a black CORE worker would have been considered outrageous and the revelation was quite noteworthy.) There is no known evidence that Manchester told the same story either to Garrison's investigators directly or to the HSCA.

Palmer's recounting of Manchester's remarkable statement is the only time anyone linked Oswald directly to CORE. As will be shown, that was the entire reason for Oswald's visit. Plans had been in the works by people close to Guy Banister to investigate CORE, along with SCEF, FPCC, and NOCPA, in a search to find Communists in their ranks, so that they could be prosecuted under the Communist Control Act.

There is no evidence the Clinton witnesses knew Oswald was destined to be the accused assassin of the president. However, their knowledge that Oswald as a part of a scheme to prove that CORE and the other integration groups were infiltrated with Communists, while not telling authorities about it, made them accessories after the fact. After the assassination, Oswald's presence in Clinton provided nothing more than a tremendous liability, not only to the town Klansmen, but also for those behind the assassination. Under that pressure, the Clinton witnesses came up with a somewhat plausible explanation for Oswald's visit to Clinton and Jackson. The story that he was there to get a job apparently was convincing enough for Garrison and the HSCA, which also bought it without reservation. They apparently did not find it odd that the wealthy Clay Shaw, who was responsible for the operation of the International Trade Mart, would spend three days sitting around in a car while Oswald was trying to get a job a long way from home.

Henry Earl Palmer and Guy Banister

Garrison's investigators suspected that the man identified as Clay Shaw in Clinton might have actually been Guy Banister, as they were of similar age and appearance. Registrar Henry

Earl Palmer did his best to keep Banister out of the Clinton story. Assistant New Orleans D.A. Andrew Sciambra interviewed Palmer on October 9, 1968, at which time Palmer told Sciambra that he and Banister were in the military together in 1944, stationed in Orlando, Florida, where, according to Palmer, Banister was doing intelligence work in the army. Palmer recounted that after that they separated when he was sent to Japan and he never saw Banister again (which turns out to be a lie, as we shall see). He said he never saw Banister in Clinton and had no knowledge of Banister and George Ratliff (more on Ratliff later) trying to organize the Klan around Clinton and Jackson.

Interestingly, Palmer said Richard Van Buskirk could give Garrison information on Banister. (Van Buskirk was never interviewed by Garrison, and was not a part of Garrison's account of the Clinton saga. Garrison investigators should have seized upon this off-the-cuff remark about Van Buskirk and Banister, but didn't.) According to a Garrison memorandum, "Palmer knew Guy Banister in the armed forces and stated he would have recognized him had he been a passenger in the black Cadillac; he was not, and Palmer was unable to identify the two occupants further, generally stating their size and hair color."[3204] Palmer was shown a picture of Guy Banister at the Clay Shaw trial, and he said he recognized Banister and knew him from their service in WWII. He recalled he had last seen Banister last around 1960 "in the Legislature," but Garrison failed to have Palmer elaborate on this remarkable, contradictory revelation. Palmer testified that Banister was not in the car in Clinton, stating, "I knew Guy Banister well enough that I would have recognized him."[3205] (Banister had attended sessions of the legislature since at least 1958, according to a letter he wrote to Willie Rainach.[3206])

Palmer lied about Banister being in the army, perhaps ignorant of the fact that Banister's FBI record reflected that he continually served in the FBI during WWII. (Unlike most citizens, Banister's position with the FBI exempted him from serving.) Banister's friend and partner in Guy Banister and Associates, Joseph Oster, told the author emphatically that Banister was never in the armed forces.[3207] Palmer also changed his story when, although initially saying that he had last seen Banister in 1944, then, under oath, saying that he had last seen Banister in the state legislature in 1960.

Evidence presented in Chapter One documented that Banister was, indeed, at the state legislature in 1960 applying for a job with the Sovereignty Commission and LUAC, two bodies investigating the Communist influence in the integration movement. As was also noted in Chapter One, Banister applied for a job with the state-run Sovereignty Commission in Baton Rouge in 1960. He wrote the Commission, "I would like to propose to Governor McKeithen a contract between Guy Banister Associates, Inc. and the State which would make available to him expert investigative help. . . . I would supervise the work of the investigators."[3208] In 1960, Guy Banister also applied for a position with Louisiana Un-American Activities Committee in Baton Rouge. While interviewing for the job, Banister told lawmakers, referring to CORE, that the "committee on racial equality [sic] operates out of New York City and is behind the troubles caused by colored students in the South." Banister said, "There has been no real exposure of subversive influence in this state, although the joint committee on segregation in the past did some work in that direction."[3209] Banister got the job and set out to remedy the lack of "real exposure of subversive influence in this state." Guy Banister had long felt the integration movement was infiltrated with Communists, stating on March 7, 1957, that, "half of Commy trained Americans were of the Negro race."[3210]

Extensive records kept by CORE in Clinton better describe Palmer's character. Most notably, Palmer displayed a small black doll, lynched and hanging by a rope around its neck, on the door to his office. He reportedly also frightened voter applicants by wearing a holstered handgun.[3211]

It's not surprising that Banister and Palmer knew each other in 1960. Palmer had become a *cause celebre* among state officials and the segregationists, as we shall see, for his well-known outright defiance of the U.S. Justice Department. Both men were dedicated to the cause of segregation. Louisiana State Attorney General Jack Gremillion came to Palmer's defense in his ongoing battle with the Justice Department. It would have been in the interest of the Leander Perez and Guy Banister operations, as well as the Sovereignty Commission and LUAC, to coach and encourage Palmer in his fight with the Justice Department for purging black voters from the voter rolls and refusing to register them. Few fanatical racists like Palmer would have missed the opportunity to attend the segregationist-led Free Electors meeting held in nearby Baton Rouge on September 4, 1963, which was attended by Guy Banister, General Walker, Richard Van Buskirk and Leander Perez.

John Manchester, Town Marshal

John Manchester testified to the HSCA that he served as Clinton town marshal from 1961 to 1970. He said that he saw the Cadillac on St. Helena Street and wrote down the names of its passengers on a note pad as Lee Harvey Oswald, Clay Shaw, and David Ferrie. He believed he asked Oswald and Ferrie their names, but did not check their identification.[3212] In another account, Manchester recalled that Palmer had asked him to check the registration on the Cadillac. He reported the "selling bananas" story to Garrison investigators. He told Palmer that the Cadillac was registered to the International Trade Mart, not the Department of Justice as some suspected. Manchester was asked to hang around the registrar's office as much as possible during the CORE demonstrations.[3213]

Manchester admitted to the HSCA that there were a lot of people in the parish who saw Oswald outside the registrar's office. Manchester told investigators, "I do know that there were plenty of people who saw him." He added, "There was a discussion around the whole parish that Oswald had been in the parish."[3214] In all, seven witnesses testified in the Clay Shaw conspiracy trial saying that they had seen Lee Harvey Oswald with David Ferrie in Clinton. Assistant D.A. Andrew Sciambra had identified "45+ potential witnesses" from the Clinton-Jackson area. Lieutenant Francis Fruge believed there were other credible witnesses from the area who would attest to the visit of Ferrie, Oswald, and Shaw.[3215]

Gloria Wilson and Mrs. Corcoran, both African Americans, affirmed that they saw Oswald get into the black Cadillac. Wilson, assuming Oswald was with CORE, told Palmer,

"Your Civil Rights workers are riding better than you are."[3216] Garrison investigators Ann Dischler and Lt. Fruge attended a CORE meeting in Clinton on August 21, 1967, held at a black church. Using a projector, they showed the attendees a group of sixty-three photos they had of Shaw, Ferrie, and Oswald. The blacks in attendance were noncommittal. According to the D.A. memorandum, they were suspicious of the white investigators.[3217] Garrison investigator Andrew Sciambra brought in an African American investigator to Clinton to question the potential black witnesses, but the black witnesses cornered him outside of a boarding house and asked him to leave.[3218]

It was not in the best interest of the white Clinton witnesses, Palmer, McGehee, Manchester, and Morgan, that Oswald's presence in Clinton, at long last, had come to the attention of investigators. However, so many saw Oswald in Clinton that it would have been suspicious and foolish for the witnesses to deny or attempt to cover up Oswald's visit. Instead, an innocent, plausible cover story was devised to protect them.

Marshal Manchester told Garrison's investigators that he had been raised in Jackson, which was twelve miles from Clinton, and had a population of about 1,500 in 1963. Interestingly, Garrison's investigators asked Manchester if he knew of any John Birch Society activity in the area, and he said there was no such activity.[3219] Garrison's investigative files made little mention of the John Birch Society. Nonetheless, as was previously presented, Guy Banister and David Ferrie had ties to the JBS. Garrison's chief investigator, Lou Ivon, when asked by the author if it were true that many of the figures in Garrison's case were members of the JBS, replied, "Yes, that is true."[3220]

When Manchester was asked to explain why he did not report seeing Oswald to federal authorities after the assassination, he gave the same excuse as the others: "If they wanted it they should have come for it."[3221] (The FBI astutely remarked on the Clinton witnesses' peculiar failure to notify them about Oswald's presence in Clinton, stating: "It seems very strange that Garrison has turned up five witnesses who now say they saw Oswald in the summer of 1963, not one of whom thought enough of the information immediately following the assassination of President Kennedy to report it at the time to an investigative agency."[3222])

Manchester, on a number of occasions, expressed his conviction that the CORE turmoil was the fault of outside agitators. On August 8, 1963, the headline of the *Baton Rouge State Times* read, "CORE Worker from New York held in Clinton." The paper quoted Manchester on the voter registration drive saying, "This thing was being conducted by outsiders, people coming in to get the people registered to vote."[3223] Manchester testified at the Shaw trial that his duties were to "just maintain law and order and to try to keep out the outside agitation that was attempting to infiltrate." He stated, "There were quite a few outsiders coming in" and "I was trying to keep out any outside agitation, keep it out of this voter registration drive being conducted."[3224]

A month after Manchester made his first remarks about "outsiders" in Clinton referring to the college CORE volunteers from the North, one famous outsider entered the town.

The State of Louisiana, the Citizens' Council, and the Black Voter Purges

Clinton was not only the hot spot in the state for CORE activities; it was also the scene of the FBI's intensive investigation efforts against the voter purges. The Justice Department's attention to Clinton, in turn, led to the strengthening of segregationist efforts in the town. The move to purge black voters from the voter rolls was vigorously encouraged by Citizens' Council stalwarts Willie Rainach and Leander Perez, while being promoted by the local Citizens' Councils in response to the *Brown* decision. After Louisiana's segregation laws were ruled unconstitutional by three federal judges (two were southerners), in New Orleans in 1956, Banister colleague Willie Rainach, who was chairman of the Joint Legislative Committee on Segregation, called for an all-out fight to maintain segregation. Rainach stated in a speech at a rally: "Moves will be met with counter moves. Decrees with laws, and political court decisions with political strategy." In that speech, he warned listeners: "The NAACP is going to get control of Louisiana—if vote officials do not stop registering unqualified negroes [sic]." Leander Perez, who was with Rainach at the rally, concurred whole-heartedly.[3225] Rainach warned the people of Lousiana, on January 25, 1956, of the "disastrous consequences" of allowing Negroes to register and vote.[3226]

At an October 23, 1956, Citizens' Council of America meeting in Jackson, Mississippi, a speaker boasted that 20,000 Negro voters had been purged from the rolls in New Orleans, alone. Delegates from other states were encouraged to do the same.[3227] At the same time, Leander Perez was busy disenfranchising black voters in Plaquemines Parish. Perez represented the parish in federal district court against a suit brought about by Albert L. Tuller, a black man who was denied registration because he was unable to pass a test on the U.S. Constitution. Judge Herbert W. Christenberry scolded Perez, saying, "If history teaches us anything, it is that dictators carry out their machinations within the framework of the law."[3228]

On September 17, 1956, citizens and nearly all the public officials of Clinton met at the Legion Hall with state senator Willie Rainach to form the Citizens' Council of East Feliciana. Rainach told them, "Stricter enforcement of voter registration requirements is one of the first things the Council can back." One of the objectives and purposes of the Citizens' Council, he stated, was to reveal "the assault which is constantly being waged upon our institutions by the Socialist and Communistic forces in this Country."[3229] On December 22, 1956, Willie Rainach announced a new campaign to rid the voter rolls of the illegally registered that he called "operation cleanup." Rainach said the campaign would begin on January 1, 1957. The press commented that Willie Rainach had played a role in every segregation-tightening law in Louisiana since 1952.[3230]

To further the voter purges, Henry Earl Palmer, was appointed Clinton voter registrar. He succeeded Charles S. Kilbourne, who had been under fire from the police jury (East Feliciana's governing commission) for writing a letter to a Memphis newspaper stating that integration was making rapid strides in the South and was only being delayed by the segregationists.[3231] Parish district attorney Richard Kilbourne told the author that Kilbourne was a very "weak" man.[3232] Under Palmer, things changed and those unable to pass the literacy tests were taken off the rolls.

On November 18, 1957, Kent Courtney spoke with Rainach, Emmet Irwin, Senator Eastland, and Leander Perez at the Citizens' Council of Greater New Orleans meeting.[3233] It's worth noting that this was just one of many times that Senator Eastland closely associated with the New Orleans hardcore underground at meetings. It might also be noted that Kent Courtney's white supremacy orientation was reflected in his 1957 opposition to Hawaiian statehood because Hawaiians were not Caucasians.[3234] Kent Courtney spoke to meeting of eight thousand members of the Citizens' Council of Greater New Orleans again on July 25, 1958, with Emmet Irwin and others urging support for the Council.[3235]

In 1958, Leander Perez backed a move to require interpretation of the Constitution for all asking to register to vote.[3236] In August 1958, the number of blacks registered to vote in East Feliciana Parish was 1,027. A year later, the number had dropped to fifty after Henry Earl Palmer assumed the Parish registrar's office in Clinton, even though the federal government took note of Palmer's malicious actions.[3237]

Not all Parish registrars approved of the voter purges. Winnfield Parish registrar Mary Flournoy became tired of Rainach's challenging of black voters for minor registration errors and "took a vacation" to prevent any further challenges by Rainach and the Citizens' Council. She charged Rainach with "creating a rabble rousing mess." Flournoy further asserted, "I'm for segregation right down the line. But I have a job to do, and I intend to be fair, or I won't be here."[3238] Governor Earl K. Long named his archrival, Leander Perez, as the one behind Rainach's attempt to purge voters from the rolls in Long's home parish of Winnfield in 1958, in order to help the election of a Long opponent to Congress.[3239]

Between February and June of 1959, the Citizens' Councils began to purge black voters from the rolls through citizen's challenges. In response, federal district judge J. Skelly Wright ordered the names of 1,377 stricken black voters to be put back on the rolls on January 1, 1960.[3240]

In 1959, the ACLU filed a complaint against Palmer and Citizens' Council leader Richard Kilbourne, and they were summoned to appear before a hearing of the U.S. Civil Rights Commission in Shreveport on July 13, 1959. Unfortunately, through the efforts of the state attorney general, the hearings were halted and never held. However, from that time on the U.S. Justice Department constantly harassed—in the eyes of the Citizens' Council—the voter registrar and the citizens of the parish, using court actions and investigations in an effort to undo the Citizen' Council and Palmer's purges. In response, in 1959, the East Feliciana Citizens' Council raised over $1,400 for the Little Rock Private School Corporation to open all white private schools.[3241]

The U.S. attorney general filed an application with the federal district courts to order Palmer to turn over the voter records for inspection on May 23, 1960. When Palmer ignored the order of the U.S. attorney general, the matter was taken to court.[3242] Palmer's ongoing defiance of the U.S. attorney general was front-page news in New Orleans.[3243] On June 29, 1960, state Attorney General Jack P. F. Gremillion began preparing a motion to halt federal examination of the East Feliciana Parish voting records, which had been ordered by U.S.

attorney general William P. Rogers under the 1960 Civil Rights Act, but Palmer refused to hand over the records.[3244] Gremillion had been an avid defender of the segregationist's efforts. In 1956, Gremillion presented the state's argument for keeping the NAACP defunct in Louisiana and had long defended the voter purges.[3245]

On June 22, 1960, Federal Judge J. Skelly Wright ordered Palmer to appear at a hearing in New Orleans concerning the inspection of the voter records.[3246] On July 18, Judge Wright ordered Palmer to make all of the voting records available to the U.S. attorney general for inspection. The action came after the U.S. attorney general again brought suit against Palmer under the 1960 Civil Right Act after Palmer again refused to produce the records.[3247] The following day, a federal court again ordered Henry Earl Palmer to make the voting records available to federal authorities, while the state attorney general advised him not to do so.[3248] The FBI finally obtained the records and reviewed them on August 8–10, 1960. The press covering the story noted that Palmer was a 46-year-old dairy farmer who had been parish registrar since February 1959. The FBI then photographed the voter records. Of 2,000 parish voters, only eighty were black, in a parish that was 60–65 percent black. Two years prior there had been 4,000 registered. Voter challenges by members of the Citizens' Council had removed 600 voters of both races. Palmer challenged more than 3,000 personally.[3249] In August 1960, the FBI held a closed conference with Clinton D.A. Richard Kilbourne, then descended upon Palmer's Clinton office as part of a court order to investigate and photograph the voting registration records of those who had failed the registration test in Clinton.[3250]

For a small rural town, the Citizens' Council of Clinton hosted some prominent speakers at its meetings. At the height of Clinton's and Palmer's defiance of the federal government, Hubert Badeaux addressed the Clinton Citizens' Council in February 1961.[3251] (As has been noted, Badeaux was the head of Guy Banister's police Red Squad and assisted in Senator Eastland's 1956 investigation of the "Soviet influence" in the integration movement. He had written Willie Rainach in 1957 and told him he was grooming an individual to infiltrate leftist groups on campus, right after Lee Harvey Oswald began to act like a Communist.) As we shall see, other familiar names in this work also came to speak in Clinton.

Leander Perez complained, in August 1961, about the FBI's appearance in the parish of Plaquemines to check on voter registration. (The Civil Rights Commission had also investigated voter rights in Plaquemines earlier in 1961.) The Plaquemines voter registrar, Ethel Fox, testified before the Commission that of the total of 4,135 non-whites in the Parish, only forty-four were registered to vote.[3252]

In October of 1961, Robert Kennedy personally ordered a federal grand jury investigation into wire tapping of integrationists in Louisiana, including a leader of the American Friends Committee, a Jewish organization, and a Baptist church. Louisiana State Sovereignty Commission leaders were called to testify.[3253]

On March 8, 1961, Federal Judge Wright ordered Henry Earl Palmer to again produce certain voter registration records for inspection.[3254] Then, on September 9, 1961, the U.S. attorney general's office asked for more records noting that many Negroes had been purged from the polls in East Feliciana; Palmer refused.[3255] In 1961, the U.S. Justice Department brought suit against the State of Louisiana to try to remove the voter registration test, which was obviously designed to deprive blacks of their right to vote.[3256]

Just prior to Oswald's visit to Clinton, the racist activities of the future Clinton witnesses to Oswald's visit to Clinton came to the attention of the FBI. They investigated both town marshal Manchester and registrar Palmer in August of 1963, based on a complaint to the Justice Department about the arrest of CORE volunteer Michael Lesser, whom Manchester had arrested for disturbing the peace after he refused to leave Henry Earl Palmer's office. The case was never prosecuted but was continued indefinitely.[3257]

On August 3, 1963, the Civil Rights Division of the U.S. Department of Justice requested that the FBI conduct inquiries concerning three employers in East Feliciana who each had fired an employee simply because the employee had registered to vote in the CORE drive. On August 5, 1963, Dr. Richard K. Munson (white) fired Georgiana S. Collins (black), and Joseph S. Breitung (white) fired Mr. Ester Lee Daniel (black). Collins and Daniel were both fired after they applied to vote on August 3, 1963. The Civil Rights Division also requested the FBI to investigate the firing of Tuler Knox, a black man, by none other than Representative Reeves Morgan, the man Oswald supposedly visited to get his help in landing a job. On August 14, 1963, it was noted that Knox's job was to deliver bulk milk from Morgan's farm to Jackson Creamery, using Knox's truck, in return for payment of two dollars per trip. Morgan refused to tell the FBI his reason for terminating Knox, but denied that it was because he was involved in the voter registration drive. The firings all took place within a week after CORE's arrival in Clinton.[3258] The FBI reported that ABC News had interviewed several Negroes who told them they had been intimidated from registering.[3259] Morgan, like the other white Clinton witnesses, was an outspoken segregationist and he even boasted about it in his campaign ads for state representative.[3260]

A Clinton constituent, Mrs. John Hobgood, wrote Louisiana senator Allen Ellender about Morgan's dealings with the FBI: "Enclosed you will find an article, and you can see just how badly the Justice Dept., CORE, and the Federal Judges are abusing the white people here." Ellender forwarded a copy of the letter to FBI Director J. Edgar Hoover.[3261]

Registrar Palmer was interviewed by the FBI on August 9, 1963, just weeks before Oswald's visit. Palmer told them that Michael Lesser, a white CORE volunteer from Newark, New Jersey, who was a graduate student at Syracuse University working for the summer with CORE,[3262] came into his office on August 6, 1963, and wanted to talk to him. Palmer told him to leave, but Lesser remained and attempted to register four Negroes. Palmer told town marshal Manchester to arrest Lesser and he would press charges against him. On August 9, 1963, the FBI interviewed Manchester, who told them he had arrested Lesser for disturbing the peace, during which, he handcuffed Lesser, put him in a police car, and took him to jail.[3263] Lesser's arrest is just one example of the arbitrary abuse of power that occurred in the South during the civil rights era. CORE litigated the case, though unsuccessfully, as East Feliciana district attorney Richard Kilbourne prosecuted Lesser. He charged Lesser with intimidating a public official in the case of *Henry Earl Palmer et al v. Michael Stephen Lesser* in Clinton.[3264]

There were several white college students from the North working for CORE in Clinton at the time of Oswald's visit. As in the case of the New Orleans Committee for Peaceful Alternatives, Oswald would have fit in seamlessly with the college students working with CORE. As the evidence presented in the last chapter showed, Oswald was groomed to infiltrate leftist student groups. His trip to Clinton served that purpose.

A third white Clinton witness, town marshal John Manchester, like Palmer and Morgan, also flagrantly violated the rights of a black man in Clinton at the time of the voter registration drive. The CORE archives contain a report that describes an incident where Manchester rode his vehicle off the road in an effort to hit a black man, Bill Brown, then arrested Brown for obstructing the highway. Manchester was constantly harassing CORE, asking for identification and arresting its members. He even arrested them while in church.[3265]

These previously undisclosed Justice Department and CORE reports are evidence of the calculated, malicious actions of three of the four Klan "witnesses," who fabricated an alibi and cover story to hide the true reason for Oswald's presence in Clinton, and to conceal the fact that Oswald was working on their side to paint CORE as Communist-influenced. Only barber Lee McGehee, the fourth white Clinton witness, failed to come under scrutiny of the FBI, as far as the author was able to discover.

In 1963, the Justice Department won an injunction against Palmer to stop using literacy tests to discriminate against black applicants. In 1964, the Department of Justice filed suit against Palmer for discriminating against black voters.[3266] Yet, in the two years after the injunction, Palmer registered only 120 blacks. Finally, in 1965, the U.S. Civil Service employees and FBI agents began registering blacks under the Voting Rights Act. Up to that time, only 187 blacks were registered, compared to 2,726 whites. Federal registrars signed up 1,595 blacks in the first week. The first black person in line was sixty-three-year-old Chris Weatherspoon, who had tried to register five times with Palmer. Each time, Palmer would say after he failed his literacy test, "Chris, you missed just one word on the test." Palmer displayed a poster of Martin Luther King, Jr. at the so-called Highlander Communist Training School on the wall behind his desk at the registrar's office.[3267] Which means that there was a second Klan witness, in addition to barber Lee McGehee, displaying this famous segregationist propaganda piece that was contrived by Joseph Milteer's colleague, Roy V. Harris.

The East Feliciana Citizens' Council

Richard Kilbourne, the district attorney for East Feliciana Parish, had headed the Citizens' Council in Clinton since its inception in 1956. Though a staunch conservative and segregationist, he was not a radical and deplored violence and the Klan. Kilbourne issued a written statement for members of the Council outlining the history of the Council and the rise of a violent faction of Klansmen trying to take it over. He wrote that, over the years, the Citizens' Council sponsored speakers in Clinton and Jackson that included Cary Daniels, a radial-right preacher from Dallas, Jack N. Rogers of LUAC, and Mary Cain, a Congress of Freedom regular. On December 22, 1961, the Citizens' Council paid for an advertisement in the local paper entitled "Will you Be Free To Celebrate Christmas In The Future," which was based on the May 29, 1957 HUAC testimony of Fred Schwarz, a noted anti-Communist, entitled "Communist Mind." In 1962, the East Feliciana Citizens' Council sponsored an essay contest on the Communist Conspiracy.

A rift developed between Kilbourne's mainstream segregationist Council faction and the violence-inclined Klan faction that tried to take it over under Judge John Rarick. Referring to Rarick and his hardcore followers, Kilbourne wrote, "'Johnny-Come Latelys' [sic] who were dishonest and dishonorable and those of their kind have attempted to take over the East Feliciana Council calling themselves the 'State Citizens' Council of East Feliciana', backed, aided and abetted by at least three directors of a state organization known as the Citizens' Council of Louisiana, Inc." As a result, Kilbourne dissolved the Citizens' Council charter to prevent Rarick's Klan group from taking it over. Kilbourne said in his statement of dissolution in 1965 that the Citizens' Council had been established to combat "the common enemy, the Communist Conspiracy in the United States."

In another letter to Citizens' Council members, Kilbourne complained that Jack Helm (a Banister colleague and Klansman), and Courtney Smith (another Klansmen) had replaced Willie Rainach and William Garrett (who helped establish the East Feliciana Citizens' Council) and had radically different ideas about the Council. The radical faction started their own unit called the State Citizens' Council of East Feliciana, which Kilbourne called a front for Ku Klux Klan activities, noting that the leaders of this group were known adherents of the Klan. A closed meeting was held for Citizens' Council members to discuss the matter at the Clinton Courthouse. On May 11, 1965, two State Citizens' Council directors, Courtney Smith and Jack Helm, spoke at the Dry Prong, Louisiana, school in Grant Parish. Smith, Helm, and Rarick were on the State Citizens' Council board and are apparently the three radical state leaders Kilbourne was referring to.

One of the State Citizens' Council board members, Jack Helm, had ties to David Ferrie. According to Klansman Jules Ricco Kimble, he was with Helm when Helm drove to Ferrie's home immediately after Ferrie's death and removed Klan documents from Ferrie's garage.[3268, 3269] Interestingly enough, Kimble is mentioned in the HSCA investigation in regards to Martin Luther King, Jr.'s murder, rather than Kennedy's. The Royal Canadian Mounted Police discovered information that Kimble was associated with James Earl Ray, in Montreal in 1967, and made daily calls to New Orleans.[3270]

In the mid-1960s, Louisiana governor John J. McKeithen hired Joseph Oster, a private detective and former Guy Banister partner, to crack down on Klan violence. The Klan was opposed to the union policies adopted in the North that led to the integration of the work force employed by businesses in Louisiana. McKeithen was worried that Klan violence against the unions was driving businesses out of the state. In the course of his investigation, Oster determined that Kimble worked closely with Klan leader Jack Helm, a Guy Banister and Leander Perez associate.[3271]

Kilbourne wrote in the letter that Rarick's attempted Council sabotage was aimed "especially at me." He wrote, "I have been somewhat in the way of JRR [John R. Rarick]." Kilbourne noted it was the FBI who told him that the KKK had infiltrated the Citizens' Council. Kilbourne discouraged people from taking part in the activities of the KKK faction. (Rarick's factions eventually began calling themselves the "Confederate Citizens' Council.") Kilbourne also suspected they might have been trying to infiltrate the John Birch Society. Kilbourne said a malicious rumor was spread that he was paid $30,000 to dissolve the Citizens' Council.[3272]

The Louisiana Un-American Activities Committee, the *Councilor*, and the Clinton Incident

Although Jim Garrison is credited with being the first to find out about Oswald's appearance in Clinton, he was not. Ned Touchstone and Jack Rogers, two far-right segregationists, began asking citizens in Clinton about Oswald's visit before Garrison did. Touchstone was the editor of the Louisiana State Citizens' Council paper, the *Councilor* and, as was noted in Chapter Fifteen, was a friend of General Walker. Touchstone served on the Citizens' Council State Board with Banister colleagues Leander Perez and George Singelmann, as well as Clinton judge John Rarick. The FBI knew Touchstone was a Klansman.

Clinton resident Gladys Palmer told Assistant D.A. Andrew Sciambra that Touchstone and Rogers interviewed her prior to the D.A.'s investigation.[3273] Touchstone investigated the Louisiana aspects of the Kennedy assassination and promoted Oswald after the assassination in the *Councilor*, as a genuine Communist who exemplified the internal threat of Communism. Rogers was the chief counsel of LUAC, the anti-Communist organization that investigated SCEF. Rogers worked as an investigator with Guy Banister, but their relationship dated back to the late 1950s when they were both engaged in the anti-Communist effort in the American Legion.

LUAC worked closely with the Mississippi Sovereignty Commission in an attempt to remove the accreditation of all-black Tougaloo College in response to sit-ins and their attempts to desegregate Mississippi's public libraries in 1961. Together, the two groups searched to tie the Communist influence to Tougaloo's primary source of funding, SCEF. Senator Eastland wrote to the Mississippi Sovereignty Commission on March 4, 1964, and said that Rogers visited him and told him that LUAC had information that SCEF was a Communist front, and that he had information on an individual formerly from Tougaloo.[3274]

The *Councilor* knew Garrison was investigating the assassination four weeks before the story broke in the *States–Item*, suggesting they (or the Citizens' Council) had an informant in the D.A.'s office. On February 20, 1967, the *Councilor* printed a front-page story with the headline "A new death probe was a-borning." They named David Ferrie in their article before the major press announced he was a suspect.

The *Councilor* also continually published false claims about Oswald after the assassination. On December 5, 1963, the *Councilor* stated that, "Oswald can be linked to New Orleans Marxists" and that David Ferrie's personal history was similar to that of Stalin; both claims were lies. On March 16, 1964, Touchstone's *Councilor* reported that an unidentified man whom he called the "Madcap aviator" from New Orleans knew Oswald and had shared mutual interests. The unidentified man reportedly flew to Laredo shortly before Oswald traveled to Mexico City, and was active in the anti-Castro effort. In 1968, the "Madcap aviator" was identified in the *Councilor* as Ferrie.

The New Orleans FBI knew Touchstone was a member of the Original Knights of the Ku Klux Klan (OKKKK) and on the date of the assassination they sought his whereabouts and ascertained that he was at home in Bossier City.[3275] The FBI obviously suspected that he might have been involved. While they were checking on Touchstone's whereabouts, General Walker arrived at Touchstone's office in Shreveport, adjacent to Bossier City, right after the assassination. (Walker had been in New Orleans on the days prior with Leander Perez, Kent Courtney and Banister employee Joe Newbrough.)

Barber Lee McGehee told the HSCA that the first person to ask him about Oswald in Clinton was Jack Rogers, whom he identified only as "a lawyer from Baton Rouge." Rogers was much more than a lawyer. McGehee failed to note that Rogers was the chief counsel for LUAC, the nefarious Louisiana Un-American Activities Committee.[3276] (Guy Banister was the chief investigator for LUAC and told the Committee, in 1960, that agitators from New York were behind the civil rights group, the Congress of Racial Equality (CORE). Banister lamented the lack of anti-subversive efforts in the state since his involvement in the investigations for the Subversion in Racial Unrest hearings in 1957.[3277])

Ned Touchstone from the *Councilor* questioned McGehee after Rogers had done so. McGehee told the HSCA that Rogers and Touchstone had heard the story of Oswald in Clinton and they both asked him about it in 1965 or 1966. McGehee told the HSCA that was the last he heard from the two men.[3278] As we will see in the final chapter of this work, Oswald's appearance in Clinton purposely preceded the October 4, 1963, raid on SCEF for violation of the state's Communist Control Act. LUAC chairman, State Representative James H. Pfister, another Banister colleague, stated that after the SCEF raid the organization was "engaged in racial agitation." Jack Rogers declared that SCEF was "the equivalent of a big holding company" and that "Communists infiltrated racial movements in Louisiana."[3279] Rogers further stated that CORE was affiliated with SCEF.[3280] As a part of their investigation of SCEF, they planned to investigate CORE.

On April 13, 1964, LUAC issued a report entitled "Activities of the Southern Conference Educational Fund, Inc., in Louisiana." Counsel Jack Rogers testified about the history of FPCC. Rogers stated: "After the horrible assassination of the president, we directed our Committee staff to make a preliminary inquiry into the connections of Fair Play for Cuba Committee here in Louisiana." The published report devoted a full page to Oswald's arrest mug shots and fingerprint sheet after his "fight" with Bringuier. Even the letterhead from FPCC bearing Carl and Anne Braden's names on it was reproduced in the LUAC report.[3281] Rogers and LUAC concluded that Oswald was a dedicated Communist and a member of FPCC who had links to Martin Luther King, Jr. and the civil rights movement. They made no mention of Oswald being in Clinton. Rogers said that SCEF was "giving us trouble all over the state" and was linked to racial demonstrations that had cropped up in various Louisiana cities. He claimed there were Communist agitators in other groups advocating racial integration, and that LUAC had several other major investigations underway.[3282]

After the SCEF raid, Kent Courtney requested that his readers read the pamphlet he had written about SCEF and encourage Congressman Edwin Willis of the House Committee on Un-American Activities to hold public hearings on the "Communist influence in the NAACP, CORE, the Student Non Violent Coordinating Committee and other organizations dedicated to racial turmoil." He stated that "in this way certain racial agitators can be officially identified as Communists or members of Communist-front groups." Copies of the letter were sent to the Friends of General Walker and various "patriotic" publications and leaders.[3283]

In 1967, Jack Rogers, summing up the SCEF matter, contacted the New Orleans office of the Central Intelligence Agency to let them know that in the 1964 hearings his committee had linked "Lee Harvey Oswald and the Fair Play for Cuba Committee with the Southern Conference Education Fund through one Carl Braden." Rogers told the CIA that he felt Oswald was a Moscow-trained agent and FPCC organizer.[3284]

The HSCA was interested in Rogers and LUAC's "investigation" into the Clinton matter. Rogers told the HSCA that LUAC conducted their investigation of Oswald beginning on November 27, 1963. He said the investigation included Oswald's visit to Clinton and the surrounding area. He told them he turned over the records to the state government when funding for his agency was cut out of the budget in 1971. His rough notes made reference to Manchester, Henry Earl Palmer, and town counsel Bill Kline.[3285] The HSCA apparently found nothing peculiar about Rogers's investigation and gave the matter little consideration. The fact that neither Rogers nor Touchstone reported to authorities their findings that Oswald had been in Clinton is suspicious, but not surprising. All of LUAC's files, like the Sovereignty Commission's, were mysteriously destroyed at some time and no longer exist.[3286]

The HSCA apparently had no knowledge of the LUAC-coordinated raid on SCEF on October 4, 1963, in conjunction with Senator Eastland's Committee's plan to not only investigate SCEF, but also the New Orleans "Fair Play for Cuba Committee and other Communist-front groups," including CORE. During the raid, LUAC also confiscated the membership list of the New Orleans Committee for Peaceful Alternatives (NOCPA). If Oswald's name, or that of his alias, Alek Hidell, showed up on the list, it would have greatly enhanced any prosecution evidence that authorities might have had against the group under the Communist Control Act.

In an interesting side note, the son of D.A. Kilbourne, Richard Kilbourne, Jr. told the author that Jack Rogers married Henry Earl Palmer's former wife, a Baton Rouge physician.[3287] Rogers probably was not investigating anything in Clinton but, more likely, was assessing the chances that the whole segregationist scheme surrounding the new Communist Control Act and the SCEF raid might be exposed by Oswald's visit in Clinton. Rogers was a friend of Judge John Rarick, the leader of the white Clinton Klan witnesses, and spoke at a meeting with Rarick at the Clinton Courthouse in 1962.[3288] Rogers was the head of the state Republican Party but, nonetheless, openly supported Rarick's Democratic congressional candidacy in 1966.[3289]

The History of CORE

The NAACP, the Southern Christian Leadership Committee (SCLC), the Student Non-Violent Coordinating Committee (SNCC), and the Congress of Racial Equality (CORE) led the civil rights protest revolution of the 1960s. CORE, which was much older than SNCC or SLC, pioneered the use of direct action tactics like boycotts in their campaigns. The Southern Conference Education Fund (SCEF) funded all of those groups.

CORE was founded in Chicago in 1942. Trying to expand their membership, they opened their ranks to members of the Trotskyist Socialist Workers Party. The move caused dissention between the non-violent CORE and the Socialist Workers Party, who espoused retaliatory violence. The factions ultimately split and the Trotskyites drifted away. CORE then made a concerted attempt to keep Communists out of its ranks. Nonetheless, some chapters of CORE had Trotskyites who advocated confrontation among their members in the 1960s. CORE was an important influence in the lunch counter sit-ins and created the Freedom Rides of 1961 (a target of the Banister operation, as was discussed in Chapter Three). In 1962, they turned their attention to voter registration and, by 1963, CORE volunteers, white and black, were descending *en masse* upon the South.[3290]

Banister's close associates George Singelmann and L. P. Davis declared, on June 2, 1961, that CORE was "Carrying the ball of the international Communist conspiracy. No less than 13 members of its national advisory board belong to numerous organizations that have been cited for Communist front activities. . . . The avowed purpose of this organization is to create incidents and excite people to violence. If their objectives are successful, the South will be a seething mass of racial strife."[3291] Leander Perez, citing Eastland's May 21, 1961, proclamation on CORE (given on the floor of the Senate and titled "Racial Agitation in the Southern States") stated: "I know that CORE is heavily infiltrated with Communists among its directors particularly."[3292] He stated: "The agent provocateurs who have descended upon the Southern states in the name of 'peace riders' were sent for the sole purpose of stirring up discord, strife and violence. 'Peace riders' is a revered Communist term, an old Communist technique. The movement was masterminded and directed by an organization known as Congress of Racial Equality, called CORE. This organization is the war department of those who sell hate, collect donations, and sow the seeds of discord in this country. Since its inception its creed has been lawlessness and its tactics have followed the pattern set by Communist agitators the world over. . . . I submit that when a person belongs to a large number of Communist-front organizations that follow the policies of the International Communist Conspiracy, that person is aiding and abetting the Communist movement in the world—a movement which, if not halted, will result in a blood bath in our own country, because the United States will fight, if necessary, in order to prevent Communist domination of our country."[3293]

CORE National Director James Farmer said the town of Plaquemine was chosen as its Louisiana headquarters in the 1963 Sixth District voter drive because it had local black support. Others, including the *Councilor* newspaper claimed CORE's choice of Plaquemine was the result of an error of geography. They maintained that CORE chose the town of Plaquemine, mistakenly, instead of *Plaquemines Parish* at the other end of the state, which had a long, publicized history of racial injustice under District Attorney Leander Perez. (In October 1961, Attorney General Robert Kennedy had asked federal courts to forbid "discrimination against Negroes" in Perez's Plaquemines Parish, and ordered the registration of qualified Negroes to vote. The Plaquemines registrar was named as a defendant in the case.[3294]) Leander Perez stood ready, nonetheless, for an invasion of demonstrators in Plaquemines Parish. He refurbished the old mosquito- and water moccasin-infested, historic Fort St. Phillip, on an island in the middle of the Mississippi River, as a prison to hold the expected CORE demonstrators.[3295] (Fort St. Phillip was built by the French in the 1700s and was located sixty miles below New Orleans. Perez had two boats equipped with cattle pens for the expected transfer of the arrested CORE workers to the island prison.[3296, 3297])

CORE in Louisiana, an Overview

In the summer of 1960, black and white CORE members, predominantly college students (some of whom later became members of NOCPA), held sit-ins at Woolworth's—and Mc-Crory's—lunch counters in New Orleans. In response, New Orleans mayor deLesseps Morrison banished CORE's activities from the city, and legal battles ensued.

A CORE chapter was formed in Baton Rouge in 1961 to integrate the dime-store lunch counters. Arrests of demonstrators under the state's newly enacted anti-demonstration law, and expulsions of students from their colleges for their participation in demonstrations, caused the Baton Rouge chapter to lose membership and fade.[3298] CORE was placed under a permanent federal court order preventing their demonstrations in Baton Rouge.[3299]

On August 28, 1961, Delphine Roberts, Guy Banister's future secretary, wrote to the new New Orleans mayor, Victor Schiro, and congratulated him for arresting CORE pickets at City Hall. She told him, "this shameful behavior of the N.O. negro [sic] is very disgraceful and it is even more so on the part of the so-called white members of this Communist organization."[3300]

The curbing of CORE activities in New Orleans and Baton Rouge essentially deprived Lee Harvey Oswald of any opportunity to infiltrate any chapters close to home. Clinton became the hot spot for CORE activities in Louisiana in 1963 and provided the essential benefit of having two Banister associates, one Leander Perez associate, and two General Walker associates among the five Klansmen in this cast of characters on the scene during Oswald's visit.

The CORE Summer Project

In response to the voter purges initiated by the segregationists after the *Brown* decision,

CORE started its Sixth Congressional District Project in 1962.[3301] CORE announced from Dayton, Ohio, that it would send voter registration workers into five southern Louisiana parishes in the summer of 1963.[3302] In Iberville Parish, CORE demanded desegregation in the town by June 15, 1963. In July 1963, CORE picketed retail establishments. On August 11, 1963, CORE members ignored segregated seating on the ferry used to cross the Mississippi. A disturbance followed, and the participants were jailed.[3303]

CORE announced that a voter registration drive would be launched, beginning with an intensified registration drive in Baton Rouge, and East and West Feliciana Parishes.[3304] Both black and white outsiders flooded the town of Plaquemine during the Louisiana Summer Project. On the night of August 15, 1963, 250 black protestors marched on the parish jail. On August 19, National CORE director James Farmer appeared in town from New York. Farmer led 800 demonstrators to City Hall, where authorities dispersed them. That night, 150 people marched on the home of the sheriff. Then, on August 30, protestors marched on the courthouse, where bricks and bottles were thrown at them before electric prods were used to disperse the crowd.[3305]

East Feliciana Parish, where Clinton is located, stood out as an extreme case of racial discrimination in voting. Although they were in the majority in East Feliciana, only 1 percent of blacks were on the rolls, while one third to one half of blacks were able to register in the other parishes, which made the Sixth Congressional District a priority for CORE. Historians took note of Henry Earl Palmer's ruthless culling of black voters from the rolls, observing, "At Clinton, the tiny East Feliciana Parish seat, the registrar's unconcealed hostility was unnerving." They noted that Palmer admitted "only one person at a time, set rigid identification requirements that few Negroes could meet, and usually flunked the few he permitted to take the tests." On the streets, registering blacks were taunted, "Boy you got to live here. Don't get pushed up to doing things against white folks."

District Judge John Rarick issued an injunction against CORE, which he called a "rabble rousing Communist front," effectively halting voter registration. Rarick claimed that the leadership of CORE had thirteen members with Communist-front ties. In response, CORE members mounted a boycott against Clinton merchants. Thirty-nine protesters were arrested on the first day. Fearing federal intervention, Rarick's injunction against CORE ended in the spring of 1964.[3306] Rarick's Twentieth Judicial District was the only district in the state where federal registrars were sent to sign up black citizens under the 1965 Voting Rights Act, reflecting its ruthlessness in disenfranchising African Americans.[3307]

The Clinton CORE Injunction

As was mentioned above, Clinton officials sought an injunction against CORE in September 1963 in Judge John Rarick's courtroom. One of their chief arguments before the court in Clinton was that CORE was "an arm of the Communist Conspiracy." During the 1961 CORE-sponsored Freedom Rides, Senator James O. Eastland had placed in the *Congressional Record* twelve pages of information on the supposed Communist connections of the thirteen national leaders of CORE, and said CORE was "carrying on the fight for Soviet America." Eastland congratulated the people of Mississippi and stated, in reference to the Freedom Riders entrance into Mississippi, "This is the first time they have come face to face with the Communist conspiracy." He cited the various hearings by the House Committee on Un-American Activities, noting that several members of the board of CORE were members of Communist fronts linked to the Communist conspiracy.[3308, 3309]

When Lee Harvey Oswald's affected relationships with FPCC, NOCPA, and CORE in 1963 are examined, a pattern emerges. Senator Eastland condemned each group as Communist-backed, and they all had ties to SCEF. Oswald began behaving like a Communist in 1956, at the same time that Guy Banister was assisting Eastland's investigation of Communists in the New Orleans civil rights movement. The segregationists' war with SCEF culminated with the October 4, 1963, SCEF raid. The raid was based on the Leander Perez-created Communist Control Act, which had been introduced to the state legislature by Jack Rogers's partner, James Pfister, who was also an associate of Guy Banister.

On August 2, 1963, CORE worker Michael Lesser was arrested for disturbing the peace while trying to register nine black individuals in Henry Earl Palmer's office, by Clinton town marshal John Manchester (this is the first major action taken by two Clinton witnesses in the Oswald affair, Manchester and Henry Earl Palmer, as they went on the offensive against CORE workers). The Department of Justice's Civil Rights Division, under John Doar, ordered an investigation into the complaint of harassment filed by CORE. The FBI described the atmosphere in Clinton in August as "tense."

On August 8, 1963, the Baton Rouge *State-Times* headline read "CORE Worker From New York Held in Clinton," emphasizing that outsiders were involved in the CORE operation. On August 9, 1963, two CORE voter registration workers were scheduled to appear before Judge John Rarick (a Klansman) on charges of disturbing the police and speeding. William Brown, an African American from Tucson, Arizona, who was working with CORE, was picked up three days later on a speeding charge. CORE national program director Gordon R. Carey said both arrests were harassment. Lesser's bond was set at $2,000; Brown's was set at $200.[3310] CORE's national vice president, Rudolph Lombard, filed a complaint with the Department of Justice after Lesser's arrest.[3311] White CORE worker Edgar Vickery announced that he planned to integrate the courtroom during Lesser's trial. In response to the arrests, a black attorney for CORE entered a motion to quash charges of disturbing the peace against the pair. A black CORE worker, accompanied by a white worker, took seats in the white section of the courtroom, while two white men wearing CORE lapel buttons sat down in the Negro section (by doing so they illegally integrated the courtroom). Judge Rarick ordered every one in the nearly full courtroom to leave, with the exception of those connected with the case—and reporters.[3312]

The press reported that, in early August, Clinton town counsel, Klansmen Richard Van Buskirk, was present at the initial meeting of a group opposed to President Kennedy's pending civil rights bill in Congress. The group raised $1,650 for the cause. Richard Kilbourne, William J. Ourso, and Van Buskirk presided over the meeting. The three had attended a similar meeting the prior week in Baton Rouge, which had been sponsored by the Louisiana Sovereignty Commission. The group planned to meet again soon in Jackson. Van Buskirk was the spokesman for the group.[3313] (It would not be surprising if Van Buskirk's relationship with Guy Banister stemmed from their mutual dealings with the Sovereignty Commission.)

At nearly the same time, on August 12, 1963, Lee Harvey Oswald supposedly infuriated Carlos Bringuier when he sat in the black section of the courtroom while the two were in court in New Orleans for charges brought about from their phony fight. Oswald's integration of the courtroom in New Orleans—two days after the press announced the CORE workers' integration of the Clinton courthouse—hardly seems coincidental. These actions suggest that Oswald and the New Orleans underground had been carefully monitoring CORE's activities in Clinton weeks prior to Oswald's journey to Clinton and were mimicking them in New Orleans.

On August 15, 1963, Parish D.A. Richard Kilbourne observed large crowds outside of the Clinton courtroom and cited newspaper stories in court that they were going to integrate the courtroom. The situation was in "such a state of alarm" that Kilbourne asked for—and was granted—a continuance in the case against CORE. No dates were set for when the trial would resume.[3314, 3315] Herbert F. Collins, CORE defense attorney, attempted to file a motion seeking desegregation of the courthouse rest rooms, drinking fountains, and gallery. Judge John Rarick called it "the most unusual motion I have ever heard in my life."[3316]

On August 19, 1963, it was announced that CORE National Director James Farmer had arrived in Louisiana to check on the voter drive. He planned to speak in Plaquemine on August 19 and Clinton on August 20.[3317]

On August 20, 1963, Plaquemine officials were reportedly forced to use tear gas to disperse an unruly mob, which had marched on City Hall late at night under the leadership of James Farmer. Plaquemine officials, at that point, reportedly were in possession of reliable information that CORE's activities in Clinton were not to be limited to voter registration but, instead, they planned "to run the whole gamut of disorderly demonstrations, marches, sit-ins, and the like, as soon as enough participants could be obtained."

Also on August 20, 1963, Judge Rarick signed a temporary restraining order late at night while a mass meeting was in progress. (National CORE leader James Farmer had been advertised as the principal speaker.) The order prohibited CORE from committing certain specific criminal acts, which had been carried out in Baton Rouge, in Plaquemine and throughout the country. The order "did not then, and does not now, limit any lawful activities of CORE or colored citizens of our community."[3318]

On August 22nd, it was reported that tensions were receding in Clinton. The East Feliciana grand jury remained in session investigating the activities of CORE.[3319]

On August 27, 1963, D.A. Kilbourne changed Michael Lesser's bond from the original $2,000 to a property bond so that he could be released from jail, where he had been since August 2.[3320] The author interviewed Miriam Feingold, a young woman from Brooklyn,

New York, who, at the time of the incidents in Clinton, was a recent graduate of Swarthmore College and part of the CORE initiative in Clinton. She related that only two other white northerners, Ed Vickery and Mike Lesser, were working with her in CORE in Clinton. Their identities were well known to town officials, who constantly followed, harassed, and—at times—arrested them. After the author told her about Oswald's visit to Clinton around September 5th, she recalled that she, Vickery, and Lesser had been jailed at the same time and wondered if that was done so they could not be witnesses to Oswald's appearance in Clinton.[3321]

On August 28, a few minutes prior to the setting of a hearing date, attorneys for CORE filed a removal petition in the United States District Court in Baton Rouge that, by law, stripped the local court of jurisdiction in the injunction hearings. The District Court remanded the case back to Clinton, however, and the case was again assigned to trial. In Clinton, CORE requested that the hearing be continued until September 30 and, later, again to October 14.[3322, 3323]

The press reported, on September 1, 1963, that the Sovereignty Commission of Louisiana had pledged funds for a statewide committee called the Louisiana Chapter for Fundamental American Freedoms, whose aim was to fight Kennedy's recently proposed civil rights bill. Speakers blasting the civil rights measure included Richard Van Buskirk and Leander Perez. Judge Rarick was present and pledged $1,000 for the group.[3324] The event was yet more evidence of an alliance between the key Oswald-in-Clinton participants, Rarick and Van Buskirk, and Perez and his operation. The idea of having Oswald show up in Clinton may have been hatched at this meeting, or at the September 4, 1963, Capitol House meeting attended by Guy Banister, General Walker, Perez, and Van Buskirk.

On Sunday, September 2, 1963, CORE members in Plaquemine defied a new federal court order and a full-scale riot broke out. Twenty state police officers were treated for injuries from thrown objects at the Plaquemine Sanitarium.[3325] In response, Leander Perez pledged, at the Citizens' Council meeting on September 5, 1963, "a different kind of reception" if civil rights demonstrators showed up in Plaquemines Parish.[3326]

On September 4, 1963, J. G. Sourwine, counsel for Eastland's SISS, held a two-day hearing on the FPCC and reportedly exposed the Communist sponsorship of the group.[3327] The case that CORE was Communist-backed could be made next in Clinton, when Oswald made his appearance in late August or early September 1963. There was no court activity involving CORE, Judge Rarick, and the town attorneys from August 28 through nearly all of September. No one was prepared for the bombshell that would be dropped next.

On Monday, September 30, 1963, special counsel for Clinton, Richard Van Buskirk, stated at the preliminary injunction hearing against CORE that the East Feliciana Parish was "met for the first time with one of the arms of the Communist conspiracy" in the Congress of Racial Equality. At the hearing, the temporary restraining order against CORE was extended to October 14, 1963. The paper reported: "Van Buskirk claimed the CORE organization has been infiltrated by left wingers throughout the history of its existence and he claimed at least one individual who is a member of a Communist front organization is working with CORE in East Feliciana Parish." Van Buskirk's comments were noted in the newspaper headline "CORE Group Termed Arm Of Red Plot." Van Buskirk claimed that CORE's actions in East Feliciana Parish constituted "criminal conspiracies, no matter how sugar coated its by-laws are with words like non-violence."

CORE lawyers asked for a recess to discuss Van Buskirk's claims. A CORE attorney asked for a delay in the hearing so they could study a written copy of the remarks. CORE argued that the prosecution was trying to prove charges far beyond those alleged in the injunction petition. Judge Rarick permitted Van Buskirk to extend his pleadings to include his opening remarks about Communism and CORE, and gave CORE a continuance until October 14. Van Buskirk said, in his opening statement, that he could prove that fourteen members of the board of directors of CORE had been cited more than 400 times with Communist-front activities: he did not mention any names in his court statement. D.A. Kilbourne added that the information was contained in reports from the Justice Department and congressional committees. The defense was surprised at the charges. Van Buskirk pledged he would prove that CORE's activities in Clinton were carefully planned actions with selected leaders drawn from New York to California. "We will show this conspiracy is directed at local government itself." Van Buskirk also said that he planned to subpoena CORE records.[3328]

The charges that CORE was Communist backed came four days before the raid on the offices of SCEF in New Orleans on October 4, 1963, which was based in charges that SCEF was also Communist backed and in violation of the Communist Control Act, which was enacted in 1962, upon Oswald's return from the Soviet Union. Given that the principals behind the SCEF raid and the Clinton injunction were tied to the same Perez and Banister segregation machinery, the timing of the Communist charges against CORE on September 25 and SCEF on October 4 were likely planned to coincide.

The Watchman on October 4, 1963, reported Richard Van Buskirk's claim that at least one Communist had infiltrated CORE in Clinton on the day of the SCEF raid in New Orleans under the Communist Control Act. The Baton Rouge *Morning Advocate*, on October 1, 1963, also reported Van Buskirk's claim that at least one Communist had infiltrated CORE in Clinton using the headline "CORE Group Termed Arm of Red Plot." Source: with permission from *The Watchman*

On October 5, 1963, Van Buskirk stated that at least one Communist infiltrator was on the scene to promote trouble in Clinton, but he declined to identify anyone. On that same day, Judge Rarick continued a temporary restraining order against CORE and issued an arrest warrant for national CORE leader Ronnie Moore for failing to appear as a witness.[3329]

On October 14, 1963, the press reported that four more Negro picketers were arrested in Clinton, bringing the total to forty-two over the weekend, despite the temporary restraining order.[3330] Hearings were to be held to make the temporary restraining order a more permanent type of court directive. Deputies then obtained a search warrant and raided CORE headquarters in Clinton. They allegedly seized books and documents and charged white CORE worker Edward Vickery with contributing to the delinquency of minors. Kilbourne reported that works by Karl Marx (who created the theories of present-day Communism) were found in a raid on the CORE house. The material was supposedly printed in English but published in Moscow, and the text was underlined. Vickery's bond was set at $5,000.[3331] Van Buskirk stated that he hoped "to prove connections between CORE's civil rights connections and the Communist movement."[3332] (CORE worker Miriam Feingold, who had also been involved in CORE's Freedom Rides, told the author adamantly that no CORE worker would have dared to keep any Communist materials among their possessions, since doing so would just have fed into the hands of their enemies.[3333])

On October 11, 1963, CORE appealed the remanding of the case back to Clinton. The next day, picketing and a boycott began against the merchants in Clinton. Thirty-nine protesters were arrested and additional arrests were made on October 13.

On October 14, the trial was set to proceed in Clinton when CORE filed motions in the United States Court of Appeals for the Fifth Circuit, in New Orleans, including a request for a stay. Judge John Minor Wisdom issued a sweeping indefinite stay order, halting the proceedings until the federal courts could decide whether it had the power to review the case. The Clinton *Watchman*, on October 18, 1963, reported, "Attorneys for CORE sought frantically to avoid a hearing which might prove connection between CORE and international Communism." Although Oswald was not in Clinton at the time, he had apparently left a memorable impression of his visit there. (The Louisiana segregationists, who enacted the Communist Control Act in 1962, specifically noted the danger of the Moscow-directed influence within the civil rights movement, which was the basis of the law, as we shall see in Chapter Twenty-three. Oswald was the only person who had been to Moscow and had also been physically present among the CORE workers in Clinton.)

On October 24, 1963, Van Buskirk, parish D.A. Kilbourne, William F. Kline, Jr. (attorney for the town of Clinton), and William E. Woodward (special counsel for East Louisiana Parish) issued a press release on CORE, declaring: "The relationship between the races in our community has been good for generations. . . . To this day there has been no interference with negro [sic] registration in Clinton. Nor have the officials sought to prevent or limit the peaceful assembly of our colored citizens."

The press reported, on November 21, 1963, that Kilbourne asked for another delay in the injunction hearing against CORE, this time due to a recent auto accident involving Van Buskirk.[3334] (Van Buskirk was seriously injured in the accident, sustaining a punctured lung and other injuries, and was taken to the East Louisiana State Hospital infirmary. He eventually recovered. Of the few files from Guy Banister that survived, one contains a news clipping of Van Buskirk's motor vehicle accident, which adds corroboration to the claim that Van Buskirk and Banister knew each other. The article reported that "R. G. Van Buskirk," special attorney for East Feliciana Parish and Clinton, in the recent civil rights litigation, was in fair condition at a Baton Rouge hospital after his station wagon had overturned. Banister wrote in the margin of the filed article, "Ban on CORE Activity."[3335])

The following day, November 22, 1963, the press reported that Van Buskirk was going to begin a probe into the Communist ties to CORE in East Feliciana Parish. He stated that two of the white Clinton witnesses in the Oswald saga, Reeves Morgan and Henry Earl Palmer, were going to assist him. Fifteen witnesses were summoned, including CORE Field Secretary Ronnie Moore, Edgar Vickery and Emmet Collins of CORE, Sheriff Arch Doughty and three parish representatives, State Representative Reeves Morgan, Henry Earl Palmer, and Dr. Richard Munson. The press reported that Attorney William Kline had shown Ronnie Moore a piece of CORE letterhead containing the names of the advisory committee. Kline told him that Senator Eastland had named twelve of the people on the letterhead as being affiliated with Communist-front organizations. Palmer testified that he had in his files false applications from black registrants. Morgan testified that he had been questioned by a representative of the Justice Department about the firing of one of his black employees, and denied knowing that the employee had attempted to register to vote in the CORE voter drive.[3336]

After the Kennedy assassination, Judge Rarick's courtroom fight with CORE began to fade. In December 1963, Rarick granted another continuance of the injunction.[3337] Another delay was granted on January 3, 1964.[3338] Finally, D.A. Kilbourne dismissed the injunction suit against CORE by the Clinton counsel in early 1964. Disgusted by Kilbourne's action, Van Buskirk refused to sign the dismissal papers and resigned from the case.[3339]

Kilbourne told the author he had marked differences with Rarick, who was infuriated by the case's dismissal. Eighty-six years old and in failing health at the time of the interview, his memory remained sharp. He said Rarick headed a particularly violent Klan group, a stance which was highlighted by a speech he made in St. Francisville, where Rarick urged a white crowd to use guns against CORE demonstrators, and whipped the crowd into a frenzy with his racist rhetoric. Kilbourne stated that there was never any Communist material seized in the raid of the CORE house as Van Buskirk had claimed, and he further told the author that Rarick and Van Buskirk fabricated the allegation.[3340, 3341]

Dan Campbell, who infiltrated the Klan for Guy Banister, told the author that Rarick's Klan involvement was common knowledge.[3342] Contemporaneous newspaper reports corroborate Kilbourne's story about the Klan violence, noting an incident where a Baton Rouge TV reporter was beaten and his life threatened when he tried to cover a KKK meeting in nearby Jackson, Louisiana. One Klansman held a pistol to the reporter's head and told him it would be the last story he would cover, while other men looked on, carrying shotguns. The reporter was driven around in a truck and, later, dropped off in the bushes.[3343]

In the end, all of Rarick and Van Buskirk's efforts to tie CORE workers in Clinton to Communism, riding on the fears of the Red Scare, failed. In the end, groups like CORE prevailed over the tactics of the segregationists in Clinton and throughout the South. After President Johnson pushed through President Kennedy's Civil Rights Act on June 2, 1964, and the Voting Rights Act in 1965, segregation was abolished.

Guy Banister, Joe Cooper, and Carl McIntire

Guy Banister met Carl McIntire at the Capitol House in Baton Rouge in or around June of 1963 according to informant and law enforcement officer William H. "Joe" Cooper. (McIntire, it will be recalled, was the Collingswood, New Jersey, radical right-wing preacher who had a nationally disseminated far-right radio program and newsletter. He was vehemently anti-Kennedy.) The meeting followed approximately one month after a similar meeting that had featured General Walker and Billy James Hargis. (Hargis and Walker spoke in Baton Rouge at the Capitol House in May, which places the McIntire-Banister meeting around June 26, 1963.)[3344, 3345, 3346]

McIntire had mentored Hargis in the 1950s, and it should be recalled from Chapter Eleven that McIntire's West Coast representative, Edgar Eugene Bradley, from California, was likely in Dallas at the time of the assassination. Walker and Banister's relationship with McIntire likely had something to do with Bradley's suspected presence in Dallas. David Ferrie's confidant, Raymond Broshears, named McIntire as a member of the assassination conspiracy (as was noted in Chapter Nineteen) and McIntire was close to General Walker, coming to his aid shortly after his return from Germany.

George Ratliff, owner of radio station WKNK in Baton Rouge, was a devotee of McIntire and sponsored McIntire's radio program "Information Hour" in the city. (Garrison's investigators found evidence that Ratliff and Clinton town counsel Richard Van Buskirk tried to take over the Klan in Clinton.[3347]) Ratliff sponsored speaking engagements for General Walker in 1963 and Carl McIntire in 1964. Guy Banister attended the September 4, 1963 Capitol House Free Electors meeting with Walker and Clinton attorney Richard Van Buskirk.

Cooper noted, in a report provided to Jim Garrison, that Ratliff, Van Buskirk, Walker, and Banister knew each other. He said Walker and Banister were close friends, and that Van Buskirk was supposedly with Banister when he died. Ratliff told Cooper that when the takeover came the FBI would be on their side. Cooper said that, before the assassination, Van Buskirk was almost killed when his car ran off the road in Clinton. In the margin of Cooper's report, Garrison wrote, "Who is Van Buskirk?"[3348] It is unfortunate that Garrison did not know who Van Buskirk was, since Van Buskirk's involvement in the Clinton incident was key to understanding it. Garrison must have known Van Buskirk's partner in crime, Judge Rarick, however, since the two attended Tulane Law School at the same time.

Notice of Cooper's appearance before the grand jury in the Garrison case was published in the Baton Rouge *State-Times* on July 9, 1968. The paper reported that Cooper had evidence pertinent to the case, calling it "definitely new evidence." The grand jury transcripts were not public record, however, and were nearly destroyed. They were eventually located in the 1990s and turned over to the Assassination Records Review Board, but the author was unable to find Cooper's reported testimony.[3349]

Cooper was a paid informant for the FBI who had penetrated the Original Order of the KKK, National States' Rights Party, and the American Nazi Party. Cooper helped foil a plot to assassinate Vice President Hubert Humphrey on April 9, 1965, when he appeared before an AFL-CIO rally in Baton Rouge. Humphrey's outspoken stand for equal rights and integration was the motive for the murder plot. The plan was to also assassinate Victor Bussie, a long-time Klan enemy and head of the Louisiana AFL-CIO, who hosted Humphrey.[3350] Jack Helm, Imperial Wizard of the Universal Klans of America, Louisiana Realm, and a fellow Citizens' Council board member with Judge Rarick, was implicated in the bombing of the Bussie's home.[3351] (Allen Campbell, who worked in Guy Banister's office "to study Communism" told the author that Banister and Helm knew each other.[3352]) A Klansman told Cooper about the Humphrey assassination plot and he obtained names and pictures of the Klansmen involved. When the two Klan gunmen entered the hall and sat down, undercover FBI and Secret Service men took them into custody; the men were questioned but never charged. Two years later, the New Orleans *States-Item* reported the assassination attempt naming only the involvement of a right-wing organization, but not the Klan.[3353, 3354] Louisiana historian Claude B. Slaton interviewed Cooper's daughter, Kathryn, who recalled that, as a child, she played in her father's Klan outfit, which he wore as an undercover informant.[3355]

In the course of informing on the National States' Rights Party and the American Nazi Party, Cooper briefly noted that Ray Leahart was a person who would do anything for George Lincoln Rockwell. He identified Leahart as a member of the New Orleans NSRP.[3356] It will be recalled from Chapter Three that a citizen, Muncey Perkins, reported to the FBI that he saw Lee Harvey Oswald with Ray Leahart in New Orleans. Moreover, an envelope from a letter addressed to Milteer from Leahart was found in Joseph Milteer's home, as was noted in Chapter Three. Guy Banister bailed Leahart out of jail after the 1961 Hate Bus incident, and Banister had a file on the Fighting American Nationalists (FAN), an American Nazi Party front group and their newspaper, which reported on CORE activities in New York in the summer of 1962, noting that New Orleans FAN leader Leahart was leading a FAN program for total racial separation.[3357] (In later years, Leahart was the best man at well-known Nazi and Klansman David Duke's wedding. Rarick was also a David Duke crony, and often gave the opening speech at Duke's rallies. Duke remains one of the countries best-known racists at the time of this writing.[3358])

According to another Garrison investigative memo, Joe Cooper, who was related to Marguerite Oswald, told Garrison's office in 1968 that he had developed a fine relationship with Marguerite, and would be glad to go to Dallas to talk to her on Garrison's behalf. Cooper stated that Marguerite told him, "Lee worked with the Civil Rights movement from time to time." Cooper stated that Sargent Pitcher, a member of the state Citizen's Council board, could give them a lot of information on Van Buskirk.[3359]

Cooper was found dead of a gunshot wound to the head, in his home in Baton Rouge, on October 16, 1974; it was ruled a suicide. However, evidence suggested that he was murdered, perhaps in retribution for his undercover work informing on the Klan and the far right. Five days before his death, Cooper had talked to reporters at a tabloid, *The Tattler*, about information he had about a flight by two men from Dallas to South America on the day President Kennedy was murdered. Cooper supposedly also had information on David

Ferrie and on arms smuggling. Cooper had been a Baton Rouge police officer for ten years and was once named outstanding policeman of the year, which lends tremendous credibility to his allegations. The evidence pointing toward murder—not suicide—included the fact that Cooper was right handed, but the .38 revolver was found on the left side of his bed. Furthermore, he had gotten up that morning and had left a pot of water boiling, which was discovered when his body was found. Based on the evidence at hand, friends and family were convinced Cooper was murdered.[3360]

Richard Van Buskirk

Clinton town counsel Richard Van Buskirk and Judge John Rarick were close friends. Van Buskirk's secretary in 1963, Mary Ann Sagely, told the author that the Van Buskirk and Rarick "were just as close as two men could be."[3361]

Years before CORE's incursion into Clinton, Van Buskirk had studied ways to fight the civil rights movement and the federal authorities' investigations into voter purges. Van Buskirk wrote Senator Allen Ellender on May 24, 1960, and told him of his concern about newspaper reports on the investigation of voter registration in East Feliciana Parish under the 1960 Civil Rights Act. (It may be worth noting that Van Buskirk was on a first-name basis with Louisiana senator Ellender's administrative assistant, George Arceneaux, Jr., which may explain how he was able to easily communicate with the senator.) Van Buskirk told Ellender that, "I . . . as a citizen and duly qualified elector of this parish, desire to make a study for the purpose of determining the most effective method of attack, independent of the efforts of local and state officers, to protect us from what I regard as unwarranted and unconstitutional federal intervention in an area so wisely reserved to the states and the people by the drafters of our constitution." Van Buskirk was interested in information he had heard about of a court granting a restraining order, which barred the FBI from inspecting voting records there. Van Buskirk's interest in the matter no doubt came from the FBI's concurrent investigation of Henry Earl Palmer. He was particularly interested in determining from which court the order was issued, the parties to the proceedings, and the name of the counsel successful in obtaining the order. Ellender's office responded on June 6, 1960, and noted that they had provided Van Buskirk with a large amount of material on the 1960 Civil Rights Act in the past. In Ellender's letter of reply, there was a mention of a state court granting a restraining order prohibiting the FBI from inspecting voter registration records in Alabama. Ellender's office promised to obtain a copy of the restraining order and forward a copy to Van Buskirk.[3362]

Van Buskirk left Clinton after his friend John Rarick's election to Congress in 1966, at which time Van Buskirk founded the American-Southern Africa Council, which had offices in Washington, D.C., and in Salisbury, Rhodesia. The office was created as a result of the closure of the U.S. Consulate in Rhodesia after U.S. sanctions were placed on Rhodesia for its position on apartheid. The *Rhodesia Herald* showed a picture of Van Buskirk flying an American flag outside the Salisbury office. The flag had once flown over the U.S. Capitol, and was sent to Van Buskirk courtesy of then-Congressman Rarick.[3363]

The far right saw Rhodesia as a model for the separation of the races. Members of the Citizens' Council and the John Birch Society, in addition to Tom Anderson and Billy James Hargis, were all admirers of South Africa.[3364] According to Jack Martin, a former Banister employee, Kent Courtney was also a supporter of Rhodesia. Martin stated that "Courtney and his followers do business with the known Neo-Nazi-right-wing-conservatives of Rhodesia, and the Union of South Africa, the Neo-Nazis-Afrikaners."[3365]

It may be worth noting that Van Buskirk was also a member of the American Lobby, a group that was formed in 1969 when five former staff members of Willis Carto's Liberty Lobby defected from the group. One was a former staffer for H. L. Hunt's *Life Lines*.[3366]

John Rarick, Leander Perez, and the Organized Resistance to Integration

John Rarick is an important figure in the Clinton incident, and at the time, his star was beginning to rise in the national hardcore underground. Unfortunately, owing to the fact that he lived somewhat in obscurity in the small town of St. Francisville, near Clinton, a lot less is known about his activities before the Kennedy assassination than after.

As has already been noted, by 1962, Clinton judge John Rarick (a close associate of Leander Perez, a colleague of General Walker and Guy Banister) had reached the upper echelon of the segregation forces in Louisiana when he was appointed to the board of directors of the Citizens' Council of Louisiana. The 1962 roster of the board of directors also included Perez, Louis P. Davis, John Garrett, Emmet Irwin, Sargent Pitcher, Jackson Ricau, Ned Touchstone, C. E. Vetter, Courtney Smith, and Jack Helm. (Davis, Perez, Ricau, and Helm were all associates of Guy Banister, noted in prior chapters.) A different, undated Council roster lists Banister associate Kent Courtney and Anthony Graffia, both of whom were active in the counter-demonstrations against NOCPA, which were noted in the last chapter. Three members of the board, Perez, Irwin and, Davis, were associates of Joseph Milteer. And Davis, Perez, and Touchstone were associates of General Walker.[3367] (Rarick's association with General Walker was reported in the press within the year after the assassination, as will be shown.)

Given that Rarick, and his close friend Richard Van Buskirk, worked on Perez's free electors bill in the state legislature in the summer of 1963, it is likely that Rarick also attended the September 4, 1963, Free Electors meeting at the Capitol House Hotel in nearby Baton Rouge. If so, he likely knew those who were known to have attended the meeting—Banister and Walker—in addition to Perez and Van Buskirk, whom he knew before the meeting.

John R. Rarick was born in Indiana, and moved to Louisiana in 1943. During WWII, he served in the army and was captured and spent three years in a Nazi prison camp. He graduated from Ball State Teacher College, then attended Louisiana State University. He received his law degree from Tulane in 1949, and practiced law in St. Francisville, before serving as a district judge from 1960 to 1965. He was urged to run for Congress in 1966 by the Ku Klux Klan and the Citizens' Council.[3368, 3369] Over the years, he became aligned with—and received awards from—the Congress of Freedom, We the People, and Liberty Lobby.[3370]

Rarick's rise to the top of the Louisiana segregation hierarchy and the national radical right likely began when he supported Willie Rainach, a close friend of Guy Banister, for governor in 1960. Correspondence between the two men revealed they were friends and supported the same segregationist and far-right causes.[3371] In 1961, Rarick campaigned for judge of the Twentieth Judicial District and vowed he would support segregation laws to the letter, stating, "I will not hesitate to jail violators of these laws whether they be local citizens or outsiders." Rarick was sworn in on June 27, 1961.[3372] In October of 1961, Rainach spoke at an opening ceremony at the Clinton courthouse, marking the beginning of Rarick's tenure as judge, along with Richard Van Buskirk (in a letter, Rainach referred to Van Buskirk as "my good friend.").[3373] Attesting to Rarick's crude racist attitude, black New Orleans attorney Lelis Ely testified under oath that Rarick, while a judge, told him "I didn't know they let coons practice law."[3374]

On October 2, 1962, Kent Courtney was scheduled to speak in St. Francisville, Rarick's hometown, on the subject of "America's Un-elected Rulers."[3375] Courtney also spoke at the Clinton courthouse, where the CORE injunction was held. His topic was the "Right to Work," in support of an anti-union movement. Richard Kilbourne, Jr. told the author that he attended the speech.[3376] Many others from the New Orleans hardcore underground, as we shall see, came off the beaten path to speak in Clinton and East Feliciana Parish.

It was announced in the press that Rarick was expected to speak on the subject of "United States or United Nations" in Clinton, sponsored by the Citizens' Council, on March 29, 1963.[3377] Then, on May 10, 1963, the press reported a Free Electors Rally was held at the Capitol House Hotel. Guy Banister was named as a representative to the First District. The Sovereignty Commission backed the Free Electors scheme.[3378] On May 21, 1963, the Unpledged Electors Bill, aimed at depriving President Kennedy of Louisiana's electors, was introduced to the Louisiana House of Representatives.[3379] On the afternoon of May 26, 1963, General Walker and Billy James Hargis spoke in Shreveport. Walker's speech was entitled "Choices before us—U.S. or U.N.?[3380] The following day, Walker and Hargis spoke to an audience of a thousand at the Capitol House Hotel in Baton Rouge. Walker stated: "It's harder every day to tell the difference between Kennedyism and Communism." Walker declared: "The front of the Cold War runs through Havana, the United Nations and the White House." Hargis stated that "three of the rankest Communists in the United States and two car loads of race agitators had recently invaded Baton Rouge," which was an apparent reference to CORE workers. (Walker earlier had appeared in the Louisiana state senate chambers, where he was applauded as he walked down the aisle. Senator Wendell Harris told the senate, Walker "will be remembered most from Oxford" and asked them to give Walker "a vote of thanks and confidence.")[3381]

On July 9, 1963, Louisiana States Rights leaders and George Shannon, head of the Free Electors movement, stated in a meeting at the Capitol House in Baton Rouge that the South must defeat the Kennedy administration in 1964 or suffer dire consequences; members of the John Birch Society, and the Citizens' Council were present. John Rarick delivered a special message for the youth, denouncing the deans of eleven southern schools who supported the decisions of the U.S. Supreme Court stating, "Where were these law deans when the Supreme Court turned eleven of the Communists loose and where were they when the same court said the Bible was an unconstitutional instrument?"[3382] On August 7, 1963, Leander Perez's newly configured Free Electors measure, which he insisted was not a free electors measure, passed in the state legislature.[3383]

The critically important relationship between Leander Perez and the two Clinton players, John Rarick and Richard Van Buskirk, was established by their presence with Perez in two meetings in 1963 in Baton Rouge around the time of Oswald's visit. The press reported, on September 1, 1963, that the Sovereignty Commission of Louisiana pledged funds for a statewide committee to fight President Kennedy's civil rights bill called the Louisiana Chapter for Fundamental American Freedoms. Speakers blasting the civil rights measure included Van Buskirk and Perez—Rarick was also present.[3384] (As was emphasized before, Rarick's closest friend, Van Buskirk, had been with Perez, General Walker and Guy Banister at the Capitol House during the Free Electors meeting on September 4, 1963. Perez was undeniably the chief architect of the Free Electors bill[3385] and Rarick and Van Buskirk helped write the Free Electors legislation in the summer of 1963.[3386]) Perez and Representative Wellborn Jack debated for the Free Electors bill resolution, which won approval in the state legislature on September 7, 1963.[3387]

The plan to have Oswald appear in Clinton among the CORE workers may have emanated from either the September 4, Capitol House meeting which Perez attended with Van Buskirk and Banister, or from around the time of the September 1 Sovereignty Commission meeting that Perez attended with Rarick. Either way, the two meetings were held right around the time that Oswald made his journey to Clinton. In Chapter Three, the allegation that Oswald was seen in Baton Rouge in the company of Kent Courtney on a number of occasions in the summer of 1963 was reported. If that is true, their presence there may have been related to either the Free Electors movement or the CORE summer project.

On October 27, 1963, Rarick wrote to Willie Rainach, less than a month before the assassination, and told him, ominously, "The only answer for the Southern and all white people is to have a secret underground army prepared to take whatever steps as are necessary to defend ourselves."[3388] (There is a suspicious gap in the correspondence between Rainach and Rarick from October 27, 1963, until July 27, 1965, when Rainach responded to a letter from Rarick asking what he thought about resettling "the Negro onto reservations within the Continental United States." Rainach approved of the idea whole-heartedly, offering that it would be even better to "repatriate them to Africa" instead.[3389])

On November 17, 1963, in a speech at a Dothan, Alabama, Civitan Club meeting, Rarick warned his audience that President Kennedy might declare martial law and postpone the next year's election if there was a chance of a conservative candidate being elected. During the same speech, he called for the resignation of Attorney General Robert Kennedy. He said President Kennedy had violated his oath to protect the Constitution, stating: "We must all understand today that the strong arm of the Communist conspiracy is among us. We must realize that a few hard-core disciplined Communists among us are using religious phrases and high sounding slogans to appeal to well meaning people and makes them their dupes and stooges."[3390, 3391, 3392]

Rarick spoke at a Citizens' Council rally in Shreveport on January 26, 1964. He was dubbed, on a flier, "The judge that 'CORE' fears most."[3393] The next month, on February 17, 1964, Rarick appeared before the Greater New Orleans Citizens' Council and said the civil rights bill was "illegal, unjust, and un-Godly and must fall." He called it a "dastardly act."[3394] CORE members picketed outside of the meeting.[3395]

Rarick then appeared with General Walker on July 4, 1964, nine months after Lee Harvey Oswald had arrived in Clinton, in Rarick's Twentieth Judicial District. The event was dubbed a "Good Old Fashioned Patriotic Rally," and was sponsored by the Calhoun, Louisiana, Citizens' Council—2,400 people gathered for the event. The July 4, 1964, appearance is the first documented association of the two men. Other honored guests included Walker's top aide, Robert Surrey, and state representative Harold Montgomery.[3396] Thus, Clinton judge John Rarick, from the backwoods of Louisiana, found himself in the presence of two Dallas Warren Commission witnesses, General Walker and Robert Surrey, both associates of Joseph Milteer, within nine months of Oswald's visit to Clinton and the murder of the president. On July 30, 1964, Leander Perez was the speaker at a Citizens' Council meeting in St. Francisville, where Rarick resided.[3397]

On Sunday, March 7, 1965, civil rights workers marched to the Edmund Pettis Bridge as a part of the historic Selma-to-Montgomery march. Dallas County sheriff Jim Clark's men, along with some state troopers, charged the protestors after they failed to disperse as ordered. The brutal beatings were shown on televisions around the world, and the incident became known as "Bloody Sunday." The protestors chose Selma because they felt sure that Sheriff Clark would overact and national reaction to what happened next would hasten the passage of the Voting Rights Act.[3398] Clark, for his part in the incident, became a celebrity among radical segregationists.

Later that spring, on May 7, 1965, Perez spoke in Bogalusa on the subject "Voting Rights Bill and the Second Reconstruction," at a United Conservative Rally and Parade, where Judge John Rarick and Sheriff Jim Clark were special guests; 10,000 people were expected to attend to protest against the federal government's policies in civil rights, and Cuban affairs. The Anti-Communist Christian Association, a camouflaged Klan group, sponsored the Bogalusa rally.[3399]

The following day, on May 8, 1965, Rarick joined George Singelmann and opened a Bogalusa rally, exclaiming, "Good evening, fellow racists." Rarick declared that the congressmen who voted for the Voting Rights Act were traitors. Jack Helm, Ned Touchstone, and Courtney Smith, who served as the state directors of the Citizens' Council, were there. Alvin Cobb spoke to the crowd, declaring, "The white race has been and always will be a superior race."[3400] (As was noted in Chapter Nine, Joseph Oster, Guy Banister's former detective agency partner, named Alvin Cobb and George Singelmann as Guy Banister's closest friends.[3401])

Alvin Cobb was a Klansman and brother of Lloyd Cobb, who was Clay Shaw's boss at the International Trade Mart. At the rally, William Simmons, who was Ross Barnett's chief advisor during the Ole Miss insurrection, announced an upcoming May 17 rally to observe the anniversary of "Black Monday" (the segregationist's term for the day the *Brown* decision was reached).[3402] Leander Perez was an announced speaker, but apparently did not make it to the engagement.[3403] Joseph Milteer's violent friend, Kenneth Adams, traveled to a Bogalusa, Louisiana, Citizens' Council- and Klan-led rally on July 23, 1965. (However, Adams had been drunk for most of the month leading up to the event and was not permitted to speak at the rally).[3404]

John Rarick also plotted against CORE in Bogalusa. Ned Touchstone "reminisced," in an article in the April 4, 1967, edition of the *Councilor*, about how Rarick, George Singelmann, and a group of Klansmen used a secret strategy called "Ingredient Four" to defeat the "Communist" CORE in Bogalusa. Touchstone wrote: "The Communists long ago began to print false credentials. But we learned that we can duplicate their letterheads, send them fake instructions, and listen in on their CB radio signals."[3405]

Jack Helm, a Banister colleague, spoke on May 13, 1965, at the State Citizens' Council of East Feliciana meeting in Clinton.[3406] On June 5, 1965, Rarick was the planned speaker at a meeting in Natchez, Mississippi, which was sponsored by Americans for the Preservation of the White Race.[3407] On July 4, 1965, Rarick, General Walker, and Jerry Festus Brown were the featured speakers at a Citizens' Council rally at the Louisiana State Capitol in Baton Rouge. (It will be recalled from the last chapter that Brown was Guy Banister's old friend and headed the American Legion.) Four Louisiana State University students from India stopped to hear them speak at the rally and were attacked; two were beaten, one (who was wearing a turban) was treated for a gash over his eye at the hospital, and two escaped and were followed—but the police found no witnesses to the incident. The rally was attended by nearly 3,500 people and rife with KKK placards—and more than 2,000 confederate flags. It concluded with a march to the governor's mansion. Before the rally, LSU students, protesting Walker's brand of patriotism, were pushed and harassed by rally followers, and one received medical attention for a piece of glass in the eye.

The 1965 rally was Walker's second straight Fourth of July appearance in Louisiana. While speaking, Walker called Kennedy's assassination a coup d'état and a complete takeover of the government. He predicted more assassinations would take place. (As was noted in Chapter Eighteen, at the same time, the FBI considered Walker a threat to the life of President Johnson.) A newspaper article reporting on the rally featured photos of Walker, Rarick, and a man they mistakenly identified as "Kent Courtney of Shreveport," who was actually Courtney Smith.[3408] A proposal was made to raise funds to determine if there were any confederates of Lee Harvey Oswald, running loose in Louisiana.[3409] A flier dubbed the event a "We—The White People Rally."[3410, 3411] George Singelmann was expected to attend with a delegation of fifty people from New Orleans. He planned to picket the governor's mansion and press for a "Statewide birth control program for Negroes on welfare rolls."[3412]

On July 12, 1965, Rarick wrote Ned Touchstone and warmly addressed him as "You ole' Christian Nazi."[3413] Then, in early September 1965, Rarick addressed a Labor Day parade held in Bogalusa by the Original Knights of the Ku Klux Klan, who were functioning under the cover name of the Anti-Communist Christian Association. (The Klan's actions around Bogalusa that year had become so extreme that a federal court, under the Civil Rights Act of 1964, issued an injunction against them from further assaults and intimidation of black and white civil rights workers.) Richard Cotton, who had a national radical-right radio program and newsletter,[3414] flew from California to join John Rarick at the rally and persuade him to run for Congress. (On September 9, 1965, the press reported that Cotton of Bakersfield, California, was an overnight guest at Rarick's home.) Minutemen leader Robert DePugh was another speaker at the event.[3415]

On January 6–7, 1966, Rarick spoke at a Liberty Lobby convention.[3416] (The board of directors of Liberty Lobby, in 1961, had included General Pedro del Valle, Harry Everingham, Billy James Hargis, Willis Carto, General Stratemeyer, and other notables on the far right.[3417])

In 1966, John Rarick resigned his position as the judge for the Twentieth Judicial District to run for Congress in the twelve-parish Sixth District against incumbent Jimmie H. Morrison. (Interestingly, when Reeves Morgan lost his seat as state representative in 1963, he had announced he would run for Congress against Jimmie H. Morrison in 1964.[3418]) After Rarick resigned as district judge and vacated his courthouse office, a burned cross, a large amount of KKK paraphernalia, homemade flare bombs, and hand grenades were found to have been left behind, discovered by Judge Ben N. Tucker, who was appointed to take his place.[3419] Leander Perez, who had a history of backing the careers of feisty racist judges for the cause of segregation, financed Rarick's campaign for Congress.[3420] (Perez's proudest accomplishment was raising an obscure Alabama Circuit Court Judge, George Wallace, to the governor's office in Alabama, and in 1968, to a candidate for president on the American Independent Party ticket.[3421] Others who ran after Wallace on the American Independent Party ticket or its successor, the American Party, were prominent John Birch Society leaders Tom Anderson and John Schmitz, and later, John Rarick.[3422])

Rarick ran a deceptive, dirty, and violent campaign, which was primarily focused on ending integration.[3423] His opponent, James ("Jimmie") H. Morrison, claimed Rarick had tapped his phone and personally harassed his campaign sound truck drivers. In perhaps one of the most ingenious and novel forms of election fraud in history, just five minutes before the filing deadline, James E. Morrison, a grocer, entered the race and, as a result, diverted the votes of 6,562 voters who probably thought they were voting for incumbent James H. Morrison. The deceptive scheme insured Rarick a victory in the ensuing run-off election.[3424]

Rarick's supporters engaged in acts of intimidation in the run-off race with James H. Morrison. The press noted, "The [Sixth] District holds those areas that have seen most of this state's racial violence including Bogalusa. Three crosses were burned last night outside Morrison's home in Hammond." Rarick denied involvement in the cross-burning incident, instead accusing Morrison for creating it to garner sympathy. The press stated that Rarick's campaign "ranks as the most vitriolic in Louisiana's history," while Rarick claimed his election was necessary to save the country from Socialism. When Morrison accused him of being in the KKK, Rarick sued him for $500,000 in damages for libel and slander.[3425] Morrison charged, in the *Congressional Record*, that Rarick had joined the Klan in 1963 and became the Exalted Cyclops in 1964. He called him "The Klan's man from Indiana."[3426] Rarick held a vendetta against Morrison, calling him responsible for bringing "federal spies" to Louisiana in the form of election observers to help those he called "illiterates" register to vote under the Morrison-backed 1965 Voting Rights Bill.[3427] One Rarick campaign flier read, "Judge John R. Rarick who stopped the Negro (CORE) from demonstrating in his Judicial District [sic], will speak at the Coushatta High Auditorium on February 7." The parish Citizens' Council invited, "All the white people, to hear the Judge."[3428] On July 6, 1966, a sound truck campaigning for Congressman Morrison was forced off the road and plastered with Rarick campaign stickers, and the driver was told to get out of the parish. In another incident, a Morrison campaign billboard was splattered with paint.[3429] Kent Courtney dedicated an entire edition of the Conservative Society of America's October 3, 1966, newsletter to praising Rarick's campaign.[3430]

A number of "Rarick for Congress" fliers were found in the personal papers of Clay Shaw who Jim Garrison accused of conspiring with Lee Harvey Oswald to kill the president. (A close friend, Jeff Bidderson, donated Shaw's papers to the Assassination Record Review Board and they reside in the National Archives.) Shaw had used the backs of the fliers to take notes during his prosecution by Jim Garrison's office.[3431]

During Rarick's tenure in Congress from January 3, 1967, to January 3, 1975, he crammed the *Congressional Record* with radical-right-wing articles that were anti-Semitic, anti-black, anti-federal government, anti-United Nations, and anti-welfare. The index to Volume 114 of the 1966 *Congressional Record* lists over 600 articles from extreme right-wing magazines that were inserted into the record for 1966 alone. Rarick was friendly with far-right national leaders Carl McIntire, Tom Anderson, and Willis Carto. When Martin Luther King, Jr. was assassinated in 1968, Rarick stated, "The untimely death of this Communist puppet occurred at the very time he had ceased to be valuable . . ."[3432] In his newsletter, Dan Smoot gave Rarick the second highest rating in Congress, and Liberty Lobby gave him a rating of 100 percent.[3433]

General Walker, Mrs. Billy James Hargis, and John Rarick in an August 7, 1967, photo (above left). John Rarick (right) with Pedro del Valle (center) and an unidentified man in Rarick's congressional office in Washington in 1968 (above right). Source: Left photo from the Edwin A. Walker Papers, Dolph Briscoe Center for American History, University of Texas at Austin; Right photo from the congressional photography office, Rayburn Office Building

In the summer of 1967, Rarick spoke at Billy James Hargis's annual Christian Crusade conference with Tom Anderson and Lester Maddox.[3434] When Rarick ran for reelection to Congress in 1968, he published his views in a small paperback book entitled *Stand Up! You are American*. Anderson, who wrote the foreword, stated, "Rarick strongly fears a Communist take over."[3435] The American Friends of John Rarick group was organized to promote Rarick's reelection to Congress and included a number of prominent national figures who are a part of the assassination story including Anderson, its chairman. Others were Walker, General Pedro del Valle, and Major Arch Roberts. An associate of Joseph Milteer, Curtis A. Dall (who presided over the 1963 Constitution Party meeting where assassination of the president was discussed), was on the national committee for Rarick. Another committee member was Richard Moran, a member of Nelson Bunker Hunt's American Volunteer Group, the so-called "kill squad," as was noted in Chapter Eleven. Other American Friends of John Rarick included Richard Cotton, J. Evetts Haley, Cleon Skousen, and General Stratemeyer, and Billy James Hargis served on the national committee.[3436]

On April 30, 1968, General Pedro del Valle visited Rarick to ask him to sign a petition and the two were photographed in Rarick's congressional office. The photo was supposed to be placed in the *Congressional Record* and the details of the event were disclosed in a letter that del Valle wrote to Wally Butterworth on May 2, 1968.[3437] (It will be recalled from Chapter Seven that Butterworth, an associate of Joseph Milteer, like del Valle, called for the killing of the president at the October 1963 Constitution Party meeting.)

In July 1968, Rarick attended a Rhodesia National Day celebration in Bethesda, Maryland, which was sponsored by the American-Southern African Council, Clinton attorney Richard Van Buskirk's outfit. On January 5, 1969, a memo noted that Rarick was helping organize the National Youth Alliance, one of Willis Carto's neo-Nazi fronts.[3438] Rarick was named a board member of the Congress of Freedom in 1970 and also received their "Man of the Year" Award.[3439] That same year, he was the chief speaker at Liberty Lobby's national convention.[3440] Rarick was also a featured speaker at a "Fourth of July Rally for God, Family, and Country" in Belmont, Massachusetts. Practically every major figure in the hardcore underground noted in this work spoke at that forum.[3441]

Rarick and Carl McIntire joined together in a "March for Victory in Vietnam" in Washington, D.C., on April 4, 1970.[3442] (As was noted in Chapter Nineteen, David Ferrie's confidant, Raymond Broshears, named McIntire as a conspirator in the assassination of the president.) In 1972 and 1973, Rarick addressed the German Volksunion in Germany.[3443] (The *Deutsche Volksunion* was a nationalist political party in Germany. It was founded by publisher Gerhard Frey as an informal association in 1971, and established as a party in 1987. Financially, it was largely dependent on Frey.[3444] It will be recalled from Chapter Fourteen that Gerhard Frey was General Walker's old friend from Germany who published the *National Zeitung* and wrote in his paper, following the assassination, that General Walker told them that Oswald had shot at him.)

Rarick went on to become the head of the Congress of Freedom in 1974.[3445] Then, in June 1977, an article written by Rarick appeared in the *Thunderbolt*.[3446] Rarick was nominated for president on the American Independent Party ticket in 1980.[3447] (George Wallace ran for president on the ticket in 1968 and made a respectable showing. Rarick did not in his 1980 run.) In 1987, Rarick supported Klansman David Duke in his election to the state house of representatives.

Up until his death in 2008, Rarick was a prominent figure in the Council of Conservative Citizens, the successor of the Citizens' Council.[3448] The author briefly interviewed Rarick in his St. Francisville law office in 1997. When asked if he planned to donate his papers to a public archive, he replied, "My enemies would only try to use them against me."[3449]

The Aftermath of the Clinton Incident

After the Kennedy assassination, Leander Perez's Greater New Orleans Citizens' Council blamed the murder on a Marxist-Communist, the Communists who dominated CORE, the NAACP, and Martin Luther King, Jr. The Council issued a statement declaring, "Our Citizens' Council leaders have consistently warned of the grave threat of Communism and its fronts who threaten the safety of every individual, and who thrust its many communities into a condition of anarchy. We stressed the nature of Communist or subversive domination of the NAACP, CORE and MARTIN LUTHER KING'S [sic] activities against peace and good order and to stir up racial strife and hatred throughout the land. . . . A victory by these evil forces who are laying in the gap, would subject our State to their further violent invasions such as was witnessed in the town of Plaquemine and nearby Clinton. . . . Now, from absolute evidence laid bare to all of us a Marxist-Communist, devoted to Cuba's Castro, has shed the blood of the president of the United States by cold-blooded assassination. In turn, the Communist assassin violated his party rule by being caught, and then his lips were sealed by liquidation, the Communist way."[3450]

It is remarkable that CORE, Plaquemine, and Clinton were mentioned in the post-assassination press release along with the "Marxist-Communist" Oswald. Perez, who controlled the Citizens' Council, presumably wrote the statement. With the additional mention of Plaquemine in the statement, it would not be surprising if Oswald had associated with, or infiltrated, the CORE headquarters in Plaquemine—and that photographic and other evidence had been generated to prove it. It is of interest to note that the mayor of Plaquemine was quoted in the newspaper on September 6, 1963, saying: "Our town was flooded with Negroes and whites too, we have never seen before."[3451]

On May 31, 1966, FBI director J. Edgar Hoover reported Clinton town marshal John Manchester to the Secret Service as a potential threat to the life of President Johnson.[3452] On March 14, 1970, Willie Holmes, a black man, was arrested on the charge of disturbing the peace. Holmes alleged that while he was being processed at the Clinton jail, Deputy Leon Reed beat him while Manchester held a gun to his head. The incident was reported to the Justice Department.[3453] However, the HSCA was apparently unaware of Manchester's involvement in either incident, when they concluded that Oswald's visit to Clinton and his encounter with the marshal and other witnesses was innocuous. In 1979, G. Robert Blakey, head of the HSCA, concluded that "the committee found that the Clinton witnesses were credible and significant. . . . [And] was inclined to believe that Oswald was in Clinton in late August, early September 1963, and that he was in the company of David Ferrie, if not Clay Shaw."[3454] In his book, *The Plot to Kill the President*, Blakey called the Clinton witnesses "honest folks."[3455]

On February 2, 1992, an interview of Reeves Morgan and Lee McGehee was published in the Baton Rouge *Morning Advocate* Sunday magazine. McGehee told the paper that the first inquiry into Oswald's visit happened around 1966 when Congressman John Rarick asked him about Oswald's appearance in the area. After that, McGehee stated that a Shreveport newspaper (likely a reference to the *Councilor*) interviewed some of the witnesses and published a story. (The author was unable to find any story in the *Councilor* about Oswald in Clinton in an extensive review of the paper.)[3456] It can be assumed that McGehee was lying about Rarick's purported inquiry about Oswald, given that Rarick was seen in the vicinity of Oswald and the registration drive, according to John Manchester. Decades later, Rarick related to a writer that he had, indeed, seen Oswald in the registration line in 1963.[3457] Rarick, McGehee's alleged Klan leader, knew all about Oswald in Clinton.

The author interviewed Reeves Morgan in 1994, before the true meaning of Oswald's visit had become apparent. At eighty-nine, Morgan was frail and at the end of life, but mentally sharp. He repeated the same story he had told Garrison and the HSCA word for word, without variation. When I asked him if he would mind if I videotaped him with my camera, he commented, "They might break it."[3458]

The author interviewed Lee McGehee in 1994 and his story, like Morgan's, was unvarying from his previous interviews.[3459] In later years, the author periodically telephoned McGehee, never revealing the author's suspicions he was lying. In one conversation, in a mocking and challenging tone, McGehee said of the many who came to interview him, "After all these years they *still* haven't figured out why Oswald was up here." On another occasion, after the recent passing of Reeves Morgan (Henry Earl Palmer had died of cancer in the 1980s, McGehee told the author), the author mentioned to McGehee that he was the last of the witnesses who had supposed direct conversations with Oswald. Again McGehee told the author, mockingly, "What did Carlos Marcello say? Two persons can keep a secret if one of them is dead. . . ." I asked him to tell me how Oswald reacted when he saw the poster of Martin Luther King, Jr. at the so-called Communist Training School hanging in his barber shop. McGehee imitated Oswald's reaction, letting out a sort of shuddering groan of surprise. I asked McGehee if he took that to mean that Oswald was bothered and surprised that the poster had revealed King's secret liaison with the Communists. He agreed that it did.[3460]

Jim Garrison provided a rather bizarre interpretation of the meaning of Oswald's visit to Clinton to support his theory that Oswald was an agent of U.S. intelligence. He wrote in his 1988 book *On the Trail of Assassins*, "The fact remained that Oswald had applied for a job at a mental institution [during his trip to Clinton], and that would have been all that his sponsors needed for another touch of sheep dipping. A few weeks of menial work there would have been enough to complete the picture of Oswald wandering haplessly from one job to another, each more obscure than the last. With a bit of luck and a little orchestration, it might even have been possible—with a switch of cards from 'employee' to 'patient'—to have the right psychiatrist at Jackson [mental hospital] describe the problems he had treating the strange outpatient named Lee Oswald." In Garrison's view, the presence of CORE in the area was insignificant. Of all the explanations for Oswald's appearance in Clinton, Garrison's is the most ludicrous.[3461]

On January 26, 1978, Willie Rainach committed suicide. Although poor health or other reasons may have been the cause, the HSCA investigation into Oswald's visit to Clinton at the time of his death may have had something to do with it. Under a more deligent investigation by the HSCA, the whole fabricated story of the Clinton witnesses might have unraveled and led them to the segregationists behind Oswald.

The HSCA had no clue as to why Oswald was really in Clinton. They concluded: "The committee believed the Clinton witnesses were telling the truth as they knew it." They admitted they were unable to reconcile Oswald, a Communist, appearing in the company of a fanatical anti-Communist, David Ferrie, noting, "The committee was puzzled by Oswald's apparent association with Ferrie, a person whose anti-Castro sentiments were so far distant from those of Oswald, the Fair Play for Cuba campaigner." They missed what is the crux of the case, a colossal misfortune for history: Oswald was not a Communist at all.[3462]

Miriam Feingold, the young CORE worker in Clinton and a former Freedom Rider, wrote in a letter home from Clinton, dated November 22, 1963, "President Kennedy is dead. I presume John Rarick and his gang of goons is gloating. . . . Last reports are that it was a Fair Play for Cuba chapter president who is prime suspect was involved. Why? Or is this a frame up? If this is true, we can expect things really to get tough down here."[3463]

Conclusions

The House Select Committee on Assassinations determined that there were four white individuals who had personal encounters with Lee Harvey Oswald in Clinton, Louisiana. They failed to appreciate that all four were members of a tight-knit Klavern led by Judge John Rarick and his close friend, town counsel Richard Van Buskirk. Van Buskirk and Rarick worked with Leander Perez in the summer of 1963 to draft the Free Electors legislation which was aimed at depriving President Kennedy of the state's electoral votes. Voter registrar Henry Earl Palmer, who also had an encounter with Oswald, was also an associate of Banister.

The HSCA further failed to note that the FBI had documented that three of the four Clinton witnesses had antipathy or a violent inclination toward the CORE workers. Rarick and Van Buskirk created the injunction against CORE, and declared that CORE had at least one individual among them who was a member of a Communist-front group—an action which was taken shortly after Oswald was seen among a group of African Americans who were registering to vote as a part of the CORE initiative.

The Congress of Racial Equality was the third Senator James O. Eastland-deemed Communist-front group that Oswald infiltrated or affected a physical relationship with, in addition to Fair Play for Cuba and the New Orleans Committee for Peaceful Alternatives. Each group had close ties to SCEF, which—as will be shown in Chapter Twenty-three—is of paramount significance.

Oswald's appearance in the CORE registration line was as phony as those in the FPCC and NOCPA sagas. The pronouncement that Reds had infiltrated CORE came four days before the raid on SCEF, when it was announced Reds had infiltrated that organization as well, suggesting that the incidents were directly related. However, none of Oswald's posturing was done with the Kennedy assassination in mind. The segregationists, with their Communist Control Act of 1962 in hand, aimed to show—through the seizure of material in the October 1963 Perez-Eastland-aided raid on SCEF—that the civil rights movement was infiltrated by Communists, like Oswald, who were Soviet directed.

As will be revealed for the first time in the final chapter of this work, Eastland planned on investigating Oswald's "product of his imagination" chapter of the FPCC before the assassination, which was tantamount to investigating Oswald. As hoped by the SCEF raid planners, an investigation of Oswald, in connection with the SCEF raid, would show that he was a Soviet agent who funded and encouraged violence in the Communist-front groups he infiltrated as a part of the World Communist Movement to defeat the United States, as was predicted in the wording of the Communist Control Act.

In October 1962, the United States was on the brink of nuclear war with the Soviet Union in the Cuban Missile Crisis. Injecting the Communist threat into the civil right movement—in effect riding the Red Scare of the time—was done in an attempt to preserve segregation by outlawing the civil rights movement and its related groups. Oswald was their ringer. With his Communist and Communist-front background well established, after President Kennedy's trip to Dallas was announced on September 12, 1963, the individuals behind Oswald who were involved in the assassination conspiracy of President Kennedy shifted a naive Oswald from the role of "ringer" to the role of "patsy."

CHAPTER TWENTY-TWO

FALSE COMMUNIST

*It was also my duty to develop and supervise those people called inform-
ers. To be more specific, we might say they were the counter spies sent
in to report on the activities of the party members. That was part of my
duties throughout the nearly seventeen years I served as Special Agent
in Charge.*

– Guy Banister

Lee Harvey Oswald began acting like a Communist in 1956 at the height of the Cold
War. The evidence as to whether or not he was a false Communist or a genuine Communist, as the Warren Commission and the HSCA concluded, will be presented in
this chapter. Essential to understanding Oswald's supposed alignment with Communism is
the history of anti-Communism, Communism, and the Red Scare and Black Scare in America, during the period when Oswald was coming of age, which will also be presented in this
chapter in relation to Oswald and the Kennedy assassination. Oswald's actions as a purported
Communist will be chronicled from their inception until his death and will be interpreted
within the context of the critical historical events of that period that shaped them.

Communism and Anti-Communism

The publishing of the *Manifesto of the Communist Party* in 1848 by Friedrich Engels and
Karl Marx was a seminal event in the emergence of Communism. The Bolshevik Revolution
of 1917 in Russia was the world's first workers' revolution and led to the establishment of a
Communist state. Vladimir Lenin led the workers' revolution that overthrew the Tsar in a civ-
il war that ran from 1917 to 1921. Lenin died in 1924 and, in 1928, Joseph Stalin succeeded
him over his rival, Leon Trotsky. Massive purges of dissidents, including the supporters of
Leon Trotsky, followed. A Stalinist agent assassinated Trotsky in 1940. After World War II,
Communism spread to Central and Eastern Europe, China, and the third world. Fascism and
Nazism emerged in Europe, in steep opposition to Communism.[3464]

The Communist Party of the United States was founded in 1919, in adherence to
the Marxist-Leninist ideology of Stalin. The Communist Party USA (CPUSA) was a bitter

rival of the Trotskyists who operated in the U.S. in the Socialist Workers Party. (Lee Harvey Oswald, it should be noted, subscribed to the newspapers of both the Communist Party (*The Worker*) and the Socialist Workers Party (*Militant*). His wife famously photographed him in his backyard, before the Walker shooting incident, holding copies of both publications, his rifle, and his pistol. An astute and genuine Communist would not likely have subscribed to both party's publications, as Oswald did.)

In the wake of World War I and the Russian Revolution, immigrants, anarchists, and labor grew increasingly dissatisfied in the U.S., which led to a series of strikes and bombings. The government countered the movement with mass arrests and the deportation of radicals in what became known as "Palmer Raids," named after Attorney General A. Mitchell Palmer, in the years around 1920. J. Edgar Hoover, his young assistant in what was then called the Bureau of Investigation, planned the raids. Thousands were arrested; most were members of the Communist Party. The raids launched J. Edgar Hoover's forty-eight-year career of Communist hunting, within what later became the Federal Bureau of Investigation.[3465]

Communism grew in popularity following the depression in 1928. While there was massive unemployment in the U.S., there was full employment in the Soviet Union under Stalin's Five-Year Plan. After the collapse of the U.S. economy, some felt capitalism was doomed in the U.S. and the ranks of the Communist Party swelled. Communism in the United States declined after WWII, and was hardly the threat that J. Edgar Hoover, the House Committee on Un-American Activities, and the radical right made it out to be. At the height of its popularity, the Communist Party membership never exceeded 140,000—in a population of 149 million. The Soviet Union's signing of the Hitler-Stalin Nonaggression Act of 1939 left many in the Communist Party disillusioned and the party was permanently reduced to a tiny sect. The Soviet's crushing of the Hungarian Revolt in Budapest in 1956 disenchanted still more in the CPUSA and membership in the party became minuscule. Nonetheless, the radical right continued to maintain that the Communist infiltration was everywhere—in the civil rights movement, the schools, the government, and the churches.

As a result of the growing anti-Communist sentiment, the Smith Act, also called the Alien Registration Act, was passed in 1940, making it a criminal offense to advocate overthrowing the government. In 1950, the McCarran Act, also known as the Internal Security Act or the Subversive Activities Control Act, was enacted, which required Communist organizations to register with the attorney general. The Subversive Activities Control Board was created to investigate those suspected of subversive activities, including Fascists and Communists. Congress passed the Internal Security Act over President Truman's veto. Truman called the act "the greatest danger to freedom of speech, press, and assembly since the Alien and Sedition Laws of 1798."[3466]

The Communist Inquisitions

Congress undertook minor committee investigations of Communism in the years that followed the Palmer Raids. In 1938, Congressman Martin Dies of Texas created the House

Un-American Activities Committee (known as HCUA or HUAC), and was its first chairman, which was first nicknamed the Dies Committee, and was the first congressional Communist-inquisition body of significance. (In his later years, Dies became a contributing editor for the John Birch Society's publication *American Opinion*. His portrait appeared on the cover of the monthly publication along with notables Taylor Caldwell, Joseph McCarthy, and others designated as "Americanist Heroes."[3467])

HUAC's chief investigator was J. B. Mathews, who served the committee until 1945. Mathews was a former Communist and supposedly belonged to a hefty twenty-eight Communist fronts. Mathews broke with the Communist Party in 1934, at a time when he operated his own private business. When his employees walked out on him in a wage dispute, he felt it was due to the influence of the Communists—a career as a staunch anti-Communist blossomed. Mathews maintained what was thought to be the largest set of private files on U.S. Communists and suspected Communists.[3468] (Later, in the years leading up to his death in 1966, Mathews worked for General Walker's friend Edgar Bundy, who inherited Mathews's massive files and kept them in a bunker protected by German Shepherd dogs and barbed wire in Wheaton, Illinois.)

HUAC and Mathews operated by recklessly engaging in character assassination and innuendo, as they accused people and organizations of being Communist influenced. One of many instances was the committee's investigation of ten-year-old actress Shirley Temple, which was instigated by J. B. Mathews. Harold Ickes, a "New Dealer" who served in President Roosevelt's cabinet, ridiculed Mathews, writing: "They've gone into Hollywood and found a great plot. They have found dangerous radicals there led by little Shirley Temple. Imagine the great committee raiding her nursery and seizing her dolls for evidence."[3469]

Mathews published the article, "Reds in our Churches" in the July 1953 *American Mercury* magazine. He claimed that Protestant ministers in the U.S. were "the largest single group supporting Communism." Reverends Billy James Hargis and Carl McIntire often repeated the charges. (General Walker later took over the *American Mercury* in 1962.) The July 13, 1953, edition of *Time* magazine called Mathews's claim against the Protestant ministers an "astounding and inherently uncheckable statement." A public uproar followed three weeks after Mathews's preposterous claims were made in the *American Mercury*, when Senator Joseph McCarthy hired him as his investigating committee's executive director. Soon after, he was let go and he went on to write for the John Birch Society's *American Opinion* magazine. However, he remained a hero to the far right and, in 1963 a portrait of Mathews was hung in the "Hall of Patriots" in Carl McIntire's Christian Admiral hotel in Cape May, New Jersey.[3470]

A 1947 HUAC investigation against ten prominent leaders in the Hollywood film industry led to their convictions for contempt of Congress and the ruin of their careers. In 1948, HUAC brought charges of espionage against New Dealer Alger Hiss, and he was convicted of perjury. Former Communists Whitaker Chambers and Elizabeth Bentley testified against him, and the case electrified the American people as fears of a growing Soviet threat spread. Congressman Richard Nixon served on HUAC in the Hiss investigation. (As a result, his career rocketed, leading to his election to the vice presidency in 1952 and presidency in 1968.) President Truman denounced HUAC in 1959 as the "most un-American thing in the country today."[3471]

Elizabeth Bentley, after renouncing Communism, served as a witness at the espionage trial of Julius and Ethel Rosenberg, as well as the perjury trial of William Remington. Bentley, from Connecticut, was called the "Nutmeg Mata Hari" after the seductive, female spy who employed sex while engaging in espionage during WWI. Bentley, a round-faced, plain, New Englander who lacked the looks of Mata Hari was the mistress of Jacob Galos, a prominent member of the Communist Party, who died in 1943. Later, Bentley walked into the New Haven FBI offices and renounced Communism because of "good old New England conscience" and embarked on a new career as an informant testifying against American Communists.[3472] Bentley testified against John Abt, naming him as a Communist, while he was serving as chief counsel of the Senate Subcommittee on Civil Liberties.[3473] (Lee Harvey Oswald, it will be recalled, requested John Abt, the famous attorney for the Communists, to defend him the day after the assassination. Oswald's request for Abt as his counsel was one way to let the world know that he was a Communist.)

Guy Banister told the press that he had been a close friend of Elizabeth Bentley shortly after she testified before HUAC in 1948 and identified Harry Dexter White and several other government officials as having Communist affiliations. In 1956, while Banister was working with Senator Eastland, hunting Communists in New Orleans, he unofficially invited Bentley to become a research analyst for the intelligence and investigation unit of the New Orleans Police Department while she was in New Orleans to visit him.[3474]

Fears about Communist infiltration by the American public rose in the wake of the Communist takeover of China, the Hiss case, and the convictions of Ethel and Julius Rosenberg. Senator Joseph McCarthy set out to exploit the nation's fears. On February 9, 1950, McCarthy gave a speech to the Republican Woman's Club of Wheeling, West Virginia, where he declared: "The State Department is infested with Communists. I have in my hand a list of 205—a list of names that were made known to the Secretary of State as being members of the Communist Party who nevertheless are still working and shaping policy in the State Department." The obscure senator won instant notoriety. (J. B. Mathews had provided him with the names.) Mathews later became an icon in the John Birch Society. In other pronouncements, however, McCarthy pared down the number considerably. Eventually, McCarthy's charges were investigated and they were determined to be "a fraud and a hoax."[3475] Undaunted, McCarthy went on to accuse a number of government organizations of being infiltrated by Communists, with little proof. J. Edgar Hoover aided McCarthy's search for Communists and William Sullivan, the number three man at the FBI, said of their role in the Communist scare: "We (the FBI) were the ones who made the McCarthy hearings possible."[3476]

McCarthy took on the International Information Agency, claiming their libraries stocked subversive books. As a result, the State Department removed controversial, pro-Communist books from its shelves. Reminiscent of the Nazi infamy, book burnings took place under McCarthy's watch. In 1953, McCarthy became the chairman of the Senate Committee on Government Operation, which included the Senate Permanent Subcommittee on Investigations, which provided him with a tool to investigate alleged Communist infiltration. McCarthy, a close friend of the Kennedy family, appointed Robert Kennedy as an assistant counsel to the committee. McCarthy's committee investigation of the Voice of America was covered on television. Insinuations, unsubstantiated claims, and the browbeating of witnesses led to the coining of the deragatory term "McCarthyism." None of the charges against the Voice of America were substantiated, but McCarthy succeeded in defaming the agency and ruining careers.

McCarthy's 1953 investigation of an alleged Communist spy ring in the United States Army Signal Corps was his eventaul undoing. Hearings failed to find any evidence of subversion. McCarthy took on the case of a dentist, Irving Peress, who was drafted into the army in 1952. Peress had refused to answer questions about his political affiliations on his enlistment application and did not disclose that he belonged to a leftist political organization. Peress was promoted to major, automatically, merited by his position as a dentist, as prescribed according to procedure. When it was revealed that he refused to disclose his political affiliations, Peress immediately requested his dismissal and was granted an honorable discharge by his commanding officer, General Ralph W. Zwicker. McCarthy called the distinguished General Zwicker to testify as to why Peress was promoted and honorably discharged, instead of being court-marshaled for failure to disclose his leftist leaning. During the hearings, McCarthy insulted and mocked the general, then declared he was "not fit to wear that uniform." The charge outraged the army, Congress, the public, and President Eisenhower.[3477]

The army countered, accusing McCarthy's chief counsel, Roy Cohn, of trying to influence the army into giving special treatment to a former McCarthy aide, G. David Schine, a recently drafted army private. The army carefully documented the McCarthy staffer's improper intrusions into army affairs. McCarthy countered that the army's charges were made in retaliation over his treatment of General Zwicker the year before. Hearings held to investigate the conflicting claims of the army and McCarthy were extensively covered by the press and were televised live. Counsel for the army, Joseph Welch, berated McCarthy for asserting that a young attorney on his staff had Red ties, stating famously: "Until this moment, senator, I think I never gauged your cruelty or recklessness . . ." When McCarthy resumed his attack, Welch cut him short, stating, "Have you no sense of decency, sir, at long last? Have you left no sense of decency?"

The Nation commented on McCarthy's technique: "He does not need to prove a charge; all he needs to do is to whisper 'Communism' and even men sworn to uphold and protect the Constitution will act like so many sheep."[3478] The American general public took it all in, live on television, in their living rooms. They witnessed McCarthy's recklessness, bullying theatrics, rude outbursts, ill-mannered interruptions, arrogance, vindictiveness, and crude personal attacks. The public opinion of McCarthy plunged. He lost his credibility and the people's respect. Senator Stuart Symington of Missouri summed up the country's impression of McCarthy, telling him: "The American people have had a look at you for six weeks. You are not fooling anyone." In December 1954, the Senate censured the beleaguered McCarthy. John F. Kennedy refused to vote for the censure of his friend, but with his political power reduced to almost nothing, the senator lived in relative obscurity until his death in 1957.

Little known about McCarthy were his connections to the radical right and the hard-core underground described in this work. Partisans on the far right saw McCarthy as a hero who had alerted the American people to the dangers of Communist infiltration. As was noted in Chapter Seven, Wesley Swift, a friend of Joseph Milteer, worked out of McCarthy's office in his campaign to defeat the nomination of Anna M. Rosenberg in 1951. (Rosenberg was appointed Assistant Secretary for Manpower and Personnel to Secretary of Defense George C. Marshall, which outraged radicals like Swift because she was obviously Jewish, a long-time friend of President Roosevelt, and a proponent of the Truman Fair Deal.)

H. L. Hunt was a great friend and backer of Senator McCarthy. Hunt had a penchant for supporting nationally known extremists like McCarthy and generals Douglas MacArthur and Edwin Walker. Hunt's relationship with McCarthy began in April 1952, when McCarthy came to Dallas to make a speech before the American Legion. The Legion, at the time, was calling for the ouster of Secretary of State Dean Acheson and the purging of Communists from the State Department, prompted by McCarthy's exaggerated pronouncements. Hunt's *Facts Forum* promoted McCarthy's appearance where Dan Smoot introduced McCarthy on the stage. Former McCarthy aides, including his future wife, Jean Kerr, became *Facts Forum* staff members.[3479] McCarthy was also a guest of Hunt's *Facts Forum* radio show. "Ex-Communist" witness, Louis Bundez, was featured on the *Facts Forum* radio show, as well, while *Facts Forum* magazine featured an article on "ex-Communist witness" Paul Crouch.[3480, 3481]

Billy James Hargis was another close friend of McCarthy and the two were pictured together in *Christian Crusade* magazine. Kent Courtney was a friend of McCarthy, as well; the attacks on McCarthy reportedly appalled Courtney and drove him into far-right politics.

Dan Smoot appeared on stage with an ill McCarthy for a rally in 1957, not long before his death. After his death, McCarthy became a martyr of the radical right movement. Rumors swirled that the Communists killed him, and his death left a void in the leadership of the far right that would not be filled until the emergence of General Walker in 1961.[3482] McCarthy became a champion of the John Birch Society and his picture graced the wall of the office of Robert Welch.[3483]

While McCarthy turned up a few former Communists in his "naming of names" here and there, his inquisitions were primarily directed at liberals, New Dealers, and moderates in the Truman and Eisenhower administrations. None who testified before McCarthy or HUAC were ever convicted of advocating the overthrow of the government of the United States.

HUAC and the Southern Conference for Human Welfare, Communist Inquisition in the Black Belt

With renewed interest in civil rights after World War II, the Southern segregationists who dominated HUAC set their sites on individuals promoting integration. Using the same effective tactics employed by McCarthy and others against alleged subversives, they aimed to curb and destroy the emergent civil rights movement. Later, Senator James O. Eastland's Senate Internal Security Subcommittee (SISS) followed the same strategy, as we shall see, utilizing Guy Banister. The Communist hearings of McCarthy and Eastland through the 1950s are relative to the coming of age of Lee Harvey Oswald and his emergence as a supposed Communist during that period. Accordingly they will be reviewed here.

In 1947, HUAC investigated the Southern integration organization called the Southern Conference for Human Welfare (SCHW). SCHW had been formed in 1937 for the purposes of improving the lot of African Americans living in the Southern states, an area which had been dubbed the "Black Belt." Hearings were held and evidence was presented aligning SCHW with the Communist Party. The notorious Mississippi congressman, racist, and anti-Semite, Representative John Rankin, led the charges.[3484] According to Rankin, "Slavery was the greatest blessing the Negro people ever had."[3485] Rankin once called reporter Walter Winchell a "Communistic little kike."[3486]

Senator Theodore Bilbo, of Mississippi, made the feelings of the South clear on SCHW. He wrote to SCHW leader James A. Dombrowski in 1945, saying: "I have just received from a friend of mine in Jackson, Mississippi, two sheets that your un-American, Negro social equality, Communistic, mongrel outfit is sending out through the country . . . If I were called on to name the Number One Enemy of the South today it would be the Southern Conference for Human Welfare."[3487]

HUAC, in their concluding report, called SCHW, "Perhaps the most deviously camouflaged Communist-front operation of the day." HUAC's report linked the SCHW to groups listed as subversive by the attorney general. They claimed the group's aim was to foment revolution and destroy democracy. They charged that SCHW favored an "Independent Negro Soviet Republic in the Southern Black Belt which in essence is a call to civil war."[3488]

HUAC issued a second report, in late 1947, on a group promoting black civil rights, entitled "Civil Rights Congress as a Communist Front Organization." Like SCHW, some members of the Civil Rights Congress were aligned with the Communist Party. Under the leadership of Georgia congressman John Wood, HUAC launched "Hearings Regarding Communist Infiltration of Minority Groups," in 1949, adding more fuel to the segregationists' fire.[3489] The October 1947 *Harvard Law Review* critiqued the HUAC-SCHW hearing, stating: "This report demonstrates not that Southern Conference is a corrupt organization but that the Committee has been either intolerably incompetent or designedly intent upon publicizing misinformation."[3490]

Paul Crouch, HUAC, and the 1949 Southern Conference for Human Welfare Hearings
In 1949, HUAC continued hearings on the Southern Conference for Human Welfare and took the testimony of their star witness, Paul Crouch, a man with an unimpeachable Communist background. James Dombrowski, who was the arch nemesis of Senator Eastland and

the New Orleans hardcore underground in Guy Banister, Hubert Badeaux, and Leander Perez, was the principal target in the investigation.

Crouch testified that he had been active in SCHW at its inception. The Committee wasted little time before asking the million-dollar question: "Was the Southern Conference for Human Welfare conceived as a Communist organization by the Communist Party itself?" Crouch replied, "It was very definitely so." Crouch explained that a small committee formed by Communist Party members conceived SCHW. Crouch claimed that Dombrowski and Virginia Durr were among them. Crouch further claimed that Earl Browder, national secretary of the Communist Party, attended a meeting of SCHW in 1937. He told them that most of the contributing editors of the SCHW's magazine, *New South*, in 1938, were officials or members of the Communist Party and their central committee in New York subsidized the publication. He testified that he knew of a member of the Communist Party who was active in the first two conferences of the SCHW, that a leading member of the group that was the precursor of SCHW was a Communist Party leader, and that Dombrowski succeeded him. Crouch testified that Durr was aware that Communists published the *New South*. Crouch said that he met with Dombrowski and Myles Horton and got the impression they were pro-Communist. (It will be recalled that it was Horton who was photographed at the Highlander Folk School with Martin Luther King, Jr. and Communist Abner Berry, who surreptitiously inserted himself into the photo.)

Crouch admitted that he did not know if Dombrowski was a member of the Communist Party. He said that he met Dombrowski at Highlander Folk School and was given the impression that he was "completely pro-Communist and anxious to collaborate with the Communist Party and follow its leadership, without taking the risk of actual Party membership." Crouch said he met Horton and that he was pro-Communist, his wife Zelphia, more so.[3491] (Zelphia Horton wrote the anthem of the civil rights movement, "We Shall Overcome," and first sang it at the 1957 Highlander meeting attended by King.[3492])

African American Manning Johnson testified on July 14, 1949, at a HUAC hearing against SCHW, that SCHW was Communist dominated. (Manning, a paid witness with significant credibility problems that emerged in later years, testified in numerous federal and state inquisitions investigating integrationists.)[3493]

Paul Crouch: Colossus of the Ex-Communist, Paid Professional Witnesses

Paul Crouch was the model for the many ex-Communists who testified at the hearings of HUAC and those of Senators Eastland and McCarthy. Without ex-Communists like Crouch, the Communist-hunting committees would have had little evidence to point the finger at and identify the alleged Communists they were trying to destroy. Many, including presidents Truman and Eisenhower, were skeptical of the witnesses. J. Edgar Hoover, however, in his book *Masters of Deceit*, wrote, "The ex-Communist is today one of our most potent weapons against Communism."[3494]

The testimony of the professional ex-Communist witnesses, in general, consisted of three parts: affirmation, renunciation, and identification. Firstly, they would affirm their initial sincere devotion to Communism (the "best" ex-Communist witnesses at one time had traveled to the Soviet Union, which alone was sufficient affirmation that they were genuine Communists)—their renunciation of Communism later followed. They would explain, in some fashion, how the inherent deviousness of Communism duped them into being true believers. Until, one day, they saw the light and vowed to fight Communism. Affirmation and renunciation out of the way, they then turned to finger pointing and the identification of fellow Communists, called before the congressional investigating bodies.

Paul Crouch's testimony in the HUAC hearings against SCHW began with his affirmation of original sincere devotion to Communism. Crouch told the Committee that he had studied Marx at age ten, growing up on a farm in North Carolina. While he was a private in the army in 1925, he was sentenced by the army to forty years for sending a letter to a friend advocating a revolutionary front. (In his defense, he claimed he wrote the letter to an imaginary friend, something he said he often did.) The Communist Party campaigned to free him, but he was sent to Alcatraz, which at the time was a disciplinary barracks, and was freed two years later.

Crouch was a member of the secretariat of the Young Communist League and editor of the *Young Worker*. He attended most meetings of the Central Committee of the Communist Party from 1927 to 1941. He became a hero to the party as a result of his arrest and was sent to Moscow's Lenin School to study Marxism at Soviet expense. He became head of the Communist Party department of infiltration of the U.S. Armed Forces, Communist Party USA representative to the Executive Committee of the Communist International in Moscow, and honorary regimental commander of the Red Army.

He told the House Committee that he toured Red Army bases with Soviet General Tukhachevsky, who had conferred with him about Russian plans to invade America. He showed them a photo of himself in a Red Army uniform, and one of him in his U.S. Army uniform. He visited the main military school of the Red Army and spoke as a guest. The reason he appeared in a Red Army uniform, he told the Committee, was to demonstrate the loyalty that all Communists, throughout the world, had to the Soviet Union. He wore the uniform for a week while inspecting Soviet troops and maneuvers. He was given very specific and detailed instruction for months on how to infiltrate Communists into the U.S. Military. Asked if he was in the U.S. Army, Crouch showed the Committee a picture of him in a U.S. Army uniform. He accused scores of Americans of being Soviet spies. What he did not tell the Committee was that he did so little studying at the Lenin School, and the Soviets found his behavior so odd, that they gave him the money to return home. He moved to the South and went on to promote the party line of "Self-Determination in the Black Belt." He moved to Oakland, California, during WWII, where his colleagues complained of his Marxist ineptitude. He spent most of his time in a bar before leaving the Party in 1942.[3495, 3496]

Crouch may well have been a key role model for the making of Lee Harvey Oswald's faux-Communist persona that emerged in 1956. Oswald and Crouch shared several key elements of their life stories as Communists. Oswald, like Crouch, supposedly studied Communism as a boy, lived in the Soviet Union, and was a member of Communist organizations or fronts. He posed in a famous photo as a Communist, as did Crouch, which left little doubt for most that Oswald was an authentic Communist. The photo of Oswald holding his pistol and the assassination rifle in his backyard, with two Communist newspapers in hand, was perhaps as striking and as persuasive as to his Communist affiliation as was Crouch's picture in the Red Army uniform.

Marina Oswald stated that her husband told her he wanted the photo of him with the gun and rifle taken so he could send it to a newspaper. After Oswald's "fight" with Carlos Bringuier, Marina testified, "I think that Lee engaged in this activity primarily for the purposes of self-advertising. He wanted to be arrested. I think he wanted to get into the newspapers so that he would be known."[3497]

With the similarities between Crouch and Oswald, Crouch's background and role as an ex-Communist witness in the hearings against the integrationists by Senator Eastland and HUAC will be detailed, below.

Paul Crouch Exposed

Paul Crouch testified prolifically and "named names" at multiple congressional hearings. In 1947, Crouch and others identified many well-known Hollywood actors and lesser-known workers in the film industry to HUAC as Communists. Crouch testified as a professional witness in 1948 and 1949 in Florida, Hawaii, and California.[3498] He testified in the Alger Hiss case on May 17, 1949, with Elizabeth Bentley and Louis Bundez.[3499] In 1950, he named Clarence F. Hiskey, an analytic chemist associated with the Manhattan Project, as a Communist Party member.[3500] Crouch also testified at a HUAC hearing in Miami in 1950.[3501] Crouch's memorandum, "Communist Infiltration in the American Armed Forces" triggered the McCarthy-Army Hearings.[3502]

Crouch testified, before McCarthy's committee in 1953, that Robert Oppenheimer, director of the Manhattan Project, was a Communist. Oppenheimer denied being a Communist, but stated that he was in accordance with some of their views. Crouch alleged that he had been at Oppenheimer's house at a meeting of top-drawer Communists. (This was a blatant lie. Oppenheimer had been in another state at the time, which was documented by the dates on x-rays taken when he sought care after he was kicked by a horse.[3503, 3504]) When accusations arose that Crouch was lying in the Oppenheimer case, J. Edgar Hoover told his agents to find evidence to back up Crouch's claims. After Crouch testified at Eastland's 1954 hearings, attacks on Crouch by columnists Stewart and Joseph Alsop put pressure on the attorney general to investigate him.[3505]

In 1951, Crouch was hired by the Department of Justice as an expert on Communism. Subsequently, he became an expert witness at congressional hearings and dozens of deportation cases and Smith Act trials. He made $9,675 over two years of testifying.[3506] He testified often, however, and contradictions began to appear. In one Smith Act trial, Crouch could not remember the things he had testified about in prior similar inquisitions. He could not recall specifics of charges he had made against indviduals in past hearings when he later claimed he knew them from the Communist Party. He testified in a deportation hearing against a *Chicago Sun–Times* cartoonist, saying he often saw him at Communist Party meetings. When asked to point him out in court, he pointed to a photographer—who didn't resemble the cartoonist. In a Philadelphia Smith Act trial, Crouch testified that he knew David Davis as a Communist. The defense pointed out that, at the perjury trial of Harry Bridges, Crouch said that he never knew David Davis. At another time, he testified that he saw Harry Bridges at a 1943 Party election, when records showed Bridges was in another part of the country at the time in question. While being cross-examined in another case, the counsel, pointing out his inconsistencies, referred to Crouch as "Mr. Stoolpigeon." The U.S. attorney general's office received several affidavits from non-Communists that contradicted parts of Crouch's testimony. As a result, the attorney general began an investigation of their own witness, Paul Crouch.[3507]

In July 1954, Crouch wrote identical letters to Senator Joseph McCarthy's Government Operations Committee and to the Senate Internal Security Subcommittee and turned on his former employer, the Justice Department. Crouch, astonishingly, charged that U.S. Attorney General Herbert Brownell had "given considerable aid and comfort to the enemies of the United States" by launching the investigation against him. Crouch reminded Brownell that, "if my reputation could be destroyed, 31 Communist leaders could get new trials, 20 immigration proceedings would be reopened." Crouch called on J. Edgar Hoover to investigate some of Brownell's aids. When Senator William Jenner, the chairman of the SISS, received the request from Crouch to investigate the Justice Department, he dismissed it, calling it "Absurd."[3508, 3509, 3510]

Author Arthur J. Sabin documented the phenomena of the paid ex-Communist in his book *The Red Scare in Court*. The number of paid professional witnesses in the 1950s has been estimated in the range of thirty-five to eighty-three. The phenomenon of paid government witnesses was unique to the Communist inquisitions.

Ex-Communist witness Harvey Matusow detailed, in his book *False Witness*, how he lied to suit the prosecutor and enrich himself. Matusow was indicted after admitting he had lied. He told reporters, "This is a good racket, being a professional witness." When asked if he thought the Communist Party was any danger to America, he said, "Frankly, no."

The practice of paying ex-Communists for their testimony has been referred to as "subsidized perjury." Paul Crouch, Manning Johnson, Louis Bundez, and Matt Cvetic were all paid witnesses in the International Worker Order case. It was well established that these paid informers did, in fact, lie. What further made them unique is that they traveled from hearing to hearing across the country. Some admired ex-Communists more than people who were never Communists. The testimonies of Johnson and Crouch were stricken from the record of the Subversive Activities Control Board for perjury at the direction of the Supreme Court.[3511]

These "ex-Communist witnesses" established their credibility as former Communists by reciting evidence that affirmed their sincere dedication to the Communist cause, before they quit the party. All Paul Crouch needed to do was flash his photo in the Red Army uniform to establish his credibility as he did at hearings. David Craute described the phenomena of the paid ex-Communist: "The informers as a group made a living out of pretending to encyclopedia knowledge of the Communist movement across the face of a vast country. On a nod from prosecutors, they sold hunches, or guesses as inside knowledge, supporting claims with bogus reports and encounters."[3512, 3513]

Exposure of the paid informers came shortly before, and continued after, the 1957 Supreme Court decision in the *Yates v. United States* case, and the practice stopped. Prosecutions under the Smith Act that resulted in the convictions of the fourteen leaders of the Communist Party in California—who had been indicted in 1951 in a federal district court for conspiring to overthrow the government—were found to be unconstitutional. As a result, the practice of hiring paid ex-Communists abated. The Supreme Court later declared that Paul Crouch was "a tainted witness."[3514, 3515] The Supreme Court struck the testimonies of Manning Johnson and Paul Crouch from the record of the Subversive Activities Control Board, after they determined the men had committed perjury.[3516]

No one would have made a better Communist witness against the defendants charged under the Communist Control Act—based on evidence obtained during the October 1963 raid on SCEF offices—than Lee Harvey Oswald. The raid, which involved Senator Eastland and his investigators, as well as local and state police—some of whom had ties to Guy Banister. Not only had they planned to investigate SCEF after the raid, they also had planned to investigate FPCC, and CORE—and, presumably, NOCPA since they confiscated NOCPA's membership list—all groups Oswald had infiltrated that had ties to SCEF. (The SCEF raid will be fully detailed in the next chapter.)

Senator Eastland, Paul Crouch, and the 1954 SCEF Hearings

Battered by the HUAC inquisition, SCHW disbanded in 1948 and reemerged as the Southern Conference Education Fund (SCEF), headed by James Dombrowski. Relocated to New Orleans, SCEF became the number one enemy of Southern segregationists, including a number of New Orleans figures tied to the assassination of President Kennedy in this work.[3517]

Senator Eastland arrived in New Orleans, in March 1954, with counsel Richard Arens and two paid informants, Paul Crouch and James Butler, in what historian Dorothy M. Zellner fittingly called, the "Redroad Show."[3518] (Lee Harvey Oswald had returned to New Orleans from his stay in New York City in January of 1954.[3519]) The Eastland hearings took place while the Supreme Court was hearing testimony in the *Brown* case, and Eastland was anticipating a negative outcome for the segregationists.

Eastland called native Southerners, and SCEF leaders, Dombrowski, Virginia Durr, Myles Horton, and Aubrey Williams to testify. Benjamin E. Smith represented Dombrowski; Clifford Durr represented Williams and Horton; and John P. Kon represented Virginia

Durr. Members of the Anti-Subversion Committee of the Young Businessmen's club of New Orleans testified that the leadership of SCEF either were Communists or followed the Communist ways. SCEF leader Dombrowski was called and told the hearing that SCEF had no members, only contributors—and denied ever being a Communist. Paid informant James Butler, however, told the committee that Dombrowski was in the upper echelon of the Communist Party. Eastland accused SCEF leaders of having an "affiliation with power abroad that has killed and maimed thousands and thousands of American boys." Eastland commented on a pamphlet that Dombrowski had written that praised the abilities of Negroes in WWII. Then he mocked Dombrowski for his non-Anglo-Saxon name, uncommon for a Southerner. Repeating the individual syllables of the defendant's name, he stated: "Fine Southern name, Dombrowski; Dom-brow-ski." Eastland viewed integration as something foreign, and viewed Dombrowski as a foreigner. (Another example of Eastland's prejudice was his comment to fellow Democratic Senator Jacob Javits of New York, a Jew, on the Senate floor: "I don't like you—or your kind.")[3520]

Eastland called Paul Crouch and he acknowledged that he was a professional witness and boasted he had spent more than 5,000 hours testifying about his history as a Communist, adding, "I am not through yet." Crouch testified about the impending Russian invasion of America and stated, under oath, that he met Dombrowski first at Highlander in 1938, and again in Miami, in 1947. He claimed that once, while they were driving together, Dombrowski talked about "the revolutionary movement" and he sang the famous Socialist song "The Internationale."

Dombrowski, for his part, denied ever having met Butler or singing, but admitted that he might have met Crouch.

Eastland permitted lawyers for SCEF members to cross-examine the slippery Crouch, who was unable to provide specifics about his claims. However, he went on to testify that the only purpose of the SCEF was to promote Communism and divide the races. Crouch identified Dombrowski as a Communist Party member, departing from his 1949 claim that Dombrowski was only "pro-Communist." SCEF attorney Clifford Durr cross-examined Crouch and succeeded in undermining his testimony. He called Crouch's claims "absolutely false," adding: "One or the other of us should be indicted for perjury."

Next, Eastland began an attack on the Highlander Folk School. Eastland called Myles Horton of Highlander and asked him if Dombrowski was associated with Highlander. Dombrowski refused to answer, and Eastland had him carried out of the room by two marshals. Crouch and Butler testified that Virginia Durr, the sister-in-law of Supreme Court Justice Hugo Black, was "under Communist discipline" and "plotted with Reds." Durr's husband, upon hearing the accusations about his wife, threatened Crouch, and said he would "kill the son of a bitch." Marshals had to separate Durr and Crouch and, in the melee, Durr suffered a small heart attack. The hearings closed,[3521] but Clifford Durr later recalled that he suspected Crouch had been an agent or informer in the Communist Party all along.[3522]

At a press conference after the hearings, Eastland seemed somewhat shaken and admitted that Crouch did not convince him that Durr or Williams, another SCEF officer, were Communists.[3523] The press viewed the hearing as an inquisition. Two hundred prominent people, including Eleanor Roosevelt, signed a petition urging the Senate to desist from any similar hearings. Lyndon Johnson and Hubert Humphrey expressed their sympathy to Aubrey Williams.[3524] Crouch was described as "one of the most brazen and colorful liars in the business" and "a political vampire."[3525] The press who covered the hearing, were polled and asked, "Which of the principals involved do you regard as the greatest menace to the American form of government and way of life?" They ranked Eastland as number one, Crouch number two, and Eastland's counsel, Richard Arens, as number three.

In the end, Crouch failed to be convincing that members of SCEF were Communists. He never testified again. One Southern newspaper called the hearings a blight on "Southern Honor." Two months later, the Supreme Court issued the *Brown* decision. Not deterred by the failure of Eastland's New Orleans hearings, the segregationists stayed their course and remained resolute in their claim that Communism was behind the civil rights movement and continued to use the supposed connection to fight the Supreme Court ruling.[3526, 3527]

Brown v. Board of Education and the Southern Reaction

Advancement of the status of African Americans had all but stagnated after the first Reconstruction, but began to accelerate after WWII. In 1951, the parents of thirteen black school children, with the help of the NAACP, filed suit against the Topeka, Kansas, Board of Education to end segregation in the public schools. On May 17, 1954, the Supreme Court, under Chief Justice Earl Warren, ruled in the case known as *Oliver Brown, et al. v. the Board of Education of Topeka, et al*, that school segregation was unconstitutional. They overturned the 1896 Court ruling in *Plessy v. Ferguson*, which had ruled that segregation was constitutional under the concept of "separate but equal." The court relied heavily on the testimony of Swedish social scientist Gunnar Myrdal, who stated that segregation resulted in a sense of inferiority in black children and affected their motivation to learn. The segregationists accused Myrdal of being a Communist. They referred to the May 17, 1954, *Brown* decision—the beginning of the end of segregation in America—as "Black Monday."

Eastland's colleague, Judge Tom P. Brady, wrote in his book *Black Monday*: "This is no time to be calm. . . . If in one mighty voice we do not protest this travesty of justice, we might as well surrender. The Supreme Court awaits our reaction."[3528] In 1954, Senator Eastland addressed the Mississippi State Citizens' Council on the subject, saying, "We've Reached an Era of Judicial Tyranny" in reference to the *Brown* decision. The speech was printed in a pamphlet and widely distributed.[3529] Eastland inserted a letter, sent to him from a South Baptist minister in the wake of *Brown*, that read, "I don't think I am too old to join with those who are willing, if necessary, to take up where Robert E. Lee left off on the memorable day at Appomattox."[3530] Eastland further responded to the *Brown* decision in a speech, stating, "On May 17, the Constitution of the United States was destroyed because the Supreme Court disregarded the law and decided integration was right. . . . You are not required to obey any court, which passes out such a ruling, in fact you are obligated to defy it." Eastland declared that the Supreme Court was pressured by groups that were colored "from the blood red of the Communist Party to the almost equally red blood of the National Council of Churches of Christ U.S.A." He declared that the Supreme Court "[had] been infiltrated and influenced by Reds."[3531] So outraged by "The Decision," segregationists were galvanized into action, and devised a number of strategies to skirt *Brown*.

One of Eastland's first initiatives after *Brown* was to establish the Federation of Constitutional Government in Memphis, Tennessee, on December 18 and 19, 1955, to preserve segregation. The group included several associates of General Walker, including Leander Perez, Willie Rainach, J. Evetts Haley, W. Scott Wilkinson, and W. J. Simmons, as was noted in Chapter Ten. (Simmons, it will be recalled, was Governor Ross Barnett's chief advisor in the integration crisis at Ole Miss.) Jim Johnson, from Arkansas, served on the board of the Federation. (More recently, Johnson led a bitter campaign against Bill Clinton when he was the governor of Arkansas and again, later, when Clinton became president.) Forty-five delegates from twelve states were sworn to secrecy at the meeting, where Eastland declared, "We are about to embark on a great crusade, a crusade to restore Americanism, and return the control of our Government to our people." Eastland's inquisitions of the integrationists, in his Senate Internal Subversive Subcommittee, were the club he would use in his battle to save the segregated South.[3532, 3533, 3534, 3535] John U. Barr, who headed the Federation, later served on the advisory committee of the New Orleans Indignation Committee in 1962, along with Guy Banister, Hubert Badeaux, and Gus LaBarre. (Directors of the Indignation Committee included George Soule and P. Cameron Terry, who were present at the infamous Congress of Freedom meeting, in New Orleans in 1963 attended by Joseph Milteer and Willie Somersett.)[3536]

Eastland stated, on December 27, 1955, at an SISS hearing, that the Communist Party would be an "isolated, insignificant sect" in the United States without its many front organizations. The SISS printed a one-hundred-page book to help alert the public to the "real nature" of the enemy. The book listed the Negro Labor Council, the Civil Rights Congress, and the National Lawyer's Guild as examples of Communist fronts.[3537]

On April 17, 1956, delegates of eleven southern states met in New Orleans to form the Citizens' Council of America. Willie Rainach was elected to run it and, later, was succeeded by Roy V. Harris, Joseph Milteer's friend.[3538]

The Greater New Orleans Citizens' Council held a rally on May 17, 1956, on the anniversary of "Black Monday." Senator Eastland and Georgia governor Griffin were to speak.[3539] When Eastland had to cancel because of Senate activities, Leander Perez spoke in his place.[3540]

In 1956, Louisiana segregation laws, enacted in the wake of *Brown*, were ruled unconstitutional by three New Orleans federal judges, two of whom were Southerners. The decision was a huge blow to the segregationists—they were running out of weapons. Violence and congressional inquisitions, like Eastland's, that equated integration to Communism were the only tools left in the fight to save segregation. Willie Rainach, chairman of the newly formed

Joint Legislative Committee on Segregation, called the *Brown* ruling, a "sorry spectacle" and pledged an all-out fight to maintain segregation. He declared *Brown* a usurpation of state powers, which he called treason. He stated: "The battle is just joined. The people of Louisiana will not integrate. We serve notice that we organize, from the grass roots to the skyscrapers." He pledged, "Moves will be met with counter moves, decrees with laws, and political court decisions with political strategy." Leander Perez added, "I concur wholeheartedly with Senator Rainach."[3541]

In early 1956, eighteen senators and seventy-seven representatives, including Senator Eastland—all but one from the states of the old Confederacy—signed a document entitled "Declaration of Constitutional Principles," which was dubbed the "Southern Manifesto." The document declared, in part, "We regard the decision of the Supreme Court in the school cases as a clear judicial abuse of power." They pledged to use all legal means to reverse *Brown*.[3542]

On March 4, 1956, a packed crowd at the New Orleans Municipal Auditorium heard Harris speak with Perez and Rainach, denouncing *Brown* and the civil rights movement as Communist directed.[3543]

Senator Eastland, on March 17, 1956, urged peaceful resistance to the court-ordered desegregation, in order to avoid returning to a "Reconstruction" government and rule by "Carpetbaggers."[3544] That same year, the Mississippi State Sovereignty Commission was established. Contemporaneously, Perez was working with Rainach to draft anti-*Brown* legislation in Louisiana.[3545]

As a result of *Brown*, a sophisticated Southern intelligence operation was developed, not only "above ground" in the Sovereignty Commission and Citizens' Councils, but also below ground in what has been described in prior chapters as the "hardcore underground."

The Eastland Committee and the Southern Strategy to Defeat Integration
Southern segregationists saw *Brown* coming and braced for it under the leadership of Senator James O. Eastland. Eastland, who became a U.S. senator in 1941, was the wealthy owner of a 5,800-acre cotton plantation in Sunflower County, Mississippi. With one of the most conservative voting records in Congress, he became a member of the powerful Senate Judiciary Committee in 1951—a committee that had tremendous influence on the passing of laws that shaped the nation, particularly civil rights bills. Over the objection of Democratic Senators Wayne Morse (from Oregon) and Herbert Lehman (from New York), who were both officers in the NAACP, Eastland was elected head of the Judiciary in 1955, based on his seniority.[3546] He consistently stalled civil rights bills, bragging, "I put a special pocket in my pants and for three years carried those [civil rights] bills around with me."[3547]

The white Southerner's anxiety over the prospect of integration, called the "Black Scare," which was left in the wake of *Brown*, melded with the ongoing national "Red Scare." Congressional Communist inquisitors like Eastland set their sites on Southern integrationists, "red baiting" them and employing the same tactics used by Dies and McCarthy to discredit them. Equating integration with Communism—the nation's biggest fear during the Cold

War—was the tactic they planned to use.

The three leading Communist-hunting congressional committees after *Brown* were all in the hands of Southern segregationists. Mississippi Senator Eastland headed the SISS; Louisiana Representative Edwin Willis headed HUAC, and Arkansas Senator John McClellan headed McCarthy's former committee, the Senate Permanent Subcommittee on Investigation. J. Edgar Hoover, who was notably anti-black, having grown up in segregated Washington, D.C., made hunting Communists in the civil rights movement a priority and furnished his findings to the inquiring bodies. Hoover's "red and black" investigations were influenced by "his dream of what America should be": a nation segregated and Communist-free.[3548] The findings of the inquisitions led many state legislatures to enact laws strengthening segregation.

There was always at least a kernel of truth supporting the congressional committees' claims that Communists were involved in the civil rights movement. There were dedicated Marxists in the movement, including Paul Robeson, Hunter Pitts O'Dell, Stanley Levison, Victor Rabinowitz, Doxey Wilkerson, and W. E. B. Du Bois. The Communist Party also appealed to some blacks due to the fact it was the first national party to call for complete social and economic equality. In 1931, the International Labor Defense, the legal branch of the Communist Party, came to the defense of nine black teenage boys accused of raping two white women on a train in Scottsboro, Alabama.[3549] As a result, in 1939, the Special Committee on Un-American Activities cited the Scottsboro Defense Committee as a Communist-front organization.[3550]

Eastland knew the profit to be gained by linking integration to Communism. He called upon the nation's leading authority on Communism, J. Edgar Hoover, to validate his claim at a January 16, 1958, SISS hearing. Hoover testified: "The Negro situation is being exploited fully and continuously by Communists on a national scale." Hoover stated that the Communist Party had declared, in 1925, "The aim of our Party in our work among the Negro masses is to create a powerful proletarian movement which will fight and lead the struggle of the Negro race against exploitation and oppression."[3551] According to one Southern news reporter, white Southerners, in large, felt blacks were "in the mass, incompetent for any good political purpose and by reason of their inexperience and racial un-wisdom, were likely to prove subversive."[3552]

Guy Banister, Robert Morris, Hubert Badeaux, and the Eastland Committee in New Orleans, 1956

In 1956, Eastland brought the SISS "Redroad Show" to New Orleans, then the home of Lee Harvey Oswald, to investigate the "Soviet influence" in New Orleans and the South. 1956 was a big year for Oswald and Guy Banister.

During his time in the Civil Air Patrol in 1955 and 1956, Oswald first began to act like a Communist. At the same time, he joined the U.S. Marine Corps, whose purpose was, ostensibly, to fight the Communists. In 1956, he told a friend he wanted to join a Communist cell. The television show "I Led Three Lives," (Oswald's favorite show about false Communist-infiltrator Herbert Philbrick) was on the air for its final year in 1956.

Banister, then the assistant superintendent of the New Orleans Police Department, began engaging in Communist hunting in New Orleans and assisted Senator Eastland in his inquisition in 1956. That year would also mark the coming together of important individuals in the radical-right power structure (who, in prior chapters, have been tied to the assassination of President Kennedy, seven years later). Eastland's chief counsel, Robert Morris, joined Eastland and Banister in the SISS hearing effort. (Morris, it will be recalled, was General Walker's close associate, advisor, and attorney, and a principal of Walker's Minutemen operation.) In the same year, Eastland's close friend Leander Perez aligned himself with the Banister operation, as we shall see. Lastly, 1956 saw the beginning of the alliance of Banister, Morris, and Perez, who were all likely accessories to the murder of President Kennedy, as the evidence presented throughout this work suggests.

As has been discussed, Oswald was a member of Captain David Ferrie's Civil Air Patrol in 1955 and 1956. (Ferrie, it may be recalled, was a fanatical anti-Communist and a close associate of Guy Banister.) Many of Ferrie's cadets had a deep affection and allegiance to him and, as was noted in Chapter One, an agent of the U.S. Border Patrol saw Ferrie and Oswald repeatedly coming and going from Banister's office. While in the Civil Air Patrol with Ferrie, Oswald began to behave as a Communist when he belonged to William Wulf's Astronomy Club, described in Chapter Nine. In preparation for a future in the marines, he read his brother's marine manual over and over. He tried to enlist at age sixteen, in 1956, with falsified enlistment documents, but was unsuccessful. On his seventeenth birthday, in October 1956, he became a marine.[3553]

The FBI reported, in an interview, "Mrs. Oswald then indicated that she was sure her son was in the employ of the U.S. government, and then said she was going to divulge information that had never before been discussed. This information consisted of a statement by Mrs. Oswald to the effect that Lee Harvey Oswald, while he was 15-1/2 years of age, was a Civil Air Patrol Cadet. She said that while he was in the Civil Air Patrol, a civilian who she believes was associated with Civil Air Patrol induced Lee Oswald to join the United States Marines."[3554] Robert Oswald recalled that his mother told him a man in a uniform came to their house and urged her to allow Lee to join the marines.[3555] That unknown man was likely Ferrie, the only man who wore a uniform in Oswald's life, at the time.

The Warren Commission documented that, when Oswald was about sixteen years old, he communicated with the Socialist Party of America, their youth affiliate the Young Peoples Socialist League (YPSL) and their newspaper, the *Socialist Call*.[3556] Banister's right-hand man, and head of the New Orleans Police Red Squad, Hubert Badeaux (who also worked with Eastland's inquisition), confided to Willie Rainach that, in early 1957, he had been grooming an individual—who fit Oswald's description—to infiltrate leftist groups on campus. The evidence suggests that the activities by the Communist hunters—Guy Banister and James Eastland—in 1956, and the emergence of Lee Harvey Oswald as a Communist during the same period were probably related.

In January 1956, the "Southern Regional Committee of the Communist Party" in St. Louis, which advocated federal investigations into recent lynchings and an end to segregated schools, supposedly sent mail to prominent New Orleans officials. Leander Perez said the mailings "prove[d] unmistakably that the fight for racial integration [was] actually the Communist Cold War home front." It is hard to believe the Communist Party would waste its time and money on the effort. It is more likely that the mailings emanated from Perez and the Southern segregationists, who were attempting to link integration to Communism.[3557] This could be why the name of the "Southern Regional Committee of the Communist Party" sounds so similar to the civil rights group, the "Southern Regional Council."

On January 5, 1956, Eastland held an SISS hearing on the "Communist Influence in the Press." Eastland subpoenaed twenty-five past or present employees of the *New York Times*. Four of them refused to say if they had ever been Communists. As a result of the hearing, one newsman was fired from his job with the *New York Daily News* and two from the *New York Times* lost their jobs. The *Times* accused Eastland of trying to harass them because their editorials views were hostile to him. The *Denver Post* called the hearings "The Big Floperoo" and a "puerile attempt . . . to smear the *New York Times*."[3558,3559]

On January 29, 1956, Eastland was a guest on television's *Meet the Press* and stated "there [was] no discrimination" in his state and that neither whites nor Negroes wanted integration.[3560] By every measure, the standard of living of African Americans in Mississippi was the worst in the nation.

In early February 1956, Banister spoke at the Post 228 American Legion in New Orleans on the topic of underground Communist activities. He told the gathering that he had no doubt that the Communist Party was trying to create dissention through segregation issues. He stated: "They [the Communists] don't give a tinker's dam for either the Negroes or the whites but they will seize upon the issue just to cause trouble." He added, "The Communists have not been very successful in conquering Negro groups." He declared that the Communists were less successful among Negroes than among whites. Banister stated, "I have no doubt that some [NAACP] local groups are Communist dominated. Communists have [ten] men supporting their cause for every one actual card-carrying member." Banister emphasized the importance of espionage as a vehicle for winning wars, stating, "The history of nations is the history of espionage."[3561] Banister's speech is one of the earliest examples that his views on the segregation issue matched those of Eastland. Banister endorsed espionage to wage the war against the Communists that he alleged were behind integration, and set up his own espionage ring in both the New Orleans Police Department and, later, in his private detective office at Camp and Lafayette Streets in New Orleans.

In 1956, during the Montgomery, Alabama, bus boycott which had begun in the prior year, Senator Eastland addressed the Montgomery White Citizens' Council, stating: "In every stage of the boycott we have been oppressed and degraded because of black, slimy, juicy, unbearably stinking niggers . . . when in the course of human events it becomes necessary to abolish the Negro race, proper methods should be used. Among theses are guns, bows and arrows, slingshots and knives. . . . All whites are created equal with certain rights, among these are life, liberty and the pursuit of dead niggers."[3562] Eastland's diatribe revealed the abject depravity of the man and the dedicated Southern segregationists who supported him. In the speech he left himself bare, devoid of the disguise of the "Southern Gentleman."

In March 1956, Eastland's subcommittee held a hearing in New Orleans, given the provocative and exaggerated title of "Scope of Soviet Activity in the United States," which was a seminal event in assassination history. This time around Eastland had to proceed without the star "ex-Communist witness" from his 1954 hearing, Paul Crouch. (Eastland must have grieved long and hard when he learned his favorite ex-Communist informant had died of lung cancer in November 1955. There would be no more witnesses like Crouch again, with his kind of impressive ex-Communist and Soviet credentials.)[3563]

The first alleged subversive called to testify was Herman Liveright, a program director for WDSU radio in New Orleans. Eastland's interest in Liveright stemmed from the volunteered testimony of ex-Communist Winston M. Burdett, a prominent foreign correspondent and radio and TV newscaster. Burdett had appeared before Eastland's Subcommittee in 1955 and had disclosed the widespread effort of the Communist Party to place people under its discipline in positions of key importance in radio, television, and the newspapers. Burdett "named names," but did not give information about Liveright at the hearing, although he probably had done so outside of the 1955 hearing.[3564]

Robert Morris, who later became a close associate of General Walker, took the testimony of Liveright on March 10, 1956. Morris went right to the punch, asking: "I will ask you, Mr. Liveright, are you now a Communist?" Liveright eloquently explained his constitutional rights to Eastland and took the Fifth. Senator Eastland took his turn, asking: "Have you ever been a member of the Communist Party?" Eastland hammered away, ordering Liveright to answer. "You refuse to state whether you were sent into the South on a secret mission by the leaders of the Communist Party in New York?" Liveright refused to answer. Eastland asked him if he was affiliated with a Communist cell in New Orleans, then Eastland told him, "Mr. Liveright, the Communist movement, with which we have information you are affiliated, sir, is a conspiracy against our country. It is conspiracy to overthrow your country." Eastland later called Liveright's wife to testify and browbeat her when she refused to tell him if she was a Communist.[3565]

Eastland, like the other congressional witch hunters, had no power to charge anyone with a crime other than perjury and contempt of Congress. Nonetheless, Eastland made Liveright pay for his supposed crimes. In the wake of the hearing, WDSU fired Liveright. (Morris later testified in federal court in Washington, D.C., on February 6, 1957, that he learned that Liveright had been sent to New Orleans from New York to take over the direction of Communist activities in the city.[3566] Liveright was found guilty on fourteen counts of contempt of Congress and sentenced to serve three months in jail and pay a $500 fine. The Supreme Court overturned the conviction on May 21, 1962.)[3567, 3568, 3569] J. Edgar Hoover wrote about the Liveright incident in his book *Masters of Deceit,* without mentioning Liveright's name. It's clear the FBI was involved in investigating Liveright in New York and his subsequent move to New Orleans, allegedly on the orders of the Communist Party.[3570]

The Liveright affair stirred up the New Orleans anti-Communists, who were convinced that the Communist menace had come to their city. On March 21, 1956, Mayor deLesseps Morrison ordered Police Superintendent Guy Banister to conduct an investigation into subversive activities in New Orleans, after the published reports of Eastland's findings that subversion flourished in city. He referred to Banister as "an expert in the field."[3571] Mayor Morrison arranged a meeting with Banister and Senator Eastland. Eastland promised to discuss the situation with Morrison and Banister thoroughly.[3572] Banister announced that he planned to add another man to the Red Squad in addition to Hubert Badeaux, the lone officer in the intelligence department.[3573]

Banister and Morrison flew to Greenwood, Mississippi, and conferred for three hours with Senator Eastland on possible subversive activity in New Orleans. They talked about the segregation stances of those who had recently run for governor of Louisiana.[3574] They also discussed cooperation between the SISS and the city in their investigation of subversive activities. Afterward, the three said they were looking forward to working together. Morrison said, "We will guide ourselves by the work being done by Senator Eastland's committee. We have established complete liaison between ourselves and the committee. . . . Mr. Banister has complete liaison with the committee's staff, which was the main object of our trip." Robert Morris and Richard Arens were the committee's staff members. Banister declared that New Orleans was a logical place for Communist infiltration.

New Orleans mayor Morrison received a letter from Leander Perez offering his aid in the probe. Morrison said he would turn the letter over to Banister.[3575] The establishment of cooperation between Perez and Banister was a seminal event in the history of the Kennedy assassination. Perez, as was discussed in Chapter Ten, was very close to Eastland, going so far as to call him "my senator." The subcommittee hearings provided Banister a "complete liaison" with General Walker's future close associate Robert Morris, as well as Perez.

On March 30, 1956, Perez asked Mayor Morrison to investigate James Dombrowski and Clarence A. Laws, of SCEF and the NAACP, respectively. Perez reported that HUAC had tied Dombrowski to various Communist-front organizations.[3576]

After the Liveright matter concluded, Mayor Morrison announced, "Ever since our initial contact with Senator Eastland two weeks ago the New Orleans police force has been quietly working with the congressional committee's staff." Morrison instructed Banister to help locate more witnesses for Eastland.[3577] The Eastland subcommittee staff members returned to the city on April 4, 1956 to question nine more witnesses. Banister met the subcommittee members as they arrived at Moisant International Airport.[3578] On April 6, 1956, when the hearings resumed, six witnesses were called who took the Fifth. Morris questioned three women in an attempt to establish that the Communist Party tried to infiltrate the Parent-Teachers Association.[3579]

Eastland's committee called Richard Feise to ask what he knew about the Southern

Conference Education Fund. He, too, refused to answer and took the Fifth. Eastland told Feise that he knew full well SCHW and SCEF served as transmission belts to bring Communism to the South.[3580] They called Fiese's wife, Winifred Feise, who was an officer in the Jefferson Parish PTA, to testify and she plead the Fifth. Five days later, a source sent a transcript of Mrs. Fiese's testimony to Clyde Tolson, assistant to J. Edgar Hoover, who noted that Benjamin E. Smith, Mrs. Fiese's lawyer "acted like a Communist" during the hearing. Tolson thought it was worthwhile to see if there was the possibility of pursuing a perjury case against Smith. Hoover directed New Orleans agents to investigate the charge of perjury, but they were unable to find evidence that Smith was a Communist. Smith, along with future SCEF officer Bruce Walzer, both members of the ACLU, would later represent Nazi leader George Lincoln Rockwell after the arrests in the 1961 Hate Bus affair in New Orleans, which was described in Chapter Three.[3581]

Eastland's prized—and most famous—target of the New Orleans hearings was African-American Hunter Pitts O'Dell. O'Dell, called "Jack" by his friends, was a former organizer for the Communist Party, which would later be a problem for him in the civil rights movement.[3582] (On June 22, 1963, Martin Luther King, Jr. met with President Kennedy at the White House. Prior to the meeting, President Kennedy and his advisor told King that having O'Dell and Stanley Levison on his staff invited the charge that his organization was Communist-influenced. Kennedy advised him to sever relations with them. With King's regrets, O'Dell resigned. O'Dell went on to work for liberal causes and, in 1984, he worked on the presidential campaign of Jesse Jackson.[3583])

In preparation for the SISS hearing, Assistant Superintendent Banister ordered Sergeant Badeaux to arrest O'Dell. When they arrived at his apartment, he was not there. Banister ordered Badeaux and Sergeant Peter Joseph Porretto to confiscate evidence from O'Dell's apartment and take it back to Banister's office. Once there, they sorted through O'Dell's papers, and then made them available to the SISS.[3584] Copies of *The Daily Worker* and the writings of Joseph Stalin were found. Banister called the library "the finest collection of Communist literature in the South that I have either seen or heard of."[3585] At the hearing, the committee counsel recited the long list of Communist literature found in O'Dell's apartment. One of the confiscated books was entitled *The Negro Question in the United States*, which had been written in 1936. Counsel Benjamin Mandel stated that the book called for "the creation of the Negro Republic in the area approximating the present Black Belt." Mandel gratuitously added, "That is an invitation to civil war in the South."[3586, 3587]

O'Dell was questioned by the SISS in Washington, D.C., on April 12, 1956, by counsel Robert Morris. O'Dell took the Fifth and refused to say if he were a Communist. Morris told the subcommittee that O'Dell was a district organizer for the Communist Party in New Orleans and said documents seized from his home by police clearly showed he was in a key position in the Communist Party. On July 30, 1958, O'Dell appeared before HUAC in Atlanta and tried to turn the hearing into a discourse on the South's mistreatment of blacks.[3588]

The committee called New Orleans Attorney Calhoun Phifer to testify. Phifer was quoted in the *Times-Picayune* as saying that even if the witnesses in Eastland's hearings denied being Communists, people would believe they were anyway; Phifer was defiant and ridiculed the proceeding. In response, Eastland told him, "We have seen Reds attempt to take over hearings." Phifer responded to Eastland's libelous assertion, saying, "You better watch what you are saying." After Eastland objected to the remark, Phifer told him, "It doesn't mean anything, sir. Your contempt for the Constitution is pretty well known, especially the [Fourteenth] Amendment." Counsel Robert Morris claimed they had evidence that Phifer was a non-dues-paying member of the Communist Party in 1954. Phifer told Eastland; "You don't bother me. I would rather take the Fifth Amendment than be a fifth rate politician." Eastland then asked him if he was taking the Fifth Amendment. Phifer told him, "I take all the amendments . . ." He continued to scoff at Eastland, "You don't scare me with your foolishness." Phifer blasted the committee, "Sir, don't give me your lecture on patriotism . . . I don't need a lecture from you." He was asked if he was a member of the Communist Party and refused to answer, taking every question as an opportunity to berate the subcommittee. Benjamin E. Smith, the SCEF and civil rights attorney, later testified and simply denied being a member of the Communist Party.

Eastland summarized the hearings' findings, vastly overstating his case: "Our evidence here in New Orleans indicates very clearly that Communist leaders in Moscow, Peking, and Bombay, and other foreign cities, through the instrumentality of their writings and party directives transmitted under discipline, are reaching down into this part of the United States from agents willing to do their mischievous work." He said the investigation uncovered a small, dedicated, active underground Communist movement in New Orleans that used code names and aliases and fabricated documents. (It's worth noting here that Lee Harvey Oswald also used an alias, Alek Hidell, on the fabricated documents for his phony FPCC chapter.) Despite the grandiose and disingenuous title of the final report of the hearing, "Scope of Soviet Activity in the United States, 1956," Eastland failed to show any evidence of Soviet activity in his hearing.

At the end of the hearings, Eastland expressed his gratitude to Guy Banister and Hubert Badeaux for setting up the hearings and taking care of the preparations for the investigation. Eastland stated, "They have spared no effort in working with us to gather evidence, develop facts, and assist in the location of witnesses." He thanked the media for televising the proceedings (which were televised at the same time Oswald was residing in New Orleans and, thus, he could have watched them).[3589]

After the proceedings, Banister announced that he would seek to have O'Dell tried under the state Communist laws, or "little Smith Acts," through the district attorney's office. The law he referred to required Communists to register. The violation carried a penalty of two to ten years hard labor and a $1,000 to $10,000 fine. Banister said others might also be charged.[3590]

Banister kept a file on Liveright (it was one of the few files that survived his death in

1964), and Jim Garrison obtained it. The file, numbered 10–66 and dated January 28, 1957, was about an individual hired at WDSU on the recommendation of Liveright. Garrison's claims that Banister's files indicated he was involved in government intelligence were false, as evidenced by Banister's Liveright file and other files described in Chapter One. However, it is proof that Banister kept files on integrationists, which is something Garrison failed to note.[3591]

On February 28, 1956, Kent Courtney appeared before the Eastland SISS hearing on Limitation of Appellate Jurisdiction of the Supreme Court. Courtney told the hearing that the Supreme Court had consistently made decisions favorable to the Communists and usurped the power of the people and of Congress.[3592] That same year, on October 18, 1956—his seventeenth birthday—Lee Harvey Oswald enlisted in the marines for a three-year stint.[3593] Then, on November 18, 1956, Soviet Premier Nikita Khrushchev heightened the Red Scare, while addressing Western ambassadors at a reception at the Polish Embassy in Moscow, when he told them, "We will bury you."[3594]

In 1957, Eastland began his investigation of "Communism in the Mid South" in Memphis, Tennessee. The hearings were again principally about SCEF and their field secretaries, Carl and Anne Braden. Subcommittee counsel recited a litany of purported evidence linking the Bradens and SCEF to the Communist Party, including the prior testimony from the deceased (and disproven) Paul Crouch. Eastland hoped the outcome of the hearing would persuade Congress to pass legislation strengthening states' rights, supposedly in an effort to outlaw sedition.[3595] In hearings in Miami, Florida, and Charlotte, North Carolina, in 1956 and 1957, SISS and HUAC again attempted to connect SCEF to the Communist Party.[3596] (There were numerous hearings of SISS and HUAC and their state counterparts and a comprehensive review of all of them is beyond the scope of this work.[3597, 3598, 3599])

Guy Banister, Hubert Badeaux, Leander Perez, and Subversion in Racial Unrest, 1957
Southern states created their own inquisitional bodies, modeled after HUAC and the SISS, as weapons against integration. The SISS and HUAC opened their case files to their state counterparts, which were dubbed "little HUACs." Many witnesses for the various state bodies were ex-Communists who had testified at congressional hearings.

Anne Braden, an officer in SCEF, ridiculed the Kentucky "little HUAC" calling it "KUAC," noting that it sounded like a duck quack. The Bradens were indicted under Kentucky's "little Smith Act" after they sold a house to a black couple in 1954.[3600] Benjamin Gitlow testified as an expert ex-Communist witness at Carl Braden's trial by the Commonwealth of Kentucky. Gitlow had been in the Communist Party since its inception in 1919. He allegedly was kicked out of the party when he refused to obey orders from Moscow.[3601] (The John Birch Society republished Gitlow's book, *The Whole of Their Lives, Communism in America—A Personal History and Intimate Portrayal of its Leaders*, in 1964.[3602])

The radical right courted ex-Communist witnesses. Benjamin Gitlow appeared with General Walker, Billy James Hargis, General Willoughby, John Rousselot, Revilo Oliver, Myers Lowman, Edward Hunter, and Strom Thurmond at a Christian Crusade Anti-Communist School in Tulsa, Oklahoma, from January 29 to February 2, 1962. He wrote two works exposing the Communist Party. Previously, he had testified against Communism before HUAC in 1939. Senator McCarthy had used his work in the field of anti-Communism at his hearings. Barbara Hartle, another ex-Communist witness was present at the Christian Crusade meeting with Gitlow.[3603, 3604, 3605] (Hartle's experiences with the Communist Party were referenced extensively in J. Edgar Hoover's book *Masters of Deceit.*) Robert Morris's Defenders of American Liberties, a sort of far-right ACLU, championed "the cause of ex-Communists who wanted to help the United States."[3606]

The Southern states also formed their own investigatory and espionage networks dubbed "little FBIs." To combat integration in Louisiana, the state government set up the Legislative Committee on Segregation, chaired by Willie Rainach. As was noted in Chapter One, Guy Banister was a part of the Louisiana segregation intelligence apparatus in LUAC and the Louisiana Sovereignty Commission, and supplied intelligence on integrationists to the Mississippi Sovereignty Commission, as well.[3607]

On March 1, 1956, the NAACP was sued in district court and an injunction was sought to dissolve the NAACP under the 1924 anti-Klan law that required filing annual membership lists to the attorney general. Attorney Sargent Pitcher, a staunch segregationist, and William Shaw, a close associate of Willie Rainach, helped prepare the suit.[3608]

In March 1957, Rainach announced that the Joint Legislative Committee on Segregation would hold hearings, declaring, "We will investigate the influences behind the sudden upsurge of serious racial troubles in the country particularly what these forces are doing in Louisiana." The U.S. Fifth Circuit Court of Appeals, the day before Rainach's announcement, had ordered the desegregation of the New Orleans Public Schools. Rainach boasted during his announcement, "I was responsible for legislation in 1954 to keep blacks out of white colleges. Louisiana was under attack for three issues, public schools, attempts to keep blacks out of state colleges, and bus seating."[3609] Rainach declared that 1957 was a "showdown" year in combating the Communist plan for integration in the state.[3610]

On March 6–9, 1957, the State of Louisiana Joint Legislative Committee held public hearings given the overstated title, "Subversion in Racial Unrest; An Outline of a Strategic Weapon to Destroy the Governments of Louisiana and the United States." Findings from an investigation by the Georgia Commission on Education were used, as well as files from HUAC and the SISS. Roy V. Harris was connected with the Georgia investigation. Leander Perez, Hubert Badeaux, and Guy Banister—first brought together during Eastland's New Orleans SISS hearings in 1956—were the star New Orleans witnesses. (Of course, it will be recalled that evidence was presented in Chapter Ten that all three men were associated with Joseph Milteer.) Robert Morris, counsel in the 1956 hearings, was not involved in the state's hearing. Joining them for the 1957 hearing were ex-Communists Zack Kornfeder and African Americans Leonard Patterson and Manning Johnson, who had all testified before HUAC and the SISS in the past and who had all once lived in the Soviet Union.[3611] Martha Edmiston, who also testified, had been a witness in an Eastland subcommittee hearing in 1955.[3612]

Rainach began the hearing with the testimony of Guy Banister. A biography of Banister's life was presented in the text of the hearing report: "Banister's work prior to and during World War II and in the Cold War following was largely committed to combating subversion. In addition to many years of actual experience in the detailed, painstaking and hazardous work of detecting and forestalling subversive activities, he also devoted considerable study to Communist history, theory, strategy and tactics." Banister testified that that he became familiar with the Communist Party through fellow agent George Starr while working in the New York office of the FBI in 1935. Starr spoke Russian fluently; his father was Russian and at one time trained horses for the Tsar. Banister testified: "George familiarized me with the problems of Communist Party work and, in fact, has been given credit for teaching the agents of the FBI how to conduct these investigations. . . . It was also my duty to develop and supervise those people called informers. To be more specific, we might say they were the counter spies sent in to report on the activities of the party members. That was part of my duties throughout the nearly seventeen years I served as Special Agent in Charge." Banister went on to say that he "regretted getting out of counter-espionage, counter-sabotage, counter-subversive activity." (In reality, Banister really never got out of the espionage business—he continued in his private detective agency after he was fired from the New Orleans Police Department. Joseph Oster, Banister's partner in his detective agency in 1957, told the author that he left Banister's detective agency because Banister was always doing things that didn't bring any money into the office. Banister continued to "supervise informants" at the time Oswald was working with him in 1963.)

Banister told the committee, "The use of spies is approved by Jehovah, and I don't see how we can well object."[3613] (Like Banister, J. Edgar Hoover himself scoured the Old Testament in search of passages that would justify spying.[3614]) Banister told the committee how he set up the New Orleans Police Department Division of Intelligence Affairs. Banister's close friend, Sergeant Hubert Badeaux, staffed the one-man "Red Squad."

Banister recounted for the committee Badeaux's 1956 raid on the house of Hunter Pitts O'Dell, the Louisiana district director of the Communist Party, which had been ordered by subpoena from the SISS. Later, when U.S. Marshals were unable to find O'Dell, they requested help from Badeaux and the New Orleans Police Department. Banister told the committee, "Every member of the Louisiana Communist Party, a component part of the Communist Party of the United States of America, is a Soviet agent. The Communist Party of the United States of America is an agency of the Soviet Government." Banister added, "I mention that Sergeant Hubert Badeaux and I—I understand he will be a witness here—are the two men, so far as I know, who are the only two officers, state or municipal, engaged in combating the Communist Party in this state."

Later, Rainach asked Banister the grand question: "Mr. Banister, in view of your over seventeen years with the FBI in assignments combating Communism, would you say that what you have learned convinces you that the Communists are attempting to use disturbances in racial relations through the ideological and organizational penetration as a means to achieve their objectives in this country?" Banister answered, "We know they have, sir. We have clear and specific directives from them in that regard."

Manning Johnson was called to testify (and likely was well paid). Johnson was the star African American witness, as he had been in a July 14, 1949, HUAC hearing against SCHW, when he testified that it was Communist-dominated. Over the years, however, Johnson, like Paul Crouch, had developed significant credibility problems. In 1950, Johnson testified for the twentieth time against Communist Party members in the trial of Harry Bridges. He stated he had met Bridges at the election of the Party's national committee in New York in 1936. Later, he claimed he had never met him. His position as a professional witness deteriorated as time went on.[3615] Johnson's image was further tarnished when he accused Ralph Bunche of being a Communist. (Bunche was a black civil rights advocate, Harvard professor and an advisor to the United Nations.) The Department of Justice and the Subversive Activities Control Board repudiated Johnson's testimony, but Johnson told the Subversive Activities Control Board he would lie under oath "a thousand times" rather than go against his instructions from the FBI. Johnson's statement led the Justice Department to investigate him and convict him for perjury.[3616] Nonetheless, Johnson's creditability problems didn't bother Rainach.

At the hearing, Johnson described his affiliation with the Young Communist League and later with the Communist Party Central Committee. He said he was an active participant in the "revolutionary plan for overthrowing the government." Johnson had graduated from the Lenin School in Moscow, where Communist agents were trained. (The fact that he had lived in the Soviet Union gave unimpeachable credibility to his credentials as a Communist, as it did for Lee Harvey Oswald.) He claimed that Communist cells were formed in churches all over the Black Belt. He told the hearing that he later felt the Communist Party did not have the black's interests at heart and he left the party.[3617] Johnson testified that, while in the Communist Party, he was: "only a tool of the devils in the Kremlin . . . to subvert my people . . . to be used as pawns in the Soviet struggle for power throughout the world . . ." He said the Communists had infiltrated the NAACP with the intent of turning whites against blacks with the expectation of "bloodshed and violence." He said he left the Communist Party after the Stalin-Hitler pact, and claimed SCEF worked to turn the Black Belt into a Communist transmission belt.[3618] (When he was no longer needed as an ex-Communist witness, Johnson later found work with the John Birch Society's speaker's bureau. They distributed his pamphlet entitled *Color, Communism and Common Sense*, and established a Manning Johnson Scholarship fund for deserving blacks in an effort to show they were not anti-black.)[3619]

African American Leonard Patterson told the Joint Legislative Committee that Communist infiltration of minority groups had started twenty-five years earlier. He claimed most of the Communist infiltration into black society occurred via the black churches.[3620] Counsel J. G. Sourwine later questioned Patterson at another SISS hearing, on February 2, 1960.[3621] (As we shall see in the next chapter, Sourwine was a key figure in the important October 4, 1963, raid on SCEF in New Orleans.)

Martha Edmiston, a white Ohio reporter, testified that "she saw within the Party the pitiless exploitation of the Negro people . . ." She identified an NAACP leader as a Communist. Edmiston and her husband had joined the Communist Party in 1940 as undercover agents for the FBI.[3622] Edmiston and her husband coached newcomer, ex-Communist witness Harvey Matusow on how to testify before HUAC. Matusow recalled that she advised him to, "Play [his] big cards one at a time. For if [he] didn't do it that way [his] life as a witness would be short." Prior to his testimony before HUAC, Edmiston helped Matusow prepare an autobiography of his life as a Communist, which he gave HUAC and the FBI. Matusow later announced that he lied at a HUAC hearing when he identified certain individuals as Communists.[3623]

Matusow had become a member of the Communist Party in 1947. He then enrolled in the Civil Rights Congress. In 1950, he became an informant for the FBI. As a reservist, he was called back to military duty in 1951. While stationed at an air force base, he was approached to testify about his former Communist connections. He testified before the Ohio Un-American Activities Committee. A month later, he testified before HUAC where he named 180 names. He went around the country as an expert witness on Communism; he exposed Communists everywhere and even made speeches on behalf of Senator McCarthy. In 1953, he wrote a letter to McCarthy stating that he was retiring as a witness. In 1954, he admitted he had been lying for the past three years at the various inquisitions and the story went public. (He wrote a book on his work, which was first called *Blacklisting was my Business*, and was later renamed *False Witness*.)[3624]

Joseph "Zack" Kornfeder, a former Communist who had lived in the Soviet Union, testified before the Joint Legislative Committee on March 7, 1957, saying "They [the Communists] aim to use the Negro—preach a doctrine of racial nationalism—in order to use the Negro for their purposes."[3625] He said that half of the approximately 600 Americans trained in Moscow colleges in the past thirty years had been black.[3626] While living in the Soviet Union, Kornfeder became a staunch opponent of Joseph Stalin after the secret police arrested his wife. He was a veteran paid "ex-Communist witness" for HUAC. (Kornfeder died in 1963 and was one of the last of the "ex-Communist" witnesses who had lived in the Soviet Union.)

Rainach's three-day hearing of the Joint Legislative Committee concluded with the testimony of Hubert Badeaux. Badeaux's testimony filled eighty pages of the 255-page hearing transcript. Badeaux was described as "an expert in [Communist] party affairs dealing with the Negro." Badeaux testified that there were "thousands of documents which support the charge of penetration of the NAACP by the Communist Party . . . enough to convince even the most skeptical." Badeaux cited the case of black teenager Emmett Till, who was brutally murdered for whistling at a white woman. Two white men were acquitted of the murder, but later admitted their involvement. Of the Till murder, Badeaux stated, "The Communists made an incident of that all out of proportion." Badeaux placed into evidence the book entitled, *The Till Case and the Negro Liberation Movement*, and other documents—most, if not all taken from the home of Hunter Pitts O'Dell—whom he called "Louisiana's top Communist."

He also presented material supposedly connecting SCHW and SCEF with the Communists. Badeaux's testimony demonstrated that he was well versed in Communism and so-called Communist-front organizations.[3627]

Badeaux had all the credentials needed to groom an individual to infiltrate the universities and leftist groups as he disclosed to Rainach in a letter in 1957. Badeaux was also a crude racist. (It will be recalled from Chapter Ten that Badeaux wrote Rainach and told him that the only Communists he ever knew were "Jews and niggers." Brady Bartlett gave Joseph Milteer a tape recording of one of Badeaux's speeches to the Citizens' Council. Badeaux stated in his the speech that, "a nigger doesn't have a lick of sense."[3628]) Lou Ivon, Jim Garrison's chief investigator during his assassination probe, told the author that Banister and Badeaux, beyond serving together in the police department, were the closest of friends.[3629] As a result of Badeaux's testimony, Rainach considered having the state legislature set up a "Red Squad."[3630]

William Shaw, a close Rainach associate, questioned Badeaux for the committee. Shaw had served on the board of the Federation for Constitutional Government, which had been inspired by Senator Eastland. Leander Perez and J. Evetts Haley, also served on the Federation board.[3631, 3632]

Plaquemines district attorney Leander Perez testified briefly at the hearing that the Field Secretary of the NAACP, Clarence Laws, maintained a close relationship with SCHW and other organizations cited as Communist fronts by HUAC. He submitted the *Congressional Record* from February 23, 1956, as evidence. (Perez had recently testified before Eastland's Committee in Washington, D.C., in regard to federal civil rights proposals, where he had also stated that the NAACP was being aided and abetted by the Communists or Communist-front organizations to destroy the nation from within.[3633])

After the hearings, Kent Courtney wrote Rainach and requested ten copies of the Subversion on Racial Unrest hearings to loan out and keep in constant circulation.[3634]

Hubert Badeaux and the Grooming of an Infiltrator

On April 27, 1957, Hubert Badeaux wrote to Willie Rainach: "I have been in contact with an out-of-town person, which I have been grooming to come here to take over the establishment of infiltration into the University and intellectual groups, I will tell you in detail about that when I see you in person. There is another matter which I discussed with Bill Simmons, in Jackson, and which I don't care to put in writing at this time." (Bill Simmons was Ross Barnett's close advisor, who orchestrated the resistance to the admission of James Meredith to the University of Mississippi—and subsequent violence.) Badeaux's letter, on Guy Banister's police department stationery, was presented in Chapter Ten.

There are a number of factors to suggest that the individual Badeaux was grooming as an infiltrator was Lee Harvey Oswald. First, Oswald was the age of a university student, a requirement for infiltrating a university group. Second, as was presented in the last chapter, while he was seen repeatedly at the office of Guy Banister in 1963, he was, in fact, infiltrating leftist organizations at Tulane University. Third, Oswald may have been recruited as an infiltrator from David Ferrie's Civil Air Patrol outfit the year prior. (Ferrie, as has been noted, was a rabid anti-Communist and a close associate Guy Banister.) Fourth, during the same period of time that Badeaux wrote Rainach that he was grooming "an infiltrator," Oswald began acting like a Communist. In 1956, Oswald told William Wulf of the New Orleans Astronomy Association that he was trying to find a Communist cell to join; and Oswald's friend at Pfisterer's Dental, Palmer McBride, recalled that, also in 1956, Oswald told him he wanted to shoot President Eisenhower for exploiting the working class. Oswald was sixteen when he requested information from the Young Peoples Socialist League (YPSL), on October 3, 1956. He wanted to know if there was a branch in the area and wanted to join it saying, "I am a Marxist and have been studying Socialist principles for well over fifteen months." He said he was very interested in the YPSL.[3635] Fifth, Rainach stated that the individual groomed as an infiltrator was out of town at the time Badeaux wrote the letter to Rainach in 1957, which fits with the fact that Oswald departed New Orleans months earlier and was stationed with the marines in Florida. Sixth, Badeaux's announcement that he was grooming an infiltrator came on the heels of Banister and Badeaux's foray into the anti-Communist and anti-integration espionage business with Senator Eastland. Seventh, Banister testified at Rainach's Subversion in Racial Unrest hearing that it was his duty while in the FBI to develop informers. Eighth, during the period of 1953 to 1956, Oswald's favorite television show was *I Led Three Lives*, which glamorized the life and times of a false Communist who infiltrated Communist cells on the behalf of the FBI. The show may have served as a model for Oswald's acting as a Communist in 1956. Ninth, if the groomed infiltrator was someone other than Oswald, he never publicly emerged among leftists groups, as Oswald did in 1963.

New leftist groups that the old guard ex-Communist witnesses were not involved with, like Fair Play for Cuba Committee, emerged in the 1960s. The former ex-Communists witnesses like Paul Crouch and Manning Johnson, who had been to the Soviet Union, had lost their credibility (or had passed away, in Crouch's case), and they could not be effectively used in the fight against them. What Senator Eastland needed was a new generation of informants, with impeccable Communist credentials, if he was going to be successful at defeating his enemies in the years to come through his SISS inquisitions. Oswald gained his credentials when he departed for the Soviet Union in 1959.

Still more evidence to suggest that Oswald was groomed to be an agent of the Louisiana segregationists (or Eastland's SISS) is the report of a conversation with Marguerite Oswald. According to a witness, in 1962, Mrs. Oswald knew her son was performing "anti-subversive work" for the government, which comports with the evidence presented herein suggesting that Oswald was posing as a Communist to be a future witness in the Eastland hearings on FPCC and other leftist groups.

On February 2, 1964, Mrs. Paine (whom the Oswalds stayed with) stated that she had heard from reporter Lonnie Hudkins of the *Houston Post* that Marguerite Oswald was working for Mrs. Linda Rosenthal as a practical nurse in Fort Worth during September and October of 1962. Oswald reportedly told Mrs. Rosenthal "her son was doing important anti-subversive work." Hudkins speculated that perhaps Oswald made a deal with the U.S. government to do work on its behalf in anti-subversive endeavors, in turn for being granted permission to return to the U.S. from the Soviet Union. Hudkins told the FBI that he was on a "fishing expedition" in his investigation of the case, to see if Oswald could have been a "Stool pigeon for the CIA or FBI." The FBI interviewed Mrs. Rosenthal and she told them she got the impression from Mrs. Oswald that Lee was working for the U.S. government in Russia.[3636]

Of all of the evidence suggesting Oswald was groomed as a false Communist to be an informant and witness, perhaps none is more important than the overwhelming evidence that Oswald was actually a member of the far right. There is no reason that Oswald would travel to the Soviet Union and masquerade as a Communist other than to be used as an informer and a witness in the Eastland hearings or similar inquisitions.

The same year Banister, Badeaux, and Perez were tying Communism to the civil rights movement, the Red Scare intensified. On October 4, 1957, the Soviet Union success-fully launched the first orbiting satellite, Sputnik I, marking the beginning of the space race.

The Highlander Folk School had held its annual meeting on Labor Day, 1957. The staged photo—detailed in Chapter Ten—and the resulting propaganda ultimately led to the closing the school.[3637] The state of Tennessee padlocked the school and confiscated $130,000 worth of property. The main building was eventually burned to the ground.[3638] The Georgia Commission on Education "exposed" Highlander as—supposedly—a Communist organiza-tion, after Rainach's hearing on Subversion in Racial Unrest.

On September 24, 1957, President Eisenhower ordered U.S. paratroopers from the 101st Airborne Division to Little Rock to enforce the federally mandated integration of Cen-tral High School. A reluctant General Walker commanded them. After Little Rock, observed Homes Alexander of the Charleston *Post and Courier*, a "new kind of Southern nationalism" emerged. The confederate flag flew everywhere. The national anthem was replaced by "Dixie" at high school football games. As historian Jeff Woods described it, Southern nationalism "had at its core a regional desire to protect 'the southern way of life'" from outside threats.

Eastland's SISS held hearings in Memphis in October 1957 as a result of the so-called Highlander expose. Testimony again centered on SCEF's Carl Braden. Robert Morris was chief counsel.[3639]

On November 18, 1957, Willie Rainach, Senator Eastland, and Leander Perez, three tireless fighters for the preservation of segregation, along with Emmet Irwin, spoke at the Citizens' Council of New Orleans.[3640]

Billy James Hargis sponsored an all-night, anti-Red radio crusade on April 18 and 24, 1958, which featured far right wingers James O. Eastland, Martin Dies, J. B. Mathews, Carl McIntire, and Charles Willoughby. The anti-Red crusade exemplified the close ties that the radical right had to the congressional Communist witch hunters in Eastland, Dies, and Mathews.[3641]

On May 6, 1958, Willie Rainach, chairman of the Joint Legislative Committee of the State of Louisiana, wrote to Guy Banister at his 434 Balter Building office address and told him, "I have heard some statements about the good program that you are initiating in New Orleans and want to congratulate you upon this move. It should serve a good cause in training the people of this state, particularly young ones, on methods of detecting and combating alien ideology."[3642]

Guy Banister and the Arkansas Legislature Hearings on Communist Ties to Racial Trouble, 1958

On December 15, 1958, the Arkansas State Legislative Council held hearings to expose the "Communistic influences" behind the racial unrest that centered on Little Rock's federally integrated Central High School. Similar hearings were held in other states. The state's attorney general testified at the hearings that the Southern Conference Education Fund, the Highlander Folk School, and the NAACP were subversive. J. B. Mathews, the former HUAC investigator and professional "ex-Communist" witness, testified that five Arkansas colleges "[had] been successfully penetrated" by Communists.[3643] Mathews, who made appearances at several state-level hearings after Senator Joseph McCarthy dropped him from his staff, further testified that Communist agents penetrated schools that were involved with the Southern Conference Education Fund. (He also testified, in Florida, that 145 leaders of the NAACP were Communists.[3644])

The Arkansas hearings mirrored those of Willie Rainach's Subversion in Racial Unrest hearings. Manning Johnson reprised his role as the African-American insider/stool pigeon. His credibility at the national level was shot, but it didn't matter to the Southern states inquisitors.

Guy Banister (who had been in Arkansas at the same time as General Walker was there to maintain order during the desegregation of the Little Rock schools) appeared before the Special Education Committee of the Arkansas Legislature on December 16–17, 1958.[3645, 3646] According to a January 17, 1959, FBI report, Banister told the Committee that the Little Rock School crisis "was started with these subversive influences in this part of the country." The news headline on Banister's testimony read, "Unrest blamed on Reds," and, later, "Half of Commy trained Americans were of the Negro race."[3647]

Communist Activities and Infiltration in the South, Atlanta, 1958

In March of 1958, HUAC held a hearing in Atlanta on "Communist Activities and Infiltration in the South." SCEF and the Bradens were, again, the principal targets. On July 30, 1958, counsel Richard Arens called Carl Braden to testify. Braden told him he was working in the integration movement in the South and was employed by SCEF, which he described as "a south wide interracial organization working to bring about integration, justice, and decency in the South." Asked if he was associated with members of the Communist Party, he responded, "My beliefs and my associations are none of the business of this committee." Braden added, "While you are investigating, Mr. Arens, you ought to investigate some of the atrocities against the Jews and Negroes in the South . . . ." Braden asked the committee, "Are you saying integration is Communism like they do in New Orleans?" Braden added, "Integration is what you are investigating. All the people here are integrationists. . . . I think you should be investigating violence: and I think you should be investigating against Jews and Negroes in the South, the bombings of synagogues, the bombing of Negro homes. That is the kind of thing you should be investigating." Carl Braden took the Fifth and refused to answer whether or not he was a Communist.[3648] (Braden was cited with six counts of contempt. He was convicted in 1959 and sentenced to a year in prison, which he began serving in 1961. The U.S. Fifth Circuit Court of Appeals upheld the conviction.[3649] He appealed his case to the Supreme Court.[3650] Braden later became an officer in FPCC.)

Hunter Pitts O'Dell testified before HUAC on July 31, 1958. (It will be recalled that Guy Banister and Hubert Badeaux had raided O'Dell's home in 1956.) When asked if he was a member of the Communist Party, he responded: "Since we are not concerned with the subversive activities as far as oppression of the Negro people is concerned, I have to rely upon all of the immunity that the Constitution of the United States gives me as a Negro, because I am concerned with subversives activities that have kept my people segregated for this long." The Committee then recited the testimony of Badeaux, regarding a document he took from O'Dell's apartment describing an alleged proposal for the takeover of the Black Belt by the Communist Party for 1955 and 1956. O'Dell denied ever seeing the document. Undaunted, the Committee recited evidence showing O'Dell was a Communist.[3651]

In a 1958 speech on a special all-night Billy James Hargis radio broadcast, Senator Eastland asserted that there were 25,000 Communists in the U.S. working diligently, day and night, as agents of a foreign power to destroy the chief stronghold of the Christian civilization—the United States.[3652] The event illustrates the early, cozy relationship Eastland had with members of the radical right, like Hargis.

Kent Courtney enjoyed a close relationship with the Communist inquisitors in Washington, D.C. He testified, in early 1958, in favor of the Jenner Bill to curb the Supreme Court, and met with Jay Sourwine and Richard Ahrens of the Senate and House Committees, respectively.[3653]

Courtney spoke to an audience of 8,000 at the Citizens' Council of New Orleans on July 25, 1958, and urged support of the Council's efforts to maintain segregation. He was joined by Emmet Irwin, a Milteer associate.[3654]

Leander Perez announced, in November 1958, "We have every research and testimony showing how the Communists went to school in Moscow and made plans for a Black Belt in America, and having failed at this, turned to infiltration."[3655] Less than a year later, Lee Harvey Oswald traveled to Moscow.

Eastland held an SISS hearing on March 18, 1959, on the subject of Red propaganda coming through the Port of New Orleans, en route to Central America. It was the third hearing on Communist activities held in New Orleans. (HUAC had held one in 1957, while Eastland had held a similar one in 1955, where he learned over a million pieces of Communist propaganda was shipped through the Port of New Orleans.)[3656] Fifteen thousand pieces of mail, allegedly from a Mexican printing plant and financed by the Soviet embassy in Mexico City, entered the U.S. through New Orleans, according to the committee's liaison officer with the post office.[3657]

Leander Perez testified at Eastland's Senate Judiciary Committee hearing in Washington, D.C., on April 29, 1959, and expressed his opposition to a civil rights bill that would give congressional approval of the Supreme Court's ruling on school integration, making it the "law of the land." Eastland was lavish in his praise of Perez, calling him a "star witness" and crediting him with the defeat of President Truman's civil rights measures. Eastland said the bill must be defeated at "all cost" and that there would be a "very, very, hard fight" over the measure.[3658] Perez told the Judiciary Committee that civil rights bills were patterned after Stalin's all-races law and that "[t]he so-called civil rights laws were reborn in Russia and have been used to enslave the Russian people." The Stalin all-race statute, he asserted, called for equality of the races and was used by Stalin to make himself the supreme dictator. Perez said that the Black Monday decision was not based on law, but, rather, the Supreme Court decision hinged on the testimony of authorities from Communist-front organizations.[3659]

On May 15, 1959, Perez testified before the civil rights unit of the Senate Judiciary Committee, saying that the Communists, their sympathizers, and their dupes initiated racial agitation. Senator Eastland said a formidable defense of the Southern point of view could be built around the legal phrases of Perez's testimony. Eastland praised Perez for establishing, irrefutably, that there had been constitutional encroachment on the rights of the states in regards to civil rights proposals.[3660]

Meanwhile, more evidence of U.S.-Soviet tensions emerged on July 24, 1959, adding to the Red Scare, when Vice President Richard Nixon visited the American National Exhibition in Moscow. While in the kitchen of a model home exhibit, Nixon and Khrushchev held an impromptu confrontational debate on the merits of their respective economic systems, dubbed the "Kitchen Debate."[3661]

During his investigation of the Kennedy assassination, Jim Garrison obtained a few of Guy Banister's investigative files. Banister's file number 10–58, dated August 27, 1959, noted that Allen Campbell, a young former marine who had worked for Banister, had surreptitiously entered James Dombrowski's SCEF office on Perdido Street.[3662]

The author interviewed both Allen Campbell and his brother Dan. Allen told the author that the reason he worked at the Banister office was to learn about Communism. He said he was a friend of David Ferrie and was eager to fly with him whenever asked, to hone his skills as a pilot. Both of the Campbell brothers told the author that they saw Lee Harvey Oswald at the Banister office at Camp and Lafayette Streets, as was noted in Chapter One. (The office was blocks away from the SCEF's Perdido Street offices, in 1963.) Allen Campbell broke into the SCEF office at Banister's request in 1959. The incident suggests that Banister, as a private investigator, may still have been working with Eastland, as he had been in 1956, in his continued quest to destroy SCEF.

On October 16, 1959, Lee Harvey Oswald arrived in Moscow by train from Helsinki, Finland.[3663] On November 15, 1959, Oswald wrote in his diary, affirming his devotion to Communism: "I have waited two years in order to dissolve my American citizenship I have seen too much hate and injustice in the U.S. . . . . I have chosen the U.S.S.R. since it is the leader of the Socialist camp and the symbolic champion of the cause of Communism. . . . In the U.S., as all know, there are many shortcomings, racial segregation and the repression of the underdog, U.S. Communist party. . . . I learned to hate the U.S. imperialistic military."[3664]

In May 1960, Willie Rainach turned down Governor Davis's offer to head the Louisiana Sovereignty Commission, a state organization created to spy on integrationists. Rainach said that Davis broke his promises to Rainach on the way he would set up the commission.[3665] Banister applied for the job of director of the Sovereignty Commission and offered the use of his files and library to the commission. In a letter to the Sovereignty Commission, Banister wrote: "I would like to propose to Governor McKeithen a contract between Guy Banister Associates, Inc. and the State which would make available to him expert investigative help. . . . I would supervise the work of the investigators."[3666]

On October 1, 1960, the Louisiana legislature set up their own "little HUAC," the Legislative Committee on Un-American Activities (LUAC). LUAC members, headed by James Pfister as chairman, met that same day to deliberate on how to best start their investigations on subversive activities. (Pfister was an admirer of high-ranking John Birch Society Council member Clarence Manion, and presented him with an American Legion "George Washington-Great American Award" on February 22, 1961.[3667]) At the meeting, Festus Brown and Jack Rogers screened a film about the May 1959 protest in San Francisco against HUAC. Pfister said, "it upsets me emotionally that we tolerate such things in this country." (Pfister, Brown, and Rogers were all associates of Guy Banister.) Harold Montgomery who was at the meeting said, "there are purposely only a few card-carrying Communists—it's the other kind who do all the damage." LUAC recommended the appointment of Jack Rogers of the American Legion Un-American Committee to the LUAC. Rogers said there were "similar dupes" at Tulane as those in the San Francisco HUAC protest group.[3668]

Guy Banister applied for a position with LUAC in 1960. Interviewing for the job, Banister told lawmakers that the Louisiana Negro sit-ins were led by white left wingers, as has been noted. He stated: "The Negro race is not capable of the leadership or organization for sit-ins, it is white people. And I might add, the Negro race never has produced a great criminal either." Banister said the "committee on racial equality [sic] operates out of New York City and is behind the troubles caused by colored students in the South. . . . There has been no real exposure of subversive influence in this state, although the joint committee on segregation in the past did some work in that direction."[3669]

An official of the Sovereignty Commission offered the use of its staff to assist LUAC. Festus Brown of the American Legion pledged their support for LUAC and mentioned several men—including Guy Banister's close friend Guy Johnson—as prospects for investigators. Johnson had been with the Office of Naval Intelligence during WWII. (It will be recalled that

Jim Garrison tried to pass off Guy *Banister* as a member of the Office of Naval Intelligence when he was not, in an effort to tie him to a purported U.S. government intelligence network he claimed was responsible for the president's assassination. It was apparently a case of "guilt by association" for Garrison. Since Johnson was formerly with the Office of Naval Intelligence, somehow Banister was too, as Garrison implied, as was discussed in Chapter Nine. In reality, what Johnson and Banister had in common was that the two were Southern racists who were interested in investigating integrationists under the created impression they were affiliated with the Communists.)[3670] As was noted in Chapter One, Guy Banister landed the job as LUAC's chief investigator.

The Louisiana Un-American Activities Committee, 1961

The Louisiana Un-American Activities Committee, chaired by James H. Pfister, held hearings entitled "The Case of Dr. Waldo McNeir" on May 8, 1961. Waldo McNeir was an English professor at Louisiana State University and a native Southerner. He drew LUAC's ire when he wrote a letter to two state representatives who were staunch advocates for segregation. He wrote them, on university stationery: "I disagree with everything you stand for. Segregation is wrong, . . . State sovereignty is dead. . . . We must live under federal law or perish. Reason must prevail." LUAC noted that McNeir was a member of the ACLU and NAACP and was active in the civil rights movement.

The university president admonished McNeir to use discretion and make it clear he was not speaking on behalf of the university. Some of his students reported to the university that McNeir continued to make statements critical of the segregationists. The university notified McNeir that charges might be brought up against him, prompting his resignation. LUAC investigated the matter, and noted that HUAC had determined in a 1948 hearing that "The American Civil Liberties Union may be definitely classified as a Communist front or 'transmission belt' organization." HUAC also pointed out that at least forty-six national officials of the NAACP each had fifteen or more Communist-front affiliations.[3671] (Oswald joined the ACLU in 1963. There is no evidence that he joined the NAACP, although he may have.)

Guy Banister and Leander Perez were active in LUAC. Banister ran for New Orleans councilman at large in the April 15, 1961, primary, favoring segregation.[3672] When he was accused of getting the facts wrong on an election issue, he conferred with Leander Perez on the matter, while attending a meeting of LUAC in Baton Rouge.[3673]

Robert Morris and the LUAC Hearings, 1962

LUAC held a hearing on April 24, 1962, entitled "Communist Propaganda Infiltration in Louisiana." They heard testimony from Robert Claitor, a bookstore owner, that his store had received unsolicited Communist propaganda in the mail from the Soviet Embassy in New York. Claitor told LUAC that he did a lively business in selling anti-Communist books. They next heard from Irving Fishman, the deputy collector of customs, who had previously testified before the SISS in 1959. Fishman told LUAC that all kinds of Communist literature entered the United States through the Port of New Orleans. He said a good deal of it came from Cuba. Robert Morris, General Walker's friend, attorney, and advisor, testified last.

Morris told LUAC that he had twice been counsel to the Eastland subcommittee. He related that he had entered the navy in 1941 as a Naval Intelligence Officer, and was put in charge of the Communist Intelligence desk. In his capacity as an intelligence officer, he heard Earl Browder, secretary general of the Communist Party, address a Communist rally in Madison Square Garden. He testified that Browder told the crowd that "Words are bullets" and that selling *The Daily Worker* on the streets of New York was as important as manning a machine gun in Stalingrad. (Oswald subscribed to *The Daily Worker* on August 9, 1962.)

Morris compared the propaganda coming into the ports to "Communist bullets." He told LUAC: "If you are looking for literature advocating the overthrow of the U.S. government you are looking for the wrong thing. The Communists are interested in the gradual encirclement of America." Morris declared that civil liberties must be forgotten when dealing with political propaganda. Morris recommended that LUAC "make a fetish out of the civil liberties when dealing with Communist propaganda." He also warned LUAC of the danger of the Fair Play for Cuba organization. Morris told LUAC that he personally knew Elizabeth Bentley, Louis Bundez, and Whitaker Chambers, who were all ex-Communist witnesses. Morris created the organization "Defenders of American Liberties," a right-winged version of the ACLU that championed "the cause of ex-Communists who wanted to help the United States."[3674]

According to the archivist of the Louisiana State Archives, most of the LUAC papers and all of Sovereignty Commission papers disappeared from the state holdings at some unknown point in time. It is possible that they were purged because they contained information about Guy Banister's use of informers and infiltrators, and were from the period of time that a large number of witnesses saw Oswald at Banister's office in the summer of 1963.

On May 22, 1962, Robert Morris returned to New Orleans to speak at the Orleans Club on the topic "One, Two, Three—surrender," an obvious reference to Kennedy's disarmament proposal.[3675] On September 22–23, 1962, Morris joined Billy James Hargis and John Rousselot as a featured speaker at the Eighth National Constitution Day Convention at the We the People meeting in Chicago.[3676]

The Communist Party was convicted by the government, on December 14, 1962, of failing to register as an agent of the Soviet Union under the McCarran Act of 1950. The party received the maximum penalty of $120,000. John Abt, whom Lee Harvey Oswald had requested to defend him after the Kennedy assassination, defended them.[3677]

Lee Harvey Oswald's Renunciation of Communism

Like the professional ex-Communist witnesses, Oswald affirmed he was a genuine Communist by his stay in the Soviet Union and other actions, even though the Soviets never saw him as a serious Communist. Remarkably, Oswald, just prior to leaving the Soviet Union in June 1962, drafted a written renunciation of Communism—the second characteristic phase of the ex-Communist witnesses' conversion before they engaged in finger pointing and the naming of names of other Communists.

The testimony of Manning Johnson illustrates the affirmation, renunciation, and identification phases of the ex-Communists. Johnson affirmed he was a genuine Communist by his travel to the Soviet Union. He then claimed to have renounced Communism when he saw the light about the evils of Communism when he realized he was "only a tool of the devils in the Kremlin . . . to subvert [his] people . . . to be used as pawns in the Soviet struggle for power throughout the world . . . ." And, finally, he went on to a prodigious and profitable career as an identifier and finger pointer.

Oswald wrote his renunciation of Communism in 1962, in the same scripted way he had previously written about the evils of capitalism and the U.S., in the Soviet diary that was discovered after his death. Oswald's renunciation is as follows (it should be noted that William Z. Foster and Helen Gurley Flynn were officers in the Communist Party USA):

> The Communist Party of the United States has betrayed itself! It has turned itself into the traditional lever of a foreign power to overthrow the Government of the United States, not in the name of freedom of high ideals, but in the servile conformity to the wishes of the Soviet Union and in anticipation of Soviet Russia's complete domination of the American continent. The Fosters and Flynns of the subsidized Communist Party of the United States have shown themselves to be willing, gullible messengers of the Kremlin's Internationalist propaganda. . . . The Communist movement in the U.S., personalized by Communist Party U.S.A., has turned itself into a "valuable gold coin" of the Kremlin.

Oswald was also critical of the U.S.S.R. for denouncing the U.S. handling of the Cuba situation and the Negro lynchings, but at the same time, hypocritically failing to denounce their own violent actions in Hungary and in East Germany. Oswald stated further: "[I have] many personal reasons to know and therefore hate and mistrust Communism."[3678]

Veteran HUAC and SISS Counsel Richard Arens commented on the scripted language and allegories ("valuable gold coin") used by the Communists: "That is what we call the Aesopian language of the Communists."[3679] J. Edgar Hoover devoted a section of his book *Masters of Deceit* to the same topic, explaining the Communist's Aesopian language.[3680]

On June 10, 1962, Oswald returned to the United States. Around June 18, 1962, Oswald retained the services of legal stenographer Pauline Bates in Fort Worth, Texas, to transcribe his renunciation. Oswald brought with him a spate of typed and handwritten notes in English and Russian on scraps of paper that he smuggled out of the U.S.S.R. Bates recalled that the notes all expressed bitterness about the working and living conditions in the Soviet Union. Oswald spent eight hours working alongside Bates, translating the notes. (Oswald's rush to have the renunciation formally typed may reflect his weariness of portraying a Communist after the ordeal of spending two years and nine months in the austere conditions of the Soviet Union. Perhaps he was looking forward to the day when he could publicly re-nounce Communism and rail against it.) He paid Bates ten dollars, which was all he could afford, suggesting the transcription was of tremendous importance to him.

Bates was of the impression that an oil engineer, probably a White Russian named Peter Gregory, was supposed to publish them as an anti-Communist book. (Gregory, a friend of George de Mohrenschildt and part of the Russian anti-Communist group Oswald associ-ated with upon his return home from the Soviet Union later denied the allegation. Gregory's father had been a member of the Old Russian aristocracy before the Bolshevik revolution.)[3681]

J. Edgar Hoover wrote a chapter in his book, *Masters of Deceit*, entitled "Why People Break With Communism." Hoover explained that the Communists were inherently evil and tricked people into believing in their cause. It was the enlightened Communists who real-ized they had been duped by the masters of deceit, quit, and then came to oppose them.[3682] Oswald never got the chance to publicly use the renunciation. He maintained his Commu-nist facade until the end. The Warren Commission and HSCA failed to explain the obvious contradiction. Despite the renunciation, Oswald continued to profess a devotion to Com-munism in his letters to the Communist Party and other groups, which was just another lie among many, as we will see later.

Eastland, the Fair Play for Cuba Hearings, and Lee Harvey Oswald

In 1960, Senator Eastland began investigating the Fair Play for Cuba Committee for the purpose of demonstrating their ties to the Communist Party, the Socialist Workers Party, and other groups that had been labeled as subversive. Five of the eight Eastland FPCC hearings were held during the time when Oswald began to communicate with the Communist Party and Socialist Workers Party and, later, the FPCC, all the while accumulating his paper cre-dentials to show that he had an active interest in Communism in the U.S.

Eastland eventually showed that the FPCC was backed and promoted by the Com-munists. During the same period, Oswald, suspiciously, wrote to the Communist Party and Socialist Workers Party and attempted to get from them, in writing, evidence that they backed or endorsed the FPCC and the American Civil Liberties Union. Neither organization took the bait. Over the years, members of both the Communist Party and Socialist Workers Party had been blacklisted, deported, and/or jailed. They were cautious as to what they would put in writing. They were wary of the Herbert Philbricks and Paul Crouches of the world. (It is somewhat surprising that they were as accommodating of Oswald as they were. This may have been—in part—due to his telling them that he had lived in the Soviet Union, which conveyed a certain level of authenticity to Oswald's claim of being one of them and set him apart from the usual false Communists continually trying to infiltrate their organizations.)

The Fair Play for Cuba Committee, which had been in operation for several months, publicly premiered when they took out a full-page ad in the *New York Times* on April 6, 1960, captioned "What is really happening in Cuba." The ad announced the formation of FPCC in New York City and declared that FPCC intended to promulgate "the truth about the revolution in Cuba" and to neutralize the distorted American press. (Castro had seized power in Cuba in January of 1960.) FPCC organized a trip to Cuba for 350 college students on the anniversary of the revolution.

On January 10, 1960, Eastland's SISS conducted hearings and determined, from the testimony of Dr. Charles A. Santos-Buch (who had become disillusioned with the organization), that FPCC had obtained funds from the Cuban Government to place the ad. The professional, paid ex-Communist witnesses, aside from their loss of credibility, were useless to Eastland's investigation of the fledgling FPCC. Instead, he relied on people like Cuban exile Santos-Buch and volunteers, Herbert Philbrick-type informants like Harry Dean, and others, to tie FPCC to the Communists. Because of this, Eastland's witnesses who testified against FPCC lacked the credentials of having been to the Soviet Union like the professional ex-Communists that testified against the left in the 1940s and 1950s.

The SISS held eight hearings on FPCC from 1961 through 1963 under the title "Castro's Network in the United States (Fair Play for Cuba Committee)."[3683] A hearing on FPCC sometime after April 1, 1964, was planned, but was never held.[3684] Many of the hearings were held in 1963, during the period when Oswald was actively promoting his one-man chapter of FPCC in New Orleans—which the Warren Commission concluded was a "product of his imagination."

On May 5, 1960, Eastland's subcommittee proclaimed that FPCC was a fraud, set up under the auspices of a concealed agent of Fidel Castro. Counsel Julius "Jay" Sourwine called FPCC a foreign-sponsored propaganda organization that was "supported and encouraged by the Communist Party."[3685] An FBI source advised that in the beginning of the FPCC's existence, there was a struggle between the Communist Party and the Socialist Workers Party when they both tried to exert their influence on FPCC, but the FPCC leadership was successful in minimizing their influence. To the contrary, another FBI informant told them that Vincent "Ted" Lee, the national office director, accepted the cooperation of the Communist Party and the Socialist Workers Party.

V. T. Lee stated that the mission of FPCC was to advocate for the resumption of U.S. diplomatic relations with Cuba and to support the rights of Cubans to manage their revolution without interference from outside.[3686] The *Tampa Times* described Lee as "a militant supporter of Castro's government" and an "exponent of the Cuban revolution." From 1959 to 1961, Lee gave speeches praising Castro's government and condemning Cuban refugees as "Batista's criminals." He told the press that he did not care if there were Communist influences in Cuba or among the local FPCC membership, and frequently attended 26th of July Movement meetings.[3687, 3688] Lee wrote in the Tampa *Fair Play* newsletter, "Castro got the cream and here in Florida are the dregs and the scum." He called the Cuban exiles "the scum of society."[3689] (Lee Harvey Oswald, as we shall see, echoed Lee's sentiment, calling the Cuban exiles "worms.") Anti-Castro Cubans forced Lee to leave Tampa under threats of violence, after the press reported on his activities. He moved the group's headquarters to New York. (On

April 19, 1963, Oswald began corresponding with FPCC and Lee.)

On April 29, 1960, Eastland's SISS interrogated officials of the Los Angeles FPCC. Eastland declared that FPCC was "substantially Communist-financed and Communist-dominated."[3690]

On May 1, 1960, Cold War tensions heightened when CIA pilot Francis Gary Powers's U-2 spy plane was shot down over the Soviet Union.

The FPCC honored Fidel Castro during his trip to the United States on September 22, 1960, at a New York reception for him. They presented him with a bust of Abraham Lincoln, saying, "Lincoln was a great American liberator and Castro is a great Cuban leader."[3691]

On April 2, 1961, Senator Eastland summed up the findings of his first hearings on FPCC: "I think it is obvious to everyone that the Fair Play for Cuba Committee is a Communist operation."[3692]

FPCC members picketed outside President Kennedy's speech in Chicago on April 28, 1961, in the wake of the Bay of Pigs fiasco, with placards saying "Peace with Cuba."[3693]

Harry Dean told the author that he infiltrated the Chicago chapter of the FPCC for the July 13 and 14, 1961, FPCC hearing and provided the information to the FBI. Dean told the FBI that the Chicago FPCC leaders, John A. Rossen and Richard Criely, were old Illinois Communist Party members who later let certain members of the Socialist Workers Party into FPCC at their approval.[3694] The FBI passed the information to Eastland's committee. (Dean had no contact with the SISS nor did he testify against his fellow FPCC members; he remained underground in the organization.) SISS counsel Julian Sourwine asked John Rossen, the chairman of the Chicago FPCC during his testimony, if he knew Harry Dean—who was listed as treasurer of the Chicago FPCC in the hearing records; Rossen refused to answer. (Eastland telephoned Dean in April of 1964 and arranged for his appearance at a California FPCC hearing. It never took place.)

In August of 1961, Eastland stated that the "seasoned Communists on the local level apparently have been assigned to push organization of Fair Play for Cuba chapters in many American cities and colleges."[3695] Eastland's committee had determined, from the study of a published work entitled "Cuba and the American Negro," that FPCC had spearheaded a campaign to popularize Cuba among blacks in the United States.[3696]

Edward Hunter, an associate of Guy Banister and General Walker, testified before Eastland's Committee on August 14, 1961, and told them that Moscow, in a memo set forth in a Kremlin manifesto issued December 5, 1960, had ordered a frontal attack on the anti-Communist movement. He claimed members of the White House entourage were Communist agents.[3697] (As has been noted, Hunter, who invented the term "brainwashing," attended Fred Schwartz's Anti-Communist School in New Orleans with Guy Banister, Robert Morris, and Herbert Philbrick on October 23–27, 1961.[3698]) Hunter spoke in New Orleans on November 21, 1961, on the Communist threat and was critical of the muzzling of General Walker. He said, "We are in a peoples war" and that President Kennedy was ridiculing the anti-Communists.[3699]

HUAC investigated FPCC on April 26–27, 1962. They determined that members of the Trotskyite Socialist Workers Party were "the concealed masterminds behind a new front organization which emerged in Los Angeles early in 1961." They called the Los Angeles FPCC "a Trotskyist front." They noted that, on December 2, 1961, Castro announced he was a "Marxist-Leninist." The summarized hearings were entitled "Communist and Trotskyist Activity with the Greater Los Angeles Chapter of FPCC."[3700]

On June 10, 1962, Lee Harvey Oswald and his wife and child arrived in Dallas after leaving the Soviet Union. He lived with his brother, Robert Oswald, in Fort Worth, Texas, for two months, then moved in with his mother. On July 16, 1962, Oswald took a job as a sheet metal worker at Leslie Welding.[3701] On August 9, 1962, *The Worker* and *Midweek Worker* received an application and two dollars for a three-month subscription from Oswald. ("Peace-Jobs-Civil Rights" was the heading on the top of *The Worker* subscription form.[3702]) On August 12, 1962, Oswald wrote to the Socialist Workers Party (SWP) and told them he wanted to find out all he could about their program. He requested an application to join the organization.[3703] Oswald, his wife and child moved into an Elsbeth Street apartment on November 2, 1962.[3704]

(It will be recalled from the last chapter that, in 1961, Guy Banister insisted that Jerry Brooks write to the Communist Party in New York. Brooks had relocated from Kansas City—where he had been a close associate of Minutemen leader Robert DePugh—to work with Banister. Banister also got Brooks to telephone the Communist Party, where he talked to a secretary. Banister persuaded him to ask about membership into the Party and to subscribe to several of their publications. Brooks was reluctant and reported the incident to the FBI. Oswald, on the other hand, enthusiastically—and often—wrote to the Communist Party and other far-left groups and subscribed to their literature, as will be shown.)

On August 17, 1962, Oswald moved to Mercedes Street in Fort Worth to be near his work at Leslie Welding, Inc. While there, the postal inspector made inquiries with the building manger about subversive mail that was being sent to Oswald's apartment. Other tenants complained that Oswald was beating his wife. They found him odd and said he never talked to anyone. He would not even return a greeting.[3705]

On August 23, 1962, the SWP sent Oswald a pamphlet describing the organization.[3706] On August 28, 1962, the SWP received an order form from Oswald for the purchase of *The Teachings of Leon Trotsky*.[3707] Oswald's request for Trotsky's teachings came four months after HUAC announced that the Trotskyite Socialist Workers Party were the masterminds behind FPCC. On September 17, 1962, Oswald purchased a four-month subscription to *The Militant*, the paper of the SWP.[3708] On September 29, 1962, the SWP notified Oswald that the book he ordered, *The Teachings of Leon Trotsky* was out of print.[3709] (It was noted by the Warren Commission that the SWP catalogue also offered the titles A Practical Program to Kill Jim Crow, and The Negro and the U.S. Army.[3710]

On October 12, 1962, Oswald began work at Jaggars-Chiles-Stovall, making photographic prints for advertisements.[3711] Oswald attempted to ingratiate himself with the Socialist Workers Party, the Communist Party, and the Socialist Labor Party by offering to do photographic work for them—no doubt using the equipment at his place of work.

On October 31, 1962, the Socialist Workers Party received an application from Oswald to join the organization. On November 5, 1962, the SWP responded to Oswald's letter and told him there would need to be at least five members before a Dallas branch of the SWP could be formed.[3712] Had Oswald been able to become the head of a Socialist Workers Party chapter in Dallas, then a link would have been established between the SWP and FPCC—which was Eastland's goal in his hearings on FPCC, when Oswald later created his one-man FPCC chapter. On November 10, 1962, Oswald wrote to the New York Labor News Co., the publishing arm of the Socialist Labor Party.[3713]

On December 13, 1962, Lee Harvey Oswald wrote a letter offering to do photographic work for the Hall-Davis Defense Committee, as he had the SWP.[3714] John Abt headed the committee, which included Gus Hall, who was general secretary of the Communist Party, USA, and Benjamin J. Davis, an African-American lawyer who defended accused Communists and was also a member of the Communist Party. Hall and Davis had been charged with violating the Internal Security Act on March 15, 1962.[3715]

On December 17, 1962, *The Militant* received a subscription request from Oswald.[3716] On December 19, 1962, Louis Weinstock, the general business manager of *The Worker*, wrote Oswald and thanked him for sending him some blowups (enlarged images). He told Oswald that the blowups would be most useful at newsstands to call attention to *The Worker*. He pledged to call upon Oswald from time to time for his work.[3717]

Around the same time, Oswald wrote James Tormey, executive secretary of the Hall-Davis Defense Committee of the Communist Party, and told him to send any material he would like duplicated and enlarged photographically, at no charge. He included two samples he had made, captioned "The Gus Hall-Benjamin J. Davis Defense Committee," in bold type and, printed below, "End McCarranism." Tormey responded on December 12, 1962, and thanked Oswald for his photo samples, promising to put them on file in the event they were needed. (Tormey testified before the Warren Commission on April 17, 1964, and was represented by John Abt.)[3718, 3719] If Tormey had agreed to accept Oswald's offer to do photographic work for the Hall-Davis Committee, then Oswald would have had, in writing, evidence that he had worked for the Communist Party. That kind of evidence would have been very powerful if Oswald were to testify against the Party in the future. All told, Oswald offered to do blow ups and photographic work surreptitiously at his job at Jaggars-Chiles-Stovall for the Communist Party, Hall-Davis Committee, and *The Worker* newspaper—as well as for their rivals, the Socialist Workers Party and the Socialist Labor Party.

On December 28, 1962, the FBI determined that FPCC leader V. T. Lee traveled from Cuba to Mexico. He returned on January 21, 1963.[3720] On January 1, 1963, Oswald ordered the pamphlets "The Coming American Revolution," "The End of Comintern" and "1948 Manifesto of the Fourth Internationale" from the Socialist Workers Party's Pioneer Publishing. He requested the English words for the song "The Internationale," and sent them thirty-five cents. (It will be recalled that, at Eastland's 1954 hearing on SCEF, Paul Crouch claimed he heard James Dombrowski sing "The Internationale" at a meeting they had attended.) A volunteer typed out the words to the song and sent them to Oswald.[3721]

On February 2, 1963, and February 7, 1963, Eastland held hearings on FPCC under the title "Castro's Network in the United States." The SISS presented two pieces of evidence linking FPCC to SCEF: 1) a letter from FPCC supporter Robert Williams to SCEF organizer Carl Braden—Williams, an African American, was broadcasting support for Castro in Cuba at the time; and, 2) an article by Williams that appeared in SCEF's *Southern Patriot* that reportedly advocated violence in the civil rights movement.[3722, 3723] Thus, it can be assumed that Oswald's activities with FPCC had as much, or more, to do with tainting SCEF as Communist-affiliated, as it did FPCC.

On February 8, 1963, Eastland held another hearing on FPCC[3724]and, on February 14, 1963, Eastland held an SISS hearing on FPCC in Washington. V. T. Lee, Oswald's pen pal, was the star witness. A pamphlet was shown that was captioned "Stop the Cold War Against Cuba" and "Hands Off Cuba!" (Oswald, that same summer, passed out leaflets captioned, "Hands Off Cuba" that bore the office building address of Guy Banister's operation.[3725]) The following day, Eastland heard the testimony of Sidney Lens[3726], and, on March 8, 1963, Eastland held another hearing on FPCC.[3727]

On March 14, 1963, the FBI learned that Oswald had been in contact with *The Daily Worker*.[3728] They were not, however, aware of the fact that two days earlier, on March 12, 1963, Oswald, under the pseudonym A. J. Hidell, had ordered a Manlicher Carcano rifle from Klein's sporting goods in Chicago.[3729]

On April 3, 1963, Eastland held another hearing on FPCC.[3730]

On April 6, 1963, Oswald was fired from his job performing photographic work at Jaggars-Chiles-Stovall in Dallas.[3731] The Warren Commission determined that Oswald might have passed out FPCC literature in Dallas in the period of April 6–24, 1963.[3732]

On April 10, 1963, the Walker shooting incident took place. A neighbor boy witnessed the aftermath and saw two cars drive away, presumably after the rifle was tossed on the back floorboards of one of the vehicles. Oswald did not drive and had no known close associates, as was noted in Chapter Fourteen. Walker, at first, said a Communist did it, and then quickly backed off the claim—perhaps after learning the neighbor boy was a witness. For all Walker knew, the boy could have recorded the license plate numbers that could be traced to Walker associates or recognized those fleeing as associates of the general and, with that information, could have exposed the ruse. Evidence presented in Chapter Fourteen suggested that Oswald was intentionally incriminating himself and wanted to get caught as a part of a scheme to promote General Walker's anti-Communist speaking tour. (Also as previously noted, *Dallas Morning News* reporter Earl Golz was told by a friend of Larrie Schmidt, that Larrie and his brother Bob drove Oswald to the shooting. Bob was a paid, live-in employee for General Walker, while Larrie was a member of the John Birch Society who frequented Walker's home.)

On April 19, 1963, Oswald sent a letter to FPCC from Dallas. He said he had made a placard with "Hands Off Cuba" and "Viva Fidel" written on it and handed out all of the fifteen or so pamphlets he had had in ten minutes time. He requested forty-nine or fifty more of the "fine basic pamphlets." The FPCC complied and sent fifty-nine pieces of literature to Oswald.[3733]

On April 24, 1963, Oswald traveled by bus and relocated to New Orleans. On April 26, 1963, Oswald wrote to Pioneer Publishing, publishers for the Socialist Workers Party.[3734]

On May 9, 1963, Oswald rented an apartment on Magazine Street.[3735] From May 19 to July 18, 1963, he worked at Reily Coffee Company as a machine oiler. Coworkers recalled that he seldom did any work and he spent a lot of time reading gun magazines next door at an auto repair shop that was operated by a member of the Minutemen.[3736]

On May 22, 1963, V. T. Lee wrote Oswald and told him he had received his change of address and was sending a catalogue of the current literature. He hoped to hear from Oswald again.[3737]

On May 26, 1963, Oswald wrote to FPCC headquarters in New York and requested formal membership in FPCC. He told them he was thinking of opening a small office, now that he was in New Orleans, and asked if they would give him a charter. He wanted to buy FPCC application forms and literature in large lots. He asked for a picture of Fidel Castro suitable for framing.[3738]

On May 28, 1963, *The Militant* office received a subscription request for their paper from Oswald, sent from New Orleans.[3739] The next day, V. T. Lee wrote back to Oswald and sent him some basic information about FPCC. He told Oswald that he did not think opening an office would be a good idea and that it would be better to operate through a post office box, to avoid the reaction of the "lunatic fringe" in the community. He told Oswald he looked forward to working with him.[3740] Oswald wrote Lee back, in an undated letter, and thanked him for his advice. He told him he had opened a post office box and, against his advice, had decided to open an office. He told him he had 2,000 pamphlets run off and enclosed a copy reading, "Hands Off Cuba" that was an invitation to join the New Orleans chapter of FPCC. He had also had an application form printed and enclosed it. He told Lee he hoped the leaflet did not appear too provocative. He pledged to send some of the membership fees to the New York office. That same day, Oswald renewed his subscription to *The Militant*.[3741]

On June 4, Oswald ordered 1,000 FPCC leaflets from Jones Printing in New Orleans, captioned "Hands Off Cuba!" under the name Lee Osborne. He distributed them in front of the carrier U.S.S. *Wasp*, docked at the Dumaine Street Warf, on June 16, and downtown, on August 9.[3742] (The Warren Commission verified Oswald's order from Jones Printing. Harold Weisberg, who was working for Jim Garrison as an investigator in 1968, took a standard mug shot book to Jones Printing, along with pictures of Oswald and his far-right-wing fellow marine Kerry Thornley. An employee identified Thornley—not Oswald—as the one who picked up Oswald's leaflets, as noted in Chapter Nine.)

On June 10, 1963, Lee Harvey Oswald sent a letter to Arnold Johnson of the Communist Party's *The Worker*, stating that he had formed a chapter of FPCC in New Orleans that he felt would be the best way to attract "the broad mass of people to a popular struggle." Oswald asked Johnson to provide him with some literature. He said "it would be very nice to have your literature among the 'Fair Play' leaflets (like the one enclosed) and pamphlets in my office." He enclosed one of his FPCC pamphlets and an honorary membership card.[3743] (Oswald was not telling the truth to Johnson. He had no office. Placing Communist Party literature with FPCC literature was a way of inferring that the Communist Party and FPCC were related, which was Senator Eastland's goal in his hearings.)

Johnson did not take Oswald's bait. Johnson honored the request and sent Oswald some literature, but told him: "We do not have any organizational ties with the Committee." However, Johnson stated they did have material that was important for anyone with concerns about Cuba. Oswald's attempt to get Johnson to affirm, in writing, a Communist Party tie to FPCC had failed. (The FBI, after the Kennedy assassination, noted that on November 27, 1962, the Subversive Activities Control Board had ordered Johnson to register under the Subversive Activities Control Act of 1950, otherwise known as the McCarran Act.[3744] Marina Oswald recalled that, after Oswald began his FPCC activity, he received a letter from a Communist leader, whom she thought was probably from New York. She noted he was very happy and felt the unnamed Communist leader was a great man. She was likely referring to Arnold Johnson.[3745])

On June 12, 1963, Oswald sent a subscription renewal to *The Militant*.[3746] On June 17, *The Militant* received a change of address from Oswald to his New Orleans address.[3747]

On June 24, 1963, Oswald applied for a passport to travel to Europe and the Soviet Union.[3748]

On July 31, 1963, Arnold Johnson of *The Worker* wrote Oswald and told him they were sending him some literature.[3749]

On August 1, 1963, Oswald wrote V. T. Lee and told him he had opened an FPCC office, but the owners had promptly closed it three days later, for reasons unclear to him. Oswald told Lee that he was sure he would understand how that kind of thing happened. (Oswald was not telling the truth—he had never opened an office.) Next, Oswald told Lee that during a street demonstration he was attacked by some "Cuban evil 'gusanos' (worms)"—another lie.[3750] Oswald told Lee that he was stirring things up in New Orleans and that it was good for FPCC. Oswald's unflattering description of the anti-Castro exiles as "gusanos" mimicked Lee, who described the anti-Castros as "dregs and the scum." (Oswald's August 1 report of the attack came eight days *before* Oswald was attacked by Cuban exile Carlos Bringuier. The letter is more evidence that the Oswald-Bringuier incident was contrived.) Oswald also told Lee that he passed out a thousand of his leaflets and "many pamphlets" that the FPCC had supplied to him. Oswald told them he picketed the fleet when it came in, a reference to the U.S.S. *Wasp*, which was true, since Oswald had leafleted the ship on June 16, 1963. He wrote that he was surprised at how many officers were interested in his materials, however, which was far fetched.[3751] (The U.S.S. *Wasp* had taken part in the blockade of Cuba from

November 2 to 19, 1962, during the Cuban Missile Crisis. Navy officers would hardly have been fans of Fidel Castro's Cuba or FPCC. Oswald's leafleting was more likely an attempt to get him into a fight with the sailors, rather than to interest them in his materials. Publicity from a fight was something Oswald may have desired.) Oswald lied twice in his letter to Lee, likely attempting to raise his stature within the national FPCC and ingratiate himself to Lee.

On August 5, 1963, Oswald allegedly entered the shop of anti-Castro Cuban Carlos Bringuier and offered to train Cubans in the fight against Castro. (Evidence was presented in Chapter Nine that Bringuier lied about the date of Oswald's store appearance.)

On August 9, 1963, Bringuier and Oswald got into a fight while Oswald was passing out FPCC materials.[3752] (Some of the leaflets Oswald passed out bore the address of Guy Banister's office building at 544 Camp Street.[3753]) Both were arrested. Bringuier went to Kent Courtney, a close associate of Guy Banister and General Walker, and asked for advice about getting a lawyer.[3754] Oswald told the police he had thirty-five members in his FPCC chapter, which was a complete lie. Police Lieutenant Martello, who—like Hubert Badeaux—was with the police Intelligence Unit, questioned the incident, stating, "[Oswald] seemed to have them set up to create an incident."[3755] As was noted in Chapter One, Oswald spoke only in Russian after his arrest. The police called an agent of the Immigration and Naturalization Service, who confronted Oswald and told him they knew he was American and not Russian, as he was pretending to be. Martello questioned Oswald at the police station and Oswald told him he became interested in FPCC in 1958, while he was in the Marine Corps. (Oswald was lying since FPCC did not come into existence until 1960.)[3756] Marina Oswald told the Warren Commission, after Oswald's arrest for the Bringuier "fight": "I think that Lee engaged in this activity primarily of the purposes of self-advertising. He wanted to be arrested. I think he wanted to get into the newspapers so that he would be known."[3757]

On August 10, 1963, Oswald gave FBI agent John Quigley a pamphlet written by Corliss Lamont called "The Crime Against Cuba," which he had distributed.[3758] Also printed on the pamphlet was a listing of other pamphlets written by Lamont, including: "To End Nuclear Bomb Tests" and "A Peace Program for the USA."[3759] Later, on September 28, 1963, Luis F. Bundez, another ex-Communist, testified before the Senate Permanent Investigations Subcommittee that Earl Browder, as head of the Communist Party, had referred to Corliss Lamont as one the "four prides" of the Communist Party, because Lamont was ready to cooperate with any Communist front or any Communist cause. Bundez stated that Lamont had been a Communist Party member at the same time he was.[3760] (Lamont had been called before Joseph McCarthy's committee on August 17, 1954, and was charged with contempt when he refused to testify. He was a member of the NAACP and the Emergency Civil Liberties Union that sought to abolish HUAC.[3761]) The *Councilor* reported that Lamont made large contributions to SCEF—the information came from LUAC, who had retained Guy Banister as their chief investigator.[3762]

David Chandler, a reporter for the New Orleans *States-Item*, told the FBI that, a couple of days after the Bringuier fight, Oswald came to his office at the newspaper and told him Bringuier was training guerillas for future fighting in Cuba. Oswald told Chandler that he would like the newspaper to do a story on his arrest—and on him, personally. Chandler told him that there was not much sympathy for FPCC, and he was not interested in doing a story.[3763]

On August 12, 1963, Oswald went to court for the fighting incident and sat in the "Negro section," in an apparent symbolic gesture of the supposed solidarity of the Communists with the black struggle. Carlos Bringuier acted appalled. Oswald was fined ten dollars.[3764] Days earlier, on August 10, 1963, the newspaper reported that CORE demonstrators had integrated the Clinton courthouse with whites sitting in the Negro section and vice versa, as was noted in the last chapter. Oswald wrote V. T. Lee and attached a news article about the incident with Bringuier and the summons naming the three Cubans involved.[3765]

On August 13, 1963, Oswald again wrote to Arnold Johnson of the Communist Party and thanked him for sending him literature for his FPCC chapter, for which he claimed to be secretary-president. Oswald told Johnson, "I am doing my best to help the cause of new Cuba, a cause, which I know, and you approve of also." He sent Johnson an FPCC honorary membership card and asked him to send literature to him from time to time. Oswald told him again that it would be nice to have Communist Party literature to place among the "Fair Play" leaflets. He enclosed the news clipping of the fight and honorary membership cards for Gus Hall and Benjamin Davis.[3766]

On August 16, 1963, with the help of men he hired from a temporary labor agency, Oswald handed out FPCC leaflets in front of the International Trade Mart on Canal Street. The media heard about it and filmed the event.[3767] John Martin, a Minuteman from Minnesota, also filmed it. He had just arrived from Dallas after first filming the bullet hole in General Walker's den. Walker had to know that the Oswald-Bringuier "fight" had been pre-planned, and directed Martin to New Orleans to film it. Kent Courtney likely told Walker about the planned fight, since he was in frequent communication with Walker and because he was involved in the "fight" to the extent that Bringuier came to him afterwards and asked him for advice on legal counsel.

On August 17, Oswald wrote V. T. Lee and told him things had been moving pretty fast since his pamphleting and arrest. He said the August 16th FPCC demonstration, with three people, was given considerable coverage on WDSU-TV and also on channel 4. Oswald told Lee that he was invited to appear on WDSU's "Latin Listening Post" after he gave a fifteen-minute taped interview to be rebroadcast later on. He asked Lee for more literature. (Oswald lied about the radio appearance. In truth, Oswald discussed the FPCC on WDSU radio, on August 17, for less than five minutes. In the letter to V. T. Lee, he also falsely claimed they were flooded with calls from people interested in joining FPCC. He had only one caller, an associate of Carlos Bringuier.)

On August 21, 1963, Lee Harvey Oswald "debated" Ed Butler and Carlos Bringuier on WDSU radio.[3768] (The debate was contrived, as was detailed in Chapter Nine.)

The day after the Kennedy assassination, Butler flew with a tape and a transcript of the "debate" to Washington, D.C., and, on Sunday, November 23, at 2:45 p.m.—the day of Oswald's murder—presented it to Eastland's SISS in a confidential session, as was discussed in Chapter Eighteen. Senator Thomas Dodd presided, with Chief Counsel J. G. Sourwine present. Senator Eastland was not in attendance. Butler told them he had met Oswald when he was invited by Bill Stuckey to appear with Oswald on a panel debate. Butler testified that he had attended Army management school and "developed a very deep interest in Communist political activities, which set the course of [his] life." He told them the motivation for Oswald's actions was "the tremendous amount of Communist indoctrination he had received."[3769] (Evidence presented throughout this work shows Oswald's phony "communist indoctrination" likely came from Guy Banister and Hubert Badeaux, with likely contributions from David Ferrie and others on the far right.) Before he left for Washington, Butler had called the FBI and told them he was scheduled to appear before Eastland's Senate Judiciary Committee on Sunday, to tell them what he knew about the presumed Communist assassin, and to say that he was concerned for the safety of his wife and children.[3770]

Carlos Bringuier helped Oswald publicly promote his membership in FPCC and the fact that he had lived in the Soviet Union, as Oswald himself had done in his radio "debate." After the debate, and before the assassination, Bringuier printed a press release stating that Oswald had declared himself a Marxist and a member of FPCC. He wrote that Oswald spent three years in the Soviet Union. Bringuier stated he felt that the name "Fair Play for Cuba Committee" should be changed to "Fair Play for Russia Committee" since Cuba was now a Russian colony. He called for a congressional investigation of Oswald and warned, "Be alert to Communist infiltration in this country."[3771] Bringuier also printed an "Open Letter to the People of New Orleans." The open letter repeated the story given in the press release, but also cited Senator Eastland's hearings on FPCC, carefully denoting the date of each of the four hearings held in 1960 and 1961.[3772]

On August 28, 1963, Oswald wrote to the Central Committee of the Communist Party, addressing the letter to "Comrades." The letter began, "Please advise me upon the problem of personal tactics" and asked them if he should go underground. He gratuitously revealed to them that he had lived in the Soviet Union from October 1956 to July 1962 and had renounced his citizenship. (He lied about the dates—he was only in the Soviet Union from 1959 to 1962.) He wrote, "Our opponents could use my background of residence in the U.S.S.R. against any cause which I join, by association, they could say the organization of which I am a member is Russian controlled etc." Oswald wrote that he was using his position with FPCC "to foster Communist ideals." He mentioned his radio debate, and that an anti-Castro Cuban had attacked him because of his residence in the Soviet Union. Oswald claimed he feared he might have compromised the FPCC because of the revelation, during the debate, of his stay in the Soviet Union.[3773] Oswald, through his letter, let the Communist Party know he was one of them, by addressing them as comrades and by the mention of "Our opponents"—the anti-Castro Cubans. Moreover, he provided the supposed evidence that he was "one of them" in revealing, albeit inaccurately, his sojourn to the Soviet Union. He may again have been hoping that they would affirm a direct tie between FPCC and the Communist Party, as he implied in his letter, as well as a shared disdain for anti-Castro Cubans, as Oswald and V. T. Lee had expressed in the past. If the Communist Party had been unwise enough to advise Oswald to go underground, then a case could have been made that the Communist Party sanctioned the underground participation of Oswald in FPCC.

On August 31, 1963, Oswald wrote to Mr. Bert, the managing editor of *The Worker*, in New York, and told Bert that he planned to relocate his family "into [his] area" in a few weeks. He told Bert that he was experienced in photography and printing and wanted to work directly for *The Worker*. He said that if there were no current openings, he hoped that they would offer him employment in the future. Oswald included some poster photographs as examples of his work, and told Bert that he had sent copies of his photographic work to Mr. Weinstock and Mr. Tormey of the Hall-Smith Committee, whom he had written to in 1962, and that they were appreciative.[3774, 3775]

On September 1, Oswald sent a letter to Arnold Johnson stating he was moving to the Baltimore-Washington area in October and wanted to know how to get in contact with the party there.[3776]

In September 1963, Oswald listed his business address as 640 Rampart Street in New Orleans, which was another lie. The address was that of the African-American newspaper *The Louisiana Weekly*. The date of Oswald's listing coincides with his appearance in a line with black voter registrants in Clinton, Louisiana, in early September, sponsored by the Congress of Racial Equality.[3777, 3778, 3779] The listing may have been another attempt to show that—since he was affiliated with the newspaper, as he was with CORE—a Communist infiltrated both organizations. *The Louisiana Weekly* also had a friendly relationship with SCEF.[3780]

On September 11, 1963, Horace Twiford, at the request of the Socialist Workers Party in New York, sent Oswald a copy of the Labor Day issue of the *Weekly People*. (Twiford was a member of the SWP and lived in Texas, according to his Commission testimony.)

On September 17, 1963, Oswald received his Mexican tourist visa in New Orleans.

On September 19, 1963, Arnold Johnson of the Communist Party told Oswald to contact him when he got to Baltimore and, at that time, he would advise Oswald on how to contact party representatives in the state. Johnson replied to the question as to whether Oswald should stay underground with respect to his stay in the Soviet Union and the effect that might have upon his association with FPCC. Johnson, not mentioning going underground, instead told Oswald it was advisable for some people to stay in the background.[3781] (It is not clear if Oswald was sincerely thinking about moving to the Baltimore-Washington area or if there was something else to be gained by making the statement. It will be recalled that Joseph Milteer told Willie Somersett that the original assassination plan called for shooting the president across the rear of the White House grounds.)

On September 23, Marina Oswald and her daughter departed New Orleans for Ruth Paine's home in Fort Worth.[3782] On September 24, 1963, Oswald moved from his New Orleans apartment owing rent.[3783]

On September 25, Lee Harvey Oswald left New Orleans, via Houston, for Mexico City. He arrived on the 27th and stayed until October 3, 1963. During that time, Oswald made three visits to the Cuban Embassy and one to the Soviet Embassy. Representing himself as the head of the New Orleans branch of FPCC, he requested a visa from the Cuban embassy in transit to the Soviet Union and said he desired to be accepted as a friend of the Cuban revolution. He told them his request for a transit visa to the Soviet Union was based on his prior stay there. He wrote on his application that he was a member of the Communist Party, which was a lie.[3784]

On September 28, 1963 Pioneer Publishing wrote a letter to Oswald.[3785]

Around October 3, 1963, Oswald telephoned Horace Twiford of the Socialist Workers Party at his home when he was out of town. Oswald spoke to Twiford's wife and told her he was a member of FPCC. Oswald told her he wanted to discuss things with her husband for a few hours before flying down to Mexico. Mrs. Twiford jotted down Oswald's name and "Fair Play for Cuba" and left the message for her husband.[3786]

Upon returning from Mexico, on October 3, 1963, Oswald stayed at the Dallas YMCA.[3787] From October 4–6, 1963, Oswald stayed with his wife at Mrs. Paine's home in Irving, Texas.[3788]

On October 10, 1963, the FBI learned that Oswald had departed New Orleans.[3789]

On October 14, 1963, Oswald moved to a room on Beckley Street in Dallas[3790] and, on October 16, 1963, Oswald started work at the Texas School Book Depository.[3791]

On October 25, 1963, Oswald attended a meeting of the American Civil Liberties Union.[3792] The ACLU had determined that Oswald later joined the organization on November 4, 1963.[3793] (After Oswald's arrest for the murder of J. D. Tippit, he met with the president of the Dallas Bar Association and told him if he could not get John Abt for an attorney, he wanted someone from the ACLU.[3794])

In a letter to Arnold Johnson dated November 1—but postmarked and received after the assassination—Oswald told him that he had changed his plans to relocate to the "Philadelphia-Baltimore" area and, instead, had settled in Dallas, Texas. He told Johnson that a friend had taken him to an ACLU meeting and there was a very critical discussion of the ultra right in Dallas. Oswald told Johnson he attended an "ultra-right meeting headed by General Edwin A. Walker" held the day after the attack on Adlai Stevenson. Oswald asked Johnson: "Could you advise me as to the general view we have on the American Civil Liberties Union? And to what degree, if any, I should attempt to heighten its progressive tendencies?" Oswald wrote him that the ACLU was in the hands of liberals, but some of them at the meeting showed "marked class awareness and insight." Johnson was surprised to get the letter after the assassination and the death of Oswald. (The reason Johnson did not receive that letter for so long after it was sent was because Oswald had written the wrong address on it.)[3795] The letter suggests that Oswald was fishing for a written admission of an ACLU-Communist Party connection, in the same way Oswald had earlier attempted to get from Johnson, in writing, the Communist Party's endorsement of FPCC, in an attempt to taint both organizations as Red.

Arnold Johnson testified before the Warren Commission on April 17, 1964, and was represented by John Abt. Johnson told the Commission that he was the director of the information and lecture bureau of the Communist Party. Right after the assassination, Johnson recalled Oswald's name and examined all of his correspondence with him and handed them over to the FBI. Johnson told the Commission that he wanted to make it clear that Oswald and the Communist Party had no formal ties to FPCC and that the literature he sent was not from the viewpoint of Fair Play for Cuba Committee. Johnson admitted that the Communist Party was sympathetic to FPCC, however. Johnson said that at no time did he have a discussion with V. T. Lee about Oswald and the FPCC, and further stated that Oswald was never a part of the Communist Party and was aware that someone could try to make a false charge about a party connection with Oswald. Johnson told the Commission he had concerns about Oswald because he attended a General Walker speech and pretended to be a pro-Castroite to Carlos Bringuier, implying that that was not the way a sincere follower of the Communist Party operated. Johnson was asked if he thought that Oswald was a Fascist. He responded that the act of the assassination indicated a Fascist-minded person. Johnson stated: "If there was a plot, it was only a rightist plot. . . . The attitude of the Communist Party toward President Kennedy was one of high regard and respect . . . ." (Johnson was the author of a book that was found with the possessions of Oswald at the Paine home, after the assassination.)[3796]

Lee Harvey Oswald was fully aware of the false Communists and the skepticism they garnered. In his Soviet diary, he wrote a rambling speech and commented on military coups, segregation, the right wing, and general criticism of the Russian and the U.S. governments. He stated: "I would never become a pseudo-professional anti-Communist such as Herbert Philbrick or MaCarthy [sic]. I would never jump on any of the many right-wing bandwagons."[3797]

After the assassination, Oswald was given permission to telephone John Abt. Oswald jotted down the telephone numbers of Abt and *The Worker* in preparation to call them. The piece of paper with the phone numbers written on them was found in Oswald's trousers after his death.[3798] He remained in character to the end.

After the Kennedy assassination, Senator Eastland announced his intention to investigate the murder in his Senate Internal Security Subcommittee. On November 28, 1963, President Johnson telephoned Senator Eastland and asked him, "This Dallas thing . . . what does your Committee plan to do on it . . . ?" Eastland replied, "Well we plan to hold hearings and just make a record of what the proof is . . . that is all. Show that this man was the assassin."[3799] The next day, on November 29, President Johnson announced the formation of the Warren Commission.

Conclusions

The congressional Communist inquisitions in the 1950s, at a time when Lee Harvey Oswald was coming of age, were used for secondary gain. Some were convened to attack those involved with President Roosevelt's New Deal and President Truman's Fair Deal policies that were felt to be Socialistic. Some hearings were held to smear President Eisenhower's moderate policies, including civil rights. The SISS hearings of Senator James O. Eastland and the HUAC hearings of Representative John Rankin were held to attack and destroy the integration movement that blossomed during the Second Reconstruction that followed the 1954 *Brown* decision. Eastland employed the same smear tactics that his colleague, the more famous inquisitor, Joseph McCarthy, had used. Eastland's hearings were completely lacking in fairness, integrity, and respect for the rule of law. Witnesses were paid for their testimony, even though many were known to be liars. The counsels for those investigated were seldom allowed to cross-examine the paid ex-Communist witnesses or challenge their accusations. The committees had no power to charge anyone with a crime other than perjury and contempt of Congress, which they did liberally. The process was corrupt and invited the creation of made-to-order Communists like Lee Harvey Oswald.

In 1954, just prior to the anticipated *Brown* decision, the SISS had launched an investigation into the Southern Conference Education Fund. SCEF, which Eastland called the southernmost outreach of the Communist Party, was located in the heart of Dixie, in downtown New Orleans, where Lee Harvey Oswald resided at the time. The SISS concluded that SCEF was Communist-dominated, largely based on the testimony of "ex-Communist witnesses" like Paul Crouch and Manning Johnson—both of whom were paid, although they were known liars. In 1949, the use of "ex-Communists" like Crouch had been effective in destroying the Southern Committee for Human Welfare, which folded and remerged under a new name, SCEF, a new leadership and a new location, in New Orleans, and continued to torment Senator Eastland and local segregationists, including Guy Banister, Leander Perez, and Kent Courtney. "Ex-Communist witnesses" were handsomely rewarded for their deeds. Many were paid substantially. Some got book deals. Herbert Philbrick, Oswald's hero, acquired a book deal and a national television show. Many wrote for the John Birch Society and spoke at their meetings. Other far-right forums used them where they gained celebrity status.

The testimony of ex-Communist witnesses was characterized by three phases: the affirmation of their devotion to Communism, their renunciation of Communism after becoming disenchanted, and their about face when they became finger pointers and identifiers, exposing their once-fellow comrades (some falsely) before the congressional and state inquisitions. Oswald affirmed his devotion to Communism in his travels to the Soviet Union. Next, he renounced Communism in his private diary in the Soviet Union and in the professionally typed account completed upon his return to the U.S. He did not live long enough to realize the third phase.

Oswald began writing to the Communist Party and Socialist Workers Party in 1962, and, later, to FPCC. Guy Banister had persuaded another young, far-right radical, Jerry Brooks, to act similarly in 1961. Oswald claimed allegiance to the groups and the cause of Communism. In his letters, he incessantly lied. He posed questions that, if the various Communist entities were to have answered in the affirmative, would have provided him with evidence, in writing, of a link between the Communist Party and both FPCC and the ACLU.

That evidence would have supported the claims of Eastland that FPCC and the ACLU were Communist-tied organizations. Had Oswald lived, he may have had the opportunity to expose fellow leftists in FPCC, NOCPA, and CORE—all groups he had infiltrated—and profit as an "ex-Communist witness." Those groups were the targets, along with SCEF who had ties to them, of a planned inquisition by Eastland in conjunction with LUAC, which was the result of a raid on SCEF headquarters, on October 4, 1963, for violation of the Communist Control Act. (The Act called for harsh penalties for any person or group shown to have a relationship with a known Communist like Lee Harvey Oswald.)

Eastland's 1956, fantastically titled inquisition in New Orleans, called the "Scope of Soviet Activity in the United States" was a seminal event in the assassination history. The inquisition brought together Guy Banister, Leander Perez, and Robert Morris, who all, later, became close associates of General Walker, the military architect of the assassination. Banister and Perez, as well as Walker, were associates of Joseph Milteer, who knew of the details of the assassination in advance and stood in Dealey Plaza—only a few feet from the passing president's motorcade—just moments before the murder.

1956 was also a pivotal year for Lee Harvey Oswald. That year, he was a Civil Air Patrol cadet under Captain Ferrie and also entered the Marine Corps. It was no coincidence that in 1956, while Banister was collaborating with Eastland and Morris to investigate Communists in New Orleans, that Oswald began acting like a Communist. Months later, in early 1957, Hubert Badeaux, the police Intelligence Division officer under Banister, divulged to Willie Rainach that he was grooming an informant to infiltrate the left and, based on the evidence at hand, Oswald was likely that person.

Eastland was challenged by the emergence of the new pro-Castro organization FPCC, which had ties to SCEF, and the rise of pro-integrationist organizations in the 1960s. He lost the weapons he used against his enemies in the past—the "ex-Communists"—when they died (in the case of Paul Crouch) or when their credibility evaporated (as happened with Manning Johnson). There are few, if any, conceivable alternative explanations as to why Oswald impersonated a Communist, other than to replace Eastland's discredited, old guard "ex-Communists." Whether or not Senator Eastland contributed to, planned, or encouraged the assassination, he likely knew that Oswald was not what he claimed to be. That alone makes him an accessory to the assassination.

It's likely that Eastland knew Oswald was a false Communist dating back to 1956, when he began to act like one. Making Eastland's involvement even more suspicious, in some way, is the fact that he was closely associated with Banister, Perez, and others in the hardcore underground of New Orleans. At the same time that Eastland was investigating FPCC and holding hearings around the country, Oswald was making a spectacle of himself, playing a Marxist and FPCC member under the noses of Eastland's associates in New Orleans.

Adding even more suspicion to Eastland's involvement was the rapid dispatch of Ed Butler, a Banister associate, to Washington, D.C., the day after the assassination, to testify in a special SISS hearing and tell them about his "debate" with Oswald wherein he professed to being a Marxist and having lived in the Soviet Union. Moreover, Eastland's attempt to commandeer the government's official investigation of the assassination, and show that Oswald had no confederates, raises further suspicions.

CHAPTER TWENTY-THREE

END GAME: THE SCEF RAID

I submit that when a person belongs to a large number of Communist-front organizations that follow the policies of the International Communist Conspiracy, that person is aiding and abetting the Communist movement in the world—a movement which, if not halted, will result in a blood bath in our own country, because the United States will fight, if necessary, in order to prevent Communist domination of our country.[3800]

— Senator James O. Easltland

Lee Harvey Oswald's return to the United States from the Soviet Union on June 14, 1962, coincided with two epic measures undertaken by the Guy Banister and colleagues' segregation operation and Senator James O. Eastland's Senate Internal Security Subcommittee. The first was the enactment of new anti-subversion laws.

Louisiana State Representative James Pfister, head of the Joint Legislative Committee on Un-American Committee (LUAC), and staff attorney Jack N. Rogers prepared two bills: the Subversive Activities and Communist Control Law and the Propaganda Control Law (henceforth simply to be referred to as the Communist Control Act), which were enacted by the legislature. The bills were the brainchildren of Leander Perez and were similar to others written by Willie Rainach that had been struck down in the 1950s. Banister, whom multiple witnesses saw with Oswald in the summer of 1963, was an associate of all involved, including Eastland, Perez, Pfister, and Rogers. Banister was also an investigator for LUAC. The laws called for years of imprisonment and huge fines for any person or organization that associated with a Communist like Oswald. Under those brutal penalties, the laws could effectively end the integration movement in the state.

The second epic measure was the October 4, 1963, raid on the Southern Conference Education Fund (SCEF). The raid took place after seventeen months of planning that began at the time of Oswald's return from the U.S.S.R. The raid was conducted under the direction of LUAC, members of Senator Eastland's staff, local police, and members of the state police working for the Sovereignty Commission. (The state police officers involved in the raid obtained Banister's files after his death in 1964 and, later, destroyed them.)

After the raid, SCEF officers James Dombrowski and Benjamin E. Smith were arrested. Also arrested was Bruce Walzer, an ACLU attorney who had at times represented SCEF. All three were charged with violating the Communist Control Act, based on the confiscated evidence. After the raid, LUAC announced that they planned not only to investigate and hold hearings on SCEF for its Communist ties, but they also planned to investigate the New Orleans FPCC, which had ties to SCEF. (An investigation of the New Orleans FPCC was tantamount to an investigation of Lee Harvey Oswald, its sole member.) LUAC would then have been able to show that an agent of the Communist conspiracy, Oswald, had infiltrated FPCC in New Orleans. (In fact, they later did show that SCEF officers were officers in the Los Angeles branch of FPCC.) LUAC also announced plans to investigate CORE and, presumably, NOCPA, since they confiscated the NOCPA membership list during the arrest of Bruce Walzer. (Oswald had joined the ACLU and FPCC and affected a relationship with CORE and NOCPA—all groups that were targeted by LUAC.)

There were two major unforeseen hitches that arose that had the potential to affect the long-planned SCEF raid. The first was President Kennedy's announcement of a sweeping federal civil rights measure on June 11, 1963, that arose a year into the planning of the operation. If Kennedy's measure passed, the plan to stifle the integration movement through the Communist Control Act would be futile. However, passage of the Civil Rights Act was far from certain. The bill would first have to make its way through Senator Eastland's Senate Judiciary Committee, where, in the past, he had been successful in killing other civil rights measures. The second possible hitch was the emergence of a plan to kill the president and to figure Lee Harvey Oswald into the scenario long after the SCEF raid had been planned. Oswald's ultimate involvement in the assassination was hardly a certainty. Any number of circumstances might have precluded Oswald's involvement.

The Law

Members of the Joint Legislative Committee on Un-American Activities announced in the press, on May 11, 1962, that they would introduce legislation making "distribution or storage of Communist propaganda," a felony. The proposed law required any "Red material" entering Louisiana be labeled as "Communist propaganda" in red ink. State representative James Pfister planned to introduce the two-part legislation immediately during the sixty-day session of the legislature. Under the bill, sheriffs would be asked to seize any illegal Communist material and padlock the premises where the material was found. Committee counsel Jack Rogers said it was the first time any state had attempted such action.[3801] (It will be recalled from the last chapter that Lee Harvey Oswald had procured a large amount of subversive literature in the mail from New York from the Communist Party, the Socialist Workers Party, and the Fair Play for Cuba Committee. Oswald, with his own funds, had had one thousand "Hands Off Cuba" handbills printed in May 1963 under the name of Lee Osborne.[3802] None was labeled as "Communist propaganda" in red ink, in violation of the law.) Just prior to the proposal of the Communist Control and Propaganda Control Laws, on April 24, 1962, LUAC held a hearing—on the same day—entitled "Communist Propaganda Infiltration in Louisiana." (Robert Morris, General Walker's friend, attorney, and advisor from Dallas, had testified before LUAC in the past about Communist propaganda, as was noted in the last chapter.)

The Communist Control statutes defined those in violation as any group that could be "construed by prosecution officials to parallel or coincide with in any manner any of the objectives of the international Communist conspiracy." The laws deemed any "citation" or "identification" of any person or group, by a committee or subcommittee of Congress, as proof of subversion. The Subversive Activities and Communist Control Law, R.S. 14:358-14:373, was a highly exaggerated, Red Scare-infused piece of legislation, directed squarely at the integration movement. The law's "legislative finding of fact and declaration of necessity" reads as follows:

> There exists a world Communist movement, directed by the Union of Soviet Socialist Republics and the other Communist bloc nations, which has as its declared objective, world control. Such world control is to be brought about by aggression, force and violence, and is to be accomplished in large by infiltrating tactics involving the use of fraud, espionage, sabotage, infiltration, subversion, propaganda, terrorism and treachery. The state of Louisiana, as a sovereign political entity under the Constitution of the United States, and as a functioning representative State government which is responsible solely to the people of this state under the constitutions of this state and nation, is a most probable and obvious target for those who seek by force, violence and other unlawful means to overthrow constitutional government, and is in imminent danger of Communist espionage, infiltration, subversion and sabotage.
>
> The agents of the world Communist movement who knowingly participate in the conspiratorial subversive work of the world Communist movement, by so doing, in effect repudiate their allegiance and loyalty to the state of Louisiana and in effect transfer their allegiance and loyalty to the foreign countries in which is vested the direction and control of the world Communist movement. By clever and ruthless tactics of espionage, sabotage, infiltration, fraud, propaganda and subversion, the agents of the world Communist movement in many instances in some form or manner successfully evade existing law. Any action organization or front organization managed, operated or controlled by Communists, no matter what outward guise, cover, or public image it may assume, is in fact an arm, or tool, or agent organization, of the world Communist move-

ment, and its continued operation is a threat and a clear and present danger to the state of Louisiana and the citizens of the state of Louisiana. The effective regulation of such organizations and the control of Communist personalities is in the best interests of the state of Louisiana because the world Communist movement is not a legitimate political effort, but is in fact a dangerous criminal conspiracy.

The world Communist movement constitutes a clear and present danger to the citizens of the state of Louisiana and is a dangerous enemy of the state of Louisiana. This makes it necessary that the Legislature, in order to protect the people of the state, to preserve the sovereignty of the state under the constitutions of the United States and the state of Louisiana, and to guarantee to the State a republican form of government, enact appropriate legislation recognizing the existence of the world Communist movement and preventing it from the accomplishment of its purposes in the state of Louisiana.

There exists a clear difference between natural persons protected by full constitutional freedoms, and organizations, which are artificial entities. With this difference in mind and considering the paramount right and interest of the state to protect itself from subversion, the issue of due process is satisfied in by the legal test of a preponderance of the evidence in a civil proceeding, R.S. 14:358-14:373 being intended as regulatory rather than punitive. The paramount interest of the state to control a clear and present danger demands the broadest possible venue provisions in such regulations. The guarantees of sovereignty and freedom enjoyed by this state and its citizens are certain to vanish if the United States and its Constitution are destroyed by the Communists, and any Communist effort or attack against the United States is and should rightly be considered an attack upon and a clear and present danger to the state of Louisiana and its citizens.

The Legislature of Louisiana does not intend that R.S. 14:358-14:373 shall in any way regulate or control race relations in the state of Louisiana, the question of race being irrelevant for the purposes of R.S. 14:358-14:373, which is written and passed solely for the purpose of regulating subversive activities directed against the state and people of Louisiana. Nothing in R.S. 14:358 to 14:373 is in any way intended to improperly infringe upon the constitutionally protected right of freedom of expression, for this right, strong though it may be, is not absolute, and falls short of the right to shout "fire" in a crowded movie theater. The protections afforded by the right to freedom of speech do not extend to acts which are by their very nature a clear and present danger to the state of Louisiana and its citizens and the carrying on of Communist propaganda activity and other Communist controlled activities in the state of Louisiana is such a danger and is therefore an intolerable abuse of the right to freedom of expression which can and should be regulated by statute for the safety of the people of this state. The public good, and the general welfare of the citizens of this state require the immediate enactment of this measure.[3803, 3804]

In summary, the Communist Control Act declared that the Soviet Union-directed agent's use of the tactics of infiltration, propaganda, force, and violence threatened the state's sovereignty (a code word for the state's right to maintain segregation). Oswald had lived in the Soviet Union, traveled to the Soviet Embassy in Mexico, and belonged to groups alleged to be or cited as Communist fronts. He made a spectacle of himself distributing Communist-front propaganda on the streets of New Orleans. He purportedly was engaged in violence in the Walker shooting incident and the fight with Carlos Bringuier. Oswald personified the threat described in the Communist Control Act, as no one else in the South did.

Eastland, LUAC and Operation Tip Top: The Planning of the SCEF Raid

The plan to raid SCEF and charge its officers under the new Communist Control Act was formulated prior to July 1962 when James O. Eastland sent an emissary, the chief of staff of the Senate Internal Security Subcommittee, J. G. Sourwine, to meet with Louisiana officials.[3805] The 1962 meeting of Sourwine and those Louisiana officials followed the April 1962 SCEF conference held in Birmingham, Alabama, where strategies to break down the walls of segregation were formulated. SCEF treasurer and attorney Benjamin E. Smith attended with other members of the National Lawyers Guild. After the bombing of the Sixteenth Street Baptist Church in Birmingham on September 15, 1963, in which four African American girls died, Governor Wallace appeared on the television show *Today*. He blamed the girls' deaths on the Supreme Court, the Kennedy administration, and outside agitators. He showed photos of SCEF officers Anne and Carl Braden and James Dombrowski at the integrated 1962 SCEF meeting and called them subversives, citing Eastland's 1954 SISS hearing in New Orleans and HUAC's 1958 hearing.[3806, 3807, 3808] (As was noted in the last chapter, Carl Braden was cited for contempt in the 1959 Atlanta HUAC hearing and was sent to prison in 1961. The Bradens also were officers of the Fair Play for Cuba Committee.)

In a LUAC "Confidential Memorandum," written on November 1, 1962, Jack N. Rogers stated that interviews with "certain ex-Communists" led to an extensive list of names they expected to tie to SCEF. The names of the "ex-Communists" were never revealed. LUAC investigator Colonel Frederick B. Alexander, Jr. was offered private financial support from an unnamed source for the investigation and hearing, which were originally planned for February or March 1963. The SISS and HUAC cooperated with the states' anti-subversive bodies and offered them the services of a long list of "ex-Communists" that they had used to point fingers in their congressional inquisitions.[3809]

In August 1963, Louisiana officials met and decided to get SCEF's list of contributors by raid instead of subpoena. They met with Sourwine to develop a procedure for removing the records from LUAC and handing them over to the SISS.[3810]

On September 30, 1963, LUAC, under James Pfister, met in executive session in Baton Rouge and recommended that the New Orleans police begin implementation of "Project 50," which was the code name for the plan to seize SCEF records from its Perdido Street office and from the homes of SCEF officials in New Orleans. New Orleans police renamed the project "Operation Tip Top."[3811, 3812, 3813]

In August or September 1963, Rogers asked Sourwine if he and Bill Mandel, research director of the SISS, would come down and help evaluate the SCEF records if he was successful in procuring them. Sourwine discussed the matter with Senator Eastland, who told him that the SISS was only interested in "material relating to Communist or Communist-front activities, especially Communist infiltration of mass organizations and the financing of Communist fronts."[3814]

Perhaps in anticipation of the SCEF raid, Eastland held Senate hearings on President Kennedy's proposed Civil Rights Act on July 31, 1963. Witnesses were called to refute Attorney General Robert Kennedy's recent statement that Martin Luther King, Jr. and other major civil rights leaders were not Communists or Communist-controlled. Mississippi state senator John C. McLauren testified that Robert Kennedy was either a liar or was ignorant when he made the statement. New Hampshire publisher William Loeb testified that Kennedy was guilty of "the most brazen cover-up job ever perpetrated on the American people." Governors Wallace and Barnett cited the pictures of King at the—supposed-Communist—Highlander training school as evidence to the contrary.[3815] On August 3, 1963, General Walker called Kennedy's civil rights bill "a new name for Communism," saying: "Communist inspiration is behind all racial disorders and racial riots." He said the solution was "to get a new president."[3816]

Senator Strom Thurmond entered the full text of ten news articles from newspapers across the country citing "the Communist connections with Negro demonstrations" in the *Congressional Record* on August 7, 1963. He cited President Kennedy's statement: "It is natural and inevitable that Communists have made efforts to infiltrate the civil rights groups and to exploit the current racial situation. In view of real injustices that exist and resentment against them these efforts have been remarkably ineffective."[3817] Thurmond, perhaps fully aware of the impending SCEF raid, declared on the Senate floor, on August 24, 1963, that he continued to find evidence of a "tie-in between Communist and Negro demonstrations." He stated that there were some people "who are sincerely carrying out the orders and aims of the Communist Party U.S.A. So I renew here today my request that this entire matter to be looked into without further delay by Congress." He inserted into the *Congressional Record* "sworn testimony of Carl Braden's Communist Party membership." He pointed out that Braden was an officer in SCEF that had ties to King. He stated that Braden was affecting racial strife throughout the country.[3818] On August 26, 1963, the SISS announced that there was a close link between Communist youth leaders in the country and FPCC.[3819]

Mississippi Senator Eastland had been trying since 1954 to obtain a copy of SCEF's list of contributors and other evidence that he might use against them. A raid would provide him with them. The announcement of a massive voter registration drive in Mississippi at the same time was additional incentive for the operation. Both the mayor of New Orleans and the governor of Louisiana endorsed the raid on SCEF.

The SCEF raid was a watershed event in the history of the civil rights movement and the Southern segregationists movement. Two attorneys close to the SCEF case and Operation Tip Top noted that it was more than just a police action against SCEF, but was a way to affect "severe intimidation of the growing southern civil rights movement . . . particularly the white collaborators as a part of an all-out effort to apply the weapons of the Cold War to the Freedom Movement all over the South."[3820, 3821, 3822]

The SCEF Raid

On October 2, 1963, the Orleans Parish District Court issued search warrants for SCEF officials James Dombrowski and Benjamen E. Smith, as well as Bruce Walzer, charging they were members of a Communist-front organization, under the Communist Control Act.

On October 4, 1963, at three o'clock in the afternoon, sirens blared on Perdido Street outside the SCEF office in the downtown business district of New Orleans. Thirteen uniformed New Orleans policemen broke into the SCEF office, with pistols drawn, and served James Dombrowski, SCEF director and attorney, with a warrant for his arrest. He was charged with "participation in the management of a subversive organization," being "a member of a Communist-front organization," and "remaining in Louisiana five days without registering with the Department of Safety," under the Communist Control Act.

SCEF treasurer Benjamin E. Smith was arrested at his home. The SCEF search warrant noted that they had informants, and that "Smith has been seen and identified on many occasions in the company of identified Communists."[3823] (As has been noted, Smith had joined the NOCPA demonstrations, as did Lee Harvey Oswald.)

Bruce Walzer—who was not an officer in SCEF but was the law partner of SCEF treasurer Smith—and Smith were both ACLU attorneys. Walzer was charged with being a member of the National Lawyers Guild (NLG), whose membership was comprised of Communists, as well as moderates, including future Supreme Court Justice Thurgood Marshall. The NLG had a long history of persecution by the FBI and Congress. In the past, the NLG had been an outspoken opponent of the FBI's tactics used against them and attempted to persuade the Truman administration to curb their domestic political intelligence activities. The FBI countered by working with Richard Nixon of HUAC to investigate the NLG. Martin Dies cited the NLG as a "Communist front" in 1943. Then, in 1950, HUAC released the "Report on the National Lawyers Guild: Legal Bulwark of the Communist Party." The FBI leaked derogatory material on the NLG from a Boston informant to Senator Joseph R. Mc-Carthy. (McCarthy's "point of order" attack on the National Lawyers Guild was his undoing in the 1954 Army-McCarthy hearings.)[3824] Senator Eastland and his chief counsel, Robert Morris, once called a prominent NLG leader before the SISS.[3825]

As a result of the raid, the New Orleans police hauled off seventy-three cartons of SCEF property, including photographs given to Dombrowski by Eleanor Roosevelt, Albert Einstein, and Mary McCloud Bethune and framed/signed letters from President Roosevelt and Albert Einstein.[3826] Leander Perez instigated the raid with the cooperation and enthusiastic support of Senator Eastland.[3827] The homes of all three men were raided. They found no SCEF or NLG materials at Bruce Walzer's house. However, and importantly, they found a mailing list for the New Orleans Committee for Peaceful Alternatives. (Evidence that Oswald infiltrated the NOCPA was presented in Chapter Twenty.) They confiscated a Hebrew Bible, which Walzer's Jewish-German wife said evoked memories of her years as a child under Hitler. The raiders also discovered papers that revealed that Walzer had had a top security clearance with the CIA during his years in Europe.[3828]

Dombrowski's lawyer, Arthur Kinoy, described the SCEF raids, saying: "They are desperate. They are going back to the weapons of the 1950s."[3829] Carl Braden said, "This sedition charge is the same old phony charge that has been used throughout the South to try to discredit integrationists."[3830]

Major Russell Willie of the Louisiana State Police Bureau of Identification and Investigation, who was assigned to the Sovereignty Commission, was involved in the raid.[3831] (It will be recalled that Major Willie purchased Guy Banister's files for the Sovereignty Commission, from his widow, after his death in 1964, and took them to Baton Rouge.[3832] When Willie left the state police, he went to work for Guy Banister's brother, Ross, in Baton Rouge.[3833]) The press failed to note Willie's connection to the Sovereignty Commission.

State police officer Joseph Cambre told the HSCA that he helped Willie obtain Banister's records from Mary Banister after his death in 1964. He said Banister had extensive records on Southern Conference Education Fund. He said he also saw files on Fair Play for Cuba Committee and a transcription of Oswald's radio debate. He recalled that the FPCC literature had an address on Camp Street and was surprised to learn that 544 Camp was the same address as Banister's office building.[3834]

Ross Banister also told investigators for Jim Garrison that Colonel Burbank obtained some of Guy's files. One of Garrison's investigators felt Ross Banister was "rather hesitant and skeptical about revealing everything that he may know or [have] access to."[3835]

Colonel Thomas D. Burbank, superintendent of the Louisiana State Police, like Major Willie, was also a state police officer signed over to the Sovereignty Commission. Burbank took custody of the SCEF files after the raid. It is noteworthy that the two members of the state police connected to the SCEF raid were also the ones who purchased Banister's files after his death in 1964 and, later, destroyed them.

Jim Garrison was aware that Banister's files later came into the possession of the state police. When he tried to obtain them in 1968, he found that most were missing. The various subjects listed on the remaining files supposedly led Garrison to believe that Banister was involved in some sort of government intelligence operation when, in fact, there was no proof that he was. (Rather, those subject titles indicated Banister's interest in civil rights groups and other leftist organizations as was noted in Chapter One.)

The HSCA interviewed Ray William Thomas, a state police officer assigned to the Sovereignty Commission, and he told them that they obtained Banister's files because they contained information on subversives. He also recalled that there were files on FPCC.[3836]

Major Presley J. Trosclair, who served under Banister during his tenure in the New Orleans Police Department, was also at the SCEF raid. An official of LUAC was also there and took charge of the cartons of documents which were removed.[3837] A news reporter saw Banister's close associate, Leander Perez, standing outside the raid.[3838]

At 11:45 p.m. on October 4, 1963, LUAC counsel Rogers said he telephoned J. G. Sourwine in Washington, D.C., and stated that LUAC had obtained "material which he believed would be of interest to the Internal Security Subcommittee." He asked for SISS counsel Ben Mandel to come down to Baton Rouge as soon as possible to assist in evaluation of the records. Sourwine and Mandel flew to Baton Rouge the next morning. Based on the nature of the documents and "the content of certain particular documents which had been procured," they concluded that there was a substantial amount of material in the SCEF records that was of interest to the SISS. (It will be recalled from the last chapter that Mandel was another counsel for Eastland's 1956 hearing in New Orleans, which Guy Banister was involved with.)

Sourwine then telephoned Eastland, who authorized him to subpoena the records for the SISS. Sourwine served a subpoena *duces tecum* (for production of evidence) on state representative James Pfister on October 5, 1963. Pfister and Rogers, along with the SCEF files, were to appear before the Senate Internal Security Subcommittee at a public hearing in Washington, D.C., the following Tuesday. Until Pfister's press conference, no one had suspected that Senator Eastland had any involvement with the raid. However, the subpoenas were actually dated October 4th, suggesting that Sourwine and Eastland had intended to subpoena the documents before both the SCEF raid and Sourwine's arrival in Louisiana. Sourwine, however, asserted that the October 4, 1963, date was a typographical error.

Sourwine arranged for Colonel Burbank of the Louisiana State Police, to hold the material as custodian for the SISS. Two staff members of the SISS brought the material to Washington. On November 8, 1963, a substantial amount of material, which was not of interest to the SISS, was shipped back to LUAC. On November 14, 1963, the SISS approved a resolution that all of the material be placed in the Subcommittee's record of reference, and—on completion of Photostatting—the originals returned to LUAC. A task force of five senators was to evaluate the material to determine if it would be placed in the record verbatim.

The SCEF Raid Aftermath

After the SCEF raid, Jack N. Rogers of LUAC held a press conference. When asked if the FBI participated in the raid, he denied it. He stated that although he had complete confidence in J. Edgar Hoover, he did not trust Attorney General Robert Kennedy. He felt that had Kennedy known about the raid, he might have tipped off "his friend, Martin Luther King." (King denounced the raid, stating it was another attempt by the hardcore racists "to equate civil rights with Communism.")

Rogers noted that the Supreme Court gave states jurisdiction in cases of sedition directed against the state. The newspaper reported that the New Orleans Citizens' Council called on the mayor and asked him to take action against SCEF, saying the Citizens' Council could supply the city with evidence.[3839, 3840] Rogers declared that SCEF was "the equivalent of a big holding company" and that "Communists infiltrated racial movements in the Louisiana."[3841]

James Pfister told reporters that SCEF "engaged in racial agitation" and that SCEF's president Fred Shuttleworth was "a close associate of Martin Luther King." Pfister stated that the raids were sparked by a recent speech of George Wallace on national television claiming Dombrowski and the Bradens were "the cause of racial agitation."[3842] (The Bradens, however, lived in Louisville, Kentucky, and were not involved in the raids.) Pfister further commented on the SCEF raid, saying: "The organization (SCEF) has engaged in open racial agitation throughout the southern part of the United States and is closely tied in with other organizations carrying on racial agitation."

The defendants asked for the help of Attorney General Robert Kennedy. The ACLU offered their assistance.[3843] James Dombrowski, after he was freed on bail, addressed a group of lawyers that were coincidentally in town to plan legal strategies for the civil rights movement. He told them about the tactics used by the segregationists: "They resorted to nullification, to interposition, to state's rights, and to force and violence. Now they are digging up the Communist conspiracy theory, if they get away with it, anything goes." If the Communist Control Act remained in force, Dombrowski felt no citizen or lawyer would come to the aid of blacks, knowing they could be convicted of subversion.

Dombrowski concluded that fighting a traditional battle with the state in trials, hearings, and appeals would ruin his health and bankrupt SCEF. Instead, his attorneys plotted a bold move recommended by civil rights attorney Arthur Kinoy, which they thought might work. They planned to seek remedies enacted after the Civil War, which permitted African Americans—in the defeated Confederate States and elsewhere—to seek immediate federal relief when state courts tried to nullify their status of emancipation. The key to their strategy was to challenge the heretofore-unassailable constitutional "doctrine of abstention," something segregationists probably were not counting on. (Abstention doctrine mandates that one court cannot intrude upon the powers of another court. It required that a citizen must exhaust all legal measures in the lower state court before turning to the federal courts. With this in mind, the segregationists, with the full force, treasure, and backing of the southern state's government, could prosecute anyone aiding the civil rights movement into oblivion, embold-ened by the fact that the Supreme Court could not to hear the case until after they exhausted their options—and the defendant's funds—in the lower courts, based on the doctrine of ab-stention.) Dombrowski feared that, if the State of Louisiana were successful in prosecuting the three men arrested in the SCEF raid under the state sedition laws, then other southern states could enact similar laws, which—by their sheer barbaric nature—would in essence preserve the sacred institution of segregation that, by 1963, faced extinction. SCEF attorney Arthur Kinoy, however, felt that he had found a way around the "doctrine of abstention."

As the legal maneuvering began it was quickly revealed that the police had a mystery informant. Major Willie refused to divulge the informant who provided him with forehand knowledge of SCEF activities.[3844] SCEF lawyers Arthur Kinoy and William Kunstler asked for a preliminary hearing, which was set for October 25, 1963. LUAC was ordered to bring all of the seized material to court. Major Willie testified at that hearing that he had an informant who provided him with evidence that SCEF was subversive, but refused to name him.[3845] The judge struck his testimony, ruling that it did not constitute evidence of subversion. LUAC failed to bring the seized evidence to court, instead only offering a witness to testify as to its contents. The judge quashed the arrests for lack of probable cause, and ruled that there was in-sufficient evidence to try the men for conspiracy. District Attorney Jim Garrison represented Orleans Parish in the case. Frank Klein, first assistant D.A., had been shown a quantity of the procured SCEF documents to determine whether to accept or reject the subversion charges based on the evidence.[3846]

Eastland subpoenaed the voluminous SCEF records from the Louisiana State Police for a hearing of the SISS in Washington, which was to be held on October 29, 1963. In re-sponse, SCEF attorneys Benjamin E. Smith and Bruce Walzer asked for a federal injunction to prevent removal of the documents from the state.[3847, 3848, 3849]

In an affidavit from J. G. Sourwine, in a later proceeding, Sourwine admitted to be-coming involved in the SCEF raid planning before July 1962. Remarkably, Sourwine told the court that he not only planned to expose SCEF's ties to Communism, but he also specifically mentioned their interest in FPCC "and other Communist-front organizations," as well.[3850] As we shall see, in the aftermath of the raid Eastland and LUAC planned to investigate all of the organizations that Lee Harvey Oswald had infiltrated: FPCC, NOCPA, and CORE.

On October 27, 1963, Colonel Burbank guaranteed a federal district judge that the SCEF evidence would remain secure in Baton Rouge. Astoundingly, the next day, Burbank notified the court that the documents had been taken to Mississippi by Eastland committee counsel J. G. Sourwine. Burbank produced a letter from Sourwine authorizing the removal of the papers to the county clerk in Woodville, Mississippi. With the SCEF files in Eastland's hands, the federal judge's ruling was moot and the matter was now outside of the jurisdiction of the federal court in Louisiana. Dombrowski filed a motion to prohibit Eastland from pos-sessing his records. Eastland successfully invoked his right to legislative immunity and denied SCEF's claim that he or Sourwine knew of the raid in advance or were part of the planning.

SCEF attorneys sued Burbank for the unlawful seizure of their records. Sourwine, an accessory who did not have Eastland's privilege of immunity, was ordered to stand trial in a case known as *Dombrowski v. Burbank*. Nonetheless, for the SCEF attorneys, the matter still appeared hopeless.

Both Jim Garrison and the HSCA interviewed Colonel Burbank in connection with their investigations of Guy Banister. They were interested in finding out what happened to Banister's files. They did not ask him about the SCEF affair, unfortunately. The HSCA showed no awareness of the SCEF raid or Burbank's participation in it. Of course, Garrison, as the D.A. during the SCEF raid and trial that followed, knew all about it. (It will be recalled from Chapter Nine that Burbank told Garrison that he purchased Guy Banister's files and hauled them away shortly after Banister's death in 1964.) Burbank was never asked why Banister's files were of interest to the state police, but it was almost certainly done to destroy evidence related to Banister and Oswald and their relationship to the SCEF affair. Nor did Garrison point out the more important fact: that Burbank was a member of the state police assigned to the Sovereignty Commission. Burbank later burned the files. (Also purged from the records of the state police was a photo of Oswald in a Canal Street parade in the summer of 1963, presumably the NOCPA parade, as was detailed in Chapter Twenty.)

It will be recalled that Lieutenant John R. Knight of the state police prepared a report on Oswald's activities in Louisiana for the Warren Commission. His completed investigation was presented to Burbank in the form of a booklet. Burbank personally presented the material to the Warren Commission. In 1969, an investigator for Jim Garrison asked Knight to look over the booklet as it appeared in the Warren Commission files and let him know if anything was missing. (Garrison got the tip that Burbank purchased Banister's files from his brother Ross Banister.[3851]) Knight told Garrison that about half of the information was missing, including a photograph of Oswald marching down Canal Street with a group of people, several pictures of Oswald in front of the International Trade Mart, and photos of Oswald's arrest on Canal Street. Burbank, therefore, committed two instances of destroying evidence relative to Lee Harvey Oswald: the removal of Guy Banister's files after his death and, later, the burning of those files; and destroying a photo of Oswald in a Canal Street parade, presumably the NOCPA parade, and others.

Two weeks after the SCEF evidence was taken from the state, LUAC counsel James Pfister presented Photostats of some of the SCEF records to an Orleans Parish grand jury. Judge Malcolm V. O'Hara instructed the grand jury to determine whether or not there was sufficient evidence to return indictments against the three men arrested in the SCEF raid for criminal conspiracy under the state's anti-subversion laws. Attorneys for SCEF saw the grand jury proceedings as an opportunity to test the constitutionality of the state anti-subversion laws, and sued for relief in federal court for the seized materials. At a November 8 hearing of LUAC, Pfister and Jack Rogers released copies of SCEF's mailing list and other documents to the press, as "proof" that SCEF was a Communist-front that was "aiding and abetting the Communist conspiracy." On November 14, the grand jury convened in New Orleans to consider the charges of violation of the Communist Control Act.

Federal Fifth Circuit Court Judge John Minor Wisdom issued a restraining order to prohibit any state indictments until a panel of three federal judges heard the challenges to the states anti-subversion laws. On January 19, 1964, the three-federal-judge panel ruled against SCEF lawyers and called the state anti-subversion laws constitutional. Judge Wisdom dissented, agreeing with SCEF lawyers that the issue of Communism was not one for the state courts to prosecute.

With the original stay vacated, the state was free to prosecute, and Dombrowski, Smith, and Walzer were indicted by the Orleans Parish grand jury. The state charged the three defendants with membership in either one or both Communist-front organizations, SCEF and the National Lawyers Guild. If convicted, Smith faced the possibility of thirty years of hard labor or a $30,000 fine for belonging to both alleged Communist-front organizations. Dombrowski faced twenty years or a $20,000 fine for belonging to SCEF. Walzer faced ten years or a $10,000 fine for belonging to the National Lawyers Guild. However because the plaintiffs filed an immediate appeal to the U.S. Supreme Court, the attorney general agreed not to prosecute the state's case until the Supreme Court had a chance consider the appeal of the three judges' ruling. The case dragged on for the next year and a half.

The United States Supreme Court agreed to hear the case on June 15, 1964. The case, *Dombrowski v. Pfister* received supporting briefs from the ACLU and the NAACP. (It is interesting to note that Martin Luther King, Jr. appeared before the court and testified on behalf of Dombrowski.[3852])

The appellants, for their part, had invoked the federal Civil Rights Act of 1871, 42 U.S.C. 1983, alleging that the state statutes, on their face, violated the First and Fourteenth Amendments, and that the threatened prosecution under them was not intended to secure valid conviction but only to harass the appellants and discourage them from attempting to vindicate the constitutional rights of the Negro citizens of Louisiana. Another section of the statute which suggested that the citation of groups as Communist-front organizations by the attorney general or any committee of Congress was "presumptive evidence" that they were Communist-front organizations, as spelled out by the Communist Control Act, was also declared invalid by the Supreme Court.[3853, 3854, 3855]

In April 1964, in a five-to-two landmark decision, the Supreme Court ruled in favor of Dombrowski. The defendants prevailed with the help of Judge Wisdom's twenty-seven-page dissent of the earlier three-judge-panel ruling. Wisdom wrote that the main issue at hand was whether the state was abusing its power—under the pretext of protecting itself from subversion—for the true purpose of harassing and prosecuting the three defendants for promoting civil rights. The Supreme Court's five-two decision, with two abstentions, found the Louisiana state subversion laws to be unconstitutional. The opinion held that the three-judge district court erred in refusing to award an injunction restraining Louisiana officials from prosecuting the appellants under the provision of the state's Communist Control Act. Supreme Court Chief Justice William Brenner, writing the majority opinion, struck down the doctrine of abstention because it had "a chilling effect upon the exercise of First Amendment rights."

LUAC counsel Jack Rogers admitted that the intended purpose of the Louisiana anti-subversion laws was to open the door to prosecuting other civil rights organizations, if they had prevailed in the SCEF case. If they had been successful, civil rights activism would have all but disappeared.

SCEF attorney Arthur Kinoy declared, after the decision, "The Supreme Court of the United States [has] kicked Louisiana and Jim Eastland right in the teeth." Dombrowski's victory was a landmark event for the civil rights movement. The decision gave a substantial boost to SCEF and was their most important contribution to the civil rights movement.

In the end, it was court decisions like *Brown v. the Board of Education,* and *Dombrowski v. Pfister* that crushed the Southern segregationists. After his death, President Kennedy's civil rights bill, first proposed on June 11, 1963, would be the final blow. After the assassination, in his first address to Congress, President Johnson stated, "No memorial oration or eulogy could more eloquently honor President Kennedy's memory than the earliest possible passage of the civil rights bill for which he fought so long."[3856]

President Johnson's skillful political maneuvering enabled the bill to bypass the Senate Judiciary Committee. Instead, the bill went straight to the Senate floor for debate and was passed on July 2, 1964.

The Plan to Investigate FPCC

James Pfister of LUAC was the first to tip his hand as to the larger intent of the SCEF raid when he announced that LUAC intended to investigate FPCC in connection with SCEF. This happened when Pfister distributed a press release on November 28, 1963, stating, in part, that there was a "clear and obvious connection between the Fair Play for Cuba Committee and the Southern Conference Educational Fund."[3857]

LUAC counsel Jack Rogers said that SCEF was "giving us trouble all over the state" and was linked to racial demonstrations that cropped up in various Louisiana cities. He claimed there were Communist agitators in other groups advocating racial integration and that LUAC had several other major investigations underway, without identifying them.[3858]

J. G. Sourwine also affirmed the true intention of the SCEF raid in his December 1964 affidavit in the *Dombrowski v. Burbank* case. He stated the SISS also planned to investigate FPCC. In the affidavit, Sourwine noted that the SISS had studied the SCEF material as "to the extent, nature, and effect of subversive activities in the United States and infiltration by people who are or may be under domination of the foreign government or organizations controlling the world Communist movement. The material is directly relevant to these matters. The material not only relates to the activities and personnel of the Southern Conference Education Fund, Inc., but also to the connections between that organization and other organizations which appear to be Communist, Communist dominated, or Communist-front organizations such, for example, as Fair Play for Cuba Committee."[3859]

Thus, both Pfister and Sourwine made it clear that the purpose of the raid was not only to investigate SCEF but also FPCC and other groups in Louisiana.

However, as it has been noted, investigating the New Orleans FPCC was equivalent to investigating Lee Harvey Oswald, its lone member. If they had investigated Oswald they would have found that he was a Communist who spent time in the Soviet Union and who had ties to a number of leftist groups, including NOCPA, CORE, the ACLU, the Communist Party, Socialist Labor Party, and other groups tied to the integration movement. They would also have found that he had received Communist propaganda from New York by mail and printed his own. He was—at least on paper—just the kind of person that the Communist Control Act declared was a clear and present danger to the people of Louisiana.

Lee Harvey Oswald, the SCEF Raid, and the Eastland Committee

The temporal milestones in Lee Harvey Oswald's false Communist career from 1956 to 1963 dovetail with those of Eastland's anti-Communism and anti-integration crusades. As has been discussed, Oswald's career as a false Communist began in 1956, the year he first began posing as one. The same year, as outlined in the last chapter, Senator Eastland brought the SISS to New Orleans to interrogate SCEF leader James Dombrowski and other integrationists in the city, in hearings entitled "Scope of Soviet Activity in the United States." (Bruce Walzer represented Dombrowski during these hearings.) Eastland failed to provide any evidence of Soviet involvement, despite the provocative title. Members of the New Orleans Police Department, Guy Banister and Hubert Badeaux, aided Eastland's hearings and Leander Perez offered his assistance as well.

In 1956, Oswald was a member of David Ferrie's Civil Air Patrol unit. Ferrie, of course, was a close associate of Banister and a fanatical anti-Communist. On October 3, 1956, at age sixteen, Oswald wrote to the obscure Socialist Party and to the tiny Young Peoples Socialist League (YPSL), its youth auxiliary, in New York City. He told them he was interested in joining the group and wondered if there was a branch in the area. He wrote: "I am a Marxist and have been studying Socialist principles for well over fifteen months."[3860]

The YPSL worked with Bayard Rustin, a leading civil rights strategist in the 1950s. In 1956, SCEF field director Carl Braden belonged to the Socialist Party and received literature from the Young Peoples Socialist League. The author found Braden's correspondence with the Socialist Party/YPSL in his personal papers, which were left to posterity at the Wisconsin Historical Society. Letters exchanged between Braden and the Socialist Party/YPSL always began with the salutation "Dear Comrade." The YPSL published stories about SCEF based on information sent to them by Carl Braden in their newspaper *The Challenge*.[3861] Dombrowski had joined the Socialist Party while he was a divinity student in New York.[3862] (The FBI had informants in the Socialist and Communist organizations in New York and surreptitiously opened their mail. The FBI shared their information about the organizations with the congressional witch hunters in Congress.)

As a teenager in New Orleans, Oswald would have had a difficult time finding out, on his own, about the existence of the Socialist Party and the YPSL in New York City. There were many Socialist parties including the Socialist Workers Party and the Socialist Labor Party. Oswald's choice of the two particular groups that Braden and Dombrowski belonged to, also in 1956, may not have been a coincidence. At the same time that Oswald was writing to the organizations, Eastland was again trying to tie SCEF to Communism in his hearings in New Orleans involving Banister and Badeaux. Oswald's choice of subversive organizations to associate with, as in the case of the Socialist Party/YPSL, was never coincidental. Another example of this was his decision to hand out Corliss Lamont's booklet, "The Crime Against Cuba," which he showed to FBI agent Quigley after his arrest for scuffling with Carlos Bringuier. Not surprisingly, LUAC had determined that Lamont had made large contributions to SCEF.[3863]

In early 1957, Badeaux wrote to his friend Willie Rainach and told him he was grooming an individual to infiltrate the leftist groups on campus. Evidence has been presented that favors Oswald as that individual. It would not be surprising if Badeaux and Banister recruited Oswald for the job when he was a cadet in Ferrie's Civil Air Patrol unit.

After a stint in the marines, Oswald traveled to the Soviet Union for a three-year stay and married a Russian woman. Although the Soviets did not take him seriously, the sojourn firmly established him as a Soviet Communist, a credential which Eastland's best ex-Communist witnesses held. Oswald's return from the U.S.S.R. to Texas where his mother and brother resided, in the summer of 1962, was contemporaneous to Eastland sending his chief counsel, J. G. Sourwine, to New Orleans to plot strategy for the SCEF raids with Louisiana law enforcement. Oswald's return to the U.S. may have been timed to coincide with the planning of the SCEF raid, or vice versa.

It was also in the summer of 1962 that Oswald began establishing paper credentials as an American Communist by writing to the Communist Party USA, Socialist Workers Party, Fair Play for Cuba Committee, and other far-left organizations, soliciting quantities of their propaganda. The phony credentials obtained for the cost of a letter and postage stamp, along with his stay in the Soviet Union, were powerfully persuasive to the Warren Commission and the HSCA—and firmly established for them that he was a genuine Communist. Undoubtedly, if Oswald had appeared before a jury in the state of Louisiana, or as a witness in an Eastland hearing, they would have been easily persuaded as to his authenticity as a Communist as well.

Upon his return to New Orleans in the summer of 1963, Oswald began his public demonstrations on behalf of his one-man chapter of the New Orleans Fair Play for Cuba Committee. At the same time that Oswald was making a spectacle of himself on the streets of New Orleans as an FPCC member, Senator Eastland was holding ongoing investigations and hearings on FPCC and cited it as a Communist-front organization. While Oswald was corresponding with FPCC chairman V. T. Lee, Eastland was grilling Lee before his committee. A month prior to the SCEF raid on September 4, 1963, J. G. Sourwine of Eastland's SISS had a two-day hearing on the FPCC and exposed the Communist sponsorship of FPCC.[3864]

Two other organizations which Oswald affected an association with in the summer of

1963, NOCPA and CORE, were groups, not coincidentally, proclaimed by Senator Eastland as Communist fronts. Both had ties to Bruce Walzer of SCEF, who was also the chairman of NOCPA. In April of 1962, Walzer and Benjamin E. Smith of SCEF defended CORE in a case that involved integration of the Tulane University student cafeteria. That same month, Smith defended CORE chairman Ronnie Moore against charges that he was illegally using a loud speaker at a rally at Southern University in Baton Rouge.[3865]

In an Eastland hearing or state court proceeding, evidence tying Oswald to CORE and NOCPA—and by extension to SCEF—would have served as proof of SCEF's ties to a Soviet Communist in the person of Oswald. Oswald's visit to the Soviet and Cuban embassy on September 20, 1963, would have provided provocative evidence of the Communist influence in SCEF, FPCC, NOCPA, and CORE, and made them ripe for prosecution under the Communist Control Act. (Reverend Fred Shuttleworth, chairman of SCEF, astutely saw the danger posed to other groups by the SCEF raid and called it the "first overt move of a carefully planned conspiracy to smash the entire Freedom Movement."

Although the Walker shooting incident was botched due to the presence of a neighbor-eyewitness, Eastland, LUAC, or a state court proceeding might have figured out a way to use it as further evidence. The incident could have served as "the proof" that the lives of segregationists—and outspoken opponents of Communism and proponents of segregation, like General Walker—were threatened by Communists like Oswald who allegedly pervaded the various civil rights and leftist groups.

Of course, Oswald never lived to become a professional ex-Communist witness to help save segregation in the South. All of his activities leading up to his early September association with CORE, and prior to the September 12 announcement of President Kennedy's trip to Dallas, would have made him a perfect witness for the Eastland hearings. The shift in strategy to involve Oswald in the assassination may have begun with his visit to the Soviet and Cuban embassies in September that further embellished his Communist credentials and, if given the chance, could have served to lay the assassination at the feet of the Cubans and Soviets. On the other hand, the embassy visits could have also enhanced Oswald's credentials as a Communist or "ex-Communist" in the planned SCEF hearings and trials.

The Banister Operation and the Congressional Inquisitions

SISS Chief Counsel J. G. Sourwine's cozy relationship with the New Orleans segregationists in Guy Banister's operation dates back to at least February 28, 1958, when he questioned Kent Courtney and John U. Barr at an SISS hearing. They testified in support of the Senate bill "Limitations of Appellate Jurisdiction of the Supreme Court," which was also known as the Jenner Bill. The hearing was called in connection with a federal judge's overthrow of the state subversive statues and the state's right to investigate subversion. Barr headed the Federation for Constitutional Government, an Eastland-promoted group that Leander Perez and General Walker's friend and advisor, J. Evetts Haley, belonged to. (The Committee also heard from Robert Chandler of the States Rights Party of Louisiana.)

Sourwine stated during the proceedings that the Supreme Court had rendered the Smith Act virtually useless against subversives. Kent Courtney testified and told the subcommittee he was "deeply perturbed by the continuing pro-Communist decisions of the Supreme Court of our Nation."[3866] (It will be recalled that Barr was also on the advisory committee of the New Orleans National Indignation Committee with Guy Banister, Hubert Badeaux, and George Soule.) On March 24, 1958, Courtney wrote Willie Rainach and told him that, on his recent trip to Washington, D.C., he had visited with Sourwine and Richard Arens of the SISS and HUAC, respectively. Courtney provided Sourwine with copies of the "Subversion on Racial Unrest" hearings that Banister, Badeaux, and Perez had testified before in 1957. Sourwine told Courtney that he would like to have five sets of Part II of the hearing. Courtney also mentioned to Sourwine that Perez's daughter had organized a series of study group on subversion.[3867]

In the November 1963 edition of his newspaper, *The Independent American*, Courtney prematurely claimed victory over the Communist conspiracy as a result of the Communist Control Act and the SCEF raids. He sent copies that featured a story on the SCEF raids "and the important issue of States Rights vs. the 'civil wrongs' of the Kennedy administration" to members of the Louisiana legislature. Courtney pointed out that there had been a slow down in the mass demonstrations in the South since the SCEF records were seized. He maintained that if every state implemented similar subversive control laws "in the same forthright and courageous manner the Communist conspiracy would be completely stopped in this country." He claimed that SCEF had provided literature and direction for racial agitation in the fourteen Southern states. He asserted that SCEF, in the past, had not been hampered in its activities because Attorney General Robert Kennedy did not see fit to act on laws passed by Congress to control subversive organizations.

Courtney sent out a "Tax Fax No. 46" pamphlet, which he published with his wife, entitled "Communist Agitation and Racial Turmoil," to 20,000 paid subscribers of *The Independent American*. He claimed that the pamphlet provided documentation that "the Communists [were] indeed behind racial agitation and turmoil." He mentioned Robert Kennedy's July 23, 1963, statement that he found "no evidence that the major civil rights groups are Communists or Communist-controlled." He called Kennedy's statement "ignorant" and provided his own evidence to the contrary. He also cited Senator Eastland's SISS hearings in New Orleans that produced evidence that Hunter Pitts O'Dell was a Communist. (As noted in the last chapter, Guy Banister and Hubert Badeaux acquired the evidence after breaking into O'Dell's home.) Courtney cited a story from an August 1963 Communist publication that reported that black attorney Benjamin J. Davis, of the Communist Party, stated the Negro Freedom movement had entered a new stage of revolution.[3868] (On December 13, 1962, it will be recalled, Lee Harvey Oswald wrote a letter offering to do photographic work for the Gus Hall-Benjamin J. Davis Defense Committee, as he had the SWP.[3869] John Abt headed the committee. Hall was the General Secretary of the Communist Party, United States, while Davis was an African-American lawyer and a member of the Communist Party who defended accused Communists. The two were charged with violating the Internal Security Act on March 15, 1962.[3870]) In the "Tax Fax No. 46" pamphlet, Courtney requested that his readers read the pamphlet and encourage Louisiana congressman Edwin Willis of HUAC to hold public hearings on the "Communist influence in the NAACP, CORE, The Student Non-Violent Coordinating Committee and other organizations dedicated to racial turmoil." He stated that "[i]n this way certain racial agitators can be officially identified as Communists or members of Communist-front groups." Copies of the letter were sent to the Friends of General Walker and various other patriotic publications and leaders.[3871]

The allegation that Oswald was seen in Baton Rouge on numerous occasions in the company of Courtney in the summer of 1963 was presented in Chapter Two. During that period of time, the state legislature was considering Perez's Free Electors legislation to deprive President Kennedy of the state's Electoral College votes. At the same time, in Baton Rouge, LUAC and the state police were preparing for the SCEF raid.

J. G. Sourwine was present when Ed Butler, a Banister colleague, appeared before a confidential executive session of the SISS in Washington, D.C., two days after the Kennedy assassination. Butler told them that he first met Oswald on August 21, 1963, during the radio debate on station WDSU. Butler handed over the tape of the debate, along with a transcript.[3872] (During the debate, Oswald had admitted he was a Marxist.)

In the wake of the assassination of the president by a Communist—as J. Edgar Hoover concluded on the day of the murder—and while the civil rights defendants were fighting in the courts in the SCEF affair, Hoover promoted the Communist ties to the civil rights movement angle. Hoover stated, on December 4, 1963: "[T]oday the Communists are engaged in a vigorous campaign to divide and weaken America from within. This is especially true in the intense civil rights movement . . ."[3873] The timing of Hoover's declaration, while the nation was absorbing the shock of the assassination and the spectacle of Lee Harvey Oswald, was strange. No one had, yet, tried to tie Oswald—the most famous Communist in the world at the time—to the civil rights movement.

Carlos Bringuier and the SCEF Affair

Carlos Bringuier, who engaged in a phony fight with Lee Harvey Oswald as he was handing out FPCC leaflets, was eager to link Oswald to SCEF, through NOCPA, after the Kennedy assassination. (It will be recalled that Bringuier also demonstrated against NOCPA with Kent Courtney.) Bringuier was an associate of Guy Banister and the Cubans who had operated out of the 544 Camp Street office—the same address which was stamped on some of Oswald's leaflets.

The FBI's interview of Bringuier after the assassination is quoted as follows: "Another individual that might be an associate of Oswald because he is connected with the New Orleans Committee for Peaceful Alternatives is Donald Savery who lives on Alta Street in Metairie. He stated he met this individual when pro-Castros were having a rally in Jackson Square, but he did not see Oswald at this rally. Bringuier stated that Bruce Walzer, New Orleans attorney, who was recently arrested by the local police in connection with a raid on the Southern Conference Educational Fund, is the New Orleans organizer for Committee for Peaceful Alternatives."[3874] (Bringuier had met Donald Savery after a NOCPA demonstration and had told him, falsely, that he was pro-Castro. Savery invited Bringuier for coffee and allegedly told him Communists would take over the United States by revolution.)

Arnesto Rodriquez, Jr. was a friend of Carlos Bringuier and a member of the Cuban Revolutionary Council and the Crusade to Free Cuba that had once operated out of the 544 Camp Street office building, above Guy Banister's office. Banister was also a member of the Crusade to Free Cuba, a small local group. As was noted in Chapter One, Rodriquez told the FBI, after the assassination, that Oswald approached him at his Modern Language School in late July or early August and asked him about taking Spanish courses. Rodriquez also told the FBI that his wife had once worked for Bruce Walzer.[3875] (In that role, Rodriquez's wife was in the perfect position to obtain confidential information on SCEF, NOCPA, CORE, and any other leftist groups Walzer associated with.)

LUAC, the American Legion, and the Banister Operation

In 1958, James Pfister, Kent Courtney, and Festus Jerry Brown, all members of the American Legion, organized a seminar to warn students about the threat of Communism. Leander Perez, Guy Banister, Douglas Caddy, and Medford Evans joined the effort.[3876] The First District of the America Legion in New Orleans proposed the establishment of a LUAC, to be modeled after HUAC. Brown, a close associate of Banister and Courtney, was the chairman of the First District Legion.[3877] (It will be recalled from Chapter Twenty that Brown counter-demonstrated on several occasions against NOCPA.) Courtney was the director of the American Legion Americanism Committee.[3878] Banister served as "special advisor" for the American Legion's Committee on Un-American Activities.[3879]

Prior to assuming the position of Chief Counsel for LUAC, Jack N. Rogers, also a Legion member, had been in search of subversives and enemies of segregationists. In 1959, Rogers told Willie Rainach that he had gathered intelligence on leftists for the America Legion to expose the American Field Service Committee, which he called "a very dangerous foe of segregation." (The American Field Service Committee was a Quaker group dedicated to peace and social justice.) Rogers condemned the ACLU for backing integration. In another letter, Rogers complained to Rainach that a member of several Communist-front groups was going to give an annual LSU law school address and that others who had addressed the law school in the past had endorsed the NAACP, ACLU, and National Lawyers Guild. He urged Rainach to investigate the matter in the legislature.[3880]

Pfister, in 1958, was the commander of the First District American Legion.[3881] He was later elected to the state house of representatives in 1960 and named chairman of the Louisiana Un-American Activities Committee that he was instrumental in creating. He hired Rogers as LUAC general counsel. Chairman Pfister stated the aims of LUAC were to identify subversives on campus or in the civil rights movement.[3882] LUAC, like its congressional counterparts, had the authority to subpoena witnesses and find them in contempt.[3883] Banister landed the job of chief investgator for LUAC. (It will be recalled that the FBI interviewed Guy Banister on February 3, 1961, and he told them he was "ferreting out subversive activities in the State of Louisiana," using student infiltrators "in connection with his interest and position in the Louisiana State organization known as the State Joint Legislative Committee on Un-American activities."[3884]) The Sovereignty Commission offered their cooperation and the use of their staff to LUAC.[3885]

In 1961, Banister attended a meeting of the LUAC in Baton Rouge with Leander Perez.[3886] Later, Pfister introduced the Communist Control Act, the creation of Perez, into the legislature, where it was passed into law in 1962.[3887, 3888]

Brown, a Legionnaire and member of the Banister operation, introduced Lawrence Melville to Banister. Melville worked in Banister's office for six to eight months and used his files to check on those involved in local integration activities. Melville told Garrison's investigators that Banister had papers on Americanism, HUAC reports on subversives, and other material.[3889]

Everyone involved with the creation of LUAC had ties to Banister and nearly everyone involved in the SCEF raid had ties to the Banister operation. Perez and Pfister, associates of Banister, created the Communist Control Act that was the basis for the raid. Banister worked closely with Senator Eastland during his 1956 hearings in New Orleans—which involved SCEF director James Dombrowski. Eastland and his investigators played a part in the raid. Eastland's chief counsel, J. G. Sourwine, worked with Banister's close colleague Kent Courtney as early as 1958. State police officers Thomas Burbank and Russell Willie, who were involved in the SCEF raid and also with the Sovereignty Commission, suspiciously scurried off with Banister's files after his death in June 1964—taking them to Baton Rouge and, later, destroying them. (The files of the Sovereignty Commission and LUAC were also, later, mysteriously destroyed.) As was noted in the last chapter, Allen Campbell, while working for Banister, broke into SCEF offices in 1959. Banister, himself, kept files on SCEF and their membership and had obtained their mailing list. The wife of Banister's Cuban associate, Ernesto Rodriquez, who admitted meeting Lee Harvey Oswald, worked for SCEF raid defendant, Bruce Walzer, perhaps as a spy.

The enemies of SCEF had an essential problem in dealing with the group. Unlike the Communist Party or FPCC, SCEF could not be infiltrated because they had no members. SCEF was financed by the donations of 3,000 subscribers to its newspaper *Southern Patriot*.[3890] SCEF had no members to participate in demonstrations, but they funded organizations that did, and promoted them in their newspaper. Jim Garrison eventually found a list of subscribers to the *Southern Patriot* in the remnants of Banister's files, which showed that Banister was listed as a subscriber.[3891] With penetration of SCEF difficult, Rogers resorted to "ex-Communists" to provide evidence against them. Major Willie testified at the LUAC hearing that he had an informant who provided him with evidence that SCEF was subversive, but refused to name him.[3892]

Virginia Durr, a SCEF officer and an Eastland target in the 1954 SCEF hearings, commented on the constant attempts to infiltrate the New Orleans SCEF office, stating: "We were always having strange young men come in saying that they wanted to be volunteers—saying their name was Joe Smith and they worked in the Post Office Department but they had a few days off and wanted to do volunteer work. As soon as they left, I would call the post office and find that no Joe Smith ever worked for the post office." Durr recalled the first thing the "volunteers" always wanted to do was get a hold of their mailing and donors list.[3893]

The author interviewed Anne Braden, FPCC officer, SCEF Field Secretary, and editor of the *Southern Patriot*. When asked her opinion of the Oswald-FPCC affair, she had absolutely no insight into the matter.[3894] If Oswald approached anyone at SCEF in the summer of 1963, they either had forgotten about it or kept quiet about it. Infiltrating FPCC and the New Orleans Committee of Peaceful Alternatives, who had shared leadership with SCEF, may have been as close as Oswald could get to infiltrating SCEF.

The LUAC Hearings on SCEF

While the SCEF raid defendants battled with Senator Eastland, J. G. Sourwine, and Colonel Thomas Burbank in the federal courts, LUAC continued to attack SCEF in hearings held in November 1963, April 1964, and January 1965. LUAC called Benjamin E. Smith and Bruce Walzer the "Communist Party's top attorneys." To make their case, LUAC enlisted the help of an "ex-Communist," Dr. William Sorum, who was a star witness in the 1957 HUAC hearings in New Orleans. Sorum testified that SCEF had been a tool and a front of the Communist conspiracy.

On November 28, 1963, the *States-Item* published a story with the headline, "Solons claim Oswald Unit, SCEF tied." The story cited LUAC's investigation that had determined Carl Braden was an officer in FPCC and a field secretary for SCEF. (By extension, that linked Oswald to SCEF.) During LUAC's hearing in March 1964, Jack Rogers stated: "The connections to the Southern Conference Education Fund through Carl and Anne Braden, these Communist Party members, stretch clear through all of these other militant organizations." Rogers listed CORE and the Student Non-Violent Coordinating Committee (SNCC) as SCEF-affiliated, as well as the Southern Christian Leadership Council (SCLC), Martin Luther King, Jr.'s organization.[3895] The *pièce de résistance* was Pfister's presentation of the letterhead showing that Braden was the "Honorary Co-Chairman" of the Los Angeles chapter of FPCC. LUAC issued a report on April 13, 1964, entitled "Activities of the Southern Conference Educational Fund, Inc., in Louisiana." Rogers stated: "After the horrible assassination of the president, we directed our Committee staff to make a preliminary inquiry into the connections of Fair Play for Cuba Committee here in Louisiana."

The published report devoted a full page to Oswald's arrest mug shots and fingerprint sheet after his "fight" with Bringuier. LUAC published a photograph, seized in the SCEF raid, of Martin Luther King, Jr. with Anne and Carl Braden and James Dombrowski. The photo was a treasured propaganda piece to show that the civil rights movements (of which King was the figurehead) had been thoroughly infiltrated by the Communists. They also produced a cancelled check from SCEF to King in the amount of $167.[3896]

FAIR PLAY FOR CUBA COMMITTEE

FPCC letterhead notes that the Bradens were officers in FPCC. Source: 124-10267-1076, The John F. Kennedy Assassination Records Collection, NARA

Since SCEF had no membership, they were not a physical force at the voter rights protests, sit-ins, and other civil rights demonstrations. However, as mentioned above, they funded those activities and publicized them in their newspaper, *Southern Patriot*. SCEF financially supported SNCC, which was targeted by LUAC, and which SCEF leaders called the "hope and heart of things."[3897] They funded SNCC's field secretaries, as well, who worked on voter registration. They also put up money to get demonstrators out of jail.[3898]

After the Kennedy assassination, LUAC's continued pursuit of SCEF was inconsequential, in light of President Johnson's announced commitment to pass Kennedy's Civil Rights Act in 1964. The battle to preserve segregation would be won or lost, not by the outcome of *Dombrowski v. Pfister* in the Supreme Court, but in the U.S. Senate.

The adverse publicity generated from Oswald's ties to FPCC after the assassination caused the national organization to fold in December 1963, as V. T. Lee told the Warren Commission in his testimony on April 17, 1964.[3899] Oswald's posing as a Communist and a member of FPCC was successful in destroying FPCC—but not SCEF or the other civil rights groups.

Carl Braden's connections to both FPCC and SCEF were played up among the far right. Dallas John Birch Society member Earl Lively wrote to Herbert Philbrick and told him, "SCEF and the FPCC are just one big ball of wax."[3900] Robert Morris, General Walker's close associate, and Philbrick aimed to fully exploit the propaganda created by Oswald's ties to FPCC.

William James Lowery, Jr. contacted the FBI and told them that a reporter (Lively) contacted him and he told Lively that he was collaborating on a book about the assassination with Morris and Philbrick. Lowery was a former Communist and an FBI informant who had testified before the Subversive Activities Control Board. Lively reportedly told Lowery he wanted to stress the FPCC connection with Oswald in the book, and wanted Lowery's assistance on the matter, since he was a former Communist.[3901]

In 1964, Billy James Hargis published the history of SCEF and its supposed Communist connections in the *Weekly Crusader*. He cited the April 13, 1964, LUAC investigation conclusion that tied Oswald to FPCC and its ties SCEF. He noted that Carl Braden had attended an FPCC banquet in New York City on April 28, 1961, and pointed out Braden's ties to SCEF.[3902]

LUAC worked with the Mississippi Sovereignty Commission and searched for ties between the historically black Tougaloo College and SCEF, the primary source of funding for student sit-ins and attempts to desegregate Mississippi's public libraries in 1961.

Senator Eastland wrote to the Mississippi Sovereignty Commission on March 4, 1964, and told them that Jack Rogers had visited him and told him that LUAC had information that SCEF was a Communist-front.[3903]

In 1967, Rogers, as LUAC counsel, summing up the whole matter, contacted the New Orleans office of the CIA to let them know that, in the 1964 hearings, his committee linked "Lee Harvey Oswald and the Fair Play for Cuba Committee with the Southern Conference Education Fund through one Carl Braden." Rogers told them that he felt Oswald was a Moscow-trained agent and FPCC organizer.[3904]

Oswald and the Two Plots

The evidence suggests that Oswald was figured into two separate—and perhaps competing—plots. The first was a plot to be used as a false-Communist operative, created to advance the New Orleans segregationists' agenda, which began in 1956, culminating with the hearings and trials of the SCEF defendants under the Communist Control Act. The second was the Kennedy assassination plot, masterminded by General Walker in Dallas. Until the assassination, no one could be sure Oswald would be involved in the Dallas plot, for any number of reasons. It was, perhaps, even a long shot up until it happened.

The Secret Service could have cancelled the motorcade, as they had done in Miami, after they learned from Willie Somersett that Joseph Milteer had told him that an assassination attempt was in the works. A rain shower would have forced the president's limousine to use its protective bubble top. A Book Depository employee deciding to watch the parade from the sixth floor would have posed significant problems. If the assassination had not happened—or had not been pinned on Oswald—the evidence presented suggests he would have likely been the star witness at the SCEF defendants' trials under the Communist Control Act, as well as the hearings by the SISS and LUAC. Oswald would have tainted SCEF, FPCC, CORE, NOCPA, and the ACLU—all of which were leftist, anti-segregationist groups that Oswald infiltrated in 1963.

The mountain of evidence showing that Oswald was an operative of the far right wing leaves few, if any, alternative explanations as to why he pretended to be a Communist. Oswald was obviously groomed as a false Communist, later to become an "ex-Communist witness" like Paul Crouch and many others, to testify against the enemies of the South and the far right to destroy them. As an "ex-Communist" witness, Oswald may have expected to enjoy the financial rewards and fame of testifying in the congressional hearings and the state inquisitions held throughout Dixie.

Midway through the long planning of the SCEF raid, the plot was significantly undermined by President Kennedy's proposal of the Civil Rights Act on June 11, 1963. If passed, the segregationists' plot to essentially outlaw the integration movement using the Communist Control Act would be futile. Further undermining the SCEF raid plot was the savvy and formidable legal maneuvering of the SCEF raid defendants in the federal courts, where they ultimately prevailed.

Given the choice as to which plot to use Oswald in, it may have ultimately been decided that eliminating the president—and thereby eliminating his civil rights bill and liberal policies—would have resulted in the more favorable outcome for the segregationists. Aside from General Walker's stand for segregation, he had his own motivation to murder the president, which the segregationists did not have. President Kennedy had relieved Walker of his command, something that had not been done since President Truman relieved General Douglas MacArthur in 1951. Under President Kennedy, Walker was arrested and detained in a federal mental facility on the charge of insurrection in the Ole Miss affair, giving him another personal motive. Ultimately, perhaps Walker's personal vendetta against Kennedy was the overriding factor in choosing to use Oswald in the assassination, rather than in the SCEF raid/Communist Control Act plots.

Conclusions

Southern segregationists tied to the Guy Banister operation planned to use the power of states rights accorded by the Constitution to essentially outlaw the civil rights movement through the use of the Communist Control Act. Lee Harvey Oswald personified the threat of the Communists working in the civil rights movement, as described in the law.

The Southern Conference Education Fund, a New Orleans-based integration group, was the first group targeted under the new law. The raid on SCEF headquarters involved close associates of Guy Banister, associates who also planned the state and congressional hearings on the supposed finding of evidence of SCEF's Communist affiliation.

SCEF officers Anne and Carl Braden were honorary chairmen of FPCC, which was also a target of the investigation. An investigation of the New Orleans FPCC would have found the supposed Soviet-directed Communist agent behind the New Orleans chapter, Lee Harvey Oswald, whom multiple witnesses saw with Guy Banister in the summer of 1963. Eastland and LUAC also planned to investigate NOCPA and CORE, two groups that Oswald had infiltrated that were also connected with SCEF.

There are few, if any, explanations as to why Oswald became a false Communist under the Banister operation, other than to serve as a false Communist "witness" against the integration movement, by way of the Communist Control Act. The practice—made popular by the far right—of using "false Communists" and "ex-Communists" in the state and congressional hearings on subversion (as a way of stifling dissent and progress in the civil rights movement) had a long history. The evidence suggests that the end game for Oswald's career as a false Communist was supposed to be through his testimony to "save the country and the Southern way of life" from the integrationists. Instead, he was used, along with his impeccable Communist credentials, as a patsy in an attempt to "save" the country from both the integrationists and the president who supported them, John F. Kennedy.

CHAPTER TWENTY-FOUR

BOOK CONCLUSIONS

We have not been told the truth about Lee Harvey Oswald.
— *Senator Richard Russell*

General Edwin A. Walker was the mastermind behind the murder of President Kennedy, as the evidence presented in this work shows. An FBI and Miami, Florida, police informant close to Walker co-conspirator Joseph Milteer provided the names of the shooters—two of whom the author has documented as close associates of Walker. The informant accurately told the FBI, thirteen days in advance, that the assassination had been planned to take place from an office building with a high-powered weapon that could be easily broken down, and that a patsy would be picked up after the murder to throw the authorities off. A mountain of additional evidence against Walker—with documented support—is also presented in this book.

Lee Harvey Oswald, the accused murderer of the president, was directly involved with Walker's radical-right operation, but he was not involved in the murder of the president—Walker set Oswald up as a fall guy. Oswald was found on the second floor of the Texas School Book Depository calmly sipping a Coke when police rushed into the building immediately after the shooting, and was most likely not on the sixth floor where the shooting took place. He made no immediate attempt to flee and had provided himself no funds to sustain flight (when he could have), further suggesting that he was not involved with the murder. Soon after the shots were fired, an unidentified man—who was likely the shooter and one of the men named by FBI informant Willie Somersett—ran out of the back door of the building. Walker also had direct ties to the New Orleans elements that were behind Oswald and Oswald's public portrayal as a Communist.

The evidence shows that Jack Ruby, who murdered Oswald, was compelled by Walker's group to silence him. Ruby knew Walker and had made visits to his home with members of the John Birch Society beginning in 1962. On the night after the assassination, Ruby became obsessed with a John Birch Society billboard and the derogatory "Welcome Mr. Kennedy to Dallas" ad that ran during the morning in the newspaper. Ruby declared that whoever was behind the ad and the billboard was behind the assassination. (He was correct: individuals close to General Walker were behind both the ad and the bulletin board.) Ruby planned to go to the FBI with his information on the Monday after the Friday assassination. Ruby also named Walker and the John Birch Society in his Warren Commission testimony, but the Commission failed to fully grasp the impact of this testimony. Ruby later claimed that the Minutemen and the Nazis (groups the author traced to Walker and his close aide Robert Surrey) used him.

After the Warren Commission released its findings in the fall of 1964 stating that Oswald had acted alone, the head of the Dallas Alcohol Tobacco and Firearms agency belatedly stated that if there had been a conspiracy, General Walker and H. L. Hunt of the Minutemen would have been directly involved.

In 1966, while awaiting a new trial, Ruby became ill and was transferred from the Dallas County jail to the hospital. Shortly thereafter, Walker told a friend (in a letter) that he was worried that Ruby might talk and the blame would be placed on the radical right. Walker vowed that Ruby would not leave the hospital alive. Walker placed Oswald's mother and his White Russian friend, George de Mohrenschildt, under surveillance—no doubt because they had knowledge about Oswald, which could be damaging to the conspirators.

According to an FBI informant, police officer J. D. Tippit, who approached and was murdered by Oswald after the assassination, was a part of the assassination conspiracy. Suspiciously, a police car with an unidentified officer in it had approached Oswald's rooming house after the assassination—according to Oswald's landlady—for no apparent reason. Shortly after that incident, Tippit was murdered by Oswald after catching up to him while Oswald was walking a mile from the rooming house. Oswald may have murdered him in self-defense. The proximity of Tippit to the rooming house where a police car had been seen parked outside was no coincidence. Instead, it strongly suggests that it was Tippit's car and, as a member of the conspiracy, Tippit was there to "silence" Oswald. The Warren Commission determined that Tippit moonlighted as a security officer at a restaurant owned by a John Birch Society member which, as the author discovered, was also a location where the Society held their meetings. The connection to the location where John Birch Society meetings were held may have been the perfect opportunity for Society members to recruit Officer Tippit and bring him into the conspiracy.

The Liaison between Oswald's New Orleans Sponsors and General Walker
In 1961, General Walker had his first contact with a member of Guy Banister's operation, Kent Courtney, who with Banister, directed Lee Harvey Oswald in New Orleans in his public demonstrations as a Communist. At the time, Walker, who had been a John Birch Society member since the 1950s, had just been relieved of his command of the 24th Infantry Division in Augsburg, Germany (for indoctrinating his troops with John Birch Society anti-Communist propaganda and accusing prominent Americans of being pro-Communist), by President Kennedy. Guy Banister's close associate, and a prominent figure on the radical right, Kent Courtney, flew to Walker's mother's ranch in Center Point, Texas, in July 1961 with a prop-

osition. He made an offer to Walker's mother to make General Walker a paid figurehead and spokesman for the radical right and wanted to fly to Germany with General Charles Willoughby to make the offer to Walker in person. (It's not known if he made the trip, but he did meet with Walker in the fall of 1961 and wrote a book about him, a seminal event in the assassination history.)

Multiple witnesses, including a member of the U.S. Border Patrol, observed Oswald either in the presence of Banister or at his office. Oswald was also seen, on multiple occasions, with Courtney, according to another credible report. Courtney's meeting with Walker marks the beginning of the connection between the Banister operation in New Orleans—which groomed Oswald as a false Communist—and General Walker, who used him to take the fall in the assassination. Medford Evans, another close associate of Banister and Courtney, joined Walker in Washington in 1961 during the hearings on his troop indoctrination program.

Walker resigned from the army in the fall of 1961 and returned to Texas as a hero to the radical right, which was engulfed in the fight against Communists at home. He gave speeches bitterly critical of President Kennedy's backing of civil rights initiatives, disarmament policies, and the handling of the Cuba situation to far-right crowds across the country.

Oswald, the False Communist

Lee Harvey Oswald's persona as a dangerous Communist was completely phony. He was raised in a conservative, anti-Jewish, anti-black family. His favorite television show in the early 1950s was *I Led Three Lives*, which was about phony Communist Herbert Philbrick, who infiltrated Communist organizations to destroy them. Oswald took on the same role. In 1955, he received indoctrination in anti-Communism in the Civil Air Patrol by the fanatic anti-Communist (and, later, White Citizens' Council and John Birch Society follower) Captain David Ferrie. Ferrie, as it has been noted, was close to Guy Banister, the former New Orleans superintendent of police and former director of the Chicago office of the FBI. In 1956, while Oswald was being schooled in anti-Communism, Banister, a rabid racist, began a well-publicized investigation into the supposed Communist influence in the racial integration movement. He worked directly with Senator James O. Eastland of the Senate Internal Security Subcommitte (SISS) on a witch hunt against the integrationists.

The South rose again in fierce opposition to the 1954 Supreme Court decision in *Brown v. Board of Education*, which abolished segregation in the public schools. General Walker and Banister eagerly joined the fight. Eastland, his close friend Leander Perez, and other prominent segregationists plotted a strategy to tie civil rights workers and integration supporters to Communism. Oswald was a part of the plan. Senator Joseph McCarthy had paved the way with reckless allegations that Communists had penetrated the highest levels of government and other areas of American life, which resulted in a new era of anti-Communism known as the Red Scare. Southern segregationists devised a strategy to tie the rising integration movement to the Red Scare and turn it into the Black Scare. Communists, they declared, were behind the civil rights movement.

After Oswald's foray into anti-Communism in the Civil Air Patrol in 1956, he began to act like a Communist, very similar to his boyhood TV hero. He told a friend he was interested in joining a Communist cell, and wrote to two Communist/Socialist organizations—the Socialist Party and Young Peoples Socialist League—expressing the same interest. Carl Braden, a leader of the New Orleans-based Southern Conference Education Fund (SCEF), which supported integration groups, belonged to these same two obscure organizations. This was not a coincidence; Braden was Senator Eastland's bitter enemy and a subject of his inquisitions, as well as an enemy of Banister, who ordered a break-in of SCEF offices in 1959. Oswald's writing to the same two organizations that Braden belonged to suggests that 1956 was the beginning of Oswald's attempt to infiltrate the enemies of Eastland and Banister's operations. A letter which was written to a prominent segregationist in early 1957 by Hubert Badeaux (the police sergeant who assisted Banister in the hunt for Communists in the integration movement), revealed the reason for Oswald acting like a Communist. The letter also explains the paradox of Oswald acting like a Communist while at the same time being under the influence of a dedicated anti-Communist in the Civil Air Patrol and preparing to join the marines—ostensibly to fight the Communists. The letter also revealed that Badeaux, under the direction of Banister, was grooming "an individual" to infiltrate leftist organizations on college campuses. The particulars of the letter favor Oswald as the one being groomed for this specific role.

The radical right courted ex-Communists and false Communists and repeatedly used them to falsely identify people they opposed as members of the Communist Party; their aim was to destroy these people and their leftist movements. The radical right defined a Communist as anyone they opposed; the list included union members, college professors, the ACLU, and integrationists. This tactic, fine-tuned by Senator McCarthy and followed by Senator Eastland, was successful. Ex-Communist witnesses took part in multiple state and congressional inquisitions in the 1950s, destroying lives and organizations. The ex-Communists and false Communists were well paid and enjoyed a celebrity status. Of course, the best ex-Communists had traveled to the Soviet Union, which made Oswald a perfect recruit.

Oswald was not brought into service as a false Communist until 1962, after spending 1956–1959 in the Marine Corps and 1959–1962 in the Soviet Union, perfecting his faux Communist credentials. During Oswald's absence, the southern legislatures had, to some extent, found a way around the federal mandates to desegregate the schools and there was no urgent need for a false Communist. Contemporaneous to Oswald's return to the U.S. in May 1962, Louisiana state representative James Pfister, who headed the Louisiana Un-American Activities Committee (LUAC)—in which Banister served as their chief investigator—enacted the Communist Control Act. Leander Perez, the brains behind the Act, was a close Banister associate, as well as being the man identified by Willie Somersett as the financier of the president's assassination. The primary underlying objective of the Communist Control Act was to destroy the civil rights movement. The Act called for penalties consisting of decades of imprisonment and massive fines for anyone in the integration movement who associated with a known Communist like Lee Harvey Oswald. The Communist Control Act, if successful, through its Draconian penalties, would have had the effect of abolishing the civil rights movement in the South.

After many months of planning, coordinated by Banister's operation and LUAC, along with Senator Eastland's investigators and the state police, plans were made to prosecute members of the SCEF. The SCEF shared officers with the Fair Play for Cuba Committee (FPCC), the ACLU, and the New Orleans Committee for Peaceful Alternative (NOCPA), and funded integrationist groups, including the Congress of Racial Equality (CORE). (Multiple book chapters have detailed Oswald's infiltration into all of those groups.) The plan was to raid the SCEF offices, arrest their officers—whom the investigators claimed had associated with a known Communist—and put them away for the better part of their lives under the Communist Control Act. The evidence supports the identification of Oswald, the false Communist, as the man who had been groomed to eventually testify in legal proceedings regarding SCEF's Communist affiliations and to destroy them and any related groups. The raid on the SCEF offices was planned for the fall of 1963.

The Rise of General Walker

By 1962, General Walker had risen to a leadership position in the radical right and was a frequent and favored speaker for the National Indignation Committee, Citizens' Councils, and other far-right organizations across the country. In June 1962, retired Major General Pedro del Valle, another politically radical, disaffected retired military officer, wrote to General Walker and suggested a plan of action to fight the establishment before resorting to violence. (The press had already reported that del Valle was close to calling for insurrection against the government in 1961.) In late 1962, FBI informant Willie Somersett revealed their plan for violence. The plan was to assassinate certain members of President Kennedy's cabinet, members of the Council on Foreign Relations (which they felt was a secret organization that controlled the government), and prominent men in business and industry, including influential Jewish figures. Five-member assassination teams would carry out the assassinations when members of the high military command gave the orders.

Retired generals Walker, del Valle, and Clyde Watts were the members of the high military command. The FBI knew all about the plot, but failed to reveal the evidence to the Warren Commission, who had investigated Walker and taken his testimony on the supposed assassination attempt made on him by Lee Harvey Oswald (which was actually a Walker-contrived sham). At the April 1963 far-right Congress of Freedom meeting in New Orleans, which was attended by Guy Banister and Kent Courtney, the FBI informant reported again that the broad-based assassination plots were serious and in the works. For some unknown reason, the FBI amazingly failed to question Walker, del Valle, or Watts in the matter. Instead, the FBI questioned low-ranking members of the conspiracy who denied the allegations, which only served to let Walker and his cronies know that they had an informant in their midst. As a result, the assassination plots were aborted.

In September 1962, Walker incited a riot at the University of Mississippi after President Kennedy ordered the admission of the first African American, James Meredith, to the then all-white school. The ensuing riot, joined by radicals tied to Guy Banister's organization and southern racists, led to two deaths and the wounding of dozens of U.S. Marshals. Walker was arrested on the orders of President Kennedy and Attorney General Robert Kennedy on charges of insurrection against the government of the United States, a charge that could have landed him in prison for decades. During Walker's subsequent trial, a Southern jury who looked favorably upon Walker's efforts to preserve segregation at the university failed to indict him.

In October 1963, informant Willie Somersett reported new plans for violence to the FBI. While attending the Constitution Party conference in Indianapolis, Somersett reported that there was serious talk of killing the president. Walker's friend, Joseph Milteer, attended with others who had been at the Congress of Freedom meeting earlier in the year, where broad-based assassination plots had initially been revealed. Pedro del Valle, a member of the high military command of the assassination plotters, also attended and revealed the plan to murder the president to Woody Kearns, a close friend of Milteer and a colleague of Walker.

Thirteen days before the Kennedy assassination, Somersett tape recorded the plan to murder the president and the FBI knew all about it. According to Somersett's recording, the assassination was to be done from an office building using a high-power rifle, with a patsy being picked up to throw the authorities off. The tape was kept from the Warren Commission investigation. After the assassination, the FBI sent an agent to question Milteer. This action served no good purpose other than to shut Milteer up. Somersett had already learned a significant amount about the plotters and was in a position to know significantly more, had the FBI not effectively silenced Milteer five days after the murder.

The Communist Posturing of Lee Harvey Oswald

Upon his return from the Soviet Union, Lee Harvey Oswald began a concerted campaign to embellish his Communist credentials for the purposes of making him an unimpeachable Communist witness against the integration forces in the South as a part of hearings to be conducted under Banister's Louisiana Un-American Activities Committee, with the assistance of Senator Eastland's Senate Internal Security Subcommittee. Oswald began the campaign in Texas, in 1962, by writing to a variety of Communist or Socialist organizations—including the Communist Party in New York—gathering literature and attempting to obtain membership cards.

Guy Banister had a history of turning young men into false Communists. In 1961, he had tried to persuade a young, high-ranking member of the Minutemen, Jerry Brooks, to write to the Communist Party in New York in an attempt to join and receive their literature. Brooks refused, however, and reported the incident to the FBI.

Oswald was also involved in five theatrical incidents in Dallas and Louisiana, each tied directly to the Banister and Kent Courtney operation. While in Texas in early 1963, Oswald and General Walker devised a scheme where Oswald would fire his rifle into a window at Walker's house and make it appear like an assassination attempt on the general's life by a known Communist. Oswald busied himself before the stunt, leaving notes behind in his apartment detailing how he planned to kill the general, as well as taking photos of Walker's home. All of that contrived evidence was clearly designed for Oswald to use to incriminate himself (he also left behind deliberately incriminating evidence on the day of the president's assassination). If the plot to "shoot" Walker went off as planned, Oswald would have been arrested; careful manipulation of the evidence—or Walker's refusal to press charges—would then have resulted in Oswald's release from custody. The incident would have further embellished Oswald's false Communist persona, while Walker would be vindicated for his often-stated position that the real threat to the nation was the Communists within. The phony scheme was aborted when Walker's men, while leaving the scene of the shooting, looked back and saw that a neighbor boy had witnessed the stunt. Earlier that year, Kent Courtney had joined Walker in Miami, Florida, for the start of a national speaking tour with Billy James Hargis, another associate of Guy Banister. After the shooting incident, Walker called Courtney and told him about it, which suggests that the shooting incident was crafted in conjunction with Courtney and the New Orleans operation.

Two days after the Kennedy assassination, Walker told a German magazine reporter that he believed Oswald was the one who had shot at him earlier that year, which he could not have known unless he was involved in the affair. (It was not until days later that Oswald's wife revealed that her husband was behind the Walker shooting.) When the Warren Commission asked Walker if he told the German paper that he felt Oswald had shot at him, he lied and vehemently denied it, understanding the trouble that admitting it could cause him.

In 1963, Oswald organized his own Fair Play for Cuba Chapter that had no members—a group the Warren Commission called "a product of his imagination." Nationally, FPCC had been under investigation since 1960 when Senator Eastland condemned it as a Communist organization. Eastland's war against FPCC went beyond the assertion that it was financed by the Communists or was pro-Castro. Two of the officers in the Los Angeles chapter of FPCC were long-time officers of SCEF—a nemesis of both Eastland and Banister. Through the SCEF connection to FPCC, Banister and Eastland aimed to show that SCEF was also Communist-affiliated in order to abolish it and imprison its officers under the Communist Control Act.

Oswald corresponded with the head of FPCC and, in the summer of 1963, began passing out FPCC literature on the streets of New Orleans, making a public spectacle of himself in the process. In August 1963, three anti-Castro Cubans feigned outrage at Oswald, and one, Carlos Bringuier, got into a halfhearted fight with Oswald—both men were arrested. Oswald was delighted by the arrest and the attention he garnered. That particular day, Oswald's FPCC leaflets bore the address of Guy Banister's office building, which was the first clue that the incident was contrived by the Banister operation. Moreover, the three Cubans had direct ties to Banister, which is further evidence of a contrived event. In total, Oswald had contact with six anti-Castro Cubans and all were tied to the Banister operation. The third piece of evidence demonstrating that Oswald's FPCC leafleting was phony was the fact that he reported the fight with the Cuban to the head of the FPCC eight days *before* it happened. After the fight, Cuban Carlos Bringuier sought a recommendation from Banister's close associate Kent Courtney for an attorney to assist him in his defense. Witnesses' accounts of seeing FPCC literature in Banister's office and in David Ferrie's home provide more evidence that Banister was behind the FPCC incident.

After Oswald's fight with Carlos Bringuier, he was invited to appear on a radio debate with Bringuier and Ed Butler. Like Bringuier, Butler was also an associate of Guy Banister and a frequent visitor to Banister's office (as was Oswald). Oswald admitted during the debate that he was a Marxist and that he had spent time in the Soviet Union, which was precisely the point of the debate. Butler was invited to play the tape before Senator Eastland's committee in Washington, D.C., on the Sunday following Kennedy's Friday assassination—the day Oswald was murdered.

Oswald also infiltrated a Tulane University leftist organization, the New Orleans Committee for Peaceful Alternatives (NOCPA), which was a ban-the-bomb group. Bruce Walzer, who was an attorney for SCEF, the ACLU and the Congress of Racial Equality, was a leader of the committee. While the group demonstrated, Kent Courtney, Carlos Bringuier, and associates of Guy Banister counter demonstrated. During NOCPA's parade on Canal Street, photos were taken of Oswald in the group. After the assassination, information on Oswald was gathered—by Louisiana authorities—for the Warren Commission, including the photos of Oswald in the parade. However, the photos of Oswald went missing and were likely purged during their transfer to the Warren Commission. (Several members of the state police, who were involved in the information-gathering process, had direct ties to Banister's operation.)

Oswald infiltrated another leftist group funded by SCEF, the Congress of Racial Equality (CORE), in August or September of 1963. Practically the whole town of Clinton, Louisiana, saw Oswald standing in a voter registration line with African Americans attempting to vote in a CORE voter drive, while the voter registrar, a Klansman, was denying them. David Ferrie and either Guy Banister or Clay Shaw drove Oswald to Clinton. At the same time, CORE had been enjoined by the town counsel and district judge and had been prohibited from demonstrating. After Oswald's visit, the town counsel declared that at least one Communist had infiltrated CORE in Clinton. It should come as no surprise that the town counsel was an associate of General Walker and Guy Banister. The voter registrar was also an associate of Guy Banister. Less than a year later, the district judge who enjoined CORE spoke with General Walker at a segregation rally in Baton Rouge, which is not far from Clinton. Similar to Oswald's infiltration of FPCC, ACLU, and NOCPA, Oswald's infiltration of the SCEF-tied CORE was intended to taint it as a Communist organization (during the hearings of Banister's Louisiana Committee on Un-American Activities in the fall of 1963), in order to help Banister's group prosecute their officers, put them in jail, and put their integration-related organizations out of business. All five of the theatrical incidents were designed by the Banister operation to enhance Oswald's credentials as a Communist in preparation for his incriminating testimony before Banister's Louisiana Un-American Activities Committee hearings to aid in the prosecution of SCEF, NOCPA, ACLU, and CORE officers under the Communist Control Act.

The Making of a Patsy: Walker's Recruitment of Oswald into the Assassination Conspiracy

While Lee Harvey Oswald and the segregationists were laying plans for—and nearing—a showdown with the integrationists by using the Communist Control Act as their weapon, the White House announced, on September 12, 1963, that President Kennedy would visit Dallas in November of 1963. General Walker must have realized that Oswald, one of his own men, with his accumulated faux Communist background and affiliations with several leftist groups, would make a superlative dupe to figure into the assassination conspiracy.

Soon after the announced trip, Oswald left Louisiana and traveled to the Cuban and Soviet embassies in Mexico City for the purported purpose of obtaining a visa to travel to the USSR by way of Cuba. When the embassies were unable to grant him a visa within his desired timeframe, Oswald reacted with a violent outburst, leaving a lasting memory of the event with the embassy staff. The FBI informant who learned in advance of the plans to kill the president, clearly stated that the plan was to lay the blame for the assassination on the Communists, which was served by Oswald's visits to the Cuban and Soviet embassies.

While there is no direct evidence related to how Walker convinced Oswald to incriminate himself as the assassin of the president, one theory best fits the known evidence. The theory postulates that Oswald was made to believe that someone would shoot a rifle from the sixth floor of the book depository and deliberately miss the president, similar to what happened in the Walker shooting incident. Oswald had been through similar theatrics before. It can be supposed that Oswald was assured that someone else would perform the sham shooting to ensure that Oswald could not be identified as the shooter. Oswald would then be picked up by the police and garner the publicity as the Communist who tried but failed to kill the president.

There are a number of scenarios by which Oswald could have been made to believe that he would be absolved of the shoot-and-miss of the president. If the shots were fired into the horizon and not recovered, there would be no ballistics match and—since no one would have seen Oswald shoot his weapon—the charges would not have stuck. In another scenario, the shooter would have assured Oswald he would use a different weapon, so that if any bullets were recovered they would not have fit the ballistic patterns of Oswald's rifle, and he would have been released. Other similar scenarios can be envisioned which could have convinced Oswald to go along with the plan.

General Walker left for New Orleans several days before the assassination and witnesses saw him with three Banister associates: Kent Courtney, Leander Perez, and a Banister employee who worked in his office in the building at 544 Camp Street, the address of which, on one occasion, appeared on Oswald's FPCC leaflets.

The Aftermath

After the Kennedy assassination, the FBI gathered reports that General Walker was plotting an overthrow of the U.S. and, by 1965, the FBI had notified the Secret Service on six separate occasions that Walker was a threat to the life of President Johnson.

In 1966, Jim Garrison, the district attorney of New Orleans, opened his own investigation into Kennedy's assassination, at least in part due to the fact that, following the assassination, Jack Martin—an employee of Guy Banister—told Garrison's office that David Ferrie, Oswald's Civil Air Patrol instructor, had a picture of Oswald at his home and that Ferrie had taught Oswald how to use a rifle. (Interestingly, on the day of the assassination, Ferrie made a suspicious trip to Houston, Texas.) Garrison questioned Ferrie and he denied the allegations; Martin then recanted, saying that he was drunk when he made the allegations against Ferrie. Later, Garrison gathered information from another source stating that Oswald and Ferrie were seen together in the summer of 1963. Garrison took Ferrie in for questioning again, in 1966, and according to Raymond Broshears, a close friend and confidant, Ferrie admitted that four associates of Guy Banister—General Walker, his financial backer H. L. Hunt, his speaking partner Billy James Hargis, and Carl McIntire—were behind the assassination.

Garrison conducted his secret investigation in 1966 using code names for his suspects: "Eddie Blue" for Edwin Walker and "Harry Blue" for H. L. Hunt. When Garrison's investigation became public in 1967 he proclaimed that the radical right, the Minutemen, and wealthy oilmen were involved in Kennedy's assassination. That allegation soon changed, however, and he dropped all references to the radical right and, instead, implicated the CIA, for which he had no credible evidence. Garrison could not have survived prosecuting the radical right, who had an underground army at their disposal that was actively committing murders of integrationists and African Americans during that era. It is worth noting that, although Garrison's public story changed, the author obtained Garrison's existing files from his family and most, if not all, pointed to the radical-right involvement in the assassination.

Three Informants

Three credible informants pointed the finger at General Walker. Joseph Milteer, who personally knew Walker, told the FBI informant about the earlier broad-based assassination plots and the high military command, including Walker, that would order them when the time came. Milteer predicted the assassination in exact detail thirteen days before it happened. Milteer appeared in a photo taken at the time of the assassination standing in Dealey Plaza beside a man who closely resembled the Klan's second in command, Melvin Sexton. After the murder, Milteer told the informant he did not do the shooting but that he did not mind watching it.

Harry Dean was a radical in the Minutemen and the John Birch Society in California and, like Oswald, infiltrated the FPCC to damage the organization. He personally knew Walker and knew he was the mastermind of the president's murder. Dean claims he told the FBI about it. In 1966, he appeared on the nationally televised late night television show, *The Tomorrow Show*, with a sack over his head and his voice disguised. He told the host that Walker, H. L. Hunt, and the John Birch Society were behind the assassination. Unfortunately, the show was never aired. Another of Dean's claims, that Ezra Taft Benson of Utah was involved in the conspiracy, suggests he had detailed inside information about those involved. (Milteer met with Benson in Salt Lake shortly before the murder. Suspiciously, Milteer also had a bank account in Provo, Utah, under an alias.)

Raymond Broshears, David Ferrie's friend and confidant, was the third person with inside knowledge implicating Walker in the murder plot.

End Game

Banister's Louisiana Un-American Activities Committee, in conjunction with Eastland's staff and state and local police, raided the SCEF offices on October 4, 1963. Three SCEF officers from the group that had ties to FPCC, the Louisiana ACLU, NOCPA, and CORE—all groups Oswald had infiltrated—were arrested and charged under the Communist Control Act. (By that time, Oswald had been figured into the assassination plans, but there was no certainty those plans would come to fruition or exclude him as a witness against the groups he infiltrated.) A huge legal battle ensued when SCEF fought back. The fight was ultimately taken to the United States Supreme Court, which ruled that the Communist Control Act was unconstitutional.

During the planning of the SCEF raid, on June 11, 1963, President Kennedy had proposed the Civil Rights Act, which would abolish segregation, and, if passed, would threaten the usefulness of the long-planned SCEF raid and related Communist Control Act as tools to maintain segregation. When the president was murdered, it was thought that the proposed Civil Rights Act would go down with him. President Johnson picked up the baton, however, and masterfully pushed the Civil Rights Act through Congress in 1964.

By the time the Civil Rights Act became law, Oswald had been murdered, Guy Banister had died of natural causes, and the attempt by General Walker and the segregationists to tie integration to Communism had failed. The battle to maintain segregation was lost forervermore.

THE DOCUMENTS

1. The Hubert Badeaux letter, 1957: The grooming of an infiltrator.

Sergeant Hubert Badeaux headed the New Orleans Police "Red Squad" under Guy Banister. Badeaux wrote the below letter to Willie Rainach in 1957. His signiture is on the letter but is not visble here. As was discussed in Chapters One, Nine, and Twenty-two, Lee Harvey Oswald fit the description of the infiltrator.[3905]

DEPARTMENT OF POLICE
2700 TULANE AVENUE

COLONEL PROVOSTY A. DAYRIES
SUPERINTENDENT

DEPUTY CHIEF ALBERT P. BLANCHER
SECRETARY

NEW ORLEANS, LA.

April 27, 1957

CHIEF GUY BANISTER
ASSISTANT SUPERINTENDENT

Sen. W.M. Rainach
P.O. Box 450
Homer, La.

Dear Senator Rainach;

I have finally completed the reading and correcting of the testimony; I am sorry to have taken so long, but the constant interruptions set me back more than once.

My trip to Doddsville and the conference with Senator Eastland, was, I believe, profitable for us. We should be getting a little more action in the near future. Mr Trice, (the Assistant D.A.) is giving me enough assistance to be considered an additional investigator which, of course, is more than welcome.

You can't imagine the effect which your Committee had on the Communist Party in Louisiana. Your stated intention to organize a State Intelligence Squad, coupled with the recent charges against members of the Party has the Daily Worker hysterical enough to come out with a tacit approval of the Smith Act! I am only sorry that the Party has become so completely demoralized that we shall have to scurry all over the countryside to collect the members for prosecution.

I have no intention, however, of relaxing my efforts in organizing and in expanding my counter-intelligence network. As small as it is now, it is still effective enough to command the respect of the Reds. I hope that you will be able to gain some sort of subsidy for my Division so that I can expand particularly in the direction of counter-attacking the Red effort to use minority groups and "liberal" fronts.

I have been in contact with an out-of-town person whom I have been grooming to come here to take over the establishment of infiltration into the University and intellectual groups. I will tell you in detail about this when I see you in person. There is another matter which I discussed with Bill Simmons, in Jackson, and which I don't care to put in writing at this time. I wish you would contact him as soon as you can so that you may be on guard.

On May 6, I will adress a group in Jackson and after the talk I will give another address on a T.V. hook-up. Bill arranged this, so you may be well aware of whom and what I propose to tear into.

You might mention to Mr. Shaw that Senator Eastland told us that this session of Congress intends to amend the Smith Act so that all of the State anti-Communist laws will be valid and operable. That will be all the more reason for having the State Squad. Let me hear from you at your convenience.

Sincerely,

2.   A letter from General Walker's mother discussing Kent Courtney and General Willoughby and their plan to visit Walker in Germany, July 23, 1961.

As was discussed in Chapter Twelve, Kent Courtney and General Willoughby planned to visit General Walker in Germany and offer him a paid position as a figurehead of the far right.[3906]

Center Point, Texas.
July 23,1961.

My very Dear Ted:

          Your note with nclosures was received and I take note that Clarke had talked on phone to Decker.I also see in the paper that Decker is going to Europe over the Berlin situation.I hope you will be given a command commensurate with your ability.To me - this is where you can be of most valuable service to our country.If the higher ups in Washington do not recognize the necessity for taking this action and you decide to resign, to keep yourself independent, you may decide is best.

          On Friday Mr. Courtney(Independent American*phoned George to say he wanted to come to Center Point to see him and his mother.They agreed that he would be met by George at the San Antonio Airport on Saturday morning.He arrived here about one fifteen and Helen had a wonderful dinner for the five of us.After much talk Mr. Courtney,he wanted to see Gen.Walker's home and family, and since having done so he felt that Gen.Walker is the man the country needs to rally the conservatives behind such a leader.When I asked just what his plan is he said-to put Gen.Walker on a salary plus commissions etc.for speaking engagements all over the country,to combat the election of liberals where ever they minght be up for election and defeat them with them conservatives.

          He said he one reason he came over here was to get George to introduce him to you by phone,that he and Gen.Willoughby planned to go to Germany to see you,next week.I asked if Gen.Willoughby had said he would go then it c came out that he wanted to line up Gen.Willoughby to do so,before having Geo. phone you.He also said that Gen Willoughby is short of funds and is under contract(with Hargis I think) till January.The inference given out was that Willoughby would be available to join him.This about Willoughby is nebulous as you can see from the above.After the above inconsistencies I said"Why don' you write your proposition to Gen.Walker?"He is quite a persuasive talker so you would get a clearer view of the situation on paper than free of his personality.After due consideration of his visit I feel that your independence would be curtailed if you joined up with his organization or any other. Lets hope you will not have to make such a vital decision as giving up your future in the Army where you have proven yourself to be of TOP value and may be needed in combat again. He said he would write you.

          Courtney said that there would be no war over Berlin,that this war scare is for the purpose of passing the Foreign Aid Bill.I said The Admenistration did not cause Kruschev to take his strong stand on Berlin.He said they always cause things to happen at the sychological moment to meet their ends.What is your opinion of Berlin question.?

          Courtney said "time is of the essence,to take advantage of your publicity".I wonder how many organizations want to use you to further their aims He mentioned that Hargis has the largest circulation of all conservative groups. He showed us your card that ended up saying "Though the (or my)(I/I, (I forget which you wrote)Heart is broken the steel is tempered".He uses this card in his speeches as a follow up of the soldier,sgt.letter of which he has a copy.

          I left him with my excuses of an engagement about four o'clock.As i came home from Coffee at the Nowlins about six I saw the Edsel leaving our entrance.Helen phoned at ten P.M. that they were staying all night with Sally and Bubs to return home in the morning.It has been raining and even a flood i San Antonio so I am glad they stayed. Aunt Bettie phoned that she and frien -s would be in to see me this morning.She certainly goes all out for you as do so many,many others. I do not know what George's reaction is to Mr. Courtney. I hope you are recovering from having gone over another heart break ridge and will come out of this experince with satisfaction in your heart,for having the intestinal fortitude to stand up for your ideals.

"Over"   greatest love always.   Mother

3. The Walker-Banister and McIntire-Banister meetings at the Capitol House Hotel.

Baton Rouge police detective Joe Cooper reported the meeting between Guy Banister and General Walker in 1963, as well as the meeting between Banister and Carl McIntire in 1964, as was noted in Chapters One, Nine, Nineteen, and Twenty-two. The third page shown in these images is the second page of a document that is missing its first page. [3907]

Botley

Baton Rouge,La.
June,12th,1968

I received your letter today concerning (A) Banister; (B)
National States Rights Party; (C) Fred Korth. On Banister I
met him at a Carl McIntire meeting in 1964. This was at the
Capitol House Hotel. I beleive he was introduced to me by Mr.
John East of Zachary La, or it was a Mr. George Ratliff of
Radio Station WYNK of Baton Rouge. I know it was one of them.
I had heard that he had a file on Oswald and I was interested
in this at that time.I am sending you some copies of some mat-
erial I had in my files on him. I also heard (not verified) that
Van Buskirk of Clinton was with him when he died. I sent Charles
Ward the material I had on him. The National States Rights Party
as far as can be determined only had a few members in Baton Rouge.
I have several of their News Papers that I am sending You to look
over. From what I read they are a wild bunch. One of the men who
puts out their lititure is Virgil Ford.He is a Vet.dog doctor and
has his office at 840 N 19th. St. Baton Rouge. A man Named Jay
Malbrough who had a T.V. show on WBRZ was a member. He wore the
States Rights Party Pin on his coat. He was called Count Ma.Cobb
on his show. Dr. Ford is also a big supporter of Dr.Carl McIntire,
and so was Ratliff. On Fred Korth I left Jim some Material on him
that I wanted back. The latest I have on him is that he left Fort
Worth shortly after the killing in Dallas. He is supposed to be
with a Law Firm in Washington D.C. He divorced his wife after 29
years of marrage. He has a girl friend who is the heir to Post
Cereal. Name is Merryweather. I am trying to verify this now.
Tell Jim I have some information on some guns that were stolen from
Houston Texas July 29th and recovered August 8th 1963 in Little Rock.
Two days later in Mandtville the F.B.I. got those You know about.
The ones in Ark. was 32 M-Rifles,parts of 7 carbines and I Machine
Gun with tripod. This was Govt.Property. Three Houston men were
arrested. Their names not known by me. I also came up with a good
picture of the two Cubens who showed up in New Orleans August 13th,
1963. I will not send this by mail,

4. Joseph Milteer, General Walker, and Robert Surrey meeting.

Joseph A. Milteer met with General Walker and Robert Surrey in Dallas in 1964.[3908]

Quitman, Ga.
June 6, 1964.

Dear Mr. Porth:

Just a few lines to let you and Mr. Smith know that I made the return trip safely and without too much tiredness.

I stopped in Dallas and talked to a Mr. R. A. Surrey, who is connected with the Johnston Printing Company, 2700 North Haskell in Dallas, Texas. Mr. Surrey and I were finishing our talk when the F. B. I. walked up and asked to speak to him. I had just given him some of my literature and he had it in his hands and then I bade him adee and went my way.

I left Mr. Surrey and went to call on Gen. Edwin A. Walker and we talked for about an hour. I left more literature with him and we exchanged different ideas of interest. One outstanding point brought out by Gen. Walker was a way and means to ruin and even destroy cars the niggers own. That is, ruin and destroy the motors so as to stop the niggers from riding. Just put a little destructive element in the crankcase when oil is added or changed that will cause the motor to " freeze-up " and be of no more use. (With-in 50 or 100 miles or so.)

I spoke to Mr. Surrey about you and your proposed books and he told me that his Company does book binding. We did not have time enough to go into details so I thought it best to write you and maybe he can help you in some way to put your books out at a reasonable figure. This you would have to work out with him. And I must add, this is merely a suggestion.

Also, may I suggest that you look at The Dan Smoot Report and see how he divides his written matter in the middle for easier reading. Using such a folder as Dan Smoot uses where-in it can be folded in the same manner as he folds his is very popular now. It makes for easy mailing and also carrying in the average pocket. And it cuts the costs way down, which is worth while in putting over you message about how to beat the Income Tax Racket, by the average person. Then by having it printed by someone connected with a large printing Company such as the one Mr. Surrey is connected with, might prove to be the advantage for you which you are looking for. All this is mentioned merely as a suggestion.

It was real nice visiting with you and Mr. Smith and the other gentlemen who dropped in while at your office. And may I again thank you for taking me to dinner (some call it lunch) and the fine food we had. I hope to repay you for your kindness in the future.

Give Mr. Smith my hearty " Hello and how are you, greeting ". Anything of interest you or Mr. Smith may have to alert me of or tell me about, please get in touch with me anytime.

I wish both of you the greatest of success and for you both to keep the good fight going, because this is our year to win and win we will with the help of a good and kind LORD and SAVIOUR JESUS CHRIST.

P. S.
The enclosed is the very latest
Mr. Surrey has put together and put
out. Just off the press.

Sincerely,

J. A. Milteer

J. A. Milteer.

5. Joseph Milteer's visit to the H. L. Hunt Company.

Joseph Milteer visited the H. L. Hunt Company, as was discussed in Chapter Eleven.[3909]

Reference copy, JFK Collection: HSCA (RG 233)

Valdosta, Ga.
May 22, 1965.

Dear Woody:

I have been notified that the Constitution Parties are having a Convention in Des Moines, Iowa, June 4th and 5th. I shall make my plans to attend although I am not certain of anything due to the small limited amount of cooperation I have received from Mr. Bert Ellis.

As I understand it, you are not going to be able to attend due to your working conditions. If there is anything you want me to bring up or call their attention to, how about writing me and outlining it to me so I can carry out your wishes.

To keep the record clear and not let it appear to be something different, I may either resign or be asked to resign after I get to the meeting. It makes little difference to me as I find it difficult to work alone and with little or no help from those you are working with. Of course I do not expect any monetary help, have not asked for any, but I did expect cooperation which I am sorry to report, has not been forthcoming. I believe had I been in or real close to Houston I would have had plenty of help. By mail it has been much different. These things I know you know all about so there is no use of me going over them.

I made a successful trip to Dallas, Texas and called on the H. L. Hunt Company and after another short trip I shall be in a position to make another report to you regarding SURVIVAL.

Anything you wish or want me to bring up at Des Moines let me know as soon as you can. I expect to leave here not later than June 2nd. driving.

Lula Belle joins with me in wishing you and your family the best of everything with GOD'S blessings.

Joe.

6.   General Walker's warning: Ruby might talk.

General Walker discussed his fear that Jack Ruby might talk when he was transferred from jail to Parkland Hospital in 1966, as was discussed in Chapter Seventeen. Walker vowed that Ruby would not leave Parkland alive.[3910]

Dec 28, 1966

Dear Billy,

Thanks so much for my wonderful briefcase. It is great and will be very useful--and I like to be carrying something from Christian Crusade. It gives me much more confidence.

I'm sorry I missed being with you, Betty and the kids for a few days as I had intended. My loss-- which I will have to make up. My plans were set--but shattered: I didn't feel it right to leave when the printer was a week late, and we did not get our Christmas publications until the 19th. After spending $1000 for print for this crash program, we had to get them out--about 3000--quite a task for us here. I believe it is timely with respect to the lawsuits and a coming Supreme Court decision. Clyde thought it was good.

Another peculiarity--with de Mohrenschildt returning to Dallas from Haiti as Rubenstein is allegedly dying with cancer (and might talk)--de M. made a front-page spread; and our informant produced his address and whom he is staying with-- not good.

A warning. When Rubenstein leaves the hospital in a box (the only way he will come out), there is no further "block" to returning the blame to the rightwing. The books and press will gradually pick it up again. RFK must have it-- it must be done, as insurance and assurance-- an RFK political necessity.

As you move toward more political freedom with the loss of tax exemption, keep in mind that political analysts and politicians are a dime a dozen. I would suggest you stay still in the field where you hurt them-- the true fundamental faith. It's full time (against NCC) and the field is wide open. Let others author your political beliefs and get them across by reprints of good editorials.

They can trap you into the political mire. This really has no day-to-day or even year-to-year solution; Christianity does. I am assuming a lot to advise you, but I see where your strength is as I travel. It is in "Christian Crusade." That is proved by their attacks.

I am convinced that there is a means by which "you represent 30 million people"-- on equal terms with E.C. Blake. You can make it work. The question is how. The answer: put those brains to work on your staff. Give them the project and tell them you want the solution.

Our thinking is the prey and victim of the church roof and building. I don't remember any building which Christ had.

7. General Walker places Marguerite Oswald under surveillance.

In 1969, during the Clay Shaw trial when Mrs. Oswald was claiming her son was framed, General Walker placed her under surveillance warning she should not be underestimated, as was discussed in Chapter Nineteen.[3911]

Fol. 1969
Jan 15-26

EDWIN A. WALKER
4011 TURTLE CREEK BLVD.
DALLAS, TEXAS 75219

Jan 15, 1969

Box 47

Marguerite Oswald being watched DL

Dear Tom,

H appy New Year to you and Caroline.

I am curious about your report on the Admiral's dining with a well known friend in Hawaii when he got word to reverse his order on taking the Pueblo back. I would like to know who the friend was--or if you had rather not, don't tell me. Or let me know whether it is in confidence.

You may not have seen this on the Scorpion. It was obvious, but I am surprised to see it in print.

Have been using a few copies of the other reprint to my lawyers, so en-close one for you. Mrs. M. Oswald should never be underestimated. We watch her moves closely. I think the Onassis marriage proved one thing--Onassis is Red. With the accusation of "extremist" on us--the Free Press outdoes us. See the enclosed and also note the ads. there in.

Republicans would emphasize the disgrace to Nixon. I, rather, put the emphasis on the disgrace to the flag.

You may find a means to a reversal of the score.... I note Bob's MOTOREDE and had heard a speech by Drake here two months ago. While I am for complete opposition and a real fight in taking the culprits to task in this area, I do not believe we should do it with words, terms and ex-pressions that are not graceful in writing or in public audiences. Other-wise, we are producing a common-ality in our own method. If our grand parents were prudes, then I like prudes.

No doubt, with the ignorance within the Wallace staff "cause-wise," there was quite a problem there that involved all of us who knew more than his help did. I can only admire his holdout against them,and those within, who would have had him play the press game in accepting the press' ene-mies.

I spent two weeks Christmas at home (county seat--Kerrville), where I visit with Dick Moran. We believe LeMay is through. Of course, I think it was way over his head, while I must admire Wallace again for the final choice. It was a choice well recognized in every foreign capital.(not here).

Of course if he is out of the effort, it is hard on Wallace to have the other half disappear in seclusion. Of course, he never made it clear why he accepted, and I don't believe he could because he didn't know enough about what the fight is all about.... All water under the dam; but still affecting the future--Wallace's future--which worries me. He sacrificed so much.
This is a bit rambling, but we have plenty to rabble through--in my opin-ion, we will have more.
    Best regards to you and Caroline.
                                      Sincerely,

                                      Ted.

8.   The allegation that Larrie Schmidt and his brother drove Lee Harvey Oswald to the shooting scene at General Walker's home.

As was discussed in Chapter Fourteen, Larrie Schmidt's brother worked as General Walker's chauffer.[3912]

TEXAS' LEADING NEWSPAPER

The Dallas Morning News

December 29, 1977

Mr. Edwin A. Walker
4011 Turtle Creek Blvd.
Dallas, Texas 75219

Dear Mr. Walker:

I received a copy of the material you sent to
Tip O'Neill and others. It may open some eyes and I hope
it does. I am especially interested in Marina's message
on the back of the photograph which you say was dated five
days before the shot fired at you by her husband.

A friend of Larry Schmidt's recently told me that
Larry and his brother, who he says was then associated with you,
had accompanied Oswald in the brother's car to the scene of
the shooting. Larry Schmidt supposedly has protected himself
since that time by placing written accounts of this story
in safe deposit boxes around the country.

I also wonder if you know there is any truth to
a story that Delessips Morrison, former New Orleans mayor,
had a hand in forcing you to retire as an army general in
West Germany. If his name rings a bell as an agent of JFK in
such a mission, this may open some new doors. Morrison was
reactivated into the military as a favor to JFK, I was told,
in an effort to get at you in the Blue Book controversy.
He was killed in an airplane explosion over Mexico about
four months after the assassination.

Yours truly,

Earl Golz

OVER

WP 9'

COMMUNICATIONS CENTER, DALLAS, TEXAS 75222, TELEPHONE (214) 745-8222

ACKNOWLEDGMENTS

Bill O'Neil made many significant contributions to this work. I relied on Bill for his expertise on the Warren Commission and general assassination literature. Bill and I traveled extensively, scouring the papers of the radical right in archives across the country.

The research of Claude B. Slaton, a Louisiana native and local historian, was vital to my understanding of Lee Harvey Oswald's visit to Clinton, Louisiana. Romney Stubbs, another Louisiana native, familiarized me with the political figures in this book, like Willie Rainach and Leander Perez, and shared his research, which was invaluable.

Head Archivist Mary Linn Wernet at Northwestern State University of Louisiana Library, went beyond the call of duty providing me with the papers of Kent Courtney on my two visits, among other materials essential to this work—Many thanks! My deepest gratitude goes to Gerald Baumgarten of the Anti-Defamation League Research Department in New York, who had an unparalleled knowledge of the radicals in this work and freely opened his files to me.

The National Archives and the Freedom of Information Act office of the FBI were as responsive, professional, and courteous as anyone could hope.

Very special thanks to my dear friend and former classmate, David H. Rubin, M. D., for his indispensible help and guidance. When the going got tough I could always count on him for an enouraging word. I am also grateful to accomplished writers Scott Lax and Ted Mooney who generously advised me on this undertaking.

I am more than grateful to Matt Tomich for the massive hours spent superbly critiquing, correcting, and formatting the book.

There were several individuals who freely and graciously provided me with the unique fruits of their labor. Thanks to Andy Kiel, Steve Roy, Dave Boylan, Thomas Becnel and Stephen Tyler for sharing your fine work with me.

Thanks to you who requested anonymity, which I understand completely. This work owes so much to you for your moral support, intellectual stimulation, and coaching at each step along the way.

Love and gratitude to Charlie Rubin who did a great job on the preliminary cover design and photo editing, and to Mathew Wagner for image formatting and other technical assistance.

NOTES

GUIDE TO CITED ARCHIVAL SOURCES

The documents from the investigation by New Orleans district attorney (NODA) Jim Garrison are found in several collections in the National Archives II, including the donated, unprocessed papers of William Wood, William Wegmann, and Lyon Garrison. William Wood often redacted the dates and the names of the investigators from the documents. Jim Garrison also furnished copies of some of his investigative reports to the House Select Committee on Assassinations (HSCA), which are indexed on the National Archives JFK Collection website.

The Brooks County Probate Court (BCPC) in Quitman, Georgia, holds nine boxes of assorted letters from Joseph Milteer's estate that were left behind by the House Select Committee on Assassinations. The author obtained a court order to view them. Information gathered from those files is simply identified by "BCPC" in the following notes.

The following conventions were used throughout the following pages:

Warren Commission Report (typically followed by a page number) refers to the actual summary report filed by the Commission.

Warren Commission followed by Roman and Arabic numerals (such as "XX, 21") refers to a volume ("XX") and page ("21") of the Commission's ancillary materials and evidence. Other Warren Commission information is listed as it was found.

Files from the House Special Committee on Assassinations (HSCA) follow the same conventions as those listed, above, for the Warren Commission.

Records from government agencies such as the John F. Kennedy Assassination Records Collection, National Archives and Records Administration (NARA) are listed by their file reference numbers (these numbers vary in length, depending upon the agency).

Listings beginning with "FBI FOIA" (or simply "FOIA") and followed by a name or search term refer to items retrieved by the author through requests to the listed agency (such as "FBI") under the Freedom of Information Act ("FOIA"), using the supplied search term.

Many of the personal papers at various archives are unprocessed, unfortunately, and there is no specific way to find them other than to search the entire collection.

Abbreviations used:

> AARC – Assassination Archives and Research Center
>
> ADL – Anti-Defamation League
>
> BCPC – Brooks County Probate Court, Quitman, Georgia
>
> FOIA – Freedom of Information Act (this indicates any files which were only made available through the eponymous federal act)
>
> HSCA – House Special Committee on Assassinations
>
> NARA – National Archives and Records Administration
>
> NODA – New Orleans District Attorney
>
> SISS – Senate Internal Security Subcommittee

Chapter 1

1   Brochure from Guy Banister Associates, Inc., deLesseps Morrison Papers, New Orleans Public Library.

2   Ken Duvio (grandson of Guy Banister), interview by the author, November 13, 2004.

3   File 12-3-2, William Wood Papers, The John F. Kennedy Assassination Records Collection, NARA.

4   *Times–Picayune*, January 5, 1955.

5   *Times–Picayune*, January 14, 1955.

6   Ibid.

7   Brochure from Guy Banister Associates, Inc., deLesseps Morrison Papers, New Orleans Public Library.

8   Letter from Provosty Dayries, June 4, 1957, deLesseps Morrison Papers, New Orleans Public Library.

9   *Times–Picayune*, March 1, 1964

10 DeLesseps Morrison Papers, New Orleans Public Library.

11 124-10193-10384, The John F. Kennedy Assassination Records Collection, NARA.

12 Lou Ivon, interview by the author, October 5, 2000.

13 Lester Ottilio, interview by the author, January 31, 1967, New Orleans district attorney (NODA).

14 180-10112-10361, The John F. Kennedy Assassination Records Collection, NARA.

15 180-10080-10204, The John F. Kennedy Assassination Records Collection, NARA.

16 Notes from Hoke May, a New Orleans *States–Item* reporter who met with Guy Banister's close friend Ivan Nitschke, May 11, 1967, NODA.

17 *Times–Picayune*, May 23, 1964.

18 Gift to the "Assassination Archives" from Earl Golz, December 30, 1986, Assassination Archives and Records Center.

19   180-10112-10373, The John F. Kennedy Assassination Records Collection, NARA.

20   180-10088-10058, The John F. Kennedy Assassination Records Collection, NARA.

21   "Record of Conversation with Robert K. Brown, July 17, 1968," NODA.

22   Robert DePugh, interviews by the author, December 17, 1999, and May 11, 2000.

23   William Wood Papers, The John F. Kennedy Assassination Records Collection, NARA.

24   Bill Turner, memo, October 4, 1967, NODA.

25   Notes from Hoke May, May 11, 1967, NODA.

26   180-10112-10367, The John F. Kennedy Assassination Records Collection, NARA.

27   180-10007-210214, The John F. Kennedy Assassination Records Collection, NARA.

28   180-10065-10330, The John F. Kennedy Assassination Records Collection, NARA.

29   S.A. BG-4951 report to the Louisiana State Police, Hale Boggs Papers, Howard-Tilton Memorial Library at Tulane University, courtesy of Romney Stubbs.

30   Mary Brengel, interview by the author, June 25, 1996.

31   Bill Boxley, memo on an interview with an unidentified informant, September 30, 1968, NODA.

32   Edward F. Wegmann Papers, The John F. Kennedy Assassination Records Collection, NARA.

33   Emile Stopper, interview by Douglas Ward, December 30, 1966, NODA.

34   180-10072-10047, The John F. Kennedy Assassination Records Collection, NARA.

35   Louise Decker McMullen, interview by HSCA, May 12, 1978.

36   Louise Decker McMullen, interview by Douglas Ward, January 31, 1967, NODA.

37   Lawrence Melville, interview by Jim Garrison, February 5, 1967, NODA.

38   180-10082-10170, The John F. Kennedy Assassination Records Collection, NARA.

39   180-10082-10166, The John F. Kennedy Assassination Records Collection, NARA.

40   *Times–Picayune*, March 9, 1962.

41   *Times–Picayune*, April 9, 1956.

42   SISS, "Scope of Soviet Activity in the United States" hearing, March 10, 1956.

43   *Times–Picayune*, March 30, 1956.

44   *Times–Picayune*, March 13, 1956.

45   *Times–Picayune*, March 22, 1956.

46   *States–Item*, March 23, 1956.

47   *New Orleans States–Item*, March 23, 1956.

48   SISS, "Scope of Soviet Activity in the United States" hearing.

49   *Plaquemines Gazette*, May 12, 1956.

50   *Time*, November 26, 1956.

51   Kent Courtney, letter to Willie Rainach, Rainach Papers, Noel Memorial Library, Louisiana State University Shreveport.

52   180-10100-10127, The John F. Kennedy Assassination Records Collection, NARA.

53   Guy Banister, letter to Willie Rainach, July 30, 1958, Rainach Papers, Noel Memorial Library, Lousiana State University Shreveport.

54   180-10096-10010, The John F. Kennedy Assassination Records Collection, NARA.

55   Guy Banister, letter to Willie Rainach, April 26, 1960, Rainach Papers, Noel Memorial Library, Lousiana State University Shreveport.

56   Sovereignty Commission Papers, Mississippi State Archives.

57   180-10097-10214, The John F. Kennedy Assassination Records Collection, NARA.

58   Louisiana Sovereignty Commission brochure, Ellender Archives, Nicholls State University, 23 FF, 1132.

59   *Plaquemines Gazette*, October 7, 1960.

60   *Times–Picayune*, April 6, 1957.

61   *Times–Picayune*, March 27, 1956.

62   Ross Banister, interview by Andrew Sciambra, February 2, 1967, NODA.

63   *States–Item*, July 19, 1959.

64   *Times–Picayune*, June 14, 1960.

65   *Times–Picayune*, March 5, 1958.

66   *States–Item*, September 22, 1960 and September 28, 1960.

67   Jack Rogers, letters to Willie Rainach, March 2, 1959, and April 6, 1959, Rainach Papers, Noel Memorial Library, Lousiana State University Shreveport.

68   Ross Banister, interview by Andrew Sciambra, February 2, 1967, NODA.

69   Record number 7810370, Agency file number 009262, HSCA, NARA.

70   180-10097-10490, The John F. Kennedy Assassination Records Collection, NARA.

71   180-10078-10371, The John F. Kennedy Assassination Records Collection, NARA.

72   180-10078-10369, The John F. Kennedy Assassination Records Collection, NARA.

73   180-10072-10214, The John F. Kennedy Assassination Records Collection, NARA.

74   Joseph Oster, interview by the author, October 14, 1999.

75   Frank Donner, *The Age of Surveillance: The Aims & Methods of America's Political Intelligence System* (New York: Alfred Knopf, 1980), 34.

76   Mary Brengel, interview by the author, June 25, 1996.

77   Donner, *The Age of Surveillance*, 23.

78   Ibid.

79   Donner, *The Age of Surveillance*, 422.

80   Robert DePugh, interviews by the author, December 17, 1999, and May 11, 2000.

81   Paul Rothermel, interview by the author, March 15, 2000.

82   Donner, *The Age of Surveillance*, footnote, 249

83   *Dallas Morning News*, July 1, 1961.

84   William Wood Papers, The John F. Kennedy Assassination Records Collection, NARA.

85   Donner, *The Age of Surveillance*, 430.

86   Donner, *The Age of Surveillance*, 419.

87   Mary Brengel, interview by the author, June 25, 1996.

88   Donner, *The Age of Surveillance*, 425.

89   Donner, *The Age of Surveillance*, xii.

90   Jim Garrison, *On the Trail of Assassins* (New York: Sheridan Square Press, 1988), 38.

91   180-10112-10373, The John F. Kennedy Assassination Records Collection, NARA.

92   Tommy Baumler, interview, May 5, 1968, NODA.

93   Mary Brengel, interview by Jim Garrison, undated, NODA.

94   *The Sign*, June 1952, cited in *Counterattack*.

95   *Counterattack*, Ohio State Historical Society

96   Ivan Nitschke, interview, May 11, 1967, NODA.

97   180-10112-10371, The John F. Kennedy Assassination Records Collection, NARA.

98   Note from David Ferrie's apartment regarding Billie Dalzell and the files, NODA.

99   Letter to "Dear Member" with enclosed 1959 Citizens' Council membership with Guy Banister's name on it, William Wood Papers, The John F. Kennedy Assassination Records Collection, NARA.

100   124-10285-10298, The John F. Kennedy Assassination Records Collection, NARA.

101   *Times–Picayune*, February 26, 1961.

102   180-10100-10127, The John F. Kennedy Assassination Records Collection, NARA.

103   D. A. White, letter to Guy Banister, undated, NODA.

104   Victor Schiro Papers, New Orleans Public Library.

105   Mary Brengel, interview by the author, June 25, 1996.

106   *Conservative Viewpoint* 2, no. 125 and 126, NODA.

107   *Shreveport Journal*, May 11, 1963.

108   *Shreveport Journal*, May 14, 1963.

109   Banister file 14-41, NODA.

110   *Times–Picayune*, October 27, 1961 and September 22, 1961.

111   180-10023-10380, The John F. Kennedy Assassination Records Collection, NARA.

112   180-10100-10127, The John F. Kennedy Assassination Records Collection, NARA.

113   Betty Parrott, interview by Andrew Sciambra, March 31, 1967, NODA.

114   180-10106-10059, The John F. Kennedy Assassination Records Collection, NARA.

115   180-10078-10414, The John F. Kennedy Assassination Records Collection, NARA.

116   Garrison, *On the Trail of Assassins*, 25.

117   *Times–Picayune*, January 21, 1962.

118   John Irion, statement, January 30, 1967, NODA.

119   "Interview with Cubans by Mr. Jim Garrison, Mr. Fowler, et al.," December 26, 1966, NODA.

120   Ronnie Caire, interview, January 23, 1967, NODA.

121   180-10141-10365, The John F. Kennedy Assassination Records Collection, NARA.

122   Warren Commission, XX, 830.

123   Warren Commission, XXII, 228–9.

124   104-10127-10088, The John F. Kennedy Assassination Records Collection, NARA.

125   104-10528-10337, The John F. Kennedy Assassination Records Collection, NARA.

126   Warren Commission, Document 87, 540.

127 124-11093-10111, The John F. Kennedy Assassination Records Collection, NARA.

128 180-10141-10365, The John F. Kennedy Assassination Records Collection, NARA.

129 Anthony Summers, *Conspiracy* (New York: McGraw-Hill, 1980), 318–319.

130 180-10091-10228, The John F. Kennedy Assassination Records Collection, NARA.

131 Arnesto Rodriguez, Jr., interview by James Alcock, February 13, 1967.

132 124-10058-10076, The John F. Kennedy Assassination Records Collection, NARA.

133 *HSCA Report*, 141.

134 180-10112-10369, The John F. Kennedy Assassination Records Collection, NARA.

135 *HSCA Report*, 141.

136 *States–Item*, May 21, 1963.

137 HSCA, X, 62.

138 Warren Commission, XXVI, 581.

139 Rudolph Ricardo Davis, interview by William Gurvich, March 22, 1967, NODA.

140 124-10369-10045, The John F. Kennedy Assassination Records Collection, NARA.

141 Robert DePugh, interviews by the author, December 17, 1999, and May 5, 2000.

142 180-10023-10380, The John F. Kennedy Assassination Records Collection, NARA.

143 George Higginbotham [sic], interview by Barbara Glancey Reid, March 12, 16, 17, 1968, NODA.

144 Anonymous, letter to Jim Garrison, undated, NODA.

145 Summers, *Conspiracy*, 326.

146 Oswald HQ File, 105-8244, Section 12, no. 89–69.

147 180-10069-10445, The John F. Kennedy Assassination Records Collection, NARA.

148 Sam Newman, interview, September 7, 1967, NODA.

149 180-10112-10369, The John F. Kennedy Assassination Records Collection, NARA.

150 180-10097-10494, The John F. Kennedy Assassination Records Collection, NARA.

151 Peter Noyes, *Legacy of Doubt* (New York: Pinnacle Books, 1973).

152 180-10082-10169, The John F. Kennedy Assassination Records Collection, NARA.

153 Sgt. Fenner Segebeer, "Special Investigation: William Guy Banister," Jan. 10, 1967.

154 Orleans Parish autopsy report, NODA

155 Warren Commission, VIII, 217.

156 Warren Commission, Document 188.

157 124-10035-10122, The John F. Kennedy Assassination Records Collection, NARA.

158 James R. Lewallen, interview by James Alcock, February 20, 1967, NODA.

159 Summers, *Conspiracy*, 150.

160 Warren Commission, Document 87, 394.

161 180-10112-10362, The John F. Kennedy Assassination Records Collection, NARA.

162 "Time and Propinquity," Smith File, January 10, 1967, NODA.

163 180-10019-10334, The John F. Kennedy Assassination Records Collection, NARA.

164 David Lewis, letters to NODA, NODA.

165 Tom Bethel, diary, William Wood Papers, The John F. Kennedy Assassination Records

Collection, NARA.

166 Tom Bethel, "Recapitulation of Actvity in New Orleans," NODA.

167 180-10117-10075, The John F. Kennedy Assassination Records Collection, NARA.

168 Summers, *Conspiracy*, 342.

169 Summers, *Conspiracy*, 332–3.

170 Earl Golz, notes, gift to the "Assassination Archives," December 30, 1986, Assassination Archives and Records Center.

171 180-10078-10089, The John F. Kennedy Assassination Records Collection, NARA.

172 179-20002-10282, The John F. Kennedy Assassination Records Collection, NARA.

173 Summers, *Conspiracy*, 325.

174 Summers, *Conspiracy*, 364–5

175 *HSCA Report*, 218.

176 180-10101-10105, The John F. Kennedy Assassination Records Collection, NARA.

177 180-10067-10294, The John F. Kennedy Assassination Records Collection, NARA.

178 Summers, *Conspiracy*, 254–6.

179 *HSCA Report*, 218.

180 Allen Campbell, interview by the author, September 22, 1996.

181 Summers, *Conspiracy*, 322.

182 Al Campbell, interview by Andrew Sciambra, May 14, 1969, NODA.

183 Dan Campbell, interview by the author, July 30, 1996.

184 Summers, *Conspiracy*, 322.

185 180-10072-10047, The John F. Kennedy Assassination Records Collection, NARA.

186 Adrian Alba, interview by HSCA, January 24, 1978.

187 *Lousiana History*, XXI, no. 1, 7–42.

188 Michael Kurtz, letter to author, March 11, 1996.

189 Ibid.

190 180-10076-10178, The John F. Kennedy Assassination Records Collection, NARA.

191 Barbara Glancey Reid, April 12, 16, 17, 1968, NODA.

192 Robert DePugh, interviews by the author, December 17, 1999, and May 11, 2000.

193 Jack S. Martin, statement, December 26, 1966, NODA.

194 180-10023-10380, The John F. Kennedy Assassination Records Collection, NARA.

195 180-10104-10278, The John F. Kennedy Assassination Records Collection, NARA, 18.

196 Record number 12110016, Agency file number 014888, Box 284, HSCA.

197 Rosemary James and Jack Wardlaw, *Plot or Politics* (New Orleans: Pelican Publishing House, 1967), 110–111.

198 United States Senate Select Committee to Study Governmental Operations with Respect to Intelligence Activities.

199 157-10014-10120, The John F. Kennedy Assassination Records Collection, NARA.

200 124-10115-10062, The John F. Kennedy Assassination Records Collection, NARA.

201   Summers, *Conspiracy*, 326.

202   Garrison, *On the Trail of Assassins*.

203   William Wood Papers, The John F. Kennedy Assassination Records Collection, NARA.

204   Garrison, *On the Trail of Assassins*.

205   180-10020-10088, The John F. Kennedy Assassination Records Collection, NARA.

206   *HSCA Report*, 140–147.

207   *HSCA Report*, 365.

208   Gaeton Fonzi, *The Last Investigation* (New York: Thunder's Mouth Press, 1993).

209   Gary Hart, speech at the Assassination Archives and Research Center Conference, November 19, 2005, Washington, D.C.

210   G. Robert Blakey and Richard Billings, *The Plot to Kill the President* (New York: Times Books, 1981), 145.

211   *HSCA Report*, 145.

Chapter 2

212   180-10121-10083, The John F. Kennedy Assassination Records Collection, NARA.

213   Brother Gregory Franz, interview by the author at Carthegena, Ohio, November 11, 1992. A former student of David Ferrie's in the 1930s, and a long-time family friend of the Ferries, Brother Greg told the author that he fondly recalled driving to a public square in downtown Cleveland on V-J Day to celebrate along with Dave and his brother. At Parmely's wedding, his bride wore the parachute that saved his life, which had been made into a dress. Dave and Brother Greg played in the orchestra. On one occasion, while driving out of the school driveway at an apparent high rate of speed, Ferrie rolled his car over.

214   *The Bennet*, Benedictine High School (Cleveland, Ohio) newspaper, October 4, 1946.

215   Summers, *Conspiracy*, 143.

216   180-10076-10017, The John F. Kennedy Assassination Records Collection, NARA.

217   Garrison, *On the Trail of Assassins*.

218   Warren Commission, Document 75, 285–297.

219   James Kirkwood, *American Grotesque: An Account of the Clay Shaw-Jim Garrison Kennedy Assassination Trial in New Orleans* (New York: Harper Perennial, 1968), 128.

220   CIA, D-001715.

221   *Playboy*, 14, no. 10, October 1967.

222   David Ferrie, interview by Frank Klein, December 15, 1969, NODA.

223   Joseph S. Newbrough, Jr., interview by NODA, William Woods Papers, The John F. Kennedy Assassination Records Collection, NARA.

224   124-10115-10060, The John F. Kennedy Assassination Records Collection, NARA.

225   Jules Ricco Kimble, interview, October 10, 1967, NODA.

226   Allen Campbell, interview by the author, September 22, 1996.

227 Citizens' Council Board roster, Ned Touchstone Papers, Noel Memorial Library, Louisiana State University Shreveport.

228 *Councilor*, May 5, 1966.

229 *Times–Picayune*, October 3, 1963.

230 Joan Mellen, *Farewell to Justice* (Dulles, Virginia: Potomac Books, 2005), 34.

231 Stephen Jaffe, memo, August 6, 1968, NODA.

232 Warren Commission, Exhibit 1413.

233 James and Wardlaw, *Plot or Politics*.

234 John Irion, statement, January 30, 1967, NODA.

235 *Baton Rouge State Times*, February 24, 1967.

236 124-10261-10071, The John F. Kennedy Assassination Records Collection, NARA.

237 Arnesto Rodriguez, Jr., interview by James Alcock and Andrew Sciambra, February 13 1967, NODA.

238 157-10014-10120, The John F. Kennedy Assassination Records Collection, NARA.

239 180-10121-10084, The John F. Kennedy Assassination Records Collection, NARA.

240 Lynn Loisel, report of phone calls from Jimmie Johnson, January 11, 1967, NODA.

241 Al Cheramie, interview by NODA, William Woods Papers, The John F. Kennedy Assassination Records Collection, NARA.

242 Thomas Compton, interview by Sergeant Tom Duffy and Ptn. Cliency Navarre, March 10, 1967, NODA.

243 Roy Tell, interview by Fenner Segebeer, February 28, 1967, NODA.

244 *Times–Picayune*, 8-29-61

245 Investigation notes, New Orleans Police Department, Juvenile Bureau, August 18, 1961, Item H-850761, NODA.

246 David William Ferrie, affadavit, NODA.

247 Robert E. Lee, memo to Jim Garrison, July 12, 1967, NODA.

248 Herbet R. Wagner, statement, December 6, 1967, NODA.

249 180-10117-10151, The John F. Kennedy Assassination Records Collection, NARA

250 Herbert Wagner, Jr., interview, December 8, 1967, NODA.

251 180-10097-10345, The John F. Kennedy Assassination Records Collection, NARA.

252 Warren Commission, Exhibit 99.

253 *Times–Picayune*, March 5, 1958.

254 Courtney Papers, Special Collections, Northwestern State University of Lousiana.

255 Kent Courtney, letter to Tom Anderson, July 29, 1959, Tom Anderson Papers, Special Collections, University of Oregon Library.

256 Mary Cain Papers, Mississippi Department of Archives and History, Box 28.

257 "New Party" flier, Courtney Papers, Special Collections, Northwestern State University of Louisiana.

258 Dan Smoot, *People Along the Way* (Tyler: Tyler Press, 1993).

259 *Summit Sun*, September 1956.

260   *The Citizen*, March 18–24, 1966, Ned Touchstone Papers, Noel Memorial Library, Louisiana State University Shreveport.

261   *The Independent American*, Wilcox Collection, RH WL Eph 2372.2.

262   *Look*, 26, no. 6, March 13, 1962.

263   Citizens' Council Board, Ned Touchstone Papers, Noel Memorial Library, Louisiana State University Shreveport.

264   *Louisiana History*, XXI, no. 1.

265   *The Independent American,* June 1963.

266   Raymond Broshears, memo to Jim Garrison, August 8, 1968, NODA.

267   "Committee to Free Cuba" flier, William Wood Papers, The John F. Kennedy Assassination Records Collection, NARA.

268   *Times–Picayune*, March 27, 1956.

269   105-82555-524, The John F. Kennedy Assassination Records Collection, NARA.

270   Kent Courtney and Jerry Ray, tape recording, Courtney Papers, Special Collections, Northwestern State University of Louisiana.

271   124-10285-1035, The John F. Kennedy Assassination Records Collection, NARA.

272   Lester Ottilio, interview by Jim Garrison, January 31, 1967, NODA.

273   Delphine Roberts, interview, January 19, 1967, NODA.

274   180-10097-10214, The John F. Kennedy Assassination Records Collection, NARA.

275   *Times–Picayune*, November 3, 1961.

276   *Times–Picayune*, December 14, 1961.

277   124-10285-10312, The John F. Kennedy Assassination Records Collection, NARA.

278   *Times–Picayune*, December 14, 1961.

279   *Times–Picayune*, November 13, 1958.

280   *Times–Picayune*, December 13, 1958.

281   *Times–Picayune*, May 7, 1960.

282   Ibid.

283   Tom Anderson Papers, Special Collections, University of Oregon Library.

284   180-10097-10214, The John F. Kennedy Assassination Records Collection, NARA.

285   Delphine Roberts, letter to the editor of the *Times–Picayune*, featured in the *Times–Picayune*, November 18, 1958.

286   *Shreveport Journal*, July 27, 1963.

287   *Times–Picayune*, August 25, 1963.

288   180-10097-10214, The John F. Kennedy Assassination Records Collection, NARA.

289   180-10113-10434, William Wood Papers, The John F. Kennedy Assassination Records Collection, NARA.

290   Summers, *Conspiracy*, 335.

Chapter 3

291   Lester Ottilio, interview, January 31, 1967, NODA.

292 Rainach Papers, April 23, 1958, Noel Memorial Library, Lousiana State University Shreveport.

293 George Lincoln Rockwell, *This Time the World* (1961), from the University of Wyoming Library.

294 Ibid.

295 A. M. Rosenthal and Arthur Gelb, *One More Victim: The Life and Death of an American Jewish Nazi* (New York: The New American Library, 1967).

296 City Directory, New Orleans Public Library.

297 Banister biography, Morrison Papers, Louisiana Division, New Orleans Public Library.

298 Joseph Oster, interview by the author, October 14, 1999.

299 John Smith, *Birch Putsch* (Domino Publications, n. pl., 1963).

300 *The Federationist*, Morrison Papers, Lousiana Division, New Orleans Public Library.

301 Rosenthal and Gelb, *One More Victim*, 106

302 180-10023-10380, The John F. Kennedy Assassination Records Collection, NARA.

303 Jack Martin, affidavit, February 20, 1967.

304 *The Citizen*, November 1956.

305 Citizens' Council Director's minutes, Touchstone Papers, Lousiana State University Shreveport.

306 George Higginbotham [sic], interviews by Barbara Glancey Reid, March 12, 16, and 17, 1968, NODA.

307 Allen Campbell, interview by the author, September 22, 1996.

308 George Higginbotham [sic] and Tom Baumler, interview, May 13, 1968, NODA.

309 Harold Weisberg, interviews by the author, September 18, 1996, and May 18, 2000.

310 *Dallas Morning News*, May 24, 1961.

311 Rosenthal and Gelb, *One More Victim*.

312 Dixiecrats roster, Mississippi Department of Archives and History.

313 FBI FOIA, George Lincoln Rockwell, file number 105-70374.

314 *Facts-274*, ADL, 1963.

315 George Higginbotham [sic] and Tom Baumler, interview, May 13, 1968, NODA.

316 FBI FOIA, Bluford Balter, file numbers: NO 157-31, BU 105-7374.

317 Warren Commission, Exhibit 1963.

318 124-10184-10329, The John F. Kennedy Assassination Records Collection, NARA.

319 Rosenthal and Gelb, *One More Victim*.

320 FBI Bufile, 157-537.

321 124-10158-10427, The John F. Kennedy Assassination Records Collection, NARA.

322 124-10184-10329, The John F. Kennedy Assassination Records Collection, NARA, 8.

323 "Probable NSRP make-up for three cities," November 5, 1967, NODA.

324 Rosenthal and Gelb, *One More Victim*.

325 *New York Times*, October 31, 1965.

326 John Roy Carlson, *Undercover* (New York: E.P. Dutton and Co., 1943).

327   Rosenthal and Gelb, *One More Victim*.

328   Patsy Sims, *The Klan* (New York: Stein and Day, 1978), 291.

329   *New York Times*, November 1, 1965.

330   180-10021-10200, The John F. Kennedy Assassination Records Collection, NARA.

331   180-10078-10023, The John F. Kennedy Assassination Records Collection, NARA.

332   FBI FOIA, Ray Leahart, file number 157-2965, AX 157-624.

333   FBI FOIA, Ray Leahart, file number 157-2965-1.

334   George Higginbotham [sic], interviews by Barbara Glancey Reid, March 12, 16, and 17, 1968, NODA.

335   *The Thunderbolt*, October 1961, Mary Cain Papers, Mississippi Department of Archives and History, JA47.

336   Willie Rainach, letter to Ray Leahart, August 31, 1961, Rainach Letters, Louisiana State University Shreveport, 11.

337   FBI FOIA, Ray Leahart, file number 157-2965.

338   Frederick J. Simonelli, *American Fuehrer: George Lincoln Rockwell and the American Nazi Party* (Champaign: University of Illinois Press, 1999), 40–41.

339   FBI FOIA, Ray Leahart, file number 157-2965.

340   Tyler Bridges, *The Rise Of David Duke* (Jackson: University Press of Mississippi, 1994), 33.

341   Ephemeral Collection, Howard-Tilton Memorial Library at Tulane University.

342   FBI FOIA, Ray Leahart, file number 157-2965 and Headquarters number 157-2965-1.

343   101-84-10329, The John F. Kennedy Assassination Records Collection, NARA.

344   FBI FOIA, Ray Leahart, March 15, 1976, file number 157-2965.

345   FBI FOIA, Bluford Balter, file number 105-HQ-70374.

346   FBI FOIA, Louis P. Davis, file number 72-1285.

347   FBI FOIA, Ray Leahart, file number 157-2965.

348   *Time*, November 1, 1967.

349   FBI FOIA, A. Roswell Thompson, file number 157-6544.

350   180-10104-10278, The John F. Kennedy Assassination Records Collection, NARA.

351   FBI FOIA, Leander Perez, file number 44-0-8149-10686.

352   180-10072-10214, The John F. Kennedy Assassination Records Collection, NARA.

353   *Times–Picayune*, October 20, 1967.

354   124-10143-10348, The John F. Kennedy Assassination Records Collection, NARA.

355   Robert DePugh, interview by the author, December 17, 1999 and May 11, 2000.

356   180-10030-10318, The John F. Kennedy Assassination Records Collection, NARA.

357   Rosenthal and Gelb, *One More Victim*.

358   180-1005-41028, The John F. Kennedy Assassination Records Collection, NARA.

359   Jim Garrison, memo to staff, September 14, 1967, NODA.

360   "Penetration and Diversification of Clandestine Operations," February 23, 1968,

NODA, 4.

361   Glenn Pinchback, letter to Jim Garrison, NODA.

362   180-100096-10027, The John F. Kennedy Assassination Records Collection, NARA.

363   Robert Oswald, *Lee: A Portrait of Lee Harvey Oswald* (New York: Coward-McCann Inc., 1967).

364   FBI file number 201-2894-8.

365   ID 1993.05.24, 08:48: 960000, The John F. Kennedy Assassination Records Collection, NARA.

366   Warren Commission, Exhibit 1962.

367   Warren Commission, Exhibit 1963.

368   Peter Noyes, *Legacy of Doubt* (New York: Pinnacle Books, 1973).

369   Warren Commission, Exhibit 1385.

370   Warren Commission, CD 87, 394.

371   *The New Yorker*, March 10, 1995.

372   Priscilla Johnson McMillan, *Marina and Lee* (New York: Harper & Row, 1977).

Chapter 4

373   Joseph A. Milteer, letter to Grady Bartlett, June 24 1961, Brooks County Probate Court (BCPC), Quitman, Georgia. The documents were obained by court order.

374   *HSCA Report*, I, 118.

375   FBI FOIA, Joseph A. Milteer. The Milteer FBI file is available online at the FBI Electronic Reading Room. The author obtained an early copy of an FOIA request courtesy of Bill Adams. That copy appears to be from the original of the Dan Christensen copy (5-5-1978 FOIA, FBI, MM 137-363) of Milteer's file, and differs from the online version. There are additional documents from the Miami Police Department in the Christense FOIA file, which are not found in the FBI online copy.

376   FBI file number 66-16458-278, March 19, 1960.

377   Letter, BCPC.

378   Letter to the editor of the *Atlanta Constitution*, October 12, 1957, BCPC.

379   Joseph A. Milteer, letter to Frank Horne, November 7, 1969, BCPC.

380   Grady Barlett, letter to Joseph A. Milteer, May 25, 1960, BCPC.

381   Roy V. Harris, letter to Joseph A. Milteer, October 20, 1960, BCPC.

382   FBI FOIA, Joseph A. Milteer.

383   Ibid.

384   Harold Weisberg, *Oswald In New Orleans: Case for Conspiracy with the CIA* (New York: Canyon Books, 1967).

385   *New York Times*, March 12, 1956.

386   *Chicago Daily Times*, March 12, 1956.

387   FBI FOIA, Kenneth Adams.

388   FBI FOIA, Joseph A. Milteer.

389   FBI FOIA, Kenneth Adams.

390   FBI file number 157-HQ-924.

391   FBI FOIA, Kenneth Adams.

392   FBI FOIA, Kenneth Adams, file number BH 157-7, 8.

393   FBI FOIA, Kenneth Adams.

394   *Facts*, ADL, May 1965.

395   FBI FOIA, Kenneth Adams.

396   FBI file number 157-370-2-345.

397   Harold Weisberg, *Frame-Up: The Martin Luther King James Earl Ray Case* (New York: Outerbridge and Dienstfrey, 1969).

398   *Facts*, ADL, January 1961.

399   FBI FOIA, Joseph A. Milteer.

400   Robert J. Groden and Harrison Livingston, *High Treason: The Assassination of President Kennedy, What Really Happened* (New York: The Conservatory Press, 1989).

401   Bernard Fensterwald, Jr., *Assassination of JFK by Coincidence or Conspiracy?* (Baton Rouge: Zebra Books, 1977), 96.

402   FBI FOIA, Joseph A. Milteer.

403   Seymour Gelber, interview by the author, June 9, 1967.

404   FBI FOIA, Joseph A. Milteer.

405   William Somersett, "The Continuing Inquiry," interview by Bill Barry, March 22, 1977, 17; A copy can be found at: 180-10103-10055, The John F. Kennedy Assassination Records Collection, NARA.

406   Dr. Edward Fields, letter to the author, November 1999.

407   FBI FOIA, Joseph A. Milteer.

Chapter 5

408   Dan Christensen, interview by the author, August 16, 1997.

409   *Miami Magazine* articles were found in the FBI FOIA, Joseph A. Milteer.

410   *HSCA Final Report*, 656. The photo of Sexton and Shelton in the New Years greeting was found inserted in the *Fiery Cross* (Tuscaloosa, Alabama: Imperial Press, undated, circa 1968). Robert Shelton was the editor. Before his death in 2003, Shelton stated in an interview, "The Klan is gone. Forever." [archive.adl.org/issue_combating_hate/uka/decline.html] Efforts to contact people connected to the Imperial Press were unsuccessful. M. Melvin Sexton is believed to have died in 1978, according to Ancestry.com.

411   FBI FOIA, Joseph A. Milteer.

412   Swift correspondence, various. Milteer visited Swift in California, BCPC.

413   *HSCA Report*, Martin Luther King.

414   HSCA, Appendix VI, 242-259.

415   The 5'8" height is given in Secret Service document CO-2-33-915 X 3-11-5563-S, the height of 5'7" came from the Miami Secret Service, File 3-11-5563-S; the height of 5'5" was written on a photo of Milteer dated 11-27-63 found via the FBI FOIA, Joseph A. Milteer; the heights of 5'4" and 5'6" are also in the FBI FOIA, Joseph A. Milteer.

416   Dr. Edward Fields, letter to the author, May 1999.

417   Dino Brugioni, letter to the author, April 9, 2000.

418   Dino A. Brugioni, *Photo Fakery* (Dulles, Virginia: Brassey's Inc., 1999), 107.

419   The author reproduced the Bell picture and photographed a person of the height of 5'8" standing where "Milteer" stood, and determined that the motorcade spectator was 5'8" high; The author is grateful for the information on the Bell and Skagg's photos, as well as the suggestion of an alternative way of determining "Milteer's" height that were provided by Gary Mack, director of the Sixth Floor Museum in Dallas, who corresponded with the author in 2004.

420   Thomas Samoluk of the Assassination Record Review Board, interview by the author, 1997.

421   William Somersett, "The Continuing Inquiry," interview by Bill Barry, Vol. 1, No. 8, 7; A copy can be found at: 180-10103-10055, The John F. Kennedy Assassination Records Collection, NARA.

422   Donald Adams, interviews by the author, October 23, 1999, June 8, 2000, February 16, 2001, and July 27, 2001.

423   180-10090-10300, The John F. Kennedy Assassination Records Collection, NARA.

424   180-10123-10039, The John F. Kennedy Assassination Records Collection, NARA.

425   124-10012-10310, The John F. Kennedy Assassination Records Collection, NARA.

426   180-10123-10039, The John F. Kennedy Assassination Records Collection, NARA.

427   Secret Service, CO-2-33, 915 X 3-11-5563.

428   FBI FOIA, Joseph A. Milteer.

429   180-100910-10198, The John F. Kennedy Assassination Records Collection, NARA.

430   124-10287-10271, The John F. Kennedy Assassination Records Collection, NARA.

431   Secret Service, CO-2-35, 588.

432   Warren Commission, Document 1347, 20.

433   80-10090-10229, The John F. Kennedy Assassination Records Collection, NARA.

434   Atlanta FBI file number105-3193.

435   FBI FOIA, Joseph A. Milteer, FBI field office file number137-608.

436   Everett Kay, interview by the author, March 6, 1999.

437   *Miami News*, February 3, 1967.

438   G. Robert Blakey and Richard Billings, *The Plot to Kill the President* (New York: Times Books, 1981), 9.

439   Ned Touchstone Papers, Noel Memorial Library, Lousiana State University Shreveport.

440 *Thunderbolt*, Paul O. Peters Papers, Special Collections, Wooster College Library, Wooster, Ohio.

441 Edward Fields, letter to the author, received (undated) in May 1999.

442 Joseph A. Milteer, letter to Frank Horne, September 7, 1969.

Chapter 6

443 FBI FOIA, Joseph A. Milteer.

444 *Warren Commission Report.*

445 Arnold Forster and Benjamin R. Epstein, *Cross Currents* (New York: Doubleday and Company Inc., 1956), 144.

446 Forster and Epstein, *Cross Currents*, 145.

447 *The American Reporter*, October 15, 1953, Paul O. Peters Papers, Special Collections, College of Wooster, Wooster, Ohio.

448 Paul O. Peters Papers, Special Collections, College of Wooster, Wooster, Ohio.

449 Flier, J. Evetts Haley Papers, Haley Memorial Library and History Center, Midland, Texas.

450 Forster and Epstein, *Cross Currents*, 160–9.

451 Paul Rothermel, interview by the author, March 15, 2000.

452 Forster and Epstein, *Cross Currents*, 160–169.

453 FBI FOIA, Wesley Swift.

454 *Summit Sun*, March 29, 1956, Paul O. Peters Papers, Special Collections, College of Wooster, Wooster, Ohio.

455 *Summit Sun*, April 1957, Paul O. Peters Papers, Special Collections, College of Wooster, Wooster, Ohio.

456 *Free Enterprise*, April 1958.

457 *Summit Sun*, April 10, 1958, Paul O. Peters Papers, Special Collections, College of Wooster, Wooster, Ohio.

458 Mary Cain Papers, Mississippi State Archives.

459 Flier, Paul O. Peters Papers, Special Collections, College of Wooster, Wooster, Ohio; a flier for the meeting is also in the author's personal collection.

460 Mary Brengel, interview by the author, June 25, 1996.

461 Gerald L. K. Smith Papers, University of Michigan, Bentley Library.

462 FBI file number 105-18057, courtesy of Andy Kiel.

463 *Summit Sun*, May, May 4, 1961, Paul O. Peters Papers, Special Collections, College of Wooster, Wooster, Ohio.

464 Audiocassette, The John F. Kennedy Assassination Records Collection, NARA.

465 180-1009-10176, The John F. Kennedy Assassination Records Collection, NARA.

466 Ibid.

467 Flier, Heinsohn Papers, Special Collections, University of Oregon, 127/1.

468 *Thunderbolt*, December 1974, Paul O. Peters Papers, Special Collections, College of Wooster, Wooster, Ohio.

469 In 1966, the Congress of Freedom (COF) was held in Shreveport, Louisiana, and featured Ned Touchstone, George Thomas, and Revilo Oliver. [Frank Capell, letter to George B. Fowler, March 7, 1966, Tom Anderson Papers, University of Oregon Library, Special Collections] Frank Capell attended. Clyde Watts was the principal speaker. [*Shreveport Times*, 10-16-66, from FBI file number 105-18057-A, AARC, courtesy of Andy Kiel] In 1972, the COF was held in Lansing, Michigan, on September 7 and 9. Congressman John Schmitz, Mary Cain, George Washington, and Captain Ken Ryker attended. [180-10095-10460, The John F. Kennedy Assassination Records Collection, NARA] Willis Carto was another involved in the founding of the Congress of Freedom. Carto was a giant in the anti-Communist and anti-Jewish far right for over half a century. (Carto was still actively promoting his anti-Jewish literature when the author met him in 2004.) Carto was an unabashed admirer of Adolf Hitler. Carto was an associate of Francis Yockey, author of *Imperium* and the last person to visit Yockey in his jail cell before he committed suicide. [Francis Yockey, *Imperium* (n. pl.: Noontide Press, 1983).] Of the meeting, Carto wrote, "I knew I was in the presence of a great force, ..." *Imperium* was a total denunciation of the Jewish race in world history. Carto wrote the forward to *Imperium* in an edition that he later republished, stating: "Hitler's defeat was the defeat of Europe. And of America. How could we have been so blind? The blame, it seems must be laid at the door of the international Jew." Carto apparently left the COF in 1955 when he was offered a seat on the board of Liberty and Property, later known as Liberty Lobby. [Mary Cain Papers, Mississippi State Archives]

470 George Soule, letters to General Walker, March 16, 1964, and April 21, 1964. Edwin A. Walker Papers, Dolph Briscoe Center for American History, University of Texas at Austin, 96-30/13.

471 FBI FOIA file numbers: 1073661-000; FBI MM 157-739, 7.

472 FBI FOIA file numbers: 1073661-000; FBI MM 157-739, 10.

473 FBI FOIA file numbers: 1073661-000; FBI MM 157-739, 18.

474 *Summit Sun*, February 14, 1963, Paul O. Peters Papers, Special Collections, College of Wooster, Wooster, Ohio.

475 *Times–Picayune*, March 31, 1963.

476 FBI FOIA, Joseph A. Milteer.

477 124-1031-10212, The John F. Kennedy Assassination Records Collection, NARA.

478 FBI FOIA, Joseph A. Milteer, file number MM 157-739, 14–5

479 Joseph A. Milteer, letter to Grady Bartlett, May 10, 1963, BCPC, Quitman, Georgia.

480 180-10099-10120, The John F. Kennedy Assassination Records Collection, NARA.

481 Flier, JBS speaker's bureau, Tom Anderson Papers, Special Collections, University of Oregon Library.

482 FBI FOIA, Joseph A. Milteer, field office file number 157-739, February 8, 1963.

483 FBI FOIA, Joseph A. Milteer, Intelligence Unit of Miami Police Department by Detective Lockhart Gracey, Jr., transcribed April 19, 1963.

484 FBI FOIA file numbers: 1073661-000; FBI MM 157-739, 16

485 FBI FOIA, Joseph A. Milteer.

486 Harry Allen Overstreet and Bonaro Overstreet, *The Strange Tactics of Extremism* (New York: W. W. Norton & Company, Inc., 1964), 219.

487 FBI FOIA, Joseph A. Milteer, Intelligence Unit of Miami Police Department by Detective Lockhart Gracey, Jr., transcribed April 19, 1963.

488 Rainach Papers, Noel Memorial Library, Louisiana State University Shreveport, Box 71.

489 FBI Miami file number 4012-63, 157-758

490 FBI FOIA, Joseph A. Milteer, Intelligence Unit of Miami Police Department by Detective Lockhart Gracey, Jr., transcribed April 19, 1963.

491 FBI file numbers: 157-758-41; 124-10331-10195, The John F. Kennedy Assassination Records Collection, NARA.

492 BCPC, courtesy of James Hall, Jr.

493 Joseph A. Milteer, letter to Woody Kearns, August 24, 1964, BCPC.

494 FBI FOIA, courtesy of Bill Adams.

495 Joseph A. Milteer, letter to Grady Bartlett, May 10, 1963.

496 FBI FOIA, file number 1073661-000, FBI Miami 157-739 to Director 157-758, June 6, 1963, 17–8.

497 A. G. Blazey, letter to Clarence Manion, April 15, 1963, Clarence Manion Papers, Chicago Historical Society, Box 8-6.

498 FBI file number MM 157-739, 9.

499 Guy Banister, letter New Orleans post of the American Legion, March 9, 1962, Courtney Papers, Special Collections, Northwestern State University of Louisiana.

500 Courtney Papers, Special Collections, Northwestern State University of Louisiana.

501 *The Jewish Voice*, August 4, 1966, California.

502 FBI FOIA, Joseph A. Milteer.

503 Joseph A. Milteer, letter to Joseph Muenzer, April 22, 1961, BCPC.

504 Joseph A. Milteer letter to Leslie Fleming, July 21, 1963, BCPC.

505 FBI FOIA, Joseph A. Milteer, Miami Police interview, April 19, 1963, 25.

506 William W. Turner, *Power on the Right* (Berkeley: Ramparts Press, Inc., 1971), 26.

507 David Wrone, interview by the author, September 21, 2006, conducted at the AARC conference.

508 Warren Commission, XV, 709–744.

509 Flier, Ned Touchstone Papers, Noel Memorial Library, Lousisana State University Shreveport.

510 Overstreet and Overstreet, *The Strange Tactics of Extremism*, 237.

511 Audiocassette, The John F. Kennedy Assassination Records Collection, NARA.

512 Letter, Grady Bartlett to Joseph A. Milteer, May 25, 1960, BCPC.

513 Warren Commission, XV, 709–744.

514 Letter, Larry Haapanen to author, 1986.

515 Warren Commission, XV, 709–744.

516 Joseph Oster, interview by the author, October 14, 1999.

517 DeLesseps Morrison Papers, New Orleans Public Library.

518 *States–Item*, March 10, 1960.

519 *Times–Picayune*, May 24, 1960.

520 *Times–Picayune*, December 12, 1962.

521 *Times–Picayune*, April 30, 1963.

522 *Times–Picayune*, September 19, 1961.

523 Audiotape, conversation between Kent Courtney and Robert Welch, 1958, Courtney Papers, Special Collections, Northwestern State University of Louisiana.

524 Jim Garrison, memo to James Alcock, February 6, 1967, New Orleans district attorney (NODA).

525 Memo, August 21, 1968, NODA.

526 *Woman Constitutionalist*, June 1, 1968. The information was reported in an FBI file, number illegible.

527 *Shreveport Journal*, June 18, 1963.

528 Letters to Senator Allen Ellender, Ellender Papers, Nicholls State University.

529 Blank stationery from Tom Anderson Papers, Special Collections, University of Oregon Library.

530 *Times–Picayune*, October 1964.

531 Flier advertising the speech, Tom Anderson Papers, Special Collections, University of Oregon Library.

532 *Times–Picayune*, August 7, 1963.

533 *Times–Picayune*, October 26, 1963.

534 Mary Brengel, interview by the author, June 25, 1996.

535 FBI FOIA, Joseph A. Milteer.

536 "Leads # 22," November 6, 1967, NODA.

537 The document about the group came from Banister's files, labeled "41–41" by Banister, NODA.

538 Garrison Memo, April 24, 1968, NODA.

539 FBI FOIA, Joseph A. Milteer, William Somersett briefing with Detective Lockhart Gracey, April 10, 1963.

540 180-10091-10245, The John F. Kennedy Assassination Records Collection, NARA.

541 180-10065-10253, The John F. Kennedy Assassination Records Collection, NARA.

542 180-10099-10166, Box 48-9, The John F. Kennedy Assassination Records Collection, NARA.

543   *Plaquemines Gazette*, January 13, 1961.

544   *Plaquemines Gazette*, May 15, 1964.

545   FBI FOIA, file numbers: 1073661-000; FBI MM 157-739, 74.

546   FBI FOIA, file numbers: 1073661-000; FBI MM 157-739, 79.

547   FBI FOIA, file numbers: 1073661-000; 157-739, 17.

Chapter 7

548   *Warren Commission Report*, 40.

549   *Warren Commission Report*, 731.

550   Willie Somersett, "The Continuing Inquiry," interview by Bill Barry, March 22, 1977; a copy is in 180-10103-10055, The John F. Kennedy Assassination Records Collection, NARA.

551   FBI FOIA, Joseph A. Milteer.

552   180-10091-10200, The John F. Kennedy Assassination Records Collection, NARA. Also found in: Secret Service, file numbers: SS CO-2-33, 915, X3-11-5563-S.

553   FBI FOIA, Joseph A. Milteer.

554   BCPC.

555   FBI FOIA, Joseph A. Milteer.

556   FBI FOIA, Edwin A. Walker.

557   The first visit by Milteer to Dallas was in June 1963, when he traveled to Dallas to persuade Dan Smoot to run for president on the Constitution Party ticket, as is noted in Chapter Four. The second stop was just prior to the Constitution Party meeting, as is noted in Chapter Seven. The third was on November 22. The fourth was on December 12, noted by Bill Barry, as is described in Chapter Five. The fifth was a visit paid to General Walker and Robert Surrey in June 1964, which is discussed later.

558   FBI FOIA, Joseph A. Milteer.

559   FBI FOIA, Kenneth Goff, file number 105-123-179.

560   FBI FOIA, Joseph A. Milteer.

561   124-10287-10273, The John F. Kennedy Assassination Records Collection, NARA.

562   FBI FOIA, Joseph A. Milteer.

563   *Constitution Press*, no. 24, October, 1957, Paul O. Peters Papers, Special Collections, College of Wooster, Wooster, Ohio.

564   *The Constitution News–Review*, Mary Cain Papers, Mississippi State Archives.

565   *Right*, no. 12, Paul O. Peters Papers, Special Collections, College of Wooster, Wooster, Ohio.

566   T. Coleman Andrew Papers, 119/17, Special Collections, University of Oregon.

567   DeLesseps Morrison Papers, New Orleans Public Library.

568   *American Reporter* 7, no. 3, Paul O. Peters Papers, Special Collections, College of Wooster, Wooster, Ohio.

569   *Summit Sun*, October 17, 1957, Paul O. Peters Papers, Special Collections, College of Wooster, Wooster, Ohio.

570   *Identity*, November 1975, courtesy of David Boylan.

571   Letter, Bard Logan to Tom Anderson, May 24, 1960, Special Collections, University of Oregon.

572   Olga Butterworth, letter to Pedro del Valle, September 11, 1972, Special Collections, University of Oregon.

573   180-10094-10188, The John F. Kennedy Assassination Records Collection, NARA.

574   Joseph A. Milteer, letter to Joseph Muenzer, April 22, 1961, BCPC.

575   *Constitution News–Review*, 3, No. 2., courtesy of David Boylan.

576   Letter, November 3, 1961, Tom Anderson Papers, 157/19, Special Collections, University of Oregon Library.

577   Dan Smoot, letter to Frank Horne, September 21, 1962, 180-10095-10452, The John F. Kennedy Assassination Records Collection, NARA.

578   *Constitution–News Review* 4, no. 2, courtesy of David Boylan.

579   Letter to Woody Kearns, July 11, 1964, HSCA, Box 49-51, The John F. Kennedy Assassination Records Collection, NARA.

580   In 1965, the Constitution Party met in Des Moines, Iowa, on June 4–5. Milteer attended and played a prominent role. [Joseph A. Milteer, letter to Woody Kearns, May 22, 1965, 180-1009-10176, The John F. Kennedy Assassination Records Collection, NARA.] The screening committee included Admiral John Crommelin representing Alabama; Milteer, Georgia; Oren Potito, Florida; and Pedro del Valle, Maryland. Del Valle recommended H. S. Riecke to represent the state of Louisiana. Riecke published a newsletter, *PRAY,* for the far-right group he headed called Paul Revere Associated Yeoman (PRAY) in New Orleans. General del Valle and Milteer made recommendations for the other state's representatives. [Tom Anderson Papers, Special Collections, University of Oregon Library, 157/18.] The 1966 Constitution Party meeting was held in Houston, Texas, and adopted the platform: "This is a Christian Nation." The retiring chairman of the meeting was Curtis Dall, the head of Liberty Lobby. Pedro del Valle was the keynote speaker. [*Facts*, 1966, ADL, 318.] In 1969, General del Valle was on the Policy Councils of the Constitution Party. W. J. "Woody" Kearns, Milteer's close friend, was the National Vice Chairman. Milteer associates Ted Billings and Frank Horne were officers, as was Myron Fagan. [Ted Billings, letter to Woody Kearns, March 30, 1969, 180-10099-10143, The John F. Kennedy Assassination Records Collection, NARA.] Woody Kearns received a letter from del Valle and suggested that the Constitution Party get together with the National States' Rights Party and the Minutemen's Patriotic Party. Milteer and Woody Kearns drew up planks for the party's platform, which del Valle felt were excellent. [Woody Kearns, letter to Joe, April 4, 1969, 180-10099-10156, The John F. Kennedy Assassination Records Collection, NARA.] One of the their planks was to "oppose anti-Christ Zionism exposed in The

Protocols of The Learned Elders of Zion . . . ." [180-10099-10150, The John F. Kennedy Assassination Records Collection, NARA.]

581 Frank Horne, letter to Joseph A. Milteer, 180-1009-10176, The John F. Kennedy Assassination Records Collection, NARA.

582 Joan Mellen, interview by the author, May 30, 2003.

583 Mary Cain Papers, C-J47, Mississippi State Archives.

584 Pamphlet, Mary Cain Papers, Mississippi State Archives.

585 Secret Service memorandum, March 10, 1967, file numbers: SS CO-2-33-915, 180-10091-10197, The John F. Kennedy Assassination Records Collection, NARA.

586 Curtis Dall, letter to Clarence Manion, September 13, 1963, Clarence Manion Papers, Box 11-13, Chicago Historical Society.

587 Olga Butterworth, letter to Joseph A. Milteer, March 19, 1963, 180-10095-10452, The John F. Kennedy Assassination Records Collection, NARA.

588 Secret Service Document, file number SS CO-2-33-915,180-10091-101201, The John F. Kennedy Assassination Records Collection, NARA

589 *Baltimore News Post*, February 10, 1950, Wally Butterworth Papers, Special Collections, University of Oregon.

590 *Newsweek*, January 30, 1950, Wally Butterworth Papers, Special Collections, University of Oregon.

591 Wally Butterworth Papers, Special Collections, University of Oregon.

592 180-10029-10277, The John F. Kennedy Assassination Records Collection, NARA.

593 *Southern Jewish Weekly*, Wally Butterworth Papers, Special Collections, University of Oregon.

594 Letters, October 15, 1969, Wally Butterworth Papers, Special Collections, University of Oregon.

595 *Atlanta Constitution*, August 11, 1962.

596 Wally Butterworth, letter to Leander Perez, July 20, 1962, Wally Butterworth Papers, Special Collections, University of Oregon.

597 Wally Butterworth, letters to friends, November 11, 1967, Wally Butterworth Papers, Special Collections, University of Oregon. From a number of letters found in Butterworth's papers in the right wing collection of the University of Oregon, it is abundantly clear that Butterworth was an anti-Jewish, anti-black extremist devoted to armed underground activities. He was in contact with others of similar views from across the country like Pedro del Valle, Admiral Crommelin, William Gale, Kenneth Goff, Gordon Winrod, Wesley Swift, and Richard Cotton. Del Valle called Butterworth, in one letter, "my dear friend." Butterworth was also in contact with Ernest Zuendel, a German neo-Nazi. Both Butterworth and Kenneth Goff were in communication with Revilo Oliver, the keynote speaker at the April 1963 Congress of Freedom meeting, who was also an advocate of violence.

598 Wally Butterworth, September 6, 1963, Wally Butterworth Papers, Special Collec-

tions, University of Oregon.

599   Wally Butterworth, letter to Vic Knight, October 11, 1963, Wally Butterworth Papers, Special Collections, University of Oregon.

600   Warren Commission, Document 304. Also found in: 180-10029-10277, The John F. Kennedy Assassination Records Collection, NARA.

601   Wally Butterworth, January 25, 1965, Wally Butterworth Papers, Special Collections, University of Oregon.

602   180-10095-1052, The John F. Kennedy Assassination Records Collection, NARA.

603   Joseph A. Milteer, note to unknown person, 180-10099-10176, The John F. Kennedy Assassination Records Collection, NARA.

604   Joseph A. Milteer, letter to Woody Kearns, July 11, 1964, 180-10099-10176, The John F. Kennedy Assassination Records Collection, NARA.

605   Woody Kearns, letter to Joseph A. Milteer in response to a October 13, 1970 letter, 180-10099-10176, The John F. Kennedy Assassination Records Collection, NARA.

606   180-10095-10495, The John F. Kennedy Assassination Records Collection, NARA.

607   Woody Kearns, letter to Joseph A. Milteer, September 22, 1967, 180-10095-10495, The John F. Kennedy Assassination Records Collection, NARA.

608   180-10099-10119, The John F. Kennedy Assassination Records Collection, NARA.

609   180-10090-10298, The John F. Kennedy Assassination Records Collection, NARA.

610   180-10090-10307, The John F. Kennedy Assassination Records Collection, NARA

611   180-10090-10298, The John F. Kennedy Assassination Records Collection, NARA.

612   180-10090-10307, The John F. Kennedy Assassination Records Collection, NARA.

613   Warren Commission, Document 39. Also found in: 180-10090-10298, The John F. Kennedy Assassination Records Collection, NARA.

614   Warren Commission, Document 1107. Also found in: 180-10090-10298, The John F. Kennedy Assassination Records Collection, NARA.

615   FBI FOIA, William Gale. Milteer attended Gale's Committee of the States meeting on February 10, 1968 in Montgomery, Alabama. Dr. Robert C. Olney invited Milteer to speak. Milteer was pleased with the meeting because "ACTION" was planned. [Joseph A. Milteer, letter to Woody Kearns, February 14, 1968, 180-10095-10486, The John F. Kennedy Assassination Records Collection, NARA.] Milteer was on a first-name basis with Gale, according to a 1971 letter, and subscribed to Gale's *Posse Comitatus* newsletter. [180-10099-10144, The John F. Kennedy Assassination Records Collection, NARA.] Woody Kearns and Pedro del Valle were connected to the Committee on the States. Two different addresses for Gale were found on a note card at Milteer's home: 1840 West Ave. K-4, phone Whitehall 2-3623, was the Gale's home address. Another Gale address was: 201 South Central Ave., Glendale, Calif. 91204. A separate notation gave Gale's address as: 1840 West Avenue K-4, Lancaster, California. The names of Colonel Ben Cameron, Lee Zane, and Ronald Reagan were haphazardly scrawled on the card. [180-10099-10176, The John F. Kennedy Assassination Records

Collection, NARA.]

616   Warren Commission, Document, 1107, courtesy of David Boylan.

617   FBI FOIA, William Gale, 157–282.

618   Cheri Seymour, *Committee of the States: Inside the Radical Right* (Mariposa: Camden Place Communications, Inc., 1991).

619   FBI FOIA, Wesley Swift, file number 62-1085916, encl. 1, 3, 4.

620   FBI FOIA, Wesley Swift, file number 100-355454-29

621   FBI FOIA, Wesley Swift.

622   Miami Intelligence Unit, October 25, 1963, 180-10090-10307, The John F. Kennedy Assassination Records Collection, NARA.

623   FBI FOIA, Joseph A. Milteer.

624   *HSCA Final Report*, June 6, 1978, 656.

625   Joseph A. Milteer, phone conversation with William Somersett, January 1, 1964, FBI FOIA, file number 66-16458.

626   BCPC, courtesy of James Hall, Jr.

627   FBI FOIA, Wesley Swift.

628   124-10330-10035, The John F. Kennedy Assassination Records Collection, NARA.

629   180-10099-10125, The John F. Kennedy Assassination Records Collection, NARA.

630   George Thayer, *The Farther Shores of Politics* (New York: Simon and Schuster, 1967).

631   Arnold Forster and Benjamin R, Epstein, *The Trouble-Makers* (Garden City: Doubleday & Company, Inc., 1952), 25–61.

632   *Identity*, Vol. 7, No. 20, January 1974, courtesy of David Boylan.

633   Seymour, *Committee of the States*.

634   Pedro del Valle Papers, Special Collections, University of Oregon Library, 157/18.

635   Seymour, *Committee of the States*.

636   Joseph A. Milteer, letter to Woody Kearns, October 26, 1971, 180-10099-10147, The John F. Kennedy Assassination Records Collection, NARA.

637   *Identity*, November 1975, courtesy of David Boylan.

638   Seymour, *Committee of the States*.

639   124-10330-10020, The John F. Kennedy Assassination Records Collection, NARA.

640   002118, Box 49, Folder 5, RG 233, The John F. Kennedy Assassination Records Collection, NARA.

641   180-10099-10124, The John F. Kennedy Assassination Records Collection, NARA.

642   180-10099-10125, The John F. Kennedy Assassination Records Collection, NARA.

643   Joseph A. Milteer, letter to Woody Kearns, March 8 1965, 180-10099-10119, The John F. Kennedy Assassination Records Collection, NARA.

644   FBI FOIA, William Gale, 157–282.

645   Daivd Boylan, "A League of Their Own: A Look Inside the Christian Defense League," *Cuban Information Archives*, last updated 2004, Cuban-exile.com/doc_026-050/doc0046.html.

646 Dick Russell, *The Man Who Knew Too Much* (New York: Carroll and Graf Publishers, Inc., 1992), 547.

647 Thayer, *The Farther Shores of Politics.*

648 Seymour, *Committee of the States*, 89.

649 Rainach Papers, Noel Memorial Library, Louisiana State University Shreveport.

650 Guy Banister and Willie Rainach, letters, Rainach Papers, Noel Memorial Library, Louisiana State University Shreveport.

651 FBI FOIA, Wesley Swift.

652 Seymour, *Committee of the States*, 228.

653 William Somersett, interview by Detective Lockhart Gracey, Jr., FBI FOIA, Joseph A. Milteer.

654 FBI FOIA, Mary Davison, MM 157-739.

655 William Somersett, interview by Detective Everette Kay, transcribed December 3, 1963, Miami Police Department, FBI FOIA, Joseph A. Milteer.

656 *Alarming Cry*, January 1, 1969, microfilm, Right-Wing Collection, University of Iowa.

657 *Common Sense*, August 1, 1957.

658 FBI FOIA, Kenneth Goff, file number 40-1618, January 20, 1964.

659 *The Defender*, June 1958, Paul O. Peters Papers, Special Collections, College of Wooster, Wooster, Ohio.

660 Overstreet and Overstreet, *The Strange Tactics of Extremism.*

661 186-10001-10183, The John F. Kennedy Assassination Records Collection, NARA.

662 FBI FOIA, Kenneth Goff.

663 *Liberty Lobby* newsletter, Wilcox Collection, University of Kansas, RH WL Eph 2212.12.

664 FBI FOIA, Kenneth Goff.

665 *The Denver Post*, August 13, 1964, FBI FOIA, Kenneth Goff.

666 *The Denver Post*, August 14, 1964, FBI FOIA, Kenneth Goff.

667 Joseph A. Milteer, letter to Woody Kearns, August 10, 1964, BCPC.

668 Joseph A. Milteer, letter to Woody Kearns, August 24, 1964, BCPC.

669 Letter, September 11, 1966, Wally Butterworth Papers, Special Collections, University of Oregon.

670 FBI FOIA, Kenneth Goff.

671 Letter, to FBI, FBI FOIA, Kenneth Goff, file number 105-123-200.

672 FBI FOIA, Kenneth Goff, file number 105-123-204.

673 FBI FOIA, Kenneth Goff, file number 105-123-911.

674 FBI FOIA, Kenneth Goff, FBI Denver file number 105-123.

675 Denver Police Offense Report, March 11, 1966, FBI FOIA, Kenneth Goff.

676 *The Denver Post*, February 10, 1966, FBI FOIA, Kenneth Goff.

677 FBI FOIA, Kenneth Goff, file number 105123-261.

678 FBI FOIA, Kenneth Goff.

679   124-10054-10409, The John F. Kennedy Assassination Records Collection, NARA.

680   Robert DePugh, interviews by the author, December 17, 1999, and May 11, 2000.

681   180-10091-10200, The John F. Kennedy Assassination Records Collection, NARA.

682   124-10331-10195, The John F. Kennedy Assassination Records Collection, NARA.

683   Melissa Fay Green, *The Temple Bombing* (Reading: Addison-Wesley, 1996).

684   Olga Butterworth, letter to Leander Perez, July 20, 1962, Wally Butterworth Papers, Special Collections, University of Oregon.

685   Sims *The Klan.*

686   William Somersett, interview by Detective Everette Kay, transcribed December 3, 1963, Miami Police Department, FBI FOIA, Joseph A. Milteer.

687   Bert Ellis, letter to Joseph A. Milteer, August 26, 1964, 180-10099-10176, The John F. Kennedy Assassination Records Collection, NARA.

688   Report of CD 20, CD 1347, 180-10090-10229, The John F. Kennedy Assassination Records Collection, NARA.

689   Curtis Dall, *F.D.R. My Exploited Father-in-Law* (Tulsa: Christian Crusade Publications, 1968).

690   Report of CD 20, CD 1347, 180-10090-10229, The John F. Kennedy Assassination Records Collection, NARA.

Chapter 8

691   William Somersett, interview by Detective Lochart Gracey, Jr., FBI FOIA, Joseph A. Milteer, 369.

692   FBI FOIA, Joseph A. Milteer.

693   William Somersett, interview by Detective Lochart Gracey, Jr., April 19, 1963, FBI FOIA, Joseph A. Milteer, file number 124-10331-10195, The John F. Kennedy Assassination Records Collection, NARA.

694   FBI FOIA, Council for Statehood, file numbers:1073661-000; FBI MM 157-739, from the *Palm Beach Post*, April 30, 1963.

695   FBI FOIA, Joseph A. Milteer, file number MM157-739.

696   124-10331-10195, The John F. Kennedy Assassination Records Collection, NARA.

697   Seymour, *Committee of the States, Inside the Radical Right*, 225.

698   FBI FOIA, Council for Statehood, file number MM 157-739, 10.

699   Letter, September 13, 1963, Paul O. Peters Papers, Wooster College, Wooster, Ohio.

700   FBI FOIA, file number 105-123-179.

701   Joseph A. Milteer visited General del Valle in his Annapolis home in 1968, followed by a meeting with Admiral Crommelin. Del Valle was impressed with Milteer's proposed group, the United States Eagles, and was pleased to be the honorary head of the movement, stating: "Yes, I shall be most happy and honored to act as head of the United States Eagles movement and glad to lend my name to such a movement." Milteer

structured the U.S. Eagles charter with himself referred to as "Colonel," "Organizer," and "Director," with del Valle as Honorary Head. He invited Woody Kearns to be the First Vice President. [Joseph A. Milteer, letter to Woody Kearns, February 12, 1968, 180-1009-10176, The John F. Kennedy Assassination Records Collection, NARA.] In 1970, del Valle suggested to Milteer that the Constitution Party join with the American Party and back their candidate. [Joseph A. Milteer, letter to Frank Horne, 180-10095-10474, The John F. Kennedy Assassination Records Collection, NARA.] Milteer complained to his friend Woody Kearns that he was not having success getting experts to help with the movement. "Gen. Del [sic] Valle is the only one we have any concrete help from so far." [Joseph A. Milteer, letter to Woody Kearns, 180-10095-10487, The John F. Kennedy Assassination Records Collection, NARA.] When Milteer was asked to speak at a 1968 meeting of the Committee of the States, he was insulted when he was asked to be the third from last speaker. He wrote a letter to the National Chairman, Dr. Robert C. Olney and stated the action "was a distinct affront to you (Kearns) and General del Valle which was not called for by any means." [Joseph A. Milteer, letter to Charles Willoughby entitled "Dear members and Friends" on the Committee of the States letterhead, Summer 1969, FBI FOIA, Joseph A. Milteer, Charles Willoughby Papers, Douglas MacArthur Archives, Norfolk, Virginia, Reel 916.]

702   FBI FOIA, Joseph A. Milteer, Miami PD Lochart Gracey debriefing of Somersett, May 4, 1963, 54.

703   Pedro del Valle Papers, Special Collections, University of Oregon Library, 157/18.

704   Ibid.

705   Donald Janson and Bernard Eismann, *The Far Right* (New York: McGraw-Hill Book Company, 1963).

706   Robert Welch, letter to Pedro del Valle, July 30, 1959, Pedro del Valle Papers, Special Collections, University of Oregon Library, 157/18.

707   Letter, October 21, 1959, Pedro del Valle Papers, Special Collections, University of Oregon Library, 157/18.

708   Wilcox Collection, University of Kansas Library, RH WL Eph 2212.115.

709   Tom Anderson Papers, Special Collections, University of Oregon Library.

710   Pedro del Valle Papers, Special Collections, University of Oregon Library.

711   Pearson article, Pedro del Valle Papers, Special Collections, University of Oregon Library.

712   FBI FOIA, Pedro del Valle.

713   FBI FOIA, Pedro del Valle. This may have been a meeting with Frank Capell.

714   FBI FOIA, Pedro del Valle.

715   Pedro del Valle Papers, Special Collections, University of Oregon Library, 157/18. The letter was originally accompanied by some "enclosures" that del Valle sent to a select group of men including J. C. Williams and his "outfit." The enclosures did not accompany the del Valle letter among his papers.

716 MacArthur Archives, Norfolk, Virginia.

717 Letter, June 28, 1962, Pedro del Valle Papers, Special Collections, University of Oregon Library, 157/18.

718 Walker Speech, Pedro del Valle Papers, Special Collections, University of Oregon Library.

719 Pedro del Valle Papers, Special Collections, University of Oregon Library.

720 Edwin A. Walker Papers, Dolph Briscoe Center for American History, University of Texas at Austin, Box 96-30/16. Also, generals Wood, Van Fleet—as well as Wedemeyer—were on the Advisory Board of H. L. Hunt's Life Line. Letter on *Life Lines* stationery dated December 19, 1967, Wally Butterworth Papers, University of Oregon Special Collections

721 Pedro del Valle Papers, Special Collections, University of Oregon Library, 157/18.

722 Frank Capell, *Treason is the Reason* (Zarepeth, New Jersey: Herald of Freedom, 1965).

723 Pedro del Valle Papers, Special Collections, University of Oregon Library, 157/18.

724 Capell, *Treason is the Reason.*

725 Boxley Summary, William Wood Papers, NARA. In the paper, Capell claimed Nazi Commander George Lincoln Rockwell was a Communist.

726 Pedro del Valle Papers, Special Collections, University of Oregon Library, 157/18.

727 FBI FOIA, Joseph A. Milteer.

728 Turner, *Power on the Right*, 133.

729 Pedro del Valle Papers, Special Collections, University of Oregon Library.

730 Letter, November 3, 1961, Tom Anderson Papers, Special Collections, University of Oregon Library.

731 Dan Smoot, letter to Frank Horne, September 21, 1962, HSCA, 180-10095-10452.

732 *Constitution–News Review* 4, no. 2, courtesy of David Boylan.

733 On August 3–5, 1962, Billy James Hargis's Christian Crusade met in Tulsa, Oklahoma. Carl Prussian, an "ex-Communist," John Rousselot, Martin Dies, General Willoughby, and General Campbell spoke. [FBI FOIA, Christian Crusade.] On September 4, 5, and 6, 1962, Kent Courtney convened a meeting to promote the Liberty Amendment in Los Angeles with Tom Anderson, Colonel Laurence Bunker, Harry Everingham, and Walter Knott as featured speakers. [Courtney Papers, Special Collections, Northwestern State University of Louisiana.] (The Liberty Amendment was a proposal by far-right Congressman James B. Utt that would have prohibited the federal government from engaging in private enterprise unless provided for in the Constitution.) On September 22–23, 1962, We the People in Chicago featured Dr. Robert Morris, Billy James Hargis, Eddie Rickenbacker, and John Rousselot as speakers. On November 17, 1962, Courtney sponsored the Cuban Liberation Rally. "Johnny Rousselot" was the featured speaker. General Walker and Tom Anderson were invited and a member of the Cuban underground, name not disclosed, was expected to attend. [Tom Anderson Papers, Special Collections, University of Oregon Library.] On January 6,

1963, Kent Courtney spoke at the New England Rally for God and Country with Billy James Hargis, Tom Anderson, and John Rousselot [*Group Research*, January 9, 1863 and *Boston Herald,* January 6, 1963.] On January 21 or 22, 1963, Gary Hemming and Eugene Hall, two anti-Castro mercenaries, visited General Walker in Dallas. [FBI FOIA, Edwin Walker.] On February 11 to 15, 1963, Billy Hargis's Christian Crusade Leadership School featured Hilaire du Berrier, who was on Kent Courtney's Conservative Society of America board of directors and also happened to be a guest at General Walker's Dallas home on the day of the assassination. Tom Anderson, General Walker's close friend and confidant, was particularly busy speaking around the time of del Valle's gap in correspondence. At one time, Joseph A. Milteer tried to get Anderson to run on the Constitution Party's Vice Presidential ticket. [BCPC.] On October 30, 1962, George Soule hosted Tom Anderson at a For America rally held at the Jerusalem Temple in New Orleans. [George Soule, letter to Tom Anderson, October 19, 1962, Tom Anderson Papers, Special Collections, University of Oregon Library.] On January 11, 1963, Tom Anderson addressed the Louisiana Press Association in New Orleans, sponsored by the American Legion Un-American Activities Committee. Kent Courtney and Guy Banister were prominent figures in the group. [Tom Anderson Papers, Special Collections, University of Oregon Library.] On April 18, 1963, Anderson met with Oswald's boyhood hero "former Communist" Herbert Philbrick at a meeting of the board of America's Future. [Tom Anderson Papers, Special Collections, University of Oregon Library.] On May 8, 1963, Anderson and John Martino spoke to Dade County Committee to Warn of the Arrival of Communist Merchandise on the Local Business Scene in Florida. [Tom Anderson Papers, Special Collections, University of Oregon Library.] Martino, who had once been jailed by Castro in Cuba, would later admit he was connected to the Kennedy assassination. He told his business associates that Oswald was set up by the anti-Castroites. Martino spoke at a September 1963 anti-Castro rally in Dallas and later spread rumors that Oswald had contacts with Cuban G-2 intelligence. [Russell, *The Man Who Knew Too Much*, 37, 539.] On June 30, 1963, a newspaper reported on a Seattle John Birch Society meeting attended by Tom Anderson and Laurence Bunker, a former MacArthur aid. [Reported in "the *Times*" (it is unknown whether this was the *New York Times* or the *Los Angeles Times*) on June 30, 1963, Tom Anderson Papers, Special Collections, University of Oregon Library.] Evidence that suggests Anderson was an accessory to the conspiracy behind the assassination of President Kennedy is presented in Chapter Nineteen. John Rousselot, a John Birch Society leader and former California Congressman, emerged as leader of the far right among members in the hardcore underground in the period of 1962–63, attending a number of meetings. On March 20, 1962, Billy James Hargis held a "secretive meeting" by invitation only in Washington, D.C. John Rousselot, General Bonner Fellers, Ed Hunter, "ex-Communist" Benjamin Gitlow, General Willoughby, Frank McGehee, and probably Arthur Blazey were at the meeting. As a result of the meeting, the League of Right Wing Organizations was formed by Rousselot. [FBI FOIA, Billy James Hargis.] As noted before, Rousselot was a key speaker in that time period at meetings of the Christian Crusade, Cuban Liberation Rally, and New England Rally for God and Country. An informant would later come forward and name Rousselot as a conspirator in the assassination of President Kennedy—the allegation is dealt with in Chapter Nineteen.

734   Russell, *The Man Who Knew Too Much*, 327.

735   Pedro del Valle Papers, Special Collections, University of Oregon Library, 157/18.

736   Pedro del Valle, letter to Meritt Newby, Pedro del Valle Papers, Special Collections, University of Oregon Library, 157/18.

737   Pedro del Valle, letter to West Wuichet, Pedro del Valle Papers, Special Collections, University of Oregon Library, 157/18.

738   Cheri Seymour, *Committee of the States, Inside the Radical Right*.

739   Wally Butterworth Papers, Special Collections, University of Oregon.

740   Pedro del Valle Papers, Special Collections, University of Oregon Library, 157/18.

741   *Warren Commission Report*, 731.

742   Pedro del Valle Papers, Special Collections, University of Oregon Library, 157/18.

743   BCPC.

744   Benjamin Epstein and Arnold Forster, *The Radical Right* (Random House, New York: 1967).

745   Pedro del Valle, letters to various recipients, March 27, 1964, April 29, 1964, and June 15, 1965, Pedro del Valle Papers, Special Collections, University of Oregon Library, 157/18.

746   Pedro del Valle Papers, Special Collections, University of Oregon Library, 157/18.

747   124-90116-10106, The John F. Kennedy Assassination Records Collection, NARA.

748   William Wood Papers, Banister File No. 14-35, The John F. Kennedy Assassination Records Collection, NARA.

749   Charles Willoughby Papers, Douglas MacArthur Archives, Norfolk, Virgina, RG, Reel 910.

750   Joan Mellen, interview by the author, May 30, 2003.

751   Pedro del Valle Papers, Special Collections, University of Oregon Library, 157/18.

752   Pedro del Valle, *Semper Fi* (Hawthorne: The Christian Book Club, 1976).

753   William C. Lemly, letter to Wally Butterworth, September 1, 1965, Wally Butterworth Papers, Special Collections, University of Oregon.

754   Joseph W. Bendersky, *The Jewish Threat: Anti-Semetic Politics of the U.S. Army* (New York: Basic Books, 2003), 303.

755   Robert Smith, *MacArthur in Korea* (New York: Simon and Schuster, 1982).

756   A newspaper interview placed in the FBI files indicated that MacArthur believed in extraterrestrial beings. In an interview, MacArthur stated that the next World War would be "by people from other planets" and that "the politics of the future will be cosmic,

or interplanetary." FBI personnel wrote in the margin, "Cannot believe this interview." [FBI FOIA file number 62-HQ-75104, electronic reading room; FBI FOIA, Edwin Walker.]

757   *Common Sense*, Paul O. Peters Papers, Special Collections, Wooster College, Wooster, Ohio.

758   *Cleveland Plain Dealer*, July 13, 2003.

759   William Manchester, *American Ceasar* (New York: Random House, 1979).

760   H. L. Hunt, letter to General MacArthur, July 5, 1952, MacArthur Archives, Microfilm Reel, 832.

761   *The Reporter*, August 19, 1952, MacArthur Archives, University of California.

762   Bendersky, *The Jewish Threat*.

763   Henry Hurt III, *Texas Rich* (New York: W. W. Norton & Company, Inc., 1981), 265.

764   Russell, *The Man Who Knew Too Much*, 582.

765   Russell, *The Man Who Knew Too Much*, 254.

766   Yaroslav Stetsko was, for a short time, a pro-Nazi premier in German-occupied Ukraine in 1941. The Anti-Soviet Bloc of Nations acknowledged that many of their members fought on the German side against the Bolsheviks. In 1983, Stetzko was invited to the White House as an honored guest of President Reagan. [Russ Ballant, *Old Nazis, the New Right and the Republican Party* (Boston: South End Press, 1988).] In another intriguing sideline, Willoughby may have had some association with Spas Raiken, the man who met Lee Harvey Oswald and his family at the Hoboken, New Jersey, port on Oswald's return by ship from the Soviet Union in 1959. The Warren Commission investigation noted only that Raiken was a representative of the Traveler's Aid Society, which had been contacted by the Department of State to assist Oswald and his family. Raiken referred them to the Welfare Department who got the Oswalds a room for the night. Raiken requested and received two hundred dollars from Oswald's brother Robert for the flight back to Texas. More importantly, Peter Dale Scott, in his book *The Assassinations*, revealed that Raiken was the Secretary-General of the American Friends of the Anti-Bolshevik Bloc of Nations, an ardently anti-Communist, pro-Fascist, and pro-Nazi organization, which Willoughby supported. [Peter Dale Scott, Paul Hoch, and Russell Stetler, *The Assassinations* (New York: Vintage Books, 1976), 366.] If the Willoughby-ABN-Raiken association were anything more than an intriguing coincidence, then it would suggest an early tie of Oswald to a member of the dissident generals in the hardcore underground. Bonner Fellers's publication, *Citizens For America Committee*, Frank Capell's *Herald of Freedom*, Hilaire du Berrier's *H. du B. Reports*, Harold Lord Varney's *Pan American Reports*, and Billy James Hargis's *Weekly Crusader* were affiliated with the *Foreign Intelligence Digest*, that had ties to the International Committee for the Defense of the Christian Culture. Hilaire du Berrier was on Kent Courtney's Conservative Society of America board. Du Berrier wrote to Willoughby in 1961 and warned him of the impending takeover by the Communists in Europe and

Africa. [Charles Willoughby Papers, Douglas MacArthur Archives, Norfolk, Virginia, Reel 908.]

767 Willoughby received a form letter from Gale's Committee of the States addressed to "Members and Friends," suggesting that he was affiliated with of the group. [Committee of the States, letter to Charles Willoughby, Summer, 1969, Charles Willoughby Papers, Douglas MacArthur Archives, Norfolk, Virginia, RG-23, Reel 916.] Willoughby was a former military editor to the anti-Semitic *American Mercury*. General Walker assumed that position in the 1960s. [*Weekly Crusader*, October 6, 1961, Willoughby Papers, Douglas MacArthur Archives, Norfolk, Virginia.] Willoughby was an associate of Brigadier General Richard B. Moran, who served on the Board of Liberty Lobby and the Christian Crusade. [Letter, September 4, 1966, Charles Willoughby Papers, Douglas MacArthur Archives, Norfolk, Virginia.] Others close to Willoughby reflected in his correspondence were John Rarick, Robert E. Wood, George Montgomery, and Minister Bob Jones. [Charles Willoughby Papers, Douglas MacArthur Archives, Norfolk, Virginia.]

768 FBI FOIA, Billy James Hargis.

769 Robert Welch, letter to Charles Willoughby, November 9, 1961, Charles Willoughby Papers, Douglas MacArthur Archives, Norfolk, Virginia.

770 Overstreet and Overstreet, *The Strange Tactics of Extremism*, 220.

771 FBI FOIA, Christian Crusade.

772 Russell, *The Man Who Knew Too Much*, 327.

773 Charles Willoughby Papers, Douglas MacArthur Archives, Norfolk, Virginia. The National Advisor Board of the YAF included Edward Hunter, Robert Morris, Herbert Philbrick, Henry Regnery, Ted Dealey, and many others.

774 Charles Willoughby Papers, Douglas MacArthur Archives, Norfolk, Virginia (Named as a board member of Young Americans for Freedom). Others on the Board in 1970 were Mary Cain, Mary Davison, Hilaire du Berrier, Richard B. Moran, and Revilo Oliver.

775 Russell, *The Man Who Knew Too Much*, 321.

776 Archibald Roberts, letter to Charles Willoughby, November 24, 1970, Charles Willoughby Papers, Douglas MacArthur Archives, Norfolk, Virginia.

777 Courtney Papers, Special Collections, Northwestern Louisiana State University. Correspondence between Courtney and Willoughby revealed that they were friends, as well.

778 Charles Willoughby, letter to Benjamin Mandel, March 25, 1959, Charles Willoughby Papers, Douglas MacArthur Archives, Norfolk, Virginia.

779 Letter, March 3, 1958, Charles Willoughby Papers, Douglas MacArthur Archives, Norfolk, Virginia.

780 Willoughby testified before the HUAC in 1951 in the Sorge espionage case. [Russell, *The Man Who Knew Too Much*, 128] Willoughby was on the board of the American Security Council, an organization that kept records on U.S. citizens felt to be

pro-Communist or Communist. Serving with Willoughby on the ASC board were Edward Teller and Claire Luce Booth. [Russell, *The Man Who Knew Too Much*; Charles Willoughby Papers, Douglas MacArthur Archives, Norfolk, Virginia.] Many in the hardcore underground, including Courtney, Banister, and Badeaux were called upon by HUAC or Eastland's SISS to testify against alleged leftist subversives. Willoughby exchanged cordial correspondence with Richard Ahrens, staff director, and Francis E. Walter, chairman of the Committee on Un-American Activities, and provided intelligence on foreign matters to the Committee. [Richard Ahrens, letter to Charles Willoughby, September 25, 1958, Charles Willoughby Papers, Douglas MacArthur Archives, Norfolk, Virginia.; Francis Walter, letter to Charles Willoughby, September 30, 1957, Charles Willoughby Papers, Douglas MacArthur Archives, Norfolk, Virginia.] Robert Morris, while chief council for Eastland's SISS, kept Willoughby apprised of the Committee's activities. [Robert Morris, letter to Charles Willoughby, February 1, 1957, Charles Willoughby Papers, Douglas MacArthur Archives, Norfolk, Virginia.]

781   Russell, *The Man Who Knew Too Much*, 123–9, 691.

782   Gerhard Frey, letter to Charles Willoughby, February 18, 1966, Charles Willoughby Papers, Douglas MacArthur Archives, Norfolk, Virginia.

783   Bendersky, *The Jewish Threat*, 238, 274.

784   General A. C. Wedemeyer served on the American Security Council 1961 with General R. E. Wood, Robert Morris, and Dr. Edward Teller. Others included Dr. Stephen Possony, Rear Admiral Chester Ward, Admiral Ben Moreel, John M. Fisher, Lloyd Wright, Admiral Felix M. Stump and Admiral Arthur Radford. [Assorted correspondence, 1962, Charles Willoughby Papers, Douglas MacArthur Archives, Norfolk, Virginia.]

785   Letter on *Life Lines* stationery, December 19, 1967, Wally Butterworth Papers, Special Collections, University of Oregon.

786   FBI FOIA, Edwin Walker.

787   Albert Wedemeyer, *Wedemeyer Reports* (New York: Henry Holt, 1958).

788   Newsletter, *Americans for Conservative Action*, August 10, 1964, Right Wing Collection, University of Iowa, microfilm.

789   Others were Lieutenant General Edward M. Almond (U.S. Army, retired), MacArthur's former chief of staff, General Mark W. Clark, Admiral Ben Moreel, and Rear Admiral Chester Ward. Clair Luce was an advisor.

790   William W. Turner, *Power on the Right* (Berkeley: Ramparts Press, Inc., 1971). Patrick J. Frawley of Los Angeles, California, was a Knight in the Order of St. Sylvester of the Sovereign Military Order of Malta. [*Covert Action Information Bulletin*, 25, Winter 1986, 27–38.] There were many far-right "Orders of Malta" and it is not clear if Frawley's group was related to the Shickshinny Knights that Frank Capell belonged to, which will be discussed later in this chapter. However, it is very likely that Frawley knew Capell. The public relations director for Capell and Frawley was indicted for

libel for allegations they made against liberal Democratic California Senator Thomas Kuchel in 1965. Frawley testified at the trial. Frawley was a major financial backer of Fred Schwartz's Christian Anti-Communist Crusade out of Long Beach, California. [*Facts*, ADL, 1966, 13.]

791 *United States Air Force*, www.airforce.com.

792 Bendersky, *The Jewish Threat*, 405–9.

793 Paul Rothermel, interview by the author, March 15, 2000.

794 Fellers incorporated For America in 1954. General Robert Wood and Dean Manion served as co-chairmen. Fellers was named the national director. The National Policy Committee included generals Wedemeyer, Mark Clark, James A. Van Fleet, George E. Stratemeyer and J. Evetts Haley. [Clarence Manion Papers, Chicago Historical Society, B-2, F2-9.] Generals Wood and Van Fleet, as well as Wedemeyer, were on the advisory board of H. L. Hunt's *Life Lines*. [Letter on *Life Lines* stationery, December 19, 1967, Wally Butterworth Papers, Special Collections, University or Oregon.] In 1956, Fellers and Stratemeyer were on a committee to elect T. Coleman Andrews and Thomas Werdel for president. Fellers was a co-chairman. Other familiar figures on the far right on the committee included Dan Smoot, Dean Manion, J. Evetts Haley and George Montgomery. [*The Cross and Flag*, November 1956, Paul O. Peters Papers, Special Collections, College of Wooster, Wooster, Ohio.]

795 Bendersky, *The Jewish Threat*.

796 *Right*, July 1956, no. 10, Paul O. Peters Papers, Special Collections, College of Wooster, Wooster, Ohio.

797 Clarence Manion Papers, Chicago Historical Society, B-2, F2-9.

798 *Common Sense*, August 1, 1957, December 15, 1957, and November 1, 1963.

799 Russ Ballant, *Old Nazis, the New Right and the Republican Party* (Boston: South End Press, 1988), 45.

800 Russell, *The Man Who Knew Too Much*, 528, 781.

801 Charles Willoughby Papers, Douglas MacArthur Archives, Norfolk, Virginia, RG 63.

802 Charles Willoughby Papers, Douglas MacArthur Archives, Norfolk, Virginia.

803 Russell, *The Man Who Knew Too Much*.

804 Russell, *The Man Who Knew Too Much*. Also, Sir Barry Edward Domvile was a right-wing extremist and anti-Semite who, in 1936, attended a rally in Germany as a guest of Joachim von Ribbentrop and met Heinrich Himmler. (Ribbentrop was hanged for war crimes after World War II. Himmler was the head of the Waffen-SS and committed suicide after his capture by the British.) Domvile was arrested in Britain and imprisoned during the war because of his pro-Nazi views. [http://www.overlordsofchaos.com/html/jewish_conspiracy__admiral_sir.html] When Major Archibald E. Roberts published his book *Victory Denied*, it was endorsed on the cover by General Charles Willoughby, Pedro del Valle, and Sir Barry Edward Domvile, all members of the Shickshinny Knights. Others who endorsed the book were Willis Carto, James Parker

Dees, and Prince Michel Sturdza. [Archibald Roberts, *Victory Denied* (Fort Collins, CO: Committee to Restore the Constitution press 1966).] Thus, Domvile establishes another link between Archibald Roberts (of the Walker faction of the high military command of the hardcore underground) to the del Valle faction and the Shickshinny Knights. Domvile published an international quarterly magazine in the 1960s called *The New Patriots* that had incorporated the publication *American Reporter*. Rear Admiral John G. Crommelin served on the editorial advisory board with Domvile and Westbrook Pegler in 1966. Crommelin was mentioned in letters to and from generals del Valle and Walker before the assassination and was close to William Potter Gale. [*The New Patriot, an International Quarterly Magazine*, 8, no. 4, December 1966, Jackson, Mississippi] Also on the advisory board were Edward Fields of the NSRP, General Pedro del Valle, and Brigadier General William L. Lee (who was a member of the board of advisors to Billy James Hargis's Christian Crusade. [George Thayer, *The Farther Shores of Politics* (New York: Simon and Schuster, 1967), 68].

805 *Covert Action*, Winter 1986, No. 25, 27–38.

806 Warren Commission, XV.

807 Capell, *Treason is the Reason.*

808 Peter Dale Scott, *Deep Politics* (New York: Vintage Books, 1976), 213.

809 Russell, *The Man Who Knew Too Much*, 528.

810 FBI FOIA, Phillip James Corso, file number: 62-HQ-110017, FBI Reading Room.

811 Capell, *Treason is the Reason.*

812 Geoffrey Perret, *Old Soldiers Never Die* (New York: Random House, 1996). In the same article, Drew Pearson noted that General del Valle was coming close to calling for armed insurrection. General MacArthur loathed Pearson, who accused him of vanity, incompetence, and disloyalty to President Roosevelt—and sued him for libel. MacArthur settled the case when MacArthur's ex-wife came forth and corroborated Pearson's story and added additional salacious details.

813 FBI FOIA, Phillip James Corso, file number: 62-HQ-110017, FBI Reading Room.

814 Gerald R. Ford and John E. Stiles, *Portrait of an Assassin* (New York: Simon and Schuster, 1965), 13.

815 Edwin A. Walker Papers, Dolph Briscoe Center for American History, University of Texas at Austin, Box 96-30/13.

816 Rear Admiral Crommelin was close to J. B. Stoner, George Lincoln Rockwell, and Edward Fields. Gale and Crommelin planned to organize a march in Washington against Congress on July 4, 1964. Crommelin was a member of the Identity movement. [Turner, *Power on the Right*, 163.] In 1968, Milteer met with Crommelin and del Valle. [Letter, February 12, 1968, 180-10099-10176, The John F. Kennedy Assassination Records Collection, NARA.] Later, Crommelin served on the advisory board of the National Youth Alliance, previously known, in 1968, as Youth for Wallace, with Pedro del Valle, Revilo Oliver, and Richard Cotton. [Turner, *Power on the Right*, 163.]

In 1968, Milteer met with Crommelin and del Valle. [Letter, February 12, 1968, 180-10099-10176, The John F. Kennedy Assassination Records Collection, NARA.] Wally Butterworth stayed at Crommelin's house in 1964. [FBI FOIA Crommelin, Field Office file number 105-380.]

817   Thayer, *The Farther Shores of Politics*.

818   FBI FOIA, John Crommelin, file number 62-HQ-91575, computer number: 998,619.

819   *Right*, November 1958, no. 38, Paul O. Peters Papers, Special Collections, College of Wooster, Wooster, Ohio.

820   *The Virginian*, January-February 1958, Paul O. Peters Papers, Special Collections, College of Wooster, Wooster, Ohio.

821   FBI FOIA, John Crommelin, file number 62-HQ-91575, computer number: 998,619.

822   Thayer, *The Farther Shores of Politics*.

823   Microfilm, Right-Wing Collection, University of Iowa. Also on the Board of the AAJ were attorney George Washington and Dr. Marque Nelson of Tulsa, Oklahoma; Washington was a featured speaker at the 1972 Congress of Freedom. [180-10095-10460, The John F. Kennedy Assassination Records Collection, NARA.]

824   FBI FOIA, John Crommelin, file number 62-HQ-91575, number: 998,619.

825   FBI FOIA, John Crommelin, file number 62-HQ-91575, number: 998,619, 157-1025-189, Ep. 1.

826   Report of the Select Committee on Assassinations of the U.S. House of Representatives: Findings in the Assassination of Dr. Martin Luther King, Jr.

827   FBI FOIA Crommelin, Field Office file number 105-380, dated March 17, 1963.

828   Tom Anderson Papers, Special Collections, University of Oregon Library.

Chapter 9

829   *Playboy*, October 1967.

830   *Warren Commission Report*.

831   Tom Bethel, diary, September 14, 1967, William Wood Papers, The John F. Kennedy Assassination Records Collection, National Archives and Records Association (NARA).

832   *Warren Commission Report*.

833   FBI New Orleans. 100-16601.

834   FBI New Orleans. 100-16601, dated December 17, 1963.

835   Andrew Sciambra, memo to Jim Garrison regarding interview of Betty Parrott held on December 18, 1967, New Orleans district attorney. Parrot told Sciambra: "Butler did know a lot about the FDC as he was always with Guy Banister and Jack Martin."

836   Allen Campbell, interview by the author, September 22, 1996. Campbell, who worked for Banister, told the author that Butler was at Banister's "all the time."

837   Warren Commission, XXII, 618-9.

838 *Playboy*, October 1967.

839 Garrison, *On the Trail of Assassins*.

840 *Playboy*, October 1967, 76.

841 *Playboy*, October 1967, 74.

842 Author Gary Shaw told the author, at a 1990s Dallas conference, that he acquired copies of Garrison's files from William Wood's widow.

843 Jim DiEugenio arranged the viewing and copying of Garrison's investigative files with Garrison's family in New Orleans in August 1994. DiEugenio wrote the book *Destiny Betrayed*, which presented Garrison in a favorable light. William Davy, author of *Let Justice Be Done*, and Peter Vea of AARC were also present.

844 Garrison, *On the Trail of Assassins*.

845 Warren Commission, Exhibit 394, XI, 325.

846 Sergeant Tom Duffy and Ptn. Cliency Navarre, memo, March 9, 1967, NODA.

847 Jim Garrison, memo, April 4, 1967, NODA.

848 180-10021-10015, The John F. Kennedy Assassination Records Collection, NARA.

849 Sergeant John J. Buccola, state police report to Lou Ivon, August 5, 1967, NODA.

850 Lou Ivon, interview by the author, October 10, 2000.

851 Garrison, *On the Trail of Assassins*.

852 Memo, statement of Aloysius Habighorst, January 23, 1968, NODA.

853 Paris Flamonde, *The Kennedy Conspiracy, An Uncommissioned Report on the Jim Garrison Investigation* (New York: Meredith Press, 1969).

854 James and Wardlaw, *Plot or Politics*.

855 Perry Russo, interview by the author, August 30, 1994.

856 James and Wardlaw, *Plot or Politics*.

857 Perry Russo, interview by the author, August 30, 1994.

858 *Councilor*, June 1967.

859 *Baton Rouge Morning Advocate*, March 15, 1967.

860 *Baton Rouge State–Times*, February 24, 1967.

861 Milton E. Brener, *The Garrison Case: A Study in the Abuse of Power* (New York: Clarkson Potter, 1969).

862 124-10039-10336, The John F. Kennedy Assassination Records Collection, NARA.

863 Press release from the New Orleans Metropolitan Crime Commission, June 22, 1967.

864 Online video interview, n.d., circa 1991. http://www.youtube.com/watch? v=2_BZk-5tkyno.

865 Harold Weisberg, interviews by the author, September 18, 1996, and May 18, 2000.

866 Perry Russo, interview by the author, August 30, 1994.

867 Ibid.

868 Flier from the Fred Schwarz Greater New Orleans School of Anti-Communism, October 23–27, 1961, Herbert Philbrick Papers, Library of Congress, Box 45:11.

869 Robert Oswald, *Lee, A Portrait of Lee Harvey Oswald* (New York, Coward-McCann,

Inc., 1967).

870 Herbert Philbrick Papers, Library of Congress, Box 19, F 5. In another episode, "Infiltration," Philbrick watched another "comrade" get slapped around and accused of being an infiltrator. Not satisfied that the "comrade" was telling the truth, he was ordered to be "taken out." Philbrick was assigned to another "comrade" that the party leaders felt might be an infiltrator who worked in an oil refinery. Philbrick told the "comrade" that there was a purge underway and that if he was not committed to the party he should leave it while he could. To show his party loyalty, the comrade exploded a bomb at the refinery.

871 Cedric Belfrage, *The American Inquisition, 1945–1960* (New York: The Bobbs-Merrill Company, Inc., 1973), 237.

872 *Daily Worker*, February 9, 1956.

873 Clarence Manion, letter to Herbert Philbrick, January 10, 1964, Herbert Philbrick Papers, Library of Congress, B134, F 4.

874 Herbert Philbrick, letter to Frank Kelley, June 4, 1951, Herbert Philbrick Papers, Library of Congress, B227, F 14.

875 Herbert Philbrick Papers, Library of Congress, B225, F 11, 158:9, 135:17.

876 Herbert Philbrick Papers, Library of Congress, B223, F 12.

877 Herbert Philbrick Papers, Library of Congress, B 279, F 9: Surrey on Board
CD 87, 349.

878 Ibid.

879 Courtney Papers, Special Collections, Northwestern State University of Louisiana.

880 Flamonde, *The Kennedy Conspiracy*.

881 Other Fascists noted were Giuseppe Gisigotti and Prince Gutierrez di Spadafora, Garrison file "For Lead File," *Pravda*, March 7, 1967, NODA.

882 William Martin, interview by Bill Boxley, May 26, 1967, NODA.

883 Raymond Broshears interview, August 9, 1968, NODA.

884 104-10170-10201, The John F. Kennedy Assassination Records Collection, NARA.

885 *HSCA Final Report*, 218.

886 Jim Garrison, memo to Andrew Sciambra, April 7, 1967, NODA.

887 179-20002-10282, The John F. Kennedy Assassination Records Collection, NARA.

888 Letter, to the San Francisco World Trade Center Directory, November 13, 1963, NODA.

889 179-20001-10432, The John F. Kennedy Assassination Records Collection, NARA.

890 Interview report of William W. Turner, March 29, 1967, NODA.

891 124-10237-10389, The John F. Kennedy Assassination Records Collection, NARA.

892 "From Sciambra, Re: Information on the NSRP and the American Nazi Party," May 13, 1968, NODA.

893 Unpublished manuscript of Harold Weisberg, *Coup D'état*, courtesy of Bill Adams, 91. (Weisberg confirmed for the author that he wrote the manuscript.)

894   Joseph Oster, interview by the author, October 14, 1999.

895   Shaw trial transcript, February 21, 1969, AARC.

896   "Notes from Alberto Fowler," undated, in Jim Garrison's handwriting, NODA.

897   Ned Touchstone Papers, Noel Memorial Library, Louisiana State University Shreve-port.

898   FBI FOIA, Alvin Cobb, file number 62102337.

899   Pedro del Valle, letters to Henry S. Riecke, March 27, 1964, Arpil 29, 1954, and June 15, 1964, Tom Anderson Papers, Special Collections, University of Oregon Library.

900   Pedro del Valle Papers, Special Collections, University of Oregon Library, 157/18.

901   Rau is mentioned in the *Councilor*, May 5, 1963.

902   Helm is mentioned in "Interview of Kimble," October 10, 1967, NODA.

903   Henry Riecke, who owned the New Orleans Cabinet Works, was a fanatical anti-Communist. He wrote Senator Allen Ellender in 1961 and urged stripping Communists of their Fifth Amendment rights as proposed in a House amendment to the Smith Act. Riecke wrote that the Communists "were like termites in the Defense Department, the CIA, the Supreme Court, the House and the Senate." In a letter on June 1, 1961, Riecke wrote Ellender: "There is a terrific, unprecedented groundswell developing in New Orleans, as people are becoming rightfully alarmed! They are joining anti-Communist organizations every day. And it's about time—that Americans wake up! The Communists already have 1/3rd of their takeover of our Government accomplished." Riecke mentioned that he attended a May 23, 1961, luncheon given by the Christian Anti-Communist Crusade, which was attended by 1,500 business leaders. (Guy Banister was an advisor to the group.) He was also impressed by a local John Birch Society meeting. [Henry S. Riecke, letter to Allen Ellender, May 22, 1961, Ellender Papers, Nicholls State University, Collection 8 FF, Box 771.] The FBI was in possession of one of PRAY's newsletters written by Riecke and sent to General Pedro del Valle, which was dated May 1, 1964. Riecke wrote that his organization, along with del Valle's Defenders of the American Constitution, Inc., had sent out an a "Alert" urging citizens to arm themselves to defeat the Communist conspiracy. [Pedro del Valle Papers, Special Collections, University of Oregon Library, 157/18.] In an April 6 letter to Robert Welch, Riecke praised Billy James Hargis, Harry Everingham, Dan Smoot, Ned Touchstone, Conde McGinley, Benjamin Freedman, and others connected with the hardcore underground who have been covered in prior chapters. Riecke proudly toed the Communism-is-Jewish line. He boasted membership of his organization in thirty-nine states and three foreign countries. [Manion Papers, Chicago Historical Society, Box 60, F 15.]

904   180-10112-10373, The John F. Kennedy Assassination Records Collection, NARA.

905   Garrison, *On the Trail of Assassins*.

906   Hale Boggs Papers, Howard-Tilton Memorial Library at Tulane University.

907   Lloyd Cobb owned a working farm in East Feliciana Parish. Curiously, when one of

Cobb's farm managers died in 1965, Cobb and Mrs. Carlos Marcello and her children attended the funeral in St. Francisville. [*The St. Francisville Democrat*, December 9, 1965.] Guy Banister and David Ferrie did research for Marcello lawyer G. Wray Gill and knew Marcello. [Joseph Newbrough, interview by NODA, undated; also: Author's interview of Mary Brengel, July 25, 1996.] David Ferrie was employed by Gill and was present in the courtroom during Marcello's trial on the day of the Kennedy assassination.

908   FBI FOIA, Alvin Cobb, file number 44-884, 18.

909   *Times–Picayune*, March 2, 1956.

910   Joint Legislative Committee on Un-American Activities for the State of Louisiana, report no. 7.

911   FBI FOIA, Joseph A. Milteer.

912   180-100801-0004, The John F. Kennedy Assassination Records Collection, NARA.

913   FBI FOIA, Alvin Cobb, file number 62102337.

914   Letter, F. Edward Herbert Papers, Political Ephemeral Collection, Howard-Tilton Memorial Library at Tulane University. Cecilia Pizzo called him "Father Alvis." She noted that Alvin Cobb was friendly with the ultra-right-wing Anna Burglass, who is mentioned in Jim Garrison's files, and also knew Klansman Roswell Thompson.

915   180-10081-10277, The John F. Kennedy Assassination Records Collection, NARA.

916   FBI FOIA, Alvin Cobb, file numbers: 62102337, 44-12611, 157-4170.

917   FBI FOIA, Alvin Cobb, on segregation rally, file number 62102337.

918   James and Wardlaw, *Plot or Politics*.

919   Garrison, *On the Trail of Assassins*, 25.

920   Joseph Oster, interview by the author, October 14, 1999.

921   Allen Ellender Papers, Nicholls State University, 1FF, Box 301.

922   AARC, FOIA request from Bernard Fensterwald to the Department of the Navy, Naval Investigative Service, March 8, 1982.

923   Garrison, *On the Trail of Assassins*.

924   180-10082-10170, The John F. Kennedy Assassination Records Collection, NARA.

925   Garrison, *On the Trail of Assassins*, 173.

926   William C. Wood, interview by George Rennar, August 31, 1971, AARC.

927   180-10082-10170, The John F. Kennedy Assassination Records Collection, NARA.

928   *States–Item* 9-22-60; *States–Item* 9-28-60. Other prospects for the job were Jack N. Rogers and George Schulz.

929   Carlos Bringuier, interview by Regis Kennedy, December 25, 1963, FBI file number 89-69-256, The John F. Kennedy Assassination Records Collection, NARA.

930   *Warren Commission Report*, 287.

931   Ibid.

932   Warren Commission, X, 32.

933   Warren Commission, XXI, 642.

934   *HSCA Final Report*, 141.

935   Carlos Quiroga's Grand Jury testimony, AARC library website (http://aarclibrary.org).

936   180-10116-10159, The John F. Kennedy Assassination Records Collection, NARA.

937   Harold Weisberg, interview by the author, November 20, 1996. Weisberg alludes to the incident on pages 284–5 in *Never Again* (New York; Carroll and Graf, 1995), but does not mention names. He related to the author that Phillip Geraci was kidnapped and interviewed by New Orleans police officers F. S. Sullivan and a Sergeant Borne (perhaps of Jefferson Parish) the day after David Ferrie died. Weisberg refers to Bringuier and Geraci in his book, not by name, but as the "Warren Commission witnesses."

938   CIA 204-10001-10005, The John F. Kennedy Assassination Records Collection, NARA. Ed Butler appeared before a confidential executive session of the SISS at 2:45 p.m. on November 24, 1963. Senator Dodd presided and J. G. Sourwine was present. Butler told them than he first met Lee Harvey Oswald on August 21, 1963, when Butler was invited to appear with him on a panel debate at WDSU. Butler told them he had a very deep interest in Communist psychological activities. He said Oswald's motivation behind his actions was the tremendous amount of Communist indoctrination that he had received. Butler handed over the taped debate, along with a transcript.

939   *HSCA Final Report*, 142.

940   "Subcommittee on International Organizations and Movements of the Committee of Foreign Affairs of the House of Representatives," September 11, 1963.

941   Summers, *Conspiracy*, 150.

942   *Times–Picayune*, November 20, 1963.

943   Allen Campbell, interview by the author, September 22, 1996.

944   Garrison, *On the Trail of Assassins*.

945   William R. Klein, letter to Jim Garrison, May 4, 1967, NODA. Garrison added in his handwriting: "Re: RADICAL RIGHT WING (Ed Butler)."

946   104-10069-10051, The John F. Kennedy Assassination Records Collection, NARA.

947   "Notes from Alberto Fowler," undated, in Garrison's handwriting, NODA.

948   Tom Bethel, diary, February 22, 1968, William Wood Papers, The John F. Kennedy Assassination Records Collection, NARA.

949   James and Wardlaw, *Plot or Politics*.

950   Marlene Mancuso, interview by Jim Garrison, March 31, 1967, NODA.

951   James and Wardlaw, *Plot or Politics*.

952   Ibid.

953   104-10406-10049, The John F. Kennedy Assassination Records Collection, NARA. In the 1967 letter to the Justice Department, the CIA noted that "Double-check" was the subject of an "erroneous" book, *The Invisible Government.*

954   Butch Bonamo, interview by the author, August 1998.

955   Lieutenant Thomas B. Casso, division of state police, memo to Jim Garrison, regard-

ing Sergeant John J. Buccola Special Investigation, March 9, 1967 through April 1, 1967, NODA.

956 John Irion, statement, January 20, 1967, NODA.

957 Marlene Mancuso, ex-wife of Gordon Novel, interview by Jim Garrison, March 31, 1967, NODA.

958 Lieutenant Thomas B. Casso, division of state police, memo to Jim Garrison, regarding Sergeant John J. Buccola Special Investigation, March 9, 1967 through April 1, 1967, NODA.

959 Tom Bethel, diary, 18, William Wood Papers, The John F. Kennedy Assassination Records Collection, NARA.

960 "Re: Testimony of Nancy M. Powell," William Wood Papers, The John F. Kennedy Assassination Records Collection, NARA.

961 Tommy Cox, interview NODA, undated.

962 Margaret McLeigh, interview December 29, 1967, NODA.

963 Marlene Mancuso, ex-wife of Gordon Novel, interview March 31, 1967, NODA.

964 Found in Novel's *Playboy* deposition. Novel sued *Playboy* over the Garrison interview. The author could not determine the source of the deposition. It may be from AARC.

965 *Times–Picayune*, December 13, 1978.

966 *States–Item*, December 15, 1978.

967 A friend of the author who was familiar with Novel's appearance believed he saw Novel on the TV news at the Waco compound at the time of the siege.

968 Summers, *Conspiracy*, 254–256.

969 *HSCA Final Report*, 218.

970 *Playboy*, October 1967, 72.

971 *Warren Commission Report*.

972 *Playboy*, October 1967, 72.

973 *HSCA Final Report*, 218.

974 William Turner, letter to the author, April 17, 2002.

975 Jim Garrison, *On the Trail of Assassins*, 45.

976 "Re: 1976 Affifavit of Kerry Thornley" appears to be Garrison's handwritten synopsis, possibly of a HSCA report on Kerry Thornley, September 20, 1976, Jim Garrison Papers, NARA.

977 180-10104-10278, The John F. Kennedy Assassination Records Collection, NARA.

978 Phillip Boatright, letter to Harold Weisberg, April 21, 1968, Jim Garrison Papers, NARA.

979 Phillip Boatright, interview by Harold Weisberg, April 3, 1968, NODA.

980 Kerry Thornley's Grand Jury Testimony, February 8, 1968, AARC online library (http://aarclibrary.org).

981 Andrew Sciambra, memo to Jim Garrison, December 9, 1967, NODA.

982 "Leads," Jim Garrison, September 6, 1967, 2.

983 Jim Garrison, memo to Jonathan Blackmer, NODA. The witnesses were Barbara Glancey Reid and Pete Diagmo. Though undated, this appears to have been written during the HSCA investigation.

984 Tom Bethel, diary, William Wood Papers, The John F. Kennedy Assassination Records Collection, NARA, 16.

985 Letter, from John Schwegmann, Jr., February 22, 1968, NODA. Another witness stated that he saw Thornley going to the grocery store with Oswald's wife so often that they thought the two were husband and wife. A Schwegmann employee saw Thornley at the Oswald residence a number of times.

986 "Re: Kerry Thornley," memo, March 14, 1968, NODA.

987 Allen Campbell, interview by Andrew Sciambra, May 4, 1969, NODA.

988 "Re: Jack Frazier," Gary Sanders memo to Louis Ivon, March 6, 1968, NODA.

989 "Re: Bernard Goldsmith," Gary Sanders memo to Louis Ivon, March 4, 1968.

990 Warren Commission, XXII, CE 1410.

991 Harold Weisberg, interviews by the author, November 18, 1996, and May 18, 2000.

992 Jim Garrison, *On the Trail of Assassins*.

993 Phillip Boatright, interview by Harold Weisberg, transcribed April 24, 1968, NODA.

994 180-10088-10485, NARA; also: affidavit of Peter Diagmo, NODA.

995 Jim Garrison, memo to Jonathon Blackmer, NODA. Though undated, this memo appears to have been written by Garrison during HSCA investigation.

996 Weisberg, *Oswald in New Orleans*, 292.

997 Harold Weisberg, interviews by the author, November 18, 1996, and May 18, 2000.

998 Jim Garrison, *On the Trail of Assassins*, 76.

999 Kerry Thornley, Grand Jury Testimony, February 8, 1968, AARC online library.

1000 Thomas Beckham, handwritten statement, 180-10100-10040, The John F. Kennedy Assassination Records Collection, NARA.

1001 *States–Item*, December 29, 1967.

1002 *States–Item*, January 3, 1968.

1003 Kerry Thornley, Grand Jury Testimony, February 8, 1968, AARC online library (http://aarclibrary.org).

1004 180-10112-10303, The John F. Kennedy Assassination Records Collection, NARA.

1005 HSCA 180-100070-10296

1006 HSCA 12110016, agency file number 014888, Box 284.

1007 180-10104-10278, The John F. Kennedy Assassination Records Collection, NARA.

1008 180-10081-10277, The John F. Kennedy Assassination Records Collection, NARA.

1009 180-10104-10278, The John F. Kennedy Assassination Records Collection, NARA.

1010 12110016, agency file number 014888, Box 284, The John F. Kennedy Assassination Records Collection, NARA.

1011 180-10070-10296, The John F. Kennedy Assassination Records Collection, NARA.

1012 180-10109-10290, The John F. Kennedy Assassination Records Collection, NARA.

1013 180-10070-10296, The John F. Kennedy Assassination Records Collection, NARA.

1014 Thomas Beckham, Grand Jury Testimony, February 8, 1968, AARC online library (http://aarclibrary.org).

1015 Jim Garrison, *On the Trail of Assassins*.

1016 Jim Lesar, interview by the author, January 9, 2012.

1017 *Times–Picayune*, December 22, 1967.

1018 Jim Garrison, *On the Trail of Assassins*, 206, 286.

1019 Peter Noyes, *Legacy of Doubt* (New York: Pinnacle Books, 1973).

1020 Bill Boxley, memo to Jim Garrison, March 19, 1968, NODA. Supplement to Bill Turner's memorandum on Edgar Eugene Bradley, dated February 16, 1968.

1021 Bill Turner, memorandum on Edgar Eugene Bradley, dated February 16, 1968.

1022 180-101-10380, The John F. Kennedy Assassination Records Collection, NARA.

1023 Edgar Eugene Bradley, interview by Steven J. Burton, May 23, 1968, NODA.

1024 *Councilor*, December 1963.

1025 180-101-10380, The John F. Kennedy Assassination Records Collection, NARA.

1026 Margaret McLeigh, interview by Jim Garrison, May 3, 1968. Gene Bradley tried to enlist people into a Minutemen group and interest them in religious activities, according to his neighbor.

1027 Noyes, *Legacy of a Doubt*, 100.

1028 *The North Valley Mail*, January 24, 1968, 180-10085-103331, The John F. Kennedy Assassination Records Collection, NARA.

1029 NODA memorandum, affidavit dated January 16, 1968:, news story by Stephen Jaffe, "Reagan Rules to Free Bradley," November 8, 1968, Sacramento, 124-10078-10381, The John F. Kennedy Assassination Records Collection, NARA. Some suggested that Max Gonzales might have confused Gene Bradley with Leslie Norman Bradley who worked at the airport.

1030 Brener, *The Garrison Case*, 198.

1031 Steven Burton, memo to Jim Garrison, March 13, 1968, NODA, Citizens Committee of Inquiry, William Wood Papers, The John F. Kennedy Assassination Records Collection, National Archives and Records Administration (NARA).

1032 *The Signal*, May 8, 1968.

1033 124-10078-10384, The John F. Kennedy Assassination Records Collection, NARA.

1034 Unknown source, "To whomever this may concern," AARC.

1035 *New York Free Press*, November 21, 1968.

1036 Bill Boxley, Garrison memo, March 19, 1968, interview of Mrs. Aydelotte, Thomas Thornhill, and Mrs. Brice. General Walker also gave a speech in Los Angeles on January 11, 1962, on the subject "Make Mine Freedom." One of Walker's detractors wrote him and told him he was better qualified to speak on "Make Mine Murder." [Herbert Holdrige, letter to General Walker, January 3, 1962, GLK Smith Collection, Bentley Library, University of Michigan, Box 55.]

1037 180-10102-1080, The John F. Kennedy Assassination Records Collection, NARA.

1038 180-10022-10452, The John F. Kennedy Assassination Records Collection, NARA.

1039 *North Valley Mail*, Vol. 6, No. 28.

1040 *Contra Mundum*, No. 6, Winter, 1993. In the 1990s, Gene Bradley stated that the original charges stemmed from four people that wanted to harm him and Carl McIntire. When Bradley, who was originally from Arkansas, was asked about his feelings about Bill Clinton's candidacy for president, a fellow Arkansan, Bradley stated that he would never vote for him because he demonstrated with the Communists during the Vietnam War and was a Rhodes Scholar "who are trained in a one-world government."

1041 Margaret McLeigh, interview by Jim Garrison, May 3, 1968, NODA.

1042 John Smith, *Birch Putsch* (Domino Publications, 1963).

1043 Janson and Eismann, *The Far Right*.

1044 Mark Stoll, *Crusaders Against Communism, Witnesses for Peace: Religion in the West and the Cold War*, http://www.colorado.edu/ReligiousStudies/chernus/4820-Nationalism/Graduate%20Readings/CrusadersAgainstCommunism.pdf.

1045 Manion Papers, 8-6, Chicago Historical Society.

1046 News clip featuring Drew Pearson, December 7, 1963, 124-10020-10204, The John F. Kennedy Assassination Records Collection, NARA.

1047 NODA memo, William Wood Papers, The John F. Kennedy Assassination Records Collection, NARA.

1048 *Thunderbolt*, December, 1969.

1049 180-10099-10176, The John F. Kennedy Assassination Records Collection, NARA.

1050 *Alarming Cry*, Sept–Oct 1954, Right Wing Collection, University of Iowa.

1051 124-10020-10204, The John F. Kennedy Assassination Records Collection, NARA.

1052 *Western Voice*, October 20, 1960, GLK Smith Papers, Box 50.

1053 180-10070-0334, The John F. Kennedy Assassination Records Collection, NARA.

1054 Letterhead of the American Council on Christian Churches found at ARCC (http://aarclibrary.org).

1055 124-10020-10204, The John F. Kennedy Assassination Records Collection, NARA.

1056 Flier, Philbrick Papers, Library of Congress, 137:7.

1057 124-10009-10088, The John F. Kennedy Assassination Records Collection, NARA.

1058 *Washington Post*, April 5, 1970. John Rarick was the featured speaker at the June 20, 1968, banquet.

1059 Flier, Heinsohn Papers, Special Collections, University of Oregon, 127:4.

1060 *Group Research*, September 10, 1970.

1061 "From Sciambra, Re: Information on the NSRP and the American Nazi Party," May 13, 1968.

1062 *States–Item*, April 13, 1968.

1063 Turner, *Power on the Right*, 106.

1064 FBI report, December 4, 1963. Also found in: Warren Commission, Document 641.

1065 *North Valley Mail*, Vol. 6, No. 28.

1066 Turner, *Power on the Right*, 108.

1067 Manion Papers, Chicago Historical Society, Box 10, File 2.

1068 Edwin A. Walker Papers, Dolph Briscoe Center for American History, University of Texas at Austin, Box 93 402/8.

1069 David Boylan, "A League of Their Own A Look Inside the Christian Defense League," *Cuban Information Archives*, last updated 2004, Cuban-exile.com/doc_026-050/doc0046.html.

1070 Secret Service CO2-26104.

1071 180-10118-1033, The John F. Kennedy Assassination Records Collection, NARA.

1072 124-10330-10035, HSCA.

1073 Woody Kearns, letter to Joseph A. Milteer, March 8, 1965, 180-10099-10119, HSCA.

1074 New Orleans newspaper, May 14, 1968. The author's notes do not make it clear if this was from the *Times–Picayune* or the *States–Item*.

1075 Thayer, *The Farther Shore of Politics*, 145.

1076 *New York Free Press*, November 21, 1968.

1077 Chester W. Warman, letter to Jim Garrison, May 10, 1968, NODA.

1078 FBI 124-10178-102006, courtesy of David Boylan.

1079 Bill Boxley, letter to Jim Garrison, March 19, 1968, NODA. Supplement to Bill Turner's memorandum on Edgar Eugene Bradley, which was dated February 16, 1968.

1080 Stephen Jaffe, letter to Jim Garrison, March 20, 1968.

Chapter 10

1081 Audiocassette, 180-10131-10099, The John F. Kennedy Assassination Records Collection, NARA.

1082 Willie Somersett, interview by Miami Police Department, transcript, November 26, 1963, 180-10090-10307, The John F. Kennedy Assassination Records Collection, NARA.

1083 180-10099-10173, The John F. Kennedy Assassination Records Collection, NARA.

1084 180-10099-10224, The John F. Kennedy Assassination Records Collection, NARA, Box 49.

1085 Barbara Glancey Reid, April 12, 16, and 17 1968, NODA.

1086 180-10076-10178, The John F. Kennedy Assassination Records Collection, NARA.

1087 180-1099-101703, The John F. Kennedy Assassination Records Collection, NARA.

1088 Guy Banister, letter to Willie Rainach, April 23, 1958, Rainach Papers, Noel Memorial Library, Lousiana State University Shreveport.

1089 HSCA, Boxed Records, boxes 48 and 49.

1090 Glen Jeansonne, *Leander Perez: Boss of the Delta* (Baton Rouge: Louisiana State University Press, 1977).

1091 Glen Jeansonne, interview by the author, 1998.

1092 Ibid.

1093 Joseph A. Milteer, letter, BCPC.

1094 Jeansonne, *Leander Perez*.

1095 *Plaquemines Gazette*, September 30, 1960.

1096 James Conway, *Judge: The Life and Times of Leander Perez* (New York: Alfred A. Knopf, 1973).

1097 *New Republic*, May 24, 1969.

1098 Jeansonne, *Leander Perez*.

1099 Adam Fairclough, *Race & Democracy: The Civil Rights Struggle in Louisiana 1915–1972* (Athens & London: The University of Georgia Press, 1995).

1100 Jeansonne, *Leander Perez*.

1101 Conway, *Judge*.

1102 *Times–Picayune*, March 27, 1959.

1103 Ibid.

1104 National Indignation letterhead, Victor Schiro Papers, New Orleans Public Library, Louisiana Division.

1105 *Memphis Commercial Appeal*, December 29, 1955.

1106 Joe Conason and Gene Lyons, *The Hunting of a President* (New York: St. Martin's Press, 2000). In 1966, Bill Clinton worked to defeat Jim Johnson's bid for governor on a States Rights platform. During the Clinton presidency, Johnson continued his assault against Clinton and was the principal hunter, revealer, and promoter of Clinton's purported immoral activity.

1107 BCPC.

1108 *Shreveport Journal*, September, 25, 1964.

1109 J. Evetts Haley Papers, The Haley Memorial Library and History Center. William Shaw, a Homer, Louisiana, attorney, was a member of the executive committee of the Federation. Shaw was the close aide of Willie Rainach, a friend of Guy Banister and also Colonel William Gale, Milteer's associate.

1110 Federation for Constitutional Government, letter to Mary Cain, April 17, 1959, Mary Cain Papers, Mississippi Department of Archives and History.

1111 FBI FOIA, Edwin A. Walker.

1112 Hubert Humphrey Oral history, Noel Memorial Library, Louisiana State University Shreveport.

1113 Conway, *Judge*.

1114 Michael Zatarain, *David Duke Evolution of a Klansman* (Gretna: Pelican Publishing Company, 1990), 77. Jack Ricau, who wrote the *Citizens' Report* that drew heavily from Guy Banister's files (as noted in Chapter One), formed the South Louisiana Citizens' Council. Ricau later headed the Louisiana Committee to Restore the Constitution, which was founded nationally by Major Arch Roberts. Roberts, as will be recalled, was General Walker's former aide de camp in the army and was a military advisor to the Council for Statehood and the Congress of Freedom. Others in the Committee included Evelyn Jahncke, a friend of Banister's love interest Delphine Roberts, and also Cameron Terry, who represented the Citizens' Council at the Congress of Freedom in New Orleans in 1963. [Flier "A Possible Dream for Our Centennial," 1974, Jim Garrison Papers, NODA.] The Committee to Restore the Constitution was located in the Maison Blanch Building.

1115 Jeansonne, *Leander Perez*.

1116 Joint Legislative Committee on Segregation letterhead, Rainach Papers, Noel Memorial Library, Louisiana State University Shreveport.

1117 Jeff Woods, *Black Struggle Red Scare: Segregation and Anticommunism in the South: 1948–1968* (Baton Rouge: Louisiana State University Press, 2004).

1118 Jeansonne, *Leander Perez*.

1119 Kent Courtney, letter to Willie Rainach, April 15, 1959, Courtney Papers, Special Collections, Northwestern State University of Louisiana.

1120 Jeansonne, *Leander Perez*.

1121 Jeansonne, *Leander Perez*.

1122 *New York Times*, March 20, 1969.

1123 Jeansonne, *Leander Perez*, 119.

1124 Conway, *Judge*.

1125 180-10097-10214, The John F. Kennedy Assassination Records Collection, NARA.

1126 Jeansonne, *Leander Perez*, 312.

1127 Jeansonne, *Leander Perez*, 314.

1128 Jeansonne, *Leander Perez*, 315.

1129 Capitol House meeting, September 5, 1960, Mary Cain Papers, Mississippi State Archives and History Center, Box 28.

1130 States Rights Party of Louisiana, letter to Friends of States Rights, March 12, 1960, New Orleans Public Library, Louisiana Division.

1131 *Alexandria Daily Town Talk*, February 22, 1960.

1132 Jeansonne, *Leander Perez*.

1133 *States–Item*, October 22, 1960 and October 23, 1960.

1134 Joseph Oster, interviews by the author, October 14, 1999, and March 20, 2000.

1135 *Plaquemines Gazette*, November 4, 1960.

1136 Jeansonne, *Leander Perez*, 325.

1137 Jeansonne, *Leander Perez*.

1138 Jeansonne, *Leander Perez*, 271.

1139 *Times–Picayune*, May 12, 1963.

1140 *Councilor*, December 5, 1963.

1141 *Councilor*, July 16, 1964.

1142 Broadcast Transcript #63-267, Courtney Papers, Special Collections, Northwestern

State University of Louisiana.

1143 *Citizens' Report*. H. L. Hunt, Jack Ricau and governors Jimmie Davis and George Wallace were there.

1144 ⁶⁴ Wellborne Jack Papers, Louisiana State University Shreveport

1145 Jeansonne, *Leander Perez*, 327.

1146 *Councilor*, December 5, 1963. Guy Banister, Delphine Roberts, Cameron Terry and C.E. Vetter were Orleans Parish elector candidates in 1963.

1147 Jeansonne, *Leander Perez*, 327.

1148 Jeansonne, *Leander Perez*.

1149 George Singelmann, interview by the author, Hubert Humphrey Oral History, Noel Memorial Library, Louisiana State University Shreveport. George Wallace was an Alabama State Judge who rose to a leadership position in the integration resistance movement. He was a sought-after speaker in the Free Electors rallies. [Jeansonne, *Leander Perez*, 315.] In 1958, Wallace demonstrated this kind of fiery Perez-like opposition to the federal government when he refused to hand over county records to the U.S. Civil Rights Commission.

1150 Jeansonne, *Leander Perez*, 329.

1151 FBI FOIA, Joseph A. Milteer.

1152 180-10095-10442, The John F. Kennedy Assassination Records Collection, NARA.

1153 *Group Research*, July 15, 1964.

1154 Conway, *Judge*.

1155 *New Republic*, May 24, 1969.

1156 *New York Times*, March 20, 1969.

1157 Letter, July 13, 1977 and June 6, 1977, Roy V. Harris Papers, Special Collections, The University of Georgia Libraries.

1158 Allen Campbell, interview by the author, September 22, 1996.

1159 *Plaquemines Gazette*, July 7, 1961.

1160 *Times–Picayune*, July 2, 1961 and July 5, 1961.

1161 *Times–Picayune*, March 16, 1961.

1162 *Times—Picayune*, March 19, 1961.

1163 *Times—Picayune*, March 4, 1956.

1164 Video of Walker and Barnett's speech to the Mississippi State Legislature are at the Mississippi State Archives and History Center.

1165 Hale Boggs Papers, Special Collections, Howard-Tilton Library at Tulane University.

1166 Jim Marrs, *Crossfire: the Plot that Killed President Kennedy* (New York: Carroll & Graf, Inc., 1989), 259.

1167 Joseph A. Milteer, letter to Roy V. Harris, September 5, 1968, 180-10099-10249, The John F. Kennedy Assassination Records Collection, NARA.

1168 Letter to Richard Cotton, February 27, 1968, 180-10099-101, The John F. Kennedy Assassination Records Collection, NARA.

1169 Letter to Woody Kearns, February 29, 1968, NARA, HSCA Box 48 or 49.

1170 FBI FOIA, Roy V. Harris, file number 157-871-2379. Harris was on the National States Rights Party membership list. Interestingly, the FBI noted that James Earl Ray was given the responsibility of guarding the national offices of the NSRP from an unknown individual who was expelled from the NSRP whom they felt might try to steal the membership list.

1171 *The Citizen*, 1956, Mississippi State Archives and History Center.

1172 *The Citizens' Council*, 6, no. 9, Mississippi State Archives and History Center.

1173 Roy V. Harris Papers, Special Collections, University of Georgia Libraries.

1174 Harris Oral History, Roy V. Harris Papers, Special Collections, University of Georgia Libraries.

1175 James Graham Cook, *The Segregationists* (New York: Meredith Press, 1962), 103.

1176 Harriet Raines, *My Soul is Rested* (New York: Penguin Books, 1986).

1177 Harris Oral History, Roy V. Harris Papers, Special Collections, University of Georgia Libraries, AVA 86-1:2 Politics, #3&4. Harris's papers are devoid of anything from 1948 to 1977 except for a few Citizens' Council pictures. (Roy Eugene Barnes, whose father was a friend of Harris, was governor of Georgia from 1999 to 2003 and was named in honor of both Roy Harris and Eugene Talmadge. Barnes, as a State Representative, voted against the Martin Luther King holiday. Later, he became more moderate and pushed for the removal of the Confederate "stars and bars" from its former prominent place on the state flag. See: *The Truth at Last*, 434, April 2002.)

1178 *Southern Digest*, April 1956, microfilm, Right Wing Collection, University of Iowa.

1179 Raines, *My Soul is Rested*.

1180 Anne Braden, interview by the author, February 3, 2001.

1181 *Councilor*, August 5, 1963, 11. The paper showed a photo taken by Ed Friend, which showed black and white participants at the Highlander School in 1957 putting their arms around each other—but not touching.

1182 Ed Friend's motion picture of the 1957 Highlander School meeting, Special Collections, University of Georgia.

1183 Earl Lively, letter to Herbert Philbrick, May 8, 1965, Herbert Philbrick Papers, Library of Congress.

1184 Raines, *My Soul is Rested*.

1185 FBI FOIA, Highlander School, FBI Reading Room website.

1186 Raines, *My Soul is Rested*.

1187 Ibid.

1188 "Communist Training School" pictured on JBS postcard, Ned Touchstone Papers, Noel Memorial Library, Louisiana State University Shreveport.

1189 HSCA Boxed Collection, Box 49.

1190 *Councilor*, September 1, 1967 and July 5, 1969.

1191 Eightieth Congress, 1st Session, Report No. 592.

1192   The New Georgia encyclopedia online, Christopher Allen Huff, Georgia Humanities Council and the University of Georgia, 2004–7 (http://www.georgiaencyclopedia. org).

1193   Harris Oral History, Roy V. Harris Papers, Special Collections, University of Georgia Libraries, 15.

1194   Rainach Papers, Noel Memorial Library, Lousiana State University Shreveport. Transcript of the speeches at the October 25–26, 1963, Annual Leadership Conference of the Citizens' Council of America in Jackson, Mississippi, including the Walker speech. This may be the only copy of Walker's speech in existence.

1195   FBI FOIA, Joseph A. Milteer, file number 66-16458, Section 4, Serials 217 through 28.7.

1196   124-10285-10310, The John F. Kennedy Assassination Records Collection, NARA.

1197   124-10285-10307, The John F. Kennedy Assassination Records Collection, NARA.

1198   124-10285-10304, The John F. Kennedy Assassination Records Collection, NARA.

1199   *Councilor*, May 5, 1963.

1200   *Times–Picayune*, Apri 26, 1962.

1201   Garrison, *On the Trail of Assassins*.

1202   *Times–Picayune*, March 6, 1962.

1203   Conway, *Judge*, 170.

1204   *Times–Picayune*, February 20, 1962.

1205   *New Republic*, May 24, 1969.

1206   *Times–Picayune*, March 3, 1962.

1207   HSCA, Vol X, 124–5.

1208   *Times–Picayune*, February 15, 1962.

1209   180-10007-210214, The John F. Kennedy Assassination Records Collection, NARA.

1210   Arthus was an "apparent harmless Protective Research subject of file CO-2-32, 791." See also: Warren Commission, XXVI, 769, 771; and HSCA X, Jack Martin interview by Lou, December 13, 1966.

1211   *Times–Picayune*, February 26, 1962.

1212   *Times–Picayune*, February 27, 1962.

1213   *Times–Picayune*, September 7, 1969. Cy Courtney was a cofounder of Kent's *Free Men Speak*. See also: *Times–Picayune*, August 28, 1959.

1214   Lou Ivon, interview by the author, October 5, 2000.

1215   *Times–Picayune*, March 31, 1962.

1216   Ellender Archives, Nicholls State University, 30:FF738.

1217   180-10099-10166, Box 48-9, The John F. Kennedy Assassination Records Collection, NARA.

1218   *Times–Picayune*, May 9, 1962.

1219   *Times–Picayune*, March 4, 1956.

1220   Willie Rainach, letter to Hubert Badeaux, September 15, 1958, Rainach Papers, Noel

Memorial Library, Lousiana State University Shreveport. Willie Rainach wrote to Hubert Badeaux on the letterhead of the Association of Citizens' Councils.

1221 *Times–Picayune*, February 15, 1956.

1222 *Times–Picayune*, March 21, 1956.

1223 *Plaquemines Gazette*, November 22, 1957.

1224 *Plaquemines Gazette*, July 27, 1958.

1225 States' Rights Party of Louisiana roster, Mary Cain Papers, Mississippi Archives and History Center, Box 28.

1226 Brenda Tucker, letter to Allen Ellender, June 23, 1969, Allen Ellender Papers, Nicholls State University, FF 22, Box 1720.

1227 *Times–Picayune*, May 18, 1960.

1228 *Plaquemines Gazette*, May 1963.

1229 *Times–Picayune*, May 24, 1963.

1230 *Times–Picayune*, May 28, 1963.

1231 *Shreveport Journal*, July 1, 1963.

1232 124-10008-10442, The John F. Kennedy Assassination Records Collection, NARA.

1233 Letter, March 9, 1962, Courtney Papers, Special Collections, Northwestern State University of Louisiana. Letter notes that Banister was a special advisor to the American Legion.

1234 HSCA 49 002118, The John F. Kennedy Assassination Records Collection, NARA.

1235 *Times–Picayune*, June 30, 1963.

1236 Joseph A. Milteer, letter to Woody Kearns and Joe Lichtburn, 180-10095-10442, The John F. Kennedy Assassination Records Collection, NARA.

1237 City Directory, New Orleans Public Library.

1238 180-10097-10345, The John F. Kennedy Assassination Records Collection, NARA. HSCA summary of FAA hearings. Also, the Richard Billings Papers at Georgetown University Library contain Guy Banister's FAA testimony.

1239 *Times–Picayune*, January 9, 1963.

1240 FBI file number 62-109060; JFK HQ File, Section 122, FBI interview with G. Wray Gill, 11-27-63: David Ferrie asked about library card: see NODA "4900 Magazine Street lead," April 11, 1969: NODA interview of Mr. and Mrs. Eames, Lee Harvey Oswald's neighbors. Ferrie came to their home and asked Mr. Eames what library card Oswald was using when he saw him at the library.

1241 HSCA X.

1242 "Outstanding Leads #17," November 14, 1967, NODA.

1243 *HSCA Final Report*, 172.

1244 180-10107-10368, The John F. Kennedy Assassination Records Collection, NARA.

1245 180-10104-10278, The John F. Kennedy Assassination Records Collection, NARA, 81.

1246 180-10104-10278, The John F. Kennedy Assassination Records Collection, NARA.

1247   180-10107-10380, The John F. Kennedy Assassination Records Collection, NARA.

1248   Ibid.

1249   180-10102-10257 The John F. Kennedy Assassination Records Collection, NARA.

1250   HSCA IX, 483, 883, 1032–4.

1251   Noyes, *Legacy of Doubt*, 44.

1252   Noyes, *Legacy of Doubt*, 21.

1253   Noyes, *Legacy of Doubt*, 24.

1254   HSCA IX, 483, 883, 1032–4.

1255   180-10107-10382, The John F. Kennedy Assassination Records Collection, NARA.

1256   Noyes, *Legacy of Doubt*, 38.

1257   180-10103-10376, The John F. Kennedy Assassination Records Collection, NARA.

1258   Noyes, *Legacy of Doubt*.

1259   Testimony of Jim Braden, May 16, 1978, HSCA, 101.

1260   HSCA X, 71.

1261   FBI Dallas 89-43, February 10, 1977.

1262   Noyes, *Legacy of Doubt*, 75.

1263   Blakey and Billings, *The Plot to Kill the President*.

1264   180-10107-10380, The John F. Kennedy Assassination Records Collection, NARA.

1265   Gerald Posner, *Case Closed* (New York: Random House, 1993).

1266   Blakey and Billings, *The Plot to Kill the President*.

1267   Blakey was asked the question at an AARC conference, November 19, 2005, Washington, D.C.

1268   A Louisiana State Police Open Records Request response noted only in a brief narrative that Singelmann was a character reference in a case against Marcello. Copies of the actual documents were not provided. State police noted that many of their records had been destroyed pursuant to law.

1269   John H. Davis, *Mafia Kingfish, Carlos Marcello and the Assassination of John F. Kennedy* (New York: McGraw-Hill Publishing Company, 1989), 337–8.

1270   Willie Somersett, *The Continuing Inquiry* 2, no. 2., part II, September 22, 1977.

1271   Nancy Powell, interview by the author, circa 1998.

1272   Glen Jeansonne, interview by the author, 1998.

1273   HSCA Boxed Collection, Boxes 48 and 49.

1274   FBI FOIA, Louis P. Davis, file number 0912224-0, FBI serial number 72-1840-111, January 30, 1969.

1275   "Outstanding Leads #17," November 14, 1967, NODA.

1276   *The Citizens' Council*, November 1956, Mississippi State Archives and History Center.

1277   *Plaquemines Gazette*, circa July 27, 1961.

1278   Barabara Glancey Reid, interviews, April 12, 16, 17, 1968, 180-10076-10178, The John F. Kennedy Assassination Records Collection, NARA.

1279   "Leads #66," November 6, 1967, NODA.

1280 Higginbotham [sic] and Baumler interview, May 13, 1968, NODA.

1281 George Higginbotham [sic], interviews by Barbara Reid, March 12, 16, and 17, 1968. Includes a notation that Jim Garrison and L. P. Davis were friends.

1282 180-100761-10178, The John F. Kennedy Assassination Records Collection, NARA. The notation that Jim Garrison and L. P. Davis were friends was deleted in this copy.

1283 *Times–Picayune*, March 1, 1963.

1284 180-10131-10103, The John F. Kennedy Assassination Records Collection, NARA.

1285 BCPC.

1286 William Gale and Willie Rainach, correspondence, Rainach Papers, Noel Memorial Library, Lousiana State University Shreveport. Gale enclosed some of his writings on British Israelism.

1287 Hubert Badeaux, letters to Rainach, January 29, 1957 and March 25, 1957, Rainach Papers, Noel Memorial Library, Lousiana State University Shreveport.

1288 Lou Ivon, interview by the author, October 5, 2000.

1289 *Times–Picayune*, November 3, 1955.

1290 *Times–Picayune*, March 20, 1965 and March 21, 1956.

1291 *Times–Picayune*, March 21, 1956.

1292 *Times–Picayune*, March 28, 1956.

1293 *Times–Picayune*, March 23, 1956.

1294 *Times–Picayune*, March 12, 1956.

1295 Rainach Papers, Noel Memorial Library, Lousiana State University Shreveport. Undated resolution from the State of Louisiana Joint Legislative Committee. The findings of the hearing were published and widely distributed across the country and sent to members of Congress.

1296 Warren Commssion, Exhibit 2716.

1297 Warren Commission, VII, 16–21.

1298 FBI DL 100-10, 561.

1299 Warren Commision, XXI, 236.

1300 *Times–Picayune*, January 30, 1959.

1301 Warren Commission, XIII, 13. Lee Harvey Oswald's friend and fellow Civil Air Patrol cadet told the Warren Commission that he had heard rumors that Oswald had started studying Communism at about age fourteen. According to the HSCA (report vol. IX), Oswald joined the CAP at age fifteen; according to Marguerite Oswald at age "15-1/2 or so."

1302 Letter, May 6, 1960, Rainach Papers, Noel Memorial Library, Lousiana State University Shreveport.

1303 Joe Vinson, note, Apirl 14, 1960, Rainach Papers, Noel Memorial Library, Lousiana State University Shreveport. Vinson also investigated the Consumer League of Greater New Orleans, who boycotted New Orleans merchants. Hugh Murray told the author that he was a leftist and once met Guy Banister while dating his daughter. [Hugh Murray, letter to author, November 11, 1996, and follow-up phone interview.]

1304 "Leads #66," November 14, 1967, NODA.

1305 Minutes of the meeting of the board of directors of the Association of Citizens' Councils, Rainach Papers, Noel Memorial Library, Lousiana State University Shreveport.

1306 *The Citizens' Council*, May 6, 1957. Film of the Citizens' Forum is available at the Mississippi State Archives and History Center. The author did not find the film of Hubert Badeaux in the collection but easily could have missed it.

1307 Hubert Badeaux, letter to Willie Rainach, May 23, 1958, Rainach Papers, Noel Memorial Library, Lousiana State University Shreveport.

1308 Hubert Badeaux, letter to Willie Rainach, November 29, 1957, Rainach Papers, Noel Memorial Library, Lousiana State University Shreveport.

1309 Hubert Badeaux, letter to Willie Rainach, March 8, 1958, Rainach Papers, Noel Memorial Library, Lousiana State University Shreveport. Hubert Badeaux mentioned being with Jack Ricau and just missing a cafe meeting with Willie Rainach and "the Pitchers" (probably Citizens' Council leader Sargent Pitcher of Baton Rouge).

1310 *Citizens' Report*, September 1960.

1311 Hubert Badeaux, letter to Willie Rainach, July 10, 1958, Rainach Papers, Noel Memorial Library, Louisiana State University Shreveport.

1312 *Times–Picayune*, December 23, 1959.

1313 Hubert Badeaux, letter to Willie Rainach, July 4, 1959, Rainach Papers, Noel Memorial Library, Lousiana State University Shreveport.

1314 *Times–Picayune*, January 30, 1959.

1315 Tom Anderson Papers, Special Collections, University of Oregon Library.

1316 *American Opinion*, September 1977, 67.

1317 CIA file number 1993.08.03.09;02:17:900060, The John F. Kennedy Assassination Records Collection, NARA.

1318 124-10369-10050, The John F. Kennedy Assassination Records Collection, NARA. The FBI report noted that a September 1, 1966 *Times–Picayune* newspaper article identified Hubert Badeaux as the personal investigator for Jefferson Parish district attorney Frank H. Langridge.

1319 104-10052-10001, The John F. Kennedy Assassination Records Collection, NARA.

1320 *Times–Picayune*, May 24, 1962.

1321 Harold Weisberg, *Case Open: The Omissions, Distortions and Falsification of Case Closed* (New York, Carroll and Graf Publishers, Inc., 1994), xvi.

1322 Posner, *Case Closed*, 139, 464.

1323 Guy Johnson, interview by Bud Fensterwald, August 24, 1967 and May 21, 1969, AARC.

1324 Michael L. Kurtz, *The JFK Assassination Debates* (Lawrence: University Press of Kansas, 2006), 219.

1325 Bernard Eble, Jr. , interview by the author, February 6, 2008. (There is little doubt that

Richard Eberle and Bernard Eble are the same person.)

Chapter 11

1326 FBI FOIA, Joseph A. Milteer.
1327 The John F. Kennedy Assassination Records Collection, NARA, HSCA Box 71.
1328 The John F. Kennedy Assassination Records Collection, NARA, HSCA Box 48-49.
1329 Smoot, *People Along the Way*, 220.
1330 Dan Smoot Papers, Cushing Memorial Library, Texas A&M University.
1331 Richard Dudman, *Men of the Far Right* (New York: Pyramid Books, 1962), 108.
1332 *San Antonio News*, March 3, 1966.
1333 Dan Smoot Papers, Cushing Memorial Library, Texas A&M University.
1334 *States–Item*, October 20–23, 1960.
1335 *Plaquemines Gazette*, November 4, 1960.
1336 Arnold Forster and Benjamin R. Epstein, *Danger on the Right* (New York: Random House, 1964), 134.
1337 Smoot, *People Along the Way*, 259.
1338 Dudman, *Men of the Far Right*, 107.
1339 *People's World*, November 11, 1963.
1340 Forster and Epstein, *Danger on the Right*.
1341 *Independent American*, October 1959.
1342 Flier, Haley Papers, The Haley Memorial Library and History Center, Midland, Texas.
1343 *The Dan Smoot Report*, 9, no. 22.
1344 *The Dan Smoot Report*, 9, no. 43.
1345 Smoot, *People Along the Way*, 275.
1346 Flier, Dan Smoot Papers, Cushing Memorial Library, Texas A&M University; Myers Lowman, Edward Hunter, and Frank McGehee were also to speak.
1347 Joseph Oster, interview by the author, October 14, 1999.
1348 *West Bank Hearld*, deLesseps Morrison Papers, New Orleans Public Library.
1349 Dan Smoot Papers, Cushing Memorial Library, Texas A&M University.
1350 180-10094-10189, The John F. Kennedy Assassination Records Collection, NARA.
1351 FBI file number MM 157-739, 10.
1352 180-10094-10189, Box 51, The John F. Kennedy Assassination Records Collection, NARA.
1353 Joseph A. Milteer, letter to Woody Kearns, May 5, 1965, 180-10099-10176, The John F. Kennedy Assassination Records Collection, NARA.
1354 Joseph A. Milteer, letter to Colonel Askins, September 30, 1965, 180-10095-10439, The John F. Kennedy Assassination Records Collection, NARA.
1355 Joseph A. Milteer, letter to Arnold Rowland, September 30, 1965, 180-10095-10438, The John F. Kennedy Assassination Records Collection, NARA.

1356 Joseph A. Milteer, letters to "George," "Jack," and "Fran," 180-10095-10493, Box 49, The John F. Kennedy Assassination Records Collection, NARA.

1357 Joseph A. Milteer, letter to Arnold Rowland, September 30, 1965, 180-10095-10438, The John F. Kennedy Assassination Records Collection, NARA.

1358 Joseph A. Milteer to "George," 180-10095-10435, The John F. Kennedy Assassination Records Collection, NARA.

1359 Hurt, *Texas Rich*.

1360 Russell, *The Man Who Knew Too Much*, 521.

1361 *New Republic*, March 29, 1954.

1362 Hurt, *Texas Rich*.

1363 *Group Research*, September 3, 1974.

1364 Hurt, *Texas Rich*.

1365 *New Republic*, March 29, 1954.

1366 *New Republic*, April 26, 1954.

1367 Hurt, *Texas Rich*.

1368 Dudman, *Men of the Far Right*, 106.

1369 Medford Evans knew Guy Banister, see: *American Opinion*, September 1977, 67.

1370 Medford Evans, letter to Noah M. Mason, April 16, 1955, Paul O. Peters Papers, Wooster College, Wooster, Ohio.

1371 *Dallas Morning News*, March 24, 1969.

1372 Hurt, *Texas Rich*, 230.

1373 Hurt, *Texas Rich*, 192.

1374 *The Jewish Voice*, December 10, 1964.

1375 Hurt, *Texas Rich*, 255.

1376 Dudman, *Men of the Far Right*, 106.

1377 Hurt, *Texas Rich*, 191.

1378 Hurt, *Texas Rich*, 194.

1379 Hurt, *Texas Rich*, 159.

1380 Hurt, *Texas Rich*, 137.

1381 Russell, *The Man Who Knew Too Much*, 584.

1382 Paul Rothermel, interview by the author, March 15, 2000.

1383 Hurt, *Texas Rich*, 137.

1384 FBI DL 89-43, 39.

1385 Russell, *The Man Who Knew Too Much*, 601.

1386 Jimmie Davis Papers, Southeastern Louisiana University.

1387 Hurt, *Texas Rich*, 234.

1388 *The Independent American*.

1389 Warren Commission, XXXV, CD 1306, 103–4.

1390 FBI DL-1039, 1.

1391 Warren Commission, XXV, CD 105, 268.

1392 FBI DL 89-43.

1393 Raymond Broshears, interview by NODA, August 9, 1968.

1394 *New York Times*, July 24, 1961.

1395 *Committee to Restore the Constitution* newsletter, 1970, Charles Willoughby Papers, Douglas MacArthur Archives, Norfolk, Virginia. Hilaire du Berrier served on the board, as well.

1396 Kent Courtney, letter to Tom Anderson, October 25, 1961, Tom Anderson Papers, Special Collections, University of Oregon Library,

1397 Russell, *The Man Who Knew Too Much*, 194.

1398 Paul Rothermel, interview by the author, March 15, 2000.

1399 Russell, *The Man Who Knew Too Much*, 193.

1400 Mary Brengel, interview by the author, June 25, 1996.

1401 FBI FOIA, Billy James Hargis.

1402 Overstreet and Overstreet, *The Strange Tactics of Extremism*, 220.

1403 *Weekly Crusader*, March 30, 1962, Charles Willoughby Papers, Douglas MacArthur Archives, Norfolk, Virginia.

1404 Russell, *The Man Who Knew Too Much*, 193.

1405 FBI FOIA, Billy James Hargis.

1406 Russell, *The Man Who Knew Too Much*, 196.

1407 FBI FOIA, Billy James Hargis; "Re: Hunt and Lewis".

1408 Russell, *The Man Who Knew Too Much*, 285.

1409 Russell, *The Man Who Knew Too Much*, 301, 395.

1410 Russell, *The Man Who Knew Too Much*, 300.

1411 Dudman, *Men of the Far Right*, 105.

1412 Tom Anderson Papers, Special Collections, University of Oregon Library, dated June 6, 1958.

1413 Glen Jeansonne, *Leander Perez: Boss of the Delta* (Baton Rouge: Louisiana State University Press, 1977), 325.

1414 Paul Rothermel, interview by the author, March 15, 2000.

1415 Hurt, *Texas Rich*, 298.

1416 FBI, DL 89-43, 39–44, February 18, 1977

1417 Clarence Manion Papers, Chicago Historical Society, Box 82.

1418 *Group Research*, January 21, 1976.

1419 Clarence Manion Papers, Chicago Historical Society, MM-61-5, dated November 23, 1965.

1420 *Group Research*, December 16, 1965. Nelson Bunker Hunt, Lamar Hunt, and Herbert Hunt owned Hunt Electronics, which advertised in the John Birch Society magazine, see *Group Research*, February 28, 1967.

1421 180-100-4104, The John F. Kennedy Assassination Records Collection, NARA.

1422 *Washington Post*, Jack Anderson column, January 1, 1975.

1423 Pedro del Valle, letter to J. Evetts Haley, February 3, 1956, Haley Papers, The Haley Memorial Library and History Center, Midland, Texas. Haley met del Valle sometime prior at a 1956 meeting in Richmond, Virginia.

1424 Bull Connor, letter to J. Evetts Haley, February 2, 1959, Haley Papers, The Haley Memorial Library and History Center, Midland, Texas.

1425 J. Evetts Haley, letter to Nelson Bunker Hunt and H. L. Hunt, September 25, 1968, Tom Anderson Papers, Special Collections, University of Oregon Library.

1426 Nelson Bunker Hunt, letter to J. Evetts Haley, September 26, 1964, Haley Papers, The Haley Memorial Library and History Center, Midland, Texas.

1427 J. Evetts Haley, letter to Nelson Bunker Hunt, July 1, 1965, Haley Papers, The Haley Memorial Library and History Center, Midland, Texas.

1428 124-90129-10032, The John F. Kennedy Assassination Records Collection, NARA.

1429 Haley Papers, The Haley Memorial Library and History Center, Midland, Texas.

1430 Flier, Haley Papers, The Haley Memorial Library and History Center, Midland, Texas.

1431 Conason and Lyons, *The Hunting of a President.*

1432 Federation flier, Haley Papers, The Haley Memorial Library and History Center, Midland, Texas.

1433 J. Evetts Haley, letter to Leander Perez, September 9, 1961, Haley Papers, The Haley Memorial Library and History Center, Midland, Texas.

1434 J. Evetts Haley, letter to Roy V. Harris, May 5, 1959 Haley Papers, The Haley Memorial Library and History Center, Midland, Texas.

1435 Tom P. Brady, letter to J. Evetts Haley, November 11, 1958, Haley Papers, The Haley Memorial Library and History Center, Midland, Texas.

1436 Kent Courtney, letter to J. Evetts Haley, November 6, 1959, Haley Papers, The Haley Memorial Library and History Center, Midland, Texas.

1437 Charles Barnett, letter to J. Evetts Haley, July 17, 1962, Haley Papers, The Haley Memorial Library and History Center, Midland, Texas.

1438 Robert B. Patterson, letter to J. Evetts Haley, July 12, 1955, Haley Papers, The Haley Memorial Library and History Center, Midland, Texas.

1439 Mary Surrey, letter to J. Evetts Haley, October 10, 1964, Haley Papers, The Haley Memorial Library and History Center, Midland, Texas.

1440 Warren Commission, V, 420.

1441 George Montgomery, letter to J. Evetts Haley, November, 10, 1961, Haley Papers, The Haley Memorial Library and History Center, Midland, Texas.

1442 J. Evetts Haley, letter to Orrin Miller, January 9, 1962, Haley Papers, The Haley Memorial Library and History Center, Midland, Texas.

1443 R. Harland Shaw, letter to J. Evetts Haley, July 11, 1962, Haley Papers, The Haley Memorial Library and History Center, Midland, Texas.

1444 Flier, Haley Papers, The Haley Memorial Library and History Center, Midland, Texas.

1445 General Walker, letter to J. Evetts Haley, September, 24, 1962, Haley Papers, The Haley Memorial Library and History Center, Midland, Texas.

1446 George Thomas, letter to J. Evetts Haley, January 3, 1963, Haley Papers, The Haley Memorial Library and History Center, Midland, Texas.

1447 J. Evetts Haley, letter to Myers Lowman, October 28, 1962, Haley Papers, The Haley Memorial Library and History Center, Midland, Texas.

1448 General Walker, letter to J. Evetts Haley, October 13, 1963, Haley Papers, The Haley Memorial Library and History Center, Midland, Texas.

1449 Warren Commission, XXVI, Exhibit 3112, 750.

1450 FBI file number 105-82555, Oswald HQ file 196, 8.

1451 General Walker, letter to J. Evetts Haley, October 14, 1963, Haley Papers, The Haley Memorial Library and History Center, Midland, Texas.

1452 FBI file number 105-82555, Oswald HQ file 196, 10.

1453 *Warren Commission Report*, 293.

1454 Harold Lord Varney, letter to J. Evetts Haley, July 31, 1963, Haley Papers, The Haley Memorial Library and History Center, Midland, Texas.

1455 Dan Smoot served on the national policy committee of J. Evetts Haley's Texans For America in the 1950s, with Haley serving as the state chairman. [Tom Anderson Papers, Special Collections, University of Oregon, Box 30.] Haley had known Smoot since 1953. For America, the national group, contained a familiar assortment of far-right figures found in the Congress of Freedom and similar groups: Mary Cain, Clarence Manion, Dan Smoot, George Montgomery, and generals Wedemeyer and Stratemeyer. On the advisory board were Roy V. Harris, Willie Rainach, Senator Eastland, and Strom Thurmond. [For America roster, Haley Papers, The Haley Memorial Library and History Center, Midland, Texas.] In the Haley papers were numerous fliers from the Constitution Party and the Congress of Freedom. [Haley Papers, The Haley Memorial Library and History Center, Midland, Texas.] Haley spoke at the 1959 Congress of Freedom in Colorado Springs with Revilo Oliver. [George Thomas, letter to J. Evetts Haley, April 28, 1959, Haley Papers, The Haley Memorial Library and History Center, Midland, Texas.] Haley was associated with the Constitution Party and was asked to run as its Senate candidate in 1960. [Wickliffe Vernard, letter to J. Evetts Haley, Haley Papers, The Haley Memorial Library and History Center, Midland, Texas; J. Evetts Haley, letter to Bard Logan, July 26, 1960, Haley Papers, The Haley Memorial Library and History Center, Midland, Texas.] Haley served on the Advisory Board of We the People, as did Dan Smoot. [Harry Everingham, letter to J. Evetts Haley, Haley Papers, The Haley Memorial Library and History Center, Midland, Texas.] Joseph A. Milteer attended the 1963 meeting of We the People. [FBI FOIA.] Haley was close to D. B. Lewis, the dog food maker, who supported Dan Smoot and many far-right causes. [Smoot, *People Along the Way*.] Haley was a Barry Goldwater supporter, attended a Goldwater rally in Los Angels, and met with "the Murphys" (perhaps the actor and California senator, George Murphy, who was championed by the far right) and

Senator Knowland. [J. Evetts Haley, letter to A. G. Heinsohn, October 1, 1963, Haley Papers, The Haley Memorial Library and History Center, Midland, Texas.] Haley was close to Robert Welch and the John Birch Society, and was involved with it early formation along with a select group of individuals. [Robert Welch, letters to J. Evetts Haley, December 14, 1959, May 5, 1960, Haley Papers, The Haley Memorial Library and History Center, Midland, Texas.] Haley was close to generals Wedemeyer and Willoughby, as is evidenced by their extensive correspondence in the Haley papers. In 1986, Haley served on the central organizational committee of Texas First with H. R. (Bum) Bright, along with Nelson Bunker Hunt and Lester L. Logue. The three were behind the "Welcome Mr. Kennedy to Dallas" ad that ran on the day of the assassination, and the group was "militantly opposed" to a Socialist or Communist bureaucracy. [Haley Papers, The Haley Memorial Library and History Center, Midland, Texas.]

1456 Russell, *The Man Who Knew Too Much*, 599.

1457 Turner, *Power on the Right*, 110. Turner noted that Medrick G. "Bud" Johnson was the chairman of the American Volunteer Group.

1458 William W. Turner, letter to the author, February 16, 2008.

1459 Russell, *The Man Who Knew Too Much*, 604.

1460 180-10099-10144, The John F. Kennedy Assassination Records Collection, NARA.

1461 Newsletter of the American Volunteer Group, Dana Point, California, Courtney Papers, Special Collections, Northwestern State University of Louisiana.

1462 FBI FOIA, John Crommelin, file number 157-12905-6 Ep. 3.

1463 FBI BH 157-864.

1464 *Summit Sun*, March 30, 1967.

1465 Charles Willoughby Papers, Douglas MacArthur Archives, Norfolk, Virginia, dated September 4, 1966.

1466 Kent Courtney, letter to Tom Anderson, March 1, 1965, Tom Anderson Papers, Special Collections, University of Oregon Library.

1467 FBI FOIA, Joseph A. Milteer.

1468 Letter, Tom Anderson Papers, Special Collections, University of Oregon Library.

1469 The Flying Tigers were eventually incorporated into the army and Scott served as their commander. He authored several books on his exploits, including *God is My Co-Pilot*, which was made into a movie. [Associated Press obituary, February 27, 2006, Fox News web site.] The information provided by William Turner stating that the American Volunteer Group was led by a former member of the original AVG is further substantiated by the AVG newsletter from the Courtney Papers.

1470 Olga Butterworth, letter to Pedro del Valle, March 9, 1972, Wally Butterworth Papers, Special Collections, University of Oregon.

1471 J. Evetts Haley, letter to E. Neel Edwards, September 26, 1967, Haley Papers, The Haley Memorial Library and History Center, Midland, Texas.

1472 Letter, "From and by H. L. Hunt," January 8, 1962, Haley Papers, The Haley Memorial Library and History Center, Midland, Texas.

1473 Russell, *The Man Who Knew Too Much*, 588.

1474 Letter in JFK Exhibit F-506, HSCA Vol IV, 337.

1475 FBI DL 89-43, 51–52.

1476 HSCA Vol IV, 337, 357–359.

1477 *Dallas Morning News*, February 6, 1977.

1478 Dallas FBI 89-43, page 46, February 7, 1977.

1479 Russell, *The Man Who Knew Too Much*, 593.

1480 Russell, *The Man Who Knew Too Much*, 592.

1481 179-200004-10108, The John F. Kennedy Assassination Records Collection, NARA.

1482 Tom Bethel, diary, William Wood Papers, The John F. Kennedy Assassination Records Collection, NARA.

1483 Paul Rothermel, interview by the author, March 15, 2000.

1484 Hurt, *Texas Rich*, 241.

1485 Paul Rothermel, interview by the author, March 15, 2000.

1486 Harold Weisberg, interviews by the author, November 18, 1996, and May 18, 2000.

1487 Hurt, *Texas Rich*, 242.

1488 Bill Boxley, memo, NODA, AARC.

1489 Joseph Oster, interview by the author, October 14, 1999.

1490 Paul Rothermel, interview by the author, March 15, 2000.

1491 Russell, *The Man Who Knew Too Much*.

1492 Paul Rothermel, interview by the author, March 15, 2000.

1493 180-10097-10398, The John F. Kennedy Assassination Records Collection, NARA.

1494 Paul Rothermel, interview by Bill Boxley William Wood Papers, The John F. Kennedy Assassination Records Collection, NARA.

1495 Memo, June 5, 1967, NODA, William Wood Papers, The John F. Kennedy Assassination Records Collection, NARA. The author mentioned Paul Rothermel's reaction to Guy Banister's death, noted in the Bill Boxley memo, to Joseph Oster, and he responded, "I would have thought Mary [Banister's wife] would have told him."

1496 Sylvia Meagher, *Accessories after the Fact* (New York: Vintage, 1992).

1497 Paul Rothermel, interview by the author, March 15, 2000.

1498 Russell, *The Man Who Knew Too Much*, 543.

1499 Warren Commission file, dated March 16, 1964.

1500 Hurt, *Texas Rich*, 223–4.

1501 Hurt, *Texas Rich*, 234.

1502 Chris Cravens, *Edwin A. Walker and the Right Wing in Dallas, 1960–1966*, Master's Thesis, Southwest Texas University, San Marcos, Texas, May 1991, 154.

Chapter 12

1503 *The Handbook of Texas* online: www.tsha online.org/handbook/handbook

1504 Cravens, *Edwin A. Walker and the Right Wing in Dallas, 1960–1966.*

1505 *Daily Oklahoman*, January 31, 1962.

1506 Ibid.

1507 Dudman, *Men of the Far Right.*

1508 Cravens, *Edwin A. Walker and the Right Wing in Dallas, 1960–1966*, 68.

1509 Cravens, *Edwin A. Walker and the Right Wing in Dallas, 1960–1966*, 64.

1510 Cravens, *Edwin A. Walker and the Right Wing in Dallas, 1960–1966.*

1511 *Times–Picayune*, November 7, 1958 and November 11, 1958.

1512 *Plaquemines Gazette*, September 27, 1957.

1513 *Times–Picayune*, October 15, 2008.

1514 *Plaquemines Gazette*, October 17, 1958.

1515 Dudman, *Men of the Far Right.*

1516 FBI interview of Walker, September 29, 1962, FBI FOIA, file number 116-16549481.

1517 *Daily Oklahoman*, January, 31, 1962.

1518 *Arkansas Gazette*, April 14, 1961.

1519 *Dallas Morning News*, June 15, 1963.

1520 *Washington Star*, September 20, 1961.

1521 Dudman, *Men of the Far Right*, 98.

1522 Overstreet and Overstreet, *The Strange Tactics of Extremism*, 147, 170.

1523 Thayer, The *Farther Shores of Politics*, 257, 260.

1524 *The Christian Fright Peddlers*, 128.

1525 Overstreet and Overstreet, *The Strange Tactics of Extremism*, 147, 170.

1526 Thayer, *The Farther Shores of Politics*, 257, 260.

1527 Forster and Epstein, *Danger on the Right*, 148.

1528 *The Journal*, Wheaton, Illinois, July 21, 1969.

1529 Janson and Eismann, *The Far Right*, 141.

1530 Robert DePugh, interviews by the author, December 17, 1999 and May 11, 2000.

1531 Janson and Eismann, *The Far Right*, 275.

1532 *Times Picayune*, September 8, 1961.

1533 *Arkansas Democrat*, December 12–16, 1958 and December 17, 1958.

1534 *Arkansas Democrat*, December 16–18, 1958.

1535 Woods, *Black Struggle Red Scare*, 77.

1536 *Times Picayune*, September 15, 1959.

1537 Dudman, *Men of the Far Right.*

1538 *Daily Oklahoman*, January 28, 1962.

1539 Dudman, *Men of the Far Right.*

1540 Cravens, *Edwin A. Walker and the Right Wing in Dallas, 1960–1966*, 68.

1541 Dudman, *Men of the Far Right.*

1542 *Dallas Morning News*, September 22, 1961.

1543 Kent Courtney and Phoebe Courtney, *The Case of General Edwin A. Walker* (New Orleans: The Conservative Society of America, 1961), 20.

1544 Courtney and Courtney, *The Case of General Edwin A. Walker*, 33.

1545 Dudman, *Men of the Far Right*.

1546 *Dallas Morning News*, April 2, 1961.

1547 *Dallas Times Herald*, April 14, 1961.

1548 *Dallas Morning News*, June 4, 1961.

1549 Dudman, *Men on the Far Right*.

1550 *Dallas Morning News*, Sepember 7, 1961.

1551 Edwin A. Walker Papers, Dolph Briscoe Center for American History, University of Texas at Austin, Box 96-30/15.

1552 FBI file number 62104401.

1553 Mike Newberry, *The Yahoos* (New York: Marzani and Munsell, 1964), 26.

1554 Edwin A. Walker Papers, Dolph Briscoe Center for American History, University of Texas at Austin, Box 96 30/15.

1555 Edwin A. Walker Papers, Dolph Briscoe Center for American History, University of Texas at Austin, Box 93-402/2.

1556 Edwin A. Walker Papers, Dolph Briscoe Center for American History, University of Texas at Austin, Box, 96-30/9.

1557 FBI FOIA, Edwin A. Walker, Dallas FBI report, December 18, 1962.

1558 Edwin A. Walker Papers, Dolph Briscoe Center for American History, University of Texas at Austin, Box, 96-30/25.

1559 Edwin A. Walker Papers, Dolph Briscoe Center for American History, University of Texas at Austin, Box 96-30/12b.

1560 *Times–Picayune*, August, 18, 1961.

1561 *Congressional Record* 107, no. 131, August 2, 1961.

1562 *Congressional Record* 107, no. 137, August 10, 1961.

1563 Cravens, *Edwin A. Walker and the Right Wing in Dallas, 1960–1966*, 74.

1564 FBI FOIA, Edwin A. Walker.

1565 *Dallas Morning News*, November 3, 1961.

1566 *Dallas Morning News*, November 4, 1961.

1567 Robert Wilonsky, *The Man Oswald Missed*. In his last interview, General Walker defended his place in history. Internet post, *Probable Cause Australia* – Double Issue 7 & 8. 2000.

1568 Cravens, *Edwin A. Walker and the Right Wing in Dallas, 1960–1966*, 77.

1569 *Dallas Morning News*, November 5, 1961.

1570 *Dallas Morning News*, November 16, 1961.

1571 Edwin A. Walker Papers, Dolph Briscoe Center for American History, University of Texas at Austin, Box 96-30/15.

1572 Edwin A. Walker Papers, Dolph Briscoe Center for American History, University of

Texas at Austin, Box 93 402/5.

1573 Edwin A. Walker Papers, Dolph Briscoe Center for American History, University of Texas at Austin, Box 30 12/A.

1574 Dudman, *Men of the Far Right*, 62.

1575 Cravens, *Edwin A. Walker and the Right Wing in Dallas, 1960–1966*, 85.

1576 *Times Picayune*, August 20, 1961.

1577 Courtney, *The Case of General Edwin A. Walker*.

1578 *Life*, 1962.

1579 Janson and Eismann, *The Far Right*, 90.

1580 Dudman, *Men of the Far Right*, 33.

1581 *Daily Oklahoman*, January 23, 1962.

1582 Ibid.

1583 *Chicago Daily Tribune*, February 8, 1962.

1584 *Dallas Morning News*, February 9, 1962.

1585 Cravens, *Edwin A. Walker and the Right Wing in Dallas, 1960–1966*, 95.

1586 Oswald, *Lee*.

1587 Strom Thurmond Papers, Clemson University.

1588 *Chicago Daily Tribune*, February 10, 1962.

1589 *Dallas Morning News*, March 2, 1962.

1590 *American Opinion*, 9-77, 67–70. Medford Evans wrote of Guy Banister: "A friend of mine it happens."

1591 *Times–Picayune*, March 5, 1958.

1592 *States–Item*, March, (day lost), 1963.

1593 *States–Item*, March 10, 1960.

1594 *Times–Picayune*, December 2, 1959.

1595 Mississippi Freedom School Curriculum, Internet article (www.educationanddemocracy.org) entitled "The Mississippi Power Structure."

1596 Dan Smoot Papers, Texas A&M University, Cushing Memorial Library.

1597 *Newsweek*, December 4, 1961.

1598 Audiotape, taken from Joseph A. Milteer's home, The John F. Kennedy Assassination Records Collection, NARA. Watts is heard speaking on tape recording at the 1963 Congress of Freedom.

1599 FBI file number 157-758-13.

1600 *American Mercury*, 1963.

1601 Flier, microfilm, Right Wing Collection, University of Iowa.

1602 *Group Research*, February 29, 1972.

1603 FBI file number 62-106572-12.

1604 *Facts*, ADL, 2, no. 6, November–December 1965.

1605 *Group Research*, December 3, 1975.

1606 Letterhead reprinted in the *Thunderbolt*, May 30, 1975.

1607 *Group Research*, February 29, 1972.

1608 *Times–Picayune*, April 5, 1962.

1609 *Dallas Morning News*, April 5, 1962.

1610 *Dallas Morning News*, April 7, 1962.

1611 *Times–Picayune*, April 6, 1962.

1612 *Dallas Morning News*, May 5, 1961.

1613 *Dallas Morning News*, April 5, 1962.

1614 *Dallas Morning News*, April 6, 1962.

1615 Dudman, *Men of the Far Right*.

1616 Nikitin Vyacheslav, *The Ultras in the U.S.A.* (Moscow: Progress Publishers, 1971), 179.

1617 Washington Capitol News Service, September 29, 1961.

1618 FBI FOIA, Edwin A. Walker.

1619 *Jackson Daily News*, January 12, 1962. President Kennedy responded after an article was published stating that air cover was planned and was later called off. He said that strikes from non-American planes had been postponed after the invading forces sustained heavy losses. [*Shreveport Times*, January 23, 1963.] Air support was not promised according to Jose A. Perez one of the leaders of the invasion. [*Jackson Daily News*, January 12, 1962.]

1620 *Times–Picayune*, November 5, 1961.

1621 Speech, typed and handwritten from General Walker, April 18, 1962, Haley Papers, The Haley Memorial Library and History Center, Midland, Texas.

1622 *Dallas Morning News*, February 10, 1962.

1623 *Dallas Morning News*, March 2, 1962.

1624 180-10078-10035, The John F. Kennedy Assassination Records Collection, NARA.

1625 Robert DePugh, interviews by the author, December 17, 1999, and May 11, 2000.

1626 Letter, Douglas MacArthur Archives, Norfolk, Virginia.

1627 Dudman, *Men of the Far Right*.

1628 Cravens, *Edwin A. Walker and the Right Wing in Dallas, 1960–1966*, 100.

1629 Dudman, *Men of the Far Right*, 174.

1630 Janson and Eismann, *The Far Right*, 108.

1631 180-10060-10033, The John F. Kennedy Assassination Records Collection, NARA.

1632 180-10060-10035, The John F. Kennedy Assassination Records Collection, NARA.

1633 180-10060-10035, The John F. Kennedy Assassination Records Collection, NARA.

1634 *Miami Herald*, November 7, 1961.

1635 Edwin A. Walker Papers, Dolph Briscoe Center for American History, University of Texas at Austin, Box 96-30/12b.

1636 *Newsweek*, IVIII, no. 23, p.18.

1637 Robert Welch, letter to W. B. Williams, November 8, 1961, Clarence Manion Papers, Chicago Historical Society.

1638 *Dallas Morning News*, November 14, 1961.

1639 *Miami Herald*, November 7, 1961.

1640 FBI file number 109-237-A.

1641 *Miami Herald*, November 15, 1961.

1642 *Dallas Morning News*, November 16, 1961.

1643 *Dallas Morning News*, November 15, 1961.

1644 *Dallas Morning News*, November 11, 1961 and November 19, 1961.

1645 FBI file number 62-107429-8.

1646 Walker was the planned speaker at a Dallas National Indignation Convention meeting on November 22–23, 1961. [*Dallas Morning News*, November 4, 1961.] On December 16, 1961, Tom Anderson was the featured speaker at a Tyler Texas NIC meeting. [*Dallas Morning News*, November 15, 1961.] Milteer's associate Revilo Oliver spoke at the national rally of the NIC on November 22–24, 1961. [*Dallas Morning News*, November 25, 1961.]

1647 *Dallas Morning News*, December 3, 1961.

1648 *Walker Speaks Unmuzzled! Complete text of three speeches of Edwin A Walker* (Dallas: American Eagle Publishing, 1962).

1649 *Time*, December 22, 1961.

1650 Ibid.

1651 Cravens, *Edwin A. Walker and the Right Wing in Dallas, 1960–1966*, 98.

1652 Cravens, *Edwin A. Walker and the Right Wing in Dallas, 1960–1966*, 86.

1653 *Dallas Morning News*, December 18, 1961.

1654 FBI file number 105-187. The individual taped General Walker's speech and planned on playing it a National States' Rights Party meeting in Little Rock on January 8, 1962.

1655 FBI file number 105-66233-705.

1656 *Times–Picayune*, January 4, 1962.

1657 *States–Item*, January 20, 1962.

1658 *Birmingham News*, January 21, 1962.

1659 General Walker spoke in Tulsa, Oklahoma, in January 1962, with his speech piped through a national phone hook-up to other National Indignation Convention meetings in the U.S. [*Daily Oklahoman*, January 19, 1962.] On January 12, 1962, Walker spoke through a phone hook-up along with Julian Williams of Christian Crusade to a National Indignation Convention in Dallas. [*Daily Oklahoman*, January 12, 1962.]

1660 *Chicago Daily Tribune*, February 9, 1962.

1661 *Dallas Morning News*, February 10, 1962.

1662 *Dallas Morning News*, January 10, 1962.

1663 *Dallas Morning News*, January 21, 1962.

1664 Pamphlet, Haley Papers, The Haley Memorial Library and History Center, Midland, Texas.

1665 *Plaquemines Gazette*, March 16, 1962.

1666 *Times–Picayune*, February 8, 1962.

1667 *Times–Picayune*, January 4, 1962.

1668 National Indignation Convention letterhead in Tom Anderson Papers, Special Collections, University of Oregon Library.

1669 Bill Boxley Papers, AARC.

1670 Janson and Eismann, *The Far Right*, 108.

1671 Janson and Eismann, *The Far Right*, 215.

1672 Robert DePugh, interviews by the author, December 17, 1999, and May 11, 2000.

1673 Video, Mississippi State Archives and History Center.

1674 *The Citizen*, January, 1962.

1675 *Dallas Morning News*, December 30, 1961.

1676 180-10080-10004, The John F. Kennedy Assassination Records Collection, NARA.

1677 FBI FOIA, Joseph A. Milteer.

1678 124-10104-10147, The John F. Kennedy Assassination Records Collection, NARA.

1679 124-10331-10195, The John F. Kennedy Assassination Records Collection, NARA.

1680 Transcript of meeting, Rainach Papers, Noel Memorial Library, Louisiana State University Shreveport.

1681 *Times Picayune*, April 23, 1961.

1682 *Plaquemines Gazette*, June 16, 1961.

1683 "The United States Program for General and Complete Disarmament in a Peaceful World," State Department bulletin 7277, September 1961, Government Printing Office.

1684 *Dallas Morning News*, August 14, 1961.

1685 FBI FOIA, Walker, file number 116-165494.

1686 Cravens, *Edwin A. Walker and the Right Wing in Dallas, 1960–1966*, 107.

1687 Manchester, *The Death of a President*, 32.

1688 *Dallas Morning News*, October 9, 1962.

1689 *Dallas Morning News*, June 9, 1962.

1690 *Dallas Morning News*, August 19, 1962.

1691 Dr. Fred Schwartz Anti-Communism School Flier, Victor Schiro Papers, New Orleans Public Library.

1692 *Times–Picayune*, March 1, 1962, p.12, sec 2, c.6.

1693 *Times–Picayune*, September 31, 1961.

1694 H. L. Hunt, letter to the editor of *Times–Picayune*, November 1, 1963.

1695 *Dallas Morning News*, May 19, 1963.

1696 *Times–Picayune*, September 19, 1961.

1697 *Dallas Morning News*, May 5, 1962.

1698 *Times–Picayune*, May 23, 1963.

1699 Allen Ellender, letter to a constituent, May 1, 1963, Ellender Papers, Nicholls State University.

1700 Edward G, White, *Alger Hiss's Looking-Glass Wars: The Covert Life of a Soviet Spy* (Oxford: Oxford University Press, 2005).

Chapter 13

1701 *Group Research*, September 19, 1962.

1702 *American Mercury*, January 1959 and others.

1703 Edwin A. Walker Papers, Dolph Briscoe Center for American History, University of Texas at Austin, Box 96-30/12a, contains the Hunt letters.

1704 Carl McIntire, letter to General Walker, Edwin A. Walker Papers, Dolph Briscoe Center for American History, University of Texas at Austin, Box 96-30/12a.

1705 FBI file number 63-4296-12-589.

1706 *Christian Crusade*, March 1962.

1707 *Dallas Morning News*, February 4, 1962.

1708 *Dallas Morning News*, February 8, 1962.

1709 *Dallas Morning News*, March 4, 1962.

1710 Robert DePugh, interviews by the author, December 17, 1999, and May 11, 2000.

1711 Dudman, *Men of the Far Right*, 176.

1712 *Dallas Morning News*, February 13, 1962.

1713 *Dallas Morning News*, March 8, 1962.

1714 *Times-Picayune*, March 14, 1962.

1715 *Times-Picayune*, May 22, 1962.

1716 *Look*, March 13, 1962.

1717 Fletcher Knebel and Charles W. Bailey, II, *Seven Days in May* (New York: Harper & Roe, 1962).

1718 Edwin A. Walker Papers, Dolph Briscoe Center for American History, University of Texas at Austin, Box 96-30/31.

1719 *Dallas Morning News*, March 17, 2002.

1720 *Dallas Morning News*, March 21, 1963.

1721 Overstreet and Overstreet, *The Strange Tactics of Extremism*, 220.

1722 *Weekly Crusader*, March 30, 1962, Charles Willoughby Papers, Douglas MacArthur Archives, Norfolk, Virginia.

1723 FBI FOIA, Billy James Hargis.

1724 *New York Times*, September 16, 1961.

1725 *Christian Crusade*, April 1962, Charles Willoughby Papers, Douglas MacArthur Archives, Norfolk, Virginia.

1726 *Weekly Crusader*, March 30, 1962, Charles Willoughby Papers, Douglas MacArthur Archives, Norfolk, Virginia.

1727 Edwin A. Walker Papers, Dolph Briscoe Center for American History, University of Texas at Austin, Box, 96-30/25.

1728 Tom Anderson Papers, Special Collections, University of Oregon Library.

1729 *Summit Sun*, February 8, 1962.

1730 *Dallas Morning News*, March 25, 1962.

1731 *Dallas Morning News*, April 1, 1962.

1732 *The Jewish Voice*, May 18, 1962.

1733 *Times–Picayune*, April 4, 1962.

1734 *Times–Picayune*, April 11, 1962.

1735 *Dallas Morning News*, April 11, 1962.

1736 *Dallas Morning News*, May 1, 1962.

1737 *Times–Picayune*, November 21, 1962.

1738 *Dallas Morning News*, April 11, 1962.

1739 *Times–Picayune*, April 17, 1962.

1740 *Dallas Morning News*, May 21, 22, 1962.

1741 *Times–Picayune*, April 20, 1962

1742 *Times–Picayune*, April 31, 1962.

1743 *Dallas Morning News*, April 28, 1962.

1744 Mary Cain Papers, Mississippi State Archives.

1745 Arch Roberts, interview by the author, 2000. Roberts may have been senile at the time of the interview. He died a few years later.

1746 *Dallas Morning News*, May 22, 1962.

1747 *Dallas Morning News*, May 3, 1962.

1748 *Dallas Morning News*, May 4, 1962

1749 180-10078-10035, The John F. Kennedy Assassination Records Collection, National Archives and Records Associaions (NARA).

1750 Tom Anderson, letter to J. Clem Barnes, Jr., May 10, 1962, Tom Anderson Papers, University of Wyoming.

1751 *Dallas Morning News*, May 8, 1962.

1752 *Dallas Morning News*, May 6, 1962.

1753 Ibid.

1754 *Weekly Crusader*, June 8, 1962.

1755 Peter Dale Scott, Paul L. Hoch, and Russell Stetler, *The Assassinations* (New York: Vintage Books, 1976), 366.

1756 *Warren Commission Report*.

1757 *Times–Picayune*, June 17, 1962.

1758 *Times–Picayune*, June 18, 1962.

1759 *Shreveport Journal*, July 5, 1962.

1760 *Dallas Morning News*, July 8, 1962.

1761 *Christian Crusade*, September 1962.

1762 124-10331-10202, The John F. Kennedy Assassination Records Collection, NARA.

1763 *Warren Commission Report*, 287.

1764 *Times–Picayune*, August 23, 1962.

1765 FBI FOIA, John Crommelin.

1766 Capell, *Treason is the Reason.*

1767 FBI file number MM 157-739, 7.

1768 FBI file number MM 157-739, 14–5.

1769 FBI file number MM 157-739, 16.

1770 Edwin A. Walker Papers, Dolph Briscoe Center for American History, University of Texas at Austin, Box 96 30/31.

1771 *Dallas Morning News*, September 15, 1962.

1772 FBI file number MM 157-739.

1773 General Walker in Council for Statehood, 124-10331-10195, The John F. Kennedy Assassination Records Collection, NARA.

1774 William Doyle, *An American Insurrection* (New York: Anchor Books, 2001), 36.

1775 Ibid.

1776 Joseph Oster, interview by the author, October 14, 1999.

1777 *Times–Picayune*, March 1, 1959.

1778 *Jackson Clarion Ledger*, January 30, 1960.

1779 Ross Barnett, letter, Rainach Papers, Noel Memorial Library, Louisiana State University Shreveport.

1780 *Times–Picayune*, August 11, 1960.

1781 *Times–Picayune,* July 13, 1960.

1782 "Strength Through Unity," pamphlet published by the Citizens' Council of Mississippi,

Sovereignty Commission Papers, Mississippi State Archives.

1783 *Jackson Clarion Ledger*, March 8, 1960.

1784 *Plaquemines Gazette*, March 11, 1960.

1785 Doyle, *An American Insurrection*, 52.

1786 Doyle, *An American Insurrection*, 53.

1787 Ibid.

1788 *Clarion Ledger*, January 17, 1960.

1789 *Jackson Daily News*, March 26, 1960.

1790 *Jackson Daily News*, February 27, 1960, and March 10, 1960.

1791 *New York Times*, July 24, 1961.

1792 *Dallas Morning News*, December 1, 1961.

1793 HSCA Boxes 48-49, The John F. Kennedy Assassination Records Collection, NARA.

1794 Doyle, *An American Insurrection.*

1795 *Jackson Daily News*, January 14, 1963.

1796 Doyle, *An American Insurrection*, 57.

1797 *Clarion Ledger*, January 13, 1960.

1798 *Jackson Daily News*, January 13, 1960.

1799 Wally Butterworth, letter, December 7, 1963, Wally Butterworth Papers, Special Collections, University of Oregon.

1800 FBI FOIA, Citizens' Council of America, October 14, 1960, file number 105-46604-45.

1801 *Plaquemines Gazette*, November 8, 1957.

1802 *Times–Picayune,* January 6, 1960.

1803 *The Citizen.*

1804 Doyle, *An American Insurrection.*

1805 Edwin A. Walker Papers, Dolph Briscoe Center for American History, University of Texas at Austin, Box 96-30/41.

1806 Doyle, *An American Insurrection*, 65.

1807 *Times–Picayune*, September 19, 1962.

1808 *Times–Picayune*, September 29, 1962.

1809 124-10285-10298, The John F. Kennedy Assassination Records Collection, NARA.

1810 Doyle, *An American Insurrection*, 12.

1811 *Times–Picayune*, September 21, 1962.

1812 FBI file number 63-429-12-622.

1813 124-10331-10030, The John F. Kennedy Assassination Records Collection, NARA.

1814 Doyle, *An American Insurrection.*

1815 *Times–Picayune*, September 23, 1962.

1816 *Times–Picayune*, September 25, 1962.

1817 124-10285-10298, The John F. Kennedy Assassination Records Collection, NARA.

1818 Doyle, *An American Insurrection*, 92.

1819 *Times–Picayune*, September 26, 1962.

1820 Ibid.

1821 Doyle, *An American Insurrection*, 86.

1822 General Walker, letter to President Kennedy, February 26, 1962, Tom Anderson Papers, Special Collections, University of Oregon Library.

1823 Doyle, *An American Insurrection*, 92.

1824 Doyle, *An American Insurrection*, 93.

1825 *Jackson Daily News*, September 23, 1962.

1826 *Clarion Ledger*, September 23, 1962.

1827 *Clarion Ledger*, September 27, 1962.

1828 Ibid.

1829 Doyle, *An American Insurrection*, 97.

1830 *Clarion Ledger*, September 27, 1962.

1831 Cravens, *Edwin A. Walker and the Right Wing in Dallas, 1960–1966*, 109.

1832 *Clarion Ledger*, September 28, 1962.

1833 Doyle, *An American Insurrection*, 93.

1834 *Times–Picayune*, September 27, 1962.

1835 Edwin A. Walker Papers, Dolph Briscoe Center for American History, University of Texas at Austin, Box, 96-30/12a.

1836 *Clarion Ledger*, September 29, 1962.

1837 *Times–Picayune*, September 28, 1962.

1838 *Times–Picayune*, September 29, 1962.

1839 FBI FOIA Ole Miss, Department of Justice, file number 1vw 11, 801 144-40-254.

1840 *Washington Evening Star*, September 29, 1963.

1841 Doyle, *An American Insurrection*, 98.

1842 Seymour, *Committee of the States, Inside the Radical Right*.

1843 Doyle, *An American Insurrection*, 98–9.

1844 *Councilor*, October 26, 1962.

1845 *Clarion Ledger*, September 30, 1961.

1846 *Washington Evening Star*, October 2, 1962.

1847 FBI FOIA Ole Miss, Department of Justice, file number 1vw 11, 801 144-40-254.

1848 *Washington Evening Star*, September 30, 1963. Cited—and information received from—an individual at Oxford. L. A. West was also with them.

1849 FBI memo, October 11, 1962, FBI FOIA, Edwin A. Walker, 157-221.

1850 Memo to John Doar, November 26, 1962, FBI FOIA Ole Miss, Department of Justice, file number 1vw 11, 801 144-40-254.

1851 *Dallas Morning News*, June 30, 1961.

1852 FBI FOIA, Ole Miss.

1853 FBI 116-165494-126.

1854 Doyle, *An American Insurrection*, 97–8.

1855 *Dallas Morning News*, September 30, 1962.

1856 *Times–Picayune*, September 30, 1962.

1857 Ibid.

1858 Ibid.

1859 Doyle, *An American Insurrection*, 110–111.

1860 *Times–Picayune*, September 29, 1962.

1861 Doyle, *An American Insurrection*, 113.

1862 *Times–Picayune*, September 30, 1962.

1863 Cravens, *Edwin A. Walker and the Right Wing in Dallas, 1960–1966*, 111.

1864 Doyle, *An American Insurrection*, 115.

1865 124-10331-10029, The John F. Kennedy Assassination Records Collection, NARA.

1866 Doyle, *An American Insurrection*, 122.

1867 Transcript of phone conversation between President Kennedy and Ross Barnett, FBI FOIA, Ole Miss.

1868 Doyle, *An American Insurrection*, 134.

1869 *Clarion Ledger*, October 1, 1962.

1870 *Times–Picayune*, September 30, 1962.

1871 "Record of Conversation with Robert K. Brown," July 17, 1968, NODA.

1872 *Times–Picayune*, October 1, 1962.

1873 *Councilor*, December 1963.

1874 *Dallas Morning News*, October 7, 1962.

1875 *Dallas Morning News*, October 13, 1962.

1876 Robert DePugh, interviews by the author, December 17, 1999, and May 11, 2000.

1877 124-10321-10043, The John F. Kennedy Assassination Records Collection, NARA.

1878 124-10331-10330, The John F. Kennedy Assassination Records Collection, NARA.

1879 180-10078-10035, The John F. Kennedy Assassination Records Collection, NARA.

1880 124-10331-10029, The John F. Kennedy Assassination Records Collection, NARA.

1881 FBI file number 105-8255, April 10, 1964.

1882 124-10331-10029, The John F. Kennedy Assassination Records Collection, NARA.

1883 Doyle, *An American Insurrection*, 134

1884 *Clarion Ledger*, September 30, 1962.

1885 Doyle, *An American Insurrection*, 154.

1886 Doyle, *An American Insurrection*, 155.

1887 *Times–Picayune*, October 2, 1962.

1888 Doyle, *An American Insurrection*, 163.

1889 *Newsweek*, October 15, 2008.

1890 Doyle, *An American Insurrection*, 124–5.

1891 *Times–Picayune*, October 3, 1962.

1892 Doyle, A*n American Insurrection*, 215.

1893 The author recalls reading a contemporaneous account of the men arrested and kept at the Lyceum. Unfortunately the source cannot be found. It was a major newspaper or magazine article on Ole Miss from the period. They described an arrested man who was "middle aged, diabetic and from Georgia" who fits Milteer's description.

1894 *Washington Star*, October 3, 1962.

1895 Doyle, *An American Insurrection*, 172.

1896 *Times–Picayune*, October 1, 1962.

1897 *Times–Picayune*, October 2, 1962.

1898 *Newsweek*, October 15, 1962.

1899 *Washington Evening Star*, October 1, 1962.

1900 *New York Times*, October 2, 1962.

1901 Doyle, *An American Insurrection*, 195–7.

1902 Doyle, *An American Insurrection*, 198.

1903 Doyle, *An American Insurrection*, 271–7.

1904 Doyle, *An American Insurrection*, 219.

1905 Doyle, *An American Insurrection*, 270.

1906 Doyle, *An American Insurrection*, 281.

1907 "Trent Lott," *Wikipedia*, last modified March 12, 2014, http://en.wikipedia.org/wiki/

Trent_Lott.

1908 Doyle, *An American Insurrection*, 267.

1909 *Times–Picayune*, October 2, 1962.

1910 Cravens, *Edwin A. Walker and the Right Wing in Dallas, 1960–1966*, 115.

1911 Doyle, *An American Insurrection*, 268.

1912 *Christian Crusade*, January 1963.

1913 Doyle, *An American Insurrection*, 268.

1914 *Times–Picayune*, October 2, 1962.

1915 David Talbot, *Brothers. The Hidden Story of the Kennedy Years* (New York: Simon & Schuster, 2008).

1916 See: John Frankenheimer and Charles Champlin, *John Frankenheimer: A Conversation* (Riverwood Press, 1995).

1917 Doyle, A*n American Insurrection*, 269.

1918 *Times–Picayune*, October 2, 1962.

1919 Doyle, *An American Insurrection*.

1920 *Shreveport Times*, December 4, 1963.

1921 Fred Schlafly, letter to Edgar Bundy, April 29, 1963, Clarence Manion Papers, Chicago Historical Society, 8–6.

1922 J. Harry Jones, Jr., *The Minutemen* (Garden City: Doubleday, 1968), 23.

1923 FBI file number 63-4296-12-622.

1924 FBI file number 62-107261-174.

1925 FBI FOIA Ole Miss, Department of Justice, file number 1vw 11, 801 144-40-254.

1926 Department of Justice, memo to John Doar, November 26, 1962.

1927 Haley Papers, The Haley Memorial Library and History Center, Midland, Texas, June 8, 1963.

1928 *Dallas Morning News*, October 3, 1962.

1929 *Times–Picayune*, October 2, 1962.

1930 *New York Times*, January 2, 1997.

1931 *Times–Picayune*, March 21, 1956.

1932 Ibid.

1933 Robert Morris, letter to Charles Willoughby, October 24, 1956, Charles Willoughby Papers, Douglas MacArthur Archives, Norfolk, Virginia.

1934 Robert Welch, letter to Robert Morris, Clarence Manion Papers, Chicago Historical Society, Box 61, Folder 7.

1935 Cravens, *Edwin A. Walker and the Right Wing in Dallas, 1960–1966*, 121–2.

1936 Liberty Lobby newsletter, November 5, 1962, Wilcox RH, WL, Eph. 2211.12, University of Kansas Library.

1937 Doyle, *An American Insurrection*, 25.

1938 *Times–Picayune*, October 2, 1962.

1939 FBI file number 116-165494.

1940 *Dallas Morning News*, October 8, 1963.

1941 Cravens, *Edwin A. Walker and the Right Wing in Dallas, 1960–1966*, 124.

1942 Clarence Manion Papers, Chicago Historical Society, Box 61, Folder 7.

1943 FBI FOIA, Edwin A. Walker, 94-56242-5, encl.,1–3.

1944 *States–Item*, October 10, 1963.

1945 *Dallas Morning News*, October 14, 1962.

1946 *Times–Picayune*, October 22, 1962.

1947 *Dallas Morning News*, November 1, 1962.

1948 *Times–Picayune*, October 29, 1962.

1949 *Times–Picayune*, January 10, 1963.

1950 FBI FOIA, Melvin Bruce.

1951 *The National Eagle*, April 1963.

1952 *Rebel Underground*, January 1963, Mississippi State Archives.

1953 *Times–Picayune*, January 6, 1963

1954 *Times–Picayune*, October 31, 1962.

1955 *States–Item*, November 13, 1962.

1956 *Independent American* – date lost.

1957 FBI FOIA, Joseph A. Milteer, report dated February 8, 1963, Field Office files 157-739.

1958 FBI FOIA, Joseph A. Milteer, MM157-739.

1959 124-10331-101195, The John F. Kennedy Assassination Records Collection, NARA.

1960 *Shreveport Times*, December 7, 1962.

1961 *Shreveport Times*, December 28, 1962.

1962 *Shreveport Times*, December 10, 1962.

1963 *Times–Picayune*, December 22, 1962.

1964 *Dallas Morning News*, November 21, 1962.

1965 FBI FOIA, Edwin A. Walker.

1966 Cravens, *Edwin A. Walker and the Right Wing in Dallas, 1960–1966*, 125.

1967 Davis, *Mafia Kingfish*, 90.

1968 *HSCA Report*.

1969 *Chicago Dailey Times*, October 9, 1967.

1970 *The Shreveport Times*, November 21, 1962.

1971 *Dallas Morning News*, May 31, 1963.

1972 *Times–Picayune*, October 2, 1962.

1973 Cravens, *Edwin A. Walker and the Right Wing in Dallas, 1960–1966*, 123.

1974 Cravens, *Edwin A. Walker and the Right Wing in Dallas, 1960–1966*, 126.

1975 Doyle, *An American Insurrection*, 282.

1976 124-10285-10298, The John F. Kennedy Assassination Records Collection, NARA.

1977 Doyle, *An American Insurrection*, 280.

1978 *Times–Picayune*, October 2, 1962.

1979 Doyle, *An American Insurrection*, 294.

1980 Doyle, *An American Insurrection*, 297.

1981 John Carpenter, *Extremism USA* (Phoenix: Associate Professional Services, Inc., 1964).

1982 President Kennedy, speech given at the Los Angeles Palladium, November 18, 1961.

1983 *Christian Crusade*, March 1963.

1984 FBI FOIA, Edwin A. Walker, file number 116-165494-47, August 5, 1963.

1985 Ibid.

Chapter 14

1986 *Christian Crusade*, January 1963.

1987 *Group Research*, January 9, 1963.

1988 *The Boston Herald*, January 6, 1963.

1989 *Boston Globe*, January 7, 1963.

1990 *Boston Globe*, January 21, 1991.

1991 FBI DL 2-05, April 5, 1963.

1992 180-101-10119, The John F. Kennedy Assassination Records Collection, NARA.

1993 *Times–Picayune*, February 9, 1963.

1994 Ned Touchstone Papers, Noel Memorial Library, Louisiana State University Shreveport, February 2, 1963.

1995 *Christian Crusade*, January 1963.

1996 *Dallas Morning News*, February 15, 1963.

1997 *Warren Commission Report*, 309.

1998 *Washington Post*, November 30, 2004.

1999 *Christian Crusade*, July 1957.

2000 Ibid.

2001 FBI FOIA, Billy James Hargis.

2002 *Christian Crusade*, June 1958.

2003 Robert Welch, letter to Granville Knight, February 1, 1965, Granville Knight Papers, University of Oregon.

2004 *Christian Crusade*, March 1959.

2005 FBI file number 100-6546-24.

2006 Mary Cain Papers, Mississippi State Archives, C-JA-47.

2007 FBI Cincinnati office to Director, April 28, 1960, CI 157-50.

2008 *National Christian American Monthly*, 13, no. 6.

2009 Archives II, Audio Room, The John F. Kennedy Assassination Records Collection, NARA.

2010 Grady Bartlett, letter to Joseph A. Milteer, May 25, 1960, BCPC.

2011 FBI FOIA, Joseph A. Milteer.

2012 Mary Brengel, interview by the author, June 25, 1996.

2013 Cravens, *Edwin A. Walker and the Right Wing in Dallas, 1960–1966*, 132–3.

2014 *Dallas Morning News*, February 17, 1963.

2015 FBI file number 116-165494-126, p. 16.

2016 FBI file number 157-66-56.

2017 FBI FOIA, Edwin A. Walker, "Racial Situation"; file number 157-4-64, February 26, 1963.

2018 FBI file number 105-66233-1015

2019 *Independent American*, March 1963.

2020 *Christian Crusade*, March 1963.

2021 FBI FOIA, Edwin A. Walker, file number 116-165494-40.

2022 FBI file number 62-101947-7.

2023 Warren Commission, IV, 441.

2024 *Christian Crusade*, March 1963.

2025 *Montgomery Advertiser–Journal*, March 10, 1963.

2026 *Greenville News*, March 12, 1963 and March 13, 1963.

2027 *Nashville Tennessean*, March 14, 1963.

2028 Warren Commission, IV, 442.

2029 *Arizonians For America* newsletter, March 1963, Manion Papers, Chicago Historical Society, 8-5.

2030 *Christian Crusade*, May 1963.

2031 FBI FOIA, Edwin A. Walker.

2032 Edwin A. Walker Papers, Dolph Briscoe Center for American History, University of Texas at Austin, Box 96-30/12a.

2033 *Times–Picayune*, March 23, 1963.

2034 FBI FOIA, Edwin A. Walker.

2035 *Christian Crusade*, May 1963.

2036 Warren Commission, Document 81b, 150.

2037 *Christian Crusade*, May 1963.

2038 *Times–Picayune*, April 3, 1963.

2039 *Christian Crusade* magazine, May 1963.

2040 Cravens, *Edwin A. Walker and the Right Wing in Dallas, 1960–1966*, 133.

2041 Edwin A. Walker Papers, Dolph Briscoe Center for American History, University of Texas at Austin, Box 96-30/12a.

2042 FBI FOIA, Edwin A. Walker.

2043 *Warren Commission Report*, 407.

2044 Cravens, *Edwin A. Walker and the Right Wing in Dallas, 1960–1966*, 134.

2045 *Christian Crusade*, February 1963.

2046 *Christian Crusade*, April 1963

2047 *Times–Picayune*, April 12 or 13, 1963: exact date is uncertain.

2048 Edwin A. Walker Papers, Dolph Briscoe Center for American History, University of

Texas at Austin, Box 96-30/12b.

2049 Edwin A. Walker Papers, Dolph Briscoe Center for American History, University of Texas at Austin, Box 96-30/12a, Broadcast #63-260.

2050 *Warren Commission Report*.

2051 Edwin A. Walker Papers, Dolph Briscoe Center for American History, University of Texas at Austin. Copies of *The Worker* were found in his personal papers.

2052 Cravens, *Edwin A. Walker and the Right Wing in Dallas, 1960–1966*, 135.

2053 *Dallas Morning News*, Early City Edition, March 12, 1963.

2054 *Dallas Morning News*, Evening Edition, March 12, 1963.

2055 Dick Russell, *The Man Who Knew Too Much* (New York: Carroll and Graf Publishers, Inc., 1992), 183.

2056 Warren Commission, XXIII, 761–762.

2057 FBI FOIA, Edwin A. Walker, DALLAS SAC, file number 1CO-10, 416 2-P, December 7, 1963.

2058 FBI BH 157-864.

2059 124-10331-10212, The John F. Kennedy Assassination Records Collection, NARA.

2060 Warren Commission, XI, 292. For information regarding dogs picking up the scent, see Warren Commission, I, 16.

2061 Edwin A. Walker Papers, Dolph Briscoe Center for American History, University of Texas at Austin, Box 96-30/9.

2062 Secret Service, letter to Jesse Curry, 12-26-63, CO-2-34-030; obtained by FOIA by Walker.

2063 Warren Commission, XI, 294–6.

2064 Warren Commission, VI, 24.

2065 Warren Commission, XI, 286.

2066 Russell, *The Man Who Knew Too Much*.

2067 FBI 116165-494, to Director, June 10, 1964.

2068 *Dallas Morning News*, April 18, 1963.

2069 *Shreveport Journal*, April 19, 1963.

2070 *Dallas Morning News*, April 25, 1963.

2071 *Dallas Morning News*, April 26, 1963.

2072 *Dallas Morning News*, April 25, 1963.

2073 *Times–Picayune*, May 3, 1963.

2074 *Shreveport Journal*, May 3, 1963.

2075 *Shreveport Journal*, May 11, 1963.

2076 *Shreveport Journal*, May 14, 1963.

2077 *Times–Picayune*, May 7, 1963.

2078 *Shreveport Journal*, May 8, 1963.

2079 William Turner, *Ramparts* magazine, September 1967.

2080 *Dallas Morning News*, April 4, 1963.

2081 *Times–Picayune*, May 21, 1963.

2082 *Times–Picayune*, May 22, 1963.

2083 *Shreveport Journal*, May 25, 1963.

2084 *Shreveport Journal*, May 25, 1963.

2085 *Councilor*, May 20, 1963.

2086 Cravens, *Edwin A. Walker and the Right Wing in Dallas, 1960–1966*, 136.

2087 *Times–Picayune*, May 28, 1963 and May 29, 1963.

2088 *Times–Picayune*, May 2, 1963.

2089 Edwin A. Walker Papers, Dolph Briscoe Center for American History, University of Texas at Austin.

2090 124-10016-1092, The John F. Kennedy Assassination Records Collection, NARA.

2091 Warren Commission, IX, 414.

2092 FBI FOIA, Edwin A. Walker, DL 100-10046.

2093 Warren Commission, IX, 414–5.

2094 Warren Commission, Exhibit 298.

2095 FBI FOIA, Edwin A. Walker, file number DL 100-10461

2096 Russell, *The Man Who Knew Too Much*, 311.

2097 Ford and Stiles, *Portrait of an Assassin*.

2098 1993.06.14.16.47:21:430000, Department of State, The John F. Kennedy Assassination Records Collection, NARA.

2099 Russell, *The Man Who Knew Too Much*, 183–7.

2100 Russell, *The Man Who Knew Too Much*, 311–4.

2101 *Warren Commission Report*, 17.

2102 1992.06.14.16.23.34:650000, Department of State, The John F. Kennedy Assassination Records Collection, NARA.

2103 124-10100-100095, The John F. Kennedy Assassination Records Collection, NARA.

2104 124-10100-100093, The John F. Kennedy Assassination Records Collection, NARA.

2105 Warren Commission, Exhibit 2389.

2106 124-10100-10093, The John F. Kennedy Assassination Records Collection, NARA.

2107 Warren Commission, Exhibit 2389.

2108 1992.06.14.16.23.34:650000, Department of State, The John F. Kennedy Assassination Records Collection, NARA.

2109 Warren Commission, Document 870, 2.

2110 Secret Service file number 00-2-34-030.

2111 124-10014-10387. The John F. Kennedy Assassination Records Collection, NARA.

2112 124-10014-10380, The John F. Kennedy Assassination Records Collection, NARA.

2113 124-10016-10118, The John F. Kennedy Assassination Records Collection, NARA.

2114 100-10461-1334, The John F. Kennedy Assassination Records Collection, NARA.

2115 1992.06.14.16.23.34:6500, Department of State, The John F. Kennedy Assassination Records Collection, NARA.

2116 Ibid.

2117 FBI file number 100-10461-133.

2118 1992.06.14.16.23.34:6500, Department of State, The John F. Kennedy Assassination Records Collection, NARA.

2119 Warren Commission, Exhibit CE 2874.

2120 124-10016-10192, The John F. Kennedy Assassination Records Collection, NARA.

2121 124-10040-10452, The John F. Kennedy Assassination Records Collection, NARA.

2122 "S", letter apparently sent to Jim Garrison, April 21, 1967, William Wood Papers, The John F. Kennedy Assassination Records Collection, NARA.

2123 Warren Commission, Exhibit CE 2874.

2124 124-10014-10387, The John F. Kennedy Assassination Records Collection, NARA.

2125 Warren Commission, Exhibit 2981.

2126 *Washington Post*, March 17, 1977.

2127 180-10086-10293, The John F. Kennedy Assassination Records Collection, NARA

2128 *Time*, February 16, 1976.

2129 Robert DePugh, interviews by the author, December 17, 1999, and May 11, 2000.

2130 "S", letter apparently sent to Jim Garrison, April 21, 1967, William Wood Papers, The John F. Kennedy Assassination Records Collection, NARA.

2131 FBI FOIA, Billy James Hargis. Speech on February 14, 1962.

2132 FBI file number 105-82555, Oswald HQ file, Section 179.

2133 Warren Commission, XI, 436.

2134 *Councilor*, December 1963.

2135 *Councilor*, April 4, 1967.

2136 FBI file number 105-82555, Oswald HQ file, Section 179.

2137 *Dallas Morning News*, November 25, 1963.

2138 FBI file number 105-82555, Oswald HQ file, Section 179.

2139 Warren Commission, Document 1543.

2140 FBI file number 105-82555-4218, dated June 26, 1964.

2141 J. Edgar Hoover, letter to Lee Rankin, August 1, 1965, FBI file number 105082555, Sec, 201.

2142 FBI FOIA, file number 116-165494-40

2143 Charles Willoughby Papers, Douglas MacArthur Archives, Norfolk, Virginia.

2144 FBI file number 105-82555.

2145 124-10022-10485, The John F. Kennedy Assassination Records Collection, NARA, 6.

2146 Richard B. Russell Papers. Richard B. Russell Library for Political Research and Studies, University of Georgia Libraries.

2147 Warren Commission, XV, 723.

2148 Russell, *The Man Who Knew Too Much*, 317.

2149 Edwin A. Walker Papers, Dolph Briscoe Center for American History, University of Texas at Austin, 96-30/37.

2150 There are twenty-four documents in the National Archives database relative to Earl Golz. The brief description in the NARA database references, mostly, the "Dear Mr. Hunt" letter. The author has not viewed them.

2151 *Look*, January 26, 2012.

2152 Warren Commission, V, 529.

2153 *Look*, January 26, 2012.

2154 Warren Commission, V, 529.

2155 Warren Commission, V, 492.

2156 Warren Commission, Exhibit 1032.

2157 Warren Commission, V, 529.

2158 Warren Commission, XXIII, 471.

2159 Warren Commission, V, 508.

2160 Warren Commission, V, 529.

2161 Warren Commission, XXIII, 471.

2162 Ibid.

2163 Warren Commission, Document 7, 701–3.

2164 Russell, *The Man Who Knew Too Much*, 320–7.

2165 John Kaplan and John R. Waltz, *The Trial of Jack Ruby* (New York: The McMillan Company, 1965), 281.

2166 Hurt, *Texas Rich*, 230.

2167 *Warren Commission Report*, 343.

2168 Warren Commission, V, 185, courtesy of Paul Trejo, from his unpublished 2012 manuscript entitled *On the Veracity of General Walker*.

Chapter 15

2169 FBI file number 94-56242-5

2170 *Warren Commission Report*.

2171 Blakey and Billings, *The Plot to Kill the President*, 357.

2172 *Facts*, May 1965, ADL.

2173 *Times–Picayune*, May 30, 1963.

2174 *Dallas Morning News*, June 2, 1963.

2175 *Dallas Morning News*, June 4, 1963.

2176 *TImes–Picayune*, June 4, 1963.

2177 *TImes–Picayune*, June 9, 1963.

2178 *Christian Crusade*, April 1963.

2179 *Times–Picayune*, June 6, 1963.

2180 Warren Commission, Document 366.

2181 124-90129-10032, The John F. Kennedy Assassination Records Collection, NARA.

2182 Russell, *The Man Who Knew Too Much*, 538.

2183 *Times–Picayune*, June 12, 1963.

2184 *Dallas Morning News*, June 12, 1963.

2185 *Shreveport Journal*, June 13, 1962.

2186 Edwin A. Walker Papers, Dolph Briscoe Center for American History, University of Texas at Austin, Box 96-30/16.

2187 *Shreveport Journal*, June 12, 1963.

2188 FBI FOIA, Joseph A. Milteer.

2189 *Dallas Morning News*, June 20, 1963.

2190 *Times–Picayune*, June 24, 1963.

2191 Rainach Papers, Noel Memorial Library, Louisiana State University Shreveport.

2192 FBI FOIA, Citizens' Council of America, file number 105-46604-53.

2193 *Times–Picayune*, June 13, 1963 and June 14, 1963.

2194 *Times–Picayune*, June 15, 1963.

2195 *Shreveport Journal*, June 15, 1963.

2196 *Dallas Morning News*, June 15, 1963.

2197 Warren Commission, Document 366.

2198 Edwin A. Walker Papers, Dolph Briscoe Center for American History, University of Texas at Austin, Box 96-30/25.

2199 *Group Research*, April 5, 1972.

2200 *Shreveport Journal*, June 17, 1963.

2201 *Times–Picayune*, June 19, 1963.

2202 Edwin A. Walker Papers, Dolph Briscoe Center for American History, University of Texas at Austin, Box 96-30/10. Others listed as attending were "Shannon, Kerschner, Rafferty, Woodbridge, Buckley," and "Rep. party."

2203 Warren Commission, Document 366.

2204 *Dallas Morning News*, June 20, 1963.

2205 *Shreveport Journal*, June 21, 1963.

2206 Warren Commission, 4, 443.

2207 *Warren Commission Report*, 412.

2208 *Dallas Morning News*, July 5, 1963.

2209 *Shreveport Journal*, July 10, 1963.

2210 *Shreveport Journal*, July 12, 1963.

2211 *Shreveport Journal*, July 15, 1963.

2212 *Shreveport Journal*, July 1, 1963.

2213 *Dallas Morning News*, July 21, 1963.

2214 *Times–Picayune*, July 26, 1963.

2215 Warren Commission, Document 81b, 156.

2216 *Shreveport Journal*, July 27, 1963.

2217 *Shreveport Journal*, August 1, 1963.

2218 *Christian Crusade*, June–July 1963.

2219 *Times–Picayune*, August 3, 1963.

2220 *Dallas Morning News*, August 4, 1963.

2221 Cravens, *Edwin A. Walker and the Right Wing in Dallas, 1960–1966*, 137.

2222 FBI FOIA, Edwin A. Walker, file number 157-158.

2223 Cravens, *Edwin A. Walker and the Right Wing in Dallas, 1960–1966*, 138.

2224 Cravens, *Edwin A. Walker and the Right Wing in Dallas, 1960–1966*, 137.

2225 *Warren Commission Report*, 407.

2226 124-103331-10147, The John F. Kennedy Assassination Records Collection, NARA.

2227 *Times–Picayune*, August 6, 1963.

2228 Warren Commission, Document 366.

2229 FBI FOIA, Pedro del Valle. This may have been a meeting with Frank Capell.

2230 Warren Commission, Document 81b, 156.

2231 Warren Commission, XXVI, 828–831.

2232 *Warren Commission Report*, 408.

2233 FBI FOIA, file number 100-16601.

2234 *Shreveport Journal*, July 26, 1963.

2235 *Shreveport Journal*, August 9, 1963.

2236 *Shreveport Journal*, August 12, 1963.

2237 *Plaquemines Gazette*, April 24, 1959.

2238 *Memphis Commercial Appeal*, December 29, 1955.

2239 Edwin A. Walker Papers, Dolph Briscoe Center for American History, University of Texas at Austin, Box 93-402/1; Speaking schedule.

2240 Edwin A. Walker Papers, Dolph Briscoe Center for American History, University of Texas at Austin, Box 96-30/20.

2241 Warren Commission, Document 366.

2242 *Dallas Morning News*, August 15, 1963.

2243 Warren Commission, Document 81b, 156.

2244 *Times–Picayune*, August 18, 1963.

2245 *Warren Commission Report*, 408.

2246 Warren Commission, Document 81b, 156.

2247 *Baton Rouge Morning Advocate*, August 20, 1963.

2248 *Times–Picayune*, August 22, 1963.

2249 *Warren Commission Report*.

2250 FBI FOIA, file number 157-970-265.

2251 FBI FOIA, file number 157-970-352.

2252 FBI FOIA, Joseph A. Milteer.

2253 FBI FOIA, file number 157-970-1018.

2254 *Baton Rouge Morning Advocate*, August 29, 1963.

2255 Warren Commission, Document 366.

2256 *Dallas Morning News*, August 23, 1963.

2257 *Jackson Daily News*, September 1, 1963.

2258 Warren Commission, Document 366.

2259 *Dallas Times Herald*, September 1, 1963, C-1.

2260 Warren Commission, Document 366.

2261 *Jackson Daily News*, September 8, 1963.

2262 *Shreveport Journal*, September 7, 1963.

2263 *Jackson Daily News*, September 4, 1963.

2264 *Times–Picayune*, November 15, 1963.

2265 *Shreveport Journal*, September 5, 1963.

2266 Kent Courtney, letter to Willie Rainach, March 24, 1958, Rainach Papers, Noel Memorial Library, Louisiana State University Shreveport.

2267 *Shreveport Journal*, September 5, 1963.

2268 *Times–Picayune*, August 21, 1963.

2269 Harold Montgomery, letter to Joe Cooper, June 2, 1964, AARC.

2270 *Jackson Daily News*, September 5, 1963.

2271 *Shreveport Journal*, September 5, 1963.

2272 Joseph Cooper, interview by Andrew Sciambra, October 2, 1968, NODA.

2273 *Shreveport Journal*, May 11, 1963.

2274 Paul Rothermel, interview by the author, March 15, 2000.

2275 Wellborn Jack Papers, Noel Memorial Library, Louisiana State University Shreveport.

2276 *Times–Picayune*, September 6, 1963.

2277 *Councilor*, September 5, 1963.

2278 *Shreveport Journal*, September 8, 1963.

2279 *New York Times*, September 7, 1963.

2280 *Jackson Daily News*, September 5–6, 1963.

2281 *Shreveport Journal*, September 9, 1963.

2282 *Plaquemines Gazette*, September 13, 1963.

2283 *Times–Picayune*, January 16, 1964.

2284 *Dallas Morning News*, September 8, 1963.

2285 *Dallas Morning News*, September 10, 1963.

2286 *Dallas Morning News*, September 11, 1963.

2287 *Shreveport Journal*, September 11, 1963. W. Scott Wilkinson was a member of the Shreveport Citizens' Council. Wilkinson and Leander Perez were members of the coordinating committee for Fundamental Freedoms, an organization founded by the Louisiana State Sovereignty Commission to fight Kennedy's civil rights bill. Wilkinson, like Perez and J. Evetts Haley, was on the advisory board, from its inception, of the Federation for Constitutional Government, a segregationist organization, as was noted earlier.

2288 *Dallas Morning News*, September 15, 1963.

2289 *Shreveport Journal*, September 16, 1963.

2290 *Shreveport Times*, September 15, 1963.

2291 United Press International, September 16, 1963.

2292 *Shreveport Journal*, September 13, 1963.

2293 *Shreveport Journal*, September 16–17, 1963.

2294 *Baton Rouge Morning Advocate*, September 16, 1963.

2295 *Times–Picayune*, September 17, 1963.

2296 Warren Commission, Document 366.

2297 *Shreveport Journal*, September 18, 1963.

2298 *Shreveport Journal*, September 20, 1963.

2299 Guy Banister, letter to Willie Rainach, Rainach Papers, Noel Memorial Library, Louisiana State University Shreveport.

2300 FBI FOIA, Joseph A. Milteer.

2301 Envelope dated December 18, 1958, no letter, Milteer Estate, BCPC.

2302 *Chicago Tribune*, September 20, 1963 and September 22, 1963.

2303 *Chicago Tribune*, September 22, 1963.

2304 Harry Everingham, letter to Clarence Manion, August 8, 1963, Clarence Manion Papers, Chicago Historical Society, 10-3.

2305 Haley Papers, 1966, The Haley Memorial Library and History Center, Midland, Texas.

2306 Herbert Philbrick Papers, Library of Congress, 218:1.

2307 *Free Enterprise*, December 15, 1956.

2308 Paul O. Peters Papers, Special Collections of Wooster College Library, Wooster, Ohio.

2309 Tom Anderson Papers, Special Collections, University of Oregon.

2310 FBI OC 100-4921, 100-424820-19, dated December 18, 1961.

2311 *Christian Crusade*, April 1960.

2312 *We the People* newsletter, September 20, 1960, Tom Anderson Papers, Special Collections, University of Oregon.

2313 *The Weekly Crusader*, October 11, 1963.

2314 Newsletter, August 12, 1964, Ned Touchstone Papers, Noel Memorial Library, Louisiana State University Shreveport.

2315 Clarence Manion Papers, Chicago Historical Society, 8-3.

2316 Courtney Papers, July-August, Special Collections, Northwestern State University of Louisiana.

2317 *We the People* newsletter, August 19, 1963, Clarence Manion Papers, Chicago Historical Society, 10-5.

2318 *Warren Commission Report*, 413.

2319 Warren Commission, IV, 446.

2320 *New York Times*, September 26, 1963.

2321 *Dallas Morning News*, September 15, 1963.

2322 Pedro del Valle Papers, Special Collections, University of Oregon.

2323 *Warren Commission Report*, 412.

2324 HSCA, III, 35, 48, 133.

2325 *Warren Commission Report*, 301.

2326 *Dallas Morning News*, November 30, 1960.

2327 *HSCA Report*, 126.

2328 *Dallas Morning News*, December 5, 1963.

2329 *HSCA Report*, 137.

2330 Warren Commission, XI, 371.

2331 HSCA, X, 32.

2332 Edwin A. Walker Papers, Dolph Briscoe Center for American History, University of Texas at Austin, Box 96-30/25.

2333 104-10103-10303, The John F. Kennedy Assassination Records Collection, NARA.

2334 HSCA, Vol. X, 22.

2335 104-10103-10303, The John F. Kennedy Assassination Records Collection, NARA.

2336 FBI DL 2-05, dated April 5, 1963.

2337 HSCA 180-101-10119, NODA.

2338 104-10103-10303, The John F. Kennedy Assassination Records Collection, NARA.

2339 *Times–Picayune*, January 3, 1968.

2340 Interview of Burton, 180-10085-10369, The John F. Kennedy Assassination Records Collection, NARA.

2341 Ibid.

2342 Record of conversation with Robert K. Brown, July 17, 1968, NODA.

2343 Citizen from Waco, Texas, letter to Jim Garrison, June 28, 1967, NODA.

2344 180-10023-10415, The John F. Kennedy Assassination Records Collection, NARA.

2345 180-10085-10365, The John F. Kennedy Assassination Records Collection, NARA.

2346 *Warren Commission Report*, 423.

2347 Russell, *The Man Who Knew Too Much*, 24.

2348 *Dallas Morning News*, October 1, 1963.

2349 *Dallas Morning News*, October 3, 1963.

2350 *Warren Commission Report*.

2351 *Dallas Morning News*, October 3, 1963.

2352 *Times–Picayune*, October 6, 1963.

2353 Russell, *The Man Who Knew Too Much*, 582.

2354 Warren Commission, Document 81b, 162.

2355 Ned Touchstone Papers, Noel Memorial Library, Louisiana State University Shreveport. Austin Flett sent a copy of the letter to Ned Touchstone.

2356 FBI FOIA, Edwin A. Walker, file number MM 105-8342.

2357 *Warren Commission Report*.

2358 *Shreveport Journal*, October 14, 1963.

2359 *Warren Commission Report*.

2360 CO-2-33, 915, 180-10091-10201, The John F. Kennedy Assassination Records Collection, NARA.

2361 *Warren Commission Report.*

2362 *Jackson Daily News*, October 21, 1963.

2363 *Dallas Morning News*, December 17, 1963.

2364 Cravens, *Edwin A. Walker and the Right Wing in Dallas, 1960–1966*, 140.

2365 *Dallas Morning News*, October 23, 1963.

2366 Cravens, *Edwin A. Walker and the Right Wing in Dallas, 1960–1966*.

2367 *Warren Commission Report*, 288, 416.

2368 Cravens, *Edwin A. Walker and the Right Wing in Dallas, 1960–1966*.

2369 *Dallas Morning News*, October 25, 1963.

2370 180-10071-9499, The John F. Kennedy Assassination Records Collection, NARA.

2371 Cravens, *Edwin A. Walker and the Right Wing in Dallas, 1960–1966*, 143.

2372 *Dallas Morning News*, October 26, 1963.

2373 *Shreveport Journal*, October 25, 1963.

2374 Robert Huffaker, William Mercer, George Phenix, and Wes Wise, *When the News Went Live, Dallas 1963* (Lanham: Taylor Trade Publishing, 2004), 116.

2375 Cravens, *Edwin A. Walker and the Right Wing in Dallas, 1960–1966*, 143.

2376 *Dallas Morning News*, October 27, 1963.

2377 Cravens, *Edwin A. Walker and the Right Wing in Dallas, 1960–1966*, 143–5.

2378 Cravens, *Edwin A. Walker and the Right Wing in Dallas, 1960–1966*, 146.

2379 Ibid.

2380 *Christian Crusade*, date unknown, probably September 1963.

2381 *Jackson Daily News*, October 24, 1963. Billy James Hargis was in Jackson, Mississippi, on October 24, 1963, to speak before the Mississippi Patriotic Network at the King Edward Hotel.

2382 *Times–Picayune*, October 26, 1963.

2383 Mary Brengel, interview by the author, June 25, 1996.

2384 *Baton Rouge Morning Advocate*, October 24, 1963 and October 27, 1963.

2385 *Baton Rouge Morning Advocate*, October 24, 1963.

2386 *Christian Crusade*, September or October 1963. The author found no details on the subject of Billy James Hargis's speeches. The cities he spoke at in Texas were: Corpus Christi on November 2; San Antonio, November 4; Houston, November 5; Austin, November 6; Kerrville, November 7; San Angelo, November 8; Coleman, November 9; Midland, November 11; Odessa, November 12; Big Spring, November 13; Amarillo, November 14; Borger, November 15; Fort Worth, November 16; and Dallas, November 17.

2387 FBI FOIA, Edwin A. Walker, FBI report dated October 27, 1963.

2388 Warren Commission, Document 81b, 162.

2389 FBI FOIA, Edwin A Walker, file number DL 89-43, October 27, 1963.

2390 *Times–Picayune*, October 26, 1963.

2391 *Jackson Daily News*, October 20, 1963, and October 26–7, 1963.

2392 Rainach Papers, Noel Memorial Library, Louisiana State University Shreveport. The speech was transcribed in a booklet.

2393 Talbot, *Brothers*, 71.

2394 Edwin A. Walker Papers, Dolph Briscoe Center for American History, University of Texas at Austin, Box, 96-30/24.

2395 *Dallas Morning News*, October 30, 1963.

2396 *Shreveport Journal*, October 29, 1963.

2397 *Baton Rouge Morning Advocate*, October 30, 1963.

2398 *Dallas Morning News*, October 13, 1963.

2399 *Shreveport Journal*, October 30, 1963.

2400 Warren Commission, V, 185.

2401 *Warren Commission Report*, 288.

2402 *Warren Commission Report*.

2403 *Warren Commission Report*, 420.

2404 *Dallas Morning News*, November 10, 1963.

2405 *Warren Commission Report*, 309, 419.

2406 *Dallas Morning News*, November 16, 1963.

2407 124-10027-10134, The John F. Kennedy Assassination Records Collection, NARA.

2408 The names "A. O. Rapellet" and "Cecil Blair" are familiar to the author as appearing in the volumes of material obtained on the free electors movement.

2409 *Hattiesburg American*, November 19, 1963.

2410 FBI FOIA, Joseph A. Milteer.

2411 *Hattiesburg American*, November 18, 1963.

2412 *Times–Picayune*, November 20, 1963.

2413 Pedro del Valle Papers, Special Collections, University of Oregon.

2414 *Warren Commission Report*.

2415 FBI New Orleans serial 89-69-56.

2416 *Times–Picayune*, November 20, 1963.

2417 Harold Lord Varney, letter to General Walker, December 22, 1963, Edwin A. Walker Papers, Dolph Briscoe Center for American History, University of Texas at Austin, Box 96-30/16.

2418 Edwin A. Walker Papers, Dolph Briscoe Center for American History, University of Texas at Austin, Box 96-30/20.

2419 John Roy Carlson, *Undercover* (New York: E.P. Dutton and Co., 1943).

2420 Pedro del Valle Papers, Special Collections, University of Oregon.

2421 Courtney Papers, Special Collections, Northwestern State University of Louisiana. Name on the Conservative Society of America letterhead; also, an audiotape of General Walker's November 21, 1963, speech is at the university.

2422 Hale Boggs Papers, report to the Louisiana State Police, Howard-Tilton Memorial Library at Tulane University, S.A. BG-4951, courtesy of Romney Stubbs. There is also evidence that Joseph Samuel Newbrough, Jr. had been arrested for homosexuality in files from NODA entitiled "Notes of Hoke May NOSI" (May was a reporter who met with a close friend of Guy Banister on May 11, 1967).

2423 180-10077-10262, The John F. Kennedy Assassination Records Collection, NARA.

2424 Tom Bethel, diary, William Wood Papers, The John F. Kennedy Assassination Records Collection, NARA.

2425 Andrew Sciambra, memo to Jim Garrison, "Shaw Leads II (Interview with Bob Guzman)," May 16, 1969, NODA.

2426 180-10097-10398, The John F. Kennedy Assassination Records Collection, NARA.

2427 180-10107-10384, The John F. Kennedy Assassination Records Collection, NARA.

2428 124-10167-10149, The John F. Kennedy Assassination Records Collection, NARA.

2429 Allen Ellender Papers, Nicholls State University, 1 FF757.

2430 180-10072-10214, The John F. Kennedy Assassination Records Collection, NARA.

2431 FBI report, DBB 75974, March 22, 1967, summarized in NARA Box 1, Segregated CIA files, D-001715.

Chapter 16

2432 Cravens, *Edwin A. Walker and the Right Wing in Dallas, 1960–1966*, 150.

2433 William Manchester, *The Death of a President* (New York: Harper & Row, 1967), 39.

2434 William Manchester, *The Death of a President* (New York: Harper & Row, 1967), 34.

2435 Cravens, *Edwin A. Walker and the Right Wing in Dallas, 1960–1966*.

2436 *Christian Crusade*, December 1963.

2437 *Dallas Morning News*, November 6, 1969.

2438 Warren Commission, XI, 434.

2439 FBI 105-82555, Oswald HQ file, sec. 22, p.148, courtesy of the Mary Ferrell Foundation.

2440 Warren Commission, XXII, 632–686.

2441 Warren Commission, XI, 434.

2442 Warren Commission, II, 210.

2443 *Warren Commission Report*, 419.

2444 *Warren Commission Report*, 420.

2445 Warren Commission, II, 210.

2446 *Warren Commission Report*, 220–1.

2447 Warren Commission, II, 210, 245.

2448 Warren Commission, II, 210.

2449 Warren Commission, XI, 345.

2450 *Warren Commission Report*, 68.

2451 Warren Commission, III, 241.

2452 Warren Commission, III, 225.

2453 Warren Commission, III, 241.

2454 Warren Commission, III, 270.

2455 *Warren Commission Report*, 154.

2456 Manchester, *The Death of a President*, 279.

2457 *Warren Commission Report*.

2458 "A Boy Named J. D.," *J. D. Tippit*, last updated 2013, www.jdtippit.com.

2459 *Warren Commission Report*, 156–176.

2460 *Warren Commission Report*, 174–9.

2461 Warren Commission, VII, 58.

2462 *Warren Commission Report*, 172.

2463 *Warren Commission Report*, 603–610.

2464 Warren Commission, IV, 202–248.

2465 Oswald, *Lee*, 143–144.

2466 *Warren Commission Report*, 239.

2467 Warren Commission, Vol. IV, 202–248.

2468 Joseph A. Milteer, letter to Grady Bartlett, May 10, 1963, BCPC.

2469 Grady Bartlett, letter to Joseph A. Milteer, April 14, 1963, BCPC. Grady Barlett recorded Clyde Watts's speech. Ted Jackman spoke for thirty-nine minutes. Bartlett brought forty tape recordings of Dr. Wesley Swift's speeches to the talk.

2470 180-10099-10120, The John F. Kennedy Assassination Records Collections, NARA.

2471 124-90129-10276, The John F. Kennedy Assassination Records Collections, NARA.

2472 *White Book of the John Birch Society* (Belmont, Massachusetts: The John Birch Society, 1962).

2473 Jackman Flier, Edwin A. Walker Papers, Dolph Briscoe Center for American History, University of Texas at Austin, 96-30/24.

2474 FBI FOIA, Joseph A. Milteer. Contains Secret Service Document SS CO-2-33, 915.

2475 *Times Picayune*, February 10, 1961.

2476 180-10080-10005, The John F. Kennedy Assassination Records Collections, NARA. R. E. Davis was a member of Dallas KKK with Carey Daniels, according to the Dallas Police.

2477 180-100801-0004, The John F. Kennedy Assassination Records Collections, NARA.

2478 *Dallas Morning News*, December 17, 1963.

2479 180-10071-9499, The John F. Kennedy Assassination Records Collections, NARA.

2480 Joint Legislative Committee on Un-American Activities for the State of Louisiana, Report No. 7.

2481 FBI FOIA, Joseph A. Milteer. (Note: The Secret Service did not provide files to the author pursuant to a FOIA request.)

2482 *Fiery Cross*, 2, no. 4, R. E. Davis editor, 3311 Glenhaven, Dallas, 11, Texas; also P.O.

Box 4384, Dallas 8, Texas, courtesy of David Boylan.

2483 Texas Department of Health, Death Certificate.

2484 180-10080-10050, The John F. Kennedy Assassination Records Collections, NARA.

2485 Meagher, *Accessories After the Fact*.

2486 *HSCA Report*, Vol. XII, 41–2.

2487 Paul Rothermel, interview by the author, March 15, 2000.

2488 Warren Commission, II, 201–205.

2489 Warren Commission, II, 205 (testimony of Euins); Warren Commission, VI, 311 (testimony of Harkness); Warren Commission, VI, 315–325 (testimony of Sawyer).

2490 Warren Commission, II, 160.

2491 Warren Commission, Exhibit 2782.

2492 *Warren Commission Report*, 68.

2493 Warren Commission, II, 143.

2494 Warren Commission, III, 61–68.

2495 Warren Commission, III, 147.

2496 Warren Commission, Exhibit 2086.

2497 Warren Commission, Exhibit 519.

2498 Warren Commission, II, 190.

2499 Warren Commission, Exhibit 313.

2500 FBI file number 100-10461-408, March 6, 1964.

2501 Blakey and Billings, *The Plot to Kill the President*, 87.

2502 *Warren Commission Report*, 46–60.

2503 Another unsubstantiated theory, contrived to explain why President Kennedy's head was driven backward from a rear shot, which was called "the jet effect," was proposed to the Rockefeller Commission that looked into some aspects of the assassination in 1975.

2504 *HSCA*, XII.

2505 Alan Adelson, *The Ruby-Oswald Affair* (Seattle: Romar Books, Ltd., 1988), 116.

Chapter 17

2506 Adelson, *The Ruby-Oswald Affair*.

2507 *Warren Commission Report*.

2508 Warren Commission, XIV, 330.

2509 *Warren Commission Report*.

2510 Warren Commission, XIII, 441.

2511 *HSCA Report*, 156.

2512 *HSCA Report*, 153.

2513 *HSCA Report*, 153.

2514 *HSCA Report*, vii.

2515 *HSCA Report*, 170.

2516 Adelson, *The Ruby-Oswald Affair*.

2517 *HSCA Report*, 333.

2518 HSCA, Vol. IX, 169–173.

2519 HSCA, Vol. XX, 49.

2520 Kaplan and Waltz, *The Trial of Jack Ruby*, 28.

2521 Warren Commission, XX1, 4.

2522 Warren Commission, XXIII, 685.

2523 FBI FOIA, Edwin A. Walker, file number 105-82553, March 28, 1964.

2524 FBI FOIA, Edwin A. Walker, file number DL 157-203, November 11, 1962.

2525 Dallas Police Department Criminal Intelligence Section, October 17, 2002. The list of members was taken from Ashland Burchwell when he was arrested for taking arms to aid General Walker at Ole Miss.

2526 Warren Commission, found in: 179-40006-10173, The John F. Kennedy Assassination Records Collections, NARA.

2527 FBI FOIA file number 105-8255, April 10, 1964.

2528 FBI SAC Dallas file number 100-10402, from S.A. James W. Bookout; also noted as file number 100-10461-203.

2529 FBI FOIA file number 63-4296-12-622, 1–3.

2530 Kaplan and Waltz, *The Trial of Jack Ruby*, 28.

2531 *Dallas Mornitng News*, December 1963.

2532 *Warren Commission Report*, 336.

2533 Seth Kantor, *The Ruby Cover-up* (New York: Zebra Books, Kensington Publishing Corp., 1978).

2534 Warren Commission, XXV, 505.

2535 Warren Commission, XIV, 164.

2536 Warren Commission, XIV, 42.

2537 Warren Commission, XV, 325.

2538 Warren Commission, XXII, 296.

2539 *HSCA*, IX, 1107.

2540 *HSCA*, IX, 1109.

2541 Warren Commission, V, 189.

2542 Melvin M. Belli, *Dallas Justice* (New York: David McKay Company, Inc., 1964), 11.

2543 Warren Commission, XV, 534.

2544 Warren Commission, XV, 484–487.

2545 *HSCA*, Vol. IX, 1107.

2546 Diane Holloway, PhD, *Dallas and the Jack Ruby Trial* (New York: Author's Choice Press, 2001), 28–29.

2547 Warren Commission, V, 188.

2548 Henry Hurt III, *Texas Rich* (New York: W. W. Norton & Company, Inc., 1981), 230.

2549   Warren Commission, Vol. XXI, 273.

2550   Warren Commission Report, 343.

2551   124-10026-10196, The John F. Kennedy Assassination Records Collection, NARA.

2552   Warren Commission, XIV, 465.

2553   Warren Commission, XIV, 503.

2554   Robert J. Groden, *The Search for Lee Harvey Oswald* (New York: Penguin Books, 1995).

2555   Kantor, *The Ruby Cover-up.*

2556   Burt Griffin and Leon Hubert, memo to Lee Rankin, March 23, 1964, "Rough Draft," 002603, NODA.

2557   Warren Commission, Exhibit 1322. The FBI copied the following notation from Ruby's notebook: "(33) back of envelope, box 1757, THOMAS HILL, 365 Concord Avenue, Belmont, Mass, EM 1-1197, DA 1-0467"

2558   Edwin A. Walker Papers, Dolph Briscoe Center for American History, University of Texas at Austin, Box 96-30/16. Both the Johnston Printing Company and the American Eagle Publishing Company received their mail at P.O. Box 750, Dallas zone 21. The Walker Defense Fund and Friends of General Walker held P.O. Box 2428 at the zone 21 post office.

2559   Elmer Gertz, *Moment of Madness* (Chicago and New York: Follett Publishing Company, 1968).

2560   Belli, *Dallas Justice*, 11.

2561   Gertz, *Moment of Madness*, 109.

2562   Kantor, *The Ruby Cover-up*, 229.

2563   Warren Commission, XIV, 504.

2564   Kantor, *The Ruby Cover-up.*

2565   Gertz, *Moment of Madenss*, 111.

2566   Warren Commission, XXV, 200.

2567   Warren Commission, XXV, 403.

2568   Kaplan and Waltz, *The Trial of Jack Ruby*, 279.

2569   Warren Commission, XIV, 469.

2570   Warren Commission, I, 77.

2571   Warren Commission, XXV, 434.

2572   *Warren Commission Report.*

2573   Warren Commission, V, 417.

2574   Gertz, *Moment of Madness.*

2575   Belli, *Dallas Justice*, 243.

2576   Kantor, *The Ruby Cover-up*, 11.

2577   Kantor, *The Ruby Cover-up*, 178.

2578   Kantor, *The Ruby Cover-up*, 20.

2579   Kaplan and Waltz, *The Trial of Jack Ruby.*

2580   Kaplan and Waltz, *The Trial of Jack Ruby*, 44.

2581 Kaplan and Waltz, *The Trial of Jack Ruby*.

2582 Kaplan and Waltz, *The Trial of Jack Ruby*, 279.

2583 Kaplan and Waltz, *The Trial of Jack Ruby*, 281.

2584 Belli, *Dallas Justice*, 39.

2585 Gertz, *Moment of Madness*.

2586 Kantor, *The Ruby Cover-up*.

2587 Warren Commission, V, 420.

2588 Warren Commission, V, 191.

2589 *The Jewish Voice*, California, August 6, 1962. Joe Crail of the Coast Federal Bank in California was one of the far-right sponsors of Project Alert where a speaker called for the hanging of Chief Justice Earl Warren in 1962. Project Alert used materials from Senator Eastland's committee and the John Birch Society. Crail published a newsletter sponsored by his bank, which featured a column by Oswald's boyhood hero, Herbert Philbrick. Crail also had ties to Dan Smoot's financial backer, D. B. Lewis.

2590 Warren Commission, V, 196.

2591 Warren Commission, V, 197–8.

2592 Leo Rosten, *The New Joys of Yiddish* (New York: Crown Publishers, 2001).

2593 Warren Commission, V, 199.

2594 Arlen Specter, address at the November 22, 2003, Duquesne University assassination conference sponsored by the Cyril Wecht Institute.

2595 Warren Commission, V, 203.

2596 Warren Commission, V, 204.

2597 Warren Commission, V, 206.

2598 Warren Commission, V, 208.

2599 Warren Commission, V, 181–211.

2600 *HSCA*, Vol. VII, 219.

2601 *Christian Crusade*, April 1964.

2602 180-10035-10430, The John F. Kennedy Assassination Records Collection, NARA.

2603 *White Book of the John Birch Society*, 78.

2604 124-10016-10335, The John F. Kennedy Assassination Records Collection, NARA.

2605 1993.05.24.08:41:54:620000, The John F. Kennedy Assassination Records Collection, NARA.

2606 124-10035-10236, The John F. Kennedy Assassination Records Collection, NARA.

2607 *Anti-Defamation League Report*, 1964.

2608 *On Target*, January 1, 1964, Ned Touchstone Papers, Noel Memorial Library, Louisiana State University Shreveport.

2609 Kantor, *The Ruby Cover-up*.

2610 Belli, *Dallas Justice*, 54.

2611 Warren Commission, XIV, 570.

2612 Warren Commission, XIV, 469.

2613 Warren Commission, XIV, 409.

2614 Warren Commission, XIV, 408.

2615 Warren Commission, XIV, 410.

2616 Mel Ayton, *Crime Magazine*, November 25, 2005.

2617 Kantor, *The Ruby Cover-up*, 26.

2618 FBI file number 442 1016-1642.

2619 Russell, *The Man Who Knew Too Much*, 684.

2620 Kantor, *The Ruby Cover-up*, 322.

2621 *Ramparts*, January 1968.

2622 Marrs, *Crossfire*, 431.

2623 Warren Commission, XXI, 321–350.

2624 *Warren Commission Report*, 364–428.

2625 180-10083-10350, The John F. Kennedy Assassination Records Collection, NARA.

2626 Commission Exhibit 2978; phone number in WC 179-40004-10169; address in 180-100491-10261, The John F. Kennedy Assassination Records Collection, NARA.

2627 C. Edward Griffin, *The Life and Words of Robert Welch* (Thousand Oaks: American Media, 1975).

2628 Robert Welch, *The Blue Book of the John Birch Society* (New York and Los Angeles: Western Islands, 1961).

2629 Warren Commission, Exhibit 1322.

2630 Griffin, *The Life and Words of Robert Welch*, 17.

2631 Robert Welch, letter to Tom Anderson, December 3, 1958, Tom Anderson Papers, Special Collections, University of Oregon. Robert Welch noted that he lived in Belmont and his phone number was Ivanhoe 4-1102; work number was IV 5057. Tom Anderson, Granville Knight, and Clarence Manion were on the council of the John Birch Society. Anderson and Knight's papers are at the University of Oregon, Special Collections. Manion's papers are at the Chicago Historical Society.

2632 FBI file number 62-104401-62.

2633 In 1960, a citizen advised the FBI that he attended a meeting in Dallas presided over by Thomas Hill. Hill, at the time, was from Dallas and was noted to be a paid coordinator for Robert Welch and the John Birch Society. The FBI had been aware of Hill's position since 1960 but it is not known if they passed the information on to the Warren Commission. William "Bill" Turner, a former FBI agent, investigating the assassination for Jim Garrison, noted in a memo to Garrison, "The name Thomas Hill, a Birch official in Massachusetts, was found in [Jack] Ruby's notebook." Garrison was aware of the Hill entry in the notebook. Garrison jotted, below Turner's memo, "*Note: Address indicated by Jack Ruby for Thomas Hill is home address of Robert Welch in Cambridge." [Bill Turner, memo to Jim Garrison, August 28, 1967, "Ferrie telephone calls," NODA.] Garrison may have beeen correct that Ruby had Welch's home address, given the fact that a post office box or street name has never appeared on any of the volumes of Birch material viewed by the author. A letter from Welch in 1954 gave Welch's home address as 810 Main Street, Cambridge, Massachusetts. [Robert Welch, letter to Clarence Manion, September 6, 1954, Clarence Manion Papers, Chicago Historical Society, Box 2, Folder 9.] Turner's claim that Ruby had Welch's home phone number in his address book has not been verified. Welch certainly would not have put his home address on the billboard. If Ruby had Welch's home address it would be suspicious.

2634 Benjamin R. Epstein and Arnold Forster, *Report on the John Birch Society, 1966* (New York: Random House, 1966), 90.

2635 *Dallas Morning News*, April 4, 1963.

2636 Letter to Clarence Manion, written on John Birch Society stationery, November 5, 1963, Clarence Manion Papers, Chicago Historical Society, Box 12-2.

2637 Bill Boxley Papers, File 1061, AARC.

2638 Bill Boxley Papers, AARC.

2639 Janson and Eismann, *The Far Right*, 34.

2640 *American Eagle*, February 6, 1964, Portland Oregon, microfilm, Right Wing Collection, University of Iowa.

2641 124-10007-10120, The John F. Kennedy Assassination Records Collection, NARA.

2642 124-10019-10017, The John F. Kennedy Assassination Records Collection, NARA.

2643 124-10029-10142, The John F. Kennedy Assassination Records Collection, NARA.

2644 Warren Commission, XIV, 334.

2645 Warren Commission, XIV, 349.

2646 Warren Commission, XIV, 353.

2647 Warren Commission, XXI, 295.

2648 Kantor, *The Ruby Cover-up*, 296.

2649 Kantor, *The Ruby Cover-up*, 306.

2650 Kantor, *The Ruby Cover-up*.

2651 180-10030-10030, The John F. Kennedy Assassination Records Collection, NARA.

2652 Kantor, *The Ruby Cover-up*.

2653 Wally Weston, interview by Gaeton Fonzi, 180-10102-10049, The John F. Kennedy Assassination Records Collection, NARA.

2654 FBI file number 105-1264-84, February 14, 1964.

2655 124-90129-10032, The John F. Kennedy Assassination Records Collection, NARA.

2656 Dallas Police Department Criminal Intelligence Section, October 17, 2002. The list of members was apparently taken from Ashland Burchwell when he was arrested for taking arms to aid General Walker at Ole Miss.

2657 Memo, September 15, 1967, NODA, William Wood Papers, The John F. Kennedy Assassination Records Collection, NARA.

2658 Patriotic Party flier, Rainach Papers, Noel Memorial Library, Louisiana State University Shreveport.

2659 FBI Director file number 157-2138-69.

2660 FBI file number 105-1264-84, February 14, 1964.

2661 Jim Garrison, memo, to lead file, August 28, 1967, NODA.

2662 Jerry Milton Brooks, memo to Bill Turner, undated, NODA. Transcript of a two-part tape recording done by Laird Wilcox of an interview of Jerry Milton Brooks on April, 18, 1966, apparently for *Ramparts* magazine, February 1967.

2663 Robert DePugh, interviews by the author December 17, 1999, and May 11, 2000. Sue Eastman, whom Jerry Milton Brooks knew by her married name, Sue Stacy, was mentioned in the transcript of an interview with Brooks that is full of gaps, in connection with an unnamed Texas state coordinator of the Minutemen, who probably was Frank McGehee. McGehee was Sue Eastman's brother, and was also the head of the National Indignation Committee, which frequently featured General Walker as a speaker. DePugh told the author that as the National Indignation Committee began to fade, Sue Eastman moved the operation to DePugh's Minutemen headquarter in Norborne, Missouri.

2664 Laird Wilcox, interview by the author, October 9, 1999.

2665 Jerry Milton Brooks, memo to Bill Turner, undated, NODA. Transcript of a two-part tape recording done by Laird Wilcox of an interview of Jerry Milton Brooks on April, 18, 1966, apparently for *Ramparts* magazine, February 1967.

2666 Allen Ellender Papers, Nicholls State University, Collection 8 FF, and Box 771.

2667 FBI HQ file number 105-12705, serial 4.

2668 FBI file number 63-4296-12-622.

2669 FBI file number 62-107261-174.

2670 124-90129-10032, The John F. Kennedy Assassination Records Collection, NARA.

2671 Warren Commission, found in 179-40006-10173, The John F. Kennedy Assassination Records Collection, NARA.

2672 FBI file number 62-107261, November 12, 1964.

2673 FBI FOIA, Edwin A. Walker, FBI memo on the Minutemen.

2674 124-90129-10112, The John F. Kennedy Assassination Records Collection, NARA.

2675 Edwin A. Walker Papers, Dolph Briscoe Center for American History, University of Texas at Austin, Box 3, Folder C.

2676 *Crime Magazine*, Mel Ayton, November 25, 2005.

2677 Adelson, *The Ruby-Oswald Affair*.

2678 Gertz, *Moment of Madness*, 469–506.

2679 Mort Sahl, interview by the author, September, 2003.

Chapter 18

2680 FBI FOIA, Edwin A. Walker.

2681 General Walker, letter to Gary Shaw (author of *Cover-Up*), September 18, 1989, Edwin A. Walker Papers, Dolph Briscoe Center for American History, University of Texas at Austin, Box 96 30/9.

2682 Warren Commission, XI, 426.

2683 General Walker, interview, January 3, 1989, Cravens, *Edwin A. Walker and the Right Wing in Dallas, 1960–1966.*

2684 *Councilor*, December, 1963.

2685 124-10236-10353, The John F. Kennedy Assassination Records Collections, NARA.

2686 Cravens, *Edwin A. Walker and the Right Wing in Dallas, 1960–1966,* 144–5.

2687 Edwin A. Walker Papers, Dolph Briscoe Center for American History, University of Texas at Austin, Box 96-30/12a.

2688 *The Jewish Voice*, California, December 26, 1963.

2689 *Dallas Morning News*, December 3, 1963.

2690 Hoover Institute Archives, Stanford University.

2691 Herbert Philbrick Papers, Library of Congress.

2692 124-10331-10202, The John F. Kennedy Assassination Records Collections, NARA.

2693 124-10016-10439, The John F. Kennedy Assassination Records Collections, NARA.

2694 Archibald Roberts, letter to Charles Willoughby, November 24, 1970, Charles Willoughby Papers, Douglas MacArthur Archives, Norfolk, Virginia.

2695 *Times–Picayune*, November 23, 1963.

2696 124-10248-10143, The John F. Kennedy Assassination Records Collections, NARA.

2697 *Plaquemines Gazette*, November 29, 1963.

2698 *Baton Rouge Morning Advocate*, November 24, 1963.

2699 Herbert Philbrick Papers, Library of Congress, Box 5, Folder 5.

2700 *Summit Sun*, December 5, 1963.

2701 Edwin A. Walker Papers, Dolph Briscoe Center for American History, University of Texas at Austin, Box 96-30/16.

2702 *Weekly Crusader*, December 6, 1963.

2703 *Dallas Morning News*, November 24, 1963.

2704 *Dallas Morning News*, December 11, 1963.

2705 *Times–Picayune*, November 28, 1963.

2706 *Times–Picayune*, November 27, 1963.

2707 *Weekly Crusader*, June 12, 1964.

2708 *Plaquemines Gazette*, December 6, 1963.

2709 *Group Research*, 2, no. 22.

2710 FBI FOIA, Edwin A. Walker, file number CG 62-6115.

2711 *Group Research*, 2, no. 22.

2712 Carl McIntire, letter to Joseph A. Milteer, November 4, 1964, BCPC.

2713 *Dallas Times Herald*, February 13, 1964.

2714 FBI FOIA, Edwin A. Walker, file number 116-165494.

2715 *Group Research*, December 13, 1963.

2716 *Bulletin*, ADL, January 1964.

2717 Leo Sauvage, *The Oswald Affair* (Cleveland: The World Publishing Company, 1966), 150.

2718 *Dollar Hollar*, December 1963, Ned Touchstone Papers, Noel Memorial Library, Lousisana State University Shreveport.

2719 FBI FOIA, Edwin A. Walker, file number 9-0-7465, 2.

2720 FBI FOIA, Edwin A. Walker, file number 9-41583.

2721 FBI FOIA, Edwin A. Walker.

2722 FBI FOIA, Edwin A. Walker, file number 9-41583.

2723 BCPC, courtesy of James Hall.

2724 Edwin A. Walker Papers, Dolph Briscoe Center for American History, University of Texas at Austin, Box 93-402/1.

2725 Tom Bethel, diary, William Wood Papers, The John F. Kennedy Assassination Records Collections, NARA.

2726 Subject on the Minutemen from Jerry Milton Brooks, October 4, 1967, NODA, from Bill Turner.

2727 *Group Research*, July 15, 1964.

2728 *People's World*, July 18, 1964.

2729 *Houston Post*, July 17, 1964.

2730 Mike Newberry, *Goldwater-ism* (New York: Marzani & Munsell, 1964).

2731 *People's World*, November 23, 1963.

2732 *The Jewish Voice*, California, August 20, 1964, and September 12, 1963.

2733 *The Jewish Voice*, California, July 9, 1964.

2734 *The Jewish Voice*, California, March 9, 1964, and July 30, 1964.

2735 *The Jewish Voice*, California, September 12, 1963.

2736 *People's World*, October 10, 1964.

2737 *Washington Daily News*, November 23, 1963.

2738 *Dallas Morning News*, November 23, 1963.

2739 124-10018-103533, The John F. Kennedy Assassination Records Collections, NARA.

2740 Cravens, *Edwin A. Walker and the Right Wing in Dallas, 1960–1966*, 155.

2741 *Dallas Morning News*, November 24, 1963.

2742 *Dallas Morning News*, December 5, 1963.

2743 *Dallas Morning News*, November 3, 1963.

2744 *Dallas Morning News*, December 4, 1963.

2745 FBI FOIA, Edwin A. Walker, FBI HQ file number 157-401, Serial 1556.

2746 124-10331-100029, The John F. Kennedy Assassination Records Collections, NARA.

2747 124-10331-10147, The John F. Kennedy Assassination Records Collections, NARA.

2748 FBI FOIA, file number 157-401, 1556.

2749 Edwin A. Walker Papers, Dolph Briscoe Center for American History, University of Texas at Austin, Box 96-30/22.

2750 180-10080-100001, The John F. Kennedy Assassination Records Collections, NARA.

2751 H. B. Kelly, letter to General Walker, April 2, 1964, Edwin A. Walker Papers, Dolph Briscoe Center for American History, University of Texas at Austin, Box 30/12A,

2752 124-10331-10029, The John F. Kennedy Assassination Records Collections, NARA.

2753 FBI FOIA, Edwin A. Walker, Jack Anderson Merry Go Round, November 25, 1969.

2754 Forster and Epstein, *Danger on the Right*, 280.

2755 FBI FOIA, Edwin A. Walker, file number 157-4-25-101, 2.

2756 *Christian Crusade*, September, 1964.

2757 Edwin A. Walker Papers, Dolph Briscoe Center for American History, University of Texas at Austin, Box 93-402-1.

2758 FBI FOIA, Edwin A. Walker, file number BH 157-864.

2759 FBI FOIA, Edwin A. Walker, file number 116-165494-126, 13.

2760 FBI file number 116-16549-97. The FBI noted, in another similar plot, as set forth in a November 2, 1964, urgent memorandum, that followers of Major General Edwin Walker planned insurrection if President Johnson was reelected. Reportedly, Klan groups would have brought about marshal law shortly after the election and Walker's followers would have started revolutions in the latter part of December 1964 or first part of January 1965.

2761 *Meet the Press*, transcript from Clarence Manion Papers, Chicago Historical Society, Box 61, Folder 6.

2762 Edwin A. Walker Papers, Dolph Briscoe Center for American History, University of Texas at Austin, Box 96-30/22.

2763 124-901116-10120, The John F. Kennedy Assassination Records Collections, NARA.

2764 124-103331-10197, The John F. Kennedy Assassination Records Collections, NARA.

2765 *Dallas Times Herald*, November 23, 1964.

2766 124-90116-10116, The John F. Kennedy Assassination Records Collections, NARA.

2767 180-10078-10035, The John F. Kennedy Assassination Records Collections, NARA.

2768 FBI FOIA, Edwin A. Walker, file number 157-2751, April 3, 1965.

2769 FBI FOIA, Edwin A. Walker, file number 116-165494-126, 14.

2770 124-90116-10120, The John F. Kennedy Assassination Records Collections, NARA.

2771 180-1009-10176, The John F. Kennedy Assassination Records Collections, NARA.

2772 Pedro del Valle Papers, Special Collections, University of Oregon Library, 157/18.

2773 March 2, 1965, 124-90116-10330, The John F. Kennedy Assassination Records Collections, NARA.

2774 *Baton Rouge Morning Advocate*, June 25, 1965.

2775 FBI FOIA Edwin A. Walker, file number 116-165494-126, 18.

2776 *Facts*, 1967, ADL, 354.

2777 FBI FOIA, Edwin A. Walker, file number 116-165494-126, 19.

2778 *Facts*, 1967, ADL, 354.

2779 FBI FOIA, Edwin A. Walker, file number 116-165494-126, 18.

2780 FBI FOIA, Edwin A. Walker, file number 116-165494-126, 19.

2781 FBI FOIA, Edwin A. Walker, Presidential Protection notification letters to the Secret Service, May 3, 7, 14, and 28, 1965; June 4, 1965, and October 2, 1965.

2782 Cravens, *Edwin A. Walker and the Right Wing in Dallas, 1960–1966*, 157.

2783 FBI FOIA, Edwin A. Walker, file number 77-51387 1820.

2784 Edwin A. Walker Papers, Dolph Briscoe Center for American History, University of Texas at Austin, Box location was lost by the author. Rayes was from Los Angeles.

2785 Edwin A. Walker Papers, Dolph Briscoe Center for American History, University of Texas at Austin, Box 96-30/15.

2786 *Group Research*, December 15, 1967.

2787 FBI FOIA, Edwin A. Walker, file number 116-165494-128.

2788 *ADL Bulletin*, April 1968.

2789 *ADL Bulletin*, February 1971.

2790 *Group Research*, October 26, 1972.

2791 CIA 1993.08.05.15:11:05:310028, The John F. Kennedy Assassination Records Collections, NARA.

2792 *New York Times*, March 17, 1977.

2793 124-102440-10343, The John F. Kennedy Assassination Records Collections, NARA.

2794 *Group Research*, November, October, 1983.

2795 Gary Cornwell, *Real Answers* (Spicewood: Paleface Press, 1998).

Chapter 19

2796 Adelson, *The Ruby-Oswald Affair*.

2797 *Warren Commission Report*.

2798 180-10045-10091, The John F. Kennedy Assassination Records Collections, NARA.

2799 180-10096-10027, The John F. Kennedy Assassination Records Collections, NARA.

2800 Warren Commission, I, 126-264, 188.

2801 1993.06.21.16.24:00:620310, The John F. Kennedy Assassination Records Collections, NARA.

2802 August 29, 1967, NODA, 180-10096-10027, The John F. Kennedy Assassination Records Collections, NARA.

2803 Jean Stafford, *A Mother in History* (New York: Pharos Books, 1965). See page 18 for her remarks on framing.

2804 Mark Lane, interview by the author, November 22, 2005, during the Wecht Institute JFK conference, Duquesne University.

2805 *Washington Post*, Jack Anderson, January 27, 1975.

2806 180-10045-10091, The John F. Kennedy Assassination Records Collections, NARA.

2807 *Councilor*, March 16, 1964.

2808 *Councilor*, 1967, month lost.

2809 *Nashville Tennessean*, January 5, 1964.

2810 J. Evetts Haley, letter to Tom Anderson, March 7, 1964, Haley Papers, The Haley Memorial Library and History Center, Midland, Texas.

2811 Nelson Bunker Hunt, letter to J. Evetts Haley, Haley Papers, The Haley Memorial Library and History Center, Midland, Texas.

2812 Ned Touchstone Papers, Noel Memorial Library, Louisiana State University Shreveport. Names of little familiarity to the author (F. Gano Chance, Charles B. Hudson, Robert B. Hughes, and Jack Ehrle) are also listed; the spitting incident was noted in an undated accompanying news clip.

2813 *Nashville Tennessean*, December 29, 1963.

2814 Robert Welch, letter to Tom Anderson, Tom Anderson Papers, Special Collections, University of Oregon.

2815 *Nashville Tennessean*, December 29, 1963.

2816 *People's World*, September 7, 1963.

2817 *Nashville Tennessean*, December 29, 1963.

2818 Tom Anderson Papers, Special Collections, University of Oregon Library.

2819 Courtney Papers, Special Collections, Northwestern State University of Louisiana.

2820 *Times–Picayune*, April 6, 1960.

2821 *Times–Picayune*, May 31, 1960.

2822 Tom Anderson Papers, Special Collections, University of Oregon Library.

2823 FBI FOIA, Billy James Hargis.

2824 *Dallas Morning News*, September 17, 1961.

2825 *Dallas Morning News*, September 16, 1961.

2826 Stuart McClendon, letter to Tom Anderson, Tom Anderson Papers, Special Collections, University of Wyoming.

2827 Emmet Irwin, letter to Tom Anderson, February 8, 1962, Special Collections, Tom Anderson Papers, University of Oregon Library.

2828 Tom Anderson, letter to Olin Johnston, Tom Anderson Papers, Special Collections, University of Oregon Library.

2829 Ted Jackman, letter to Tom Anderson, Tom Anderson Papers, Special Collections, University of Wyoming.

2830 Tom Anderson, letter to J. Clem Barnes, Jr, May 10, 1962, Tom Anderson Papers, Special Collections, University of Wyoming.

2831 Carlos Marcello, letter to Tom Anderson, Tom Anderson Papers, Special Collections, University of Oregon Library.

2832 *Group Research*, April 5, 1972. Also noted in a news clipping in Joseph A. Milteer's materials at BCPC.

2833 *American Progress*, Nov-Dec. 1962, microfilm, Right Wing Collection, University of Iowa.

2834 General Walker, letter to President Kennedy, Tom Anderson Papers, Special Collections, University of Oregon Library.

2835 *Nashville Tennessean Magazine*, December 29, 1963 and January 5, 1964.

2836 Robert Welch, letter to Tom Anderson, November 1962, Tom Anderson Papers, Special Collections, University of Oregon Library.

2837 Kent Courtney, letter to Tom Anderson, Tom Anderson Papers, Special Collections, University of Oregon Library.

2838 *Dallas Morning News*, October 14, 1962.

2839 *Times–Picayune*, October 31, 1962.

2840 *Christian Crusade*, June-July 1963.

2841 *Group Research*, January 9, 1963.

2842 *Boston Herald*, January 6, 1963. Billy James Hargis and Kent Courtney were present.

2843 *Boston Globe*, January 7, 1963. Ezra Taft Benson and Josef Mlot-Mroz were present.

2844 *Shreveport Times*, January 12, 1963.

2845 *Nashville Tennessean*, March 14, 1963.

2846 Tom Anderson Papers, Special Collections, University of Oregon Library.

2847 *The Examiner*, Birmingham, Alabama, December 12, 1963.

2848 *Nashville Tennessean*, December 29, 1963.

2849 *Dallas Morning News*, June 2, 1963.

2850 *Group Research*, April 5, 1972.

2851 *Dallas Morning News*, July 21, 1963.

2852 Stanley Drennan, letter to Tom Anderson, August 20, 1963, Tom Anderson Papers, Special Collections, University of Wyoming.

2853 Tom Anderson, letter to Stanley Drennan, August 29, 1963, Tom Anderson Papers, Special Collections, University of Wyoming.

2854 *Chicago Tribune*, September 22, 1963.

2855 Curtis Caine, letter to Tom Anderson, Tom Anderson Papers, Special Collections, University of Oregon Library.

2856 Vic Knight, letter to Tom Anderson, Tom Anderson Papers, Special Collections, University of Oregon Library.

2857 William Voit, letter to Anderson, Tom Anderson Papers, Special Collections, University of Oregon Library.

2858 In the February 1965, *American Opinion* Tom Anderson wrote that "the right to discriminate is the right to choose and the right to choose is the essence of liberty." [*Facts*, 1967, ADL, 354.] At the June 30 to July 4, 1973, New England God and Country rally, General Walker was honored at dinner. Among those present were Clyde Watts, Archibald Roosevelt, Robert Montgomery, Curtis Dall, Tom Anderson, and Laurence Bunker. [Herbert Philbrick Papers, Library of Congress, 151:4.] On October 19–21, 1973, at the Liberty Lobby Survival Strategy meeting, Curtis Dall, Tom Anderson, Willis Carto, Ned Touchstone, Pedro del Valle, and Robert DePugh were participants. [Microfilm, Right Wing Collection, University of Iowa.]

2859 Epstein and Forster, *Report on the John Birch Society, 1966.*

2860 Taylor Caldwell, letter to Tom Anderson, October 2, 1958, Tom Anderson Papers, Special Collections, University of Wyoming.

2861 Willis Carto, letter to Tom Anderson, Tom Anderson Papers, Special Collections, University of Oregon Library.

2862 Newberry, *The Yahoos*, 20.

2863 FBI FOIA, Taylor Caldwell. Available online at the FBI Reading Room, file number 65-10492-145. Generals Willoughby and Wedemeyer also served on the board of governors of the Federation of Conservatives.

2864 FBI FOIA, Taylor Caldwell, file number 100-836-7.

2865 FBI FOIA, Taylor Caldwell, file number 62106941-5

2866 *The Wanderer*, October 31, 1963, Herbert Philbrick Papers, Library of Congress, Box 140, Folder 5.

2867 *The Wanderer*, 33, no. 48.

2868 *Group Research*, June 15, 1966.

2869 Edwin A. Walker Papers, Dolph Briscoe Center for American History, University of Texas at Austin, Box 96-30/13.

2870 *The Wanderer*, October 31, 1963, Herbert Philbrick Papers, Library of Congress, Box 140, Folder 5.

2871 Letter, Roberts to Morris, September 30, 1963; Clarence Manion Papers, Chicago Historical Society, Box 11, Folder 5. The letter mentions Oliver.

2872 *Detroit Free Press*, December 19, 1963.

2873 FBI FOIA, Taylor Caldwell, file number 100-836-19.

2874 FBI FOIA Taylor Caldwell, file number 44-38861-4690. Also of interest is a letter to Jim Garrison from Irma Stewart of California, dated June 11, 1968. Six days after the murder, Stewart, a staff member of the *Angry Voice*, who was familiar with Garrison's California investigator, sent him a letter telling him of a letter she had received from a reader, Lee Irvin. She quoted the letter: "Do you remember the American-Nazi, pro Arabs, Cuban exiles, and Minutemen types in the groups that annoyed the Peace Marchers on June 23rd (1967) and of August 6th last year? If someone has film of that, I feel sure they would see that this man—Zirhan Zirhan [sic] (as he was listed at the time—I remember the double name)—was in one (or maybe both) of those incidents." Irvin did not feel it was worthwhile notifying the police because he felt they were anti-Kennedy. The letter stated that further investigation might "lead back to Minutemen and Cuban exiles in Louisiana and Texas in 1963." Film was taken of the incident, but it is not known if anyone every identified Sirhan in it.

2875 *Bulletin*, ADL, July 1968 and June 1964.

2876 *Danger: Extremism*, ADL, New York, 1996.

2877 Tom Anderson Papers, Special Collections, University of Oregon Library.

2878 Willis Carto, letter to Ned Touchstone, October 11, 1965, Ned Touchstone Papers, Noel Memorial Library, Louisiana State University Shreveport.

2879 David Duke Euro Conference, New Orleans, August 2004.

2880 Wilcox Collection, University of Kansas Libraries, RH WL Eph 2212.115.

2881 Herbert Philbrick Papers, Library of Congress, 129:14.

2882 *New York Times*, December 18, 1981.

2883 www,publiceye.org

2884 Bernard Fensterwald, *Coincidence or Conspiracy* (New York: Zebra Books, 1977).

2885 www.publiceye.org

2886 Oliver Stone and Zachary Sklar, *JFK: The Book of the Film* (New York: Applause Books, 1992).

2887 Bellant, *Old Nazis, the New Right, and the Republican Party.*

2888 Memo to Jim Garrison, "Re: Raymond Broshears," August 8, 1968, NODA.

2889 Citizens' Council Board roster, Ned Touchstone Papers, Noel Memorial Library, Louisiana State University Shreveport.

2890 William Gurvich, memo to Jim Garrison, February 14, 1967, regarding seizures of explosives, Lacombe, Louisiana, August 1962, NODA.

2891 180-10086-10453, The John F. Kennedy Assassination Records Collections, NARA.

2892 180-10102-10168, The John F. Kennedy Assassination Records Collections, NARA.

2893 District attorney's interview with Barbara Glancey Reid, April 12, 16, and 17, 1968, 180-10076-10178, The John F. Kennedy Assassination Records Collections, NARA.

2894 Robert DePugh, interviews by the author, December 17, 1999, and May 15, 2000.

2895 Memo entitiled, "Record of Conversation with Robert K. Brown, July 17, 1968," NODA.

2896 *Chicago Tribune*, November 30, 1965.

2897 Hale Boggs Papers, Howard-Tilton Memorial Library at Tulane University.

2898 Memo to Jim Garrison, "Re: Raymond Broshears," August 8, 1968, NODA. A third page—and possibly more pages—is/are missing.

2899 Raymond Broshears, interview by Steve Jaffe, James Alcock, and Louis Ivon, August 8, 1968, NODA. There may be additional pages to the available twenty-one-page interview.

2900 FBI FOIA, Raymond Broshears, Secret Service, file number 127-CO2-0042269-1.

2901 Edwin A. Walker Papers, Dolph Briscoe Center for American History, University of Texas at Austin, Box 30/12A

2902 Edwin A. Walker Papers, Dolph Briscoe Center for American History, University of Texas at Austin, Box 93-402/1

2903 *Facts*, ADL, 234.

2904 Christian Admiral Hotel staff member, letter to Tom Anderson, September 11, 1963, Tom Anderson Papers, Special Collections, University of Oregon Library.

2905 Raymond Broshears, interview by Steve Jaffe, James Alcock, and Louis Ivon, August 8, 1968. There may be additional pages to the available twenty-one -page interview.

2906 180-10086-10453, The John F. Kennedy Assassination Records Collections, NARA.

2907 180-10102-10168, The John F. Kennedy Assassination Records Collections, NARA.

2908 Memo from Bill Turner, Subject on the Minutemen from Jerry Milton Brooks, October 4, 1967 NODA.

2909 180-10086-10453, The John F. Kennedy Assassination Records Collections, NARA.

2910 180-10102-10168, The John F. Kennedy Assassination Records Collections, NARA.

2911 Jack Martin, interview by HSCA, November 22, 1977, 180-10080-10202, The John F. Kennedy Assassination Records Collections, NARA.

2912 Jack Martin, affidavit, 180-10023-10380, The John F. Kennedy Assassination Records Collections, NARA.

2913 180-10086-10453 The John F. Kennedy Assassination Records Collections, NARA.

2914 180-10102-10158, The John F. Kennedy Assassination Records Collections, NARA.

2915 Hal Verb, letter to the author, February 5, 2005.

2916 *Time*, October 8, 1973.

2917 124-10293-10376, The John F. Kennedy Assassination Records Collections, NARA.

2918 124-10031-10293, The John F. Kennedy Assassination Records Collections, NARA.

2919 124-10293-10376, The John F. Kennedy Assassination Records Collections, NARA.

2920 124-10031-10293, The John F. Kennedy Assassination Records Collections, NARA.

2921 CIA file number 104-10404-10046.

2922 Harry Dean (presumed), phonecall to Jim Garrison, undated, NODA dictation, sent to Bernard Fensterwald on April 8, 1968 by Tom Bethel of the NODA, AARC.

2923 180-10102-10201, The John F. Kennedy Assassination Records Collections, NARA.

2924 W. R. Morris, letter to the author, May 10, 1996.

2925 W. R. Morris, *The Men Behind the Guns* (Reagan: National Booksellers, 1975).

2926 R. B. Cutler and W. R. Morris, *Alias Oswald* (Manchester: GKG Partners, 1985), Box 1465.

2927 Kathy Meadows, Morris's widow, interview by the author, November 30, 2000.

2928 Edwin A. Walker Papers, Dolph Briscoe Center for American History, University of Texas at Austin. Box 96-30/18 contains a copy of *Alias Oswald*.

2929 W. R. Morris, *The Secret Papers of Harry Dean* (Reagan: National Booksellers, 1994). Morris died circa 1997.

2930 Harry Dean, interviews by the author via correspondence, 2009 to 2012.

2931 180-10090-10245, The John F. Kennedy Assassination Records Collections, NARA.

2932 *Between the Lines*, March 8, 1977, Valley Publications.

2933 Drive Against Communist Aggression newsletter, February 23, 1963, Special Collections, Hoover Institute. The Drive Against Communist Aggression newsletter, on February 23, 1963, noted their offices were in Whittier, California, and Calle Carmen # 8 Mexico, D. F. The newsletter announced a luncheon to honor Lieutenant Colonel Fuentes Gallegos, Chief of Security for Baja, California, held at Knott's Berry Farm. Dignitaries present were James B. Utt, Walter Knott, and Dr. Tirso del Junco. Max Skousen was the keynote speaker. The aim was to keep Mexico free of Communism.

Kay Fleischman was an officer in the group.

2934 Loran Hall, interview by NODA, May 6, 1968, 180-10094-10242, The John F. Kennedy Assassination Records Collections, NARA.

2935 Harry Dean, *Crosstrails* (Hesperia, California: Probe News, 1991).

2936 Harry Dean, interviews by the author via correspondence, 2009 to 2012.

2937 Flier, Victor Schiro Papers, New Orleans Public Library.

2938 *Baton Rouge Morning Advocate*, September 6, 1963.

2939 Harry Dean, *Crosstrails*.

2940 Harry Dean, interviews by the author via correspondence, 2009 to 2012.

2941 Flier, Special Collections, Hoover Institute.

2942 Harry Dean, *Crosstrails*.

2943 Harry Dean, interviews by the author via correspondence, 2009 to 2012.

2944 FBI FOIA, Joseph A. Milteer.

2945 BCPC.

2946 Press Release, We the People, August 25, 1962, Tom Anderson Papers, Special Collections, University of Wyoming.

2947 John Rousselot, letter to Tom Anderson, August 13, 1963, Tom Anderson Papers, Special Collections, University of Wyoming.

2948 *Times–Picayune*, September 1963, date lost, probably between 12 and 21, 1963.

2949 *Group Research*, 5, no. 15.

2950 Barbara Shell Stone, *The John Birch Society in California*, Doctoral dissertation, University of Southern California, 1968.

2951 Epstein and Forster, *Report on the John Birch Society 1966*, 66.

2952 *Dallas Morning News*, April 2, 1961.

2953 Kent Courtney, letter to General Walker, September 15, 1961, Edwin A. Walker Papers, Dolph Briscoe Center for American History, University of Texas at Austin, Box 96-30/25.

2954 *New York Times*, November 20, 1961.

2955 *Times–Picayune*, December 4, 1961.

2956 Janson and Eismann, *The Far Right*, 108.

2957 Courtney and Courtney, *The Case of General Edwin A. Walker*.

2958 *The Jewish Voice*, California, November 1, 1962.

2959 Dudman, *Men of the Far Right*, 29.

2960 Overstreet and Overstreet, *The Strange Tactics of Extremism*, 220.

2961 *Weekly Crusader*, March 30, 1962.

2962 FBI FOIA, Billy James Hargis.

2963 *Christian Crusade*, September 1962.

2964 Tom Anderson Papers, Special Collections, University of Oregon.

2965 *Christian Crusade*, April 1963, microfilm, Right Wing Collection, University of Iowa Rightwing Collection.

2966 *Christian Crusade*, January 1963.

2967 *Group Research*, January 9, 1963.

2968 *Boston Herald*, January 6, 1963.

2969 *Boston Globe*, January 7, 1963.

2970 *People's World*, February 23, 1963.

2971 *People's World*, March 12, 1963.

2972 *Nashville Tennessean*, March 14, 1963.

2973 Cravens, *Edwin A. Walker and the Right Wing in Dallas, 1960–1966*, 133.

2974 John Birch Society flier promoting rally with Tom Anderson and John Rousselot, Tom Anderson Papers, Special Collections, University of Wyoming.

2975 *Dallas Morning News*, October 30, 1963.

2976 *Baton Rouge Morning News*, October 31, 1963.

2977 *White Book of the John Birch Society*.

2978 Joseph A. Milteer, letter to Grady Bartlett, May 10, 1963, BCPC.

2979 Epstein and Forster, *Report on the John Birch Society, 1966*, 90.

2980 Epstein and Forster, *Report on the John Birch Society, 1966*, 72–3.

2981 Newberry, *Goldwater-ism*.

2982 Epstein and Forster, *Report on the John Birch Society, 1966*, 72–3.

2983 Epstein and Forster, *Report on the John Birch Society, 1966*, 39.

2984 *Dallas Times Herald*, October 29, 1965.

2985 *The Jewish Voice*, California, August 4, 1966.

2986 Epstein and Forster, *The Radical Right*.

2987 *The Jewish Voice*, California, January 12, 1967.

2988 Joseph A. Milteer, letter to Grady Bartlett, May 10, 1963, BCPC.

Chapter 20

2989 *Subversion in Racial Unrest: An Outline of a Strategic Weapon to Destroy the Governments of Louisiana and the United States*, Louisiana State Legislature, 1957, Courtney Papers, Special Collections, Northwestern State University of Louisiana.

2990 Robert DePugh, interviews by the author, December 12, 1999, and May 11, 2000.

2991 FBI file number 62-109060-6057, 22.

2992 Jones, *The Minutemen*, 12.

2993 Robert DePugh, interviews by the author, December 12, 1999, and May 11, 2000.

2994 *Congressional Record*, May 25, 1961, 69, 89.

2995 124-90023-10017, The John F. Kennedy Assassination Records Collections, NARA.

2996 124-90023-10026, The John F. Kennedy Assassination Records Collections, NARA.

2997 Mary Brengel, interview by Cliency Navarre and Kent Simms, June 1, 1967, NODA.

2998 180-10117-10075, The John F. Kennedy Assassination Records Collections, NARA.

2999 James and Wardlaw, *Plot or Politics*, 152.

3000 Summers, *Conspiracy*, 506.

3001 Noyes, *Legacy of Doubt*, 128.

3002 Jack Martin, affadavit prepared for the HSCA, 180-10080-10209, The John F. Kennedy Assassination Records Collections, NARA.

3003 Bill Boxley, summation of the Garrison case, NODA, William Wood Papers, The John F. Kennedy Assassination Records Collections, NARA.

3004 Warren Commission, XXIII, 738.

3005 Warren Commission, X, 54.

3006 Warren Commission, XXV, 729.

3007 Warren Commission, XXVI, 774, 22:828ff, Exhibit 1414ff.

3008 Warren Commission, Exhibit 826.

3009 Warren Commission, XXVI, 784.

3010 Warren Commission, XXVI, 705.

3011 Warren Commission, X, 58.

3012 Warren Commission, XXIII, 738.

3013 Warren Commission, XXVI, 767.

3014 Mailing list of *Southern Patriot*, NODA, William Wood Papers, The John F. Kennedy Assassination Records Collections, NARA.

3015 Myers Lowman Papers, Hoover Institute, Box 76, SCEF folder.

3016 Warren Commission, XXVI, 762–3.

3017 FBI file number 124-10285-10301.

3018 Hugh Murray, letter to the author, November 11, 1996. The *Councilor* was the official newspaper of the Citzens' Council of Lousiana, Inc. Attempts to locate people connected to the Council or the newspaper were not successful. Editor Ned Touchstone died on July 27, 1988. His personal papers are at Lousiana State University at Shreveport, Noel Library Special Collections. Hardcopies of the *Councilor* are at Lousiana Tech University, Ruston, Lousiana, which graciously furnished the author with a copy from the original.

3019 Hugh Murray, interview by the author via phone, 1996.

3020 Hugh Murray, letter to the author. See also: Hugh Murray in *The Fourth Decade* 3, no. 5, July 1996.

3021 Mailing list of *Southern Patriot*, NODA, Banister file.

3022 Hugh Murray, letter to the author, November 11, 1996.

3023 Hugh Murray, interview by the author via phone, 1996.

3024 Warren Commission, XXVI, 791–2.

3025 Warren Commission, VIII, 147, 170.

3026 Warren Commission, XXIII, 723, 726, 728.

3027 Warren Commission, XXV, 729

3028 Warren Commission, XXVI, 766, 791.

3029 Warren Commission, XXVI, 766.

3030 Warren Commission, VIII, 147, 170.

3031 Warren Commission, X, 68.

3032 Warren Commission, II, 491–2.

3033 Warren Commission, XI, 210.

3034 Warren Commission, Gray Exhibit No. 1.

3035 Warrren Commission, Document 75, 232–3.

3036 124-10285-10311, The John F. Kennedy Assassination Records Collections, NARA.

3037 124-90023-10026, The John F. Kennedy Assassination Records Collections, NARA.

3038 Mary Brengel, statement made in preparation for HSCA interview, March 19, 1979, AARC.

3039 Mary Brengel, interview by Cliency Navarre and Kent Simms, June 1, 1967, NODA.

3040 Mary Brengel, interview by the author, June 25, 1996.

3041 Louise Decker, interview by Douglas Ward, January 31, 1967, NODA.

3042 Mary Brengel, interview by the author, June 25, 1996.

3043 Mary Brengel, interview by Cliency Navarre and Kent Simms, June 1, 1967, NODA.

3044 124-00023-10009, The John F. Kennedy Assassination Records Collections, NARA.

3045 124-00023-10010, The John F. Kennedy Assassination Records Collections, NARA.

3046 124-00023-10011, The John F. Kennedy Assassination Records Collections, NARA.

3047 124-00023-10014, The John F. Kennedy Assassination Records Collections, NARA.

3048 124-00023-10025, The John F. Kennedy Assassination Records Collections, NARA.

3049 *Times–Picayune*, March 27, 1956.

3050 124-90023-10026, The John F. Kennedy Assassination Records Collections, NARA.

3051 124-00023-10009, The John F. Kennedy Assassination Records Collections, NARA.

3052 124-00023-10010, The John F. Kennedy Assassination Records Collections, NARA.

3053 124-00023-10011, The John F. Kennedy Assassination Records Collections, NARA.

3054 124-00023-10014, The John F. Kennedy Assassination Records Collections, NARA.

3055 124-00023-10025, The John F. Kennedy Assassination Records Collections, NARA.

3056 124-00023-10026, The John F. Kennedy Assassination Records Collections, NARA.

3057 *States–Item*, June 11, 1963.

3058 FBI New Orleans file number 89-69-256.

3059 124-10248-10159, The John F. Kennedy Assassination Records Collections, NARA.

3060 *Times–Picayune*, March 5, 1958.

3061 *Times–Picayune*, September 22, 1960.

3062 FBI FOIA Edwin A. Walker.

3063 Banister was on the advisory committee of Dr. Fred Schwartz's Greater New Orleans School of Anti-Communism from October 21 to 27, 1961. Festus Brown was one of the school's local advisors. Serving on the faculty were national figures on the far right Herbert Philbrick, Robert Morris, Phyllis Schlafly, and W. Cleon Skousen. [deLesseps Morrison Papers, New Orleans Public Library.]

3064 February 5, 1967, NODA, The John F. Kennedy Assassination Records Collections,

NARA. Four of nine pages on the Festus Brown interrogation are missing in the author's copies.

3065 Mary Brengel, interview by Cliency Navarre and Kent Simms, June 1, 1967, NODA.

3066 Interviews of Nitschke, May 11, 1967, NODA.

3067 Ross Banister, interview by Andrew Sciambra, February 2, 1967, NODA.

3068 DeLesseps Morrison Papers, New Orleans Public Library.

3069 Hugh Murray, *The Fourth Decade* 4, no. 3, 25, 27.

3070 *States–Item*, June 11, 1963.

3071 Vereen Alexander, interview by the author, October 12, 1999.

3072 FBI Atlanta file number 105-3193.

3073 Don Adams, letter to the author, July 1, 2010.

3074 Robert Reinders, interview by the author, February 17, 2002.

3075 124-90023-10009, The John F. Kennedy Assassination Records Collections, NARA.

3076 Robert Reinders, interview by the author, February 17, 2002.

3077 FBI file number 62-109060 JFK HQ File, Section 132, 49.

3078 Warren Commission, Document 20.

3079 Warren Commission, Document 40, 14.

3080 Andrew Sciambra, memo to Jim Garrison, April 23, 1969, "Shaw Leads II," NODA, 41.

3081 Warren Commission, XXII, 810–828.

3082 Warren Commission, XXII, 809

3083 HSCA record number 7810370, Agency file number 009262.

3084 180-10078-10371, The John F. Kennedy Assassination Records Collections, NARA.

3085 180-10097-10490, The John F. Kennedy Assassination Records Collections, NARA.

3086 180-10082-10179, The John F. Kennedy Assassination Records Collections, NARA.

3087 Smith investigation, "Visit to Ross Banister," February 1, 1967, NODA.

3088 Warren Commission, XXVI, 826.

3089 Warren Commission, XXVI, 828–831.

3090 Harold Weisberg, *Oswald in New Orleans* (New York: Canyon Books, 1967), 362.

3091 180-101120-10369, The John F. Kennedy Assassination Records Collections, NARA.

3092 180-10097-10494, The John F. Kennedy Assassination Records Collections, NARA.

3093 180-10112-10371, The John F. Kennedy Assassination Records Collections, NARA.

3094 Notes of Hoke May, *States-Item* reporter who met with close friend of Banister, Ivan Nitschke, May 11, 1967, NODA.

3095 *HSCA Final Report*, 141.

3096 Quiroga's Grand Jury testimony, arclibrary.org/publib/jfk/garr/grandjury/Quiroga/html/Quiroga_0001a.htm.

3097 180-10116-10159, The John F. Kennedy Assassination Records Collections, NARA.

3098 Courtney Papers, Special Collections, Northwestern State University of Louisiana.

3099 FBI transcription of Bringuier's memorandum to Garrison, 62-109060-4514, AARC;

Same as 124-10050-10376, The John F. Kennedy Assassination Records Collections, NARA.

3100 Carlos Bringuier, *Red Friday* (Chicago: Halberg and Co., 1969), 25.

3101 Harold Weisberg, *Never Again* (New York: Carroll and Graf, 1995), 284–5.

3102 Fredrick O'Sullivan, a member of the police vice squad, is mentioned in *Warren Commission* XIII, 27–31.

3103 Warren Commission, Document 75, 320, 341–2, 491.

3104 Rosemary James and Jack Wardlaw, *Plot or Politics* (New Orleans: Pelican Publishing House, 1967), 158.

The author is not certain of the correct spelling of the name "Bourne."

3105 *HSCA Report*, 145–6.

3106 FBI, NO 89-69-256.

3107 124-90023-10002, The John F. Kennedy Assassination Records Collections, NARA.

3108 124-10058-10076, The John F. Kennedy Assassination Records Collections, NARA.

3109 Taperecording, March 1969, Courtney Papers, Special Collections, Northwestern State University of Louisiana.

3110 Christian Crusade brochure, Ned Touchstone Papers, Noel Memorial Library, Louisiana State University Shreveport.

3111 FBI, NO 100-1660.

3112 *Christian Crusade*, March 1964.

3113 Hugh Murray, interview by the author, 1996.

3114 Letter, Hugh Murray to author, November 11, 1996.

3115 *The Fourth Decade*, Vol 3, No. 5.

3116 *The Fourth Decade*, Vol 4, No. 3.

3117 *The Fourth Decade*, Vol 1, No. 5.

3118 Clark Rowley, interview by the author, February 17, 2002.

3119 *The Fourth Decade*, Vol 3, No. 5.

3120 Robert Reinders, interview by the author, February 17, 2002.

3121 *Councilor*, September 12, 1968.

3122 Clarence Manion Papers, Chicago Historical Society, Box 12-6.

3123 Guy Banister, letters to Willie Rainach, September 30, 1958 and August 7, 1958, Rainach Papers, Noel Memorial Library, Louisiana State University Shreveport.

3124 *Times–Picayune*, March 5, 1958.

3125 Guy Banister's Citizens' Council membership card and newsletter, William Wood Papers, The John F. Kennedy Assassination Records Collections, NARA.

3126 House of Representatives, 85 Congress, Second Session, March 15, 1958.

3127 Edward Hunter, *Brain-washing in Red China: the Calculated Destruction of Men's Minds* (New York: Vanguard Press, 1951). An inscribed copy of *Brain-washing in Red China* is in the author's collection.

3128 Banister file 10-60, William Wood Papers, The John F. Kennedy Assassination Records Collections, NARA.

3129 Warren Commission, XXVI, 575.

3130 *Christian Crusade*, March 1962.

3131 *Weekly Crusader*, March 30, 1962, Willoughby Papers.

3132 Overstreet and Overstreet, *The Strange Tactics of Extremism*, 220.

3133 FBI FOIA, Billy James Hargis.

3134 *Christian Crusade*, April 1962.

3135 *Weekly Crusader*, March 30, 1962.

3136 *Group Research*, December 13, 1963.

3137 Hunter, *Brain-washing in Red China*.

3138 *The Citizen*, Vol. 9. No. 2.

3139 Barbara Reid, report to Jim Garrison, June 12, 1968, NODA.

3140 Andrew Sciambra interview with George Higginbotham [sic] and Tommy Baumler, March 14, 1968, NODA.

3141 Guy Banister, letter to Guy Johnson, January 5, 1959, William Wood Papers, The John F. Kennedy Assassination Records Collections, NARA.

3142 William Wegmann Papers, The John F. Kennedy Assassination Records Collections, NARA.

3143 Allen Campbell, interview by the author, September 22, 1996.

3144 Banister file number 10-197-1, William Wood Papers, The John F. Kennedy Assassination Records Collections, NARA.

3145 180-10100-10127, The John F. Kennedy Assassination Records Collections, NARA.

3146 Bill Boxley, memo, William Wood Papers, The John F. Kennedy Assassination Records Collections, NARA.

3147 180-10100-10127, The John F. Kennedy Assassination Records Collections, NARA.

3148 Michael Kurtz, *Crime of the Century* (Knoxville: University of Tennessee, 1982).

3149 Michael Kurtz, letter to Congressman Louis Stokes, March 15, 1978, 180-10108-10427, The John F. Kennedy Assassination Records Collections, NARA.

3150 Michael Kurtz, AARB testimony, March 28, 1995, The John F. Kennedy Assassination Records Collections, NARA.

Chapter 21

3151 *Congressional Record*, May 25, 1961, 8349–8363.

3152 *The New Yorker*, September 25, 2011, 42.

3153 *Felicianas*, Tourist brochure, Louisiana State University Library, Special Collections.

3154 The author first published portions of the evidence presented here in an article in *The Fourth Decade*, entitled "New Evidence in the Clinton Incident," published by the State University of New York, Fredonia, November 1996, under the pseudonym "William Holden."

3155 William C. Wood, interview by George Rennar, NODA.

3156 *Times–Picayune*, September 12, 1963.

3157 The State Citizens' Council rosters, Ned Touchstone Papers, Noel Memorial Library, Louisiana State University Shreveport. The Wellborn Jack papers note Judge John Rarick and Richard Van Buskirk's work on the Free Electors bill during the summer session of the legislature in 1963. The board later decided to use the money raised at the September 4 Free Electors meeting to fund Rarick's congressional campaign. [Wellborn Jack Papers, Noel Memorial Library, Louisiana State University Shreveport.]

3158 Warren Commission, Document 366.

3159 Warren Commission, IV, 446.

3160 179-20003-10218, The John F. Kennedy Assassination Records Collections, NARA.

3161 124-10298-10133, The John F. Kennedy Assassination Records Collections, NARA.

3162 124-10298-10132, The John F. Kennedy Assassination Records Collections, NARA.

3163 Richard Kilbourne, Sr., interview by the author, August 6, 1996.

3164 Jimmie H. Morrison Papers, Southeastern Louisiana University archives.

3165 Andrew Sciambra, memo to Jim Garrison, April 3, 1969, NODA.

3166 *St. Francisville Democrat*, December 9, 1965.

3167 *St. Francisville Democrat*, April 1, 1965. Lloyd Cobb owned Marydale Farm.

3168 Sarah Brown, *Standing Against Dragons: Three Southern Lawyers in the Era of Fear* (Baton Rouge: Louisiana State University Press, 1998), 205. Ben Smith had become a target of both Senator Eastland and James Pfister of LUAC.

3169 180-10024-10264, The John F. Kennedy Assassination Records Collections, NARA.

3170 180-10024-10268, The John F. Kennedy Assassination Records Collections, NARA.

3171 180-10066-10298, The John F. Kennedy Assassination Records Collections, NARA.

3172 180-10108-10003, The John F. Kennedy Assassination Records Collections, NARA.

3173 Andrew Sciambra, memos, January 31, 1968 and October 26, 1967, NODA.

3174 180-10102-10316, The John F. Kennedy Assassination Records Collections, NARA.

3175 Agency file number 015044, HSCA record number 11710074, The John F. Kennedy Assassination Records Collections, NARA.

3176 Andrew H. Dunn affadavit to Lieutenant Francis Fruge, July 13, 1967, NODA.

3177 Henry H. Burnell, notarized affidavit, September 12, 1967, NODA.

3178 Edwin Lea McGehee, testimony in Clay Shaw trial in the Jim Garrison case Grand Jury, February 6, 1969, Mary Ferrell Foundation, www.maryferrell.org.

3179 180-10085-10248, The John F. Kennedy Assassination Records Collections, NARA.

3180 Edwin Lea McGehee, interview by Andrew Sciambra, June 17, 1967, NODA.

3181 *The Watchman*, Clinton, Louisiana, August 2, 1963.

3182 Edwin Lea McGehee, interview by the author, June 30, 1996.

3183 *Councilor*, September 1, 1967.

3184 *The Watchman*, Clinton, Louisiana, June 21, 1963.

3185 Edwin Lea McGehee, interview by the author, June 30, 1996.

3186 Mary Cobb Bloch, interview by the author, July 3, 1996.

3187 *Times–Picayune*, May 1, 1968 and May 2, 1968.

3188 Andrew Sciambra and Lieutenant Francis Fruge, report, May 29, 1967, NODA.

3189 Reeves Morgan, interview by Lieutenant Francis Fruge, January 29, 1968, NODA.

3190 180-10085-10248, The John F. Kennedy Assassination Records Collections, NARA.

3191 179-20003-10218, The John F. Kennedy Assassination Records Collections, NARA.

3192 Andrew Sciambra and Lieutenant Francis Fruge, report, May 29, 1967, NODA.

3193 Bobbie Dedon, interview by Andrew Sciambra, January 29, 1968, NODA.

3194 Maxine Kemp Drane, interview, 180-10102-10316, The John F. Kennedy Assassination Records Collections, NARA.

3195 Thomas Williams, interview by C. J. Navarre, March 17, 1967, NODA.

3196 Thomas Williams, interview by the author, July 31, 1996.

3197 Andrew Sciambra, report, May 29, 1967, NODA.

3198 Joan Mellen, interview by the author, May 30, 2003. Mellen struck up a friendship with Judge John Rarick while investigating the Clinton incident for her book. She called him "my buddy." She believed Rarick and the other Clinton witnesses were nothing but upstanding individuals.

3199 Andrew Sciambra, memo, May 29, 1967, NODA.

3200 180-10102-10316, The John F. Kennedy Assassination Records Collections, NARA.

3201 180-10102-10317, The John F. Kennedy Assassination Records Collections, NARA.

3202 180-10085-10248, The John F. Kennedy Assassination Records Collections, NARA.

3203 Henry Earl Palmer, interview by Andrew Sciambra, part II, January 22, 1968, NODA.

3204 180-10102-10316, The John F. Kennedy Assassination Records Collections, NARA, 2.

3205 180-10089-10041, The John F. Kennedy Assassination Records Collections, NARA.

3206 Guy Banister, letter to Willie Rainach, May 6, 1958, Rainach Papers, Noel Memorial Library, Louisiana State University Shreveport.

3207 Joseph Oster, interview by the author, October 14, 1999.

3208 180-10096-10010, The John F. Kennedy Assassination Records Collections, NARA.

3209 *Plaquemines Gazette*, October 7, 1960.

3210 *Baton Rouge Morning Advocate*, March 7, 1957, 180-10100-101277, The John F. Kennedy Assassination Records Collections, NARA.

3211 CORE Archives, the State Historical Society of Wisconsin.

3212 180-10085-10248, The John F. Kennedy Assassination Records Collections, NARA.

3213 John Manchester, affidavit, 1967, New Orleans, NODA.

3214 180-10089-10049, The John F. Kennedy Assassination Records Collections, NARA.

3215 Agency file number 015044, record number 11710074, The John F. Kennedy Assassination Records Collections, NARA.

3216 Summary of Clinton investigation, May 25, 1967, NODA.

3217 Andrew Sciambra, memo to Jim Garrison, August 23, 1967, NODA, 180-10102-10316, The John F. Kennedy Assassination Records Collections, NARA.

3218 William Wood Papers, NODA, The John F. Kennedy Assassination Records Collections, NARA. Bill Boxley removed all of the titles and dates from his documents from the Garrison investigation.

3219 180-10089-10049, The John F. Kennedy Assassination Records Collections, NARA.

3220 Lou Ivon, interview by the author, October 5, 2000. (The author held multiple phone interviews with Ivon in 2000.)

3221 180-10085-10248, The John F. Kennedy Assassination Records Collections, NARA.

3222 180-10102-10316, The John F. Kennedy Assassination Records Collections, NARA.

3223 180-10089-10049, The John F. Kennedy Assassination Records Collections, NARA.

3224 Jim Garrison, trial transcript, February 6, 1969, 180-10118-10068, The John F. Kennedy Assassination Records Collections, NARA.

3225 *Plaquemines Gazette*, February 18, 1946.

3226 *Times–Picayune*, January 26, 1956.

3227 FBI file number 105-46604-19, October 31, 1956.

3228 *Times–Picayune*, March 15, 1956.

3229 *The Watchman*, Clinton, Louisiana, June 11, 1965.

3230 *Plaquemines Gazette*, December 29, 1956.

3231 *Baton Rouge State Times*, March 12, 1957.

3232 Richard Kilbourne Sr., interview by the author, August 6, 1996.

3233 *Plaquemines Gazette*, November 22, 1957.

3234 Kent Courtney, letter to Willie Rainach, March 22, 1957, Courtney Papers, Special Collections, Northwestern State University of Louisiana.

3235 *Plaquemines Gazette*, July 27, 1958.

3236 *Times–Picayune*, June 30, 1958.

3237 *Times–Picayune*, June 30, 1960.

3238 *Times–Picayune*, August 4, 1959.

3239 *Times–Picayune*, September 12, 1958.

3240 *New York Times*, January 12, 1960.

3241 *The Watchman*, Clinton, Louisiana, June 11, 1965.

3242 *Times–Picayune*, June 14, 1960.

3243 *Times–Picayune*, June 14, 1960.

3244 *Times–Picayune*, June 30, 1960.

3245 *Times–Picayune*, October 5, 1956.

3246 *The Watchman*, Clinton, Louisiana, June 17, 1960.

3247 *Times–Picayune*, July 19, 1960.

3248 *Baton Rouge Morning Advocate*, July 30, 1960.

3249 *Times–Picayune*, January 18, 1961.

3250 *The Watchman*, Clinton, Louisiana, August 12, 1960.

3251 *The Watchman*, Clinton, Louisiana, February 24, 1961.

3252 *Times–Picayune*, August 9, 1961.

3253 *Times–Picayune*, October 8, 1961.

3254 *Times–Picayune*, March 7, 1961.

3255 *Times–Picayune*, January 18, 1961.

3256 *Dallas Morning News*, December 30, 1961.

3257 179-20003-10218, The John F. Kennedy Assassination Records Collections, NARA.

3258 August Meier and Elliott Rudwick, *CORE: A Study in the Civil Rights Movement 1942–1968* (Oxford: Oxford University Press, 1973).

3259 124-10294-10254, The John F. Kennedy Assassination Records Collections, NARA.

3260 *The Watchman*, Clinton, Louisiana, October 2, 1959.

3261 J. Edgar Hoover, letter to Senator Allen Ellender, August 30, 1963, Ellender Papers, Nicholls State University. The letter was in response to an October 21, 1963, letter Senator Ellender had received from Mrs. John Hobgood of Clinton, Louisiana.

3262 *Baton Rouge State Times*, August 3, 1963.

3263 180-10102-10317, The John F. Kennedy Assassination Records Collections, NARA.

3264 124-10182-10376, The John F. Kennedy Assassination Records Collections, NARA.

3265 CORE Archives, State Historical Society of Wisconsin.

3266 *Times–Picayune*, March 27, 1964.

3267 *Wall Street Journal*, August 27, 1965.

3268 Jim Garrison, memo, September 6, 1967, NODA.

3269 Jules Rico Kimble, statement, October 10, 1967.

3270 Report of the HSCA, Government Printing Office, 392.

3271 Joseph Oster, interview by the author, October 14, 1999.

3272 "Dissolution of the Citizens' Council of East Feliciana," Tom Anderson Papers, Special Collections, University of Wyoming. John Rarick sent his friend Tom Anderson a copy of the letter presented here that included a history of the Council's formation, which is also found in *The Watchman*, Clinton, Louisiana, June 11, 1965.

3273 Henry Earl Palmer, interview by Andrew Sciambra, August 25, 1967, NODA.

3274 *The Wooster Daily Record*, March 19, 1998, AP Story.

3275 124-10236-10353, The John F. Kennedy Assassination Records Collections, NARA.

3276 180-10089-10049, The John F. Kennedy Assassination Records Collections, NARA, 13.

3277 *Plaquemines Gazette*, October 7, 1960.

3278 180-10089-10049, The John F. Kennedy Assassination Records Collections, NARA, 13.

3279 *States–Item*, October 6, 1963.

3280 Pamela Turner, *Civil Rights and Anti-Communism in New Orleans, 1946–1965*, Master's Thesis, University of New Orleans, August 1981.

3281 124-10267-1076, The John F. Kennedy Assassination Records Collections, NARA.

3282 Jack M. Peebles, *Subversion and the Southern Conference Education Fund*, Thesis, Louisiana State University in New Orleans, 1970, 59.

3283 Kent Courtney, letter to the Friends of General Walker, New Orleans Public Library, Louisiana Division.

3284 124-10039-10385, The John F. Kennedy Assassination Records Collections, NARA.

3285 180-10082-10167, The John F. Kennedy Assassination Records Collections, NARA.

3286 Archivist at Louisiana State Archives, Baton Rouge, interview by the author.

3287 Richard Kilbourne, Jr., interview by the author, August 6, 1996.

3288 *The Watchman*, Clinton, Louisiana, October 12, 1962.

3289 *The Conservative Society of America Newsletter*, October 3, 1966, Courtney Papers, Special Collections, Northwestern State University of Louisiana.

3290 Meier and Rudwick, *CORE*.

3291 *Times–Picayune*, June 3, 1961.

3292 *Plaquemines Gazette*, July 17, 1964.

3293 *Congressional Record*, 107, no. 88.

3294 *Times–Picayune*, October 17, 1961.

3295 *Councilor*, July 16, 1964.

3296 Jeansome, *Leander Perez*, 272.

3297 Robert Sherill, *Gothic Politics in the Deep South* (New York: Ballantine Books, Inc., 1968).

3298 Meier and Rudwick, *CORE*.

3299 *Times–Picayune*, September 8, 1963.

3300 Victor Schiro Papers, New Orleans Public Library, Louisiana Division.

3301 Meier and Rudwick, *CORE*.

3302 *Shreveport Journal*, July 1, 1963.

3303 Meier and Rudwick, *CORE*.

3304 *Times–Picayune*, July 25, 1963.

3305 *The Plaquemine Story, A Question of Law and Order*, Louisiana State Sovereignty Commission, courtesy of Claude B. Slaton.

3306 Meier and Rudwick, *CORE*.

3307 *Washington Close-Up*, Jimmie H. Morrison Papers, Southeastern Louisiana University archives.

3308 *Congressional Record*, May 25, 1961, 89, 58.

3309 Anne Braden, *HUAC: Bulwark of Segregation*. From the Universty of Texas at Arlington Libraries. Braden cited a complaint filed in federal court by the Clinton Movement and CORE entitled Collins v. Jimmie Davis, as the source of Eastland's claim.

3310 *Baton Rouge States Times*, August 9, 1963.

3311 FBI file number 44-22889-5.

3312 *Baton Rouge States Times*, August 10, 1963.

3313 *Baton Rouge States Times*, August 6, 1963.

3314 180-10102-10316, The John F. Kennedy Assassination Records Collections, NARA.

3315 FBI file number 44-22889-5.

3316 *Baton Rouge States Times*, August 16, 1963.

3317 *Baton Rouge Morning Advocate*, August 19, 1963.

3318 Press release on CORE, Rainach Papers, Noel Memorial Library, Louisiana State University Shreveport.

3319 *Baton Rouge Morning Advocate*, August 22, 1963.

3320 180-10102-10316, The John F. Kennedy Assassination Records Collections, NARA.

3321 Miriam "Mimi" Feingold, a.k.a. "Mimi Real," interview by the author, June 24, 1996.

3322 Press release on CORE, Rainach Papers, Noel Memorial Library, Louisiana State University Shreveport.

3323 See also: *Baton Rouge Morning Advocate*, August 28, 1963.

3324 *Baton Rouge Morning Advocate*, August 1, 1963.

3325 *Times–Picayune*, September 8, 1963.

3326 *Baton Rouge State Times*, September 6, 1963.

3327 *Shreveport Journal*, September 5, 1963.

3328 *Baton Rouge Morning Advocate*, October 1, 1963.

3329 *Times–Picayune*, October 6, 1963.

3330 *Times–Picayune*, October 15, 1963.

3331 *Baton Rouge Morning Advocate*, October 14, 1963.

3332 *Councilor*, December 5, 1963.

3333 Miriam "Mimi" Feingold, a.k.a. "Mimi Real," interview by the author, June 24, 1996.

3334 *Baton Rouge Morning Advocate*, November 21, 1963.

3335 William Wood Papers, NODA, The John F. Kennedy Assassination Records Collections, NARA.

3336 *Baton Rouge Morning Advocate*, November 22, 1963.

3337 *Baton Rouge Morning Advocate*, December 11, 1963.

3338 *Baton Rouge Morning Advocate*, January 3, 1964.

3339 John Rarick, letter to Ned Touchstone, April 5, 1964, Ned Touchstone Papers, Noel Memorial Library, Louisiana State University Shreveport.

3340 Richard Kilbourne, Sr., interview by the author August 6, 1996.

3341 *States–Item*, October 21, 1963. The FBI photographed the demonstrations between the Klan and CORE in St. Francisville.

3342 Dan Campbell, interview by the author, July 30, 1996.

3343 *Times–Picayune*, April 20, 1964.

3344 *Councilor*, May 20, 1963.

3345 *Shreveport Journal*, May 25, 1963.

3346 Andrew Sciambra, memo on National States' Rights Party and American Nazi Party, May 13, 1968, NODA.

3347 Ibid.

3348 Joseph Cooper, interview by Andrew Sciambra, October 2, 1968.

3349 Grand Jury records, Mary Ferrell Foundation Archives, www.maryferrell.org.

3350 *Tattler*, June 8, 1975, courtesy of Claude B. Slaton.

3351 Jack Nelson, *Terror in the Night* (Jackson: University Press of Mississippi, 1996), 93.

3352 Allen Campbell, interview by the author, September 22, 1996.

3353 *Tattler*, June 8, 1975, courtesy of Claude B. Slaton.

3354 Claude B. Slaton, interviews by the author, 1994 and subsequent years.

3355 The reader is directed to Claude B. Slaton's comprehensive review of Cooper's life and death in *The Fourth Decade* entitled "Joe Cooper," State University of New York at Fredonia, *The Fourth Decade* 4, no. 2, January 1997.

3356 Andrew Sciambra, memo on National States' Rights Party and American Nazi Party, May 13, 1968, NODA.

3357 William Wood Papers, NODA, The John F. Kennedy Assassination Records Collections, NARA.

3358 Tyler Bridges, *The Rise of David Duke* (Jackson: University Press of Mississippi, 1994), 33, 177.

3359 Joseph Cooper, interview, October 14, 1968, Baton Rouge, Lousiana, NODA.

3360 *Tattler*, December 8, 1974, courtesy of Claude B. Slaton.

3361 Mary Ann Sagely Robertson, interview by the author, July 3, 1996.

3362 Allen Ellender Papers, Nicholls State University, 1 FF, 757.

3363 *Rhodesia Herald*, May 29, 1970, Rainach Papers, Noel Memorial Library, Louisiana State University Shreveport.

3364 H. J. van deer Merwe, letter to Tom Anderson, January 5, 1968, Tom Anderson Papers, Special Collections, University of Oregon. Billy James Hargis visited Johannesburg on January 4, 1968.

3365 Jack Martin, affadavit, 1968, NODA, 180-10023-10380, The John F. Kennedy Assassination Records Collections, NARA.

3366 *Group Research*, October 31, 1969.

3367 Citizens' Council rosters, Rainach Papers, Noel Memorial Library, Louisiana State University Shreveport.

3368 Biographical Directory of American Congress, 1774–1971.

3369 Elizabeth Blum and Arthur Magida, *John R. Rarick Democratic Representative from Louisiana, Ralph Nader Congress Project* (New York: Grossman Publishers, 1972).

3370 Judge John Rarick biography sheet, Haley Papers, The Haley Memorial Library and History Center, Midland, Texas.

3371 John Rarick and Willie Rainach, correspondence, Rainach Papers, Noel Memorial Library, Louisiana State University Shreveport.

3372 John Rarick, letter to Willie Rainach, August 2, 1961, Rainach Papers, Noel Memorial Library, Louisiana State University Shreveport.

3373 Willie Rainach, letter to John Rarick, October 9, 1961, Rainach Papers, Noel Memorial Library, Louisiana State University Shreveport.

3374 Blum and Magida, *John R. Rarick Democratic Representative from Louisiana.*

3375 *St. Francisville Democrat*, April 18, 1963.

3376 Richard Kilbourne, Jr., interview by the author, August 6, 1996.

3377 *St. Francisville Democrat*, October 4, 1962.

3378 *Shreveport Journal*, May 14, 1963.

3379 *Times–Picayune*, May 22, 1963.

3380 *Shreveport Journal*, May 25, 1963.

3381 *Times–Picayune*, May 28, 29 1963.

3382 *Shreveport Journal*, July 10, 1963.

3383 *Times–Picayune*, September 8, 1963.

3384 *Baton Rouge Morning Advocate*, August 1, 1963.

3385 *Times–Picayune*, September 12, 1963.

3386 Wellborn Jack Papers, Noel Memorial Library, Louisiana State University Shreveport.

3387 *Times–Picayune*, September 8, 1963.

3388 John Rarick, letter to Willie Rainach, October 27, 1963, Rainach Papers, Noel Memorial Library, Louisiana State University Shreveport.

3389 Willie Rainach, letter to John Rarick, July 27, 1965, Rainach Papers, Noel Memorial Library, Louisiana State University Shreveport.

3390 *The Watchman*, Clinton, Louisiana, September 22, 1963.

3391 *Dothan Eagle*, December 22, 1963.

3392 *Congressional Record*, July 25, 1966.

3393 Flier, Tom Anderson Papers, Special Collections, University of Wyoming.

3394 *Plaquemines Gazette*, February 21, 1964.

3395 *St. Francisville Democrat*, July 30, 1964.

3396 *Councilor*, July 16, 1964.

3397 *St. Francisville Democrat, February 20, 1964.*

3398 Frye Gaillard, *Cradle of Freedom: Alabama and the Movement that Changed America* (Tuscaloosa: University of Alabama Press, 2004).

3399 *Facts*, ADL, 20, no. 2.

3400 *Baton Rouge Morning Advocate*, May 8 1965.

3401 Joseph Oster, interview by Robert Buras, 180-10080-10203, The John F. Kennedy Assassination Records Collections, NARA.

3402 *Baton Rouge Morning Advocate*, May 8, 1965.

3403 *Times–Picayune*, April 28, 1965.

3404 FBI FOIA, Kenneth Adams.

3405 *Councilor,* April 4, 1967.

3406 Tom Anderson Papers, Special Collections, University of Wyoming.

3407 *Summit Sun*, June 3, 1965.

3408 *Baton Rouge Morning Advocate*, July 5, 1965.

3409 FBI HQ 105-44534, July 12, 1965.

3410 Flier, reproduced in *Good Government News*, August 1966, Jimmie H. Morrison Papers, Southeastern Louisiana University Archives.

3411 *Baton Rouge Morning Advocate*, June 25, 1965.

3412 *Shreveport Journal*, July 3, 1965.

3413 John Rarick, letter to Ned Touchstone, Ned Touchstone Papers, Noel Memorial Library, Louisiana State University Shreveport.

3414 *Francisville Democrat*, September 9, 1965.

3415 *Facts*, ADL, November 1971.

3416 Jim Garrison, file on John Rarick, AARC.

3417 Library of Congress, Herbert Philbrick Papers, 129:14.

3418 *Baton Rouge Morning Advocate*, January 14, 1964.

3419 *Good Government News*, August 1966, Jimmie H. Morrison Papers, Southeastern Louisiana University Archives.

3420 Jeansonne, *Leander Perez*, 173.

3421 George Singelmann, interview transcript in the Hubert Humphrey Oral History collection, Noel Memorial Library, Louisiana State University Shreveport

3422 Tom Anderson Papers, Special Collections, University of Oregon.

3423 Blum and Magida, *John R. Rarick Democratic Representative from Louisiana*.

3424 *Washington Close-Up*, Jimmie H. Morrison Papers, Southeastern Louisiana University Archives.

3425 *Detroit News*, September 25, 1966.

3426 *Good Government News*, August 1966, Jimmie H. Morrison Papers, Southeastern Louisiana University Archives.

3427 *Detroit News*, September 25, 1966.

3428 Flier, Ned Touchstone Papers, Noel Memorial Library, Louisiana State University Shreveport.

3429 *Baton Rouge Morning Advocate*, July 26, 1966.

3430 Courtney Papers, Special Collections, Northwestern State University of Louisiana.

3431 Clay Shaw Papers, The John F. Kennedy Assassination Records Collections, NARA.

3432 Blum and Magida, *John R. Rarick Democratice Representative from Louisiana*.

3433 Haley Papers, The Haley Memorial Library and History Center, Midland, Texas.

3434 *Group Research*, August 14, 1967.

3435 John McComb, *Stand Up! You are American* (Vienna: Founders Press, 1968).

3436 Friends of Rarick pamphlet, Tom Anderson Papers, Special Collections, University of Oregon.

3437 Pedro Del Valle Papers, Special Collections, University of Oregon Library.

3438 Chronicle of John Rarick's activities, NODA.

3439 *The Woman Constitutionalist*, December 12, 1970, Mississippi State Archives.

3440 *Facts*, ADL, September 1971.

3441 Turner, *Power on the Right*, 21.

3442 G. L. K. Smith Papers, Bentley Library, University of Michigan, Box 50, 9.

3443 John Rarick Biography sheet, Haley Papers, The Haley Memorial Library and History Center, Midland, Texas.

3444 "Gerhard Frey (politician)," *Wikipedia*, last updated March 6, 2014, http://en.wikipedia.org/wiki/Gerhard_Frey_(politician).

3445 *Congress of Freedom News*, November 11, 1976, Wilcox Collection, Special Collections, University of Kansas, RH WL G 537 V. 5:1.

3446 *Thunderbolt*, Paul O. Peters Papers, Special Collections, Wooster College Library, Wooster, Ohio.

3447 Rarick obituary, *Baton Rouge Morning Advocate*, September 16, 2009.

3448 *The Citizens Informer*, 2009.

3449 John Rarick, interview by the author, May 28, 1996.

3450 *Plaquemines Gazette*, December 6, 1963.

3451 *Baton Rouge Morning Advocate*, September 6, 1963.

3452 124-10298-10133, The John F. Kennedy Assassination Records Collections, NARA.

3453 124-10294-10263, The John F. Kennedy Assassination Records Collections, NARA.

3454 Report of the HSCA, Government Printing Office, 142–145.

3455 Blakey and Billings, *The Plot to Kill the President*.

3456 *Baton Rouge Morning Advocate*, February 2, 1992.

3457 Joan Mellen, interview by the author, May 30, 2003.

3458 Reeves Morgan, interview by the author, August 27, 1994, arranged courtesy of Claude B. Slaton.

3459 Edwin Lea McGehee, interview by the author, August 27, 1994, arranged courtesy of Claude B. Slaton.

3460 Edwin Lea McGehee, interview by the author, July 1, 1996, and subsequent phone calls from 1966 to 2000.

3461 Garrison, *On the Trail of Assassins*, 108.

3462 Report of the HSCA, Government Printing Office, 145.

3463 Miriam Feingold Papers, CORE Archives, the State Historical Society of Wisconsin.

Chapter 22

3464 James D. Forman, *Communism from Marx's Manifesto to 20th Century Reality* (New York: Watts, 1972).

3465 Edwin P. Hoyt, *The Palmer Raids, 1919–1920: An Attempt to Suppress Dissent* (New York: Seabury Press, 1969).

3466 Michal Belknap, *Cold War Political Justice: The Smith Act, the Communist Party, and American Civil Liberties* (Westport: Greenwood Press, 1977).

3467 Epstein and Forster, *The Radical Right*.

3468 *Time* magazine, July 13, 1953.

3469 Walter Goodman, *The Committee: The Extraordinary Career of the House Committee on Un-America Activities* (New York: Farrar, Straus and Giroux, 1968), 39.

3470 Forster and Epstein, *Danger on the Right*, 105.

3471 Walter Goodman, *The Committee.*

3472 *Dallas Morning News*, December 4, 1963.

3473 James Rorty and Moshe Decter, *McCarthy and the Communists* (Boston: The Beacon Press, 1954).

3474 *Times–Picayune*, April 9, 1956.

3475 David M. Oshinsky, *A Conspiracy so Immense: The World of Joe McCarthy* (New York: The Free Press, 1983).

3476 R. Andrew Kiel, *J. Edgar Hoover, Father of the Cold War* (Lanham: University of America Press, 2000), 68.

3477 Oshinsky, *A Conspiracy so Immense.*

3478 *The Nation*, March 6, 1954.

3479 Hurt, *Texas Rich.*

3480 Ardis Burst, *The Three Families of H. L. Hunt* (New York: Weidenfeld & Nicholson, 1988), 36.

3481 *Facts Forum*, circa 1955, Dan Smoot Papers, Texas A&M.

3482 Daniel Cohen, *Joseph McCarthy, The Misuse of Political Power* (Brookfield: Millbrook Press, 1996.)

3483 Epstein and Forster, *The Radical Right.*

3484 Jeff Woods, *Black Struggle Red Scare.*

3485 Griffin Fariello, *Red Scare* (New York: W. W. Norton & Company, 1995).

3486 Anne Braden, *House Un-American Activities Committee, Bulwark of Segregation* (Los Angeles, National Committee to Abolish HUAC, 1963).

3487 Frank T. Adams, *James A. Dombrowski: An American Heretic, 1897–1983* (Knoxville: University of Tennessee Press, 1992).

3488 House Committee on Un-American Activities, 592, *Hearings, Southern Conference on Human Welfare, 1947.*

3489 Jeff Woods, *Black Struggle Red Scare.*

3490 *Harvard Law Review*, LX, no. 8.

3491 House Committee on Un-American Activities, 592, *Hearings, Southern Conference on Human Welfare, June 16, 1947 and May 6, 1949.*

3492 Anne Braden, interview by the author, February 3, 2001.

3493 House Committee on Un-American Activities, 592, *Hearings, Southern Conference on Human Welfare, 1947.*

3494 J. Edgar Hoover, *Masters of Deceit* (New York: Holt, Rinehart, Winston, 1958), 117.

3495 Belfrage, *The American Inquisition 1945–1960.*

3496 House Committee on Un-American Activities, 592, *Hearings, Southern Conference on Human Welfare, 1947.*

3497 Warren Commission, I, 15, 24.

3498 Brown, *Standing Against Dragons.*

3499 Richard M. Fried, *Nightmare in Red: The McCarthy Era in Perspective* (Oxford: Oxford

University Press, 1990).

3500 Goodman, *The Committee*, 298.

3501 Belfrage, *The American Inquisition 1945–1960*.

3502 John A. Salmond, *The Great Southern Commie Hunt* (South Atlantic Quarterly, 1978), 433.

3503 Fried, *Nightmare in Red*.

3504 Martin J. Sherwin, *American Prometheus* (New York: Alfred A. Knopf, 2005).

3505 Brown, *Standing Against Dragons*.

3506 *Time*, July 19, 1954.

3507 Belfrage, *The American Inquisition 1945–1960*.

3508 *Time*, July 19, 1954.

3509 Belfrage, *The American Inquisition 1945–1960*.

3510 Paul Crouch, testimony before HUAC, May 6, 1949, 81st Congress, first session.

3511 Herbert L. Packer, *Ex-Communist witnesses: Four Studies in Fact Finding* (Palo Alto: Stanford University Press, 1962).

3512 Arthur J. Sabin, *Red Scare in Court* (Philadelphia: Universities of Pennsylvania Press, 1993).

3513 Harold Josephson, "Ex Communists in Crossfire: A Cold War Debate," *The Historian*, 44, 1 (Winter 1981), 69.

3514 Belfrage, *The American Inquisition 1945–1960*.

3515 Paul Crouch, testimony before HUAC, May 6, 1949, 81st Congress, first session.

3516 Packer, *Ex-Communist Witnesses*.

3517 Adams, *James A. Dombrowski*.

3518 Dorothy M. Zellner, "Red Roadshow: Eastland in New Orleans, 1954," *Louisiana History* 33, 1992, 31–60.

3519 *Warren Commission Report*, 383.

3520 Robert A. Caro, *The Years of Lyndon Johnson, Master of the Senate* (New York: Alfred A. Knopf, 2002), 103.

3521 House Committee on Un-American Activities, 592, *Hearings, Southern Conference on Human Welfare, 1947*.

3522 Virginia Durr, *Outside the Magic Circle* (The University of Alabama Press, 1985), 262.

3523 John A. Salmond, "The Great Southern Commie Hunt," *South Atlantic Quarterly*, autumn, 1978, 433.

3524 Brown, *Standing Against Dragons*.

3525 Sabin, *Red Scare in Court*, 141.

3526 Belfrage, *The American Inquisition 1945–1960*.

3527 Adams, *James A. Dombrowski*.

3528 Hodding Carter, III, *The South Strikes Back* (New York: Doubleday & Co., 1959).

3529 Patricia Webb Robison, Louisiana State University, Master's Thesis, 1976.

3530 *Congressional Record*, May 25, 1961, 11525.

3531 Carter, *The South Strikes Back*.

3532 Federation for Constitutional Government, letter to Mary Cain, April 17, 1959, Mary Cain Papers, Mississippi Department of Archives and History.

3533 Newsletter, Mississippi Department of Archives and History.

3534 *Times–Picayune*, December 30, 1956.

3535 Conason and Lyons, *The Hunting of a President*.

3536 National Indignation Committee letterhead, Victor Schiro Papers, New Orleans Public Library.

3537 *Times–Picayune*, December 28, 1956.

3538 *New Orleans Item*, April 9, 1956.

3539 *Plaquemines Gazette*, May 12, 1956.

3540 *Plaquemines Gazette*, May 19, 1956.

3541 *Plaquemines Gazette*, February 18, 1956.

3542 Cook, *The Segregationists*.

3543 Adams, *James A. Dombrowski*.

3544 *Times–Picayune*, March 18, 1956.

3545 Adams, *James A. Dombrowski*.

3546 *Plaquemines Gazette*, March 10, 1956.

3547 Patricia Webb Robison, Louisiana State University, Master's Thesis, 1976.

3548 Kenneth O'Reilly, *Racial Matters* (New York: The Free Press, 1989).

3549 Woods, *Black Struggle Red Scare*.

3550 *Congressional Record*, May 25, 1961, 8957.

3551 Medford Evans, *Civil Rights Myths and Communist Realities*, Conservative Society of America, 1965.

3552 Woods, *Black Struggle Red Scare*.

3553 Oswald, *Lee*.

3554 Warren Commission, Document 480 A, 3.

3555 Oswald, *Lee*.

3556 Warren Commission, X, 115.

3557 *Plaquemines Gazette*, January 14, 1956.

3558 *Time*, January 15, 1956.

3559 *Times–Picayune*, January 6–7, 1956.

3560 *Times–Picayune*, March 20, 1956.

3561 *Times– Picayune*, February 9, 1956.

3562 Caro, *The Years of Lyndon Johnson, Master of the Senate*, 767.

3563 Senate Internal Security Subcommittee, *Scope of Soviet Activity in the United States*, March 10, 1956.

3564 Herman Liveright, Appellant, v. United States of America, Appellee, United States Court of Appeals District of Columbia Circuit. - 280 F.2d 708; argued Feb. 15, 1960. Decided June 18, 1960.

3565 *Times–Picayune*, March 30, 1956.

3566 *States–Item*, February 7, 1957.

3567 *New York Times*, February 8, 2001.

3568 *Plaquemines Gazette*, February 16, 1957, and March 30, 1957.

3569 *Times–Picayune*, May 22, 1962.

3570 Hoover, *Masters of Deceit*.

3571 *Times–Picayune*, March 13, 1956.

3572 *Times–Picayune*, March 21, 1956.

3573 *Times–Picayune*, March 22, 1956.

3574 *States–Item*, March 23, 1956.

3575 *Times–Picayune*, March 23, 1956.

3576 *Plaquemines Gazette*, March 31, 1956.

3577 *Times–Picayune*, April 1, 1956.

3578 *Times–Picayune*, April 3, 1956.

3579 *Times–Picayune*, April 7, 1956.

3580 Senate Internal Security Subcommittee, *Scope of Soviet Activity in the United States*, March 10, 1956.

3581 Sarah Hart Brown, "Redressing Southern 'Subversion': The Case of Senator Eastland and the Louisiana Lawyer," *Louisiana History*, 43:3 (2002): 295–314.

3582 *Times–Picayune*, October 26, 1962.

3583 Nick Kotz, *Judgment Days: Lyndon Baines Johnson, Martin Luther King, Jr., and the Laws that Changed America* (Boston: Houghton Mifflin Books, 2005).

3584 *Scope of Soviet Activity in the United States*, Hearings Before the Subcommittee to Investigate the Administration of the Internal Security Act and Other Internal Security Laws, Committee on the Judiciary, Part 12, Senate, 84th Congress, 3rd Session, April 5, 6, 1956.

3585 *Times–Picayune*, March 31, 1956.

3586 Senate Internal Security Subcommittee, *Scope of Soviet Activity in the United States*, March 3–10, 1956.

3587 *Times–Picayune*, March 12, 1956.

3588 *Times–Picayune*, October 26, 1962.

3589 *Scope of Soviet Activity in the United States*, Hearings Before the Subcommittee to Investigate the Administration of the Internal Security Act and Other Internal Security Laws, Committee on the Judiciary, Part 12, Senate, 84th Congress, 3rd Session, April 5, 6, 1956

3590 *Plaquemines Gazette*, May 12, 1956.

3591 180-10112-10373, The John F. Kennedy Assassination Records Collections, NARA.

3592 U.S. Congress, February 28, 1956, Senate Internal Security Subcommittee, *Limitation of Appellate Jurisdiction of the Supreme Court*.

3593 Warren Commission, Document 82.

3594 *Time*, November 26, 1956.

3595 Adams, *James A. Dombrowski.*

3596 Brown, *Standing Against Dragons.*

3597 *Communism in the Mid-South*, Hearings Before the Subcommittee to Investigate the Administration of the Internal Security Act and Other Internal Security Laws, Committee on the Judiciary, United States Senate, 85th Congress, 1st session, October 28 and 28, 1957.

3598 Sarah Hart Brown, "Redressing Southern 'Subversion': The Case of Senator Eastland and the Louisiana Lawyer," *Louisiana History*, 43:3 (2002): 295–314.

3599 *Scope of Soviet Activity in the United States*, Hearings Before the Subcommittee to Investigate the Administration of the Internal Security Act and Other Internal Security Laws, Committee on the Judiciary, Part 12, Senate, 84th Congress, 3rd Session, April 5–6, 1956.

3600 Fariello, *Red Scare.*

3601 Benjamin Gitlow, notarized statement, December 4, 1954, Haley Papers, The Haley Memorial Library and History Center, Midland, Texas.

3602 Benjamin Gitlow, *The Whole of Their Lives, Communism in America* (Boston: Western Islands, 1965).

3603 FBI file number 100-424820-19.

3604 Flier, Courtney Papers, Special Collections, at Northwestern State University of Louisiana.

3605 *Weekly Crusader*, March 30, 1962.

3606 Herbert Philbrick Papers, Library of Congress, B140, F5.

3607 Sovereignty Commission Papers, Mississippi State Archives.

3608 *Times–Picayune*, March 15, 1956.

3609 *Baton Rouge State Times*, March 4, 1957.

3610 *Plaquemines Gazette*, February 2, 1957.

3611 The State of Louisiana Joint Legislative Committee, *Subversion in Racial Unrest; An Outline of a Strategic Weapon to Destroy the Governments of Louisiana and the United States*, March 6–9, 1957.

3612 *Strategy and Tactics of World Communism, the Significance of the Matusow Case*, Senate Internal Security Subcommittee, April 20, 1955.

3613 The State of Louisiana Joint Legislative Committee, *Subversion in Racial Unrest; An Outline of a Strategic Weapon to Destroy the Governments of Louisiana and the United States*, March 6–9, 1957.

3614 Kenneth O'Reilly, *Hoover and the Un-Americans, The FBI, HUAC and the Red Menace* (Philadelphia: Temple University Press, 1983), 239.

3615 Belfrage, *The American Inquisition 1945–1960.*

3616 Woods, *Black Struggle Red Scare.*

3617 *Baton Rouge State Times*, March 8–9, 1957.

3618 The State of Louisiana Joint Legislative Committee, *Subversion in Racial Unrest; An Outline of a Strategic Weapon to Destroy the Governments of Louisiana and the United States*, March 6–9, 1957.

3619 Epstein and Forster, *Report on the John Birch Society, 1966*.

3620 *Baton Rouge State Times*, circa March 8–9, 1957. The exact date is unknown.

3621 *Times–Picayune*, February 3, 1960.

3622 The State of Louisiana Joint Legislative Committee, *Subversion in Racial Unrest; An Outline of a Strategic Weapon to Destroy the Governments of Louisiana and the United States*, March 6–9, 1957.

3623 Robert M. Lichtman and Ronald D. Cohen, *Deadly Farce: Harvey Matusow and the Informer System in the McCarthy Era* (Urbana: University of Illinois Press, 2004).

3624 *New Republic*, March 7, 1955.

3625 Medford Evans, *Civil Rights Myths and Communist Realities* (Conservative Society of America, 1965).

3626 *Baton Rouge State Times*, March 8, 1958.

3627 The State of Louisiana Joint Legislative Committee, *Subversion in Racial Unrest; An Outline of a Strategic Weapon to Destroy the Governments of Louisiana and the United States*, March 6–9, 1957.

3628 Audiotape, Hubert Badeaux, audio department of the National Archives II.

3629 Lou Ivon, interview by the author, October 5, 2000.

3630 *Plaquemines Gazette*, March 16, 1957.

3631 Letter to Mary Cain, April 17, 1959, Federation for Constitutional Government.

3632 Newsletter, Mississippi Department of Archives and History.

3633 The State of Louisiana Joint Legislative Committee, *Subversion in Racial Unrest; An Outline of a Strategic Weapon to Destroy the Governments of Louisiana and the United States*, March 6–9, 1957.

3634 Kent Courtney, letter to Willie Rainach, March 24, 1958, Rainach Papers, Noel Memorial Library, Louisiana State University Shreveport.

3635 Warren Commission, XI, No. 1, Gray Exhibit, 210.

3636 124-10025-10170, The John F. Kennedy Assassination Records Collections, NARA.

3637 Adams, *James A. Dombrowski*.

3638 Anne Braden, *HUAC: Bulwark of Segregation*, undated, self-published book from the University of Texas at Arlington Libraries.

3639 Woods, *Black Struggle Red Scare*.

3640 *Plaquemines Gazette*, November 22, 1957.

3641 *Christian Crusade*, June 1958.

3642 May 6, 1958, Rainach Papers, Noel Memorial Library, Louisiana State University Shreveport.

3643 *Arkansas Democrat*, December 16–18, 1958.

3644 Woods, *Black Struggle Red Scare*.

3645 *Arkansas Democrat*, December 16–18, 1958.

3646 Woods, *Black Struggle Red Scare*, 77.

3647 180-10100-10127, The John F. Kennedy Assassination Records Collections, NARA.

3648 Hearing before the House Committee on Un-American Activities, House of Representatives, 85th Congress, 2nd session, July 29–31, 1958, *Communist Activities and Infiltration in the South*.

3649 *Times–Picayune*, December 11, 1959.

3650 Catherine Fosl, *Subversive Southerner* (New York: Palgrave Macmillan, 2002).

3651 Hearing before the House Committee on Un-American Activities, House of Representatives, 85th Congress, 2nd session, July 29–31, 1958, *Communist Activities and Infiltration in the South*.

3652 *Christian Crusade*, August 1958.

3653 Kent Courtney, letter to Willie Rainach, March 24, 1958, Rainach Papers, Noel Memorial Library, Louisiana State University Shreveport.

3654 *Plaquemines Gazette*, July 27, 1958.

3655 *Plaquemines Gazette*, November 14, 1958.

3656 *Times–Picayune*, March 14, 1959.

3657 *Plaquemines Gazette*, April 3, 1959.

3658 *Plaquemines Gazette*, April 3, 1959, and April 24, 1959.

3659 *Plaquemines Gazette*, May 8, 1959.

3660 *Times–Picayune*, May 16, 1959.

3661 *New York Times*, July 24, 1959.

3662 Banister's file number 10-58, August 27, 1959, Wegmann Papers, The John F. Kennedy Assassination Records Collections, NARA.

3663 *Warren Commission Report*.

3664 104-10434-10012 The John F. Kennedy Assassination Records Collections, NARA.

3665 *Times–Picayune*, June 1, 1960.

3666 180-10096-10010, The John F. Kennedy Assassination Records Collections, NARA.

3667 *Times–Picayune*, February 23, 1961.

3668 *Times–Picayune*, October 2, 1960.

3669 *Plaquemines Gazette*, October 7, 1960.

3670 *States–Item*, September 22, 1960, and September 28, 1960. Other prospects were Jack N. Rogers and George Schulz.

3671 LUAC, Waldo McNeir Hearing, Courtney Papers, Special Collections, Northwestern State University of Louisiana.

3672 *Times–Picayune*, February 26, 1961.

3673 *Times–Picayune*, March 16, 1961.

3674 Flier from the school, October 23–27, Herbert Philbrick Papers, Library of Congress, 1961, B140, F11.

3675 *Times–Picayune*, May 22, 1962.

3676 *Weekly Crusader*, October 19, 1962.

3677 *Shreveport Times*, December 18, 1962.

3678 Warren Commission, XVI, 422–425.

3679 Sarah Hart Brown, "Congressional Anti-Communists in the South." *Georgia Historical Quarterly*, LXXX. no. 4, winter 1996, 801.

3680 Hoover, *Masters of Deceit*.

3681 Warren Commission, VIII, 330–343.

3682 Hoover, *Masters of Deceit*.

3683 Part 1, February 14, 1963; Part 2, July 13 and 14, 1961; Part 3, June 15, 1961, April 10, 1962; Part 4, April 3, 1963; Part 6, February 8, 1963; Part 7, February 15, 1963; Part 8, March 8, 1963 and April 3, 1962. There may have been more hearings. It is not known why the dates and part numbers are not in a temporal sequence, or why Part 5 was not able to be located.

3684 Senator Eastland, letter to Harry Dean, 124-10293-10376, The John F. Kennedy Assassination Records Collections, NARA.

3685 *Congressional Record*, February 16, 1961, 2228.

3686 124-10285-10011, The John F. Kennedy Assassination Records Collections, NARA.

3687 *Castro's Network in the United States*, Part one, February 14, 1963, Senate Internal Security Subcommittee Hearings.

3688 *Tampa Times*, May 22, 1963.

3689 *Congressional Record*, March 15, 1961, 4318.

3690 *Castro's Network in the United States*, April 9, 1960, Senate Internal Security Subcommittee Hearings.

3691 *Times–Picayune*, September 23, 1960.

3692 *Dallas Morning News*, April 3, 1961, and April 4, 1961.

3693 *Times–Picayune*, April 29, 1961.

3694 Harry Dean, interview by the author, November 18, 2009.

3695 *Times–Picayune*, August 24, 1961.

3696 *Times–Picayune*, August 28, 1961.

3697 *Dallas Morning News*, August 15, 1961.

3698 Herbert Philbrick Papers, Library of Congress, B45:F11.

3699 *Times–Picayune*, November 22, 1961.

3700 HUAC's Executive Hearing on the Los Angeles FPCC, 87th Congress, 2nd session, April 26 and 27, 1962.

3701 Warren Commission, XXII, 161.

3702 Warren Commission, Exhibit 1172.

3703 Warren Commission, X, 110.

3704 Warren Commission, XXII, 157–60a.

3705 Warren Commission, XXII, 156.

3706 Warren Commission, XIX, 576.

3707 Warren Commission, X, 119.

3708 Warren Commission, X, 112.

3709 Warren Commission, X, 109.

3710 Warren Commission, XIX, 572.

3711 Warren Commission, XXII, 161.

3712 Warren Commission, X, 110.

3713 Warren Commission, XXI, 681–82.

3714 Warren Commission, Document 366.

3715 Warren Commission, XXII, 172.

3716 Warren Commission, XIX, 567.

3717 Warren Commission, XXI, 721.

3718 Warren Commission, XXI, 674–677.

3719 Warren Commission, X, 107.

3720 104-10408-10383, The John F. Kennedy Assassination Records Collections, NARA.

3721 Warren Commission, X, 108–109.

3722 *Castro's Network in the United States*, Part 6, dated February 8, 1963, Senate Internal Security Subcommittee Hearings.

3723 LUAC report on the SISS hearing, 124-10267-1076, The John F. Kennedy Assassination Records Collections, NARA.

3724 Lyle Stuart, testimony, *Castro's Network in the United States*, Part 6, February 8, 1963, Senate Internal Security Subcommittee Hearings.

3725 *Castro's Network in the United States*, Part 1, February 14, 1963, Senate Internal Security Subcommittee Hearings.

3726 *Castro's Network in the United States*, Part 7, February 15, 1963, Senate Internal Security Subcommittee Hearings,.

3727 Waldo Frank, testimony, *Castro's Network in the United States*, Part 8, March 8, 1963, Senate Internal Security Subcommittee Hearings.

3728 Warren Commission, IV, 422.

3729 *Warren Commission Report*.

3730 *Castro's Network in the United States*, Part 4, April 3, 1964, Senate Internal Security Subcommittee Hearings.

3731 Warren Commission, XXII, 159.

3732 *Warren Commission Report*, 407.

3733 Warren Commission, XX, 511.

3734 Warren Commission, X, 112.

3735 Warren Commission, XXII, 159.

3736 Warren Commission, XXII, 162.

3737 Warren Commission, XX, 517.

3738 Warren Commission, XX, 512.

3739 Warren Commission, XIX, 567.

3740 Warren Commission, XX, 514.

3741 Warren Commission, X, 109.

3742 *Warren Commission Report*, 407.

3743 Warren Commission, XX, 257.

3744 Warren Commission, XXII, 172.

3745 Warren Commission, I, 23.

3746 Warren Commission, X, 109.

3747 Warren Commission, XIX, 569.

3748 Warren Commission, IV, 433.

3749 Warren Commission, XXII, 166, 167.

3750 *Warren Commission Report*, 407.

3751 Warren Commission, XX, 524–525.

3752 Warren Commission, Documents 81b and 156.

3753 *Warren Commission Report*, 408.

3754 Courtney Papers, Special Collections, Northwestern State University of Louisiana.

3755 *Warren Commission Report*, 407.

3756 Warren Commission, X, 54.

3757 Warren Commission, VI, 24.

3758 Warren Commission, XXVI, 774.

3759 Warren Commission, XXVI, 784.

3760 Warren Commission, Exhibit 826.

3761 Corliss Lamont, *A Lifetime of Dissent* (New York: Prometheus Books, 1988).

3762 *Councilor*, May 29, 1864.

3763 FBI file number 100-16601.

3764 *Warren Commission Report*, 408.

3765 Warren Commission, XX, 527.

3766 Warren Commission, XXII, 167.

3767 Warren Commission, XX, 409.

3768 Warren Commission, Documents 81b and 157.

3769 180-10031-10326, The John F. Kennedy Assassination Records Collections, NARA.

3770 124-10248-10143, The John F. Kennedy Assassination Records Collections, NARA.

3771 Warren Commission, XIX, 175.

3772 Warren Commission, XIX, 176.

3773 Warren Commission, XXII, 168. (Oswald's spelling errors were corrected by the author.)

3774 Warren Commission, XXII, 16.

3775 Warren Commission, X, 95, 102.

3776 Warren Commission, XX, 270.

3777 Warren Commission, XXIII, 708.

3778 Warren Commission, Exhibits 1906 and 1907.

3779 Warren Commission, Documents 75 and 57.

3780 *Louisiana Weekly*, letter to SCEF, Anne and Carl Braden Papers, Wisconsin Historical Society.

3781 Warren Commission, XX, 265.

3782 *Warren Commission Report*, 413.

3783 Warren Commission, XXII, 159.

3784 *Warren Commission Report*, 412.

3785 Warren Commission, X, 109.

3786 Warren Commission, X, 179.

3787 Warren Commission, XXII, 159.

3788 Warren Commission, XXII, 161.

3789 Warren Commission, IV, 446.

3790 Warren Commission, XXII, 161.

3791 Warren Commission, XXII, 162.

3792 Warren Commission, XX, 273.

3793 FBI file number 100-10461-966.

3794 *Warren Commission Report*, 201.

3795 Warren Commission, XX, 273.

3796 Warren Commission, X, 95–107.

3797 Warren Commission, XV1, 442.

3798 Warren Commission, Exhibit 2073.

3799 President Johnson, phonecall to Senator Eastland, November 28, 1963, transcript, LBJ Presidential Library.

Chapter 23

3800 *Congressional Record*, Vol. 107, No. 88.

3801 *Times–Picayune*, May 12, 1962, S2, 4.

3802 Warren Commission, Document 7, FBI DL 89-43.

3803 The Subversive Activities and Communist Control Law is La. Rev. Stat. 14:358 through 14:374 (Cum. Supp. 1962).

3804 The Communist Propaganda Control Law is La. Rev. Stat. 14:390 through 14:390.8 (Cum. Supp. 1962).

3805 J. G. Sourwine, affidavit in *Dombrowski v. Colonel Thomas D. Burbank*, December 1963, Carl and Anne Braden Papers, Wisconsin Historical Society, Call number: Mss. 6: Box 24, Folder 3.

3806 Brown, *Standing Against Dragons*.

3807 Adams, *James A. Dombrowski, 1897–1983, An American Heretic*.

3808 *American Bar Association Journal*, June 1965.

3809 Louisiana State Archives. Colonel Alexander was hired as staff director of LUAC in

1961. At the time he was serving as an Army ROTC instructor at Louisiana State University, according to the *Times–Picayune*, July 12, 1961.

3810 Peebles. *Subversion and the Southern Conference Education Fund*, 54.

3811 Brown, *Standing Against Dragons*.

3812 Adams, *James A. Dombrowski*.

3813 *American Bar Association Journal*, June 1965.

3814 Adams, *James A. Dombrowski*.

3815 *Times–Picayune*, July 31, 1963.

3816 *Times–Picayune*, August 4, 1963.

3817 *Congressional Record*, August 7, 1963, p.14455, JFK quoted, 14462.

3818 *Times–Picayune*, August 24, 1963.

3819 *Times–Picayune*, August 27, 1963.

3820 Brown, *Standing Against Dragons*.

3821 Adams, *James A. Dombrowski*.

3822 *American Bar Association Journal*, June 1965.

3823 Search warrant for Benjamen E. Smith, Braden Papers, Wisconsin Historical Society, 24-4.

3824 Athan G. Theoharis, *Beyond the Hiss Case: The FBI, Congress and the Cold War* (Philadelphia: Temple University Press, 1982).

3825 O'Reilly, *Hoover and the Un-Americans*, 146.

3826 Adams, *James A. Dombrowski*.

3827 Sarah Hart Brown, "Redressing Southern "Subversion': The Case of Senator Eastland and the Louisiana Lawyer." *Louisiana History*, 43:3 (2002), 307.

3828 Brown, *Standing Against Dragons*, 219.

3829 Adams, *James A. Dombrowski*.

3830 *Times–Picayune*, October 5, 1963.

3831 Adams, *James A. Dombrowski*, 263.

3832 180-10096-10010, The John F. Kennedy Assassination Records Collection, NARA.

3833 180-10097-10490, The John F. Kennedy Assassination Records Collection, NARA.

3834 180-100781-0371, The John F. Kennedy Assassination Records Collection, NARA.

3835 Visit to Ross Banister, Ben E. Smith investigation, February 1, 1967, NODA.

3836 180-10078-10369, The John F. Kennedy Assassination Records Collection, NARA.

3837 Adams, *James A. Dombrowski*.

3838 *Times–Picayune*, October 5, 1963.

3839 *Baton Rouge Morning Advocate*, October 5, 1963.

3840 *Times–Picayune*, October 5, 1963.

3841 *States–Item*, October 6, 1963.

3842 Brown, *Standing Against Dragons*.

3843 *States–Item*, October 17, 1963.

3844 *Times–Picayune*, October 26, 1963.

3845 Peebles, *Subversion and the Southern Conference Education Fund.*

3846 *Times–Picayune*, October 13, 1963.

3847 See also: Brown, *Standing Against Dragons.*

3848 *American Bar Association Journal*, June 1965.

3849 Adams, *James A. Dombrowski.*

3850 J. G. Sourwine, affidavit in *Dombrowski v. Colonel Thomas D. Burbank*, December 1963, Carl and Anne Braden Papers, Wisconsin Historical Society, Call number: Mss 6: Box 24, Folder 3.

3851 Visit to Ross Banister, Ben E. Smith investigation, February 1, 1967, NODA.

3852 MLK court transcript, Carl and Anne Braden Papers, Wisconsin Historical Society, Box 24-4.

3853 Adams, *James A. Dombrowski.*

3854 *American Bar Association Journal*, June 1965.

3855 Brown, *Standing Against Dragons.*

3856 *Year in Review*, Part One, United Press International, 1963.

3857 124-10010-10152, The John F. Kennedy Assassination Records Collection, NARA.

3858 Peebles. *Subversion and the Southern Conference Education Fund*, 59.

3859 J. G. Sourwine, affidavit in *Dombrowski v. Colonel Thomas D. Burbank*, December 1963, Carl and Anne Braden Papers, Wisconsin Historical Society, Call number: Mss 6: Box 24, Folder 3.

3860 Warren Commission, XI, 210, Gray Exhibit No. 1.

3861 Young Peoples Socialist League, letter to Carl Braden, September 20, 1957, Carl and Anne Braden Papers, Wisconsin Historical Society, Call number: Mss 6: Box 58, Folder 4.

3862 Adams, *James A. Dombrowski*, 40.

3863 *Councilor*, May 29, 1964.

3864 *Shreveport Journal*, September 5, 1963.

3865 Brown, *Standing Against Dragons*, 205.

3866 Senate Internal Security Subcommittee Hearings, February 28, 265-289.

3867 Kent Courtney, letter to Willie Rainach, March 24, 1958, Courtney Papers, Special Collections, Northwestern State University of Louisiana.

3868 *Independent American*, November 5, 1963, Courtney Papers, Special Collections, Northwestern State University of Louisiana.

3869 Warren Commission, Document 366.

3870 Warren Commission, XXII, 172.

3871 *Tax Fax No. 46*, Courtney Papers, Special Collections, Northwestern State University of Louisiana.

3872 Senate Internal Security Subcommittee, 204-10001-10005, The John F. Kennedy Assassination Records Collection, NARA.

3873 UPI release, 12-4-63, FBI file number 116-65494-58.

3874 FBI file number 105-8255, Oswald HQ File, Section 12; NO 89-69, Interview November 25, 1963.

3875 124-10058-10076, The John F. Kennedy Assassination Records Collection, NARA.

3876 *Times–Picayune*, March 5, 1958.

3877 *Times–Picayune*, April 6, 1957.

3878 *Times–Picayune*, March 27, 1956.

3879 Weisberg, *Oswald in New Orleans*, 329.

3880 Willie Rainach, letter to Jack N. Rogers, March 2, 1959 and April 6, 1959, Rainach Papers, Noel Memorial Library, Louisiana State University Shreveport.

3881 *Times–Picayune*, October 23, 1958.

3882 *Times–Picayune*, October 2, 1960.

3883 *Times–Picayune*, May 19, 1960.

3884 180-10100-10127, The John F. Kennedy Assassination Records Collection, NARA.

3885 *Times–Picayune*, October 2, 1960.

3886 *Times–Picayune*, March 16, 1961.

3887 Peebles, *Subversion and the Southern Conference Education Fund*, 49.

3888 For information on the creation of the Communist Control Act, see Adam Fairclough, *Race & Democracy: The Civil Rights Struggle in Louisiana, 1915-1972*.

3889 Lawrence Melville, interview, February 5, 1967, NODA.

3890 John A. Salmond, "The Great Southern Commie Hunt," *South Atlantic Quarterly*, autumn, 1978, 433.

3891 SCEF mailing list, NODA.

3892 Peebles, *Subversion and the Southern Conference Education Fund*.

3893 Durr, *Outside the Magic Circle*, 188.

3894 Anne Braden, interview by the author, February 3, 2001.

3895 Turner, *Civil Rights and Anti-Communism in New Orleans, 1946–1965*.

3896 124-10267-1076, The John F. Kennedy Assassination Records Collection, NARA.

3897 Adams, *James A. Dombrowski*, 253–261, 274.

3898 Transcript, "Conversation Carte Blanche," WDSU radio, October 31, 1963, Carl and Anne Braden Papers, Wisconsin Historical Society, Call number: Mss. 6: Box 24, Folder 4.

3899 Warren Commission, X, 87.

3900 Earl Lively, letter to Herb Philbrick, May 8, 1965, Herbert Philbrick Papers, Library of Congress, Box 223, F 9.

3901 124-10275-10011, The John F. Kennedy Assassination Records Collection, NARA.

3902 *Weekly Crusader*, June 12, 1964.

3903 *The Wooster Daily Record*, March 19, 1958, AP Story.

3904 124-10039-10385, The John F. Kennedy Assassination Records Collection, NARA.

The Documents

3905 Rainach Papers, Noel Memorial Library, Louisiana State University Shreveport.

3906 Edwin A. Walker Papers, Dolph Briscoe Center for American History, University of Texas at Austin, Box 96-30/9.

3907 William Wood Papers, The John F. Kennedy Assassination Records Collection, NARA.

3908 180-10094-10189, The John F. Kennedy Assassination Records Collection, NARA.

3909 180-10099-10176, The John F. Kennedy Assassination Records Collection, NARA.

3910 Edwin A. Walker Papers, Dolph Briscoe Center for American History, University of Texas at Austin, Box 3, Folder C.

3911 Tom Anderson Papers, Special Collections, University of Oregon Library, Box 47.

3912 Edwin A. Walker Papers, Dolph Briscoe Center for American History, University of Texas at Austin, 96-30/37.

INDEX

and McCarthy, 704

Miami assassination plot, 457

and military muzzling, 323

on military subordination to civilian control, 321

motorcade route, 456-457

and the National Guard troops, 421, 435

and Ole Miss, 351-364

and the radical right, 141, 143

and the South, 326

and the Stevenson incident, 452

and the United Nations, 343

and voting rights, 379

and Walker, 60, 198, 286, 301, 311, 318, 364, 459, 778, 781

wounds of, 490-492

Kennedy, Regis, 24-25, 34, 36, 42, 45, 79, 199, 204-205, 212-213, 617, 624

Kennedy, Robert F.

on the American Communist Party, 342

and Barnett, 353

and the Birmingham riot, 432

and Caldwell's prediction, 576-577

and Capell, 17

and civil rights, 344, 425, 759

and Cobb, 215

and Crommelin, 196

enemies, actions against, 369

and the Freedom Riders, 350, 352

and Goff, 169-170

and integrationist protection, 73-74

and the JBS, 317, 328, 607

and Marcello, 6, 268

and McCarthy, 703

and Meredith, 348

and the National Indignation Committee, 328

and Ole Miss, 354-355, 358, 364, 556

and Oswald, 402

presidential campaign announced, 539

as responsible for JFK's murder, 111

and the SCEF raid, 763

and the Senate Commerce Committee, 425

and voting rights, 342, 676

and Walker, 297, 364, 370, 595

and the Walker shooting, 404, 407

and Wallace, 387

warnings about the assassination, 466

and wiretapping of integrationists, 668

Kerr, Jean, 704

Key Records, 161, 572-573

Khrushchev, Nikita, 10, 315, 431, 437, 521, 531, 722, 732

Kilbourne, Charles S., 666

Kilbourne, Richard, 655, 666-674, 678-683, 688

Kimble, Jules Ricco, 53, 232, 671

King, George, Jr., 240

King, John, Jr., 369

King, Martin Luther, Jr.

and Adams, 107

assassination of, 693

and Birmingham, 436-437

and Brown, 108

and the Highlander Folk School, 376

and the Highlander School poster, 256-257, 279, 424

and JFK, 437

and Robert Kennedy, 74

and the LUAC report, 775-776

and the March on Washington, 425, 428-430, 484

murder investigation of, 46, 48, 65, 78, 112, 123, 154, 164, 197, 510

and O'Dell, 9, 720

photo, 257

and the SCEF raid, 763

and the State Commerce Committee, 425

and the Student Non-Violent Coordinating Committee, 158

threats against and insults, 67, 86, 103, 107-108, 115-116, 120, 144, 156, 171, 269, 272, 454, 535, 555, 759

Kinoy, Arthur, 761, 763-764, 767

Kissinger, Henry, 558

the Klan, 38, 53, 74-75, 78, 82, 84, 92-98, 106-108, 113-116, 119, 122-123, 127, 132, 135, 144, 157, 160, 165, 167, 172, 214-215, 214-216, 215, 252, 352-356, 371, 429, 484-485, 535, 548, 553-556, 652-655, 663, 670-673, 683, 690-692

Klein, Frank, 764

Klein, William R., 224, 262-263

imprisoned after Ole Miss incident, 365-371

and the insurrection plot, 524, 551-554, 556, 789

and integration, 4, 77

and Jackman, 483

and Jews, 550

and JFK, 24, 188-189, 198, 238, 258-259, 286, 311, 325-327, 343, 354, 378, 397, 436-437, 459, 778

and the John Birch Society, 22

and Johnson, 556

and Robert Kennedy, 311, 364, 370, 556

and Key Records, 161

and King, 171, 554

and the Klan, 554-556

in later years, 556-559

lawsuits for libel and slander, 435, 555

letter about becoming head of far right, 792

and the letter to Touchstone, 564-565

and Little Rock, 313, 553

and the March on Washington, 425, 429-431

as the mastermind behind the JFK murder, 780

and McIntire, 239, 684

military career of, 313-314

and the military muzzling, 311, 315-326

military underground, 174-175

and the military underground, 369

and Milteer, 285-286, 312, 794

and the Minutemen, 307-308, 380, 419-420, 500, 531, 554

and Moran, 300

and Morris, 295, 575

and the National Indignation Committee, 327-330

and *National-Zeitung*, 402-406, 542

Nazi connection, 73

in New Orleans, 254, 458-459

NSRP member, 77

on the Nuclear Test Ban Treaty, 436

and Ole Miss, 107, 170, 236, 297-298, 337-373, 377-378, 785

and Operation Alert, 387-389

and Operation Midnight Ride, 140, 375-381, 389

and Oswald, 6, 298, 329, 520, 547-548, 603, 781-782, 788-789

and Marguerite Oswald, 561-563, 797

and the Oswald-Bringuier fight, 201

and Perez, 254-255, 454, 459-460

photo, 175, 313, 316, 337, 380, 693

and Potito, 377

pre-assassination meetings in New Orleans, 459-463

propaganda of, 337-340, 542-551

psychiatric evaluation of, 297, 320, 364-367, 370

and Rarick, 690

and Ratliff, 684

reinstated by Army, 558

relieved of command by JFK, 60, 301, 317, 778, 781

resignation from army, 321, 782

rise of, 312-315, 784-785

and Roberts, 343

and Rockefeller, 436

on Eleanor Roosevelt, 316-317

and Ruby, 399, 404, 413, 515-516, 520-524, 536-539, 796

and Sauvage, 548-549

and school integration, 782

and Shaw, 564

shooting incident, 34, 374-417, 548-549, 742, 786

and sovereignty, 423

speaking tours, 149, 373-381, 387-389, 427-428, 688

and the Special Armed Services Committee, 325-326

and Stevenson, 450-452, 457

and the Student Revolutionary Directorate, 449

and the Supreme Court, 425

and Surrey, 380, 418, 794

on Thurmond, 436

and the top-secret strategy meeting, 423

and Touchstone, 542, 673

and Truman, 24, 60, 158, 316-317

and the United Nations, 323, 388, 425, 436-437, 457-458

and Varney, 458

and Wallace, 457

and *The Wanderer*, 575

and the Warren Commission findings, 511

and Watts, 283, 296-297

and Wedemeyer, 191

and We the People, 438